Hillforts, Warfare and Society in Bronze Age Ireland

William O'Brien and James O'Driscoll

Archaeopress Archaeology

ARCHAEOPRESS PUBLISHING LTD
Gordon House
276 Banbury Road
Oxford OX2 7ED

www.archaeopress.com

ISBN 978 1 78491 655 8
ISBN 978 1 78491 656 5 (e-Pdf)

Cover: James O'Driscoll

Front Cover: Brusselstown Ring, Baltinglass, Co. Wicklow.
Back Cover: Bronze Age spearheads from Ireland, Clashanimud Co. Cork, aerial view and reconstruction.

For John Waddell,
in acknowledgement of his major contribution to research on the Irish Bronze Age.

Printed in England by Oxuniprint, Oxford
This book is available direct from Archaeopress or from our website www.archaeopress.com

Contents

List of Figures

All of the figures for this volume were produced by the authors unless otherwise stated.

Acknowledgments

We wish to thank the Irish Research Council for a major grant in 2011 to develop this project, and a subsequent doctoral scholarship provided to James O'Driscoll. We also wish to acknowledge the support of the National Monuments Service, Department of Arts, Heritage and the Gaeltacht for funding the Clashanimud excavation, through a grant in 2004–6 administered by the Royal Irish Academy. We are grateful for the continuing support of the Department of Archaeology, University College Cork, and also thank the Department of Archaeology, National University of Ireland Galway, where WO'B was employed during the Clashanimud excavation. For that excavation, we wish to thank the core team for help and support over three seasons: Michelle Comber, Elizabeth Gill, Liam Hickey, Nick Hogan, Noel McCarthy, Margaret Murphy, and Paul Naessens, and the site supervisor, Madeline O'Brien, in addition to many student volunteers from Cork and Galway. For the other hillfort excavations, many thanks to the site supervisor, Nick Hogan, and archaeologists Alan Hawkes, Caen Harris, Kevin Kearney, Barry Lacey, Liam O'Brien, and Niall O'Sullivan.

Nick Hogan and James O'Driscoll provided most of the illustrations in this monograph, with some provided by Patsi Bates, Michelle Comber and Angela Gallagher. Madeline O'Brien edited and proof-read the final text, and contributed to the discussion of the excavation results. Thanks to Katharina Becker for supervision of James Lineen's spearhead thesis and to Barry Cunliffe for advice and support. The late Pauline van Rijn provided charcoal data, with radiocarbon results supplied by the Groningen laboratory. Specialist contributions were also made by Rose Cleary (pottery), Kevin Kearney (Bayesian analysis) and Susan Lyons (charcoal), while Tim Mighall (University of Aberdeen) assisted with the Clashanimud landscape study. Many thanks to the National Museum of Ireland for support; to Ordnance Survey Ireland, the Geological Survey of Ireland, and the Environmental Protection Agency for providing data-sets used in GIS analysis; and Gary Lock and Ian Ralston for inviting us to contribute to the *Atlas of Hillforts in Britain and Ireland.*

We also wish to express our appreciation to the respective landowners for permission to survey and excavate at these ten hillforts. Many thanks to David Davison and the team at Archaeopress for believing in the publication, and to the College of Arts, Celtic Studies and Social Sciences in UCC for a grant towards publication costs. Finally, a special thanks to Nick Hogan who made a major contribution to the project, to Alan Hawkes who spent several months assisting with survey and excavation work, and to our respective families, Madeline, Michael, Donal and Liam, and Martha, Bob, Margaret and Aaron.

1

Introduction

War and conflict have been a harsh reality of human existence in recent world history. Archaeological sources reveal this was also the case in prehistory, going back to the very origins of humankind. The Bronze Age provides some of the most striking examples of early warfare, organized on a significantly greater scale than in earlier periods. The evidence in Europe includes large numbers of fortifications, mass production of weaponry, and the evidence of physical trauma on human remains. The representation of the male warrior in Bronze Age rock art evokes images of a heroic culture, such as that portrayed by Homer in his epic tales of the Trojan War. While Bronze Age warfare is often presented as limited and ritualized, the recent discovery of a battlefield site at Tollense, north-east Germany, along with evidence of massacres from other parts of Europe, is a reminder that these conflicts had very serious consequences in terms of human life and social upheaval.

This is also evident in Ireland for the centuries after 1500 BC, when defensive considerations in settlement and the production of weaponry increased to a level where warfare and political instability can be inferred from the archaeological record. While acknowledging conflict as an active agent of social change, many Irish prehistorians continue to avoid explicit consideration of warfare, emphasizing the more peaceful aspects of settlement and economy, social roles and other ideological aspects of society. This unconscious pacification of the past is part of a Golden Age 'noble savage' understanding of the Bronze Age, a reaction in part to the terrible realities of recent European history. The same is true of Bronze Age research in Ireland, an island with its own troubled history and colourful origin legends that feature waves of invaders and internecine strife.

1.1 The Hillfort Phenomenon

Hillforts are the largest monumental constructions of the Bronze Age and Iron Age in Europe. That alone testifies to the great significance these central places held for prehistoric societies in economic, political and other terms. The label 'hillfort' is problematic in that it includes sites of different form, location, date, and cultural associations in various regions. While such variability undermines any notion of a single phenomenon, referring to these sites as hillforts does convey two essential features: a prominent location in the landscape, and the physical demarcation of a large space to which access was controlled by physical barriers. This was achieved by natural and artificial means, where one or more lines of earthworks, stone walls or timber palisades were built individually or in combination to take advantage of elevation and topography. Most hillforts are very large enclosures on or near the summit of a prominent hill, low mountain, ridge, plateau, inland promontory, spur or cliff. In some parts of Europe, they occur on eminences in lowland settings or were built adjacent to major rivers. In all cases the natural setting presents a tactical advantage in terms of enclosure and defence, but also a landscape perspective that seems to be strategic in intent.

The imposing nature of hillforts is also a product of their immense size - sites that are often so large that their entire extent can only be viewed from the air, which obviously was not possible for their builders (Figure 1.1). While examples under one hectare are known, the majority are up to 20ha in enclosed area, with exceptionally large variants up to 100ha, and sometimes more, in parts of Europe. In most cases the scale of construction was well beyond the capabilities of individual families, while the size of the enclosed areas suggests use by larger population groups. These 'forts' were regarded as central places in their respective societies, formal settings for the expression of power and warrior culture. For this reason, narratives of competition and control, aggression and warfare have been to the fore, perspectives that have been tempered somewhat in recent consideration of other roles and symbolic meaning.

The building of hillforts was part of a wider phenomenon of enclosure of land, settlement and ritual space, which in Ireland extends back some six millennia to the earliest Neolithic farmers. A connection with farming is relevant as the creation of fields and animal enclosures was an important feature of agricultural intensification and land management. This had a broader significance in terms of the assertion of land ownership and territorial rights. The building of hillforts was a further affirmation of those rights. The element of protection was a consideration in hillfort design and location, tied to a basic human need for security of life and property.

In a broad sense, the purpose of enclosure was to define or segregate space, and to afford physical or spiritual protection for whomever or whatever was enclosed from the outside world (Harding 2012: 6). Harding adds that

Figure 1.1: Aerial view of Clashanimud hillfort, Co. Cork.

the purpose of enclosure may have been less to underline the distinction between 'them' and 'us', and more to emphasise something that was special for the group in question. The idea of retaining dangerous supernatural forces can be applied in Ireland to henge enclosures of the later Neolithic, or to internally ditched 'royal' enclosures of the Iron Age. While hillforts are in a different category with their records of permanent occupation, many had defined areas of 'ritual space' in their interiors. Others were built on hills where there were older burial mounds, an explicit referencing of the past tied up with the creation of identity and the legitimization of power.

1.2 The Hillfort in Ireland

There are approximately 100 sites in Ireland that might be properly termed hillforts, though this number varies depending on the criteria chosen. Their function and cultural significance is a much-debated topic in Irish archaeology. Raftery's (1994: 62) comment that hillforts remain 'enigmatic' relates to their origins and cultural connections, but also to their use and broader meaning for prehistoric societies. Waddell (1998) considered the 'hillfort problem' in similar terms, and like Raftery drew attention to the long history of hill-top enclosure in Ireland, from Neolithic to medieval times, and to the absence of secure dating evidence for most hillforts. Part of the 'problem' relates to morphology and classification. Hillfort morphology is generally adapted to topographic setting, and while certain standardised types can be identified, there is no chronologically specific form. Small hillforts, and those examples under 1ha in size known as hill-top enclosures, can be difficult to distinguish from medieval ringforts, of which there may originally have been up to 60,000 examples in Ireland.

The history of hillfort studies in Ireland will be considered in Chapter 2. Some general observations may be made to understand the research context of this volume. The basic identification of the monument type owes much to the surveys of Thomas Westropp in the early 20th century. The first scientific investigation of an Irish hillfort was undertaken by Gerhard Bersu in 1948–9 at Freestone Hill, Co. Kilkenny. That excavation was subsequently published by Barry Raftery (1969), the leading Irish Iron Age scholar of the modern era. Raftery devised the current classification of Irish hillforts, separating those examples with a single enclosure (Class 1) from those with two or more widely spaced defences (Class 2), with a separate category of inland promontory forts (Class 3), but excluding coastal promontory forts (Raftery 1970; 1972).

In 1969, the same year he published the 'Iron Age' hillfort at Freestone Hill, Raftery commenced excavation at Rathgall hillfort, Co. Wicklow. This project was undertaken at a time when Irish hillforts were regarded as Iron Age, heavily influenced by research in Britain where hillforts such as Maiden Castle were the classic monuments of the period. The Rathgall results were to change that perception, as excavations over the next five years uncovered a high-status settlement and ritual complex of the Middle to Late Bronze Age (Raftery 1970; 1973; 1976; see also Becker 2010). While that project remains to be fully published (Raftery and

Becker in prep.), the results from Rathgall are very significant for our understanding of Class 2 hillforts in Ireland. This was reinforced by subsequent excavations, beginning with Haughey's Fort in the Navan landscape, Co. Armagh (Mallory 1995), followed by investigations conducted by the Discovery Programme at Mooghaun, Co. Clare (Grogan 2005) and Dún Aonghasa, Inishmore, Co. Galway (Cotter 2012). These projects are very important, as the significance of those hillforts was contextualised within a wider cultural landscape, thus broadening our understanding of their place in regional societies of the Irish Bronze Age.

Gaps in knowledge

While the 'problem' of the Irish hillfort can be overstated, there are still significant weaknesses in our understanding of these monuments. The first of these relates to chronology, and specifically to the origins, development and demise of different hillfort traditions. The overall dating of hillforts in Ireland remains weak, due largely to a lack of detailed excavation projects and radiocarbon programmes. Only around ten hillforts have been excavated in the modern era, to varying degrees of detail, along with a small number of Neolithic hill-top enclosures and 'royal sites' of the Iron Age. While many hillforts were occupied during the Bronze Age and later periods, there are few reliable dates for construction and abandonment, or for the sequence of occupation. In that respect the Irish research lags significantly behind that in Britain, though there is enough evidence to now demonstrate the two islands have very different hillfort traditions.

The chronology of different types of hillfort in Ireland is not well understood. The dating of Class 1 (univallate) examples is particularly poor, with very few investigations of these sites. The same is true of Class 3 (inland promontory) hillforts, while the relationship of coastal promontory forts to these sites is not established. As mentioned above, there are some important excavation records for Class 2 (multiple enclosure) hillforts, yet much remains to be learnt about their overall chronology (Figure 1.2). There are few reliable dates for the construction or abandonment of individual sites, while the temporality of occupation is often poorly understood. Each hillfort had its own unique history, the fine detail of which can only be understood through large-scale archaeological excavations of a type that is now rarely undertaken in Ireland. The chronology of hillfort clusters is also poorly understood, with the complementary investigations of Haughey's Fort and Navan Fort in Co. Armagh unique in that respect.

The origins of the Irish hillfort continue to be questioned. Once connected to invading hordes of Celts, the emphasis in recent research has shifted to an understanding of internal processes in the regional societies of the Middle to Late Bronze Age. With parallel developments in Britain and mainland Europe, external influences cannot be discounted, particularly given the extensive trade and other connections of hillfort groups in Ireland during the second millennium BC.

As in many parts of Europe, there is a Neolithic background to the hillfort phenomenon in Ireland. This centres on a small number of hill-top enclosures of fourth millennium BC date, sites such as Lyles Hill and Donegore Hill in Antrim. Some of these fall into the category of causewayed enclosures of the southern British type, but others have a more explicit element of fortification and permanent occupation. A direct connection with hillforts of the later Bronze Age is problematic given an interval of some two millennia between the two traditions. That said, the building of Bronze Age hillforts, or at least their location, may have been partly inspired by a memory or physical traces of older enclosures in the landscape.

The sequence of hillfort construction during the Bronze Age remains to be clarified, and also the circumstances by which individual sites were abandoned. The apparent collapse of hillfort society around the eighth century BC is a major issue for research. The use of hillforts in Ireland during the ensuing Iron Age (600 BC–400 AD) can only be described as enigmatic. No classic hillforts seem to have been built in the Irish Iron Age, even though activity from that period is recorded in older examples of the Bronze Age. In a sense, that was the real 'problem' of the Irish hillfort for Barry Raftery: how a major monument type so distinctive of the British Iron Age could be absent in Ireland during the same period. The internally-ditched enclosures built in some 'royal sites' during the late first millennium BC are not hillforts in the narrow definition, but rather ceremonial centres more akin to henges of the later Neolithic. Harding (2012: 284) argued that these sites may lie at the end of the hillfort spectrum, as their importance to Iron Age groups was such they would have been actively defended when threatened.

If the Iron Age hillfort is an enigma in Ireland, the same is true of medieval examples. There is no evidence that large sites on the scale of hillforts were built during the later first millennium AD, a period when there was a proliferation of ringfort-type enclosures, often built on low eminences or prominent hills. There is, however, abundant evidence for the re-occupation of Bronze Age hillforts, at sites such as Dún Aonghasa, Mooghaun, Rahally and Rathgall. The significance of this later activity is unclear, as are aspects of the mythological and folkloric associations of prehistoric hillforts to the modern era.

Class 2 Hillforts: Definite*/Likely

1. Haughey's Fort, Armagh*
2. Dún Aonghasa, Galway*
3. Kilskeagh (Cahermore), Galway
4. Rahally, Galway*
5. Ballycurragh, Offaly
6. Cumber Lower, Offaly
7. Kill Hill, Kildare
8. Hughstown, Wicklow
9. Tinoran, Wicklow*
10. Rathnagree, Wicklow*
11. Rathcoran, Wicklow
12. Brusselstown Ring, Wicklow
13. Rathgall, Wicklow*
14. Knockeen, Wicklow
15. Toor More, Wicklow *
16. Knigh, Tipperary
17. Formoyle Beg, Clare*
18. Mooghaun, Clare*
19. Ballylin, Limerick*
20. Curradobbin, Waterford
21. Carn Tighernagh, Cork
22. Clashanimud, Cork*
23. Glanbane, Kerry*

** = Dated hillfort*

Class 2 Hillforts: Possible

24. Carrowreagh (Grianán of Aileach), Donegal
25. Lisbancarney, Tyrone
26. Lisbanroe, Armagh
27. Drumnagranshy, Sligo
28. Carrownrush, Sligo
29. Hill of Ward, Meath*
30. Common of Lloyds, Meath
31. Boley, Laois
32. Ballinkillin, Carlow
33. Liss, Tipperary
34. Rathcannon, Limerick
35. Caherdrinny, Cork
36. Rath, Cork
37. Knockanacuig, Kerry

FIGURE 1.2: DISTRIBUTION OF CLASS 2 HILLFORTS IN IRELAND, SHOWING LOCATION OF SITES SURVEYED AND EXCAVATED IN THIS PROJECT.

Hillfort construction and design

There are several questions in regard to the design and building of hillforts in Ireland. A considerable degree of planning is apparent in these major construction projects. This is indicated by their seemingly coherent design, the execution of which over very large areas, with restricted visibility in places, reflects some basic principles of measurement and surveying. The question must always be asked as to whether the hillforts we see today are the product of a single design executed over one phase of construction, or created over a longer period, in a process involving repair and re-building, adjustments to size, enhanced fortification and other structural changes.

While hillfort morphology is adapted to specific topographic settings, there are strong elements of purposeful design for sites of a similar tradition over a wide geographical area. This is true of Class 2 (multiple enclosure) hillforts in Ireland, which have a broad consistency of form across the range. Why such hillforts vary in size is unclear. This may have some connection to the size of the hillfort population in terms of the capacity to build such large enclosures, but it cannot be simply about accommodating that number of people. Some design features of Class 2 hillforts in Ireland also require explanation, such as the division of space created by their wide concentric enclosures.

The scale and logistics of hillfort construction is often staggering, involving extensive land clearance and the building of many kilometres of artificial defences. The rock-cut ditches, dump ramparts, stone walls, timber palisades and other enclosing elements represent a massive commitment of time, resources and energy. This involved the coordinated effort of a large group working to an agreed design and a clear vision of what was intended. This communal effort required careful coordination and strong leadership, which is some cases may have had a coercive element. The nature of that leadership is a key question in understanding the social and political context of hillforts.

Function and use

The function of hillforts is a much debated topic, with opinion often divided between those who regard them as defensive strongholds, and those who argue for wider meaning in social and economic terms. These viewpoints need not be in opposition, as there is enough evidence to indicate that hillforts served a multiplicity of roles in their respective communities. The intention was to create an enclosed space that would serve as a central place in that society. The physical barriers represent a control of access that could be defended if necessary, but that does not tell us what the space inside was used for in times of peace. Hillforts vary widely in form, location, age and cultural context, and so it is not surprising that their use and meaning was variable across different prehistoric societies. As Cunliffe (2006) has observed, 'there may be no such thing as a typical hillfort'. Those meanings would have evolved over time, as hillforts acquired new significance though habitual use, and as economic and socio-political circumstances changed in their respective societies.

As the name suggests, military and defensive considerations loom large in any discussion of hillforts. The basic and widely held definition of a hillfort is 'a site fortified so as to be defensible against human attack' (Avery 1976: 30). This was achieved by creation of physical barriers, such as the types listed above, and by the tactical use of natural terrain at locations that enjoyed a commanding position in the landscape. Despite these important features of hillfort design, the defensibility of many sites can be questioned in terms of their overall size and extended perimeters, restricted visibility, limited water supply and exposed locations. The 'refuge' theory of hillfort use is problematic for the same reasons. This is only an issue if we consider hillfort design in terms of passive defence, when it is unlikely that siege warfare was ever practised at these sites.

The defensive potential of each hillfort needs to be assessed on its own merits, allowing for topographical location, the size and layout of the enclosure(s), the strength of the enclosing element(s), and the form of the entrance(s). Even then, there is the uncertainty of what constituted the active force of defenders, and the possibility that the real defensive value of a hillfort was one of deterrence. Understanding the nature of hillfort warfare is further complicated by the likelihood that many confrontations took place some distance away from these sites. Depending on the outcome, the hillfort itself may have become a strategic target, as a place of final resistance and refuge, a store of wealth that could be pillaged, and as a symbol of group identity chosen for punitive destruction.

While more investigations are required, there is enough excavation evidence to confirm that some, but perhaps not all, hillforts in Ireland were used for permanent occupation. While elite residence is suggested in most cases, the size and composition of the group concerned is generally unclear. Unlike later hillforts in Britain and the Continent, the Irish evidence does not indicate a proto-urban layout or a large residential community. There is also the phenomenon of the 'empty hillfort', and whether this is connected to original site use or to limited archaeological investigation.

Who lived inside these hillforts is a major research question. The controlling aspect of their location and design points to the powerful in society and most hillforts are interpreted with reference to the presence of a chief or leader, living there with family and retinue, separate from or as part of a large community. In some cases, the special character of structures and artifacts in the hillfort is consistent with elite residence and with conspicuous consumption of material wealth and exotica. The source of this chiefly power is always contentious. This is often attributed to core economic functions of hillforts, such as centralised storage and redistribution of commodities, trade in raw materials and exotica, and patronage of specialist crafts such as metalworking. Each site needs to be assessed separately, as there is obvious variability in terms of environmental circumstances and economic priorities.

Excavation and environmental records suggest that farming was also a critical resource, with most hillforts part of a wider landscape of agricultural settlement. This may be a consideration in the size and design of Class 2 hillforts in Ireland, which may have been used as compounds for livestock in addition to other uses. The importance of cattle and cattle-raiding is well attested in Irish epic literature (Lucas 1989), which may preserve oral tradition that extends back to the later Bronze Age.

The basis of chiefly power may lie in other areas. Warfare and aggression are obvious candidates to explain the expansion of hillfort power. The emergence of these sites is often explained as a consequence of growing political instability during the Bronze Age in Europe. This is tied to militarist tendencies in society, represented by the increased output of specialized weapons such as bronze swords and spearheads, which in turn reflect the rise of a warrior class. In this model the status of leaders derives from prowess in battle and necessarily involves belligerent relations with other hillfort warlords.

The ceremonial aspects of hillfort use must also be considered. Given their prominence in the landscape, it is likely that these locations were important places of assembly. Harding (2012: 282) makes a distinction between different types of assembly for the related or dependent community. This includes social (seasonal festivals, marriages etc), economic (markets, craft centres etc), political (inauguration, alliances etc), and ritual (funerals, votive displays etc) assembly, many of which were mutually embedded with multiple meanings for the group in question. Such roles are not well understood in the Irish record, partly because of a lack of large-scale excavations, but also because many such gatherings may have left little archaeological evidence.

Excavation confirms that many hillforts contained areas of ritual space and religious observance. These elevated locations may have had liminal significance, where the world of the living met the supernatural. This was given added significance by the presence of older burial mounds in many sites. The high status of their occupancy explains the presence of elite funerary complexes and ritual deposition of material culture within or close to the hillfort. These associations added significantly to the importance of hillforts over time, and were an important resource for the exercise of social power.

Some of the most interesting hillfort questions centre on details of their use and eventual abandonment. Each hillfort had its own unique history of occupation, the details of which were contingent on local and wider historical and environmental circumstances. The occupation of hillforts was affected by many inter-linked variables, such as environmental change, population pressure, cycles of economic expansion and decline, religious prescription, and social relations within and outside of the group in question. The latter is of particular interest to this volume, as it includes the role that warfare played in the political relations of regional hillfort groups in southern Ireland. These changes in social organization may also explain the development of hillforts over a long period from their emergence in the Middle Bronze Age to the collapse of their society around the eighth century BC.

Hillforts, landscape and society

Though often considered as discrete monuments, no hillfort was an island, in that these great enclosures were connected to a wider cultural landscape of farms and fields, route-ways and settlements, and places of religious significance. Understanding these archaeological landscapes is an important focus of modern research, from local investigations to the regional scale in studies such as the Danebury Environs Project in southern England (Cunliffe 2000 *et seq.*), or the North Munster Project in Ireland (Grogan 2005). Chronology was a major concern for these projects, in terms of distinguishing settlements and other cultural features that were contemporary with the main periods of hillfort use from the larger palimpsest of activity in the landscape. More research is also required into the environmental context of hillforts; for example, to examine how these sites relate to different types of anthropogenic impact in the pollen record. While the construction of most hillforts is unlikely to register as such, the large amount of wood required for some defensive arrangements makes this a possibility. Most pollen impacts will come from agricultural activity associated with the hillfort and its associated settlement, though any disturbance or collapse of these economic systems through warfare has the potential to be recorded. There has been some research in this area in Ireland (Molloy 2005; Plunkett 2006), but more needs to be done.

The building of a hillfort had a significant symbolic impact in terms of its imposing presence in the landscape. This promoted a sense of group identity by controlling access to a central place and by the exclusion of outsiders. In that sense the building of hillforts was important in the symbolic construction of community and was a striking physical affirmation of tribal power. This is not to suggest that the act of construction was more important that its intended use, as the latter is borne out by the evidence of prolonged occupation in many sites.

In conclusion, hillforts have much potential to inform us about the organization of prehistoric societies. They are often placed at the apex of a settlement hierarchy that extends far into the surrounding landscape. This perspective is based on the imposing nature of these central places, the evidence of elite residence, and the highly visible concentration of wealth under the control of a particular individual or group. The 'rise of the privileged' is a broad social phenomenon with origins in the Chalcolithic, which has its strongest expression in the chiefdom societies of the European Bronze Age (Kristiansen 1999; Kristiansen and Larsson 2005). This model has been criticised in recent years (e.g. Brück and Fontijn 2013), with alternatives to the power paradigm including the use of hillforts as community assembly locations with a range of communal functions and religious associations.

1.3 Hillforts, Warfare and Society in Bronze Age Ireland

This project developed out of earlier research that examined different aspects of late prehistoric landscapes in south-west Ireland. The Local Worlds project (2002–4) was a study of early hill farming in the Beara Peninsula of West Cork (O'Brien 2009). This involved analysis of a series of important landscape records of ancient fields and settlement features preserved under blanket bog. The study examined the land-use dynamics of these upland locations to explore themes of settlement continuity and change from the Bronze Age to medieval and early modern times.

This was followed in 2004 by the Iverni Project, with research designed to examine themes of continuity and change from the Bronze Age to the Iron Age (O'Brien 2012). While the latter has often been connected to external agency ('the coming of the Celts'), the absence of a significant La Tène material culture in south Munster highlighted the importance of the indigenous populations, and the possibility that a regional Iron Age culture was marked by significant continuity from the Late Bronze Age.

One of the key elements of the Iverni Project was the investigation of a large hillfort in Co. Cork in its local landscape setting (Figure 1.1). The investigation of Clashanimud hillfort (8ha) was a significant undertaking, with some 37 trenches excavated over three seasons in 2004–6 (O'Brien 2016a). The site history is interesting as there is no evidence of significant occupation, while the strong fortifications there were destroyed by fire not long after the hillfort was built around 1100 BC (Figure

FIGURE 1.3: ARCHAEOLOGICAL EXCAVATION OF DEFENCES TO INNER ENCLOSURE, CLASHANIMUD HILLFORT, SUMMER 2005.

1.3). The circumstances of this destruction raised several issues concerning the prevalence of warfare in Late Bronze Age Ireland, questions that ultimately led to this project.

Project Design

In 2011 the author received major funding from the Irish Research Council for a study of hillforts, warfare and society in Bronze Age Ireland. The project is designed to examine the archaeological evidence for warfare and inter-regional conflict during the later Bronze Age (1500–700 BC). This includes a consideration of weapons, fortifications, metal hoarding and burials in local and regional landscape contexts. The focus is the strategic role of Class 2 hillforts in the political landscape of that period (Figure 1.2), considered with reference to models of chiefdom organization, competition and territoriality, communication and exchange.

The following are the research aims, along with objectives and methodologies designed to achieve these outcomes:

1. To create a revised data-base of prehistoric hillforts in Ireland. *This required a review of hillfort morphology and classification, using available site information in combination with aerial survey and fieldwork data.*

2. To increase knowledge of hillfort morphology through remote sensing survey. *This involved geophysical and lidar survey of selected hillforts in southern Ireland.*

3. To achieve greater understanding of hillfort design, use-history and abandonment. *This involved analysis of excavation results from Clashanimud hillfort, Co. Cork.*

4. To produce a new chronology of prehistoric hillforts in Ireland. *Along with the Clashanimud results, sample excavation was undertaken at nine other hillforts to recover radiocarbon and other dating evidence.*

5. To explore possible connections between hillforts and warfare in Bronze Age Ireland. *This involved a detailed analysis of the defences at ten excavated hillforts, in terms of their original design and the evidence of deliberate destruction possibly linked to warfare.*

6. To investigate the cultural landscape setting of an individual hillfort. *A study of the environs of Clashanimud hillfort, Co. Cork.*

7. To examine the landscape context of a major cluster of prehistoric hillforts. *This involved a GIS-based analysis of the Baltinglass complex of hillforts in Co. Wicklow, using results of field survey and excavation in combination with remote sensing data.*

8. To assess the current condition and protection of prehistoric hillforts in Ireland. *Fieldwork and analysis of aerial imagery was undertaken to identify major impacts on the archaeological resource.*

The project provides a synthesis of information on hillforts and warfare, dealing with fortifications and weaponry, burials, settlement territory, frontier zones and routeways. This will consider whether hillforts could have provided effective protection for their occupants in the face of military onslaught. The study examines the relationship of Late Bronze Age weapon finds (swords, spearheads etc) to hillfort strongholds and associated frontier zones. This will hopefully lead to a better understanding of the strategic role of hillforts in Bronze Age societies. The wider context of this militarism is considered in relation to current models of chiefdom society. The overall aim is to understand the rise and collapse of those regional hillfort societies and their political relations.

Methodology

There is a strong fieldwork element in this project. This centred on detailed survey and excavation of nine prehistoric hillforts in southern Ireland, in addition to the major excavation conducted at Clashanimud, Co. Cork (Figure 1.2). These include Glanbane, Co. Kerry; Ballylin, Co. Limerick; Formoyle, Co. Clare; Toor More, Co. Kilkenny; and five sites in the Baltinglass complex, namely Spinans Hill 1, Rathnagree, Sruhaun, and Tinoran in Co. Wicklow, and Hughstown, Co. Kildare. Geophysical survey was also conducted at the hillforts of Knigh, Co. Tipperary, and Rathcoran, Co. Wicklow. The fieldwork programme involved the following:

- Fieldwalking and descriptive survey of selected hillforts.

- Lidar survey to map hillfort morphology and terrain setting, used in combination with conventional aerial survey and GPS/total station mapping on the ground (Figure 1.4).

- GIS analysis of hillfort landscapes, with 3-D visualization of their strategic setting.

- Geophysical survey to investigate the interior and enclosing elements of selected hillforts (Figure 1.5).

- Sample excavation to examine the form and history of the defences at selected hillforts (Figure 1.6).

While excavation of the physical defences provides some insight into the history of these hillforts, it does not shed much light on the community or activities therein. The project addressed this with large-scale excavation at

Clashanimud hillfort, and through blanket geophysical survey at other hillforts.

Project Team

The Principal Investigator (WO'B) had overall responsibility for the design, conduct and completion of this research project. He directed the excavation programme, and overall analysis of the project results and this publication. Dr James O'Driscoll was the lead research assistant on the project, with responsibility for the hillfort database, and for geophysical survey at selected hillforts, assisted in the field by Dr Alan Hawkes. In 2013 he commenced doctoral research, separately funded by the Irish Research Council, looking at the Baltinglass complex of hillforts in south-west Wicklow (O'Driscoll 2016). The excavation programme was supervised by Nick Hogan, who assisted with computing applications and provided many of the illustrations in this volume. He also conducted geophysical surveys at Clashanimud hillfort and Formoyle hillfort, working with Liam Hickey at both sites. The various excavation projects were supported by Dr Alan Hawkes and Dr James O'Driscoll, and by Caen Harris, Kevin Kearney, James Lineen, Liam O'Brien and Sean Sharpe.

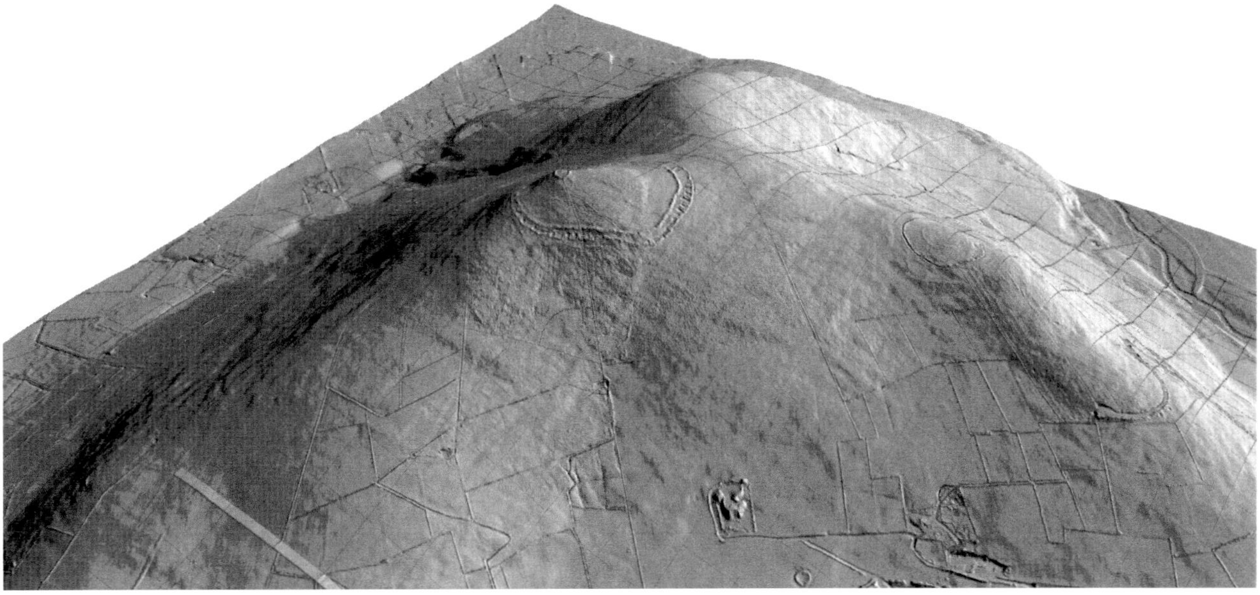

FIGURE 1.4: LIDAR IMAGE OF PREHISTORIC HILLFORTS ON TUCKMILL HILL, BALTINGLASS, CO. WICKLOW.

FIGURE 1.5: GEOPHYSICAL SURVEY (MAGNETIC GRADIOMETRY) AT KNIGH HILLFORT, CO. TIPPERARY.

FIGURE 1.6: SAMPLE EXCAVATION AT HUGHSTOWN HILLFORT, CO. WICKLOW, SUMMER 2016.

Project Schedule

Stage 1: Background research and database, 2011–12
Work on this project began with a review of the relevant literature on prehistoric hillforts and ancient warfare in Ireland, with reference to parallel developments in Britain and the Continent. Consultation of published sources and State inventories made it possible to revise the existing database of hillforts in Ireland. The analysis of this data provides information on the average size, form and landscape setting of these monuments. Lists of Middle and Late Bronze Age swords, shields, hoards and other metalwork were compiled for comparison with hillfort distributions.

Stage 2: Hillfort surveys, 2012–13
Detailed surveys were undertaken by James O'Driscoll at ten hillforts in this project, namely Ballylin, Co. Limerick; Glanbane, Co. Kerry; Formoyle, Co. Clare; Knigh, Co. Tipperary; Toor More, Co. Kilkenny and the sites of Rathnagree, Sruhaun, Tinoran, Rathcoran and Hughstown in the Baltinglass area, Co. Wicklow. The interiors and enclosing elements of these hillforts were mapped using GPS and/or lidar survey. Geophysical survey was also undertaken, either of the entire enclosure or those parts that were accessible. The surface and sub-surface mapping is supported by descriptive recording, topographic profiling and ground photography. The Clashanimud and Formoyle hillforts were surveyed by Nick Hogan and Liam Hickey. Airborne lidar surveys were commissioned for the Ballylin and Rathcoran sites from a Coleraine-based company, Fugro-BKS Ltd (Figure 1.4). Where available, lidar data and aerial photographs for the other sites were obtained from Ordnance Survey Ireland.

Stage 3: Sample hillfort excavations, 2012–16
Sample excavation was undertaken at nine hillforts in this project (Figure 1.2). This work commenced in summer 2012 with investigations at Ballylin, Co. Limerick; Glanbane, Co. Kerry, and Formoyle, Co. Clare. This was followed in summer 2013 by investigations at Toor More hillfort, Co. Kilkenny. Sample excavation was conducted over the next three summers at five sites in the Baltinglass complex of south-west Wicklow (Figure 1.6), namely Spinans Hill 1, Rathnagree, Sruhaun, Tinoran, culminating in a second season of excavation in July 2016 at Hughstown, Co. Kildare.

Stage 4: Postgraduate research 2013–17
PhD project: James O'Driscoll 'The Prehistoric Hillforts of Co. Wicklow'
On-line publication: http://hdl.handle.net/10468/3532

This study, completed in 2016, examined the cultural significance of a unique cluster of large hillforts in the Baltinglass area of south-west Wicklow, described by some as 'Ireland's hillfort capital' in the west Wicklow

Mountains. This is the first detailed study of any hillfort cluster in Ireland, and the first application of archaeological remote sensing and conventional survey methods to what is an exceptional group of nine hillforts, including some the largest examples in Ireland. The cultural significance of these sites was examined, using an interpretative framework of landscape archaeology to consider the socio-political, economic and ideological importance of these sites in their contemporary societies. The form, function, economy and strategic positioning of these monuments was analysed using a combination of desk-top research, GIS (Geographic Information Systems), LiDAR (Light Detecting and Ranging), geophysical surveying techniques and conventional fieldwork.

MPhil project: The Bronze Age spearheads of Ireland (Lineen 2017) On-line publication: https://independent.academia.edu/JimLineen

The project also supported a study of bronze spearheads, one of the best-known weapon types of the Irish Bronze Age. The adoption of these weapons at different times during the second millennium BC in Europe coincided with the emergence of a warrior identity and a more explicit manifestation of warfare in the archaeological record. The work provides an overview of the introduction and development of the bronze spearhead in Ireland c.1600–600 BC, based on the first comprehensive catalogue of these weapons in Ireland. The study, completed in 2017, examined contextual aspects of spearhead use and deposition during the Middle and Late Bronze Age, in an effort to understand the changing use and perception of these weapons in contemporary landscape contexts, from hunting to warfare, to their symbolic value in military and religious settings.

Stage 5: *The Atlas of Hillforts of Britain and Ireland* https://hillforts.arch.ox.ac.uk/
The study also contributed to this four-year project directed by Professors Gary Lock (University of Oxford) and Ian Ralston (University of Edinburgh), with funding from the UK Arts and Humanities Research Council. This ambitious project involved the collection and collation of data on some 4000 recorded hillforts across Britain and Ireland, to create an interactive online database and a published atlas. In 2015–17 James O'Driscoll and Alan Hawkes compiled the Irish section of the Atlas, using information from published sources and State inventories, as well as data presented in this volume.

Stage 6: Project completion 2015–17
The final stages of research involved post-excavation analysis of the Clashanimud project, and the compilation of a detailed archive report (O'Brien 2015). Post-excavation analysis was also undertaken of the nine hillforts sampled in this project, with final reports submitted to the licensing authority. Doctoral research on the Baltinglass hillfort landscape (O'Driscoll 2016), was completed, as was the study of Bronze Age spearheads (Lineen 2016). A series of peer-reviewed journal articles were published, presenting the results of different aspects of the project (O'Brien 2016a; O'Brien 2016b; O'Brien, Hogan and O'Driscoll 2014–15; O'Brien, O'Driscoll and Hogan 2016; O'Brien, Hogan and O'Driscoll 2016; O'Driscoll 2017). Final reports on licensed geophysical survey and excavation work were submitted to the National Monuments Service in Ireland. The project concluded with preparation of this monograph, with other research articles planned for publication in coming years.

1.4 This Volume

The project hopes to highlight the important role warfare played in shaping Bronze Age societies in Ireland, with specific reference to the hillfort. The study commences with a general overview of the prehistoric hillfort in Ireland (Chapter 2). The distribution and landscape of these enclosures is presented, with details of classification, morphology and size. The history of research is examined, with reference to past excavations and landscape research, and an overview of chronology.

This background information is followed by the results of the 2004–6 excavation of Clashanimud hillfort in Co. Cork (Chapter 3). The details of that project are presented, including excavation strategy, stratification, analysis of assemblage materials, and radiocarbon dating. This is followed by an examination of the hillfort environs and wider cultural landscape. The next chapter deals with sample excavations conducted in 2012–3 at four Class 2 hillforts in southern Ireland (Chapter 4). These include Glanbane, Co. Kerry; Ballylin, Co. Limerick; Formoyle, Co. Clare; and Toor More, Co. Kilkenny. The enclosing elements of those hillforts are examined, with details of their construction and abandonment supported by radiocarbon records.

This is followed by the first of three chapters dealing with an important complex of hillforts in Baltinglass, Co. Wicklow (Chapter 5). The form, distribution and landscape setting of sites in what is described as 'Ireland's hillfort capital' (Condit 1992) is presented. This includes the results of LiDAR and geophysical survey undertaken for the project (Figure 1.4). Chapter 6 presents the results of sample excavations conducted in 2014–6 at five of these Baltinglass hillforts. These include (east to west) Spinans Hill 1, Rathnagree, Sruhaun, and Tinoran in Co. Wicklow, and the nearby site of Hughstown, Co. Kildare. Again, the focus is on the enclosing elements, their structural details and history, supported by radiocarbon results.

The next chapter is a review of the chronology of

hillforts in Ireland in light of the results from these ten new hillfort investigations (Chapter 7). The dating of the construction and destruction/abandonment of individual hillforts is discussed, with detailed analysis of the Clashanimud chronology. The dating of the important Baltinglass complex is discussed, and a chronological model presented for the evolution of this hillfort landscape. This provides dating control for a GIS-based landscape analysis, the first such study ever undertaken for prehistoric hillforts in Ireland (Chapter 8). The study examines the topographic siting and visibility of nine hillforts and enclosure sites located on five hills in the Baltinglass area, looking at aspects of access and routeways.

The final two chapters bring together the results of these hillfort investigations to discuss their significance for the research aims of the project. This includes a consideration of hillfort destruction in relation to the conduct of warfare among the hillfort polities of Middle and Late Bronze Age Ireland (Chapter 9). The tactical siting of hillforts, their defensibility and practical use as enclosures, is examined. The evidence of warfare in the wider landscape is assessed, with reference to weapon finds and burials. The volume concludes by discussing the origins and development of the hillfort in Ireland (Chapter 10). There is also a discussion of broader themes of hillfort use, such as trade and communication, as well as a review of different models of social organization.

Finally, this research provides information that can contribute to the public presentation of prehistoric hillforts as major heritage attractions in Ireland. The knowledge presented will provide an informed public with detailed information about the chronology, construction, function and cultural context of these important sites. The sharing of field survey data-sets with State heritage agencies and community groups allows for hillforts to be presented through information plaques, walking trails and heritage tourism web-sites. This includes the development of a proposed heritage park at Clashanimud hillfort, funding for which is now being sought. Another objective is to increase awareness of ongoing threats to the preservation of prehistoric hillforts in Ireland. A very significant number of these sites have been damaged by forestry and the construction of telecommunication masts, windfarms etc. The hillfort surveys presented in this volume will assist in the future management of these important monuments. At the very least, this field information should raise major concerns among State heritage bodies as to the current state of protection of hillforts in Ireland.

2

Prehistoric Hillforts

This chapter will review archaeological evidence for hillforts and hilltop settlements in Bronze Age Europe.

2.1 Hillforts in Prehistoric Europe

In Europe, the concept of enclosing hilltop sites is a recurring feature from the Neolithic period onwards. However, during the later part of the Early Bronze Age, fortified hilltop settlements became more common (Harding 2007a). Hillforts were mainly constructed in three periods: during the transition between the Early to Middle Bronze Age (1800–1600), Middle to Late Bronze Age (1300–1000) and Late Bronze Age/Early Iron Age (800–600). Jockenhövel (2013: 740) has discussed this cyclical fluctuation in terms of the German evidence and has connected it to changing social, economic, and ecological conditions. In many instances, there is no settlement continuity, particularly after the first cycle of hillfort construction, where hilltop settlements were almost completely abandoned throughout Europe (*ibid.*: 740).

The beginning of the Late Bronze Age, around 1300 BC, brought about the most intensive building cycle, when there was a significant increase in hilltop fortification throughout Urnfield and Atlantic Europe (Harding 2000: 296). Considering this prolonged period of construction, and despite the problems of classification and terminology, Ralston (2006) has suggested that there may be up to 30,000 hillforts in Europe. Their distribution is concentrated in Central Europe, in Britain, France, Germany, Spain, Austria, Switzerland, Poland, Slovakia, Hungary and the Czech Republic, although distributional variability occurs across the three identified construction phases. Considering the number of hillforts in Europe, it is not surprising that a definitive distribution map has not been produced and only regional data-sets are available.

Early/Middle Bronze Age

Early hillforts were often built near natural resources or in areas that could control the flow and distribution of such materials. A fort may have been a visible means of both protecting the natural resources and projecting the ownership of these raw materials through the use of monumental architecture. In many cases, artefacts indicative of metalworking are found within these sites. Early hillforts are rare in western countries such as France or Germany and are generally concentrated in the Alpine region, although some 'castros' are found in the Early Bronze Age in some parts of north-west Spain and Portugal (Pardo *et al.* 2009).

The fortified settlement at Bruszczewo, Poland is positioned at a spur of high ground overlooking a lake-shore to the east. It comprises a ditch up to 4m in depth and up to 21m wide, with two palisade trenches immediately inside, and encloses an area of approximately 1.5ha (Czebreszuk and Müller 2004; Müller and Czebreszuk 2010). Dendrochronological dates place the construction and early occupation of the site to around 1800–1700 BC. The occurrence of metalworking at the site, and the distribution of contemporary monuments in its environs, led Müller and Czebreszuk (2010: 395) to interpret Bruszczewo as a central place strategically positioned to control trade and communication. In fact, connections between hillforts and low-land settlements may have been common during this period. Primas (2002: 45) has suggested that the material assemblage of hilltop sites along the Danube and in the Slovakian mountains indicate that they were linked to lowland settlement, sites such as the 'Tells' of the Hungarian Plain.

Other early hillforts occur in Slovakia at Spišsky Štvrtok and Nitriansky Hrádok, both of which comprise substantial stone walls. Spišsky Štvrtok is located in eastern Slovakia and has been dated to the later part of the Early Bronze Age. The site has a total footprint of 6.6ha (Gogâltan 2008: 52). The western part of the settlement abuts a steep natural slope and was protected by a palisade with stone footing. An external ditch measuring 6m wide and 2m deep was identified on the eastern side. In the northern and southern section, an earthen bank with internal and external stone facing was constructed. Another stone wall was built inside and parallel to the latter. A single entrance flanked by two round towers is visible to the east (*ibid.*: 52). Nitriansky Hrádok is of similar construction, although the entire settlement was surrounded by a ditch and the entrance did not incorporate flanking towers (Točík 1981). Spišsky Štvrtok was destroyed by fire, while Nitriansky Hrádok was abandoned with no traces of destruction (Gogâltan 2008: 52). Primas notes that sites with strong ramparts with an internal structure of wooden beams evolved during the Early Bronze Age in eastern parts of Europe (Primas 2002: 44).

In the Alpine region, large numbers of hillforts, positioned in strategic locations, date to this period (Della Casa 2013: 714; Jiráň *et al.* 2013: 791; Krause 2008: 65). Krause interprets these hillforts as central places that controlled smaller neighbouring sites and copper ore deposits in the vicinity. In Germany, Early Bronze Age hillforts are confined to the regions influenced by the Middle Danube Culture in southern Germany, in the plains north of the Alps (Jockenhövel 2013: 740). This may be connected, at least in part, to a need to control the flow of copper near its source (Kienlin 2013: 424). The numerous finds from higher elevations and mountain passes, indicates the intensive use of these routes for exchange and communication between the inner Alpine valleys (Krause 2007: 120; Krause 2008: 65; Della Casa 2002).

In Austria, early hillforts in the Alpine region, such as Götschenberg at Bishofshofen (Lippert 1992) and St Veit Klinglberg in the Salzach Valley (Shennan 1995), were constructed around 1600 BC, in areas close to sites of mineral extraction. The Klinglberg hillfort was built at the edge of a mountainous spur in a strategically positioned part of the Danube Valley, overlooking the River Salzburg and positioned close to sources of copper, gold, iron and salt (Shennan 1995: 23). The enclosing elements were constructed after an initial phase of open settlement. Excavation revealed the enclosing elements consisted of a rubble stone wall approximately 2m in width and up to 2.5m high. This wall was approximately 100m in length and protected the western, most accessible approach. Radiocarbon dates and the distribution of pottery suggest that the wall was built around 1685–1400 BC (*ibid.*: 281). A number of domestic structures were excavated within the interior and a large pottery assemblage was recovered (*ibid.*: 283). The vast majority of the assemblage is tempered with copper slag (*ibid.*: 253; 283). Ceramic analysis suggests that some of this pottery may have been imported from the nearby hillfort at Götschenberg (see Lippert 1992). Metal items represent the most common non-ceramic finds from Klinglberg, the majority comprising small fragments and lumps of raw cast metal (Shennan 1995: 285). These were all made of copper, rather than bronze, which may indicate the settlement was involved in the production and control of raw copper. Shennan (1995: 287) suggests that the small animal bone assemblage and lack of evidence for cereal cultivation near the site may indicate food stocks were imported and possibly traded for raw copper.

A similar situation occurred at the contemporary hillfort of Götschenberg. The latter is situated on an impressive rock outcrop, with extensive views of the Salzach valley and the Mitterberg mining district. Early activity associated with copper mining was abandoned by the end of the fourth millennium BC. The site was re-occupied around 2000 BC and after a period of open settlement, an enclosure was constructed using stone walls to cut off the northern and north-western approach. Shennan (1995: 290) suggests that the abandonment of the site may be associated with the expansion of centralised control in the Mitterberg-Pongau region, where a single centre controlled the mines and copper trade of the entire region.

A recently discovered hillfort at Bartholomäberg, in the Friaga Wald in Montafon, Austria, can also be linked with early mining activity. The site is located in the Alps above the Sole and Schruns Valleys, where the Litz River flows out of the Silbertal into the Ill River. This is a strategic position with extensive views of the surrounding valleys (Krause 2003: 219). The hillfort was probably constructed at the beginning of the Middle Bronze Age. It comprises a promontory separated from the landward side by a 2–3m wide stone bank that could have stood up to 2–3m, and rock cut ditch (*ibid.*: 216–217). The fort was divided by an internal wall that dates to the beginning of the Middle Bronze Age (*ibid.*: 214). The excavator suggests a similar date may be proposed for the outer wall. The presence of copper and iron ores at the site may indicate that prospecting and exploration of ores occurred prior to construction of the hillfort. Krause (2008: 79) has argued that hillforts such as Bartholomäberg were at the summit of a hierarchy of Bronze Age settlements in Montafon, with a structured society and governing leadership that probably controlled mining and metal production.

During this period, many hillforts produce evidence for craftworking of various types. An excellent example is Sotciastel hillfort in the southern Italian Alps. The site is positioned on a mountain spur in a commanding position overlooking a prominent north–south running valley. A stone wall protects the most accessible approach and occupation of the interior dates to the end of the Early Bronze Age (Tecchiati 1998). Metal objects and a mould for casting axes were found during excavation. This hillfort was not directly involved in copper ore mining, as the site is too far from copper sources. However, a bead of blue glass paste and a number of leaf-shaped clay tablets, which have a widespread distribution throughout the Alpine region, indicate that the hillfort was embedded in a wider network of communication and trade (Primas 2002: 47).

Hillforts were built for a variety of functions during this early period, though it is clear that the control of trade and communication routes was a paramount concern. Della Casa (2013: 714) has identified a concentration of largely undated hillforts in the Alpine Rhine Valley between Chur and Bregenz. The sites are usually positioned in commanding hilltops along the edges of the valley and Della Casa (2007; 2013: 715) has suggested their importance as trans-Alpine routeways. He argues that such sites are positioned on natural obstacles in order to control access and transit. Ochsenberg hillfort, near Wartau, Switzerland has a similar topographical position. This hillfort comprises a stone wall constructed along the eastern face of a hilltop at the edge of the Rhine valley. This enclosing element was built at approximately 1800 BC and preceded earlier habitation (Primas 2002: 49). The discovery of numerous storage pits within the interior is notable (*ibid.*: 49). Della Casa (2013: 714–715) suggests that the site holds an excellent strategic position, which must have been a key factor in the location of the hillfort.

Primas (2002: 44) notes that a common feature of Early Bronze Age hillforts is their excellent visibility at potential routes of traffic, cross-roads, or river crossings. However, open settlements on hilltops also occupied such strategic positions in the landscape. An excellent example is a settlement on Frauenberg hilltop, near Weltenburg, Germany. The site is in a commanding position that overlooks the Danube River before it cuts through a mountain ridge. The hilltop was settled in the Early Bronze Age, but was probably not enclosed until 1200 BC. The importance of this natural routeway is further attested in the location of the Early Bronze Age hillfort on the Michelsberg near Kelheim, Germany, positioned at the other end of the mountain pass.

Middle/Late Bronze Age

During the Middle Bronze Age hilltop settlements were almost completely abandoned, and construction ceased across Central Europe (Jockenhövel 1990: 219; 2013:740). It is not until the beginning of the Late Bronze Age (around 1300 BC) that hilltops began to be fortified in different parts of the Continent, with a highly structured method of enclosure in place involving considerable natural and human resources (Harding 2000: 298). The sudden intensification of hillfort construction during this period has been described as unprecedented (Primas 2002: 50). Jockenhövel (2013: 740) notes as estimated 100 examples of hillforts in southern, central and eastern Germany from this period, while Primas (2002: 43) states that hillforts with radiocarbon-dated enclosing elements in this area seem to be a Late Bronze Age phenomenon. This construction phase was highly dispersed, with hillforts being built throughout Atlantic and Urnfield Europe. It is during this period that the first known hillforts in Britain and Ireland were constructed.

Härke (1979: 31) has noted that a large number of German hillforts such as Glauberg and Bliebeskopf at the Wetterau loess basin, or Dommelberg overlooking the Neuwied basin, among others, are associated with densely settled fertile areas. Although it is likely that this topographical relationship can be applied to other regions, the importance of controlling natural routeways seems to be a continuing concern for hillfort builders. Jockenhövel (1975: 57) points out that many German hillforts of the Urnfield period were located along important long-distance routes. The enclosing elements usually comprise an unsophisticated layout with simple entrance features (Jockenhovel 2013: 741; Härke 1979:30; 166–167), a trend apparent in hillfort layout throughout Europe, including Britain and Ireland (Lynch *et al.* 2000:15). There is often dense settlement in the interiors, which may indicate increasing population (Jockenhövel 2013: 741; Härke 1979: 30), although there are also examples where well defended hillforts show low levels of settlement activity, an example being Thinsberg hillfort in northern Switzerland. Interestingly, there is a notable increase in the evidence for violence at these sites and traces of destruction are not uncommon (Thorpe 2013: 240). Harding (2001: 334) and Bogucki (2004: 88–89) both suggest that 'almost all' of the Urnfield hillforts in Central Europe were rapidly destroyed, with artefact assemblages often indicating a single phase of occupation that rarely exceeded one hundred years. Similarly, Härke (1979: 33) has noted the presence of burnt destruction layers at many German hillforts. An excellent example of this is Biskupin hillfort in Poland, where up to three phases of Late Bronze Age settlement was destroyed and rebuilt in rapid succession (Harding 2001: 335).

The hillfort at Velim, Bohemia, Czech Republic, was destroyed soon after construction and there is substantial evidence indicating that this site was attacked. Positioned on a low hill, Velim overlooks an old branch of the Labe River, believed to be a significant prehistoric communication route (Harding *et al.* 2007: 154). The fort was constructed around 1400 BC and comprises an inner ditch and palisade, and an outer ditch and palisade, with isolated pits dispersed irregularly across the site (*ibid*: 144). Almost all of these pits contained human bone, with the remains being haphazardly deposited. Evidence of peri-mortem trauma is apparent and some crania were found separated from other remains with evidence for attempted decapitation. In part of the ditch, a minimum of thirty individuals were discovered with traces of cutting, breaking and chopping. Twenty six socketed bronze arrowheads were found on site, although the precise locations are unknown. This evidence might indicate that a hostile attack on the site, although other explanations cannot be discounted. The site was abandoned after a catastrophic burning event that destroyed the entire fort. There is a similar site, also dating to the Late Bronze Age, at Cezavy Hill near Blucina in Moracia, Czech Republic. There, incomplete skeletons were often deposited with bronze artefacts that could have been produced onsite (Jiran *et al.* 2013: 792). Cezavy Hill is interpreted as a religious centre on a commanding height, where cult rituals were repeatedly carried out in association with the production of metal goods (*ibid.*: 792).

The Heunischenburg hillfort near Kronach, Bavaria, Germany, is located on a high mountain spur near the summit of the Bergsporn des Wolfsbergs. The site was possibly positioned to control copper and tin resources in the area. The landward approach at the north-east was protected by a palisade built around the first half of the 10th century BC, before being replaced by a 2.6m wide and 3.5m high stone wall. A substantial wooden gateway was positioned at the eastern edge of the wall. A wooden fence probably surrounded the remainder of the site, which was already protected by naturally steep slopes (Abels 2002). The later phase of the site was destroyed by fire. Bronze weapons, including a large number of arrowheads, some of them burnt, fragments of swords, spearheads and possibly armour, may be indicative of a hostile attack (Thorpe 2013: 240).

The site of Bernstorf, near Freising, Germany is situated on a hilltop overlooking the River Amper. The enclosing element comprises a bank with a palisade at its crest (Moosauer and Bachmaier 2000). Radiocarbon dates from burnt wooden posts indicate that the enclosing elements were constructed *c.*1675–1330 BC and a dendrochronological date gave a *terminus post quem* of 1360 BC for construction (Primas 2002: 51). Amber artefacts and an impressive assemblage of gold may indicate that Bernstorf functioned as a means of controlling trade routes and high status goods in the region. Excavation suggests that the wooden palisade was systematically destroyed (Moosauer and Bachmaier 2000). Although there is no evidence to suggest that the fort was destroyed in a hostile attack, this remains a possibility.

The Late Bronze Age hillfort at Limberg, Austria, was also destroyed when its box rampart was burnt down (Schindler 1968; 1974: 435). The Bullenheimer Berg in northern Barvaria, Germany is another example of a large hillfort with timber enclosing elements destroyed by fire (Diemer 1995). Across Europe at this time, there is a notable increase in the incorporation of wood into the defences of hillforts (Primas 2002: 50), and their destruction by fire may indicate that there was a well-known way of destroyed these sites. This has also been noted in Britain, at sites such Rams Hill, England (Bradley and Ellison 1975; Needham and Ambers 1994), Taplow, England (Allen *et al.* 2009), Thwing, England (Manby 2007) and Springfield Lyons in England (Buckley and Hedges 1987), among others. Cunliffe (1991: 313) has suggested that in Britain, the earliest type of hilltop enclosure of hillfort proportions was the palisaded enclosure. Earthen hillforts were also constructed during this period in Britain, such as Camp Gardens, Stow-on-the-Wold, England, dated to 1400–990 BC (Parry 1999) and Fairfield, Stotfold, England, built at 1250–1000 BC (Webley *et al.* 2007). Allen *et al.* (2009: 191) suggest that the dating evidence implies that the floruit for these early hillforts seems to have begun around 1100 BC and continued to around 900 or 800 BC.

There is growing evidence to suggest that by the Late Bronze Age metalworking and specialized craftworking was taking place within or immediately outside some hillforts. Lull *et al.* (2013: 612) have highlighted that all of the excavated hilltops sites in Portugal, such as Senhora da Guia de Baiões in Beira Alta, have produced evidence for metalworking, while Härke (1979: 30) has suggested similar evidence is often found on German hillforts during this period. Jiran *et al.* (2013: 792) have noted that crafts, and especially metalworking, were concentrated at hillforts and their environs in Austria the Czech Republic. Vandkilde (2004: 32) suggests that all of these sites should be interpreted as protected centres of crafts and trade that were presided by local elites. Although it is important to note that craft-working was not confined to these locations, there is a clear concentration of such activities at hillforts in Late Bronze Age Europe.

An excellent example is the hillfort at Várvölgy–Nagy-Lázhegy, Hungary, which has recently been excavated. The enclosing elements comprise a stone wall that surrounds an area of 160ha, which survives to a height of 5m in places (Müller 2006: 189–190). A large area excavated in 2003–2006 produced an estimated seven tons of ceramics, indicating intensive settlement. A considerable assemblage was retrieved from 43 large pits which Müller has interpreted as grain storage pits. A number of stone hammers, 51 moulds and 102 crucible fragments attest to on-site bronze working. Twelve bronze and one gold hoard, together comprising 620 objects, were recovered from the interior (Müller 2012). The distribution of the artefacts suggests a bilateral internal division, with bronze craftsmen and merchants occupying the northern section, and individuals involved in processing and preparing bronze at the southern end (Müller 2006: 191).

Markova and Ilon (2013: 831) have noted that metallurgical centres appear at fortified settlements during the Late Bronze Age and have suggested that the discovery of foreign goods could indicate they functioned as inter-regional and intercultural trade centres. An excellent example is the heavily occupied hillfort at Pod, Bosnia and Herzegovina, constructed during the beginning of the Late Bronze Age (Terzan 2013: 847). The site sits on a plateau on the slopes of Mt. Koprivnica overlooking fertile land and north–south routeway. The hillfort comprises a stone wall and probably a palisade. Evidence for bronze and iron working suggest that the site played an important role in the manufacture of metal products for a broad region (*ibid.*: 847). Terzan stresses the exceptionally strategic position of the site, the dense internal occupation and metalworking activities, which together make this hillfort a central settlement.

The Hunenburg hillfort near Waterstedt, Germany, built around 1100 BC, revealed evidence for a possible metal workshop where cast objects include swords and high-quality hanging bowls (Jockenhövel 2013: 741). Interestingly, aerial photography has identified a subsidiary settlement outside the hillfort that is considerably larger. Excavations by Heske *et al.* (2010) recovered evidence for metalworking activities for the production of bronze tools and weapons. The excavations did not reveal an obvious class distinction between the hillfort and open settlement (Heske *et al.* 2010: 186). Conversely, at the Late Bronze Age hillfort of Ormož, Slovenia, a densely occupied interior with evidence for metalworking and craft activities was separated from external habitation with no evidence of such (Dular and Tomanič Jevremov 2010; Teržan 2013: 847). A similar pattern of ancillary settlement was identified at Feadvar hillfort in Serbia.

The Late Bronze Age phases of the French hillforts at Fort-Harrouard at Sorel-Mousel (Mohen and Bailloud 1987) and Saint-Pierre-en-Chastre at Vieux-Moulin both produced large numbers of bronze objects, as well as evidence for metalworking (Mohen and Bailloud 1987: 140). Mould fragments from Fort-Harrouard constitute the largest assemblage of such material in France and indicates the large-scale production of weapons. In total, 1252 metal objects were recovered. Approximately 18% of the bronze artefacts are weapons and 29 swords were found. Moulds for at least 39 swords were also recovered. Approximately 46% of the moulds were used to create ornaments. The location of the artefacts at the site allowed the excavators to identify specific areas of specialisation, such as zones where spearheads were created (Mohen and Bailloud 1987: 138). At Saint-Pierre-en-Chastre, 78% of the bronze artefacts were ornaments, while 58 % of the moulds found were used to create weapons. The evidence indicates that the hillforts at Fort-Harrouard and Saint-Pierre-en-Chastre were centres for the intensive production of prestige goods. Other sites with evidence for dedicated craft-workshops include Mont Beuvray, France. There, a large hillfort of 135ha was internally divided with enamel and metal-working areas located near the main entrance (Ralston 2006). Burgess and O'Connor (2008: 46–48) have noted that an unusually large proportion of Late Bronze Age metal artefacts have come from the Spanish and Portuguese castros, with sites such as Nossa Senhora da Guia de Baiões, Viseu, in central Portugal (González-Ruibal 2004: 290; Kalb 1978; Silva 1979) producing evidence for the on-site manufacture of objects.

Reflecting the situation on the Continent, some Late Bronze Age hillforts in Britain produce evidence for metalworking. Examples in England include Mucking (Jones and Bond 1980), Thwing (Manby 1980), Springfield Lyons, (Buckley and Hedges 1987) and South Hornchurch (Guttmann and Last 2000: 344).

It is interesting that at many hillforts where metalworking is recorded, large pits possibly used for storing grain have also been identified. Várvölgy–Nagy-Lázhegy and the Hunenburg hillforts are excellent examples. Storage pits have also been identified at the Late Bronze Age hillfort of Burgberg, near Burkheim in south-west Germany, where hundreds of round pits were discovered. Storage pits were also found at the Late Bronze Age hillfort at Feudvar and at Btuszczewo in west-central Poland. The identification of storage pits may be an indication of centralized storage of agricultural produce (Czebresuk and Müller 2004), or perhaps storage of excess produce to sustain craftsmen.

Although Osgood and Monks (2010: 66) suggest that by the end of the Late Bronze Age, much of the production of goods seems to have taken place at fortified sites, important craft production centres also occurred in low-land settings. The best known example is Frattesina in northern Italy, where glass-working and/or production was taking place (Brill 1992; Henderson 1988). Similarly, important settlement sites were constructed in low-lying areas which incorporated large, monumental enclosing elements. Corneşti-Iarcuri, a Late Bronze Age multiple enclosure nearly 6km wide, had a dense occupation and some evidence for destruction by fire. Szentmiklosi *et al.* (2011: 819) argued that this site may be one of the largest single prehistoric settlement in Europe.

Final Late Bronze Age/Early Iron Age to Late Iron Age

A final construction phase occurs at the Late Bronze Age/Iron Age transition, although in a more confined region spanning southern Britain, northern France, Belgium, southern Germany, the Czech Republic and Slovakia. Härke (1979: 33; 261–263) argues that the end of the Urnfield culture (800 BC) coincided with the abandonment of hillfort sites in much of Europe during Hallstatt C1 (800–650 BC). While this seems to be the case in regionalized areas such as southern Germany (Gerlach 1998; Rind 1999; Metzner-Nebelsick 2012, 425), north-west France (Delrieu 2013: 144) and eastern parts of Hungary and Slovakia (Matuz and Nováki 2002), there is also some occupation of hillfort sites in western Hungary, north-east Austria and western Slovakia (Metzner-Nebelsick 2012: 425). Ralston points out that in eastern Germany, hillforts built during this period are generally larger, although less densely inhabited (Ralston 2006: 14). Markova and Ilon (2013: 831) have noted a similar pattern in Slovakia and this may be extrapolated for much of this European hillfort zone.

Larger hillforts began to be constructed at a similar period in Britain, around the end of the 10th century BC. Examples include The Breidden (Musson 1991), Dinorben (Savory 1971), Grimthorpe (Stead 1968), Beeston Castle (Ellis 1993), Balksbury Camp (Ellis and Rawlings 2001), Castle Hill (Allen *et al.* 2009: 193), Thrapston (Hull 2000) and Wolstonbury (Hamilton and Manley 1997). These sites are still characterized by a basic design and simple entrance features. At Balksbury Camp, for example, the main enclosure consisted to a single ditch less than 7.3m wide and at least 0.9m deep, with an internal bank averaging 3–3.5m wide and simple entrance gap (Wainwright and Davis 1995: 10). This simple enclosure defined a roughly triangular area approximately 18ha in extent (Ellis and Rawlings 2001: 84). These sites precede the more widespread construction of hillforts in the 8th century (Allen *et al.* 2009: 193).

Primas (2002: 51) has suggested that a considerable number of hillforts were occupied in Central Europe between 1000–800 BC, but by the 8th/7th centuries BC most had been abandoned. However, in regional zones such as southern Germany, hillfort construction was at its height during the 6th and early 5th centuries BC (Cunliffe 2001: 341–352). This period saw the emergence of a limited number of small hillforts with signs of elite occupation (Ralston 2006: 22). Known as Fürstensitze, or princely seats, these sites often produce very elaborate brooches and in some cases, such as Mont Lassois in Burgundy, Heuneburg in southern Germany and Châtillion-sur-Glâne in Switzerland, Mediterranean luxury goods have been found (Cunliffe 2001: 346). At Heuneburg, the original defences consisted of a wall of unfired mudbrick up to 5m high with an external V-shaped ditch up to 14m wide and 6m deep (Fernández-Götz and Krausse 2012). An entrance with a gatehouse and the remains of forward-projecting rectangular bastions, both of mudbrick construction, were also identified. Evidence suggests that the hillfort was the subject of repeated attacks as the walls were rebuilt on numerous occasions (Ralston 2006: 78). A wider study of the environs of the hillfort provided even more spectacular results. There is evidence of dense settlement over a 100ha area in the immediate vicinity, which Fernández-Götz and Krausse (2012: 31) suggest represented a population of approximately 5000 at its height. The site was abruptly abandoned around the mid-5th century BC, around the same time the hillfort at Glauberg in southwestern Germany was becoming more important (*ibid.*: 34).

In northwestern Spain and Portugal, Pardo *et al.* (2009) argued that the majority of hillforts were constructed and occupied between the 8th century BC to the 2nd century AD. Two major construction phases occur around 800 and 450 BC. The length of occupation varies, with some hillforts such as Torroso, Penalba or Penarrubia constructed and abandoned between 800–450 BC, and A Graña, for example, having a long history of occupation, beginning around 800 BC and continuing until the turn of the millennium. A general abandonment of these sites occurs from the 3rd–4th centuries AD, although intermittent occupation occurs at some examples into the historic period (*ibid.*: 96).

The development of the hillfort in Europe culminates in the enormous 'oppida' that can be broadly dated to the final stages of the pre-Roman Iron Age, around the 2nd and 1st centuries BC. These monuments are confined to a broad band that extends from Hungary through temperate Europe, west to Atlantic France and north into southern England (Ralston 2006: 14). However, massive fortifications occurred as early as the Late Bronze Age, and size should not be the defining factor of an oppida. For example, the low-land promontory of the Fossé Saint Philibert at Yainville and Jumiéges (Seine Maritime) encloses an area of approximately 2000ha and has been dated to the Late Bronze Age (Ralston 2006: 29).

The major phase of hillfort construction in Britain began during the Late Bronze Age/Iron Age transition around 800–600, and continued until the Roman invasion around the turn of the millennium. In rare cases, sites were still in use during the Early Medieval period. Some of the Early Iron Age hillforts can be connected with river valleys (Corney 2006: 134) and may have been sited to control such natural routeways. Examples include the Avon, and its tributaries, the Wylie and the Bourne and the Stour in Dorset. Sharples (2007: 66) has questioned this assumption, noting some important rivers that are not associated with hillforts. He also observed that hillforts built during this period are often located on prominent hilltops or at the edges of inland escarpments. Cunliffe (2013: 304–305) interprets this in territorial terms, where the hillfort is a controlling presence in an area defined by natural boundaries such as river valleys.

In Wessex, the well known sites of Danebury and Maiden Castle (Figure 2.1) were constructed within a densely populated zone of hillforts, known as the 'hillfort dominated zone' (Figure 2.2). This extended from southeastern coast of England to north Wales (see Cunliffe 2013: 304; 1991: 312). The excavation evidence indicates that most of these hillforts were built during the 6th and 5th centuries BC, the forts themselves characterized by a rampart and ditch of 'defensive' proportions and two opposing entrance features (Cunliffe 2013: 304). Evidence of occupation varies from one hillfort to another. At one extreme, there are hillforts which were never occupied and show little trace of sustained use, while some were intensively occupied by a permanent population throughout the length of their life, such as Maiden Castle or Danebury (Cunliffe 2013: 305; Harding 2012: 206; Mytum 2013: 10). Sharples (2007: 120) has noted that there may be a link between the complexity of the enclosing elements and more intensive occupation of the interior.

For the period 450–200 BC, the mobilisation of resources for boundary construction is considered the principal medium for elite competition (Sharples 2007: 120). This manifests in the evolution of the hillfort through the substantial enhancement of enclosing elements and creation of complex entrance features. These forts are termed 'developed hillforts'. An excellent example is Maiden Castle in Dorset. This is one of the most extensively studied hillforts in southern England (Sharples 1991: 257). Positioned in a commanding position at the eastern edge of an east–west running ridge, the earliest phase incorporated the remains that date to around 600 BC and com-

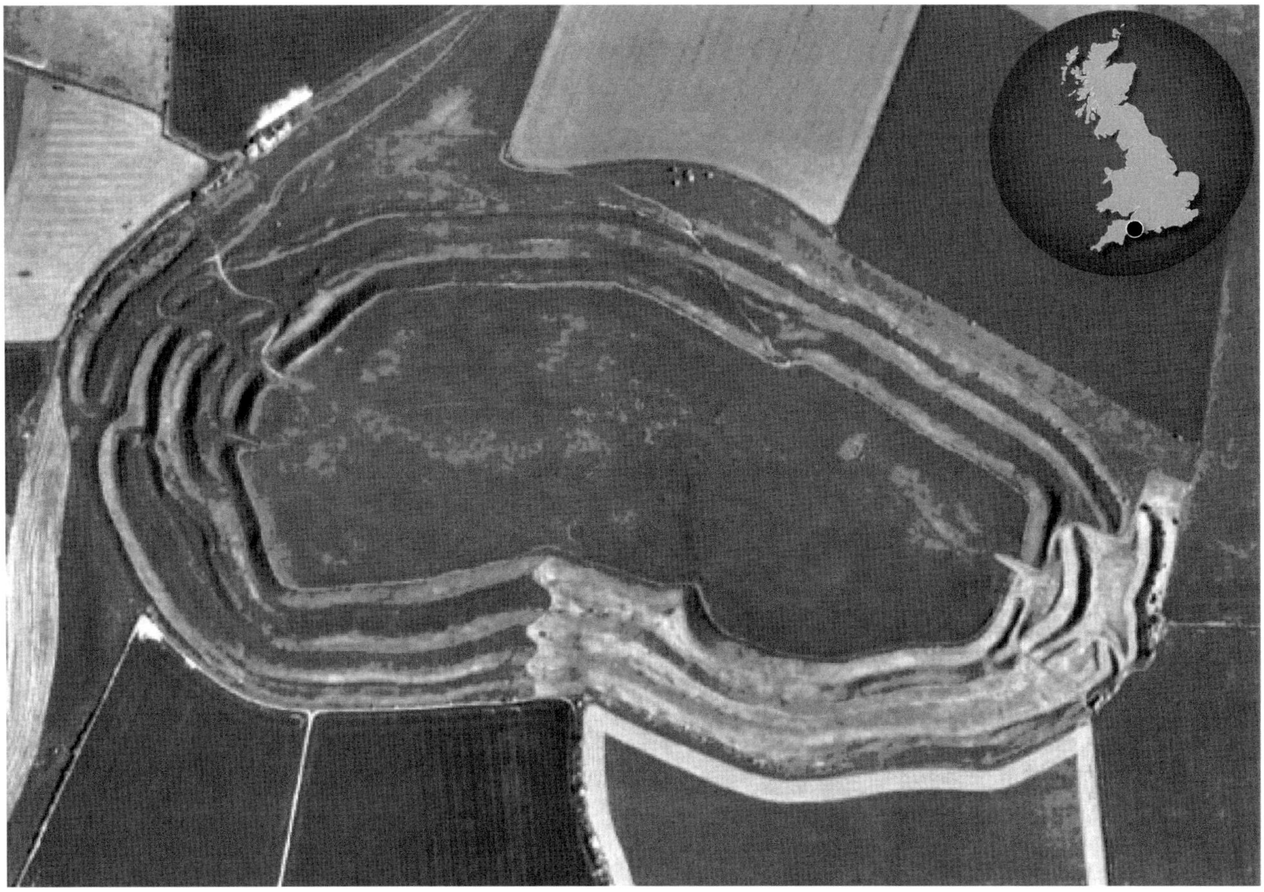

FIGURE 2.1: MAIDEN CASTLE, DORSET (GOOGLE EARTH 2017).

prised a bank and external V-shaped ditch up to 6.5m in depth. It enclosed an area of 6.47ha at the eastern summit of the hilltop. There are two opposing entrances at the east and west. Around 450 BC, the enclosing elements were dramatically refurbished and the hillfort extended to the west to enclose an area of approximately 17.22ha. Throughout this period, there is sustained development of the enclosing elements with the addition of ramparts and ditches, a significant increase in the scale of these earthworks and the gradual development of complex entrance features (Sharples 1991: 63). In total, the hillfort occupied an area of approximately 45.28ha. The interior appears to be densely occupied throughout this period, with evidence for dense clusters of domestic structures and large storage pits. Analysis of the surrounding landscape indicates that contemporary settlements and hillforts were abandoned, and the inhabitants may have been absorbed into the hillfort at Maiden Castle (*ibid.*: 260). The hillfort was largely abandoned at the end of the 1st century AD (Sharples 1991).

This trend is apparent elsewhere in Britain, such as at Danebury and may be seen as a sign of the increasing importance of these developed hillforts (Sharples 2007: 76). Cunliffe (2013: 306) considers this as evidence for the amalgamation of individual polities to create larger social units. This led to the decline of once-active hillforts, while others took on a greater significance to serve a larger territory. Storage pits are a key feature of the Wessex hillforts, and particularly the developed hillforts of that area. Sharples (2007: 122) noted that the storage capacity at many of these sites could have provided resources for communities much larger than those occupying the interior. He linked this increased storage capacity to the construction and development of the enclosing elements, suggesting that the success of a hillfort construction event depended not only on available labour and resources, but also on the ability to keep everyone content by supplying food.

Danebury hillfort was constructed in the late 6th or early 5th century BC and continued in use until around 100 BC. The original enclosure comprised an earth-filled box-structure of wood backed by a chalk rampart, with external ditch and two opposing entrance gaps at the east and south-west (Cunliffe 2011: 47–53). The east entrance was refurbished up to three times during the first-phase of defences. The back slope of the rampart was subsequently heightened with chalk rubble, the material deriving from a series of shallow, discontinuous quarry hollows within the interior. At this time, the east entrance was widened and remodelled. These early phases were associated with four-post structures interpreted as raised granaries, and with a dense distribution of storage pits and circular hut structures. At the beginning of the 3rd century BC the hillfort was extensively refurbished. This

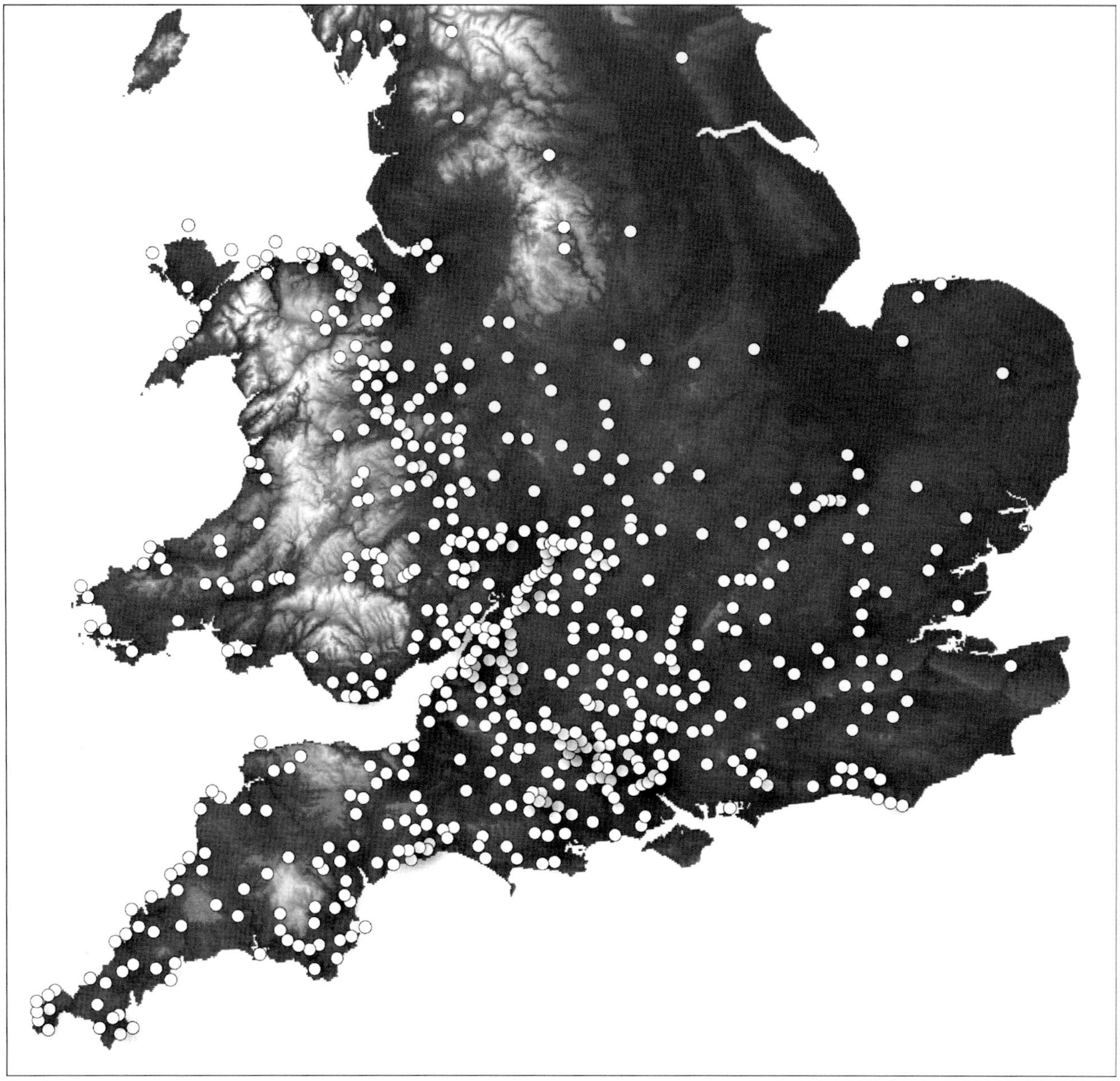

FIGURE 2.2: DISTRIBUTION OF ENGLISH AND WELSH HILLFORTS OVER 1.2HA (AFTER PAYNE 2006 FIG. 1.2).

involved further heightening of the rampart, an extension of the ditch, and the addition of complex forward-projecting hornworks. The north and east side of the rampart was substantially increased, the material being dug from a deep continuous quarry, 10m wide, abutting the interior of the rampart. The ditch was re-dug into a deep V-shaped profile, 11–12m wide and 6m in depth. Subsequent maintenance of the ditch resulted in the creation of a 2m high and 7m wide bank. This phase of use is characterized by a dramatic increase in the internal population as indicated by the dense, structured layout of roundhouses and storage pits. At this time, contemporary hillforts at Bury, Woolbury and Quarley Hill, located in the environs of Danebury, were abandoned (Cunliffe 2000: 166). This intensive occupation continued for more than two centuries. Around 100–50 BC, the eastern gate was destroyed by fire and the fort was largely abandoned (Cunliffe 2011: 64).

Broxmouth, Scotland, is one of the most comprehensively dated hillforts in Britain (Armit and McKenzie 2013), with a total of 158 radiocarbon dates from 101 archaeological deposits providing an excellent sequence for chronicling the evolution from palisaded enclosure to developed hillfort (Hamilton *et al.* 2013; Armit and McKenzie 2013). The site is situated on the East Lothian coast and commands views across the North Sea, the First of Forth, and along the coastal routeway leading south to the Tweed Basin (Armit and McKenzie 2013: 494). The development of the enclosing elements began around 640–570 BC with the construction of a palisaded enclosure. After this initial enclosure was removed, a number of large roundhouses were built. This open settlement was enclosed by a single rampart and external ditch around 490–430 BC. Two opposing entrance gaps at the east and west were recorded. The enclosing elements were later elaborated with the addition of a second rampart and external ditch that incorporated a monumental wooden entrance corridor. Around 395–375 BC, this entrance was blocked and a new entrance was built at the south-west. Successive phases saw the creation of a third enclosing element at the west. By 295–235 BC, the settlement had expanded over the enclosing elements and a number of hut structures were built over the infilled ditches. The settlement contracted around 235–210 BC and a small inhumation cemetery was created north of the hillfort. The final phase of the hillfort began around 100–60 BC and comprised a compact agglomeration of hut structures surrounded by a low bank. This settlement continued for a number of generations, with the hillfort finally abandoned around AD 155–210. This sequence of hillfort evolution is a pattern which is beginning to emerge throughout Britain (*ibid.*: 11).

Another excellent example is Dinorben hillfort in Wales (Gardner and Savory 1964; Savory 1971). There, the earliest palisaded enclosure, dating to the Late Bronze Age, preceded a series of Iron Age earthworks that evolved from a simple box rampart to a complex multivallate hillfort with an embellished entrance and elongated passage. For a more comprehensive discussion on the evolution of hillfort defences in Britain see Cunliffe (1991: 313–329).

Summary

There is well-established evidence for the chronology and design of hillfort construction in Britain and the Continent during the Bronze Age and Iron Age. Although not uniform in distribution, the hillfort phenomenon flourished in three distinct phases: the Early Bronze Age/Middle Bronze Age transition, the Middle Bronze Age/Late Bronze Age transition and the Late Bronze Age/Early Iron Age transition. It is interesting to note that construction of hillforts generally occurred at transition periods, possibly indicating that social upheaval may be a cause for these construction events. Evidence for the initial construction phase during the Early Bronze Age/Middle Bronze Age transition can often be associated with copper sources and a need to control natural resources and routeways. The hillforts at Götschenberg and St Veit Klinglberg were probably built to convey ownership of copper resources in the immediate environs and to control the flow of this metal. The excellent visibility at potential routes of traffic, cross-roads or river crossings has been noted by Primas (2002: 44), and others. The concentration of early hillforts in areas close to the Alpine region may indicate an increasing need to control the flow of copper near its source (Jockenhövel 2013: 740; Kienlin 2013: 424).

During the Middle Bronze Age, hilltop settlements were almost completely abandoned (Jockenhövel 1990: 219; Jockenhövel 2013: 740). It is not until the Middle Bronze Age/Late Bronze Age transition that hillforts re-emerge with an 'unprecedented' intensification in construction (Primas 2002: 50). This construction phase was much more dispersed than previously, with hillforts being built in many parts of Urnfield and Atlantic Europe. The importance of controlling natural routeways and highly visible locales continues to be an important facet of hillfort location during this period. This may be due to the increasing reliance on long-distance trading for high status materials such as bronze. A need to control the flow of exotic goods or attract traders with this material may be an undercurrent for the construction of hillforts and so explain their dense distribution during this phase. A notable increase in the evidence for violence at these sites and traces of destruction, exemplified at Velim hillfort, may be an indication of increasing competition to control these routeways.

A final construction phase occurs at the Late Bronze Age/Early Iron Age transition, although only in specific regions of the Continent. Again, these are largely associated with natural routeways. This period also saw the emergence of the 'princely seat', a type of hillfort that can be associated with the production of high status goods and elite occupation. In Britain, the hillfort phenomenon partly reflects the situation in mainland Europe where a significant construction phase is evident at the beginning of the Late Bronze Age. Construction continues into the later part of the 1st century BC, when some hillforts were still being intensively occupied. Many of the British sites were built between 800–450 BC, in contrast to the Continent, where a small number of 'princely seats' were constructed with most hillforts largely abandoned. The hillfort phenomenon culminated with the construction of large enclosures (oppida) both in Britain and the Continent during the 2nd and 1st centuries BC.

2.2 Hillforts in Ireland

The term 'hillfort' is perhaps a misnomer, attributed to a category of monuments that can vary considerably in morphology, landscape setting, chronology and function. First introduced by Hawkes in 1931, the term is now used loosely by some to describe a wide variety of hilltop sites that are surrounded and enclosed by banks, walls, palisades, fences and ditches, with little regard to function or place in prehistoric or later society (Brown 2009: 7). The term implies a distinct and pervasive need for defence. This has been perpetuated by researchers such as Hogg, who defines a hillfort as 'an enclosure, apparently fortified, and so placed as to gain some defensive advantage from its position' (Hogg 1975: 15). Similarly, Avery (1976: 3) describes these sites as 'fortified so as to be defensible against human attack...[and which] exploits the natural terrain so as to give the defenders an advantage of height over those approaching the site'. In a later publication he suggested that 'all hillforts are connected by the fact that each was in one way or another used for defence of the community which built it' (Avery 1993: 1). Similarly, Barry Raftery, one of the seminal researchers in Ireland, considered hillforts as 'hilltop enclosure[s] of considerable size and strength, which deliberately exploit the natural properties of the situation for defensive purposes' (Raftery 1994: 38). Recently, Grogan (2005b: 111) has defined Irish hillforts as 'large hilltop sites that take advantage of the natural defensive properties of the topography'. Today, the use of the term 'hillfort' is viewed as an over-simplification, but is nonetheless widely used by archaeologists (Harding 2004).

These militaristic connotations have been challenged in recent years (Brown 2009: 7; Harding 2012: 1). A post-processual backlash has downplayed the defensive role of hillforts without providing a revised definition that adequately encompasses this new stand-point (see Armit 2007). Harding (2012: 1–5) concluded that the label 'hillfort' is problematic and views it more as a term of convenience. He instead suggests that the act of 'enclosure' is a key element, both physically or conceptually demarcating an area to which access is restricted or controlled. This is achieved by the construction of a rampart and ditch, stockade or fence and by the incorporation of topographical and natural features such as cliffs or promontories. The scale of the enclosing works may range from a relatively modest barrier to massive earthworks. These enclosing elements may be located around hilltop contours, or on cliff-edges, ridges or promontories, spurs, hill slopes, in river bends, or across variable terrain. The enclosed area may range from under a hectare to 20ha and more, with the territorial or terrain oppida of the late pre-Roman Iron Age approximately 300ha in size (*ibid.*: 1–5). This broad definition can have regional interpretations, such as in Ireland, where coastal and low-lying inland promontory forts, the latter viewed as a sub-set of the 'hillfort' class in Britain, are a distinct monument type in cultural and chronological terms.

There are approximately 108 confirmed hillforts in Ireland (Figure 2.3). The Irish definition distinctly refers to monuments on or near hilltops, cliff edges and spurs and generally does not include enclosures outside this remit. This contrasts with the situation in Britain, where hillforts are not restricted topographically to hills (Harding 2012: 4). Irish hillforts are often identified by their size. One definition places them over 1ha in internal area, with smaller examples classified as 'hilltop enclosures' (Grogan 2005b: 116–117). Grogan has listed some 200 examples of this site type, although a large number are more likely to be Early Medieval ringforts. A review of that list reveals that approximately 73 sites can be properly termed 'hilltop enclosures', only one of which has been excavated. The example at Clenagh, Co. Clare, did not produce any dates or artefacts that could date either construction or occupation (Grogan 2005a). These small hilltop sites in Ireland are distinct from the British 'hilltop enclosure', which is usually larger than 15ha and dates to the Early Iron Age (Cunliffe 2013: 300).

There are approximately 274 recorded coastal promontory forts in Ireland. Nine of these have been excavated and date mainly to the Medieval period, although a single Late Bronze Age date from Dunbeg in Co. Kerry, may indicate an early attempt at delimiting that promontory. Approximately 82.8% of these sites are under 1ha and only 5.8% are comparable to the size of an average hillfort, although large sites such as Ballynacarriga and Downmacpatrick in Co. Cork can measure up to 84ha. Considering this morphological and chronological distinction, coastal promontories are not considered as 'hillforts' in this work. Similarly, inland promontory forts positioned in low-land areas such as river bends or not topographically dominant locations will not be considered. Promontories positioned in dominant positions, such as Caherconree or Faha, Co. Kerry, or Castle Gale in Co. Limerick, are categorised as hillforts in this study.

A separate problem in Ireland is the large number of ringfort enclosures of Early Medieval date, many of which are sited on low hills or otherwise elevated ground. There are over 47,000 extant examples of this monument, with possibly as many more now destroyed. Recent developer-led excavations (Clarke 2002; Clarke and Carlin 2008; McConway 2002; Kinsella 2008) emphasize the use of these monuments during the Early Medieval period and do not indicate earlier origins. The dating and function of ringforts is therefore not as 'contentious' as Harding (2012: 172) suggests. More importantly, the archaeological evidence strongly suggests that ringforts are unlikely to be chronologically or culturally associated with hillforts, though there can be later associations, an excellent example being the stone ringforts inside the hillforts at Mooghaun, Co. Clare and Rathgall, Co. Wicklow.

It could be argued that the large 'royal' enclosures of Rath na Rioga, Tara, Co. Meath, Dún Ailinne, Co. Kildare, Rathcrogan, Co. Roscommon and Navan Fort, Co. Armagh, are also hillforts. Three of these have been dated to the Iron Age. Dún Ailinne produced Iron Age material and an Iron Age radiocarbon date was returned from material recovered below the bank (Johnson and Wailes 2007; Wailes 1990: 20). Roche (1999) has confirmed that the Tara enclosure, Rath na Rioga, was constructed around the first century BC, while Mallory (2000) places the construction of Navan Fort during the first century BC. The morphological layout of these enclosures is also somewhat distinct. Tara, Dún Ailinne and Navan Fort have substantial internal ditches, a deliberate feature that Warner (2000) has interpreted as a defence against the

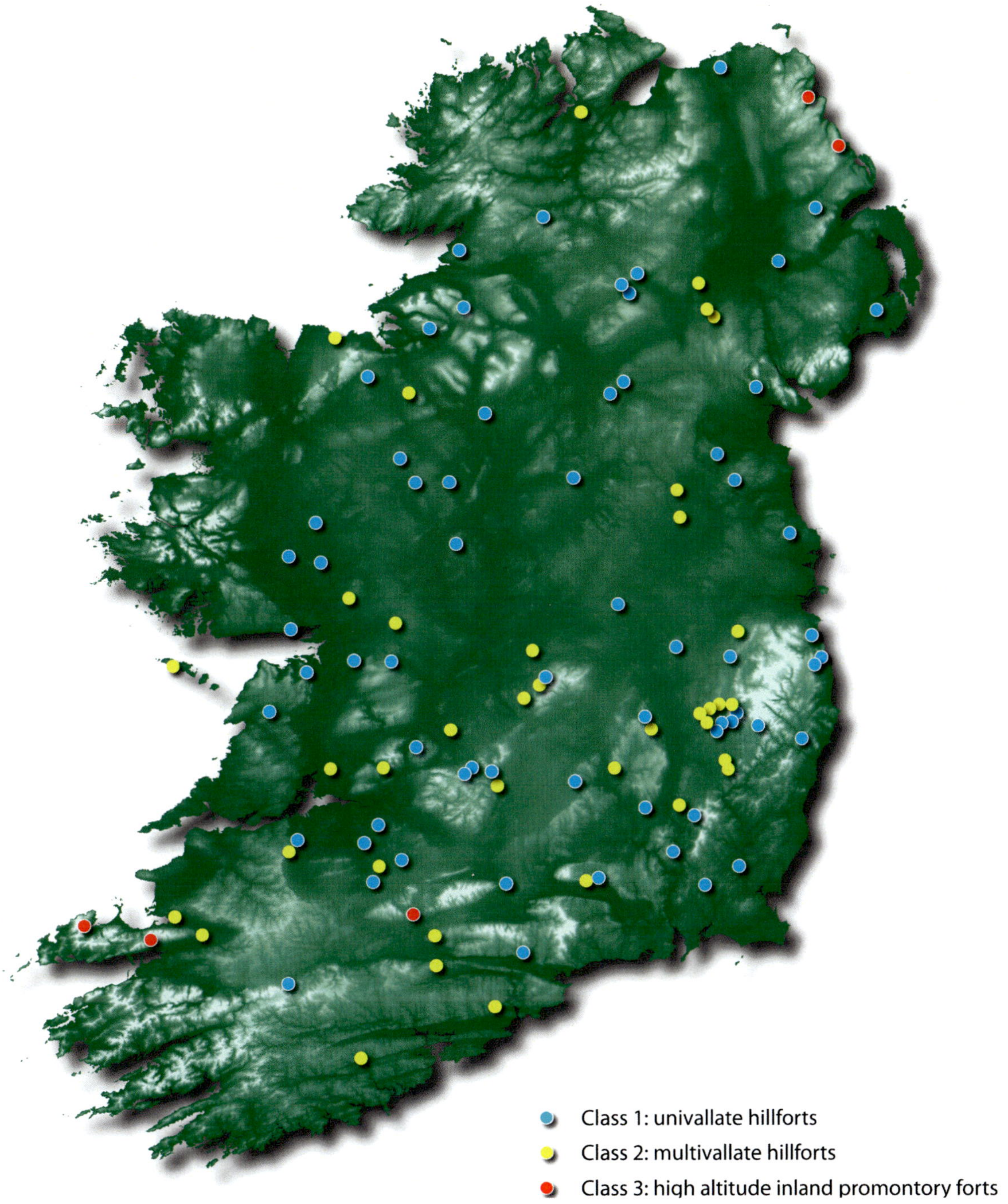

Figure 2.3: Distribution of prehistoric hillforts in Ireland.

chaotic otherworld emanating from inside the enclosure. The distinct morphological differences and the chronological gap between these enclosures and 'true' Irish hillforts may suggest that these cannot be considered as hillforts proper. Examples with substantial internal ditches, such as Kedra, Co. Tipperary, may therefore be more appropriately categorised with Iron Age royal sites, however, further research is needed. A further complication is the category of large internally-ditched enclosures that may belong to the Neolithic henge tradition.

The term 'hillfort' tends to be more loosely applied in Britain than in Ireland. More than half of the total number of hillforts in Britain enclose an area under 1.2ha (Harding 2012: 9). Halliday and Ralston (2009: 467) note that the majority of the 1305 hillforts in Scotland are 'tiny enclosures'. For Britain, Cunliffe (1991c: 312) proposes that that these small enclosures may legitimately be considered as a separate phenomenon. There is also the situation where many southern English hillforts are not located on high ground, but in lowland settings. Irrespective of terminology, there are also important differences in respect to chronology, with Brown (2009: 12) highlighting many of the dating issues. The difference between hillforts and smaller enclosures cannot be seen as 'an issue of semantics' as Harding (2004: 50) suggests. To help distinguish between these site types, Sharples (2010: 61) suggests that dominance over the landscape, as well as the monumentality of the monument, should be considered. However, Brown (2009: 12) remains cautious of this approach, suggesting that substantial variations in these aspects can exist.

The subjectivity surrounding definition and the constraints of applying blanket terminology ignore the fact that 'hillforts' defy rigid classification. Coupled with this, the process of enclosure can have multiple connotations and purposes at different times and places (Brown 2009: 7; Harding 2004: 298; Halliday and Ralston 2009: 467), meaning that a 'hillfort' built in the Late Bronze Age might be constructed for very different reasons than a 'hillfort' built in the Later Iron Age, even if the two are morphologically comparable with a similar landscape setting.

Hillforts in Ireland: a history of research

The study of hillforts in Ireland began with the work of Thomas Westropp in the early 20th Century. Westropp was one of the most celebrated Irish antiquarians and he had a specific interest in forts, particular the impressive sites in County Clare (Ashe FitzGerald 2000). Many of the almost 300 papers he published were used to discuss the subject. His most important work, '*The Ancient Forts of Ireland*', published in 1902, was the first significant attempted to classify monument types in Ireland that fell within the blanket term 'fort' (Westropp 1902a). He identified eleven classes (although never identified hillforts as a separate group) and examined the morphology and distribution of these groups, discussing for the first time their wider European context. This provided an excellent framework for subsequent research, one that was not surpassed until the publication of Ó Ríordain's '*Antiquities of the Irish Countryside*' in 1943 (Cotter 2012a: 11). Even before the invention of absolute dating techniques, Westropp posited that the majority of Irish forts were Early Medieval and that larger examples such as Mooghaun and Dún Aonghasa were built prior to the introduction of Christianity. Although cautious when considering the chronology of these large forts, using documentary sources and evidence from stray finds, Westropp (1902: 725) concluded that forts 'originate at least 1200 years before our era (i.e. 1200 BC) and 'by their simplicity and elasticity held their own till many centuries of our era had passed away'. Remarkably, this coincides with modern dating evidence that indicates the emergence of hillforts *c.*1400–1200 BC and the established dating of Early Medieval enclosures, *c.*400–1200 AD.

Westropp was the first to criticize the mythological origins of these forts, which was widely accepted by nineteenth-century scholars such as John O'Donovan, George Petrie and Eugene O'Curry. O'Donovan (1839) and Petrie (1972: 256–257) linked the origins of Dún Aonghasa (Figure 2.4) and the forts in western Ireland to the mythical invasion of the Firbolg, an ancient tribe originally located in Scotland. This origin tale recounts how the sons of the Firbolg chief fled from the territory of the Picts in Scotland and attempted to settle at Tara and Newgrange (Stokes 1894). The sons were unable to afford the tribute required to settle in these territories and advanced farther west, where they encountered Maeve, the Queen of Connaught, who suggested that they settle outposts farther to the west. There they built the elaborate stone forts of Dún Aonghasa and Dún Conor, among others. Rather than accept that 'excessively improbable' explanation, Westropp saw these forts as part of a series of monuments stretching all across Europe (Ashe FitzGerald 2000: 56). Even at this early stage, Westropp saw beyond the defensive paradigm and acknowledged that ritual and ceremonial interpretations should be considered when interpreting these large monuments (Westropp 1911: 347).

The premises of Westropp's publications were to record monuments for future scholars who would have the resources for field survey and scientific excavation (Ashe FitzGerald 2000: 56; Westropp 1896: 143). An excellent example is Westropp's survey of Mooghaun hillfort in Co. Clare (Westropp 1893; 1902a; 1902b; 1908). Grogan (2005a: 107) describes these surveys as the best published descriptions of the site prior to his own study. Several excellent drawings of the monument accompanied Westropp's publications, the most detailed published in 1908. Prior to this, the only scale plan of the site was that contained in the 1st edition Ordnance Survey maps published in 1840. The detail of Westropp's survey is evident, with a number of possible entrances and small structures recorded.

Westropp published various plans and descriptions of hillforts both in Ireland and abroad. He described ten of the Irish sites in his '*The Ancient Forts of Ireland*', including a number of the Baltinglass hillforts in Wicklow (see Chapter 4), although many of these were defined as large ringforts. Considering that around 40 hillforts had been identified by Raftery by 1972, the number of hillforts described by Westropp is remarkable. One of the most famous sites Westropp recorded was Dún Aonghasa in Co. Galway. Westropp published various sketches (Westropp 1897; 1898; 1910) and plans (Westropp 1910) of the hillfort, adding to a wealth of investigations undertaken by several other eminent antiquarians. George Petrie (in Stokes 1868: 18) and John O'Donovan (1839) both visited the site and published descriptions and plan drawings. These are particularly important as they were undertaken prior to the restoration works undertaken by the Office of Public Works in the late nineteenth century.

FIGURE 2.4: DÚN AONGHASA HILLFORT IN CO. GALWAY (GOOGLE EARTH 2017).

The size and imposing nature of some Irish hillforts encouraged other antiquarians to study these monuments, although not to the same extent as Westropp. O'Donovan and O'Curry were both employed with the Ordnance Survey, and recorded various details of hillforts such as Mooghaun and Dún Aonghasa. A more focused study of the hillforts at Rathgall and Knockeen (Figure 2.5), Co. Wicklow, was undertaken by Orpen in 1911. The latter was the first to record the morphological layout of Rathgall hillfort, comparing it to Dún Aonghasa and the large stone forts in the west of Ireland (Orpen 1911: 143). Orpen interpreted Rathgall as the centre of political power in south Leinster, and connected it with some of the early kings of Okinselagh. While this places the hillfort at the beginning of the Early Medieval period around 400 AD, high status settlement is attested by the large cashel at the centre of the earlier hillfort. In a later paper, Orpen (1916: 42) tentatively identified Rathgall as the Dun Galion marked on Ptolemy's map of Ireland, describing the hillfort as a primitive *oppidum munitum*.

There are no recorded amateur/antiquarian excavations at any Irish hillforts. This contrasts with the extensive evidence for such at British hillforts. The first archaeological excavation of an Irish hillfort was undertaken by Bersu at Freestone Hill in Co. Kilkenny and subsequently published by Raftery in 1969. This was quickly followed by Proudfoot's excavations at Downpatrick in Co. Down (Proudfoot 1954; 1955a). Both sites produced distinctive pottery now known to date to the Late Bronze Age, although at Freestone Hill important high status Roman finds were recovered from a central enclosure initially suggesting to the excavator that the site was Iron Age (Raftery 1969). These excavations became the foundation for the first major synthesis of Irish hillforts by Raftery (1970a; 1970b; 1972) and his subsequent excavation at Rathgall hillfort in Co. Wicklow. Although this excavation has not been published in full, the significance of the site is indisputable. Raftery identified much evidence of specialist craft-working, as well as exotic items indicative of long-distance trade with the Continent. Unfortunately, the dating of the enclosing elements of the hillfort remains problematic, although the majority of the internal activity is securely Late Bronze Age (Becker 2010). Similar dating problems were encountered by Warner (2009) when excavating the defences of Clogher hillfort in County Tyrone during the 1970s. The discovery of coarse ware pottery within and underneath the hillfort bank at Clogher strongly implies a Late Bronze Age date.

Mallory (1995) discovered exotic items indicative of

FIGURE 2.5: RATHGALL (FOREGROUND) AND KNOCKEEN (BACKGROUND) HILLFORTS IN CO. WICKLOW (CAMBRIDGE AERIAL PHOTOGRAPHIC COLLECTION).

long-distance trade at Haughey's Fort in Co. Armagh. A recent revaluation of the site by Mallory and Baban (2014: 26) suggests that the occupants of the site were also producing prestige goods. A large central post structure was partially excavated, and this has been interpreted as evidence supporting the primarily ritual character of the fort. Importantly, secure radiocarbon and dendrochronological samples were recovered from the enclosing elements, which for the first time in Ireland scientifically dated the defences of the hillfort to the Late Bronze Age. Environmental analysis undertaken at the site revealed that the construction of the hillfort coincided with an intensive landnam event that cleared the site and surrounding area of forest (see Weir 1987a; 1987b; 1994).

Subsequently, a number of important investigations by the Discovery Programme were undertaken at Mooghaun hillfort in Co. Clare (Grogan 2005a; 2005b) and at Dún Aonghasa in Co. Galway (Cotter 2013a; 2013b). These supported the Late Bronze Age dates obtained from Haughey's Fort and paralleled the environment evidence, revealing extensive clearance of the hilltops prior to the construction of the enclosing elements. Other significant investigations include the extensive excavation of Rahally hillfort in Co. Galway in advance of road development (Mullins 2008) and the research excavations at Knockdhu in Co. Antrim (Macdonald 2016).

Despite this research, hillfort studies in Ireland have not advanced significantly, due in part to a lack of dating information and to problems of classification. In total,

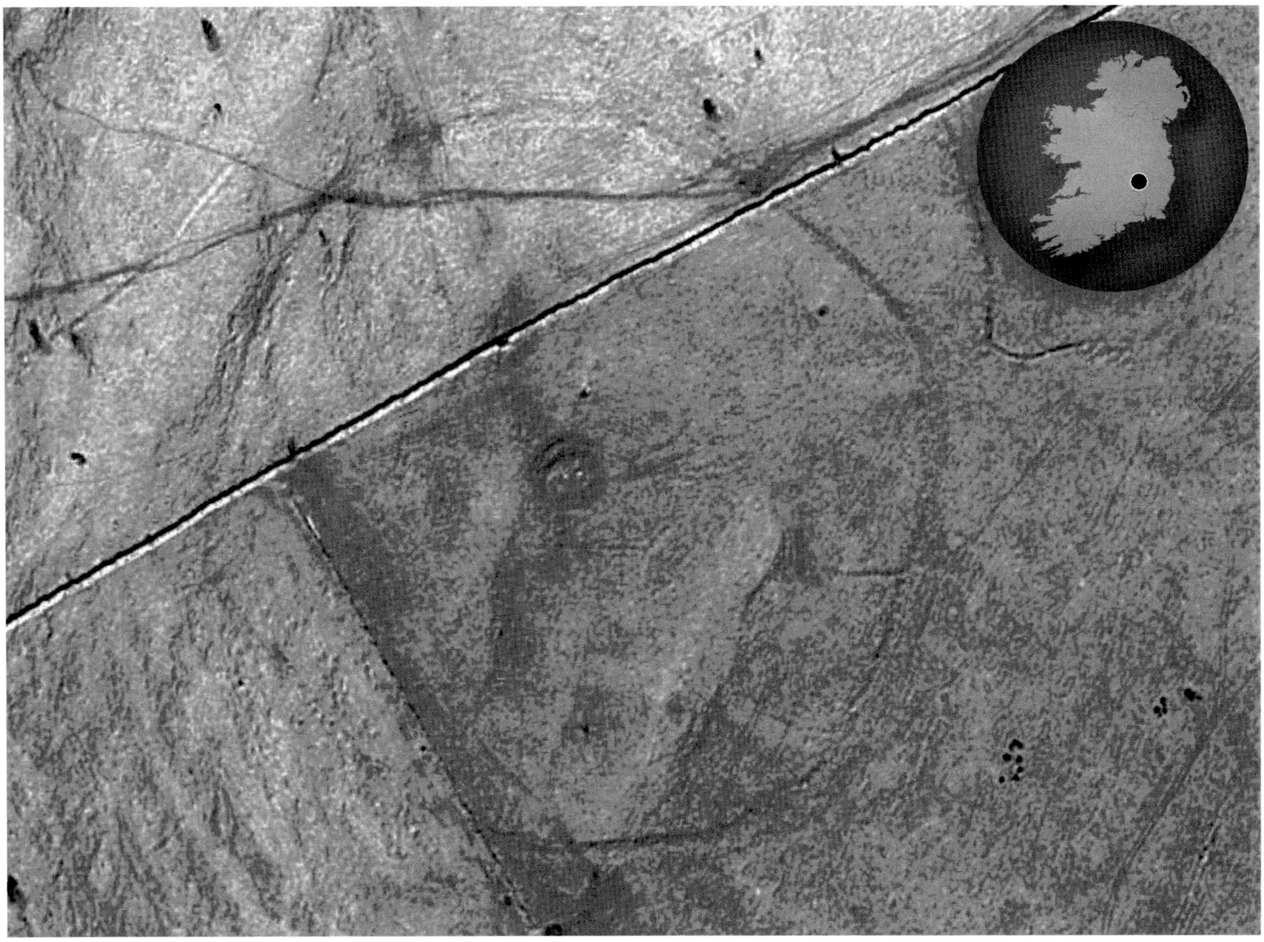

FIGURE 2.6: THE CLASS 1 HILLFORT AT CLOMANTAGH, CO. KILKENNY (GOOGLE EARTH 2017).

twenty one hillforts have been excavated in Ireland, with only five having more extensive investigations of their interiors. This has resulted in a poor understanding of the function and economy of these monuments and a tentative chronology. This contrasts with British hillfort studies, where numerous monuments have been subject to detailed excavations and multi-disciplinary studies. The lack of site information has pushed Irish researchers to rely heavily on data from British and continental studies, which has its limitations given the distinctive character of Irish hillforts.

Hillforts in Ireland: classification, morphology and distribution

Raftery (1972: 39) proposed the first classification of Irish hillforts, dividing 40 known examples into three groups. Class 1 hillforts comprised univallate sites such as Clomantagh, Co. Kilkenny (Figure 2.6). Class 2 sites were defined as widely-spaced, multivallate defences on (a) hill-tops, e.g. Toor More, Co. Kilkenny (Figure 2.7), and (b) cliff-tops such as Dún Aonghasa, Co. Galway. Class 3 included inland promontory forts such as Knockdhu, Co. Antrim and Caherconree, Co. Kerry (Figure 2.8). Since Raftery's (1972) publication, the number of identified hillforts in Ireland has risen to approximately 108 examples.

Almost 55% of Irish hillforts are univallate, 40% widely-spaced multivallate, with the remainder inland promontory forts. There is no archaeological distinction between Class 1 and 2 hillforts other than overall size and the number of enclosing elements. Both classes are sited in similar topographical positions and height above sea level. Class 1 hillforts are sited on average at 167m OD and Class 2 are 178m OD. Only three hillforts are positioned above 410m OD. Grogan (2005b: 121) concluded that elevation was not an absolute factor in hillfort location and suggests that extensive views over specific parts of the local landscape were more important. It is certainly the case that most Irish hillforts have commanding views. An estimated 69% of Class 1 hillforts have panoramic views (360°), with a further 20% having extensive (approximately 270°) visibility of the surrounding landscapc. Class 2 hillforts generally have more extensive viewsheds, approximately 80% having panoramic views and 15% have extensive visibility.

More notable differences occur when analysing the area enclosed, with Class 2 sites (7.39ha on average) enclosing nearly twice that of Class 1 sites (4.2ha on average).

Figure 2.7: Class 2 hillfort at Toor more, Co. Kilkenny (Google Earth 2017).

Approximately half of all univallate sites are under 2ha in comparison to 15% of widely-spaced multivallate sites. Half of the widely-spaced multivallate sites are over 5ha, in contrast to approximately 25% of univallate sites. About 27% of widely-spaced multivallate sites are over 10ha in size, compared to approximately 9% of univallate examples. Grogan (2005b: 112) has proposed a revised classification of Irish hillforts that amalgamates Raftery's Class 1 and 2 and divides the combined monuments by size, Class 1 becoming hillforts under 5ha and Class 2 represented by sites over 5ha. The merits of this approach are unclear and it is obviously problematic at the lower end of the scale in relation to the status of hilltop enclosures.

The separate classes of hillfort in Ireland do not have mutually exclusive distributions. All three of Raftery's classes of hillfort occur widely throughout Ireland. Gaps may occur in hillfort distribution where sites in agriculturally rich areas have been destroyed. The recently discovered Rahally hillfort, Co. Galway is an excellent example. Situated at the summit of a low-rise hill, the large widely-spaced multivallate hillfort has been completely levelled and was only discovered prior to construction of the N6 Galway to East Ballinsloe road scheme (Mullins 2008). While hillforts mostly occur in isolation, there are a number of pairs, such as the Friarstown group in Co. Limerick (Figure 2.9), and Rathgall and Knockeen hillforts in Co. Wicklow. There is an exceptional group of up to nine examples on the western edge of the Wicklow Mountains, overlooking the town of Baltinglass.

Further classification of class 2(a) hillforts is possible. An estimated 51% of this class could be categorized as having widely spaced enclosing elements, the separation between these always being over 55m, an excellent example being Kill Hill hillfort, Co. Kildare. About 18% have more closely spaced enclosing features, separated by no more than 30m (on average 20m), such as Rathcoran hillfort, Co. Wicklow. There are three sites that fit both categories; Hughstown, Co. Kildare, Rathgall, Co. Wicklow, and Haughey's Fort, Co. Armagh. The remainder of sites comprise closely spaced multivallation with no intervening gap between enclosing elements, such as Ballinkillin, Co. Carlow. Many of these, however, may be misclassified, and the outer defensive elements may instead consist of an external counter-scarp, as at Rathnagree or Ballylin hillforts. Raftery (1994: 57–58) has suggested that sites with little or no space between enclosing elements provided defence in depth, where those that are widely spaced offered space to regroup and fall back on inner ramparts. Wailes (1982) suggests the outer

FIGURE 2.8: THE CLASS 3 HILLFORT (INLAND PROMONTORY FORT) AT CAHERCONREE, CO. KERRY.

enclosures of a hillfort may have been a 'token' element of ritual or symbolic significance, while most would regard multivallation as a statement of power and status.

Approximately 25% of Irish hillforts have recorded cairns or mounds and three hillforts surround recorded megalithic tombs (Figure 2.10). About 34% of sites surround some form of burial monument (i.e. a barrow, mound, cairn etc.). The incorporation of earlier burial monuments may be a symbolic attempt to both venerate the past and legitimate power and control of the landscape. The significance placed on these monuments by the hillfort builders is implied by the number of examples that survive. This is attested at Freestone Hill, where the hillfort builders carefully avoided an earlier cairn before Iron Age occupants destroyed it (Raftery 1969: 7). The hillfort enclosures themselves may also represent a definition of sacred space giving rise to a need to defend that space (Finney 2006: 88–89).

Thirty one hillforts have surface evidence for settlement activity, but only nine have more than ten visible structures in their interiors. A small number of these have been excavated, making it difficult to establish whether those hut sites are contemporary with the construction and occupation of the hillfort in question. Brown (2009: 195) notes that the very presence of a hillfort on a prominent topographical feature would have been enough of a status enhancement not to warrant elaborate internal features and could explain the seeming 'absence of life' at some sites. In some instances, the limited evidence for settlement might also be explained by seasonal, rather than permanent occupation and/or activity. The inaccessibility of certain hillforts did not preclude them from extensive settlement. For example, 600m to the east of Turlough hillfort, Co. Clare, an extensive upland settlement comprising over 150 hut structures is positioned on the opposing summit of Oughtmama Mountain and is easily accessible from the hillfort. A smaller group of seven hut structures is visible at Caherconree, Co. Kerry, an inaccessible inland promontory fort positioned on a western facing spur of Gortaleen Mountain at 659m OD (Figure 2.11). Conversely, easily accessible hillforts such as Rahally, Co. Galway reveal very limited settlement activity. This is despite that fact that 50% of the interior of Rahally was excavated (Mullins 2008). It must also be noted that not all settlements were enclosed during the Late Bronze Age, as evidenced by the extensive

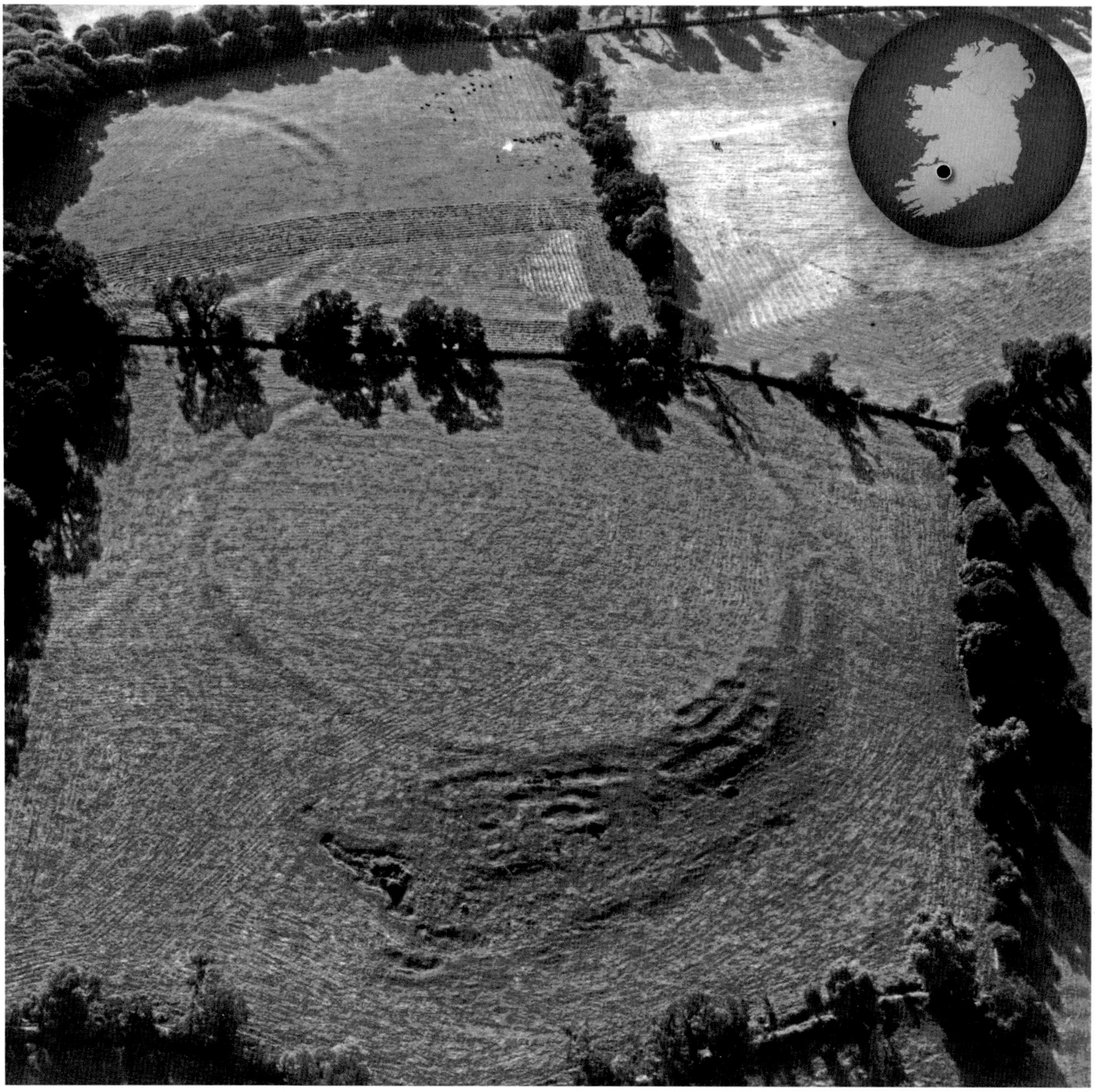

FIGURE 2.9: A PAIR OF HILLFORTS AT FRIARSTOWN, CO. LIMERICK (CAMBRIDGE AERIAL PHOTOGRAPHIC COLLECTION).

settlement at Corrstown, Co. Derry (Ginn and Rathbone 2011).

Hillforts in Ireland: the excavation record

Twenty one hillforts have been examined by excavation in Ireland, ten of which were investigated as part of this project. The majority of these excavations comprise small-scale examinations of enclosing elements, with limited investigation of interiors. Despite this, the evidence obtained from these excavations indicates the diverse nature of the Irish hillfort, with varying degrees of evidence relating to internal settlement, industrial and craft-working activity and ritual action.

As already mentioned, the earliest recorded excavation was undertaken at Freestone Hill in Co. Kilkenny (Figure 2.12). The site was excavated by Bersu between 1948–1949 and later published by Raftery (1969). The hillfort comprises a single low bank with an external ditch, enclosing an oval area of 1.52 ha. The enclosing elements do not follow the contours of the hill, rather the hillfort slopes partially to the south. The interior rises steeply towards a flat centre where the partial remains of a circular wall 18m in diameter was surrounded by a larger 37m by 30m oval enclosure (Raftery 1969: 6). The remains of a Bronze Age cairn was identified underneath these enclosures.

Excavation revealed that the hillfort ditch at Freestone Hill was rock-cut and had an irregular profile that var-

FIGURE 2.10: A LARGE CAIRN AT THE SUMMIT OF THE CLASS 2 HILLFORT OF CARN TIGHERNAGH, CO. CORK.

FIGURE 2.11: HUT STRUCTURE AGAINST OUTER FACE OF THE ENCLOSING WALL AT CAHERCONREE, CO. KERRY.

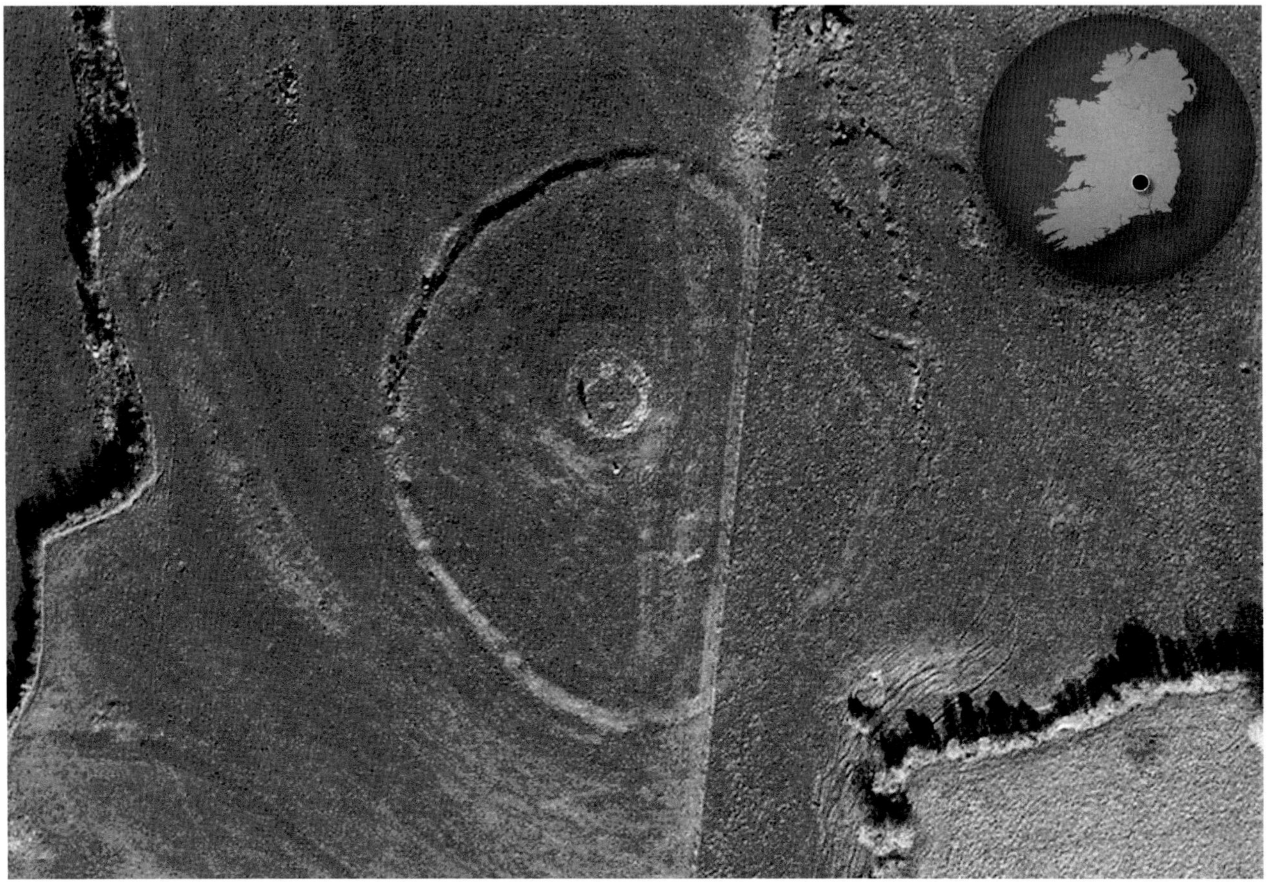

FIGURE 2.12: FREESTONE HILL, CO. KILKENNY (GOOGLE EARTH 2017).

ied from V-shaped to flat-bottomed. It is approximately 1.3–2.5m wide (averaging 2m) and 0.75m–2m in depth (Raftery 1969: 33). The bank is composed of stone and gravel. It is 2.5m–4m wide at its base, rising 0.5m–1m above the old ground surface. Large stones in the ditch suggest some form of stone facing. A potential post-hole was identified on the crest of the bank; however, Raftery (1969: 34–35) suggests that it is unlikely to form part of a larger wooden palisade. Coarse ware pottery of Bronze Age type was discovered underneath the bank and within the ditch fill. Excavation of the interior revealed no discernible structures, although shallow depressions excavated within the larger enclosure at the centre contained spreads of artefacts and 'dark' soil, and so may be considered occupation areas. Raftery (1969: 41) identifies four similar features that remain unexcavated and recent aerial photography has identified up to ten further examples. Excavation of the central area revealed the truncated remains of an Early Bronze Age cairn. This measured 23m in diameter and was probably contained by a kerb of stones, with a second concentric band of stone 3m inside this. Three inhumations (a child, a young adult, possibly female, and an unidentified example), thirteen cremations and two possible cremations were excavated within or immediately outside this cairn. South of the cairn, at least five Food Vessels of Early Bronze Age date and a 'considerable number' of worked flints were identified (*ibid.*: 9–16).

Surrounding the cairn was a large circular enclosure that Ó Floinn (2000) suggests may have been contemporary with the hillfort. Later Iron Age occupants built a smaller enclosure within this and dismantled the central cairn (Raftery 1969: 7). Freestone Hill was originally dated to the Iron Age due to the recovery of Roman artefacts within the smaller central enclosure (Raftery 1969; Bateson 1973: 45). While these finds indicate a strong Iron Age presence, coarse ware underneath the hillfort bank, in the ditch fill and within occupation areas implies that the original construction and occupation of the hillfort dates to the Late Bronze Age (Raftery 1969: 91; 1976: 58–59). Ó Floinn (2000) suggests that the ceramic assemblage, as well as other artefacts such as four blue glass beads (Henderson 1988: 442), date the construction and occupation of the hillfort to the Late Bronze Age. A single radiocarbon date (810–550 BC) from an occupation layer confirms Late Bronze Age/Early Iron Age occupation (Raftery 1995; Waddell 1998: 270).

Downpatrick hillfort in Co. Down was excavated between 1954 and 1995 by Proudfoot (1955a; 1957). It comprises a single enclosing element, visible on aerial photographs, which surrounds the historic cathedral. A 3m by 45m trench was excavated in 1954 over the enclosing elements at the south-west. Several phases of construction were noted by Proudfoot (1954: 97–98), potentially ranging from the Late Bronze Age to Medieval period. Excavation revealed a ditch/bank/ditch arrangement, although Proudfoot (1955a: 66) suggests that the inner ditch is of slightly later date. Coarse ware pottery was recovered from both the ditch and underneath the bank (Proudfoot 1954: 99). More pottery of this type was recovered from the interior. Proudfoot suggests that these sherds are similar to the Late Bronze Age pottery from crannógs at Ballinderry 2, Knocknalappa and Lough Gara. Raftery (1969: 93–94) describes the Downpatrick and Freestone Hill pottery assemblages as 'superficially comparable' and dated Downpatrick to the Late Bronze Age (Raftery 1976: 351). Three Late Bronze Age gold hoards from the interior of the hillfort further attest to Late Bronze Age activity. A series of post-holes at the edge of the bank face suggests a palisade was used to contain an earthen bank (Proudfoot 1954: 98–99). No charcoal was present inferring the palisade had decayed *in situ*. A similar setting of post-holes abutting the inner face of the bank was linked to the outer row of posts by a series of shallow traverse trenches and could be interpreted as the bedding trenches for tie-beams (Proudfoot 1955a: 59). The palisades suggest that the bank was originally 6.5m wide. A single oval structure discovered within the interior may be contemporary with the hillfort. More than a dozen clay or wattle and daub-lined pits of varying size were excavated in the interior (*ibid.*: 98).

The stratification of the ditch suggests that there was a significant period where the enclosing elements at Downpatrick were not maintained. Following this, there was a distinctive Early and Late Medieval presence, identified by the recovery of souterrain ware and glazed pottery. This period of occupation saw a re-use of the enclosing elements, with the construction of a wooden palisade on a newly formed bank and the use of the partially infilled outer ditch for an iron bloomery. Later trial excavations led Hamlin and Lynn (1988: 61–64) to suggest the hillfort is Early Medieval, but this remains to be resolved.

Coarse ware may also date the univallate hillfort at Clogher, Co. Tyrone, to the Late Bronze Age (Waddell 1998: 270). This hillfort is enclosed by a single earthen bank and a wide external ditch, which surrounds a ring-barrow and an Early Medieval ringfort. This palimpsest of monuments has complicated the dating of the site, as almost all contexts earlier than the Early Medieval period are disturbed (Warner 2009: 512). However, some radiocarbon dates confirm occupation of the hilltop during this period (Waddell 1998: 270; 277). Excavations of the bank produced evidence for wooden lacing and an association with coarse ware pottery (Warner 2009: 509), the latter pointing to Late Bronze Age occupation. Coarse ware may be associated with the construction of the hillfort and large pits containing this pottery discovered at the centre of the monument are possibly Late Bronze Age (Warner 1972; 1974). A recent publication by Warner (2009) suggests that the hillfort is Iron Age, despite the author conceding that dating evidence for the earthwork itself is poor. This is in contrast to earlier summary excavation reports that suggest a Late Bronze Age date (Warner 1971 *et seq.*).

Lyles Hill in Co. Antrim (Figure 2.13) is a pear-shaped univallate enclosure, comprising an earthen bank 9m wide and 1m high, over an area of 6.25ha. The site was originally dated to the Neolithic by Evans (1953) based on Neolithic artefacts in the bank core. Later excavations by Gibson and Simpson (1987; Simpson and Gibson 1989) produced a Late Bronze Age date of 1396–1162 BC from charcoal within the bank. The old ground surface directly underneath the bank is dated to 1526–1326 BC. Evidence for the re-use of the monument in the Late Iron Age was revealed by radiocarbon dates from the gravel capping of the bank (138 BC–AD 122) and a post-hole at the top of the bank (99–209 AD) (*ibid.*: 215). Further excavation of the interior revealed two roughly parallel lines of palisade trenches placed 3–6m apart, approximately 40m inside the Late Bronze Age bank. These palisades would have a diameter of 70m and 110m respectively (Cooney 2002: 71). Charcoal from the inner palisade is dated to 3330–2920 BC and the outer example to 2600–2350 BC (Simpson and Gibson 1989: 215). The clear evidence for Neolithic occupation at the site suggests the hilltop was an important landscape feature throughout prehistory.

Neolithic activity is also recorded at Knockacarrigeen and Knockdhu hillforts. A univallate hillfort was excavated at Knockacarrigeen Hill, Co. Galway, prior to the construction of a reservoir. Large areas of the interior and the enclosing elements were investigated. The hillfort is 4.85ha in size and surrounds a small cairn and stone enclosure (Carey 2002: 61). The enclosing elements comprise a drystone wall 6–7m in width with a maximum height of 1m. Dates obtained from a small stone built enclosure inside the hillfort (2121–1913 BC, 2173–1828 BC, 2600–2484 BC, 2860–2460 BC) indicate that the hilltop was occupied during the Neolithic and/or Early Bronze Age. Although there is no useful dating information for the excavated hillfort bank, Carey (2002) notes that this is 'remarkably similar' to the drystone banks at the Late Bronze Age hillfort at Mooghaun, Co. Clare.

Mooghaun hillfort comprises three widely spaced limestone rubble banks, occupying a total area of 11.05ha. The inner enclosing element surrounds a sub-circular area of 0.76ha. The stone bank varies from 6–9m in width and is on average 1.5m in height, although the apparent height of the banks from the exterior varies from 0.8–3.5m (Grogan 2005a: 118). There are no apparent ditches associated with this bank. A single radiocarbon date for animal bone in the inner bank material is dated to 922–813 BC. The middle enclosing element is roughly concentric and occupies an area of 2.88ha. The bank is 8–11m wide and rises to a height 2m and of 3.5m externally. Again, there is no apparent ditch feature. A series of radiocarbon dates were attained for the middle

Figure 2.13: Lyles Hill, Co. Antrim (Google Earth 2017).

enclosing element (see Grogan 2005a: Table 6.1) dating the original construction of the bank to 1125–918 BC, with subsequent alterations occurring between 1000 BC to 800 BC. The outer enclosing element is oval and encloses an area of 11.05 ha. It comprises a large inner bank, 12–15m wide, an intervening ditch 5m in average width, and a smaller outer bank. A charcoal sample from a burnt surface directly underneath the bank dates its construction to 1255–917 BC (*ibid.*: 121–188).

Grogan (2005a: 128) suggests that broadly similar radiocarbon dates from the three enclosing elements of the hillfort (ranging 1255–813 BC) imply that they were likely constructed as a unit during the Late Bronze Age. Grogan (2005a: 238–239) has argued for a construction date around the final two decades of the tenth century BC, although the radiocarbon dates for the middle and outer enclosing elements could potentially be earlier. Contemporary occupation evidence and coarse ware pottery was identified in numerous excavated areas, corroborating the radiocarbon evidence (*ibid.*: Figure. 7.10). Two hut structures abutting the middle enclosing element may be associated with pre-rampart construction or the initial building of the rampart (*ibid.*: 183–184). Grogan suggests that a 'small compact settlement' occupied the middle and inner enclosing elements, although, considering only a small proportion of the hillfort was excavated, it is likely that more extensive occupation evidence exists. There is a strong Early Medieval presence within the hillfort, visible as two large cashels, a number of smaller enclosures and several excavated hut structures (*ibid.*: 161).

The famous cliff-top fort of Dún Aonghasa, on Inishmore, Aran Islands, Co. Galway, is dated to the Late Bronze Age based on radiocarbon results and artefact finds. The hillfort comprises three main drystone walls, built of limestone blocks, which surround a cliff edge to the west. These enclose an area of 5.8ha. Two main construction phases were identified. The first relates to the construction of three of the enclosing elements and dates to the Late Bronze Age. The second comprised the construction of a fourth enclosing element and *chevaux de frise* which remains undated (see Cotter 2012a: 55, Figure 3.7; Warner 2012). The inner wall survives to a height of 4.9m and varies from 3.5m to 5.8m in width at its base. This has been rebuilt in relatively recent times, with the addition of external buttresses. The wall has two internal tiers, with access provided by a number of steps which are built into the wall (Cotter 2012a: 54). A sample of animal bone from an occupation layer deposited 'soon' after the construction of the abutting inner enclosing element returned a date of 980–810 BC (Cotter 2012a: 158–163; Warner 2012: 224). Underneath this layer, another occupation surface is dated 1070–890 BC (Cotter 2012a: 158; Warner 2012: 224).

Up to ten structures were identified in the interior of Dún Aonghasa fort (Cotter 2012a: 262–272). Two were dated, namely structures 8 (930–810 BC) and 5 (350–1 BC) (Cotter 2012b: 230). The middle enclosing element survives to a height of 4m and varies from 1.6m to 3.8m in width at its base. Two radiocarbon dates from occupation refuse underneath the lower terrace returned dates of 1300–1050 BC and 1250–1000 BC. Samples obtained from contexts later than the enclosure construction returned dates of 1080–510 BC (Cotter 2012a: 64; Warner 2012). Sherds from a minimum of 340 coarse ware vessels were recovered from the excavations, primarily from contexts dated to 1000–800 BC (Cleary 2012: 9). This corresponds well with a cumulative probability density curve that indicates a distinct peak in activity between *c.*1000–800 BC (Warner 2012: 224). Other likely Late Bronze Age finds include 460 fragments of clay crucibles and moulds (O'Carroll 2012a). Approximately 40 bronze objects, including many of Late Bronze Age type, and 17 pieces of amber (Feeney-Johnson 2012: 93) were recovered mainly from the interior. Numerous stone (Clarke 2012), bone (Mullins 2012; FitzGerald 2012a; O'Brien 2012a; Fitzgerald 2012b) and iron (Fitzgerald 2012c) implements were also recovered, which together with fourteen blue glass beads attest to Iron Age or Early Medieval occupation (Fitzgerald and Warner 2012). A large animal bone assemblage was recovered, although 95% of the material was too fragmented to identify (McCormick and Murphy 2012: 155). Cattle and sheep dominated the assemblage. Small quantities of pig, red deer, fox and grey seal were also apparent. The fish bone assemblage is the largest found in Bronze Age Ireland (McCarthy 2012: 172).

Radiocarbon samples from the three ditches at Haughey's Fort, Co. Armagh, have produced broadly contemporary results ranging 1300–900 BC (Mallory 1995: 75). Haughey's Fort is a trivallate hillfort that occupies a large area, 10.42ha in size. Originally, the hillfort was thought to be univallate, until aerial photography, and subsequent archaeological excavations, confirmed two further enclosing elements. All three ditches are approximately V-shaped and measure 2.3–3.2m in depth (Mallory 1995: 74). There is no surviving bank material, although Mallory (1995: 74) suggests the ditch fill sequence indicates there were originally internal banks. Large stones found at the bottom of the inner ditch may have formed an external revetment (Mallory 1988: 14). The inner enclosure was further enhanced by a small palisade beyond the lip of the ditch (Mallory 1995: 75). Aitchison (1998: 31) has suggested that radiocarbon dates from the three enclosing ditches indicate that Haughey's Fort was constructed *c.*1150–1050 BC and abandoned shortly afterwards. The features discovered within the site can also be assigned to this general period (Mallory 1995: 84). A dendro-date from a piece of waterlogged wood at the base of the inner ditch has precisely dated the latter to 1166 BC (Ballie and Brown 1991; Ballie and Brown 1998). Excavation of the middle and outer enclosing elements are broadly contemporary with the inner example, and date to around 1200–800 BC. Occupation activity within the hillfort is largely contemporary with its construction (Mallory 1995: 75; 78; Mallory and Warner 1988). Large pits were excavated, containing substantial amounts of carbonized grain as well as Late Bronze Age coarse ware pottery, fragments of quern stones, metal artefacts and fragments of gold and bronze. The majority of these pits were positioned within a large (25–30m) built structure comprising an arc of three lines of stakes set outside larger postholes. Two post-holes are dated to 1250–900 BC, and Mallory (1995: 84) has suggested that this could have been a ritual structure.

Rahally hillfort, Co. Galway, is a large (14.24ha) trivallate hillfort situated on a low glacial ridge (Figure 2.14). Overall, 53% of its interior and approximately 30% of the entire hillfort has been excavated. The ditches of the hillfort are U-shaped, up to 4m wide and 1.5m deep, with the outer and inner elements being more substantial than the middle example (Mullins 2008: 26). Sherds of Late Bronze Age coarse ware and a damaged polished stone axe were recovered from the inner ditch, from where a radiocarbon date of 994–827 BC is available for charcoal found at the base. Although there was no surviving bank material, the ditch fills indicate that banks formed part of the inner and middle enclosing elements (*ibid.*: 26). A charcoal sample from the basal layer of the middle ditch returned a date of 790–520 BC (Mullins 2008: 26). The outer enclosing element of the hillfort comprises a ditch-bank-ditch arrangement. A charcoal sample from the base of one of the ditches returned a date of 1090–900 BC (*ibid.*: 26). Although a large portion of the hillfort was excavated, there was a distinct lack of Late Bronze Age artefacts and/or contemporary settlement evidence, although Early Medieval settlement in the form of ringforts is well attested. A 30m gap in the northern section of the inner enclosing element incorporates a wet marshy area that extended northwards. A late La Téne artefact, possibly some horse equipment, was recovered from this context, suggesting a possible votive pond. Somewhat similar evidence is found close to Haughey's Fort, where an artificial pool known as the Kings Stables, was constructed at the same time as the hillfort and was used for depositing bronze artefacts and human remains (Lynn 1977).

The important excavations conducted by Barry Raftery at the quadravallate hillfort at Rathgall, Co. Wicklow, are still awaiting publication, and only a limited number of published dates are available. The inner enclosure is likely to be an Early Medieval ringfort (Waddell 1998: 270). Excavation of the two closely spaced middle enclosing elements was inconclusive but suggested that

FIGURE 2.14: RAHALLY HILLFORT, CO. GALWAY DURING EXCAVATION (SOURCE: MARKUS CASEY).

the intervening ditch had been substantially backfilled by the Late Iron Age (see Raftery 1988: 79). A recent listing of 55 radiocarbon dates from Rathgall (Chapple 2013) includes 47 of Late Bronze Age date. Although these lack contextual detail prior to their publication, a number of these can be used to date the enclosing elements to the Late Bronze Age. Settlement activity is well attested and is dated to the Late Bronze Age (Raftery 1976: 341; 350). A substantial assemblage of crucible and clay moulds fragments, as well as various bronze, gold and amber objects, attest to the intensive production of prestige goods and long-distance trading at Rathgall during the Late Bronze Age. Contemporary burials were also recovered in the interior. Iron Age and Early Medieval re-occupation of the hillfort is also attested (Becker 2010).

Recent excavations have been conducted at the substantial inland promontory fort at Knockdhu, Co. Antrim (Macdonald 2008). The monument uses cliff edges to the north, east and south as a natural barrier. The western approach is protected using a series of three banks and two ditches. Macdonald (2008) notes that although the enclosing elements are visually impressive, the three banks are relatively slight features that have been carefully positioned to exploit the promontory's natural topography and maximise the impact of their appearance.

Excavation revealed two main phases of construction. The excavator has argued that the inner and middle banks were probably contemporary, stating that the latest dates derived from a sample obtained from buried soil beneath the inner bank (1409–1221 BC) is superseded by the latest date derived from a sample taken from buried soil underneath the middle bank (1008–858 BC). The latest date from the outer bank was obtained from a sample taken from buried soil underneath the bank and dates to (1426–1293 BC). Although all three banks could be contemporary, there was no stratigraphic evidence to validate this assumption. The excavation awaits its full publication, with only a limited number of radiocarbon dates available. The second phase of activity is represented by an extension of the inner bank and the re-cutting of its associated ditch after it had accumulated a substantial amount of silt. The latest radiocarbon date obtained near the base of this re-cut provides a *terminus ante quem* of 740–389 BC.

The entrance to this Class 3 hillfort comprises a simple corresponding gap in the enclosing elements at the southern end. Excavation of the break in the inner bank revealed a roughly cobbled surface overlaying polished bedrock that was 1.9m wide. A large post-hole 0.4m wide, was revealed underneath 0.55m from the edge of the entrance. This feature is likely to be associated with the original entrance. A radiocarbon date from twigs recovered from the fill of the post-hole dates the dismantling of the structural wood to 1118–930 BC. Sealing the post-hole, a series of heat-modified clay deposits contained charcoal indicate a surface subjected to intense burning (Macdonald 2008). There was no date from this surface. This feature may be associated with the burning of the wooden palisade. Although no obvious post-holes were associated with this feature, the narrow trench may not have been large enough to reveal possible palisade features.

Five circular structures or platforms were excavated within the interior of the hillfort. There have been approximately 70 possible hut structures identified within the interior, the majority recently being revealed by high-resolution LiDAR commissioned by the Northern Ireland Environmental Agency (McNeary 2012). The majority of excavated structures appear to date to the Late Bronze Age and may be broadly contemporary with the construction and occupation of the hillfort (Macdonald 2008). One structure dates to the Late Neolithic/Early Bronze Age (dates from a hearth range 2425–2201 BC and 2459–2206 BC, and a charred hazelnut from a wall-slot returned a date of 2459–2206 BC), indicating that the promontory was periodically exploited prior to the construction of the enclosing elements.

Neary (2004) excavated Commons of Lloyd hillfort in Co. Meath, a trivallate hillfort visible in aerial photography comprising three non-concentric ditches. A narrow trench approximately 0.5m in width was excavated on the northern side of the interior and over the enclosing elements, prior to the laying of an electrical cable. The trench was not bottomed and features were not resolved, with excavation extending only to the depth of the cable. Cremated animal bone deposited in a pit close to the summit of the hillfort returned a Late Bronze Age date (1130–910 BC).

A bivallate hillfort at Knockanacuig, Co. Kerry, was partially excavated prior to development of the site (Dunne and Bartlett 2009). The hillfort has a total area of 7.21ha. It is heavily disturbed and only a small portion of the outer enclosure is extant. The external bank measures 12m in width and 0.5m in height. Excavation revealed an external ditch comprising two phases of activity, the initial construction was V-shaped, 5.2m wide and 2.2m deep, with steeply sloping sides and a rounded base, and a second re-cut was U-shaped, 6.1m in maximum width and 1.2m in depth, with gradually sloping sides and a flat base. A sample from the basal layer of the primary ditch cut returned a date of 90 BC–79 AD, while an internal pit is dated 398–544 AD. The excavation has not been fully published, and without further contextual information these radiocarbon dates cannot conclusively date the construction of the hillfort to the Iron Age.

Trial excavations at Downshill hillfort, Co. Wicklow, produced no datable finds or radiocarbon evidence and remain unpublished (O'Neill 2007). Similarly, monitoring of reconstruction works at Grianán of Aileach, Co. Donegal did not produce any artefacts or radiocarbon evidence to date the construction or occupation of the hillfort (Moore 2006; 2007).

Ongoing excavations at the Hill of Ward (Tlaghta) in Co. Meath has identified a large series of enclosing elements surrounding the summit. Although there are currently no publications relating to the site, dates from the enclosing elements range 1100–800 BC (steve Davis pers. comm.). The size and dating of the monument is consistent with other Class 2 hillforts in Ireland.

Hillforts in Ireland: the environmental evidence

Environmental studies have highlighted the intensive clearance and exploitation of land immediately surrounding Irish hillforts. At Mooghaun, woodland was almost completely removed and replaced by pasture and some cereal cultivation during the Late Bronze Age (Molloy 2005: 284). A clearance event in the period 1400–1100 BC was of such severity that pollen representation of trees and tall shrubs fell from 83–94% to 18% (O'Connell *et al.* 2001; Molloy 2005: 285–286). Cattle were the dominant species, followed by pig and sheep/goat, which suggests that animal husbandry was the principal form of agriculture (McCormick and Murray 2005: 304). This may explain the absence of storage pits at Mooghaun, though the limited extent of excavation there must also be considered.

Weir's (1987a, 1987b, 1993, 1994) extensive analysis of the palaeo-environment surrounding Haughey's Fort has revealed a major clearance episode around 1400–1000 BC. Cereal pollen makes up 6% of the open landscape. This is amongst the highest known from prehistoric Ireland and indicates that arable agriculture was an important component of the economy (see Plunkett 2006: 65). Animal bone from the hillfort indicates a mixed economy based on cattle and to a lesser extent pig (McCormick 1991: 31). This is confirmed by lipid analysis of pottery from the site, which has found positive traces of cattle meat (Mallory 1995: 82). The major clearance phase ended by *c.*1000 BC, broadly contemporary with the abandonment of Haughey's Fort (Mallory 1995: 79). Plunkett (2006: 65) suggests that the environmental data indicates that Haughey's Fort and Mooghaun hillfort were supported by 'thriving economies'.

At Rahally, Co. Galway, the environs of the hillfort was cleared of deciduous woodland during the Late Bronze Age, with fewer trees and a rise in clearance indicators implying an increase in pastoral farming contemporary with the construction of the hillfort (Mullins and Bermingham 2009: 71). A reliance on cattle rearing is evident in the recovered faunal remains, which like Mooghaun, may explain the absence of pit features.

At Lyles Hill, Co. Antrim, pollen evidence suggests that the landscape was already being exploited immediately prior to the construction of the hillfort, when barley was being cultivated (Simpson and Gibson 1989: 215). This was succeeded by hazel scrub and grassland, the latter indicating the importance of animal husbandry. Raftery (1969: 99) suggests that snail remains found in the ditch fill at Freestone Hill, Co. Kilkenny, are characteristic of dry fauna and infer that the sides of the hilltop were covered with patches of hazel scrub and open grassland. Pollen analysis undertaken near a potential hillfort on Croghan Hill, Co. Offaly, shows Late Bronze Age activity in that area. Plunkett (2009: 274) has noted extensive woodland clearance comparable with other hillforts, with the absence of arable weeds suggesting that pastoral farming dominated. Plunkett (2006: 65–66) cites Ballylin hillfort, Co. Limerick as another example where an agricultural expansion occurs near a hillfort in the Late Bronze Age. This is more tenuous as the pollen core was taken from a bog 7km from this Late Bronze Age hillfort. Analysis suggests that an intense phase of clearance began *c.*1200 BC and 'flourished' from the 11th century BC, the pattern and duration of activity being reminiscent of that recorded at Mooghaun (Plunkett 2006: 66). A pollen core 3.5 km from Lurigethan hillfort, Co. Antrim, indicates an intensification of activity during the Late Bronze Age, attested by a major woodland clearance (Weir 1993: 21–23). The very low levels of tree pollen suggests that the local area was probably almost entirely clear at that time.

In summary, the environmental evidence indicates that the immediate environs of Irish hillforts were being exploited for agricultural purposes. In certain instances, where more extensive excavation of the interior has been undertaken, features associated with the storage of agricultural produce have been identified. For example, at Haughey's Fort, Co. Armagh, large pits within a substantial structure at the centre of the hillfort contained considerable amounts of carbonized grain. At Downpatrick, Co. Down, wattle-lined pits within the hillfort have been interpreted as grain silos (Proudfoot 1954: 98). Geophysical survey at Toor More, Co. Kilkenny and Ballylin, Co. Limerick, has revealed substantial numbers of possible pits near the summit of the hillforts. This is important, as Yates (2007: 2–4) suggests that wealth in the Late Bronze Age resulted from the successful management of available resources, particularly agricultural produce, with intensive farming possibly leading to rapid economic growth. Cunliffe (2013: 252) also considers control of agrarian surplus as connected to the maintenance and expansion of elites, used for feasting purposes or to acquire high status goods outside the local territory (Cunliffe 1995: 90; Cunliffe 2013: 257–258). Hillfort societies can be described as 'decentralised stratified societies' where the upper echelons of the community exploit farming communities through tribute and taxation (Kristiansen 1993: 19–20). Importantly, Kristiansen (1993) argues that these 'archaic states' developed in regions where surplus can be generated and controlled before being converted into large-scale ritual activities such as building ceremonial centres, organization of craft production, and centralized trade. In Kristiansen's model, the accumulation of surplus agricultural produce is central to hillfort societies. The intensification of land exploitation surrounding Irish hillforts, therefore, corresponds with this model, and could be seen as an attempt by hillfort communities to protect important agricultural land and produce excess produce to support large-scale building projects and long-distance trade.

Summary

Irish hillforts consist of large enclosures strategically positioned on prominent topographic positions. These sites were often located near natural routeways or in commanding positions in the landscape. There are approximately 108 examples in Ireland and these are somewhat evenly distributed throughout the country. The site type known as the hilltop enclosure may be contemporary, though the dating of these is problematic, which is why they are not considered in this study. Irish hillforts are on average around 5ha in size, with some examples well in excess of 20ha. The available evidence suggests that hillforts were built and occupied in the Middle to Late Bronze Age, with a particular flourish occurring during the Late Bishopland and Roscommon phases *c.*1300–900 BC. Excavation of some hillforts has uncovered artefacts indicative of long-distance trade, as well as evidence for the on-site production of prestigious metalwork. This suggests that Irish hillforts may have functioned as central places of redistribution controlled by an elite. There is varying evidence for settlement at the Irish sites, with some examples such as Knockdhu in Antrim revealing dense internal settlement, and other sites such as Rahally in Galway showing no contemporary habitation. A ritual/ceremonial element is also apparent at these sites. For example, the artificial pool known as the King's Stables, close to Haughey's Fort, was used as an area for ritual deposition. The different types of widely-spaced multivallation may also be related to ritual activity, where it was necessary to have the enclosing elements spaced a certain distance apart. Unfortunately, so few Irish hillforts have been extensively investigated, that it is difficult to confidently assess the broader aspects of function.

3

Clashanimud Hillfort, Co. Cork

Our analysis of Bronze Age hillforts in Ireland begins with the site of Clashanimud (Cashel), Co. Cork. This is a fine example of a Class 2a hillfort, where an area of almost nine hectares is surrounded by two widely spaced concentric enclosures in a prominent landscape setting. The scale of construction is impressive, with a total defensive perimeter of 1.74km, and each enclosure protected by a bank with wooden fence and external ditch. Our investigations suggest the hillfort was built as a single design *c.*1250–1050 BC, but may have been destroyed after only a brief occupation. That calculated act provides an insight into the political climate of the Middle/Late Bronze Age transition in Ireland, and the consequences of inter-regional warfare that was prevalent at that time.

The following is a detailed account of the archaeological excavation undertaken at Clashanimud hillfort over three seasons in 2004–6.

3.1 Landscape Setting

This hillfort is located on the northern side of Clashanimud townland near the small village of Knockavilla, in the parish of Innishannon (ITM 552189, 561391), 14km to the south-west of Cork city (Figure 3.1). The northern side forms part of the boundary of the baronies of Kinalea and East Muskerry, with the boundaries of East Carbery and Kinalmeaky baronies located 1–2km to the south and west respectively. The site lies on a small spur off the southern edge of a prominent anticlinal ridge that extends west from Cork Harbour (Figure 3.2). There are steep to moderate slopes on the southern, western and northern sides, with more level terrain approaching the hillfort on the eastern side (Figure 3.3). The summit (179m OD) is a low rise on the south-eastern side of the interior, marked today by a low cairn.

The hillfort overlooks a broad valley to the immediate

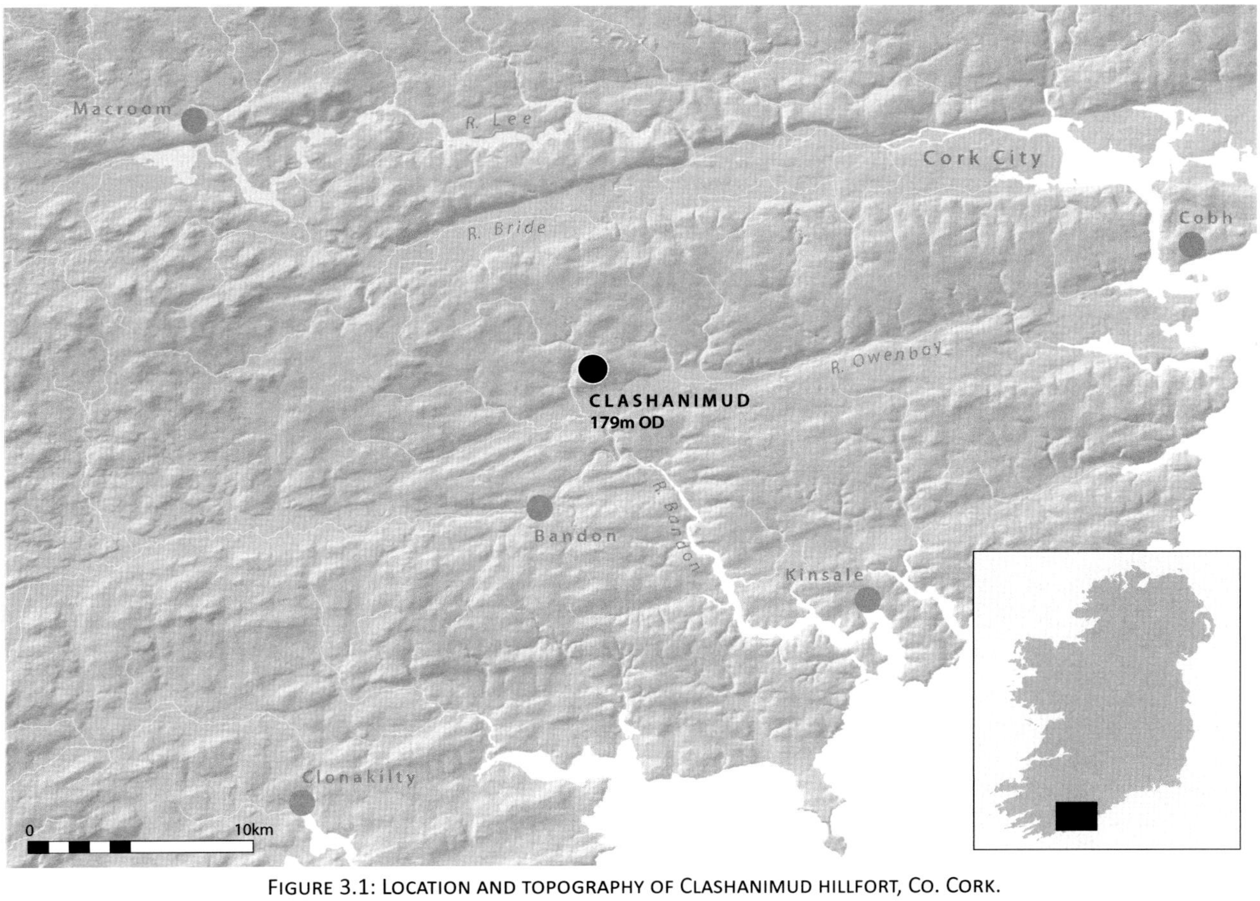

FIGURE 3.1: LOCATION AND TOPOGRAPHY OF CLASHANIMUD HILLFORT, CO. CORK.

FIGURE 3.2: AERIAL VIEW OF LANDSCAPE SETTING OF CLASHANIMUD HILLFORT.

south, with panoramic views across a wide part of the ridge and valley topography of Mid and West Cork. While the overall elevation is low, the site does have a strong visibility relative to the surrounding landscape, particularly when seen from the south and west. The interior is presently overgrown by bracken and gorse, apart from two small pasture fields on the southern side of the outer enclosure. The northern side is bordered by coniferous forestry first planted in the 1970s. The only bedrock exposures are those produced by quarrying in the modern era, mostly along the eastern slopes. This is basal Carboniferous geology of the Kinsale Formation,

FIGURE 3.3: VIEW OF CLASHANIMUD HILLFORT FROM NORTH-WEST.

a mud-dominant series of sedimentary rocks with subordinate sandstones, deposited around 350 million years ago.

3.2 Recent History

The earliest record of the hillfort is contained in the first edition of the Ordnance Survey six-inch mapping (1:10,560), surveyed in 1841 and published in 1845 (Cork sheet 96). This map depicts two concentric oval enclosures with the generic name 'Cashel Fort'. The inner defences are shown as a hachured bank with an external line indicating the presence of a ditch. The outer defences only show a hachured bank, probably because an external ditch was already infilled by the mid nineteenth century. There is no indication of any entrance to the inner enclosure, while the only access shown to the outer enclosure is a short track that presently connects the eastern side of the hillfort to the adjacent road. The 1845 six-inch map also depicts a sub-division of the outer hillfort enclosure by six radiating field banks, four of which are on the south-east side, with one each on the northern and western sides.

The 1845 Ordnance Survey recorded three irregular quarry pits on the eastern side of the inner enclosure, and one example bordering the outside of that enclosing element on the north-east side. This confirms that stone quarrying was already underway by 1841, which is significant as there is a local tradition that the adjacent road was built as a famine relief project in the nineteenth century (Irish Folklore Commission *Schools' Folklore Scheme* 1937–8: 287; 329). The map evidence confirms this road was already built by the time of the Great Famine of 1845–9, so either it was re-surfaced then or else this tradition relates to earlier famine relief.

The Ordnance Survey revised the first edition of the six-inch mapping in 1904, based on a more detailed survey conducted in 1901 at a scale of 25 inches to one mile. There are only minor changes on this second edition map, notably the addition of two extra radiating fences/walls in the outer enclosure, on the north-east and south sides respectively, and the omission of the quarry pits from the interior. It is likely that stone quarrying was still in progress as a new access track to those pits is shown connecting the eastern side of the hillfort to the adjacent road. Local information indicates this quarrying continued to the 1950s, which accounts for the extensive pitting now evident along the eastern slopes of the hillfort.

The earliest description of the hillfort comes from a visit made in 1856 by the well-known Cork antiquarian, John Windele. His description of 'the great fort of Cashel', known locally as the Caher, includes the following:

'The summit of the hill, which is 597 feet in height, consists for a considerable space of a wild uncultivated heath, considerably flat at the western side, and somewhat steep at the east. Around this elevation is drawn a fosse, at present varying in breadth from six to ten feet, the earth excavated from which being thrown up, forms a rampart about ten or twelve feet high from the bottom of the fosse, and on the inside but a few feet in elevation and much abraided. Very much in character of the ordinary earthen forts.

The space enclosed is several acres in extent, and of very unequal surface, flat towards the west, and steep at the east side, the whole ground having been left in its natural state by its original fortifying possessors. There are no remains of any kind whatsoever within, no appearance to indicate subterranean structures or constructions' (in O'Mahony 1908: 80; from Windele MS 12. I. 10, Royal Irish Academy).

The site featured in a lecture given in the summer of 1864 to the Bandon Young Men's Society by another Cork antiquarian, Richard Caulfield, who was accompanied on that occasion by the well-known British archaeologist, Colonel Lane Fox (later General Pitt-Rivers). In a publication of that talk, Caulfield noted:

'Cashel Fort, near Inishanon, Co. Cork, is perhaps the largest in Ireland; it is of oval form and in two lines, the outer being 900 feet by 1,140 feet; the inner line is at a distance of 150 feet from the other, which is quite exceptional. The fort is on the crest of a high hill, and commands the county for miles around' (Caulfield 1865: 707).

Some 30 years later, Thomas Westropp, mentioned the site in a survey of ancient Irish forts, and included a sketch plan based on the 1845 Ordnance Survey (Westropp 1896/1901: 691–3). This drawing shows an oval feature, around 30m in length, on the north-east side of the inner enclosure, now recognized as one of the large quarry pits recorded on the 1845 Ordnance Survey.

While these antiquarian reports provide only minimal description of the hillfort, the following historical association was made by the historian Canon O'Mahony:

'The Hill-Fort of Cashel is in the part of Kinalea which was originally known as Musgry Mitine, and must therefore have been a stronghold of the Muscraighe, the chief branch of the Ernai (Iverni), whom Duald Mac Firbis and the compilers of the Book of Ballymote trace to a name-giving ancestor, Erainn of the line of Mile' (O'Mahony 1908: 79).

Professor Sean P. Ó Ríordáin of University College Cork visited the hillfort in the early 1930s, and published a short description accompanied by a sketch profile of the inner defences (Ó Ríordáin 1935: 49). The site was listed by Raftery (1972: 45) as an example of a Class 2a hillfort (widely spaced, multivallate, hill-top enclosure), and is mentioned in subsequent reviews of Irish hillforts (e.g. Raftery 1994; Grogan 2005b, table 7.1; Waddell 2010). A short description in the *Archaeological Inventory of County Cork* refers to the former existence of a folly ('Hawke's Tower') on the summit of the hill, as well as an association with an ancient Celtic festival (Power *et al.* 1994: 66). Both assertions are incorrect, based on a misreading of Máire MacNeill's 1962 work *The Festival of Lughnasa*, which refers to a hill known as the 'Peakeen', five miles to the south-west of Bandon (Clashanimud hillfort lies to the north north-east of that town). This is confirmed by a discovery there in 1991 of the remains of a tower in the townland of Cashelmore, which was erected in 1852 by one Zacheria Hawkes (Connolly 2001: 81, with photographs).

There is no record of any archaeological excavation or antiquarian digging at the hillfort. Today, the site is known by archaeologists as 'Cashel Fort' following the 1845 Ordnance Survey, while local people refer to it as the 'Caher'. The Irish Folklore Commission recorded some popular legends during the School Survey of 1937–8. These include references to a 'treasure' buried by the 'Danes', to strange lights seen on the hill, and to subterranean passages connected to other forts in the locality (*Schools' Folklore Scheme* 1937–8: 254–5; 292). Mention should be made of the townland name, Clashanimud (Clais an Adhmaid: 'Trench/Ravine of the Timbers'; or possibly Clós an Adhmaid: 'wooden enclosure'), and the locality name, Knockavilla (Cnoc a'Bhile: 'Hill of the Sacred Tree'), both of which may have significance in relation to the hillfort. There is a folk tradition that the tree in the Knockavilla place-name was formerly in the middle of the hillfort, where a notorious landlord, Sean Dearg Nash, is supposed to have hanged several people (*ibid.*: 298–9).

3.3 Hillfort Morphology

The hillfort is comprised of two concentric oval enclosures (Figure 3.4), measuring 365m (east–west) by 305m (north–south), with an overall area of 8.88ha (including enclosing elements). The inner enclosure measures 230m (east–west) by 170m (north–south), with an internal area of 3.3ha (4.07ha including enclosing elements). The inner defences are 0.69km long and comprise a large earthen bank, outside which there is a large ditch with a low counterscarp bank. The bank averages 5.4m wide (range 3.6–7m), with an average internal height of 0.4m (range 0.1–0.9m), and an external height of 1.5m (range 0.5–2.3m). The ditch averages 3.1m in upper width (range 2–5.1m), with an average external depth of 0.9m (range 0.6–1.5m). The counterscarp bank averages 2.1m in width (range 1.5–3.6m) and 0.5m in external height (range 0.2–1.1m). The

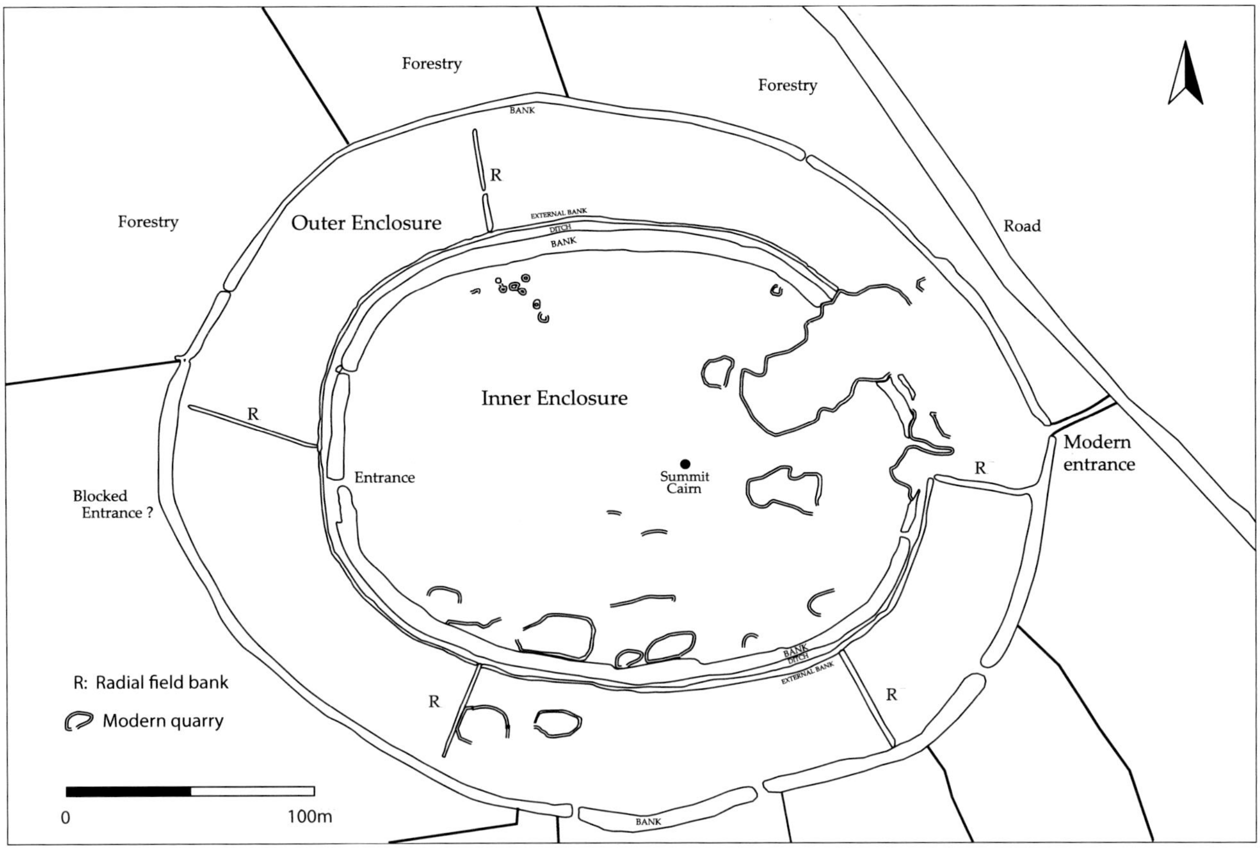

FIGURE 3.4: SURFACE FEATURES OF CLASHANIMUD HILLFORT.

latter was re-built in places, particularly on the southern side of the inner enclosure, probably in the early modern era.

There are few features visible in the interior of the inner enclosure, which is now heavily overgrown by bracken and gorse (Figure 3.5). These include a small cairn at the summit, and numerous modern quarry pits on the eastern and southern slopes. The original entrance to the inner enclosure is located on the western side, though this was not apparent before excavation.

The outer enclosure is positioned 48–55m from the bank of the inner enclosure, and is also overgrown by bracken and gorse. It has an internal area of 3.96ha (4.81ha including enclosing elements), and is bounded by a stone-faced earthen bank re-built in the modern era (Figure 3.6). The outer bank has a perimeter of 1.05km, with an average width of 4.1m (range 3.1–6.3m), an internal height of 1.2m (range 1.1–1.3m), and an external height of 2.3m (range 1.7–2.8m) except where re-built in the early modern era. The external ditch is entirely infilled along the enclosure perimeter, except on the west north-west side where there is a 4m wide depression with a slight counterscarp bank. The original entrance(s) to the outer enclosure is not clearly defined. The most likely location is on the western side, where a break in the bank is now closed with large boulders. This is directly opposite the original entrance to the inner enclosure that was identified by excavation.

Today, the inner and outer enclosing elements are connected by four radial boundaries, three of which create two small pasture fields on the southern side of the hillfort. These are earthen banks with drystone facing on both sides, averaging 1–1.4m in height with shrub cover. Up to eight such radial walls are recorded in the historic mapping of the Ordnance Survey. These field banks are likely to be early modern in date, based on their extant profile and some excavation evidence (see below).

3.4 Archaeological Investigation

The objective of the Clashanimud project was to obtain dating evidence and stratigraphic records for the construction, occupation and abandonment of the hillfort, as well as information pertaining to the subsequent site history. A further objective was to recover information on the hillfort defences and entrance arrangements, and to understand the organization of settlement and ritual/ ceremonial space inside the hillfort. The intention was to examine different aspects of settlement economy through the excavation of specific activity areas, artifacts and environmental remains. The project also explored the wider significance of the hillfort within a local and regional cultural landscape setting.

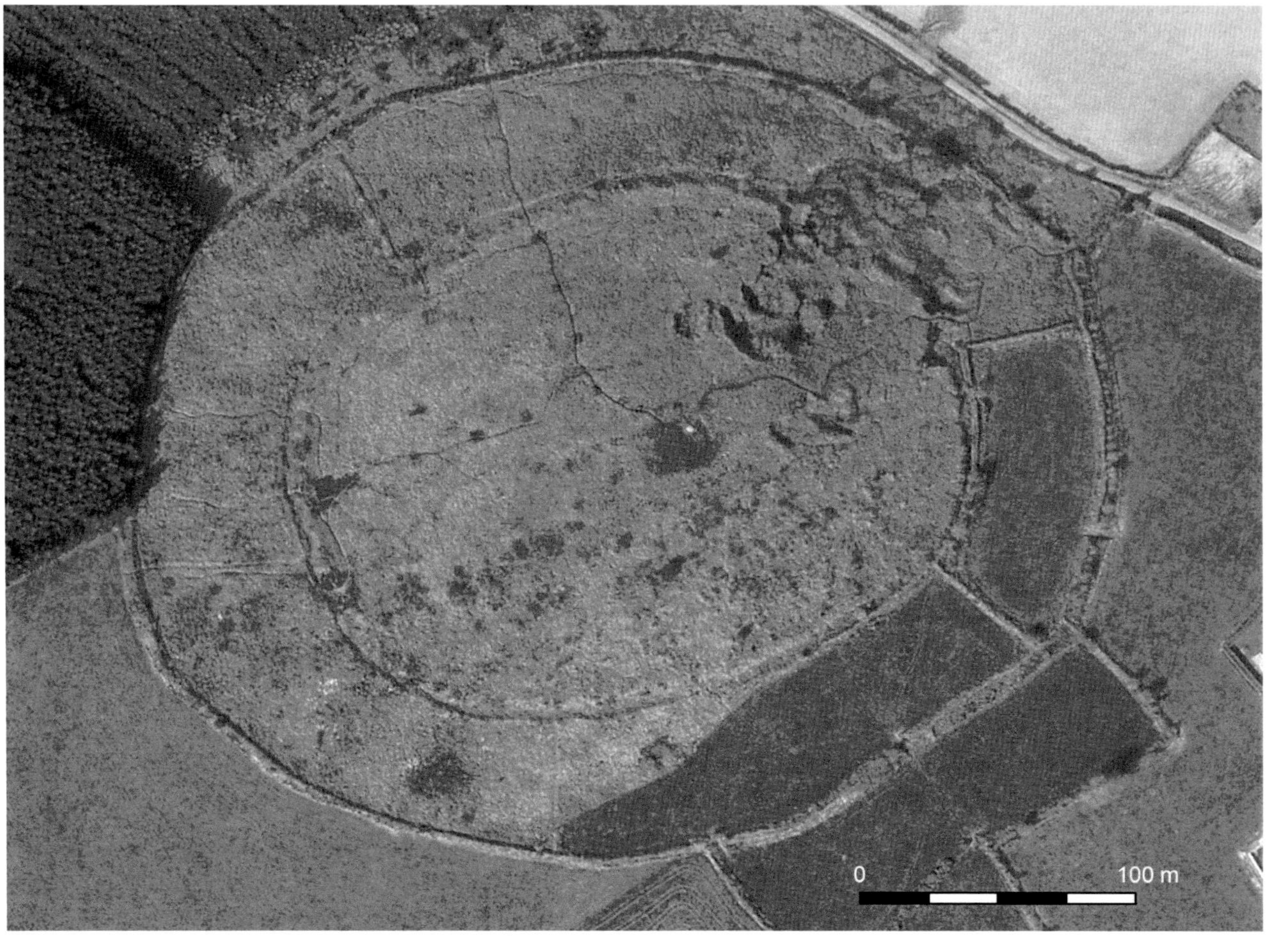

FIGURE 3.5: VERTICAL AERIAL VIEW OF CLASHANIMUD HILLFORT, 2011. NOTE EXTENSIVE QUARRYING IN NORTH-EAST SECTOR (UPPER RIGHT), AND RADIAL FIELD BANKS IN OUTER ENCLOSURE.

FIGURE 3.6: AERIAL VIEW OF CLASHANIMUD HILLFORT, TAKEN *C.*1970, LOOKING SOUTH (SOURCE: DAPHNE POCHIN MOULD). NOTE CULTIVATION FEATURES INSIDE OUTER ENCLOSURE (LOWER RIGHT).

Fieldwork commenced in 2004 with two weeks of total station survey and geophysical prospection. This provided a detailed topographic survey of the hillfort, as well as a magnetic and electrical resistivity survey of the north-west part of the inner enclosure. The latter provided a number of targets for excavation in that area. Further geophysical survey was subsequently undertaken on the hillfort summit and along the defences of the inner enclosure, as well as in fields adjacent to the hillfort (see below).

The initial season of excavation was of four weeks duration in 2004 (Figure 3.7). The focus was on the northern side of the inner enclosure. The objectives were (a) to sample the defences of the inner enclosure (Trench 1); (b) to examine some surface hollows regarded as possible hut-sites (Trench 2), and (c) to test-pit geophysical survey anomalies (Trenches 3–5).

A second season of excavation was conducted over 17 weeks in 2005. There were three main objectives: (a) the investigation of a small cairn and some geophysical survey anomalies at the summit area (Trenches 6–8); (b) sampling of the north-west quadrant of the inner enclosure where a series of eight 4m² test-pits (Trenches 11–18) were excavated on a 20m grid spacing; (c) the hillfort defences were examined on the western side of the inner enclosure (Trenches 9, 10 and 19), and the north-west side of the outer enclosure (Trench 21).

A third and final season of excavation was conducted over 15 weeks in 2006. There were two major objectives: (a) to continue grid sampling of the inner enclosure to locate evidence of occupation (Trenches 23–37); and (b) to investigate a possible original entrance to the inner enclosure on the western side of the hillfort (Trench 22).

The total area excavated amounts to 1059m², which represents 1.19% of the hillfort (8.88ha). While this is a small sample, the excavation of 37 trenches does represent an extensive investigation of the hillfort, in particular its defences. The grid sampling strategy across the inner enclosure, involving 4m² test-pits spaced 20m apart, represents a reasonably thorough investigation of the interior (Figure 3.8). Those parts of the inner enclosure not excavated were those least likely to have been used for occupation, such as the steeper eastern slopes where quarrying was undertaken in the modern era. The least representative results are for the outer enclosure, where considerably less excavation was conducted. This was partly due to its size, but also because of poor archaeological preservation caused by cultivation in the early modern era.

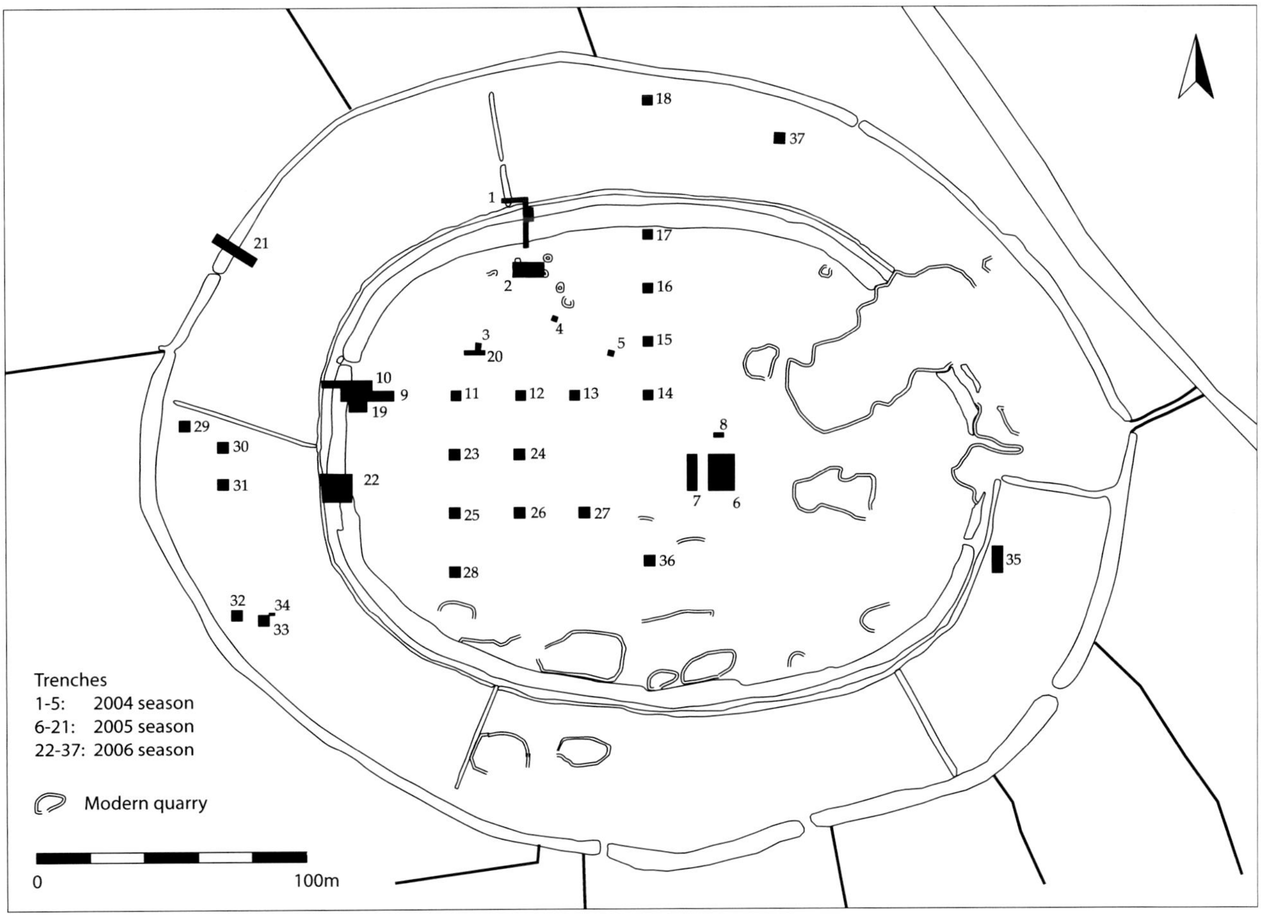

Figure 3.7: Plan of Clashanimud hillfort showing location of 37 excavation trenches.

FIGURE 3.8: TEST-PIT EXCAVATION IN NORTH-WEST PART OF INNER AND OUTER ENCLOSURES, CLASHANIMUD.

Substantial clearance of fern and gorse growth was required before excavation could proceed in different areas of the hillfort. This clearance facilitated total station survey of the hillfort topography, as well as geophysical survey in selected areas. Excavation was carried out by hand, to the highest possible standards of recovery, stratigraphic recording and context investigation. This involved the use of spades to de-sod the excavation trenches, followed by coarse and fine trowelling of the exposed surfaces. Archaeological features were excavated and recorded on a single context basis, with composite planning, section drawing and photography. No sieving was carried out on site due to the absence of a water source. Bulk samples were taken for laboratory sieving to extract macro-plant remains. The trenches were backfilled by hand on completion of excavation, with some partial reconstruction of the defences for public presentation.

Archaeological preservation

The overall conditions of aerobic preservation were not good, due to a combination of factors. High soil acidity caused by podzolisation of thin lithosols across the interior militated against the preservation of bone and other organic material. The well-drained nature of the stony glacial till, and the near-surface bedrock in some areas, meant that there were no contexts with waterlogged preservation. Finally, the shattered nature of the near-surface bedrock led to poor stratigraphic resolution in many parts of the site.

Excavation revealed a similar pattern of soil development across the inner enclosure (Figure 3.9). The thin skeletal soils there could be classed as lithosols. This is typically a thin organic soil overlying a heavily podzolised subsoil, with well defined zones of leaching/eluviation (E-horizon) and precipitation/illuviation (B-horizon). The latter can be generally divided into a Bh-horizon of humus precipitation overlying a Bs-horizon of iron enrichment. At Clashanimud, the B-horizon is occasionally formed on pockets of glacial till (C-horizon), but in most cases occurs on weathered bedrock.

The following is a typical soil profile in the inner hillfort enclosure:

O-horizon. Thin rooty sod (C.01), free of stones; often with fern rhizomes.

A-horizon. Dark brown humic silt (C.02) with numerous small to medium stones.

E-horizon. Grey sandy silt (C.04) with leached appearance, very compact with frequent small to medium stones and occasional larger stones.

FIGURE 3.9: NATURAL SOIL PROFILE IN THE INNER ENCLOSURE OF CLASHANIMUD HILLFORT.

Bh-horizon. Compact silt or sandy silt (C.359) with variable dark colour (mid to dark brown to black), with numerous small to large stones, some of which can be decayed.

Bs-horizon. Compact layer of red-brown or orange-brown silt or sandy silt (C.360), with visible iron enrichment, frequent small to large stones. Contains iron, manganese and aluminium sesquioxides.

C-horizon. Pockets of hard white-grey silt (C.361) between bedrock, with numerous small to large stones.

Eroded bedrock (C.362). The result of periglacial frost-shattering of near-surface bedrock in late Pleistocene times, combined with glacial scouring, and some solifluxion-type movement.

Variants include the occasional occurrence of a thin spread of dark grey silt (C.03) at the base of the organic soil, transitional to underlying B-horizon. Similarly, there can be lenses or a thin layer of grey-brown silt (C.05) at the base of the E-horizon (C.04) in areas of high stone density, transitional to underlying B-horizon.

While this is the general soil profile across the hillfort, there is local variability depending on such factors as agricultural activity, drainage and depth to bedrock. Soil podzolization was most intense in the inner enclosure where there had been no cultivation in the early modern era. Lazy-bed cultivation in the outer enclosure in the early modern era had an effect on soil development, removing the leached E-horizon and contributing to the build-up of organic soil. The same is true of modern agricultural practices in the two pasture fields located within the southern side of the hillfort. The thickness of organic soil (C.01/C.02) in the inner enclosure is only 0.07–0.18m, increasing to 0.27m in those parts of the outer enclosure affected by modern agriculture.

In conclusion, soil quality within the hillfort is very poor, comprising a mix of peaty podzols and lithosols. This contrasts with surrounding agricultural land where fertile brown earth soils support intensive cereal cultivation and high quality pasture.

3.5 The Hillfort Defences

The enclosing elements of the hillfort were investigated in six excavation trenches (Figure 3.7). These were located on the northern (Trench 1) and western sides (Trenches 9, 10 and 19, and Trench 22) of the inner enclosure, as well as the north-west side of the outer enclosure (Trench 21). The results from five of these excavation trenches are presented here (details of Trench 22 at the entrance to inner enclosure are presented in the next section).

Inner enclosure: Trench 1

The first of these was located on the northern side of the inner enclosure, where a single trench was opened in 2004 across the bank-and-ditch defences (Figure 3.10). This was extended to include a cutting through a radial field bank that crossed the outer hillfort enclosure. There were four separate areas of investigation in Trench 1, as follows:

- Trench 1A: 10m (N–S) by 2m (E–W) cutting across the inner hillfort bank
- Trench 1B: 4.5m (N–S) by 4m (E–W) cutting, widened for the purpose of excavating the ditch
- Trench 1C: 4.5m (N–S) by 2m (E–W) trench across a low (counterscarp) bank along the outer edge of the ditch
- Trench 1D: 8m (E–W) by 2m (E–W) trench across a radial bank outside these defences.

Trench 1 represents a total excavation area of 63m^2, the investigation of which was completed in the 2004 field season.

Main bank

Today, the main bank has a low rounded profile, approximately 7m wide, with a maximum eroded height of 0.95m above the pre-bank surface. The exterior (northern) side slopes more steeply into the adjacent ditch, with no intervening berm. The eroded bank lies mostly on a 5m wide stretch of level ground, with the northern part lying on a 2–2.5m wide slope on the inside of the ditch. The original bank was around 4m wide, with an external stone facing and a possible wooden revetment on the inside (Figure 3.11). The collapse of these revetments led to the slumping of bank material on both sides. The original bank height is unlikely to have

FIGURE 3.10: GENERAL VIEW OF TRENCH 1 (2004) ON NORTHERN SIDE OF INNER ENCLOSURE, SHOWING EXCAVATION OF RADIAL BANK OF OUTER ENCLOSURE (FOREGROUND).

FIGURE 3.11: EXCAVATION OF INNER ENCLOSURE BANK, TRENCH 1, CLASHANIMUD (1M SCALE). NOTE STONES OF OUTER REVETMENT (FAR RIGHT) AND POSTHOLE OF INTERNAL REVETMENT (TOP LEFT).

exceeded 1.5–2m, based on the amount of slip excavated from the adjacent ditch.

The drystone facing on the outer side of the bank was built of large angular blocks of grey sandstone, laid horizontally to a height of at least 1m. This was not exposed prior to excavation. The remains of this stone facing were discovered 0.75m inside the inner edge of the ditch. There was no equivalent stonework on the inside of the bank, where a single posthole might indicate some form of wooden revetment. This feature will be discussed further in relation to similar bank structures excavated in Trench 9/10 (see below).

Bank stratification

The bank is of dump construction, made up of broken stone of variable size mixed with stony silt sediment of subsoil origin (Figure 3.12). This material came from the adjacent ditch, where B- and C-horizon subsoil was extracted, along with shattered bedrock. The bank seems

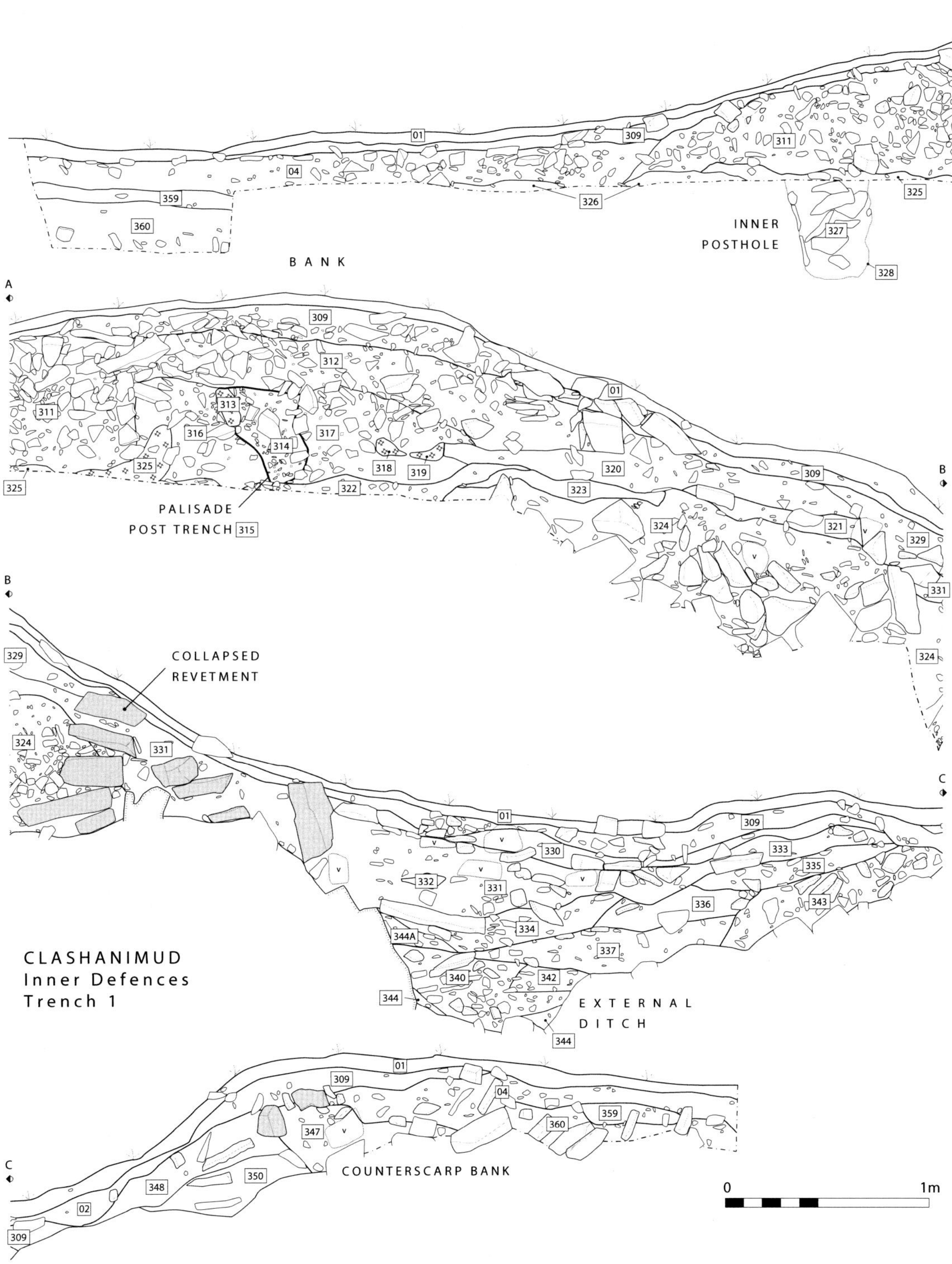

Figure 3.12: Stratification of bank/ditch/counterscarp bank, Trench 1, Clashanimud.

to have been built as a single event, with no definite evidence of either pre-bank activity or later modification. Excavation revealed the following stratification:

The removal of a 0.05–0.07m thick sod (C.01) revealed a stony surface (C.309) extending 7.5m in width across Trench 1A. This comprised a 0.05–0.17m thick layer of loose angular stones (grey sandstone). These stones occur within a matrix of organic rooty silt, where the bank surface was altered by modern soil development.

The body of the bank was made up of a loose deposit (contexts 311 and 312) of stones and re-deposited subsoil. This comprised angular pieces of grey sandstone in a matrix of silty sediment, which varied in colour from mid brown on the inside (C.311) to darker brown on the exterior (C.312). This material was not in its original position, having slumped in both directions following the collapse of the original bank revetments.

Excavation revealed a probable palisade trench in the lower central area of the eroded bank. There were indications of a 0.45m deep slot (C.315) cut into the lower bank deposits. This slot measured 0.2–0.4m wide, and was filled with loose stony silt (C.314) with an orange fire-reddened colour. A concentration of charcoal (C.313) on the upper inner side seemed to be part of a burnt timber in this palisade trench. The C.313 charcoal is radiocarbon dated 3050±20 BP (GrN-29046).

The C.315 slot cut into a deposit of stony sediment that formed the base of the bank (Figure 3.13). This comprised stony orange sediment (C.316) on the southern side, with a red-orange stony deposit (C.317) on the northern side. Both of these deposits were oxidised as a result of exposure to intense heat. Context 317 contained pockets of dense charcoal (contexts 318 and 319), with indications of timbers burnt *in situ*. Charcoal from C.319 is radiocarbon dated 2965±20 BP (GrN-29045).

Excavation on the exterior of the bank exposed deposits of stony silt along a broken rock surface sloping towards the inner edge of the ditch. These include a deposit of orange sandy silt (C.329) over a layer of orange-brown stony sediment (C.320). This, in turn, overlay a layer of grey-brown silt with some charcoal (C.321) and a thin spread of grey-white silt (C.323). These layers overlay a dump of re-deposited subsoil and broken stone (C.324) that was part of the original bank construction. This material backed up against a partly collapsed drystone wall (C.310), which served as a revetment for the bank. The wall consisted of horizontally laid slabs of grey sandstone, with 4–5 courses surviving to a height of approximately 0.7m. This walling was secured at the base by projecting pieces of broken bedrock.

The lower part of the bank contained a large spread of charcoal-rich silt (C.325) on a fire-reddened subsoil (C.326). Context 325 contained several small concentrations of charcoal, one of which is radiocarbon dated 3000±20 BP (GrN-29044). This charcoal spread extended across the central bank area, 0.3m south of the C.315 slot, as far as the edge of the eroded bank (Figure 3.14). The northern end of C.325 rises up against the basal bank deposit (C.316) in a manner that indicates the collapse of burnt timbers from the adjacent slot trench. This indicates that the latter may have been close to the inner edge of the original bank, which would have been much narrower than it is today.

The C.325 charcoal spread overlay a small posthole (C.328) beneath the southern edge of the eroded bank (Figure 3.15). This sub-circular cut measured 0.5m (N–S) by 0.34m, with a central depth of 0.48m. It was filled with mid–dark brown silt (C.327) containing much charcoal, a sample of which is radiocarbon dated 3075±20 BP (GrN-29043). This posthole was located 0.7m south of the C.325 charcoal spread, and so is more likely to have been part of an inner bank timber revetment than the main palisade. Further excavation is required to clarify the significance of this posthole. In the absence of same, a comparison can be made with the inner post row in the Trench 9/10 bank (see below).

Bank contexts, Trench 1

C.309 Stony surface of bank mixed with organic soil (C.02); 0.05–0.17m thick layer of loose angular stones in the <0.1–0.2m size range. This layer extended across the top of the fill of adjacent ditch.

C.310 External revetment of bank, partially collapsed. Arrangement of large stones (grey sandstone), 0.2–0.46m in size (average 0.3–0.35m), roughly laid in 4–5 horizontal courses to an extant height of 0.7m.

C.311 Upper part of bank. A <0.2–0.7m thick deposit of mid–dark brown stony silt on inner side of bank. Contains numerous angular fragments of grey sandstone, <0.1–0.35m in size.

C.312 Upper part of bank, coeval with C.311 layer. A 0.2–0.38m thick deposit of light brown stony silt on centre/upper exterior side of bank. Contains numerous angular fragments of grey sandstone, <0.1–0.35m in size.

C.313 Burnt timber in bank. Concentration of charcoal representing a burnt stake in upper fill (C.314) of palisade trench (C.315). This charcoal is radiocarbon dated 3050±20 BP (GrN-29046).

C.314 Fill of possible palisade trench. Deposit of loose gravelly sediment, with numerous pebbles and small stones, and occasional larger examples in 0.1–0.2m size range.

Figure 3.13: Detail of bank stratification in Trench 1, showing fragments of burnt wood (C.313 centre left and C.319 lower right), heat-altered sediment and fire-reddened stone.

Figure 3.14: Fragments of charred wood in burnt spread (C.325) within lower bank, Trench 1, Clashanimud.

FIGURE 3.15: POSTHOLE (C.328) CONNECTED TO POSSIBLE REVETMENT ON INNER SIDE OF BANK, TRENCH 1, CLASHANIMUD.

C.315 Cut of possible palisade trench. A 0.45m deep cut in lower bank material (C.316 on southern side; C.317 on northern side), 0.4m wide on top, 0.2m at base, inclined to south.

C.316 Lower bank deposit. A 0.5m thick deposit of orange sandy silt with numerous small–large angular stones in 0.06–0.12m size range, many of which are fire-reddened.

C.317 Lower bank deposit, similar to C.316. A 0.3–0.45m thick deposit of red-orange sandy silt with numerous small–large angular stones in 0.05–0.10m size range. Fire-reddened and contained charcoal deposits (C.318 and C.319).

C.318 Charcoal deposit, 0.08m in thickness, within C.317, central bank area.

C.319 Charcoal deposit, 0.06m in thickness, within C.317. This charcoal is radiocarbon dated 2965±20 BP (GrN-29045).

C.320 Deposit on lower exterior of bank. Layer of orange-brown silt, 0.06–0.26m in thickness, with few stones and occasional fragments of charcoal.

C.321 Deposit on lower exterior of bank. Layer of grey-brown silt, 0.06–0.11m in thickness, with occasional small–large stones up to 0.19m, stones and occasional fragments of charcoal.

C.322 Spread of white-grey sandy silt at base of bank; possibly redeposited subsoil (E-horizon).

C.323 Thin layer of grey-white sandy silt at base of bank; possibly redeposited subsoil (E-horizon) similar to C.322.

C.324 Deposit on lower exterior of bank. Deposit of orange stony sediment on inner side of C.310 revetment. Very stony deposit, up to 0.65m in thickness, on broken bedrock. Compact deposit of orange silt with gravelly texture, numerous small to large stones up to 0.25m.

C.325 Discontinuous spread of charcoal-rich silt on fire-reddened surface (C.326) at base of bank. This extended across a 1.9m (N–S) wide area in centre of bank. The deposit included several large fragments of carbonised wood, which are radiocarbon dated 3000±20 BP (GrN-29044) and 2940±35 BP (GrA-42683).

C.326 B-horizon subsoil at base of bank on inner side. Compact spread of yellow-orange silt with occasional pebbles and small stones. Fire-reddened over a 2m wide section of central bank area, where this surface was overlain by a large spread of charcoal (C.325)

C.327 Fill of posthole (C.328). Loose deposit of mid-dark brown silt containing small to medium stones; frequent inclusions of charcoal, including one large lump at base that is radiocarbon dated 3075±20 BP (GrN-29043).

C.328 Posthole on inner side of bank. Sub-circular cut in subsoil, measuring 0.45m (N–S) by 0.32m (E–W), narrowing to 0.3m at base, with a vertical depth of 0.45.

C.329 Sediment slip on exterior of bank. Deposit of creamy-orange sandy silt, 0.05–0.25m in thickness, with some small to medium stones up to 0.13m in length.

Ditch

The soil and stone used to build the bank of the inner enclosure came from an external adjacent ditch. This had an asymmetrical profile, with a steeper inner (southern) side and a rounded to irregularly flat narrow base (Figure 3.16). The ditch measured 3.4–3.6m wide (top) and 1.6–2m (centre), narrowing to 0.65–0.8m at the base, with a central depth of 1.8m. The upper part was dug through B-horizon subsoil into a compact grey-white, sandy silt (C.361 C-horizon) over a shattered bedrock surface. The latter was quarried to a depth of one metre or so, where bedded ribs of coarse grey sandstone with a 50° southerly dip were removed (these were exposed on inner side of the ditch). There were no tool marks visible on the ditch cut.

Fill sequence

Prior to excavation the ditch was visible as an approximately 3m wide depression, 1m or less in external depth, which was almost entirely infilled (Figure 3.12). The fill consisted mostly of sediment that eroded from the bank over a long period (Figures 3.17 and 3.18). This began with a thin deposit of white-grey silt (C.344) at the base of the ditch, which represents primary erosion of the lower ditch sides, mostly as a result of rainwash. The basal silt contained small amounts of charcoal, derived from the burning of the bank palisade. A sample of that charcoal is radiocarbon dated 2920±50 BP (GrN-29042). The ditch itself was free-draining, which partly explains the absence of organic deposits at the base.

The lower ditch contained a deposit of grey-brown stony silt (C.340), with lighter (C.341) and darker (C.342) fractions of the same sediment. There were occasional lenses of grey silt containing charcoal (C.338 and C.339) within this lower fill. There was also an early deposit of sediment along the exterior slope of the ditch, consisting of loose, dark brown silt with occasional stones (C.343).

The next stage in the infilling of the ditch was a substantial deposit of grey-brown sandy silt (C.337). This varied in compaction and contained numerous small-to-large stones and some flecks of charcoal. The deposit ranged in thickness from 0.1–0.22m on the western side of the ditch to <0.3–0.6m on the eastern side. Context 337 was overlain on the western side of the ditch by a deposit of

Figure 3.16: Post-excavation view of inner enclosure ditch, Trench 1, Clashanimud.

FIGURE 3.17: WEST-FACING STRATIGRAPHIC SECTION OF DITCH, TRENCH 1, CLASHANIMUD.

FIGURE 3.18: EAST-FACING STRATIGRAPHIC SECTION OF DITCH, TRENCH 1, CLASHANIMUD.

red-brown clayey silt (C.336).

The upper part of the ditch was filled by a series of orange-brown sandy silt deposits, up to 0.5m in overall thickness (Figure 3.12). These represent an influx of subsoil-like sediment into the ditch, mostly derived from erosion of the main bank. They include a deposit of compact, orange-light brown, stony sediment (C.334). This was overlain by a looser deposit of light brown-orange silt (C.331), which contained some large stones but no small clasts. There was similar influx of subsoil-like sediment on the exterior side of the ditch, in the form of orange-brown sandy silt with numerous stones (C.335). Some of that sediment may derive from the collapse of a low bank along the exterior edge of the ditch (see below).

Context 335 was overlain by a thin deposit of compact white-grey silt with some small stones (C.333). The orange silt deposits in the upper ditch were overlain by a layer of grey-brown sandy silt (C.330) up to 0.15m in thickness, with numerous stones. This, in turn, was overlain by a thin spread of stony silt (C.309), which was part of the A-horizon.

Ditch contexts

C.330 Deposit in upper fill of ditch. Layer of grey-light brown silt, 0.03–0.15m in thickness, with some large stones 0.1–0.15m in length.

C.331 Deposit in upper fill of ditch, inner side. Compact deposit of orange-light brown sandy silt, 0.2–0.53m in thickness, free of pebbles but containing numerous small to large stones in 0.08–0.16m range. This deposit represents bank slip forming the main upper fill of ditch.

C.332 Small lens of compact white-grey silt within C.331 deposit.

C.333 Deposit in upper fill of ditch, outer side. Layer of compact white-grey silt, 0.06–0.18m in thickness, with occasional small to large stones up to 0.26m.

C.334 Deposit in central fill of ditch, inner side. Compact layer of orange-light brown silt up to 0.18m in thickness, with numerous small–large angular stones.

C.335 Deposit in central fill of ditch, outer side. Compact deposit of orange-brown sandy silt, 0.16–0.33m in thickness, with numerous small–medium stones up to 0.1m.

C.336 Fill in ditch, outer side. Compact deposit of red-dark brown clayey silt, 0.13–0.18m in thickness, with a few large stones.

C.337 Lower fill in ditch. Compact deposit of grey-light brown sandy silt, 0.1–0.22m thick on west side, increasing to 0.6m thick in central area of ditch where there were numerous large angular stones in 0.15–0.25m range. Occasional flecks of charcoal.

C.338 Thin lens of light grey silt with frequent charcoal, overlying C.337 on inner side of lower ditch.

C.339 Thin lens of yellow-grey silt with frequent charcoal, under C.337 on inner side of lower ditch.

C.340 Stony fill at base of ditch. A 0.23–0.34m thick deposit of small to large angular stones, 0.05–0.25m in size, with numerous small voids. Becoming more compact towards base, with a matrix of grey-dark grown silt.

C.341 Primary slip at base of ditch on inner side. Compact deposit of yellow sandy silt with gravelly texture.

C.342 Sediment in lower fill of ditch, outer side. Compact deposit of dark brown silt with frequent pebbles and small stones.

C.343 Sediment on lower side of ditch. Loose deposit of dark brown silt, 0.15–0.23m in thickness, on broken bedrock forming upper exterior cut of ditch. Frequent small to large stones up to 0.16m in length.

C.344 Basal sediment in ditch. Compact spread of white-grey clayey silt, <0.03–0.08m in thickness on bedrock base of ditch. Primary erosion of ditch sides. Contained a small amount of charcoal, radiocarbon dated 2920±50 BP (GrN-29042).

C.345 Cut of ditch (see description in main text).

Counterscarp bank

Excavation in Trench 1C uncovered the base of a low wall (C.349), running parallel to and approximately 1m out from the exterior edge of the ditch (Figure 3.19). This measured 0.8–1m wide and 0.4–0.6m high; the original height is unlikely to have exceeded 1m. The wall was built of large stones laid in a rough horizontal coursing and covered by re-deposited subsoil. This created a low bank designed to prevent an influx of material into the open ditch.

The wall was built on a stony B-horizon surface (C.360), on which there was re-deposited subsoil from the adjacent ditch. This included a compact yellow-orange silt (C.350) directly outside the edge of the ditch, overlain by a deposit of orange silt (C.348). These deposits served to create a level surface for the wall, around which there was a further build-up of compact stony silt (C.347). Following its collapse, the bank was

FIGURE 3.19: EXCAVATION OF COUNTERSCARP BANK, TRENCH1, CLASHANIMUD.

overlain by a leached soil layer (C.04) beneath organic soil (C.01 and 309).

Counterscarp bank contexts
C.347 Sediment fill around wall stones. Compact deposit of mid brown stony silt, up to 0.35m in thickness, with few stones.

C.348 Sediment on southern side of wall stones. Compact deposit of orange silt with no pebbles or small stones but some larger examples.

C.349 Collapsed stone wall along outer edge of ditch. Concentration of large stones, 0.4–0.8m in length, laid in rough horizontal coursing to form a low wall, 0.08–1m wide by 0.4–0.6m extant height.

C.350 Sediment under C.348 on southern side of wall stones. Compact deposit of yellow-orange silt, 0.1–0.23m in thickness, with occasional pebbles and a few large angular stones up to 0.22m in length.

Radial field bank and drain

The northern end of Trench 1was extended 90° west for a distance of 8m (Trench 1D). The aim was to investigate a low field bank dividing the outer enclosure of the hillfort. Excavation uncovered a stone-faced earthen bank and adjacent field drain (Figure 3.20), both of which are likely to be of early modern date.

The bank stands 0.55–0.64m high above the old ground surface, with a basal width of 1.52m narrowing to 0.86m at the top. The western side is stone faced (C.355), with four extant courses of horizontally laid field stones. The eastern side was similarly constructed, with the original facing stone partially collapsed into an adjacent drain. Excavation revealed an old sod layer beneath the bank, preserved as a band of dark grey silt (C.358). The bank was built using soil upcast from digging of the adjacent drain. The core was comprised of orange silt (re-deposited Bs-horizon) with numerous small–large stones (C.354). This was overlain by re-deposited topsoil, in the form of brown-grey organic soil (C.353), with a sod layer on top (contexts 01 and 02).

A shallow drain was found at the base of the radial bank feature on its eastern side. This was a hand-dug trench (C.357) with steep sides and an irregular base, ranging 0.98m (top) to 0.45m (base) in width and a central depth of 0.7m. The drain was almost entirely infilled, where a thin sod overlay a homogenous fill of dark brown organic silt (C.356) containing large stones 0.1–0.4m in size. Some of the stones may have been placed for drainage purposes, though their position along the western side of the drain probably points to a collapsed facing of the adjacent radial bank.

FIGURE 3.20: EXCAVATION OF RADIAL FIELD BANK AND ADJACENT DRAIN (TRENCH 1), OUTER ENCLOSURE, CLASHANIMUD.

There are no artifact finds from this bank or drain. The condition of the bank, with its intact stone facing on the western side, as well as the preservation of the pre-bank sod layer and the undifferentiated nature of the drain fill, taken together suggests these features are likely to be of early modern date. This is supported by the fact that they are stratigraphically later than the leached soil horizon (C.04), which in turn post-dates the hillfort bank in Trench 1A. As already mentioned, the bank and drain were probably built in recent centuries, as part of a radial sub-division of the outer enclosure recorded on the 1845 Ordnance Survey.

Radial bank contexts

C.353 A 0.05–0.13m thick layer of brown-grey silt in upper part of radial bank.

C.354 A 0.35–0.4m thick layer of stony orange silt forming core of radial bank. The stones were 0.05–0.18m in length, mostly sub-rounded clasts of subsoil origin.

C.355 Stone facing on western side of radial bank. Four courses of horizontally laid stones, 0.1–0.17m in length, survive to a height of 0.35m. Most were sub-rounded to sub-angular field stones.

C.356 Fill of drain (C.357) on eastern side of radial bank. Loose deposit of dark brown organic silt, containing numerous small–large stones, the largest 0.2–0.42m in length.

C.357 Cut of drain (see main text for description).

C.358 Old ground surface beneath radial bank. A 0.06–0.10m thick layer of dark grey organic silt with no clasts.

Trench 1: summary

Excavation of Trench 1 confirmed that the hillfort bank is of dump construction, made with upcast subsoil and quarried stone from the adjacent ditch. There is evidence of an external stone revetment that subsequently collapsed into the ditch. Several charcoal features within the bank suggest burnt posts connected to a central palisade. The main postholes of this wooden fence were not discovered, though part of an associated slot trench (C.315) was found. It is possible that this narrow excavation cutting may have passed between two of the main palisade postholes, which based on the evidence from Trenches 9 and 10 (below) were spaced approximately 2m apart. With inclined sections required to support the stony bank material, the investigation in Trench 1A ended up only 0.8–1m wide at the base. A single post-hole on the inner side of the bank was probably connected to an internal wood revetment comparable to that found in Trench 9/10.

The adjacent ditch was dug into glacial till subsoil, with some quarrying of bedrock. The ditch has a V-profile, measuring 4.1m wide at the top with a central depth of 1.8m. The ditch was mostly infilled by bank collapse, with thin deposits of charcoal at the base derived from the burning of the bank palisade. A low wall along the outer edge of the ditch seems to have been a primary feature. This may be the stone facing recorded by Ó Ríordáin (1935) on the inner side of the ditch. Finally, a low bank with adjacent field drain extended north across the outer hillfort enclosure at right angles to the ditch. It is likely that this bank was built in recent centuries, as part of a radial sub-division of the outer enclosure recorded on the Ordnance Survey historic mapping.

No artefacts of any type were discovered during the Trench 1 excavation. The construction, use and abandonment of the inner hillfort defences can only be dated using the radiocarbon method. Five charcoal samples were selected for this purpose from stratified contexts in the bank-and-ditch section. The radiocarbon results are discussed below.

Inner enclosure: Trenches 9, 10 and 19

Three parallel trenches were excavated across the defences of the inner enclosure on the western side of the hillfort (Figure 3.7). They include Trench 10, a 19m (E–W) by 4m (N–S) cutting that extended across the external ditch, the bank and 7.5m further into the interior of the enclosure. Adjacent to this is Trench 9, a 20m (E–W) by 4m (N–S) cutting that extended 16.5m from centre of the bank into the interior. Finally, Trench 19, a 7m (E–W) by 4m (N–S) cutting, was excavated on the inner side of the hillfort bank.

Bank

Excavation confirmed that the main bank is of dump construction, comprised of stony subsoil and quarried bedrock upcast from the ditch. A line of four large postholes, 0.6–0.9m in diameter and 0.45–0.91m in depth, spaced 1.9m apart, was found under the centre of the bank (Figure 3.21). These large rock-cut pits held wooden posts of 0.2–0.4m diameter, which provided the main supports for a stout wooden palisade. The bank material was heaped around this line of upright posts as they were erected. A narrow slot was dug into the upper surface of the bank between each pair of main posts. This provided a foundation trench for a fence of smaller upright posts secured with packing stones.

The exterior of the bank was originally faced with large stones, arranged in rough horizontal coursing up to 1m

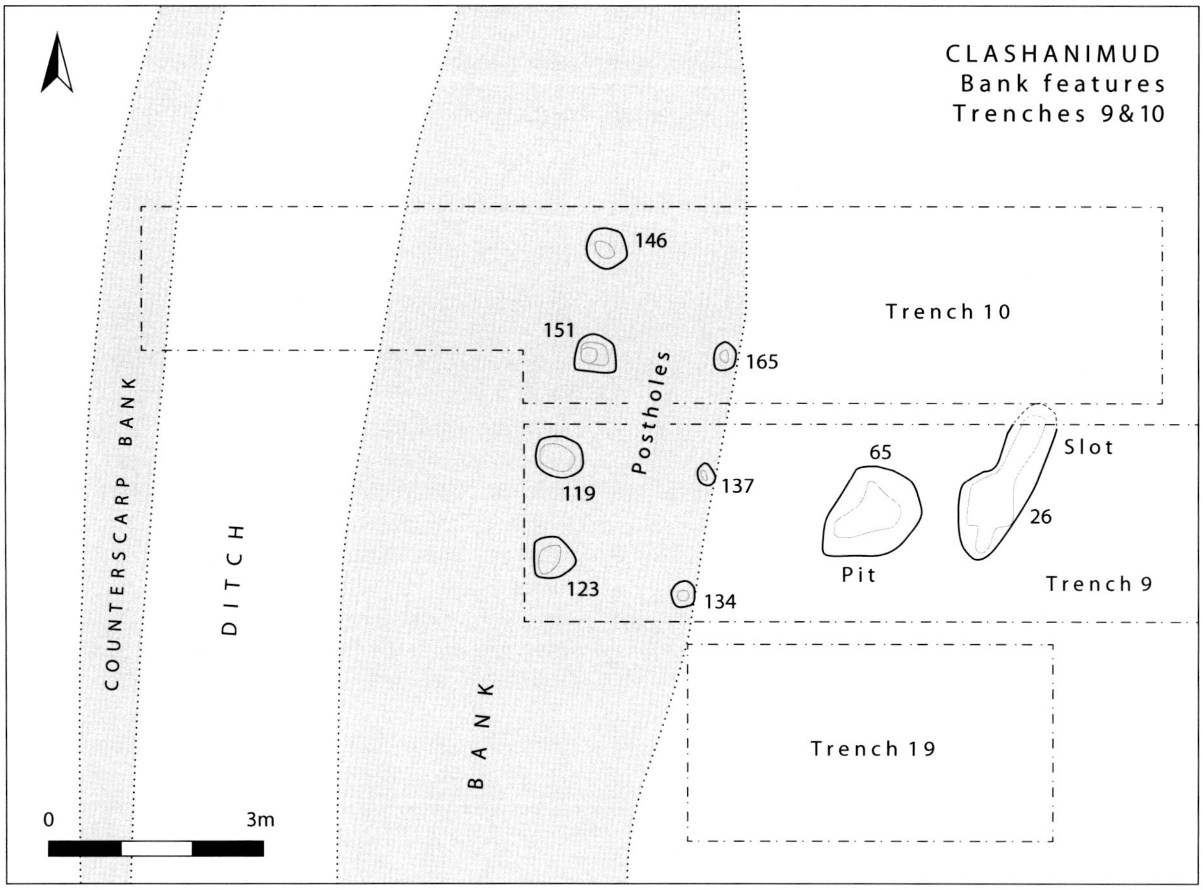

Figure 3.21: Schematic plan of excavated features in defences of inner enclosure, Trenches 9/10/19. Note row of central palisade postholes, the three stakeholes of inner revetment, and two pit features inside the bank.

high (Figure 3.22). The purpose was to retain loose soil and broken stone in the bank, to prevent slippage into the ditch. When excavated, the stone facing had mostly collapsed, with a jumble of large stones along the lower slope of the bank. A wooden revetment, supported in places by a low stone footing, originally retained the inner side of the hillfort bank. The former seems to have been constructed approximately 2m east of the main palisade fence, where a line of smaller vertical posts, spaced 1.7m apart, supported a stack of horizontal timbers against the inner side of the bank. This is confirmed by the discovery of a line of three postholes along the inner edge of the bank, with an average diameter of 0.45m and depth of 0.27–0.44m. There is some evidence of wattlework in the core of the bank, possibly used to consolidate loose soil and stone in the construction process.

Stratification (Figures 3.23, 3.24 and 3.25)

The bank sequence in Trenches 9 and 10 may be summarised as follows (from modern surface to old ground level):

• Sod layer (C.01) over organic soil (C.02) mixed with upper layer of bank stones (C.36), overlying

• Upper slip layers on inner (eastern) side of bank (C.37 and C.109) overlying

• Main bank deposits (*in situ*). These include Trench 10 (north section): C.36 over C.109 over C.64 over C.86 (with C.110) over C.161 over C.152 over C.376; Trench 9 (north section): C.36 over C.156 over C.43 over C.105 over C.62 over C.70; Trench 9 (south section): C.36 over C.43 over C.105 over C.62 over C.59 over C.135

• Palisade slot on crest of bank (C.29 over C.22 with C.158 in C.23 cut)

• Main posts of palisade (north to south): C.146 posthole with fills C.144 and C.145; C.151 posthole with fills C.149 and C.150; C.119 posthole with fills C.111, C.114, C.157, C.115 and C.116; C.123 posthole with fills C.121, C.120, C.122 and C.124

• Burnt deposits and charred wood on inner slope of bank. In section drawings: C.38, C.47, C.75, C.76 and C.142, in addition to burnt sediments C.70 and C.147; not in section drawings: C.30, C.32, C.35, C.45, C.46, C.48, C.49, C.50/51, C.55, C.56, C.57, C.58, C.59/60, C.63, C.66, C.67, C.73, C.79, C.80, C.81, C.87, C.88, C.106, C.140, C.141, C.143, C.148, C.153, C.154, C.158 and C.164

• Inner bank slip sediments (below C.37), namely Trench 10 (north section): C.378 over C.377 over C.147 and C.155; Trench 9 (north section): C.160 over C.68; Trench 9 (south section): C.31 over C.68

FIGURE 3.22: STRATIFICATION OF INNER ENCLOSURE BANK, LOOKING SOUTH, TRENCH 10, CLASHANIMUD. NOTE EXTERNAL STONE REVETMENT (LOWER LEFT) AND POSTHOLE OF CENTRAL PALISADE.

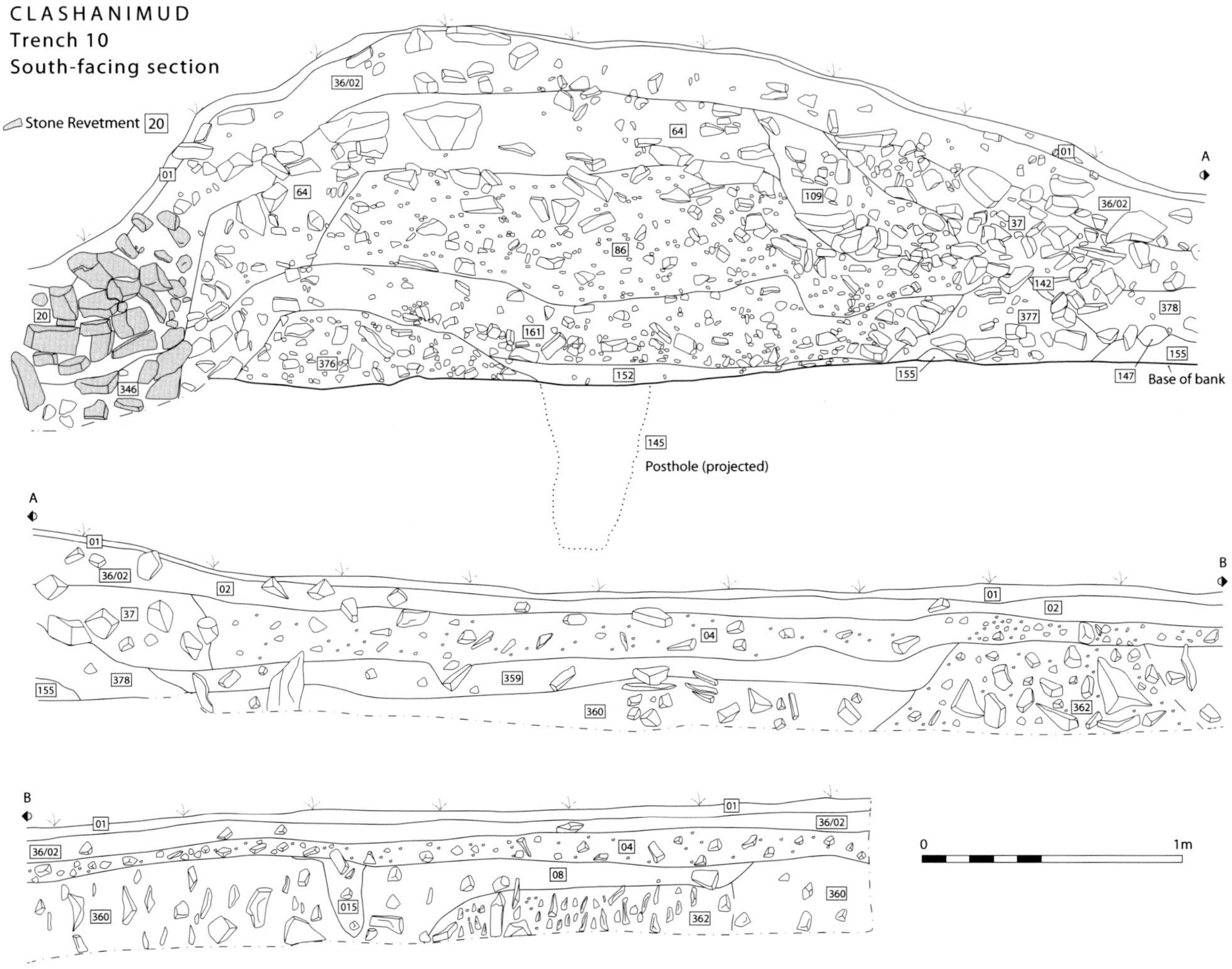

FIGURE 3.23: STRATIFICATION OF INNER ENCLOSURE BANK, LOOKING SOUTH, TRENCH 10, CLASHANIMUD.

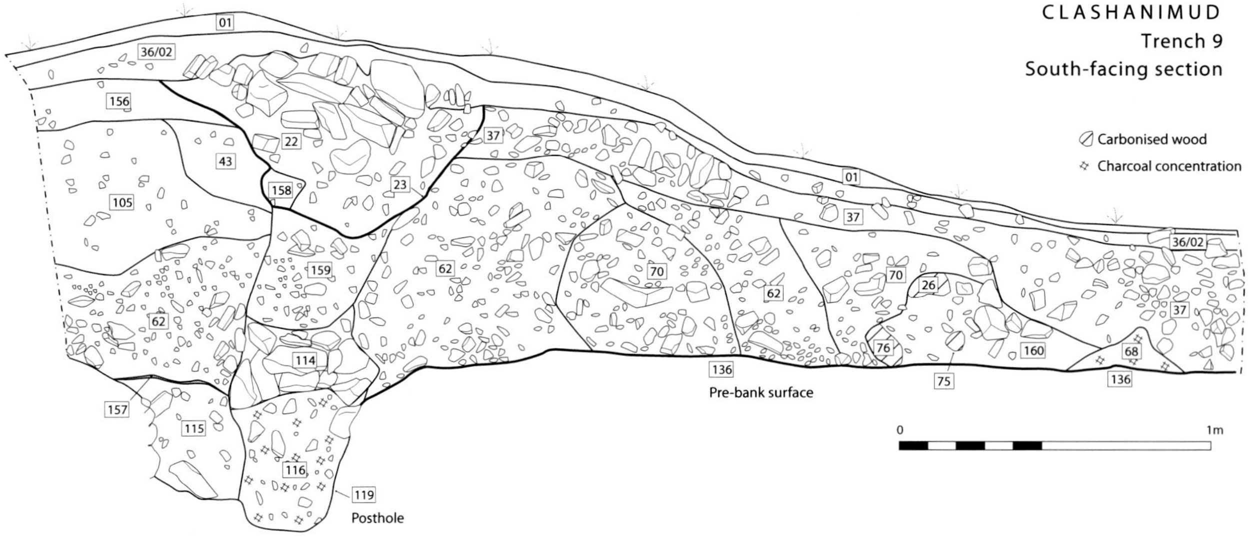

FIGURE 3.24: STRATIFICATION OF INNER ENCLOSURE BANK, LOOKING SOUTH, TRENCH 9, CLASHANIMUD.

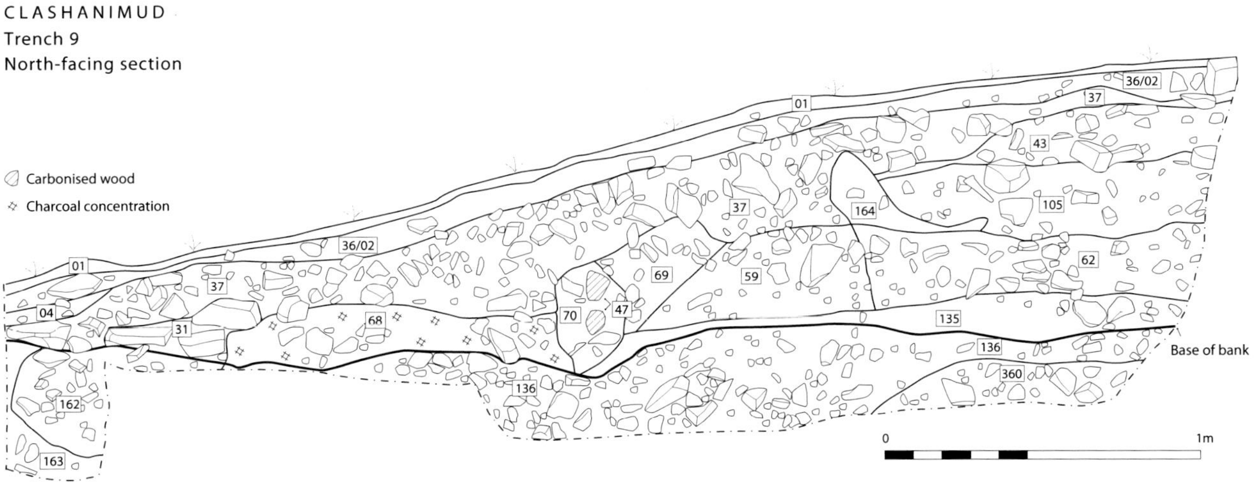

Figure 3.25: Stratification of inner enclosure bank, looking north, Trench 9, Clashanimud.

•Bank revetments. Inner line of stakeholes (north to south): C.165 with fill C.44, C.137 with fill C.379 and C.134 with fill C.54; in addition to C.82 posthole with C.79 fill. Inner stone walling: C.31 with stone collapse C.33 and C.34. External stone walling: C.20.

Bank excavation

The removal of a sod layer (C.01), 0.02–0.08m in thickness, in Trenches 9 and 10 exposed a stony surface across the upper part of the bank. This comprised a mix of medium to large stones (C.36) in a matrix of dark brown organic silt (C.02). This layer was 0.15–0.25m in thickness on the northern side of Trench 10, thinning to 0.03–0.14m in Trench 9. A shallow trench (C.23) was cut into this stony layer along the crest of the bank.

The removal of A-horizon (C.02) along the inner slope of the bank exposed a deposit of brown silt with angular fragments of fire-reddened stones (C.37), ranging in thickness 0.15–0.32m in Trench 10, to <0.05–0.4m in Trench 9 (Figure 3.26). This upper layer was the first indication of significant burning in the bank. The removal of C.37 exposed the main body of bank material. The coarse nature of these stony deposits meant they were poorly differentiated across the Trench 9/10 excavation surface, with some only evident in vertical section.

The sequence in Trench 10 (south-facing section) comprised the surface deposit of large stones (C.36) overlying the C.37 fire-reddened stones and an underlying deposit of dark brown stony silt (C.109) on the inner side of the bank. These upper deposits overlay a 0.2–0.4m thick layer of orange-yellow stony silt (C.64), representing subsoil from the external ditch. This, in turn, overlay a 0.3–0.44m thick layer of yellow-brown silt (C.86), which was also upcast Bs-horizon from the ditch. The excavation of C.86 revealed a small spread of grey sandy silt with numerous stones and charcoal flecks (C.110). It also exposed the lower layers of the bank in Trench 10. The first of these was a compact deposit of brown-orange sandy silt (C.161), 0.16–0.35m in thickness, with contained numerous small to medium stones. This overlay a 0.03–0.08m thick spread of orange-brown silt (C.152), which was removed to reveal a small dump of grey-white sandy silt (C.376) on the western side. The latter represents a dump of E-horizon subsoil, upcast from either the external ditch or, more likely, the C.146 post-hole.

There was no indication of a buried sod layer beneath the bank representing an old ground surface. The lowest bank material was removed to white-grey sandy silt (C.136) with numerous small to medium stones, similar in composition to C.376. This pre-bank surface represents leached subsoil (E-horizon), the equivalent of C.04 in the hillfort interior.

The variability in bank composition is evident in the stratification on either side of Trench 9, which differs in several respects to that in Trench 10. In the south-facing section the sod layer (C.01) covered a spread of surface stones (C.36 mixed with C.02 A-horizon) thinner than that in Trench 10. On the western side of the bank C.36 was removed to expose a thin layer of brown silt (C.156) overlying a deposit of orange-yellow silt with charcoal flecks (C.43). These sediments were removed to reveal a deposit of mid brown stony silt (C.105), up to 0.5m in thickness. This, in turn, overlay a 0.34–0.48m thick deposit of yellow silt with a gravelly texture (C.62) that comprised the core of the bank. That material was altered in places by intense heat coming from the burning of the bank palisade. Two pockets of bright orange silt with charcoal (C.70) were identified within C.62 on the inner side of the bank.

FIGURE 3.26: STONY SURFACE OF BANK, TRENCH 10, DEFENCES OF INNER ENCLOSURE, CLASHANIMUD.

The sequence on the southern side of Trench 9 is broadly similar. The removal of a thin spread of stony A-horizon (C.02/36) exposed a deposit of stony orange-yellow silt (C.43), 0.13–0.18m in thickness, on the crest of the bank. This overlay a 0.2–0.24m thick layer of mid brown stony silt (C.105) on top of yellow gravelly silt (C.62), 0.16–0.26m in thickness. The latter was coeval with a 0.28m thick deposit of mid brown stony silt (C.59). Context 59 was overlain on the eastern side by a deposit of orange-yellow silt with charcoal flecks (C.69), which, in turn, overlay a spread of bright orange fire-reddened silt (C.70) that contained charred wood (C.47 below). These deposits overlay a basal bank layer of orange-yellow sandy silt (C.135), similar in character to C.152 in Trench 10.

Bank slip

Most of the sediment deposits on the lower inner slope of the bank were exposed to the high temperatures of the palisade burning (Figures 3.23, 3.24 and 3.25). These include oxidised sediments with a red-orange colour, containing fire-reddened stone and charcoal. The highest of these was a general spread of loose brown silt (C.37) with fire-reddened stones across the upper bank surface in Trenches 9 and 10. A number of other sediment deposits were discovered on the lower inner side of the bank. In Trench 10 these include a build-up of organic silt (C.378) representing an old A-horizon along the slip edge of the bank. Context 378 overlay a deposit of dark brown stony silt (C.377), and also an area of fire-reddened sediment (C.147), beneath which there was charcoal-rich silt (C.155). The latter sediments are the direct result of the palisade fire and the collapse of burning posts along the inner bank surface.

Equivalent sediments on the inner bank slope of Trench 9 include the layer of fire-reddened stone (C.37) overlying a deposit of grey brown silt (C.160). The latter overlay a spread of dark brown silt (C.68), rich in charcoal, which occurred at the same level as several burnt timbers (see below).

Trench 9/10 bank layers

C.29 Silt deposit in upper slope of bank, Trench 9 and 10. A 0.01–0.02m thick linear (east–west) deposit of grey-black silt, with occasional pebbles and flecks of charcoal, with small pockets of dense charcoal. Produced by down-slope rain wash on upper bank surface.

C.36 General deposit of stones on top of bank exposed on removal of sod layer, Trench 9 and 10. Loose spread of medium to large stones in 0.05–0.25m range, with matrix of dark brown humic silt. Very similar to fill (C.22) of foundation trench C.23.

C.37 Deposit of stony silt on inner slope of bank, Trenches 9 and 10. A layer of loose mid to dark brown silt of variable <0.05–0.4m thickness, containing frequent angular, fire-reddened stones in 0.03–0.1m range.

C.43 Upper bank deposit. A spread of orange-yellow silt with numerous small to large stones across bank in Trenches 9 and 10. Frequent flecks of charcoal.

C.59 Lower bank deposit in Trench 9 (south section). Deposit of loose, mid brown, stony silt, with frequent small to medium stones and occasional examples up to 0.24m.

C.62 Deposit of gravelly sediment on inner slope of bank in Trench 9. Yellow silt with frequent pebbles up to 0.05m.

C.64 Upper bank deposit. A 1.63m wide (N–S) spread of orange-yellow sandy silt, 0.2–0.3m in thickness, of varying compaction. Contained frequent small to large stones in 0.01–0.3m range; the larger ones were angular.

C.68 Deposit on inner slope of bank, southern side of Trench 9. A spread of loose dark brown silt with frequent small to medium stones in 0.05–0.1m range. Rich in charcoal, with frequent small pieces of carbonised wood.

C.69 Deposit on inner slope of bank, southern side of Trench 9. Compact spread of orange-yellow silt with numerous small stones and pebbles; flecks of charcoal.

C.70 Inner bank deposit in Trenches 9 and 10. A 0.07–0.1m thick spread of bright orange silt on the inner slope of bank in Trench 9. Loosely compacted with frequent small stones, many of which were fire-reddened, giving it a gravelly texture. Occasional inclusions of charcoal. Heat-altered version of C.62 bank layer.

C.86 Upper bank deposit in Trench 10. Layer of yellow-brown silt, 0.3–0.44m in thickness, with numerous small to medium stones, and occasional large stones up to 0.2m. Mix of sub-rounded, sub-angular to angular clasts.

C.105 Upper bank deposit. Irregular spread of mid brown silt along crest of bank in Trench 9, extending into Trench 10. Compact with frequent small stones, but no charcoal.

C.109 Deposit on inner slope of bank. Dark brown silt with angular stones.

C.110 Sediment within C.86 bank layer in Trench 10. Irregular east–west spread of light grey sandy silt with frequent small to medium stones in 0.01–0.1m range. Frequent flecks of charcoal.

C.135 Basal bank deposit, Trenches 9 and 10. Compact spread of orange-yellow silt with occasional pebbles but no larger stones. The eastern extent of this sediment may mark the inner line of the original bank.

C.136 Pre-bank surface, Trenches 9 and 10. Continuous spread of loose, white-light grey, sandy silt with frequent small to medium stones. This represents the pre-bank leached E-horizon (variant of C.04).

C.147 Deposit of fire-reddened sediment on inner slope of bank, Trench 10. Compact spread of red-orange silt, 0.15m in thickness, with occasional small to large angular stones in 0.05–0.2m range. Occasional flecks of charcoal. This sediment only occurs around the charred timbers (C.140–3), and is a heat-altered version of C.152.

C.152 Basal sediment in central area of bank. Spread of light orange-brown silt above pre-bank surface (C.136/04).

C.155 Basal sediment of inner slope of bank, Trench 10. Thin spread of charcoal-rich silt under fire-reddened silt (C.147) on pre-bank surface (C.136/04). Residual spread of finely divided charcoal from overlying burnt timbers.

C.156 Upper bank deposit, Trench 9. A 0.12–0.15m thick layer of brown silt with occasional pebbles, but no larger stones.

C.157 Thin layer of black organic silt in Trench 9, possibly representing an old ground surface beneath the bank.

C.159 Bank sediment in Trench 9. Spread of loose grey silt with gravelly texture due to numerous small to medium stones.

C.160 Bank sediment in Trench 9. Spread of brown-grey silt with small pebbles.

C.161 Lower bank sediment in Trench 10. Compact deposit of brown-orange sandy silt (C.161), 0.16–0.35m in thickness, with contained numerous small to medium stones.

C.162 Bank sediment in Trench 9. Spread of orange silt, many small to medium stones.

C.163 Bank sediment in Trench 9. Spread of mid to dark brown silt.

C.376 Lower bank sediment in Trench 10. Deposit of compact grey-white stony silt, 1.1m wide (E–W) by 0.3m thick, on top of pre-bank natural (C.136). This may represent redeposited leached soil (C.136 E-horizon) from digging of adjacent posthole (C.145). It may also represent redeposited subsoil from the adjacent ditch.

C.377 Deposit on lower inner side of bank, Trench 10. Deposit of looser dark brown silt, 0.8m wide (E–W) by 0.35m thick, on top of pre-bank natural (C.136). Contains small-medium stones up to 0.15m in size.

C.378 Deposit on lower inner side of bank, Trench 10. Deposit of loose dark brown silt with no stones. Build-up of organic soil on lower edge of bank slip.

Bank structures: Palisade

Excavation revealed that a palisade of oak posts formerly existed along the central axis of the bank. This was built in two stages at the same time as the bank construction. A line of main posts, spaced approximately 2m apart, was initially erected, followed by the insertion of smaller upright posts in the intervening spaces to create a continuous fence. This is indicated by a line of four postholes found under the bank in Trenches 9 and 10, and by a shallow foundation trench discovered between these post positions along the top of the bank.

Four substantial pits used to contain some of the main posts of the palisade were discovered in a line spaced 1.9m apart (from centre of each posthole) along the crest of the bank. These postholes were circular to sub-circular cuts in the pre-bank surface (C.136), measuring 0.6–0.9m in diameter and 0.45–0.91m in depth, with the lower part cut into bedrock. They include the following (north to south):

C.146 Sub-circular cut though subsoil (C.136) into bedrock, measuring 0.74m (E–W) by 0.67m (N–S), with a central depth of 0.69m. Filled with sediment (C.144) packed around a post-pipe (C.145), 0.3m in diameter with a high charcoal content.

C.151 Circular cut, 0.73m in diameter, with a central depth of 0.91m from pre-bank surface. Near-vertical sides cut through subsoil (C.136) into bedrock. The cut narrowed at a depth of 0.55m to a circular post setting, 0.38m in diameter, with a post-pipe (C.149) containing charcoal surrounded by fill (C.150). A charred timber (C.140/C.87) was found overlying the western side of posthole.

C.119 A sub-oval cut in the pre-bank surface (C.136), measuring 0.9m (E–W) by 0.59m (N–S), with vertical sides and a depth of 0.34m. The charred remains of a post (C.116) survived to a depth of 0.45m on the eastern side of the posthole. This post had been placed in a circular cut, 0.37m in diameter and 0.11m deep, the base of which was broken bedrock. The upper fills of the posthole included displaced packing stones (C.114) and charcoal-rich sediment (C.111 and C.115).

C.123 Sub-circular cut through pre-bank subsoil (C.136) into bedrock, measuring 0.67m (E–W) by 0.63m (N–S), with a maximum depth of 0.65m (Figure 3.27). The base

FIGURE 3.27: POSTHOLE (C.123) OF BANK PALISADE, SHOWING C.23 FOUNDATION TRENCH IN UPPER PART OF ADJACENT SECTION, TRENCH 9, CLASHANIMUD.

of the posthole sloped gently from the north side to a central post setting, 0.14m (E–W) by 0.09m (N–S) by 0.15m deep, with a rounded base. This contained a post-pipe comprised of grey silt (C.121) with a high charcoal content, which extended up through the bank surrounded by packing stones (C.120) and by sediment containing fire-reddened stones (C.122).

The main posts of the palisade were placed upright in these pits and secured with packing stones and soil. The bank was then constructed around the standing posts, which meant that the lower 2–3m of these timbers was firmly secured in the ground (allowing for a reduction of approximately 1m in the original bank height). The original length of these main posts is uncertain, but was probably in the order of 4–6m, assuming that the palisade height above the bank may have been 2–3m.

The palisade was finished on completion of the bank, when a narrow trench (C.23) was dug into the upper surface between each pair of posts (Figure 3.27). This provided a foundation trench for a line of smaller upright posts used to complete the final fence structure. A 3.5m length of this trench in Trench 9/10 survived as a truncated feature due to erosion of the upper bank surface. This trench averaged 0.5m in width and had steeply sloping sides to a maximum depth of 0.79m. It was filled with stony sediment (C.22) containing small amounts of charcoal (e.g. C.158).

External bank revetment

Excavation confirmed that the exterior (western) side of the bank was originally faced with large stones (C.20), roughly arranged in horizontal coursing up to 1m high. This wall was built partly on a slip of orange-brown sediment (C.346) and partly on the pre-bank ground surface, which suggests it is more likely to be a primary feature of the bank construction. The purpose was to retain loose soil and broken stone making up the bank, to prevent slippage into the ditch. When excavated, the stone facing had mostly collapsed, surviving as a jumble of large stones along the lower bank slope.

Internal bank revetment

The inner side of the hillfort bank was originally supported by a wooden revetment, with a stone-built wall of possible later date on the outside. The former seems to have been constructed approximately 2m east of the main palisade fence, where a line of smaller vertical posts, spaced 1.7m apart, supported an arrangement of horizontal timbers (Figure 3.21). This is confirmed by the discovery of three postholes in a line along the inner edge of the bank. These had an average diameter of 0.45m and depth of 0.27–0.44m. They include the following (north to south): C.165 circular cut, 0.45m in diameter, filled with charcoal-flecked silt (C.44) to a depth of 0.44m; C.137 sub-circular cut measuring 0.45m by 0.31m, filled with charcoal-rich silt (C.379) to a depth of 0.27m; C.134 sub-circular cut measuring 0.44m by 0.32m, filled with charcoal-rich silt (C.54) to a depth of 0.29m, with possible packing stone along northern edge.

A small posthole (C.82) was discovered 1m east of the C.119 palisade posthole and 1.1m west of the C.137 inner posthole. This circular cut in lower bank material (C.62 on west side; C.70 fire-reddened material on east side), was 0.19m in diameter with a depth of 0.38m. The remains of a charred post (C.79) were found in a fill that also contained packing stones.

This wooden revetment subsequently burnt down, causing the bank to collapse inwards over some of the charred timbers (see below). The base of a stone wall (C.31) was found along the immediate eastern side of the revetment postholes (C.165, C.137 and C.134). Though substantially collapsed, at least two courses of large stones were found, placed horizontally along the inner edge of the C.37 bank slip. Also relevant is a 4m wide deposit of large stones and small boulders (C.33) crossing Trenches 9, 10 and 19, on the eastern side of the bank. These stones may represent tumble from the stone walling (C.31), which would indicate a wall of 1m or more in height.

The proximity of C.31 to the inner line of postholes suggests this wall may have been a primary feature of the bank construction, acting as a support for the timber revetment. It is also possible that the stone wall was built following the burning of the palisade, in an attempt to limit the subsequent collapse of the bank. The fact that most of the C.37 bank slip did not extend beyond the stone wall indicates that this was successful. This remains speculative, which is unfortunate as any such re-building would indicate a re-occupation of the site following the destruction event.

Trench 9/10 Bank palisade and revetment contexts
Wooden palisade
C.22 Upper 0.38m fill of foundation trench (C.23) on eroded crest of bank, Trenches 9 and 10. Exposed directly below modern sod as an east–west band of medium to large stones in a matrix of loose dark brown silt. The stones ranged 0.05–0.35m, with some larger stones, as well as numerous voids and occasional flecks and concentrations of charcoal.

C.23 Foundation trench on top of bank in Trenches 9 and 10. Linear cut measuring 3.5m (east–west) across Trench 9/10. Truncated due to erosion of bank surface. This feature in Trench 9 had a central width of 0.5m, 0.55m on the northern side, narrowing to a rounded point at southern end. There were two internal depressions, the northern of which was 0.79m deep. The sides were steeply sloping, and also irregular due to the stony nature of the surrounding bank material (contexts 37, 43 and 64).

C.79 Fill of posthole C.82. Loose brown silt with gravelly texture due to numerous pebbles and small stones, with three medium stones around upper edges used as packing. Remains of charred post in upper part of fill.

C.82 Cut of posthole on lower inner slope of bank, Trench 9. Circular cut in bank material (C.62 on west side; C.70 fire-reddened material on east side), measuring 0.19m in diameter with a maximum central depth of 0.38m. Vertical sides to an irregularly flat base that reached the pre-bank surface (C.136).

C.111 Upper fill of posthole (C.119) on crest of bank, Trench 9. Loose deposit of mid to dark brown silt with frequent pebbles and some small stones. Frequent inclusions of charcoal.

C.114 Second fill of posthole (C.119). Loose jumble of medium to large stones with frequent voids. Some influx of silt and fine charcoal from overlying C.111.

C.115 Third fill of posthole (C.119). Loose gravelly sediment with frequent small stones and occasional medium stones in orange-brown silt matrix. This fill surrounds post-pipe (C.116).

C.116 Charred remains of post in posthole (C.119). Exposed as a circular 0.34m by 0.33m deposit of brown-grey sandy silt with frequent pebbles and small stones, many of which were fire-reddened. Frequent flecks and small lumps of charcoal. Excavated to a vertical depth of approximately 0.5m in this posthole.

C.119 Cut of posthole on crest of bank, Trench 9. Sub-oval cut exposed at base of bank, (though post-pipe extends through the latter), measuring 0.9m (E–W) by 0.59m (N–S), with vertical sides and a central depth of 0.34m. A circular cut measuring 0.37m in diameter and 0.11m deep, with vertical sides and an irregularly flat base, was discovered at the base on the eastern side.

C.120 Packing stones of posthole (C.123) on top of bank, Trench 9. Square arrangement of five stones, measuring 0.38m (N–S) by 0.32m (E–W), set on edge around upper fill (C.121) of posthole. These stones range 0.13–0.2m in length, 0.07–0.25m in width and 0.03–0.08m in thickness.

C.121 Post-pipe in posthole (C.123). Circular deposit of loose grey silt with frequent pebbles and occasional small to medium stones. High charcoal content, both finely divided and small lumps. Exposed as a circular deposit, 0.1m in diameter, between the packing stones (C.120), widening to 0.39m by 0.35m lower down in posthole. The post-pipe continued into posthole fill for a depth of 0.65m from pre-bank surface, but also extended through the overlying bank.

C.122 Fill surrounding post-pipe (C.121) in posthole (C.123). Compact deposit of orange silt to depth of 0.5m in posthole. Frequent pebbles and small to large stones, many fire-reddened, with several voids. Some of larger stones may have been used as packing.

C.123 Posthole on top of bank, Trench 9. Sub-circular cut through subsoil (C.136/04) into bedrock, measuring 0.67m (E–W) by 0.63m (N–S), with a maximum depth of 0.65m. The base of the posthole sloped gently from the north side to a central post setting, 0.14m (E–W) by 0.09m (N–S) by 0.15m deep, with a rounded base.

C.54 Fill of posthole (C.134). Dark brown silt, compact with frequent pebbles and fire-reddened small stones. High charcoal content with numerous lumps.

C.134 Small posthole on western side of stone revetment (C.31), lower inner side of bank, Trench 9. Sub-circular cut, 0.44m (E–W) by 0.32m (N–S), with a central depth of 0.29m. Sloping sides to an irregularly pointed base, with protruding stones from subsoil on eastern side. There was a possible packing stone (not numbered) along northern edge of posthole.

C.379 Fill of small posthole (C.137). Loose deposit of dark brown silt with frequent pebbles and occasional fire-reddened small stones. Occasional flecks and small lumps of charcoal.

C.137 Small posthole on western side of stone revetment (C.31), lower inner side of bank, Trench 9. Sub-circular cut, 0.45m (N–S) by 0.31m (E–W), with a central depth of 0.27m. Irregular profile due to stony cut, with steeply sloping north side, more gentle slope on south side to a flat base.

C.144 Fill of posthole (C.146). Compact deposit of orange-brown silt, with frequent pebbles and small stones. Packed around post-pipe (C.145).

C.145 Post-pipe in posthole (C.146). Circular 0.32m by 0.3m spread of loose grey silt with frequent pebbles and small stones. High charcoal content.

C.146 Large posthole on top of bank, Trench 10. Sub-circular cut though subsoil (C.136/04) into bedrock, measuring 0.74m (E–W) by 0.67m (N–S), with a central depth of 0.69m. Southern side was near-vertical, while the northern side sloped steeply to slightly rounded base.

C.149 Post-pipe in posthole (C.151) on top of bank, Trench 10. Exposed as a circular spread of mid brown-grey silt, 0.42m in diameter, loose with frequent small angular stones in 0.01–0.05m range, and occasional large angular stones in 0.06–0.13m. Frequent flecks of charcoal. The charred timber (C.140/C.87) was found overlying the western side of posthole.

C.150 Fill around post-pipe (C.149) in posthole (C.151). Loose deposit of light orange-brown silt with frequent small rounded pebbles and occasional angular stones in 0.03–0.1m.

C.151 Large posthole first exposed on top of bank, 1.33m south of C.145 posthole, Trench 10. Circular cut, 0.73m in diameter, with a central depth of 0.91m from pre-bank surface. Upper sides were near-vertical cut through subsoil (C.136/04) into bedrock. The cut narrowed at a depth of 0.55m to a circular post setting, 0.38m in diameter.

C.44 Fill of posthole (C.165). Loose dark brown silt with frequent angular stones in 0.04–0.1m range. Occasional flecks of charcoal on surface, becoming more numerous at a depth of 0.2m, changing the fill to a black-brown colour with same texture.

C.165 Cut of small posthole on eastern side of main palisade postholes, Trench 10. Circular cut, 0.45m in diameter, in pre-bank surface (C.136), ranging in depth from 0.44m on west side to 0.2m on east side.

External stone revetment

C.20 Stone walling on lower external side of bank, exposed in Trench 10. A 0.6m (E–W) wide deposit of angular to sub-angular stones, 0.13–0.24m in length, within a matrix of dark brown humic silt (C.02). These stones were loosely arranged with indications of rough horizontal coursing.

Internal stone revetment

C.31 Remains of stone wall on inner side of bank in Trench 9. Though substantially collapsed, at least two courses of medium to large stones survive, laid horizontally along inner edge of bank collapse. This wall was built parallel to inner side of bank, but curved outwards at northern end of Trench 9. The stones range 0.3–0.85m in length, 0.15–0.23m in width and 0.07–0.17m in thickness. This wall was built 0.5m east of the original edge of bank, to contain the bank slip (C.37).

C.33 A 4m wide deposit of large stones and small boulders was exposed beneath the sod layer (C.01), on the east side of the C.31 revetment in Trenches 9, 10 and 19. These stones ranged 0.15–0.3m, with a smaller number in the 0.3–0.5m range. The origin of these stones is uncertain, but one possibility is that they represent tumble from the inner bank walling (C.31).

C.34 Stony spread under C.33 on eastern side of inner bank revetment (C.31), Trenches 9 and 10. The stones were smaller than those in C.33, mostly pebbles and small to medium clasts up to 0.15m, with some larger examples. These were contained in a matrix of mid brown silt in a natural hollow east of bank.

Burnt deposits and bank destruction

Excavation in Trenches 9 and 10 uncovered evidence of intense fires that affected the bank at varying depths from the old ground level to the present surface. This prolonged burning occurred within a 2.2m wide space between the main palisade and the inner row of smaller postholes, but was particularly concentrated directly inside the latter. These fires destroyed three wooden structures, namely the main palisade and a possible wattle structure within the bank, and a plank/post revetment on the inner edge. The evidence of this destruction is as follows:

1. There was a high incidence of charcoal (e.g. C.158) within the main postholes of the palisade and in the associated foundation trench.

2. The upper sides of the main post-holes were oxidised red-orange as a result of exposure to intense heat.

3. Each of the main postholes contained a post-pipe made up of charcoal-rich sediment (Figure 3.27). They included (north to south) C.149 in C.151 posthole; C.116 in C.119 posthole; C.121 in C.123 posthole, and C.145 in C.146 posthole. These post-pipes formed where the burning of the upright post extended into the posthole.

4. There were significant amounts of fire-reddened stone, in some cases semi-vitified, in the bank, in particular the surface layer (C.37).

5. Some of the finer bank sediments were oxidised red-orange as a result of exposure to high temperatures (e.g. C.70 and C.147).

6. There was a general incidence of finely divided and lump charcoal through these same fire-reddened sediments.

7. Several small spreads of finely divided charcoal were found within the lower inner bank, where larger pieces of carbonised wood were crushed by the slip of stony bank material (e.g. C.30, C.32, C.153, C.158 and C.164).

8. Numerous lengths of carbonised wood (intact, but

fully charred) were found within the inner bank (Figure 3.28). Most of these represent timbers and posts used in the inner bank revetments. A total of 34 pieces of carbonised wood were found within a 1–1.6m (E–W) wide space on the immediate inside of the inner post row (C.134, C.137 and C.165). These include 21 fragments found in Trench 9 and 13 from Trench 10. They range in length from as little as 0.03–0.08m up to the five largest examples, namely C.75 (1.2m), C.140 (1.26m), C.142 (1.16m), C.143 (1.79m) and the largest C.141 (2.14m). The total length of these 34 pieces of carbonised wood is approximately 16.5m.

Some of these carbonized wood fragments had a curved surface, which suggests the use of complete roundwood (e.g. C.106). Others had a flatter profile, which suggests some form of rough planking produced from split roundwood. These include three large examples found in Trench 10 (C.141, C.142 and C.143). The charred remains of these timbers ranged 1.16–2.14m in length, 0.28–0.4m in width and 0.04–0.1m in thickness (Figures 3.29 and 3.30). The upper surfaces of both C.141 and C.143 were concave, with a flat lower surface lying horizontal on burnt bank material (C.147).

Most of these carbonised wood fragments were found lying horizontal in a north–south direction within the inner side of the bank. Many were originally part of the same timber, which in some cases can be reconstructed based on alignment. Three parallel rows of carbonised wood, spaced 0.1–0.5m apart in a north–south direction, were discovered on the inner side of the bank. They include the following:

The outermost row was represented in Trench 10 by a charred timber (C.143) and a spread of charcoal (C.153), which seem to have fallen outwards from the burning revetment. The latter was defined by a middle row of charred timbers that includes (south to north) C.45, C.50, C.51 and C.38 in Trench 9, continuing in Trench 10 as C.148, C.141 and the large timbers C.141 and C142. These occurred on the immediate inside of the revetment postholes (C.134, C.137 and C.165), in a manner suggesting the latter held vertical uprights that braced a stack of horizontal timbers, represented by the charred timbers of the middle row.

An inner row within the bank itself was made up of slender fragments of charred wood, some of which had a twisted appearance. When joined together there is evidence of a 3.2m length of slender wood, partly twisted, made up of six fragments (C.47, C.48, C.57, C.58, C.59 and C.60) extending south to north in Trench 9. The base of a burnt stake (C.79) placed upright in a small posthole (C.82) was discovered along the line of this western row. A second upright stake along the same line was found in Trench 9, represented by a charred wood fragment (C.73). That wattle structure may possibly be traced into

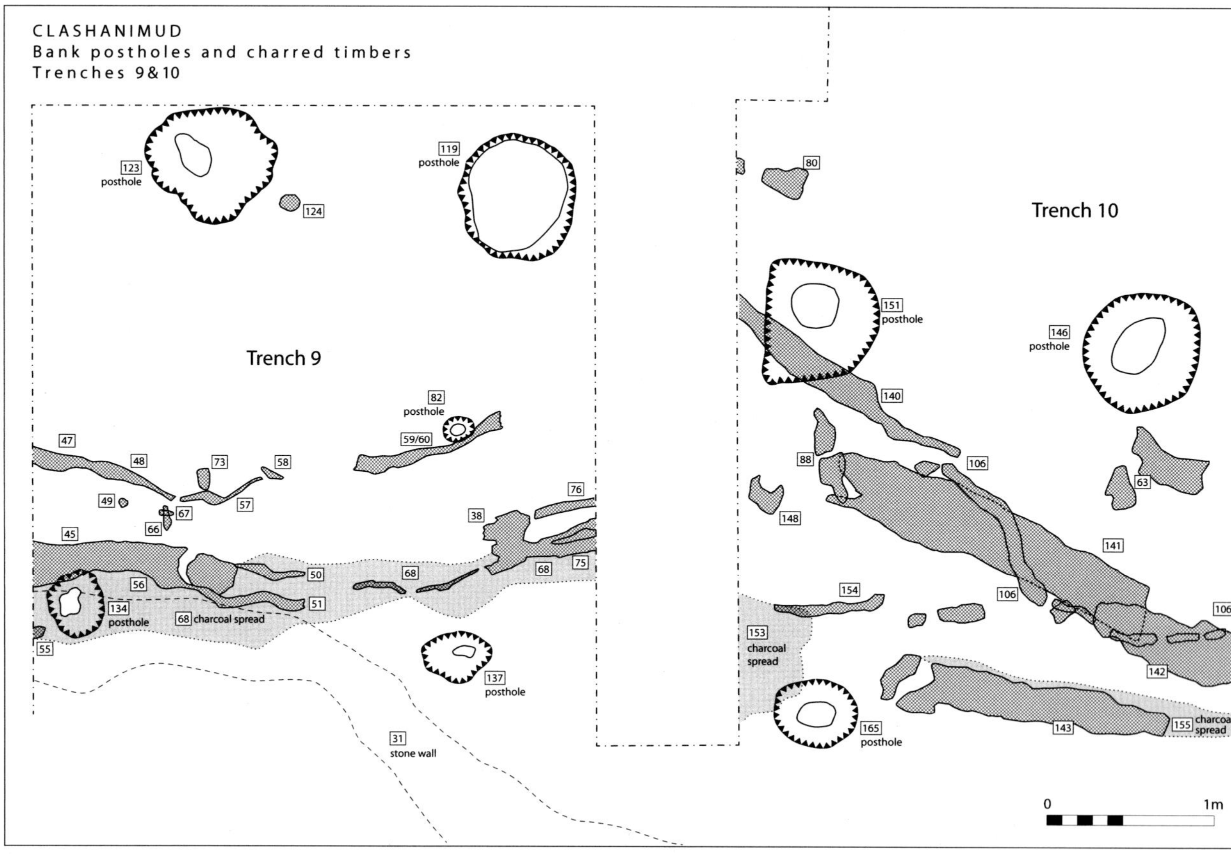

FIGURE 3.28: DISTRIBUTION OF CHARRED TIMBERS AND CHARCOAL DEPOSITS IN RELATION TO POSTHOLES OF MAIN PALISADE AND STAKEHOLES OF INNER REVETMENT, TRENCHES 9 AND 10, CLASHANIMUD.

FIGURE 3.29: CHARRED TIMBERS (C.143 LOWER RIGHT; C.141 CENTRE LEFT) IN TRENCH 10, CLASHANIMUD.

FIGURE 3.30: DETAIL OF CHARRED TIMBERS C.141 AND C.142 (RIGHT) AND C.143 (LEFT) IN TRENCH 10, CLASHANIMUD.

Trench 10 (C.87, C.140 and C.106). Context 106 is a 2.42m length of charred twisted wood, with a diameter of 0.02–0.09m. The fact that this length of twisted roundwood fell outwards over large timbers (C.141 and C.142) is significant, as it demonstrates that the wattle structure and post revetment were contemporary, and not that one replaced the other. The most likely scenario is that the wattle structure was built to retain bank material during construction, with more substantial planking acting as a permanent revetment on the inner side.

Finally, the inner side of the bank was also supported by a wall of horizontally laid stones (C.31; see above) located on the immediate outside of the revetment post row (C.134, C.137 and C.165). This walling curved outwards from the line of the post row as it extended from Trench 9 into Trench 10. This suggests the wall may have been a later addition, built at a time when the wooden revetments were failing to retain the bank material, possibly because they were destroyed by fire. The fact that none of the C.31 wall stones were fire-reddened supports the idea that this wall was a later addition. If this could be proven, it would indicate some re-occupation and repair of the hillfort following its destruction by fire.

Trench 9/10 Charcoal concentrations and carbonised wood within bank.

C.30 Deposit of charcoal-rich sediment on lower inner edge of bank, southern side of Trench 9. A sub-circular spread of dark brown-black silt, measuring 0.36m (E–W) by 0.34m (N–S) with a maximum thickness of 0.05m, with frequent pebbles and occasional small stones. High charcoal content, finely divided and small lumps.

C.32 Small deposit of charcoal on lower inner edge of bank, southern side of Trench 10 extending into Trench 9. Dark brown-black silt, loosely compacted, with some small stones and frequent flecks and small lumps of charcoal.

C.35 Carbonised wood fragment on inner slope of bank Trench 9.

C.38 Short length of carbonised wood on inner slope of bank, Trench 9. Lying horizontal within C.43 bank sediment, this piece of wood measured 0.68m (N–S minimum) by 0.4m (E–W), with a thickness of 0.08–0.1m. Found at same level as other charcoal deposits on inner slope of bank.

C.45 Short length of carbonised wood on inner slope of bank, Trench 9. Lying horizontal within bank sediment (C.43), this piece of wood measured 0.16m by 0.07m, with a thickness of 0.05m. Joins with carbonised wood fragments contexts 50, 51 and 56.

C.46 Small fragment of carbonised wood on inner slope of bank, Trench 9. Horizontal piece of burnt wood, 0.08m by 0.06m by 0.01m thick.

C.47 Small fragment of carbonised wood on inner slope of bank, Trench 9. Very fragmentary, measuring 0.09m by 0.03m by 0.015m thick.

C.48 Small fragment of carbonised wood on inner slope of bank, Trench 9. Very fragmentary, measuring 0.03m by 0.02m by 0.05m thick.

C.49 Small fragment of carbonised wood on inner slope of bank, Trench 9. Very fragmentary, measuring 0.08m by 0.07m by 0.01m thick. Contexts 45, 47, 48 and 49 all found in close proximity and may be part of same burnt timber.

C.50 Small fragment of carbonised wood on inner slope of bank, Trench 9. Lying horizontal on bank material (C.43), measuring 0.53m by 0.09m by 0.1m thick. Joins with C.51.

C.51 Small fragment of carbonised wood on inner slope of bank, Trench 9. Lying horizontal on bank material (C.43), measuring 0.28m by 0.09m. Joins with C.50.

C.55 Small fragment of carbonised wood on inner slope of bank, Trench 9. Measures 0.06m by 0.05m and found at same level as contexts 38, 50–1 and 56–60.

C.56 Small fragment of carbonised wood on inner slope of bank, Trench 9. Curved piece, measuring 0.4m by 0.01m, extending from C.50 carbonised wood C.50 to C.54 stakehole. Possible wattle?

C.57 Small fragment of carbonised wood on inner slope of bank, Trench 9. Measures 0.6m by 0.03m. Possible wattle?

C.58 Small fragment of crushed carbonised wood on inner slope of bank, Trench 9. Measures 0.12m by 0.02m.

C.59 Small fragment of carbonised wood on inner slope of bank, Trench 9. Crushed, measuring 0.1m by 0.03m; joins with C.60.

C.60 Small fragment of carbonised wood on inner slope of bank, Trench 9. Crushed, measuring 0.07m by 0.01m; joins with C.59.

C.59/60 was a single length of carbonised wood measuring 0.41 in length, 0.29m wide and 0.02m thick, which extended north–south along inner slope of bank, Trench 9.

C.63 Large piece of carbonised wood within C.64 material in upper bank, Trench 10. In two fragments: the largest measuring 0.52m (N–S) by 0.2m (E–W) by

0.04 thick, with a smaller piece on the south-east side measuring 0.18m by 0.12m by 0.06m.

C.66 Short length of carbonised wood extending east–west on inner edge of bank, Trench 9. Measured 0.18m by 0.09m, with a thickness of 0.08m. Lay at right angles to main parallel lengths of carbonised wood in that area.

C.67 Small fragment of carbonised wood on inner edge of bank, Trench 9. Measures 0.1m by 0.05m at right angles over C.66.

C.73 Small fragment of carbonised wood on inner slope of bank, Trench 9. Sub-circular in cross-section, measuring 0.1m (E–W) by 0.07m, and found at 70° slope. Possible remains of upright post in bank revetment that was burnt *in situ*.

C.75 Length of carbonised wood, very crushed, on inner slope of bank, Trench 9. Horizontal piece measuring 1.2m long, 0.07m wide by 0.04m thick. Joins with C.50 fragment.

C.76 Small fragment of carbonised wood, measuring 0.4m by 0.1m, on inner slope of bank, Trench 9. Joins with C.38 carbonised wood.

C.79 Short length of carbonised wood, measuring 0.07m by 0.04m, on inner edge of bank, Trench 9. Found between two medium sized stones, possibly used as packing for upright post.

C.80 Small fragment of carbonised wood, measuring 0.22m by 0.16m by 0.02m, aligned north–south on inner slope of bank, southern side of Trench 10.

C.81 Carbonised wood in Trench 10.

C.87 Charcoal deposits within C.22 fill of foundation trench (C.23), Trench 10. Joins with C.140 carbonised timber.

C.88 Length of carbonised wood on bank slope close to southern side of Trench 10. Fragmented, measuring 0.46m (E–W) by 0.18m (N–S) with a thickness of 0.02m, lying broken on fire-reddened angular stones (C.37) in bank. Numerous flecks of charcoal within a 0.2m radius.

C.106 Length of carbonised wood on inner slope of bank, northern side of Trench 10. Fragmented, measuring 2.42m (N–S) by 0.09m wide with a thickness of 0.015m, lying broken on fire-reddened angular stones (C.37) in bank.

C.124 Small deposit of charcoal on edge of posthole (C.123), top of bank in Trench 9. A 0.18m by 0.17m spread of crushed charcoal on pre-bank leached surface (C.136/04).

C.140 Length of burnt wood on inner slope of bank, southern side of Trench 10. 1.26m long (north-east/south-west) by 0.24m wide by 0.09m thick, lying on its side at 45° and extending northeast from C.151 posthole.

C.141 Large burnt timber aligned north north-east/south south-west within inner slope of bank, Trench 10. This timber measured 2.14m long by 0.4m wide by 0.1m thick. The upper surface was slightly concave, with a flat lower surface lying horizontal on burnt bank material (C.147).

C.142 Length of burnt timber within inner bank slope, northern side of Trench 10. This timber measured 1.16m (N–S) by 0.38m wide by 0.08m thick, lying horizontal on burnt bank material (C.147), partly over the larger C.141 timber.

C.143 Large burnt timber lying horizontal on eastern side of C.141 and C.142 timbers on inner bank slope, Trench 10. This timber measured 1.79m long by 0.18–0.28m wide by 0.04m thick. The upper surface was concave, with a flat lower surface lying horizontal on burnt bank material (C.147). The southern end of C.143 was crushed to loose charcoal.

C.148 Concentration of charcoal at southern end of C.141 timber, southern side of Trench 10. This 0.2m by 0.16m by 0.02m thick deposit of charcoal lay on the pre-bank surface (C.136/04).

C.153 Sprcad of black silt containing charcoal on eastern side of C.154 burnt timber, inner slope of bank, Trench 10. This 0.76m (E–W) by 0.65m (N–S) by 0.06m thick deposit lay on the pre-bank surface (C.136/04).

C.154 Length of burnt timber on inner edge of bank, southern side of Trench 10. This timber measured 0.72m by 0.08m by 0.03m, and was found lying on its side slightly twisted in a north–south direction.

C.158 Charcoal-rich deposit in C.23 foundation trench. A 0.14m (E–W) by 0.11m thick concentration of carbonised wood on the lower western side of the C.23 palisade trench.

C.164 Charcoal-rich deposit, 0.5m (E–W) by 0.23m thick, in upper part of bank, which was exposed in southern section of Trench 9.

Ditch

Excavation directly outside the bank revealed a steep-sided U-shaped cut, measuring 2.2–2.8m wide at the top and 0.65–1.1m wide at the base, with a central depth of 1.6–1.8m (Figure 3.31). This ditch was cut through stony B-horizon subsoil into compact C-horizon silt and fractured bedrock. The latter is well drained, which explains the absence of waterlogged sediments in the ditch. There were no visible tool marks on the sides or base of the ditch.

The infilling of the ditch commenced with a 0.35–0.5m thick deposit of dark grey-brown stony silt (C.368) at the base (Figure 3.32). The basal fill contained a small amount of charcoal, but no fire-reddened clasts and not enough charcoal to connect this context with the palisade destruction. This was followed by an influx of light grey silt (C.367) coming in from the exterior (western) side of the ditch. Context 367 was overlain by a thicker layer of stony silt (C.366), which was brown-dark grey in colour. The influx of sediment from the exterior side of the ditch continued with an influx of stony brown-orange silt (C.365). These lower ditch sediments (contexts 265, 366 and 367) were archaeologically sterile, with a notable absence of charcoal.

The next stage in the fill sequence involved a 0.17–0.25m thick deposit of grey-brown silt (C.364) on the eastern

FIGURE 3.31: ROCK-CUT DITCH OF INNER ENCLOSURE, LOOKING NORTH-EAST, TRENCH 10, CLASHANIMUD.

FIGURE 3.32: STRATIFICATION OF DITCH, TRENCH 10, CLASHANIMUD.

side of the ditch (Figure 3.33). This was overlain on the eastern side by a thin layer of mid brown silt (C.363). The influx of sediment from the bank side of the ditch continued with a thin layer of orange silt (C.352). This was overlain by a deposit of stony yellow-orange silt (C.351), which contained some large slabs collapsed from the bank revetment. A continued influx of sediment from that direction is represented by a thin layer of grey-brown silt (C.346).

The final stage in the infilling of this ditch involved an accumulation of large stones in the central ditch area. These include a deposit of stones with a yellow-grey silt matrix (C.289), overlain by a deposit of similarly sized stones in dark brown humic silt (C.288) beneath the modern sod.

It is difficult to interpret the Trench 10 ditch sequence due to the stony nature of its various fills, the small amount of charcoal recovered and the absence of dating material. The ditch was filled by a series of lenticular deposits of stony silt, the result of natural erosion of the inner hillfort bank and also the small counterscarp bank. The tip lines indicate that some of the early infill came from the exterior (western) side of the ditch. The fact that these deposits (contexts 368, 367 and 366) were very stony suggest some contribution from the bank side in addition to external material. The stone-free orange silt (C.365) may represent some erosion of the counterscarp bank, but this is not certain.

The later infill (C.364 upwards) mostly comprised collapsed stone and eroded sediment from the inner bank. Some collapsed stone from the bank revetment was identified in C.351, but it was difficult to distinguish this material in the overall ditch fill. The absence of any significant amount of charcoal that might be connected to the burning of the bank palisade is notable. This suggests that most of this burnt material fell inwards, possibly due to prevailing westerly winds.

There were two artifact finds from the excavation of this ditch. The first is a collection of 19 sherds from a single vessel of glazed brownware (04E1038:08:01–19). These were found at the base of the organic soil (C.02) in the central ditch area. The significance of this find is uncertain. It may be linked to a possible use of the infilled ditch as a convenient trackway around the interior of the hillfort in recent centuries. This could be connected to stone quarrying or to lazy-bed cultivation in the north-west side of the outer enclosure (see Trench 21 inner).

The only early artifact from the ditch is a crude axehead or wedge (04E1038:09), made of fine sedimentary rock,

Figure 3.33: Stratification of ditch, Trench 10, Clashanimud.

triangular in shape, with a worn cutting edge (Figure 3.67 below). This implement was found in the basal fill (C.168) of the ditch, 0.08m above the base. It was possibly used to split roundwood during construction of the bank palisade and revetment.

Trench 10 ditch

C.288 Deposit of large angular stones, 0.08–0.16m in size, centre of ditch beneath modern sod.

C.289 A 0.15–0.35m thick deposit of large stone with a matrix of yellow-grey silt; mostly medium to large angular stones in 0.1–0.18m range.

C.346 A 0.05–0.12m thick layer of grey-brown silt with frequent pebbles and roots.

C.351 A 0.15–0.28m thick layer of yellow-light orange silt with frequent pebbles and small stones, occasional larger stones up to 0.1m, and a few large slabs up to 0.4m.

C.352 A 0.06–0.2m thick layer of orange silt with occasional pebbles and small stones, with an accumulation of large stones, 0.1–0.18m in size, in central ditch area.

C.363 Thin layer of mid brown silt on eastern upper side of ditch, mostly free of stones.

C.364 A 0.17–0.25m thick layer of grey-brown silt with frequent pebbles and small stones, and a few examples up to 0.12m.

C.365 A 0.25m thick deposit of brown-orange silt on exterior side of ditch, thinning to 0.1–0.2m at base This sediment contained frequent pebbles but no larger stones, except in central ditch area where there were examples in 0.04–0.1m range.

C.366 A 0.08–0.2m thick layer of brown-dark grey silt with frequent small to large stones up to 0.07–0.19m in size.

C.367 A 0.06–0.12m thick layer of light grey silt, with numerous pebbles and small stones in 0.03–0.07m range and a few larger examples up to 0.15m.

C.368 Loose dark grey-brown silt with small to medium stones in 0.05–0.1m range and some larger examples up to 0.22m, loosely arranged with numerous voids.

C.369 Thin spread of light brown silt with some small stones, overlying eroded bedrock in space between inner edge of counterscarp bank and the outer edge of ditch.

C.374 Cut of ditch formed in light grey sandy silt (C.361 C-horizon in eroding bedrock).

External bank

A low counterscarp bank was discovered along the outer edge of the ditch (Figure 3.32). Today, this feature is approximately 1m wide and does not exceed 0.6m in height. The bank was composed of humic soil (contexts 02 and 371) overlying re-deposited subsoil (contexts 372 and 373) that was upcast from the ditch. There were also indications of a collapsed stone facing (C.370) on the inner side, reminiscent of that recorded by Ó Ríordáin (1935). This bank overlay a buried sod/old ground surface (C.375) on top of a podzolic subsoil (contexts 04, 359 and 360). The extant bank has a thickness of 0.37m from the old surface.

The date of this external bank is uncertain. It may have been part of the original hillfort defences, designed to reduce infilling of the ditch. The intact nature of the drystone facing suggests it may have been built, or possibly re-built, during the early modern era. This could have occurred if the infilled ditch was used as a trackway to facilitate stone quarrying or lazy-bed cultivation (see above).

Trench 10 counterscarp bank

C.01 Sod.

C.02 Dark brown humic silt, occasional stones. A-horizon.

C.370 Drystone facing on inner side of bank. Tumble of large field stones, 0.15–0.23m in length, with irregular sub-rounded shape.

C.371 Thin layer of brown humic silt, 0.07m in thickness, frequent roots. Part of A-horizon.

C.372 Upper layer of bank. Light brown-yellow silt with gravelly texture, 0.07–0.16m in thickness.

C.373 Basal layer of bank. Grey silt with occasional pebbles, 0.04–0.07m in thickness.

C.375 Dark brown humic silt; buried sod layer 0.01–0.02m in thickness.

C.04 Grey silt with numerous small–medium stones; leached E-horizon.

C.359 Light brown-grey silt with numerous small to large stones; thin Bh-horizon.

C.360 Brown-orange iron-enriched silt, numerous small to large stones; Bs-horizon.

Trench 9/10 defences: summary

The original defences of the inner enclosure comprised a strong palisade of upright posts, securely erected within a bank of dump construction. The soil and stone used to build the bank came from an external rock-cut ditch, which had a low counterscarp bank along its outer edge. The main bank had an external stone facing, and an internal revetment of horizontal timber planking held in place with vertical posts, inside which there was a wattle revetment in the core of the bank.

These defences of the inner enclosure were partly reconstructed at the end of the 2006 excavation season (Figure 3.34). This work was carried out in Trench 9/10 and in the adjacent entrance area (Trench 22). The bank in Trench 9/10 was re-built to its pre-excavation size and profile, with some of its original features reconstructed for public presentation. The timber palisade was partially re-built (main posts only), to give some impression of the scale of the original hillfort defences. Four large timber posts, approximately 5m in length and 0.3m in diameter, were placed upright in the original palisade postholes

HAULAGE OF MAIN POST OF PALISADE

ERECTION OF MAIN POST

USE OF PACKING STONES TO SECURE POST.

BUILDING OF EXTERNAL BANK REVETMENT.

PILING OF EARTH AND LATER STONE AROUND MAIN POST

COMPLETED BANK WITH MAIN POSTS IN POSITION READY FOR COMPLETION OF PALISADE FENCE.

FIGURE 3.34: PARTIAL RECONSTRUCTION OF DEFENCES OF INNER HILLFORT ENCLOSURE, CLASHANIMUD.

discovered beneath this bank. The bank was then restored around these posts to a height of approximately 2m using original soil and stone. The four posts stand vertically to a height of 2.5m above the restored bank and are spaced 1.5m apart. The original stone revetment was partially reconstructed as a drystone wall facing the lower exterior side of the bank. The rock-cut ditch outside this enclosure bank had to be backfilled because of safety concerns.

While the final result represents a partial reconstruction, it does illustrate how formidable the original defenses of the inner enclosure were, with a height of at least 6–7m from the base of rock-cut ditch to the top of the palisade.

Outer enclosure: Trench 21

The outer defences of the hillfort were investigated on the north-west side of the site (Figure 3.7). An 18m (NW–SE) by 4m wide cutting (Trench 21) was excavated across the line of the extant bank (Figure 3.35). This exposed an early bank and ditch (Period 1) that was re-built in the modern era (Period 2), and damaged by recent forestry (Period 3).

The Period 1 bank consisted of a low, flat-topped, earthen bank, 0.6–0.8m in height, with an original basal width estimated at 4m (Figure 3.36). The bank was comprised of subsoil taken from the external ditch. This material was largely undifferentiated, with a loose sandy silt texture and occasional small stones. No dating material or artifacts were recovered within the bank. Charcoal from the old ground surface is radiocarbon dated 3160±40 BP (GrA-42678), providing a *terminus post quem* for this bank. There is evidence for a light wooden fence, in the form of two rows of opposing stakeholes, totaling 7–8 in number, along the top of the Period 1 bank. Unlike the stronger palisade of the inner enclosure, this fence does not seem to have been burnt down.

Excavation on the outside of the bank revealed an adjacent ditch that was not visible before excavation. This had a V-section profile, measuring 2.85m wide at the top with a central depth of 1.7m. It contained a series of sediment deposits with variable amounts of stone. There are no artifacts finds, but a radiocarbon date (GrA-42677) for charcoal from the basal fill does provide a *terminus ante quem* for the digging of this ditch (see below).

The bank was subsequently re-built (Period 2) to create a field wall for farming purposes. This was achieved by digging into the base of the bank for a short distance on both sides, with the resulting soil piled on top of the central bank area. Both sides of this Period 2 bank were faced with drystone walling. The fact that much of this stone facing is still intact indicates this rebuilding occurred in recent centuries. A small field drain was also dug on the inner side of the bank. There is also evidence of more recent activity (Period 3), where the ground

FIGURE 3.35: GENERAL VIEW OF TRENCH 21, NORTH-WEST SIDE OF OUTER ENCLOSURE. THE OUTER BANK OF HILLFORT IS VISIBLE, ALONG WITH CULTIVATION FEATURES IN FOREGROUND.

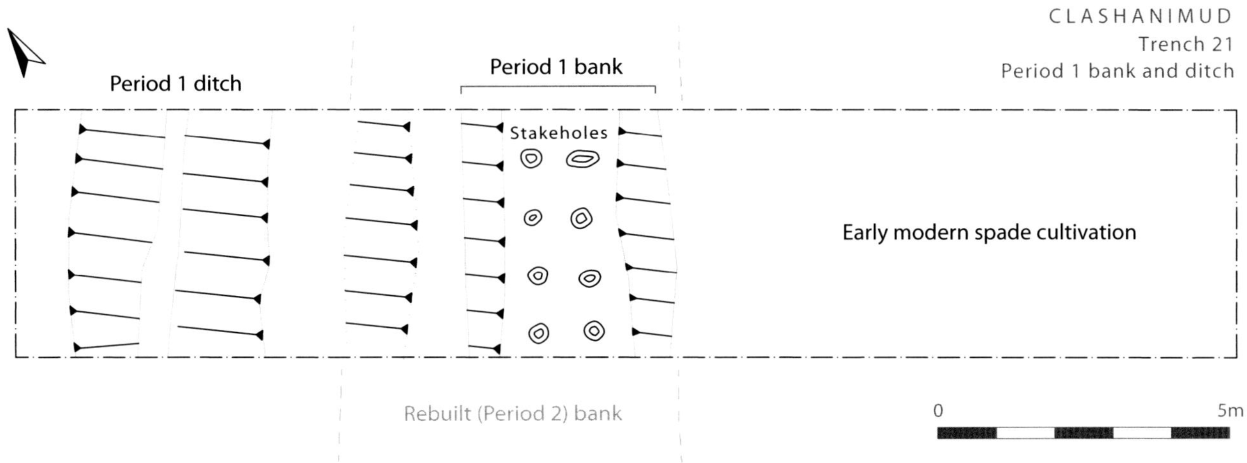

FIGURE 3.36: SCHEMATIC PLAN OF EXCAVATED FEATURES, TRENCH 21, OUTER HILLFORT ENCLOSURE, CLASHANIMUD.

surface outside and against the base of the re-built bank was scraped by machine. This occurred during clearance of the area outside the bank in preparation for recent forestry plantation.

Period 1 bank

This survives as a flat-topped earthen bank, measuring 1.8–2m wide at the top, and 2.8–2.9m at the base (Figures 3.37 and 3.38). It had an extant height of 1.1m on the outer side, reducing to 0.7m on the inner side, in both cases taken from the old ground level to a buried sod layer on the bank surface. The bank is of dump construction, composed of soil and stones extracted from the external ditch. This began with a compact spread of bright orange silt (C.173), which was deposited to a thickness of 0.28m on the ditch side, thinning to 0.03m on the inner side of the bank (Figure 3.39). The initial upcast from the ditch was deposited on a grey-white, sandy silt surface (C.04), with occasional flecks of charcoal. In the absence of a humic palaeosol, this leached soil horizon represents the old ground surface.

Context 173 was overlain by the main bank material (C.172), which comprised loose, light brown, sandy silt with numerous small-to-large stones, creating a gravelly texture. This, in turn, was overlain by a more compact deposit of bright orange silt with occasional large stones (C.171). These two contexts represent dumps of redeposited subsoil from the adjacent ditch. They were overlain by a thin layer of compact orange-brown silt with stones (C.95).

The exposure of this layer revealed seven definite stakeholes and one possible example (latter not numbered). They were arranged in opposing pairs to form two parallel rows, placed 0.56–0.74m apart along the axis of the bank (Figures 3.36 and 3.40). The inner row included four stakeholes (contexts 104, 107, 112 and 113) placed 0.42–0.62m apart, while the outer row (contexts 131, 133 and 139) had a similar spacing. These irregular cuts were sub-circular to sub-rectangular in plan, ranging 0.24–0.56m in width and 0.17–0.38m in depth. There were arrangements of small stones around some examples, interpreted as packing for a vertical stake/post. There is no evidence that these uprights rotted or were burnt *in situ*, with the pit fills indicating that they had been removed. Four of these (contexts 104, 107, 112, 113) were filled with a black silt (C.103) that occurred as discrete spreads on the C.95 surface. The other three examples (contexts 131, 133 and 139) had their own separate fills. It is not entirely certain whether these cuts represent truncated post-holes or large stake-holes, but they were certainly part of a fence arrangement on the top of the Period 1 bank. Their size indicates that this was a lighter structure than the oak palisade of the inner hillfort enclosure.

These post settings and the C.103 silt spreads were overlain by a 0.09–0.14m thick layer of grey leached sediment (C.118), which represents the development of a thin E-horizon in the upper bank. This, in turn, was overlain by a thin A-horizon consisting of a 0.02–0.06m thick layer of dark brown-black humic silt (C.91). That buried sod marks the boundary of the Period 1 and 2 bank structures.

Period 1 bank contexts

C.91. Buried sod. Thin compact layer of rooty dark brown-black humic silt with a peaty texture; occasional fine pebbles, but no larger clasts.

C.95. Compact layer of dark brown sandy silt (purple tinge), very stony with numerous pebbles and small stones.

C.103. Three discrete deposits of black sediment on C.95 bank surface. Thin spreads of black sandy silt with mottles of orange-yellow decayed sandstone; frequent pebbles and occasional larger stones. Rare flecks of

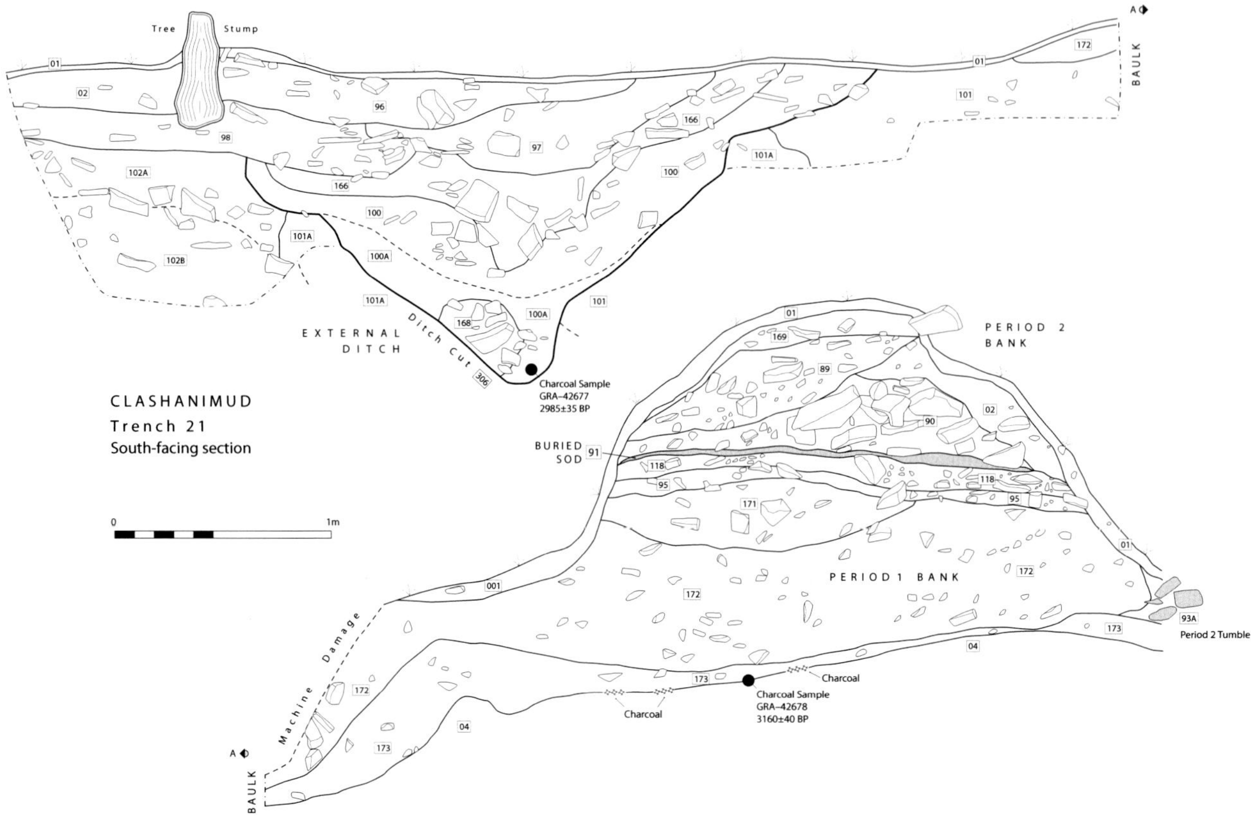

FIGURE 3.37: BANK AND DITCH STRATIFICATION (TRENCH 21), OUTER ENCLOSURE.

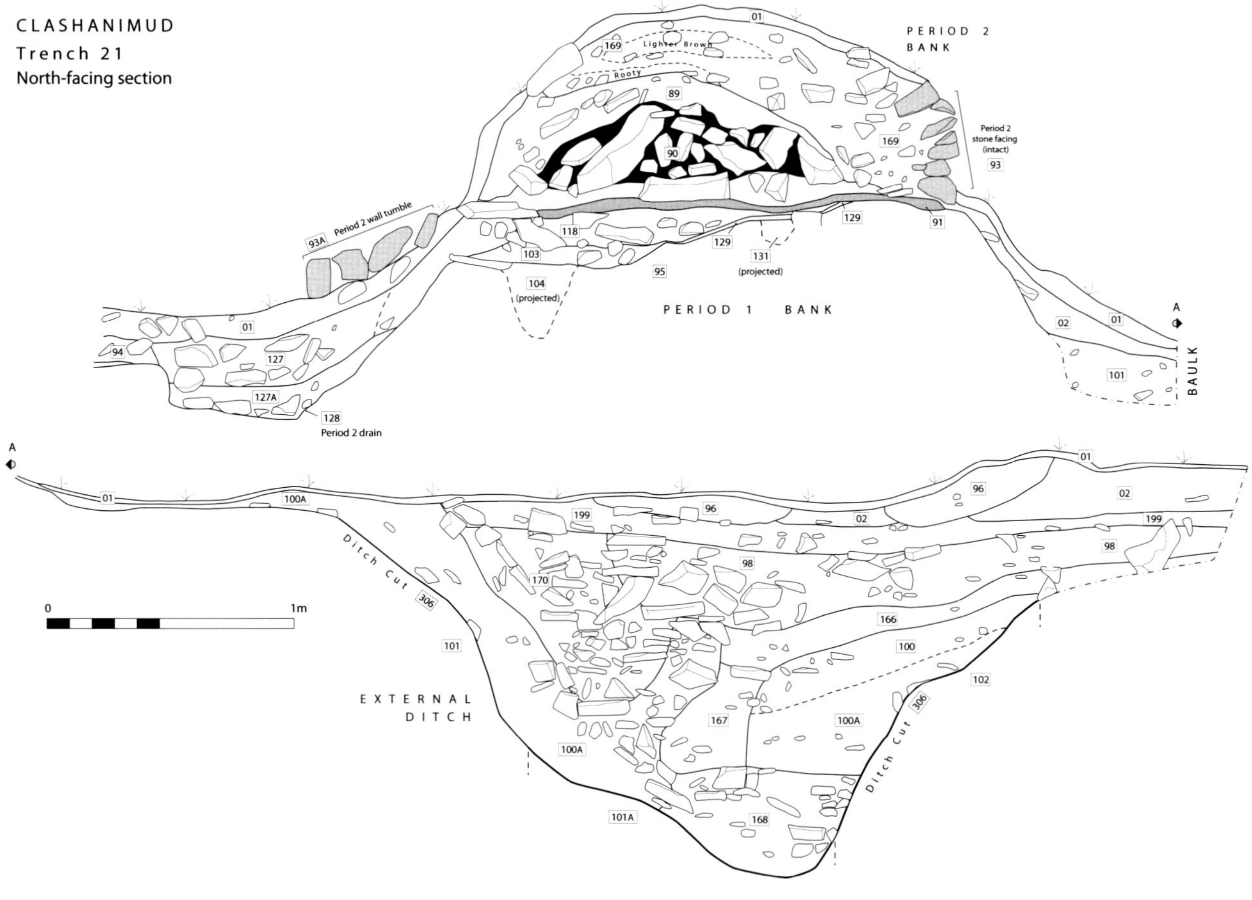

FIGURE 3.38: BANK AND DITCH STRATIFICATION (TRENCH 21), OUTER ENCLOSURE.

Figure 3.39: South-facing section of bank (Trench 21), showing Period 2 re-building of Period 1 bank (lower).

Figure 3.40: North-facing section of Period 2 bank in Trench 21. The surface of the underlying Period 1 bank is exposed, with two rows of large stakeholes visible.

charcoal, but no indication this is a burnt deposit. This sediment forms the fill of post-hole contexts 104, 107, 112 and 113.

C.104. Post-hole. Sub-circular cut, 0.35m wide by 0.38m deep, with steeply sloping sides to a rounded base. Slightly inclined to west. Filled with black silt (C.103).

C.107. Post-hole. Circular cut, 0.35m in diameter and 0.24m deep, sloping sides to a flat base, Filled with C.103 silt.

C.112. Posthole. Sub-rectangular cut, 0.56m by 0.4m, with a depth of 0.29m; steeply sloping sides to a flat base. Filled with C.103 silt, with some packing stones.

C.113. Post-hole. Sub-rectangular cut, 0.5m by 0.28m, with a depth of 0.29m; steeply sloping sides to a pointed base. Filled with C.103 silt; large stones arranged around the edge of this pit represent post packing.

C.118. Upper layer of Period 1 bank. Compact deposit of grey sandy silt, with frequent fine pebbles and occasional larger stones up to cobble size. Leached appearance.

C.129. Thin compact deposit mid-light brown silty sand, with frequent pebbles and small-to-large stones.

C.130. Fill of post-hole C.131. Loose deposit of dark brown silt with occcasional fine pebbles (no charcoal).

C.131. Post-hole. Sub-circular cut, 0.24m by 0.21m, with a depth of 0.17m; steeply sloping sides to a pointed circular base.

C.132. Fill of post-hole C.133. Loose deposit of dark brown sandy silt with a few small stones (no charcoal). Large stones around the edge of this pit may represent post packing.

C.133. Post-hole. Sub-rectangular cut, 0.3m by 0.26m, with a depth of 0.26m; steeply sloping sides to a flat base.

C.138. Fill of post-hole C.139. Loose deposit of light brown silt with occasional pebbles and small stones (no charcoal). Numerous small stones around the edge of this pit may represent post packing.

C.139. Post-hole. Sub-circular cut, 0.27m by 0.26m, with a depth of 0.24m; steeply sloping sides to an irregular base.

C.171. Compact deposit of orange-brown silt, confined to exterior upper side of Period 1 bank.

C.172. Loose deposit of light brown sandy silt, with numerous pebbles and small-to-large stones.

C.173. Compact deposit of bright orange silt; no pebbles, but occasional larger stones.

Period 2 bank

The bank of the outer hillfort enclosure was re-built for farming purposes in the early modern era. The precise date of this re-building is not known, but it certainly occurred long after a natural soil (C.91 sod and C.118 E-horizon) formed on the surface of the Period 1 bank (Figures 3.37 and 3.39). This involved the piling of loose stony sediment (C.90) on top of the buried sod (C.91). Context 90 contained a number of very large stones mixed with loose dark brown silt. This stony material was consolidated by the dumping of organic soil (C.02) against the eastern side of the bank, with an overlying deposit of yellow-brown stony silt (C.89). The upper part of the re-built bank was composed of dark brown humic silt (C.169) beneath the modern sod.

Both sides of the Period 2 bank were faced with rough drystone walling (C.93). The latter was constructed as the re-building took place and explains the steep profile of the bank today. The stone facing is intact elsewhere along the inner bank face, but not in Trench 21 where the bank facing has collapsed. This is indicated by large stones (C.93A) piled at the base of the bank. Part of the outer bank revetment does survive in the form of 3–4 courses of rough stone.

Excavation uncoved a shallow field drain at the base of the Period 2 bank, probably dug when the latter was being re-built (Figure 3.37). This consisted of a shallow trench (C.128), 0.5–0.7m in width and 0.16m deep, dug into the underlying B-horizon. This feature contained numerous field stones in a 0.25–0.5m size range, irregularly placed within a matrix of organic silt (C.127). The collapsed facing stones (C.93A) from the Period 2 bank overlay the infilled drain.

Period 2 bank contexts

C.02. Dark brown humic silt, very rooty, with a few small and large stones (including C.93A wall tumble at the base).

C.89. Loose deposit of yellow-light brown sandy silt; numerous pebbles and small-to-large stones (not as stony as underlying C.90).

C.90. Loose deposit of small-to-large angular and rounded stones within a matrix of dark brown silt. Numerous voids between the larer stones.

C.93. Intact stone facing on exterior of Period 2 bank. Visible in north-facing section as 3–4 horizontal courses of large field stones in 0.14–0.35m size range.

C.93A. Collapsed stone from C.93 bank facing. Best exposed as tumble on inside of bank, with stones in 0.15–0.3m size range; not discernible on exterior side due to recent forestry clearance in that area.

C.169. Compact deposit of rooty, dark brown, humic silt with frequent pebbles and small stones beneath modern sod.

Field drain

C.127. Fill of shallow trench C.128. Deposit of rough field stones in 0.25–0.5m size range, irregularly placed in trench with a later build-up of rooty, dark brown, humic silt, which was lighter brown towards the base.

C.128. Cut of drain. Shallow trench, 0.5–0.7m wide on top, 0.3–0.35m wide at base, ranging 0.11–0.16m in depth. Gently sloping sides to a rounded base cut into the upper B-horizon

Period 1 ditch

Prior to this project there was no indication of an accompanying ditch at any point along the perimeter of the outer hillfort bank. Excavation at the western end of Trench 21 confirmed the presence of a substantial ditch that was completely infilled by agriculture and later forestry in the modern era. This earth-cut ditch provided the main source of soil and stones to build the adjacent Period 1 bank.

The ditch consists of an irregular V-shaped cut (C.306), measuring approximately 2.8m wide at the top, with a central depth of 1.41–1.56m from the modern ground surface (Figure 3.41). Both sides are steeply sloping to a narrow rounded base. The ditch is cut into a natural subsoil consisting of very compact yellow-light brown silt (C.101), which is grey in places (C.101A). This is a fluvio-glacial sediment with relatively few clasts. Part of the ditch cut on the western (exterior) side is formed by a loose gravelly silt (C.102) with a yellow-orange colour, that is dark brown in places (C.102A). This seems to be natural gravel deposit within the C.101 silt, also of fluvio-glacial origin. There was no bedrock exposure in the ditch.

Fill sequence

The ditch seems to have been open for a substantial period, when a deposit of up to 0.45m of dark brown silt (C.168) accumulated at the base (Figures 3.37 and

FIGURE 3.41: SOUTH-FACING SECTION OF OUTER ENCLOSURE DITCH, TRENCH 21, CLASHANIMUD.

3.38). The latter remained dry during the archaeological excavation, which explains why no waterlogged sediments were found (Figure 3.42). The initial sedimentation was followed by an influx of orange silt on both sides of the ditch (C.100). This iron-enriched sediment on the inner (eastern) side of the ditch was similar to natural B-horizon subsoil, and was probably the result erosion of the Period 1 bank. The source on the outer (western) side is less obvious, with one possibility being the erosion of a former counterscarp bank.

Following the influx of C.100 sediment, there followed a series of further deposits in the upper part of the ditch. These are mostly lenticular deposits of silty sediment with a variable stone content (contexts 167, 167 and 170 in sequence), after which the ditch was substantially infilled. This probably occurred some time before the Period 2 farming, as these upper ditch sediments were overlain by a build-up of natural soil (contexts 98, 97 and 99 up to C.02). The A-horizon was disturbed when the ground surface was levelled by machine during the recent conifer plantation. This resulted in a spread of subsoil-like sediment (C.96) across the ground surface, some of which was scraped off the hillfort bank.

Period 1 ditch contexts

C.96. Compact deposit of orange-light brown silt below sod, <0.1–0.23m in thickness, with frequent pebbles and occasional large stones.

C.97. Discrete deposit of stony humic silt in upper central area of ditch, with maximum thickness of 0.33m. Very loose black-dark brown silt with frequent small stones (best exposed in south-facing section).

C.98. Compact layer of stony silt of western side of upper ditch fill, 0.15–0.32m in thickness. Dark brown (grey tinge) silt with frequent pebbles and occasional larger stones.

C.99. Compact layer of silt, <0.05–0.13m in thickness, in the upper ditch fill. Mid-brown in colour, with occasional pebbles and small stones. Similar texture, but not as dark, as the overlying lower A-horizon (C.02).

C.100. Substantial deposit of iron-enriched silt forming lower fill of ditch on both sides. Loose sediment with bright orange colour, very few pebbles and occasional small-to-large stones. The lower part of this deposit (C.100A) is less visibly iron-enriched and greyer in colour.

FIGURE 3.42: NORTH-FACING SECTION OF DITCH, TRENCH 21, CLASHANIMUD.

C.101. C-horizon subsoil forming main cut of ditch (C.306). Compact deposit of yellow-light brown silt (slight green tinge), with orange (iron oxide) mottles. Mostly free of stones. This sediment had a greyer colour (C.101A) on the lower sides of the ditch, due to reducing iron oxide precipitation with depth.

C.102. Discrete deposit of stony silt forming part of ditch cut on western (exterior side). Loose stony sediment with a mid brown (orange tinge) silty matrix, that is darker brown in places (C.102A). Natural gravelly sediment within C-horizon subsoil (best exposed in north-facing section).

C.166. Layer of dark brown sandy silt in central fill of ditch. Very compact with numerous pebbles and small-to-large stones.

C.167. Discrete deposit of compact, mid brown silt in lower ditch fill; frequent pebbles but no larger clasts (only exposed in north-facing section).

C.168. Basal sediment of ditch. Compact deposit of dark brown silt with numerous small-to-large stones. A small amount of charcoal collected from this sediment, 3cm above base of ditch, was submitted for radiocarbon dating (GrA-42677).

C.170. Discrete deposit of stony silt on upper east side of ditch. Compact, with dark brown colour, and numerous stones up to 0.22m in size (only exposed in north-facng section).

No attempt was made to reconstruct the defences of the outer enclosure as exposed in Trench 21. This is because the type of stake fencing used on that bank would have been difficult to maintain. The adjacent ditch had to be backfilled for safety reasons.

3.6 The Hillfort Entrances

The original entrances to Clashanimud hillfort were not known prior to excavation. Today, access to the hillfort is from the eastern side, where a narrow embanked path from an adjacent road leads into the outer enclosure. This opening is likely to be of early modern date, as are a number of small gaps at various locations across the inner and outer enclosures. While extensive quarry damage on the eastern side may have removed original entrances, the steeper slopes there make this a less likely approach to the hillfort.

A survey of the hillfort identified a possible original entrance on the western side of the inner enclosure (Trench 22; Figure 3.7). The clearance of surface vegetation revealed a 3m wide break in the enclosing bank, and what appeared to be a causeway across an external ditch (Figure 3.43). Excavation confirmed that this was indeed the original entrance to the inner enclosure. The equivalent entrance to the outer enclosure may be located opposite this opening on the western side, where a possible break in the bank is now closed with large boulders. This could not be excavated as that gap is permanently closed by agricultural fencing.

FIGURE 3.43: EXPOSED ENTRANCE TO INNER HILLFORT ENCLOSURE PRIOR TO EXCAVATION.

Inner entrance: Trench 22

Excavation confirmed the entrance to the inner hillfort enclosure was originally closed by a stout wooden gate, attached to a palisade built into the bank on both sides. A causeway across the external ditch led to a narrow passageway between the bank terminals. Large post-holes were discovered on either side of this opening. The palisade and gate were subsequently burnt down.

Entrance passage

Excavation on the western side of Trench 22 confirmed the presence of an uncut stretch of ground crossing the hillfort ditch. This causeway measured 6.5m (N–S) wide between the two ditch terminals. The latter have an irregularly rounded shape, though the southern example is much less distinct. The removal of organic soil across this causeway revealed a very stony surface with protruding ribs of bedrock. This levelled off towards the entrance gap in the bank where a roughly metalled surface was found (Figure 3.44). This consisted of a compact spread of small to large stones (C.174), set within a matrix of fine sandy silt (C.300) on top of B-horizon subsoil. The bank opening measured 2.6m at its narrowest point, taken from inside two opposing postholes on the outside (C.185 on northern side; C.245 on southern side) that were part of a gate feature (Figure 3.45). This gate was approximately 3m wide and was connected to a strong wooden palisade along the crest of the banks on either side of the entrance (Figure 3.46).

The bank passage was flanked on both sides by a low stone wall retaining the bank terminals (C.266 on northern side; C.272 on southern side). The metalled surface was confined to the passageway between these two revetments. The removal of C.174 exposed a stony B-horizon surface in that area, with several small exposures of bedrock. No wheel ruts were identified. The significance of a small deposit of dark silt (C.195) contained in a depression inside the entrance passage is unknown.

Trench 22 entrance passage

C.174 Metalled surface of entrance passageway, extending from the western side of the ditch causeway to inside the bank (the eastern limits extend beyond the limit of excavation). This consisted of a compact spread of stones (C.174), ranging 0.05–0.15m in size, set firmly in an spread of sandy silt (C.300). The stones within the bank itself were smaller in size, ranging 0.03–0.08m. A considerable number of these stones were vitrified, having a glassy surface caused by the extreme heat of the palisade burning.

C.300 Spread of light brown-grey sandy silt within and under stones of the C.174 surface. Occasional flecks of charcoal.

FIGURE 3.44: SURFACE OF ENTRANCE PASSAGE PRIOR TO EXCAVATION, TRENCH 22, CLASHANIMUD.

FIGURE 3.45: EXCAVATION OF ENTRANCE TO INNER ENCLOSURE, TRENCH 22, CLASHANIMUD. POSITION OF GATE POSTS MARKED BY VERTICAL POLES.

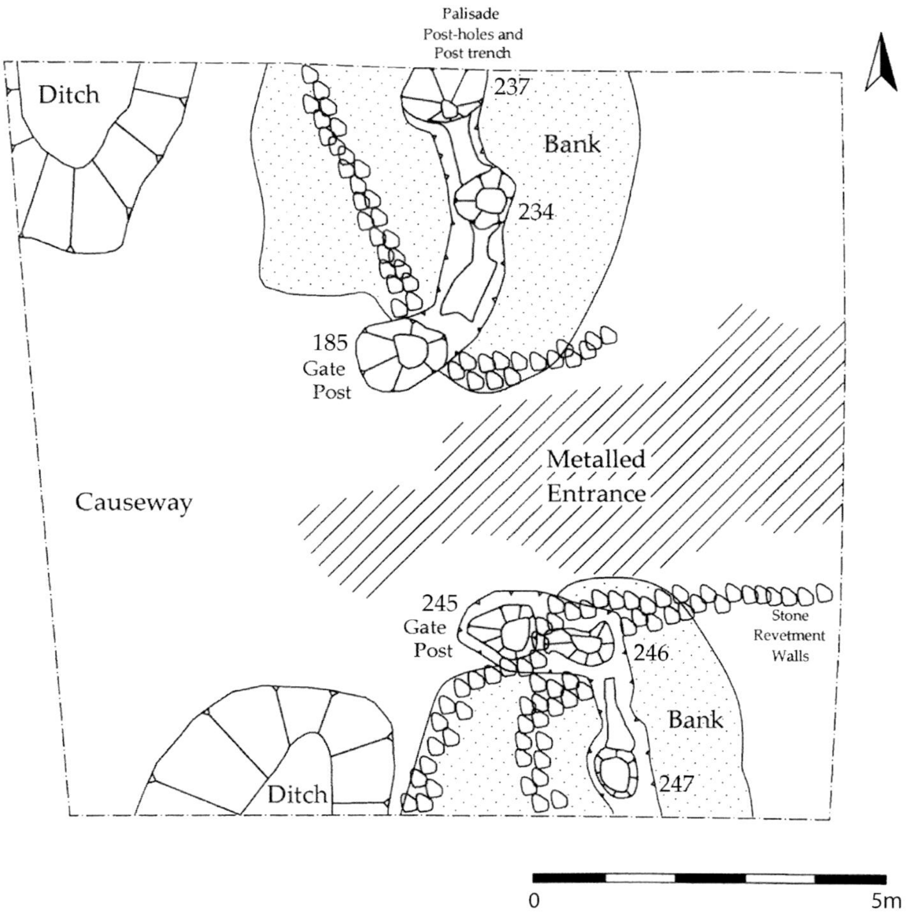

FIGURE 3.46: SCHEMATIC PLAN OF EXCAVATED FEATURES, ENTRANCE TO INNER ENCLOSURE, TRENCH 22, CLASHANIMUD.

C.195 Discrete spread of dark brown silty sand on inner side of entrance passage, east side of Trench 22. Occasional pebbles, but no clasts larger than 0.3m. Flecks of charcoal on surface, but not within the sediment. This sediment occurred within an irregular oval depression measuring 0.36m (north–south) by 0.3m (east–west), with an uneven base 0.06m in depth. There was no indication that this was a deliberate cut.

Northern bank terminal

Excavation confirmed the existence of a low bank on the immediate inside of the hillfort ditch. The bank was of dump contruction, where subsoil and broken stone extracted in the ditch was piled on its inner side (Figure 3.47). Excavation confirmed that the exterior (western) side of the bank was originally retained by a low stone wall, which curved around the southern end of the bank. There are no definite revetment features on the inner side; however, some wooden posts were built into the main body of the bank for retention purposes. Excavation also uncovered the foundations of a wooden palisade along the centre of the bank. Three large postholes connected by a slot trench were examined (Figure 3.46). The former held the main posts of a wooden palisade, which was completed using smaller posts and timbers placed upright in the slot trench. The latter curved as it approached the entrance, ending with a large posthole that held one of two gate posts in the entrance passage.

The bank palisade was burnt down in antiquity, probably not long after it was built. This led to a partial collapse of the bank on both sides. The overall width today is aproximately 6m, from the upper edge of the ditch to the base of the inner slope on the eastern side. The original bank would have been narrower, extending approximately 3m from the exterior stone revetment to 1m or so inside the palisade. This indicates a 2m wide gently sloping space between the exterior bank revetment and the inner edge of the ditch. This does not represent a deliberate berm (see below). The eroded bank has a central thickness of 1m or so from the old ground surface, but would originally have been at least a metre higher.

Construction

The bank was constructed directly on top of an old ground surface (Figure 3.48). Excavation revealed a thin spread of dark silt (C.296) at the base of the bank, in the space between the external stone revetment and the palisade trench/postholes. This represents a buried sod overlying a grey leached subsoil (C.04). This palaeosol did not survive in the area between the bank and upper edge of the ditch, nor on the inner side of the bank where a spread of brown-yellow sandy silt (C.259) may be part of the natural Bs-horizon (C.360).

Excavation exposed a layer of red-orange silt (C.257)

FIGURE 3.47: GENERAL VIEW OF EXCAVATED BANK AND OUTER DITCH, NORTHERN SIDE OF TRENCH 22, CLASHANIMUD.

Figure 3.48: Stratification of bank and ditch on northern side of Trench 22, Clashanimud.

overlying C.296 at the base of the bank on the outer (western) side, deposited between the palisade trench and the external bank revetment. Three lengths of burnt roundwood/timber (contexts 291, 292 and 293) were found lying horizontal on the C.257 surface. The stratigraphic position of these timbers suggests they did not form part of the vertical palisade fence, but were horizontally laid within the bank for revetment purposes during construction. Other contexts at the same level included a spread of dark brown silt (C.301). This and the burnt timbers were overlain by a layer of dark brown stony silt (C.305). Both C.257 and C.305 represent an initial piling of subsoil taken from the ditch. This was followed by the use of broken stone quarried in the lower ditch to build the upper part of the bank. The fire-reddened stone and significant amounts of charcoal in this upper bank deposit (C.242) is a consequence of the palisade destruction.

The primary bank layers on the eastern side of the palisade trench are more difficult to establish as there has been significant slip on the inner side of the bank. The old ground surface (C.296) is absent, and the bank instead overlies a possible Bs-horizon subsoil (C.259). The base of the bank is represented by a deposit of red-orange stony silt (C.257), overlain by a layer of orange-brown sandy silt (C.256) and a related deposit of brown silt (C.255). Context 256 did not contain much charcoal, nor did an overlying layer of brown-yellow sandy silt (C.252), though the latter did have fire-reddened stones. The upper bank surface was formed by a layer of fire-reddened brokenstone (C.242), with some large unburnt stones (C.180) in places.

Structural features: revetments

The loose nature of the bank material meant that various forms of revetment were required to consolidate this structure. This included the use of roundwood branches (contexts 291, 292 and 293) placed horizontally within the bank. The exterior and southern end of the bank were revetted by a low wall built of large stones (C.294 on western side; C.266 at southern end), laid horizontally in a rough coursing (Figure 3.49). This stone facing had partly collapsed, with tumble at several points, including a pile of such stones (C.276) at the south-west end. No such revetment was confirmed on the inner (eastern) side of the bank where excavation did uncover a significant amount of large stones. These include a surface spread of large stones (C.179), and a similar deposit at a lower level (C.240). These stones could have formed part of an internal bank revetment; however, no footing was found for such a feature.

Structural features: palisade

The removal of organic soil (C.02) and some of the C.242 stone in the upper bank exposed the foundations

FIGURE 3.49: PALISADE POSTHOLES (GATE POSTHOLE AT TOP) AND BANK REVETMENT WALL, NORTHERN SIDE OF TRENCH 22, CLASHANIMUD.

of the original bank palisade. This comprised a line of three postholes connected by a narrow slot trench that curved to the south-west along the crest of the bank (Figures 3.49 and 3.50). They include (north to south) postholes C.237, C.234 and the gate posthole C.185, with the intervening slot trenches C.235 and C.234.

These were substantial postholes, measuring 1m or so in upper width, with a depth of 1.58m (C.237), 1.27m (C.236) and 0.95m (C.185) respectively. The upper portion of each posthole was formed in stony bank material, with the lower part cut into bedrock. The fills were also similar, reflecting the history of these features. The lower fill comprises loose silty soil with varying amounts of charcoal (C.227 and C.222 in C.237 posthole; C.226 and C.220 in C.236 posthole; C.238 in C.185 posthole). Evidence of *in situ* burning was found in the C.237 posthole, where the fill included a concentration of charcoal (C.223) suggestive of a post-pipe, with fire-reddened sediment on the eastern (C.225) and western (C.224) sides. A concentration of charcoal (C.239) was also observed in the C.236 posthole, again indicative of the burning of an upright post. This was not observed in the case of the entrance gate posthole (C.185), which might suggest some dismantling prior to the burning event. Given the evidence for the lighting of fires on top of the bank it is possible that partly burnt posts were subsequently pulled out of the postholes. The upper bank material (C.242) was intensely fire-reddened with a large amount of charcoal. Similar burnt stone is found in the upper part of postholes C.236 and C.237, namely contexts 218 and 221 respectively. The upper fill (C.184) of the gate posthole (C.185) has significantly less burnt stone and charcoal than the other two examples.

The fill deposits contained in two short lengths of slot trench (contexts 234 and 235) connecting these three postholes were also similar. In both cases, the lower fill comprised a silty soil with only a few flecks of charcoal (C.233 in C.234; C.230 in C.235). This was overlain by a thin layer of rooty matter (C.232 in C.234; C.229 in C.235), with an upper fill of fire-reddened stones (C.231 in C.234; C.228 in C.235). The former is of interest as it represents a thin sod that developed in the partly infilled trench. Similar root-matted layers (C.219 and C.263) were found in the fills of the C.236 and C.237 postholes respectively. The development of a thin sod suggests some interval between the burning of the palisade and the influx of burnt stones from the top of the bank that finally filled in the postholes and slot trench.

Charcoal deposits

Excavation exposed a significant amount of charcoal, fire-reddened stone and oxidised soil in and around the palisade trench and postholes. This is indicative of intense heat from the burning of a substantial palisade, which charcoal analysis indicates was built of mature oak posts (see below). In addition to the remains of a burnt post (C.223) found in the C.237 posthole, and similar evidence (C.239) from the C.236 posthole,

FIGURE 3.50: PALISADE POSTHOLES AND SLOT TRENCH, NORTHERN SIDE OF BANK, TRENCH 22, CLASHANIMUD. NOTE GATE POSTHOLE (TOP CENTRE).

concentrations of charcoal were found at other locations in that area. These include a small deposit of charcoal (C.261) from the base of the C.235 slot trench, and a length of charred wood (C.262) in the C.237 posthole. Excavation on the immediate eastern side of the palisade trench uncovered a short length of charred wood (C.241) within the upper bank layer of fire-reddened stone (C.242). A deposit of charcoal (C.260) was also found within another layer of fire-reddened stone (C.257) in the same area.

Excavation at the southern end of the bank identified two burnt timbers directly inside the partly collapsed revetment (C.266). These include a deposit of finely divided charcoal (C.264), which was adjacent to a 1.56m long carbonised stake (C.265) that seems to have fallen inwards from the palisade trench.

Bank erosion

The burning of the palisade was followed by a gradual erosion of the bank structure over a long period. This was a slow process that reduced the overall bank height by as much as 1m. The results are evident on both the inner and exterior sides of the bank, and also at the southern end bordering the entrance passage. This included a partial collapse of the C.294 revetment, stones (C.175) from which accumulated with charcoal-rich sediments in the fill of the adjacent ditch (the influx of bank sediment into the ditch is discussed below). Stone tumble from the C.294 revetment is also recorded at the south-west end of this walling, in the form of a pile of large stones (C.276). The partial collapse of this external revetment led to a slip of bank material into the berm area. This began with a layer of brown sandy silt (C.275) on top of bedrock, overlain by a deposit of yellow-brown gravelly sediment (C.303) that, in turn, was covered by a dark brown silt (C.302).

As stated previously, it is difficult to distinguish primary bank material from slip deposits occurring on the inner side of the bank. The latter includes part of a layer of orange-brown sandy silt (C.256) with numerous large stones that extends 2.5m east from the palisade trench. This was overlain by a spread of stony brown silt (C.253). The upper bank slip on this side of the bank comprised a thin layer of the C.242 fire-reddened stone.

Trench 22 (northern bank terminal): Context descriptions (in stratigraphic sequence)
Pre-bank
C.259 Pre-bank surface on inner side. A 2.12m (N–S) by 0.8m (E–W) spread of light brown-yellow sandy silt on inner side of bank. Compact with frequent medium to large stones up to 0.2m in size (not fire-reddened). Rare flecks of charcoal, with one small concentration of charcoal.

C.296 Buried sod at base of bank. A 1.05m (E–W) spread of dark silt at base of bank, extending 2.35m south from northern side of excavation trench. This 0.01–0.03m thick layer had occasional small stones, but no visible charcoal.

Main bank layers
C.240 Stone deposit on inner side of bank. Spread of loose stones extending 2.1m (north–south) by 1.2m (east–west) along inner edge of bank. Mix of medium to large stones up to 0.35m in length. Tumble deposit with no obvious coursing.

C.242 The upper part of the bank was formed of coarsely broken, fire-reddened stone. This was loose on the surface with greater compaction at depth. The stones were mostly angular, ranging 0.02–0.25m in length (majority 0.08–0.12m). Small amounts of mid brown silt between stones. Frequent fragments of charcoal/partly charred wood. C.242 is identical to C.37 in Trench 9, with both deposits consisting of broken stone quarried from the base of the adjacent ditch and piled to form the upper part of the bank.

C.252 Layer on inner slope of bank. Deposit of light brown-yellow sandy silt, very loose with minor roots. Frequent pebbles and small to medium stones in 0.04–0.1m range, most of which are angular and fire-reddened. Rare flecks of charcoal.

C.253 Layer on inner slope of bank. A 0.35m (E–W) wide spread of mid brown silt (green tinge) extending 0.48m (N–S) from north section, averaging 0.12m in thickness. This loose deposit contained frequent small stones in 0.03–0.06m range, with some flecks of charcoal.

C.254 Layer on inner slope of bank. Small deposit of mid–dark brown silt on east side of C.237 posthole. Contains rounded pebbles and small stones of subsoil origin, as well as some angular, fire-reddened clasts. Compact with some flecks of charcoal. Context 254 seems to represent a mix of C.242 and C.252.
C.255 Layer on inner slope of bank. Deposit of mid brown silt with frequent stones in 0.03–0.08m range. Loose with some flecks and lumps of charcoal. Stratigraphically coeval with C.256, a similar layer of stony and burnt material.

C.256 Layer on inner slope of bank. A 0.15m thick deposit of orange-brown silt on inner side of C.237 posthole. Very loose with frequent small to medium stones in 0.03–0.08m range. Minor roots with rare flecks of charcoal.

C.257 Thin layer at base of bank on inner side. Red-orange silt with frequent small to medium stones in 0.03–0.1m range, with occasional larger stones up to 0.15m. Many of the stones are fire-reddened. Very loose with minor roots and rare flecks of charcoal.

C.258 Thin layer at base of bank on inner side. Dark brown-black silt with frequent small stones in 0.02–0.05m, with some larger examples up to 0.15m. Stratigraphically coeval with C.257, with a greater charcoal content.

C.275 A 0.25–0.3m thick deposit of mid brown (orange tinge) sandy silt, piled against the external bank revetment (C.294). Compact with frequent small to medium stones in 0.05–0.1m range.

C.276 A 0.2m thick deposit of loose stones extending 1m (E–W) by 0.8m (N–S) outside the south-west corner of the external bank revetment (C.294), on northern side of gate posthole (C.185). Mostly angular stones in 0.05–0.4m size range, with a matrix of mid–dark brown silt. Probable tumble from C.294 stone revertment, with some broken stone from underlying bedrock.

C.301 Deposit of dark brown silt on exterior (western) slope of bank. This thin 0.32m by 0.15m spread contained small amounts of fire-reddened angular stone.

C.302 Deposit of dark brown silt on exterior bank slope. This thin 0.9m by 0.15m spread contained small amounts of angular stone up to 0.15m in size.

C.303 Deposit of yellow-brown silty sediment with gravelly texture on exterior bank slope. Loose deposit with frequent small to medium stones.

C.305 A 1.3m long deposit of dark brown silt on exterior bank slope, averaging 0.3m in thickness. Numerous small stones and some large examples, mostly sub-angular.

Bank revetments

C.266 Stone revetment on exterior of bank terminal. A line of large stones extending east from palisade trench (C.234) for a distance of 1.65m bordering north side of entrance passage. Partly collapsed wall crudely built with medium to large stones in 0.28–0.4m range, horizontally placed with no regular coursing. Most of the stones are angular to sub-angular, with some fire-reddened examples. Some of this collapsed stone overlay a burnt timber (C.265) on north side.

C.294 Stone-built revetment on exterior (western) side of bank. A crude drystone wall extending south from northern side of excavation trench, before curving south-east towards the palisade trench (C.234), and beyond this as C.266. Partly collapsed wall crudely built with medium to large stones in 0.15–0.55m range, horizontally placed with no regular coursing. Most of the stones are angular to sub-angular, with some fire-reddened examples.

Palisade

C.184 Upper fill of C.185 posthole. Dark brown humic silt with frequent small to medium stones, and some larger examples up to 0.2m. Approximately 20% of stones are fire-reddened and angular, with numerous voids and occasional flecks of charcoal. A whetstone (04E1038:10) was discovered in the upper part of the fill.

C.238 Lower fill of C.185 posthole. Compact deposit of mid brown (orange tinge) silt with frequent small to medium stones, and small to large pieces of charcoal. The compaction is due to weight of overlying stony fill (C.184).

C.185 Posthole used for gate post on northern side of entrance passage. Sub-oval cut measuring 1.19m (east–west) by 0.87m (north–south); near-vertical sides, except on steeply sloping western side, with a central depth of 0.95m. Lower sides and uneven base cut into bedrock. The upper north-east side is cut by the C.234 palisade trench, the base of which is 0.7m higher than bottom of posthole.

C.218 Upper fill of C.236 posthole. Loose deposit of angular stones, 0.1–0.3m in size, most of which are fire-reddened. Some matrix of dark brown silt with numerous voids between stones. This context represents a tumble of C.242 bank stones into the partly open posthole following the burning of the bank palisade.

C.219 Second fill of C.236 posthole. Orange-brown sandy silt with rooty fibrous matter. No stones or charcoal. Buried sod within the upper fill of posthole.

C.220 Third fill of C.236 posthole. Loose deposit of dark brown-black silt with minor roots. Frequent stones in 0.05–0.1m range (generally smaller than stones in C.218), most of which were fire-reddened. Frequent inclusions of charcoal.

C.226 Basal fill of C.236 posthole. Deposit of loose mid-dark brown silt with minor roots. Frequent stones in 0.03–0.1m range, with occasional examples up to 0.15m. Significant amount of charcoal.

C.239 Concentration of charcoal along eastern side of C.236 posthole. Possible remains of post-pipe.

C.236 Posthole in northern bank. Sub-circular cut measuring 0.86m (north–south) by 0.75m (east–west) on the surface; 0.47m (north–south) by 0.54m (east–west) in centre; and 0.4m (north–south) by 0.38m (east–west) at the base, with a central depth of 1.27m. The upper part of this vertical cut was formed in stony bank material, with the lower 0.7m quarried into bedrock. Near-vertical sides with an irregularly flat base.

C.221 Upper fill of C.237 posthole. Deposit of loose small to medium stones, with occasional large stones. Numerous voids between stones with frequent roots. Similar to upper fill (C.218) in C.236 posthole.

C.262 Fragment of charred wood from upper east side of C.237 posthole. Found at base of upper fill (C.221), partly embedded into underlying C.263 buried sod. Short length of charred wood measuring 0.12m (north–south) by 0.08m (east–west) by 0.03m in thickness.

C.263 Second fill of C.237 posthole. Spread of mid brown silty with root fibrous texture, 0.01-0.08m in thickness, with a few pebbles. Buried sod on upper north-east side of posthole.

C.222 Third fill of C.237 posthole. Deposit of loose dark brown silt with numerous small stones and a few larger examples. Confined to north-west side of posthole. Small amounts of charcoal.

C.223 Fourth fill of C.237 posthole. Dark grey-black silt beneath the stony C.221 at a depth of 0.51m in posthole. Frequent lumps of charcoal indicate a possible post-pipe.

C.224 Fifth fill of C.237 posthole. Spread of fire-reddened sediment on western side of posthole. Red-orange in colour, with silt texture and occasional small to medium stones.

C.225 Sixth fill of C.237 posthole. Spread of fire-reddened sediment on eastern side of posthole, stratigraphically coeval with C.224. Pink-orange in colour, with silt texture and occasional small stones. Occasional flecks of charcoal.

C.227 Basal fill of C.237 posthole. Orange brown silt with numerous small to large stones, and flecks of charcoal.

C.237 Posthole in northern bank. Sub-circular cut measuring 1.3m in diameter, reducing with depth to 0.74m (centre) and 0.25m (base), with a maximum depth of 1.58m. Vertical through stony bank material, with lower half cut through the old ground surface (C.296) into bedrock. The base was irregularly flat.

C.228 Upper fill of C.235 palisade trench. Loose deposit of angular stones, 0.1–0.25m in size, several of which are fire-reddened, with matrix of dark brown silt. Similar to upper fills (contexts 218 and 221) of C.236 and C.237 postholes.

C.229 Fill of C.235 palisade trench. Deposit of light brown-orange silt with fibrous rooty texture. Similar to C.219 in C.236 posthole, C.263 in C.237 posthole, and C.232 in C.234 trench. Buried sod.

C.230 Basal fill of C.235 palisade trench. Dark brown silt, loose with frequent small stones and occasional flecks of charcoal.

C.261 Small concentration of charcoal at base of C.235 palisade trench. Compact with some pebbles; 0.04m in thickness.

C.235 Palisade trench on top of bank. Stone-lined slot extending 0.75m between C.236 and C.237 postholes, averaging 0.3m in width and 0.33–0.41m in depth. Near-vertical sides to a flat base in stony bank material. Indications of packing where a number of large stones, 0.1–0.2m in size, were found in a near-vertical position along the sides of the trench, while others of similar size were displaced along the edges.

C.231 Upper fill of C.234 palisade trench. Loose deposit of small to large angular stones. No charcoal.

C.232 Central fill of C.234 palisade trench. Deposit of light brown humic silt with fibrous rooty texture. Occasional small stones and flecks of charcoal. Buried sod.

C.233 Lower fill of C.234 palisade trench. Deposit of loose dark brown-black silt with occasional small to medum stones, and a few flecks of charcoal.

C.234 Palisade trench on top of bank. Stone-lined slot that extends 1.75m between the C.236 and C.185 postholes, averaging 0.5m in width and 0.4m in depth. Near-vertical sides to an uneven base that slopes south towards C.185 gate posthole. Upper part of trench is formed in stony bank material; base is cut into white stony silt representing leached subsoil (C.04). Numerous angular stones along both edges of trench, including several vertical stones that represent original packing stones.

Charcoal/charred wood on inside (east) of palisade trench

C.241 Length of charred wood on inner side of C.237 posthole, at a depth of 0.4m below the modern ground surface on top of the bank. This fragment lay in a horizontal north–south position within a layer of fire-reddened stone (C.242). It measured 0.16m (north–south) by 0.13m (east–west) with a thickness of 0.07–0.1m.

C.260 Linear deposit of charcoal along eastern edge of C.235 palisade trench and C.237 posthole. An alignment of six small concentrations of charcoal, 0.08–0.27m in length, all part of the same branch/timber burnt during the destruction of the palisade.

C.264 Linear spread of dark brown-black silt extending east–west from eastern side of C.234 palisade trench.

This 0.08–0.1m thick deposit contained some finely divided and lump charcoal. Located on immediate north side of C.265 burnt timber, with some fire-reddened stones in vicinity.

C.265 Burnt timber in bank. Charred remains of a single branch or post extending east from palisade trench (C.234). Slightly curving, with overall length of 1.56m. Located on inner (north) side of stone revetment (C.266), with the C.264 burnt deposit on other side.

Charcoal/charred wood on outside (west) of palisade trench

C.291 Burnt timber/post on bank surface. Linear deposit of charcoal measuring 1.7m (N–S) by 0.4m wide, with a maximum thickness of 0.22m, lying horizontally on inner (eastern) side of external bank revetment (C.294). Located 0.4m west of a parallel burnt post (C.292).

C.292 Burnt timber/post within C.242 bank material. A curving 0.2m wide line of charcoal in upper part of C.242 stony bank material, extending 1.54m south from edge of C.237 posthole to the inner side of C.294 stone revetment.

C.293 Short length of burnt wood within C.242 bank material. A 0.7m long piece of charred wood, 0.12m in diameter, extending north-east/south-west across southern end of another burnt branch (C.292), on western side of C.236 posthole.

Northern ditch terminal

Excavation on the north side of Trench 22 uncovered the terminal of a substantial ditch that provided soil and stone to build the adjacent bank (Figure 3.51). The inner edge of the ditch was approximately 2m out from the external revetment of the bank; however, this stretch of gently sloping ground should not be considered a deliberate berm. The upper part of the ditch was dug through B-horizon subsoil, with the lower half cut into solid bedrock. The ditch cut (C.211) had a U-shaped profile, ranging 2.2m (top) to 1.4m (base) in width, with a central depth of 1.3m below modern ground level. The upper western side was not fully exposed; both this and the eastern side of the ditch were steeply sloping (45°), while the southern end was somewhat steeper (60°). There were no obvious toolmarks on the quarried rock surfaces and no indication that fire-setting was used in that process.

Fill sequence

The infilling of the northern terminal commenced with an influx of primary silt (C.210) from the exterior side of the ditch (Figure 3.48). This was probably due to rainwash on the external (counterscarp) bank, which was mainly composed of soil. There followed a minor slip of stony silt (C.209) from the main bank, again probably due to rainwash. The first substantial infilling in the ditch is represented by a deposit of large stones

FIGURE 3.51: DITCH STRATIFICATION, NORTHERN SIDE OF TRENCH 22, CLASHANIMUD.

in brown-orange silt (C.196). This 0.4m deep deposit accumulated prior to an influx of charcoal and stones from the bank revetment, suggesting some interval between construction and destruction of the entrance defences. The latter is represented by deposits of charcoal-rich sediment (C.190 and C.191) from the burning of the bank palisades. This was accompanied by the partial collapse of a stone revetment (C.294) on the bank exterior, marked by large stones (C.175) within the charcoal-rich sediments. A layer of stony silt (C.194) on the western side of the ditch is stratigraphically coeval with the C.191 burnt layer, but was distinguished by the absence of C.175 stones and charcoal, the influx of which was confined to the inner side of the ditch. The possibility that these C.175 stones represent the collapse of a second bank revetment located outside C.294 should be considered in light of a similar arrrangement in the southern bank terminal (see below). This would remove any suggestion of a deliberate berm between bank and ditch.

The next stage in the fill sequence involve a slow accumulation of stony silt on the western side of the upper ditch. The origin of this sediment (C.192 and overlying C.208) is unknown, but may derive in part from erosion of the counterscarp bank. These contexts were overlain by a mid brown sandy silt (C.193), with some continued erosion of main bank (C.302). This was followed by a large deposit of stones (C.189) in the central ditch area, overlain by a smaller deposit of loose stones (C.181). Context 189 occurs as an apparent intrusion in the upper fill sequence; however, the circumstances in which this material was deposited are uncertain. The presence of some fire-reddened stone connects C.189 to erosion of the burnt bank surface. The possibilty that the C.189 and C.181 stones served to level the ditch surface for use as a farm track in the early modern era should be considered.

Trench 22 (northern ditch terminal): Context descriptions (in stratigraphic sequence)
C.211 Cut of northern ditch terminal.

C.210 Thin compact deposit of grey-brown silt (green tinge) on lower outer (west) slope and base of rock-cut ditch. Rare inclusions of pebbles, small stones and flecks of charcoal.

C.209 Small build-up of stony silt against lower inner side of ditch, overlying the basal silt (C.210). Moderately compact deposit of mid–dark brown gritty silt with frequent pebbles and small stones.

C.196 Deposit of stones in lower part of ditch. Very looose mix of small to medium stones in 0.05–0.15m size range, with a matrix of brown-orange silt. Some voids between larger stones and minor root activity. Many of stone surfaces were discoloured black due to water seepage.

C.175 Deposit of large stones in central fill of ditch on inner (eastern side). Large angular stones, 0.25–0.55m in size, found within C.191 and in the lower part of the overlying C.190, both of which are charcoal-rich deposits. The C.175 stones represent a partial collapse of the exterior bank revetment (C.294). This occured at the same time as the palisades were burnt, even if the C.175 stones were not fire-reddened.

C.191 Layer of orange–brown sandy silt in central fill of ditch on inner side. Moderately compact with high charcoal content, both finely divided and small to large lumps. Frequent small stones, as well as large stones (C.175) from the external bank revetment.

C.194 Layer of orange–brown sandy silt in central fill of ditch on outer side. Compact with small–medium stones. Similar in texture to C.191, except that it does not contain charcoal.

C.190 Deposit of mid brown sandy silt in central fill of ditch on inner side. Moderately compact with frequent small to medium stones in 0.05–0.15m range. High charcoal content, both finely divided and small to large lumps, as well as pieces of partly charred wood.

C.192 Deposit of orange–yellow silt in upper fill of ditch on outer side. Loose with numerous large stones, angular in shape, with frequent voids between the stones.

C.208 Deposit of compact orange silt in upper fill of ditch on outer side. Frequent small to medium stones with occasional large stones.

C.193 Small deposit of mid brown sandy silt in upper fill of ditch on outer side. Compact with frequent small to medium stones. A lead musket/pistol shot (04E1038:11) was found in upper part of this context, close to interface with O-horizon.

C.189 Deposit of stones in upper fill of ditch. Loose mix of small to large stones with a matrix of mid-dark brown silt with humic content. Mostly angular stones, some of which are fire-reddened, in 0.05–0.2m size range. Numerous voids between stones.

C.181 This spread of small to medium stones across upper fill of ditch, directly below organic soil.

O-horizon. Thin sod (C.01) overlying a 0.03–0.07m thick layer of dark brown humic silt (C.02).

Southern bank terminal

Excavation on the southern side of Trench 22 confirmed the existence of a low bank on the immediate inside of a shallow ditch (Figure 3.45). The bank was of dump contruction, where subsoil and broken stone extracted in the ditch was piled on its inner side, with no intervening berm. The exterior (western) side of the bank was retained by a low stone wall, which curved around the northern end of the bank to line the entrance passage (Figure 3.52). There was no obvious revetment on the inner side of the bank. Excavation uncovered the foundations of a wooden palisade along the centre of the bank, with three large postholes connected by a slot trench. These postholes held the main posts of a large wooden palisade that was completed using smaller posts placed upright in the slot trench. The latter took a turn to the west at its northern end, ending at a large posthole that originally held the southern gate post of the entrance (Figure 3.53).

The exterior revetment was re-built following an initial collapse of the bank, an event that pre-dated the burning of the palisade. The latter led to a further collapse of the bank and its revetment walls. The overall width of the bank today is 6–7m, but it would originally have been narrower, possibly extending 3m from the exterior revetments to a metre or so inside the palisade. The eroded bank has a central thickness of 0.8m from the old ground surface, but would originally have been at least 1m higher.

Construction

The bank was built directly on top of the old ground surface (Figure 3.54). Excavation did not uncover any palaeosol/buried sod under the bank, which instead overlay a stony orange-brown subsoil that was part of the natural Bs-horizon (C.360). The bank was of dump construction, where stony subsoil and broken bedrock extracted in the adjacent ditch was piled inside a revetment of large stones (C.270). This included a dump of stony orange-brown silt (C.298), overlain by a deposit of yellow-brown stony sediment (C.267) on the inside. These loose deposits made up the core of the bank, and were poorly differentiated due to their coarse stony composition, with colour variation mostly the result of the bank burning and post-depositional processes.

Structural features: revetments

As with the northern bank, various forms of revetment were required to consolidate this bank. These may have included the use of roundwood branches (C.297) placed horizontally within the bank (see below). The exterior and northern end of the bank were revetted by a low wall built of large stones (C.270 and C.272 respectively), laid horizontally in a rough coursing. The exterior revetment (C.270) was initially built by placing wedge-shaped stones on the sloping ground surface to create a level base for low wall of rough horizontal coursing (Figure 3.53). This revetment had to be re-built after a partial

FIGURE 3.52: EXCAVATION OF SOUTHERN TERMINAL OF BANK, TRENCH 22, SHOWING STONE REVETMENTS AND ONE OF PALISADE POSTHOLES.

FIGURE 3.53: POSTHOLES OF BANK PALISADE (GATE POSTHOLE TOP LEFT) AND STONE REVETMENTS, SOUTH SIDE OF TRENCH 22, CLASHANIMUD.

collapse of the bank, represented by a stony deposit (C.273) on the lower slope. A second wall facing (C.271) was built on top of this slip at a lower level, 0.7m to the west. The revetment at the northern end of the bank, extending along the entrance passage, was found to be almost entirely collapsed. No evidence of any internal bank revetment was found.

Structural features: palisade

The removal of organic soil (C.02) and burnt stone (C.176) in the upper bank exposed the foundations of the original bank palisade. This comprised a line of three postholes connected by a narrow slot trench along the crest of the bank (Figures 3.46 and 3.53). They include (north to south) postholes C.245, C.246 and C.247, with the intervening slot trenches C.249 and C.251. These were substantial postholes, measuring 0.7–1.4m in upper width, and were near-vertical to a depth of 0.5–0.9m (C.245), 1.25m (C.246) and 1.16 (C.247). The upper portion of each posthole was formed in stony bank material, with the lower part cut into bedrock. The fills were broadly similar, reflecting the history of these features. The lower fill generally comprised loose silty soil with varying amounts of charcoal (C.183 in C.245 posthole; C.199 in C.246 posthole; C.206 and C.207 in C.247 posthole). With the exception of C.247, there were no concentrations of charcoal in these postholes to indicate post-pipes burnt *in situ*. Given the evidence for the lighting of fires on top of the bank it is possible that partly burnt posts were subsequently pulled out of the postholes. Flecks of charcoal were common in the stony fill of the intervening palisade slots (contexts 234 and 235), but again not enough to indicate *in situ* burning of upright posts.

Excavation confirmed the use of packing stones in these postholes. This included two large slabs (C.179) found in the gate posthole (C.245), as well as large stones (C.180) in the C.246 posthole, and a lining of large slabs (C.308) around the lower part of the C.247 posthole.

Palisade destruction

As with the northern side of the entrance, excavation revealed a significant amount of charcoal, fire-reddened stone and oxidised soil in and around the palisade trench and postholes of the southern bank terminal. The upper bank material (C.176) was intensely fire-reddened with variable amounts of charcoal. This extended into the core of the bank to contexts 203, 267 and 298. Much of the stone in those deposits was fire-reddened, the result of intense heat penetrating the core of the bank during the prolonged burning of the oak palisades.

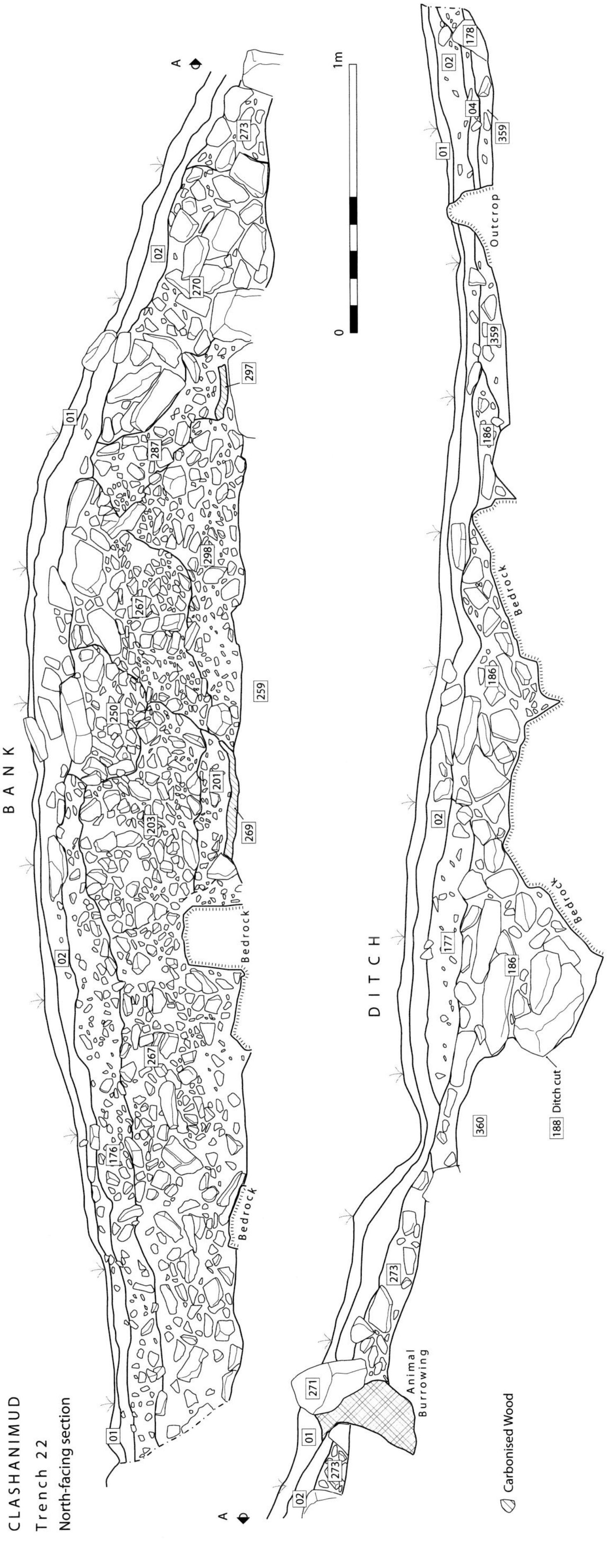

Figure 3.54: Stratification of bank and ditch on southern side of Trench 22, Clashanimud.

As well as a general incidence of charcoal in the bank material, excavation identified some short lengths of charred wood at varying depths within the bank. Examples on the inner (eastern) side include contexts 268, 274 and 290, as well as the burnt spread C.269. These mostly derive from collapse of the burning palisade. Of particular interest is a 1.26m length of burnt wood (C.297) found on the immediate inside of the C.270 revetment on the bank exterior. This was part of a horizontal branch/post that was charred *in situ* at the base of the bank, similar to what occurred in contexts 291–3 in the northern bank terminal of Trench 22. This suggests that some branches of wood were occasionally laid horizontally within the bank during construction, for the purpose of retaining the piles of loose soil and broken stone. Somewhat different is a 1.78m long charred post (C.304) found outside the C.272 revetment on north side of bank. This may represent a fallen post from the palisade bordering the southern side of the entrance passage.

Bank erosion

The burning of the palisade was followed by a gradual erosion of the bank structure over a long period. This was a slow process that reduced the overall height of the bank by as much as 1m. The results are evident on both the inner and exterior sides of the bank (Figure 3.54), and also at the southern end bordering the entrance passage.

It is difficult to distinguish primary bank material from slip deposits occurring on the inner side of the bank. The main deposit there was C.267, a 0.3–0.4m thick deposit of fire-reddened stones that extended as much as 3m inside the palisade trench. On the exterior side, the final collapse of the bank revetments is marked by the accumulation of large stones (C.186) in the adjacent ditch. The fact that these stones were overlain by a deposit of finer fire-reddened stone (C.177 west) suggests that the revetments may have collapsed in a significant way when the palisade was burned down.

Trench 22 (southern bank terminal): Context descriptions (in stratigraphic sequence)
Main bank layers
C.201 Sediment deposit on inner (eastern) side of C.247 posthole. Loose angular stones, 0.04–0.16m in size. Frequent voids in upper 0.16m, with matrix of mid brown sandy silt in lower part.

C.203 Stony sediment in central part of bank. A 0.45m thick (max.) deposit of tightly packed angular stones, 0.08–0.2m in size, with a matrix of mid–dark brown silt. Many of the stones were fire-reddened in a deposit that contained frequent charcoal.

C.267 Stony sediment in central part and eastern side of bank. Compact deposit of yellow-brown sandy silt, with numerous small to large angular stones, many of which were fire-reddened.

C.298 Deposit of orange-brown coarse sandy silt with numerous small stones, 0.04–0.07m in size, as well as a few larger stones up to 0.1m.

Bank revetments
C.270 Upper line of external stone revetment of bank. A low wall built into the exterior bank slope, using flat angular stones, 0.2–0.3m in length, with some up to 0.55m, placed in a rough horizontal coursing. The revetment was initially built by placing wedge-shaped stones on the sloping ground surface to create a level base for the revetment wall. The partial collapse of this revetment was represented by a deposit of loose stones (C273) on the exterior side.

C.271 Lower line of external stone revetment of bank. A low wall built into the lower bank slope, again using flat angular stones, 0.2–48m in length in a rough horizontal coursing. This was built of top of collapsed stone (C.273) from the original revetment.

C.272 External revetment of bank on inside of entrance passage. This was a continuation of the C.270 and/ or C.271 walling on western side of bank, along the northern side of the bank terminal. This revetment was mostly collapsed, but seems to have originaly comprised large tabular stones, 0.15–0.3m in length, with some up to 0.6m, roughly placed in horizontal coursing.

Palisade

C.179 Packing stones in C.245 posthole. The posthole was divided by two large slabs arranged north–south across the western side of cut, leaning towards the east. These were quarried stones, measuring 0.3m by 0.25m by 0.13m and 0.25m by 0.23m by 0.1m respectively, which were carefully selected as packing for the gate post. The latter is unlikely to have been placed on the western side of these stones as this had a maximum depth of only 0.5m. The post was probably positioned in the larger eastern space, where a depth of 0.9m offered a more secure footing.

C.182 Upper fill of gate posthole (C.245). Loose, mid brown, sandy silt with occasional small–medium stones in 0.08–0.15m range. Some larger stones, up to 0.25m in size, may be slip from the overlying C.176 deposit. Frequent flecks of charcoal.

C.183 Lower fill of gate posthole (C.245). Loose yellow-orange silt with gravelly texture, frequent small stones and occasional medium–large stones in 0.15–0.2m range. Some flecks of charcoal.

C.245 Southern posthole of entrance gate, located at end of palisade trench. Pear-shaped cut measuring 1m (east–west) by 0.55–0.9m (north–south), widening towards the east. The upper sides had an irregular profile, formed by stony bank material (C.267) and revetment stones (C.272). The lower part was cut into bedrock, with the base sloping west to east. The posthole ranged in depth from 0.5m on the west side to 0.9m on the east side. The sides were near-vertical.

C.198 Upper fill of C.246 posthole. The upper part of this fill comprised a deposit of loose stones 0.15–0.35m in size, with numerous voids and some light brown sandy silt. The stone size decreased with depth to 0.05–0.15m, with the matrix becoming sandier and more compact. Rare flecks of charcoal, mostly at base of fill; with some recent rodent burrows.

C.199 Upper fill of C.246 posthole. A 0.45m thick deposit of fine silt with a gravelly texture due to numerous small stones in 0.04–0.07m range. This sediment was yellow-brown on the surface, but became darker brown with depth, due mainly to the increased incidence of charcoal. The lower 0.07m of this sediment was rich in charcoal.

C.180 Packing stones in C.246 posthole. A number of large stones, 0.2–0.3m in size, loosely arranged within the C.199 lower fill.

C.246 Central posthole in excavated palisade trench. Sub-circular cut measuring 0.7m (east–west) by 0.9m (north–south), narrowing to 0.36m (east–west) by 0.26m (north–south) at the base, with near-vertical sides to an overall depth of 1.25m. The upper third was formed in stony bank material (C.267) on the east and west sides, and by stones of the bank revetment (C.272) on the northern side, with the cut opening into the C.249 and C.251 palisade trenches. The mid-section of the posthole cut through a compact orange-brown B-horizon (C.360) down to an irregularly flat base in bedrock.

C.200 Upper fill of C.247 posthole. A 0.3m thick deposit of mid brown sandy silt of moderate compaction. Frequent large stones, 0.15–0.3m range, in upper part, with numerous voids; smaller stones, 0.05–0.1m, at base. Moderate compaction, with occasional flecks of charcoal.

C.204 Second fill of C.247 posthole. A 0.04m thick deposit of loose, grey-brown silt with some fine sand. Numerous small stones in 0.06–0.08m range, with frequent flecks of charcoal.

C.205 Third fill of C.247 posthole. A 0.07m thick deposit of orange-brown silt with slight gravelly texture due to numerous small stones in 0.03–0.07m range. Occasional flecks of charcoal.

C.206 Lower fill of C.247 posthole. A 0.14m thick deposit of dark brown silt, loose with frequent stones in 0.01–0.07m range. This occurred as a dark coloration on the northern side of the posthole. The sediment had a similar texture and stone content to C.205, the main difference being a high charcoal content, and that several larger stones were fire-reddened.

C.207 Basal fill of C.247 posthole. A 0.07m thick deposit of yellow-brown stony silt, becoming darker near the base of the posthole. Frequent small–medium stones in 0.08–0.12m range, with larger packing stones (C.308) around the sides. Occasional flecks and small lumps of charcoal, with the lower 0.05–0.1m of this fill densely packed with charcoal. Possible post-pipe, with *in situ* burning of post.

C.308 Packing stones in C.247 posthole. Thin stone slabs, averaging 0.4m by 0.2m by 0.1m in size, arranged around lower sides of posthole.

C.247 Posthole at southern end of excavated palisade trench. Oval cut measuring 1.4m (north–south) by 0.6m (east–west), narrowing with depth to a circular 0.5m (north–south) by 0.6m (east–west) cut. The posthole has a depth of 1.16m, where the upper 0.48m was formed by stony bank material (C.267), and the lower 0.68m cut through eroded rock into solid bedrock. The east and west sides were near-vertical; the north and south sides were stepped to an irregularly flat base.

C.248 Fill of C. 249 palisade trench. A stony deposit contained within the short slot connecting the C.245 gate posthole with the C.246 posthole. The depth of this fill ranged 0.7m on the west side to 1.1m to the east. Upper portion consisted of large stones in 0.1–0.25m range, as well as smaller stones in 0.07–0.1m range, loosely arranged with numerous voids with some dark brown silt matrix. Some of the larger stones near surface may represent collapse from the C.272 bank revetment. The context was more compact with depth, also becoming light brown in colour. Frequent flecks of charcoal throughout, but not enough concentration to indicate *in situ* burning of palisade timbers.

C.249 Short palisade trench between C.245 gate posthole and C.246 posthole. Narrow cut in bank material and underlying subsoil, measuring 0.7m (east–west) in length, 0.85m wide on top and 0.4m wide at base, ranging in depth from 0.7m on the west side to 1.1m to east. Near-vertical sides with slightly rounded base. The original width was probably around 0.4m, as the upper northern side has widened due to partial collapse of C.272 bank revetment.

C.250 Upper fill of C. 251 palisade trench, connecting the C.246 and C.247 postholes. Deposit of loose, red-brown, silt sand with frequent small to medium stones in 0.05–0.12m range, many of which are fire-reddened. Occasional flecks of charcoal close to base.

C.251 Short palisade trench between C.246 and C.247 postholes. Narrow cut in bank material down to old ground surface, measuring 0.9m (east–west) in length, 0.35–0.44m wide and 0.12–0.34m deep, with steeply sloping sides and a flat base.

C.197 Possible stakehole on upper surface of bank, western side. Cut was formed in stony bank material (C.267) and measured 0.12m (north–south) by 0.09m (east–west), with a central depth of 0.14m. Filled with loose dark brown silt containing flecks of charcoal and occasonal small stones inder 0.02m.

Charcoal/charred wood on inside (east) of palisade trench

C.268 Short length of charcoal within C.269 burnt spread, 0.6m east of C.246 posthole. Single piece of charred wood measuring 0.25m (north–south) by 0.08m wide by 0.04m thick. A similarly sized spread of finely divided charcoal on the southern side was probably part of the same branch/post, which was crushed by overlying bank material (C.267).

C.269 Spread of grey-black sediment beneath C.201 on inner side of C.251 palisade trench and C.246/247 postholes. A 0.05–0.07m thick deposit of loose sediment with fine sandy silt texture and frequent small stones in 0.04–0.08m range. High charcoal content, both finely divided and lumps in 0.02–0.04m range. Most of this dark silt was contained within a shallow depression on the inner (eastern) side of the palisade trench. This was a natural depression in the old ground surface, measuring 1.6m (north–south) long by 0.15–0.35m wide by 0.03–0.12m deep. Some of the C.269 sediment extended beyond the edges of this depression.

C.274 Short length of charred wood on inner side of bank.

C.290 Short length of charred wood inside bank in the south-east corner of Trench 22. A 0.22m (north-west/south-east) long by 0.05m wide by 0.04m thick piece of burnt wood lying on eroded bedrock. Scatter of charcoal flecks and small lumps in general vicinity.

Charred wood on outer (western) side of palisade trench

C.297 Length of charred wood lying horizontal directly inside the C.270 revetment wall. A 1.26m (north–south) length of charcoal, ranging 0.06–0.11m in width, heavily fragmented due to weight of overlying bank material.

FIGURE 3.55: TERMINAL OF DITCH, SOUTHERN SIDE OF TRENCH 22. POSITION OF GATE POSTHOLES MARKED BY RANGING POLES (TOP LEFT AND TOP CENTRE).

Part of a horizontal branch/post that charred *in situ* at base of bank. Similar to contexts 291–3 in the northern bank terminal of Trench 22.

C.299 Length of charred wood in space between C.251 palisade trench and C.270 revetment wall. Small piece of burnt wood measuring 0.11m by 0.07m by 0.04m.

Charred wood in entrance passage

C.304 Charred remains of post on exterior side of C.272 revetment wall. A line of charcoal, 1.78m (east–west) long, 0.07–0.15m wide and up to 0.03m in thickness, present in two concentrations on southern side of a low rib of bedrock marking the edge of entrance passageway.

Bank slip on inner (eastern) side of bank

C.176 Spread of loose fire-reddened stone beneath sod layer along inner surface of bank. Majority of stones in 0.01–0.07m range, occurring in a matrix of brown-grey silt. Similar to C.177 in upper fill of adjacent ditch.

Bank slip on outer (western) side of palisade trench

C.273 Bank collapse on outer (western) side. A 0.2–0.35m deposit of loose stony sediment found between and outside the C.270 and C.271 stone revetments. Large angular stones in 0.25–0.4m range, loosely arranged with smaller clasts and frequent voids.

Southern ditch terminal

Excavation on the southern side of the entrance causeway in Trench 22 revealed a second terminal of the main hillfort ditch (Figure 3.55). A 1.85m (north–south) length of this ditch (C.11) was exposed on the immediate outside of the hillfort bank. This was cut into near-surface bedrock, averaging 1.7m wide (east–west), and ranging in depth from 0.3m (northern end) to 0.85m (southern section, Trench 22). The western side was near-vertical, while the eastern side sloped steeply towards the bank, with no intervening berm. Projecting ribs of bedrock served to separate the northern end of the ditch from the adjacent causeway. Overall, the ditch had an irregular profile, where the rock extraction was controlled by bedding and joint planes. There were no obvious toolmarks on the exposed rock surfaces and no indication that fire-setting was used to extract bedrock.

Fill sequence

The infilling of the southern ditch terminal began with a thin deposit of silt (C.187), probably the result of rainwash on the adjacent surface (Figure 3.54). This was followed by an influx of large stones (C.186), most of which were fire-reddened, coming from the inner bank. These stones can be linked to the burning of the hillfort defences, though charcoal was noticeably absent at this level. The upper part of the ditch fill contained a loose spread of fire-reddened stones (C.177), representing slip off the main bank.

Trench 22 (southern ditch terminal): Context descriptions (in stratigraphic sequence)

C.11 Cut of ditch (see main text).

C.187 Basal fill of ditch. Compact deposit of mid to dark brown silt, with maximum thickness of 0.15m. Frequent small and medium stones ranging 0.05–0.25m. Small amounts of charcoal (not shown in southern section).

C.186 Central fill of ditch. Loose deposit of small in 0.05–0.7m size range, in a matrix of grey brown humic silt. Approximately 60–70% of stones are fire-reddened.

C.177 Upper fill of ditch comprising a spread of fire-reddened stone in 0.01–0.07m size range, within a matrix of brown-grey silt. Similar deposit (C.178) on upper surface of adjacent bank.

O-horizon Thin sod (C.01) over very thin layer of dark bown humic silt (C.02).

External bank

As elsewhere in the perimeter of the inner enclosure, there are indications in Trench 22 of a low bank following the outer edge of the ditch (Figure 3.54). This is a slight feature along the outer edge of the ditch in the southern side of Trench 22, approximately 1m in width with an external height of only 0.3m. The inner part was exposed along the western side of Trench 22; however the bank was not fully sectioned. Excavation did uncover some large stones (C.178), ranging 0.18–0.35m in length, along the inner side of this bank. These may represent tumble from a low wall that served to prevent material accumulating in the hillfort ditch. This feature did not continue across the entrance causeway on the west side of Trench 22.

Discussion: Entrance to inner enclosure

The excavation of Trench 22 provides much detail concerning the original entrance to the inner hillfort enclosure.

Pre-hillfort activity

No evidence of any earlier site occupation was found in

this part of the hillfort. The possibility that burnt wood at the base of the bank (contexts 291, 292 and 293 north of entrance; contexts 297 and 299 south of entrance) pre-dates the defences was considered, but can be dismissed. Those finds represent buried wood in the bank that was charred as a result of intense heat created by the prolonged burning of the oak palisade. This heat passed through the coarse bank material, reddening much of its broken stone in the process.

Construction

The hillfort entrance has a basic design and was built as a single construction event. No phasing is evident in the arrangement of the defensive features. These included a stout wooden gate conected on both sides to a palisaded and stone-faced bank, with a causeway across the adjacent ditch. The relationship of the palisade to the enclosing bank may also be clarified. It is very unlikely that this feature was inserted into the bank either when the latter was finished or at some subsequent time. The main reason is the depth of the postholes when taken from the top of the bank. Allowing that the latter would originally have been at least 1m higher, it would have been necessary to dig those postholes 3m down through the top of the bank into bedrock. This could not have been done without a massive disturbance to the bank.

The stratigraphic position of the palisade postholes indicate that this feature and the enclosing bank were built together in the following sequence:

1. A line of postholes was dug through subsoil into bedrock.

2. The main posts of the palisade were placed upright in these postholes and secured with stone packing.

3. A ditch was dug outside the palisade, soil from which was piled around the posts to form a bank.

4. Continued digging of the ditch into bedrock provided broken stone to form final bank layers, in which the main palisade posts were buried to a depth of 2–3m.

5. A narrow slot was dug into the upper bank material between each pair of main posts. This held small wooden uprights, which were secured to the main posts to complete the palisade fence.

6. The palisade slot trench curved outwards at both bank terminals, ending with a large posthole on either side that held gateposts for the entrance.

7. A rough stone facing of horizontally laid stones was built as a facing on the outer (western) side of the bank. This low revetment continued around the bank terminals along both sides of the entrance passage.

FIGURE 3.56: PARTIAL RECONSTRUCTION OF ENTRANCE TO INNER ENCLOSURE, TRENCH 22, CLASHANIMUD. NOTE THE MAIN POSTS OF PALISADE AND GATE IN THEIR ORIGINAL POSTHOLES, AS WELL AS LOW STONE WALLING ON EXTERIOR OF BANK AND ENTRANCE PASSAGEWAY.

In this way the bank served to support the palisade, with the main posts buried to a depth of 2–3m. No evidence of any revetment was found on the inside of the bank, which is where the most significant collapse occurred.

A partial reconstruction was undertaken in Trench 22 of the entrance to the inner enclosure (Figure 3.56). Three stout timber posts were inserted into original posthole positions along the palisade trench on both sides of the entrance gap. These six posts were smaller than those used in the Trench 9–10 bank reconstruction, ranging 2–3m in overall height and 1.5-2.m in exposed height after the bank was re-built. This was necessary because the enclosure bank on either side of the entrance was significantly thinner than in Trench 9/10 and thus would not have supported taller posts in a safe manner. Two of these posts mark the position of the original gate-posts in the inner enclosure entrance. The ditch sections on either side of the entrance causeway outside this gate were backfilled for safety reasons. Finally, the entrance passage inside this causeway was restored to approximately 0.1m below the pre-excavation level, exposing some of the original metalled surface.

Early use (pre-burning)

There are some indications of a significant interval between the building and destruction of the hillfort entrance. The first is the large amount of fill (C.196) that accumulated in the northern ditch prior to an influx of charcoal-rich sediment (C.190 and C.191) and collapsed revetment stone (C.175) from the palisade burning. The second is an apparent rebuilding of the external bank revetment (C.270 to C.271) on the southern side of the entrance following its partial collapse. There is no evidence that the palisade was ever re-built prior to or following its final destruction. The entrance passage itself had the appearance of a trampled surface, with numerous small stones compacted into the B-horizon. While there were no indications of wear or wheel ruts, this does indicate some traffic through the entrance.

The only artifact finds associated with the early use of this entrance are a whetstone (04E1038-10) found in the fill of the northern gate post (Figure 3.67 below), and the tip of another possible whetstone (04E1038:12) from the entrance passage (not illustrated). The former comes from a closed context, and was possibly used to sharpen swords, or perhaps axes or knives used to build the palisade and gate.

Palisade destruction

There was a high incidence of charcoal within the collapsed bank, including a number of charred fragments of the posts used in that structure. The analysis of this charcoal confirms that that palisade was also built entirely of oak. The burning of such a massive structure must have been both intense and prolonged to explain the fire-reddening of the bank deposits. The heat penetrated the coarse bank material, reddening the broken stone and charring any wood therein. The intensity of these fires is evident in the large number of small stones from the entrance area that have vitrified glassy surfaces.

Abandonment

There is no evidence that any attempt was made to rebuild the bank or the palisade following their destruction by fire. Instead, the excavation record indicates a slow weathering of the exposed bank surface, resulting in the gradual infilling of the ditch. The presence of a thin sod (contexts 219, 229, 232 and 263) in the partly filled postholes and palisade trench on the northern side of the entrance suggests a brief interval between the burning event and the final collapse of the bank. The stony fill in the upper part of both ditch terminals indicates a significant influx of bank stone, connected in part to a gradual failure of the external revetment. Bank collapse was more severe on the inner side where no revetment was recorded during excavation.

3.7 The Inner Enclosure

A total of 25 trenches were excavated inside the inner enclosure of Clashanimud hillfort (Figure 3.7). The importance of that space for the hillfort builders is obvious from the considerable effort taken to build the enclosing fortification. The excavation of some hillforts in Ireland confirms that the inner enclosure was often used for high-status occupation and ceremonial activities, with evidence of timber-built structures, specialized craftworking and ritual deposits, as well as significant amounts of material culture.

Summit: Trenches 6–8

The summit of any hillfort is potentially an area of archaeological importance. This is where the presence of an older monument had a special significance, such as the Neolithic passage tomb at Rathcoran hillfort, Co. Wicklow, or the Bronze Age burial cairn at Freestone Hill, Co. Kilkenny, or where timber structures ('temples') are the focus of complex rituals as at Dun Ailinne, Co. Kildare and Navan Fort, Co. Armagh (see Raftery 1994; Waddell 2010). For this reason, it was decided to conduct an extensive investigation of the summit of Clashanimud, to examine whether that area was used as ceremonial space at different times.

Following clearance of vegetation, geophysical survey was undertaken over a 900m2 area across the summit.

FIGURE 3.57: EXCAVATION OF SUMMIT AREA, LOOKING SOUTH, TRENCH 6, CLASHANIMUD. NOTE ORDNANCE SURVEY CAIRN ERECTED IN 1841 (CENTRE RIGHT).

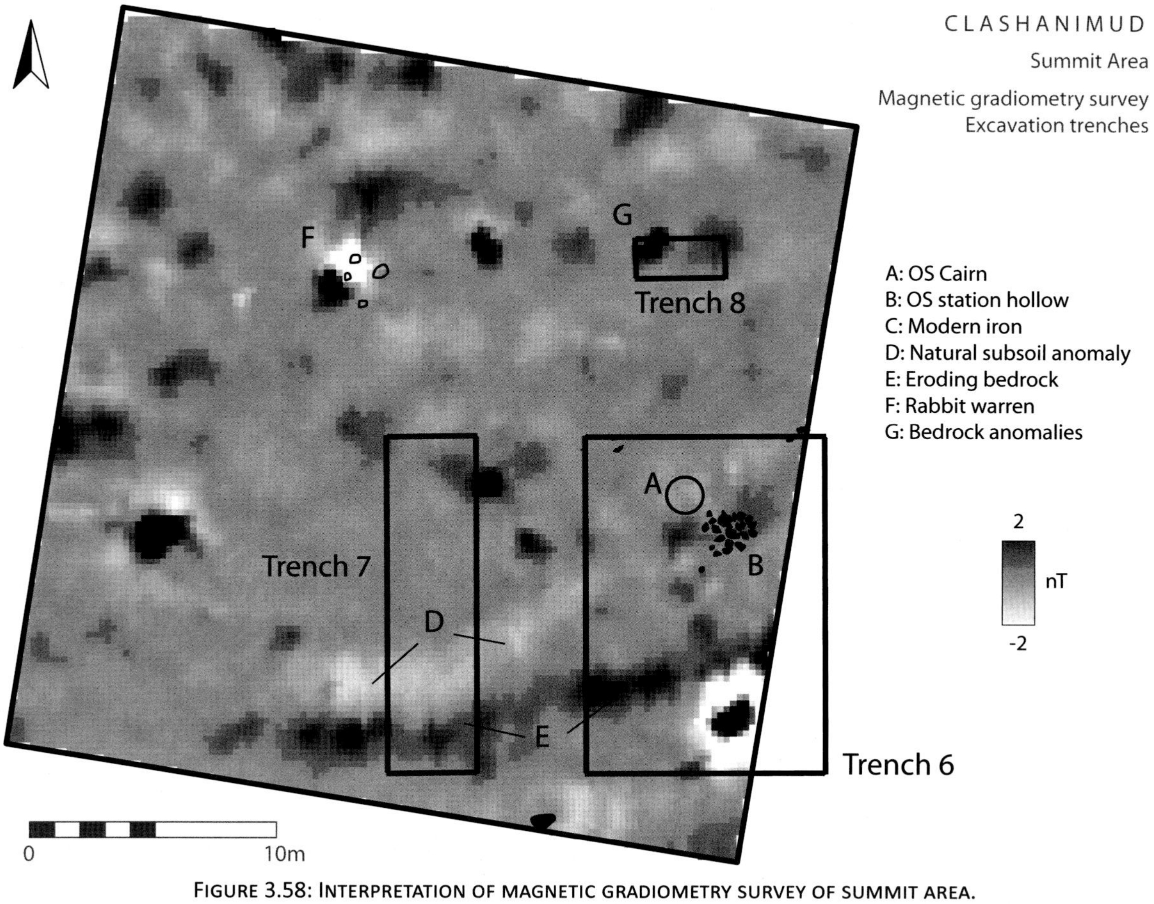

FIGURE 3.58: INTERPRETATION OF MAGNETIC GRADIOMETRY SURVEY OF SUMMIT AREA.

The results of the electrical resistivity and magnetic susceptibility surveys were inconclusive. Magnetic gradiometry identified a number of point anomalies suggesting pit features, while curving arcs of high and low gradiometry readings hinted at a possible enclosure encircling the summit, measuring c.20m in diameter, with a funnel-shaped opening to the east. The clearance of vegetation exposed a number of surface features. These included a small cairn of loose stones, 2.1m by 1.7m in diameter and c.0.6m high, and two nearby surface hollows. A small rabbit warren to the west of this cairn is the likely source of a significant dipole effect in the gradiometry survey.

Three trenches were excavated at the summit over an area of 204m2 (Figure 3.7). A 10m by 14m cutting (Trench 6) was initially excavated to investigate the cairn and adjacent hollows, and to test the south-east side of the 'enclosure' feature suggested by magnetic gradiometry (Figure 3.57). A second cutting (Trench 7), measuring 4m by 14m, was excavated 4m to the west of Trench 6. This also examined the southern side of the 'enclosure', as well as a number of gradiometry point anomalies (Figure 3.58). Finally, a 2m by 4m cutting (Trench 8) was excavated 6m to the north of Trench 6, to examine a row of possible pits indicated by the geophysical survey.

The excavation of those trenches removed a thin organic soil (O-horizon; contexts 01 and 02) across the summit area. This 0.05–0.08m thick layer overlay a grey leached surface (E-horizon; C.04). This was removed to expose a humus-enriched subsoil (Bh-horizon) that graded from light brown (C.05) to dark brown (C.359) with depth, with an underlying layer of iron-enriched subsoil (Bs-horizon; C.360) of variable thickness. The B-horizon overlay a broad rib of eroded bedrock across the southern half of Trenches 6 and 7, extending into Trench 8. This loose spread of coarsely broken stone was excavated carefully over three weeks. It was unclear for some time whether the stony deposit represented the base of a robbed-out cairn, or was possibly connected to quarrying in the modern era. Eventually, it was discovered that the surface is of natural origin, produced by periglacial frost-shattering of near-surface bedrock in late Pleistocene times, with the possibility of some glacial scouring, and solifluxion-type movement. This was confirmed by the exposure of ribs of *in situ* bedrock, striking east–west with a steep northerly dip, underneath the stony surface (Figure 3.59). There is a broad correlation in Trenches 6 and 7 between this band of broken bedrock and the gradiometry anomaly that formed the southern side of the so-called 'enclosure'. An investigation of other gradiometry anomalies in these trenches did not reveal any archaeological features.

Archaeological features

Excavation at the northern end of Trench 6 exposed the extent of the small cairn (C.16) marking the summit of the hill. This sub-circular mound of loose stone measured 2.8m by 2.7m, with a maximum height of 0.45m. It is made up of small to large stones up to 0.6m in length, piled loosely on a buried sod layer (C.17). The

FIGURE 3.59: POST-EXCAVATION VIEW OF BROKEN BEDROCK SURFACE, TRENCH 6, CLASHANIMUD (SCALE 2M).

FIGURE 3.60: RECONSTRUCTION OF SUMMIT CAIRN FOLLOWING EXCAVATION.

dismantling of this cairn uncovered a small amount of broken glass, china pottery and fragments of corroded iron, all of early modern date (04E1038:05). A large piece of corroded iron found under a boulder near the base of the cairn confirms the latter is of early modern date. A small pit (C.08) on the north-west edge of the cairn contained a large slab (C.10), measuring 0.59m by 0.32m by 0.12m in thickness, lying flat at ground level. The upper surface has a crudely pecked arrow with an indentation at the point. This stone and the adjacent cairn mark the location of a trignometrical station shown on the 1845 Ordnance Survey. The presence of modern glass and pot sherds around the cairn may be explained by visits made to the summit by local people over the years. Following excavation, this cairn was reconstructed and the trignometrical stone replaced in the original pit (Figure 3.60). The cairn now measures 2.7m (east–west) by 2.55m (north–south), with a maximum height of 0.6m.

No other archaeological features or finds were identified in Trench 6, or in the adjacent Trenches 7 or 8 where the removal of sod and organic soil exposed a thin B-horizon on shattered bedrock.

Discussion

In the absence of relevant artifacts or archaeological features, there is no evidence to indicate that the summit of this hillfort was used either for occupation or ceremonial activity in prehistory or in later periods. The Ordnance Survey erected the small summit cairn in 1841, using an inscribed stone in an adjacent pit to mark the position of a trigonometrical station. The discovery of modern glass and pottery sherds around the cairn is connected to periodic visits by local people.

Excavation was able to resolve the significance of a number of geophysical anomalies in the summit area. The 'pits' and 'enclosure' identified by magnetic gradiometry were produced by natural weathering of near-surface bedrock. These anomalies have no connection to a large oval feature marked on Westropp's 1901 plan, which is likely to be one of the large quarry pits marked on the 1845 Ordnance Survey.

Test-excavation of inner enclosure

The 2004 season of excavation included an investigation of possible hut-sites (Trench 2) in the northern part of the inner enclosure, just inside the hillfort bank (Figure 3.7). This was accompanied the same year by investigation of geophysical survey anomalies in that same area using 2m^2 test-pits (Trenches 3, 4 and 5, and the extension Trench 20). The strategy shifted in 2005 to systematic test-pitting, where 4m^2 test-pits were excavated on a north–south/east–west grid (Figure 3.8). A total of 14 such test-pits were eventually excavated (Trenches 11,

FIGURE 3.61: STONY SURFACE WITH DEPRESSIONS, TRENCH 2, CLASHANIMUD.

12, 13, 14, 15, 16, 17, 23, 24, 25, 26, 27, 28 and 36). Together with the results from the inner side of Trenches 9, 10 and 19, this represent a total of 22 excavation trenches within the inner enclosure of the hillfort. The following is a summary of the main findings, with stratigraphic details for each trench available in the site archive report (O'Brien 2015).

Test-pitting of surface hollows (Trench 2)

Survey in 2004 identified a number of surface depressions inside the hillfort bank on the northern side of the inner enclosure (Figure 3.7). Geophysical survey recorded a number of resistivity and magnetic anomalies in the same area. A 10m (east–west) by 4m excavation area (Trench 2) was opened 6m inside the inner bank to investigate these depressions as possible hut-sites. Deturfing exposed a general spread of coarsely broken sandstone across the entire trench. Several surface depressions were identified in this stone spread, roughly circular in shape and measuring 2–3m across (Figure 3.61). Further excavation identified a loose deposit of broken stone, at least 1m in thickness, across the entire excavation area. The discovery of part of a china tableware vessel (04E1038:1) at a depth of 0.8m indicates considerable disturbance of this stony deposit. This is probably connected to rock quarrying activity in the modern era. There were no other finds, and the excavation of Trench 2 was eventually abandoned due to the likely extent of that quarry disturbance.

Test-pit sampling of geophysical survey anomalies (Trenches 3–5)

These three $2m^2$ test-pits were excavated in the north-west part of the inner hillfort enclosure. They were located on magnetic gradiometry anomalies recorded during geophysical survey in 2004. It was hoped that these test-pits would identify occupation features for further excavation. Trenches 4 and 5 contained no archaeological features or finds, and the geophysical anomalies there are probably the result of high bedrock. The significance of a deep cut in Trench 3 was not resolved, even though the excavation area was extended (Trench 20; see O'Brien 2015 for details).

Systematic test-pitting of inner enclosure (Trenches 11–17; 23–28; 36)

An important objective of the 2005 excavation season was to test the inner hillfort enclosure for evidence of early occupation. With no surface indications of same, it was necessary to conduct a systematic sampling of the interior. The 2004 work confirmed the limited value of geophysical survey in an environment of high bedrock. It also suggested that $2m^2$ test-pits were not especially

FIGURE 3.62: EXCAVATION OF 4M SQUARE TEST-PITS IN THE INNER ENCLOSURE OF CLASHANIMUD HILLFORT: (CLOCKWISE FROM TOP LEFT) TRENCHES 11, 12, 15, AND 16.

useful in detecting evidence of occupation in the interior. For 2005 it was decided to initiate a systematic sampling of the enclosure using 4m by 4m test-pits spaced at approximately 20m intervals (Figures 3.7 and 3.8). The decision to increase the size of the test-pits was made to maximise the recovery of archaeological features and finds, and to detect large structural features (Figure 3.62).

An east–west line of four test-pits (Trenches 11–14) was excavated east from Trench 9, with a further three test-pits (Trenches 15–17) extending north from Trench 14 (Figure 3.7). These seven test-pits, together with the three examples excavated in 2004, provide a comprehensive sampling of the northwestern quadrant of the inner enclosure. In 2006, sampling was extended to the south-west quadrant, where seven test-pits (Trenches 23–28 and 36) were excavated using the same strategy.

Excavation revealed a podzolised soil profile in all of these test-pits. This comprised a thin organic soil (C.01 O-horizon and C.02 A-horizon) overlying a stony leached layer (C.04 E-horizon). This, in turn, overlay a stony B-horizon with separate zones of humus (C.359 Bh-horizon) and iron (C.360 Bs-horizon) precipitation. In most cases this B-horizon subsoil was directly on eroded bedrock (C.362), though a C-horizon subsoil of primary fluvio-glacial silt is recorded in places.

The results of this test-pitting are mostly negative, with no occupation deposits, built structures or artifacts found. While the acidic soil environment, high bedrock and drainage of the inner enclosure are not conducive to archaeological preservation, the small amount of charcoal from these test-pits is notable. This includes rare flecks found in Trenches 12, 16 and 26, with the only large charcoal deposit (C.41) coming from Trench 17, where it can be linked to burning of the adjacent bank palisade. This is supported by high magnetic gradiometry readings along the inner bank slope in that area. Excavation exposed spreads of large stones under the organic soil in several of these test-pits (e.g. C.12 in Trench 11; contexts 52 and 53 in Trench 16; contexts 39 and 40 in Trench 17; C.06 in Trench 23). Some of this derives from recent quarrying, while other stone deposits are connected to the inward collapse of the hillfort bank.

Inner side of Trenches 9, 10 and 19

Excavation was also conducted directly inside the hillfort bank on the western side of the inner enclosure. The area concerned was the eastern side of Trenches 9 and 10, and all of Trench 19. As elsewhere, the thin organic soil overlay heavily leached subsoil, with areas of frost-shattered bedrock near the surface. Excavation uncovered a 4m wide spread of large stones (C.33) that probably represent tumble from a low stone facing (C.31) along the inner side of the bank (Figure 3.63).

Figure 3.63: Spread of stones (C.33) on inner side of bank, inner enclosure, Clashanimud.

Figure 3.64: Stone slab (C.24) placed upright in pit/slot (C.26), Trench 9, inner enclosure of Clashanimud hillfort.

These overlay a stony spread (C.34) filling a natural hollow in that area.

Further excavation in that area exposed two cut features possibly related to built structures on the inner side of the hillfort bank. The first was a narrow slot (C.26), measuring 3.09m in length, 0.64m in width and 0.3m deep, which extended in a north–south direction across Trench 9. The central part of this trench widened to a sub-circular pit (C.26a), 1.2m wide and 0.65m deep (Figure 3.64). A large stone slab (C.24) was set upright in this pit and secured with fill (C.25). This slab was carefully chosen to serve as a packing stone for a timber upright, though no trace of the latter was found. There were no finds or charcoal in the pit or extended slot trench.

A 1.17m wide spread of redeposited subsoil (C.27) on the western side of C.26 represents upcast from the digging of that pit. Excavation on the western side of C.27 exposed a second feature that may also have contributed to this redeposited subsoil. This was a sub-triangular pit (C.65), 1.9m by 0.4–1.4m across and 0.55–0.85m deep, located 0.65m west of the C.26 trench. This contained a loose stony fill, similar to broken bedrock in that area. There were no artifacts, charcoal or other datable material in the pit.

C.24 Large stone slab set on edge, north–south across centre of C.26 pit. Sub-triangular slab of grey sandstone, 0.8m long by 0.2–0.52m wide by 0.17m thick, flat surfaces and rectangular in cross section. Possibly quarried for use as packing stone; no tooling marks.

C.25 Stony fill of pit C.26. Loose deposit of dark brown silt, with numerous small to large stones, averaging 0.25m in length, with small voids.

C.26 Slot trench with central posthole extending north–south across Trench 9. A narrow slot trench with near-vertical sides, 0.64m wide and 0.3m deep. This extended 0.5–0.6m out from northern and southern sides of a sub-circular pit (C.26a), 1.2m (N–S) by 1.1m (E–W) and 0.65m deep, with steeply sloping sides to an uneven rounded base.

C.27 Spread of redeposited subsoil on immediate western side of C.26 slot trench/posthole. A 1.17m wide (E–W) by 0.1–0.15m thick deposit of orange silt, with frequent pebbles and small to medium stones.

C.61 Stony fill of pit C.65. Loose deposit of dark brown-black sandy silt with frequent small to medium stones up to cobble size; voids between some stones. Overlain by stone spread C.33 (see Section 2b for details of contexts 31, 34 and 34).

C.65 Triangular pit, 1.9m by 0.4–1.4m across by 0.55–0.85m deep, cut into Bs-horizon subsoil. Straight edged on two sides with curving western side. Near-vertical sides to irregularly flat base.

Inner enclosure: Discussion

The results of excavation in the inner hillfort enclosure are mostly negative, with no occupation deposits, built structures or early artifact finds from these 22 trenches. While the acidic soil environment, high bedrock and drainage of the inner enclosure is not conducive to archaeological preservation, the small amount of charcoal from these test-pits is notable. In total, this amounted to rare flecks found on the C.359 surface in Trench 12; rare flecks within C.04 and underlying C.359 in Trench 16; and flecks of charcoal within C.04 in Trench 26. The only charcoal find of any significance are some flecks in C.04, Trench 17, probably connected to burning of the adjacent hillfort bank. This is supported by high gradiomery readings from the inner bank slope in that area.

Excavation did reveal spreads of large stones directly under the organic soil in several of these trenches. In most cases, the origin of this stone is not known. Some may derive from recent quarrying, while others may be connected to the inward collapse of the hillfort bank. The likely quarry residues include C.52 and C.53 in Trench 16. The C.40 stones in Trench 17 was also probably connected to quarrying, as was the C.07 deposit in Trench 25. The C.39 stone spread in Trench 17 represents collapse from the inner hillfort bank. This is also likely for the spread of stones found at the base of the same bank in Trenches 9/10. The origin of the the C.28 stone spread in Trench 11 is not known.

It was hoped that these test-pits would provide targets for more extensive excavation of occupation features. This happened in only one instance, when a subsoil cut in Trench 3 was found to continue into Trench 20 as a shallow trench-like feature. There were no finds or occupation residues in the fill of this 'trench', and further excavation is necessary to clarify the significance of what seems to be a deliberately dug feature.

The only other structural features identified in the inner enclosure are the C.65 pit and adjacent slot trench with posthole (C.26) in Trench 9. The discovery of these features raised the possibility of a built structure on the inner western side of the hillfort bank. Following careful excavation over five weeks, no other evidence for a possible structure was found. There is no indication of a house 'floor', nor any hearth features, charcoal or artifact evidence to suggest the presence of a building. The most likely interpretation of the slot trench and pits in Trench 9 is that they were somehow connected to the hillfort construction, but probably not to occupation of this site.

FIGURE 3.65: EXCAVATION IN TRENCH 35, SHOWING LINEAR CULTIVATION MARKS ON STONY SUBSOIL.

3.8 The Outer Enclosure

The creation of two separate enclosures was an important element of the original hillfort design. These concentric spaces are likely to have had different functions and use history, as reflected in the different nature of their enclosing elements, with much stronger fortification evident around the inner enclosure.

A total of eleven trenches were excavated in the outer enclosure. Trenches 18 and 37 examined the northern side of the enclosure (Figure 3.7). Trench 35 investigated the south-east side, including some circular anomalies identified by geophysical survey in that area (Figure 3.65). Trenches 32 and 33 (with an extension Trench 34) tested the south-west side. Trenches 29, 30 and 31 examined the western side between the confirmed entrance to the inner enclosure (Trench 22) and the likely entrance to the outer enclosure. Finally, the inner part of Trench 21 investigated the north-west side of the outer enclosure. The stratigraphic details for these trenches are summarised here, with further details available in the site archive report (O'Brien 2015).

The results confirm that archaeological preservation in the outer enclosure of the hillfort was adversely affected by farming and stone quarrying in recent centuries. The outer enclosure was divided by radial banks into a series of small fields in the early modern era. Two of these are still in use as farm pasture on the southern and south-east sides of the hillfort. Aerial photographs show cultivation ridges across the north-west sector of the outer enclosure (Figure 3.6). Evidence of cultivation was confirmed by excavation, including plough furrows in Trench 35, the lazy-beds and earlier furrows in Trenches 21 (C.83, 85, 108, 125 and 126), 26 (C.214), 30 (C.215 and C.217), and 37 (contexts 285–289), and possible furrows in Trench 31, all of which are likely to be of early modern date (Figure 3.66). A trackway excavated inside the hillfort bank in Trench 21 was probably connected to this farming in the outer enclosure.

No archaeological investigation was undertaken on the eastern side of the outer enclosure due to the extent of modern rock quarrying. Spreads of broken stone found in Trenches 32 (C.244), 33 (Figure 3.66) and 34 (C.307) may be connected to some limited quarrying on the western side of the hillfort, possibly in an area of ground disturbance on the southern side of the entrance to the inner enclosure. The few finds from the outer enclosure come from Trench 35, where a small collection of broken glass, china and brown ware pottery, as well as clay pipe and iron fragments (11E110:14) was discovered in the A-horizon topsoil.

No features or artifacts were found that can be connected to the occupation of the hillfort. The significance of three pits (contexts 279, 281 and 283) found in Trench 35 is

Figure 3.66: Some of the 4m square test-pits excavated in the outer enclosure of Clashanimud hillfort (clockwise from top left): Trenches 29, 30, 33, and 37.

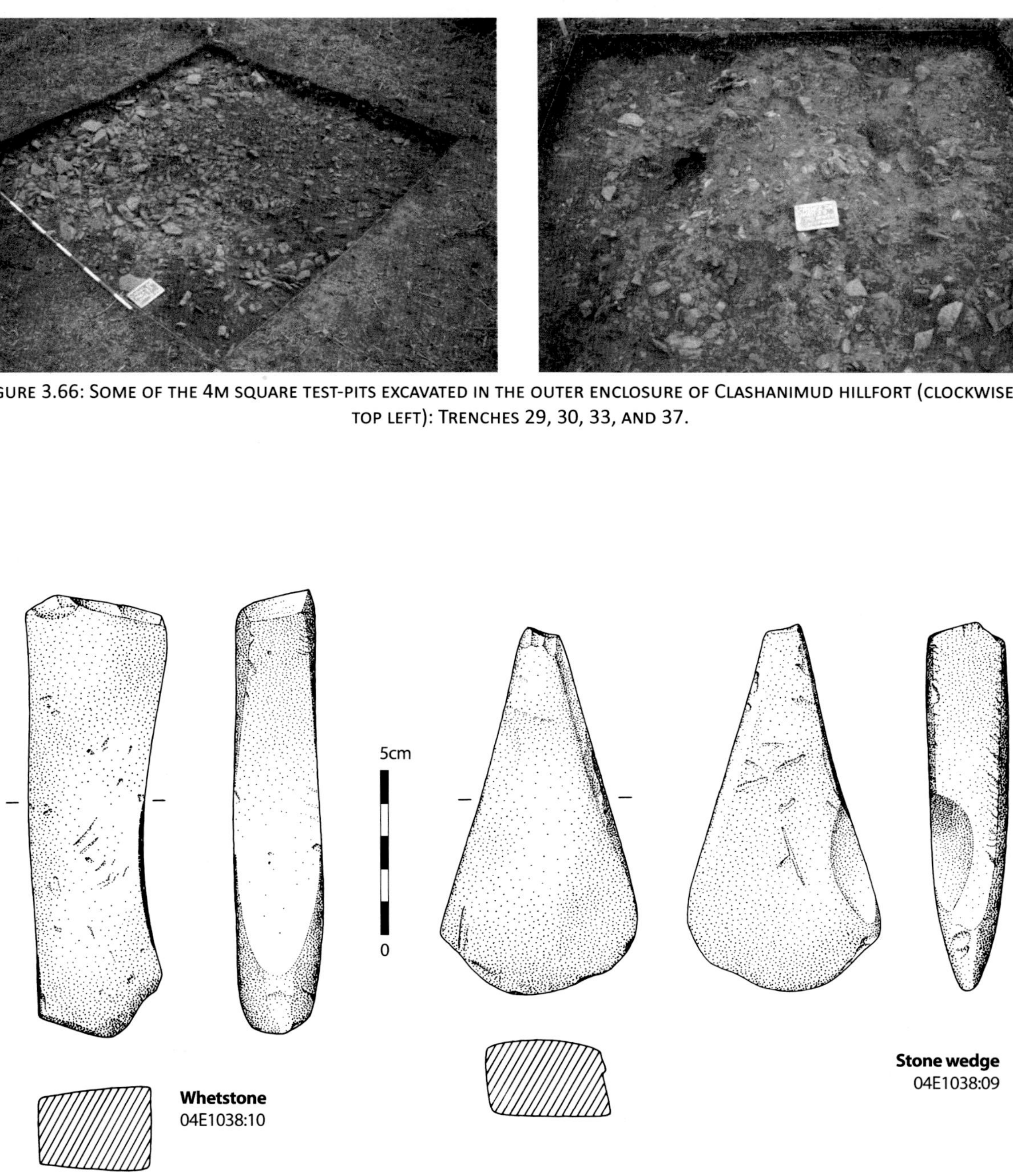

Figure 3.67: Stone artifacts from Clashanimud hillfort excavation.

not known, but are probably recent in date. Charcoal recorded from Trenches 18 (C.42); 29 (C.04); 21 (C.84 and furrow fills); 30 (furrow fills); 32 (C.04); 33/34 (C.243), and 37 (lazy-beds) probably derives from scrub burning in the early modern era. One significant find is the discovery of a small hearth found in Trench 37 on the northern side of the inner enclosure (Figure 3.7). This comprised a deposit of charcoal-rich sediment (C.284) contained within a shallow oval depression (C.295) measuring 0.64m (east–west) by 0.52m (north–south) at the top, 0.25m by 0.3m at the base, with a central depth of 0.13m (Figure 3.66). A sample of charcoal from C.284 is radiocarbon dated 3735±35 BP (GrA-42687), several centuries before the hillfort was built (see below 3.10).

3.9 Finds

The excavation of Clashanimud hillfort is disappointing in terms of finds, with only three artifacts of probable early date from three seasons of excavation. These include a stone wedge (04E1038:09) found at the base of the inner enclosure ditch (Trench 10); a small whetstone (04E1038:10) used to sharpen metal blades from the fill of a gate-post in the inner enclosure entrance (Trench 22); and the tip of another possible whetstone (04E1038:12) from the same area (Figure 3.67). None of these can be closely dated; however, the find contexts of the first two artifacts indicate some association with the construction phase of the hillfort.

04E1038:09. Stone wedge or axehead from base of ditch (C.368), inner defences of hillfort (Trench 10). Sub-triangular in shape, slightly asymmetrical in profile. 109mm long; 12mm wide and 22mm thick at butt end, which is an irregularly flat point; 39mm wide and 23mm thick in centre; 59mm wide at broad end, with a convex cutting edge, 18mm in depth. Face 1 is very smooth with light scratches, but no obvious wear and slightly curved. Face 2 is also smooth with light scratches, and no obvious wear apart from a 38mm by 15mm flake detached off the lower side. Side 1 is smooth apart from this flake; Side 2 is smooth with irregular ridge along upper part. Green fine-grained sandstone or siltstone. Possibly used to split timbers in palisade construction.

04E1038:10. Whetstone found in fill (C.184) of gatepost (C.185), northern side of entrance to inner hillfort enclosure (Trench 22). Sub-rectangular stone, 133mm in length. End 1 is 42mm wide by 19–23mm thick; centre is 35mm wide by 20–26mm thick; End 2 is 38mm wide by 12–22mm thick. Both faces roughly smooth with some light scatches but no use-wear. Broad end is irregularly smooth; narrower end is smooth and slightly pointed. Side 1 is slightly convex, very smooth with obvious wear. Side 2 is deeply concave, very smooth and heavily worn. Green fine-grained sandstone or siltstone.

04E1038:12. Broken tip of possible whetstone from entrance area to inner hillfort enclosure (Trench 22). Coarse sedimentary rock, with sub-rounded sides and flattened end, measuring 48mm by 29mm by 19mm.

The excavation also uncovered a small number of early modern artifacts mostly from the summit area (Trench 6) and outer enclosure (Trench 35). These include sherds of white and coloured china, glazed and unglazed brown earthenware and bottle glass, as well as a few clay pipe fragments and corroded iron objects, and a lead musket ball, as well as items of more recent date such as shotgun cartridges, bottle glass and plastic.

Charcoal analysis

Pauline van Rijn

The discovery of a burnt timber palisade in the defences of the inner enclosure at Clashanimud provided a large number of charcoal samples for analysis. This was an opportunity to consider the species of wood selected to build the palisade and associated timber revetments, and also what type of fuel was used to burn these structures down. Another important objective of the charcoal study was to extract samples of sapwood for AMS-radiocarbon dating, and to investigate the potential of charcoal ring sequences for dendrochronology. Details of the methods used and the data collected are available in the site archive report (see van Rijn in O'Brien 2015, appendices 1 and 2).
Charcoal was sampled from the following excavation areas:

- Trench 1: defences on the northern side of the inner enclosure; 11 samples of charred wood from the bank and loose charcoal from the base of the ditch.

- Trenches 9 and 10: defences on the western side of the inner enclosure; 27 samples of charred wood from bank.

- Trench 22: the original gated entrance to the inner enclosure; 16 samples of carbonised wod and loose charcoal from bank and ditch.

- Trench 37: charcoal from a small hearth (C.284) in the northern side of the outer hillfort enclosure.

Results

Wood taxa were identified for 573 fragments of charcoal in this study. The most striking result of this analysis is that all of the samples of burnt wood from the inner enclosure defences, namely the bank palisade, bank revetment and entrance gate-posts, contained only oak wood (*Quercus*). This is consistent across three points of excavation (Trenches 1, 9/10 and 22), which indicates the bank palisade and entrance gate were probably built entirely of oak. Only a few examples of this charcoal were suitable for ring counting. A sequence of approximately 70 rings in Sample 124 included a series of some 20 narrow rings that indicate a period of strongly repressed growth. This was also recognized in Sample 127, which had approximately 60 rings. The rings on a number of other fragments were also counted, but the sequences were too short to make any sensible observation on the growth pattern.

All the charcoal from the ditch sediment in Trench 22, namely C.190 (sample 87) and from under C.191 (sample 88), consisted of oak. The same is true for charcoal from a small hearth (C.284) in the outer enclosure (sample 123, Trench 37), with all those fragments in the form of heartwood. Almost all charcoal examined in this study showed signs of heavy cindering, not only by the metallic shine but often the cell walls were melted and the anatomical structure was deformed. In almost all fragments the cell walls showed the effects of 'puffing', mostly along the edges of the ray cells and fibers.

Only one sample, coming from the base of the ditch on the north side of the enclosure (Sample 19, Trench 1), contained charcoal that could be interpreted as the remains of brushwood or fire starter. This sample contained one oak twig whose growth ended in the summer season), many fragments of oak tree knots, and also many fragments of willow (Salix). This assemblage would have formed excellent fuel for starting a fire. The willow fragments all showed signs of fungi. This is an indication that dead wood was collected for that purpose.

Charcoal/charred wood samples were also selected for AMS-radiocarbon dating. For the palisade timbers this included only those samples that contained fragments likely to be from the sapwood part of the tree. The results of the radiocarbon dating programme are presented in the following section. Samples 124 and 127 from Trench 22 each contained a few large fragments of charred wood with 60 or more rings, possibly enough to attempt a dendrochronological analysis. Sample 80 (with 31 rings) can be added to this list. Assuming a more or less simultaneous felling of the oak trees used for these three timbers, the different series could perhaps result in lengthening the ring sequence to provide a site chronology. The samples were sent to the Dutch dendrochronological laboratory RING for trial measuring and dating analysis. The results, unfortunately, were negative.

The main result of this study is that mature oak was exclusively used to build the palisade defences and gate of the inner hillfort enclosure. With the exception of one sample, the absence of younger wood of different species used as brushwood to burn down this palisade is notable. Much of that fuel is likely to have been consumed in the intense fires that ensued. With such a limited range of wood taxa, it is difficult to say anything about the environment around the hillfort at the time of construction, except that the builders had access to large stands of mature oak. The choice of this wood was deliberate in terms of a desire to build a strong palisade that would last for a significant period of time.

3.10 Radiocarbon Dating

In the absence of useful artifact evidence, radiocarbon analysis is the only way to date the construction, occupation(s) and abandonment of Clashanimud hillfort. A total of thirteen radiocarbon dates are available for securely stratified contexts from this excavation (Figure 3.68). Twelve of these relate to the hillfort defences, with the remaining result (GrA-42687) connected to an earlier hearth dated 2277–2030 BC. The results are as follows:

Trench 1
Site sample CD2004-1 Charcoal (willow and oak) from basal sediment (C.344) in ditch, west-facing section. Submitted to provide terminus ante quem for ditch digging.
GrN-29042; 2920 ± 50 BP

CD2004-2 Charcoal (mixed oak) from posthole fill (C.327) beneath inner side of bank. Submitted to examine possibility of pre-bank phase.
GrN-29043; 3075 ± 20 BP

CD2004-3 Charcoal (mixed oak) from charred timber that was part of a burnt spread (C.325) at base of bank. Submitted to examine possibility of pre-bank activity.
GrN-29044; 3000 ± 20 BP

FIELD NO.	LAB NO.	C-14 BP	∂13C	95.4% CALIBRATION
CD2004-01	GRN-29042	2920±50	-26.50	1263–976 BC
CD2004-02	GRN-29043	3075±20	-25.40	1409–1280 BC
CD2004-03	GRN-29044	3000±20	-23.88	1371–1130 BC
CD2004-04	GRN-29045	2965±20	-24.42	1260–1116 BC
CD2004-05	GRN-29046	3050±20	-25.16	1396–1231 BC
CD2008-01	GRA-42677	2985±35	-24.67	1378–1089 BC
CD2008-02	GRA-42678	3160±40	-24.83	1511–1303 BC
CD2008-03	GRA-42683	2940±35	-24.18	1258–1027 BC
CD2008-04	GRA-42682	2910±35	-24.81	1214–1006 BC
CD2008-05	GRA-42679	3105±35	-26.11	1442–1273 BC
CD2008-06	GRA-42684	2915±35	-26.78	1216–1008 BC
CD2008-07	GRA-42687	3735±35	-25.39	2277–2030 BC
CD2016-01	GRA-67392	2745±35	-24.07	976–815 BC

FIGURE 3.68: RADIOCARBON DATES FOR CLASHANIMUD HILLFORT (CALIBRATION AFTER OXCAL V.4.2.4).

CD2004-4 Charcoal (mixed oak) from burnt deposit (C.319) within bank. Secure sample to date bank construction.
GrN-29045; 2965 ± 20 BP

CD2004-5 Charcoal (mixed oak) from burnt timber (C.313) in trench feature (along crest of bank. Submitted to date possible palisade.
GrN-29046; 3050 ± 20 BP

CD2008–3 Charcoal (oak sapwood) from burnt timber (C.325) within bank of inner hillfort defences. To date construction of inner hillfort defences.
GrA-42683; 2940±35 BP

CD2016–1 Charcoal (willow) from basal sediment (C.344) in ditch. Submitted to date burning of hillfort.
GrA-67392; 2745 ± 35 BP

Trench 21
CD2008–1 Charcoal (oak; 1.4g) from base of ditch (C.168), outer hillfort defences. Terminus ante quem result for construction of outer hillfort defences.
GrA-42677; 2985±35 BP

CD2008–2 Charcoal (oak; 2.7g) from beneath bank (C.173), outer hillfort defences. Terminus post quem result for construction of outer hillfort defences.
GrA-42678; 3160±40 BP

Trench 10
CD2008–4 Charcoal sample (oak sapwood; 2.5g) from burnt timber within bank of inner hillfort defences. Excavation area 10; Context 143. To date construction of inner hillfort defences.
GrA-42682; 2910±35 BP

Trench 22
CD2008–5 Charcoal sample (oak sapwood; 2.35g) from posthole (C.207) within bank at entrance to inner hillfort enclosure. To date construction of inner hillfort defences.
GrA-42679; 3105±35 BP

CD2008–6 Charcoal sample (oak sapwood; 2g) from posthole (C.239) within bank at entrance to inner hillfort enclosure. To date building of inner hillfort defences.
GrA-42684; 2915±35 BP

Trench 37
CD2008–7 Charcoal sample (oak sapwood; 0.3g) from small hearth (C.284) in outer enclosure. To date occupation activity inside hillfort.
GrA-42687; 3735±35 BP

There are ten dates from three separate points of excavation along the defences of the inner enclosure. Four of these (GrN-29043–6) come from bulk samples of mature oakwood, dated by conventional radiocarbon analysis to the period c.1409–1116 BC. To minimize the sample age effect, four samples of oak sapwood were subsequently dated by the AMS radiocarbon method. The results allow the date range for the palisade to be reconciled at two-sigma calibration to 1214–1027 BC (GrA-42682–4), with one outlier at 1442–1273 (GrA-42679).

There are two radiocarbon dates for charcoal samples from the ditch of the inner enclosure (Trench 1). A date range of 1263–976 BC (GrN-29042) for mixed charcoal from the base of the ditch is of interest, as this sample may include remnants of fuel used to burn down the defences. The fact that this result is younger than the other dates indicates an interval between the building and destruction of the hillfort, probably a century or so in duration.

This was examined further in 2016 when a sample of willow charcoal from the same lower ditch sediment was submitted for radiocarbon dating. That charcoal may come from brushwood fuel used to burn the hillfort palisade. A more likely scenario is that represents shrub willow growth in the ditch, which caught fire as the burning palisade collapsed on the adjacent bank. In either case, the dating of this willow charcoal to 976–815 BC (GrA-67392) can probably be connected to the hillfort burning. When compared to dates for the burnt palisade (above), there is a suggestion of a greater interval, possibly one to two centuries, between the building and destruction of the hillfort. This will be examined further in Chapter 7, when the Clashanimud radiocarbon dates are analysed using Bayesian statistical methods.

Finally, there are no radiocarbon samples available for the light wooden fence that formed part of the outer enclosing element of the hillfort. The latter was probably built sometime between 1511–1089 BC, based on a *terminus ante quem* radiocarbon date for oak charcoal from the base of the ditch (GrA-42677), and a *terminus post quem* result from beneath the bank (GrA-42678).

3.11 Discussion

Radiocarbon dates confirm that Clashanimud hillfort was probably built in the twelfth or eleventh centuries BC, during the transition from the Middle to Late Bronze Age in Ireland. The substantial nature of the enclosing elements reflects a desire to create an imposing stronghold in the landscape of Mid Cork. The outer line of defence consisted of an earthen bank, topped by a stake fence, inside a V-shaped, soil-cut ditch. The

Figure 3.69: Partial reconstruction of defences of inner hillfort enclosure, Trench 10, Clashanimud. Note rock-cut ditch, bank with external stone revetment, and main posts of central bank palisade. The eroded bank would have been at least 1m higher when originally built. The height of the posts shown here is 2m above that original bank height.

defences of the inner enclosure were more substantial, where a palisaded bank was built inside a deep rock-cut ditch, using large oak posts and smaller timbers along with stone and timber revetments (Figure 3.69). This represented a 6–7m high barrier protecting the inner enclosure (assuming a 2–3m high palisade fence above the original bank height). The size and construction of that bank and ditch arrangement, the associated wooden palisade and gated entrance, points to a strong defensive element rather than a symbolic feature or animal enclosure.

The construction of the inner defensive line involved the following stages:

1. The digging of large postholes, spaced 1.5m apart, around the entire 0.69km perimeter of the inner enclosure bank.

2. Large upright timbers, probably 0.3–0.4m in diameter and 4–5m in height, were placed in these postholes and held upright by packing stones. These posts comprised the main support timbers for a wooden fence palisade running along the top of the bank.

3. The palisade foundations were secured by the dumping of bank material in and around the upright posts. The bank material comprised a mixture of natural soil and quarried rock from the external ditch. The soil and broken rock was carefully packed around the posts and consolidated by roughly built walls of larger stones placed within the bank and used as external stone facing. There is also evidence of an internal timber revetment in the Trench 9/10 bank, possibly to create a walkway along the top.

4. The bank palisade was completed by digging a shallow trench along the top of the bank, to allow the insertion of small posts between the main palisade posts.

The evidence of timber palisading from Clashanimud is particularly important as this feature is not well documented in Irish hillforts. Assuming the palisade was continuous, and allowing for a 10m break for an entrance, it is likely that as many as 354 wooden posts of 0.2–0.3m diameter were used in this impressive structure, in addition to several thousand smaller posts and other fencing materials. Charcoal analysis suggests the wood used was possibly entirely oak. The palisade must have been an impressive sight, visible from a considerable distance across the landscape. The hillfort is located in the townland of Clashanimud ('Trench of the Timbers'), raising an intriguing possibility that this place-name may preserve a folk memory of wooden defences that stood for a brief time some 3000 years ago.

Excavation confirmed that Clashanimud hillfort was burnt down in what seems to have been a single deliberate act. The evidence for this comes from three separate locations (Trenches 1, 9/10 and 22), where charcoal deposits and burnt timbers were found within the collapsed inner bank. The stones of this bank were intensely fire-reddened, with numerous vitrified examples in the entrance area (Trench 22). There is no evidence that the wooden fence of the outer enclosure was burnt down, though that structure was much slighter than the palisade of the inner bank.

The destruction of the inner hillfort defences must have been deliberate, as any accidental burning of a heavy oak palisade along a perimeter of 0.69km can be ruled out. This would have taken considerable effort, requiring a considerable amount of tinder and brushwood was required to ignite the heavy fencing, possibly aided by the smearing of animal fat. Much of this starter fuel burnt out in the intense fires that ensued. The presence of willow charcoal in the Trench 1 ditch does indicate the use of brushwood for that purpose, with other wood species likely to have been used.

Excavation did not uncover evidence of occupation inside Clashanimud hillfort. There is no evidence to indicate the summit was of special significance. The extent of the test-pit investigation, combined with the paucity of archaeological finds, suggests that there was no significant residential occupation of the inner enclosure during the Bronze Age. The same may be argued for the outer enclosure, though less excavation was carried out as there was considerable ground disturbance caused by agriculture and quarrying in early modern times. While the latter might explain the absence of early occupation evidence, it is notable that a small hearth pre-dating the construction of this hillfort was discovered in Trench 37, in an area of early modern spade cultivation. The discovery of this hearth suggests that any occupation of the site for a prolonged period should have left some physical record. In the absence of such evidence, it is reasonable to conclude the hillfort was not occupied to any significant extent during the Bronze Age.

Clashanimud hillfort was effectively abandoned after it was burnt, with no attempt to re-build the defences. The fact that this prominent location was not re-used in later times may indicate the site held some negative associations for the early inhabitants of Cork. The wider implications in terms of warfare during the Bronze Age will be discussed in Chapter 9.

Landscape context

An examination of the wider cultural landscape during the period 1200–800 BC is essential to understanding who built and occupied Clashanimud hillfort. This landscape context must be considered at a local level, and then on a regional scale within county Cork and the

FIGURE 3.70: RECONSTRUCTION OF CLASHANIMUD HILLFORT IN THE MODERN LANDSCAPE SETTING.

wider Munster region. The local picture should take into account the considerable changes to the environment over the past 3000 years. Today, the hillfort is located in an area of fertile farmland, surrounded by large fields created in modern times for cattle pasture and cereal cultivation. The intensive nature of this farming, in particular the plough zone to the immediate east of the hillfort, probably resulted in the removal of many prehistoric sites (Figures 3.2 and 3.70). This makes it difficult to reconstruct the local settlement landscape contemporary with the hillfort occupation.

Despite its low elevation (179m OD), Clashanimud hillfort occupies a prominent position in the ridge and valley topography of Mid Cork. The hillfort is highly visible over a wide distance, with panoramic views deep into West Cork and as far north as the Boggeragh mountains. To the south, the hillfort overlooks the broad valleys of the Owenboy and Bandon rivers, in what could be considered a strategic location in terms of territorial boundary (Figures 3.1 and 3.3). It is unlikely that this was to do with control of movement along those east–west synclinal valleys, as the latter were poorly drained and heavily wooded during the late prehistoric period. The distribution of extant sites and monuments suggests that Bronze Age settlement was concentrated on higher ground along the intervening anticlinal ridges (O'Brien 2012), which includes the location of Clashanimud hillfort.

Contextualising this landscape is not easy, due to an absence of settlement archaeology and palaeoenvironmental data. With no local vegetation records, a programme of pollen analysis was undertaken in 2006 and 2007 involving a collaboration with Dr Tim Mighall, University of Aberdeen. Several lake sediments and peat bogs in this area were sampled to obtain a vegetation history for the late prehistoric period. The results (unpublished) from the first site, Annagh More bog near Crossbarry, represent an early Holocene record from a 3m deep bog that must have been cut over in historic times. The sequence there is too early to be relevant to Clashanimud hillfort. Pollen cores were also taken in two local lakes, namely Castlenalact Lake 4km west of the hillfort, and Brinny Lake 1.3km to the south. Examination of these cores confirmed that both lakes are of early modern origin, which is corroborated by historical research. Further field survey was undertaken to identify local bogs suitable for pollen analysis, but no suitable coring locations were identified close to the hillfort.

Few prehistoric sites have been excavated within a 10km radius of Clashanimud, which makes it difficult to identify settlements or ritual sites during the period of construction and use of the hillfort (*c.*1200–900 BC). To address this, a fieldwork programme directed by Nick Hogan examined the immediate vicinity of the hillfort, employing a combination of fieldwalking, geophysical prospection and aerial survey in a search for associated settlement. The results are poor, with no new prehistoric sites or artifacts. The geophysical survey did locate two circular enclosures, now levelled, on the western and northern sides of the hillfort respectively (Figure 3.71). These are possibly ringforts of early medieval date, settlements that may be connected to a single sherd of B-ware pottery found in a ploughed field to the immediate east of hillfort (Fig. 3.72). This type of pottery was imported as part of a trade in wine and other goods from the late Roman Empire during the 4th/5th century AD. Similar pottery is recorded at Garranes ringfort in Templemartin, 5.5km to the north-west of the hillfort (Ó Ríordáin 1942). That trivallate ringfort has been identified as Rath Raithleann, the seat of a branch of the ruling Eóganacht dynasty who dominated the political landscape of south Munster over several centuries of the early medieval period.

Figure 3.71: Geophysical survey (magnetic gradiometry) of environs of Clashanimud hillfort (Nick Hogan).

FIGURE 3.72: FIELDWALKING IN PLOUGHED FIELD, EASTERN SIDE OF CLASHANIMUD HILLFORT (BACKGROUND). THIS IS THE LOCATION WHERE A SINGLE SHERD OF ROMAN AMPHORA (B-WARE) WAS FOUND.

The Bronze Age landscape

Clashanimud hillfort is in a part of county Cork that has numerous field monuments of the later Bronze Age (O'Brien 2012), few of which have been investigated by archaeologists. The hillfort lies on the southern margin of a major concentration of prehistoric burnt mounds (*fulachtaí fia*) in the mid-Cork area (Figure 3.73 and Figure 3.74). These water-boiling sites have a long chronology in the late prehistoric period, with many of the Cork examples likely to be Bronze Age (Hawkes 2014). While there is no direct connection to the hillfort, burnt mounds are a general indicator of the density of Bronze Age settlement in the region (Figure 3.73). There are no extant examples adjacent to the hillfort, as the land there is well-drained and heavily cultivated in modern times. Three burnt mounds are recorded 1.3–1.5km east of the hillfort in the townlands of Kill (RMP CO097-002) and Lissanisky (CO097-003 and CO097-004).

The same is true of a scattered distribution of standing stone monuments that occur within a 5km radius of the hillfort, mostly located to the west and north west (Figure 3.74). The erection of standing stones, either singly or grouped into circles and alignments, is a distinctive feature of Bronze Age ritual in the Cork and Kerry. Two types of standing stone alignments are known in this region: stone pairs and rows of 3–6 stones built on a general north-east/south-west axis. (Ó Nualláin 1988). There are some 77 rows and 91 pairs in Co. Cork. These are often found in proximity to stone circles, single monoliths, boulder-burials and radial stone cairns, part of what is termed the 'stone circle complex' of Cork and Kerry.

The largest stone row in county Cork is located in Castlenalact townland, 3.5km west of the hillfort (Ó Nualláin 1988; O'Brien 2012). It consists of four upright stones in a north-east/south-west alignment, measuring 13.4m in length, reducing in height from 3.4m to 1.9m (Figure 3.75). There are several single standing stones in the environs of the hillfort, including a 1.25m high example in Russel Hill townland (CO096-066), 0.7km north of the hillfort, and examples in Kilnagnady townland (CO096-022, -024 and -077) 1.8–2.3km to the west/south-west (Figure 3.76). Single standing stones are numerous in the Cork region, with some 1372 examples recorded. The date of those near Clashanimud has not been established, but the taller examples are likely to be prehistoric (see O'Brien 2012 for discussion).

Boulder-burials are another important element of the 'stone circle complex'. A total of 84 examples are recorded in county Cork alone, mostly along the coastline of West Cork and its immediate hinterland. They consist of a rough stone boulder, usually a rounded glacial erratic, placed on three or more supporting stones that barely protrude above ground level. They are

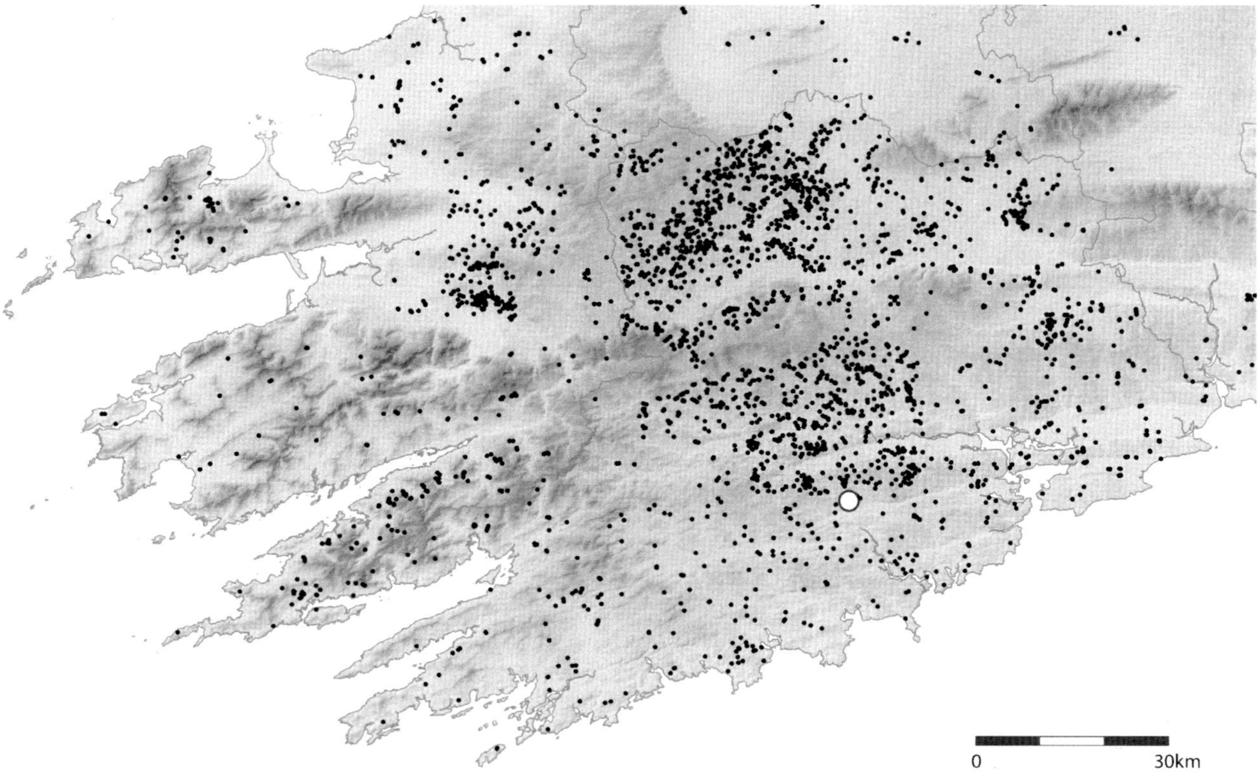

FIGURE 3.73: DISTRIBUTION OF BURNT MOUNDS (*fulachtaí fia*) IN CO. CORK (OPEN CIRCLE: CLASHANIMUD HILLFORT).

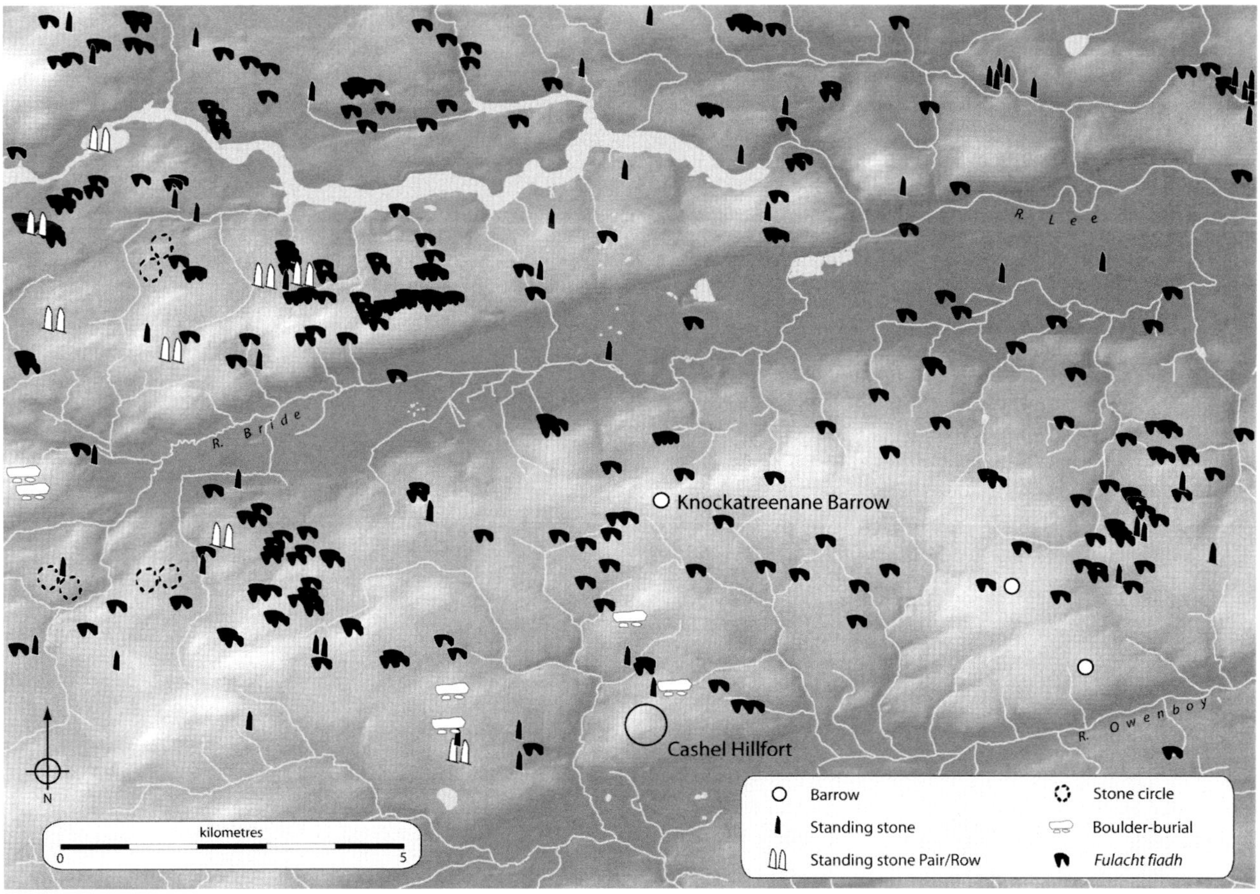

FIGURE 3.74: MAP SHOWING DISTRIBUTION OF PREHISTORIC SITES AND MONUMENTS IN THE VICINITY OF CLASHANIMUD HILLFORT, CO. CORK.

Figure 3.75: Castlenalact stone row, Co. Cork.

regarded as a form of monumental grave marker, based on the discovery of a pit containing cremated bone at Bohonagh near Rosscarbery (Fahy 1961). While other excavated examples have not contained human remains (O'Brien 2012), the close association in the landscape of boulder-burials with stone rows and pairs, stone circles and radial stone cairns, points to some funerary and/or commemorative significance.

There is a small concentration of boulder-burials within 1–4km of Clashanimud hillfort (Figure 3.73). These include an example on the boundary of Knockaphreagane and Raheen townlands (CO084-111), 2km north/north-east of the hillfort (Hawkes 1931; Hartnett 1939: 264–6; Ó Nualláin 1978: 85, no. 5; Power *et al.* 1997: 21, site 6500). A boulder-burial in Castlenalact townland (CO096-012), 3.7km west of the hillfort, had been destroyed by 1983 (Ó Nualláin 1978: 86, no.9; Power *et al.* 1992: 31, site 109). A fine example survives in Garranes townland (CO096-012), 4.2km west/north-west of the hillfort (Figure 3.77; Power *et al.* 1992: 32, site 121).

Also relevant is the record of a 'Giant's Stone' originally located 250–300m west of the hillfort. This stone was moved when surrounding fields were enlarged in the modern era. Local informants recall a low rounded boulder, as opposed to a standing stone(s) (information: Michael Lynch). This is confirmed by an unpublished source that records an oval boulder, approximately 1.6m by 1m in size, with surface markings viewed by local people as the handprint of a giant who supposedly hurled the stone from the hillfort (information: Irish Tourist Association survey (Innishannon parish, Co. Cork), 1942; Cork County Library). The stone may survive built into one of the remaining field boundaries in that area (information Naomi Barry), though this is not certain. The significance of the stone is uncertain, and it is interesting to speculate that it was part of a Bronze Age boulder-burial. Another possible boulder-burial (Figure 3.77) has been identified in Russel Hill townland (RMP CO096-067), 0.7km north/north-east of the hillfort (Power *et al.* 1997: 21, site 6502).

These boulder-burials and stone rows, and the associated stone circles in Cork, date to the Middle/Late Bronze Age transition (O'Brien 1992; 2012). Several examples have cremation burials that are broadly contemporary with Clashanimud hillfort. They include the boulder-burial (1259–1024 BC) and stone circle (1371–1055 BC) at Bohonagh, standing stone pairs at Clogagh (1200–1050 BC) and Barrees (1261–996 BC), and the stone circles at Drombeg (1115–791 BC) and Reanascreena South (1253–835 BC) (O'Brien 2012: 182).

Turning to material culture, there are no significant artifact finds from the vicinity of Clashanimud hillfort. Some early gold finds from Mid Cork may be broadly contemporary with the hillfort. These include penannular gold rings, such as an example from nearby Crookstown, and bracelets of the type in the Cappeen hoard (Cahill 2006; O'Brien 2012: fig. 248). There are no finds of bronze weaponry from the vicinity of the hillfort, though depositional and recovery processes must be considered.

Figure 3.76: Kilnagnady townland standing stones, Co. Cork (hillfort in background in three examples on right).

Figure 3.77: Garranes boulder-burial, Co. Cork.

Some socketed spearheads and swords from the wider Cork area may be contemporary, though this remains to be established (see Chapter 9 for further discussion on hillforts and weaponry).

While no examples are known near the hillfort, Bronze Age settlements of similar date have been excavated on recent road and pipeline projects in other parts of Cork. They include Middle to Late Bronze Age house sites at Ballynacorra, Ballyvergan West, Curraheen (Site 2), Ballynamona (Site 2), Careysville, Killydonoghue (Site 7), Gortnahown (Sites 1 and 3) and Gortore (Site 1b) Mitchelstown (Site 1). They were mostly farm settlements with a small number of roundhouses and other built structures, as well as activity areas connected to food processing and craftworking (see O'Brien 2012; O'Brien 2013; Cleary 2015 for details).

While no such discoveries have been made near Clashanimud, the hillfort was almost certainly part of a cultural landscape that included agricultural settlements of different form and size, as well as *fulachtaí fia*, and ritual monuments such as barrows and elements of the stone circle complex such as boulder-burials, stone rows and pairs. These sites were inter-linked components of a contemporary settled landscape, made up of communities who regarded the hillfort as a central place in a common tribal identity. Whether this corresponds to a hierarchy of settlement organization, the apex of which was elite residence in the hillfort, remains to be confirmed.

This is a subject that will be taken up in Chapter 9, where hillforts and warrior graves form part of a consideration of Bronze Age warfare in Ireland. The focus will be on a large earthen barrow in Knockatreenane townland, located on a prominent ridge overlooking the Bride river valley, 5km to the north of Clashanimud hillfort. Excavation there in 2007 uncovered the cremation burial of an adult male dated 901–811 BC (O'Brien 2010). It was initially thought that this burial post-dated the Clashanimud occupation by several centuries (O'Brien 2016a: 22), but the possibility of overlap in the early ninth century BC can now be considered in light of a recent radiocarbon result of 976–815 BC (GrA-67392) connected to the burning of that hillfort.

4

Other Bronze Age Hillforts in Munster/south Leinster

Following completion of the Clashanimud project, a second stage of research commenced in 2012 focusing on comparable hillforts in southern Ireland. This led to the investigation of four Class 2 examples, one of which (Toor More, Co. Kilkenny) is in south Leinster, with the remaining three (Glanbane, Co. Kerry; Ballylin, Co. Limerick; Formoyle, Co. Clare) in Munster (Figure 4.1). The methodology in each case involved analysis of aerial LiDAR and satellite data, followed by ground survey, geophysical prospection, and sample excavation. The focus of the latter was to examine the defences of each hillfort, and to recover finds and radiocarbon samples for dating purposes. The results confirm that like Clashanimud these hillforts were important central places in their respective regions during the Middle to Late Bronze Age transition, *c.*1300–1000 BC.

4.1 Glanbane, Co. Kerry

This large enclosure lies on the summit (86m OD) of a prominent ridge at the eastern end of the Sliabh Mis mountain range in west Kerry (Figure 4.2). It is located in Glanbane townland, some 5km north of Farranfore, on the western side of the main Killarney/Tralee road (ITM 492287, 608520). The hillfort overlooks the valleys of the rivers Lee and Maine, with panoramic views of the Castleisland and Killarney lowlands to the east and south respectively.

There are no early records of this hillfort, despite its size (6.43ha) and the fact that it was partially extant until the 1960s. It is not shown as an antiquity in the historic mapping of the Ordnance Survey of Ireland. The inner enclosure is represented on first and second editions of the six-inch (1:10560) maps as a sub-ovoid field, measuring 237m (north–south) by 227m (east–west). This enclosed seven fields on the first edition (1846) of the six-inch survey, reduced to four fields on the second edition (based on the 1893 1:2500 mapping). There are no indications of the outer hillfort enclosure in these historic maps.

Local information confirms the hillfort was levelled during agricultural improvements in the late 1960s. This resulted in the removal of 15 small fields of early modern date to create a single field, 23.7ha in size, which is now sub-divided by electric fencing for pasture management. No trace of the original hillfort survives in the modern field pattern, apart from a short section on the southern side where the line of the outer enclosure follows the rebuilt field bank for a distance of c.75m. The entire site is now listed in the *Record of Monuments and Places* for Co. Kerry (RMP KE039-065).

The original extent of the hillfort is best viewed on aerial photographs. The site was first brought to attention in 1994 when Raftery (1994) identified it as a Class 2 hillfort, based on an aerial photograph taken by Daphne Pochin-Mould that showed soil and vegetation marks of a 'double ramparted fort' (Figure 4.3). Recent aerial photographs, including satellite imagery, confirm the presence of two concentric enclosures on the hill (Figure 4.4). There are no visible entrances to the hillfort, nor any upstanding features in the interior. Satellite imagery indicates some low-relief features in the central area of the hillfort, where there is a possible curvilinear enclosure. This measures approximately 65m (north-east/south-west) by 52m (north-west/south-east), and is not clearly visible on the ground.

Archaeological investigation

A geophysical survey was carried out at Glanbane by James O'Driscoll over a three-week period in February 2012 (O'Driscoll 2012a). The open nature of this farm pasture made it possible to investigate the entire monument. An area of 7.2 hectares was surveyed using the magnetic gradiometry technique (Figure 4.5). This demonstrated that the hillfort was originally sub-circular in plan, consisting of two concentric sub-oval enclosures, spaced 20–25m apart, with an overall extent of 290m (north–south) by 280m (east–west) over 6.43ha. The inner enclosure was 240m (north–south) by 230m (east–west), 4.74ha in area, with a perimeter of 790m (592m of which is clearly discernible on the geophysical survey). The perimeter of the outer enclosure is estimated at 932m (684m clearly discernible on the geophysical survey).

Geophysical survey indicates the former presence of a single bank and ditch around both enclosures. The ditches are imaged as a dark band of high gradiometry readings, inside which there is a white band of low readings suggesting the former bank. The weakening of the responses on the eastern side of the hillfort may be related to a substantial fall in ground level affecting soil drainage in that area. A line of high gradiometry readings

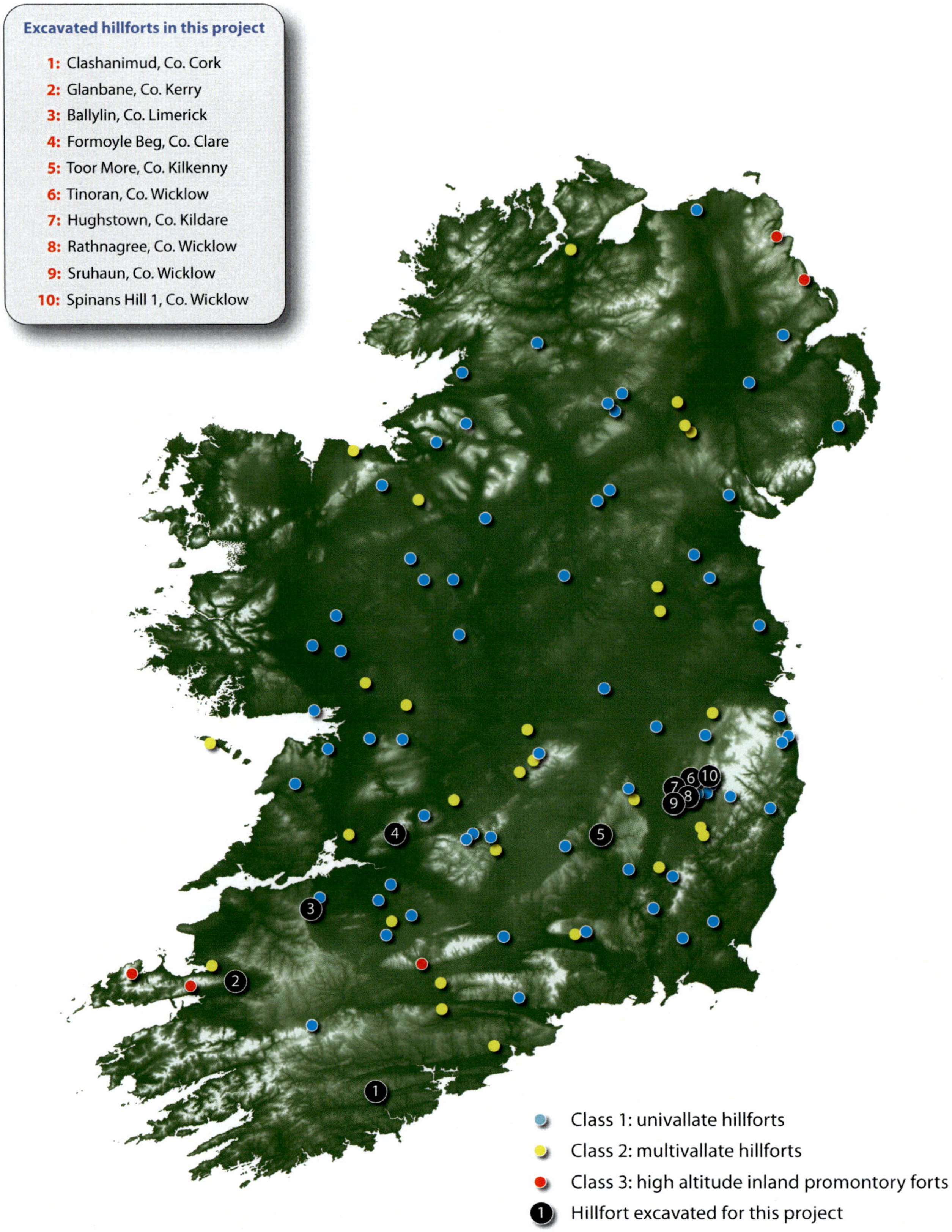

Figure 4.1: Hillforts excavated in this project.

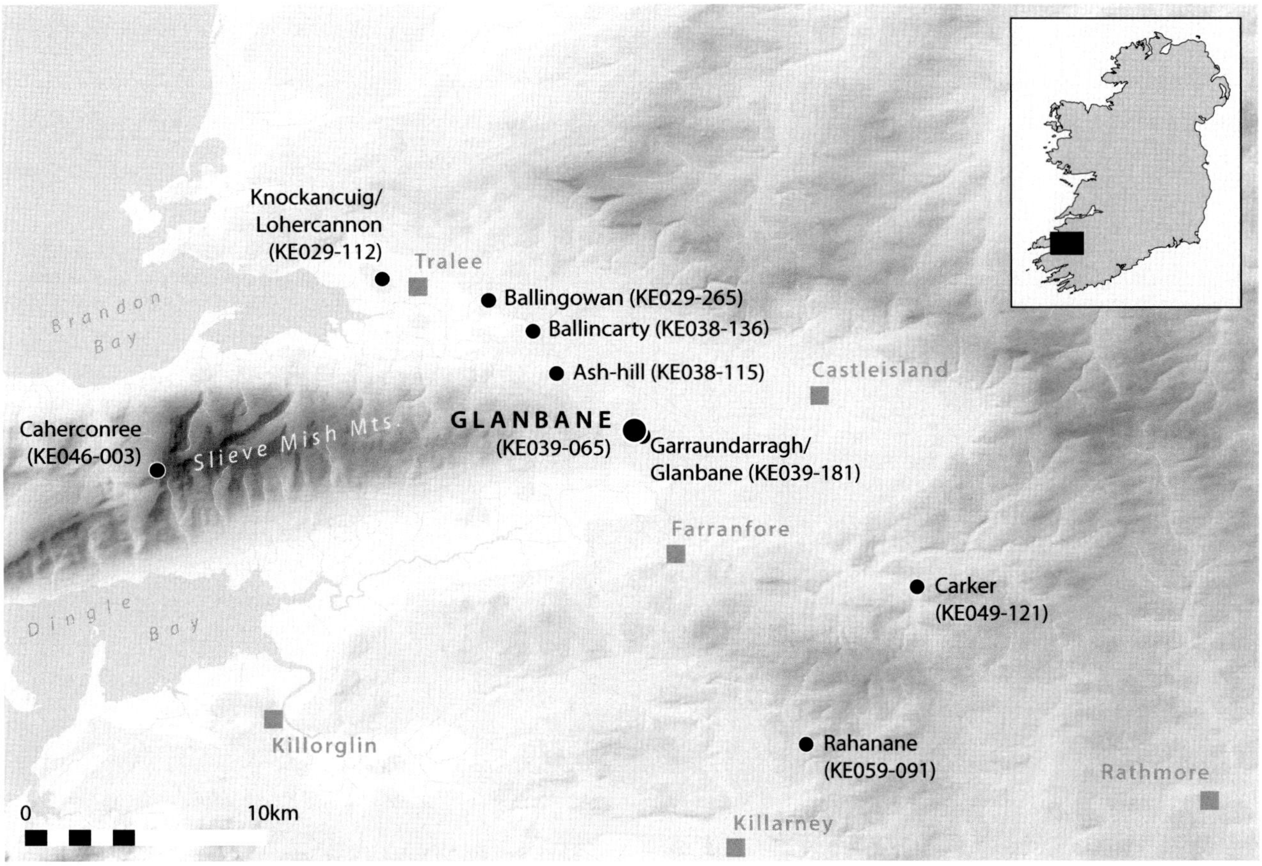

FIGURE 4.2: LOCATION AND LANDSCAPE SETTING OF GLANBANE HILLFORT, CO. KERRY, SHOWING LOCATION OF OTHER HILLFORTS AND HILLTOP ENCLOSURES IN CO. KERRY.

FIGURE 4.3: OBLIQUE AERIAL PHOTOGRAPH OF GLANBANE HILLFORT, 1970S (COURTESY: DAPHNE POCHIN MOULD).

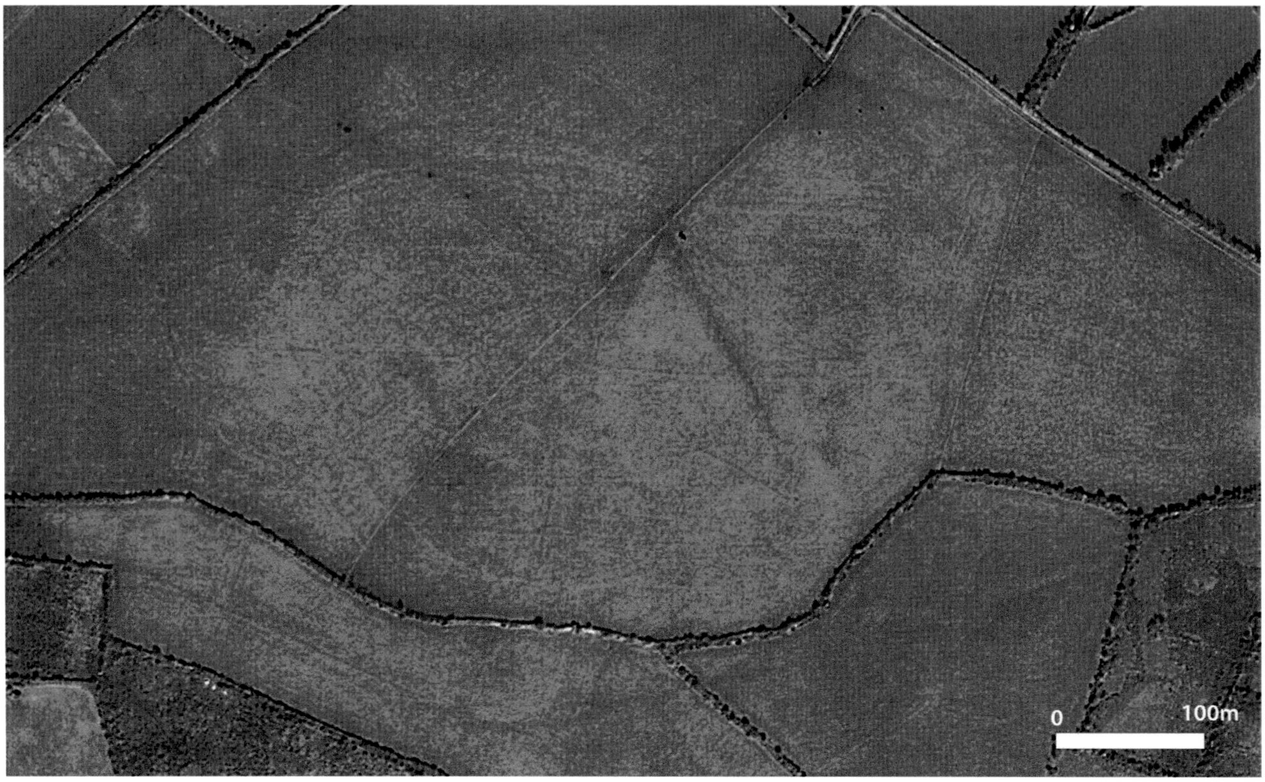

FIGURE 4.4: SATELLITE PHOTOGRAPH (2006) OF GLANBANE HILLFORT (SOURCE: GOOGLE EARTH).

inside the bank of the inner enclosure was confirmed by excavation to be a later field drain (see below).

The gradiometry reveals numerous small gaps in the inner and outer enclosing elements, none of which have been confirmed as original entrances. There is a possible original entrance on the north-east side of the hillfort, where the two enclosing elements are only 7m apart, and where the bank-and-ditch terminals may turn slightly outwards. This opening is approximately 30m wide, but originally could have been narrower. There is considerable magnetic disturbance in that area, probably caused by iron objects of unknown age.

In addition to the two main enclosures, there are indications of a small enclosure in the summit area of the hillfort. This is visible as a faint discontinuous band of enhanced magnetic readings, forming a curvilinear feature that measures 112m (east–west) by 124m (north–south). The geophysical response is not conclusive, as the anomaly does not comprise a complete enclosure. While it could be a later field pattern, this feature occurs close to, and may at least partly enclose, a number of other structures.

The magnetic survey suggests that there may have been a large number of built structures in the central area of the hillfort (Figure 4.6). Twelve anomalies, measuring 9–16m in diameter, may represent roundhouse structures. These are distributed across the inner enclosure, with one example in the outer enclosure on the eastern side. Of the other five possible structures, three are 20–27m in diameter, with two examples 38m and 46m in diameter respectively. Four of the largest structures are located within the possible small enclosure in the summit area. The two largest structures are located at the highest point of the interior. The first measures 46m in diameter, and is visible as a wide, curvilinear magnetic response, surrounded by faint negative readings. This may represent a cut feature such as a ditch. A number of possible pits (postholes?) on the western side may be incorporated into the structure. A concentration of dipolar responses at the centre of the anomaly may be indicative of ferrous material of unknown date.

The southeastern side of the 46m structure appears to be truncated by another large circular feature, approximately 38m in diameter. This may have been built of wood, as there are indications of large postholes in the results. As with the 46m structure, there are a series of dipolar anomalies at the centre. Two sub-parallel lines of possible pits radiating from the interior of the 38m structure may lead to an entrance on the western side. The size and location of the 38m and 46m structures suggests they may have been the central focus of the hillfort occupation. There are no indications of internal postholes in the gradiometry survey, which would be expected if either structure were roofed.

Finally, geophysical survey identified the line of several field banks, now levelled, recorded by Ordnance Survey mapping in the modern era. The outer enclosure of the

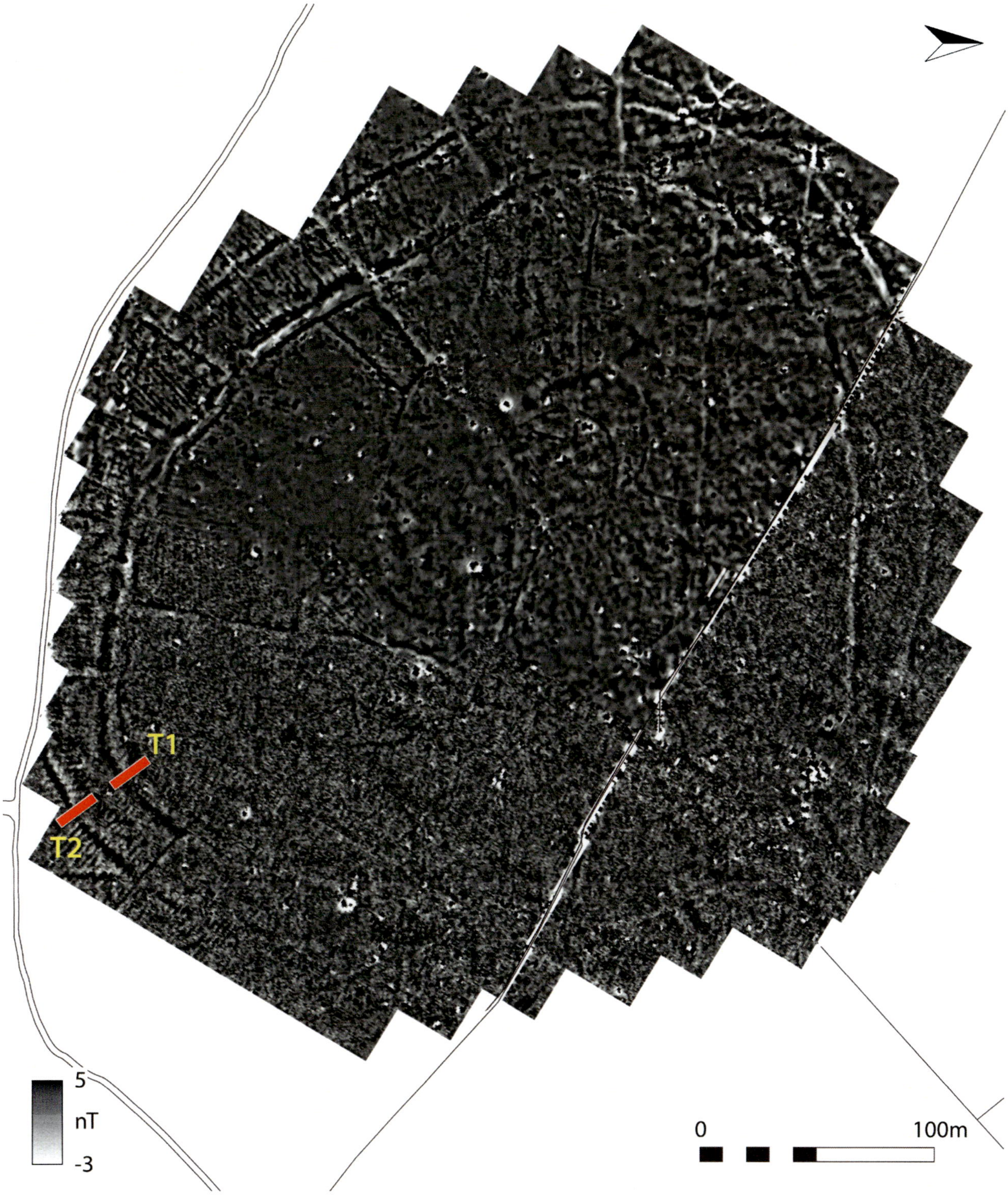

Figure 4.5: Geophysical survey (magnetic gradiometry) of Glanbane hillfort.

hillfort seems to have been divided by as many as ten radial field banks. There are indications of ridge-and-furrow cultivation, possibly spade-dug lazy-beds, within and outside these small radial fields on the eastern and southern side of the hillfort.

Archaeological excavation

Excavation work was conducted at Glanbane over a two-week period in July 2012 (O'Brien 2012a). The objective was to obtain information on the physical form of the enclosing elements and the methods and materials em-

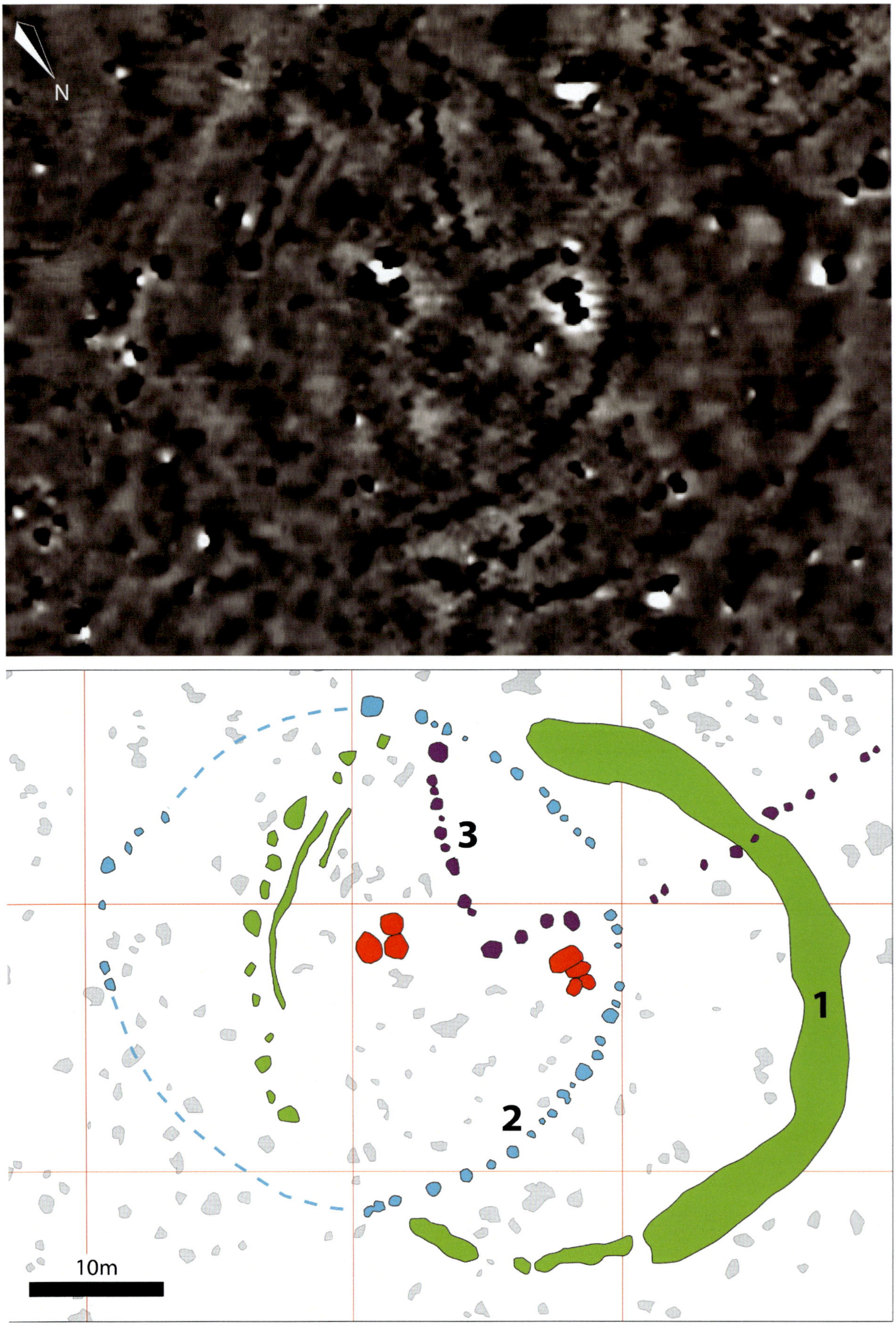

Figure 4.6: Magnetic survey results from summit area, Glanbane. 1: 46m structure with central dipole anomaly. 2: 38m pit structure with central dipole anomaly. 3: Rows of possible pit features.

ployed in their construction. It was also hoped to obtain dating evidence for construction, occupation and abandonment of the hillfort, as well as material culture and environmental evidence relating to the history of the site.

Two trenches were excavated: Trench 1 was located on the southern side of the inner enclosing element; Trench 2 directly opposite across the defences of the outer enclosure (Figure 4.7). Prior to excavation the hillfort ditches were visible at both trench locations as low-relief features, with no trace of associated bank(s). Both trenches were de-turfed and the topsoil removed by machine. This was justified on the basis that the entire field was levelled by bulldozers in the late 1960s (landowner information). Subsequent excavation was carried out by hand using small digging equipment. On completion of work the trenches were back-filled by machine and the ground surface restored.

The natural soil is a brown podzol, which is well-drained, moderately acidic and free of large stones. The profile comprised a thin sod (C.01) over a 0.14–0.3m thick humic A-horizon (C.02a and C.04). This organic soil, in turn, overlay a bright orange, stony silt (C.21), with moderate to strong iron oxide enrichment in the upper part, reducing with depth to a yellow stony silt (C.22). This combined B-horizon (C.21/C.22) was 0.2–0.6m in thickness, and directly overlay weathered bedrock (C.23).

Excavation results: Trench 1

This 18m (north-west/south-east) by 4m cutting was excavated to a depth of 0.3–0.45m (excluding ditch) across the defences of the inner enclosure on its southern side (Figure 4.5). The removal of organic soil revealed two features of archaeological interest on the B-horizon surface. The first was a 4m wide band of dark organic sediment across the southern side of the trench. Excavation identified this as the upper fill of a rock-cut ditch (Figure 4.8). The second feature was a 0.5–0.7m wide band of dark silt that extended in a east–west direction across the trench, 4.85m north of the ditch. This was excavated to expose a shallow field drain of probable modern date.

Ditch

Excavation revealed a curving length of ditch (C.18) extending east–west across Trench 1 (Figure 4.9). The upper part of this ditch cut through a thin layer of B-horizon subsoil, with the lower two-thirds quarried into the Devonian (Old Red Sandstone) bedrock. The latter is highly laminated, with both sides of the rock-cut ditch broken along a closely spaced cleavage plane.

The upper part of the ditch measured 2.4–3.1m in width, with the top of the bedrock cut 1.8–2m wide. The base of the ditch is 0.6–0.7m wide and irregularly flat. The rock-cut portion varies 0.9–1.05m in depth along the inner (northern) side, and 0.4–0.9m on the exterior (southern)

Figure 4.7: General view of two excavation trenches at Glanbane, with partial reconstruction of stone bank revetments (outer enclosure Trench 2 centre; inner enclosure Trench 1 top left).

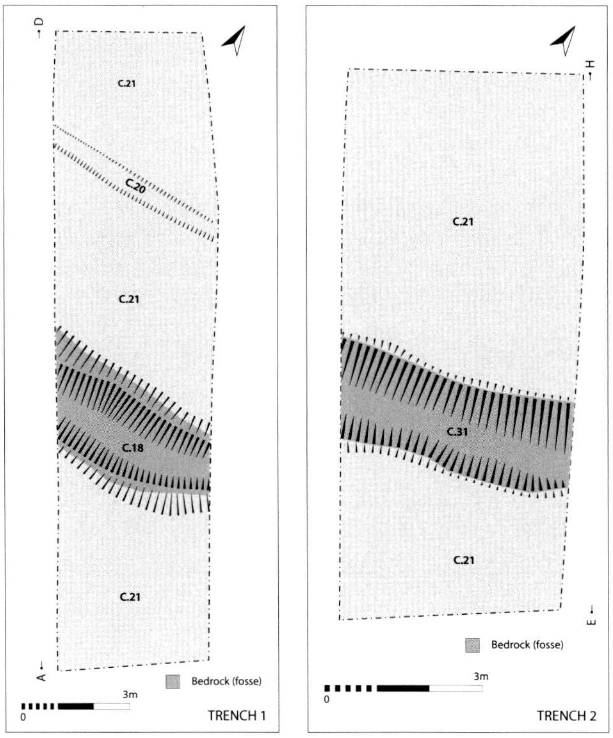

FIGURE 4.8: POST-EXCAVATION FEATURES IN TRENCHES 1 AND 2, GLANBANE.

side. Taken from the top of the subsoil cut, the overall depth of the ditch is 1.15–1.35m on the inside and 0.9–1.05m on the exterior.

The following fill sequence was recorded (Figure 4.10):

Primary sediments
The filling process commenced shortly after the ditch was dug. There is evidence for weathering of the friable rock-cut sides, with stony sediments forming at the base (C.10) and along the inner side (C.09) of the ditch. This was followed by silting into the waterlogged base of the ditch, resulting in yellowish/light brown deposits (contexts 07 and 08 on the western side; contexts 15, 16 and 17 on the eastern side). There are no artifact finds from these lower silts, nor did they contain charcoal apart from some flecking in C.15.

The early silting of the ditch was accompanied by an influx of large stones (C.06) that collapsed from a wall retaining the adjacent bank (see below). This was a gradual process that began with stones accumulating in a matrix of loose brown silt (C.14).

Secondary silting
The collapse of the bank revetment continued over a long period, with some of its stones present in the upper silt of the ditch (Figure 4.11). One of these silt deposits (C.05) was heavily iron-enriched, with a low clast content. There is some organic content with charcoal flecks in the upper silts of the ditch (C.12 and C.13).

FIGURE 4.9: DITCH OF INNER ENCLOSURE AFTER EXCAVATION, TRENCH 1, GLANBANE.

Organic soil
The silt deposits in this ditch were overlain by a 0.65–0.75m thickness of organic soil (A-horizon; Figures 4.12 and 4.13). The lower part was a loamy organic silt (C.04), overlain by a spread of dark silt with orange mottles (C.03a) that extended south-east to become a thin orange silt with dark brown mottles (C.03b). Both of these layers were beneath the upper A-horizon (C.02). Context 03 represents a mixture of organic soil and re-deposited subsoil, resulting from the levelling of the adjacent bank in the 1960s. The discovery of a sherd of modern china pottery at a depth of 0.6m confirms the entire A-horizon is disturbed by cultivation and field clearance.

Bank and revetment
Excavation uncovered 95 large stones at various depths within the lower ditch fill. These were mostly blocky stones of Old Red Sandstone geology, 0.24–0.37m in length and 0.11–0.23m in width. Their uniform size, shape and water-rolled appearance suggests these stones had been carefully selected for use, probably from fields in the general vicinity of the hillfort. They were not quarried in the adjacent ditch, where the extracted rock would have been much smaller and more angular.

These stones were part of a revetment to retain a bank

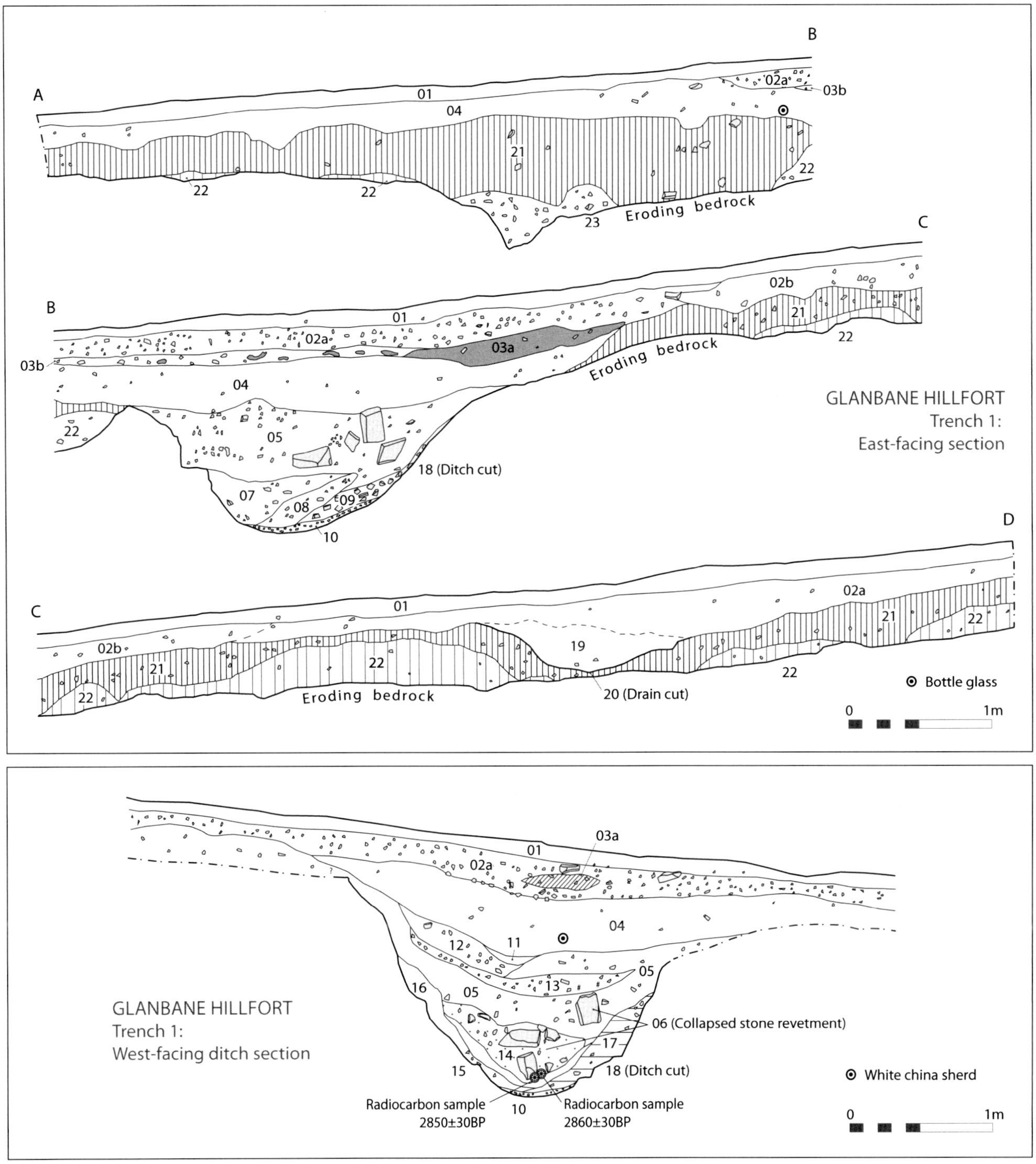

FIGURE 4.10: STRATIGRAPHIC SECTIONS (TRENCH 1), INNER ENCLOSURE, GLANBANE.

of soil and broken stone that had been built on the inner (northern) side of the ditch (Figure 4.14). Based on the quantity in the ditch, these stones may have been laid horizontally in four or five courses to a height of around 0.6m. Their position in the ditch fill suggests that the bank facing collapsed gradually over a period of time. Little trace of the accompanying bank was discovered in the excavation. The stratigraphic sections indicate a slightly raised B-horizon (contexts 21 and 22) in the area between the inner edge of the ditch and the C.20 drain feature (Figures 4.10 and 4.15). There is also evidence for some admixture of subsoil with the lower A-horizon in that area (C.02b), possibly connected to clearance of the bank.

Shallow trench

Cleaning of the B-horizon surface exposed a narrow linear feature extending east–west across the northern side of Trench 1. It corresponds to a line of enhanced magnetism inside the levelled bank that extends for approximately 228m on the southern side of the inner enclos-

FIGURE 4.11: STONES OF COLLAPSED BANK REVETMENT IN DITCH FILL, TRENCH 1, GLANBANE.

ure (Figure 4.5). Excavation revealed a shallow trench (C.20) containing a fill of dark brown humic silt (C.19), with few stones, no artifacts or charcoal (Figure 4.8). The trench measured 0.5–0.7m in upper width and 0.4–0.6m wide at the base, averaging 0.05–0.12m in depth along the exposed length. The base was irregularly flat, with no evidence for stake settings or other structural features.

Based on the geophysical results, this feature was initially interpreted as a possible palisade trench on the inside of the hillfort bank. The excavation confirmed it is more likely to be a field drain, dug at the base of the extant bank probably in the early modern era.

List of excavation contexts, Trench 1, Glanbane

Context 01: Sod layer; stone-free humic silt.

C.02a: Mid brown humic silt; loamy texture with pebbles. Upper A-horizon.

C.02b: Yellow/light brown humic silt, very mottled with frequent pebbles.

C.03a: Dark brown/black silt with orange mottles; west side of infilled ditch.

C.03b: Bright orange silt with dark brown/black mottles, east side of infilled ditch.

C.04: Mid brown humic silt across upper part of ditch area. Lower A-horizon.

C.05: Bright orange silt, iron-enriched with few stones; silting of upper ditch.

C.06: Large stones from collapsed bank revetment, mostly within C.05.

C.07: Yellow/orange silt in lower ditch, mostly free of stones, charcoal flecks.

C.08: Light brown/white silt in ditch, similar to C.07; few stones, low iron content.

C.09: Loose deposit of small angular stones in dark brown silt in lower ditch.

C.10: Loose sediment with small angular stones in fine grey silt at base of ditch.

C.11: Lense of white/light brown fine silt in upper ditch fill.

C.12: Yellow/light brown silt with many pebbles, inner side of ditch, northern end.

Figure 4.12: East-facing section across rock-cut ditch of inner hillfort enclosure, Trench 1 (scale: 20cm divisions). Note some large stones from the collapsed bank revetment (C.06).

Figure 4.13 West-facing section across rock-cut ditch of inner hillfort enclosure, Trench 1. Note large stones from the collapsed bank revetment (C.06).

Figure 4.14: Ditch of inner enclosure, Trench 1, with revetment of former bank reconstructed using original stones found in ditch (scale: 20cm divisions).

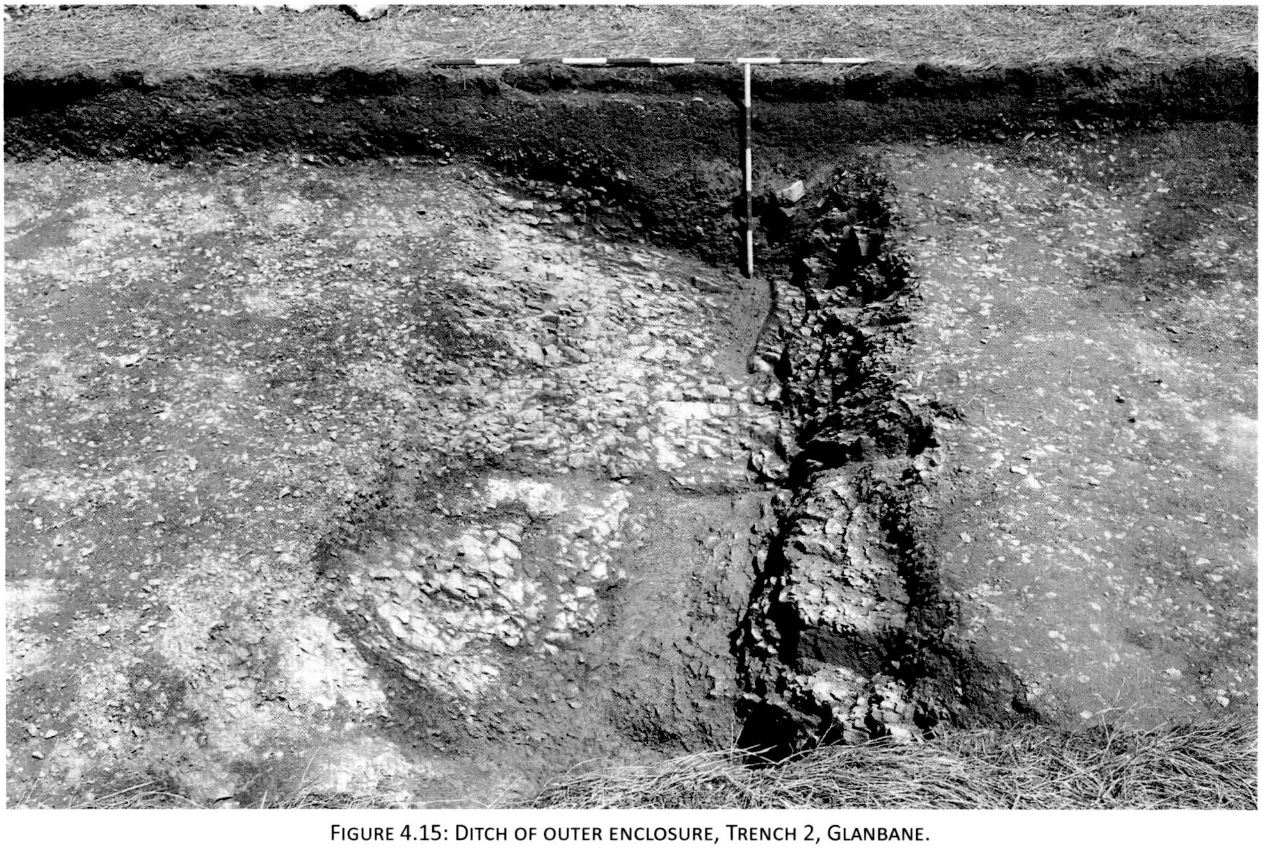

Figure 4.15: Ditch of outer enclosure, Trench 2, Glanbane.

C.13: Dark brown organic silt in upper ditch, many pebbles and some charcoal flecks.

C.14: Loose grey/brown organic silt around lower stones of C.06 in lower ditch.

C.15: Yellow/white clayey silt with bright orange mottles in lower ditch; no clasts.

C.16: Yellow/orange silt along lower inner side of ditch; no clasts. Similar to C.07.

C.17: Green/light brown silt with orange mottles, no stones, lower ditch.

C.18: Cut of ditch, inner enclosure.

C.19: Dark brown soft organic silt; few stones. Fill of possible field drain C.20.

C.20: Shallow trench with irregularly flat base. Probable field drain.

C.21: Bright orange silt with frequent small stones; iron-enriched. Upper B-horizon.

C.22: Yellow/orange silt, fewer stones and iron oxides than C.21. Lower B-horizon.

C.23: Loose deposit of small angular stones in green/grey silt; weathered bedrock.

Excavation results: Trench 2

This 10m (north-west/south-east) by 4m cutting was excavated to a depth of 0.4–0.7m (excluding ditch) across the defences of the outer enclosure on its southern side (Figure 4.5). Following removal of organic soil, the cleaning of the orange B-horizon (C.21) revealed only one feature of archaeological interest, namely a 3m wide band of dark sediment representing the upper fill of a ditch.

Ditch

Excavation uncovered a curving length of ditch (C.31) extending in east–west across the southern side of Trench 2 (Figure 4.8). The ditch is cut into bedrock, and through a thin layer of B-horizon subsoil along the inner northern side. The bedrock is highly laminated, consisting of a closely spaced cleavage dipping to the north, as well as widely spaced joint and bedding planes (Figure 4.15). The ditch is 1.8–2.05m wide at the top, and 0.4–0.6m wide at the irregularly flat base. The rock-cut portion has a central depth of 0.61–0.7m, with the maximum depth of 0.8m from the top of the subsoil cut.

Excavation recorded the following fill sequence (Figure 4.16):

Primary sediments

The process of infilling seems to have commenced soon after the ditch was dug. There is evidence for weathering of the rock-cut sides, with stone-rich sediments forming at the base (C.30) and along the inner (C.27 and C.28) and outer (C.29) sides (Figure 4.17). This was followed by silting into the waterlogged base, represented by bright orange silt (C.24a) containing stones from the weathered ditch sides. There are no artifacts from these lower silts, but there were occasional flecks of charcoal.

Revetment stones and secondary silting

The early silting was followed by an influx of large stones (C.25) that collapsed in from a low wall retaining a bank that had stood on the inner side of the ditch. This was a gradual process with the majority of stones accumulating in the upper fill of the ditch (C.24). This bright orange deposit comprised water-lain silt that was heavily iron-enriched. The lower part also contained small clasts derived from weathering of the bedrock sides of the ditch (C.24a).

Organic soil

The infilled ditch was overlain by a 0.45–0.55m thickness of A-horizon topsoil (C.02), with a uniform sod layer (C.01) over this. The lower part of this organic soil (C.02a) over the ditch had a significant amount of charcoal flecking.

Bank and revetment

As stated, excavation uncovered a number of large stones (C.25) within the central to lower fill (C.24/24a) of the ditch. These were mostly blocky stones of Old Red Sandstone geology, 0.18–0.25m in length, with some examples up to 0.25–0.37m. As with the stones in Trench 1, these are probably field stones collected in the general vicinity of the hillfort. Their size, shape and rolled appearance indicates they were not quarried from the ditch.

These stones were part of a revetment that was built at the time of the hillfort construction, to retain a bank of soil and quarried stone that had stood directly inside the ditch (Figure 4.7). The size, shape and number of stones found suggests these were laid horizontally, in perhaps three or four courses to a height of 0.35–0.4m. Their position in the ditch confirms this stone facing collapsed gradually over a period of time. No trace of the original bank was discovered in the excavation.

List of excavation contexts, Trench 2, Glanbane

Context 01: Sod layer; stone-free humic soil.

C.02a: Mid brown humic silt with small stones, charcoal flecks at base. A-horizon.

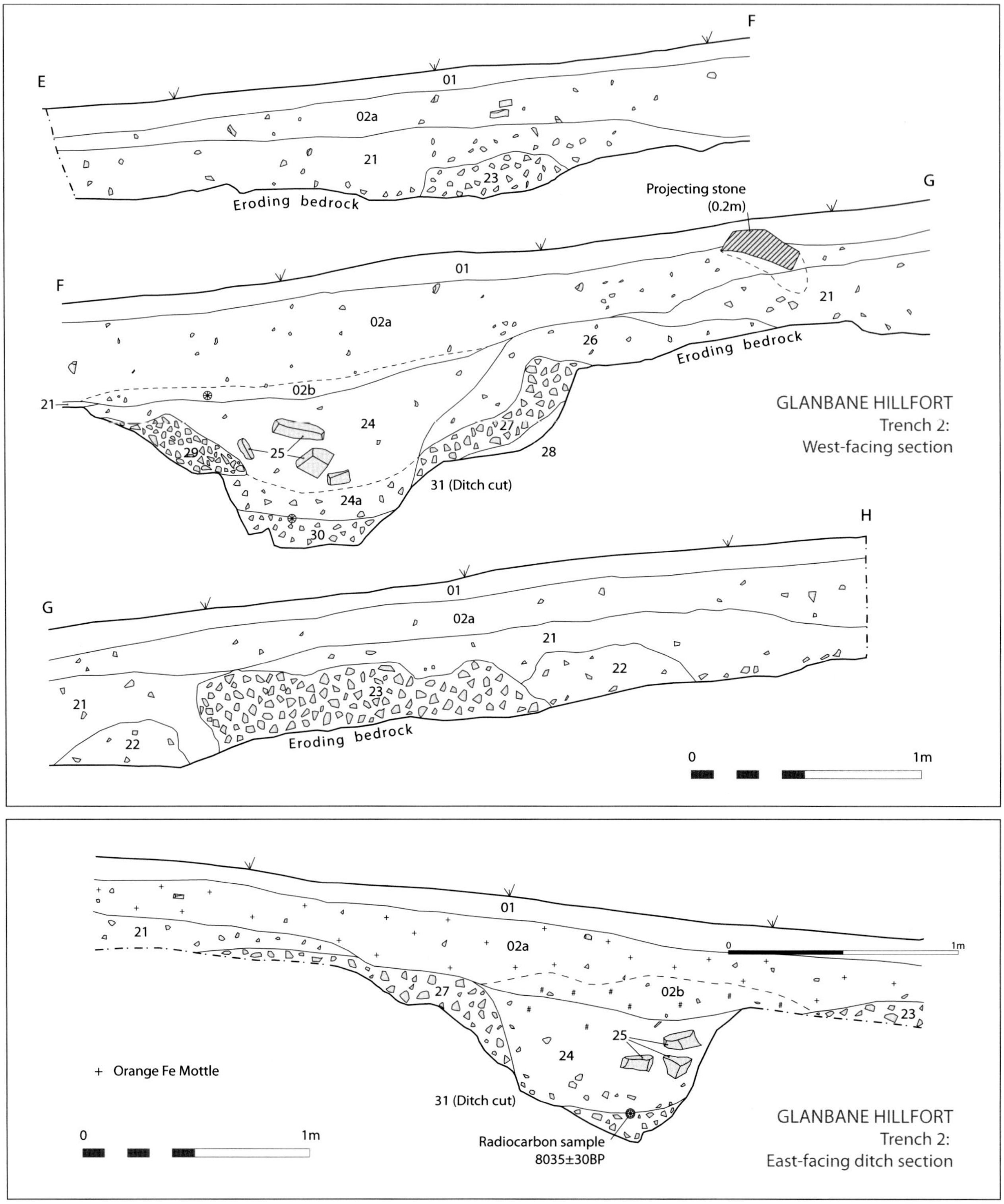

Figure 4.16: Stratigraphic sections, Trench 2, outer enclosure, Glanbane.

C.21: Bright orange silt with frequent small stones; iron-enriched. Upper B-horizon.

C.22: Yellow/orange silt, fewer stones and iron oxides than C.21. Lower B-horizon.

C.23: Loose deposit of small angular stones in green/grey silt; weathered bedrock.

C.24: Bright orange silt in central ditch; soft texture, iron-enriched with few stones.

C.24a: Same as C.24 except for small angular clasts from eroded sides of ditch.

C.25: Stones from collapsed bank revetment.

Figure 4.17: West-facing section of ditch of outer enclosure, Trench 2, Glanbane.

C.26: Loose red/brown silt with stones on western side of upper ditch.

C.27: Loose angular stones along western upper side of ditch.

C.28: Thin deposit of yellow/orange silt. Primary ditch sediment.

C.29: Loose angular stones in grey/light brown silt along upper eastern side of ditch.

C.30: Deposit of small angular stones with loose white/ grey silt at base of ditch.

C.31: Cut of ditch, outer enclosure.

Finds and dating

No early artifacts were found in this excavation. Four objects of modern date were recovered in the topsoil of Trench 1. These include a fragment of heavily corroded iron, probably part of an agricultural tool, from the upper A-horizon (C.02). Three sherds of white china tableware were found in the lower A-horizon (C.04) at different locations. There are no artifact finds from Trench 2.

In the absence of significant finds, the dating of this hillfort relies on the radiocarbon method. Three charcoal samples were submitted for AMS radiocarbon dating to the Centre for Isotope Research, University of Groningen. The sample details and results are as follows (calibration based on OxCal v.4.2.4; 95.4% confidence):

Trench 1 (inner enclosure ditch)
Sample GB2012-02: Charcoal from under large stone of collapsed bank revetment (C.06), sampled approximately 0.10m above base of ditch at northern side of trench. Wood species: hazel.
GrA-54508; 2850±30 BP. Calibrated 1111–927 BC (95.4% confidence; OxCal 4.2.4) (∂^{13}C -26.84).

Sample GB2012-03: Charcoal from around same stone of collapsed bank revetment (C.06). Wood species: hazel.
GrA-54509; 2860±30 BP. Calibrated 1118–929 BC (95.4% confidence; OxCal 4.2.4) (∂^{13}C -27.24).

Trench 2 (outer enclosure ditch)
Sample GB2012-01: Charcoal from basal ditch sediment (C.30).
GrA-54507; 8035±40 BP. Calibrated 7079–6813 BC (95.4% confidence; OxCal 4.2.4) (∂^{13}C -26.65).

The radiocarbon results from Trench 1 are significant, as the presence of this charcoal at the base of the ditch suggests a fire event close in date to the early occupation of the hillfort. Assuming that residuality from earlier activity can be ruled out, this indicates a date range of 1118–927 BC during or before which the ditch of the inner enclosure was dug. The occurrence of this charcoal underneath and around stones of the collapsed revetment points to some interval between bank construction and collapse. Whether the latter is directly connected to fire and a possible destruction event remains to be proven.

The charcoal from Trench 3 has a calendar date range 7079–6813 BC, placing this material in the early Holocene, the period of the earliest human colonization of Ireland. Mesolithic sites are recorded at several locations in south-west Ireland, the best known being Ferriter's Cove in the Dingle Peninsula, Co. Kerry (Woodman, Anderson and Finlay 1999). In the absence of relevant cultural material, such as stone tools, the Glanbane charcoal cannot be taken as evidence of Mesolithic human settlement at that location. It is not unusual to have early Holocene radiocarbon dates for charcoal found in later prehistoric sites (*op. cit.*: 140–1; see also O'Brien 2004: 167–8). Where cultural material is absent this is more likely to be connnected to natural fire events. The Glanbane charcoal probably belongs to this category. Confirmation of this comes from the immediate outer side of the ditch in Trench 2, where excavation recorded small amounts of charcoal within the upper B-horizon. Some of this charcoal must have been displaced during hillfort construction, and washed into the open ditch.

Discussion

Though limited in extent, the Glanbane excavation has yielded important information on the defences of this Bronze Age hillfort. The form of both enclosing elements, and the methods used in their construction, were very similar. This involved the digging of a steep-sided ditch through thin subsoil into bedrock. The ditch of the inner enclosure was the larger of the two, averaging 1–1.3m in depth, which suggests that the adjacent bank did not exceed 1.5m in height. The ditch of the outer enclosure was around 0.8–1m in depth, with the adjacent bank probably not much higher than 1m.

The soil and rock extracted from these ditches was piled directly on the inside surface to form a bank. The original size and shape of this bank is uncertain, but may have been 3.5–4m wide. The loose composition of these banks required the building of a low stone wall to prevent this material slipping into the ditch. There is no evidence for a wooden palisade or stake fence accompanying either bank. In their absence the overall defensive height of the inner enclosure (base of ditch to top of bank) was 2.5–3m, while that of the outer enclosure was closer to 2m.

Though the defences are somewhat slight, the scale of construction is impressive over the entire extent of the hillfort. The perimeter of the inner enclosure is 790m, while that of the outer enclosure in 932m, creating some 1.7km of built defences. While the ditch size may have varied over this distance, depending on geology and other factors, the effort involved in construction may be gauged from an assessment of the amount of material used. The rock quarried from the ditch of the inner enclosure is estimated at 1626.87 tonnes. This is based on a total ditch volume of 1162.88m^3 (perimeter length of 790m by average ditch depth of 1.15m and width of 1.28m) and an estimated rock density of 1.399 tonnes per m^3. The total number of field stones used in the 0.5–0.6m high revetment of the inner hillfort bank is estimated at 15,010 (based on the recovery of 95 stones over a 5m length in Trench 1).

Comparable estimates for the outer hillfort defences indicate some 1017.02 tonnes of quarried rock. This is based on a total ditch volume of 726.96m^3 (perimeter length of 932m by average ditch depth of 0.65m and width of 1.2m) and an estimated rock density of 1.399 tonnes per m^3. The total number of field stones used in the revetment of the outer hillfort bank is estimated at 17,708 (based on Trench 1 stone data).

Taken together, the total estimate of rock extraction for both enclosure ditches at Glanbane is 2643.9 tonnes, with an estimated 32,718 stones required to build the associated bank revetments. These are approximate figures, but they illustrate the effort required to build this hillfort. This must have been a laborious process requiring pick-like tools of wood and/or bone, but not fire-setting. The fact that the former were not found may be explained by poor organic preservation in these ditches. The ditch quarrying was helped by the laminated structure of the bedrock and its friable weathered surface.

The excavation did not identify evidence for the occupation of this hillfort. No artifacts, food residues or structural remains were recovered in the excavation. This is due to the limited area of investigation, as geophysical survey indicates several possible built structures in inner hillfort enclosure (Figure 4.5). These may include several small roundhouses used for domestic residence, as well as at least two larger structures of possible ceremonial/ritual significance.

Aerial photographs, geophysical survey or surface features indicate the presence of built structures at an estimated 31 prehistoric hillforts in Ireland. Nine of these, including Glanbane, have more than ten probable structures within their interiors. Only a small number have been excavated, making it difficult to establish their relationship to the hillfort in question. Many are comparable in size to the smaller structures (roundhouses?) at Glanbane.

The two large structures identified by geophysical survey in the central area of Glanbane are some the largest examples found in an Irish hillfort. The only comparable site is the partially excavated structure at the centre of Haughey's Fort in Co. Armagh. The occupation of this triple enclosure hillfort is dated c.1150–1050 BC (Mallory and Baban 2014). A 25–30m structure, comprising an arc of three lines of stakes set outside larger postholes, is broadly contemporary with the hillfort. It is associated with a number of large pits that contained substantial amounts of carbonized grain, as well as coarse ware pottery, fragments of quern stones, and gold and bronze objects of Late Bronze Age date. The excavator asserted that the structure had a ritual function (*ibid.*). The Glanbane structures would seem to be significantly larger than the Haughey's Fort example, or the large roundhouse excavated at the centre of the Late Bronze Age hillfort at Rathgall, Co. Wicklow (Raftery 1994: plate 16). A comparison could also be made with large timber structures found in the Iron Age 'royal sites' of Dún Aillinne and Navan Fort (*ibid*: plate 21). Though the significance of the Glanbane structures remains to be established by excavation, their presence lends further weight to suggestions that this was an important political and ceremonial centre in south-west Ireland.

The abandonment of Glanbane hillfort is evident in the gradual silting of the ditch and the collapse of the bank revetment. Both seem to have occcured over a long period, with no evidence for maintenance of either feature. The removal of the banks occurred long after both ditches were silted to almost modern ground level. Portions of these banks may have been re-built as field boundaries in the early modern era, before they were finally removed by bulldozers during field clearance in the late 1960s.

Cultural Landscape

While no detailed study has been undertaken, some general observations may be made on the cultural landscape context of Glanbane hillfort. Today, Glanbane hillfort overlooks extensive lowlands to the north, east and south, with farmscapes of small and large fields used mostly for animal pasture. While there are no pollen records from the locality, it is likely there have been considerable changes to this lowland environment over the past 3000 years, brought about by deforestation, land drainage and soil improvement connected to agriculture. This would have led to the destruction of many prehistoric settlements and ritual monuments connected to the hillfort.

The *Record of Monuments and Places* for Kerry lists a number of archaeological monuments close to the hillfort. These include several ringforts and 'enclosures', most of which are likely to be medieval in date. Of greater interest is the large number of prehistoric burnt mounds (*fulachtaí fia*) in the Farranfore area. These include a burnt mound (KE039-067) in marshy ground at the bottom of Glanbane hill, 0.5km south-east of the hillfort. There is also a concentration of these water-boiling sites in Garraundarragh townland, 0.9km south-east of the hillfort (RMP KE039-211; KE039-190–4), with other examples in the wider area. Some of the Garraundarragh examples were excavated in 2004–5, as part of the N22 road development (Kiely 2007; O'Callaghan 2007). Charcoal from one of those *fulachtaí fia* is radiocarbon dated 1000–790 BC, while a second site is dated 1530–1400 BC. These results confirm that *fulachtaí fia* were used in large numbers in this locality during the period of hillfort occupation at Glanbane.

It is likely that Glanbane hillfort was part of a settlement landscape that included small farms with roundhouses, ritual monuments such as barrows and standing stone monuments, as well as *fulachtaí fia*. There have been several discoveries of Bronze Age sites on recent road schemes in the Tralee area. These include occupation sites at Clogher II, Ballyvelly I, Buntalloon II, and Mount Hawk I (Kiely and Dunne 2005: table 1). While full details on these sites are not available, they attest to widespread settlement of Middle and Late Bronze Age date in the area of the Lee valley (reviewed by Connolly 2008).

Glanbane is one of only two hillforts listed in the Record of Monuments and Places for Co. Kerry, the other being an unconfirmed example at Rahanane (KE059-091) near Kilcummin. The much-damaged site at Knockanacuig/Lohercannon, on the western outskirts of Tralee (KE029-112) may also be a Class 2 hillfort, having two or possibly three enclosures over a 7.2ha area. Recent rescue excavation obtained Iron Age radiocarbon dates, but it is not certain how these relate to the construction or primary occupation of the hillfort (Dunne and Bartlett 2009). Also to be considered are the inland promontory hillforts of Caherconree (KE046-003) and Faha (KE034-048) on the Dingle Peninsula of Co. Kerry (Figure 4.2). These are the highest known hillforts in Ireland, occurring at elevations of 659m OD and 777m OD respectively. Neither site has been excavated and so their relationship to Glanbane cannot be established.

The Record of Monuments and Places lists five hill-top enclosures in Kerry, found in an area extending south-east from Tralee towards Ballycarty, Farranfore and Scartaglin (Figure 4.2). They include the sites at Ballingowan (KE029-265), Ash-hill (KE038-115), Ballycarty (KE038-136), and Carker (KE049-121). There is a record of a possible example at Garraundarragh/Glanbane (KE039-181) on the eastern slope of Glanbane hill, some 50m below the outer enclosure of the hillfort (Connolly 2008). This could not be confirmed by the current project, as there are no relevant surface features or geophysical responses at the location.

Turning to material culture, there is no obvious concentration of Bronze Age weaponry in the vicinity of Glanbane hillfort, though such finds do occur in the wider Kerry region. A total of eight swords of Late Bronze Age date are recorded from Kerry (Eogan 1965). These include extant finds from Aghadoe, Aughrim, Ballinclemesig, Valencia, and 'Co. Kerry', with records of three other examples, from Aughrim, Cool, and Killarney. All but one of these are of Eogan's Class 4 type, the earliest use of which occurred *c.* 1300–1000 BC. Other weapon finds from Kerry include five side-looped socketed spearheads of Middle Bronze Age type, and five rivet-hole variants of the Late Bronze Age (information: James Lineen). Also relevant is the discovery of eight socketed bronze axeheads in the county, most coming from North Kerry or the Dingle Peninsula (Eogan 2000).

One of these axeheads was found in 1944, along with a peg-hole spearhead, two plain penannular bracelets and a knobbed penannular bracelet (all bronze), at Kilmurry, 14km north east of Glanbane (Eogan 1983: no. 90). Four other hoards of Late Bronze Age metalwork are recorded from Kerry. These include the hoards of bronze horns found at Clocherclemin and near Killarney, and the associated find of a bronze socketed knife and a gold ring from Oghermong near Cahersiveen (Eogan 1983: nos 87–91). The final example is the discovery in 1940 of three penannular gold bracelets and a gold dress fastener in a wooden box from a bog at Kilmoyly North, near Ballyheigue, north Kerry. Cahill (2005) lists a total of thirteen gold objects from this period in Kerry. They include nine penannular bracelets, two dress fasteners, an ear-spool and a gold bar (*ibid.*: table 1). Most of these are likely to be Dowris phase, and so possibly later than the hillfort occupation. The bracelets from Carhan Upper near Cahersiveen and Toureen near Tralee may date as early as the Bishopsland phase of the Middle Bronze Age (*ibid.*: 15). While there is no direct association, these gold objects testify to the wealth of certain individuals and communities in the Kerry region around the time Glanbane hillfort was occupied.

4.2 Ballylin, Co. Limerick

This hillfort is on the summit of a prominent hill on the eastern edge of the Mullaghareirk mountain range in west Limerick (Figure 4.18). The 'Black Hill', as it is known locally, falls steeply to the east, with a panoramic view from the summit (243m OD) over the plains of central Limerick. The hill slopes more gently to the north, with the lower Shannon estuary visible in the distance. There is mountainous terrain to the west and south, facing Kerry and Cork respectively. The site is located in Ballylin townland, with a portion extending into the adjoining townlands of Kerrikyle and Glenville, 2km north-west of the village of Ardagh (ITM 525750/639520).

Despite its immense size (20.5ha), this hillfort only came to attention in 1981 when the Ordnance Survey of Ireland were conducting aerial reconnaissance in west Limerick (Figure 4.19). Their archaeologists surveyed the

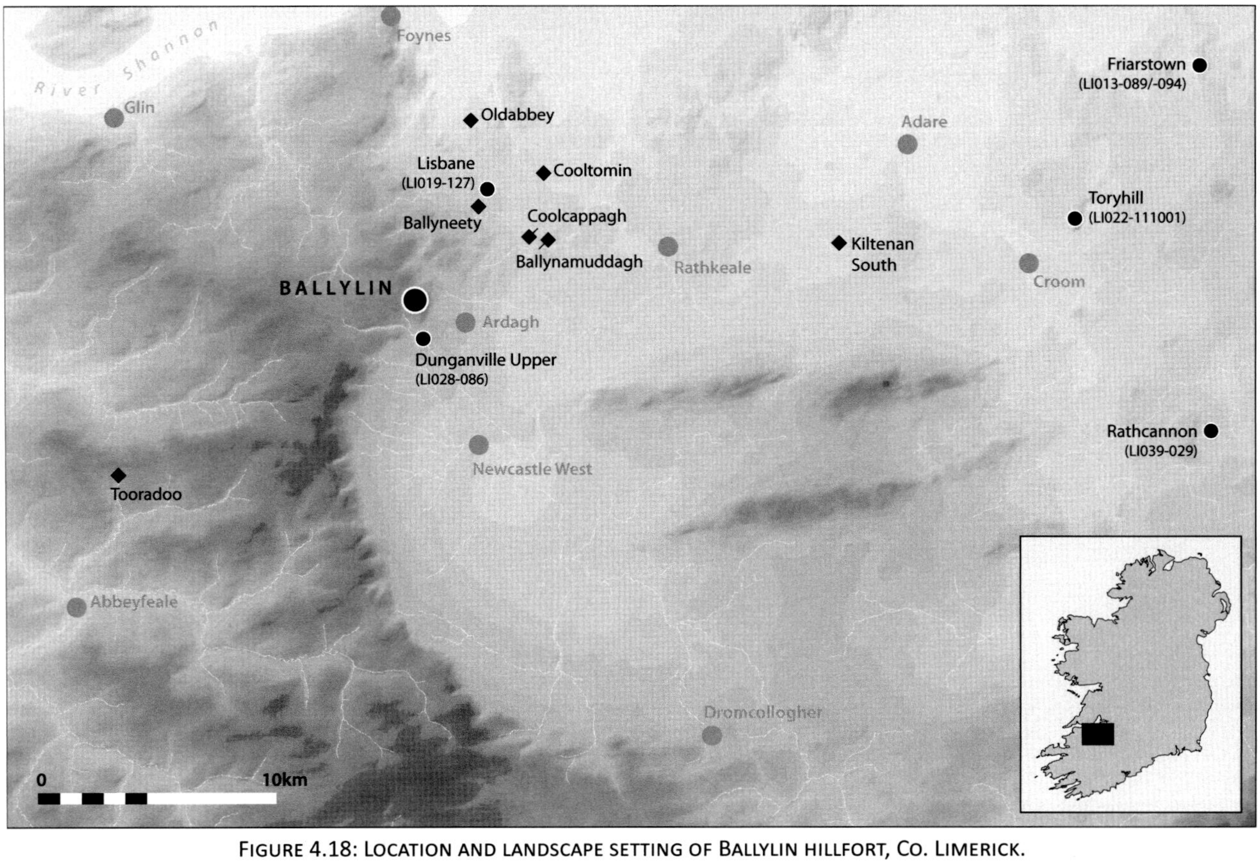

FIGURE 4.18: LOCATION AND LANDSCAPE SETTING OF BALLYLIN HILLFORT, CO. LIMERICK.

FIGURE 4.19: SATELLITE PHOTOGRAPH (2010) OF BALLYLIN HILLFORT (SOURCE: GOOGLE EARTH).

site, and the results were published that same year in the *Journal of the Royal Society of Antiquaries of Ireland*. This included a description of the surface features of the hillfort, supported by a contour plan, aerial photograph, and surface profiles across the 'defences' of both enclosures (Cody 1981: figs 13–15). The latter are described as consisting of a shallow ditch inside a low bank, with indications of an inner bank in places. Cody also identified a possible original entrance on the eastern side of the inner enclosure (*ibid*.: figure 14c).

The 1981 survey did not record any early features inside the hillfort. This is partly because the interior is overgrown by bog vegetation, particularly on the northern side of the outer enclosure. Three circular features, each about 10m in diameter, were recorded near what is probably a later field bank in the north-west part of the outer enclosure (*ibid*.: 78). They are not visible today due to vegetation cover. No surface features are visible inside the inner enclosure, where an Ordnance Survey trigonometric pillar marks the summit of an otherwise flat area covered by thin blanket peat.

Arising from these findings, Ballylin hillfort was registered in the *Record of Monuments and Places* for Co. Limerick (RMP LI028-085). This also lists a small mound adjacent to the exterior of the outer enclosure on the eastern side of the hillfort (LI028-173). The significance of that mound remains to be established. No other fieldwork was conducted at Ballylin prior to the present project. The site features in a general analysis of Bronze Age landscapes in North Munster (Grogan 2005b).

Archaeological investigation

A LiDAR survey of Ballylin hillfort was commissioned for this project (Figure 4.20). This is a remote sensing technique particularly suited to surveying large areas of ground. The process involves the transmission of laser light energy from a unit mounted on an aircraft, and analysing the duration of flight and strength of the returning pulses to create a detailed three-dimensional model of the ground surface. As an archaeological tool LiDAR has the ability to rapidly map low-relief sites and landscapes, even those masked by trees and overgrowth given a sufficiently high survey resolution. The Ballylin survey was carried out by BKS Ltd. who supplied a final bare-earth model dataset for the Ballylin study area covering 6 square km and amounting to some 24 million data points, which equates to a ground reading every 0.5m. The LiDAR survey, supported by aerial and satellite pho-

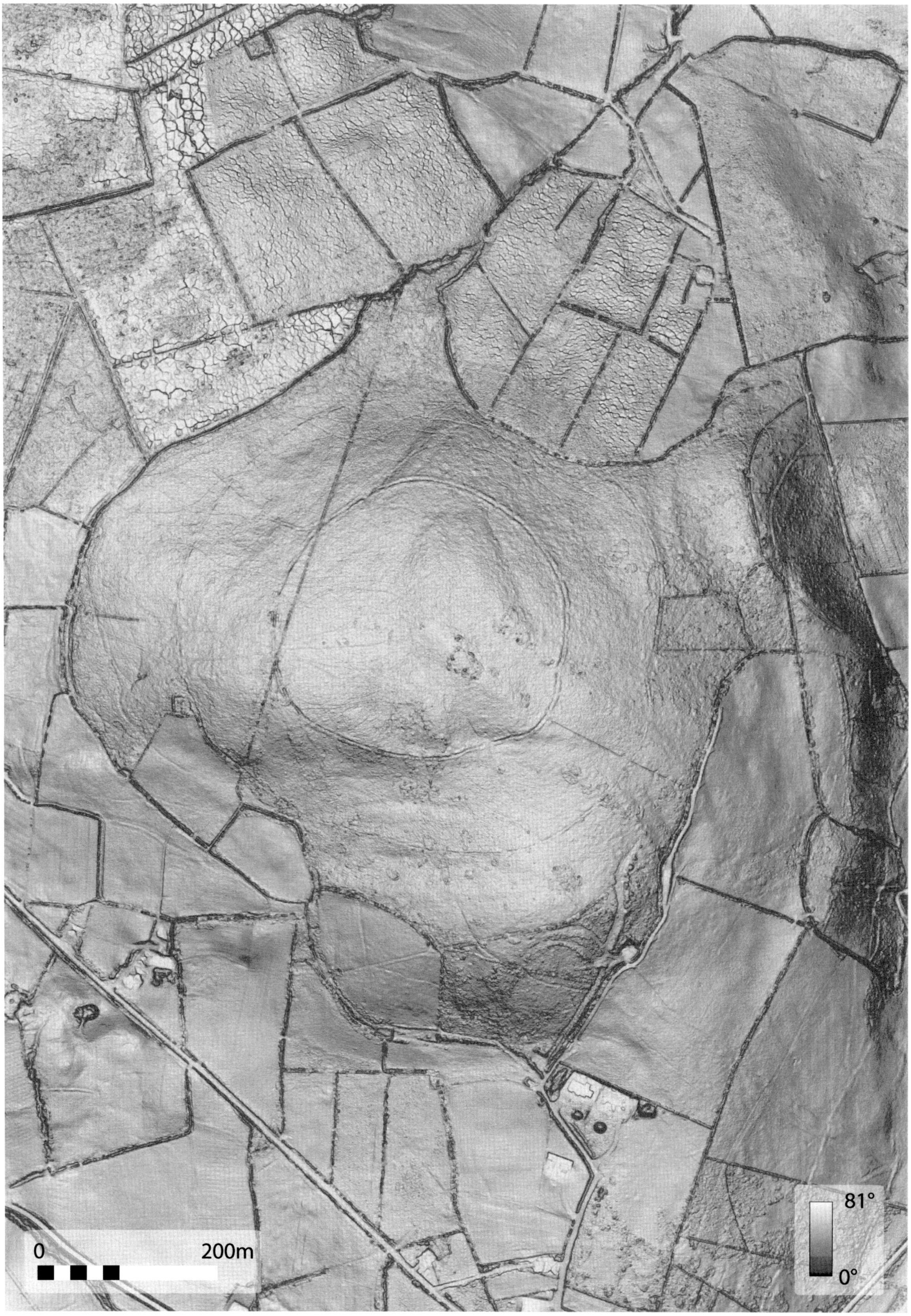

Figure 4.20: Slope model derived from LiDAR data showing Ballylin hillfort and environs.

tographs, followed by fieldwalking, confirms the basic description of this hillfort provided by Cody (1981). The hill is surrounded by two roughly concentric enclosures, placed 80–120m apart, each defined by a bank and ditch arrangement (Figure 4.21). These earthworks survive as low-relief features accentuated by vegetation growth (Figure 4.22). The inner enclosure is intact, and measures 300m by 315m over an area of 7.5ha (18.5 acres). The outer enclosure is 500m by 525m over 13.5 hectares (33.4 acres), but is damaged by forestry on the north/north-east side, with the south-west side incorporated into modern field banks.

With a total area of 21 hectares (almost 52 acres), Ballylin is the largest prehistoric hillfort in Munster, and one of the most impressive in Ireland. Despite this, neither enclosure is depicted on the various editions of the Ordnance Survey six-inch (1:10,560) mapping. Cody discussed the possibility of a third enclosure, represented on those maps and in aerial photography by curving field banks outside and concentric with the northern, western and southern sides of the second enclosure (*ibid.*: 78, fig. 13). Archaeological excavation would be required to examine whether these are later field boundaries following the lower contours of the hill. Should a third enclosure be confirmed at Ballylin, which is probably unlikely, the hillfort might have a total site area of some 37ha.

The LiDAR survey confirmed Cody's identification of an entrance opening on the eastern side of the inner enclosure (Figure 4.21). No corresponding entrance to the outer enclosure can be identified. The LiDAR does not indicate archaeological features in the interior of the hillfort, where dense heather growth hindered the ability of the technique to map the ground surface (Figure 4.22). Some circular features in the LiDAR results, particularly in the southern half of the site, are the result of thick pockets of gorse.

A magnetic gradiometry survey was carried out at Ballylin hillfort (O'Driscoll 2012b). Owing to dense heather and gorse growth this was limited to a 3ha

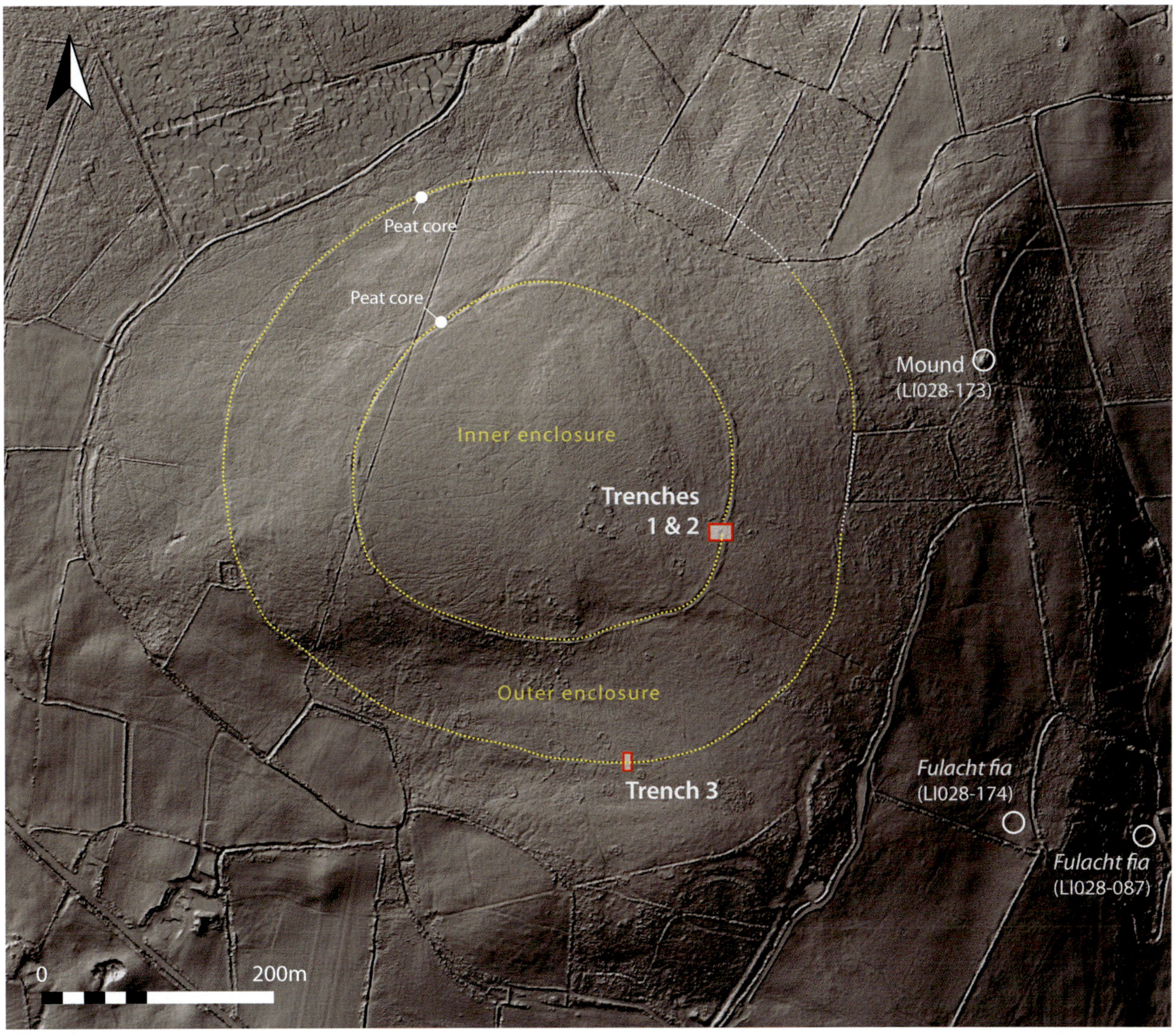

FIGURE 4.21: ANNOTATED HILLSHADE MODEL SHOWING MAIN FEATURES OF BALLYIN HILLFORT, EXCAVATION TRENCHES, AUGERED PEAT SAMPLES, AND RECORDED ARCHAEOLOGICAL SITES IN VICINITY.

FIGURE 4.22: NORTHERN SIDE OF BALLYLIN HILLFORT, LOOKING NORTH-WEST FROM INNER (FOREGROUND) TO OUTER (ARROW) ENCLOSING ELEMENTS.

area (14% of the site), extending east from the summit to include the entrance to the inner enclosure, as well as a transect across the outer enclosure. The enclosing elements are imaged as contrasting bands of high and low magnetic responses, as is the inner entrance (Figure 4.23). Some of the numerous point anomalies, particularly within the inner enclosure, may represent signatures of burning activity, or dug features such as pits and postholes. This remains, however, to be confirmed by excavation.

Archaeological Excavation

Three trenches were excavated at Ballylin hillfort over a four-week period in late summer 2012 (O'Brien 2012b). Trenches 1 and 2 were located on the southern side of the aforementioned entrance to the inner enclosure (Figure 4.21). Trench 3 was excavated across the line of the outer enclosure on the southern side of the hillfort. Prior to excavation both enclosing elements appeared to comprise a shallow ditch with indications of low banks on either side.

All three trenches were de-turfed by spade. An estimated 18m3 of peat was removed from Trenches 1 and 2, with some 2.25m^3 from Trench 3. Subsequent excavation was carried out by hand, using small digging equipment. This involved detailed stratigraphic excavation and context-based recording, with full written descriptions, photography and scale drawings. On completion of this work the trenches were back-filled by hand and the ground surface restored.

Further investigation included the sampling of peat from the ditches of the inner and outer enclosures on the northern side of the hillfort (Figure 4.21). This was done using a russian auger to sample peat at a depth of 0.7–0.75m in these ditches (Figure 4.24). It was hoped to obtain radiocarbon results for this peat growth to serve as *terminus ante quem* dates for the ditches (see below).

Excavation Results: Inner Enclosure

A 10m (east–west) by 5m (north–south) cutting (Trench 1) was excavated across an original entrance on the eastern side of the inner enclosure (Figures 4.25 and 4.26). A second cutting (Trench 2), measuring 2.5m square, was excavated as an extension to the northern side of Trench 1. There was a continuous growth of blanket peat across the entrance area, ranging 0.33–0.5m in thickness at the western side to 0.3–0.35m on the eastern side (Figure 4.27). This comprised a mid brown fibrous peat, supporting *calluna*, *molinia* and other blanket bog vegetation (C.01), overlying a more humified dark brown peat (C.02). The removal of this peat exposed a thin gley surface (C.03) across the eastern end of the trench, formed

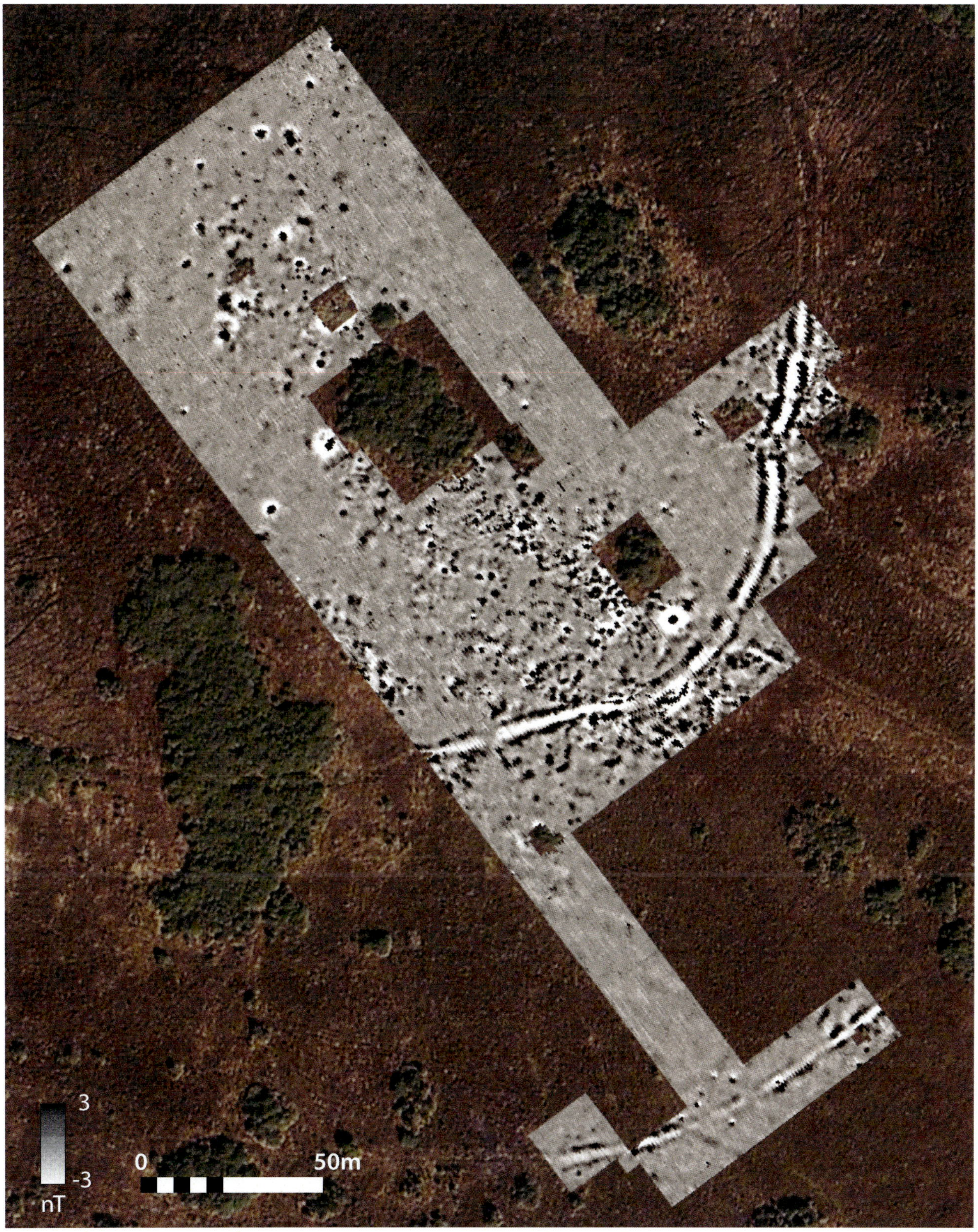

FIGURE 4.23: GEOPHYSICAL SURVEY (MAGNETIC GRADIOMETRY) OF BALLYLIN HILLFORT.

by soil podzolization in acidic waterlogged conditions. The same leaching action led to the precipitation of iron oxides in the underlying stony B-horizon (C.23). This bright orange subsoil overlay broken (C.24) or solid bedrock.

Excavation beneath the inner bank and around the outer edges of the ditch exposed a thin layer of white/grey silt (C.22) with charcoal flecks in places. This represents an old ground surface that existed immediately prior to the hillfort construction.

FIGURE 4.24: AUGERING OF DITCH, NORTHERN SIDE OF INNER ENCLOSURE, BALLYLIN.

Enclosing Elements

The excavated features in Trenches 1 and 2 include two low banks and an intervening ditch forming the southern side of the entrance, part of the ditch causeway and entrance passage, and two large postholes that were possibly part of a wooden gate arrangement (Figure 4.25).

The inner bank was created with subsoil and quarried bedrock extracted from the ditch (Figure 4.28). It measured 2.05m in width, with a maximum central height (eroded) of 0.35m. There is no evidence of stone facing, nor any indication of an associated palisade/fence. The bank was composed of five separate deposits overlying the old ground surface (Figure 4.27). The upper part of the bank was gleyed, creating a hard surface (C.04). This overlay three successive deposits of broken stone (contexts 11, 12 and 13) extracted from the ditch and intermixed with silt sediment. The removal of C.13 exposed a deposit of orange/light brown silt (C.14), which formed the lower part of the bank. Context 14 contained very little broken stone, as it represents upcast from the upper part of the ditch where the latter was dug through B-horizon subsoil (C.23). There was some erosion on the inner (western) side and northern end of the bank, with a mixed deposit of light to dark brown stony silt (C.10) derived from slip of the main bank deposits (C.11 and C.12).

A 2.3m length of ditch terminal with a rounded end was fully excavated on the southern side of Trench 1 (Figure 4.25). The ditch (C.21) is 3.5m wide at the surface and 1.6m at the base, with a depth of 0.89m to the modern surface (Figure 4.28). It was dug through 0.2–0.3m of orange B-horizon, with the lower part cut into bedrock. One unusual feature was a narrow channel, measuring 0.5–0.58m wide by 0.08–0.1m deep, along the centre of the ditch (Figure 4.29). This was deliberately cut into bedrock, sloping downwards from the lower side of the terminal to extend along the flat base of the ditch.

The fill sequence of this ditch began with a thin deposit of stony sediment (C.20) at the base (Figure 4.27). It is not certain whether this represents erosion of the bedrock cut or a slippage of bank material. It was overlain by thin deposits of stony silt (C.19) along the western slope, probably caused by erosion of the bank. This was followed by a slow and uninterrupted accumulation of peat in the ditch to a central thickness of 0.63m.

There are indications of a low bank outside the ditch. Excavation in Trench 1 identified a deposit of soil and broken rock that had been extracted from the ditch around its northern and eastern sides (Figure 4.27). This commenced with a spread of orange re-deposited B-horizon (C.06), overlain by dark brown stony silt with broken stone (C.05). Together, these deposits form a low

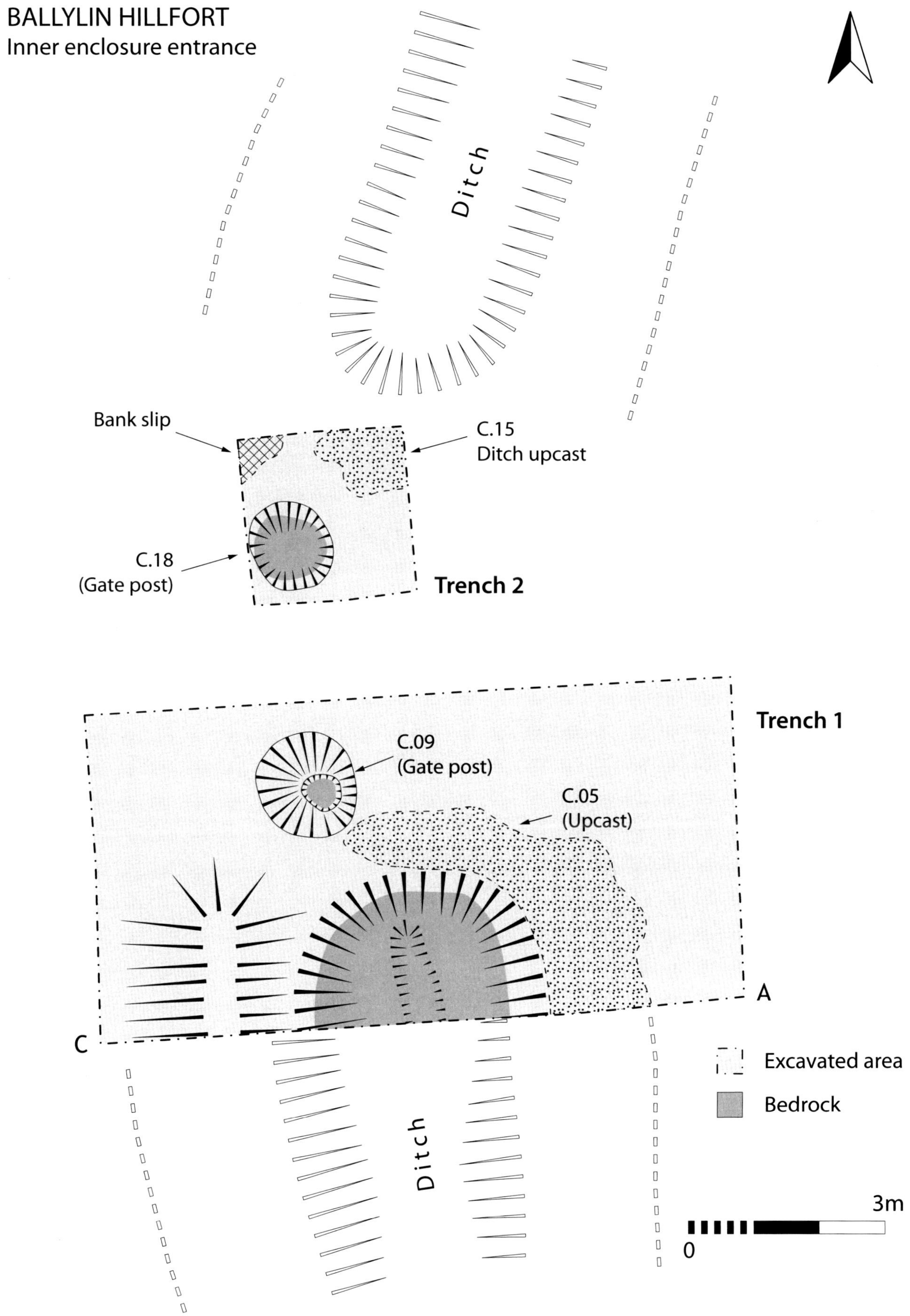

Figure 4.25: Post-excavation plan of entrance to inner hillfort enclosure, Ballylin.

FIGURE 4.26: EXCAVATION OF TRENCH 1, ENTRANCE TO INNER ENCLOSURE, BALLYLIN. NOTE THE DITCH TERMINAL (CENTRE RIGHT) AND FILL OF SOUTHERN POSTHOLE (CENTRE LEFT). PANORAMIC VIEW OF LOWLANDS OF CENTRAL LIMERICK IN BACKGROUND.

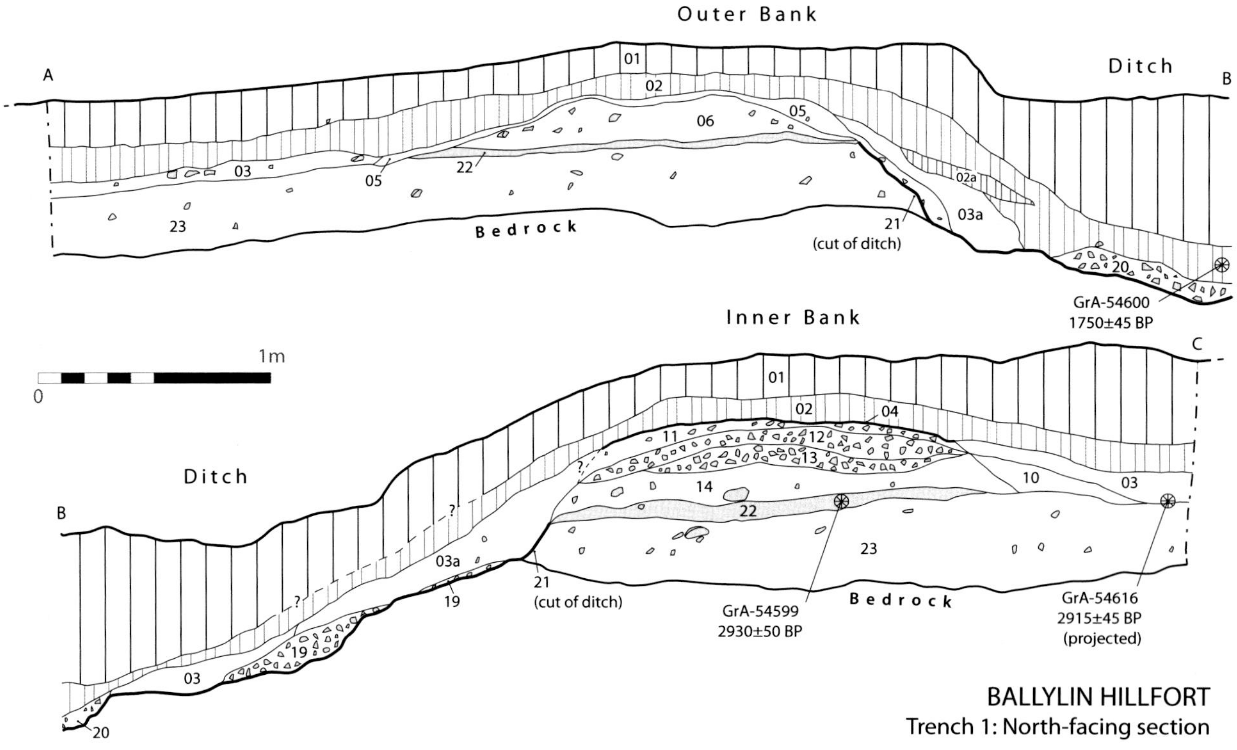

FIGURE 4.27: NORTH-FACING SECTION, ENTRANCE TO INNER ENCLOSURE, BALLYLIN HILLFORT.

Figure 4.28: Excavation of Trench 1, Ballylin (looking south), showing southern posthole and ditch terminal with low banks on either side (scale: 0.2m divisions).

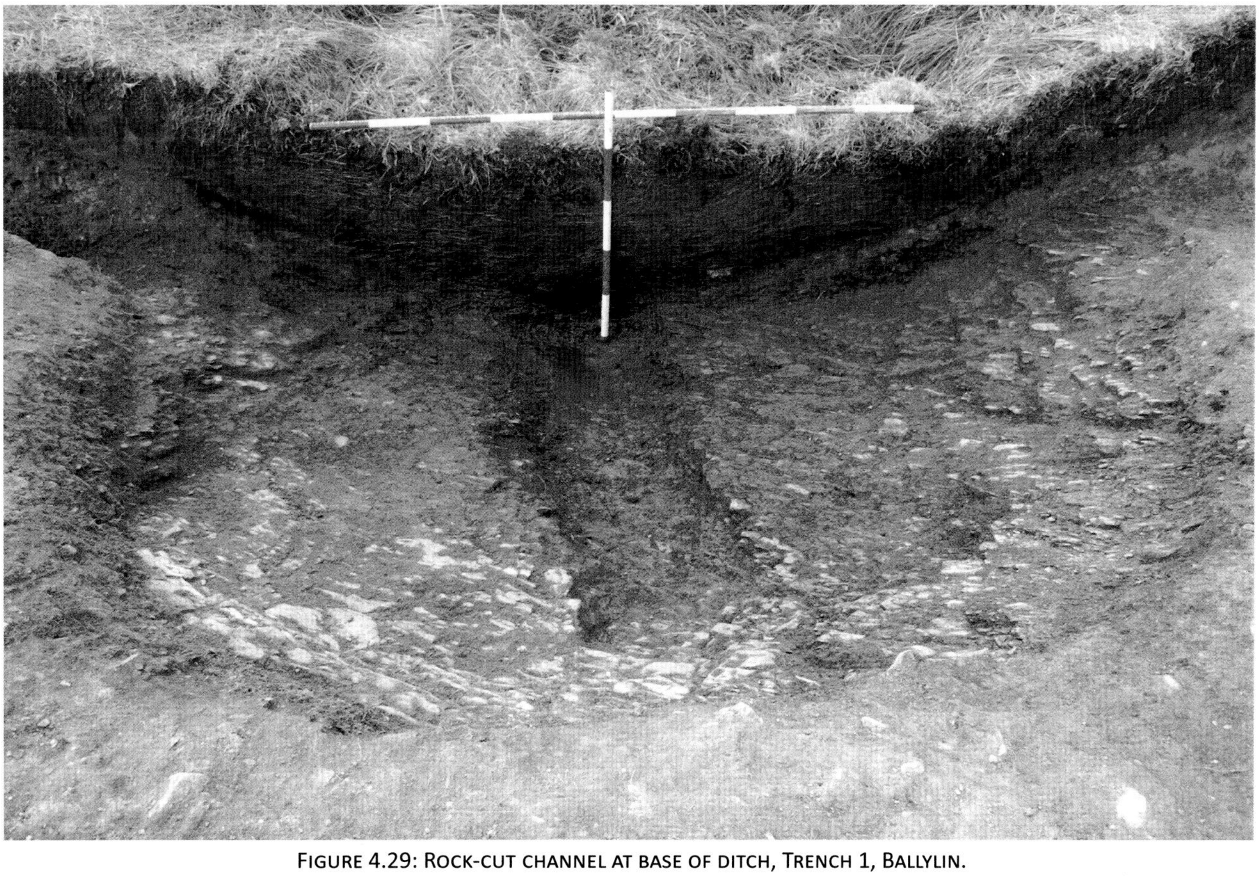

Figure 4.29: Rock-cut channel at base of ditch, Trench 1, Ballylin.

bank on the outer edge of the ditch. There is probably a similar feature on the other side of the entrance, where a spread of dark brown stony sediment (C.15) was exposed along the northern side of Trench 2. This was similar in appearance to C.05, and probably represents the same type of ditch upcast forming a low external bank.

An examination of the material used to build the two banks confirms that they were constructed at the same time as the ditch. In both instances the lower bank material (C.06 outer bank; C.14 inner bank) comprised redeposited subsoil from the initial digging of the ditch. The upper bank deposits (C.05 outer bank; C.11, C.12 and C.13 inner bank) contained a significant amount of broken stone from the extraction of bedrock in the lower ditch. The presence of only minor amounts of slip in the ditch (C.21) indicates that these banks remained relatively stable after construction. There is no evidence of a stone revetment, probably because the banks were never substantial.

Entrance Passage

Two pits were discovered inside the ditch terminals in the entrance passage (Figure 4.25). The southern example (C.09) was 1.2m from the north-west side of the southern ditch (Figure 4.28). It consisted of a vertical D–shaped cut in the B-horizon subsoil, measuring 0.55m (north-east/south-west) by 0.53m (north-west\south-east), with a central depth of 0.54m (Figure 4.30). The fill (C.07) consisted of loose stony silt with only a few fragments of charcoal. The upper portion contained 19 large stones (C.08), many of which were inclined along the sides of the pit, as if used as packing for an upright post.

The northern posthole (C.18) was 2.1m from the edge of the northern ditch terminal (Figure 4.31). This fea-

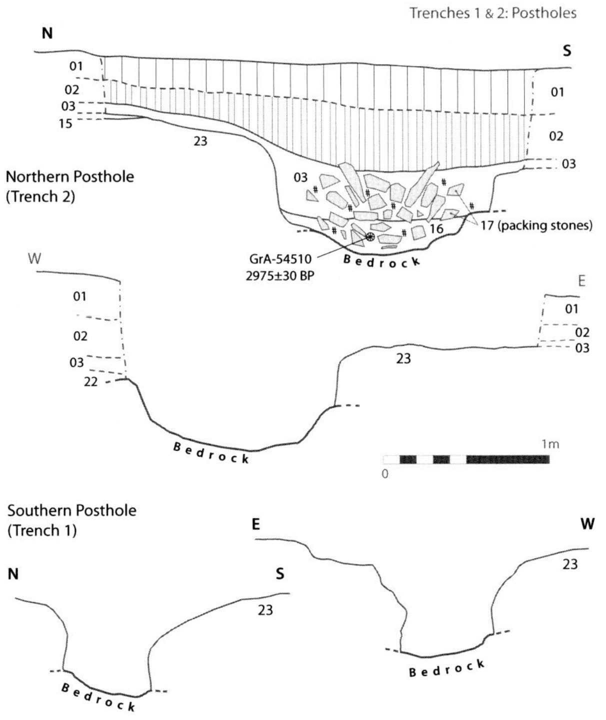

Figure 4.30: Profiles across entrance postholes, Trenches 1 and 2, Ballylin.

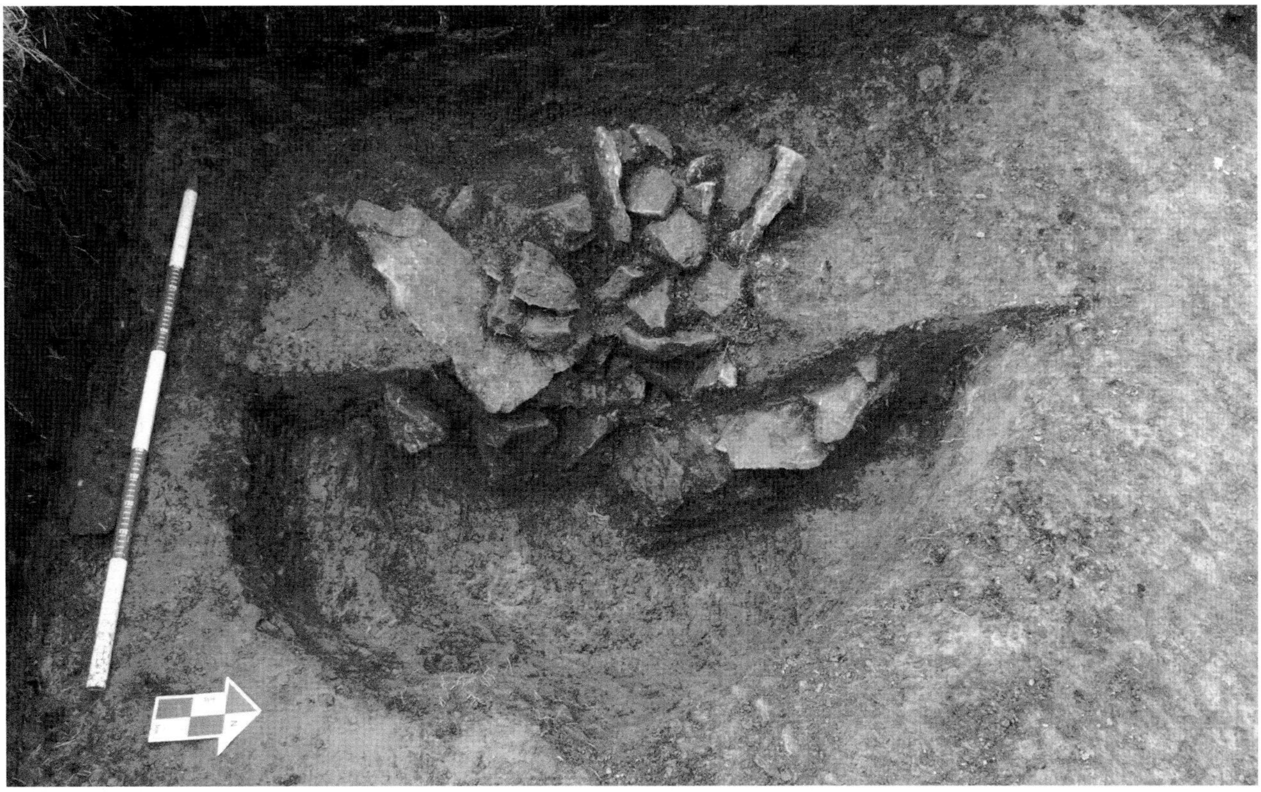

Figure 4.31: Northern entrance posthole, Trench 2, Ballylin.

ture was sub-circular in plan, with steeply sloping sides and an irregularly flat base. The posthole measured 1.45m (north–south) by 1.33m, with a central depth of 0.6m (Figure 4.30). It was dug through orange B-horizon (C.23), with the lower part cut into bedrock. The fill consisted of loose stony silt (C.16) with numerous flecks and small fragments of charcoal. It also contained 107 small to large sized stones (C.17) used as post packing. These stones were concentrated in the central area of the posthole, and the loose arrangement suggests they were displaced by removal of the northern gate post.

Occasional flecks of charcoal were found on the pre-peat gleyed surface (C.03) in the inner part of the entrance passageway. Three small concentrations were identified in the north-west corner of Trench 1, but there was no indication of a hearth or burnt surface. Charcoal from C.03, and from the old ground surface (C.22) under the bank slip (C.10), were sampled for radiocarbon dating (see below).

List of excavation contexts, Trenches 1 and 2, Ballylin hillfort

Context 01. Mid brown fibrous peat with blanket bog vegetation.

C.02. Lower peat, dark brown/black, well humified and less fibrous than C.01.

C.02a Lens of black peat, similar texture to C.02.

C.03. Gleyed surface across trench; green/blue compact silt with charcoal flecks.

C.03a Same as C.03, except looser with visible iron oxide enrichment.

C.04. Gleyed surface of bank; thin layer of hard, dark brown, stony silt, with mottles.

C.05. Dark brown stony silt along exterior edge of ditch; many small angular stones.

C.06. Orange silt with grey mottles under C.05 on edge of ditch. Redeposited subsoil.

C.07. Main fill of posthole (C.09); stony silt with broken stone and some charcoal. C.08. Packing stones from posthole (C.09); angular stones, 0.11–0.32m in length. C.09. D-shaped cut of southern posthole in subsoil, vertical sides and flat base.

C.10. Dark brown stony silt; eroded from inner side and northern end of bank.

C.11. Dark brown silt in upper part of bank; root-matted with some angular stones.

C.12. Deposit of mid brown stony sediment under C.11 in upper part of bank.

C.13. Green/light brown sandy silt under C.12 in lower bank, many angular stones.

C.14. Orange/light brown silt forming lower part of bank; occasional rounded stones.

C.15. Dark brown stony silt on north side of Trench 2; ditch upcast similar to C.05.

C.16. Main fill of posthole (C.18); loose grey/ brown stony silt, with some charcoal.

C.17. Packing stones from posthole (C.18); angular stones, average length 0.12m.

C.18. Sub-circular cut of northern posthole, steeply sloping sides to flat base.

C.19. Thin deposit of stony silt on western slope of ditch; primary slip of bank.

C.20. Thin deposit of stony silt at base of ditch; contained small angular stones.

C.21. Cut of ditch (see main text for description).

C.22. Spread of white/grey silt under bank slip, charcoal flecks; old ground surface.

C.23. Orange, iron-enriched, stony silt forming B-horizon over broken bedrock.

C.24. Patches of broken bedrock beneath B-horizon (C.23).

Excavation Results: Outer Enclosure

This investigation was conducted 205m south/south-west of Trench 1 on the southern side of the hillfort (Figure 4.21). An 8m (east–west) by 3m (north–south) cutting (Trench 3) was excavated across the line of the outer hillfort enclosure (Figure 4.32). This was visible before excavation as a 1.8m wide by 0.3m deep ditch, with a low bank (<0.4m high) on either side.

There was a continuous growth of blanket peat, ranging 0.55–0.6m in thickness at the western end to 0.25–0.3m on the eastern side of the trench (Figure 4.33). As with Trench 1, this comprised an upper layer of mid brown, fibrous peat and surface vegetation (C.01), and a lower formation of more humified black peat (C.02). Removal of the peat exposed a thin gley surface (C.25) across the

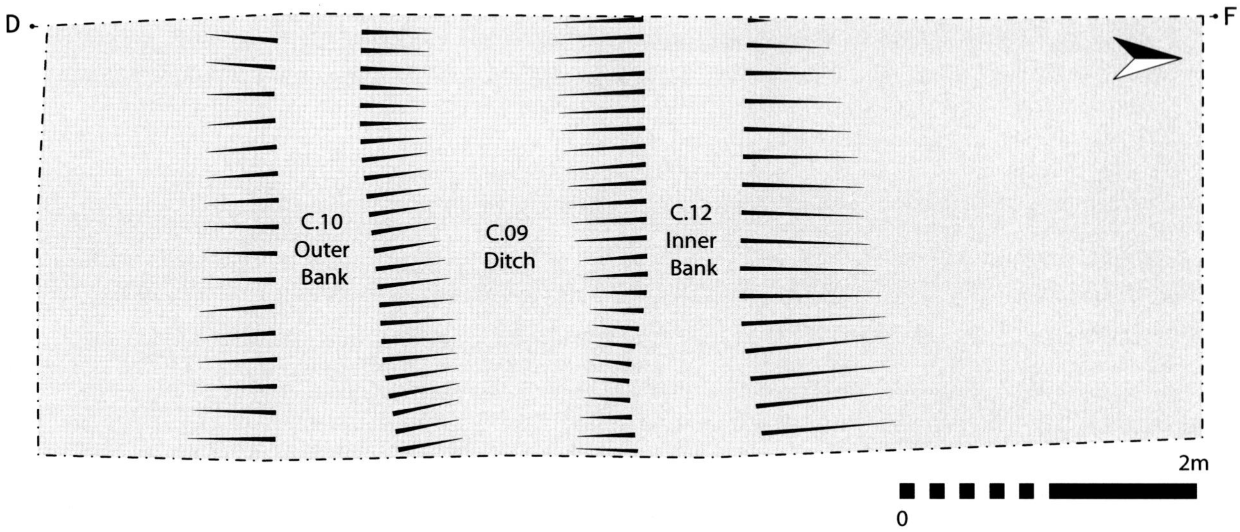

Figure 4.32: Post-excavation plan of outer enclosing element, Trench 3, Ballylin hillfort.

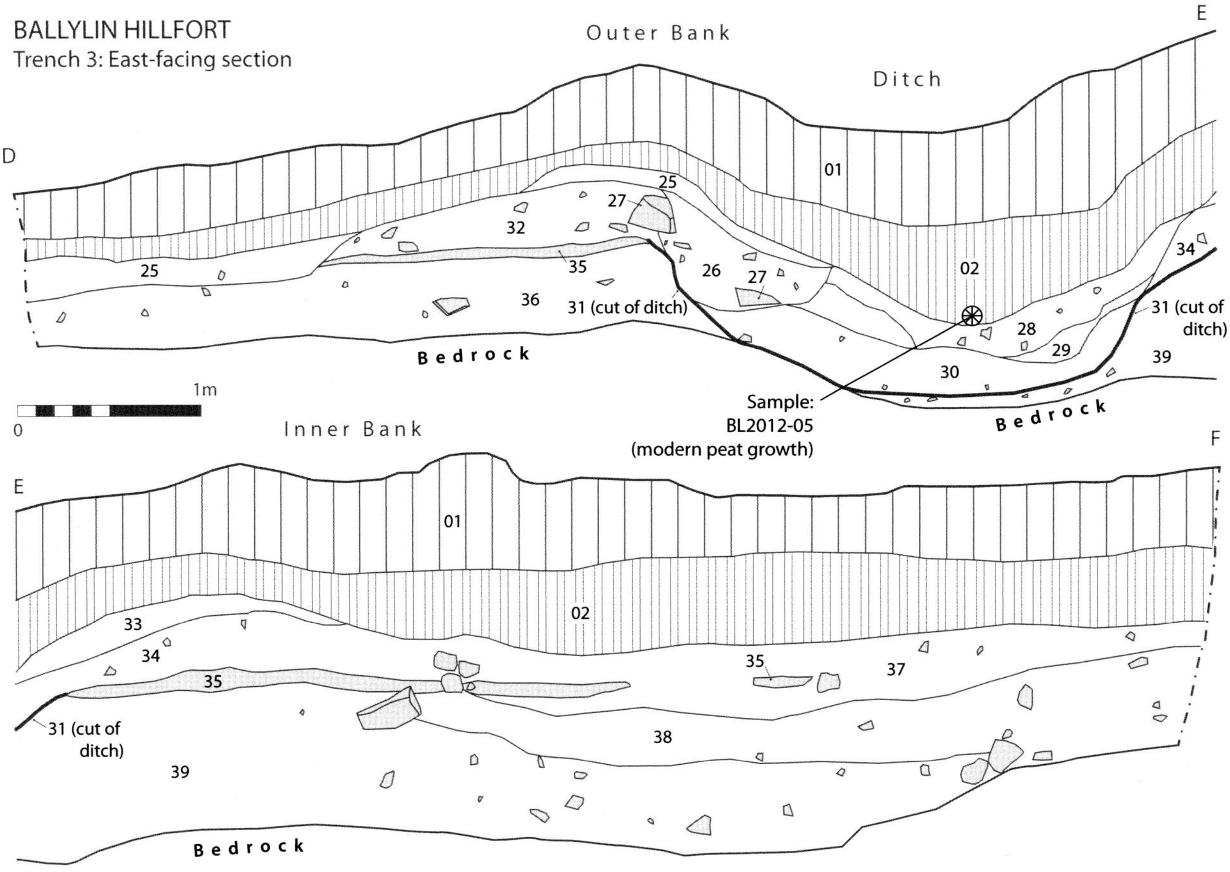

Figure 4.33: Stratigraphic section, outer enclosing element, Trench 3, Ballylin.

eastern end of the trench. This surface formed as a result of soil podzolization in acidic waterlogged conditions, leading to precipitation of iron oxides in the underlying stony B-horizon (C.36). It is notable that the B-horizon at the western end of the trench (C.38) was not visibly iron-enriched. The gley surface (C.25) was absent in that area, and instead there was a silt layer with a peaty texture (C.37). The reasons for this subsoil variation are unknown, but may be a consequence of impeded drainage due to the presence of the inner bank.

Excavation beneath both banks uncovered a thin layer of grey/white silt (C.35) representing an old ground surface pre-dating the hillfort construction. There was no charcoal nor any archaeological features visible in this surface. Outside of the banks, this surface had become incorporated into the gleyed layer (C.25) at the eastern end, and the peaty silt layer (C.37) at the western end.

Enclosing Elements

The archaeology of Trench 3 consists of a shallow ditch with low banks on both sides, but no other features (Figure 4.34). The inner bank was 1.3m (southern side) to 1.6m (northern side) wide, with a central height (eroded) of 0.23m (southern end) to 0.35m (northern end). It was created using redeposited subsoil (C.34) extracted from the ditch, which was deposited on the old ground surface (C.35). The upper part of the bank had become gleyed, creating a hard surface (C.33). The core of the bank was mostly composed of soil, with only a few small stones. There is no evidence of a stone facing in this bank.

Excavation of a 2.9m length of the ditch across the centre of Trench 3 revealed it had steeply sloping sides and a rounded base. The ditch measured 1.4–1.8m in width, with a central depth of 0.85m from the modern ground surface. It was dug from the old ground surface (C.35) through the underlying subsoil (C. 36 and C.39). The base was formed by the latter, except along the eastern side where bedrock was exposed in places. There is no indication that the bedrock was quarried to any extent, which explains the absence of broken stone in the adjacent banks.

The fill sequence of this ditch began with a build-up of grey/white silt (C.30) from the weathering of C.39 along the lower ditch sides (Figure 4.33). This 0.08–0.2m thick deposit of primary silt was followed by an inwash of iron-enriched silt (C.29), as well as slip from the exterior bank (C.26). It was followed by deposition of organic silt (C.28) that marked the transition from minerogenic to organic sedimentation. This culminated in the build-up of blanket peat in the ditch to a central thickness of 0.62m.

Excavation exposed a low bank of redeposited subsoil (C.32) bordering the exterior of the ditch (Figure 4.32). This feature was 1.1m wide with a central (eroded) height of 0.15–0.17m. A low revetment of field stones (C.27), some 2–3 courses high, was built along a 0.3m wide ledge on the inner (western) side of the bank. A few of these stones were *in situ*, but most had fallen into the ditch.

List of excavation contexts, Trench 3, Ballylin

C.25. Hard gley at eastern end of trench; grey/light brown fibrous silt with rare stones.

C.26. Dark brown silt with orange mottles on upper eastern side of ditch; bank slip.

Figure 4.34: Excavation of Trench 3 (looking south-east), showing ditch with low banks on either side (scale: 0.2m divisions).

C.27. Deposit of 26 large stones along exterior slope of ditch; collapsed revetment.

C.28. Inwash of mid brown silt under peat in centre of ditch; no stones or charcoal.

C.29. Thin deposit of orange silt in lower ditch; inwash of fine sediment from bank.

C.30. Compact grey/white silt with orange mottles, base of ditch; primary inwash silt.

C.31. Cut of ditch (see main text for description).

C.32. Compact light brown mottled silt; redeposited subsoil forming outer bank.

C.33. Upper gleyed surface of inner bank; 0.02–0.06m in thickness.

C.34. Compact grey/brown silt (green tinge) forming the main layer of inner bank.

C.35. Thin layer of grey/white fine silt under both banks; old ground surface.

C.36. Compact orange stony silt across east end of trench; iron-enriched B-horizon.

C.37. Light brown peaty silt underlying peat (C.01/02) at western end of trench.

C.38. Mid brown silt, with some stones; B-horizon subsoil, west end of trench.

C.39. Layer of grey stony fine silt, west end of trench; C-horizon over bedrock (C.24).

Finds and Dating

No artifacts were recovered, and so the dating of the excavated features must rely on the radiocarbon method. Seven samples were submitted for AMS radiocarbon dating to the Centre for Isotope Research, University of Groningen. The sample details and results are as follows (Figure 4.35; calibration based on OxCal v.4.2.4; 95.4% confidence):

Trenches 1 and 2 (inner enclosure entrance)
Sample BL2012-01: Charcoal from fill of northern gate posthole (C.16). Wood species: oak.
GrA-54510; 2975±30 BP.

Sample BL2012-02: Charcoal from pre-bank surface (C.22). Wood species: hazel.
GrA-54599; 2930±50 BP.

Field No.	Lab No.	C-14 BP	$\partial^{13}C$	95.4% calibration
BL2012-01	GrN-54510	2975±30	-24.99	1368–1059 BC
BL2012-02	GrN-54599	2930±50	-29.93	1279–980 BC
BL2012-03	GrN-54600	1750±45	-27.28	141–393 AD
BL2012-04	GrN-54616	2915±45	-25.44	1258–979 BC
BL2012-05	GrN-54953	118.8±0.4% C	-28.74	Modern peat
BL2012-06	GrA-54954	915±30	-28.82	1030–1189 AD
BL2012-07	GrA-54955	315±30	-28.90	1484–1648 AD

Figure 4.35: Radiocarbon dates for Ballylin hillfort (calibration after OxCal v.4.2.4).

Sample BL2012-03: Peat sample from base of peat infill in ditch of inner hillfort enclosure.
GrA-54600; 1750±45 BP.

Sample BL2012-04: Charcoal from passageway of inner enclosure entrance (C.03). Wood species: willow.
GrA-54616; 2915±45 BP.

Comment: Radiocarbon dates are available for three significant contexts in the entrance of the inner enclosure. These include similar results for charcoal found beneath bank slip (GrA-54599), in the northern post-hole (GrA-54510), and in the entrance passage (GrA-54616) of Trench 1. Taken together, the three results indicate a calibrated date range of 1258–1059 BC for the hillfort entrance. While the source and 'own age' of the charcoal is unknown, some connection is likely to the occupation, and possibly construction, of this hillfort. The calibrated date range of 141–393 AD for peat growth in the lower ditch (GrA-54600) indicates a time when the hillfort was probably abandoned.

Trench 3 (outer enclosure ditch)
Sample BL2012-05: Peat sample from base of peat infill in ditch of outer hillfort enclosure (east-facing section).
GrA-54953; 118.8±0.4% Act. C.

Comment: This result points to peat growth in this ditch during the modern era. The fact that this sample was taken at a depth of 0.65m from the modern surface could suggest that the growth of peat in this ditch is of recent date, but it is more likely to result from root contamination.

Augered peat samples
Sample BL2012-06: Peat from lower part of inner enclosure ditch (0.7–0.75m below modern ground) on

north/north-west side of hillfort.
GrA-54954; 915±30 BP.

Sample BL2012-07: Peat from lower part of outer enclosure ditch (0.7–0.75m below modern ground) on the north/north-west side of hillfort.
GrA-54955; 315±30 BP.

Comment: The peat samples provide *terminus ante quem* age ranges for the hillfort ditches. The GrA-54954 result confirms the ditch of the inner enclosure is likely to be pre-medieval. GrA-54955 confirms the ditch of the outer enclosure must pre-date the sixteenth century AD. While not very informative, due probably to root contamination of the sample, this result does indicate the outer enclosure was built before the modern era.

Discussion

Based on current knowledge of Irish hillforts, Cody (1981: 79) proposed an Iron Age date (500 BC–400 AD) for Ballylin. In that context, the presence of what he regarded as internal ditches around both enclosures was significant, drawing comparisons with various 'royal sites' of the Iron Age, such as Ráth na Ríogh, Tara, Emain Macha (Navan Fort), Co. Armagh, and Dún Ailinne, Co. Kildare. This is not supported by the recent investigation at Ballylin, which confirms the site is earlier than those Iron Age enclosures, and should not be regarded as an internally ditched enclosure.

The 2012 excavation yielded important information on the defences of the hillfort and one of its original entrances. Both enclosing elements were similar, comprised of a shallow ditch with a low bank on either side, and no indication of wooden fencing. The ditch of the inner enclosure was the larger of the two, averaging 3.5m wide and 0.9m in depth. It consisted of a wide shallow trench with sloping sides and a flat base. The significance of a narrow rock-cut channel along the base is unclear, but it would have been too shallow to serve as a footing trench for fence posts. The regular shape suggests a drainage feature, however it is difficult to understand how this would have been effective at the bottom of a ditch, unless connected to the collection of drinking water in a sump feature located outside the excavation area.

The soil and broken rock extracted from the ditch was piled on the inside to create a low bank, now *c.*2m wide and 0.35m high. The absence of a significant amount of bank slip at the base of the ditch suggests that this feature was not significantly higher when first built. The same material was used to raise the northern and eastern edges of the ditch, in what might be termed an outer bank. The excavation of both bank features did not reveal evidence of palisade posts or other fencing features.

The ditch of the outer enclosure was only around 1.9m wide by 0.85m deep, with the low bank on either side not exceeding 0.35m in height. As the overall height of the enclosure was only 1–1.2m from base of ditch to top of the inner bank, this did not constitute a functional barrier in the sense of a fortification or animal enclosure. Despite their slight nature, the construction of these enclosures was labour intensive. The inner enclosure has a perimeter of 1.01km, the outer enclosure 1.65km, giving a combined length of some 2.65km of earthworks. The techniques used in the construction of this earthwork are unknown. This was a laborious process involving digging with wood and/or bone implements, none of which were found during excavation. There were no tool marks or traces of fire-setting on the bedrock surfaces of either enclosure ditch.

Excavation revealed important details about the entrance to the inner hillfort enclosure. This took the form of a narrow ditch causeway leading to a 5.5m wide opening in the bank. Two large postholes, spaced 2.2m apart, may have held posts for a wooden gate. The presence of packing stones in both pits indicates that they once held upright posts. The northern posthole (C.18) was significantly larger than its southern counterpart, which might indicate a larger post used to hang a gate. That said, it is difficult to see how a gate would have been functional with no palisade in the adjacent banks. As an alternative, upright posts may have been used to formally mark the hillfort entrance without any need for a gate. Whatever structure was used, the absence of post-pipes from *in situ* decay, or significant amounts of charcoal from burning, together with the jumbled arrangement of packing stones, indicates these posts were removed.

The excavation did not uncover evidence for the occupation of this hillfort, apart from some charcoal deposited at the entrance to the inner enclosure. No artifacts, food residues or structural remains were found. This is due to the limited area excavated. There is no information on the abandonment of the hillfort or its subsequent history. The former is represented by the deliberate removal of two wooden posts at the entrance to the inner enclosure, and by the uninterrupted growth of blanket peat in the hillfort ditches.

Cultural Landscape

Some general observations may be made on the cultural landscape context of Ballylin hillfort. The site overlooks a modern farmscape of fertile farmland in the central plain of Co. Limerick. This lowland environment has changed considerably over the past 3000 years, as a result of deforestation, drainage and soil improvement connected to agriculture. This would have resulted in the destruction of many prehistoric settlements and ritual monuments, some of which may have been contemporary with the hillfort.

While pollen records are not available for the Ballylin area, Plunkett (2006) has presented results from a small bog at Moyreen, 7km to the north-west of the hillfort. There are indications of intensified agriculture in that area during the twelfth and eleventh centuries BC, at a time of fluctuating climatic conditions. Plunkett suggests this may be connected to a concentration of settlement in the hinterlands of Ballylin, an interpretation supported by the new dating evidence for the hillfort. She also observed a reduction in arable agriculture at Moyreen during the tenth century BC, corresponding to an apparent deterioration of climate (Plunkett 2006: 66, fig. 3).

There are few recorded sites or monuments of Bronze Age date in the environs of Ballylin hillfort. The *Record of Monuments and Places* for Co. Limerick lists 14 archaeological monuments within one kilometre of the hillfort. These include seven ringforts that are likely to be Early Medieval, and three enclosures of unknown age, but also possibly later than the hillfort. There is an unclassified (and undated) barrow (LI028-178) at the summit of a hill in Dunganville Upper townland, 1.25km to the south/south-west of the hillfort (Figure 4.18). Also significant is a RMP record of four *fulachtaí fia* (LI028-087, LI028-089, LI028-174 and LI028-175) on the southeastern slopes of Ballylin hill. These water-boiling sites have a long chronology, with the majority now dated to the Bronze Age (Hawkes 2014). One of the Ballylin examples (LI028-174) was excavated in the 1980s, in the course of reclamation of fields directly below the hillfort. While there are no details, a radiocarbon analysis of 3400±60 BP (Grn-13153) was obtained for charcoal from one of three troughs at the site (information in Brindley *et al.* 1989/90: 7). The result is calibrated to 1881–1534 BC, placing this burnt mound in the Early Bronze Age, several centuries older that the nearby hillfort.

While no Bronze Age settlements are recorded close to Ballylin, a number were excavated on the 2002 Bord Gáis Pipeline to the West project (Grogan, O'Donnell and Johnston 2007). These include two structures of possible Late Bronze Age date at Ballincurra (*ibid.*: 238), and Middle Bronze Age occupation at Kiltenan South (ibid., 289–90) and Knockuregare (*ibid.*: 293–7). A roundhouse dated 1620–1461 BC is recorded at Garryduff near Newcastle West. While this pre-dates Ballylin hillfort by several centuries, there are dates of 1381–1132 BC and 1371–1060 BC for two burnt mounds excavated at the same location (Delaney 2014). These are just some of a number of Middle and Late Bronze Age sites discovered in development-led archaeology projects in Limerick in recent years. Older excavations include the two enclosures excavated in 1974 at Aughinish Island, which are associated with coarse ware pottery and bronze metalwork of the Dowris phase (Kelly 1974). Bronze Age settlements are recorded at Lough Gur, including the Circle K and L enclosures (Grogan and Eogan 1987; Cleary 2003), with occupation also of unenclosed house sites on Knockadoon (Ó Ríordáin 1954; Cleary 1995).

Ballylin is the only prehistoric hillfort listed in the *Record of Monuments and Places* for Co. Limerick. A site at Lisbane, 6km to the north/north-east, listed as a hilltop enclosure (RMP LI019-127) is regarded by Raftery (1972) as a small Class 2 hillfort (Figure 4.18). Lisbane comprises two concentric oval enclosures, spaced 15–23m apart, with a overall diameter of 70m by 60m. Both enclosing elements consist of a single stone-faced earthen bank with a shallow external ditch (Westropp 1916–17: 29). The size and overall features of Lisbane question whether this is a prehistoric hillfort, comparable to sites such as Ballylin. The same is true of Dunganville Upper (LI028-086), 2km to the south of Ballylin, listed by Grogan (2005b: fig 4.7; table 7.6) as a hilltop enclosure, but possibly an early medieval ringfort. There are similar questions for sites in east Limerick (Figure 4.18), where the identification of hillforts at Rathcannon (LI039-029), Knockainy (LI032-139), Tory Hill (LI022-111001), and Friarstown (LI013-089 and LI013-094) remains uncertain (*ibid.*: table 7.1). A site that is likely to be of Bronze Age date is the inland promontory fort of Castle Gale (LI059A001) in Darragh More townland, Co. Limerick (Doody 2008: 540–1). Until such sites are excavated, Ballylin remains the only confirmed Class 2 hillfort in Limerick and, as such, is of particular significance for the Bronze Age prehistory of the region.

In terms of material culture, a review of published catalogues of swords (Eogan 1965), bronze hoards (Eogan 1983), gold (Eogan 1994) and socketed axeheads (Eogan 2000) of Middle to Late Bronze Age date does not indicate many significant finds within a 5km distance from the hillfort. This cannot be taken at face value, as such records are heavily influenced by circumstances of discovery and recording, as well as by the original depositional practices. Grogan (2005b: fig. 4.5) lists several examples of bronze metalwork in the general vicinity of Ballylin. These include a flanged axehead from Ardagh 2km to the east; while 5km to the north-east there are records of a rivet-hole spearhead from Ballynamuddagh, a socketed axe from Coolcappagh, and a chisel from Ballyneety. The Ardagh axe is likely to pre-date Ballylin hillfort, while the other objects could be contemporary or slightly later in the Bronze Age. There is an apparent concentration of Middle to Late Bronze Age metalwork in the Oldabbey area near Shanagolden, 7km to the north of Ballylin, where a palstave, two socketed axeheads, and a socket-looped spearhead, among other objects were found in a bog (Eogan 1965: 72; Eogan 2000: 77).

There are no hoards of Middle or Late Bronze Age metalwork recorded in the vicinity of Ballylin. The most significant find is from Tooradoo, 16km south-west of the hillfort close to the Kerry border (Figure 4.18; Eogan 1983: 104, fig. 58a). This contains four penannular 'hair rings' of lead covered by gold foil, four plain bronze rings, two bronze rings with buffer-shaped projections, a lignite bead, and a necklace of 105 graduated amber beads. The Tooradoo hoard is likely to be Dowris phase (900–750 BC), and so probably later in date than Ballylin, though this is not certain as the full chronology of the hillfort occupation is not known. The absence of Bronze age goldwork in the area is notable, though a bar-twisted gold torc (National Museum of Ireland SA1926:49) of Bishopsland Phase is recorded from Cooltomin, 7km north-east of the hillfort (Figure 4.18; information: Mary Cahill).

In conclusion, available records indicate that Ballylin hillfort was probably part of a settlement landscape that included small farm holdings with roundhouses, *fulachtaí fia* used for feasting on special occasions, and monuments such as barrows and standing stones connected to funerary practice. The relationship of these different site types has been explained in terms of stratified societies corresponding to a hierarchy of settlement organization, at the apex of which is the hillfort (Grogan 2005b). While it is not possible on present knowledge to propose a similar model for Ballylin hillfort, exotic finds of the Cooltomin and Tooradoo type reflect the wealth of some local groups during the Late Bronze Age.

4.3 Formoyle, Co. Clare

This hillfort is situated 5km south–east of Broadford village in south-east Clare, and 10km west of Killaloe town. The hillfort is located on the southern side of the Glenomra Valley, which crosses the southern slopes of the Slieve Bernagh Mountains in an east–west direction (Figure 4.36). This broad valley was a natural routeway in ancient and historic times, connecting the lakeland region of south-east Clare with the crossing of the Shannon at Killaloe, south of Lough Derg. The significance of this landscape in prehistory has been highlighted by Condit and O'Sullivan (1996), with reference to the strategic siting of the hillfort.

The hillfort lies on the summit of Formoyle Hill (242m OD), a north-east/south-west ridge divided along its length by a boundary between the townland of Formoyle Beg to the south/south-west and Cloonyconry More to the north (Figures 4.37 and 4.38). There are extensive views from the hillfort, the siting of which is very conspicuous in the landscape. The western and southern slopes are gentler than the northern and eastern slopes which fall sharply to the valley bottom. The slope is most regular on the western side, whereas natural depressions and rock outcrop create a more irregular profile on the eastern and southern slopes. The summit area has a flat profile with broken topography (Hickey and Hogan 2005).

FIGURE 4.36: GENERAL VIEW OF FORMOYLE HILLFORT (ARROW), LOOKING ACROSS GLENOMRA VALLEY TO SOUTH.

FIGURE 4.37: AERIAL VIEW OF FORMOYLE HILLFORT, CO. CLARE (SOURCE: GOOGLE EARTH).

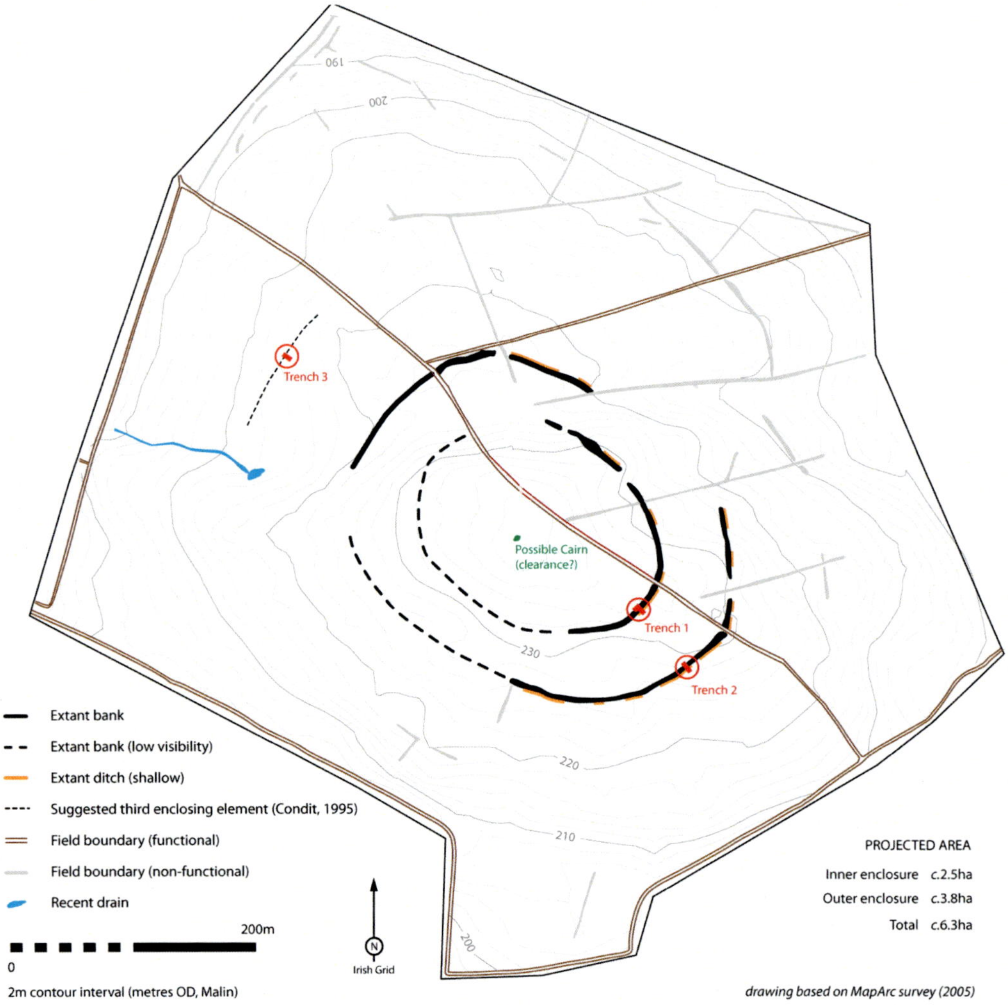

FIGURE 4.38: PLAN OF FORMOYLE HILLFORT SHOWING OUTLINE OF TWO HILLFORT ENCLOSURES, ALONG WITH THE LOCATION OF GEOPHYSICAL SURVEY PANELS AND EXCAVATION TRENCHES.

Much of the hill is covered by thin blanket bog, particularly on the south-west side in Formoyle Beg townland where the hillfort enclosures are most visible. There was extensive peat-cutting in that area in modern times. The north-west side of the hillfort in the same townland was levelled in 2005 during land reclamation. The land on the northern side in Cloonyconry townland was also reclaimed over the centuries, with indications of lazy-bed furrows in several areas. Much of that area is today covered by gorse, interspersed with areas of rough grazing.

Site history

There are no antiquarian references to this site, which also does not feature in the research of Thomas Westropp, who wrote extensively on ancient forts in east Clare (Westropp 1912; 1916). It is not recorded in the historic mapping of the Ordnance Survey of Ireland, which depict a number of smaller ringforts and megalithic monuments in the immediate vicinity. There is no historical name for the site, which for convenience here is referred to as 'Formoyle hillfort', though strictly should be called 'Formoyle Beg/Cloonyconry More hillfort'. The presence of a 'fort' on the hill is well known locally, with the summit area on referred to as 'holy ground', reputedly the site of several burials marked by large stones. There is no evidence of such features today.

The hillfort was first identified on aerial photographs by Tom Condit, who published a brief description of the surface features, and considered its significance in the cultural landscape of east Clare (Condit 1995; Condit and O'Sullivan 1996; 1999). Condit identified three concentric enclosures around the summit of this hill (Condit 1995; Grogan 2005a: table 7.1). Two of these ramparts survive intact, separated by a distance of some 40–60m (Figures 4.37 and 4.38). Condit argued that the remains of a third enclosure were traceable on the north–west side of the hill, where a shallow ditch was exposed over a length of c.120m, at a distance of c.100m from the middle enclosure.

The site was surveyed in 2005 following the destruction of the north-west side of the hillfort during reclamation of agricultural land over an area of 10.2ha (Hickey and Hogan 2005). This survey involved fieldwalking, total station mapping and analysis of aerial photographs, which have provided a basic plan of the site (Figure 4.38). Some geophysical prospection (magnetic gradiometry) was carried out in the levelled area, however the results were mostly negative.

Site morphology

The inner enclosure measures 200m (north-west/south-east) by 145m (north-east/south-west), and has a perimeter of 580m and an internal area of approximately 2.57ha. The middle enclosure measures 315m (north-west/south-east) by 230m (north-east/south-west), with a perimeter of 920m and an internal area of 3.85ha. The third enclosure proposed by Condit and O'Sullivan (1996; 1999) measures approximately 490m (north-west/south-east) by 365m (north-east/south-west), based on projecting a number of short ditch lengths. The perimeter of that third enclosure is estimated at 1450m, over an area of 9.7ha. This represents an overall hillfort area of 16.1ha (reduced to 6.4ha taking only the inner and middle enclosures). There are no entrances to any of these enclosures obvious on the ground or in aerial photographs.

The enclosing elements are best exposed on the southern side of the hillfort, where the banks are 2–4m wide and 0.2–0.5m high, with the adjacent ditch 1.5–3m wide and 0.2–0.4m deep. The latter can vary depending on slope, with the maximum height from base of ditch to top of inner bank estimated at 1–1.2m (Hickey and Hogan 2005). There are no recorded archaeological features in the interior of this hillfort, apart from a small cairn near the summit. It is not known if the latter is of any antiquity, as it may be a clearance feature connected to recent turf cutting, or possibly an early Ordnance Survey marker similar to that found at Clashanimud hillfort (Figure 3.60). The summit is over-grown today, with no clear indication of either the cairn, or a low earthwork that Condit (1995: 37) also recorded in that area.

Archaeological investigation

The main purpose of the Formoyle excavation was to obtain information on the enclosing elements of the hillfort, including their original size and form, and the methods and materials employed in construction. It was also hoped to date the construction sequence, and the chronology of site occupation and abandonment. This required the recovery of radiocarbon samples, artifacts and environmental evidence.

Three trenches were excavated over a three-week period in late August 2012 (Figure 4.38). Trench 1 was located across the inner enclosing element; Trench 2 across the middle example, and Trench 3 across that of the proposed outer enclosure (O'Brien 2012c). Prior to excavation these 'defences' were visible as low-relief depressions indicating a ditch with an internal bank.

All three trenches were de-turfed by spade. Subsequent excavation was carried out by hand using small digging equipment. This involved detailed stratigraphic excavation and context-based recording, with full written descriptions, photography and scale drawings. On completion of work the trenches were back-filled by hand and the ground surface restored.

Excavation Results: Trench 1

An 8m (N–S) by 3m (E–W) trench was excavated across the line of the inner enclosure on the southern side of the hillfort (Figure 4.38). This was subsequently extended with a 2.5m by 2.4m cutting at the north-west corner, to give a total excavation area of 30m2. The only features visible in Trench 1 prior to excavation were a shallow ditch with a low bank on either side (Figure 4.39).

There is a continuous growth of blanket peat across the trench area. This ranged in thickness 0.15–0.18m at the northern end, to 0.04–0.15m over the inner bank, 0.26–0.3m at the base of the ditch, 0.08–0.14m over the outer bank and 0.05–0.07m at the eastern end of the trench. The variation in peat thickness is partly because this part of the hill was cut for turf in the modern era (local information). There are indications of old turf banks adjacent to the excavation area.

The removal of peat at the southern end of Trench 1 exposed a typical stagnopodzol profile. The extreme acidification and leaching of this soil resulted in the formation of a gleyed layer (C.03) beneath the peat. This overlay an orange-brown, stony layer (C.14) with iron sesquioxide precipitation. This B-horizon subsoil overlay either eroding (C.15) or solid bedrock.

The subsoil profile at the northern end of the trench, inside the inner bank, differed in two respects. A layer of compact brown peat sediment (C.02) containing small stones and charcoal flecks was discovered directly beneath the peat. This overlay the gleyed surface (C.03), beneath which there was a stony B–horizon (C.14) with reduced iron precipitation on eroding bedrock.

The gleying process extended over the surface of the inner bank as a thin layer (C.03) overlying an even thinner band of iron pan (C.08). The excavation of this bank exposed an old ground surface, comprising a thin layer of grey-brown organic silt (C.12). This overlay a leached horizon (C.13), which was not subjected to a gleying process due to the overlying bank, and so was not as compact as the C.03 gley.

Archaeological Features (Trench 1)

Excavation revealed a shallow ditch with a low earthen bank on either side (Figure 4.40). A line of stakeholes on the inside of the inner bank provides evidence of wooden fencing in the original enclosure. There is no indication of any activity in this area pre-dating the hillfort, with the possible exception of charcoal flecks discovered on the pre-bank old ground surface (C.12).

FIGURE 4.39: SURFACE EXPOSURE OF BANK/DITCH/BANK DEFENCES OF INNER ENCLOSURE, FORMOYLE, PRIOR TO EXCAVATION.

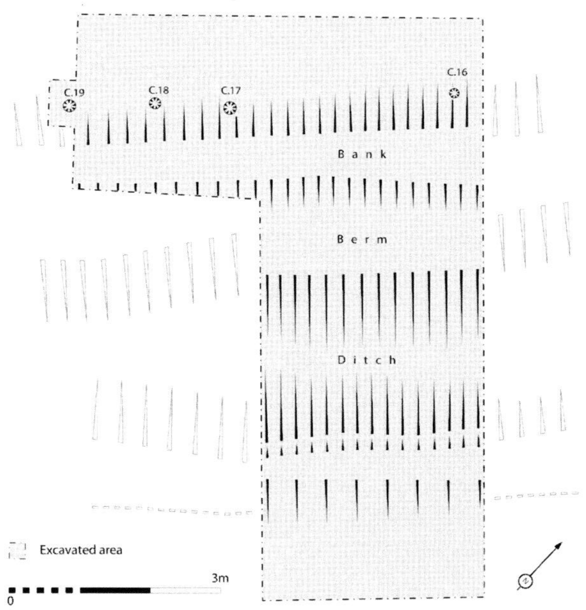

FIG. 4.40: PLAN OF TRENCH 1 FEATURES AT FORMOYLE HILLFORT, SHOWING LINE OF STAKEHOLES ON INNER SIDE OF MAIN BANK.

Inner bank

This comprised a small dump of redeposited subsoil on the northern side of the ditch, separated from the latter by a 0.9m wide sloping berm (Figure 4.41). The bank measured 1.4–1.8m in width, with a central (eroded) height of 0.3–0.35m. It was composed of a single deposit of orange sandy silt (C.10) containing fragments of broken stone. This material was originally extracted from the ditch, where B-horizon subsoil and a small amount of bedrock was removed. There was some sediment slip (C.09) on the immediate inside and exterior of the bank. That erosion was limited by the onset of gleying (C.03) and iron panning (C.08), both of which stabilised the bank surface. There is no evidence of any stone revetment used in this bank.

Stake fence

Excavation identified a line of stakeholes on the inside of the inner bank (Figure 4.40). Five definite and two possible stakeholes, spaced 0.5–1.15m apart, extended in an east–west line along the inner edge of the bank (Figure 4.42). These include (from east to west) contexts 11, 16, 17, 18 and 19. These were all produced by driving pointed roundwood stakes, measuring 0.11–16m diameter, into the subsoil to a depth of 0.17–0.39m. Also relevant is a shallow depression on the B-horizon surface 0.4m west of C.16, and a similar example 0.4m to the west of that. These two features (no context numbers assigned) cannot be confirmed as stakeholes, but it is significant that they occur along the same line as the context 11/16/17/18/19 stake row.

Ditch

Excavation exposed a shallow cut 0.9m outside the inner bank (Figure 4.40). This ditch averaged 2m in width from the top of old ground surface cut, while the central depth from the crest of the adjacent banks was 0.6–0.65m. The ditch cut through the B-horizon subsoil down to the bedrock surface (Figure 4.43). Some of the latter was removed, probably to a depth of less than 0.2m. The southern side of the ditch is more gently sloping than the inner side. The base is gently rounded, with a irregular profile due to haphazard removal of bedrock.

The ditch was infilled to a depth of 0.35–0.38m (Figure 4.41). The upper 0.26–0.3m comprised blanket peat (C.01), the surface of which may have been cut over during turf extraction in the twentieth century. The C.01 peat overlay a deposit of stony grey silt with charcoal flecks (C.04), which represents an early phase of organic silting. There was a thin deposit of sterile fine silt (C.05) at the base of the ditch, mostly occuring in the crevices of the broken bedrock.

Outer 'bank'

Prior to excavation there was some indication of a low counterscarp bank bordering the exterior of the ditch. This was a small deposit of subsoil overlying an old ground surface, measuring 1.05m in width and up to 0.16m high (Figure 4.41). This soil was placed along the ditch edge to prevent inwash of extraneous material.

Charcoal deposits
Excavation on the inside of the bank uncovered a peaty surface (C.02) with occasional charcoal flecks (Figure 4.41). The age of this charcoal is not known, nor its relationship to the hillfort occupation.

List of excavation contexts, Formoyle hillfort

Context 01. Mid-brown fibrous peat with *Molinia* and *Calluna* vegetation; no stones.

C.02. Thin layer of root-matted peat under C.01 inside bank, with small stones and charcoal.

C.03. Gleyed surface under peat; compact grey-brown silt, small stones and charcoal flecks.

C.04. Lower ditch sediment; grey-brown rooty silt with broken stones and flecks of charcoal.

C.05. Thin deposits of fine green-grey silt at base of ditch in contact with bedrock.

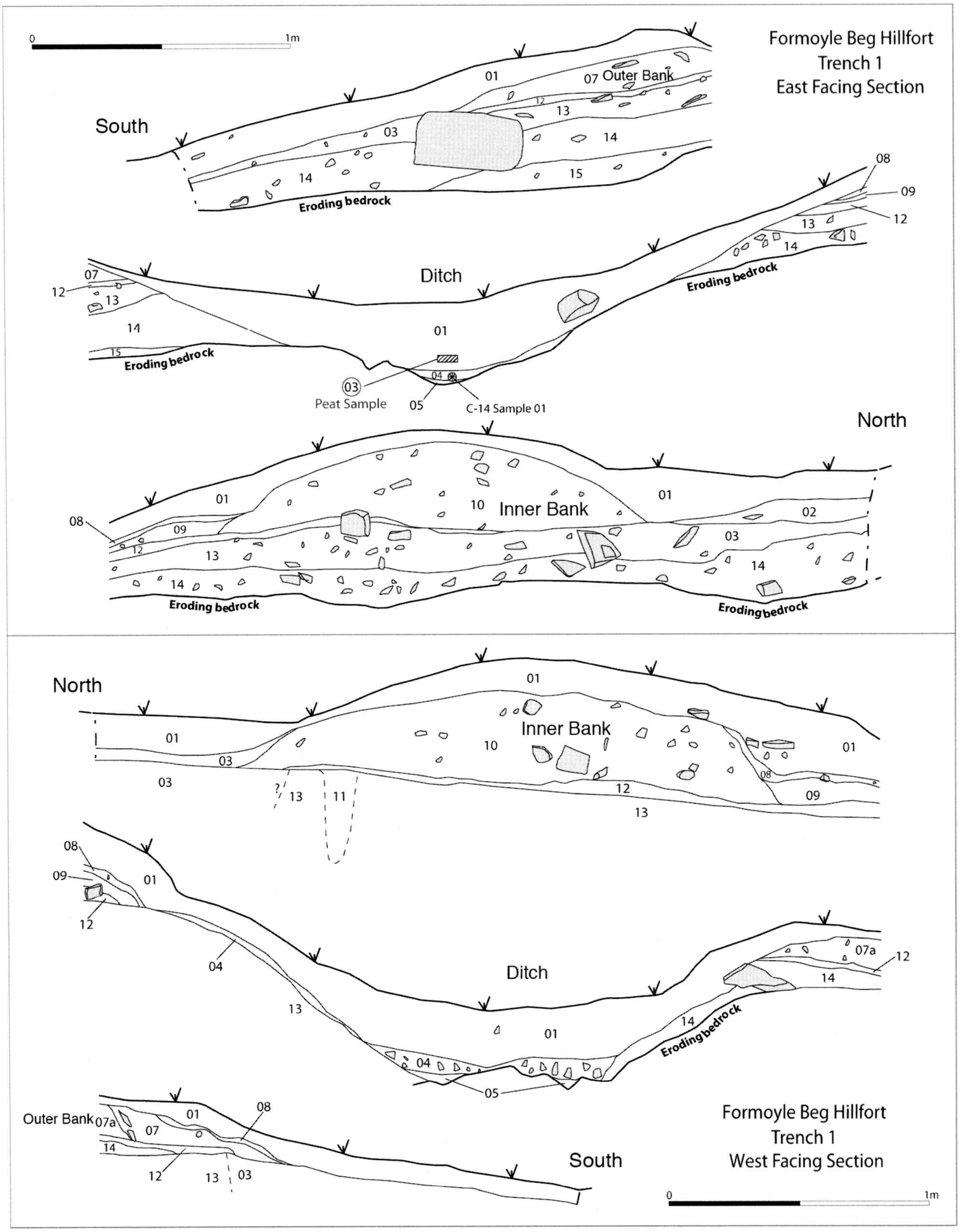

FIGURE 4.41: STRATIGRAPHIC SECTIONS ACROSS ENCLOSING ELEMENTS IN TRENCH 1.

Figure 4.42: Excavation of stakeholes on inner side of main bank, Trench 1, Formoyle.

Figure 4.43: Main bank (section) and ditch of inner enclosure after excavation, Trench 1, Formoyle.

C.06. Cut of ditch (see main text).

C.07. Exterior 'bank' of loose orange-brown silt with small broken stones (see main text).

C.08. A 2–3cm thick band of orange-red iron pan on lower exterior slope of inner bank.

C.09. Slip deposit of loose orange silt, some stones, on exterior side of inner bank.

C.10. Inner bank of bright orange sandy silt, loose with broken stone (see main text).

C.11. Stakehole inside main bank; sub-circular cut, 0.11m by 0.13m, vertical to depth of 0.36m with point; fill of loose orange-grey silt with a few small stones, but no charcoal.

C.12. Old ground surface under banks; thin layer of grey-brown fine silt, charcoal flecks.

C.13. Leached layer beneath banks; grey-light brown silt with some small stones.

C.14. Bs-horizon subsoil; compact bright orange silt with numerous stones; iron-enriched.

C.15. Eroding bedrock.

C.16. Possible stakehole 0.53m west of C.11 stakehole. Circular 0.14m cut, with vertical depth of 0.17m. Filled with loose, bright orange silt; no charcoal.

C.17. Stakehole inside main bank; exposed on old ground surface (C.12). Circular 0.15m cut, with vertical depth of 0.34m; filled with loose blue-grey silt with small stones; no charcoal.

C.18. Stakehole on C.12 surface inside main bank, 1m west of C.17. Sub-circular 0.13m by 0.11m cut, vertical depth of 0.39m; fill of loose grey silt, small stones, flecks of charcoal.

C.19. Stakehole under C.03 gley inside main bank, 1.15m west of C.18. Sub-circular 0.16m by 0.14m cut, vertical depth of 0.17m; fill of loose grey-brown silt, small stones, no charcoal.

Excavation Results: Trench 2

This 9m (north–south) by 3m (east–west) cutting was excavated across the line of the second enclosure at Formoyle, 60m to the south/south-east of Trench 1 (Figure 4.38). As with Trench 1, there is surface evidence that blanket peat growth across this area was cut in the modern era (Figure 4.44). The surviving peat ranges in thickness from 0.23–0.27m at the northern end, 0.2–0.4m over the bank, 0.25–0.31m in the ditch and 0.09–0.27m

FIGURE 4.44: GENERAL VIEW OF TRENCH 2 LOOKING SOUTH, SHOWING BANK/DITCH/BANK ARRANGEMENT.

at the southern end of the trench. This comprised an upper layer of dark brown fibrous peat (C.20) overlying more humified black peat (C.21). The peat was removed to expose a gleyed surface (C.22) across the entire trench area. This ranged in thickness from 0.1–0.15m at the northern end, to 0.05m over the bank, up to 0.12m in the lower ditch and up to 0.15m at the southern end of the trench. A band of red-orange iron pan, 2–4cm in thickness, was discovered on the surface of the inner bank underneath this gley, and in some other parts of the trench.

Excavation revealed a thin old ground surface (C.46) beneath the bank in this trench (Figure 4.45). Traces of this surface were also visible on the inside of the bank, where there was a thin band of grey-brown fibrous silt (C.47) at the base of the C.22 gley. The natural subsoil at the southern end of the trench comprised an upper B-horizon of stony, yellow-brown silt (C.48) over a lower B-hori-

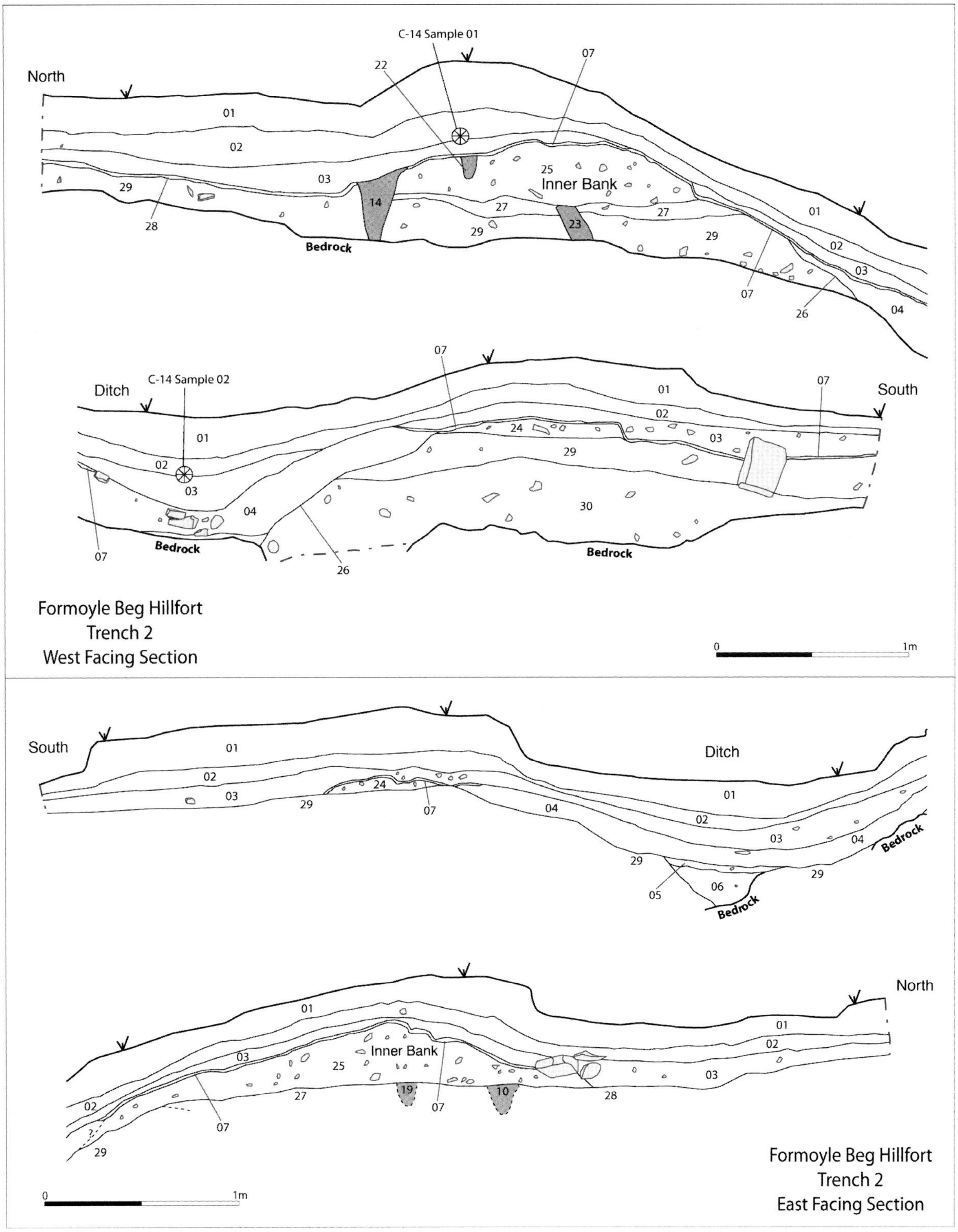

FIGURE 4.45: STRATIGRAPHIC SECTIONS ACROSS BANK-AND-DITCH IN TRENCH 2, FORMOYLE.

zon of orange-brown colour (C.49), both with obvious iron enrichment. This subsoil overlay eroding bedrock, which is obviously high in that area as a low outcrop of rock is visible a few metres to the west of Trench 2.

Archaeological Features

Excavation uncovered a single bank and ditch arrangement with evidence for an associated stake fence on the inside of the bank (Figure 4.46). There is no evidence of any activity pre-dating this hillfort, apart possibly from some charcoal flecking on the pre-bank ground surface.

Inner bank

A low bank on the immediate northern side of the ditch measured 1.7m in width with a central eroded height of 0.34m (Figure 4.45). This was composed of a single deposit of loose, iron-enriched, stony silt (C.44), which included some broken stone as well as rounded clasts. The outer (southern) side of the bank was eroded, with sediment slip (C.23) into the adjacent ditch. The upper surface of the bank was consolidated by a thin layer of iron pan (C.26) and gley (C.22). There is no indication of any stone revetment in this bank.

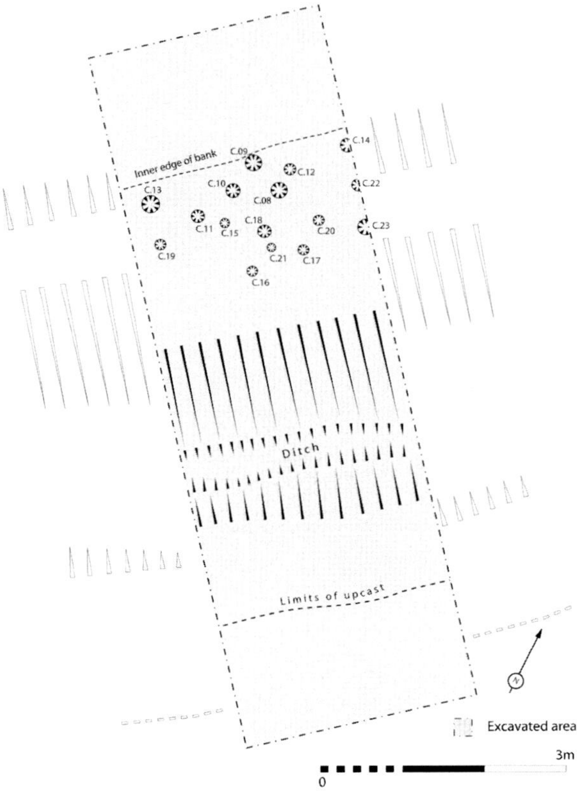

Figure 4.46: Plan of excavated features in Trench 2, Formoyle, showing band of stakeholes within the inner bank of the outer hillfort enclosure.

Stake fence

Excavation identified an arrangement of 16 stakeholes (C.27–42) along the inner side and slope of the bank (Figure 4.45). This includes three examples exposed in the west-facing section (Figure 4.47). Some of these were first visible on the inner surface of the bank, while others were only exposed on the underlying old ground surface once the bank was removed (Figure 4.48). This is because the original wooden stakes had been pulled out, and the cuts of some examples were not well exposed against the bank material that infilled the resulting voids.

These stakeholes range 0.07–0.2m in width and 0.12–0.51in depth. Most had pointed ends and were driven vertically, with the exception of C.42 placed at a 60° angle. The majority penetrated the old ground level (C.46) down to the bedrock surface, however at least five examples (contexts 34, 35, 36, 37 and 41) were driven into the bank material (C.44), but not into the underlying old ground surface.

The stakeholes were arranged in a broad east–west band along the inner side of the bank (Figure 4.46). This relates to a light wooden fence that was partly supported by the bank material. The irregular distribution of stakeholes is probably due to the replacement of some individual stakes in this fence over time.

Significant amounts of charcoal were found in only three of these 16 stakeholes (contexts 27, 28 and 41). Only one of these (C.27) contained enough charcoal to indicate that the stake was burnt *in situ*. The other stakeholes had silty fills with a low organic content, indicating the original stakes had been removed during the dismantling of this fence.

Ditch

This shallow cut on the immediate outside of the bank was c.2.7m wide and c.0.7m deep, with a gently rounded base (Figure 4.46). It was dug through the subsoil horizon (C.48/C.49), with bedrock exposed at the base and along the northern side. The ditch sides are gently sloping, with an irregular 0.3–0.4m wide channel at the bedrock base (Figure 4.49).

The ditch was infilled to a maximum depth of 0.65m (Figure 4.45). The upper 0.25–0.31m consisted of peat (C.20/C.21), which overlay a gley layer (C.22) to a maximum thickness of 0.12m. The removal of this gley exposed three thin sediments at the base of the ditch. The

FIGURE 4.47: STAKEHOLES EXPOSED IN WEST-FACING SECTION, TRENCH 2, FORMOYLE.

FIGURE 4.48: STAKEHOLES ON INNER SIDE OF MAIN BANK, TRENCH 1, FORMOYLE.

FIGURE 4.49: DITCH OF FORMOYLE SECOND ENCLOSURE DURING EXCAVATION.

first of these was an orange sandy silt (C.23), probably representing inwash of eroded bank material. This overlay a thin deposit of light brown silt with some charcoal flecks (C.24), representing an early phase of organic sedimentation in the lower ditch. Finally, a thin deposit of green-yellow silt at the base of the ditch probably derived from primary erosion of the ditch sides.

Exterior 'bank'

A small deposit of loose brown silt (C.43), measuring 0.8m wide by <0.1m in thickness, was identified along the exterior edge of the ditch (Figure 4.45). This counterscarp feature represents subsoil from the ditch placed along its exterior edge to prevent inwash of extraneous sediment.

List of excavation contexts, Trench 2, Formoyle hillfort

Context 20. Dark brown fibrous peat with *Molinia* and *Calluna* vegetation; no stones.

C.21. Compact black peat, more humified and less rooty than overlying C.20. No stones.

C.22. Gley layer beneath peat, very compact fine grey silt, with fibrous texture. No stones.

C.23. Upper fill of ditch under C.22 gley; loose orange-brown fine silt with few stones.

C.24. Lower ditch sediment; loose dark brown silt, no stones, with flecks of charcoal flecks.

C.25. Compact fine grey-yellow silt on bedrock base of ditch; no stones or charcoal.

C.26. A 2–4cm thick layer of red-orange iron pan on top of the inner and exterior banks.

C.27. Stakehole under C.22 gley, inner side of main bank. Sub-circular 0.19m by 0.18m cut, vertical to depth of 0.47m; filled with large charcoal over mid-brown silt with small charcoal.

C.28. Stakehole driven into C.44 bank, 0.32m west of C.27. Sub-circular 0.22m by 0.18m cut, vertical to 0.31m depth; fill of large charcoal over orange-brown silt with small charcoal.

C.29. Stakehole on inside of main bank, 0.36m south-west of C.28. Circular 0.11m cut, vertical to depth of 0.51m; filled with loose mid-brown silt containing pebbles; no charcoal.

C.30. Stakehole under C.22 gley on inner side of main bank. Sub-circular 0.22m by 0.17m cut, vertical to depth of 0.34m; fill of orange-brown silt with pebbles; charcoal in upper fill.

C.31. Stakehole on inside of main bank, north of C.27. Circular 0.12m cut, vertical to depth of 0.33m; filled with loose light brown silt, some pebbles and rare charcoal flecks.

C.32. Stakehole on inside of main bank, 0.48m north-west of C.30. Sub-circular 0.15m by 0.11m cut, vertical to depth of 0.16m; fill of orange-brown silt with pebbles; no charcoal.

C.33. Stakehole on inside of main bank, west-facing section. Circular 0.16m cut, vertical to depth of 0.36m; fill of loose mid-brown silt with some pebbles; no charcoal.

C.34. Stakehole under C.22 gley on inside of main bank, 0.42m south of C.29. Sub-circular 0.11m by 0.1m cut, vertical depth 0.16m; fill of orange-brown silt with pebbles; no charcoal.

C.35. Stakehole on crest of main bank, 0.4m south-east of C.34. Circular 0.09m cut, vertical to depth of 0.17m; fill of loose orange-brown silt with some pebbles; no charcoal.

C.36. Stakehole on crest of main bank to east of C.35. Sub-circular 0.1m by 0.07m cut, vertical to depth of 0.3m; fill of loose light brown silt with some pebbles; no charcoal.

C.37. Stakehole on inside of main bank, 0.34m south of C.27. Sub-circular 0.17m by 0.13m cut, vertical to depth of 0.16m; fill of light brown silt with some pebbles and charcoal flecks.

C.38. Stakehole on west side of inner slope of inner bank. Sub-circular 0.12m by 0.1m cut, vertical to depth of 0.15m; fill of light brown silt with some pebbles; no charcoal.

C.39. Stakehole on inside of main bank, south-east of C.27. Sub-circular 0.09m by 0.07m cut, vertical to depth of 0.13m; fill of light brown silt with some pebbles; no charcoal.

C.40. Stakehole on crest of main bank between C.35 and C.36. Sub-circular 0.1m by 0.08 by 0.12m deep cut, slight incline to north; fill of light brown silt, some pebbles; no charcoal.

C.41. Stakehole under C.22 gley on inside of main bank, west-facing section. Circular 0.07m cut, vertical to depth of 0.19m; fill of loose dark brown silt with numerous flecks of charcoal.

C.42. Stakehole on crest of main bank, west-facing section. Circular 0.07m cut, 60° to depth of 0.27m; fill of loose light brown silt with a few pebbles and flecks of charcoal.

C.43. Counterscarp bank; loose deposit of light brown silt with some small stones.

C.44. Inner (main) bank; loosely compacted orange-brown silt with frequent broken stones.

C.45. Cut of ditch (see main text).

C.46. Old ground surface under inner bank; yellow-grey fine silt, orange mottles, no stones.

C.47. Old ground surface inside inner bank; thin layer of grey-brown fibrous silt; no stones.

C.48. Upper B-horizon subsoil. Layer of compact yellow-brown stony silt.

C.49. Lower B-horizon on eroding bedrock. Compact orange-brown stony silt, iron-enriched.

Excavation Results: Trench 3

This 6m (north-west/south-east) by 2m trench was excavated across the line of a shallow ditch on the north-west side of the hillfort (Figure 4.38). That feature had previously been interpreted as part of a third enclosure) of the hillfort (Condit 1995).

The area around Trench 3 was deep-ploughed in 2005 as part of agricultural land improvement on this hill. No trace of this ploughing is visible on the ground surface today, where there is light grass and rush growth. Excavation revealed a continuous layer of peat (C.50) across the trench area, ranging 0.2–0.25m in thickness at the north-west end to 0.18–0.28m on the south-east side (Figure 4.50). Deturfing revealed some oblique cuts through this peat, however it was otherwise undisturbed across the trench area.

This peat overlay a compact layer of gley (C.51), ranging 0.14–0.18m in thickness. This was underlain by a stony, iron-enriched B-horizon (C.55), on top of eroding bedrock, across the southern two-thirds of the trench. At the northern end of the trench, the C.51 gley overlay a spread of grey clayey silt (C.54) on top of the B-horizon. The origin of this C.54 sediment is not known, but it is believed to be of natural origin.

Archaeological features

Excavation identified only one feature of archaeological

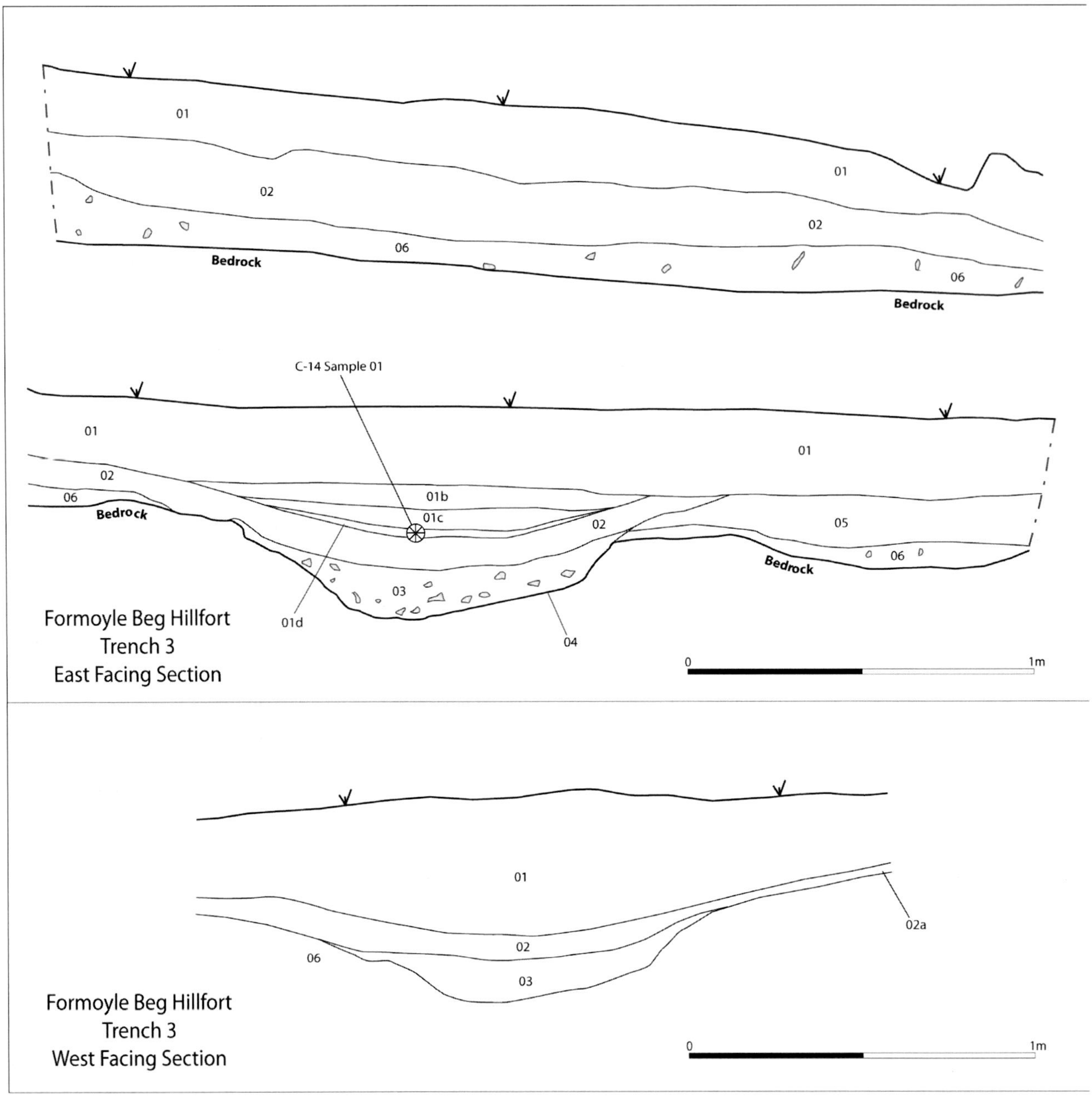

FIGURE 4.50: STRATIGRAPHIC SECTIONS, TRENCH 3, FORMOYLE.

interest in Trench 3. This is a shallow ditch, measuring 1.15–1.3m wide by 0.3–0.33m deep, which extended across the northern end of the trench in an east–west direction (Figure 4.51). This shallow cut (C.53) has gently sloping sides and a rounded base (Figure 4.52). It was sealed by a gleyed layer (C.51), but cut though the B-horizon (C.55), and also the C.54 layer. The western end of the excavated trench was cut into the eroding bedrock surface, whereas the eastern end did not (note: during excavation it proved difficult to distinguish the base of the B-horizon from the top of the eroding bedrock in that area).

This ditch was infilled to a depth of c.0.6m from the modern ground surface (Figure 4.50). The upper 0.36m consisted of peat (C.50) overlying a 0.12m thick gley layer (C.51). The peat infill was banded in the following sequence: C.50a dark brown fibrous peat overlying C.50b more humified black peat, over C.50c grey peat, over C.50d black peat. A thin deposit of grey silt (C.53) at the base did not contain charcoal or other archaeological material. Finally, there was no indication of a bank feature on either side of this 'ditch'.

List of excavation contexts, Trench 3, Formoyle hillfort

Context 50. Dark brown to black fibrous peat with

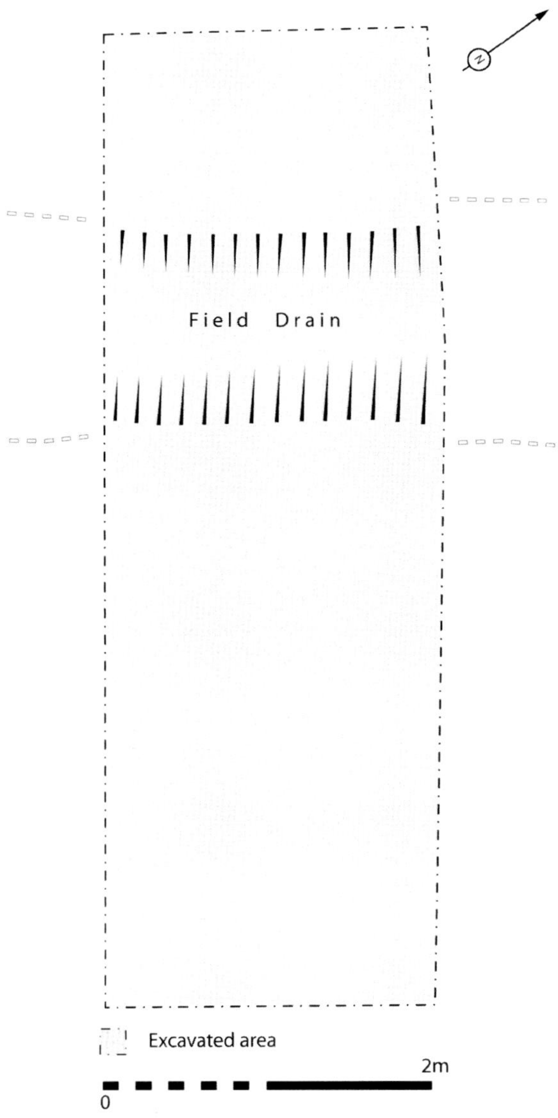

FIGURE 4.51: EXCAVATED FEATURES, TRENCH 3, FORMOYLE.

Molinia and *Calluna* vegetation.

C.51. Gleyed layer of grey fine silt; small stones and charcoal at contact with overlying peat.

C.52. Thin deposit of compact fine grey silt at base of ditch (C.04); occasional pebbles.

C.53 Cut of ditch (see main text).

C.54. Deposit of grey clayey silt at northern end of trench; fine sticky texture; no stones.

C.55. Layer of compact to loose, orange-brown silt, with frequent stones. Natural B-horizon.

Finds and dating

There are no artifact finds of any type from this excavation project.

Radiocarbon dating

In the absence of culturally significant finds, the dating of the excavated features at Formoyle must rely on the radiocarbon method. Eleven samples were submitted for AMS radiocarbon dating to the Centre for Isotope Research, University of Groningen. The sample details and results are as follows (Figure 4.53):

Sample FM2012-01: Charcoal from C.02 sediment at base of peat inside inner bank, inner hillfort enclosure. Wood species: hazel.
GrA-54956; 2840±30 BP

Sample FM2012-02: Charcoal from C.04 sediment at base of ditch, inner hillfort enclosure. Wood species: hazel.
GrA-54957; 2890±30 BP

Sample FM2012-03: Charcoal from old ground surface (C.12) at base of inner bank, inner hillfort enclosure. Wood species: ash.
GrA-54958; 3125±35 BP

Sample FM2012-04: Peat sample from base of peat infill in ditch of inner hillfort enclosure (east-facing section).
GrA-54959: 116.5±0.4% C (modern peat)

Sample FM2012-05: Charcoal from C.27 stakehole on inside of inner bank, second hillfort enclosure. Wood species: ash.
GrA-54961; 2880±30 BP

Sample FM2012-06: Charcoal from C.28 stakehole on inside of inner bank, second hillfort enclosure. Wood species: hazel.
GrA-54963; 2900±30 BP

Sample FM2012-07: Charcoal from C.41 stakehole on inside of inner bank, second hillfort enclosure. Wood species: hazel.
GrA-54964; 2880±30 BP

Sample FM2012-08: Charcoal from old ground surface (C.46) at base of inner bank, second hillfort enclosure. Wood species: hazel.
GrA-54965; 2920±35 BP

Sample FM2012-09: Peat sample from base of peat infill in ditch of second hillfort enclosure (west-facing section).
GrA-54966; 101.0±0.4% C (modern peat)

Sample FM2012-10: Peat sample from directly above surface of bank, second hillfort enclosure (west-facing section).
GrA-54967; 106.7±0.4% C (modern peat).

FIGURE 4.52: EXCAVATION OF PROBABLE FIELD DRAIN, TRENCH 3, FORMOYLE.

FIELD NO.	LAB NO.	C-14 BP	∂13C	95.4% CALIBRATION
FM2012-01	GRN-54956	2840±30	-27.75	1108–917 BC
FM2012-02	GRN-54957	2890±30	-26.72	1195–978 BC
FM2012-03	GRN-54958	3125±35	-28.18	1494–1289 BC
FM2012-04	GRN-54959	116.5±0.4% C	-29.16	MODERN PEAT
FM2012-05	GRN-54961	2880±30	-27.05	1192–939 BC
FM2012-06	GRA-54963	2900±30	-27.70	1207–1004 BC
FM2012-07	GRA-54964	2880±30	-28.08	1192–939 BC
FM2012-08	GRA-54965	2920±35	-26.07	1219–1011 BC
FM2012-09	GRA-54966	101.5±0.4% C	-29.54	MODERN PEAT
FM2012-010	GRA-54967	106.7±0.4% C	-28.90	MODERN PEAT
FM2012-011	GRA-54968	108.2±0.4% C	-28.81	MODERN PEAT

FIGURE 4.53: RADIOCARBON DATES FOR FORMOYLE HILLFORT (CALIBRATION AFTER OXCAL V.4.2.4).

Sample FM2012-11: Peat sample from base of peat infill in ditch of supposed third hillfort enclosure (possible agricultural drain).
GrA-54968; 108.2±0.4% C (modern peat)

Radiocarbon dating of charcoal (GrA-54957) from the base of the ditch in Trench 1 provides a *terminus ante quem* of 1195–978 BC for the digging of that feature. This can be usefully combined with calibrated date ranges of 1108–917 BC (GrA-54956) for charcoal from the ground surface inside the bank, and a *terminus post quem* result of 1494–1289 BC (GrA-54958) for charcoal under the bank. This suggests a construction date for the inner enclosure broadly centred on 1100 BC.

Turning to Trench 2, the most significant results are for charcoal samples taken from stakeholes connected to the bank fence. These have calibrated date ranges of 1207–1004 BC (GrA-54963), 1192–939 BC (GrA-54961) and 1192–939 BC (GrA-54964). When combined with a pre-bank charcoal result of 1218–1011 BC (GrA-54965), this points to occupation of the second enclosure during the eleventh century BC. Taken together, these radiocarbon results suggest that both enclosures were broadly contemporary, and may have been built at the same time.

Finally, the results for peat samples from the hillfort

ditches in Trenches 1 (GrA-54959) and 2 (GrA-54966) indicate that this peat growth is relatively recent, or has been contaminated by root activity. The modern date (GrA-54958) obtained for peat in Trench 3 relates to the upper part of the ditch fill, and so does not provide a reliable indication of age for that feature. As this 'ditch' is only 1.15–1.3m wide by 0.3m deep, the likelihood is that it is an agricultural drain of early modern date.

Discussion

The major aims of the 2012 excavation at Formoyle hillfort were achieved, namely to investigate the form and construction of the hillfort defences and recover samples for radiocarbon dating. The results of the latter provide an indication of when the hillfort was built, but do not clarify its occupation history. No evidence was discovered of any human activity pre-dating the hillfort, nor is there any information as to later activity on the hill before the early modern era.

Hillfort construction

The most significant results relate to the original hillfort defences, which radiocarbon dating indicates were built *c.*1100 BC. The excavation suggests the hillfort was bivallate, with a third enclosure identified by Condit (1995) unlikely to be an original feature. The physical form of the inner and second enclosing elements were similar, as were the methods used in their construction. In both cases this involved the digging of a shallow ditch through thin subsoil slightly into the bedrock surface. The ditch of the inner enclosure averaged 2.4m in width and 0.6m deep. The adjacent bank did not exceed 0.35m in (eroded) height. The ditch of the second enclosure was only around 2.7m wide by 0.7m deep, with the adjacent bank again not more than 0.35m in (eroded) height. Both enclosure banks were reinforced by wooden fences built using light roundwood stakes.

The techniques used in ditch quarrying and bank construction are not known. This must have been a laborious process involving pick-like tools of wood and/or bone, and possibly hammerstones. The miners were assisted in their efforts by the thin deposit of glacial till across this hillside, and also by the friable nature of the sub-surface bedrock. Fire was not employed in the quarrying of either hillfort ditch.

The ditch feature in Trench 3 is too small to be considered part of the original hillfort defences. The small size, and the radiocarbon result for peat infill, suggest it is more likely to be a field drain of early modern age.

Occupation and abandonment

The excavation did not produce any evidence for the occupation of this hillfort, apart from some charcoal deposition inside the bank of the inner enclosure. No artifacts, food residues or structural remains were uncovered. This is probably due to the limited area of investigation. Geophysical prospecting conducted by the project team in 2005 did not uncover evidence of built structures in the interior, though it should be noted that only a small portion of the interior was surveyed due to vegetation cover.

The 2012 investigation at Formoyle did not yield information on the final occupation of the hillfort nor its subsequent history. The abandonment of the site is marked archaeologically by the deliberate removal of the stakes used to fence off the inner and outer enclosures. It is also represented by the subsequent, and apparently uninterrupted, growth of blanket peat over the bank-and-ditch defences.

Cultural Landscape

The Broadford Gap is a natural routeway connecting the lowlands of south-east Clare to the Shannon River, with its important fording points at Killaloe, O'Brien's Bridge and Castleconnell. Condit and O'Sullivan (1999) have reviewed the prehistoric archaeology of this region, drawing attention to the large number of artifacts of Mesolithic to Iron Age date found at Killaloe. These include at least ten Bronze Age spearheads and swords, among other items of bronze metalwork, some of which could be contemporary with Formoyle hillfort (*ibid.*: 36).

No early artifact finds are recorded close to the hillfort itself. The *Record of Monuments and Places* (RMP) for Co. Clare lists a number of archaeological sites in the vicinity (source: archaeology.ie). These include two wedge tombs (RMP Cl044-051 and Cl044-053) and a megalithic structure (Cl044-052) within a 0.75km distance north of the hillfort. There are no recorded monuments on the eastern side of the hillfort, while to the south is an enclosure (Cl044-054) at the base of the hill. Five other enclosures (Cl044-046, -047, -048, -049, -050) are recorded within a 1km distance on the western side of the hillfort, with a wedge tomb (Cl044-045) located 1.3km to the south-west. It is notable that no burnt mounds (*fulacht fia*), standing stone monuments, funerary barrows or other late prehistoric monuments are recorded in the environs of the hillfort.

Wedge tombs were built at various times during the Chalcolithic and earliest Bronze Age (*c.*2500–1800 BC), with numerous examples in south-east Clare extending into the area of the Broadford Gap. While these monuments pre-date Formoyle hillfort, as tombs of the ancestors they may have had a special meaning for that community. The significance of the six enclosures within a kilometre of the hillfort is unknown. Some may be ringforts of the early medieval period, while others could be earlier or indeed later in date. Further research on these sites, involving detailed field survey, excavation and palaeoenvironmental studies, is required before any connection can be made to the hillfort.

4.4 Toor More, Co. Kilkenny

This hillfort is located on the western side of Toor More townland, with part of the outer enclosure extending into the neighbouring townland of Donaghmore, 2km east of Ballyragget village, Co. Kilkenny (Figure 4.54; ITM 647590, 671040). The site lies on the highest point (253m OD) of a north-west/south-east ridge, which overlooks a broad expanse of lowland stretching south from Ballyragget to Freshford, and south-east along the river Nore as far as Kilkenny city (Figure 4.55).

The hillfort is comprised of two sub-circular, concentric enclosures, separated by a distance of 105m (Figure 4.56). The diameter of the inner enclosure is approximately 145m (N–S) (130m internally) by 160m (E–W) (140m internally), over an area of 1.72ha (Figure 4.57). The outer enclosure is 320m (N–S) (305m internally) by approximately 340 (E–W), over an area of 7.22ha; the entire hillfort covers 8.94ha. The enclosing elements in both cases are visible as low relief banks, with no exposed ditches or other defensive features. There are no obvious archaeological features in the interior of the hillfort. The outer enclosure was cleared for grassland pasture in the modern era, apart from the north-west side which is now planted with conifers. The western half of the inner enclosure is also under pasture, while the eastern side is covered by scrub vegetation. This includes the summit area where recent disturbance was caused by the erection of a broadband mast.

Site history

There is no record of Toor More hillfort in the nineteenth-century mapping of the Ordnance Survey of Ireland. The north-west side of the outer enclosing element is evident in the field pattern depicted on the first edition (1840) of the six-inch survey. The earliest reference to the site is contained in Rev. Carrigan's History and Antiquities of the Diocese of Ossory, published in 1905. This refers to the hill of Corrandhu ('the Black Cairn') in the townland of Toor More, on the summit of which is a narrow rocky plateau where an ancient mound of stones may have once stood. This was surrounded by two oval ramparts of earth and stone, parts of which were already levelled when Carrigan made the following observation:

'Calcined human bones have been found on the fringe of the plateau, while quarrying operations were being carried on there; also in the inner rampart, within a square enclosure formed of flags; and also in glazed urns upturned while levelling part of the outer rampart, at the

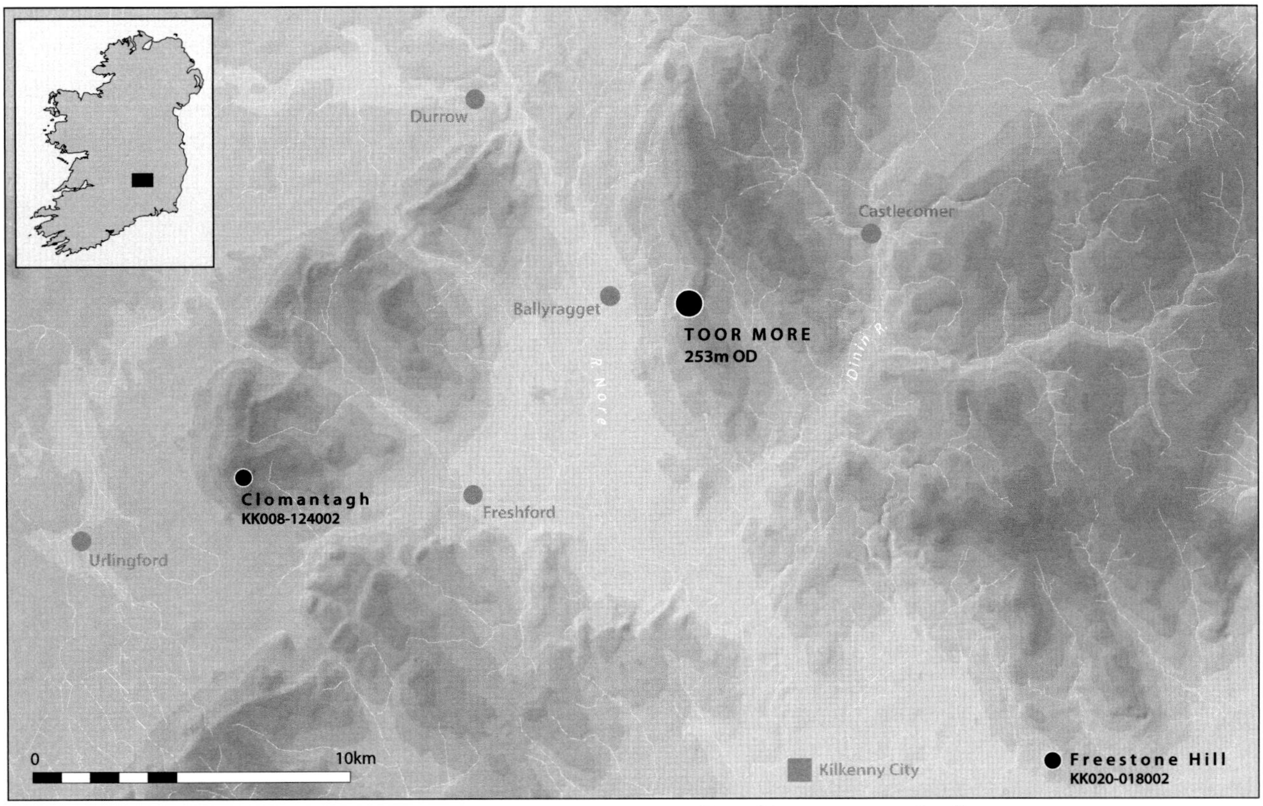

FIGURE 4.54: LOCATION AND LANDSCAPE SETTING OF TOOR MORE HILLFORT, CO. KILKENNY.

FIGURE 4.55: GENERAL VIEW OF TOOR MORE HILLFORT, LOOKING SOUTH.

west side. From this it may be assumed that Corrandhu was a favorite place of interment in pagan times, that it was, in fact, a pagan cemetery'.

The 'square enclosure formed of flags' may be located in the summit area, where lidar survey shows a rectangular enclosure, measuring approximately 135m (N–S) by 115m (E–W). This may be a burial ground of later date than the hillfort, though this remains to be confirmed by excavation.

Carrigan suggested that Corrandhu might be '...the last resting place of the celebrated champion, Lughaidh Mac na d-tri Con, who flourished about the commencement of the Christian era'. Citing an entry in the Book of Leinster that records his death at the hand of Conall Cearnach, Carrigan argued that the cairn on Corrandhu in the territory of Magh Argat-Ros is the most likely location of Lughaidh's grave. Another interpretation of the place-name (Corrandhu: 'the black sickle') might refer to the curve of that ridge extending south-east from Ballyraggett towards Castlecomer (Figure 4.54).

Condit and Gibbons (1988) brought Toor More hillfort to attention in the modern era, using aerial photographs to locate the two enclosures recorded by Carrigan. Arising from this, the site was listed in the *Record of Monuments and Places* for Co. Kilkenny (KK010-00701), along with the record of a 'burial' (KK010-00702).

Archaeological investigation

In 2013 James O'Driscoll carried out a geophysical survey at Toor More hillfort. A total of 7.1ha, approximately 80% of the hillfort area, was surveyed at 0.5m traverse and 0.125m sample intervals using a Bartington Grad 601 magnetic gradiometer (Figure 4.58). This revealed distinctive anomalies along both enclosing elements, as well as some evidence for built structures and pits in the interior. The hillfort defences are imaged as bands of high and low magnetic readings, the former following the crest of the partially levelled banks, with lower readings on either side. There is some variation at the northern side of the outer enclosing element, where there are two positive responses at the crest of the bank. A band of strong magnetic disturbance on the outside of the banks of both enclosures represents an external ditch that is now infilled (O'Driscoll 2013).

The magnetic survey revealed several narrow breaks in the inner enclosing element. Some of these may relate to agricultural drainage in the modern era. A 14m wide gap on the northern side may represent an original entrance (Figure 4.58: no. 1). There are strong responses from two pit-like features within this gap, which may represent gate posts destroyed by fire. There are indications of a possible entrance on the south-east side of the outer enclosing element, where a central anomaly within a 7m wide break may also be a gate-post (Figure 4.58: no. 3). The identification of both entrances remains to be confirmed by excavation. It is notable that they are

Figure 4.56: Satellite photograph of Toor More hillfort (source: Google Earth 2017). Location of two excavation trenches marked.

not aligned, though this can occur in Class 2 hillforts in Ireland.

There are limited geophysical responses for occupation in the interior of the hillfort. A number of possible structures are visible in the results, the largest being a possible sub-circular structure 22m outside the suggested entrance to the inner enclosure (Figure 4.58: no. 2). The general absence of structural features suggests the hillfort was not occupied over a long period. There are a significant number of large point anomalies in the inner enclosure, which may represent pits or areas of burning rather than built structures. These features may indicate a concentration of activity in the inner enclosure, but this remains to be confirmed by excavation. Finally, the eastern half of the inner enclosure could not be surveyed as it is covered by thick gorse. Therefore, it was not therefore possible to investigate the possible burial ground ('square enclosure formed of flags') recorded by Carrigan.

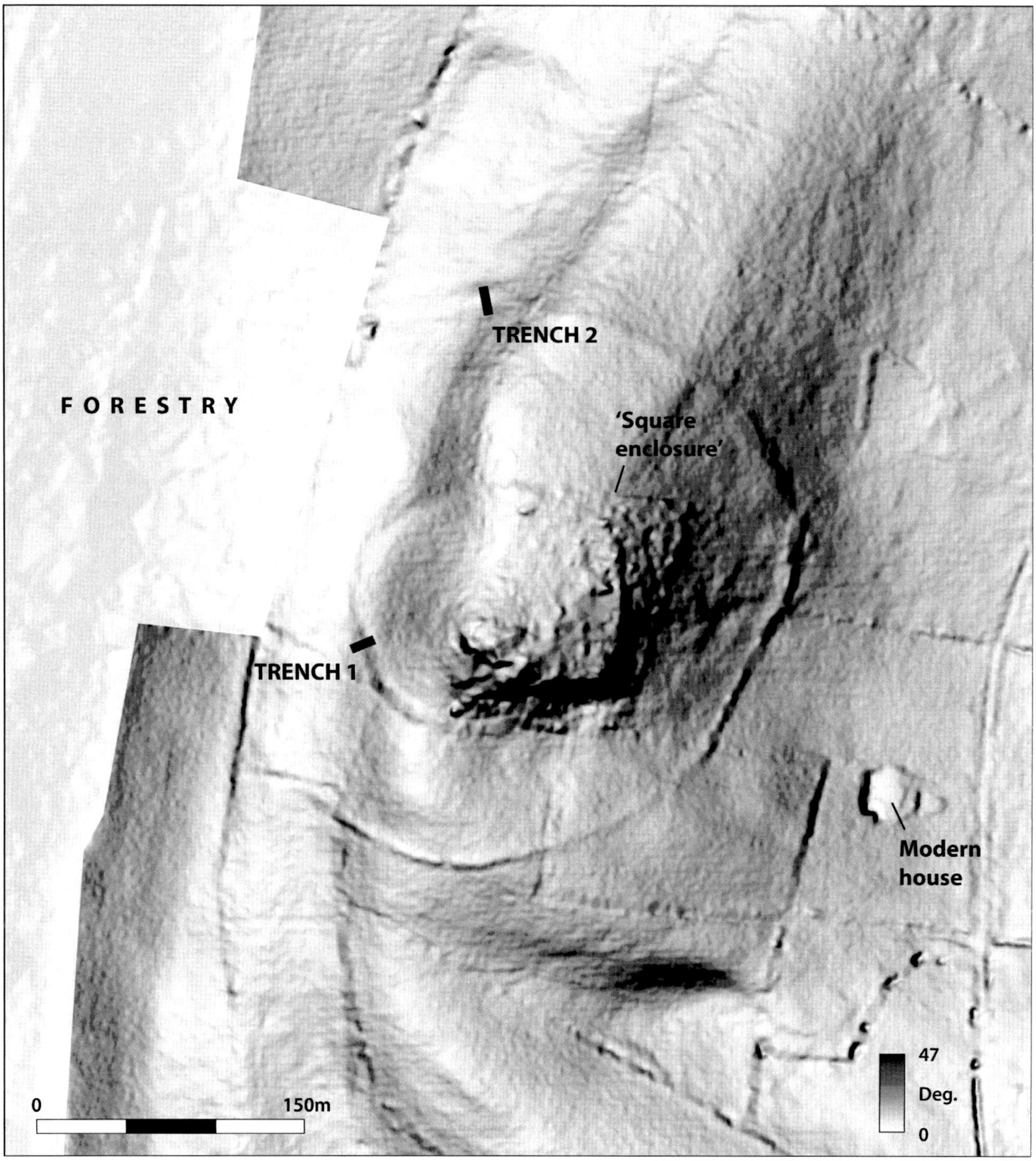

Figure 4.57: Slope model of aerial Lidar data, Toor More hillfort, showing excavation across defences of inner (Trench 1) and outer (Trench 2) enclosures, as well as location of Carrigan's 'square enclosure'.

Excavation strategy

Two trenches were excavated at Toor More hillfort in a four-week period in August 2013 (Figure 4.57). Trench 1 was located on the western line of the inner enclosure, with Trench 2 across the outer enclosure on the northern side (O'Brien 2013). The main purpose of the excavation was to obtain information on the defences of the hillfort. This includes details of their design and the methods and materials employed in construction. It was hoped to obtain evidence for the date(s) of construction and abandonment of the hillfort based on the history of these defences. There was also a possibility of recovering artifacts and environmental evidence relating to the occupation of the site.

Inner enclosure (Trench 1)

A 13m (E–W) by 2.5m trench was excavated across the

Figure 4.58: Results of magnetic gradiometry at Toor More hillfort, showing location of possible entrances to inner [1] and outer [3] enclosures, as well as possible built structure [2].

western defences of the inner enclosure (Figure 4.59). Excavation revealed a thin organic soil overlying a silty clay subsoil of fluvio-glacial origin. The topsoil is free of large stones, having been ploughed, drained and fertilised for grassland pasture in the modern era. Bedrock was exposed at a depth of 0.7–0.9m, at the base of the hillfort ditch. This is an eroded marine shale with lenses containing small nodules of iron oxide.

The excavation of Trench 1 revealed a levelled earthwork comprised of an earthen bank with stone facing, and an external ditch. A slot trench used for a wooden palisade was discovered on the inside of the bank. These features are described as follows:

Ditch

The removal of 0.3m of organic soil at the western side of the trench exposed a deposit of large stones in the up-

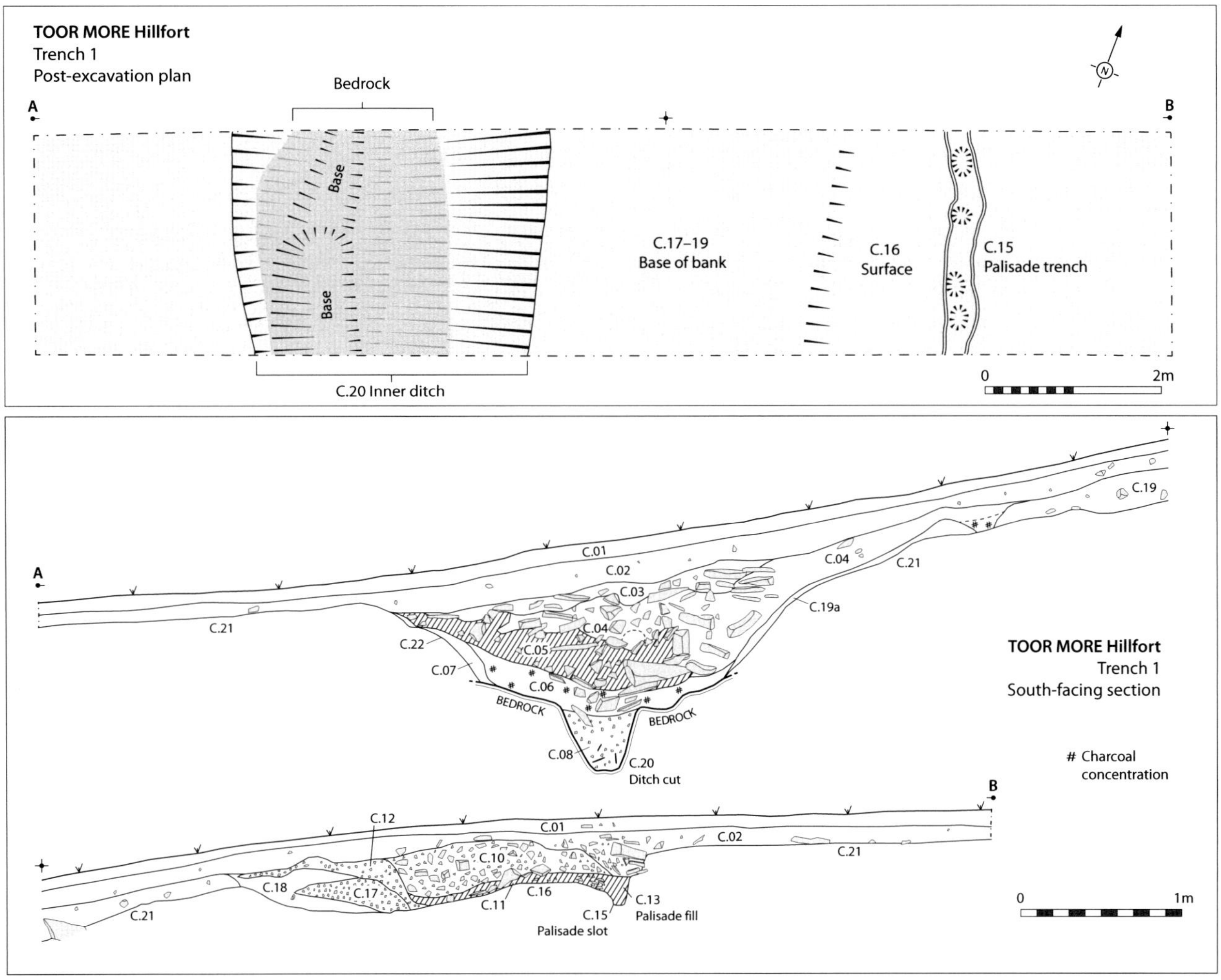

FIGURE 4.59: POST-EXCAVATION PLAN AND STRATIGRAPHIC SECTION ACROSS DEFENCES OF INNER ENCLOSURE, TRENCH 1, TOOR MORE.

per part of the ditch. The removal of this fill exposed a 2.4m length of ditch (C.20), the upper part of which was cut into an iron-stained B-horizon (C.21) to a depth of 0.4m. Below this level the ditch cut through a 0.3m thick layer of glacial clay (C-horizon; C.22) to a further depth of 0.6–0.8m into bedrock.

The ditch is V-shaped in cross section, with steeply sloping sides (Figure 4.60). The upper part (top of B-horizon cut) ranges 3.2–3.6m in width, narrowing to 1.85–1.95m in the mid section (top of bedrock cut), with a 0.3–0.4m wide gully at the base. The ditch ranged in depth (top of B-horizon cut) from 1.2m on the north side to 1.5m on the south side, with a 0.55–0.8m depth of bedrock extracted at the base.

The inner (eastern) side of the ditch has a steeply sloping profile, extending from the top of the B-horizon to a depth of 0.3–0.35m where it is almost vertical. The lower slope is entirely in bedrock with a rotten appearance, the result of water flowing down the ditch sides. The exterior of the ditch has a steeper profile, with two irregular ledges 0.5m and 0.7m respectively above the base.

The upper fill of the ditch comprised several deposits of small and large stones, with finer clay and silt sediments at the base (Figure 4.59). The infilling process began soon after the ditch was dug, when a 0.3–0.4m thick deposit of finely broken shale in a clayey matrix (C.08) accumulated within the gully at the base. This contained a few large sandstone slabs, but was otherwise free of large stones. A small quantity of waterlogged wood in the lower part of C.08 included twigs and young roundwood stems, as well as pieces of what may be worked wood, none of which were charred.

The basal sediment is the result of an influx of eroding bank material that occurred early in the history of the enclosure. This comprised finely broken shale extracted from the lower ditch, along with an inwash of clay and silt from the bank. Some primary erosion (C.07) was identified along the upper exterior slope of the ditch. The next stage in the ditch fill is represented by a 0.1–0.2m thick deposit of grey clay with iron oxide mottles (C.06). This sediment was washed into the open ditch, along with a significant amount of charcoal and a large number of tabular sandstone slabs. Context 06 derives from the

FIGURE 4.60: DITCH OF INNER ENCLOSURE, TRENCH 1, TOOR MORE HILLFORT.

burning of a nearby palisade, followed soon after by the collapse of the stone wall or revetment associated with the bank.

This destruction led to further deposition of large stones (C.04 and C.05) into the ditch, some of which sank into the C.06 silt (Figure 4.61). These were mostly tabular slabs of coarse sandstone, 0.2–0.55m in length and 0.05–0.12m in thickness, with a small number of blockier examples. None of these were fire-reddened or had any man-made markings. It was initially thought they came from the ditch, but geological examination revealed a different rock type (sandstone) than the local marine shale. The stones seem to have been brought from elsewhere for use in the bank walling (see below), mainly because the friable shale in the lower ditch was unsuitable for that purpose. Though slightly weathered, the regular shape suggests they are more likely to have been quarried than collected as field stones.

The rapid accumulation of stone in the ditch occurred at a time when that feature was open. As stated, the lower stones were partly embedded in the charcoal-flecked silt (C.06) linked to the palisade burning. The upper stones (C.04 and C.05) were very loose, with numerous voids and pockets of white sticky clay (C.22) that represents inwash of fine sediment from the bank. The upper part of the stony deposit (C.04) also had a silty clay matrix, again probably connected to bank erosion.

FIGURE 4.61: STONES FROM COLLAPSED BANK REVETMENT IN UPPER FILL OF EXTERNAL DITCH, TRENCH 1, TOOR MORE.

Bank

Prior to excavation this feature was visible as a low rise in the field, with no indication of an external ditch. The base of the bank survived to a maximum height of 0.35m, averaging 0.1–0.15m across a 3.3m wide area inside the inner edge of the ditch (Figure 4.59). The original form of the bank may be reconstructed from this surviving base, and from erosion deposits in the adjacent ditch. The builders created a platform made of clay and silty clay subsoil and finely broken shale upcast from the ditch. The main bank deposit (C.18 and C.19) was comprised of subsoil (C.21) extracted from the ditch. This was piled directly on B-horizon subsoil with no indication of a buried sod layer. There was some charcoal flecking on the pre-bank surface, but not enough to indicate pre-hillfort activity.

The main bank deposit was overlain on the inner (eastern) side of the bank by a deposit of finely broken stone (C.17) derived from the lower ditch bedrock. The original height of the bank is not known, but is unlikely to have exceeded 1–1.5m given the amount of soil and rock from the ditch. The presence of a large number of sandstone slabs in the upper and middle fill of the ditch can be linked to a stone wall or revetment built on or within the bank (Figure 4.62). Excavation did not clarify whether this was built at the same time as the bank, or at a later date. No portion of the stone wall has survived, and it seems to have either been pushed or collapsed into the open ditch as part of the destruction event, or soon afterwards. In terms of construction, the tabular form of the stones used suggests that regular coursing may have been employed, possibly bonded with sticky clay (C.22) extracted from the ditch.

Palisade

Excavation of an area 1.1m inside the inner (eastern) edge of the bank revealed a narrow slot trench with several post settings (C.15). This feature ran parallel to the bank, but seems to have been a separate structure (Figure 4.59). A 2.4m long section of this slot was excavated, measuring 0.2–0.3m in width, dug into the B-horizon (C.21) to a depth of 0.27–0.36m. Four post positions were identified in this slot, marked by circular depressions with rounded bases, around which there were small packing stones (C.14). The shape of the slot indicates a line of closely placed wooden posts, approximately 0.2m in diameter, which provided a frame for either smaller fencing posts and/or interwoven wattle.

The shallow depth of this slot trench is surprising given its exposed position on the hill. This suggests that the fence was not free-standing, but may have been braced using timbers placed at an angle between the upright posts and the inner base of the bank. This cannot be confirmed as post settings were not identified along the bank edge, where the surface was damaged by fire (C.12). The

FIGURE 4.62: DEFENCES OF INNER ENCLOSURE AT TOOR MORE, WITH DITCH AND PARTIAL RECONSTRUCTION OF STONE-FACED BANK AND PALISADE.

chronological relationship of the palisade to the bank and ditch is not certain. The bank is likely to have been present when the palisade was built, with both features possibly built at more or less the same time. The possibility must be considered that the palisade relates to a re-building or strengthening of the hillfort defences, or is earlier than the bank and ditch.

The excavation of Trench 1 did not recover any firm evidence for the occupation of the inner enclosure. Tiny fragments of unidentified bone around the palisade slot may represent food residues, but could be associated with either the construction or occupation of the hillfort.

Destruction event

Excavation uncovered evidence of intense burning along the inner side of the bank. The bank surface was fire-reddened with small deposits of charcoal (C.12). The same was observed in a 1m wide space between the inner bank edge and the palisade slot. Excavation in that area uncovered a fire-reddened surface (C.16), overlain by a 0.05m thick spread of charcoal and ashy soil (C.11). A charred timber on this C.16 surface was in a position that suggests it fell from the burning palisade (Figure 4.63). This charred wood and charcoal was preserved by an overlying spread of heat-shattered stone (C.10) in that area. Most of that stone was part of the inner face of the destroyed wall of the hillfort bank, as well as some packing material at the base of the palisade. The C.10 burnt stones covered the C.11 burnt layer to a depth of 0.25–0.3m (Figure 4.59).

List of excavation contexts, Trench 1, Toor More hillfort.

Context 01. Sod layer; mid brown loamy silt with very few clasts.

C.02. Lower A-horizon. Grey–light brown humic silt with some pebbles.

C.03. Loose tabular stones (<0.1–0.48m in length) in upper ditch fill.

C.04. Loose stones (<0.1–0.4m), with pockets of grey sticky clay in upper ditch.

C.05. Loose tabular stones (<0.1–0.35m) in white clay, in upper fill of ditch.

C.06. Deposit of grey clayey silt with charcoal in lower fill of ditch.

FIGURE 4.63: BURNT TIMBER NEXT TO PALISADE OF INNER ENCLOSURE, TRENCH 1, TOOR MORE.

C.07. Thin lens of grey clayey silt with charcoal flecks, upper east side of ditch.

C.08. Deposit of grey clayey silt, with waterlogged wood, at base of ditch.

C.09. Spread of broken stones (<0.1–0.3m) across eastern side of trench.

C.10. Band of fire-reddened stone (0.03–0.15m) in centre of C.09 stone deposit.

C.11. Charcoal surface under C.10, with charred timber, eastern side of trench.

C.12. Fire-reddened surface with charcoal on inner (eastern) side of bank.

C.13. Dark sandy silt with some charcoal and burnt bone, fill of C.15 slot trench.

C.14. Packing stones (0.19–0.34m) placed vertically or inclined in C.15 slot trench.

C.15. Cut of palisade slot on inner side of bank (see main text for description).

C.16. A 1.2–1.34m wide fire-reddened depression between slot trench and bank.

C.17. Broken shale forming inner slope of bank, with reddened surface (C.12).

C.18. Thin compact deposit of light brown silt with some shale in bank.

C.19. Orange silty-clay sediment, some stones, forming base of original bank.

C.19a. Slip of same into upper east side of ditch.

C.20. Cut of ditch (see main text for description).

C.21. Compact, orange/brown, silty clay, some large stones; B-horizon subsoil.

C.22. Hard orange clay, few stones; C-horizon subsoil of fluvio-glacial origin.

Outer enclosure (Trench 2)

A 14m (N–S) by 2.5m trench was excavated across the defences of the outer enclosure on the northern side of the hillfort, 201m to the north of Trench 1 (Figures 4.57 and 4.64). This revealed a large ditch with an internal bank, inside which there was a smaller ditch, and beyond this a separate slot for a light wooden fence (Figure 4.65).

FIGURE 4.64: EXCAVATION OF OUTER ENCLOSURE, TRENCH 2, TOOR MORE.

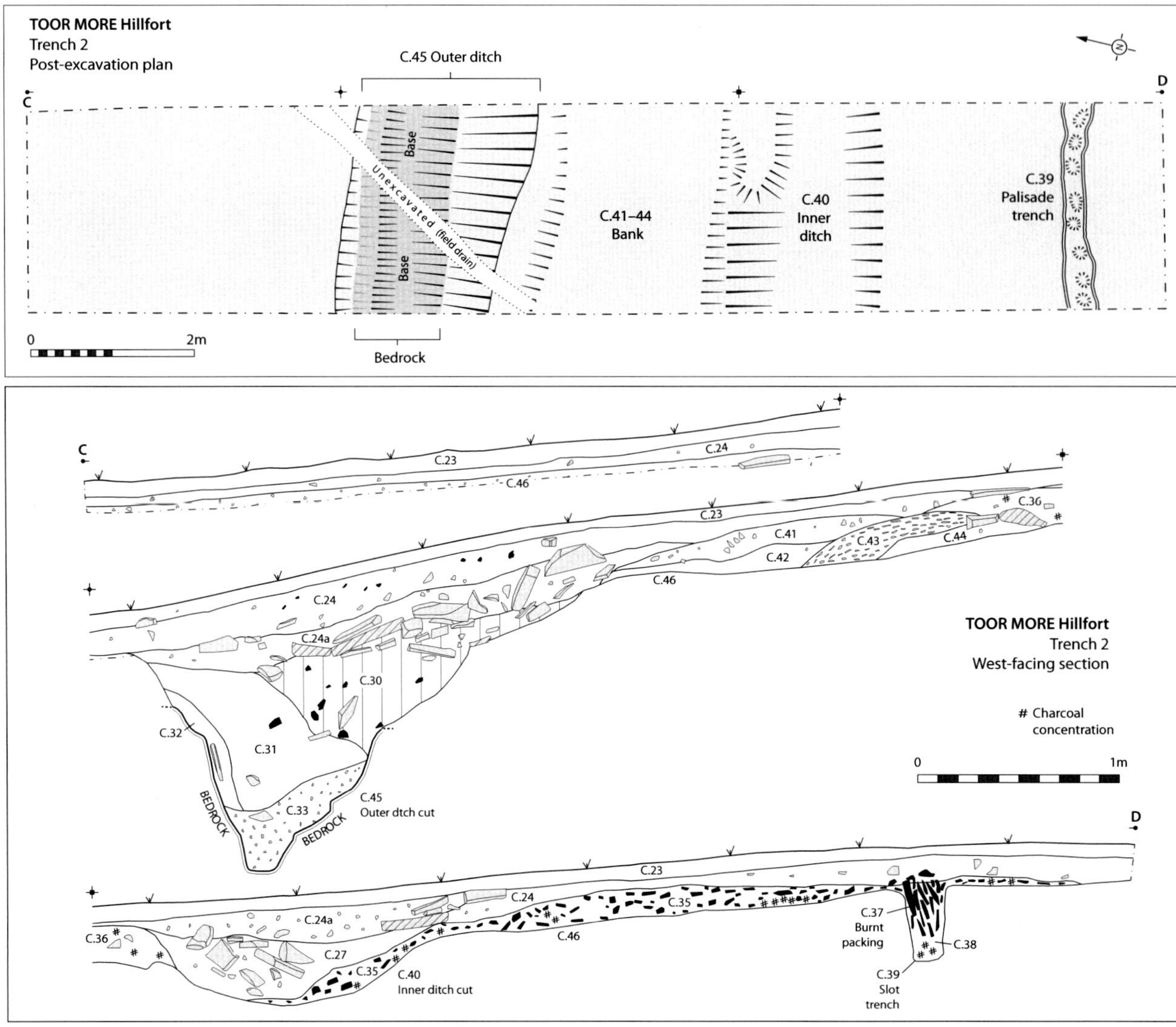

FIGURE 4.65: POST-EXCAVATION PLAN AND STRATIGRAPHIC SECTION ACROSS DEFENCES OF OUTER ENCLOSURE, TRENCH 2, TOOR MORE.

Outer ditch

This feature was first exposed on removal of 0.3m of topsoil at the western side of the trench. Excavation revealed a deposit of large stones in the upper part of the ditch, overlying finer sediments at the base. The removal of this fill exposed a 2.4m length of ditch, the upper part of which cut through 0.25–0.4m of subsoil (C.46 and C.47) into a weathered shale bedrock (Figure 4.66). The ditch had a V-shaped profile with steeply sloping sides, with a upper width of 1.8–2m (from top of B-horizon), a central width of 0.85–0.9m (top of bedrock cut), and a basal width of 0.2–0.3m. The ditch depth was 1.35–1.45m from the modern ground surface, or 1.05–1.22m from the top of the B-horizon. The inner (southern) side had a 45° slope, while the bedrock cut on the outer side was near-vertical.

The infilling of the ditch began soon after it was dug, with up to 0.3m of finely broken shale (C.33) accumulating at the base (Figure 4.65). This represents primary erosion of the lower ditch sides, with some inwash of silt. Context 33 did not contain large stones, suggesting that the bank wall had not collapsed at that stage. This is confirmed by the absence of charcoal, which indicates an interval of time between the build-up of this sediment and the burning of the adjacent palisade (see below).

The next stage in the infilling of the outer ditch is represented by a 0.45m thickness of clayey silt (C.31) overlying C.33. This was overlain on the inner side by a second deposit of silty clay (C.30). These deposits represent inwash of sediment eroded from the adjacent bank. The absence of charcoal and large stones indicates that the stonework on the adjacent bank had not collapsed by that stage of the ditch infilling.

This silting was followed by the deposition of large stones (C.29) in the ditch. These were mostly tabular slabs of sandstone, 0.15–0.4m in size, with slightly weathered surfaces. They may be explained by the collapse of a wall built on or within the adjacent bank. This seems to have occurred at a relatively late stage, when the ditch was substantially infilled. There is no obvious

Figure 4.66: External ditch of outer enclosure, Trench 2, Toor More hillfort.

connection with the destruction of the internal palisade, as the stones were not fire-reddened or associated with charcoal deposition. The stones from the wall/revetment may have been pushed into the upper ditch when the field was levelled for agriculture in modern times.

Bank

Prior to excavation the outer bank of the hillfort was visible as a low rise in the field, with no indication of the external ditch. The base of the original bank survived to a maximum thickness of 0.25m, extending over a 2m wide area from the inner edge of the ditch (Figure 4.65). The bank seems to have been of dump construction, comprised silty clay subsoil and finely broken shale extracted from the ditch (contexts 36, 41, 42, 43 and 44). The height of the original bank is unknown, but based on the amount of soil and rock taken from the ditch it is unlikely to have exceeded 1–1.5m. There was no buried sod or pre-bank features, apart from some flecks of charcoal, but not enough to indicate earlier occupation at the site.

The large number of sandstone slabs in the upper fill of the ditch indicates the presence of a stone wall within or on top of the bank. The excavation did not clarify whether the wall was built at the same time as the bank, or was added subsequently. The amount of stone in the ditch indicates it may have been 1–2m in height. The construction technique is unknown; however, the tabular form of the sandstone used suggests that regular coursing may have been employed. As with similar examples in Trench 1, these stones were brought from elsewhere for use in bank construction, because the friable shale bedrock extracted in the lower ditch was not suitable for that purpose.

Inner ditch

Excavation along the southern (inner) side of the bank revealed a shallow subsoil cut (C.40), approximately 2m wide, with gently sloping sides and rounded base to a depth of 0.25–0.3m (Figures 4.65 and 4.67). The basal fill consisted of a thin layer of fire-reddened stone (C.35). It was part of a larger spread of similar burnt material extending south towards a palisade slot (C.39). Within the inner ditch the burnt stone was overlain by a deposit of large stones (C.28), around which there was an accumulation of silt (C.27). These stones represent some inward collapse of the bank wall into the ditch.

Palisade

Excavation of an area 2.3m inside the inner ditch exposed a narrow slot (C.39) cut into the B-horizon surface (Figure 4.65). This slot was 0.22–0.34m wide,

Figure 4.67: Inner ditch (centre) and palisade slot (top left) of outer enclosure, Trench 2, Toor More.

with a basal width of 0.13–0.16m, and vertical sides to a depth of 0.28–0.34m. Excavation identified eight separate post-settings at the base of the trench, visible as oval to circular shaped depressions (Figure 4.68). The upper part of the slot was filled with vertically placed stones (C.37), which were heat-shattered *in situ*. These were packed tightly, along with a fine silty sediment containing charcoal (C.38). This indicates a line of wooden posts, approximately 0.15m in diameter and spaced 0.1–0.15m apart, which may have provided a frame for smaller fencing posts and/or interwoven wattle.

The chronological relationship of the enclosing elements is not certain. It is possible that the palisade and inner ditch were part of a later re-building of the hillfort defences. This cannot be confirmed, however excavation indicates a possible interval between the digging of both ditches. The evidence is tenuous, based on the absence of charcoal or fire-reddened stone in a 0.3m thick deposit of sediment (C.33) at the base of the outer ditch. No such sediment was found at the base of the inner ditch, where the lower fill contains fire-reddened stone connected to the burning of the palisade. This may be explained by the presence of the intervening bank, which prevented charcoal from the burnt palisade entering the outer ditch.

Excavation confirmed that this wooden palisade was burnt down as a single event and it was not replaced. Evidence is provided by the heat-shattered packing stones found within (C.37) and outside (C.35) of the slot trench, and by deposits of charcoal (C.34) in the spread of burnt stones (C.35) extending from the slot trench into the inner ditch. This points to an intense fire that burnt down the palisade, with some burnt timbers falling into the space between the bank and the palisade trench.

List of excavation contexts, Trench 2, Toor More hillfort

Context 23. Sod layer; mid brown loamy silt with few clasts.

C.24. Light brown humic sandy silt, frequent small clasts; A-horizon topsoil.

C.25. Loose stone and soil in trench with plastic drain pipe, overlying outer ditch.

C.26. Machine-cut trench for plastic field drain overlying upper fill of outer ditch.

C.27. Deposit of dark brown humic silt in upper part of inner ditch.

C.28. Deposit of sandstone slabs (0.09–0.22m long), upper side of inner ditch.

C.29. Deposit of tabular and blocky stones (0.15–0.4m),

FIGURE 4.68: SLOT TRENCH OF BURNT PALISADE OF OUTER ENCLOSURE, TRENCH 2, TOOR MORE.

upper part of outer ditch.

C.30. Compact yellow/brown clayey silt, upper south side of outer ditch.

C.31. Grey compact deposit of clayey silt; central fill of outer ditch.

C.32. Compact lens of orange silty clay along upper northern side of outer ditch.

C.33. Compact deposit of grey broken shale in silty clay; lower fill of outer ditch.

C.34. Charcoal deposition in C.35, in area between C.39 palisade and inner ditch.

C.35. Spread of fire-reddened sandstone forming basal fill of inner ditch (C.40).

C.36. Burnt sediment with charcoal along upper north side of inner ditch.

C.37. Heat-shattered stones (0.05–0.2m) from packing of slot trench (C.39).

C.38. Orange/brown fine silt with charcoal; lower fill of palisade slot (C.39).

C.39. Cut of palisade slot on inner side of bank (see main text for description).

C.40. Cut of inner ditch (see main text for description).

C.41. Thin spread of yellow/orange stony silt on surface of surviving bank.

C.42. Compact deposit of bright orange silt under C.41 in bank.

C.43. Deposit of broken shale (<0.03–0.1m) under C.42, inner side of bank.

C.44. Compact deposit of orange/brown silt under C.43 in bank.

C.45. Cut of outer ditch (see main text for description).

C.46. Compact grey to yellow/brown stony silt; B-horizon subsoil.

C.47. Hard grey clay with iron oxide mottles on surface; C-horizon subsoil.

Dating

The only artifacts from this excavation are four sherds of

modern china pottery found in topsoil in the central part of Trench 2. In the absence of early finds, the site chronology relies entirely on radiocarbon analysis of samples recovered from Trenches 1 and 2. There are seven radiocarbon results available for waterlogged and charred wood, charcoal and burnt bone. This includes two charcoal results from the defences of the outer enclosure and five results (two charcoal, two waterlogged wood and one bone) for those of the inner enclosure. These dates can be associated with either the construction, early use, or burning of the hillfort defences (Figure 4.69):

Trench 1 (inner enclosure)
GrA-58572; 2970±30 BP: Charcoal sample (TM2013-01) from burnt timber (C.11) next to palisade slot trench. Ash charcoal.

GrA-58614; 2845±35 BP: Charcoal sample (TM2013-02) from lower ditch sediment (C.06). Hazel charcoal.

GrA-58575; 2935±35 BP: Waterlogged wood sample (TM2013-03D) from basal ditch sediment (C.08). Oak sapwood/bark.

GrA-58574; 2945±30 BP: Waterlogged wood (TM2013-04) from basal ditch sediment (C.08). Alder twig with 4-year growth.

GrA-59103; 2975±35 BP: Burnt bone from fill (C.13) of slot trench (sample TM2013-05). Not identifiable to species.

Trench 2 (outer enclosure)
GrA-58576; 2920±35 BP: Charcoal sample (TM2013-06) from palisade post setting (C.38F). Alder charcoal.

GrA-58577; 3000±30 BP: Charcoal sample (TM2013-07) from burnt deposit (C.34). Ash charcoal.

The results for the inner enclosure (Trench 1) include dates for charcoal and bone from the palisade trench (GrA-58572 and GrA-58713) calibrated to 1281–1058 BC, as well as combined calibrations of 1257–1049 BC for two wood samples (GrA-58574–5) from the base of the adjacent ditch. These four dates indicate that the enclosing elements of the inner enclosure were built and destroyed some time between approximately 1270–1050 BC. A further date is available for the inner enclosure, for a charcoal sample (GrA-58614) from the base of the ditch, which gave a calibrated result of 1114–917 BC.

The two charcoal results (GrA-58576–7) from the defences of the outer enclosure (Trench 2) are both connected to the wooden palisade inside the bank and ditch arrangement. These provide calibrated results of 1377–1126 BC and 1218–1011 BC respectively, which overlap with the date range for the inner enclosure, and probably place the construction of the hillfort in the twelfth or eleventh centuries BC.

Field No.	Lab No.	C-14 BP	$\partial^{13}C$	95.4% calibration
TM2013-01	GrN-58572	2970±30	-26.21	1281–1058 BC
TM2013-02	GrN-58614	2845±35	-24.33	1114–917 BC
TM2013-03	GrN-58575	2935±35	-27.12	1257–1019 BC
TM2013-04	GrN-58574	2945±30	-28.22	1258–1049 BC
TM2013-05	GrN-59103	2975±35	-26.40	1369–1056 BC
TM2013-06	GrA-58576	2920±35	-27.16	1218–1011 BC
TM2013-07	GrA-58577	3000±30	-28.29	1377–1126 BC

Figure 4.69: Radiocarbon dates for inner and outer defences, Toor More hillfort.

Discussion

The excavation at Toor More yielded important information on the design and construction of the hillfort defences. Both enclosing elements were similar in form, comprising a shallow rock-cut ditch, inside which there was a low bank with a stone wall, with an internal wooden fence. The construction of those defences was a major undertaking, which raises the question as to why there is no occupation evidence from the hillfort. Caution, however, is necessary given the limited extent of excavation, and the impact of land reclamation on the geophysical responses.

The fencing around both enclosures seems to have burnt down as a single event and they were not rebuilt. In both cases, some of the burning posts fell into the space between the fence and the inner edge of the bank, where charcoal deposits, large pieces of charred wood, and heat-shattered packing stones were found. It is not known whether the hillfort was completely abandoned following the destruction of the defences, but these were certainly not re-built.

Cultural Landscape

There is no significant occurrence of prehistoric sites in the immediate vicinity of Toor More hillfort (source: www.archaeology.ie). The number of potential Bronze Age sites does increase within a 2–5km radius of the hillfort, including several *fulachtaí fia*, barrows, ring ditches and unclassified mounds. This includes a possible ring ditch cemetery in Connahy townland, 3km south-east of the hillfort (Condit and Gibbons 1998). There is also a concentration of prehistoric burnt mounds (*fulachtaí fia*) in the Castlecomer area, 5km north east of the hillfort (Gibbons 1990). This is the same area where an impressive necklace of amber and gold beads of Late Bronze Age date was found at Cruttenclough (Eogan 1994: 41).

In terms of other material culture, available records for swords (Eogan 1965), bronze hoards (Eogan 1983), goldwork (Eogan 1994), socketed axeheads (Eogan 2000), and bronze spearheads (Lineen 2016), do not reveal any significant Middle or Late Bronze Age finds near the hillfort. This cannot be taken at face value, as those find records are heavily influenced by circumstances of discovery and recording, as well as by the original depositional practices. Attention may be drawn to a number of Bronze Age finds in the wider landscape. These include four bronze objects discovered in the Ballyraggett area, for which there are no find details (National Museum of Ireland reg. 1939: 64–7). They include a palstave, a flanged axe, and two dirk/rapiers, which probably predate Toor More hillfort. Farther north, there is a notable concentration of Late Bronze Age hoards at different locations in the neighbouring county of Laois. These include examples at Ballytegan, Blackhills, Money Lower, and Maryborough, Portlaoise (Eogan 1983, hoards 94–7). All four hoards contain metalwork of the Dowris phase (900–700 BC), and so are likely to post-date the occupation of the hillfort.

Toor More is one of three known prehistoric hillforts in Kilkenny, the others being Clomantagh 15km to the west/south-west, and Freestone Hill 19km to the south-east (Figure 4.54). These are univallate enclosures of Raftery's Class 1 type, and so may be different in age, function and cultural associations to Toor More hillfort. The excavation of Freestone Hill by Gerhard Bersu in 1948–9 revealed a complex ritual site, where an Early Bronze Age cemetery mound was modified by Late Bronze Age occupation and a later Iron Age enclosure with Roman material (Raftery 1969; Ó Floinn 2000). A number of other hill-top enclosures in Co. Kilkenny have not been dated (see Gibbons 1990). This means that Toor More is the only confirmed Class 2 hillfort in Kilkenny, and so is of particular significance for the Bronze Age prehistory of the region.

4.5 Some Conclusions

Though limited in extent, these site investigations provide important information on the morphology and defences of the hillforts concerned, and their chronological position. The radiocarbon results confirm the four sites were broadly contemporary with the Clashanimud example in Cork, placing these Class 2 hillforts in the twelfth or eleventh centuries BC. The Glanbane dates are the least helpful, as they only provide a *terminus ante quem* for the defences of the inner enclosure. The radiocarbon results for Ballylin relate to use and possible dismantling of the gated entrance to the inner enclosure, with a prehistoric date likely (though not confirmed) for the outer enclosure. The results for burnt stakes in the defences of the outer enclosure at Formoyle are likely to date that construction, with a similar time frame indicated by pre-bank and lower ditch dates from the inner enclosing element. The Toor More dates relate to the burning of wooden elements in the defences of both enclosures, with some evidence from burnt bone of occupation in the same period.

Each of these sites is a typical example of a Class IIa hillfort, having two concentric widely spaced enclosures, ranging in area 6.4–8.8ha in the case of Glanbane, Formoyle and Toor More, to a massive 20.5ha at Ballylin. Their landscape setting is also typical, located on prominent hills or ridges, at elevations of 242–253m OD in the case of Ballylin, Formoyle and Toor More. While Glanbane is at a lower elevation (86m OD), the setting is still prominent relative to the surrounding lowland. In all cases, these sites seem to have been positioned to overlook extensive tracts of lowland, with high visibility to and from the hillfort in most directions.

The hillfort defences are also broadly similar, comprising a single earth and stone-built bank, often with a stone facing (Glanbane and Toor More), an external soil and rock-cut ditch, and occasionally a low counterscarp bank. There is evidence of wooden fencing at two sites, made of light stakes on the inner side and crest of the banks at Formoyle, or heavier posts in slot trenches inside the banks at Toor More. The absence of fencing at Glanbane may be explained by the use of stone walling in the banks of both the inner and outer enclosures. At Ballylin it was different, as neither stone walls or palisade fencing were used, even though the entrance was formally marked by a wooden 'gate'. The latter differs from the example excavated at Clashanimud, which was connected to bank palisades on either side of the entrance. This might indicate that the Ballylin 'gate' was more symbolic than functional, in an enclosure surrounded by a rather slight bank and ditch.

With such large perimeters, the scale of construction at these hillforts is impressive. This is particularly true for Ballylin, where the two enclosures have a combined defensive circuit of 2.65km. That said, the defences in these hillforts could not be described as formidable, with the enclosing elements generally under 3m in overall height, possibly reaching 5m or so at Toor More. This, combined with the large size of these hillforts and the wide spacing of their two enclosures (20–25m apart in case of Glanbane; 40–60m at Formoyle; 105m at Toormore, and 80–120m at Ballylin), would have limited their effectiveness as defensive strongholds. Whether that was their primary function will be discussed in Chapter 9.

With the focus of excavation on the defensive elements, it is not surprising that there is little evidence of occupation from these hillforts. The absence of material culture is notable, with not one early artefact recovered from these four excavations. The geophysical surveys are not particularly informative, with the exception of the central area at Glanbane where a number of large built structures of unknown date were identified. Similar occupation features are absent from the other three sites, though in all cases the ground conditions were not ideal for magnetic gradiometry survey. There are a number of possible structures at Toor More, but as with the point anomalies at Ballylin, these require excavation to resolve their significance. This phenomenon of the 'empty hillfort', if proven to be correct, will be discussed further later in relation to the significance these places held for Bronze Age societies.

In the absence of excavation, the overall settlement history of these hillforts remains to be clarified. Evidence of deliberate destruction was found at Toor More, and possibly Formoyle, while the circumstances of the abandonment of Glanbane and Ballylin are unclear. There is no evidence that any of these defences were re-built, or that the hillforts were re-occupied at any time. The apparent collapse of some hillfort communities during the eleventh century BC will be explored in later chapters of this book.

5

The Baltinglass Hillfort Landscape of County Wicklow

The Baltinglass cluster of hillforts comprises nine of the largest examples in Ireland, situated in an area with numerous other monuments from many periods of prehistory (Figure 5.1). The landscape has been described by Condit (1992) as 'Ireland's hillfort capital', having the single largest concentration of these monuments in Ireland. Although its importance has been noted by many researchers, there had been no significant study of this hillfort landscape prior to the present study.

5.1 Natural Landscape

These hillforts overlook the town of Baltinglass and the Slaney River, on the highest points of a series of prominent hills off the southwestern part of the Wicklow Mountains (Figure 5.2). Despite being dwarfed by this mountain range, the Baltinglass hills are highly visible against the low-lying landscapes to the north, west and south. They divide these regions and overlook areas with diverse natural resources and excellent agricultural lands on either side of the meandering Slaney River.

Two distinct landforms are apparent in the study area: the Wicklow Mountains to the east and north-east, and the flat plains to the south and west. The Wicklow Mountains are the predominant landscape feature. These are mostly igneous geology and form part of the largest mass of granite in north-west Europe (Figure 5.3). This formation extends into the flat landform of Co. Carlow, which is surrounded by a relatively thin band of metamorphic rock (Jackson *et al.* 2010; Williams and Harper 1999). These were formed over millions of years, when large amounts of mud, silt and sand accumulating on the floor of the Iapetus Ocean were compressed into rock. The mountains began to be formed at the end of the Silurian period, approximately 443–415 million years ago, when the Iapetus Suture closed as the North American and European plates collided, forcing these rocks out of the Iapetus Ocean at the start of the Devonian period around 415–358 million years ago (Williams and Harper 1999: 23–28). The heat from the collision metamorphosed the mudstone and sandstone into schists and also created what Whittow (1975: 261) describes as Ireland's most significant metalliferous belt, with evidence for minerals including copper, sulphur, lead, zinc, iron, gold and silver. Underlying this, the molten layer of the earth's crust was also raised and this subsequently cooled to form granite (Holland 2003: 29). Between 2.6 million–11,700 years ago, Pleistocene glaciation eroded much of the overlying metamorphic rock to reveal the underlying granite (*ibid.*: 29). A small ice dome formed over the Wicklow Mountains forcing the pattern of glaciation to occur in an outward direction from the centre (see Sleeman *et al.* 2004: 111). This glaciation also created the deep U-shaped valleys that characterise the edges of the mountain range and contained a number of lakes, such as those found at Glendalough (*ibid.*: 30).

The Baltinglass hillforts are positioned just off the northern edge of the granite mass that extends into the southern plain occupying most of Co. Carlow. At this contact point, a number of different Lower Palaeozoic geologies meet. The hillforts at Hughstown and Tinoran are located on a large formation of Silurian sandstone, greywacke and shale that extends northwards to the southern edge of Dublin City. The three hillforts on Tuckmill Hill (Rathnagree, Rathcoran and Sruhaun) are on a Lower/Middle Ordovician slate formation that extends 14km to the north-east. The central portion of Rathcoran sits on a small ridge of granite within this geology. Spinans Hill 1 and the northern and western portions of Spinans Hill 2 lie on the same granite formation. Brusselstown Ring and the southern and eastern portion of Spinans Hill 2 are positioned on a small formation of andesite and andesitic tuff formed in the Lower/Middle Ordovician period, a consolidated volcanic rock that belongs of the igneous type.

The mountains to the east are characterised by a series of peaks and ridges that broadly extend north–south. The largest of these is Lugnaquilla Mountain (925m OD), a granite massif and foothills that surround the Glen of Imaal to the west. The mountain environment primarily consists of heathland and thin blanket bog of mid-to-late Holocene ages (Nairn and Crowley 1998: 20). Prior to this, the habitat was likely covered in deciduous forest (*ibid.*: 20). The predominant soil types in Wicklow are brown earths at lower elevations and brown podzols with a skin of peat, blanket bog and lithosols at higher elevations (Figure 5.4). At the foothills of the Wicklow Mountains, a mixture of shallow lithosolic and podzolic soils with peaty topsoil dominates. All of the Baltinglass hillforts are sited on similar poor quality soils only suitable for rough grazing, while the lower hill slopes and surrounding landscape hold shallow well-drained mineral soils. The underlying geology of Carboniferous slates, shales, schists and igneous rock types tend to pro-

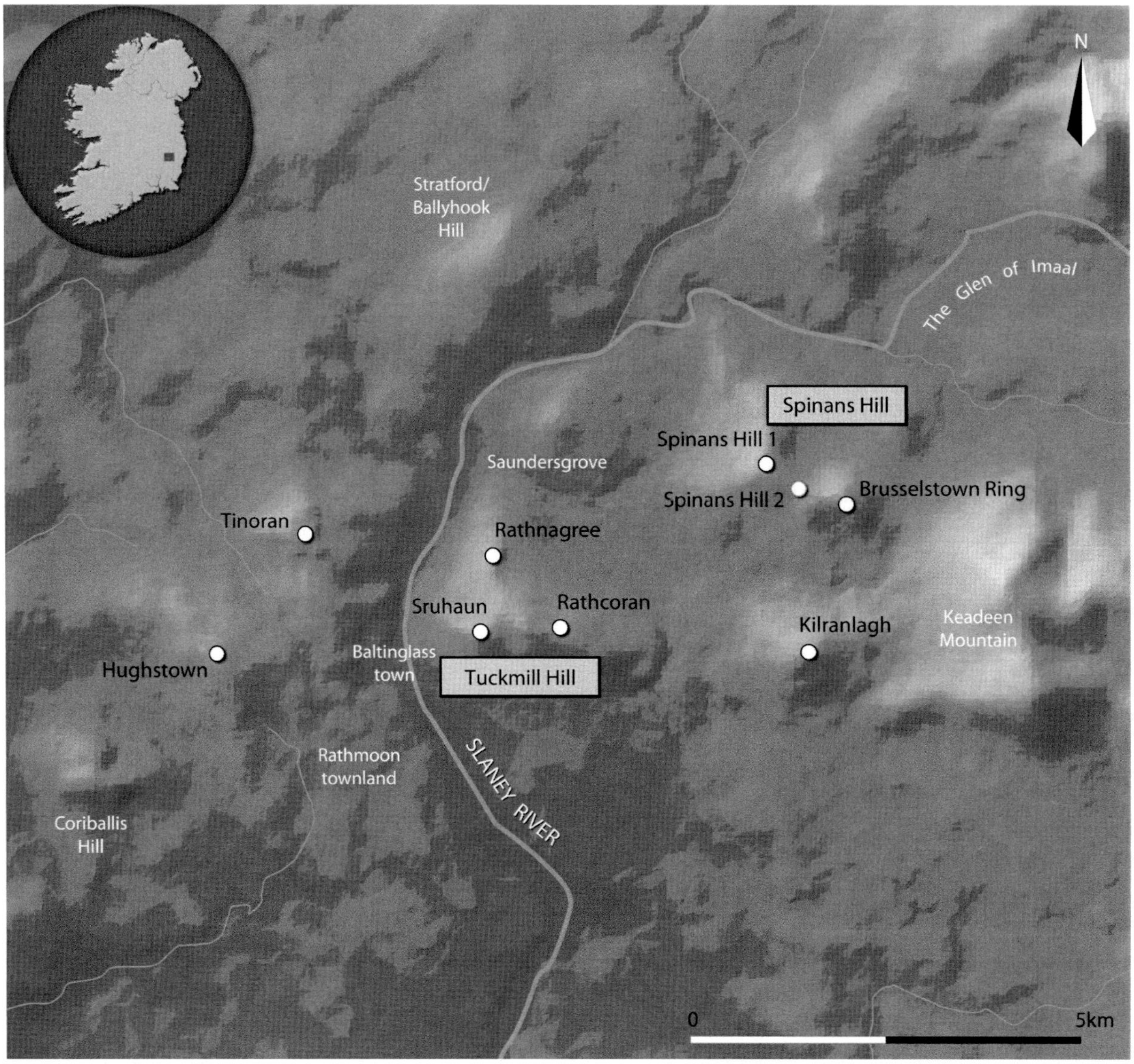

Figure 5.1: The Baltinglass hillfort cluster, Co. Wicklow, with hillforts marked by circle.

duce well drained mineral brown podzols appropriate for intensive farming. The wider study area comprises a mixture of brown and grey-brown podzolics and brown earths of varying depth and drainage, with alluvium terraces near river edges. This provides excellent quality soil cover suitable for various agricultural regimes.

The Wicklow Mountains are the source of several major river systems, including the rivers Liffey, Slaney and Avoca. The Slaney flows westward from Lugnaquilla Mountain towards Baltinglass town where it curves and runs south towards Wexford Harbour. The Avoca River is fed by a number of small tributaries which originate in the southern Wicklow Mountains. In 1795, gold was discovered in the Avoca Valley, 32km to the east of Baltinglass. Around 80kg was extracted from alluvial placer deposits by locals, including a nugget weighting 682g, the largest discovered in Britain or Ireland. The British government subsequently seized the mine workings and opened Ireland's only commercial gold mine and extracted approximately 300kg of gold (Vines 2007). Copper was also commercially mined at Avoca between 1720 and 1983, with a total output of 16 million tons of copper ore (Sleeman *et al.* 2004: 36).

5.2 History of Research

There has been relatively little work conducted on the Baltinglass hillforts. The published research is largely descriptive and no scientific survey or excavation was undertaken prior to this project. The first researcher to take an interest in these hillforts was Liam Price, a barrister and amateur historian, who visited the Baltinglass hillforts on numerous occasions during the early–mid twentieth century. His field notes have been published by Corlett and Weaver (2002a; 2002b) and are an important source even though they provide little in the way of interpretation or critical analysis. Price was the first to identify and record the cairns at the summit of

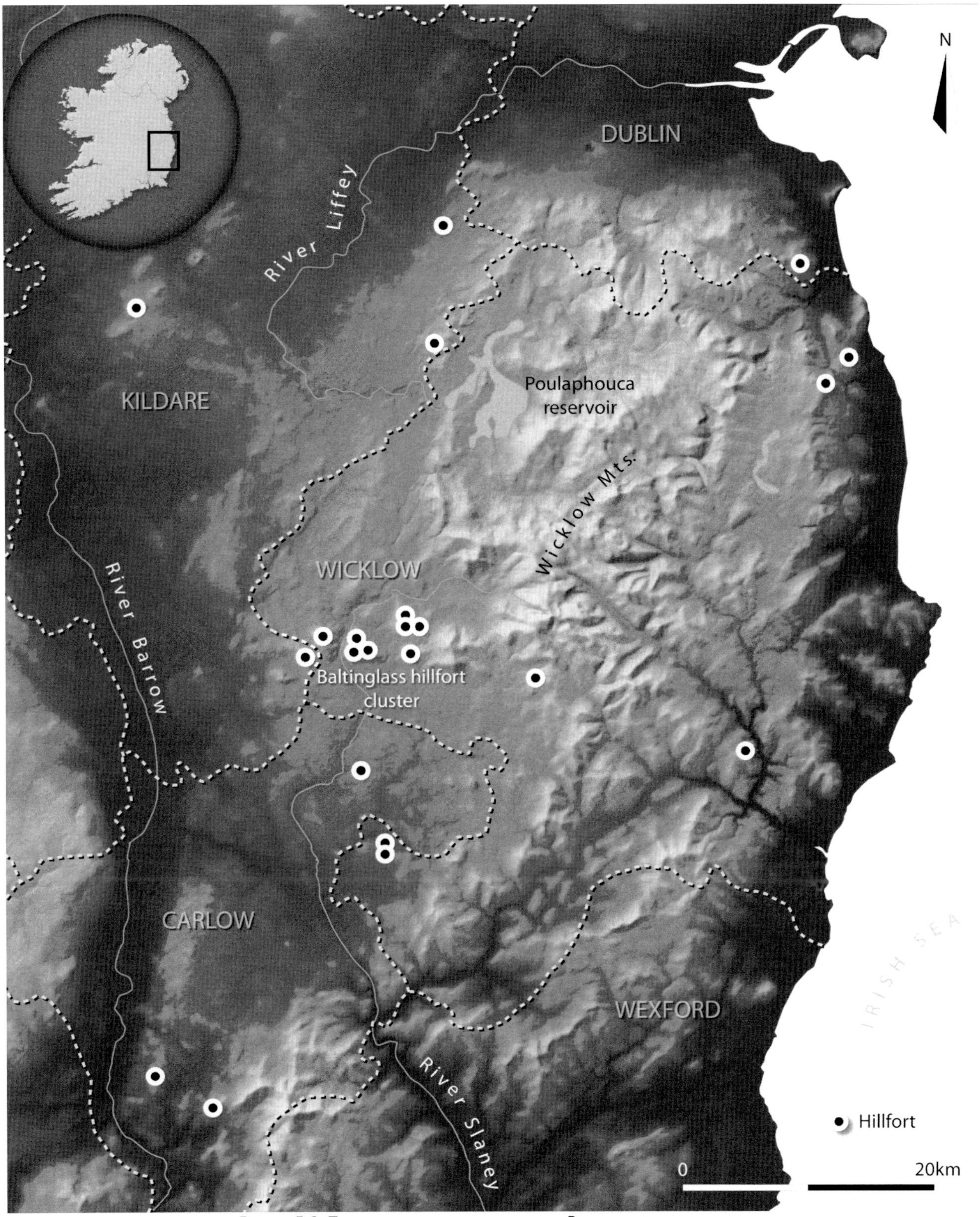

FIGURE 5.2: THE PHYSICAL LANDSCAPE OF THE BALTINGLASS STUDY AREA.

Spinans Hill 1 and also identified a large enclosure at the northeastern base of Kilranlagh Hill (Corlett and Weaver 2002b: 539–540).

The most comprehensive study of these monuments was undertaken by Tom Condit (1992, 1998). These provide descriptions and basic ground plans of some of the hillforts, together with a short discussion placing them in the wider context of Irish hillforts. His 1992 article was the first to highlight the importance of the Spinans Hill 2 contour fort. Condit summarised the morphology of these monuments, discussing the phenomenon of hillfort pairs and briefly considered the available evidence with reference to Mitchell and Ryan's (1997: 240) interpret-

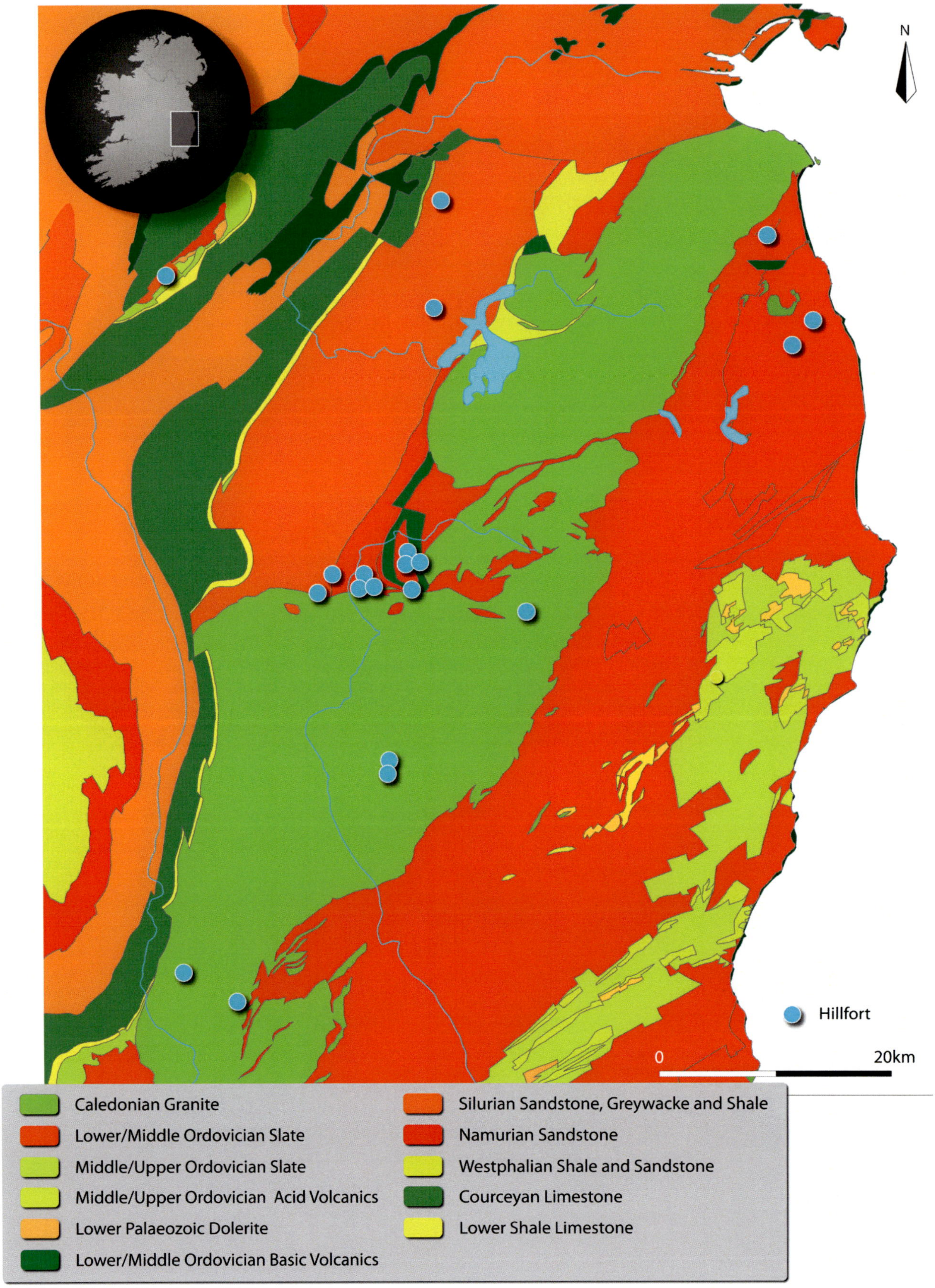

Figure 5.3: Geology (1:500,000 scale) of the Baltinglass study area. Data taken from www.gsi.ie.

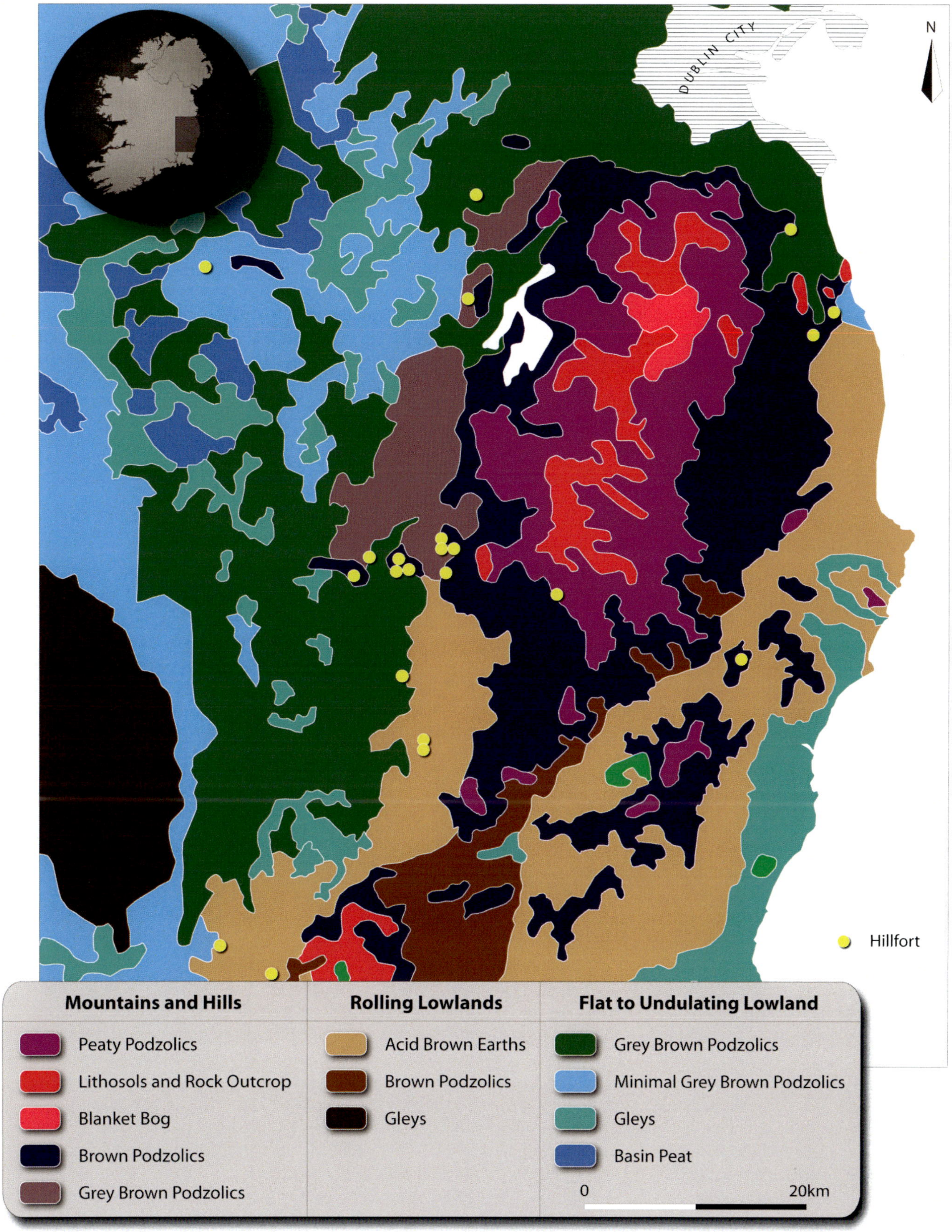

Figure 5.4: Soils (1:575,000 scale) of the Baltinglass study area. Data based on the Ordnance Survey 'General Soils Map' (second edition).

ations. The latter suggested two models to explain this unique concentration of sites. The first is that the hillforts were assembly places or defensive structures on either side of the Slaney River erected by two adjacent polities, essentially 'rival works inspired by competitive emulation between political groups'. The second suggests that the hillforts represent the successive replacement of a single tribal centre over a period of time. Waddell (1998: 356) commented briefly on this 'remarkable concentration'. He favours the latter interpretation and considers the hillforts as representing 'a sequence of activity over a long period of time'. Conversely, Grogan (2005b: 124) supported the former, stating 'their location is suggestive of the confrontational siting of forts belonging to rival neighbouring territories'. Neither author supported their interpretations with evidence and so no definitive conclusions could be reached.

There has been much commentary on the Spinans Hill complex due to the large size of the enclosure. It has been speculated that Spinans Hill 2, a massive contour fort of approximately 131ha, could have been used to delimit an area of tribal assembly or may be comparable to the Dorsey 'enclosure', Co. Armagh, which represents a series of cross-dykes rather than an actual enclosure (Raftery 1994: 63). Condit (1998: 22) stressed caution in such an interpretation. The Dorsey in Co. Armagh and the Dun of Drumsna, Co. Roscommon, likely functioned as defensive dykes protecting multiple fording points in rivers (Condit and Buckley 1989). While these enclosures compare with Spinans Hill 2 in terms of size, Condit (1998: 23) points out that Spinans Hill 2 encloses a hilltop and 'is not a gateway in the fashion of the Dorsey and the Dun of Drumsna'. We must also note the comparably large size of the nearby Tinoran hillfort, which may be up to 84ha in size. More recently, Flood (2009: 83) proposed Knocknarea Mountain in Co. Sligo as a more likely parallel to Spinans Hill 2. Bergh (2000) discovered a system of discontinuous banks on the eastern summit of the mountain, which effectively blocked the flat summit area from the lower eastern shoulder. These features have been tentatively dated to the Neolithic (Bergh 2000), while the date of Spinans Hill 2 remains uncertain. Similar parallels could be made with the large areas enclosed on the hillforts of Knocknashee, Co. Sligo, or Turlough Hill in Co. Clare.

Raftery (1994: 63) questioned the defensive function of Spinans Hill 2, suggesting that it could never have functioned as a single defended settlement. Whatever its function, it is clear that the enclosure represents a huge and concentrated effort by a significant number of people and that Spinans Hill was a place of exceptional importance (*ibid.*: 63). This is supported by limited fieldwork undertaken by Grogan and Kilfeather (1997: 41) who identified up to 24 hut structures within Spinans Hill 2. Waddell (1998: 356–357) suggests that the complex was likely conceived of and constructed as a unit.

5.3 Spinans Hill

The Spinans Hill complex is on the eastern edge of the Baltinglass hillfort cluster (Figure 5.5). It comprises three hillforts, namely Brusselstown Ring (*Record of Monuments and Places*: WI027-018), Spinans Hill 1 (WI027-078002) and Spinans Hill 2 (WI027-078001). All three lie on this broad north-east/south-west ridge that has two distinct summits. The northern summit rises to a maximum height of 406m OD and is surrounded by Spinans Hill 1 hillfort. The southern summit, at 386m OD, is surrounded by Brusselstown Ring, with Spinans Hill 2 enclosing the entire hill.

The following is a summary of the main features of these three large enclosures based on field survey and GPS mapping undertaken by the author, as well as LiDAR survey. It was not possible to use geophysical prospection in this survey, due to the igneous geology of the hill and the high bedrock exposure.

Brusselstown Ring

Brusselstown Ring (WI027-018) comprises a large bivallate hillfort, with widely spaced stone walls, occupying a total area of 32.43ha (Figure 5.6). It is located in the townlands of Brusselstown and Castlequarter, with the southern portion of the inner enclosing elements forming part of the townland boundary. The site is recorded on both the first and second editions of the Ordnance Survey six-inch maps. There are excellent views from the summit of Brusselstown Ring (402m OD), with particularly striking views of the Glen of Imaal to the north-east. The interior is a mixture of open pasture on the eastern side of the interior, with dense bracken and gorse on the southern and western side, and lighter growth in all areas between the inner and outer enclosing elements.

The inner enclosure closely follows the 370m contour, deviating by less than five metres along its 824m perimeter. A stone bank of varying width (5.3m–11.7) surrounds a natural oval terrace within an area of 4.63ha (Figure 5.7). A modern wall was built on the inner face. The large sub-rounded stones of andesite and andesitic tuff that make up the bank suggest that it was constructed from field clearance. Loose stone and boulders scattered on the immediate lower slopes suggest the original bank was more extensive. Price identified some coursed stone facing on the north-west side (in Corlett and Weaver 2002: 466), and this survey recorded a 98m length of stone facing to the south (Figure 5.8). An estimated 61 small circular depressions were recorded on top of the inner bank mostly visible on the southern side. These features measure 1.5–2.7m in diameter and could represent the remains of large post-holes. To the south, there is an alignment of 17 of these features, spaced on average 0.7m apart. No such features are apparent in the outer

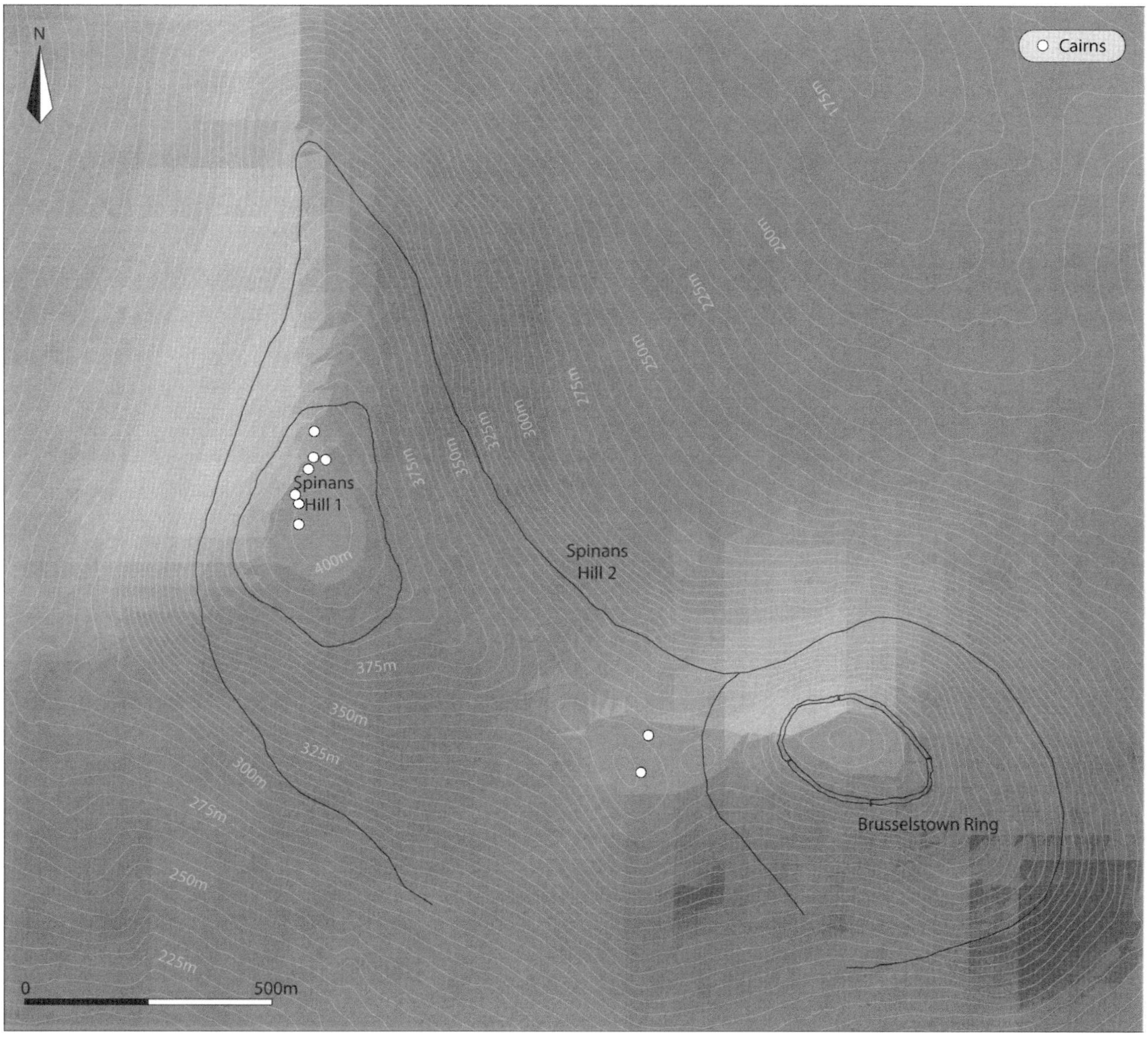

Figure 5.5: GPS survey of hillfort complex on Spinans Hill, Co. Wicklow, with location of possible prehistoric cairns shown.

enclosing element, although this is more denuded than the inner example and partially obscured by vegetation.

Four possible entrances were identified at the north, south, east and west sides of the inner bank (Figure 5.8). There were no corresponding entrances identified in the outer bank, although, vegetation may obscure such features. The entrances are morphologically similar and consist of narrow breaks ranging 1.7–2.6m in width. In each example, there is a short avenue or 'funnel' of stones extending from the terminals that measure up to 4m in length. This may have been used to highlight the position of the entrances to outsiders but are more likely to have been created in recent centuries, where gaps in the bank were created by pushing stones outwards.

The outer rampart is located 124–305m outside the inner rampart, but unlike the latter, does not follow the contours of the hill, varying from 366–298m OD. It comprises a less substantial stone bank, the eastern and south-eastern section of which is incorporated into modern field systems. This is best preserved to the north, where the stone bank averages 10.2m in width and is more comparable in size to the inner enclosing element. There is no obvious ditch associated with this bank.

There are numerous rock outcrops in the interior of Brusselstown Ring. The largest is located at the centre of the inner enclosure, where it forms a prominent rise overlooking most of the interior. There are records of two structures in that area and 24 examples immediately outside that rampart to the south (Grogan and Kilfeather 1997). Recent survey by the author identified a total of 288 possible hut sites, 25 within the inner enclosure and a further 263 are located between the inner and outer defences (Figure 5.9). These features consist of flat, circular areas, on average 3–12m in diameter, often defined by a band of grass-covered stone at its outer edge.

A settlement area was recorded by Condit (1992: 16–20)

Figure 5.6: Brusselstown Ring, viewed from Spinans Hill 1 looking south-east.

Figure 5.7: Inner enclosing stone bank of Brusselstown Ring, Co. Wicklow.

Figure 5.8: GPS plan of the inner enclosure of Brusselstown Ring with distribution of possible hut sites.

immediately to the north-west of the outer defences. This is reported to contain enclosures, hut sites and field walls over an area of 320m by 145m. The majority of this settlement has been forested and could not be surveyed further.

Spinans Hill 1

Located on the northern summit of this ridge, Spinans Hill 1 (WI027-078002) consists of a sub-quadrangular enclosure defined by a peat-covered earthen bank surrounding an area of 11.11ha (Figure 5.10). An east-west field bank crossing the interior forms the boundary between Spinans Hill and Ballyhubbock Upper townlands. The bank is best preserved at the north and east, but is largely levelled over the remainder of its perimeter (Grogan and Kilfeather 1997: 40–41). It is not recorded in either edition of the Ordnance Survey, and was first identified through aerial photography (Condit 1992). The full outline of the site was not recorded until the present study. Price had previously noted some features of the site but did not identify it as a hillfort (in Corlett and Weaver 2002: 538–539). There are panoramic views from the summit (409m OD), although visibility to the south-east is somewhat obscured by the hilltop on which lies Brusselstown Ring.

The hillfort has a perimeter of approximately 1.29km. On the eastern side, the enclosing elements comprise a bank/ditch/counterscarp bank arrangement. The bank measures 7–9m in width and is approximately 2.8m above the current level of the external ditch. It is approximately 0.8m in internal height and has an external stone facing. The ditch is 7–9m wide. The eastern section of the enclosing elements is broadly straight and follows the con-

Figure 5.9: Possible hut site in the interior of Brusselstown Ring.

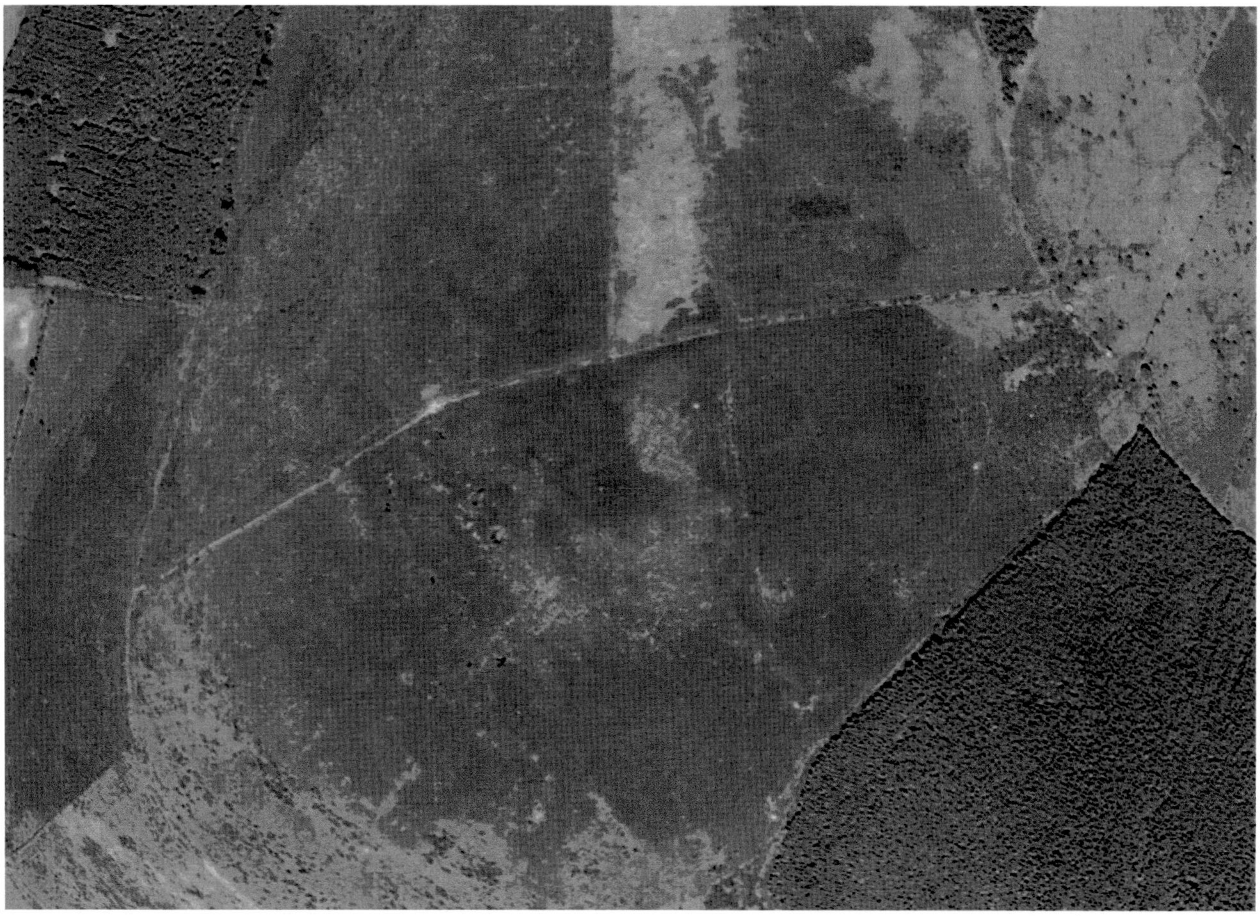

Figure 5.10: Satellite image of Spinans Hill 1, Co. Wicklow (Google Earth 2017).

FIGURE 5.11: LOW-RISE BANK ON NORTHERN SIDE OF SPINANS HILL 1, APPARENT AS A VEGETATION MARK ON THE SURFACE.

tours of the hilltop. The northern and north-eastern side is apparent as a low-rise bank, 8–10m wide and up to 0.4m in height (Figure 5.11). It can be differentiated by grass growth on the drier bank contrasting with heather growth across the boggy interior of the hillfort. There is no clear indication of an associated ditch on that side of the hillfort. This vegetation pattern continues around the perimeter at the west and as a low scarp at the south-west. At the south, the enclosing elements comprise an earthen bank 1.1m high and 2.1m wide. This may be the remains of a later field boundary that followed the line of the bank and incorporated elements of same. The western and southern section of the bank is more influenced by the topography and largely follows the contours of the hilltop. There is no obvious entrance to this enclosure.

There is no visible evidence for habitation in the interior, where heather growth on blanket peat makes identification of ground features difficult. Condit (1992: 19–20) recorded six cairns at the centre of the hillfort. These include a large central cairn (WI021-080004), 30m in diameter, at the summit, surrounded by five smaller examples (WI021-080003, WI021-080006, WI021-080007, WI021-080008, and WI021-080009). A seventh cairn was recorded by the author (Figure 5.5). This group of cairns was interpreted by Condit (1992: 20; 1998: 20) as a possible passage tomb cemetery, but this has yet to be confirmed. Price identified ruined cists (Figure 5.12) in several of these robbed out cairns (in Corlett and Weaver 2002: 467). For a more detailed description of these features see O'Driscoll (2016).

Spinans Hill 2

Spinans Hill 2 (WI027-078001) is an extensive earthwork with a 5.46km perimeter that surrounds an area of 131ha including both Brusselstown Ring and Spinans

FIGURE 5.12: POSSIBLE CENTRAL CIST STRUCTURE WITHIN CAIRN, INTERIOR OF SPINANS HILL 1.

FIGURE 5.13: ENCLOSING ELEMENTS AT THE NORTHERN SIDE OF SPINANS HILL 2, CO. WICKLOW.

Hill 1 (Figure 5.5). The site was first discovered by Condit (1992) using aerial photographs to identify what he believed to be the largest hillfort in Ireland. The northern section of the enclosing elements delimits the boundaries of Ballyhubbock Upper and Spinans Hill, while the southern half is divided between Brusselstown, Castlequarter and Moorstown townlands. Visibility to and from the site varies considerably due to the size of the hillfort and the topography of the hill. There are generally excellent views from most parts of the interior. Due to its size, there is variable preservation in the interior, with a large section of mature forestry at its centre causing significant damage.

Over the course of the perimeter, the enclosing elements vary from 295–368m OD, being on average 330m OD, with the highest point in the interior being 409m OD. The defences are best preserved at the north and north-west where it comprises a bank/ditch/counterscarp arrangement (Figure 5.13). It is most visible on the northern side, where the internal bank ranges 5–8m in width and comprises mostly stone and boulders, capped in places with soil. Some sections comprise entirely of large boulders and this may be where the builders took advantage of natural erratics. The external ditch ranges 7–10m in width, is 1.4m deep externally and up to 2.4m below the crest of the inner bank. The external counterscarp bank measures 4–5m wide and up to 1.1m in height. In places, the total width of the defences is up to 23m. At the north- west, the defences are built along the edge of a steep drop. A modern fence incorporates the internal bank as a boundary, but the original defences are not otherwise altered. The internal bank is up to 1.2m high internally, whereas the external ditch takes advantage of a steep fall of up to 3.6m. A small counterscarp bank is visible in places has been affected by land reclamation and other agricultural processes. The south-eastern section of the contour fort integrates a large portion of the outer enclosing element of Brusselstown Ring. Condit (1992: 19) noted that there are 'a number of breaches' to the north of Spinans Hill 2, which he suggested may be original entrances. Bersu identified a possible roadway to the hillfort at the south-west corner of Brusselstown Ring (in Corlett and Weaver 2002: 504).

As already stated, a large portion of Spinans Hill 2 is under forestry, and so potential habitation structures and other monuments are not well exposed. Examples in-

FIGURE 5.14: KILRANLAGH HILL, CO. WICKLOW, VIEWED FROM BRUSSELSTOWN RING LOOKING SOUTH.

clude a cairn (WI027-078004) discovered on the southern side of the enclosure. A 17m diameter circular enclosure (WI027-078005) 50m to the north-east on level ground between two natural mounds has been interpreted as a possible ritual monument (Condit 1992: 20). These features have not been dated and so their relationship to the hillforts is unknown.

5.4 Kilranlagh

A possible hillfort was discovered by the author on the summit of Kilranlagh (385m OD), in the townland of Colvinstown, a prominent hill 5km to the east of Baltinglass town. The site occupies a total area of approximately 5.33ha, most of which is now under conifer forestry and thick gorse growth. There are panoramic views from the summit, with particularly striking scenes of the lowlands to the south and south-west. Igneous bedrock prevented the application of geophysical survey, with the survey carried out using GPS mapping and aerial photographs.

The enclosing element comprises a stone bank, approximately 14m wide and up to 0.6m high on the west and south-west sides. The outer side of this bank is revetted with large stone slabs placed horizontally. A change in vegetation immediately outside the bank may indicate the presence of an outer ditch, approximately 6m wide. This section of the enclosing elements extends for approximately 140m in length and continues into forestry to the north, abutting a 3–6m high cliff face which forms the southern portion of the hillfort defences. The eastern section is under dense vegetation and is not visible on the ground. A curving field pattern recorded in the 1910 edition of the Ordnance Survey may represent the remains of the enclosing elements in this area.

There are no obvious internal features, although these may be obscured by thick heather and scrub growth in some areas. Bedrock is close to the surface in some areas of the interior. The south-west section of the hillfort perimeter abuts the outer edge of a large cairn (WI027-036). Two other cairns (WI027-035 and WI027-037) are recorded on the western slopes of the hillfort. A stone circle (WI027-039) and a barrow (WI027-040) are recorded on the lower eastern slopes.

FIGURE 5.15: WESTERN SECTION OF EXPOSED BANK OF KILRANLAGH.

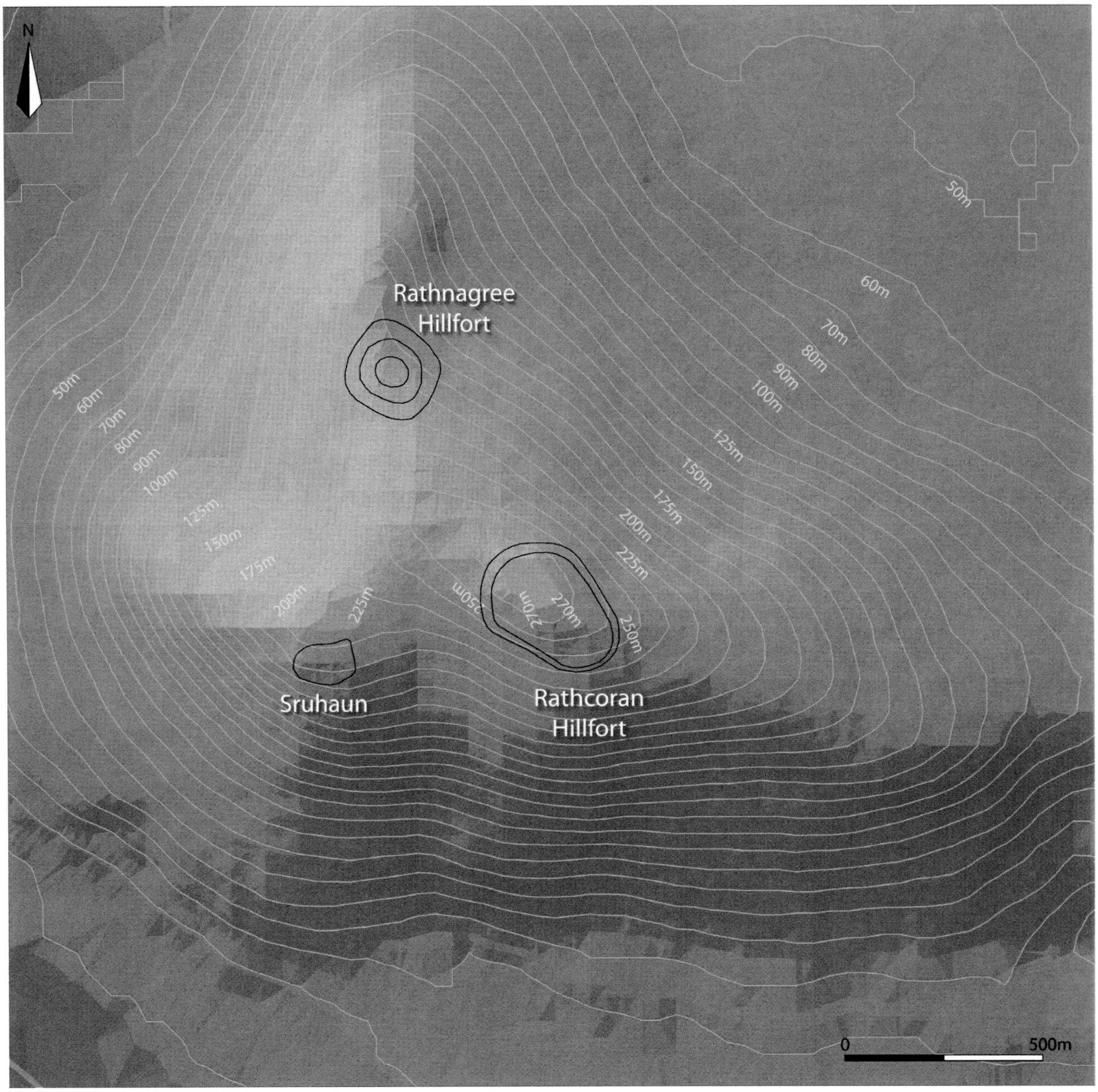

FIGURE 5.16: HILLFORTS ON TUCKMILL HILL, BALTINGLASS, CO. WICKLOW.

5.5 Tuckmill Hill

There are three hillforts on Tuckmill Hill, a prominent hill of tribolate shape at the centre of the Baltinglass cluster (Figure 5.5). Tuckmill Hill overlooks the modern town of Baltinglass directly to the south. The northern summit (318m OD) is surrounded by Rathnagree hillfort (WI027-027010). The south-east summit (378m OD) is enclosed by Rathcoran hillfort (WI027-026001). The author discovered a previously unrecorded hillfort in Sruhaun townland, on the western summit (315m OD). The entire hill was surveyed by high resolution LiDAR (16 points per metre) in work undertaken by Furgo–BKS Ltd for this project. The resultant Digital Terrain Model (DTM) provides an opportunity to map these hillforts in detail and visualise the landscape setting.

The LiDAR survey has identified a complex pattern of unrecorded fields on this hill, many of which are not recorded on the historic Ordnance Survey mapping (Figure 5.17). This suggests that many field systems were destroyed before the middle of the 19th century. There is a notable absence of field walls on the upper slopes and summit of Tuckmill Hill. There may have been practical reasons for this, with upland environments presenting challenges for farming, with difficult topography and accessibility, as well as exposure to high winds and rainfall contributing to poor soil fertility. However, ancient field systems survive particularly well in upland environments, such as in the Burren, Co. Clare (Jones 1998) and the Céide Fields in Co. Mayo (Caulfield 1978; 1983). The possibility that some of the Tuckmill Hill field patterns are ancient cannot be dismissed. Shallow ridge and

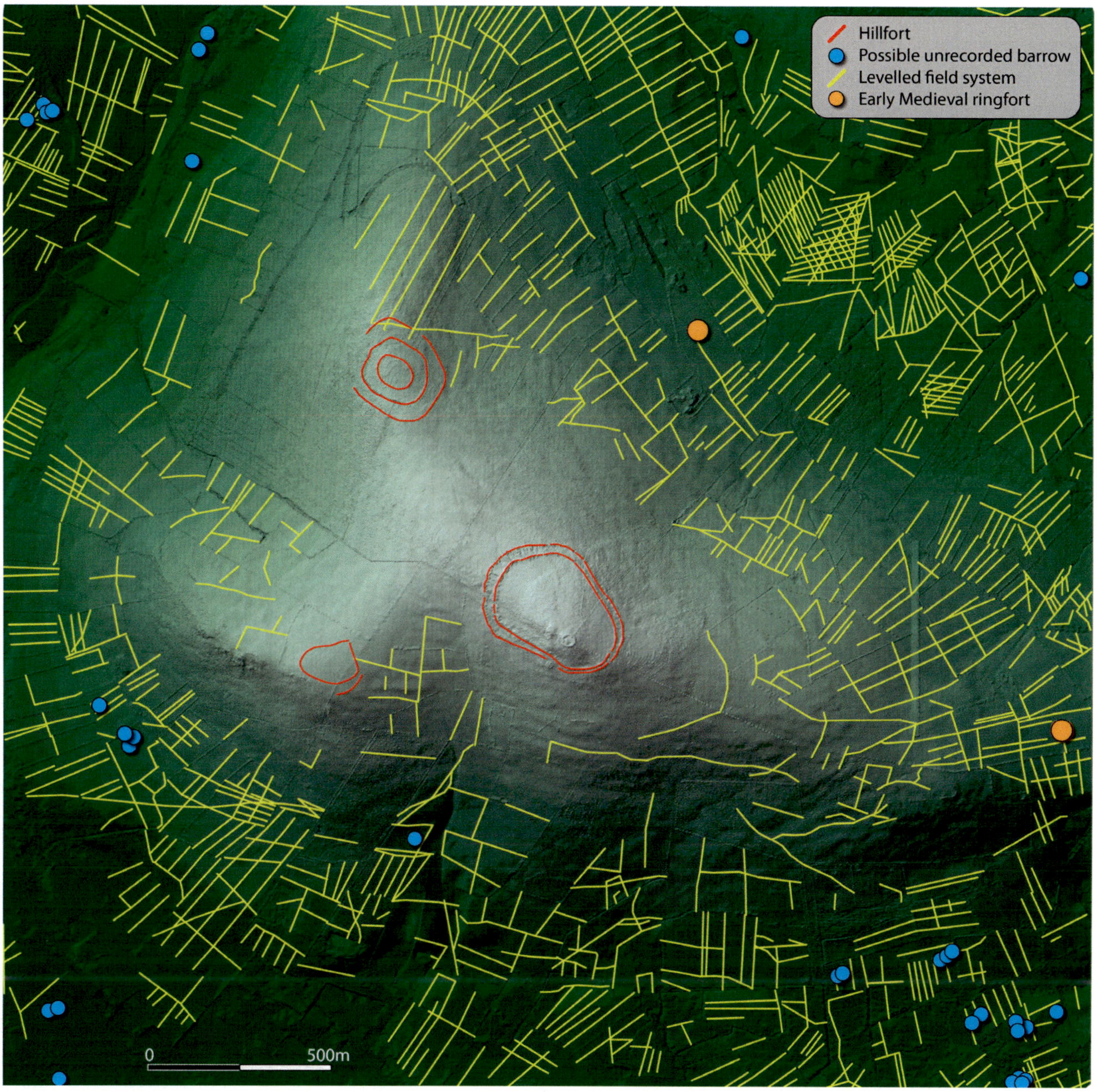

Figure 5.17: Unrecorded field systems, agricultural features and possible barrows identified by LiDAR on Tuckmill Hill.

furrow marks are apparent on near the summit on the western slopes indicating some form of cultivation in the past. The LiDAR also recorded a number of Medieval ringforts in this area, as well as up to 32 possible ring-ditches/barrows.

Rathcoran

Rathcoran is the largest of the three hillforts on Tuckmill Hill (Figure 5.18). The name probably refers to a large prehistoric cairn at its centre ('fort of the cairn'). A field pattern running through the hillfort divides the interior into three. This forms the boundary between the townlands of Coolinarrig Upper, Pinnacle and Tuckmill Hill. The monument was identified prior to the first edition Ordnance Survey mapping of 1835, with Lewis (1837: 174) recording that a hoard of gold coins were discovered in one of the enclosing banks. This explains why the hillfort was known locally as the Golden Fort. Westropp (1902a, 81), however, suggested that this hoard was recovered from the interior of the nearby hillfort of Rathnagree. Rathcoran is recorded in the second edition Ordnance Survey map, while Westropp (1902a) has also published a sketch plan of the hillfort. There are panoramic views from the summit (378m OD). The hilltop itself is prominent within the local landscape, particularly to the south. The interior is covered by dense heather and peat growth, and is grazed today by cattle and sheep.

Rathcoran is a pear-shaped bivallate hillfort that occupies a total area of 10.06ha (Figure 5.19). The shape is

FIGURE 5.18: AERIAL PHOTOGRAPH OF RATHCORAN HILLFORT, CO. WICKLOW (CAMBRIDGE AERIAL PHOTOGRAPHIC COLLECTION).

dictated by the topography of the hill which the enclosing elements largely follow. The inner rampart lies between 353–363m OD and the outer example 347–361m OD. Waddell (1998) and Condit (1998) interpreted Rathcoran as an unfinished hillfort, due to the seemingly incomplete nature of the enclosing elements and intervening quarry features. The enclosing elements are most complete at the north and north-west, where the inner example is 16m in width and up to 3.1m high, while the outer defences are up to 2.2m high and 8m wide. Both comprise a mixture of earth and stone and are separated by approximately 28–35m, with no evidence of associated ditches.

In this area, geophysical survey (Figure 5.20 and Figure 5.21; O'Driscoll 2014a) revealed a series of strong magnetic anomalies along the crest of the inner bank (Figure 5.22) on the north-west side (**G1a**). These may represent an intensive burning event, related to the destruction of a wooden palisade. Similar geophysical responses over the enclosing elements at Clashanimud Co. Cork, Toor More, Co. Kilkenny and Hughstown, Co. Kildare were confirmed by excavation to relate to destruction by fire. Considering the responses at Rathcoran are confined to the top of the bank, the posts may have been burnt *in situ*. As the bank reduces in size to the east the responses become diffuse and less intense (**G1b–G1e**). These more modest responses may also represent post-holes associated with a palisade. **G1e** represents a series of evenly spaced pit-like features. These are placed at the centre of the low-rise bank which forms the inner defensive element at the south of the hillfort. Placed approximately 15m apart, these may represent post-hole features. These may have marked out the perimeter of the site prior to the building of the bank proper. The evidence from the geophysical survey may suggest that a possible palisade associated with the enclosing elements was built in stages corresponding with the construction of the bank.

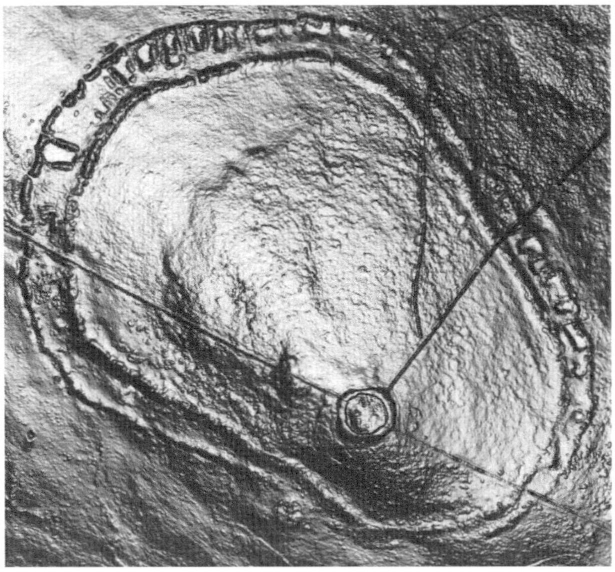

FIGURE 5.19: SLOPE ANALYSIS OF LIDAR DATA OBTAINED FOR RATHCORAN HILLFORT.

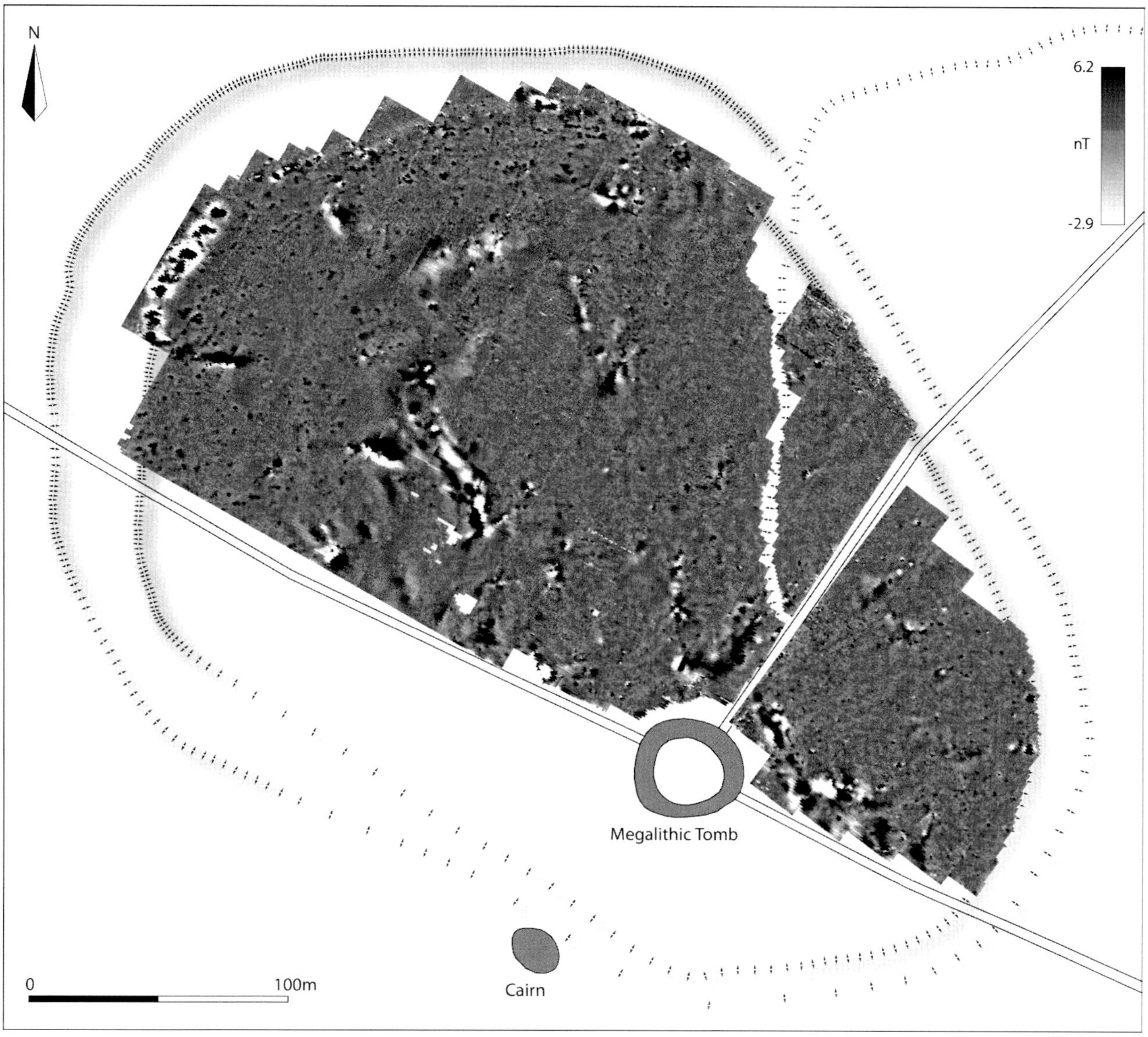

Figure 5.20: Results of geophysical survey at Rathcoran hillfort.

Apart from this north and north-west section, the enclosing elements are mainly composed of small and large granite boulders and are slighter in dimension. The inner enclosing element averages 0.8m in internal height and almost 3m externally. Similarly, the outer enclosure has an internal height of 0.4m and is 2.1m high externally. To the south, a 185m long section of the enclosing elements are more closely spaced and smaller, with the inner bank 0.2m high and 0.4m wide, and the outer example 0.4m high and 0.45m wide.

The enclosing elements seem to have been built in sections up to 70m in length, visible as varying lengths of bank with different composition, alignment and size. This could be interpreted as evidence for gang-working, but could also indicate seasonal construction by the same group over a prolonged time. This feature is recorded at other hillforts in Ireland, such as Mooghaun (Grogan 2005a: 129), as well as numerous hillforts in Britain, such as Cherbury Camp, Oxfordshire (Bradford 1940), Chiselbury in Wiltshire (Pugh and Crittall 1957) and Mere Hill, Herefordshire (Ray and Hoverd 2000), among others.

A total of 39 breaks in both enclosing elements have been identified at Rathcoran. These are narrow, simple gaps in the bank, approximately 2m in average width. They are often positioned on either side of the rectangular pits located between the two banks (Figure 5.23). They probably represent modern breaks to allow animal access to the interior. A corresponding 3.2m wide break in the inner and outer enclosing elements on the northern side may represent an original entrance. This is orientated on the most accessible approach to the summit of Tuckmill Hill and Rathcoran hillfort.

A 4–7.2m wide level terrace is apparent along the inner edge of both hillfort banks (Figure 5.23). This feature extends along most of the perimeter and is most evident in the north and north-east. A similar 4–6m wide

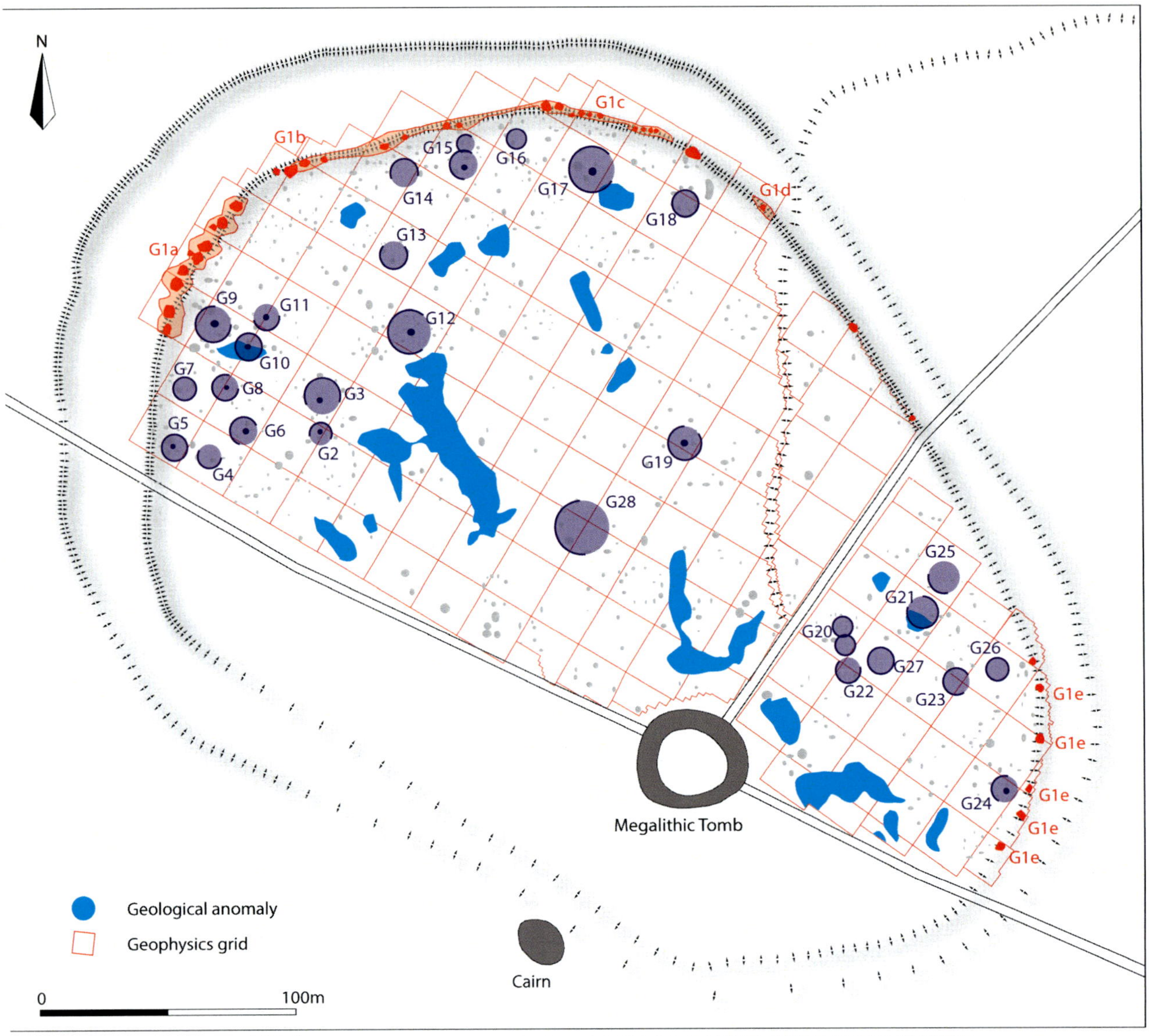

FIGURE 5.21: INTERPRETATION OF RESULTS FROM GEOPHYSICAL SURVEY AT RATHCORAN HILLFORT.

level platform was identified along the inner edge of the middle rampart at Mooghaun hillfort, Co. Clare (2005a: 164). These platforms may have been used to provide a level area to begin building the defences and to mark the intended circuit of the defences. The platform could also be interpreted as levelled ground used for habitation purposes, although no structures have been identified in the areas immediately abutting the bank at Rathcoran.

A total of 23 pits have been identified in the area between the two banks of the hillfort, in the north-western, northern and south-eastern sides (Figure 5.23). They comprise shallow rectangular depressions that mostly abut the inner side of the outer bank. They range in length from 14m–22m, in width 8–14m, with a depth variation of 0.2m–0.9m below modern ground level. In most cases, these are quarry features dug into the naturally sloping ground to create a level surface. They occur in groups at the north/north-west, east and south-east sides, with some isolated examples in the west. At the north/north-west, the pits are surrounded by low banks, the largest measuring 1.2m high and 6m wide. The eastern and south-eastern examples do not have associated banks. Where the pits occur the opposing banks are larger, with the size and depth of the pits often reflecting the size

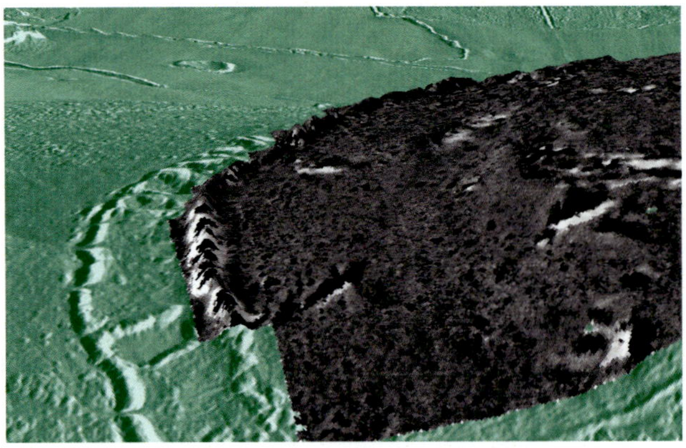

FIGURE 5.22: GEOPHYSICS RESULTS OVERLAYED ON LIDAR DATA, HIGHLIGHTING THE STRONG ANOMALIES AT THE CREST OF THE INNER BANK OF RATHCORAN AT THE NORTH-WEST.

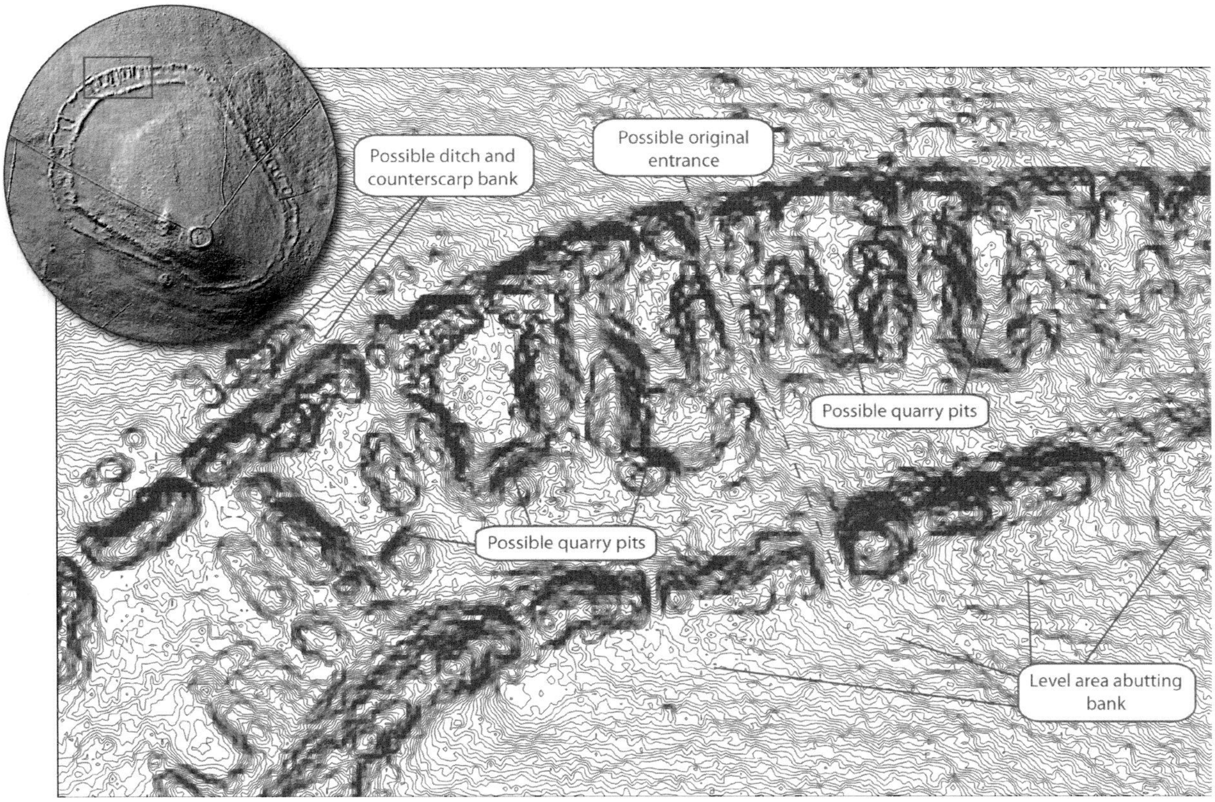

FIGURE 5.23: CONTOUR LINES DERIVED FROM LIDAR DATA HIGHLIGHTING EXAMPLES OF POSSIBLE QUARRY PITS, LEVEL PLATFORM, AND POSSIBLE ORIGINAL ENTRANCE.

of the opposing enclosing elements (larger and deeper pits often abut larger and wider sections of bank). This may establish a connection between the amount of stone taken from these quarry pits and the building of the hillfort banks, suggesting that both are likely to be contemporary. The partial remains of two largely completed quarry pits are apparent at the north-west, abutting the external face of the most substantial section of the inner bank. These quarry pits may have been used to gather material for constructing the banks, although loose stone and glacial erratics in the interior may also have been used.

The interior of the hillfort rises towards a rock outcrop at the south-east corner of the site, with the surface covered by significant heather growth, loose stone and glacial erratics. The summit of the hillfort is crowned by a large passage tomb excavated in the 1930's (Walshe 1941). The stone that originally covered the monument now forms a protective wall around the tomb and is often mistaken for the hillfort. A second cairn (WI027-076) abuts the exterior of the outer enclosing element to the south. There are three previously recorded hut structures (WI027-026002, WI027-026004, WI027-026007) within the hillfort.

This project has identified approximately 124 possible hut sites in the interior of Rathcoran, using a combination of LiDAR, GPS and geophysical survey (G2–G28). LiDAR survey revealed that the majority of these sites comprise circular terraces cut into the natural slope, a feature apparent in GIS slope analysis. These are often outlined by a circular setting of large stones, and range from 6–14m in diameter. Some structures are visible in the geophysical results as circular/curvilinear sets of pit-like features, which often correspond with the circular platforms on the surface. The imaging of these possible hut-sites using geophysical methods is variable probably due to the variable depth of blanket peat at the site.

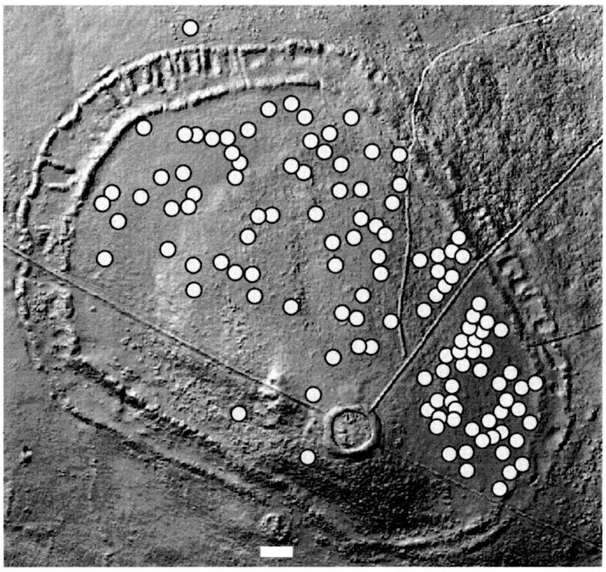

FIGURE 5.24: POSSIBLE HUT SITES RECORDED BY A COMBINATION OF GEOPHYSICAL SURVEY, GPS AND LIDAR.

Rathnagree

Rathnagree is a trivallate hillfort (Figure 5.25) positioned on a northern spur (318m OD) of Tuckmill Hill, 400m north/north-west of Rathcoran (Figure 5.16). The name translates as 'fort of the king'. The hillfort is located in the townlands of Tuckmill Hill and Tuckmill Upper, with the eastern section of the middle enclosing elements forming the boundary. The site occupies a total area of 5.78ha. There are excellent views from the interior, with visibility to the south-east restricted by the higher ground of Rathcoran hillfort. The interior is under a mixture of pasture on the southern side, gorse at the centre and forestry to the north. The latter also encroaches upon the hillfort at the north-east side.

In contrast to Rathcoran, the enclosing elements do not follow the contours of the hill, but disregard topography to form three circular enclosures. The inner and middle enclosing elements are separated by approximately 37m, while the middle and outer examples are 35m apart. The inner rampart comprises a low-rise stone bank with no corresponding ditch. The bank is on average 0.2m in height and 5.5m wide. Two entrances to the north/north-east and north may be original. There are no surface features to suggest habitation, but there is extensive vegetation cover inside the enclosure. The outer enclosing element is similar in composition where visible. It is denuded and remains in forestry or actively farmed areas, but is visible from the south where it is 0.2m high and 5m wide. The outer defences are more irregular in shape than the innermost example which may be a reflection of the local topography.

The middle enclosure is the most impressive of the three defensive elements. It comprises a well preserved bank with outer ditch and a counterscarp bank on the southern and eastern side. The bank and counterscarp seem to be composed mainly of earth with indications of stone facing. The height of the bank ranges 2.4m–0.5m and is on average 7m wide. The ditch ranges from 2.9m–1.3m in depth and is on average 7m wide. The counterscarp bank is 0.4m–0.9m in height and is on average 3m wide. There are a number of small breaks along the perimeter, although there is no clear indication of an original entrance(s).

Geophysical survey (Figure 5.26 and Figure 5.27; O'Driscoll 2014b) revealed strong magnetic anomalies over the perimeter of the inner and outer defences (**G1a–G1d** and **G4**). These are unlikely to derive from the type of stone comprising the banks, which mainly consist of non-magnetic sandstones and granite. Similar to the response at the crest of the north-western section of the inner bank at Rathcoran, the magnetic anomalies probably reflect a wooden palisade destroyed by fire. The sustained heating and subsequent cooling of the stones would have significantly increased their magnetic signature, making them visible in the geophysical results. The results suggest that the slight nature of the inner and outer enclosures, as evidenced from the surface remains, were much more substantial. Survey undertaken over the middle enclosure did not record features that could be interpreted as a palisade. The anomaly G2, which runs adjacent to the middle bank, represents the response associated with a post and barbed wire fence.

FIGURE 5.25: RATHNAGREE HILLFORT, WITH EXCAVATION OF THE MIDDLE ENCLOSURE (CENTRE RIGHT).

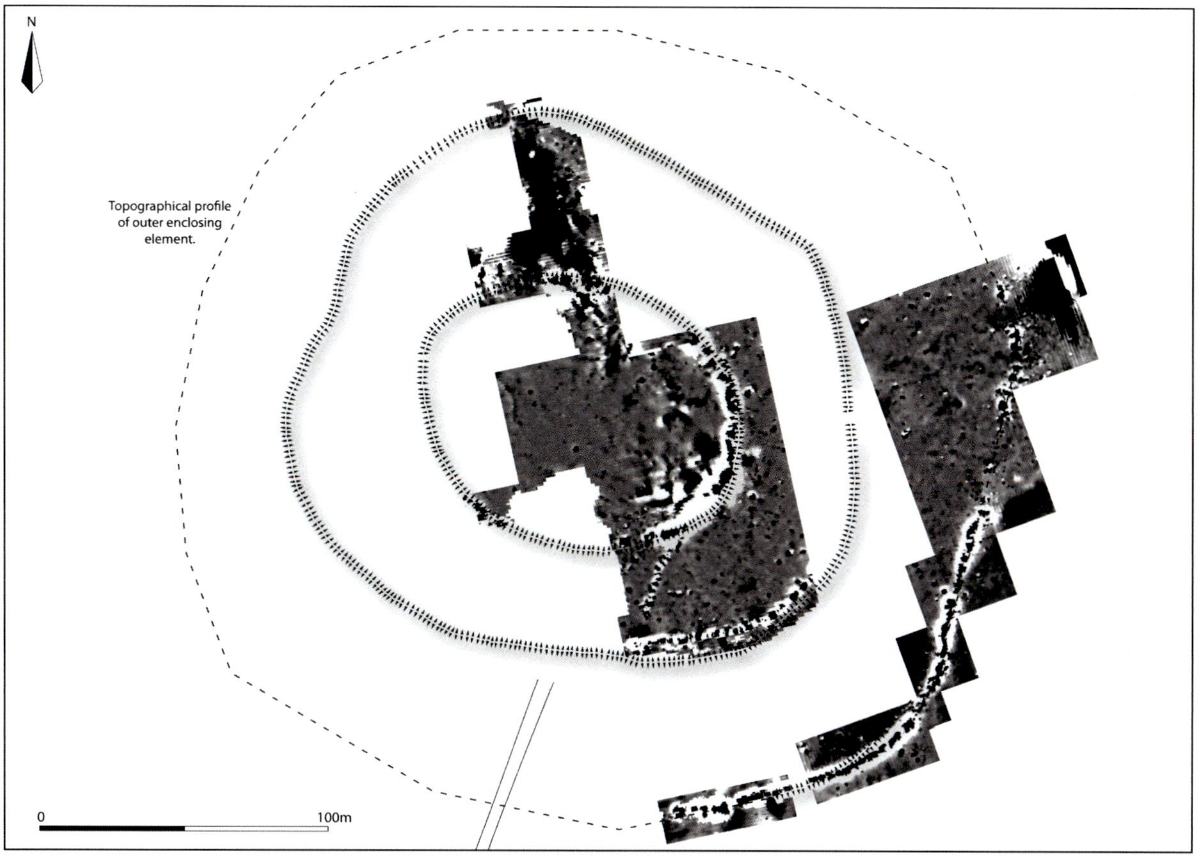

FIGURE 5.26: RESULTS OF GEOPHYSICAL SURVEY AT RATHNAGREE HILLFORT.

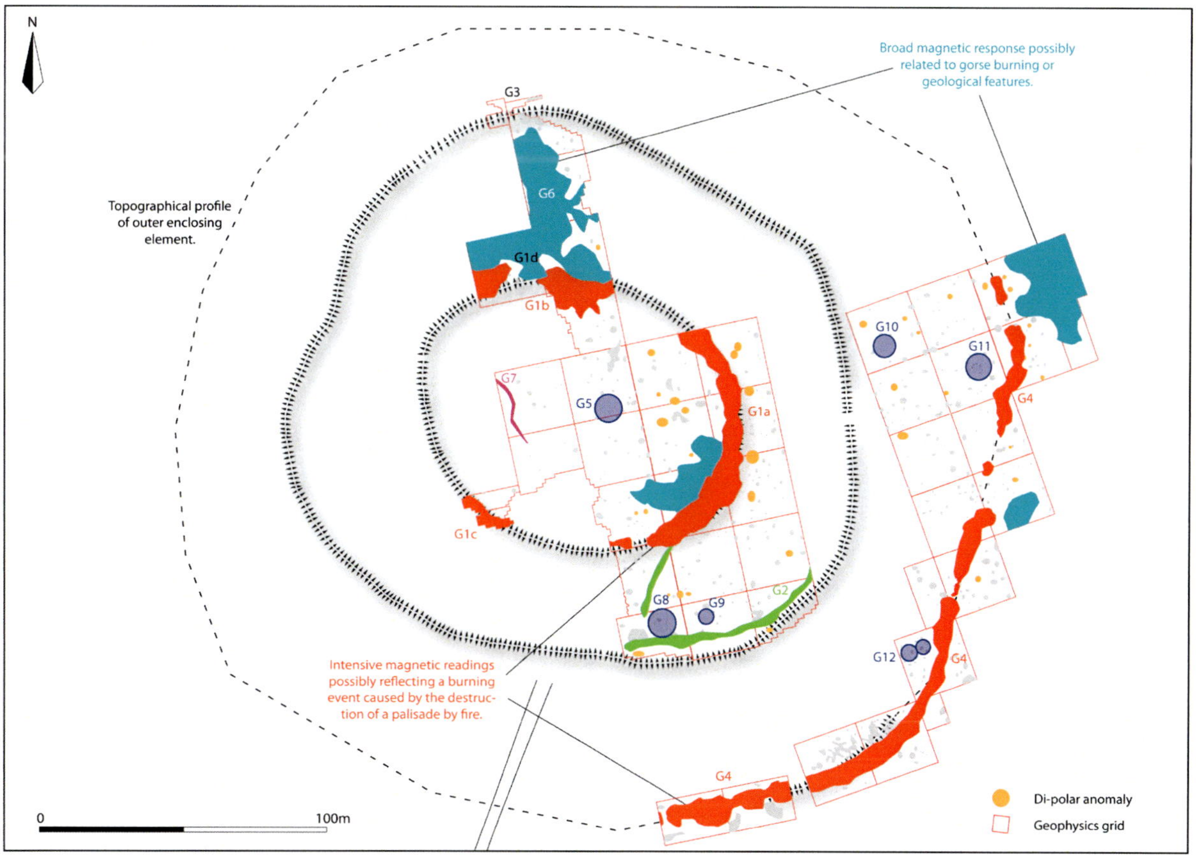

FIGURE 5.27: INTERPRETATION OF RESULTS FROM GEOPHYSICAL SURVEY OF RATHNAGREE HILLFORT.

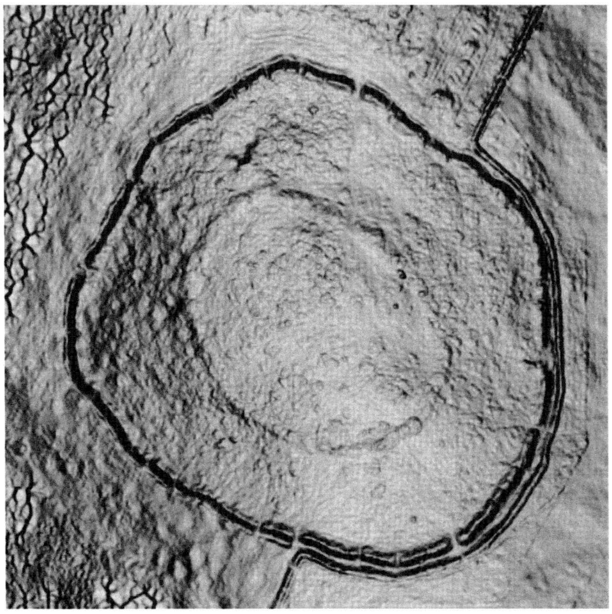

FIGURE 5.28: SLOPE ANALYSIS HIGHLIGHTING BREAKS AND DEPRESSIONS IN MIDDLE ENCLOSURE AT RATHNAGREE.

Similar to Rathcoran, up to 25 openings or depressions have been identified in the middle bank of Rathnagree (Figure 5.28 and Figure 5.29). The majority are small gaps less than 2m wide, although they are often not complete breaks and could be described as depressions between more substantial portions of the bank. Some of these could relate to gang working or seasonal building, but because many do not have corresponding causeways they are likely to be caused by modern farming. Four substantial breaks with possible causeways could be original entrances. They are positioned at the north, south, east and west of the perimeter and measure between 2.8–6.1m. The eastern example is the most substantial, where GPS survey identified a small internal avenue of boulders and stones extending from the edge of the bank terminals that may have formed a formal entrance. This broadly corresponds with the geophysical results of the outer enclosing elements where there are a number of possible breaks in the strong anomalies associated with this feature. The possible northern entrance comprises a 2.3m break in the middle enclosure and this corresponds with the geophysical results which do not indicate the former presence of a bank of ditch in this area (**G3**).

A level platform approximately 4m in width abuts the inside of the middle enclosing element (Figure 5.29). This is most prevalent at the north-east and west where the steep natural slope of the hilltop emphasises this feature. A similar feature was identified at Rathcoran and Mooghaun, and may be a construction feature.

The LiDAR and GPS surveys revealed up to 19 possible hut structures in the interior of Rathnagree hillfort Figure 5.30). These are apparent as circular terraces cut into the natural slope of the hilltop and are concentrated at the west and south-west. The slopes in those areas are much steeper, which has made the terraces more apparent. Additional structures may be present that are not visible

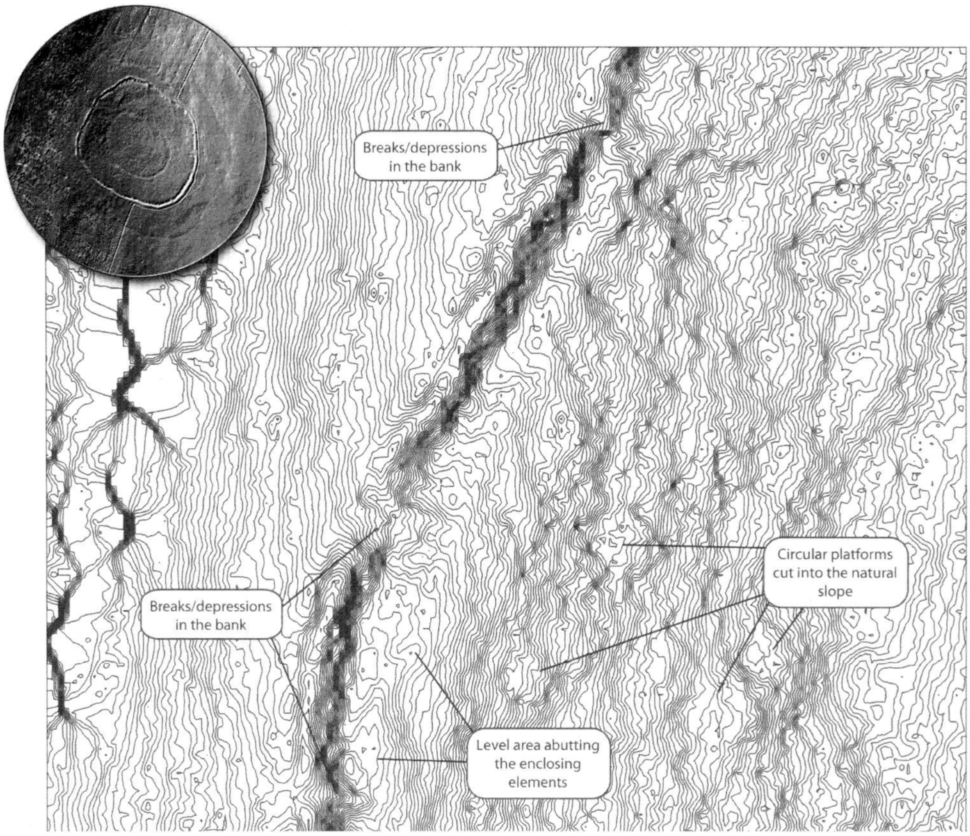

FIGURE 5.29: CONTOUR LINES DERIVED FROM LIDAR DATA OF MIDDLE ENCLOSURE OF RATHNAGREE.

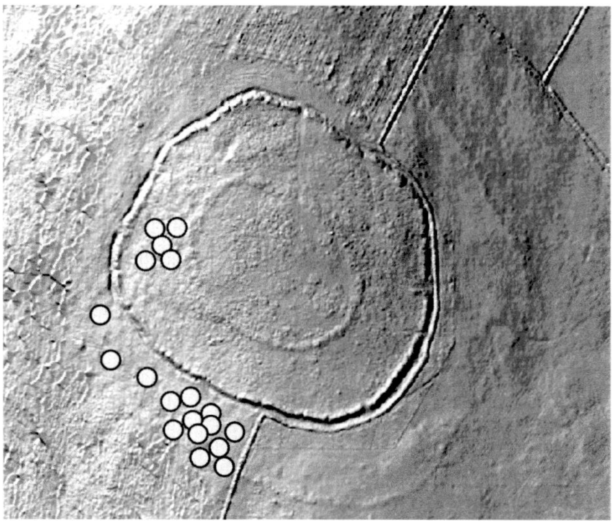

FIGURE 5.30: POSSIBLE HUT SITES RECORDED BY GPS AND LIDAR AT RATHNAGREE.

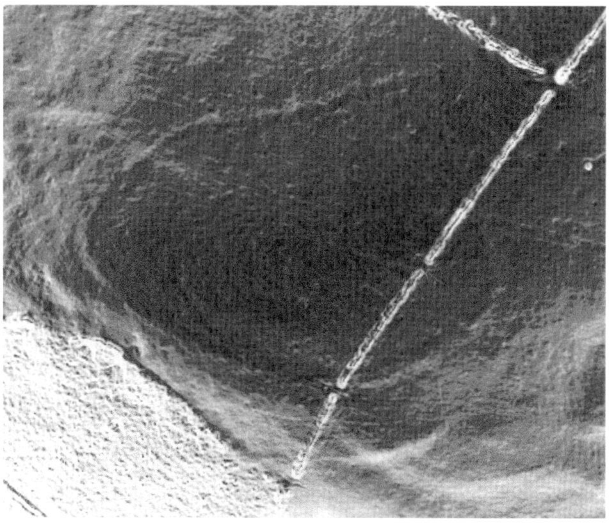

FIGURE 5.31: SLOPE ANALYSIS OF LIDAR DATA OBTAINED FOR SRUHAUN HILLFORT.

in the LiDAR data. This is suggested by the results of geophysical survey, which identified up to seven additional structures between the inner and middle enclosing elements. These range 6–12m in diameter and are apparent as circular or curvilinear arcs of pit-like features that could represent post-holes.

Sruhaun

A sub-circular univallate hillfort was identified by the author in Sruhaun townland on the south-west spur of Tuckmill Hill. This new site was identified by analysis of LiDAR data, but is not clearly visible on most aerial photographs (Figure 5.31). The site is located on a level terrace with steep slopes to the south and east. There are excellent views of the lowlands to the west and south, although visibility to the east is obscured by Tuckmill Hill itself.

The enclosure comprises a single low-rise bank approximately 4.5m wide, occupying a total area of 1.43ha. The slight nature of the bank makes it difficult to identify at ground level. There is a single 10m wide break in the enclosing elements at the north-east, which extend outwards toward the summit of Tuckmill Hill and Rathcoran hillfort, 375m to the north-east. A modern field bank runs through the eastern side of the interior. There are no obvious internal features visible on the ground or in the LiDAR data. The presence of occasional outcrop indicates that bedrock is close to the surface in some areas of the interior.

The entire 436m perimeter of the hillfort is apparent in the geophysical survey (Figure 5.32 and Figure 5.33; O'Driscoll 2014c) as an intense band of magnetism (**G2**). The results are similar to those found at Rathcoran and Rathnagree and may be suggestive of a prolonged burning event. The 'noise' extending beyond some of responses comprising **G2** are similar to that found at Toor More or at *fulachtaí fia*, suggesting this represents heat affected stone. This, in turn, implies that the enclosing elements comprised a low stone wall with wooden elements that were destroyed by fire. There are no obvious structural features visible in the geophysical results with little evidence for any form of internal activity. **G3** represents a 6m wide break in the enclosing elements at the northwestern side and this could represent an original entrance. There are no obvious pit-like features that might represent stake- or post-holes indicative of a gate feature, although these may be masked by the collapse of the wall terminal.

There are no obvious internal features that might represent structures or other settlement features. **G1** represents a series of broad magnetic anomalies that likely represent geological features such as close to surface rock outcrop. There is a notable lack of pit-like features (these can sometimes be archaeological features, as well as geological or modern) suggesting this enclosure may not have been built for settlement, unlike Rathcoran or, to a lesser extent, Rathnagree. This is an important outcome, as it has a significant impact on how we interpret the function of this enclosure. Considering the lack of internal features, the enclosure may have had a practical function as a cattle corral. Conversely, considering its strategic topographic position at the edge of a hillspur in a highly visible location, the enclosure may have been positioned to overlook routes to the summit of Tuckmill Hill, as well as acting as a defensive-looking enclosure from afar.

5.6 Tinoran

This impressive hillfort is located near the western edge of the Baltinglass area and is divided equally between two townlands, Tinoran Hill North and Tinoran Hill

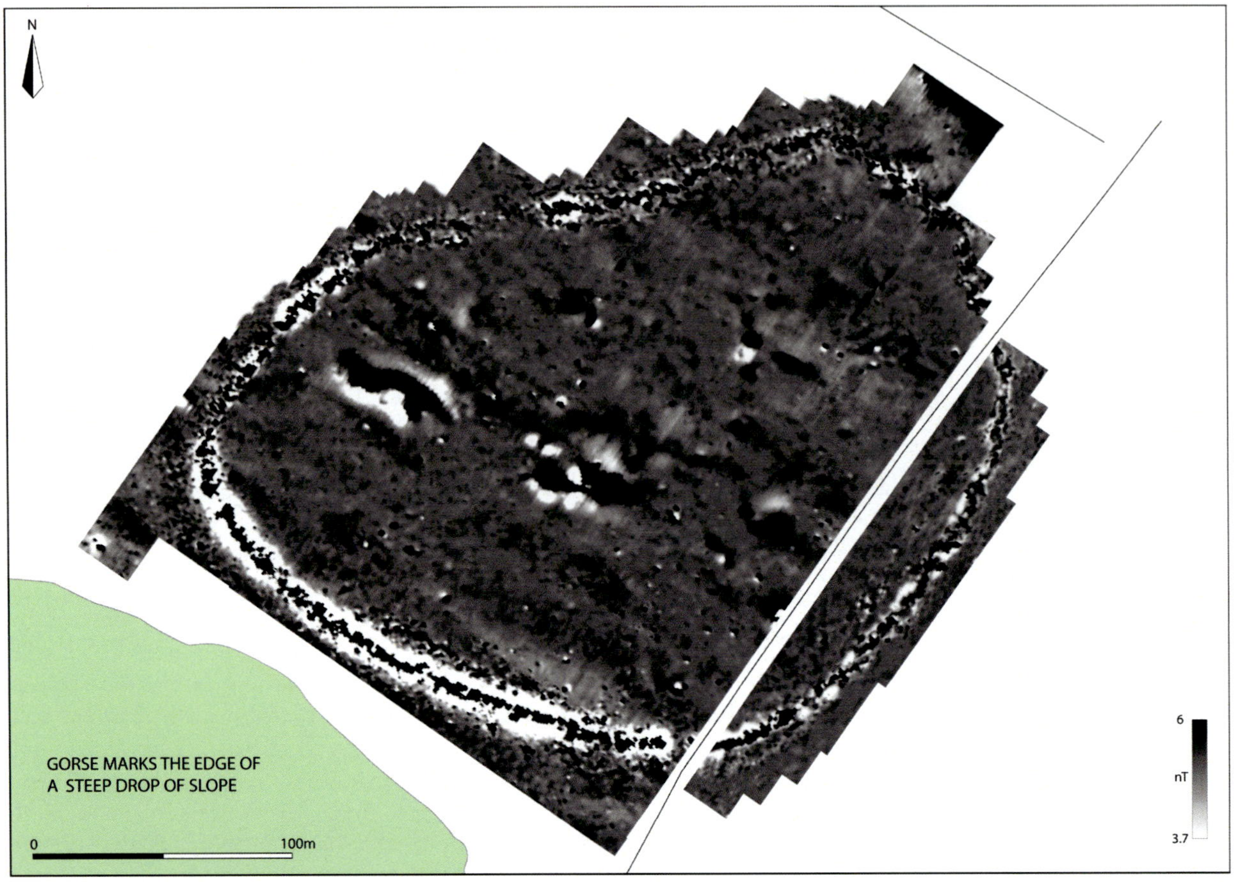

FIGURE 5.32: RESULTS OF GEOPHYSICAL SURVEY (MAGNETIC GRADIOMETRY) AT SRUHAUN HILLFORT.

FIGURE 5.33: INTERPRETATION OF RESULTS FROM GEOPHYSICAL SURVEY OF SRUHAUN HILLFORT.

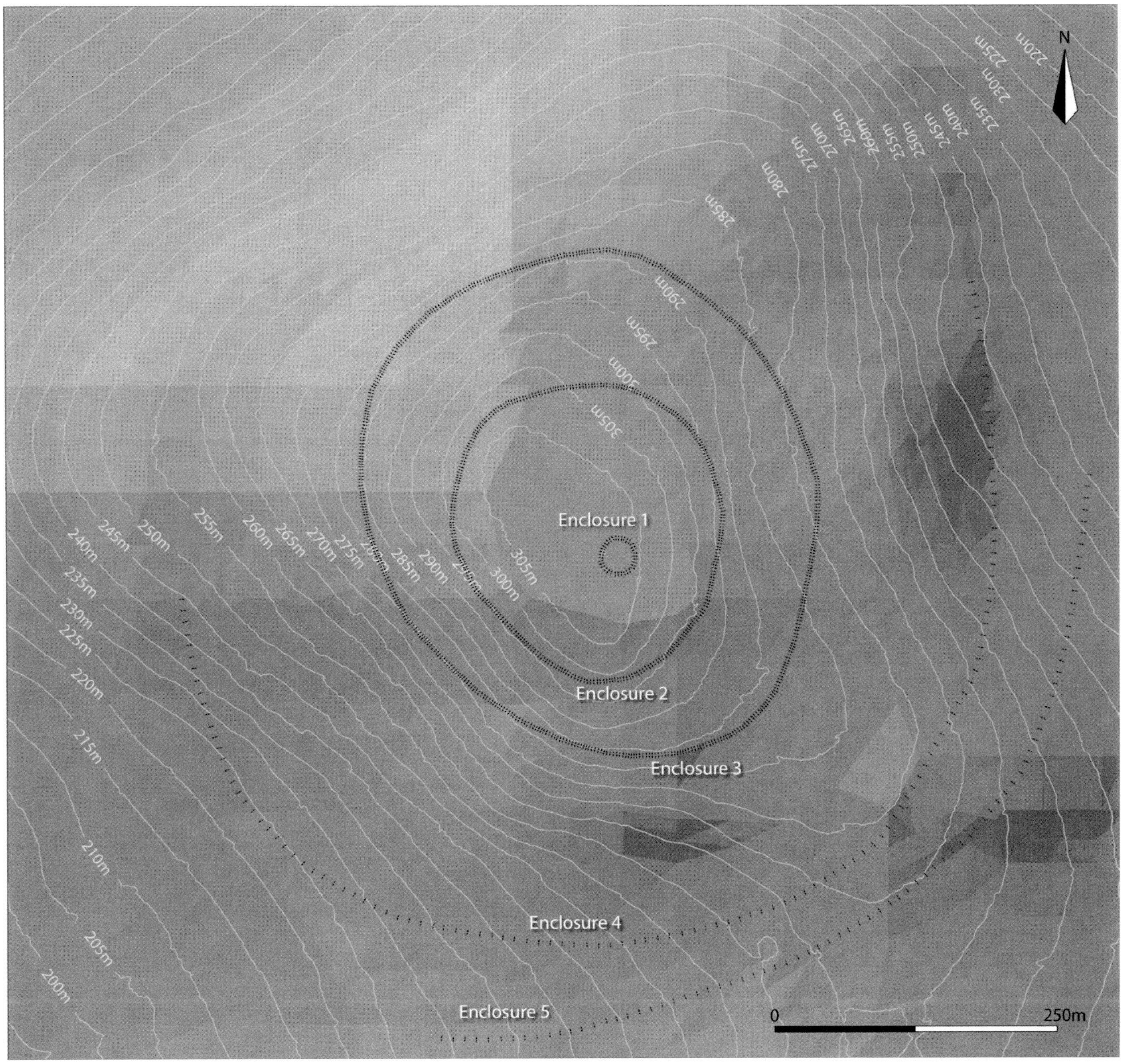

FIGURE 5.34: PLAN OF HILLFORT ON TINORAN HILL, CO. WICKLOW.

South (Figure 5.34 and Figure 5.35). It is the second largest hillfort in Ireland (WI026-004), occupying a total area of 84.03ha. There are four widely spaced enclosing elements, with a fifth small enclosure at the summit that probably belongs to the later ringfort class which date to the Early Medieval period (312m OD). There are panoramic views from the summit with particularly excellent visibility to the north, north-west and east. Tinoran can be translated as 'house of Odhrán'. Most of the hillfort was forested in the modern era, with resulting destruction to large parts of the interior. This forestry continues to be harvested and replanted. Portions of the outer two enclosing elements at the south-eastern side of the hill are in farmland pasture.

Due to the extent of forestry, the majority of Tinoran hillfort could not be surveyed with GPS or using geophysical techniques (Figure 5.35). LiDAR survey was obtained at 0.5m resolution, making it possible to record the hillfort enclosures in some detail despite the forestry cover, with the exception of the innermost enclosure (Figure 5.36).

The inner enclosure comprises an earth and stone bank, 2.2m in average width, and 0.9–1.2m in height, enclosing an area of 0.06ha. This is named as the 'Round O' on the first and second editions of the six-inch Ordnance Survey. The exterior face of this bank has a stone revetment. There is a ditch immediately outside this, measuring 1.6m wide and 0.8m deep, which is best preserved on the south/south-west side. The age of this small enclosure is unknown, however the form of the enclosing elements suggests it may be a ringfort of Early Medieval date.

The second enclosing element is oval in shape and surrounds an area of 4.67ha. This is depicted on the second

Figure 5.35: Satellite image of Tinoran hillfort, Co. Wicklow (Google Earth 2017).

edition Ordnance Survey map and follows the 300m contour varying from 304–296m OD. This bank is now incorporated into modern field boundaries. It is best preserved on the south-west side as an 8m wide bank of boulders and stones with an external height of 2m. This was built on a relatively steep slope using boulders and large stones. There is no indication of an associated ditch. Immediately inside the southern section of the bank there is a possible hut structure (WI026-004001), consisting of a D-shaped platform measuring 14m by 12m, cut into the hillslope. This is defined on the north and east slope by a boulder wall, 1.2–1.3m in width, and a steep scarp 0.8m in height to the south. Other occupation features are difficult to identity due to forest cover.

The third enclosing element is located 65–127m outside of the second enclosure. It is somewhat oval in shape and follows the 280m contour, ranging 276–284m OD over

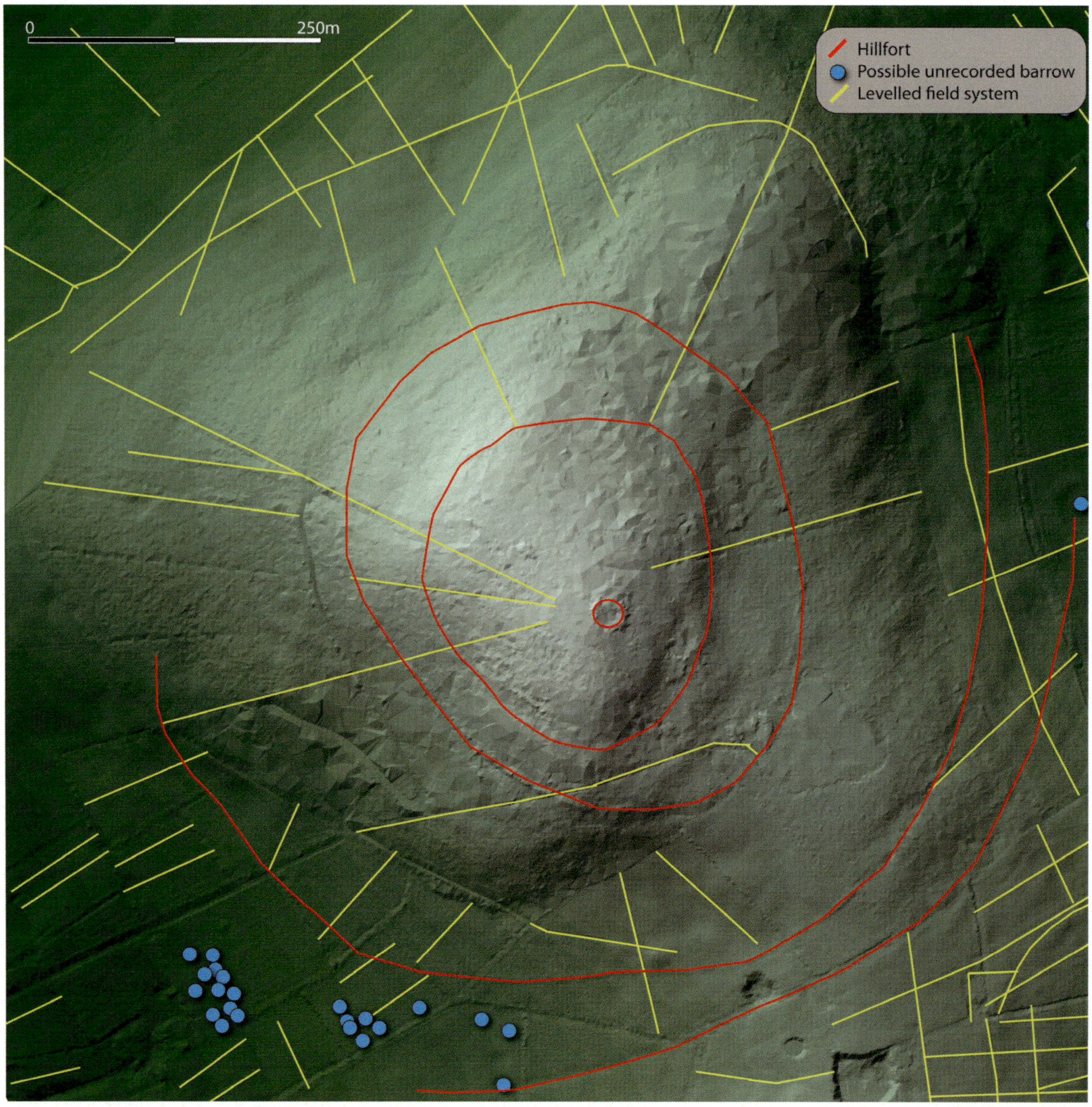

Figure 5.36: Unrecorded field systems and possible barrows identified by LiDAR on Tinoran Hill.

a perimeter of 1.37km. This enclosure occupies an area of 14.46ha. The southern half of the enclosing elements is now incorporated into a field wall. The original bank survives best at the south-west where it is under dense gorse growth. It is of similar construction to the second enclosure, comprising a low-rise bank of boulders and large stones measuring approximately 6m wide and 3.2m in external height. There is no indication of an associated ditch.

The partial remains of a fourth enclosing element were identified through aerial photography (Condit 1998: 15). The southern side of this enclosure survives as a low-rise bank feature in agricultural land, and measures approximately 6m wide and up to 0.3m high. There is a slight indication of an outer ditch. When projected, the enclosure occupies an area of 55.74ha, with the bank following an elevation of 221–244m OD. A large ring-barrow (WI026-005) abuts the enclosure on the eastern side. This has a low domed interior, 16–22m in width and 0.4m in height, surrounded by a ditch, 7–9m in width, with an outer bank 11–18m in width and 0.3m in average height. The barrow is approximately 55m in diameter.

The author identified a possible fifth enclosure using LiDAR, located 50–97m outside the former example (Figure 5.34). This is best preserved on the southern side where it survives as a low-rise bank with an external ditch 8.2–11.6m wide and up to 1.2m deep. When projected, this fifth enclosure may enclose an area of 84.03ha.

The LiDAR survey also revealed a considerable number of relict field patterns surrounding the hilltop. Most of the levelled examples are likely to pre-date the completion of the first edition Ordnance Survey mapping programme in 1842. Up to 29 possible ring-ditches/barrows were also recorded using this technique.

5.7 Hughstown

This is the westernmost hillfort of the Baltinglass cluster. It is located on the border between counties Kildare and Wicklow in the townland of Hughstown (KD038-025001). The site has been levelled by modern agricultural activity and is currently used for cattle grazing Figure 5.37 and Figure 5.38). There is excellent visibility from the site, with panoramic views from the summit (295m OD).

The fort has been recorded as a bivallate enclosure with a small enclosure of probable later date at the summit of the hill. The latter comprises a large boulder bank with no corresponding ditch feature. Condit (1998: 16) recorded a 2m wide entrance gap to the north that may be original. A large circular setting of stones, 17m in diameter, is visible near the centre of the enclosure. No other structural features are visible on the surface, although Condit (1998: 16) notes 'circular arrangements' of boulders, indicating more than one such feature was visible in the past. There is a recorded mound (KD038-025002) within

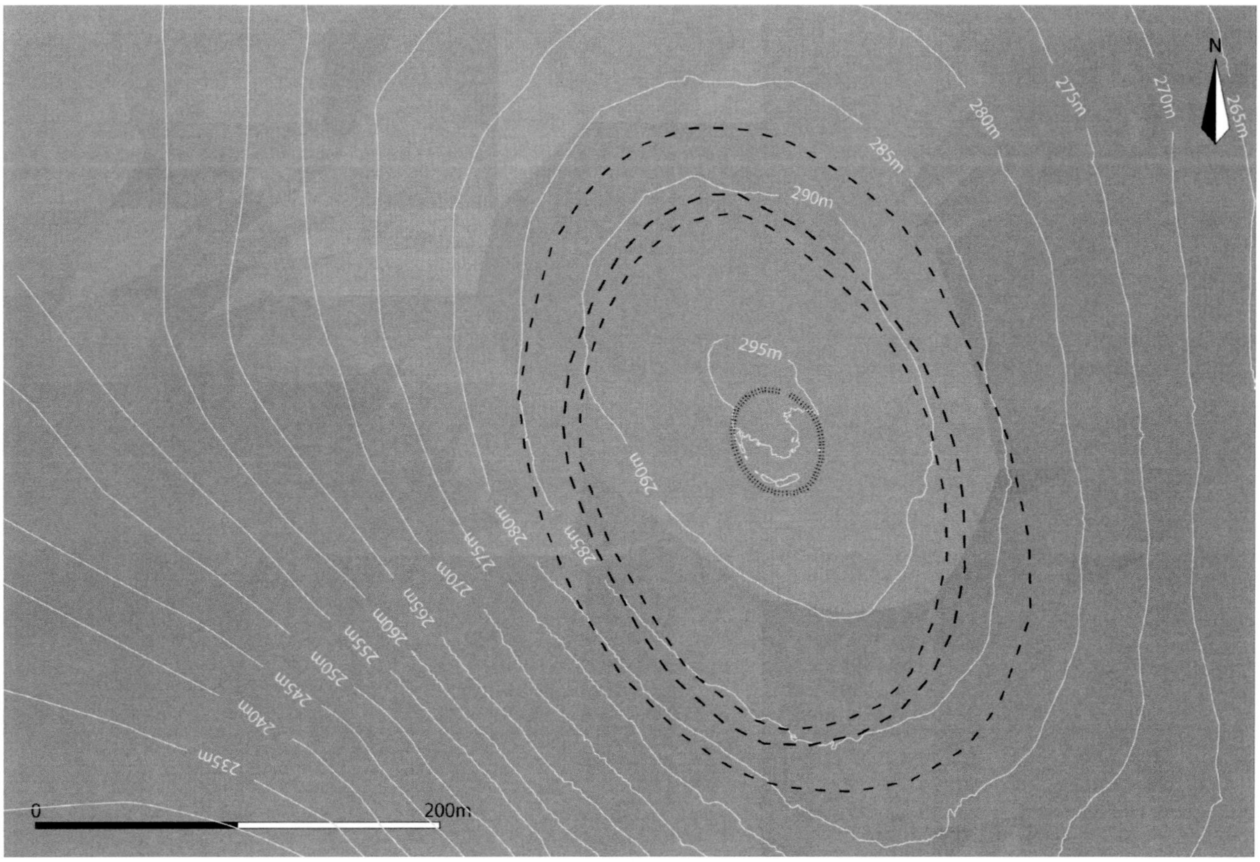

Figure 5.37: Plan of hillfort at Hughstow, Co. Kildare.

FIGURE 5.38: SATELLITE IMAGE OF HUGHSTOWN HILLFORT (GOOGLE EARTH 2017).

FIGURE 5.39: HUGHSTOWN FORT. NOTE THE VEGETATION GAPS IN THE OUTER ENCLOSING ELEMENTS, POSSIBLY INDICATING BREAKS IN THE ORIGINAL ENCLOSURE (CAMBRIDGE AERIAL PHOTOGRAPHIC COLLECTION).

this enclosure although this cannot be identified today. That feature may instead be located 180m to the north of the hillfort, where there is a 1.5m high mound of earth, 12m in diameter.

Outside of this central enclosure, Irish Army Air Corp and Cambridge University aerial photographs (Figure 5.39) reveal two enclosing elements as parch-marks, separated by a distance of 23–48m. These are not recorded on the Ordnance Survey mapping of the nineteenth century. The second enclosing element lies at 288–274m OD, and the third example at 292–285m OD, which means they generally follow the contours of the hill. Condit (1998: 16) suggests these defences both consisted of a bank with an external rock-cut ditch. However, survey by the author has revealed a more complex arrangement of up to four enclosing elements.

Geophysical survey (Figure 5.40 and FIgure 5.41; O'Driscoll 2014d) revealed the second enclosing element as a series of up to four concentric features (**G5a** and **G5b**). These appear prominently in the geophysical survey as two concentric sets of strong magnetic anomalies, although the features are disrupted throughout their lengths, possibly indicating the presence of numerous causeways/breaks. The strong magnetic readings appear to represent areas of burning that could be interpreted as evidence for the destruction of these defences. Each set comprises concentric annular features approximately 1.8–3.1m apart. There is some evidence for associated pit-like features that could represent post-holes and these are mostly apparent at the north-east, where they are spaced approximately 1.2m apart. Both sets of features are concentric and produced a similar geophysical response, possibly indicating they may be contemporary.

Cambridge University aerial photographs reveal a broad parch-mark over the circuit of these features, possibly indicating that stone was incorporated in the complex design of the defences. The four concentric anomalies could represent two moderately spaced enclosing elements, each of which consists of a stone bank and external ditch. Both banks could have contained wooden elements that were destroyed by fire. Subsequent erosion of this material into the ditch may explain the presence of two closely spaced magnetic features.

The outer enclosing element (the third enclosure recorded by Condit) is partially preserved at the north-east, where it comprises a curving field bank of large boulders in line with vegetation marks revealed in aerial photographs. Geophysical survey confirmed this bank continued along the north and north-west side where it is approximately 5–7m wide (**G7**). There is no clear geophysical indication of a ditch feature, although LiDAR data suggests the presence of an in-filled external ditch. This slight topographical feature continues along its path and is visible in the LiDAR data at the west and south-west. It is particularly evident at the west where it is up to 8.5m in width. Vegetation marks on Irish Air Corp aerial photographs suggest this may be a ditch feature. It is notable that the outer enclosing element produced a notably different geophysical response than the multiple enclosing elements that represents Condit's enclosure. It is also apparent that the outer defences are not concentric with the latter.

There is no clear evidence in the geophysical survey for an entrance in any of the enclosing elements at Hughstown. However, there are a considerable number of breaks throughout the perimeter of the enclosing elements. This may have been a morphological feature of the enclosing elements, or it could be related to the destruction of the monument by agricultural activity such

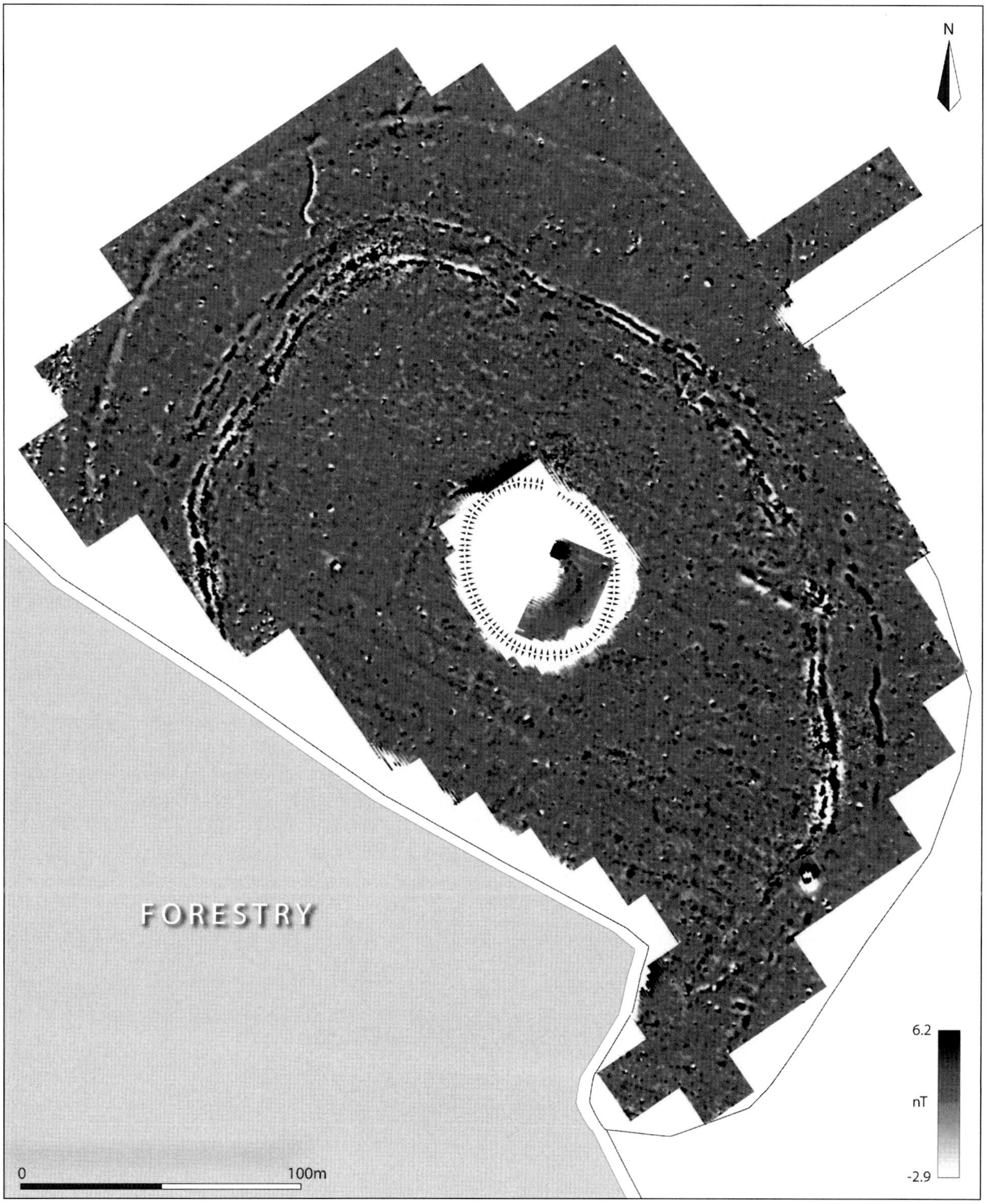

Figure 5.40: Results of geophysical survey (magnetic gradiometry) at Hughstown fort.

as ploughing. A linear arrangement of strong readings indicative of an area of burning is visible at the north (**G4b**). This could have marked a formal entrance to the interior, which does not align with the entrance of the summit enclosure probably because this was built at a later date.

The geophysical results identified 41 ephemeral circular anomalies in the interior of Hughstown that are tentatively interpreted as hut structures (**G10–G50**). These range from 6m to 17m in diameter, and appear as faint circular bands of magnetic readings. A single structure is positioned inside the enclosure at the summit of the hillfort. This is the largest hut site and is visible on the ground as a circular setting of stones, approximately 17m in diameter (**G50**). The stone setting is approximately

FIGURE 5.41: INTERPRETATION OF RESULTS FROM GEOPHYSICAL SURVEY OF HUGHSTOWN HILLFORT.

0.6m wide and up to 0.4m high. High magnetic readings in the geophysical results suggest this may have been a footing for a wooden palisade that was subsequently destroyed by fire. There is no obvious entrance feature visible on the surface or in the magnetic data, although a portion of the structure has been truncated by recent activity within the centre of the enclosure.

LiDAR survey on the eastern slopes of Hughstown reveals a series of unrecorded relict field boundaries (Figure 5.42). None of these are apparent in historic mapping, and therefore may be of pre-nineteenth century date. They comprise elongated fields with boundaries spaced 15–28m apart. On the southwestern edge of Hughstown, in an area of newly planted forestry, a pair of extant banks are separated approximately 26m

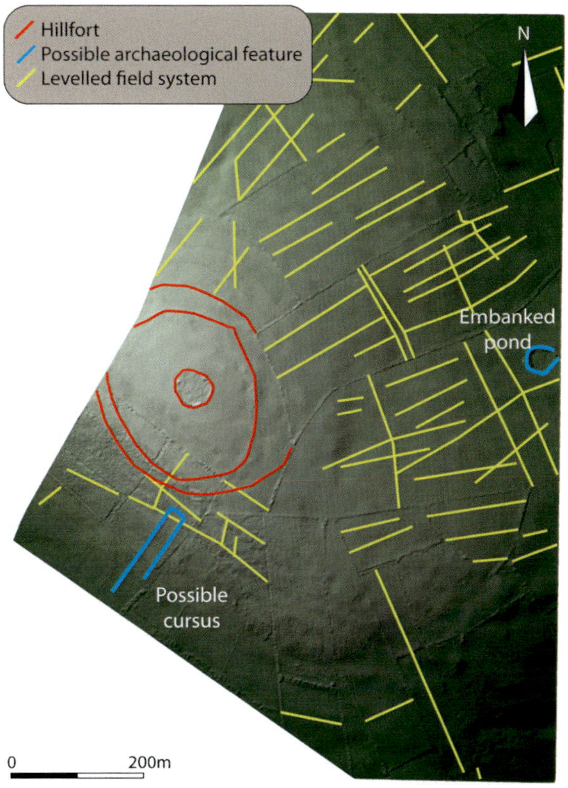

FIGURE 5.42: UNRECORDED FIELD SYSTEMS, EMBANKED POND AND POSSIBLE CURSUS IDENTIFIED BY LIDAR NEAR HUGHSTOWN FORT.

FIGURE 5.43: EMBANKED POND EAST OF HUGHSTOWN FORT.

apart. These banks are larger than most field boundaries and measure 9–12m in width and extend north-east to south-west for approximately 155m. These features are recorded by the Archaeological Survey of Ireland as a pair of parallel banks approaching the outer rampart on the south-west side of the hill (KD038–026). This is interpreted as a possible cursus, based on the width of the banks and apparent absence of an associated ditch, but this remains to be confirmed by excavation.

Also relevant is a large embanked pond 350m to the east of the hillfort. The western side of this feature is approximately 4m beneath the modern ground surface. The pond appears on early Ordnance Survey maps and is likely to have been constructed before 1842. Today, water is continually drained from the pond to prevent flooding, with the source likely to be a natural spring. Another large pond is positioned on the eastern side of the hilltop about 70m from the hillfort. Approximately 150m to the south-east is an unrecorded ring-barrow. The monument is approximately 18m in diameter and comprises a 4m wide band of stone, 0.3m high, with a low-rise central mound.

5.8 The Wider Landscape

Other prehistoric monuments are recorded in the Baltinglass area. They include the stone circles of Castleruddery, Co. Wicklow (WI021-032), located at the northern base of Spinans Hill (Figure 5.44), and Boleycarrigeen Co. Wicklow (WI027-029), situated on a plateau immediately to the east of Kilranlagh Hill (Figure 5.45). Boleycarrigeen comprises eleven stones, 1.3–1.94m in height, with a diameter of 15m. The stones rise in height from an entrance opening on the south-west side. A low-rise bank, 0.4m in height and approximately 2m in width, surrounds and abuts the outer edge of the stones. While there is no direct dating evidence, multiple stone circles in south-west Ireland broadly date to the period 1400–800 BC (O'Brien 2012a: 182) and a similar date could be ascribed to the Wicklow group. O'Brien (2004) has discussed the potential 'fusion' of ritual tradition in the West Cork region (stone circles with barrow monuments). The site at Reanascreena South in Co. Cork is somewhat comparable with Boleycarrigeen, comprising an embanked circle of 13 stones dated to 1253–835 BC (O'Brien 2012a).

The embanked stone circle at Castleruddery, Co. Wicklow, sits near the northern base of Spinans Hill, overlooking the Slaney River to the south. It comprises a series of 29 large boulders and stones and is approximately 30m in diameter. The entrance at Castleruddery is marked by two large quartz boulders marking a gap approximately 1.5m in width. An earthen bank on average 5m wide and 1m in height abuts the exterior face of the stone circle. A break in the bank corresponds with the entrance, where two large quartz boulders flank the terminals. Two enclosures, 50m and 80m in diameter, are visible surrounding the stone circle on aerial photographs. This is comparable with the possible stone circle on Brewel Hill in Co. Kildare, which is surrounded by a circular ditch approximately 60m in diameter.

The chronology of embanked stone circles is uncertain. The pottery assemblage from the embanked circle at Grange, Co. Limerick, prompted Ó Ríordáin (1952) to consider a later Neolithic date. Roche (2004) argued for a Late Bronze Age date, however, recent dating of this

Figure 5.44: Embanked stone circle at Castleruddery, Co. Wicklow.

Figure 5.45: Booleycarigeen stone circle, Co. Wicklow, with Keadeen Mountain in the background.

monument confirmed that it was constructed in the Late Neolithic (Cleary and O'Driscoll 2014; O'Driscoll and Cleary 2016). A similar date could be argued for Castleruddery, but again this cannot be confirmed in the absence of excavation.

There is a concentration of up to 14 stone circles at the edge of the mountain range to the north and west of the Baltinglass hillforts, of which Boleycarrigeen stone circle is the southernmost example (Figure 5.46). These circles are typically large and incorporate a considerable number of stones. The example at Tornant Upper, Co. Kildare (KD015-037) is up to 37m in diameter with some 20 stones. Broadleas Commons, Co. Kildare (KD029-023) is approximately 31m in diameter with up to 48 stones. Significantly, six of these stone circles are

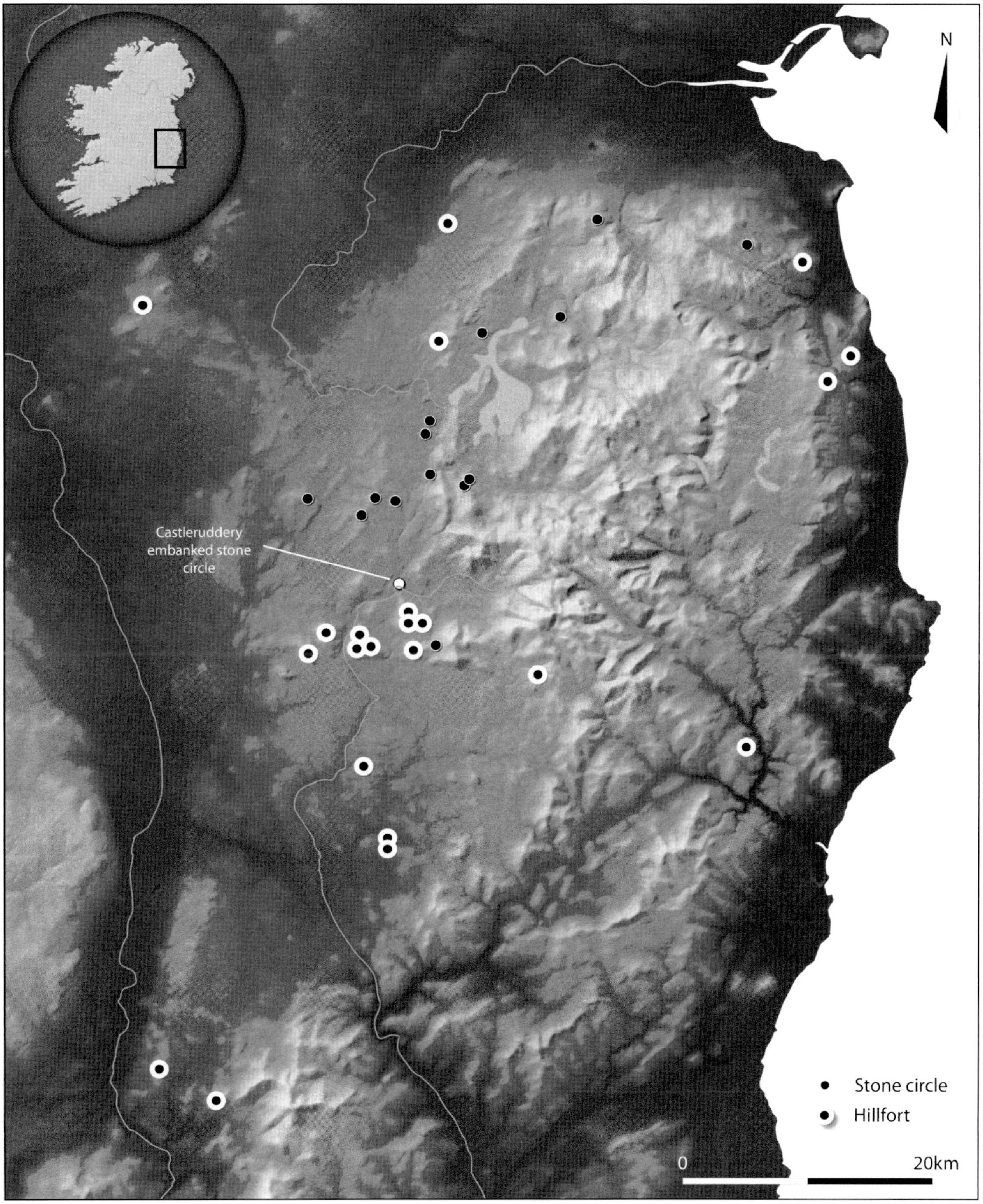

FIGURE 5.46: STONE CIRCLES IN THE BALTINGLASS STUDY AREA.

within an enclosure of some form or have small embankments abutting the face of the stone circle. They include Boleycarrigeen, Co. Wicklow; Brewel Hill, Co. Kildare (KD032-026002); Tornant Upper, Co. Kildare (KD015-037); Plezica, Co. Wicklow (WI015-088); Athgreany, Co. Wicklow (WI015-010), and Whiteleas, Co. Kildare (KD029-032). Burl (2000) has compared this group of stone circles in Wicklow to similar sites in Cumbria, England.

There is also a concentration of standing stones and standing stone pairs at the western foothills of the Wicklow Mountains (Figure 5.47). These monuments function as burial markers, indicators of routeways or boundaries and generally date to the Late Bronze Age. Like the aforementioned circles, they may be contemporary with the Baltinglass hillforts. Four standing stones are recorded within the immediate environs of the hillforts, none of which have been excavated. One

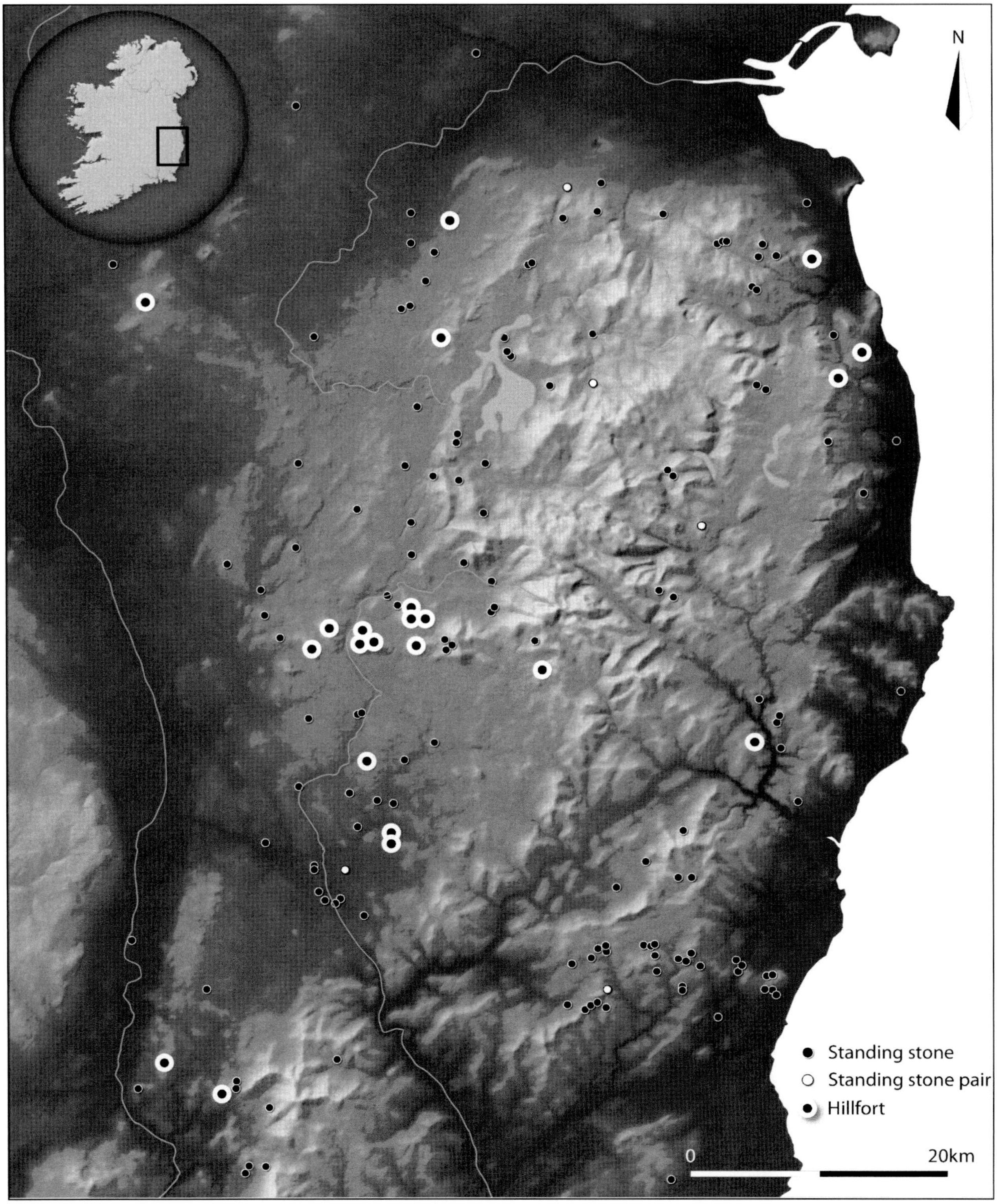

FIGURE 5.47: STANDING STONES IN THE BALTINGLASS STUDY AREA.

of these (WI027-043002) is positioned at the centre of a large enclosure at the base of Keadeen mountain (Figure 5.48). This enclosure was identified through aerial photography (Corlett 2004) and comprises a collapsed stone wall 1.5–1.8m in width and 0.5m in average height (*ibid.*). Seven hut structures were identified within the interior. Corlett (2004, 90) compares this enclosure with the hillforts on top of the surrounding hills, stating 'this enclosure may belong to the general family of hillforts in the area in as much as representing a political symbol of tribal strength'. While the size of the enclosure (2.75ha) is somewhat comparable, the siting and morphology suggest it probably did not function in the way a hillfort did. More comparable are a number of other large enclosures at the base Corballis, Hughstown, Tinoran and Tuckmill Hill.

The example at Rathmoon, a levelled enclosure located near the base of Hughstown, is classified by Grogan (2005b: 117) as a hilltop enclosure (WI026-009), despite its low-lying location. It is one of four large enclosures in the Baltinglass area positioned at the base of hilltops in inconspicuous lowland settings (Figure 5.48). The enclosure is depicted in the first and second edition Ordnance Survey 6 inch map as a univallate enclosure approximately 1.14ha in area. Aerial and satellite imagery reveal a more complex system of up to three somewhat concentric enclosing elements, all of which have been levelled (Figure 5.49).

Geophysical survey at Rathmoon revealed a complex system of enclosure and internal features that may be prehistoric (Figure 5.50 and Figure 5.51; O'Driscoll 2014e). The enclosure is sub-rectangular, comprising a series of widely-spaced enclosing elements measuring 160m (east–west) by 120m (north–south) occupying a total area of 1.71ha. The enclosing elements are spaced between 15–22m apart. The two outer enclosures (**G2** and **G4**) do not form complete circuits and are appended to inner enclosures. The responses from the geophysical survey suggest that these are ditch features, measuring

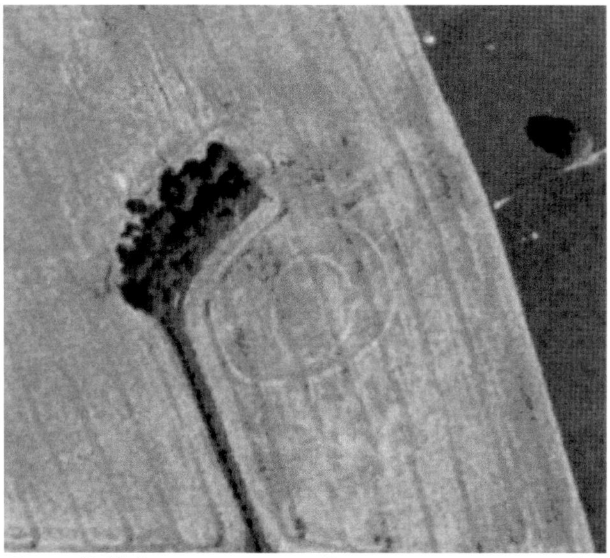

Figure 5.49: Satellite image of Rathmoon enclosure in Co. Wicklow (Google Earth 2017).

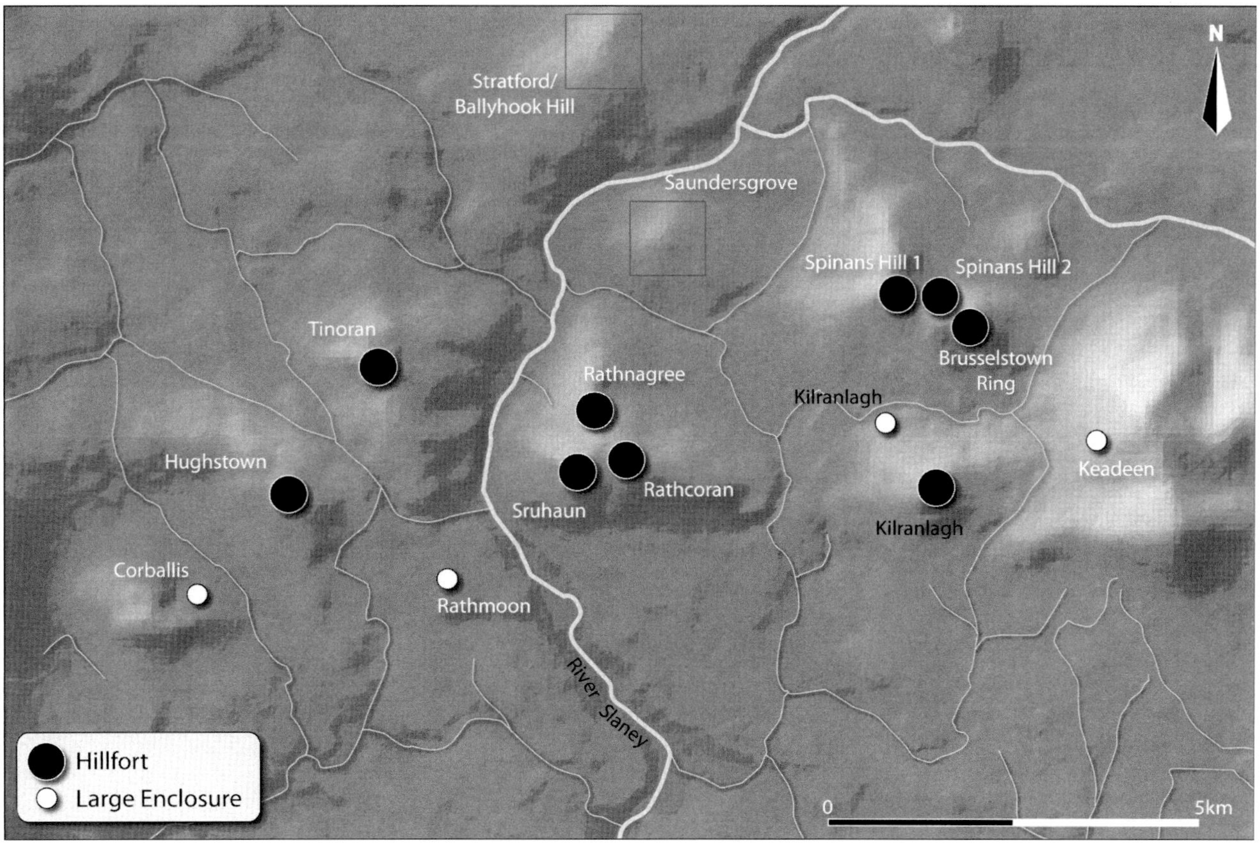

Figure 5.48: Distribution of hillforts and other large low-lying enclosures in the Baltinglass area.

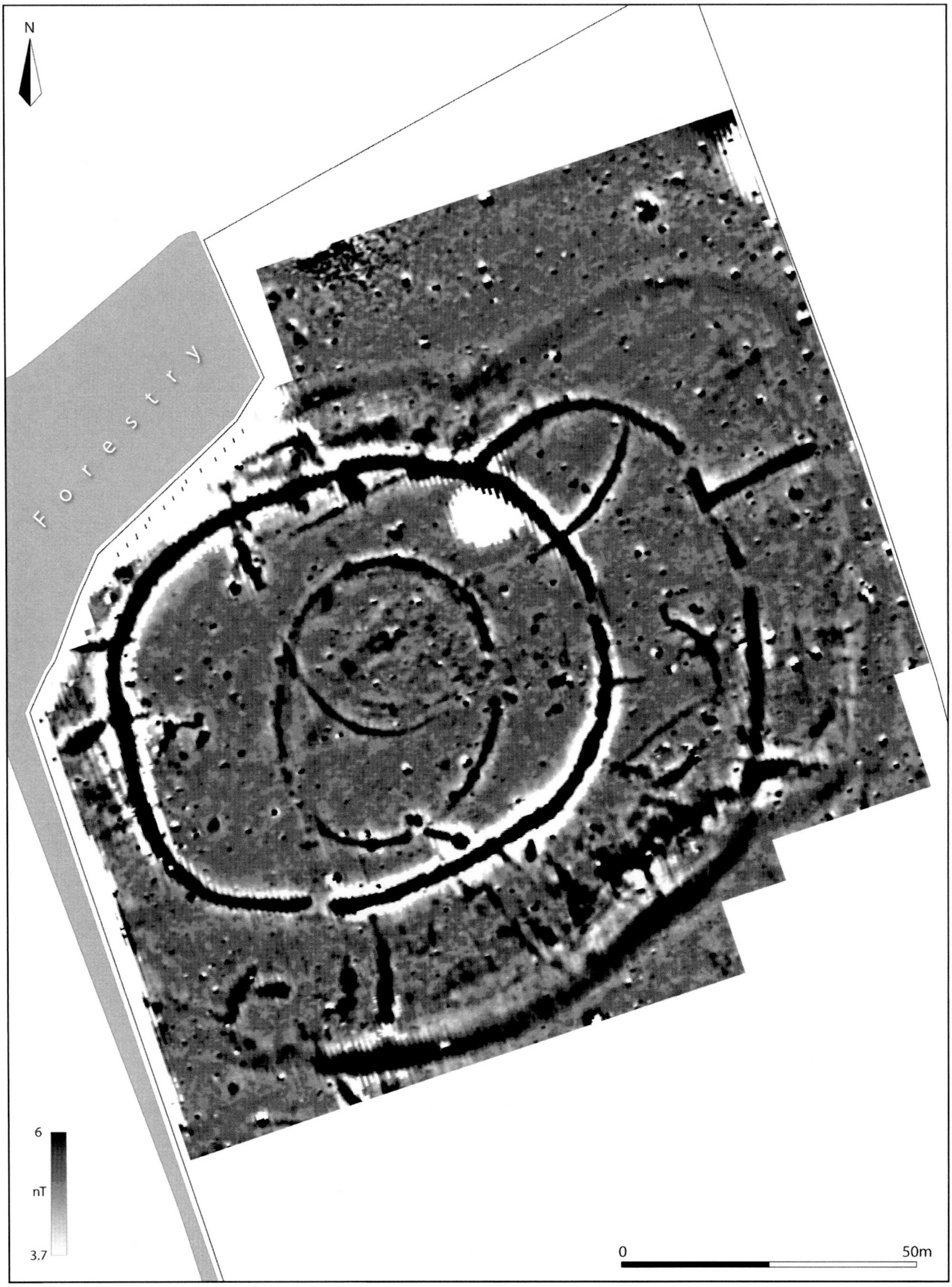

Figure 5.50: Results of geophysical survey (magnetic gradiometry) at Rathmoon.

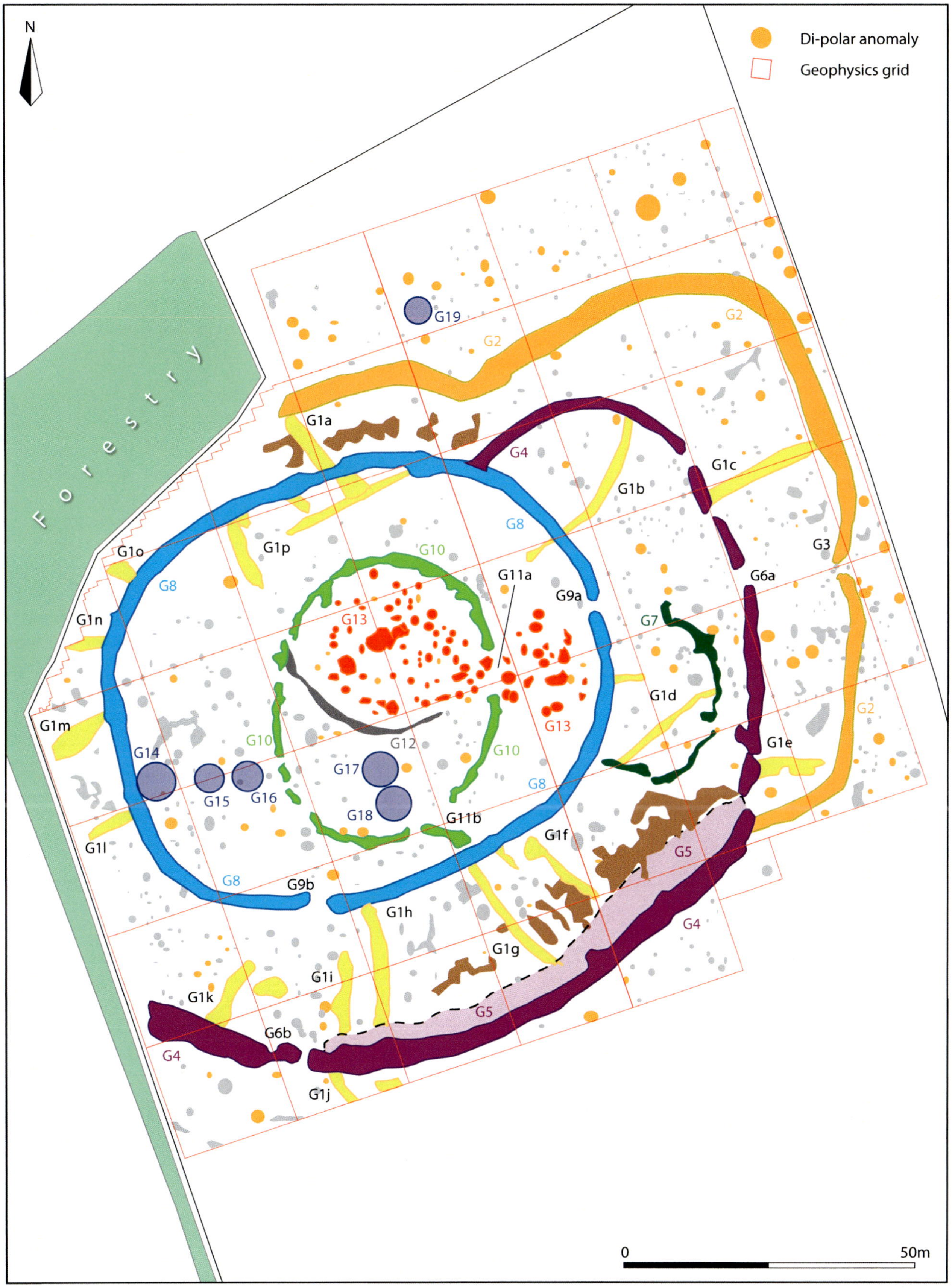

Figure 5.51: Interpretation of results from geophysical survey of Rathmoon.

up to 8m wide. These probably had internal banks (**G5**) and geophysical responses suggest that these were up to 9m wide. A series of radial banks between the outer two enclosures (**G1a–G1o**) were probably created in the early modern era for cultivation and animal grazing. The anomalies that define the two inner enclosures (**G8** and **G10**) are distinct from the latter examples and comprise a series of high magnetic responses 1.5–4m in width (although not high enough to be regarded as *in situ* burning). Considering these enclosures are apparent in the aerial and satellite imagery as probable ditch features, it is likely that they form ditches filled in with highly magnetic material. The inner enclosure is sub-divided by an annular band of magnetism (**G12**), probably a shallow ditch.

At the east, where the enclosures overlap, there is a corresponding entrance in each of the enclosing elements (**G3**, **G6a**, **G9a** and **G11a**), suggesting that all four enclosures were in use at the same time. These openings range from 6–2.3m in width. They probably formed a formal entrance to the site. It is notable that this is the only side of the enclosure where all four enclosing elements overlap. This may have been a deliberate attempt to monumentalise the entrance area. The entrance of the inner enclosure is slightly staggered, which may have been a purposeful arrangement to conceal visibility of the interior on approach. There are two other corresponding entrance breaks at the south (**G6b** and **G9b**).

Two faint circular features (**G17** and **G18**) were identified within the inner enclosing elements and a further three examples (**G14**, **G15** and **G16**) were identified between the inner two enclosures. These 6–8m in diameter and could represent levelled hut structures. Within the northern part of the inner enclosure and immediately outside the entrance area, there is a concentration of pit-like features (**G13**), as well as a strong number of magnetic responses at the centre. With no clear indication of domestic habitation, the composite monument could be regarded as a funerary complex, possibly similar to the so-called cemetery settlements found in Ireland.

Reference must also be made to a number of hill-top cairns in the Baltinglass area (Figure 5.52), many of which are likely to be of prehistoric date. These include the passage tomb on Rathcoran, now known to be of Early/Middle Neolithic date (Schulting per. comm.). Spinans Hill 1, Spinans Hill 2 and Kilranlagh hillforts each have cairns within or close to the enclosing elements. The acceptance of these monuments by the hillfort builders and their subsequent survival suggests that these were important to the hillfort communities.

There are also a significant number of earthen barrows of prehistoric date in the Baltinglass area (Figure 5.53). Within the area visible to the Baltinglass hillforts, there is a clear increase in the distribution of these burial monuments, although this may simply reflect more intensive agricultural activity in the midlands. Analysis of LiDAR and aerial imagery has revealed up to 105 possible barrows and/or enclosures in the area (Figure 5.54 and Figure 5.55). Most of these are positioned in low-lying areas, on the lower slopes of hilltops or near rivers and streams. There are two notable clusters; at the southern base of Tinoran and the southeastern base of Tuckmill Hill.

A total of 32 possible ring-ditches or levelled/low-relief ring-barrows were revealed by LiDAR surrounding Tuckmill Hill. These are visible in the data as faint circular banks surrounding slight central mounds. These generally occur in groups, although there are a number of isolated examples. They range in size from 4.8–18.6m in diameter, averaging 7.3m. This corresponds well with available data for later prehistoric Irish ring-ditches (McGarry 2009; also see Ahern 2012). McGarry (2009: 415) states that Irish examples average 11m in diameter, although there are a considerable number that measure less than 7m. There are also three recorded cist burials positioned at the northern and northwestern base of Tuckmill Hill that, when grouped with the possible barrows recorded in the LiDAR survey, surrounded the base of the hilltop on all sides.

As many as 29 possible ring-barrows were identified at Tinoran hillfort. Three of these are at the north-east base of the hilltop. The remainder are clustered at the south/south-east side, between the fourth and fifth enclosing elements of the hillfort. The majority comprise circular terraces, approximately 8–13m in diameter, cut into the natural slope defined by narrow banks with internal low-rise mounds. Caution is needed as modern farming can produce similar low-relief features.

5.9 Excavations and Finds in the Baltinglass Environs

Neolithic

The only scientific excavation undertaken in the Baltinglass hillfort complex was at the passage tomb (WI027-026003) within Rathcoran hillfort on Tuckmill Hill (Figure 5.56: No. 1). This was excavated in 1934–1936 by Walshe (1941). The monument consists of a kerbed cairn measuring 27m in diameter. Underneath this, five structures were identified, as well as an inner kerb of smaller stones. Three stones are inscribed with passage tomb art, two within the inner kerb and another in the outer kerb. The main tomb (Figure 5.57) consists of a 3.2m long passage leading to a 2m wide chamber roofed by slabs at the northern side of the cairn. This chamber has three recesses, one of which contains a large ornamented stone basin. The only other examples of such stone basins are from the famous passage tombs in the Boyne Valley, Co. Meath. A second chamber was found in the southern

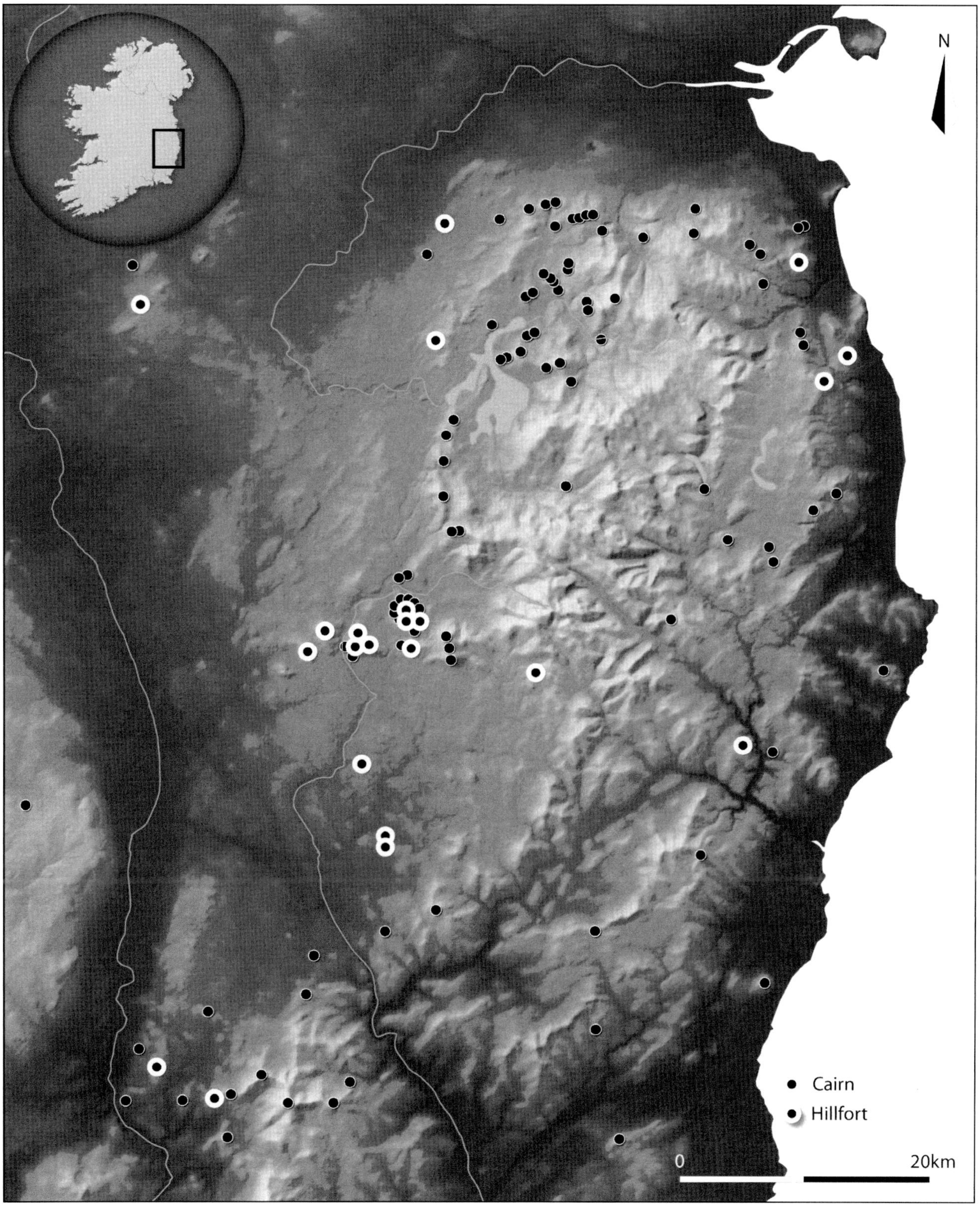

FIGURE 5.52: CAIRNS IN THE BALTINGLASS STUDY AREA.

section of the cairn, although no associated passage was identified. This chamber was similar to the former example, comprising three compartments. A third chamber is located to the north-east of the cairn with no associated passage. Two further structures were revealed during excavation consisting of a 'small cist-like' feature and a corbelled structure. The remains of at least three adults and one child were recovered. A number of artefacts associated with the use of the tomb include flint scrapers, bone pins and Carrowkeel ware pottery (Walshe 1941). A stone axe and a flint javelin-head are among the most notable pre-cairn artefacts recovered. Condit (1992: 20) records the find of a polished stone axehead from within the Spinans Hill 2 enclosure (Figure 5.56: No. 2). A per-

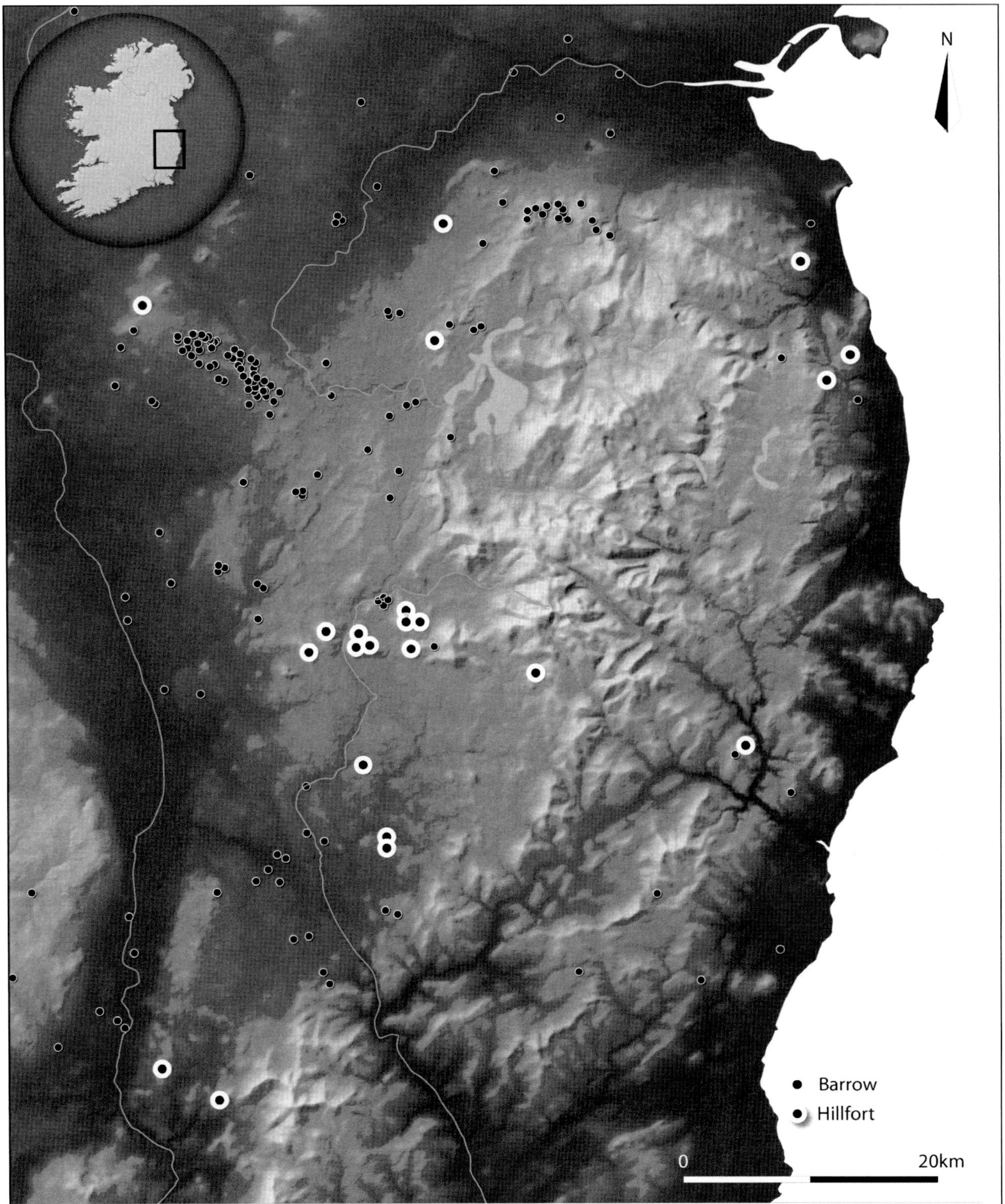

FIGURE 5.53: BARROWS LISTED IN *RECORD OF MONUMENT AND PLACES* FOR STUDY AREA.

forated stone axe-hammer was found in 1947 just over 1km to the east of Tuckmill Hill (Figure 5.56: No. 3).

At the north-western base of Spinans Hill in Ballintruer More townland, the investigation of a circular mound 24m in diameter and 2m in height (WI021-057) produced one pit burial containing the remains of an adult male and part of a second inhumation (Ryan 1973) (Figure 5.56: No. 4). A second burial contained two adolescent inhumations protected by a polygonal cist. One of these had a simple Neolithic bowl and a piece of lignite, with a crouched burial dated 3338–2910 BC. Although Raftery (1973) has argued that the burial is consistent with the Linkardstown burial tradition, Brindley and

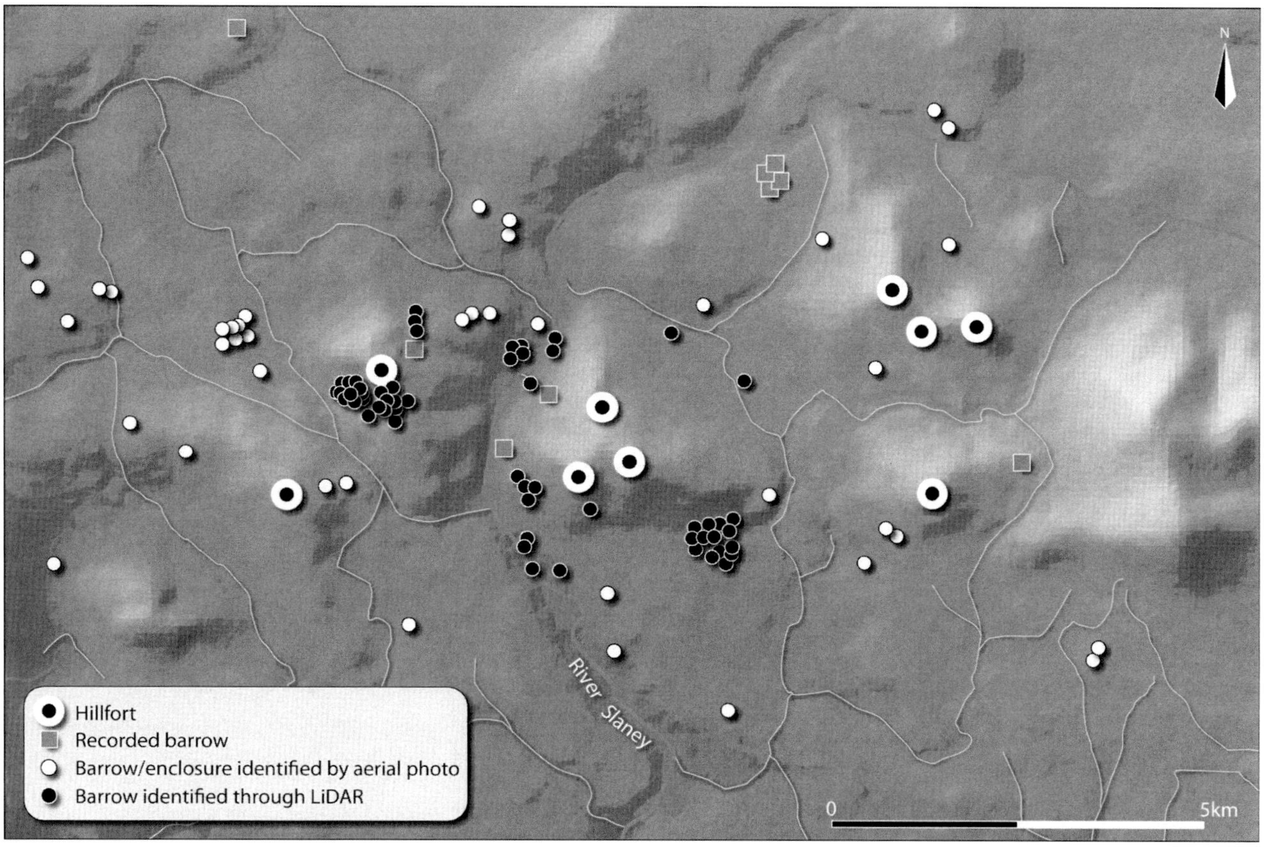

Figure 5.54: Possible barrow monuments identified by this project in the Baltinglass area.

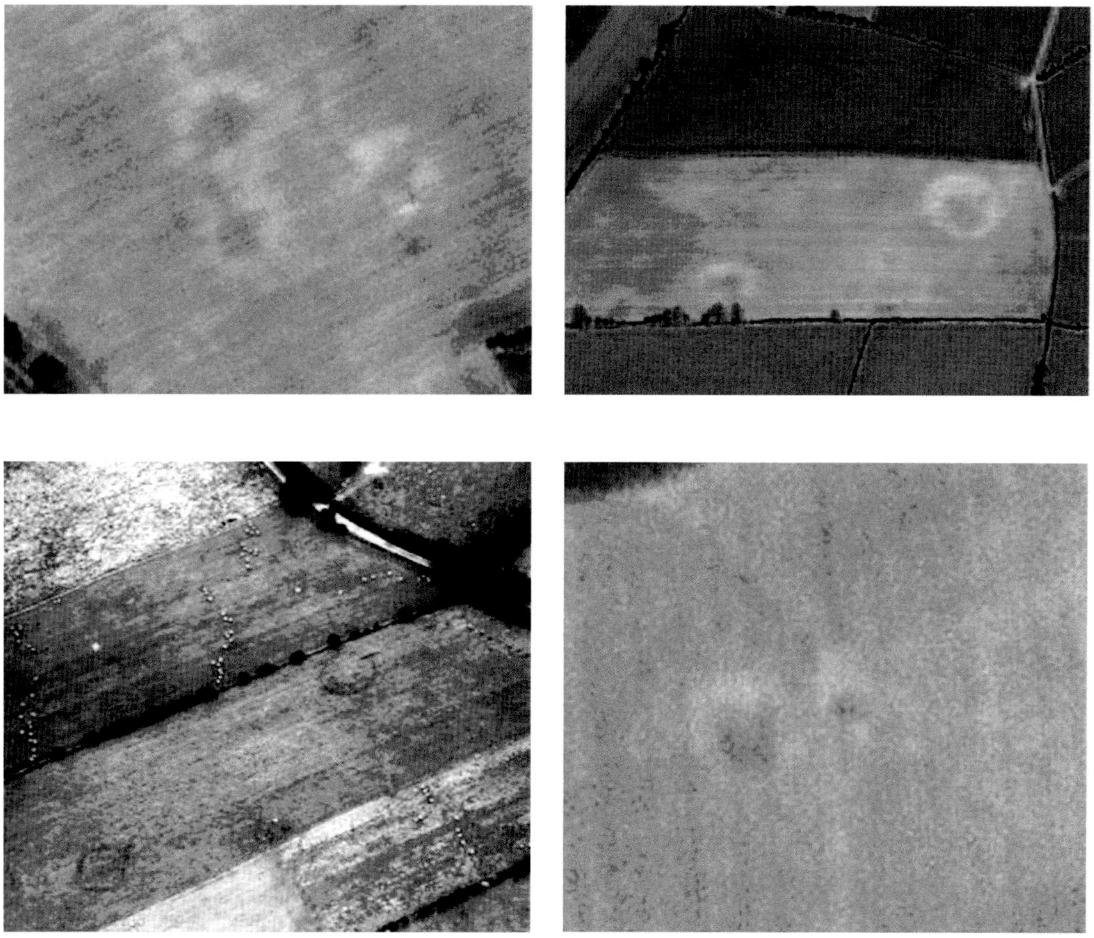

Figure 5.55: Examples of possible levelled barrows in Baltinglass area visible in aerial photography (Google Earth 2017).

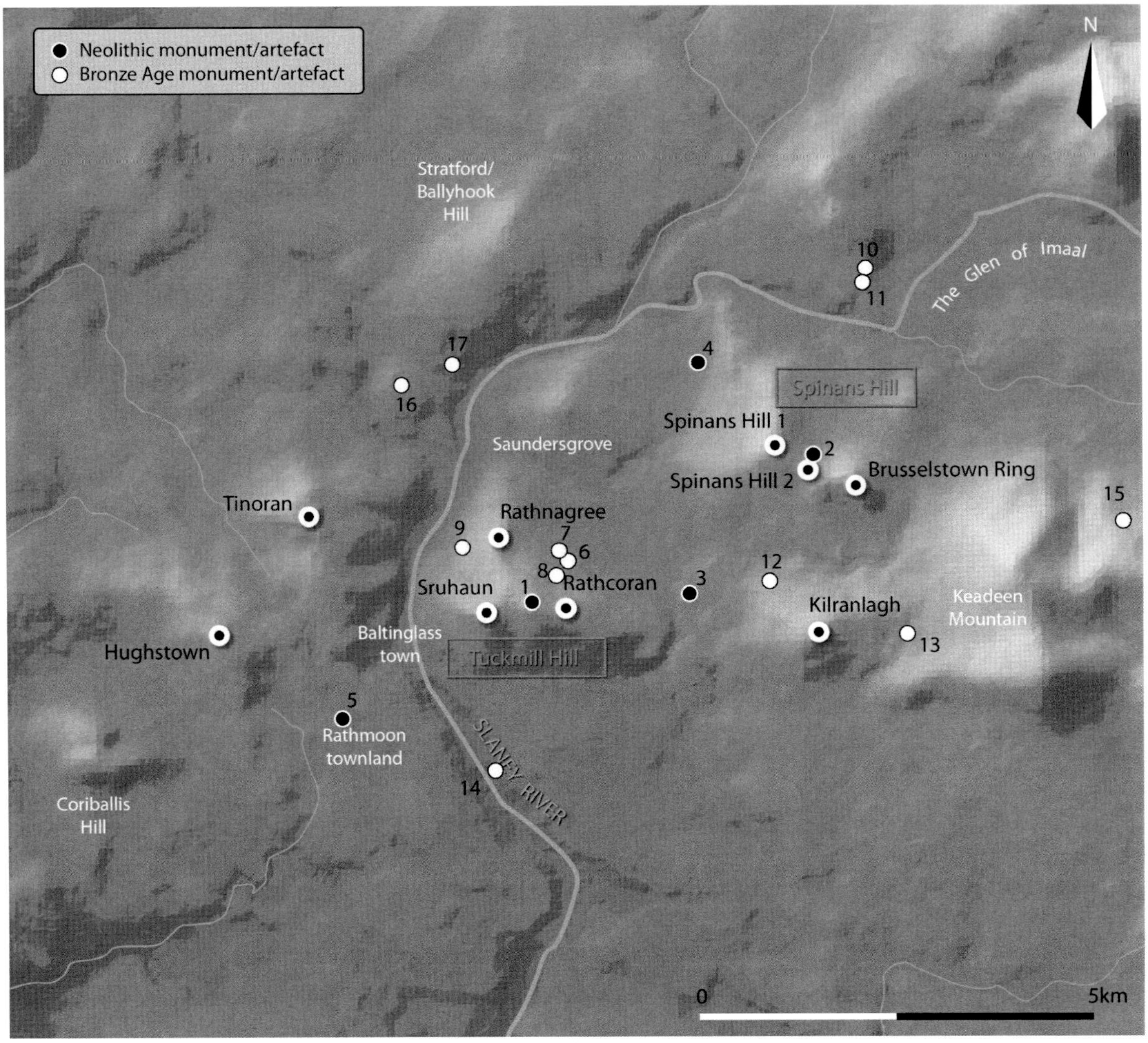

FIGURE 5.56: LOCATION OF PREHISTORIC SITES AND ARTEFACTS MENTIONED IN TEXT.

FIGURE 5.57: MAIN CHAMBER OF PASSAGE TOMB AT SUMMIT OF RATHCORAN.

Lanting (1990: 3) have suggested that this date is later than that burial type and belongs to a different tradition. Immediately to the north-west, in the same townland of Ballintruer More, is a cluster of unclassified barrows (WI021-054001–004), visible in aerial photographs.

Another mound (WI026-006001) in Rathmoon townland, 1.3km west of Baltinglass town and 1km to the south of Hughstown hillfort, has produced cremated remains (Figure 5.56: No. 5). Price described the monument as a circular mound 26m in diameter and 3.9m high standing on the crest of a hill (Corlett and Weaver 2002a: 175). The lower part of the mound formed a terrace just over 1m wide, with a central dome-shaped mound rising out of this. The monument may have originally had an outer bank. During the destruction of the mound in 1958, a rectangular cist was recorded near the southern edge, measuring 0.8m by 0.45m, and 0.5m deep. Lucas (1960: 86) notes that the top of the cist was probably at the old ground surface. The cist contained a 'very considerable' amount of cremated bone (*ibid.*: 87). The number of individuals was estimated to be three adult females and two adolescents, one newly born and another aged 6–8 years. A leaf-shaped arrowhead of Early/Middle Neolithic type was the only artefact recovered from the deposit. It was found within the cist with the cremated bone, and showed signs that it had been burnt. No radiocarbon dates have been retrieved from the burial.

Early/Middle Bronze Age

A number of cist burials have been discovered in the Baltinglass area as a result of agricultural activities in the last century. There is a concentration of these monuments around the base of Tuckmill Hill. On the eastern side, a cist burial (WI027-074) (Figure 5.56: No. 6) containing two sherds of Early Bronze Age food vessel pottery with cremated bone was found 9m from a pit burial (WI027-074001) (Figure 5.56: No. 7) also containing cremated bone (Ó Ríordáin 1972). A third possible cist burial is recorded 450m to the east of Rathcoran hillfort, approximately 500m from the aforementioned examples (Figure 5.56: No. 8). This is described as a possible destroyed cist which contained human remains (http://www.heritagecouncil.ie/heritage-maps/heritage-maps/). At the north-western base of Tuckmill Hill, a cist burial (WI027-008002) (Figure 5.56: No. 9) containing an inhumation was discovered within a now destroyed ring-barrow comprising a low circular mound 19m in diameter and 0.5m in height (Price 1934: 46–47). This was located 400m to the west of Rathnagree.

Two cist burials (WI021-036; WI021-036001) are recorded in Kelshamore townland, 2km north/north-east of Spinans Hill have been dated to the Early Bronze Age (Figure 5.56: No. 10 and 11). One example was heavily disturbed, but produced sherds of a food vessel. The second contained the cremated remains of an adult, a food vessel and a plano-convex flint knife (Hartnett 1952: 153–160). Price recorded a possible cist burial at the base of Kilranlagh Hill within a levelled enclosure in Kilranlagh townland (Corlett and Weaver 2002b: 540) (Figure 5.56: No. 12). He also noted a small cairn, 6.6m in diameter and 0.6m in height, at the east side of this enclosure, and questioned whether this was the location where the owner of the land had previously found a 'Late Bronze Age urn' (*ibid.*: 540). Another possible cist (WI027-040) was discovered within the centre of a mound barrow, 75m north-west of a stone circle on the eastern side of Kilranlagh Hill in Boleycarrigeen townland (Figure 5.56: No. 13). The finds database of the National Museum of Ireland highlights other cist and cremation burials in the Baltinglass landscape (Figure 5.56: No. 14 and 15). Although the artefacts and pottery often associated with these burials imply that indicates are significantly older than the hillforts, it is important to note the significance placed on the hilltops in this area prior to construction of the latter.

There have been relatively few archaeological excavations in the Baltinglass area in modern times. Within a 10km radius of the town there have been 15 excavations since 1969. Eight of these yielded no features of archaeological significance and four revealed activity dating to the Early Medieval or later. Two *fulachtaí fia* (WI021-085; WI021-086) were excavated approximately 3.5km north of Baltinglass town (Figure 5.56: No. 16 and 17). One of these has a Middle Bronze Age date c.1607–1570 BC. Excavation of the nearby M9 motorway indicates that the absence of visible *fulachtaí fia* in the Baltinglass area is a false representation of the archaeology. A 50km length of this motorway 10km to the east of Baltinglass town, uncovered 55 *fulachtaí fia*. This concentration is typical of many parts of Ireland and is an indication of the dense settlement of the landscape throughout the Bronze Age (Figure 5.58).

Several finds of copper and bronze objects also attest to Early Bronze Age activity in the general area of Baltinglass. An hoard of six flat axheads and two ingots was recovered near Tullowbeg, Co. Carlow, approximately 15km to the south of Baltinglass town (Figure 5.59).

Late Bronze Age

Two Middle/Late Bronze Age unenclosed settlements have been identified at Mullamast, Co. Kildare, and at Burtown Little, Co. Kildare, 11km and 12km north-west of Baltinglass town respectively. These sites highlight the diversity of settlement during the Bronze Age and confirm that some settlements were not enclosed.

Middle/Late Bronze Age axes are more numerous than their earlier counterparts in the area, with one palstave,

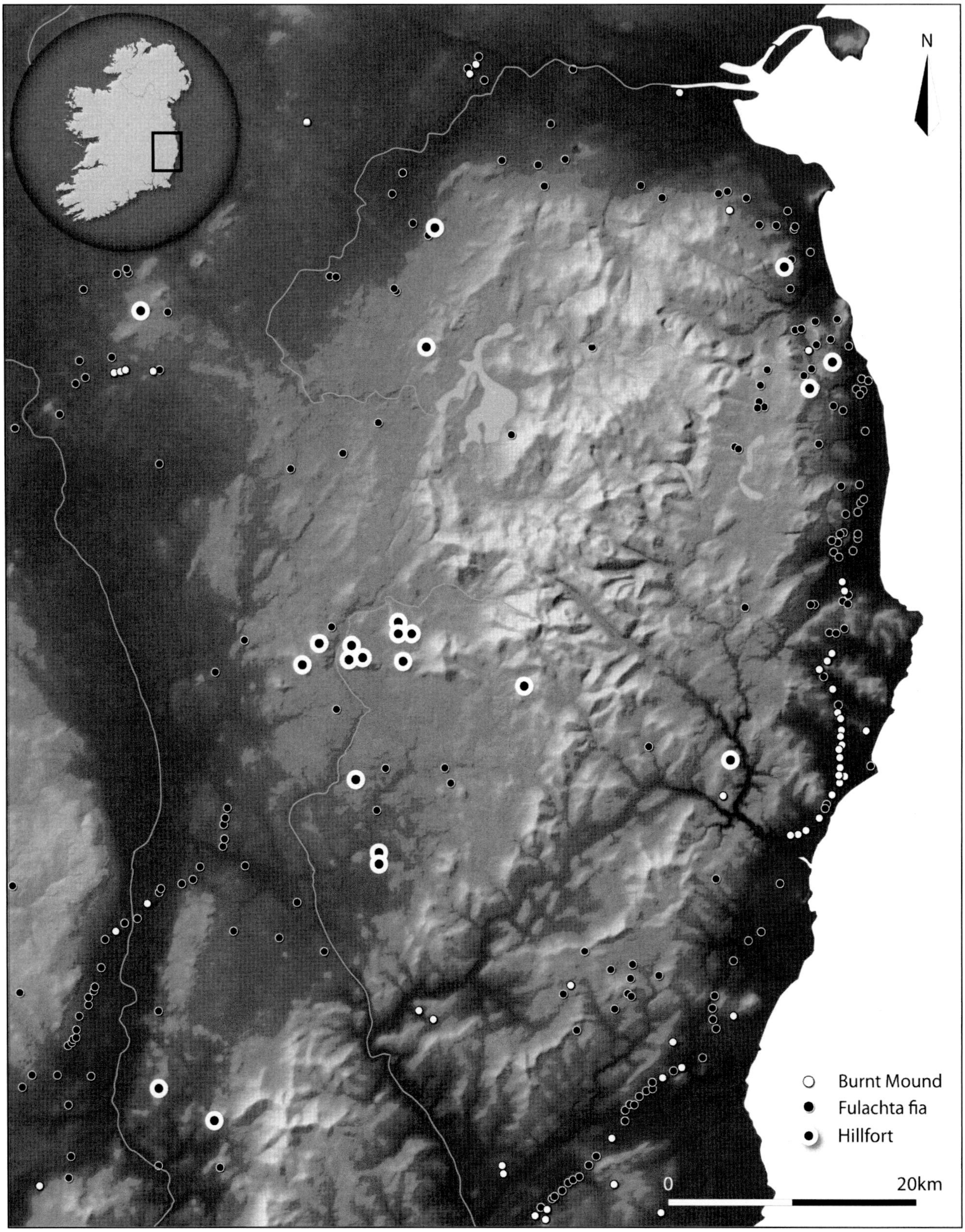

FIGURE 5.58: *FULACHTAÍ FIA* IN THE BALTINGLASS STUDY AREA. NOTE THE LINEAR DISTRIBUTIONS PATTERNS CREATED BY EXCAVATION OF ROAD SCHEMES.

two bronze axes with stop ridges, and sixteen socketed axes discovered within 25km of Baltinglass town (Figure 5.59 and Figure 5.60). Ten of the socketed axes are of Eogan's (2000) Class 11 type which are the most common type in Ireland. The majority were recovered from the flat plain to the south of Baltinglass. At Ballytegan, Co. Laois, two socketed axes were deposited in a shallow pit with ornaments including an annular bracelet, a disc-headed pin, a small cylindrical-shaped bronze object, part of a sheet bronze hook and up to 53 rings of

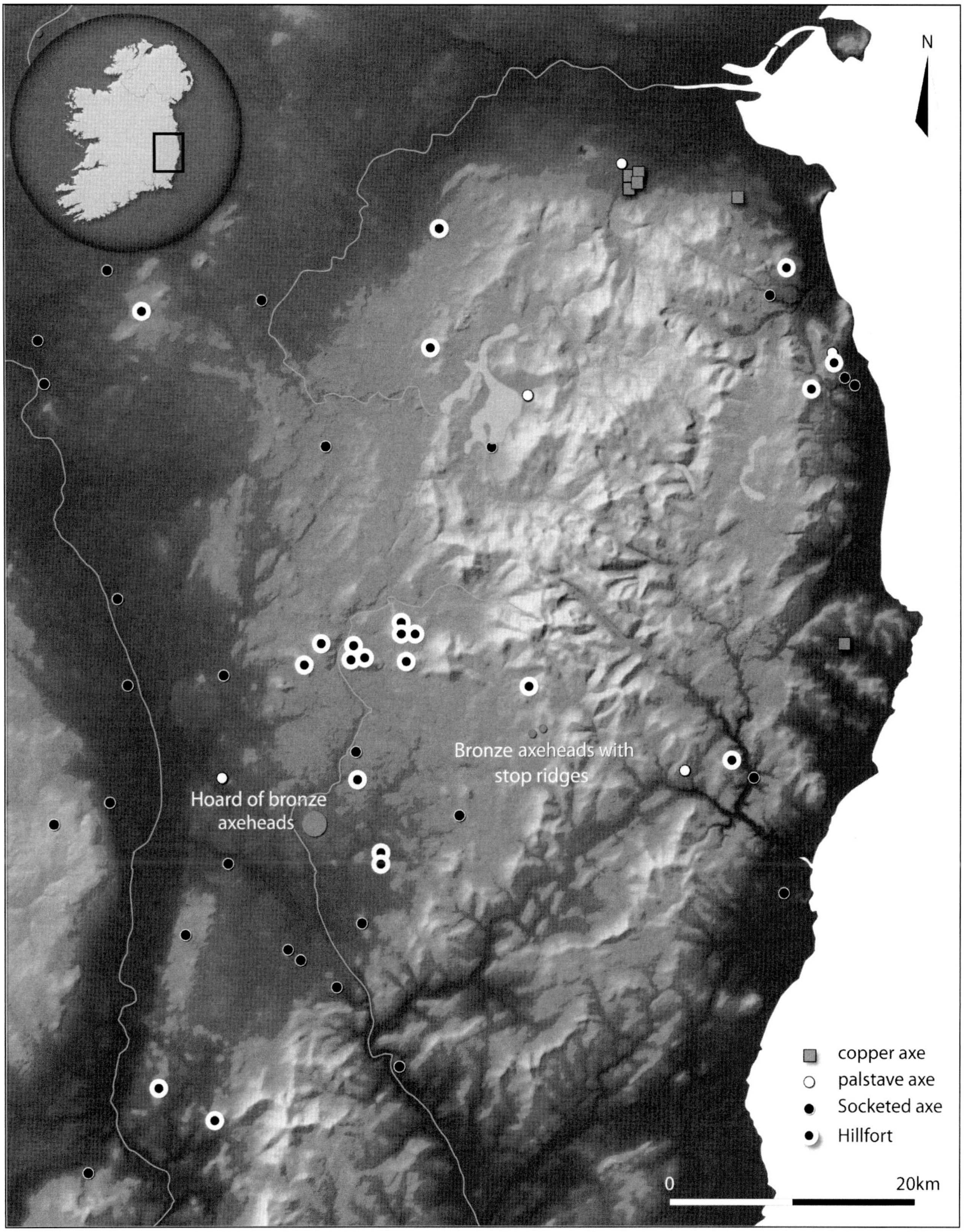

Figure 5.59: Copper and bronze axes recovered within the study area (sources: Harbison 1969; Eogan 2000; with additions).

various size and decoration (Figure 5.60). Two other Late Bronze Age hoards have been recovered in the local area and have produced similar ornamental objects. A hoard discovered in a field at Saintjohns, near Castledermot, Co. Kildare, comprises five gold ornaments, including a bracelet, two twisted armlets and two pieces of decorated sheet gold. A Late Bronze Age sword was recovered less than 0.5km to the south. At Coolmanagh Upper, Co. Carlow, a flanged torc and ribbon torc were deposited on a knoll projecting into marshy land. The

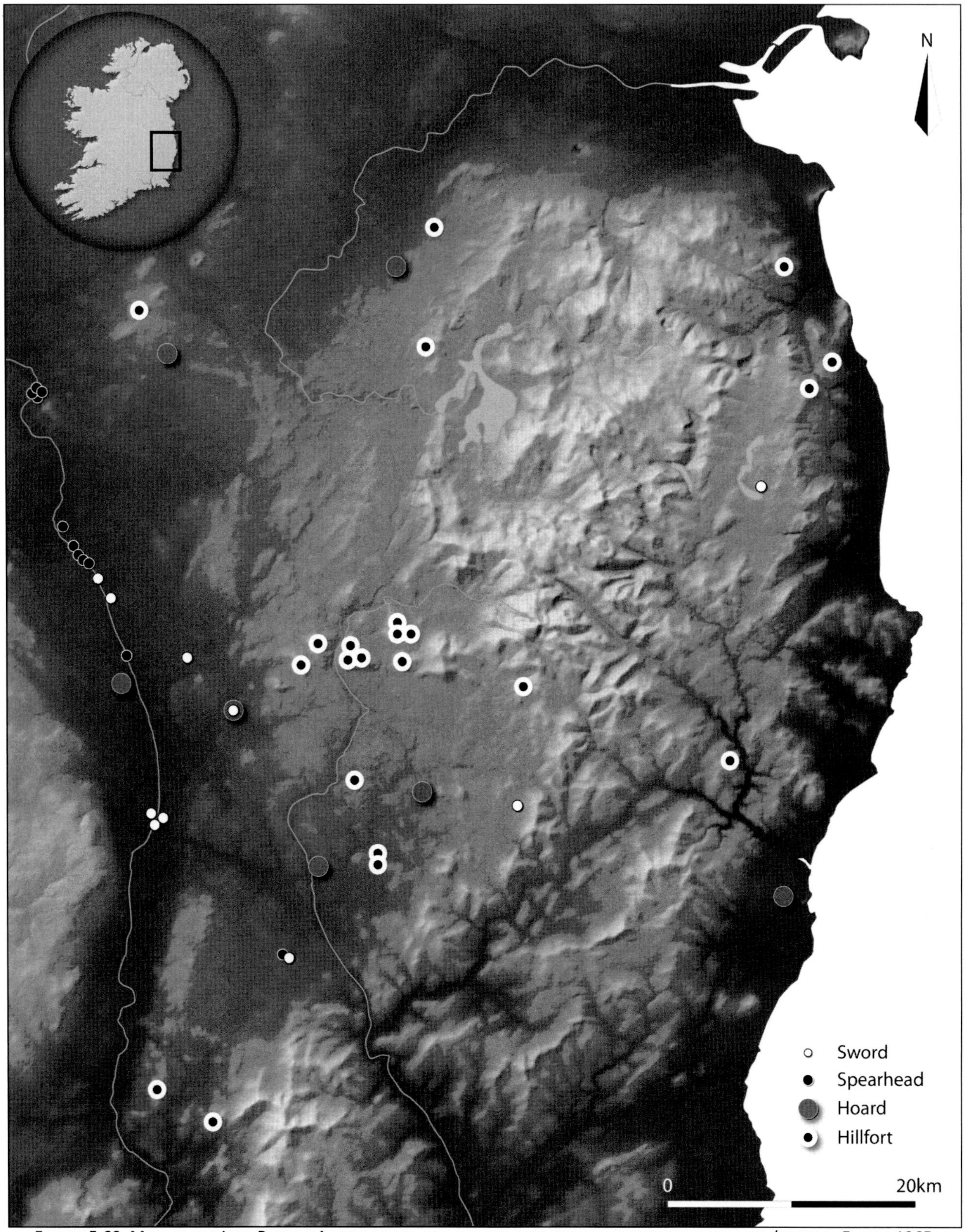

Figure 5.60: Middle and Late Bronze Age weapons and hoards recovered within the study area (source: Eogan 1965; Eogan 1983; Lineen 2017).

famous Bishopsland hoard from Co. Kildare was found less than 20km to the north of Baltinglass.

A kite-shaped bronze spearhead with side loops and decoration was found in the Baltinglass area (per comm Jim Lineen). No radiocarbon dates are available although this type of spearhead generally dates to the Killymaddy/Acton Park Phase of the Middle Bronze Age (1500–1350). The large number of this type suggests a prolonged period of use possibly extending beyond the Killymaddy phase. It is probably of Irish origin. There have been no other weapons finds near the Baltinglass hillforts.

5.10 Conclusions

The mountainous terrain of Wicklow had a significant bearing on the geography of early settlement in the region (Figure 5.2). This is reflected in the distribution of monuments from the historic and prehistoric periods. This shows an intensive occupation of the buffer area between the mountainous uplands and the flat plains to the south and west. This was probably a deliberate attempt to exploit the resources of a number of diverse ecozones. The uplands would have provided excellent hunting grounds, while there was significant potential for agriculture in the fertile low-lying plains around Baltinglass. The well-drained brown earth and podzolic soils have allowed farmers in modern times to undertake cattle and sheep rearing for dairy and meat production, as well as tillage farming. The Slaney River also holds good stocks of trout and salmon, and the surrounding valley produces a variety of edible plants and berries. Woodland would have been readily available in this area, while other resources such as mineral deposits may also have been exploited.

For these reasons the physical environment of the Baltinglass area would have been attractive for early settlement. The earliest evidence of a human presence extends back some 5500 years. Numerous cairns and possible passage tombs line the edge of the mountainous zone and extending into the low-lying areas on hills such as Tuckmill Hill. Linkardstown burials are also indicative of Neolithic settlement and there is a notable concentration of this burial type around the Baltinglass area. The most intensive period of human settlement probably occurred during the Middle/Late Bronze Age, when many of the recorded hillforts seem to have been constructed, along with other ritual and settlement sites.

The individual forts in the Baltinglass area are notably different in their design, which probably reflects different traditions in this type of monumental enclosure over a long period of time. The building of different enclosing systems may have been a visible display of the esoteric knowledge attained by the community through long-distance contract, and could have been used as another element of competitive display.

Tinoran hillfort is unique in the number of possible enclosing elements incorporated into its design, with up to five concentric enclosures occupying a total area of 84.03ha. The total composite length of the defences is approximately 7.68km, comprising the longest combined length of enclosing works in the Baltinglass group. The construction of the enclosing elements would have been an enormous task requiring a large workforce over an extended period of time. Only the high altitude inland promontory fort of Lurigethan in Co. Antrim incorporates more enclosing elements (six), although these are closely spaced and have a composite length of approximately 1.2km.

Kilranlagh hillfort comprises a stone bank with a possible external ditch and is morphologically similar to Brusselstown Ring. At both sites, the banks are about 14m in average width. Stone facing has been identified on the lower, outer façades, suggesting this is likely to have been the original thickness of the walls at both sites. These wide stone walls again are a unique form in the Baltinglass area. Wide stone rubble walls have been noted at other Irish hillforts such as Mooghaun, Co. Clare.

The cluster of sites on Tuckmill Hill are distinctly different in form, comprising a univallate enclosure with stone bank and tentative evidence for a palisade or other wooden elements (Sruhaun), moderately spaced bivallate site with earth and stone bank and possible palisade (Rathcoran) and a trivallate site consisting of three widely spaced enclosing elements with possible evidence for wooden features (Rathnagree). There close spacing may suggest that they are broadly contemporary and were built by a single community. The use of timber at Late Bronze Age hillforts in Britain and the Continent has already been discussed, and the possible use of this material at some of the Baltinglass hillforts is interesting.

The close grouping of three hillforts on Spinans Hill is somewhat analogous with Tuckmill Hill. The Spinans Hill hillforts could be also broadly contemporary. Two large hillforts surround the eastern and western summits of Spinans Hill respectively, both of which are enclosed by an extensive earthwork. Somewhat like the hillforts on Tuckmill Hill, each fort on Spinans Hill incorporates different construction details. Brusselstown Ring comprises two widely spaced stone banks. The western summit of Spinans Hill is surrounded by Spinans Hill 1, a large univallate earthen bank with external ditch in places. Both sites are surrounded by the larger earthwork of Spinans hill 2. Where the latter earthwork survives best, it is a massive construction that would have been imposing to outsiders. This impressive enclosing element would have been an excellent way of communicating the power and prestige of the community as well as the resources and workforce they could generate. Hillfort groups, generally consisting of a pair of sites, are not uncommon in Ireland. They have been interpreted as contemporary communities competing for control over a routeway or resources. This will be discussed in detail in Chapter 10.

Finally, there are a number of prominent hilltops in the Baltinglass area that have no visible features to suggest the presence of a hillfort. Corballis Hill is 2.2km south-west of Hughstown and is the westernmost hilltop in the series of prominent hills extending westward from the Wicklow Mountains. The hill is extensively forested, which limits the application of GPS and geophysical techniques, and there is no LiDAR available for the area. Aerial photography reveals no clear features of archaeological interest, but the prominence of the hilltop marks it as important landscape feature. At the eastern base of Corballis, a large enclosure 1.05ha in size is marked in the first and second edition Ordnance Survey maps (Figure 5.48). This enclosure comprises a bank and ditch measuring up to 33m wide (Flood 2009: 97). The size of the enclosure and the enclosing elements, as well as its similarities in layout and position to other large enclosures in the vicinity, could suggest a prehistoric date.

Similarly, Saundersgrove Hill is a prominent hilltop visible from all of the Baltinglass hillforts (Figure 5.61). It is located 1.5km north-east of Tuckmill Hill and 2.2km west of Spinans Hill. There is a cluster of four recorded barrows (WI021-054-001–004), two standing stones (WI021-027, WI021-079) and a Linkardstown burial (WI021-057) at the north-eastern base of the hill. Up to six levelled enclosures have been identified on the south-western slopes (WI021-048, WI021-049, WI021-050, WI021-052, WI021-053, WI027-013). While these are probably Early Medieval in date, the fact that three of these are under 25m in diameter may suggest they could be prehistoric barrows. LiDAR data obtained for the area at 0.5m resolution identified a discrete annular earthwork at the western base of the hill (Figure 5.62). This is apparent as a bank up to 12.2m wide and 0.3m high, visible on the northern side as a 14m wide depression. The

Figure 5.61: Satellite image of Saundersgrove Hill, Co. Wicklow (Google Earth 2017).

Figure 5.62: Unrecorded field systems and possible archaeological features identified by LiDAR at Saundersgrove Hill, Co. Wicklow. (see Figure 5.48 for location).

earthwork is approximately 343m in length and varies between 181–184m OD. It is positioned at the margin of slope where undulating terrain meets a more severe incline. If projected, the earthwork has an approximate diameter of 510m that would enclose an area of 19.63ha. However, the landscape position does not correspond with other hillforts in the area and interpreting this site as a hillfort is unconvincing at present.

Stratford (Ballyhook Hill) is another prominent hilltop visible from all of the Baltinglass hillforts (Figure 5.63). It is approximately 3.6km north-west of Spinans hill and 3.3km north of Tuckmill Hill. There are no obvious archaeological features at the site, although a circular mound 2.3km south-west of the summit produced human remains, including three skulls, during sand extraction in the early 20th century. There are no features of potential archaeological significance visible in aerial or satellite imagery. LiDAR data was obtained at 0.5m resolution and revealed no features related to a possible hillfort (Figure 5.64).

The concentration of numerous large and elaborate monuments indicates that the Baltinglass area was of considerable importance during the prehistoric period. Beginning as early as the Neolithic period, when Linkardstown burials, passage tombs, cairns and cursus monuments were built, the landscape was seemingly

FIGURE 5.63: SATELLITE IMAGE OF STRATFORD HILL (GOOGLE EARTH 2017).

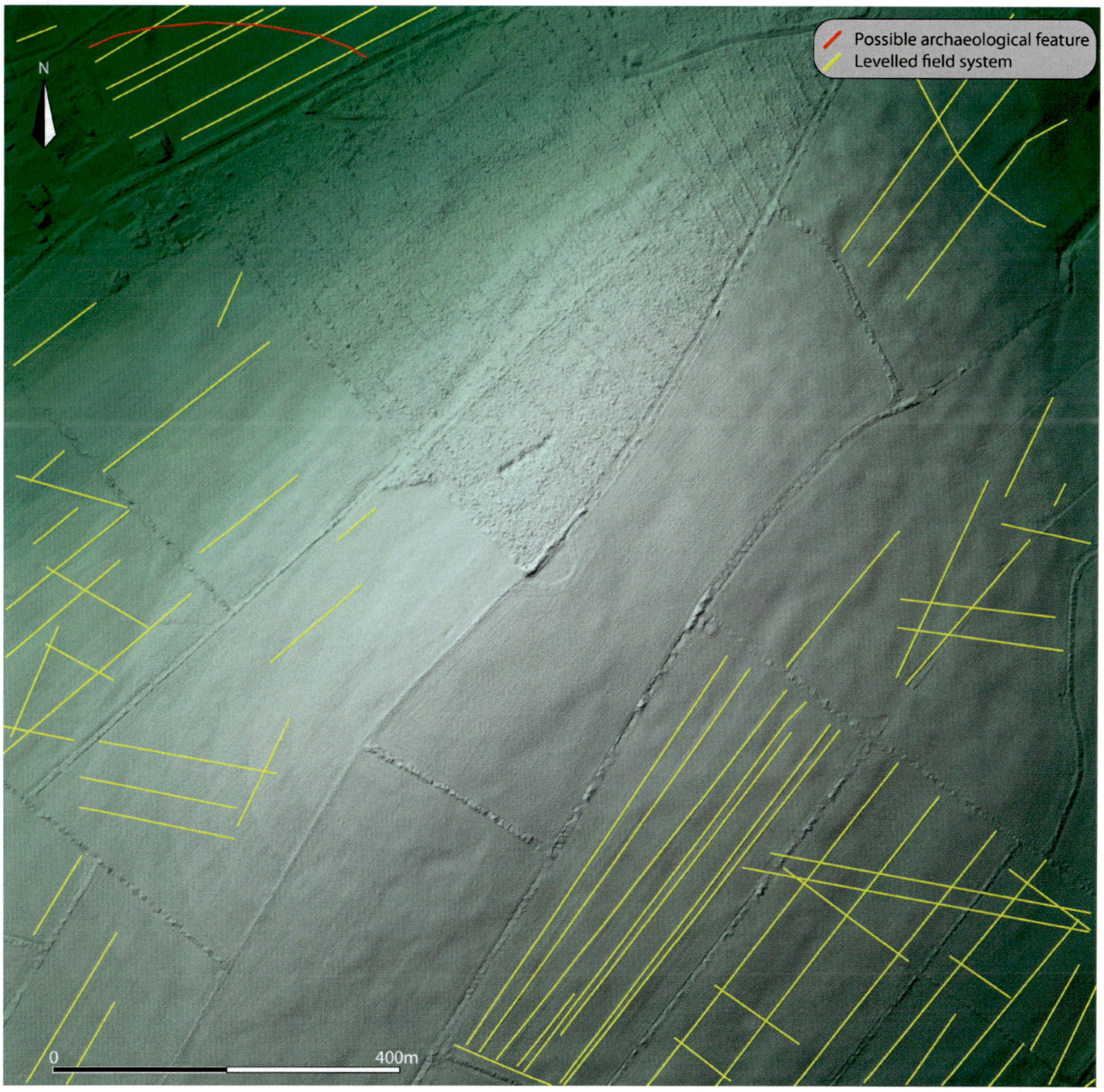

FIGURE 5.64: UNRECORDED FIELD SYSTEMS AND POSSIBLE ARCHAEOLOGICAL FEATURES IDENTIFIED BY LIDAR AT STRATFORD (SEE FIGURE 5.48 FOR LOCATION).

densely populated. However, during the Middle to Late Bronze Age, there was a notable increase in the construction of monumental features, including hillforts, stone circles, ring-ditches/barrows and standing stones, among others. The building of hillforts at that time required significant amounts of time, people and natural resources to complete. In other locations throughout Ireland, hillforts were also being constructed. However, it is the size, complexity and concentration of hillforts at Baltinglass that separates this area from others as a unique and significant area during this period of Irish prehistory.

6

The Baltinglass Hillfort Excavations

This survey of the Baltinglass hillforts was followed in 2014–6 by sample excavation at five sites (Figure 6.1). These include three Class 2 (multiple enclosure) hillforts (Rathnagree, Tinoran, and Hughstown), and two Class 1 (univallate) examples (Sruhaun and Spinans Hill 1). The excavations had a specific purpose, namely to obtain information on the enclosing elements of the hillforts concerned, their size and original form, and the methods and materials employed in construction. It was also hoped to obtain dating evidence, artifacts and environmental evidence connected to the construction, occupation and of abandonment of these sites.

6.1 Spinans Hill 1, Co. Wicklow

As discussed in Chapter 4, this univallate enclosure lies on the summit of Spinans Hill (410m OD), on a broad shelf of blanket bog terrain in the townlands of Ballyhubbock Upper and Spinans Hill (ITM 691957, 691590). It consists of a sub-quadrangular enclosure measuring c.550m (north–south) by 320m (east–west), with a perimeter of 1.29km enclosing an area of 11.11ha (Figure 6.2). In July 2016 a single trench was excavated across the enclosing element on the northern side of the hillfort (Figure 6.3). The surface features consisted of a low bank, 3.7m wide with an external height of 0.95m and inner height less than 0.2m (Figure 6.4). The 11m (east–west; 160–340°) by 2m trench was excavated to a depth of 0.4–0.85m across the exposed bank (O'Brien 2016b).

The natural soil is a blanket peat on a heavily podzolised glacial till subsoil. The peat (C.02) varied in thickness from 0.24–0.32m at the southern end of the trench, 0.25–0.3m at the north end, to 0.09–0.15m over the centre of the bank. Beyond the bank limits this peat overlay a compact layer of mid brown humic silt (C.03), with numerous small to large stones, including collapsed stones from both sides of the bank (Figure 6.5). This was removed to reveal a thin layer of iron pan (C.10) across the

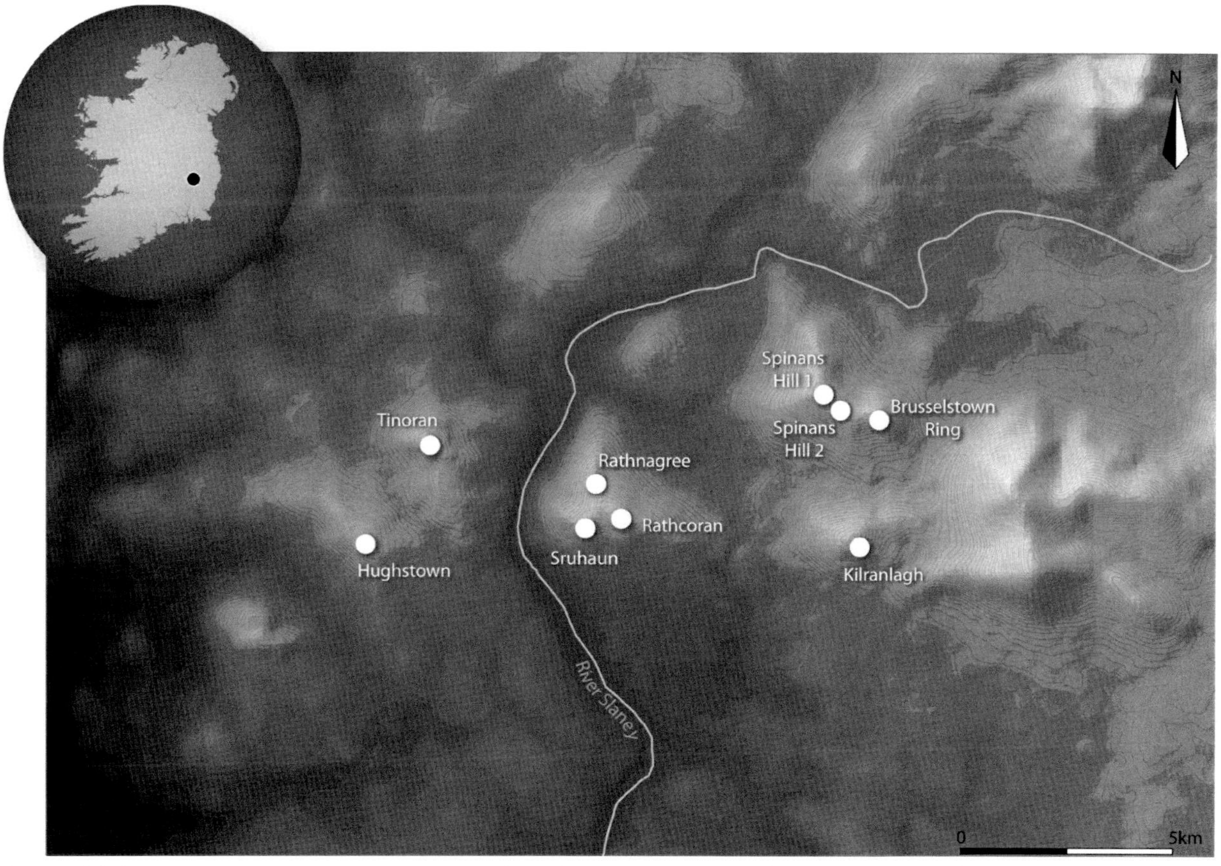

FIGURE 6.1: LOCATION OF FIVE EXCAVATED HILLFORTS IN THE BALTINGLASS COMPLEX (FROM EAST TO WEST): SPINANS HILL 1, RATHNAGREE, SRUHAUN, TINORAN AND HUGHSTOWN.

Figure 6.2: Aerial view of Spinans Hill, showing two enclosures.

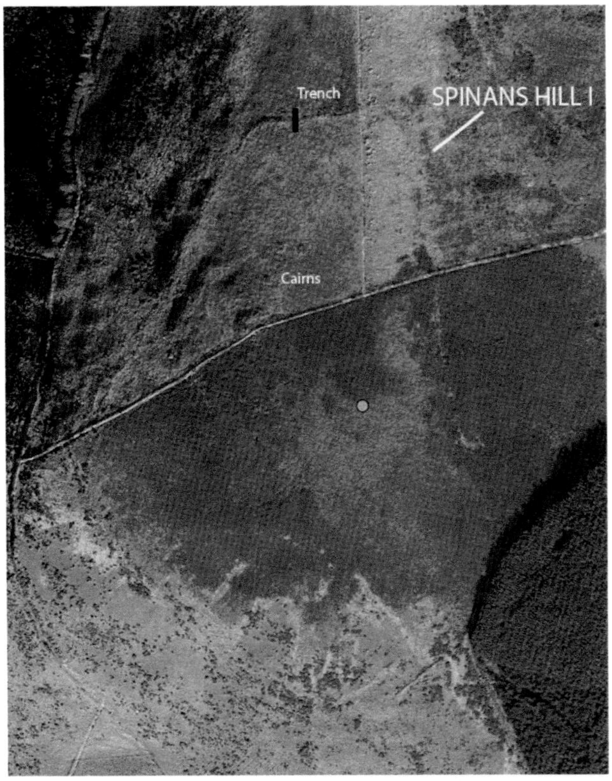

Figure 6.3: Aerial view of Spinans Hill 1 hillfort, with location of excavation trench and cairns (source: www.archaeology.ie).

excavation area, ranging in thickness 1–3cm under bank to 3–5cm at both ends of trench. The natural subsoil was a bright orange Bs-horizon (C.11), which was very compact with frequent pebbles and small to large stones. Excavation at the lower northern end of the trench exposed part of the underlying Bh-horizon (C.12), comprised of loose small to large angular/sub-angular stones with voids in dark brown sandy silt under the Bs-horizon.

Archaeological features

There was only one significant archaeological feature in the trench. This was a bank (C.04) of large stones piled loosely along a gentle slope (Figure 6.6). The bank was collapsed over a length of 7.15m, with the original width estimated at 2.8m, and approximately 2.1m of tumble on the inner (south) side and 2.25m on the outer side (Figure 6.7). The extant bank had a maximum thickness of 0.75m on the west side of the trench, and 0.66m on the east side. The height of the original bank was probably not greater than 1–1.5m.

The bank stones were 0.15–0.55m in length, with many large examples from 0.25–0.4m, as well as smaller stones. The stones were irregular tabular to blocky in shape, with water-rolled surfaces indicative of a drift sources rather than quarried stone. The majority were intact, with only a few broken examples.

There was no obvious structure in the bank, with no coursing or careful revetment (Figure 6.8). Excavation revealed some vertical stones on the inner side, and small boulders on the outer side, which helped to retain the loose core of the bank. The eastern side of the excavated bank was piled between a low outcrop of bedrock on the outside, measuring 0.8m (north–south) by 0.45m (projecting west), and a natural subsoil boulder on the inside. In general, the bank stones were piled in a loose fashion

FIGURE 6.4: LOCATION OF SPINANS HILL 1 EXCAVATION TRENCH, LOOKING WEST TO TINORAN HILLFORT (TOP LEFT).

FIGURE 6.5: STONE BANK OF SPINANS HILL 1 ENCLOSURE AFTER REMOVAL OF BLANKET PEAT.

with numerous voids, partly filled with humic silt (C.05) and root matting. There was a deposit of compact dark brown silt (C.06) with small amounts of charcoal in the lower part of the bank, possibly the result of rain-wash through the loose stones (Figure 6.9).

The bank was built on an old ground surface that survives today as a thin layer of compact blue-grey silt (C.07) with occasional flecks of charcoal (Figure 6.10). This was removed to an orange Bs-horizon surface with no definite archaeological features. Excavation revealed a sub-circular cut (C.09), measuring 0.16m by 0.15m by 0.21m deep, under the centre of the bank. This was filled with dark brown silt with numerous small to large stones. The pit was irregular in shape, and could be a natural stone socket rather than a stakehole or post setting. The former seems likely as the C.08 fill was overlain by silt (C.07) of the pre-bank surface.

List of excavation contexts, Trench 1, Spinans Hill 1.
Context 01: Sod layer; stone-free humic silt.

C.02: A 0.09–0.32m thick layer of well humified black peat.

C.03: Layer of mid brown humic silt below C.02 peat, with numerous stones, including bank collapse.

C.04: Stone bank; see main text for details.

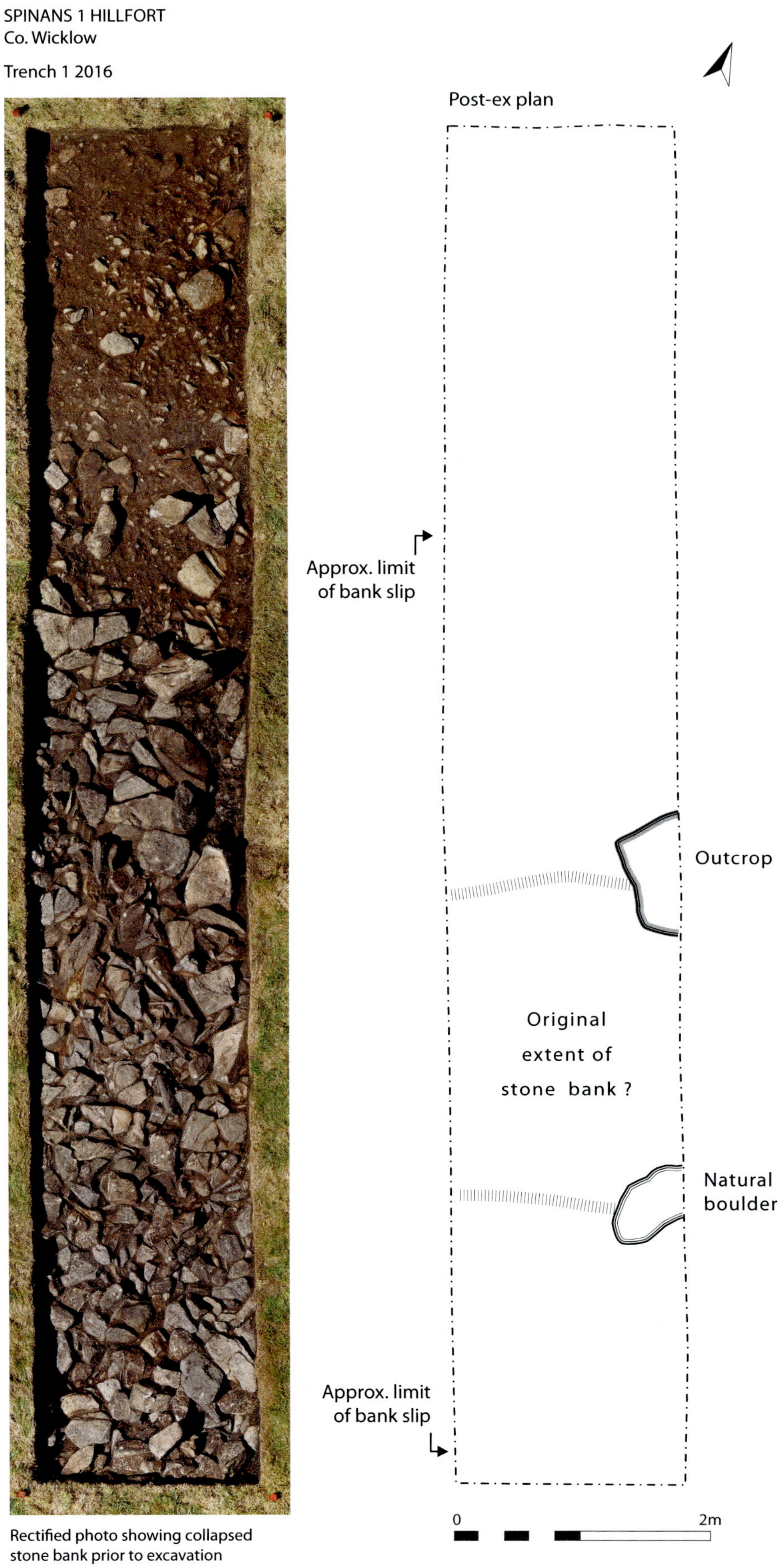

FIGURE 6.6: PLAN OF EXCAVATED FEATURES, TRENCH 1, SPINANS HILL 1.

FIGURE 6.7: COLLAPSED STONES ON OUTER SIDE OF BANK AFTER REMOVAL OF PEAT, SPINANS HILL 1.

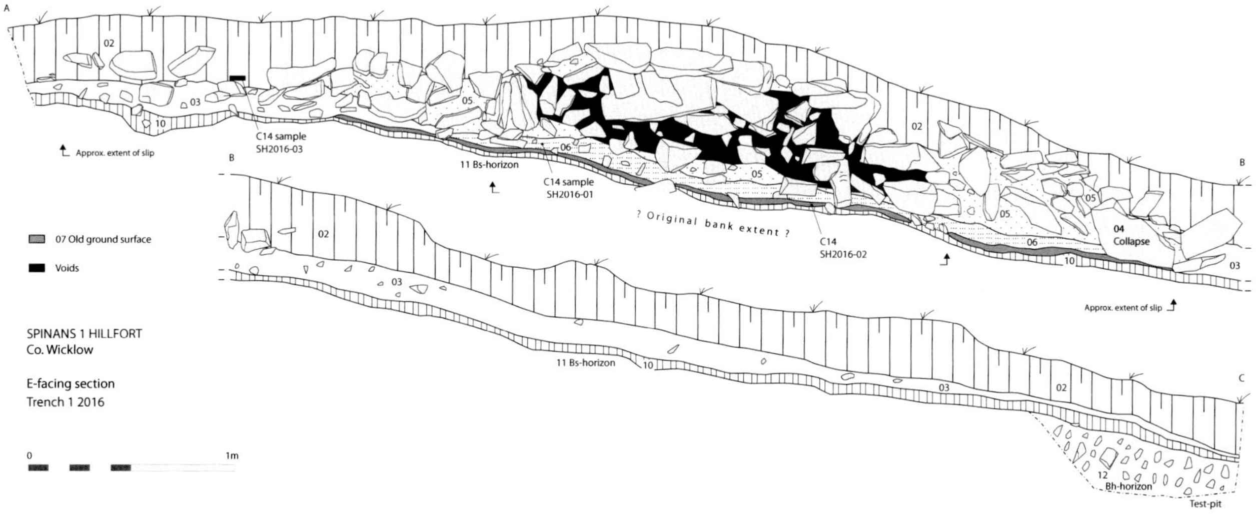

FIGURE 6.8: STRATIFICATION OF TRENCH 1, SPINANS HILL 1.

C.05: Loose deposit of mid brown, root-matted, humic silt between stones (C.04) of bank.

C.06: Compact dark brown silt between lower stones (C.04) of bank. Charcoal flecks in places.

C.07: Compact 1–3cm thick spread of blue-grey fine silt under C.06 at base of bank; charcoal flecks.

C.08: Loose deposit of dark brown silt with numerous sub-angular stones, in an irregular pit (C.09).

C.09: Sub-circular cut with C.08 fill in Bs-horizon, 0.16m by 0.15m by 0.21m deep.

C.10: A 1–5cm thick hard layer of red/orange/brown iron pan on Bs-horizon.

Figure 6.9 Silt with charcoal flecks (C.07; centre lower) at base of bank. Note vertical stones (left) at what may have been the original inner edge of bank.

Figure 6.10: Spread of blue-grey silt (C.07) representing an old ground surface under bank.

C.11: Bs-horizon. Compact bright orange silt under iron pan; frequent small to large stones.

C.12: Bh-horizon. Loose layer of angular/sub-angular clasts in dark brown sandy silt.

Finds and dating

There are no artifact finds of any type/date from this excavation. Three samples were selected for radiocarbon dating in the University of Groningen (wood identifications: Susan Lyons). The results are as follows (Figure 6.11):

Site sample SH2016-01 Single lump of alder charcoal from dark brown silt (C.06) on top of some lower stones (C.04) of bank, western side of trench.
GrA-67387 4835±35 BC

SH2016-02 Alder charcoal from blue-grey silt (C.07), old ground surface under bank.
GrA-67389 4835±35 BC

SH2016-03 Peat sample overlying collapsed stones on inner side of bank.
GrA-67391 102.13±0.35 activity corr. (%)

Field No.	Lab No.	C-14 BP	∂13C	95.4% calibration
SH2016-01	GrA-67387	4835±35	-25.96	3697–3527 BC
SH2016-02	GrA-76389	4835±35	-26.11	3697–3527 BC
SH2016-03	GrA-67391	102.13±0.35 C	-27.87	Modern peat

Figure 6.11 Radiocarbon dates for Spinans Hill 1 (calibration after OxCal v.4.2.4).

Discussion

This sample excavation revealed details of the form and construction of the enclosing bank at Spinans Hill 1. That feature was built by piling stones, probably gathered from surrounding hill slopes, to create a bank not exceeding 1.5m in height. This can hardly be described as a fortification, but more excavation is required to clarify the function and occupation history of the site. Any consideration of the enclosure cannot be separated from an understanding of other elements of the Spinans Hill complex, notably the larger enclosure of Spinans Hill 2 and the nearby hillfort of Brusselstown Ring.

In the absence of artifacts, the dating of this enclosure relies on three radiocarbon dates obtained from the 2016 excavation. Peat growth on top of collapsed stones on the inside of the bank is dated (GrA-67391) to the modern era. This may be explained by contamination of the peat sample by modern roots. The dating of two samples of charcoal-flecked silt (GrA-67387 and -67389) at the base of the bank gave identical date ranges of 3697–3527 BC. Neither radiocarbon sample can be connected directly to the bank construction, or to occupation of the enclosure. Given the possibility of surface burning connected to earlier activity, the dating of this bank remains to be confirmed by further excavation. Until this is undertaken, it is reasonable to propose an Early Neolithic date for the Spinans Hill 1 enclosure as a working hypothesis for the chronology of the Baltinglass complex.

6.2 Rathnagree, Co. Wicklow

As outlined in the previous chapter, Rathnagree is one of three hillforts on Tuckmill Hill, a prominent hill (365m OD) overlooking the town of Baltinglass to the south (Figure 6.1). The site is located on the northern spur of the hill, at an elevation of 315m OD (Figure 1.3). It comprises three concentric circular enclosures, measuring 294m by 273m in total, extending over an area of 5.59ha (Figure 6.12).

Three trenches were excavated at Rathnagree in July 2014 (Figure 6.13). Trench 1 was located across the line of the inner enclosure on the southern side; Trench 2 across the middle enclosure on the eastern side, while Trench 3 was placed on the southern side of the outer enclosure. Samples were recovered for radiocarbon dating from all three trenches, with an important find of Bronze Age pottery from Trench 2 (O'Brien 2014a).

Inner enclosure (Trench 1)

The inner enclosure at Rathnagree measures 104m (N–S) by 93m (E–W), with a perimeter of 296m and a total area of 0.63ha. It is surrounded by low bank of what appears to be loose stones, some of which are exposed. The bank averages 0.2m in height and 6m in width. There are no indications of an accompanying ditch.

A 8m (N–S) by 2m (E–W) trench was excavated across this bank on the southern side of the enclosure (Figure 6.13). Trench 1 was excavated to a depth of 0.2–0.3m down to natural subsoil. This revealed a thin growth of blanket peat, ranging in thickness from 0.2–0.23m at the northern end of the trench to 0.08–0.12m over the bank itself (Figure 6.14). This peat was part of a podzolic soil profile, where a thin leached E-horizon (C.05) overlay an iron-enriched Bs-horizon (C20). The podzolization was less developed at the southern end of the trench, where there was no visible leaching and considerably less iron precipitation on the B-horizon surface.

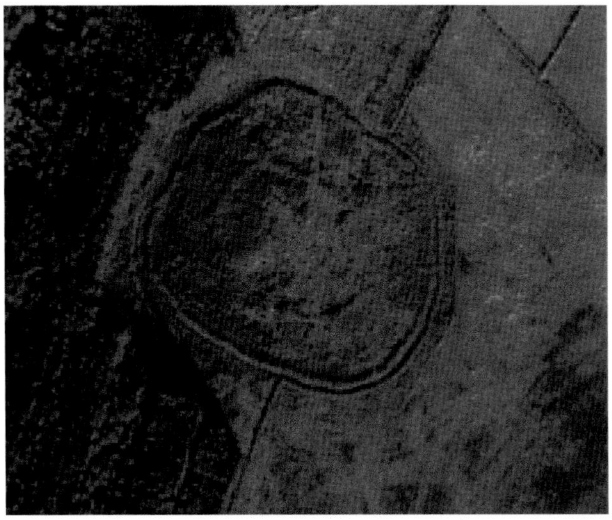

Figure 6.12: Aerial photograph of Rathnagree hillfort, Baltinglass, Co. Wicklow (top: north).

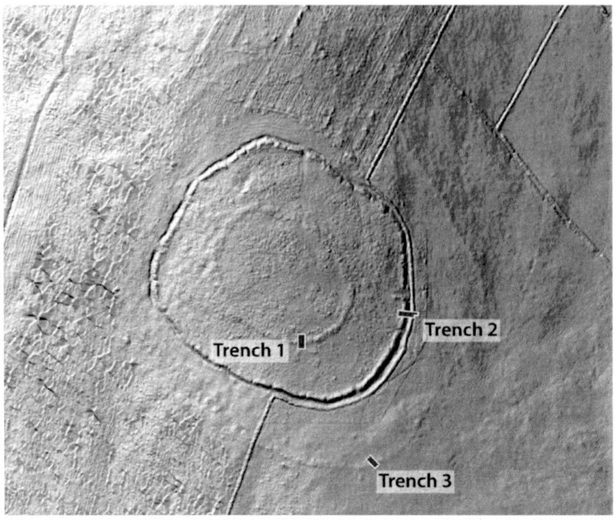

Figure 6.13: Lidar image of Rathnagree hillfort showing location of three excavation trenches (top north).

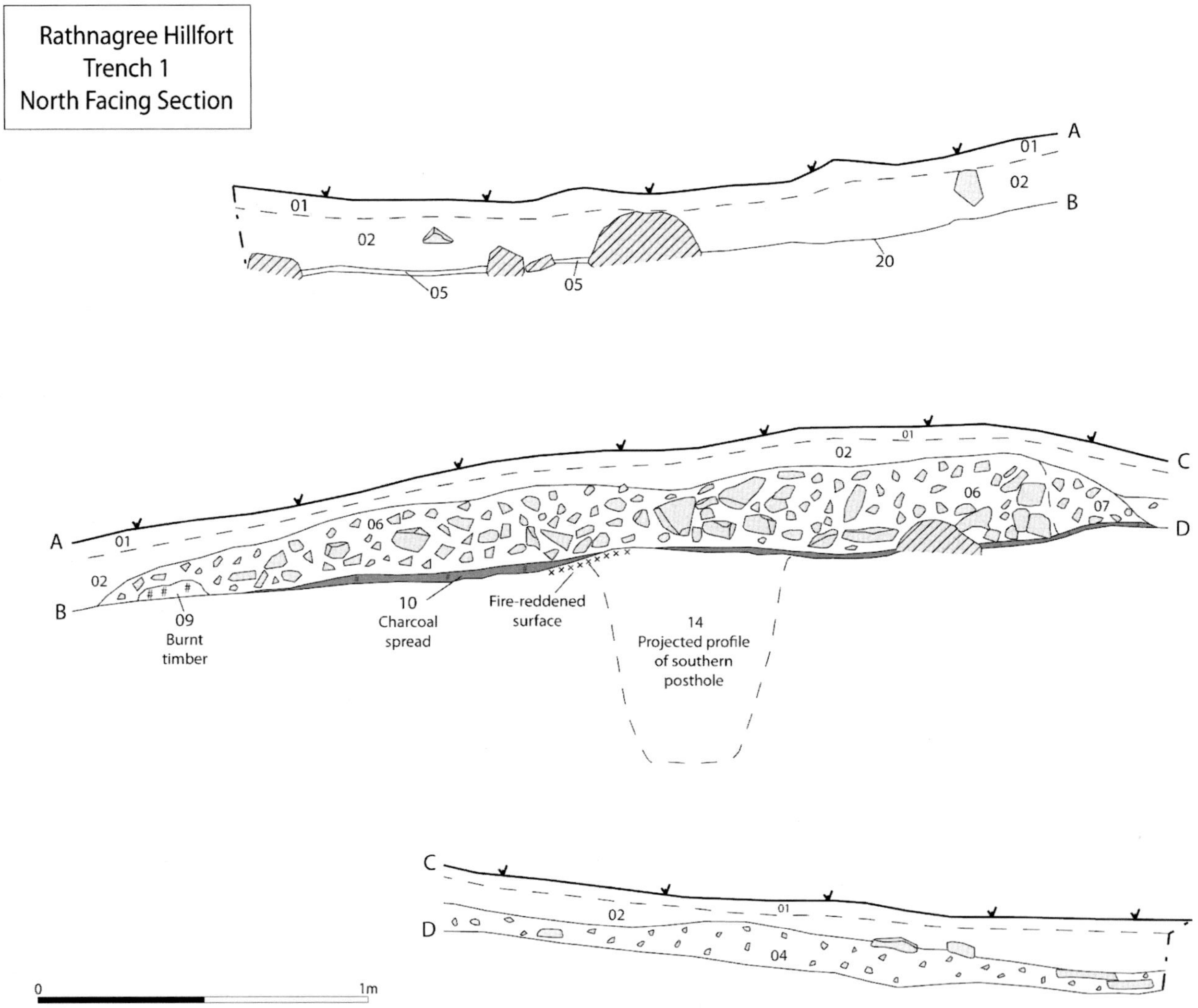

Figure 6.14: Stratification of Trench 1, Rathnagree.

Excavation revealed a spread of loose stones (C.03) in the lower part of this peat at the northern end of trench. The largest stones were in the 0.35–0.45m range, with smaller stones of 0.15–0.25m. None of the stones were fire-reddened, and so are unlikely to be connected to the hillfort bank. They may derive instead from later field clearance.

Archaeological features

De-sodding revealed a 2.8m wide bank of stone across the central part of the trench (Figure 6.15). This comprised a loose deposit of small to large stones (C.06) within a matrix of dark brown/black humic silt, having a maximum thickness of c.0.25m at the centre. The stones range <0.05–0.32m in size, with most in the 0.1–0.2m range. These were angular in appearance with light-to-strong reddening, both the result of fire shattering. A number of larger stones were broken in situ, though there was relatively little charcoal within the bank itself.

The excavation of heat-shattered stone on the bank surface exposed a tightly packed arrangement of large stones (C.07), set in a vertical to steeply inclined position along the outer (southern) side of the bank (Figures 6.16 and 6.17). These stones were 0.18–0.4m in size, and were blocky in shape with some fire reddening. They were placed on the natural subsoil (C.20) to form an exterior facing to the bank.

The removal of this stone deposit exposed a spread of charcoal-rich sediment (C.10) on the northern (inner) side of the bank (Figure 6.14). The underlying subsoil surface was fire-reddened in places, confirming a large fire at this location. The excavation of C.10 exposed two lengths of burnt branch (contexts 08 and 09), one of which was sampled for radiocarbon dating (sample RNG2014-05). Context 08 was a single piece of burnt wood, 0.43m in length and 0.12m in diameter, which extended into the excavation section. It was exposed at a depth of 0.32m below the modern ground surface, on removal of a 0.21m thickness of fire-reddened stone (C.06) that slipped from the original bank. Context 09 was a 0.24m long piece of burnt wood, extending into section on the eastern side of the trench. It was exposed at a depth of 0.22m below the modern ground surface, on removal of a 0.11m thickness of fire-reddened bank stone (C.06).

The removal of the stone bank exposed two postholes on the subsoil surface (Figure 6.17). These were large pits placed c.0.5m apart, in which vertical posts were secured with packing stones. The eastern posthole (C.14) measured 0.59m (E–W) by 0.56m (N–S), narrowing to 0.28m (E–W) by 0.25m (N–S) at the base, with a depth of 0.71m. There was a rim of intense fire-reddening on the northern side of this posthole (Figure 6.18). Several large stones in the lower fill (C.13) may be displaced post packing. The western posthole (C.18) measured 0.58m (E–W) by 0.54m (N–S), narrowing to 0.25m (E–W) by

FIGURE 6.15: STONE DEPOSIT (C.03; BOTTOM RIGHT) AND STONY BANK (C.06; CENTRE) EXPOSED BENEATH PEAT, TRENCH 1, RATHNAGREE.

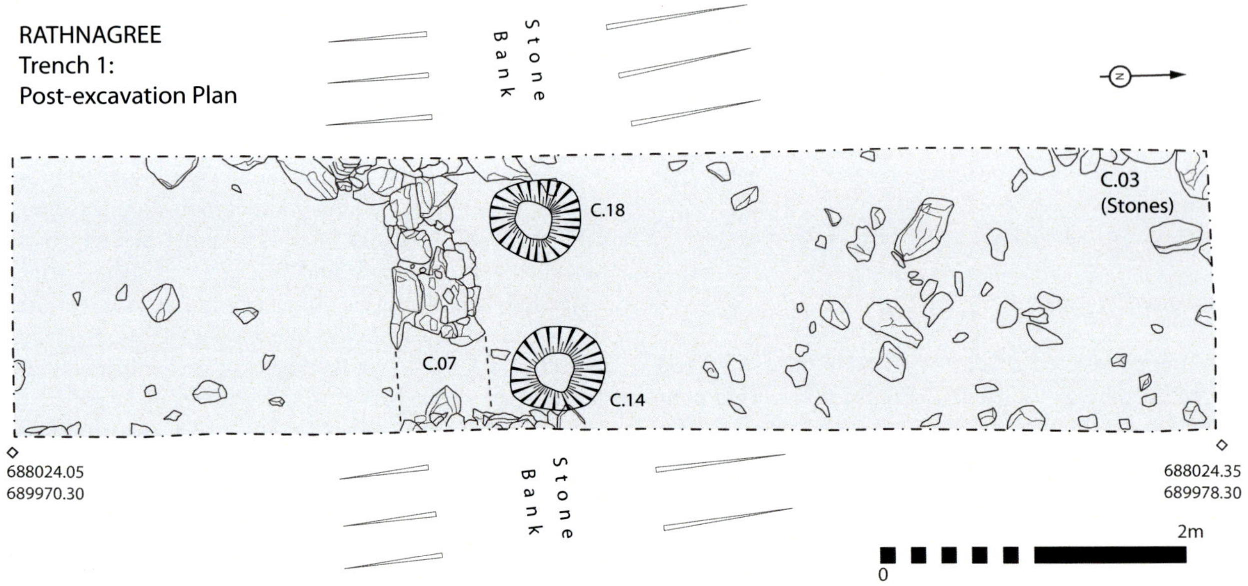

FIGURE 6.16: POST-EXCAVATION PLAN OF TRENCH 1, RATHNAGREE.

FIGURE 6.17: POST-EXCAVATION PHOTOGRAMMETRY, TRENCH 1, RATHNAGREE.

0.34m (N–S) at base, with a depth of 0.77m. There were several large packing stones (C.17) around the upper edges, including a rectangular slab measuring 0.31m by 0.17m by 0.11m, set on edge against the western side.

Finds

A single flint flake (14E227:01) was found near the base of the lower A-horizon (C.02) at northern end of trench. This is a primary flake, measuring 23mm by 13mm, with no cortex or obvious retouch. It may have been produced using a bipolar technique, but cannot be dated or connected to any flint-working activity on the hill. See below for details of radiocarbon dates from Trench 1.

Trench 1: summary

Excavation confirmed that the inner enclosure of the hillfort was originally surrounded by a wooden palisade, supported at the base by a low stone wall. This fence was probably constructed using large roundwood posts of 0.2–0.25m diameter, set upright in individual pits dug to a depth of 0.7–0.8m, and secured with stone packing. Further support was provided by the building of a stone revetment against the front of this palisade (Figure 6.19).

With the evidence from Trench 1 indicating a spacing of *c.*0.5m, it is possible that some 592 main posts were used in the perimeter of the enclosure. There was no indication of a slot trench or other post/stake-holes between these posts, which suggests that the intervening timbers may have been set into the surface of the bank.

The evidence of intense burning in this bank, in the form of charcoal spreads and heat-shattered stone, confirms the wooden palisade was burnt down some time after construction. While there were no charred post-pipes, the burnt rim around each posthole indicates the wooden uprights were burnt *in situ*. There is no evidence of any attempt to re-build the palisade or stone bank following its destruction.

Figure 6.18: Two postholes (C.14 left; C.18 right), Trench 1, Rathnagree. Note burnt surface around C.14.

Figure 6.19: Reconstruction of stone bank around C.18 posthole, Trench 1, Rathnagree.

List of excavation contexts, Trench 1, Rathnagree.
Context 01: Sod layer; mid brown, root-matted peaty soil, 4–5cm in thickness; no stones.

C.02: Black fibrous peat, 0.2–0.23m thick at north end of trench, thinning to 0.08–0.12m over bank.

C.03: Loose stones, 0.15–0.45m in size, within C.02 peat at north end of trench. Field clearance.

C.04: Grey/brown humic silt with small–medium stones at south end of trench. Lower A-horizon.

C.05: Thin (<2–3cm) spread of compact grey/white silt under peat at north end of trench. E-horizon.

C.06: Loose deposit of small–large angular stones, fire-reddened; charcoal in lower part of bank.

C.07: Line of large stones, 0.18–0.4m in length, set vertically along outer (south) side of bank.

C.08: Burnt wood, 0.43m long by 0.12m thick, under fire-reddened stone on western side of trench.

C.09: Burnt wood, 0.24m long into section on west side of trench, under fire-reddened bank stone.

C.10: Thin 0.95m by 0.6m spread of charcoal-rich black silt on inner (north) side of stone bank.

C.11: Small concentration of charcoal on upper east side of C.14 posthole. Part of C.10 burnt spread.

C.12: Upper fill of C.14 posthole; loose silty sediment with burnt stones, 0.1–0.15m in size.

C.13: Lower fill of C.14, loose orange/brown silt, with many 0.14–0.2m long stones; some charcoal.

C.14: Eastern posthole; sub-circular subsoil pit, 0.59m by 0.56m, with a depth of 0.71m.

C.15: Upper fill of C.18 posthole; loose burnt stone with humic silt and rare charcoal.

C.16: Lower fill of C.18; loose orange/yellow brown silt, some charcoal, with a few large stones.

C.17: Large packing stones around upper edges and sides of C.18 posthole.

C.18: Western posthole; sub-circular subsoil pit, 0.58m by 0.54m, with a depth of 0.77m.

C.19: Old ground surface. Thin spread of brown silt under stone bank.

C.20: Bs-horizon; compact orange/brown silt, with 0.2–0.3m stones, and patches of brown iron pan.

Middle enclosure (Trench 2)

The middle enclosure at Rathnagree measures 198m (N–S) by 182m (E–W), with a total area of 2.27ha (Figure 6.13). The enclosing element is the most impressive of the three in this hillfort, comprising a prominent inner bank with an outer ditch and counterscarp bank along a perimeter of 549m (Figure 6.20). The bank is 3–5m in width, with an internal height of 0.1–0.3m and an external height of *c.*2m to the bottom of the adjacent ditch. The inner side is gently sloping to a rounded top, while the exterior falls steeply into a round-bottomed ditch with a maximum width of 2.9–3.1m. The depth of this ditch was accentuated by the presence of a counterscarp bank with an external height of around 1m and an average width of 3m. This feature has a flat-topped profile and external stone facing, which suggests re-building in modern times for agricultural purposes.

A 9m (E–W) by 2.5m (N–S) trench, with a 3m (E–W) by 1m (N–S) extension, was excavated across these defences on the eastern side of the middle enclosure (Figures 6.21 and 6.22). The excavation of Trench 2 revealed a similar podzolic soil to that in Trench 1, where a thin peaty A-horizon (C.01 sod over C.02 peat/humus) overlay an iron-enriched Bs-horizon (C.20). Excavation at the base of the ditch revealed pockets of a grey/white silt (C.25) representing a thin C-horizon subsoil on bedrock. Though not exposed on the modern ground surface, excavation confirmed that bedrock occurs at a depth of 0.3–0.4m in the area of this trench.

Archaeological features

There were five areas of excavation within Trench 1 (from west to east): directly inside the main bank; the bank itself, the external ditch; a counterscarp bank on the edge of that ditch; and finally, the area outside that bank (Figure 6.21)

1. Inner bank area

Excavation at the western end of Trench 1 exposed a spread of large stones (C.26) within a thin layer of peat (Figure 6.23). These stones probably represent slip from stone walling placed on the top of the Phase 2 bank (see below). The removal of these stones revealed grey-brown, root-matted, humic silt (C.27) extending on to the adjacent bank. This overlay a slip of orange/brown stony silt (C.27) off the same bank. The removal of this bank slip exposed a spread of compact yellow/brown silt

FIGURE 6.20: LOCATION OF TRENCH 2, DEFENCES OF MIDDLE ENCLOSURE, RATHNAGREE HILLFORT.

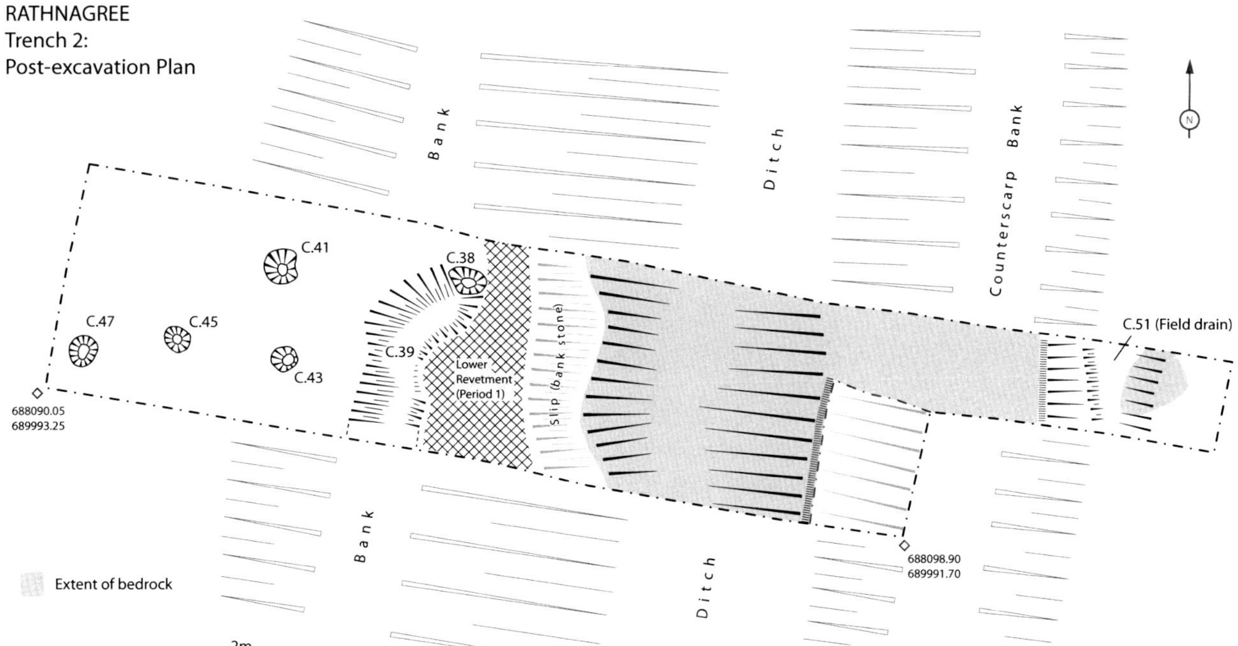

FIGURE 6.21: PLAN OF EXCAVATED FEATURES, TRENCH 2, RATHNAGREE.

with heavy charcoal flecking (C.31) across the south-west corner of the trench. This may be the continuation of a burnt layer (C.30) under the main bank. The Bs-horizon adjacent to this spread in the north-west corner was also flecked with charcoal at the same level (C.32).

Further excavation revealed two postholes (contexts 45 and 47), the cuts of which were partly surrounded by the C.31 charcoal-flecked silt (Figure 6.21). It is not clear from excavation whether the latter built up around the standing posts, or instead pre-dates the postholes (see below).

2. Bank

The removal of a thin peaty sod (C.01) exposed the surface of the inner bank. This consisted of a compacted layer of grey/brown, root-matted, silt (C.27). This was removed to expose a deposit of orange/brown stony silt (C.28). This was redeposited subsoil from the digging of adjacent ditch, which overlay the top and inner slope of the bank to a maximum thickness of 0.5m (Figure 6.23). The removal of this orange soil revealed the core of the bank to be made up almost entirely of medium to large stones with numerous voids (C.29) and rootlets, as well as some inwash of grey/brown humic silt (Figure 6.24). These bank stones had a sub-rounded form, suggestive of gathered field stone rather than quarried material. It is notable that they were not fire-reddened or heat-shattered, with no charcoal recorded in the core of the bank. The external (eastern) side of the bank was supported by a line of large boulders packed together with smaller stones. While the upper portion of this bank revetment had collapsed into the ditch, the lower part was largely intact.

Pre-bank features

The stone core (C.29), and the overlying orange bank sediment (C.28) on its inner side, were removed to expose a thin spread of dark brown/black silt with much charcoal (C.30) under the bank (Figure 6.23). This was more or less continuous, except where interrupted by large stones in or on the underlying subsoil surface (Figure 6.24). This charcoal spread represents a burning event that pre-dates the overlying bank, which had no indications of fire. Excavation of the C.30 burnt layer revealed the underlying surface and some of surface stones to be fire-reddened. Context 30 extended as far as the outer edge of the bank, where it seems to have been truncated by the later ditch. The burnt layer thinned considerably on the western side, where it can be con-

FIGURE 6.22: POST-EXCAVATION PHOTOGRAMMETRY, TRENCH 2, RATHNAGREE.

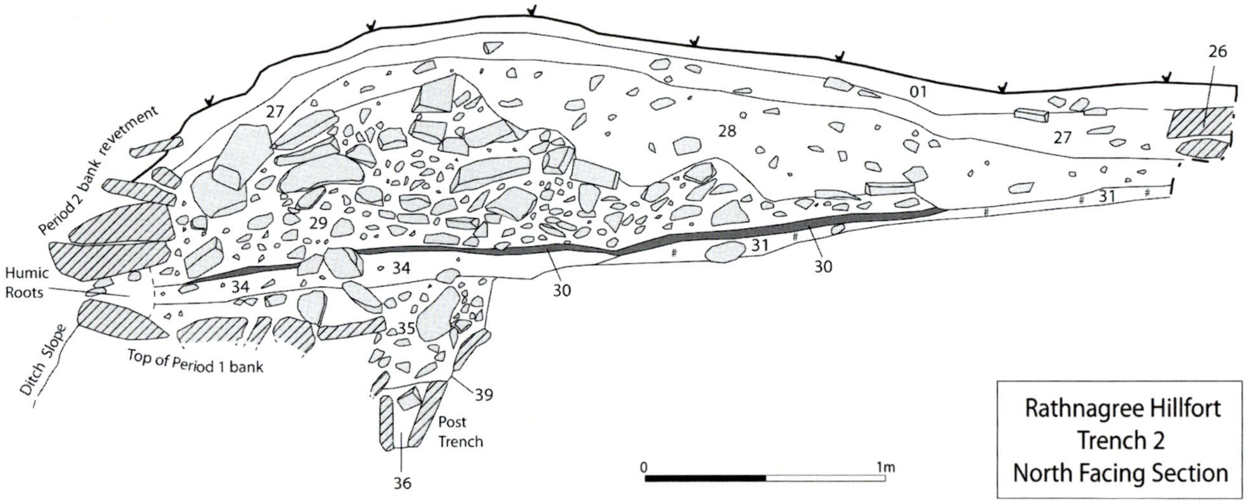

FIGURE 6.23: STRATIFICATION OF BANK, TRENCH 2, RATHNAGREE.

FIGURE 6.24: NORTH-FACING SECTION OF MAIN BANK, WITH UNDERLYING POSTHOLES (C.41 AND C.43) AND PART OF PRE-BANK BURNT SPREAD (C.30; FAR LEFT).

nected to a spread of charcoal-flecked silt (C.31) in the south-west corner of the trench, and possibly to charcoal flecking (C.32) on the Bs-horizon surface in the north-west corner.

The removal of C.30 burnt layer exposed a thin layer of orange sandy silt (C.34) up to 0.1m in thickness. This was excavated to reveal the stony fill of a foundation trench (C.39) extending in a north–south direction beneath the core of the later bank (Figure 6.23). The upper fill (C.35) of this trench was a loose deposit of small-to-large rounded/sub-rounded stones, 0.05–036m length, in grey/brown sandy silt with voids. These were mostly sub-rounded field stones, some of which were broken, but no fire-reddened examples or charcoal. The removal of this stony fill exposed a dark silt (C.36) at the base of the slot, which contained only a few flecks of charcoal. The removal of this fill at the southern end revealed several thin slabs placed against both sides of the C.39 slot as packing stones.

The slot trench (C.39) itself measured 0.5m (north end), 0.55m (centre) and 0.65m (south end) in width, with a corresponding depth of 0.3m, 0.45m and 0.68m in the natural subsoil (Figures 6.25 and 6.26). The western side was near-vertical to steeply inclined, whereas the eastern side was formed by large stones forming an exterior revetment. The southern end was V-shaped in profile, with some thin stones placed against the western side as post packing. Excavation at the northern end revealed a small post-setting (C.38), filled with grey/brown sandy silt with charcoal flecks (C.37). This contained a 0.18m long thin slab, placed vertically as a packing stone against the southern edge of the posthole. The central area of the slot trench had a rounded profile, which suggests this feature may have held upright posts spaced c.1.5m apart.

Further excavation identified four small postholes and a single stakehole on the ground surface west of the C.39 slot (Figure 6.25). Two of these postholes with packing stones (contexts 41 and 43) were parallel to the C.39 slot trench, and so may be connected to the Period 1 palisade (Figure 6.21). This may also apply to the C.57 stakehole found on the western edge of the slot trench. Two other postholes (contexts 45 and 47) were discovered at the western end of Trench 2 on a different orientation. This may indicate a built structure comprising all four postholes, and possibly others outside the area of excavation, close to the inner edge of the Period 1 palisade. While the two western postholes (contexts 45 and 47) were covered by slip from the bank (C.28), their stratigraphic position is unclear due to their uncertain relationship to a spread of charcoal-flecked silt (C.31) from the Period 1 activity in the same area. The two easterly postholes (contexts 41 and 43) were both beneath the C.30 burnt spread, which in turn was overlain by the

FIGURE 6.25: POST-EXCAVATION VIEW OF SLOT TRENCH (C.39; CENTRE LEFT) UNDER BANK. FOUR POSTHOLES (CONTEXTS 41, 43, 45 AND 47) TO RIGHT OF SLOT TRENCH).

FIGURE 6.26: SOUTH-FACING SECTION OF MAIN BANK, SHOWING SOUTHERN END OF C.39 SLOT (FAR RIGHT) WITH POSTHOLES (C.41 AND 43; CENTRE).

Period 2 bank. If all four postholes were part of the same structure, this indicates that the two western examples (contexts 45 and 47) also date to Period 1. This cannot be confirmed without further excavation to reveal the nature of this putative structure.

3. Ditch

The removal of a thin sod (C.01) exposed the upper fill of the ditch (Figure 6.27). This consisted of a 0.12–0.2m thick layer of humic silt (C.27), which was heavily root-matted and contained a few small to large stones. This context represents the development of A-horizon organic soil in the ditch following the collapse of the bank revetment. The latter is represented by a deposit of large stones (C.21) within the lower ditch area at the base of the main bank. This deposit had a maximum thickness of 0.4m, and comprised large stones in a dark brown sandy silt with numerous voids. This represents the collapse of stone walling from the Phase 2 bank into the open ditch. The stones had an angular blocky appearance in a 0.3–4m size range, as well as slab-like stones measuring from 0.15m up to 0.7m. They are the same lithology as the bedrock exposed at base of ditch, where these stones had been quarried. The position of the stones in the upper ditch fill indicates the collapse of a stone wall that formerly existed on top of the adjacent bank. Some of the C.21 stones on the eastern (outer) side of the ditch may derive from partial collapse of the internal revetment of the counterscarp bank.

The removal of this C.21 stone deposit exposed a thin layer of dark brown silt (C.22) on the inner slope of the ditch. This overlay a deposit of orange silt (C.24), that was removed to reveal grey mottled silt (C.25) on quarried bedrock. The stony deposit (C.21) was removed to expose a thick layer of compact bright orange silt (C.23) on the lower exterior slope of the ditch. This overlay mid brown orange silt (C.33), on top of mottled silt (C.25), on bedrock. The lower part of C.23, as well as the underlying C.33, contained 18 sherds of coarse ware pottery of later Bronze Age type (see below).

The removal of these lower sediments exposed the base of the ditch (Figure 6.28). This has an irregularly rounded profile, with exposed ribs of bedrock separated by pockets of compact sterile silt (C.25) that had some flecks of

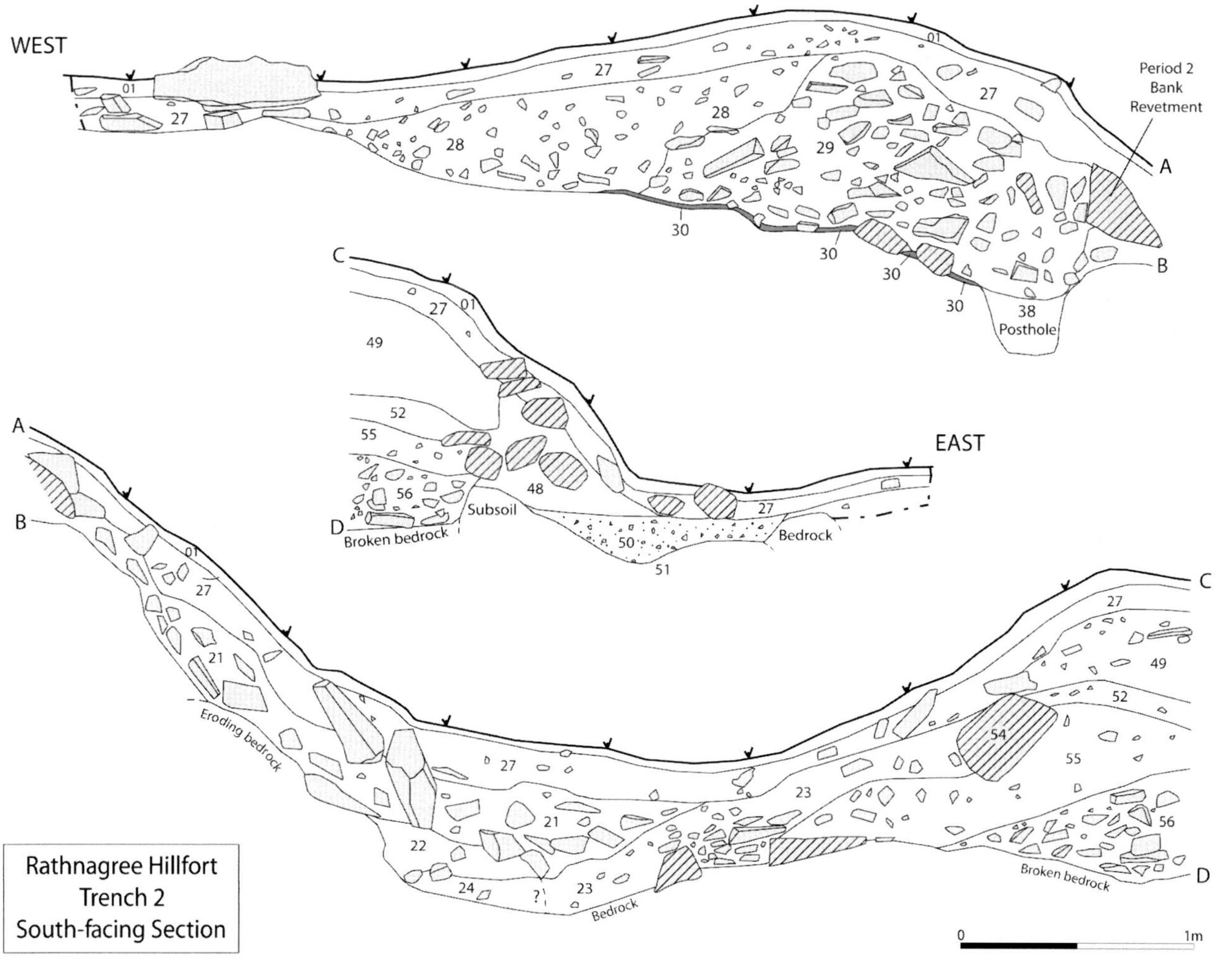

FIGURE 6.27: STRATIFICATION OF BANK, DITCH AND COUNTERSCARP BANK, TRENCH 2, RATHNAGREE.

Figure 6.28: Post-excavation view of ditch, with exposed bedrock at base.

charcoal. The upper width of the ditch was 2.6–2.7m, with a lower width of 1.1–1.2m, and a central depth of 0.7–0.8m below modern grass surface.

4–5. Counterscarp bank and external area

The outer edge of the ditch is raised today by a flat-topped earthen bank, which ranges 1.2m (top) to 1.7m (base) in width (Figure 6.29). The central height of the bank after rebuilding is 1.35m, while the original height was around 0.7m. Excavation of a thin sod (C.01) and peaty layer (C.27) on the immediate exterior of this bank revealed a deposit of large stones (C.48) within lower A-horizon soil. This represent the collapse of stone facing, the lower part of which survives in the bank (Figure 6.27). The removal of these stones exposed a shallow trench (C.51) at the base of the bank, cut into subsoil with bedrock on lower outer edge. This feature was filled with dark brown silt (C.50), with no cultural material or samples for dating. It is probably a field drain, dug when the counterscarp bank was re-built in the early modern era.

Excavation revealed a deposit of orange/brown sandy silt (C.49) forming the upper part of counterscarp bank. Some of this soil is probably upcast from digging of the C.51 drain, when the counterscarp bank was re-built. This re-building is confirmed by the discovery of a 0.04–0.15m thick buried sod layer (C.52) separating the original bank material from the overlying C.49 soil. Excavation of this buried sod exposed a loose deposit of bright orange silt (C.55) piled to a thickness of 0.25m to form the primary counterscarp bank. This was retained on both sides by large stones forming a roughly coursed revetment (C.53 exterior facing; C.54 inner facing). The inner stone facing was built on the lower edge of this C.55 deposit, some of which extended into the adjacent ditch. This inner stone facing had partly collapsed into the open ditch. Some lower stones of the external bank facing (C.53) survived in situ to a height of 0.5m, while the upper portion was re-built (and subsequently collapsed; C.48) in modern times. The C.53 stones had an angular blocky appearance similar to stones in the upper ditch fill (C.21), suggesting they were also quarried from the ditch.

Context 55 represents redeposited subsoil forming the upper part of the primary counterscarp bank (Figure 6.27). It overlay a deposit of broken stones with numerous voids (C.56) at the base of the bank. This broken stone was piled up on a shattered bedrock surface that was created during digging of the adjacent ditch. No dating material or artifacts were recovered from the primary counterscarp bank, however the stratigraphy indicates it was built at the same time as the adjacent ditch. As previously stated, this was necessary because the counterscarp bank was necessary to raise the depth of that ditch given the slope on that eastern side of the hillfort.

FIGURE 6.29: EXTERIOR REVETMENT STONES (C.53) OF COUNTERSCARP BANK, WITH EXTERNAL FIELD DRAIN.

Finds

The only artifacts found in the excavation of Trench 2 is a small collection of prehistoric pottery sherds from the ditch of the middle enclosure (Figure 6.30).

Rathnagree Pottery (Rose M. Cleary)

The assemblage comprises 18 sherds (153.7g) and of these 17 sherds (nos 2–13; 15–19) were recovered from the basal sediment of the ditch of the middle enclosure of the hillfort and one sherd (no. 20; 9.7g) was from a burnt spread under the bank of Period I defences. Radiocarbon analysis (GrA-63008; 3170 ± 35 BP) of carbonised residue on a sherd (14E227-8) returned a date of 1495–1415 BC. The fabric suggests a single vessel from the ditch fill. A sherd (no. 20) from the pre-bank burnt spread is the same fabric as the sherds from the ditch but is more-evenly fired.

Description

The assemblage from the basal ditch fill comprises two rim fragments (2, 17), one base fragment (18), one body/base fragment (16), body sherds (3, 7–10, 12 and 15) and four minute fragments (4, 6, 11 and 19). The number of sherds suggests one vessel from the ditch fill and as few rim and base sherds were recovered it is likely that the pottery was fragmentary when deposited (Figure 6.30). The vessel is a small squat, flat-based pot with an estimated rim diameter of 14cm, base diameter of 11cm and height of *c.*14cm (Figure 6.31). The rim is bevelled internally. Vessel wall sherd thickness is on average 13mm and the base is *c.*20mm thick. The pottery is well-made and coil-constructed evidenced by a distinctive fracture pattern. Coil manufacture is usual in Irish prehistoric pottery for the production of medium-large sized vessels (Cleary 2000: 130). The internally bevelled rim may indicate that the pot had a cover seated on the rim. The cover may have been of wood or a flat stone as there is no evidence for a ceramic lid.

Soot accretions are visible internally in the upper body and rim areas whereas the extant basal sherds do not have charred residues. The external vessel wall is partially blackened from contact with a smoke. The pottery is richly tempered with crushed stone macroscopically identified as granite and the inclusions are generally ≥3mm with larger fragments up to 7mm. The granite contains quartz, feldspars and large tourmaline crystals (Richard Unitt pers. comm.). The clay has visible quartz and mica and is sandy textured. The pottery was fired externally to reddish brown (Munsell 5YR5/4) and has a very dark grey (Munsell 5YR3/1) core. Sherd No. 20 from the burnt spread is a 12mm thick body sherd evenly fired throughout to reddish yellow (Munsell 5YR6/6).

FIGURE 6.30: SHERDS OF BRONZE AGE POTTERY FROM TRENCH 2, RATHNAGREE.

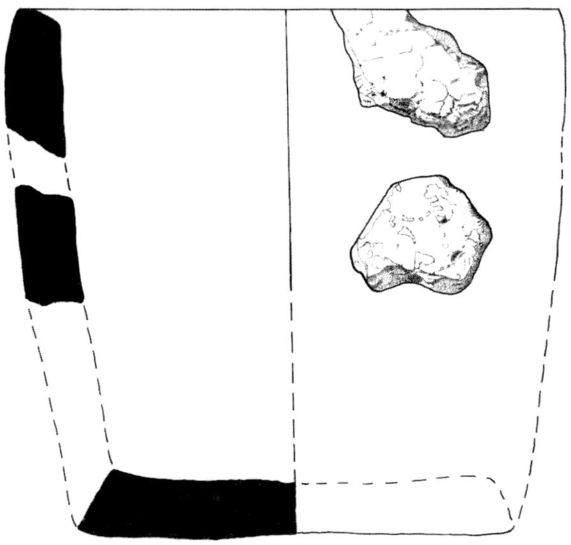

FIGURE 6.31: RECONSTRUCTION OF POTTERY FROM TRENCH 2, RATHNAGREE (DIAMETER 14CM, BASE DIAMETER 11CM, HEIGHT 14CM).

The vessel was tempered with crushed granite (≥3mm) and made from mica-rich clay, similar to the pottery from the ditch.

Discussion

There is evidence of weathering on the external surface of the basal sherd from the ditch and the probability is that the vessel was upturned and exposed to some physical weathering from the elements prior to being covered by subsequent infill layers. *In situ* weathering suggests a break in the infill of the ditch. The vessel from the ditch sediment is incomplete and the likelihood is that the vessel was broken prior to deposition and some fragments were thrown into the ditch. The sherd from the pre-bank burnt layer is also weathered on one surface and was exposed to the elements prior to being covered by soil. The interval between the accumulation of the burnt layer and subsequent bank construction may not however have been great but long enough to abrade the sherd surface.

The crushed stone used as temper (added to the clay) was macroscopically identified as granite and the clay contains visible mica. Rock samples collected from modern stone field boundaries around the hillfort have been identified as of similar geological origin and the source of the temper was probably in the locale (Richard Unitt pers. comm.). The clay used for pottery manufacture has visible mica and includes the same minerals (feldspar, quartz, hornblende[?]) as the granite temper fragments. The clay also contains fragments of rounded grey sandstone(?) and rounded quartz/quartzite crystals suggesting a fluvially derived source. The clay source was probably local from residual clays developed over the granite bedrock and would normally be extracted along river valleys.

The beneficial effect of the use of volcanic rocks as pottery temper has been discussed elsewhere (Cleary 2008: 257; 2011). Good quality vessels suitable for use over a fire and repeated re-heating are produced when clays are tempered with rocks that include silicates, feldspars and mica. The use of granitic rocks which are acidic rocks lessens the probability of cracking due to thermal shock during repeated re-heatings, but are not as effective as more basic rocks (basalts, gabbros, etc.) with lower thermal expansion rates. The use of large temper fragments probably resulted in a porous vessel suitable for resisting thermal shock from use over an open fire (Shepard 1963: 26; 52–53), but may have made the vessel brittle as large temper fragments may cause cracking where clay has insufficiently bonded during firing. Externally soot blackened rims and some body sherds suggest that the vessel was used over an open fire perhaps to heat the contents. The relatively small size of the pot may indicate limited use for bulk cooking.

The fired colour of the Rathnagree vessel assemblage is even and a reddish yellow hue. The evenness of the colour indicates some control over the firing temperature and the pottery was probably fired in a primitive kiln rather than an open bonfire (Tite 1995). The sherd from the pre-bank burnt spread is very evenly fired. By the Bronze Age temperature control is confirmed by the productive of an extensive range of metal artefacts by sophisticated metallurgical production processes and this technology was undoubtedly applied to pottery production. The blackish cores suggest the pottery was rapidly-fired and oxidization did not occur throughout the sherds (Cleary 2008). This does not make a less durable pottery and as the cores are not seen when the vessels are whole, has little effect on the aesthetic appearance of the vessels.

The vessel shape is relatively small and bucket-shaped. Bucket-shaped vessels are common on Middle–Late Bronze Age domestic sites and are amply represented on excavations on Knockadoon Hill, Lough Gur, Co. Limerick (Ó Ríordáin 1954; Grogan and Eogan 1987; Cleary 1995 and 2003). Pottery from Knockadoon termed 'Class II' ware was flat-based and bucket-shaped with estimated rim diameters of *c.*20–26cm and heights of *c.*26–29cm (Ó Ríordáin 1954: 333) and significantly larger than the Rathnagree vessel. The difference may be related to functionality and the Rathnagree vessel may have been 'tableware' to contain rather than cook food and this is confirmed by the absence of residues on the basal sherds. Other Lough Gur Middle–Late Bronze Age sites produced smaller vessels pottery which had average rim diameters of 14cm (Cleary 1995; 2003) and are of similar size to the Rathnagree vessel. A Middle Bronze Age (*c.*1500–1200 BC) settlement at Chancellorsland, Co. Tipperary also produced a range of flat-based bucket-shaped pots including some of similar size to that from Rathnagree (Cleary 2008, fig. 2.5.2:12). Nine vessels from a Middle Bronze Age settlement dated to 1510–1220 BC and 1130–850 BC (O'Kelly 1989: 222) within the enclosure at Carrigillihy, Co. Cork (O'Kelly 1951: fig. 8) were also relatively fine and small-sized with rim diameters of *c.*16cm. Vessels from the environs of Late Bronze Age hut sites within the stone fort at Dún Aonghasa, Inis Mór, Aran Islands included a number of small bucket-shaped pots (Cleary 2012: fig. 8.6) similar to the vessel from Rathnagree. Small vessels were also recorded on a number of Bronze Age sites (Grogan and Roche 2009: 42).

Trench 2: summary

The excavation of Trench 2 identified three periods of construction in the defences of the middle enclosure:

Period 1 (prehistoric): post palisade with revetment wall; possible post-built structure on inside.

Period 2 (prehistoric): earthen/stone bank topped with stone walling, with an external ditch and a counterscarp bank. This re-building occurred immediately after burning of period 1 palisade.

Period 3 (early modern): Rebuilding of the counterscarp bank.

Period 1: Palisade

The discovery of a slot trench (C.39) with post settings underneath the bank indicates an earlier enclosure on this side of the hillfort. This slot trench seems to have held upright posts, spaced approximately 1.5m apart, which were secured with packing stones and by a low revetment of large stones on the immediate outside. The discovery of four postholes (contexts 41, 43, 45 and 47) on the western side of the slot trench may indicate a post-built structure on the immediate inside of the palisade. It is also possible that two of these postholes (contexts 41 and 43) were part of the palisade, along with a single stakehole (C.57) nearby.

This arrangement of a post-built fence supported by low stone walling is similar to that in the inner enclosure (Trench 1), and also the outer enclosure (see Trench 3 below), the main difference being the use of a slot trench rather than individual postholes to hold the main posts. With a perimeter of 549m and a 1.2m main post spacing, the middle enclosure required as many as 458 such posts to construct this palisade, in addition to a considerable amount of smaller roundwood necessary to complete the fencing. Also similar is the destruction of the palisade by fire, represented in the case of the middle enclosure by a burnt layer (C.30) beneath the later bank. This burning event probably included the posts held in the four postholes inside the slot trench. Radiocarbon dating of this destruction level indicates that the Period 1 defences were either built or destroyed in the period 1535–1126 BC (see below).

Period 2: Walled bank-and-ditch

Unlike the other two hillfort enclosures, the middle enclosure was restored probably soon after it was burnt. This took a different form to the earlier palisade, with the building of an earth and stone bank, on top of which was a wall of coursed stone. The material used came from an external ditch, the lower part of which was in bedrock. The soil (C.28) and drift stones (C.29) used in the bank core came from the upper part of the ditch. The blocky stone used in the bank wall was quarried at the base of the ditch. The fact that this bank and ditch were constructed on a slope required the building of a low earthen and stone bank on the immediate outside of the ditch so as to deepen the latter.

The subsequent collapse of this bank wall into the ditch (C.21) does not seem to have been a deliberate act. There were no radiocarbon samples available for the building of these Period 2 defences or their abandonment. The significance of pottery found in the lower ditch fill is discussed below.

Period 3: re-building of counterscarp bank.

Excavation confirmed that the eroded counterscarp bank was re-built for agricultural purposes some time in the early modern era. This involved the digging of an external field drain, soil from which was piled to raise the Period 2 bank, with additional stones added to the external revetment. Though there has been some collapse of this revetment, this re-building explains the regular, flat-topped, profile of the counterscarp bank today.

List of excavation contexts, Trench 2, Rathnagree.
Context 01: Sod layer, mid brown, root-matted peat, no stones, with grass vegetation.

C.02: Thin layer of rooty peat, frequent small–medium stones. Flecks of charcoal flecks from periodic hill burning.

C.20: Bs-horizon. Orange sandy silt with small–large stones; iron-enriched but no iron pan.

C.21: Central fill of ditch. Large angular stones, 0.15–0.7m long, in dark brown silt with voids.

C.22: Compact dark brown silt, some small–large stones

and charcoal flecks, inner slope of ditch.

C.23: Compact bright orange sandy silt on lower exterior slope of ditch; contains pottery.

C.24: Orange silt under C.22 on inner side of ditch; few stones, some boulders from bank revetment.

C.25: Thin pockets of grey/white mottled silt within broken bedrock at base of ditch.

C.26: Spread of sub-rounded stones, 0.15–0.4m long, inside main bank, west end of Trench 2.

C.27: A-horizon in ditch. Grey/brown humic silt, up to 0.2m thick, with some small–large stones.

C.28: Orange/brown stony silt forming upper part of main bank. Frequent pebbles, few large stones.

C.29: Large stones forming core of main bank, with voids and inwash of grey/brown humic silt.

C.30: Burnt layer beneath main bank. Spread of dark brown/black silt with much fine/lump charcoal.

C.31: Spread of yellow/brown silt with charcoal flecks at south-west end of trench.

C.32: Compact orange stony silt with charcoal flecks, north-west end of trench. Bs-horizon.

C.33: Pockets of red/brown silt on bedrock, lower exterior side of ditch. Contains pottery.

C.34: Compact spread of bright orange sandy silt with small pebbles under C.30 burnt spread.

C.35: Upper fill of C.39 trench. Loose mix of sub-angular stones in 0.05–0.36m range, some broken.

C.36: Lower fill of C.39 trench. Similar stone content to C.35 fill, in loose dark brown humic silt.

C.37: Fill of posthole (C.38). Loose grey/brown sandy silt, some stones and rare charcoal.

C.38: Posthole at north end of C.39 slot. Sub-circular vertical cut, 0.42m by 0.3m by 0.22m deep.

C.39: Cut of irregular slot trench under main bank. See main text for details.

C.40: Fill of posthole (C.41). Loose grey/brown silt with several large stones (displaced packing).

C.41: Posthole. Vertical cut, 0.47m by 0.4m by 0.31m deep, with small boulders around edge.

C.42: Fill of posthole (C.43). Loose grey/brown silt; five stones, 0.16–0.22m, around eastern edge.

C.43: Posthole. Circular cut, 0.18m in central diameter, with vertical depth of 0.38m to a point.

C.44: Fill of posthole (C.45). Loose grey/brown sandy silt with on edge suggestive of packing.

C.45: Posthole. Circular cut, 0.17m wide by 0.41m deep, slight incline, with stones around edges.

C.46: Fill of posthole (C.47) at west end of Trench 2. Loose grey/brown silt with large stones.

C.47: Posthole. Sub-circular vertical cut, 0.3m by 0.28m, with vertical sides to 0.45m depth.

C.48: Blocky stones, 0.12–0.5m in length, in C.02; collapsed exterior of re-built counterscarp bank.

C.49: Deposit of loose orange/brown sandy silt with large stones; upper part of counterscarp bank.

C.50: Fill of field drain (C.51) at base of re-built counterscarp bank. Dark brown silt with pebbles.

C.51: Field drain. Shallow trench with rounded profile, 0.7m wide and 0.2m deep.

C.52: Buried sod layer under C.49 in outer bank. Dark brown sandy silt, 0.04–0.15m in thickness.

C.53: Outer revetment of primary outer bank. Blocky 0.2–0.55m stones, rough horizontal coursing.

C.54: Inner revetment of primary counterscarp bank. Blocky stones in 0.2–0.55m size range.

C.55: Upper part of primary outer bank. Compact, 0.25m thick, bright orange silt with small stones.

C.56: Deposit of loose angular stones, <0.05–0.5m, in orange sandy silt, base of primary outer bank.

C.57: Stakehole. Oval vertical cut, 0.1m by 0.7m by 0.28m deep. Grey/brown silt fill with charcoal.

Outer enclosure (Trench 3)

The outer enclosure measures 294m (N–S) by 273m (E–W), a perimeter of 873m and a total area of 2.69ha (Figure 6.13). The enclosing element has a similar appearance to the inner enclosure, comprising a low denuded bank of stones, some of which are exposed. There is no surface indication of an accompanying ditch (Figure 6.32). The bank is most visible on the southern side

FIGURE 6.32: SURFACE OF STONE BANK (C.60), CENTRAL AREA OF TRENCH 3, RATHNAGREE.

of the enclosure where it is 0.1–0.3m high and 3m wide. A 7m (N–S) by 2m (E–W) trench was excavated across the line of the bank on that side.

Excavation at the northern end of the trench (inside the hillfort bank) revealed a 0.1–0.15m thick A-horizon, consisting of a thin sod (C.01) over black fibrous peat (C.02). A number of large stones (C.58) at the base of this peat represent tumble off the bank (Figure 6.33). The removal of this peat at the southern end of the trench exposed a compact layer of grey-brown, root-matted silt (C.59). This overlay an iron-panned surface (C.69) on bright orange subsoil (C.20) that forms the Bs-horizon.

Archaeological features

Excavation of the outer enclosing element revealed a low bank of stones with large postholes, which were originally part of a wooden palisade (Figures 6.34 and 6.35).

The removal of a thin peaty sod exposed a band of small to large stones across the centre of Trench 3 (Figures 6.32 and 6.33). The surface was heavily root-matted and compacted (C.59). The underlying stone bank (C.60) had an overall width of 2.35–2.45m, with a maximum thickness of 0.3m on the eastern side and 0.35m on the western side. None of the bank stone had the angular profile of quarried rock, with the prevalence of sub-rounded forms indicating the use of gathered field stone. Most were in the 0.1–0.2m size range, with the largest up to 0.43m long and fewer intact stones under 0.1m. There was no obvious fire-reddening on the upper stones of this bank, possibly due to surface weathering. This did occur on the heat-shattered stones forming the lower part of the bank. It was particularly evident on the northern (inner) side of the bank where the lower stones overlay a spread of charcoal-rich sediment (C.61; Figure 6.33) in which a burnt branch was discovered (radiocarbon sample RNG2014-05).

The absence of fire reddening on the surface of the bank suggest that some of this stone may have been added after the burning event. This is also suggested by the fill of the western posthole (C.67), which contained a tightly packed arrangement of four large stones, placed side by side in a vertical position. It is not certain whether these were original packing or a possible re-building of the stone bank. The former seems more likely, and so any evidence for the re-building of this bank is tenuous.

Excavation of the C.61 burnt surface revealed the position of two postholes placed 0.7m apart on the outer side of the stone bank (Figures 6.34 and 6.35). The eastern posthole (C.64) measured 0.51m (N–S) by 0.38m (E–W), with a vertical depth of 0.72m (Figure 6.36). When excavated this posthole was filled with stony silt (C.62) that contained a small amount of charcoal, though

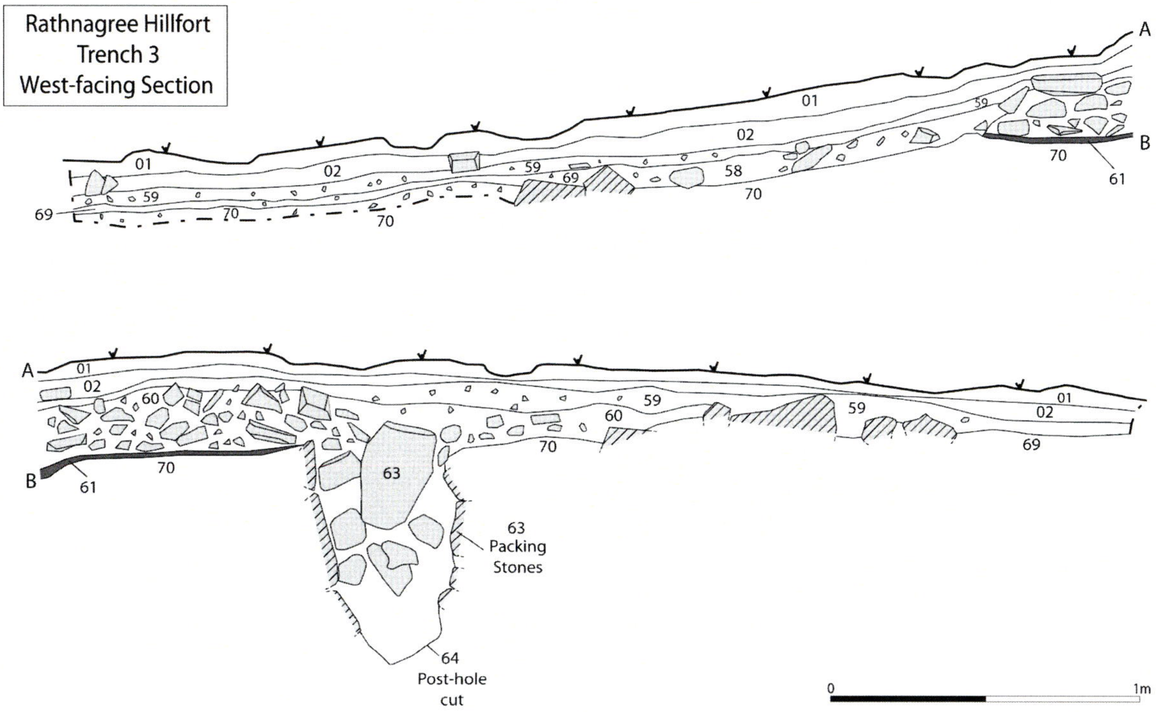

Figure 6.33: Stratification of Trench 3, Rathnagree.

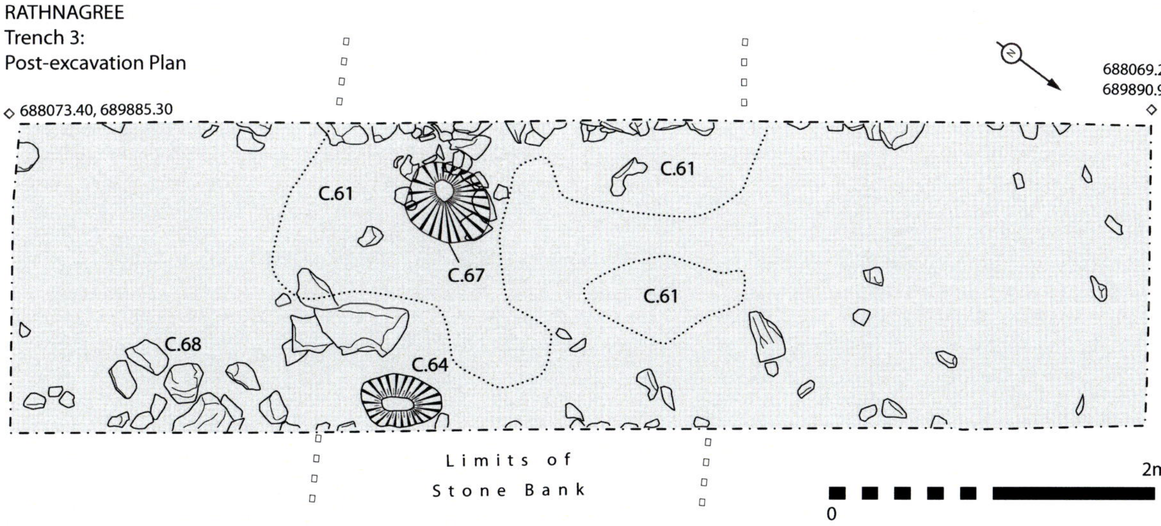

Figure 6.34: Post-excavation plan of Trench 3, Rathnagree.

Figure 6.35: Post-excavation photogrammetry of Trench 3, Rathnagree.

not enough to indicate the burning of this post in situ. The overlying bank stone (C.60), some of which was fire-shattered and reddened, extended into the upper part of the posthole. The removal of C.62 fill revealed an arrangement of large packing stones (C.63) lining the sides of the posthole. These included an arrangment of six stones in the upper 0.25m, beneath which there there were at least eight slabs down to the base. These stones seem to have been jammed down the sides of the posthole once the post was erected, and remained in this position following its removal. The width of the lower cut suggests the original post had a diameter of approximately 0.25m.

The western posthole (C.67) was circular in shape, narrowing from 0.66m (N–S) at the surface to 0.34–0.4m at the base, with a central depth of 0.48m (Figure 6.36). The upper part was filled with heat-shattered bank stone (C.60), beneath which there was a red/dark brown silty fill containing charcoal (C.65). This became blacker towards the base where there was a significant amount of charcoal. The removal of a horizontal stone, measuring 0.33m by 0.28m by 0.13m, exposed a 0.1m thick deposit of charcoal-rich silt at the base of the posthole (radiocarbon sample RNG2014-06). There was not enough charcoal in the fill to indicate the original post was burnt in situ. Several vertical packing stones (C.66) were identified in this posthole fill. The largest measured 0.59m by 0.16m by 0.11m, and had been deliberately pointed for use as a packing stone (Figure 6.37). This was part of a tightly packed arrangement of five other stones, ranging 0.19–0.29m in length.

Finds

There are no artefact finds from Trench 3. See below for details of radiocarbon dates.

Trench 3: summary

The results from Trench 3 indicate that a wooden palisade, supported by a low bank of stones, delimited the outer enclosure of the hillfort. This consisted of upright posts, probably complete roundwood 0.2–0.25m in diameter, spaced 0.7m apart. With a perimeter of 873m, the outer enclosure required as many as 1247 such posts to construct this palisade, in addition to a large amount of smaller roundwood necessary to complete the work. As with the inner enclosure, there is no evidence for a slot trench between the main posts, suggesting that any intervening posts were either set into the surface of the stone bank and/or lashed horizontally or obliquely to form the palisade. The size of that fence is unknown, but given the depth of the excavated postholes (0.48m and 0.72m) it must have been at least 2–3m in height. The stone piled at the base of these posts probably did not exceed 1m in height, and so should be considered a fence revetment rather than a wall.

The discovery of fire-reddened and heat-shattered stone in the lower bank deposit, together with a spread of charcoal overlying an oxidised surface around the postholes, confirms that the palisade was burnt down. There is no evidence to suggest these defences were ever re-built.

FIGURE 6.36: TWO POSTHOLES EXCAVATED IN TRENCH 3 (C.64 RIGHT; C.67 LEFT). NOTE PACKING STONE ARRANGEMENT IN C.67.

FIGURE 6.37: DELIBERATELY SHAPED PACKING STONE USED IN C.67 POSTHOLE, TRENCH 3, RATHNAGREE.

List of excavation contexts, Trench 3, Rathnagree.
Context 01: Sod layer, 3–5cm in thickness; root-matted peat, free of stones.

C.02: Thin layer of peat inside bank. Root-matted, frequent small-to-medium stones, charcoal flecks.

C.20: Bs-horizon. Bright orange sandy silt with small–large stones; iron-rich with C.69 iron pan.

C.58: Stone tumble off bank, north end of trench. Sub-rounded field stones, 0.15–0.38m in size.

C.59: Compact layer of grey/brown, root-matted, stony silt under A-horizon.

C.60: Deposit of burnt and unburnt field stones forming low bank. See main text for details.

C.61: Spread of dark brown silt, with much fine and lump charcoal, over fire-reddened stones.

C.62: Fill of eastern posthole (C.63). Brown/orange silt with <0.05–0.2m size stones, some charcoal.

C.63: Packing stones in eastern posthole (C.64). Some 14 thin slabs in the 0.2–0.3m range.

C.64: Eastern posthole. Oval cut, 0.51m by 0.38m, with a vertical depth of 0.72m to a round point.

C.65: Fill of western posthole (C.67). Loose broken stone over red/dark brown silt with charcoal.

C.66: Packing stones in western posthole (C.67). Six vertical stones, 0.19–0.59m in length (Figure 6.37).

C.67: Western posthole. Circular cut, 0.66m wide by 0.48m deep, to a 0.34m by 0.4m wide flat base.

C.68: Natural stones in subsoil (C.20) near eastern posthole. Sub-rounded stones, 0.2–0.34m in size.

C.69: Patches of hard, red/brown, iron pan on C.20 surface.

Rathnagree radiocarbon results

A total of eight radiocarbon dates are available from the 2014 excavation season at Rathnagree hillfort. These include two samples from the enclosing elements of the inner enclosure (Trench 1); four from those of the middle enclosure (Trench 2); and two from those of the outer enclosure (Trench 3). The results are as follows (Figure 6.38; calibration to 95.4% confidence, Oxcal v4.2.4).

Trench 1 (inner enclosure)
Sample RNG2014-01: Charcoal from burnt timber (C.08) next to palisade posts. Identified as ash (*fraxinus excelsior*) with wide growth ring pattern.
GrA-60925; 3045 ± 40 BP

Sample RNG2014-02: Charcoal from basal fill (C.16) of posthole (C.18). Identified as sessile oak (*quercus cf petraea*).
GrA-60927; 3055 ± 40 BP

Trench 2 (middle enclosure)
Sample RNG2014-03: Charcoal from Period 1 burnt spread (C.30) under Period 2 bank. Mix of hazel, sessile oak, willow and ash.
GrA-60929; 3050 ± 40 BP

Sample RNG2014-04: Charcoal from fill of Period 1 stakehole (C.57) under Period 2 bank. Not identified to wood genus.
GrA-60930; 3015 ± 40 BP

Sample RNG2014-07: Charcoal from Period 1 burnt spread (C.30) under Period 2 bank. Identified as frag-

ment of hazel (*corylus avellana*); twig with less that 10 growth rings and some sapwood adhering.
GrA-63007; 3240 ± 35 BP

Sample RNG2014-08: Pottery sherd residue. From one of the pot sherds found at base of ditch of middle hillfort enclosure.
GrA-63008; 3170 ± 35 BP

Trench 3 (outer enclosure)
Sample RNG2014-05: Charcoal from burnt timber (within C.61) next to palisade posts. Identified as sessile oak (*quercus cf petraea*) with wide growth ring pattern.
GrA-60931; 3020 ± 40 BP

Sample RNG2014-06: Charcoal from lower fill (C.65) of posthole (C.67). Identified as sessile oak (*quercus cf petraea*).
GrA-60932; 3035 ± 40 BP

FIELD NO.	LAB NO.	C-14 BP	∂13C	95.4% CALIBRATION
RNG2016-01	GRA-60925	3045±40	-24.59	1414–1135 BC
RNG2016-02	GRA-60927	3055±40	-25.50	1417–1213 BC
RNG2016-03	GRA-60929	3050±40	-25.19	1417–1208 BC
RNG2016-04	GRA-60930	3015±40	-25.68	1395–1126 BC
RNG2016-05	GRA-60931	3020±40	-25.18	1397–1128 BC
RNG2016-06	GRA-60932	3035±40	-25.59	1411–1131 BC
RNG2016-07	GRA-63007	3240±35	–	1535–1450 BC
RNG2016-08	GRA-63008	3170±35	–	1495–1415 BC

FIGURE 6.38: RADIOCARBON DATES FOR RATHNAGREE HILLFORT (CALIBRATION AFTER OXCAL V.4.2.4).

Discussion

The major aims of the 2014 excavation at Rathnagree hillfort were achieved, namely to investigate the form and construction of the hillfort defences and recover samples for radiocarbon dating. Radiocarbon dates for the inner (1417–1135 BC), middle (1535–1126 BC), and outer palisaded enclosures (1411–1128 BC) indicate that Rathnagree hillfort was built some time between 1400–1200 BC. The results do not clarify the history of hillfort occupation, except perhaps to indicate when the site may have been abandoned. No evidence was discovered of any human activity pre-dating the hillfort, nor is there any information as to later activity on the hill before the early modern era.

The radiocarbon results from Trench 2 are supported by the discovery of coarse ware pottery of Bronze Age type in the ditch of the middle enclosure. While this is a Period 2 context connected to re-building of the defences, the pottery find is probably residual from Period 1 activity. This is supported by the discovery of a sherd of similar pottery (14E227-20) in a burnt layer (C.30) under the Period 2 bank. Also, a radiocarbon result of 1495–1415 BC for organic residue (unknown type) from one of the pot sherds overlaps with the earliest date (1535–1450 BC) from the same burnt layer.

Hillfort construction

The most significant results relate to the initial hillfort defences. The radiocarbon results suggest that all three enclosing elements are likely to have been contemporary. Their physical form is similar, as are the methods used in construction. There were three widely spaced lines of strong wooden palisade, the main posts of which were set in individual postholes (inner and outer enclosures) or a slot trench (middle enclosure). This fencing was supported in each case by a low bank of stones. It is estimated that as many as 2297 large roundwood posts were required for these three palisades, as well as several thousand smaller posts and lashing. All together, this represents a substantial work effort in the clearance of woodland and preparation of the palisade timbers.

Hillfort occupation

The excavation of the inner (Trench 1) and outer (Trench 3) defences did not uncover any evidence for occupation of this hillfort. No artifacts, food residues or structural remains were uncovered. The paucity of occupation evidence can be explained by the limited extent of excavation. There is some evidence from Trench 2 where traces of a post structure were found inside the Period 1 palisade of the middle enclosure, with use of coarse ware pottery at the same location. This admittedly slight evidence of occupation is supported by surface indications of what are possible hut sites elsewhere in the hillfort (see Chapter 5). Further excavation is required to clarify the nature and duration of that settlement.

Abandonment

The evidence from Trench 2 confirms the defences of the middle enclosure at Rathnagree were re-built after the early palisade was burnt down. While no radiocarbon dates are available for the Period 2 defences, this re-building probably occured immediately after the burning event. This is suggested by the preservation of a distinct destruction layer (C.30) beneath the later bank. Finally, the excavation did not yield information on the final abandonment of the hillfort or to any subsequent activity at the site.

6.3 Sruhaun, Co. Wicklow

This is the second of three enclosures on Tuckmill Hill, located 650m south of Rathnagree in the townland of Sruhaun, partly extending into the adjacent townland of Pinnacle (Figure 6.1; ITM 687824, 689216). It lies on the southern spur of the hill at an altitude of 310m OD, enclosing an area of 1.43 hectares of fairly level ground, with steep slopes to the south and west, and rising ground to the north and east. The location is striking, directly overlooking the town of Baltinglass, with extensive views of the lowlands of south Wicklow, east Kildare and Carlow.

As discussed in Chapter 4, LiDAR survey and geophysical prospection revealed a levelled univallate enclosure, measuring approximately 129m (north-east/south-west) by 152m (north-west/south-east). The site is sub-circular in plan, with a rounded profile that rises gently to a point on the north-east side, facing the summit of Tuckmill Hill with Rathcoran hillfort 375m in the distance. The enclosing element is visible today as a low-relief bank, approximately 4.5m wide and up to 0.2m high, surrounding a total area of 1.43ha. The slight nature of the bank makes it difficult to identify this feature at ground level. There are indications of an internal ditch, visible as a shallow depression inside this bank. The magnetic gradiometry survey does not clearly differentiate the bank and ditch, but instead indicates a continuous line of strong magnetic readings indicative of burning (Figure 6.39).

The geophysical survey revealed a 10m wide opening on the northern side of the enclosure. It may be an original entrance, but this remains to be confirmed. The eastern side of the enclosure is crossed by a modern field boundary, comprising an older wall of smaller stones now covered by boulders from recent field clearance.

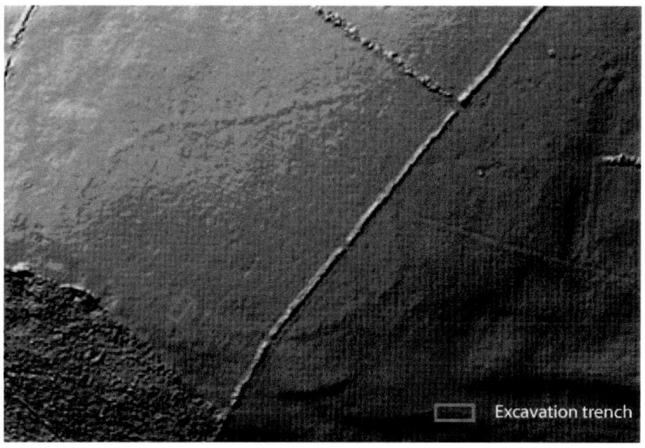

FIGURE 6.39: LIDAR SURVEY OF SRUHAUN ENCLOSURE, SHOWING LOCATION OF EXCAVATION TRENCH.

There are no features in the interior of the Sruhaun enclosure, apart from a few large boulders. There are no obvious internal features visible in either the geophysical results or the LiDAR data. The landowner confirmed the site was levelled in modern times, which removed all surface stones. As a consequence, the interior is mostly level, with a slight rise to the north. This area is used today for cattle and sheep grazing, as part of open-field pasture across the southern slopes of Tuckmill Hill.

Archaeological excavation

A single excavation trench was excavated across the enclosing elements on the southern side of Sruhaun hillfort (Figure 6.39; O'Brien 2015a). This 8m by 2m trench was aligned north north-east/south south-west across the line of the enclosure (Figure 6.40). Excavation commenced with the removal of a thin grass sod (C.01), 0.07–0.12m in thickness, overlying an A-horizon of grey/brown humic silt with occasional stones. This organic soil covered a thin layer of red/brown iron pan (C.14) in the southern third of the trench, which was removed to an iron-enriched subsoil (C.25; Bs-horizon).

There were three areas of archaeological interest in this trench (Figure 6.41):

1. A double ditch in the northern third of the trench.

2. The remains of a stone bank/wall in the central area.

3. A number of structural features, including a pre-enclosure slot, in the southern area.

The removal of A-horizon topsoil exposed a spread of yellow/brown sandy silt (C.03) across the entire trench (Figure 6.42). This deposit was thickest over the inner ditch area (0.15–0.24m), thinning to north (0.05–0.06m over extension trench) and south (0.06–0.08m over bank). The cleaning of this C.03 surface exposed several patches of dark brown silt (C.05) at the northern end of the trench. These were initially investigated as possible pits or postholes. Further excavation revealed the presence of two parallel ditches placed close together (Figure 6.43).

Inner ditch (C.15)

This feature was cut into the Bs-horizon subsoil (C.25), approximately 1.8m inside the parallel enclosure bank (Figure 6.41). It had a U-shaped profile, ranging in depth from 0.8m on the eastern side, rising to only 0.2m on the western side (Figure 6.43). The top of the ditch was 1.6–1.65m wide, narrowing to 1.3–1.4m at the base. The lat-

FIGURE 6.40: POST-EXCAVATION VIEW OF SRUHAUN TRENCH (LOOKING NORTH-WEST), SHOWING PILES OF BANK STONES REMOVED FROM THE TWO DITCHES (VERTICAL 2M POLE).

ter was irregularly smooth and free of protruding stones, apart from three flat slabs, 0.4–0.7m in length, embedded in the base of the ditch on the eastern side. The presence of these natural boulders may explain the variation in the depth of the ditch.

The infilling of the inner ditch began with an accumulation of peat accompanied by an influx of large stones (Figure 6.42). Excavation revealed a deposit of black peat (C.08) at the base of the ditch, ranging in thickness from 0.55m on the eastern side to 0.08m on the western side. This peat was well humified with no obvious banding. It was waterlogged at the base, with visible plant fibres and rootlets, but no fine minerogenic content.

This peat contained numerous large stones (C.07) infilling the upper part of the ditch (Figure 6.44). There was no obvious arrangement to these loose stones, with some lying on edge, while others were inclined or flat. They seem to have been thrown into the open ditch, with heavier examples sinking into the lower peat formation. Peat continued to accumulate around the uppermost stones, with voids forming in several places.

The C.07 stones were mostly angular to sub-angular in shape, with only a few sub-rounded examples. The majority were 0.3–0.45m in length, with some examples as large as 0.6–0.7m. There was a significant number in the 0.15–0.3m size range, but very few under 0.15m. The majority were fractured to some degree, while a few examples seem to have been deliberately pointed. Approximately half of these stones had a reddened appearance, possibly connected to fire, which would explain why so many were broken. This is not certain, however, as the reddening of this stone may be a weathering feature with iron oxide induration. These stones were thrown into the open ditch at an early stage in its infilling, as the lowest examples were close to the base.

This stone/peat deposit in the inner ditch was overlain on the northern side by a deposit of orange/brown silt (C.06). This sediment represents slip off the upper edge of the ditch cut. The entire ditch fill was sealed by a 0.05–0.08m thick layer of peaty silt (C.05). This represents a buried sod that formed in the ditch depression prior to the main spread of redeposited subsoil (C.03) across that area.

Outer ditch (C.16)

Excavation confirmed the presence of a parallel ditch on the immediate southern side of the inner ditch, separated by a narrow ridge of Bs-horizon subsoil (Figure 6.41). This ditch was dug into the latter to a depth of 0.38–0.42m (0.58–0.74m from modern ground surface). It had a V-shaped profile, ranging in upper width from 1.62m (east side), 1.5m (centre) to 1.65m (west side). The sides

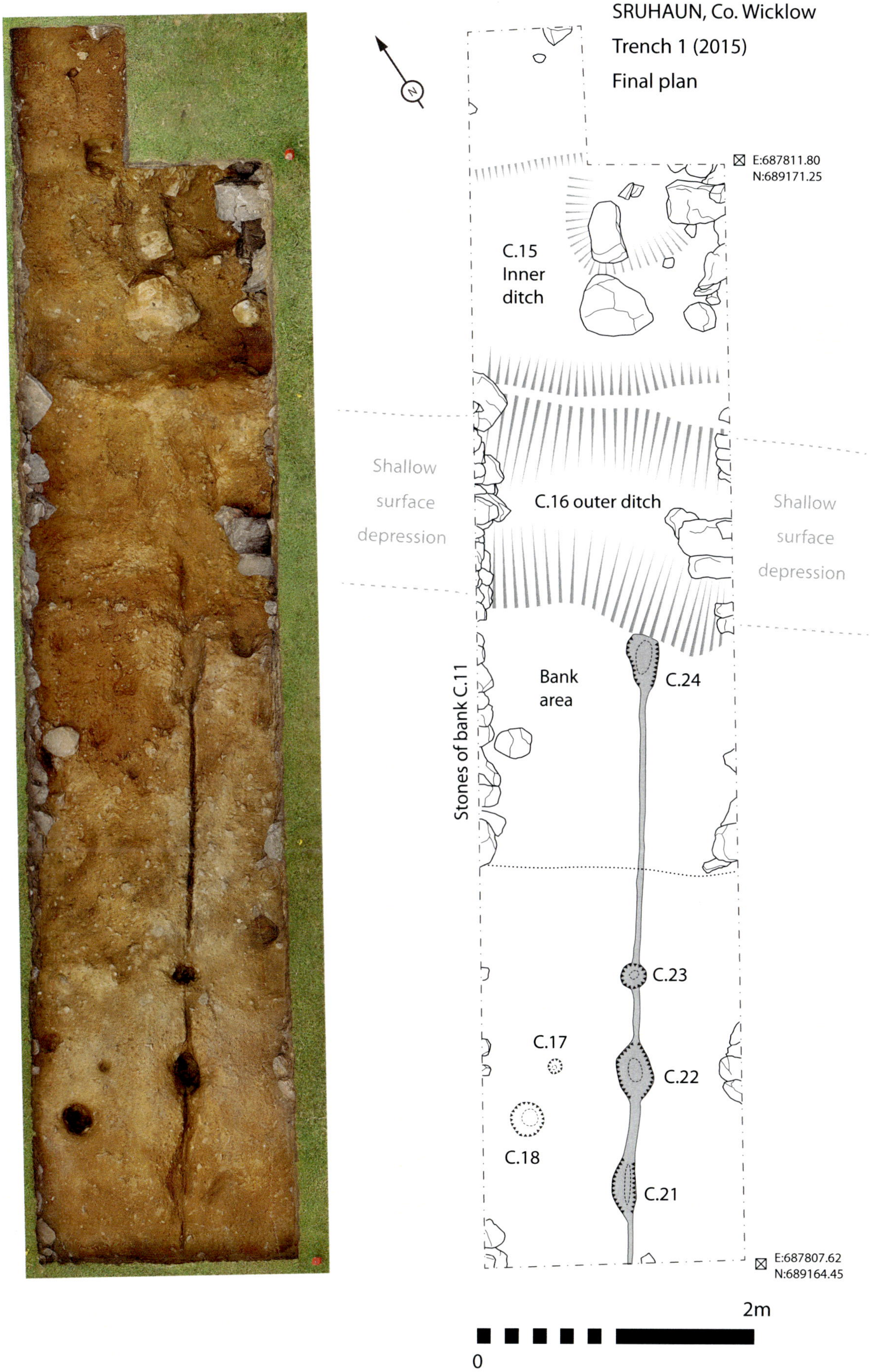

Figure 6.41: Post-excavation plan with photogrammetry, Sruhaun trench.

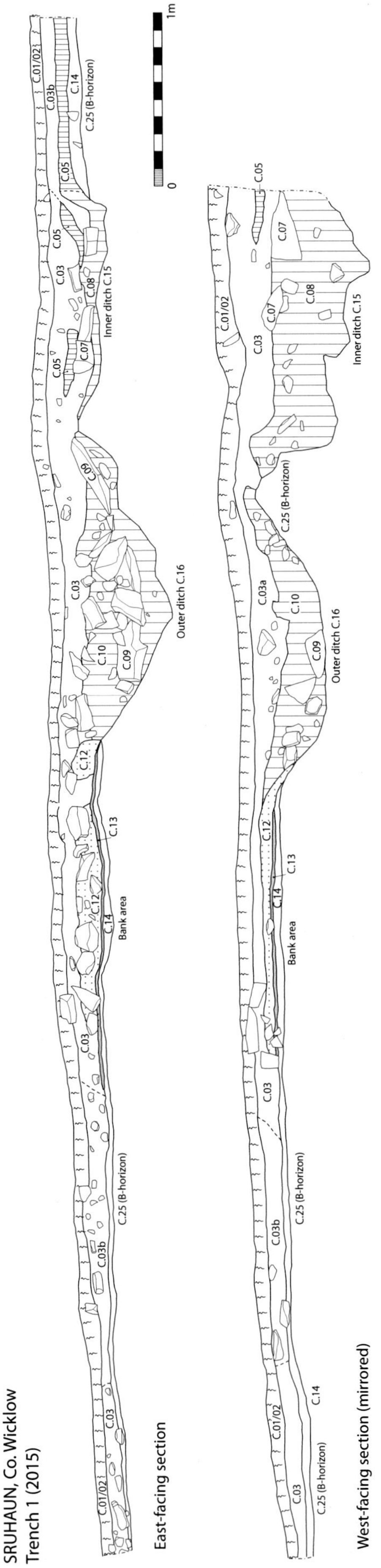

FIGURE 6.42: STRATIFICATION OF SRUHAUN TRENCH.

Figure 6.43: Post-excavation view of outer ditch (C.16; left) and inner ditch (C.15; right).

Figure 6.44: Stratification of inner ditch, west-facing section, showing large stones (C.07) in lower peaty fill (C.08), overlain by spread of redeposited subsoil (C.03).

were smooth, with few exposed stones (Figure 6.43).

Excavation revealed a similar fill sequence to the inner ditch (Figure 6.42). The primary sediment was a well-humified peat (C.10), 0.2–0.4m in thickness and slightly waterlogged at the base. There was no visible banding and no fine mineral content. As with the inner ditch, there was a deposit of large stones (C.09) within this peat formation. These were mostly angular to sub-angular in shape, often fractured and reddened (Figure 6.45). They averaged 0.15–0.25m in length, with some up to 0.3–0.45m. These stones seem to have been part of the same deposit as the C.07 stones in the outer ditch. The C.09 stones and C.10 peat deposit were overlain by the C.03 spread of redeposited subsoil that also covered the inner ditch.

Bank

Prior to excavation this feature was visible as a low rise in the field, with slight indications of an internal ditch. While the ground surface had been levelled in modern times, excavation was able to uncover the base of the original bank. The removal of A-horizon topsoil exposed a 2.6m wide spread of medium–large stones (C.11) across the central area of the trench, extending south from the edge of the outer ditch (Figure 6.42). These stones were arranged loosely with no obvious coursing, though some examples were piled two or three high. While the surface stones were loose, the base of this deposit was very compact. The individual stones were angular to sub-angular, with very few rounded examples. The majority were 0.15–0.25m in length, with some up to 0.3m, and many as small as 0.07–0.15m. The deposit was 0.12–0.18m in overall thickness, with the uppermost stones only 0.1m or less beneath the modern ground surface. A large proportion of these stones had reddened surfaces. Geological examination suggests this is iron oxide staining produced by weathering (Richard Unitt pers. comm.).

Excavation revealed a thin deposit of black silt (C.12) with lenses of granular quartz, between the lower stones of C.11 deposit. This probably represents rainwash through these stones and did not contain charcoal. Context 12 was removed to expose a spread of compact black silt (C.13), with few stones but much charcoal (Figure 6.46). This black silt extended over most of the bank area, and included several concentrations of oak charcoal (radiocarbon sample SR2015-01). With no charcoal content in the C.11 stone deposit, the charcoal in C.13 may derive from the burning of an earlier wooden structure (see C.20 below). Context 13 was removed to reveal a hard stony surface (C.14), 1–3cm in thickness and red/brown in colour, which extended to the southern end of the trench. This thin layer represents iron pan on top of the natural Bs-horizon.

FIGURE 6.45: FILL OF OUTER DITCH, WEST-FACING SECTION. DEPOSIT OF LARGE STONES (C.09) FROM DESTROYED OUTER BANK/WALL, OCCURRING WITHIN PEAT (C.10), OVERLAIN BY REDEPOSITED SUBSOIL (C.03) FROM LEVELLED INNER BANK.

FIGURE 6.46: SPREAD OF CHARCOAL-RICH SEDIMENT (C13) UNDER C.11/C.12 BANK MATERIAL.

Southern end of trench

The removal of A-horizon topsoil in the south-east corner of the trench revealed a deposit of dark brown organic silt (C.04) within a shallow depression. Elsewhere, the stratigraphic sequence at this end of the trench consisted of A-horizon (C.01/C.02) over a thin layer of redeposited subsoil (C.03 and C.03b), over the iron pan (C.14) on top of Bs-horizon (C.25).

The removal of iron pan at this end of the trench revealed a number of cut features in the Bs-horizon subsoil (Figure 6.41). These include a possible stakehole (C.17) filled with light brown silt that contained small fragments of burnt stone and flecks of charcoal . A small pit (C.18) 0.23m to the west of C.17 contained a similar fill. This 0.29m wide by 0.23m deep cut may also be a stakehole, but this cannot be confirmed.

Pre-bank feature

The excavation of C.04 and iron pan (C.14) at the southern end of the trench exposed a narrow slot (C.20) cut into the Bs-horizon subsoil (Figure 6.47). This perfectly straight feature extended north-west (aligned 030–210°) from the southern end of the trench for a distance of 4.5m. It continued under the spread of bank stones (C.11) as far as the edge of the outer ditch (C.16), which cut across the slot as a later feature (Figure 6.48). The slot was best preserved beneath the C.11 bank, where it averaged 4–5cm wide and 6–9cm deep. The sides were vertical to a 1–2cm wide, slightly pointed, base. The slot was not as well preserved south of the bank area. The fill consisted of tightly packed burnt stones (C.19), many of which were set upright and seem to have been heat-shattered in situ.

The slot widened at four points to form possible stakeholes (contexts 21–24; Figure 6.41). These had a similar fill to the slot, consisting of light brown to dark brown/black silt with fragments of burnt stone and some flecks of charcoal. If confirmed, the presence of stake settings suggests the slot may be the foundation of a wooden fence structure that pre-dated the enclosing bank and ditches.

List of excavation contexts, Trench 1, Sruhaun.
Context 01: Sod layer; 0.07–0.12m thick, mostly free of stones.

C.02: A-horizon topsoil; grey/brown humic silt with occasional pebbles and small stones.

C.03: Spread of yellow/brown silty sand, with small–medium stones; redeposited subsoil.

C.03a: Lens of orange/brown silty sand, more iron-enriched and mottled than C.03.

C.03b: Lens of grey/brown/orange silty sand.

Figure 6.47: Post-excavation view of narrow slot (C.20) with stake settings, and small pit (C.18; bottom centre).

Figure 6.48 Post-excavation view of Sruhaun trench, showing C.20 slot truncated by ditches at northern end of trench. Note piles of bank stones removed from the two ditches.

C.04: Dark brown mottled silt with stones, in subsoil depression in south-east corner of trench.

C.05: Buried sod, north of inner ditch. Dark brown peaty, with lenses of granular quartz; no stones.

C.06: Thin deposit of orange silt with small stones, along outer edge of inner ditch.

C.07: Stone fill of inner ditch. Loose deposit of broken stones in C.08 peat, 0.3–0.45m in length.

C.08: Peat in inner ditch. Black peat, well humified, 0.55m thick on east side, 0.08m on west side.

C.09: Stone fill of outer ditch. Loose deposit of broken stones in C.10 peat, most 0.15–0.25m long.

C.10: Peat deposit in outer ditch. Black peat, well humified, 0.2–0.45m thick, with voids.

C.11: A 2.6m wide band of 0.07–0.3m long stones across centre of trench, with no obvious coursing.

C.12: Thin spread of black silt between the C.11 stones; no charcoal. Possible rainwash sediment.

C.13: Spread of black silt under C.12 at base of bank; few stones, but much charcoal.

C.14: Thin layer of iron pan across southern part of trench. Red/brown, hard and stony.

C.15: Inner ditch. U-shaped profile, 1.6m wide on top, 1.3–1.4m at base, with depth of 0.2–0.8m.

C.16: Outer ditch. V-shaped profile 1.5–1.65m wide on top, with variable depth of 0.58–0.74m.

C.17: Possible stakehole, south end of trench. Circular sloping cut, 0.13m wide by 0.06m deep.

C.18: Sub-circular subsoil cut, 0.29m by 0.27m, with a vertical depth of 0.23m.

C.19: Fill of pre-bank slot (C.20). Small angular pieces of heat-shattered stone, packed tightly in cut.

C.20: Narrow slot extending 4.5m from south end of trench, under the bank to edge of outer ditch.

C.21: Possible stakehole, south end of C.20 slot, A 0.4m long by 0.24m wide by 0.1m deep cut.
C.22: Possible stakehole 0.45m north-east of C.21. A 0.4m long by 0.3m wide by 0.25m deep cut.

C.23: Possible stakehole 0.4m north-east of C.22. A circular 0.23m wide cut, 0.17m in depth.

C.24: Possible stakehole 2.05m north-east of C.23, A 0.3m long by 0.25m wide by 0.17m deep cut. C.25: Bs-horizon subsoil. Bright orange silt, very compact with pebbles, but mostly free of stones.

Finds

No artifacts were found in the Sruhaun excavation.

Dating

The following two samples were submited for radiocarbon dating:

SR2015-01 Oak charcoal with sapwood rings, sampled from black silt (C.13) under C.11 bank (wood identification: Susan Lyons).
GrA-64430; 3030 ± 35 BP (∂^{13}C -23.34)
Calibrated to 1405–1132 BC at 2-sigma (95.4% confidence) calibration (OxCal 4.2.4).

SR2015-02 Sample of peat (C.08) from base of infill of inner ditch.
GrA-64432; 126.73 ± 0.39 BP (∂^{13}C -29.31)
Modern peat growth.

The charcoal sample (SR2015-01) is probably (but not definitely) derived from burning of the pre-enclosure fence (C.20), and so should provide a *terminus post quem* for the outer bank of the enclosure. The fact that this charcoal was only preserved beneath the spread of bank material (C.11) suggests the latter was deposited soon after the burning of that fence. The second result (SR2015-02) may indicate that peat growth in the inner ditch is early modern, or that the sample is containated by modern root activity. It is likely that both ditches are of much later date than the external bank.

Discussion

The excavation yielded important information on the construction and history of the Sruhaun enclosure. The remains of an external bank of stones were found on the outer side of two shallow ditches, the soil from which was probably used to build a now-destroyed inner bank. This unusual arrangement of stone bank/double ditch/ earthen bank can be explained by the re-building of this enclosure on one or more occasions. The following sequence can be proposed:

Pre-enclosure (Period 1)
• A light wooden fence, probably one of many such examples, was used in land division on this side of Tuckmill Hill.

• This fence was eventually burnt down.

Enclosure (Period 2)
• An outer bank of stones was built very soon afterwards, overlying charcoal from the burnt fence

Enclosure (Period 3)
• One or both ditches were dug inside the Phase 1 bank at a much later date

• The soil from these ditches was possibly used to build an inner bank.

Abandonment and destruction
• Peat started to form in the two waterlogged ditches

• The outer bank was levelled, and large stones thrown into the adjacent ditches

• Peat formation continued in ditches

• The inner bank of soil was levelled over the aforementioned features.

In terms of absolute chronology, the GrA-64430 result is the only radiocarbon date available for the Sruhaun enclosure. A second result obtained for peat from the adjacent ditch is of modern date. The stratigraphic position of this charcoal sample is not entirely secure as it may derive from the burning of the pre-bank field fence, but could also come from the burning of a wooden palisade in the bank. There is no excavation evidence for the latter, but such a burnt structure might be inferred from the high magnetic survey responses along the perimeter of the Sruhaun enclosure (Figure 6.39). Whatever the source of the GrA-64430 charcoal, the stratigraphic evidence does not indicate a significant interval of time between the burning of the C.20 slot and the overlying C.11 bank, making it likely that the enclosure was built in the period 1375–1225 BC. The burning of this enclosure was broadly contemporary with the destruction of Rathnagree (Period 1).

Pre-enclosure activity

This relates to the discovery of a narrow slot (C.20) extending 4.5m from the southern end of the excavation trench under the C.11 bank as far as the edge of the cross-cutting ditches. This perfectly straight slot widened in four areas to four possible stake settings. The most likely interpretation is a wooden fence connected to an animal stockade on that side of Tuckmill Hill, which was later replaced by a banked enclosure. The presence of fire-shattered stone in the slot indicates the fence was burnt down prior to construction of the enclosure bank. A spread of charcoal (C.13) on either side of this slot may be connected to the burning and collapse of that fence.

Enclosure

The results from this excavation indicate four closely spaced enclosing elements at Sruhaun. These include:

1.A now-destroyed outer bank of stones with no soil component. The base of this feature survives as a spread of broken stone (C.11). Some of the original stones may be present in the adjacent ditches (contexts 07 and 09), but this is not certain.

2.An outer ditch (C.16) directly inside the C.11 bank.

3.An inner ditch (C.15) directly inside the C.16 ditch.

4.A now-destroyed inner bank of earth and possible some stone, located on the inside of the C.15 ditch. The existence of such a bank, built using soil upcast from the ditches, is indicated by a spread of redeposited subsoil (C.03) over the latter.

Radiocarbon dating confirms that these were not contemporary features, and so some re-building of the enclosure must have occurred on one or more occasions. The inner bank is likely to be contemporary with one or both of the ditches from where that bank material derived. The two ditches seem to be much later than the outer bank, as they do not contain any fine sediment derived from erosion of the latter. This is supported by the late date (GrA-64432) for the commencement of peat growth in these ditches.

The original height of the inner and inner banks is uncertain. Based on the amount of soil extracted from both ditches, and the amount of stone dumped there subsequently, neither bank/wall is likely to have exceeded a metre in height.

Occupation

The excavation did not produce any evidence for the occupation of this hillfort. No artifacts, food residues or structural remains were uncovered, mainly due to the limited area of excavation. It should be noted that geophysical survey does not indicate the presence of built structures inside the Sruhaun enclosure. This, together with the slight nature of the outer bank, suggests the site should not be regarded as a hillfort as there is no evidence of fortification. The fact that this enclosure was broadly contemporary with the nearby hillfort of Rathnagree does raise interesting questions as to their functional relationship. One interpretation is that Sruhaun was an enclosure for livestock, used by the occupants of Rathnagree hillfort.

Abandonment

The Sruhaun excavation did not yield much information on the final use of this enclosure. While the geophysical survey records high magnetic gradiometry readings along the enclosing element, there is no definite evidence for deliberate destruction by fire. In the absence of postholes or stake settings associated with the bank, there is no evidence of any wooden fencing that might have been destroyed by fire.

The stones used to build the outer bank/wall were subsequently dumped into the outer and inner ditches. This means that both ditches must have been open when the outer bank/wall was destroyed. The radiocarbon dating of peat in the lower ditch suggests this may have happened in the early modern era. The destruction of the proposed inner bank occurred some time after this, as levelled soil from that feature was spread over both ditches that were already partially infilled with peat and stone from the outer bank. This occured during agricultural clearance in the modern era (landowner information). This means that the destruction of the outer bank/wall must have been an earlier event.

6.4 Tinoran, Co. Wicklow

Sample excavation was also conducted at Tinoran hillfort in the Baltinglass complex. This Class 2 hillfort is located on the highest point of a prominent hill (312m OD) in the townlands of Tinoranhill North and Tinoranhill South, 2km north/north-west of the Baltinglass town (Figure 6.1; ITM 685175, 690581). As discussed in Chapter 4, Tinoran is one of the largest hillforts in Ireland, with four or possibly five enclosures extending over an area of 84.03ha.

In August 2015 two trenches were excavated across the defences of the third and fourth enclosures respectively on the southern side of the hillfort (Figure 6.49).

Trench 1 (Fourth enclosure)

A single trench, measuring 10m by 2m, was excavated across the line of a levelled bank on the south-east side of the hillfort (Figure 6.50). This trench was located on the eastern side of a large pasture field, which was cultivated at various times in the modern era. The bank is visible as a low slope over a distance of 4m, with no exposed stones or visible ditch (O'Brien 2015b).

Excavation confirmed the natural soil at this location is a brown podzol. A 0.1m thick sod (C.01) overlay a A-horizon of dark brown organic silt with some stones (C.02), with a greater depth and mid brown colour (C.06) over the central part of the ditch (Figure 6.51). The removal of this organic soil exposed a thin hard layer of red/brown iron pan (C.26), overlying a bright orange stony silt Bs-horizon (C.27) inside the bank and outside the ditch. The C-horizon subsoil was exposed in the lower ditch, comprised of hard grey/light brown silt with numerous stones (C.28).

The absence of a leached layer (E-horizon) in this podzol profile may be explained by modern cultivation in this field. The landowner confirmed there was cultivation of oats in this field some decades ago. The former existence of a leached layer is indicated by the degree of

FIGURE 6.49: AERIAL PHOTOGRAPH OF TINORAN HILLFORT, SHOWING LOCATION OF EXCAVATION TRENCHES (SOURCE: GOOGLE EARTH).

FIGURE 6.50: TRENCH 1, TINORAN, FOLLOWING CLEANING OF BS-HORIZON (C.27). THE INFILLED DITCH IS VISIBLE AS A DARK BAND ACROSS CENTRE OF TRENCH, BEYOND WHICH THE LEVELLED BANK IS EXPOSED AS AN AREA OF LIGHTER COLOURED SOIL (LOOKING NORTH-WEST).

iron oxide precipitation (C.26) on the Bs-horizon surface (C.27). This is confirmed by the discovery of a thin layer of light brown/grey silt (C.25) beneath the remaining bank material, which represents a pre-bank E-horizon (Figure 6.51).

Archaeological features

Excavation revealed three significant features in this trench. These include a large earth-cut ditch, inside which there was the base of a levelled bank, on the inner side of which was an isolated pit (Figure 6.52).

Ditch

Excavation revealed a ditch (C.18) with a U-shaped profile cut into natural subsoil (Figure 6.53). The top of the ditch was 1.7–1.8 wide, narrowing to 0.4–0.5m at the base, with a cut depth of 0.6–0.8m (maximum depth of 0.9m from modern ground level). The sides were gently sloping (45°) and smooth, with the upper portion formed in Bs-horizon (C.27) and the base in C-horizon (C.28). The lower inner slope of the ditch was interrupted by a narrow flat-bottomed ledge (C.22) that contained separate fills from the main ditch (Figure 6.54). This channel-like feature was approximately 0.4–0.5m wide and 0.1–0.15m in depth. It was part of the primary ditch cut, though its purpose is unknown.

When this ledge is included, the overall width of the ditch was approximately 3.3m, with a central cut depth of 0.8m.

Fill sequence

There were four stages in the infilling of this ditch (Figures 6.52, 6.55 and 6.56):

- Early fill sequence (contexts 11–17)
- Fill of ledge on lower inner slope of ditch (contexts 19–21)
- Break in ditch fill (C.10)
- Levelling of bank into ditch (contexts 06–09).

Early fill sequence

The filling of the ditch commenced with a thin deposit of bright orange silt (C.17), derived from primary erosion of the ditch cut. The basal sediment contained numerous flecks of charcoal (radiocarbon sample TN2015-01). This was overlain by a thin deposit of mottled orange/brown silt (C.16), also with flecks of charcoal. It was followed by deposition of compact mid brown silt (C.15), again with flecks of charcoal. The next layer was a compact grey silt (C.14) containing lenses of red/orange iron pan, overlain by a deposit of mid brown silt (C.13) with flecks of charcoal forming the upper fill of the ditch. The latter included a lens of black compact silt (C.12) overlain by a small deposit of grey/brown silt (C.11) on the western side of ditch. There are no artifact finds from these ditch sediments.

Fill of ledge on lower inner slope of ditch (contexts 19–21)

Excavation revealed a thin deposit of yellow/dark brown mottled silt (C.21) at the base of the narrow ledge on the lower inner side of ditch (Figure 6.52). This sediment contained flecks and small lumps of charcoal. The upper fill of the ledge consisted of orange/brown sandy silt (C.20), overlain on eastern side of the trench by a lens of mid brown silt (C.19).

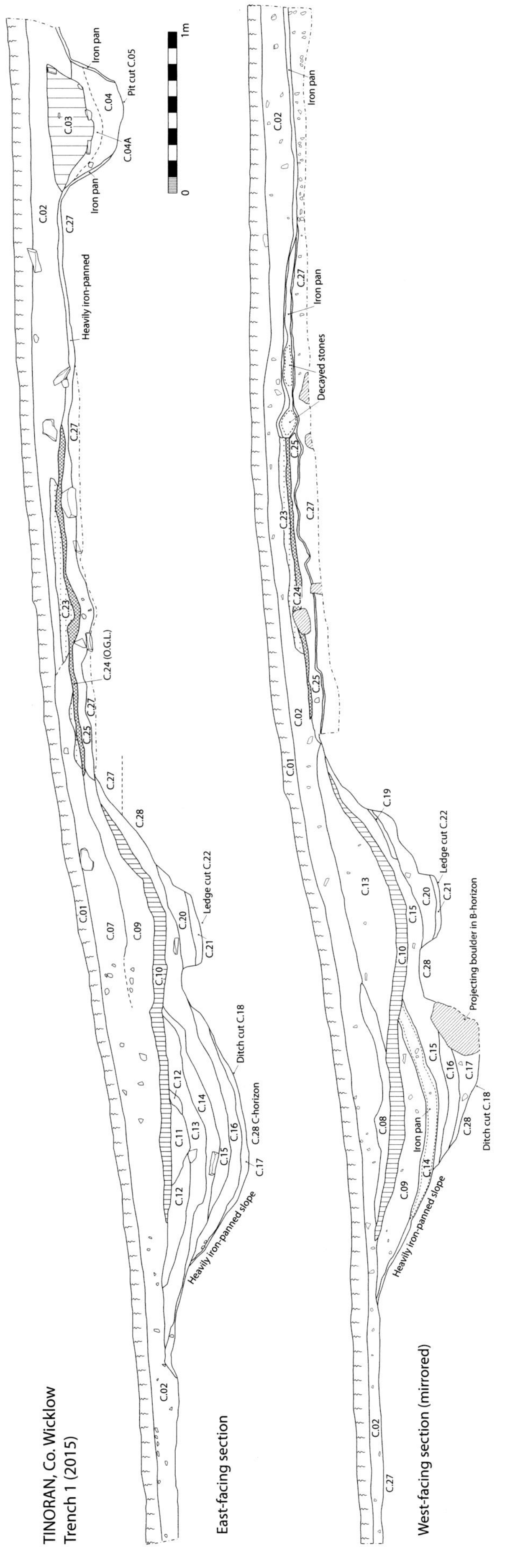

FIGURE 6.51: STRATIFICATION OF TRENCH 1, FOURTH ENCLOSURE, TINORAN.

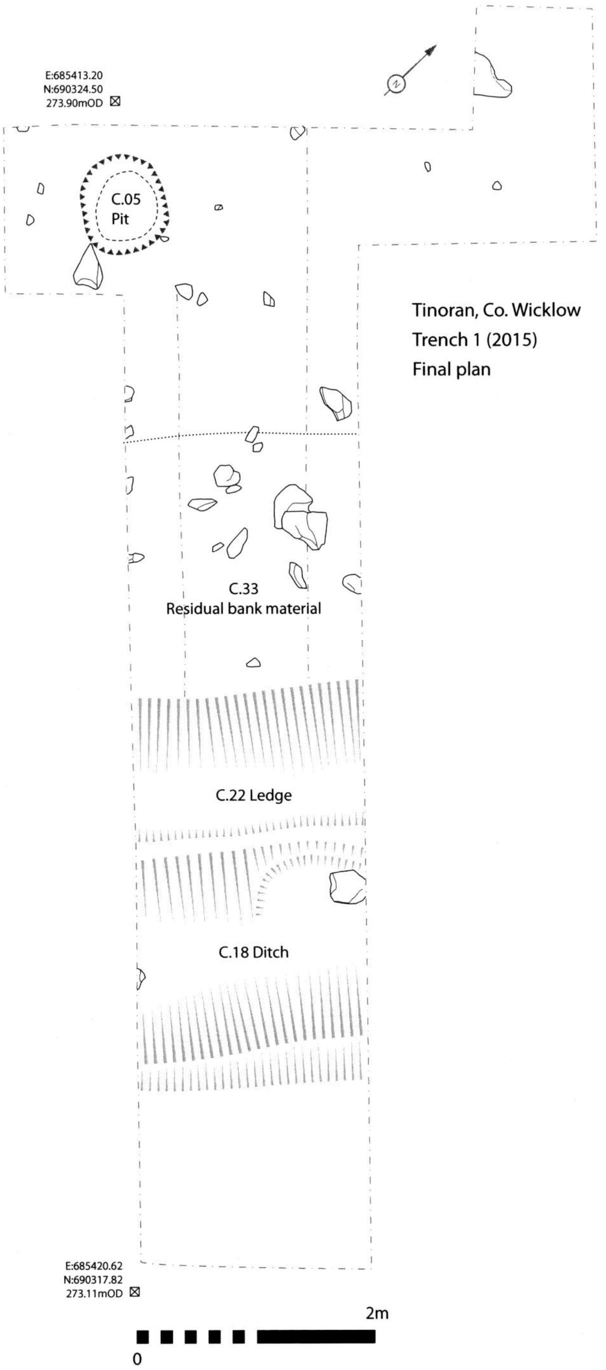

FIGURE 6.52 POST-EXCAVATION PLAN, TRENCH 1, TINORAN.

Break in ditch fill

The infilling of the main ditch cut was interrupted by the formation of a sod layer (C.10) that separates early deposits from those created by the levelling of the adjacent bank (Figure 6.52). This buried sod is represented by a 0.05–0.09m thick layer of grey/brown organic silt (C.10). There are no charcoal or artifact finds from this buried sod layer.

Levelling of bank into ditch (contexts 06–09)

The final stage in the ditch fill is represented by a deposit of dark brown sandy silt (C.09) over the inner side of ditch (Figure 6.42). This sediment derived from the levelling of the adjacent bank c.1955 (landowner information). The original subsoil core of that bank may in part be represented by a thin deposit of yellow/light brown silt (C.08) on the eastern side of the trench. This was overlain by a thickness of up to 0.3m of organic soil (contexts 06 and 07) beneath the modern sod.

Bank

The excavation results point to the former presence of a bank on the inner side of the ditch. The landowner, Mr Victor O'Neill, confirmed that this bank was levelled by agriculture in the modern period. He recalled that his father employed a local man *c.*1955 to level by spade a 'three foot high bank' into an adjacent ditch depression.

The removal of a 0.15–0.18m thickness of organic soil (contexts 01 and 02) exposed a spread of residual bank material (C.23), the southern limit of which was approximately 0.7m inside the ditch (Figure 6.52). This compact deposit of orange sandy silt measured 1.2–1.4m wide by 0.02–0.05m thick (up to 0.09m in places), and contained only a few small stones. None of these had a reddened appearance, and there was no charcoal in the spread.

The residual bank material overlay a thin layer of black organic silt containing few clasts (C.24). This 0.02–0.04m thick layer extended 1.8–2.2m from the inner edge of the ditch. It represents a sod layer buried beneath the former bank (Figure 6.57). This old ground surface contained a few flecks of charcoal, but no archaeological material to indicate pre-enclosure activity at that location. It overlay a grey leached layer (C.25), 0.05–0.08m in thickness, which respected the width of the buried sod layer (C.24) and formed part of the pre-bank natural soil.

Pit

Excavation revealed a small circular pit (C.05) inside the bank in the north-west corner of the trench (Figures 6.50 and 6.58). This measured 0.87m (north–south) by 0.85m (east–west) on top and 0.6m (north–south) by 0.55m (east–west) at base, with steeply sloping sides to an irregularly flat base at a depth of 0.46m. The sides and base of the pit were covered by a thin layer of red iron pan (C.26). A large stone, 0.4m by 0.22m by 0.1m, on the southern edge of the pit was probably of natural ori-

Figure 6.53: Post-excavation view of ditch, Trench 1 (looking south). Note ledge (C.22) on inner slope of ditch (lower centre).

Figure 6.54: Detail of C.22 ledge on inner lower slope of ditch, Trench 1, Tinoran.

FIGURE 6.55: WEST-FACING SECTION OF MAIN DITCH (C.18) AND C.22 LEDGE (FAR LEFT), TRENCH 1, TINORAN.

FIGURE 6.56: EAST-FACING SECTION OF MAIN DITCH (C.18) AND C.22 LEDGE (FAR RIGHT), TRENCH 1, TINORAN.

Figure 6.57: Stratification of bank area, Trench 1. Removal of sod/A-horizon exposed stony bank sediment (C.23), overlying a buried sod layer (C.24), over a grey leached layer (C.25) on top of iron pan (C.26) and Bs-horizon (C.27).

Figure 6.58: C.05 pit (bottom centre) in relation to excavated bank (top centre) and ditch (top right), Trench 1, Tinoran.

gin, as it was found embedded in the Bs-horizon subsoil. There were two separate fills in this pit (Figure 6.52). The upper fill (C.03) consisted of black organic silt with occasional small stones and some flecks of charcoal on the surface. The lower fill (C.04) of grey/light brown sandy silt did not contain charcoal or other archaeological material.

List of excavation contexts, Trench 1, Tinoran.
Context 01: Sod layer, 0.1m in thickness, no stones.

C.02: A-horizon. Dark brown organic silt, friable, some pebbles and small stones.

C.03: Upper fill of C.05 pit. Black organic silt, a few small stones with charcoal flecks in upper part.

C.04: Lower fill of C.05 pit. Grey/light brown sandy silt, some iron oxide mottles and small stones.

C.05: Cut of circular pit inside bank, 0.86m wide and 0.46m deep, steeply sloping sides to flat base.

C.06: A-horizon over ditch. Mid brown organic silt, lighter colour than C.02, many small stones.

C.07: A-horizon on inner side of ditch. Light brown sandy silt with pebbles. From levelled bank.

C.08: Lens of yellow/light brown silt over centre of ditch. Redeposited subsoil from levelled bank.

C.09: Dark brown sandy silt with frequent small stones over inner side of ditch. From levelled bank.

C.10: Buried sod in upper fill of ditch. Grey/brown organic silt, compact with no clasts.

C.11: Deposit of grey/brown silt with orange iron oxide mottles in upper fill, western side of ditch.

C.12: Deposit of black compact silt with no clasts in upper fill on western side of ditch.

C.13: Layer of mid brown silt in upper part of ditch; many small stones and some flecks of charcoal.

C.14: Compact grey silt in central fill of ditch. Thin lenses of iron pan on upper and lower surfaces.

C.15: Layer of mid brown silt in lower fill of ditch; compact with rare clasts, some charcoal flecks.

C.16: Lower fill of ditch. Thin deposit of orange/brown silt with grey mottles and flecks of charcoal.

C.17: Basal sediment in ditch. Orange silt with many flecks of charcoal. From erosion of ditch cut.

C.18: Cut of ditch (see main text).

C.19: Lens of mid brown silt in upper fill of the C.22 ledge on inner side of ditch.

C.20: Deposit of orange/brown sandy silt in fill of the C.22 ledge.

C.21: Thin deposit of yellow/dark brown mottled silt with charcoal, base of C.22 ledge.

C.22: Cut of ledge on lower inner side of ditch (see main text).

C.23: Thin spread of orange sandy silt with many pebbles and small stones. Residual bank material.

C.24: Buried sod. Thin spread of black organic silt under C.23 bank material; no clasts or charcoal.

C.25: Thin layer of light brown/grey silt with some pebbles. Pre-bank leached subsoil (E-horizon).

C.26: Layer of red/brown iron pan, 1–3cm thick, on top of Bs-horizon (C.27) under and inside bank.

C.27: Bs-horizon. Compact bright orange silt, with occasional pebbles and small to large stones.

C.28: C-horizon. Hard grey/light brown silt with many small–large stones, and some small boulders.

Finds

The only artifacts from Tinoran Trench 1 are a sherd of white china and a sherd of brown glazed china, neither of which was retained. These fragments of modern pottery were found in agricultural topsoil (C.02) inside the bank area.

Radiocarbon dating

A single sample of charcoal was selected from Tinoran Trench 1 for AMS radiocarbon dating (wood identification: Susan Lyons, UCC). The result is as follows:

Site sample TN2015-01: Sample of oak charcoal from basal sediment (Context 17) in ditch of fourth enclosure. GrA-64438; 2600 ± 30 BP

Trench 1: summary

Excavation confirmed that the fourth enclosure of this hillfort was surrounded by a single bank and ditch, which was levelled in the modern era. No evidence of pre-enclosure activity was found. The enclosing element consisted of a shallow earth-cut ditch, the soil from which was dumped on the inside to form a low bank. No stone was used in the construction of this bank, nor is there any evidence of wooden fencing. Based on the ditch size, the original height of the bank is unlikely to have exceeded 1.5m, with a combined bank/ditch height of perhaps 2–2.5m.

There are few details as to the occupation or abandonment of the hillfort. The ditch remained open for a long period, with primary erosion of the cut accompanied by an influx of organic silt, as well as eroded sediment from the bank. A small amount of charcoal was found in the basal fill of the ditch. Radiocarbon dating suggests this can be linked to continued occupation of the hillfort into the Late Bronze Age (see below). There is no evidence of any deliberate destruction of the defences.

The only other archaeological feature in this trench was a large pit (C.05) inside the bank. The excavation trench was extended 1m to the east to investigate the possibility that this feature was one of a line of similar pits connected to a wooden palisade inside the bank. No other pits were identified in this 3m wide space east of the C.05 pit. Magnetic gradiometry survey was also undertaken over a 20m distance to the west of this pit in search of similar examples. The results were negative, and so the excavated pit remains an isolated feature of uncertain significance.

Trench 2 (Third enclosure)

A single trench was excavated across the visible bank on the south-west side of the third enclosure at Tinoran hillfort (Figure 6.49). Prior to excavation the bank was visible as 4–5m wide band of ferns crossing an area of heavy gorse growth (Figure 6.59). The excavation trench measured 4m (NW–SE) by 3m (NE–SW), with a 5m by 1m extension cutting across the bank on the southern side (Figures 6.60 and 6.61).

Excavation began with the removal of a thin grassy sod (C.01) across the hillfort bank. The tops of some large stones in the bank were visible before excavation; otherwise, this sod was intact across the trench area. The underlying A-horizon on the inner side of the bank consisted of a dark brown organic silt (C.30) with numerous small stones (Figure 6.63). On the bank itself there were pockets of organic peat (C.29) among the uppermost stones. The A-horizon along the lower exterior slope of the bank was a dark brown organic silt (C.42), which contained stones (C.37) tumbled from the bank (Figure 6.62). The natural Bs-horizon subsoil across the trench area was a bright orange compact silt containing numerous stones (C.44). Pockets of white silt (C.43) overlying this Bs-horizon on the inner side of the bank may represent the remains of a former leached layer (E-horizon).

FIGURE 6.59: THE BANK OF THE THIRD HILLFORT ENCLOSURE IS VISIBLE AS BAND OF FERN GROWTH ACROSS SOUTHERN SLOPE OF TINORAN HILL. TRENCH 2 WAS LOCATED IN CENTRE OF PHOTOGRAPH.

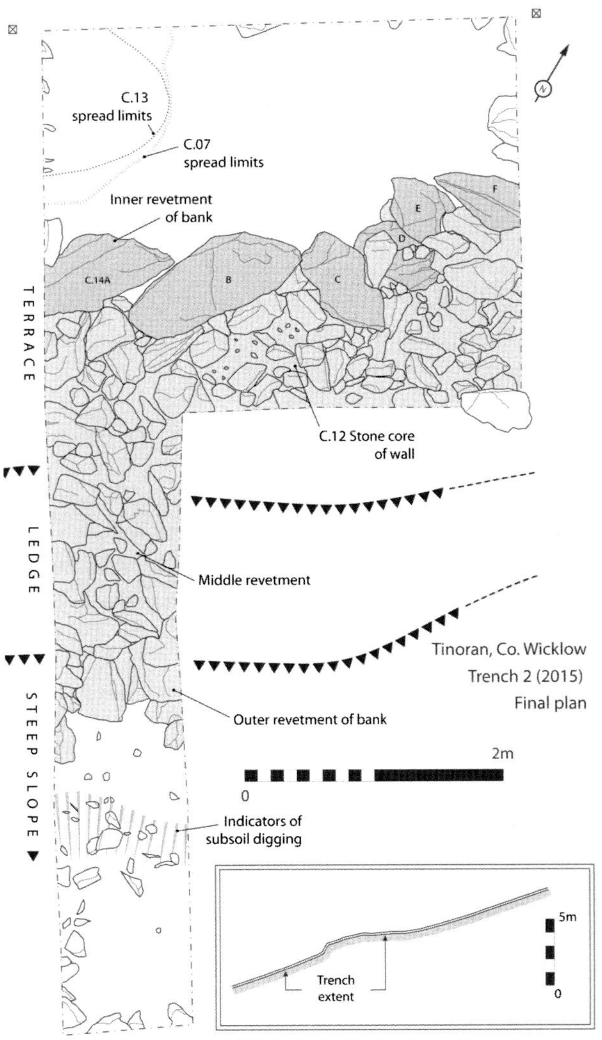

Figure 6.60: Post-excavation plan, Trench 2, Tinoran.

Figure 6.61: Post-excavation photogrammetry, Trench 2, Tinoran.

Archaeological features

Bank construction

Excavation revealed two layers of sediment on the inner side of the bank and also continuing under this feature (Figure 6.62). This material seems to have been deliberately deposited to create a terrace along this slope as a level surface for construction of the bank. This dumping began with a deposit of grey/light brown silt (C.36) that contained some charcoal (radiocarbon sample TN2015-04). This layer was 0.12m in thickness at eastern end of trench thinning to 0.08m under the hillfort wall. Finds include a collection of coarseware sherds (15E0321:02–106), probably from a single vessel, which were trampled into the upper surface of C.36 on the inner side of the bank. A whetstone (15E0321:01) was also discovered in the upper part of this deposit, close to where the pottery was found.

Context 36 was overlain by a layer of orange/brown stony sediment (C.35), also occurring on the inner side and beneath the hillfort bank (Figure 6.64). This sediment contained numerous small stones of slaty form, possibly derived from soil dug from the slope below and outside the bank (Figure 6.65). This material was spread on top of the C.36 deposit to further level the slope for bank construction.

The bank itself was built entirely of large boulders and smaller stones, with no soil component. The inner side comprised a line of large boulders (C.41), mostly placed in a recumbent position, either contiguously or with a slight overlap (Figure 6.66). The excavation revealed six of these boulders on the pre-bank levelled surface (contexts 35 and 36), These ranged 0.72–1.47m in maximum length, and were sub-rectangular to sub-ovoid in cross section with a weathered appearance and no fractured surfaces. They were mostly placed horizontally, and in some cases were propped underneath by smaller stones. The details are as follows (from north to south):

C.41 Boulder A: 1.1m by 0.54m by 0.3m; sub-rectangular in cross-section, projecting into west section, placed

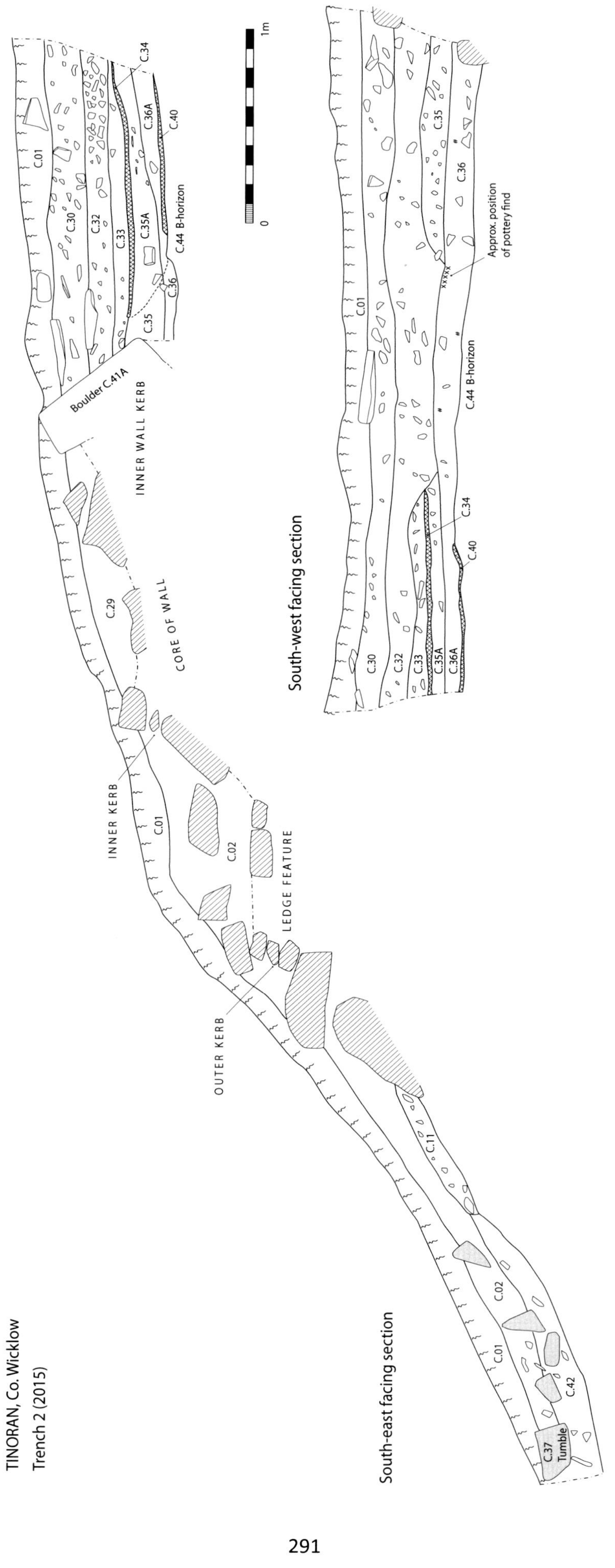

Figure 6.62: Stratification of Trench 2, third enclosure, Tinoran.

FIGURE 6.63: GENERAL VIEW OF C.03 SURFACE IN TRENCH 2, TINORAN (LOOKING SOUTH), FOLLOWING REMOVAL OF ORGANIC SOIL. NOTE STONE TUMBLE (C.04) FROM BANK (TOP LEFT CORNER).

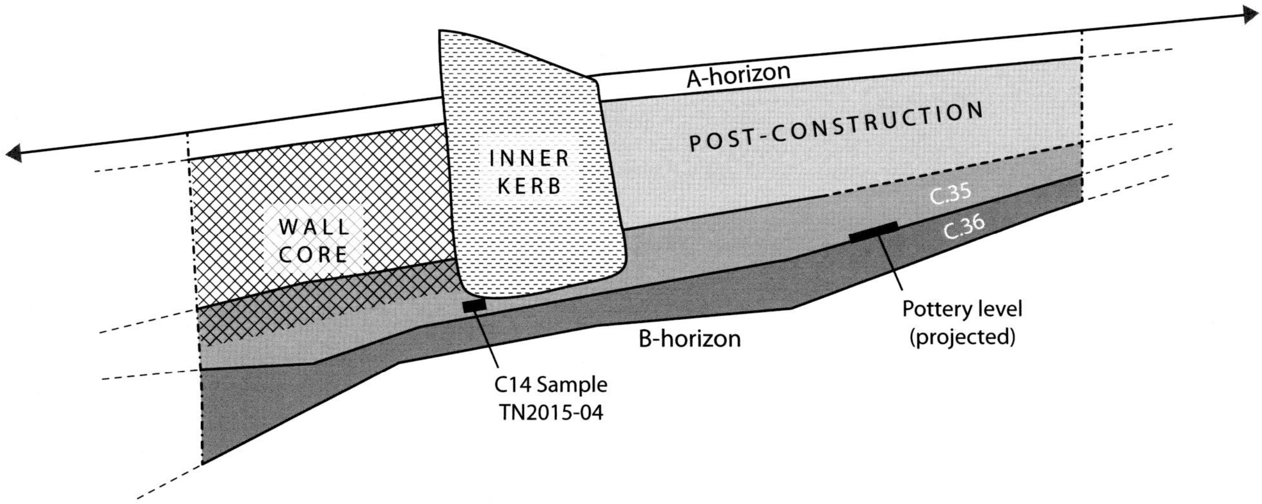

FIGURE 6.64: SCHEMATIC SECTION ACROSS HILLFORT BANK, TRENCH 2, TINORAN.

Figure 6.65: Stratification under stone bank, Trench 2. The stones forming core of bank are visible, with a kerb boulder (right). These stones overlie two pre-bank layers: an orange/brown layer (C.08) over a grey/brown slaty sediment (C.09) on top of subsoil.

Figure 6.66: Line of boulders (C.14) forming inner kerb on stone bank, Trench 2, Tinoran.

on side with slight incline to west.

Boulder B: 1.47m by 0.48m by 0.4m; sub-rectangular in cross-section placed on side.

Boulder C: 0.94m by 0.38m by 0.3m; irregular stone originally set upright, but now leaning heavily to west.

Boulder D: 0.72m by 0.41m by 0.29m; sub-oval stone lying recumbent with slight lean to west.

Boulder E: 0.89m by 0.47m by 0.16m; flattish pointed stone leaning to west, with two overlying smaller boulders.

Boulder F: 0.79m by 0.52m by 0.18m; sub-triangular stone projecting into east section.

The core of the bank consisted of grey sandstone clasts (C.39) of weathered appearance, having an average length of 0.33m. These stones were piled loosely inside the boulder kerb with no obvious coursing. They were retained by two possible kerbs of small boulders within the centre and outer side of the bank (Figure 6.67). This seems likely, but is difficult to confirm given that the excavation trench was only a metre wide at this point. Excavation also revealed a small amount of redeposited subsoil (C.38) against the lower exterior side of bank, probably placed there as part of the construction process.

Post-construction activity

Excavation uncovered a thin spread of dark silt (C.34) inside the bank in the north-east corner of the excavation trench (Figure 6.68). This burnt sediment contained charcoal and fragments of burnt bone (radiocarbon sample TN2015-02), which derived from a small hearth in the vicinity where some cooking may have occurred. The C.34 sediment directly overlay a layer of orange/brown stony sediment (C.35) on which the bank was built. This overlay a lower hearth deposit (C.40) in the same corner of the excavation trench (Figure 6.62). That 1–3cm thick spread of dark brown/black fine silt had a similar high charcoal content with small fragments of burnt bone (radiocarbon sample TN2015-03).

Early slopewash deposits on inner side of wall

The C.34 fire was followed by a prolonged period of natural slopewash on the inner side of the hillfort bank. A layer of light brown silt (C.33), overlain by a layer of mid brown silt (C.32), were deposited to a combined thickness of 0.15–0.28m (Figure 6.62). There was no archaeological material in this sediment.

Bank erosion/collapse

The processes of natural sedimentation continued with

FIGURE 6.67: LARGE STONES FORMING OUTER FACING OF STONE BANK (C.12), TRENCH 2, TINORAN.

Figure 6.68: Charcoal spread with fragments of burnt bone (C.07) inside stone bank, Trench 2, Tinoran.

a build-up of organic silt (C.30) on the inner side of the bank. This A-horizon contained a number of large stones (C.31) that represent tumble from the bank (Figure 6.53). A similar tumble of large stones (C.37) was excavated in organic soil (C.42) along the lower slope on the outer side of the bank.

List of excavation contexts, Trench 2, Tinoran.
Context 01: Sod layer, 0.08–0.18m in thickness across trench; no stones.

C.29: Peaty sediment between upper stones of bank. Loose dark brown/black humic sediment.

C.30: A-horizon inside bank. Dark brown organic silt with many small stones. Slopewash sediment.

C.31: Tumble of stones within A-horizon (C.30) on inner side of bank. Same size range as C.12.

C.32: Layer of mid brown silt, with small slaty stones, under C.30 and C.31, inner side of bank.

C.33: Layer of light brown silt under C.32 on inner side of bank. Compact with many small stones.

C.34: Thin spread of dark brown/black fine silt, much charcoal and some burnt bone, inside bank.

C.35: Spread of orange/brown sandy silt with small slaty stones, inside and under C.12 bank.

C.35a: Very similar to C.35; less compact.

C.36: Spread of stony grey/light brown silt with charcoal, inner side and under bank. Pottery finds.

C.36a: Very similar to C.09; less compact.

C.37: Collapsed bank stones in peat (C.29) upper slope; in dark brown silt (C.42) lower slope.

C.38: Build-up of orange silt (redeposited C.44) with small stones against exterior base of bank.

C.39: Core of bank. Loose deposit of grey sandstone sub-angular clasts, 0.18–0.56m in length.

C.40: Hearth. Thin spread of dark brown/black fine silt, much charcoal and burnt bone, under C.36.

C.41: Line of contiguous boulders forming inner side of hillfort bank (see main text).

C.42: A-horizon, base of slope below bank. Dark brown rooty organic silt, and C.10 stone tumble.

C.43: Thin white silt under grey silt (C.36) and over

Bs-horizon (C.44), inner side of bank.

C.44: Natural Bs-horizon. Bright orange compact silt with numerous small-medium stones.

Finds

The only artifacts from Tinoran Trench 2 are a whetstone, and a small collection of prehistoric pottery sherds from the upper surface of the C.36 layer, concentrated in a 0.24m by 0.3m area inside the hillfort bank.

Whetstone

A probable whetstone (15E0321:01) was found in the upper part of the C.36 layer inside the stone bank. This object is a cuboid, almost perfectly rectangular measuring 127mm by 41mm by 38mm, with flat ends and very smooth surfaces (Figure 6.69). The lithology is a grey, fine-grained, micaceous sandstone. Three of the four sides are slightly concave, with obvious wear connected to use as a sharpening stone.

Tinoran pottery (Rose M. Cleary)

The pottery was recovered from a construction layer (C.36) in the defences of the third enclosure. A radiocarbon analysis (GrA-64440) of organic sediment on the inner surface of a pottery sherd returned a date of 1155–1020 BC. The assemblage comprises 108 sherds (605.2g) from a single vessel which represents about 20% of the entire pot. The sherds are from the rim (9), base (3), base and lower body (11), body sherds (85), as well as crumbs.

FIGURE 6.69: WHETSTONE FROM TRENCH 2, TINORAN.

Description

The vessel is thin walled, bucket-shaped with a flat rim and slightly footed base (Figure 6.70). A row of perforations *c.*7mm below the rim are *c.*30mm apart, 3mm in diameter externally and taper to 1mm in diameter internally (Figure 6.71). The perforations are punched through from the outside. The estimated dimensions are rim diameter 20cm, base diameter 14cm and height *c.*19cm. The wall thickness is 9–11mm, being thickest at the base. The vessel can be considered as 'fine' ware in that it is thin-walled with medium amounts of temper.

Temper was macroscopically identified as granitic with grain sizes of ≥3mm with larger fragments up to 7mm. The clay has visible mica and includes the same minerals (feldspar, quartz) as the granite temper fragments. The surface is tactilely slightly grainy as the clay has shrunk during firing leaving some of the temper grains in relief. The vessel is evenly fired reddish yellow (Munsell 5YR6/6) on the external and internal surfaces and has a dark reddish grey (Munsell 5YR4/2) core. The uniform vessel colour suggests temperature control and the use of a primitive kiln (Tite 1995). The fracture pattern shows coil construction.

Apart from an outer surface of one basal sherd which is weathered, the surface condition shows little abrasion from the elements and the surfaces are very well-pre-

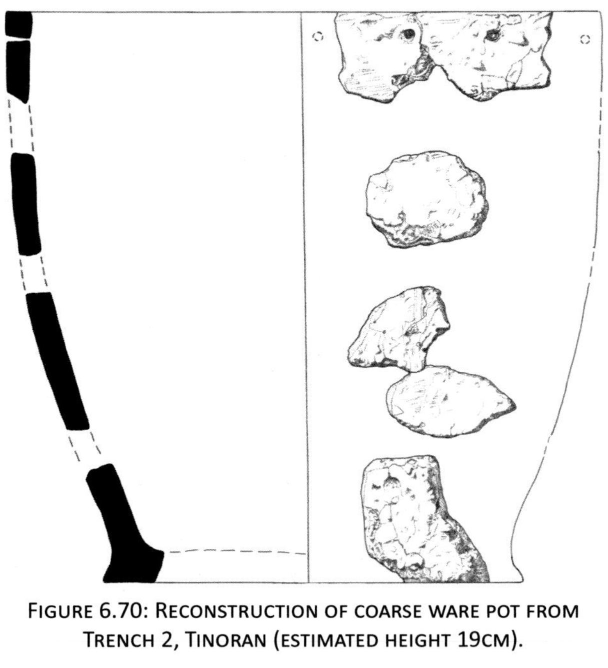

FIGURE 6.70: RECONSTRUCTION OF COARSE WARE POT FROM TRENCH 2, TINORAN (ESTIMATED HEIGHT 19CM).

FIGURE 6.71: SHERDS OF BRONZE AGE POTTERY, WITH RIM PERFORATIONS, TRENCH 2, TINORAN.

served. It is likely that part of the vessel was deposited where it was found and as the fractures are fresh and it may have been further broken in situ and subsequently covered over with soil. Internal charred residues are relatively substantial and very well-preserved and occur around the rim and upper body rather than at the base.

Discussion

Radiocarbon dating (GrA-64440; see below) confirms a Late Bronze Age date for the Tinoran vessel. The shape of the vessel is a relatively large flat-based, bucket-shaped and thin walled pot. The fabric of the Tinoran vessel is fine-textured, although larger fragments of crushed granitic temper were used but in sparse amounts. The granitic temper and mica-rich clay indicate a likely local manufacture. Perforations occur below in single rows just below the rim. These may have been decorative or functional to allow steam to escape if the vessel was used as a lidded cooking pot although the absence of external soot or surface blackening on the pots suggests it was not used over an open fire for cooking. The perforations may also have been used to suspend the vessel.

Perforations below the rim were recorded on pottery from the hillfort at Rathgall, Co. Wicklow (Grogan and Roche 2009: 41). There is as yet no available contextual information from the Rathgall excavations but it may have been a contemporary site with the hillfort at Tinoran. Pottery similar to that from Tinoran was recovered by Bersu in his 1948–49 excavation of Freestone Hill hillfort in Co. Kilkenny (Raftery 1969). About 700 sherds were recovered from Freestone Hill and many of these were heavily weathered. The pottery was recovered from a black habitation layer in the central area, around 'hut sites' and in occupation material inside, underneath and mixed in layers within the bank of Freestone Hill (Raftery 1969: 91). The pottery was undecorated flat-based vessels grouped into four units (A–D) relative to colour, fabric, coarseness, etc. but the divisions were arbitrary. Group A had in the main rounded or flat rims, 11–12mm thick vessel walls and perforations of 3–4mm diameter located 7–10mm below the rims and set *c.*17mm apart (Raftery 1969: 88). Group A pottery from Freestone Hill provides a close parallel for the Tinoran vessel. Raftery's (1969: 91) dating of the Freestone Hill pottery to the 4th century A.D. was based on a recorded association with a Roman coin, an interpretation that may be revised in light of the radiocarbon results from Tinoran.

Similar 'coarse wares' to the Tinoran vessel were recovered from Navan Fort (McCorry 1997). Around 800 sherds representing up to 92 vessels were found in a habitation layer in Phase 3 and some of the pottery assemblage had perforations below the rims (McCorry 1997: 72; figs 32 and 36). Of interest is that the clay and temper used in the Navan Fort pottery was not local and the pottery was probably imported onto the site.

Further afield, excavations on Knockadoon, Lough Gur, Co. Limerick have produced similar pottery with perforations below the rim. The Knockadoon flat-based, bucket-shaped pottery has been given the all-embracing nomenclature of Class II ware (Ó Ríordáin 1954) or coarse flat-bottomed ware (Grogan and Eogan 1987) but includes Late Neolithic Grooved Ware and Middle/Late Bronze Age domestic pottery. Pottery with perforations below the rim was recovered from within the enclosure at Circle L and from the enclosure wall fill at Circle K (Grogan and Eogan 1987: figs 7 and16). A review of dating these enclosures on Knockadoon suggests they were constructed in the Middle Bronze Age (Cleary 2003: 144–146). Pottery with perforations below the rims from an enclosed site on Knockadoon is dated to c. 1400–1100 B.C. (Cleary 2003: figs 20–21). Excavations at Sites C and D, Knockadoon also produced pottery with perforations below the rims (Ó Ríordáin 1954: figs 19 and 34) and these vessels identified as 'Class II' are also likely to be Middle/Late Bronze Age. Indeed, Raftery (1969: 92) drew close parallels between the pottery from Freestone Hill and the pottery with sub-rim perforations from Site C and suggested that the vessels were almost indistinguishable in terms of profile and fabric.

The radiocarbon result for the Tinoran vessel allows for a re-dating of assemblages from other sites, including Freestone Hill and Lough Gur.

Radiocarbon Samples

Four samples were selected from Trench 2, Tinoran, for AMS radiocarbon dating (wood identifications: Susan Lyons, UCC. The results are as follows (Figure 6.72):

TN2015-02: Sample of burnt bone from burnt spread (Context 34) inside bank of third enclosure.
GrA-64571; 2685 ± 30 BP

TN2015-03: Sample of burnt bone from burnt spread (Context 40) inside bank of third enclosure.
GrA-64572; 2640 ± 30 BP

TN2015-04: Sample of oak charcoal from sediment (Context 36) from under Boulder B of bank of third enclosure.
GrA-64439; 2865 ± 35 BP

TN2015-05: Sample of organic sediment from inner surface of pottery sherd from surface (C.36) inside the bank of third enclosure.
GrA-64440; 2905 ± 35 BP

FIELD NO.	LAB NO.	C-14 BP	∂13C	95.4% CALIBRATION
TN2015-01	GRA-64438	2600±30	-22.89	826–763 BC
TN2015-02	GRA-64571	2685±30	–	899–803 BC
TN2015-03	GRA-64572	2640±30	–	893–786 BC
TN2015-04	GRA-64439	2865±35	-26.21	1188–923 BC
TN2015-05	GRA-64440	2905±35	-26.89	1214–1001 BC

FIGURE 6.72: RADIOCARBON DATES FOR TINORAN HILLFORT (CALIBRATION AFTER OXCAL V.4.2.4).

Trench 2: summary

Pre-bank activity

There are no definite indications of activity at this location prior to construction of the hillfort bank.

Bank construction

Excavation confirmed that the third enclosure at Tinoran hillfort was surrounded by a single bank of stones. This was built on a slight break of slope along the steeply inclined south-west slope of the hill. The steepness of this slope required a level platform on which the bank could be constructed. This was achieved by digging into the slope to create a shallow ledge approximately 1.3m in width (Figure 6.73). The soil/subsoil and broken rock removed in this way was piled on the upslope side of the ledge, to create a 3–4m wide stretch of reasonably level ground. The wall was then built on this platform in the following sequence:

1. A contiguous line of massive boulders (C.41) was arranged on top of the introduced layers on the platform. This formed the inner kerb of the bank, with the aim of reducing slopewash erosion of this structure.

2. A central facing of large stones and some small boulders was stacked against the inner side of the ledge. This served to consolidate the loose stony core of the bank.

3. A facing of similarly sized stones was stacked on the outside of the ledge to form the outer kerb of the bank. A small amount of redeposited subsoil (C.38) was piled against the base of these facing stones.

4. The spaces between these three structures were then filled with medium to large stones (C.39). These stones were packed tightly together, but were not coursed. The end result was a stone bank measuring 3.5–3.7m in width, with an internal height of 0.6–0.8m that was probably 1m so originally.

All of stones used were surface drift material, probably gathered from the surrounding hill slope, with no evidence of any quarried material. The large boulders of the inner kerb were probably rolled downslope into position, a process that required considerable effort. No soil was used in the bank, which is also consistent with the ab-

FIGURE 6.73: EXCAVATION OF SLOPE BELOW STONE BANK, TRENCH 2, TINORAN. THIS SLOPE WAS ORIGINALLY DUG INTO AT TWO LEVELS (CENTRE AND TOP OF PHOTOGRAPH) TO CREATE A PLATFORM FOR THE BANK CONSTRUCTION.

sence of an associated ditch.

Radiocarbon dating indicates a date of 1155–980 BC for construction of the third enclosure of Tinoran hillfort (Figure 6.72). This is based on the dating of pottery residues from the construction surface (sample TN2015-05), and charcoal from construction sediment directly below the stone bank (sample TN2015-04).

Post-bank activity

A small fire connected to the cooking of food was lit directly inside the stone bank at some stage during the early occupation of this hillfort. This is represented by two spreads of charcoal and burnt bone overlying each other in the northern corner of the trench. The lower spread (C.40) lay directly on the natural Bs-horizon, which was fire-reddened in places indicating *in situ* fire. This C.40 burnt spread was overlain in the northern corner of the trench by a spread of grey silt (C.36a), covered in turn by a thin spread of orange-brown silt (C.35a). The latter was then covered by a second spread of charcoal and burnt bone (C.34). This overlay the extent of the C.40 deposit, but was slightly wider in extent.

Initially, it was considered that the two fire events were separate in time, with C.40 possibly representing a pre-bank hearth and C.34 a later hearth. The fact that both burnt spreads are similar in extent and composition suggested another possibility. Both fires may have been lit within a shallow pit, dug through the C.35 and underlying C.36 construction layers for a depth of 0.15–0.18m, down to the surface of the Bs-horizon subsoil. The initial fire in this hearth pit, represented by the C.40 sediment, was used for cooking, as indicated by the presence of burnt bone. This burnt sediment was subsequently covered by two spreads of sterile soil derived from the initial digging of the hearth pit. This explains why the sides of this hearth pit were not clearly visible in excavation, as the fill (C.35a and C.36a) and cut (C.35 and C.36) material was very similar.

A second cooking fire was lit soon afterwards at this location, represented by the charcoal and burnt bone in the C.34 spread. Both fire events in this hearth pit are likely to have been close in time, possibly lit over a matter of days. Radiocarbon dating of burnt bone from C.34 and C.40 (samples TN2015-02 and TN2015-03) indicate a date range of 890–795 BC for this hearth. This is significant as it indicates an occupation of the hillfort several centuries after it was built.

Abandonment

Excavation revealed a gradual accumulation of slopewash silt on the inner side of the bank. Some of these contained stone tumble from the bank. This sediment did not contain any other archaeological material, and so there are no details of the occupation history or abandonment of the hillfort. There is also evidence for partial collapse and erosion of the bank exterior, consistent with natural erosion over a long period of time.

Discussion

The aim of the Tinoran excavation was to examine details of the defences of the third and fourth enclosures of this hillfort, and to recover samples for scientific dating. In that respect, the project was successful, and the final results provide important dating evidence for an important prehistoric settlement in eastern Ireland. This information will also strengthen the case for the future protection of the hillfort, or at least the portion that has survived the devastation caused by modern forestry.

The defences of both enclosures are notably different in character. The third enclosure is surrounded by a carefully built stone bank, while a bank made with soil from an external ditch was used for the fourth enclosure. This might indicate the enclosures were built at different times, but could also reflect the different topography at the respective locations. The stone bank of the third enclosure was built on a very steep slope, where an earthen bank and accompanying ditch would have been difficult to maintain. The latter was feasible on the less steeper slopes of the fourth enclosure. Other factors may explain the different construction methods, such as the availability of stone, and the visual significance attached to different enclosures in this hillfort.

The Tinoran excavation did not produce significant evidence for the occupation of this hillfort. The small hearth inside the bank in Trench 2 is connected with continued occupation of the site *c.*890–795 BC. The crushed pottery vessel and whetstone are connected to occupation activity during the construction of the stone bank enclosure, *c.*1155–980 BC.

Finally, neither excavation trench yielded information on the final abandonment of this hillfort. There is no evidence from either trench for deliberate destruction connected to warfare.

6.5 Hughstown, Co. Kildare

This is the most western hillfort in the Baltinglass group, located 2km west of that town, just inside the border of Co. Kildare (Figure 6.1; ITM 684004, 688930). The hillfort encloses an area of 8.22 hectares on Hughstown Hill (298m OD), where steep to moderate slopes lead to a rounded summit on which there is a small earthwork enclosure. As discussed in Chapter 5, a magnetic gradiometry survey was undertaken in 2012 across the entire site. When combined with aerial photographs and LiDAR data, this revealed a multiple enclosure hillfort, measuring approximately 356m (north-west/south-east) by 261m (north-east/south-west) in overall extent (Figure 6.74). There are four widely-spaced enclosing elements. The only one of these that is fully extant is a small circular enclosure at the summit, measuring 54m (north-west/south-east) by 50m (north-east/south-west). Outside this, the geophysical survey recorded a large sub-oval enclosure, measuring 248m (north-west/south-east) by 197m (north-east/south-west), visible in places as a low-relief feature. The third enclosing element is 23–48m outside and concentric with the second enclosure, and measures 290m (north-west/south-east) by 228m (north-east/south-west). The outermost (fourth) enclosure measures 356m (north-west/south-east) by 261m (north-east/south-west). Though mostly levelled, a portion does survive as a curving field bank along the north-east side of the outer enclosure.

Sample excavation was conducted at Hughstown in August 2015 and July 2016 (O'Brien 2015c; 2016c). The objective was to obtain information on the outer three enclosures, all of which are now substantially levelled. Guided by magnetic gradiometry readings, a single trench was excavated across each of these enclosing elements on the western side of the hillfort (Figure 6.74).

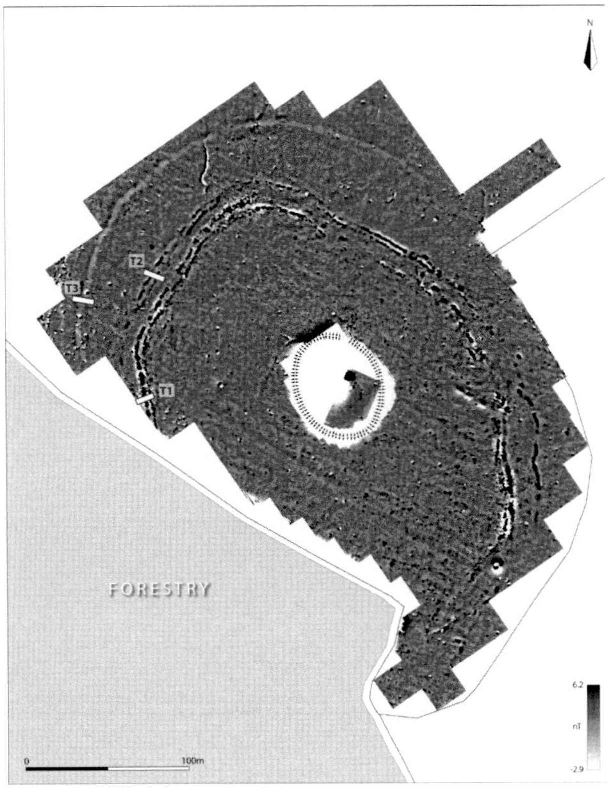

FIGURE 6.74: MAGNETIC GRADIOMETRY SURVEY OF HUGHSTOWN, SHOWING LOCATION OF EXCAVATION TRENCHES.

Trench 1

In August 2015 a single trench was hand excavated on the western side of the second enclosure of the hillfort. This 10m by 2m trench was aligned approximately east–west across the line of the enclosure (Figure 6.75). The natural soil is a brown podzol, where a thin sod (C.01) overlay an 0.07–0.2m thick A-horizon (C.02) of dark brown sandy silt with frequent small stones. This organic soil overlay a compact Bs-horizon surface (C.36) of yellow/orange sandy silt with many stones. The underlying C-horizon (C.37) was exposed on the lower ditch sides as a hard grey/white fluvio-glacial silt, with pebbles and occasional large angular stones of shale and sandstone.

Archaeological features

There were two separate areas of archaeology in this trench (Figures 6.76 and Figure 6.77):

1.A large earth-cut ditch occupying the western half of the trench.

2.The remains of a stone-faced bank of soil, which incorporated a slot trench with stake settings, in the central area.

Ditch (C.34)

Excavation revealed a large ditch with a V-shaped profile cut into the Bs-horizon subsoil (C.36). The top of the ditch was 2.8–3m wide, narrowing to 0.5–0.6m at the base, with a central depth of 1.5–1.6m (Figure 6.77). The sides were steeply sloping (45°) and smooth, with the upper portion formed in Bs-horizon and the base in C-horizon (C.37). A sharp break of slope 0.4m above the base served to create a channel-like profile at the bottom of the ditch (Figure 6.78).

There were four significant events in the infilling of this ditch (Figures 6.79 and 6.80):

1. Early fire event

Excavation exposed a thin deposit of charcoal (C.33) at the base of the ditch. This was present as small lumps and flecks in direct contact with the cut of the ditch. A radiocarbon date for this material (sample HT2015-01) should be close in time to the digging of the ditch, even if the source of this charcoal is unknown. The latter does not seem to be connected to any burning event inside the ditch or in the adjacent bank, as neither the underlying cut nor the stones directly overlying the charcoal were fire-reddened. The occurrence of this charcoal indicates a small fire in the vicinity of the ditch, close in time to when the latter was dug.

FIGURE 6.75: TRENCH 1, HUGHSTOWN. SURFACE BENEATH A-HORIZON ORGANIC SOIL (LOOKING WEST), SHOWING DARK BANK OF UPPER DITCH FILL (TOP LEFT) AND BASE OF FORMER BANK (CENTRE).

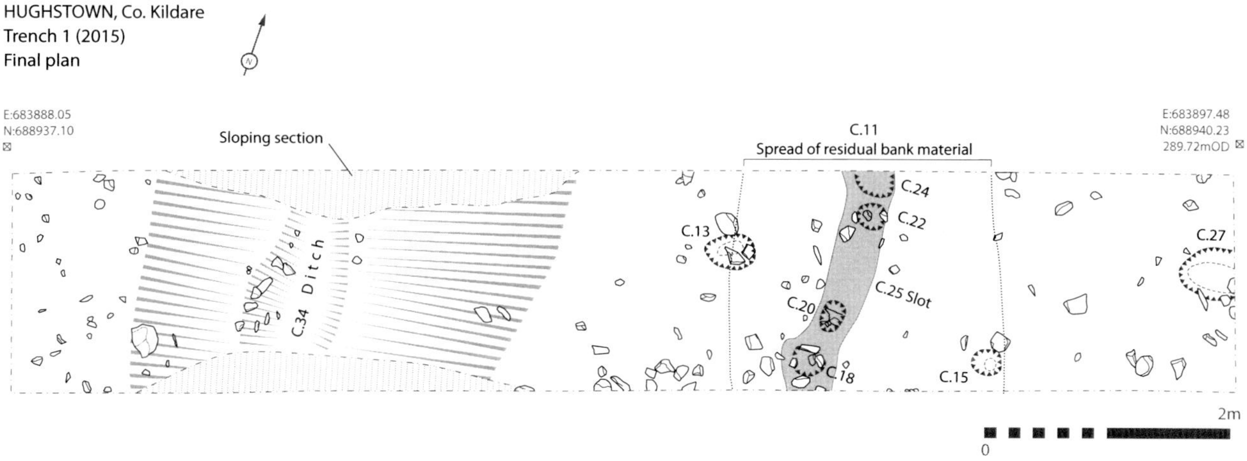

FIGURE 6.76: POST-EXCAVATION PLAN OF TRENCH 1, HUGHSTOWN.

FIGURE 6.77 POST-EXCAVATION PHOTOGRAMMETRY OF TRENCH 1, HUGHSTOWN.

FIGURE 6.78: POST-EXCAVATION VIEW OF DITCH, HUGHSTOWN (LOOKING SOUTH-WEST).

The C.33 deposit may be related to a minor occurrence of charcoal along the mid outer slope of the ditch. Excavation removed thin pockets of red/brown silt (C.32) containing charcoal, which were in direct contact with the ditch cut. If C.32 and C.33 were connected, it would indicate a source for this charcoal from outside the ditch, rather than the bank area.

2. Bank erosion

The infilling of the ditch began with an accumulation of yellow/brown silt (C.31) along the inner base and lower slope (Figure 6.79). This primary sediment continued up the inner slope of the ditch as a grey/brown silt (C.09). Both sediments had a number of small to large stones, with C.09 containing some large inclined slabs (C.06) that seem to have fallen into the open ditch. This probably represents a collapsed stone facing on the exterior of the adjacent bank (Figure 6.80). These stones were mostly of grey coarse sandstone, with no obvious fire-reddening. The majority were 0.1–0.25m in length, with some larger examples up to 0.3–0.45m, as well as five examples in 0.6–0.7m (largest was 0.81m by 0.43m by 0.14m). They were mostly angular to sub-angular in shape, with many broken surfaces. Some had a slightly rolled appearance to indicate a drift source.

Contexts 09 and 31 represent primary erosion of the bank connected to the failure of this revetment. This eventually resulted in an influx of significant amounts of bank material, represented by large stones and dark brown silt (C.30) with numerous voids in the lower part of the ditch. It is notable that none of these stones were fire-reddened, and so cannot be linked to any deliberate destruction of the bank. There was also an influx of orange gravelly sediment (C.29) from outside the ditch, which might represent the erosion of a low counterscarp bank.

3. Break in ditch infill

The infilling of this ditch slowed considerably following collapse of the adjacent bank. This is marked by the development of a thin sod layer in the half-filled ditch. This was visible as a thin lense of organic silt (C.08) overlying the C.30 stones in the centre of the ditch (Figure 6.79). This buried sod continued as C.07 on the upper outer edge of the ditch.

4. Agricultural clearance

Local sources confirm that the remaining bank was levelled some 20–30 years ago during land reclamation for agricultural purposes (landowner information). This is recorded in the upper ditch stratification as a layer of bright orange stony silt (C.05), overlain by a layer of brown/orange stony silt (C.04). These sediments represent redeposited subsoil derived from the ditch, which originally formed the core of the adjacent bank (Figure 6.79). The levelling of the latter into the ditch depression was followed by deposition of a mid brown organic silt

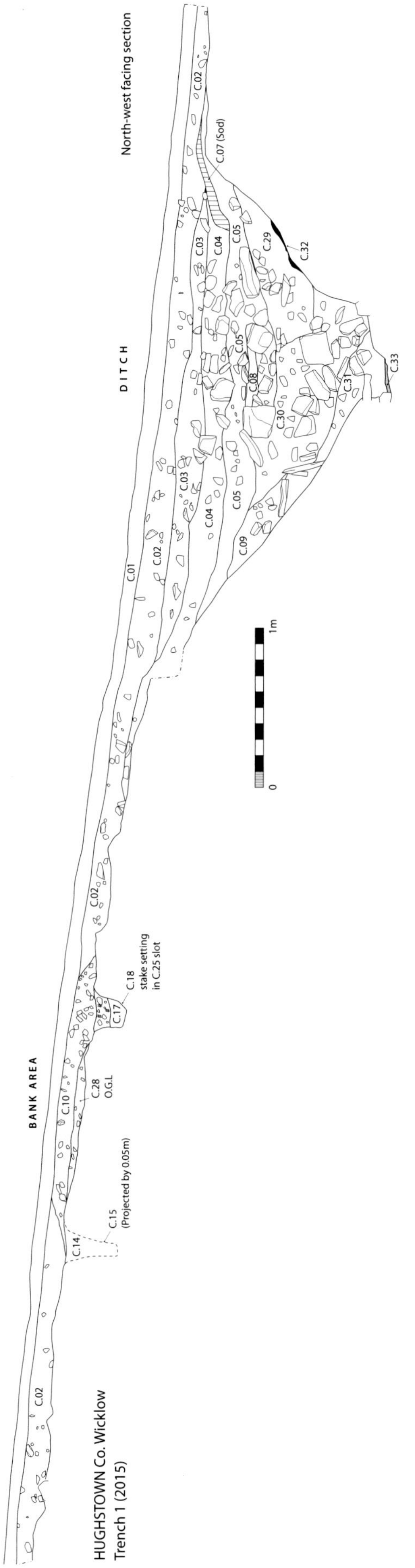

Figure 6.79: Stratification of Trench 1, Hughstown.

FIGURE 6.80: STRATIFICATION OF DITCH, TRENCH 1, HUGHSTOWN (NORTH-WEST FACING SECTION).

(C.03) with some small reddened stones, overlain by the A-horizon (C.02).

Bank

The excavation results point to the former presence of a bank on the inner side of the ditch (Figure 6.75). This feature was not visible prior to excavation, and landowner information indicates it was levelled by agriculture in the modern period. The removal of A-horizon topsoil exposed a spread of residual bank material (C.10), measuring 1.9–2.5m wide by 0.05–0.1m thick, located 2m inside the ditch (Figure 6.79). This compact deposit of yellow/brown silt contained broken stones, 0.04–0.1m in size, many of which had a reddened appearance. The latter is probably due to iron oxide weathering rather than heat-reddening, and it is notable there was no significant occurrence of charcoal in the C.10 spread.

Excavation revealed a deposit of larger stones (C.11) at the base of the A-horizon (C.02), located between the western margin of the C.10 deposit and the inner edge of ditch. These loose stones were 0.15–0.35m in length, mostly sub-angular clasts with slightly rolled appearance. They probably represent bank material, possibly related to the stones of the collapsed bank revetment (C.06) occurring within the inner side of the ditch.

Old ground surface

Excavation of the residual bank material exposed a thin spread of fine black silt (C.28) underneath and respecting limits of C.10 stone deposit (Figure 6.79). This represents an buried sod layer beneath the former bank. This old ground surface contained a few flecks of charcoal, but no other archaeological material to indicate construction or pre-enclosure activity at that location.

Stake features

Excavation uncovered a number of small features cut into the Bs-horizon subsoil, within or adjacent to the location of the former bank (Figure 6.76). These include (from west to east) a possible stakehole (C.13), a slot trench (C.25) with four possible stake settings (contexts 18, 20, 22 and 24), a large stakehole (C.15) and a small pit (C.27).

The C.11 stones overlay a small pit (C.13) that may be a large stakehole. This D-shaped feature measured 0.38m (east–west) by 0.3m (north–south), with a depth of 0.27m. There were two large stones along the western side, measuring 0.21m by 0.16m by 0.05m and 0.15m by 0.09m by 0.09m respectively. The east and north sides of the pit were vertical, with other sides sloping steeply to an irregularly flat base with a central depth of 0.27m. It was filled with a mid brown sandy silt (C.12) that contained the same type of reddened angular stone as the C.10 bank material. The lower part of C.12 was grey/brown sandy silt containing charcoal that is radiocarbon dated (sample HT2015-03).

The removal of the residual stony bank material (C.10) exposed a narrow curving band of dark sediment within the underlying old ground surface (C.28). The excavation of this dark brown silt (C.16) revealed a 1.74m length of slot trench (C.25) cut through C.28 into the Bs-horizon (Figure 6.81). This feature had a slight curve, measuring 0.25–0.36m in upper width and 0.1–0.14m at base, with a depth of 0.07–0.11m (outside of stake settings). It was filled with a compact deposit of dark brown silt that contained frequent small angular and reddened stones similar to those in the C.10 bank deposit. The C.16 fill also contained a small amount of charcoal, a sample of which was submitted for radiocarbon dating (sample HT2015-02).

The investigation of this slot trench revealed four possible stake settings (from south to north: contexts 18, 20, 22 and 24). These ranged 0.23–0.35m in maximum length and 0.14–0.21m in depth, and were filled at the base by a light brown sandy silt (contexts 17, 19, 21 and 23 respectively) that did not contain charcoal. There was also some use of packing stones, as in the case of C.20 where two large stones on the east and west sides created a 0.13m by 0.07m space for an upright stake. The upper fill of the slot trench (C.16) was composed of similar stony sediment to the C.10 spread, suggesting that these stakes stood with, and were supported by, the original bank. The diameter of these possible stake settings within the C.25 slot trench indicates this may have been a light roundwood fence.

Excavation on the inner side of the C.10 bank material revealed a large stakehole (C.15) close to southern side of trench (Figure 6.76). This sub-circular feature measured 0.27m by 0.25m, with a depth of 0.34m. The fill (C.14) consisted of a yellow/brown silt with occasional angular and reddened stones in 0.04–0.13m range, similar to those in the C.10 spread from which they probably derive.

Finally, a small pit (C.27) was discovered extending into section at eastern end of trench (Figure 6.76). This irregular cut measured 0.41m by 0.4m (extending out of eastern section), with an irregularly flat base at a depth of 0.09–0.13m. The fill (C.26) consisted of a mid brown silt with occasional small stones and flecks of charcoal. The significance of this feature is not known, and it cannot be stratigraphically linked to the enclosing element.

List of excavation contexts, Trench 1, Hughstown.
Context 01: Sod layer; 0.07–0.1m in thickness; compact

FIGURE 6.81: POST-EXCAVATION VIEW OF BANK AREA (LOOKING SOUTH) SHOWING C.25 SLOT WITH CONTEXTS 18, 20, 22 AND 24 STAKE SETTINGS (CENTRE RIGHT), AND ADJACENT SMALL PITS C.13 (FAR RIGHT) AND C.15 (FAR LEFT).

and free of stones.

C.02: A-horizon. Dark brown organic soil, friable sandy silt, frequent pebbles and small stones.

C.03: Organic soil over ditch. Mid brown silt, 0.06–0.19m thick, with small angular stones.

C.04: Upper fill of ditch. Orange brown silt, 0.1–0.2m thick; C.06 revetment stones on inner side.

C.05: Upper fill of ditch. Compact orange silt, 0.1–0.28m thick, with large stones in centre of ditch.

C.06: Collapsed stones from bank revetment along mid to upper inner side of ditch (see text).

C.07: Buried sod. Dark brown peaty silt, 0.03–0.06m thick, on upper outer edge of ditch.

C.08: Buried sod. Dark brown peaty silt, 0.04–0.08m thick, in central area of ditch.

C.09: Compact light brown silt, up to 0.2m thick, around C.06 stones on mid inner slope of ditch.

C.10: Residual bank. A 1.9–2.5m wide by 0.05–0.1m thick layer of small broken stones inside ditch.

C.11: Spread of small–large stones in 2m wide area between inner edge of ditch and bank (C.10).

C.12: Fill of C.13 pit, inner side of ditch. Grey/brown sandy silt with small stones and charcoal.

C.13: Cut of D-shaped pit, 0.38m by 0.3m by 0.27m deep, with two large stones on western side.

C.14: Fill of C.15 stakehole. Yellow/brown fine silt with 0.04–0.13m size angular reddened stones.

C.15: Stakehole. Sub-circular vertical cut, 0.27m by 0.25m by 0.34m deep, to irregularly flat base.

C.16: Upper fill of slot trench (C.25) in bank. Compact, dark brown, stony silt with some charcoal.

C.17: Lower fill of stake setting (C.18), south end of C.25 slot. Light brown sandy silt, rare charcoal.

C.18: Possible stake setting, south end of C.25 slot. Sub-oval shape, 0.23m by 0.2m by 0.2m deep.

C.19: Lower fill of stake setting (C.20), south side of C.25 slot. Light brown sandy silt with pebbles.

C.20: Possible stake setting, south side of C.25 slot. Sub-oval shape, 0.25m by 0.18m by 0.2m deep.

C.21: Lower fill of stake setting (C.22), north side of C.25 slot. Light brown sandy silt with pebbles.

C.22: Possible stake setting, north side of C.25 slot. Sub-oval cut, 0.25m by 0.22m by 0.17m deep.

C.23: Lower fill of stake setting (C.22), north end of C.25 slot. Light brown sandy silt with pebbles.

C.24: Possible stake setting, north side of C.25 slot. Oval cut 0.35m by 0.13m by 0.08–0.14m deep.

C.25: Shallow slot trench in Bs-horizon, with four stake settings (see main text).

C.26: Fill of pit (C.27). Mid brown silt with some pebbles, small stones; frequent charcoal flecks.

C.27: Small irregular pit, 0.41m by 0.4m by 0.09–0.13m deep to an irregularly flat base.

C.28: Old ground surface. Spread of fine black silt under limits of C.10 bank; some charcoal flecks.

C.29: Deposit on outer slope of ditch. Compact bright orange stony silt with gravelly texture.

C.30: Stone deposit in lower centre of ditch, 0.15–0.4m in length, within dark brown sandy silt.

C.31: Compact yellow/brown silt on lower inner slope of ditch, with many small to large stones.

C.32: Small pockets of red/brown sandy silt on mid outer slope of ditch; small amounts of charcoal.

C.33: Deposit of lump and fleck charcoal at base of ditch.
C.34: Cut of ditch (see main text for details).

C.36: Bs-horizon. Compact orange/yellow sandy silt, frequent pebbles and small–large stones.

C.37: C-horizon, lower sides of ditch. Hard grey/white silt, with pebbles and some large stones.

Trench 2

This 12m (east–west) by 2m trench was hand excavated across the line of the third enclosure on the western side of the hillfort (Figure 6.74). The ground surface is managed pasture, with a moderate westerly slope. There are no surface features to indicate the now levelled enclosure (Figure 6.82). For that reason, the trench location was determined by magnetic gradiometry survey. This revealed a positive magnetic anomaly, alongside traces of a weaker linear anomaly, crossing the eastern and central sides of the trench respectively (Figure 6.74). The excavation trench was aligned at right angles (110–290°) to these anomalies.

The sod layer was removed by spade, followed by coarse trowelling of the organic soil, with fine trowelling to a subsoil surface. The natural soil is a brown podzol, where a 0.1m thick sod (C.01) overlay an A-horizon topsoil (C.02) of dark brown/black loamy silt with frequent pebbles. This organic soil overlay a thin layer of hard iron pan (C.35) on a compact Bs-horizon surface (C.36) of orange, stony, sandy silt. The underlying C-horizon (C.37) was exposed on the lower ditch sides as a hard grey/white fluvio-glacial silt, with pebbles and some large angular stones of shale and sandstone, on broken bedrock.

The removal of the organic soil revealed a pattern of closely spaced plough furrows exposed on the Bs-horizon surface (Figure 6.82). These parallel cultivation marks criss-crossed the western half of the trench in a north–south (C.49) and north-west/south-east (C.50) direction, cutting the top of the Bs-horizon surface to a depth of 2–5cm. They were eventually removed down to the lower Bs-horizon subsoil.

While the C.49 furrows were confined to the western third of the trench, the C.50 examples partly extended over the fill of the central ditch. It is notable that neither set of furrows were visible at the eastern end of the trench. While that area is rising ground, there is no obvious reason why the plough marks did not extend across the entire trench. Neither set of furrows is dated; however, the north-west/south-east examples are likely to be of modern/early modern date as they overlie the final ditch fill.

There were two significant features in Trench 2 (Figures 6.83 and 6.84). The terminal of a small earth-cut ditch was discovered in the central area, with the corresponding end of a slot trench 2.6m inside that feature. The slot trench contained large amounts of charcoal and heat-shattered packing stones, possibly connected to the burning of a wooden palisade. There was no trace of any accompanying bank, though it is likely that one did exist in the space between the ditch and palisade trench.

Ditch (C.55)

This feature was first exposed on removal of a thin layer of iron pan (C.37) in the central trench area. Further excavation revealed the terminal of a shallow ditch, exposed to a length of 1.55m from the southern side of the trench (Figure 6.83 and Figure 6.84). The ditch had an irregular U-shaped profile, with a straight northern end. The upper part had a maximum width of 2.35m on southern side of trench, narrowing to 1.8m in the centre, and 0.95m at the flattened northern end. There were corresponding depths of 0.72m, 0.54m and 0.44m from the B-horizon subsoil, with a maximum depth of 1.03m from modern

FIGURE 6.82: GENERAL VIEW OF TRENCH 2 AFTER REMOVAL OF A-HORIZON ORGANIC SOIL; CULTIVATION FURROWS VISIBLE, WITH C.51 STONES IN FOREGROUND (LOOKING WEST).

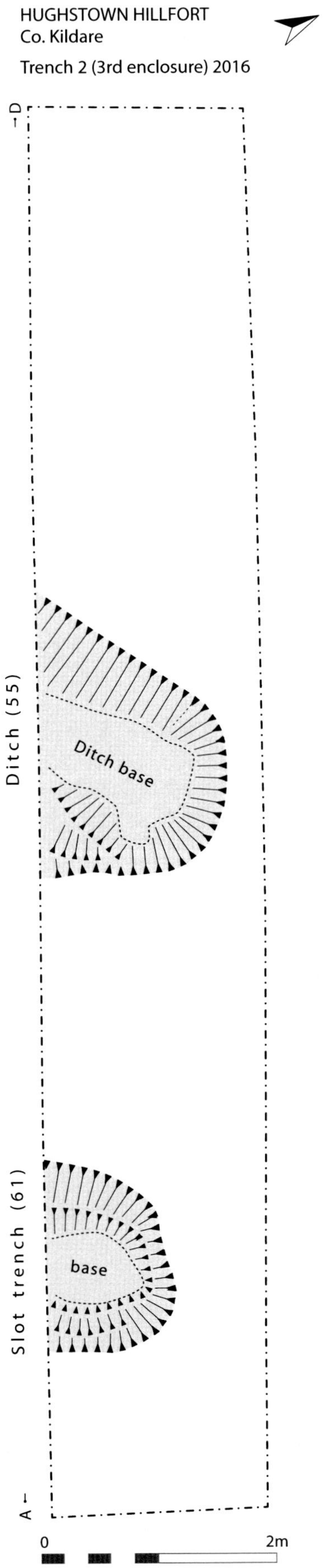

FIGURE 6.83: POST-EXCAVATION PLAN OF TRENCH 2, HUGHSTOWN.

FIGURE 6.84: POST-EXCAVATION PHOTOGRAMMETRY OF TRENCH 2, HUGHSTOWN.

ground surface (Figure 6.85). The irregular eastern side was steeply sloping in places, less so in other parts. The western side had a uniform 45° slope, while the northern end was near-vertical. The base was 0.5–0.55m wide, and irregularly flat, except on the south-east side where the cut was narrower. The ditch cut through subsoil (contexts 36 and 37), with some ribs of bedrock exposed at the base. It is unlikely, however, that much bedrock was removed during the digging of this ditch (Figure 6.86).

There were two significant fills in the ditch terminal, along with a significant number of stones (Figure 6.87). The upper fill (C.52) was a loose deposit of orange/mid brown silt with frequent small to medium stones, and only rare charcoal. The lower fill (C.53) was a compact yellow/light brown silt that contained a large number of broken stones (C.54), but also frequent flecks of charcoal. The upper fill may represent the levelling of a low bank on the inside of the ditch in the modern era. The lower fill (C.53 and stone content C.54) may represent the erosion of that bank over a long period, as well as an influx of small amounts of charcoal (radiocarbon sample HT2016-03) from the burning of an adjacent wooden structure (see below).

Slot trench (C.61)

This was first exposed as a 0.15–0.25m wide band of dark silt and charcoal (C.59) at the eastern end of the trench. Further excavation revealed the terminal of a small trench 2.6m east of the ditch (Figure 6.83 and Figure 6.84). This had a rounded U-shaped profile, with steeply sloping sides cut into subsoil to an irregularly flat base (Figure 6.88). The lower northern side was interrupted by a small exposure of broken bedrock. The cut had an exposed length of 1.15m from the southern side of the trench, narrowing from 1.58 wide on the southern side to <1.1m at the rounded northern end. The maximum depth from the modern ground level is 0.94m, or 0.68m from the B-horizon cut.

Excavation revealed four separate deposits in the infilling of this slot trench (Figure 6.87). The earliest was a charcoal-rich sediment (C.59) containing fire-reddened and heat-shattered stones. This deposit of loose dark brown/black fine silt was first exposed on the western upper side of the C.61 trench. It extended under the upper fill (C.56), covering the lower western sides and base of this cut to a thickness of 0.2–0.27m. The deposit was very rich in charcoal, both finely divided and small to large lumps, which was sampled for radiocarbon dating (samples HT2016-01 and HT2016-02). Most of the charcoal is alder, with a small amount of willow also present (Susan Lyons pers. comm.). The deposit contained numerous small to large stones (C.60), many of which were fire-reddened and heat-shattered. These were mostly sub-rectangular to sub-triangular in shape. The largest were 0.3–0.4m in length (5%), with examples in 0.25–0.3m (20%), 0.18–0.25m (45%) and 0.1–0.18m

FIGURE 6.85: POST-EXCAVATION VIEW OF DITCH (C.55), SHOWING STONES IT CONTAINED (LOOKING NORTH).

Figure 6.86: Post-excavation view of ditch terminal (C.55) (looking south).

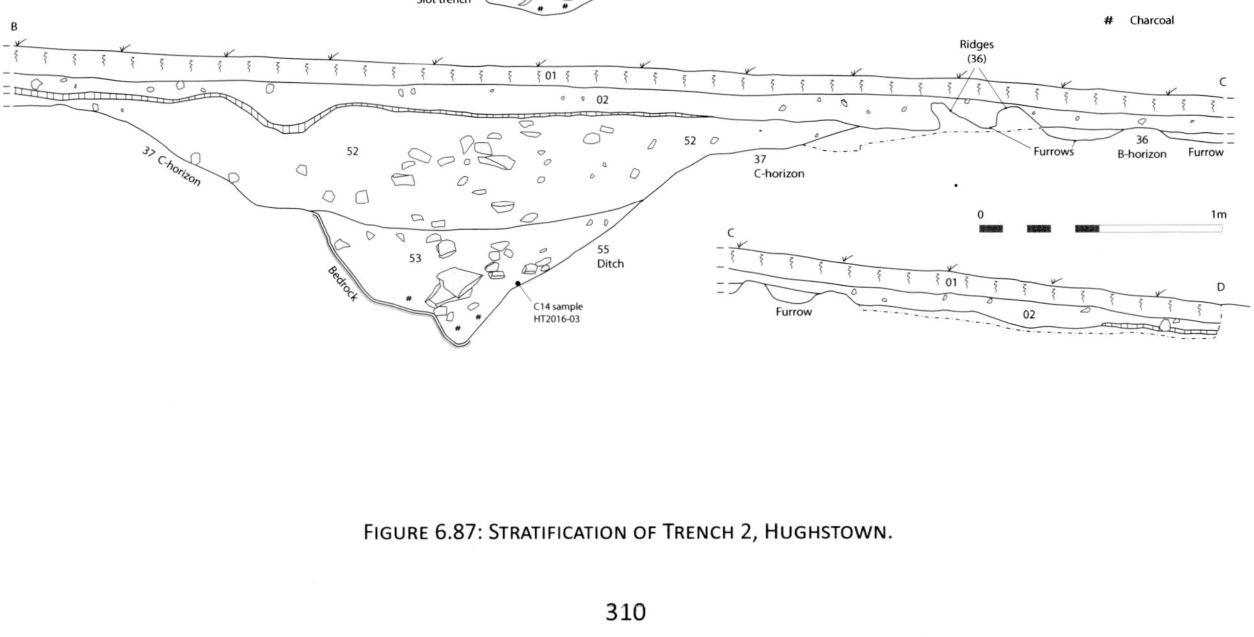

Figure 6.87: Stratification of Trench 2, Hughstown.

FIGURE 6.88: POST-EXCAVATION VIEW OF SLOT TRENCH, EAST END OF TRENCH 2, WITH C.60 STONES.

(30%) range.

The presence of large fragments of alder charcoal, along with large stones probably used as packing, points to the burning of a wooden structure (fencing?) in this slot trench. The possibility of a gate post cannot be dismissed given the limited extent of excavation. The unusual occurrence of the burnt deposit (C.59), concentrated along the base and western side of the cut, suggests a burning structure may have collapsed in that direction. Notwithstanding that the cut itself was not fire-reddened, the presence of some lenses of red oxidised sediment at the base of C.59 does indicate *in situ* burning of wood. Whether this represents burning wood that fell into an open trench, or the firing of an upright post secured with packing stones in that feature, remains to be established. The latter is more likely given the large number of fire-reddened stones and the primary position of the charcoal deposit, but further excavation is required to confirm the presence of a palisade.

This burnt deposit was overlain by a small deposit of redeposited subsoil (C.58) on the lower eastern side of the slot. The upper part of the slot trench was filled with mid brown silt that had few clasts and only rare charcoal (C.56). A thin lens of charcoal-flecked silt (C.57) at the base of C.56 probably derived from weathering of the C.59 burnt deposit as the slot trench silted in over a period of time.

List of excavation contexts, Trench 2, Hughstown.
Context 01: Compact sod, 0.09–0.1m in thickness, dark brown humic silt with no clasts.

C.02: A-horizon. Dark brown/black organic silt, 0.09–0.1m thick, frequent pebbles and small stones.

C.35: Iron pan. Thin layer of hard red/brown/yellow iron oxide on Bs-horizon across trench.

C.36: Bs-horizon. Compact orange/light brown sandy silt, frequent pebbles, with small–large stones.

C.37: C-horizon. Compact to hard grey/light brown sandy silt with frequent small–large stones.

C.49: Parallel north–south furrows, 0.2–0.24m apart, 0.2–0.27m wide and 2–4cm deep.

C.50: Parallel north-west/south-east furrows, 0.15–0.2m apart, 0.2–0.25m wide and 3–5cm deep.

C.51: Line of stones, 0.1–0.2m in size, within A-horizon close to eastern edge of slot trench (C.61).

C.52: Upper ditch fill. Loose orange/mid brown silt with small stones; larger stones (C.54) at base.
C.53: Lower ditch fill. Compact yellow/light brown silt with broken stones (C.54), and charcoal.

C.54: Large stones in C.53 and C.54 ditch fills, 0.1–0.18m up to 0.63m, mostly angular and broken.

C.55: Cut of ditch (see main text for details).

C.56: Upper fill of slot trench. Compact orange/brown silt with few clasts, some flecks of charcoal.

C.57: Thin band of charcoal-flecked mid brown silt, 0.06–0.08m thick, at base of C.56 in slot trench.

C.58: Small deposit of light brown silt on lower eastern side of trench. No charcoal.

C.59: Burnt deposit at base of C.61 slot trench (see main text for details).

C.60: Deposit of small–large stones within C.59 sediment in lower/western part of C.61 slot trench.

C.61: Cut of slot trench (see main text for details).

C.62: Loose dark brown silt with fine charcoal in 0.18m wide by 0.09m deep cut, 0.9m east of ditch.

Trench 3

This 12m (east–west; 287–107°) by 2m trench was hand excavated across the levelled defences of the fourth enclosure at Hughstown (Figure 6.74). This is the same field as Trench 2, consisting of managed pasture on a gentle westerly slope. There are no surface features apart from a slight 3–4m wide depression across the western half of the trench, suggestive of an infilled ditch. The position of the trench was determined by magnetic gradiometry survey. This revealed a linear response across the trench, consisting of a band of low magnetic readings with high readings on either side. The excavation trench was aligned across this anomaly, leaving a 3m wide space on either side.

The trench was deturfed by spade, with coarse troweling of organic soil followed by fine troweling to expose the underlying Bs-horizon surface and any archaeological features therein. The latter include a series of closely spaced cultivation furrows at the eastern end of the trench, with one such example at the western end. These parallel features averaged 0.12–0.18m in width and were approximately 0.1–0.15m apart. They followed a north-west/south-east direction, but swung sharply to the south-west as they approached the location of the ditch.

The natural soil is similar to that in the nearby Trench 2, namely a brown podzol consisting of a 0.1m thick sod (C.01), overlying an A-horizon (C.02) of 0.06–0.1m thickness, increasing to 0.18m thick over the central ditch area. This topsoil was composed of dark brown/black loamy silt, friable with numerous pebbles and some larger stones up to cobble size. This organic soil overlay a layer of hard iron pan (C.35) averaging 1–3cm in thickness across the trench, with a less compact 3–5cm in thickness over the central ditch area. This iron pan was removed to expose a compact Bs-horizon (C.36) of bright yellow/orange sandy silt with frequent pebbles, and occasional larger stones. The underlying C-horizon (C.37) was a hard grey/light brown sandy silt, with numerous pebbles and some large angular stones of shale and sandstone. The deposit also contained numerous small fragments of decayed shale. It was exposed in contact with eroded bedrock in the lower ditch cut.

Excavation exposed a *c.*3m wide band of dark brown/black soil across the central area of the trench. This was excavated to reveal a large rock-cut ditch (C.48), inside which there were faint traces of a former bank (Figure 6.89).

FIGURE 6.89: GENERAL POST-EXCAVATION VIEW OF TRENCH 3 SHOWING DITCH (LOOKING SOUTH-WEST).

Ditch (C.48)

This was a deep parallel-sided cut across the central part of Trench 3, dug through subsoil (contexts 36 and 37) with the lower part cut into bedrock (Figure 6.90). It had a U-shaped profile, with an irregularly rounded base on broken bedrock (Figure 6.91). The eastern side had a 45° slope with projecting ribs of bedrock in the lower part. The western (outer) side was near vertical to steeply sloping in the upper part, rounding towards the base. The ditch ranged in width from 3.08m on the southern side to 3.18m on the north side, with a width of 1.08m and 0.96m respectively at the base. It has a central depth of 1.58m from the B-horizon surface (1.75m from the modern ground level).

Prior to excavation the ditch was entirely infilled, with only a slight depression visible on the modern ground surface. The removal of a thin layer of iron pan (C.35) at the base of the organic soil, exposed the upper fill of the ditch (Figure 6.92). This comprised a 0.6–0.68m thick deposit of orange/brown silt (C.45) with some stones, but no charcoal. The lower fill (C.47) was a compact deposit of grey/light brown sandy silt with a central thickness of 0.55m (Figures 6.93 and 6.94). This sediment contained many small angular fragments of weathered shale, as well as larger stones in the 0.12–0.55m range. The latter were not fire-reddened or broken. Context 47 contained a small amount of charcoal, which was sampled for radiocarbon dating (HT2016-05), as was a 3–5cm lens of charcoal (C.46; sample HT2016-04) at the interface of C.45 and C.47 on the lower south-west side of the ditch.

List of excavation contexts, Trench 3, Hughstown.
Context 01: Sod layer, 0.08–0.1m in thickness, compact dark brown silt with no stones.

C.02: A-horizon. Dark brown/black loamy silt, friable with numerous pebbles and some large stones.

C.35: Thin layer of hard iron pan, base of A-horizon. Very hard yellow/brown/red surface.

C.36: Bs-horizon. Hard surface under iron pan, bright yellow/orange sandy silt with small stones.

C.37: C-horizon. Compact deposit of grey/light brown sandy silt, with small–large angular stones.

C.38: Cultivation furrow, 0.15–0.25m wide by 3–5cm deep, on Bs-horizon, western end of trench.

C.39: Cultivation furrow, 0.14m wide by 0.06m deep, with dark brown silt.

C.40: Cultivation furrow, 0.16m wide by 0.08m deep, filled with dark brown silt.

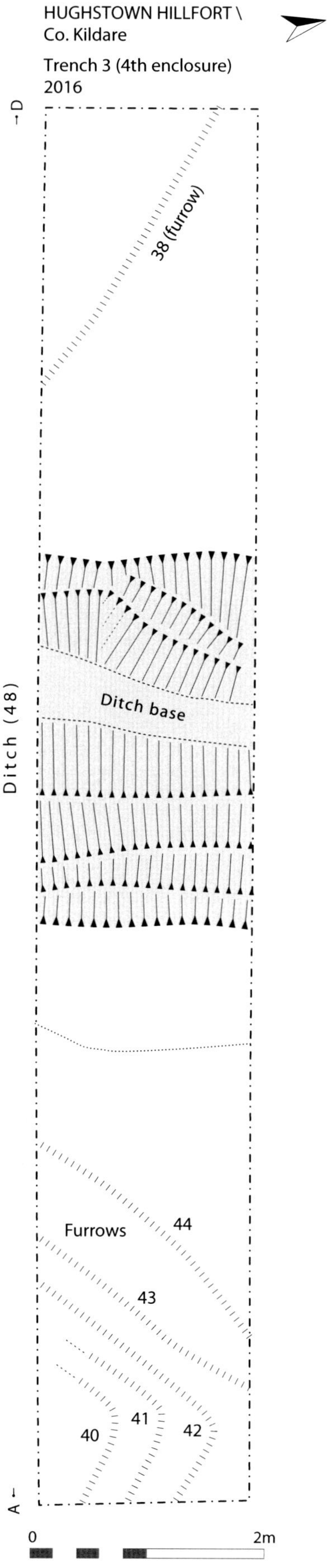

FIGURE 6.90: POST-EXCAVATION PLAN OF TRENCH 3, HUGHSTOWN.

Figure 6.91: Post-excavation view of ditch, Trench 3 (looking south-west).

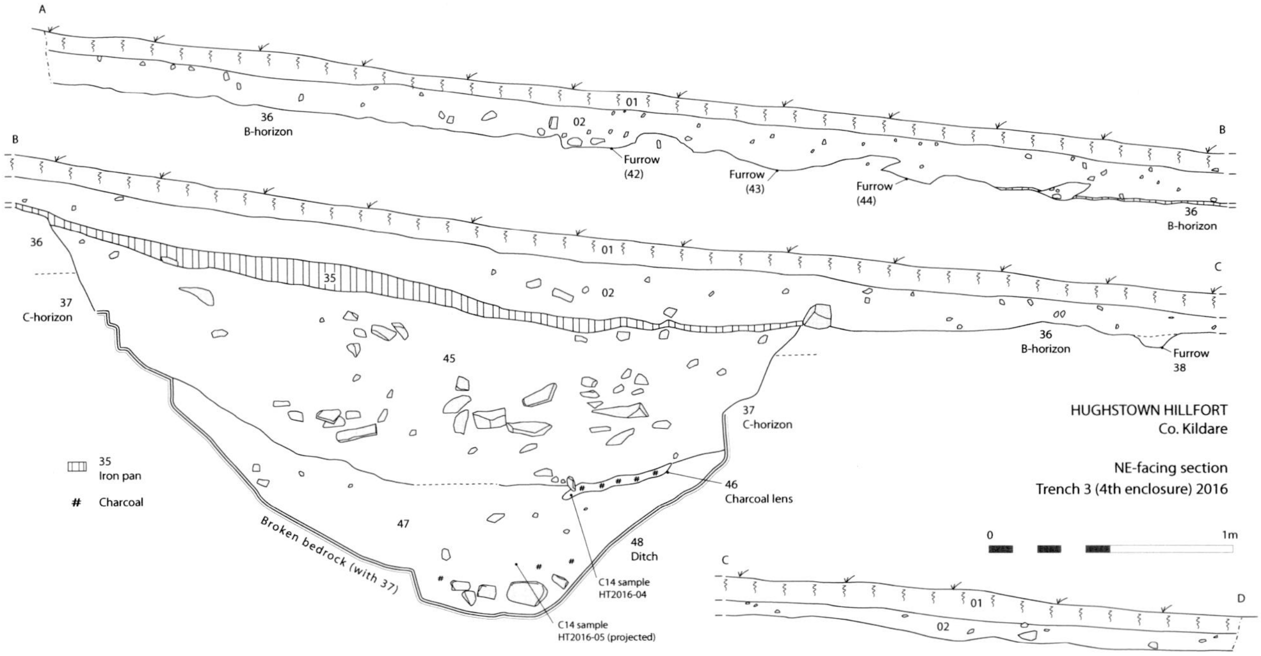

Figure 6.92: Stratification of Trench 3, Hughstown.

Figure 6.93: Stratification of C.48 ditch (north-facing section). Note two white tags (centre right) marking location of HT2016-04 and HT2016-05 radiocarbon samples.

Figure 6.94: Stratification of C.48 ditch (south-facing section).

C.41: Cultivation furrow, 0.16m wide by 0.07m deep, filled with dark brown silt.

C.42: Cultivation furrow, 0.15m wide by 0.09m deep, filled with dark brown silt.

C.43: Cultivation furrow, 0.18m wide by 0.1m deep, filled with dark brown silt.

C.44: Cultivation furrow, 0.17m wide by 0.11m deep, filled with dark brown silt.

C.45: Upper fill of C.48 ditch; 0.6–0.68m thick deposit of orange/mid brown silt with small stones.

C.46: A 3–5cm thick lens of charcoal in light brown silt on lower south-west side of ditch.

C.47: Lower fill of ditch. Compact grey/brown sandy silt, with weathered shale and larger stones.

C.48: Cut of ditch (see main text for details).

Pottery (Rose Cleary)

The only artifact find of any significance from Hughstown is a single sherd of Neolithic pottery found in Trench 1 (second enclosure). This find (15E322:01) is a well-preserved body sherd (12.2g), which was recovered from organic soil (C.02) over the bank area. This is a cultivation-disturbed context, and so the find cannot be directly associated with the enclosing elements. The closest parallels are with burnished wares of the Early/Middle Neolithic, an identification consistent with the radiocarbon results from Trench 1 (see below).

The sherd has a slight convex curvature and was probably from the neck area of a Carinated Bowl (Figure 6.95). The sherd thickness (*c.*9mm) suggests a fairly sturdy vessel. The sherd has a burnished external surface which is characteristic of Early Neolithic pottery. The sherd surface was rubbed with a stone or perhaps leather before firing and the fired surface has a lustre. The facture pattern suggests coil construction which is the norm for large prehistoric pottery vessels. The sherd is evenly fired to reddish brown (Munsell 2.5YR4/4) with a brown core (Munsell 7.5YR5/4). The evenness of the firing indicates some control of the firing temperature as Irish Neolithic pottery is frequently blotchy. The pottery was made from a mica-rich clay which originated in a volcanic area; the temper is identified in hand specimen as crushed granite(?) also sourced in a volcanic region. The absence of any weathering suggests the sherd was buried soon after discard.

Radiocarbon Samples

The following samples were selected from the Hughstown charcoal for AMS radiocarbon dating The results are as follows (Figure 6.96; wood identifications: Susan Lyons, UCC):

Trench 1
HT2015-01 Sample of alder charcoal (heartwood) from sediment (Context 33) at base of ditch of second enclosure.
GrA-64434; 4815 ± 35 BP

HT2015-02 Sample of willow charcoal (heartwood) from upper fill (Context 16) of slot trench (Context 25) inside bank of second enclosure.
GrA-64437; 4825 ± 35 BP

HT2015-03 Sample of alder charcoal (heartwood) from fill (Context 12) of small pit (Context 13) inside bank of second enclosure.
GrA-64436; 4850 ± 35 BP

Trench 2
HT2016-01 Sample of alder charcoal from basal fill (Context 56) of slot trench (C.61), third enclosure of hillfort.

FIGURE 6.95: SHERD OF NEOLITHIC POTTERY (15E322:01) FROM TRENCH 1, HUGHSTOWN.

GrA-67382; 4725±35 BP

HT2016-02 Sample of willow charcoal from basal fill (Context 56) of slot trench (C.61), third enclosure of hillfort.
GrA-67383; 4690±35 BP

HT2016-03 Sample of alder charcoal from lower fill (Context 53) of ditch (C.55), third enclosure of hillfort.
GrA-67384; 4710±35 BP

Trench 3
HT2016-04 Sample of charcoal (no identification) from charcoal lens (Context 46), from a depth of 1.1m on central western side of ditch (C.48), fourth enclosure of hillfort.
GrA-67385; 4730±40 BP

HT2016-05 Sample of holly charcoal from lower fill (Context 47), from lower western side of ditch (C.48), fourth enclosure of hillfort.
GrA-67386; 4685±35 BP

Field No.	Lab No.	C-14 BP	∂13C	95.4% calibration
HT2015-01	GrA-64434	4815±35	-26.29	3661–3521 BC
HT2015-02	GrA-64437	4825±35	-26.73	3694–3523 BC
HT2015-03	GrA-64436	4850±35	-26.25	3704–3533 BC
HT2016-01	GrA-67382	4725±35	-25.06	3635–3376 BC
HT2016-01	GrA-67383	4690±35	-23.44	3629–3369 BC
HT2016-01	GrA-67384	4710±35	-26.19	3362–3373 BC
HT2016-01	GrA-67385	4730±40	-29.04	3636–3376 BC
HT2016-01	GrA-67386	4685±35	-26.74	3627–3369 BC

Figure 6.96: Radiocarbon dates for Hughstown hillfort (calibration after OxCal v.4.2.4).

Discussion

The aim of the Hughstown excavation was to investigate the age, form and construction of the defences of the second, third and fourth hillfort enclosures of this hillfort. Radiocarbon dating of charcoal suggests that construction and/or use of the second enclosure at Hughstown occurred during the Early Neolithic, *c.*3694–3533 BC (Figure 6.96). A result of 3661–3521 BC (GrA-64434) provides a *terminus ante quem* for the digging of the enclosure ditch, while a similar date range of 3694–3523 BC (GrA-64437) for charcoal in the slot trench is probably (but not certainly) part of the same construction event, as is the result of 3704–3533 BC (GrA-64436) for an adjacent pit (posthole?). These radiocarbon dates are supported by the discovery of a single body sherd of prehistoric pottery (15E0321:01), with parallels to burnished wares of the Early or Middle Neolithic.

Radiocarbon dating of charcoal from the C.61 slot trench (GrA-67382 and -67383) suggests that the third enclosure at Hughstown was built *c.*3629–3376 BC (Figure 6.96). This is supported by a date range of 3632–3373 BC (GrA-67384) for charcoal from the lower fill of the adjacent ditch. Radiocarbon dating of charcoal from the lower ditch (GrA-67385 and -67386) suggests that the fourth enclosure at Hughstown was dug during or before 3627–3376 BC (Figure 6.96).

Hillfort construction

The excavation yielded important information on the defences of the second enclosure at Hughstown. This involved the digging of a substantial ditch, the soil from which was piled on the inside to form a bank. The discovery of numerous large stones in the ditch fill suggests that the bank was faced with drystone walling (Figure 6.97). Based on the depth of the ditch (1.5–1.6m from modern ground level), the original height of the earthwork defences at this location is extimated at 3m.

The excavation also provides information on the construction of the third enclosure. This involved the digging of a small ditch, soil from which was probably (but not certainly) piled on the inside to form a bank. A slot trench on the inside of that putative bank contained the burnt remains of what may have been a fence. The discovery of the corresponding terminals of the ditch and slot trench indicates the southern side of an original entrance gap to the third enclosure (Figure 6.98). The full extent and structural details of that opening remain to be clarified by future excavation.

Excavation of the fourth enclosure (Trench 3) revealed a substantial rock-cut ditch, approximately 3m wide and 1.75m deep. There are some indications that the soil and broken rock from this ditch was piled on the inside to form a bank. As with the putative banks of the second and third enclosures, that feature was probably levelled in the early modern era, with much of this material used to infill the adjacent ditches.

Hillfort occupation

The excavation did not produce significant evidence for the occupation of this hillfort. The discovery of charcoal residues at the base of the ditches of the second and fourth enclosures may be connected to early occupation

Figure 6.97: Reconstructed appearance of the exterior stone facing in the bank of the second enclosure at Hughstown, using original stones (C.06) excavated from the ditch in Trench 1.

Figure 6.98: Possible entrance opening to third enclosure at Hughstown, after excavation of terminals of ditch (top) and slot trench in Trench 2 (looking west).

of the hillfort, but there are no details available. The discovery of a single sherd of Neolithic pottery in Trench 1 is also relevant, though this find lacks contextual information.

The excavation did not produce any evidence for the occupation of either the third or fourtth enclosures of the hillfort. This reflects the limited area of excavation, but also the levelled nature of the ground surface, with considerable damage caused by cultivation in the modern era. Geophysical survey identified potential structures at various locations inside the hillfort (Figure 6.74), but none of these have been confirmed by excavation.

Abandonment

The Hughstown excavation did not yield information on the final occupation of this hillfort. Geophysical survey indicates high magnetic gradiometry readings along the defences of both the second and third enclosures. Excavation did not confirm deliberate destruction by fire of the defences of the second enclosure. There is a broad correspondence between the higher gradiometry readings and both the ditch and palisade slot trench, but neither of the latter can be associated with definite burning events. Excavation was able to confirm a major burning event in the slot trench of the third enclosure, possibly connected to deliberate destruction of the defences and site abandonment. No such evidence was found for the fourth enclosure.

7

Chronology

Along with questions of site function, dating is central to what is often called the 'hillfort problem' in Ireland. This is partly because hillforts were not fully recognized as a separate monument type here until the second half of the twentieth century (see Cotter 2012a: 7–15). The first archaeological excavation was conducted in 1948 (Freestone Hill, Co, Kilkenny), and it would be another two decades before the Rathgall project established the reality of Bronze Age hillforts. In the intervening years, the study of Irish hillforts was still reliant on the scholarship of Thomas Westropp (1902 *et seq.*), while their dating was heavily influenced by research in Britain where these monuments have long been associated with the Iron Age. As one commentator observed of the Irish examples, 'these hill-forts are presumably related to the enormous Iron Age hill-top camps of Britain, though, since none have been excavated in this country, we cannot speak with certainty of their date.' (Ó Ríordáin 1942: 2). The notion of Iron Age hillforts became ingrained in the minds of Irish archaeologists, with some disquiet caused by earlier dates proposed for hill-top enclosures at Lyles Hill, Co. Antrim (Evans 1953; also O'Kelly 1956), and Downpatrick, Co. Down (Proudfoot 1954). The possibility of a Bronze Age date was raised by Westropp (1902), who speculated that these monuments may date as far back as 1200 BC (see Chapter 2), and also by Macalister when he proposed an association between Mooghaun hillfort and a large hoard of Late Bronze Age gold (the Great Clare Find of 1954) (Macalister 1928: 82, fn 5).

The Iron Age connection was supported by Barry Raftery's interpretation of Freestone Hill as a Late Iron Age fort built in the fourth century AD, which he considered to be '..a product of an indigenous Celtic group having close contacts with the Roman world, but continuing a tradition of hillfort-building, which had been going on unbroken in Ireland for some considerable period beforehand.' (Raftery 1969: 102). Soon after, he commented on the dating of Class 2 hillforts that '…it is not possible to assign any positive dating to the multivallate sites and rather than suggest a date which would be almost entirely conjecture, it is better to leave the matter completely open pending further definite information.' (Raftery 1972: 53). This was the uncertain climate of hillfort chronology in Ireland around the time Raftery commenced the Rathgall project. The dating of that Wicklow hillfort to the Late Bronze Age (Raftery 1973; 1976) was followed by similar findings from hillforts excavated in the 1990s at Haugheys Fort, Co. Armagh (Mallory 1995), Mooghaun, Co. Clare (Grogan 2005) and Dún Aonghasa, Co. Galway (Cotter 2012). There was a parallel development in Britain where research in the modern era led to the identification of Bronze Age hillforts in several regions (summarised in Brown 2009: 28–33; Harding 2012: 154–6).

7.1 What is the 'Date' of a Hillfort?

Though categorised as a monument *type*, each hillfort had its own unique history from construction to abandonment. This was contingent on many inter-related factors, from natural environment and resources, to cultural context and historical circumstances. Understanding the temporality of a hillfort is more than a chronometric exercise; rather it seeks to explain the interaction of processes that occurred over the course of short-term events and longer-term cycles of political, socio-economic, demographic and environmental change. No hillfort was a self-contained entity, and no matter how powerful these centres became in their respective societies, they were always part of a cultural landscape that ultimately shaped their history.

These questions may be examined using three scales of analysis. The first examines the emergence of a hillfort 'tradition' as a long-scale temporal process, where sites of similar design and purpose were built within a defined period and geographical distribution. Each such 'tradition' must be considered in terms of specific trajectories of origins, duration, and demise. Not all hillforts in any area were built at the same time, nor was their occupation always contemporaneous, which means that sequence must be considered as part of a hillfort 'tradition'. This was not the same as the spread of a belief system manifested in the building of ritual monuments. Hillforts certainly had ritual and ceremonial uses, but their origins are better viewed in social evolutionary terms where the use of such central places was connected to the emergence of early complex societies with hierarchical power structures. Differences in social context may be the main distinction between the Neolithic hillfort and its Bronze Age counterpart, an issue to be considered in the final chapter of this volume.

The second scale of temporal analysis considers the phenomenon of hillfort clusters within a particular landscape. This requires some understanding of the relationships that developed over time between hillforts occupied at the same time in a particular region. These relationships were broad ranging, from economic exchanges to different interactions in the socio-political sphere. They also include various disputes leading to conflict and warfare, which is a particular concern for this project. These interactions are explored in the following two chapters, beginning with a landscape study of an important cluster of sites in the Baltinglass complex, followed by a consideration of hillfort warfare at an inter-regional level in southern Ireland.

The final scale of temporal analysis deals with the chronology of individual hillforts in respect of their life-cycle and historicity. This involved processes of short or long duration that operated on a continuous or episodic basis. These include the construction and subsequent occupation of the hillfort, its destruction and abandonment, any re-building and secondary occupation, ending with final abandonment. Details of pre-hillfort activity and more recent activity at the site must also be considered.

A hillfort was a permanent presence on the landscape long after it was 'abandoned' from its original use or subsequent occupation. These locations acquired different meanings and associations over time. How to measure those engagements is difficult, as they were more often mythologized associations in the landscape rather that physical evidence in the ground. The circumstances of abandonment, whether forced or voluntary, organized or rushed, are important to an understanding of hillfort histories. How this is measured in time is another matter. This includes a consideration of warfare as a critical factor in hillfort abandonment, a subject explored in the next chapter. Understanding the re-use of hillforts by the original community or their descendants, or by a new community arising out of conquest, must also be considered. Many Bronze Age hillforts in Ireland were re-occupied in the early medieval period, with the building of ringfort-type enclosures in their interior (e.g. Rathgall, Mooghaun, Rahally, and possibly Tinoran).

The results from older excavations of hillforts in Ireland, at sites such as Dún Aonghasa, Mooghaun, Haughey's Fort and Rathgall, highlight the problem of obtaining secure dates for the construction, modification and abandonment of hillfort defences. The available dates come from either pre-rampart or ditch contexts and at best provide *terminus ante/post quem* statements on the construction of these hillforts. The problems are considerable, and it should be noted that some excavations in recent times have been unable to obtain dating evidence for the construction or primary occupation of the hillfort; for example, the Class 2 hillfort at Knockanacuig, Co. Kerry (Dunne 2006).

Understanding hillfort chronology is also complicated by the multi-period and prolonged occupation of many sites. This is a significant feature of hillforts excavated in Ireland before the present project, beginning with the complex record from Freestone Hill in Kilkenny that is still not fully resolved. There are similar problems at Clogher, Co. Tyrone, and also at Lyles hill, Co. Antrim and Downpatrick, Co. Down. The most detailed history of prolonged occupation comes from the excavation at Rathgall, Co. Wicklow, the details of which are not fully published.

7.2 This Project

For the reasons discussed above, chronology is a major concern of hillfort research in Ireland. This project addressed the subject in two ways. First, by building a chronology for one hillfort, Clashanimud, Co. Cork, using large-scale excavation and scientific dating to examine the history of this site from construction to abandonment. Second, through sample excavation and radiocarbon dating at nine other hillforts across southern Ireland. The objective was to obtain secure dates for the construction and abandonment of Class 1 and Class 2 hillforts by reconstructing the history of their defences. In some cases information was obtained on site occupation, but in most cases this was not possible because of the targeted nature of those excavations.

The dating of prehistoric hillforts relies entirely on archaeological sources, with an emphasis on diagnostic material culture and the scientific dating of securely stratified material connected to significant events in the history of these sites. The absence of artefacts is a notable feature of the site investigations in this project partly related to the aforementioned excavation strategy. The exception is Clashanimud, where very few artefact finds were made despite a comprehensive sampling exercise. There are no early artefacts from Ballylin, Formoyle, Glanbane, Spinans Hill 1, Sruhaun, or Toor More. The most significant finds come from the Baltinglass complex, and include individual vessels of Bronze Age coarse ware from Rathnagree and Tinoran, as well as a single sherd of Neolithic pottery from Hughstown. While the Rathnagree and Tinoran pots are representative of later Bronze Age coarse ware, their age is established independently by radiocarbon dating of organic residues on both vessels. The Hughstown find, albeit a single sherd, provides useful confirmation of Neolithic occupation in that site.

Radiocarbon dating

Various scientific techniques are available to provide absolute dates in solar calendar years BC/AD for different episodes in the life of a hillfort. Many of these are not easily applicable for reasons of sample availability or the chronological resolution possible. Tree-ring dating should have important applications given the large-scale use of wood in many hillfort defences, but it is rare to recover suitable samples from waterlogged contexts in these sites. An exception is the dendro-date of 1166 BC available for a wood sample from the base of the inner ditch at Haugheys Fort, Co. Armagh, believed to be close in time to the construction of that hillfort (Ballie and Brown 1991; Ballie and Brown 1998). Tree-ring dating was also attempted by this project for charred oak timbers from the inner defences of Clashanimud hillfort, but this was not successful (see Chapter 3).

While scientific methods such as luminescence dating and archaeomagnetic dating have potential for the dating of pottery or burnt defences in these hillforts, they have not been used in Ireland because of the availability of another technique. Radiocarbon dating has transformed the understanding of hillfort chronology here ever since it was first applied on a large-scale at Rathgall hillfort. The scientific independence of this radiometric technique, combined with flexibility of use and acceptable chronological resolution, mean that it is now the principal means of dating prehistoric hillforts in Ireland. This is particularly important given the limited artifact record from many of these sites, and the problematic ceramic record of the later prehistoric period. Radiocarbon dating has been applied to all hillfort excavations in the modern era, with varying degrees of success depending on sample background. It has also been used in the re-dating of some older excavations, notably Downpatrick, Co. Down, Lyles Hill, Co. Antrim, and to a lesser extent, Freestone Hill, Co. Kilkenny. The largest database for a single hillfort comes from Rathgall, where there are 55 radiocarbon dates awaiting final publication.

The method is not without its problems in respect of statistical uncertainty, the need to calibrate results due to fluctuations in atmospheric radiocarbon, issues of sample quality, and the degree of chronological resolution achievable with single or multiple dates. For these reasons it is important to adopt a source-critical approach to the interpretation of individual dates, and not to exceed the limitations of the available results.

Samling strategy

A total of 67 radiocarbon dates were obtained for ten hillforts investigated in this project. These include 55 results for samples of charcoal (48), bone (3), pottery residues (2), and waterlogged wood (2) from primary or secondary contexts in these sites (Figure 7.1). The total number of dates was determined by sampling opportunities during excavation, but also by financial constraints within the project. These provide direct dates, or dating in relative terms (before or after which), for different episodes of hillfort construction, occupation and abandonment. In addition, there are two radiocarbon dates for pre-hillfort activity, namely an Early Bronze Age hearth at Clashanimud, and natural fires of the early Holocene at Glanbane. The remaining ten dates are for peat growth overlying banks and ditches at Ballylin (4), Formoyle (4), Spinans Hill 1 (1) and Sruhan (1). To ensure laboratory consistency, all of these samples were dated by Centre for Isotope Research in the University of Groningen.

Sample context

It is important to consider the degree of certainty by which measured radiocarbon samples are associated with the archaeological contexts that they are intended to date. Following criteria established by Waterbolk (1971) and others, radiocarbon samples can be classified by their degree of association into full certainty, high probability, probability and reasonable possibility. For this project there are instances where a close functional and contextual relationship can be established between the measured sample and different events in the history of a hillfort. Examples of 'full certainty' include Clashanimud, Formoyle, Toor More and Rathnagree hillforts, where burnt wooden elements of the original hillfort defences were excavated in situ. The dating of organic residues on pottery at Rathnagree and Tinoran also falls into this category in respect of episodes of hillfort occupation. There is a 'high probability' of association in the case of a burnt spread from palisade destruction sealed under the later bank of the middle enclosure at Rathnagree, and for a charcoal deposit in a palisade slot trench of the third enclosure at Hughstown.

A 'probability' of association can be assumed for the dating of burnt bone from the palisade trench of the inner enclosure at Toor More, and for the inner enclosure at Glanbane where charcoal deposits occur with stones of a collapsed bank facing. There is a 'reasonable possibility' of association in the case of small amounts of charcoal from the palisade trench of the second enclosure at Hughstown. The same can be argued for three charcoal deposits from the entrance area at Ballylin hillfort, and for charcoal-flecked silt from the base of the stone bank at Spinans Hill 1, though in the latter case the possibility of pre-enclosure activity cannot be entirely ruled out. The Ballylin results are given weight by comparison with dates for other Class 2 hillforts in Ireland, while those from Spinans Hills 1 have parallels with the Early Neolithic record from nearby Hughstown.

Several of these hillforts have radiocarbon dates for charcoal obtained from enclosure ditches. The samples mostly come from the basal fill, close in time to the original cut. They include ditch samples from both enclosures at Clashanimud; the inner enclosure at Glanbane; both enclosures at Toor More; the fourth enclosure at Tinoran, and the three enclosures at Hughstown. The results provide *terminus ante quem* age (TAQ) ranges for

Hillfort	Lab No.	C-14 result BP	95.4% calibration	Sample context	Site sample No.
Clashanimud, Cork	GrN-29042	2920±50	1263–976 BC	Charcoal at base of ditch, inner enclosure	CD2004-01
	GrN-29043	3075±20	1409–1280 BC	Palisade post charcoal, bank of inner enclosure	CD2004-02
	GrN-29044	3000±20	1371–1130 BC	Palisade post charcoal, bank of inner enclosure	CD2004-03
	GrN-29045	2965±20	1260–1116 BC	Charcoal layer within bank of inner enclosure	CD2004-04
	GrN-29046	3050±20	1396–1231 BC	Palisade post charcoal, bank of inner enclosure	CD2004-05
	GrA-42677	2985±35	1378–1089 BC	Charcoal at base of ditch, outer enclosure	CD2008-01
	GrA-42678	3160±40	1511–1303 BC	Pre-bank charcoal, outer enclosure	CD2008-02
	GrA-42683	2940±35	1258–1027 BC	Palisade post charcoal, bank of inner enclosure	CD2008-03
	GrA-42682	2910±35	1214–1006 BC	Palisade post charcoal, entrance to inner enclosure	CD2008-04
	GrA-42679	3105±35	1442–1273 BC	Palisade post charcoal, entrance to inner enclosure	CD2008-05
	GrA-42684	2915±35	1216–1008 BC	Palisade post charcoal, entrance to inner enclosure	CD2008-06
	GrA-67392	2745±35	976-815 BC	Charcoal at base of ditch, inner enclosure	CD2016-01
Glanbane, Limerick	GrA-54508	2850±30	1111–927 BC	Charcoal at base of ditch, inner enclosure	GB2012-02
	GrA-54509	2860±30	1118–929 BC	Charcoal at base of ditch, inner enclosure	GB2012-03
Ballylin, Limerick	GrA-54510	2975±30	1368–1059 BC	Charcoal from gate posthole, inner enclosure	BL2010-01
	GrA-54599	2930±50	1279–980 BC	Charcoal beneath bank slip, inner enclosure	BL2010-02
	GrA-54616	2915±45	1258–979 BC	Charcoal from entrance passage, inner enclosure	BL2010-04
Formoyle, Clare	GrA-54956	2840±30	1108–917 BC	Charcoal from inside bank of inner enclosure	FM2012-01
	GrA-54957	2890±30	1195–978 BC	Charcoal at base of ditch, inner enclosure	FM2012-02
	GrA-54958	3125±35	1494–1289 BC	Pre-bank charcoal, inner enclosure	FM2012-03
	GrA-54961	2880±30	1192–939 BC	Charcoal from stake fence, outer enclosure bank	FM2012-05
	GrA-54963	2900±30	1207–1004 BC	Charcoal from stake fence, outer enclosure bank	FM2012-06
	GrA-54964	2880±30	1192–939 BC	Charcoal from stake fence, outer enclosure bank	FM2012-07

	GrA-54965	2920±35	1218–1011 BC	Pre-bank charcoal, outer enclosure	FM2012-08
Toor More, Kilkenny	GrA-58572	2970±30	1281–1058 BC	Palisade trench charcoal, inner enclosure	TM2013-01
	GrA-58614	2845±35	1114–917 BC	Charcoal at base of ditch, inner enclosure	TM2013-02
	GrA-58575	2935±35	1257–1019 BC	Waterlogged wood at base of ditch, inner enclosure	TM2013-03
	GrA-58574	2945±30	1258–1049 BC	Waterlogged wood, base of ditch, inner enclosure	TM2013-04
	GrA-59103	2975±35	1369–1056 BC	Burnt bone from palisade trench; inner enclosure	TM2013-05
	GrA-58576	2920±35	1218–1011 BC	Palisade trench charcoal, outer enclosure	TM2013-06
	GrA-58577	3000±30	1377–1126 BC	Charcoal from burnt spread, outer enclosure	TM2013-07
Rathnagree, Wicklow	GrA-60925	3045±40	1414–1135 BC	Charcoal from palisade timber, inner enclosure	RNG2014-01
	GrA-60927	3055±40	1417–1213 BC	Palisade post charcoal, inner enclosure	RNG2014-02
	GrA-60929	3050±40	1417–1208 BC	Charcoal spread, middle enclosure (Period 1)	RNG2014-03
	GrA-60930	3015±40	1395–1126 BC	Charcoal in burnt stake, middle enclosure (Period 1)	RNG2014-04
	GrA-60931	3020±40	1397–1128 BC	Charcoal from palisade timber, outer enclosure	RNG2014-05
	GrA-60932	3035±40	1411–1131 BC	Palisade post charcoal, outer enclosure	RNG2014-06
	GrA-63007	3240±35	1535–1450 BC	Charcoal in spread under Period 2 bank, Trench 2	RNG2014-07
	GrA-63008	3170±35	1495–1415 BC	Residue from pot sherd. Base of ditch, Trench 2	RNG2014-08
Sruhaun, Wicklow	GrA-64430	3030±35	1375–1225 BC	Charcoal from burnt spread beneath bank	SR2015-01
Tinoran, Wicklow	GrA-64438	2600±30	805–785 BC	Charcoal from base of ditch, Trench 1	TN2015-01
	GrA-64571	2685±30	890–805 BC	Burnt bone from hearth spread, Trench 2	TN2015-02
	GrA-64572	2640±30	825–795 BC	Burnt bone from hearth spread, Trench 2	TN2015-03
	GrA-64439	2865±35	1110–980 BC	Charcoal from beneath stone bank, Trench 2	TN2015-04
	GrA-64440	2905±35	1155–1020 BC	Carbonised residue from pot sherd, Trench 2	TN2015-05
Hughstown, Kildare	GrA-64434	4815±35	3645–3535 BC	Charcoal from base of ditch, second enclosure.	HT2015-01

	GrA-64437	4825±35	3655–3535 BC	Charcoal from fill of slot trench, second enclosure	HT2015-02
	GrA-64436	4850±35	3690–3540 BC	Charcoal in small pit in bank area, second enclosure	HT2015-03
	GrA-67382	4725±35	3635–3376 BC	Charcoal in basal fill of slot trench, third enclosure	HT2016-01
	GrA-67383	4690±35	3629–3369 BC	Charcoal in basal fill of slot trench, third enclosure	HT2016-02
	GrA-67384	4710±35	3632–3373 BC	Charcoal in lower fill of ditch, third enclosure	HT2016-03
	GrA-67385	4730±40	3636–3376 BC	Charcoal from enclosing ditch, fourth enclosure	HT2016-04
	GrA-67386	4685±35	3627–3369 BC	Charcoal from enclosing ditch, fourth enclosure	HT2016-05
Spinans Hill 1, Wicklow	GrA-67387	4835±35	3697–3527 BC	Charcoal from silt on lower stones of bank	SH2016-01
	GrA-67389	4835±35	3697–3527 BC	Charcoal from old ground surface under bank	SH2016-02

Figure 7.1: Radiocarbon dates from Irish hillfort excavations in this project. Calibration based on OxCal v.4.2.4. Results for ten peat samples from Ballylin, Formoyle, Sruhaun, and Spinans Hill 1, as well as pre-hillfort activity (early Holocene charcoal from Glanbane, and an Early Bronze Age hearth at Clashanimud) are not included.

construction of the defences at those sites, which have a greater value when combined with dates from other contexts. This was possible with the outer defences at Clashanimud, and also the inner enclosure at Formoyle, where a broad date range for construction was established using charcoal results from pre-bank and lower ditch contexts. Caution is required with ditch samples, as problems of residuality and admixture can arise. This occurred with charcoal from the ditch of the outer enclosure at Glanbane, which is dated to the early Holocene, and also with a residual find of Period 1 pottery in the Period 2 ditch of the middle enclosure at Rathnagree.

Problems can also arise with radiocarbon dates for charcoal from old ground surfaces beneath hillfort banks. In most cases the origin and 'own age' of the charcoal is unknown, and so the results must be viewed with caution. These dates provide a broad *terminus post quem* (TPQ) for the bank construction, which as in the aforementioned examples can be combined with TAQ results from an accompanying ditch.

Sample quality

There are several areas of concern, including the age of the sample before human use, and the possibility of contamination and admixture. The former can be minimised by the use of samples with a limited 'own age', as opposed to material such as the heartwood of long-lived tree species, where the time difference may amount to several centuries. The first five results in this project, taken from the 2004 excavation of the inner defences at Clashanimud, are conventional radiocarbon dates (GrN-29042 to -29046) obtained for bulk charcoal samples with no botanical identifications. The subsequent identification of this charcoal raised a concern as to the implications for radiocarbon dating of the use of mature oak posts in the palisade defences. This was addressed by dating a second series of samples from similar contexts (GrA-42679, 42682–4), using the AMS radiocarbon method to date individual fragments of oak sapwood to minimise the sample age effect. Where possible, all subsequent dates from Clashanimud and other hillforts in the project were obtained using AMS-dating of short-lived sample material.

The possibility of contamination and admixture with younger or older material was minimised by careful excavation of samples from closed contexts, and by the selection of individual fragments of charcoal, bone and wood as opposed to bulk samples. Multiple samples were dated where available, again within the financial constraints of the project. Where possible, a combination of sample materials were used to date primary contexts. This was most successful for the inner defences at Toor More, where samples with a limited own age were dated, namely ash branch charcoal from a burnt palisade and burnt bone from associated occupation. These results are combined with AMS dates for charcoal (short-lived hazel growth) and waterlogged wood (alder twig and oak sapwood samples) from an adjacent ditch, to provide a broad chronology of those defences from construction to abandonment. In the same way, AMS dates for bone and pottery residues from Tinoran are combined with the charcoal results for the defences of the third enclosure at this hillfort.

A final issue in relation to sample quality relates to the dating of peat growth at several hillforts, primarily to obtain TAQ markers for specific elements of the defences. These include results from Ballylin, Formoyle, Sruhaun, and Spinans Hill 1. In most cases the peat sample is dated to the modern era, which is somewhat surprising given that the samples were taken at some depth, either from the upper fill of a ditch or else from beneath in situ or collapsed bank material. This can be explained by contamination of the peat sample by modern roots, which might have been minimised had separate humin and humic fractions of the peat samples been dated. The peat results are not without value, as those from Ballylin establish that the ditches of both enclosures pre-date the medieval period, while one from an outer ditch at Formoyle probably rules out a third enclosure at that hillfort.

Radiocarbon calibration

Radiocarbon dates are not dates at all, but rather measurements of an isotope ratio that requires some form of statistical probability analysis using a calibration curve to convert them to calendrical time (Bronk Ramsey 2009). This process of calibration is essential to date the history of these hillforts. Some events, such as construction and destruction, occurred over a short time period, whereas the occupation of a hillfort might extend over centuries, with the excavation record representing a time-averaged palimpsest of information. This can be analysed in more detail where stratigraphic sequences are available, but a further problem is that radiocarbon results generally only have an accuracy of 25 years or more, making it difficult to focus in on events of short duration. This may not be significant in terms of longer-term processes in these sites, but is an issue in establishing absolute chronology of events such as warfare that operated over very short time-scales.

The radiocarbon results for each hillfort in this project are converted to calendrical time using the OxCal software (v.4.2.4) that works with the IntCal13 calibration curve. The probable age range for each result is presented at two-sigma (95.4%) confidence level. The results from each site are then visually compared using multiple plots.

Bayesian analysis (Kevin Kearney)

Bayesian statistical modelling is used to consider a series of radiocarbon dates in combination with relative archaeological information ('prior information'), such as stratigraphic and contextual details of the samples used. This can create formal date estimates that are often much more precise than single calibrations. It can also provide robust probability distributions for specific boundary events within the constructed models. The boundaries are estimated probabilities which usually correspond to the beginning and ending of archaeological phases. A general introduction to the Bayesian approach in radiocarbon calibration is provided by Buck *et al.* (1996), with the methods used to build these chronologies in archaeology outlined in Bayliss *et al.* (2007) and Bayliss (2007).

Six hillforts, Clashanimud, Formoyle, Rathnagree, Tinoran, Toor More and Hughstown, were initially selected as having potential for Bayesian analysis. Rathnagree and Tinoran were subsequently excluded due to a lack of viable radiocarbon dates for this type of statistics. Bayesian analysis of the other four sites was undertaken to refine the construction date of these hillforts. The radiocarbon dates were calibrated using the datasets published by Reimer *et al.* (2013) and the computer program OxCal 4.2.4 (Bronk Ramsey 1995, 1998, 2001, 2009). The calibrated date ranges cited are quoted in the form recommended by Mook (1986), with the end points rounded outward to 10 years and calculated according to the maximum intercept method (Stuiver and Reimer 1986). The resuts are cited at two sigma (95.4% confidence) unless stated otherwise. The ranges quoted in italics are posterior density estimates, derived from Bayesian modelling. The probability distributions are derived from the probability method (Stuiver and Reimer 1993). A minimum of five securely dated radiocarbon determinate are required for each Bayesian model (Whitehouse *et al.* 2014). In the absence of short-lived, single entity material, all dates used in the models are derived from charcoal samples. Samples which were residual in their context or were composed of material with an in-built age-offset were only included in the models as providing a *terminus post quem* for its context or for any stratigraphically later deposits. Additional residual material, or those from samples which potentially contain long-lived material, could not be used as *terminus ante quem* in the chronological models (Bayliss *et al.* 2011).

7.3 Results

Clashanimud

A total of thirteen radiocarbon dates are available for this Class 2 hillfort (Figure 7.1). Twelve of these relate to the hillfort defences, with one result (GrA-42687) connected to an earlier hearth dated 2277–2030 BC. There are no samples for a light wooden fence that was part of the bank of the outer enclosure. The latter was built *c.*1511–1089 BC, based on a TAQ date from the base of the ditch (GrA-42677), and a TPQ result from beneath the bank (GrA-42678).

There are ten dates from three separate points of excavation along the defences of the inner enclosure (Figure 7.2). Four of these (GrN-29043–6) come from bulk samples of mature oakwood, dated by conventional radiocarbon analysis to the period *c.*1409–1116 BC. To minimize the sample age effect, four samples of oak sapwood were subsequently dated by the AMS radiocarbon method. The results allow the date range for the palisade to be reconciled at two-sigma calibration to 1214–1027 BC (GrA-42682–4), with one outlier at 1442–1273 BC (GrA-42679).

There are two radiocarbon dates for charcoal samples from the ditch of the inner enclosure (Trench 1). The first is an age of 1263–976 BC (GrN-29042) for unidentified charcoal from the base of the ditch, a sample that may include oakwood from the bank palisade mixed with fuel used to burn those defences. A second result from the same ditch context is more useful, as it comes from willow charcoal that represents either brushwood fuel used to burn the defences, or shrub growth in the ditch that caught fire as the burning palisade collapsed from the bank. In either case, the dating of this willow charcoal to 976–815 BC (GrA-67392) may relate with some certainty to the destruction event, which therefore occurred one to two centuries after the hillfort was built (Figure 7.3).

Bayesian analysis

Based on the requirements for Bayesian models, only the radiocarbon dates for the palisade defences of the inner enclosure are suitable for analysis. Four of these (GrN-29043, GrN-29044, GrN29045 and GrN-29046) were obtained from bulk samples of charcoal. As these are from palisade posts of mature oak, and so likely to be produce a large offset due to the 'old wood' effect, they were excluded from the model and treated as a *terminus post quem* date for construction of the inner palisade. Three statistically consistent radiocarbon dates, GrA-42682, GrA-42683 and GrA-42684 (X2-Test: df=2; T'=0.4; T'(5%)=6.0), obtained for oak sapwood from the same palisade, were included in the model. Another result, GrA-42679 (X2-Test: df=3; T'=21.226; T'(5%)=7.8) for oak sapwood from the same palisade is statistically inconsistent, and so was excluded from the model.

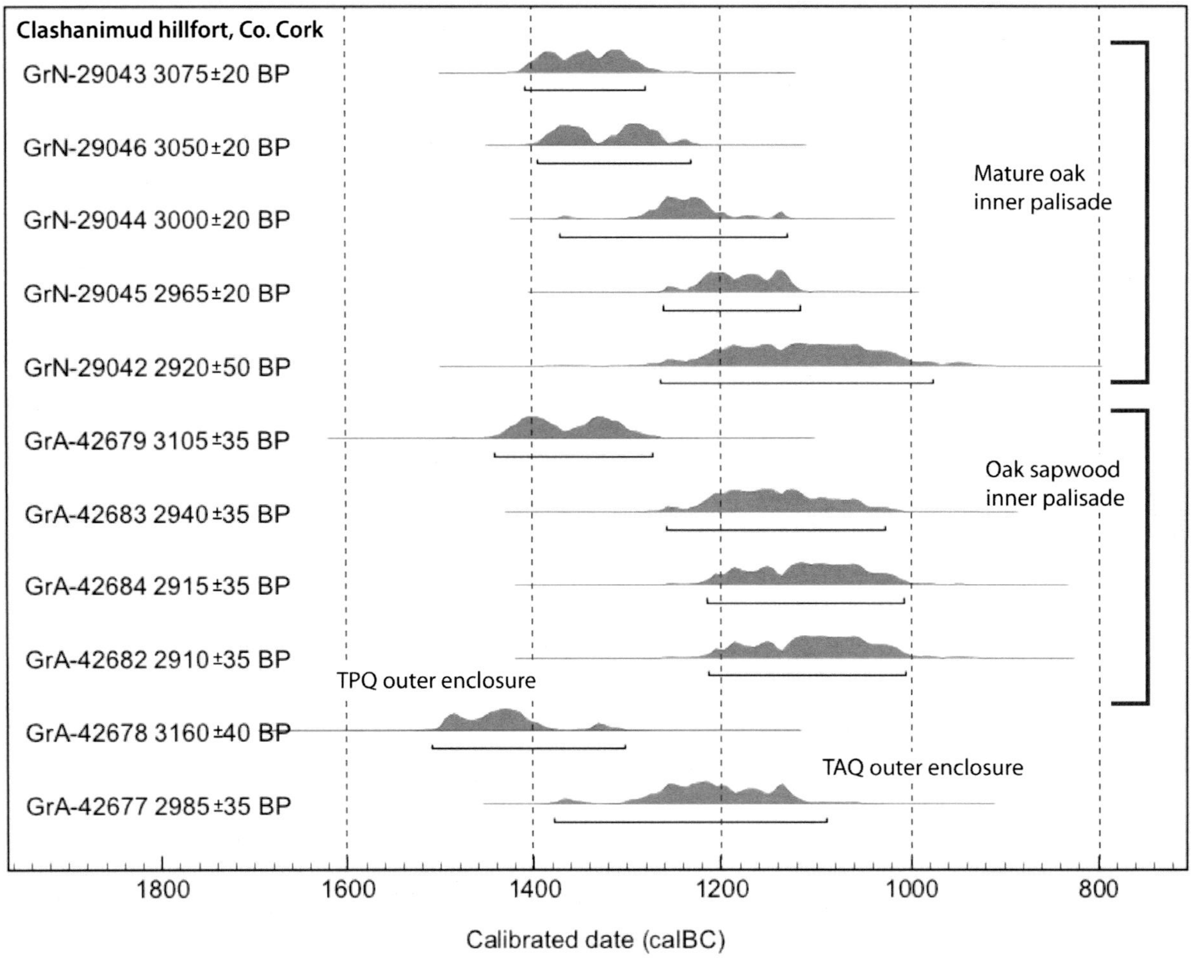

FIGURE 7.2: RADIOCARBON DATES FOR ENCLOSING ELEMENTS OF CLASHANIMUD HILLFORT, CO. CORK (CALIBRATION AFTER OXCAL V.4.2.4).

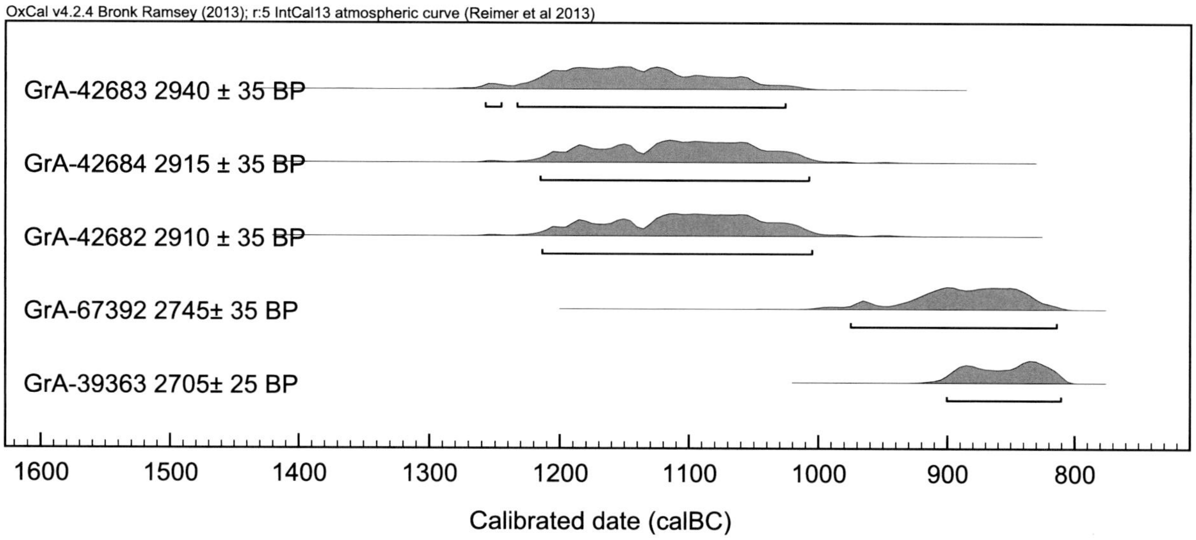

Figure 7.3: Comparison of calibrated dates for construction (GrA-42682, -42683 and -42684), and burning (GrA-67392) of Clashanimud hillfort, Co. Cork. The result (GrA-39363) for the primary cremation burial at Knockatreenane barrow is also shown (calibration after OxCal v.4.2.4).

These dates were plotted using OxCal 4.2.4 (Bronk Ramsey 2009) to propose refined dates for the construction of the palisade of the inner enclosure at Clashanimud (Figure 7.4). Bayesian modelling returned a date range of 1510–1040 BC (95% probability), 1240–1080 BC (68% probability) for the construction (Aoverall=106.1).

Glanbane, Co. Kerry

There are three radiocarbon results from this Class 2 hillfort (Figure 7.1). Two of these (GrA-54508 and -54509) are for samples of charcoal from the base of the ditch of the inner enclosure. Together, they indicate a TAQ of 1118–927 BC during or before which the ditch was dug (Figure 7.5). The charcoal was found with stones from a collapsed facing on the adjacent bank. Whether this relates to a possible destruction event is unclear, as the charcoal cannot be linked to any wooden component in the original bank structure. The third result from Glanbane (GrA-54507) is 7079–6813 BC for charcoal that probably derived from natural fires during the early Holocene.

Ballylin, Co. Limerick

There are seven radiocarbon results from this Class 2 hillfort (Figure 7.1), three of which are significant results from the entrance of the inner enclosure. These are broadly similar results for charcoal found beneath bank slip (GrA-54599), in the northern gate posthole (GrA-54510), and in the entrance passage (GrA-54616). Together, the three results indicate a calibrated date of 1258–1059 BC for use of the inner entrance of the hillfort (Figure 7.6). While the source and 'own age' of the charcoal is unknown, some connection is very likely to the occupation of this hillfort. The calibrated date of 141–393 AD for peat growth in the lower ditch (GrA-54600) indicates a time when the hillfort was abandoned. There is also a result of 1030–1189 AD for a peat core (GrA-54954) from the same ditch on the north/north-west side of the hillfort.

The chronology of the outer enclosure at Ballylin is less clear, as no radiocarbon samples were obtained from primary contexts in the Trench 3 excavation. The lower peat fill in that ditch is dated to the modern era (GrA-54953), while a peat sample from the ditch on the north/north-west side of the hillfort is dated 1484–1648 AD (GrA-54955). Though not very informative, the latter does indicate the outer enclosure was built before the modern era.

Formoyle, Co. Clare

There are eleven radiocarbon results from this Class 2 hillfort (Figure 7.1). The dating of charcoal (GrA-54957) provides a TAQ of 1195–978 BC for the ditch of the inner enclosure. This can be combined with calibrated date ranges of 1108–917 BC (GrA-54956) for charcoal from the ground surface inside the adjacent bank, and a TPQ of 1494–1289 BC (GrA-54958) for charcoal under the bank (Figure 7.7). Taken together, this suggests construction and use of the inner enclosure in or around the eleventh century BC.

This is consistent with results for the defences of the second (outer) enclosure. Charcoal from burnt stakes

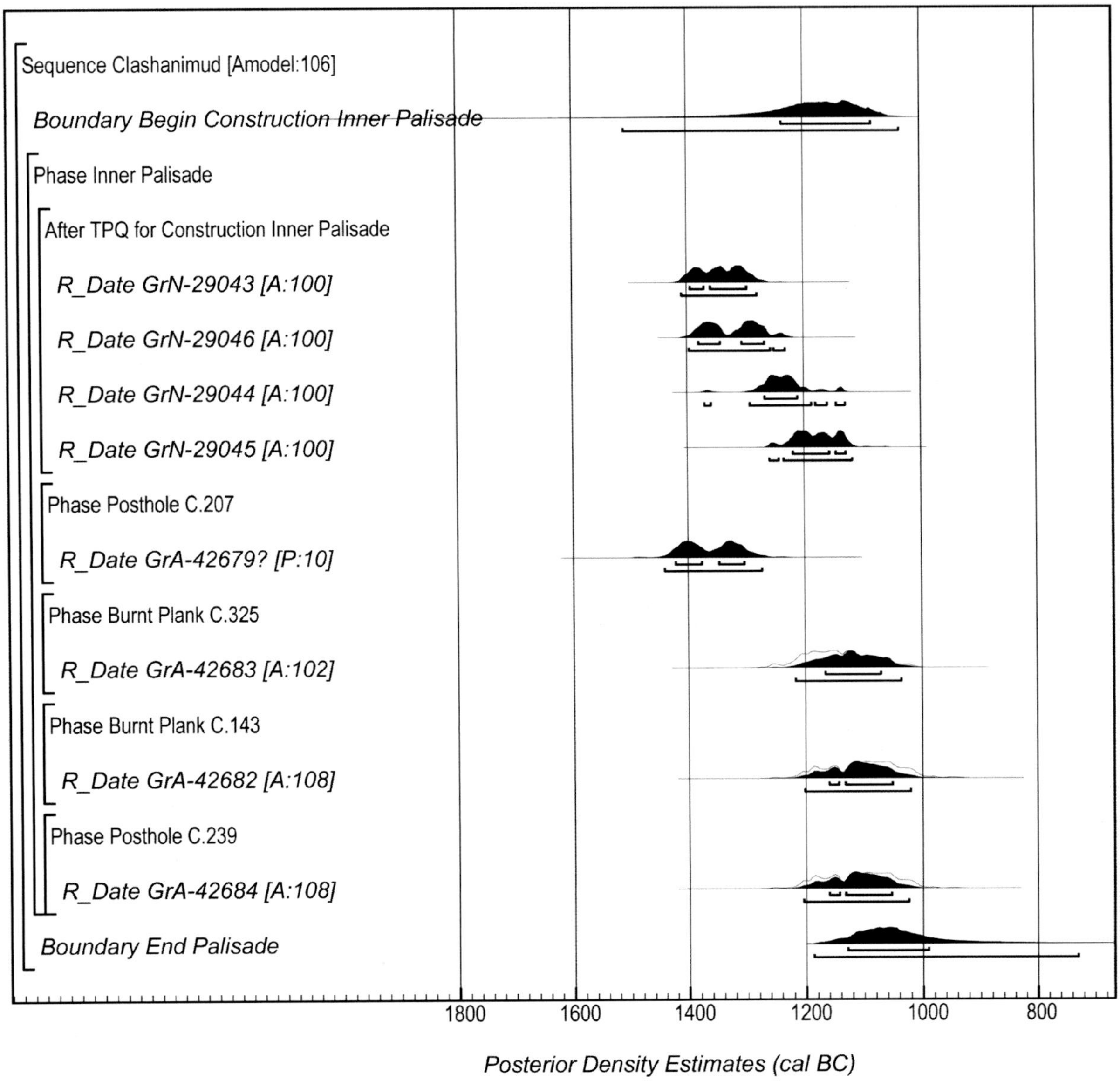

FIGURE 7.4: BAYESIAN MODEL FOR DEFENCES OF INNER ENCLOSURE AT CLASHANIMUD HILLFORT, CO. CORK (COURTESY KEVIN KEARNEY).

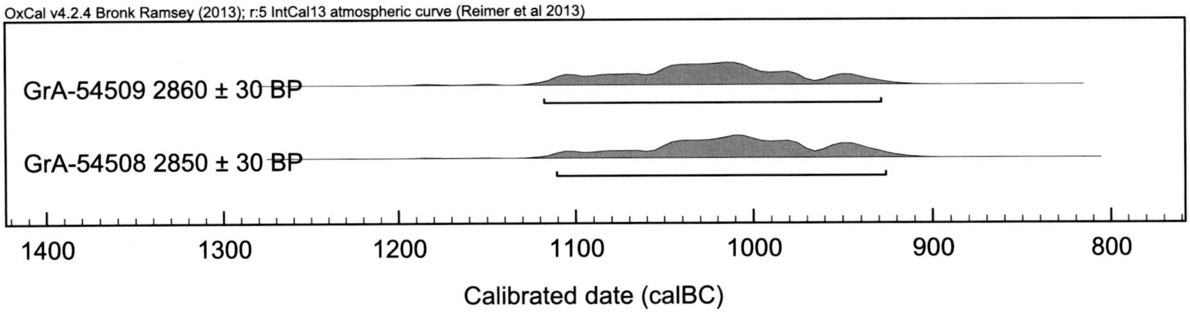

FIGURE 7.5: RADIOCARBON DATES FOR CHARCOAL IN DITCH OF INNER DEFENCES OF GLANBANE HILLFORT, CO. KERRY (CALIBRATION AFTER OXCAL V.4.2.4).

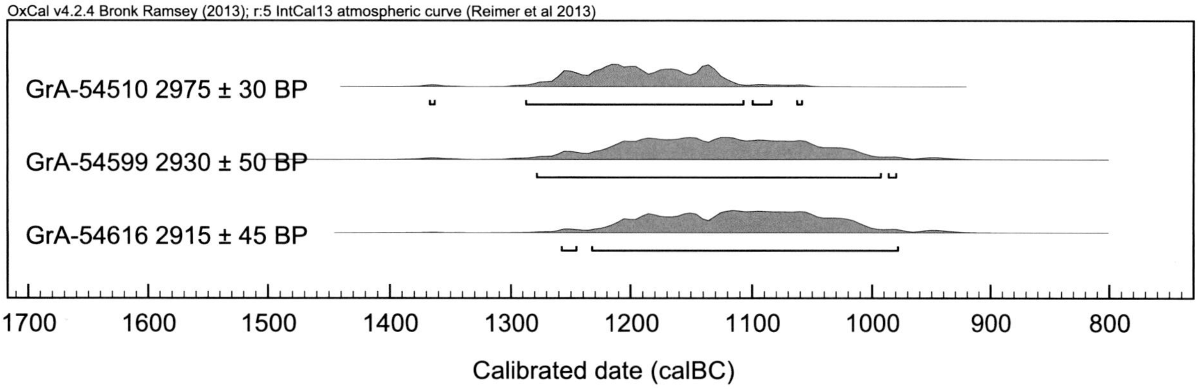

FIGURE 7.6: RADIOCARBON DATES FOR ENTRANCE AREA TO INNER ENCLOSURE OF BALLYLIN HILLFORT, CO. LIMERICK (CALIBRATION AFTER OXCAL V.4.2.4).

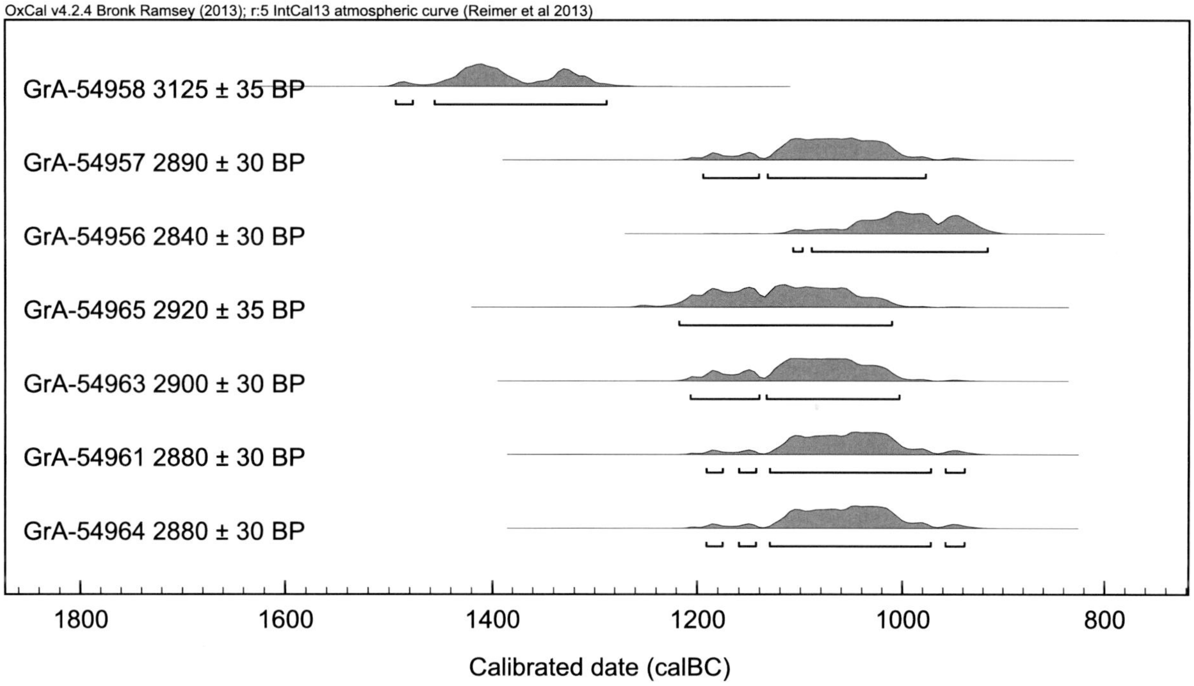

FIGURE 7.7: RADIOCARBON DATES FOR DEFENCES OF THE TWO ENCLOSURES OF FORMOYLE HILLFORT, CO. CLARE (CALIBRATION AFTER OXCAL V.4.2.4).

within that bank have calibrated date ranges of 1207–1004 BC (GrA-54963), 1192–939 BC (GrA-54961) and 1192–939 BC (GrA-54964) respectively. Combined with a pre-bank charcoal result of 1218–1011 BC (GrA-54965), this also points to occupation of the second enclosure around the eleventh century BC.

Bayesian analysis

Three radiocarbon dates (GrA-54956, GrA-54957 and GrA-54958) are available for the defence of the inner enclosure at Formoyle, with four results (GrA-54961, GrA-54963, GrA-54963 and GrA-54965) for that of the second enclosure. GrA-54956 was obtained from hazel charcoal recovered from the base of peat inside the inner bank, GrA-54957 from hazel charcoal recovered from the basal ditch fill, while GrA-54958 was obtained from ash charcoal recovered from beneath the inner bank and can be treated as a *terminus post quem* date for construction of the inner palisade. Three statistically consistent radiocarbon determinates, GrA-54961, GrA-54963 and GrA-54964 (X2 Test df:=2; T'=0.3; T'(5%)=6.0) were obtained for burnt stakes in the bank of the second enclosure. An additional radiocarbon date, GrA-54965, recovered from beneath the bank of the second enclosing element was excluded from the model and treated as a *terminus post quem* date for construction of the second enclosure.

These dates were plotted using OxCal 4.2.4 (Bronk Ramsey 2009) to propose refined dates for Formoyle (Figure 7.8). Bayesian modelling returned a date range of 1230–1010 BC (95% probability), 1140–1040 BC (68% probability) for the construction (Aoverall=121).

Toor More, Co. Kilkenny

There are seven radiocarbon results from this Class 2 hillfort (Figure 7.1), including five for the defences of the inner enclosure and two from those of the outer enclosure. The results for the inner enclosure include dates for charcoal and bone from the palisade trench (GrA-58572 and GrA-59103) calibrated 1281–1058 BC, as well as combined calibrations of 1257–1049 BC for two wood samples (GrA-58574–5) from the base of the adjacent ditch (Figure 7.9). These four dates indicate that the enclosing elements of the inner enclosure were built and destroyed some time approximately 1270–1050 BC. A further date is available for the inner enclosure, for a charcoal sample (GrA-58614) from the base of the ditch, which gave a calibrated result 1114–917 BC.

The two charcoal results (GrA-58576–7) from the defences of the outer enclosure are both connected to the wooden palisade inside the bank and ditch arrangement. These provide calibrated date ranges 1377–1126 BC and 1218–1011 BC respectively, which overlap with results for the inner enclosure to place the construction of the hillfort in the twelfth or eleventh centuries BC.

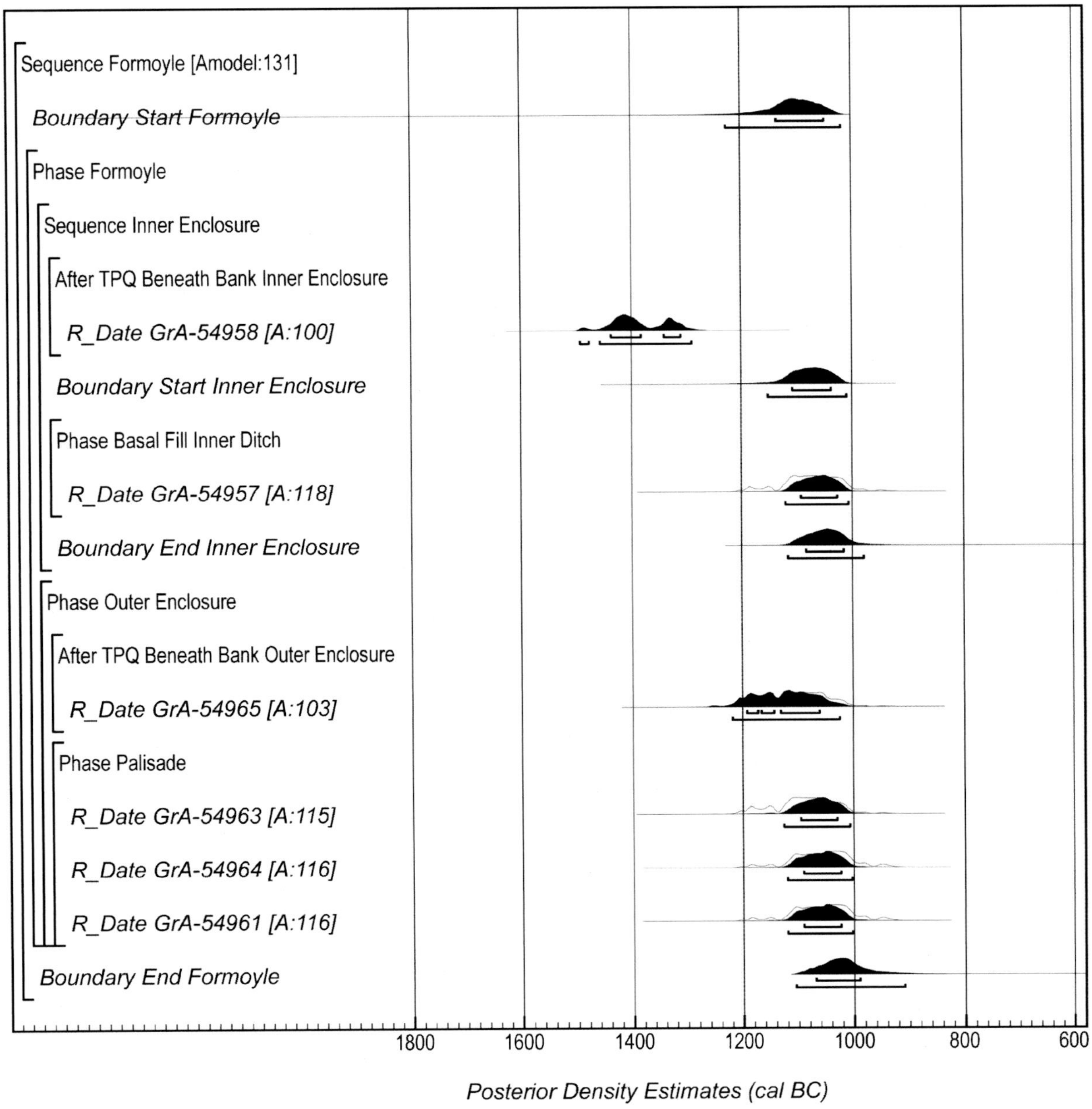

FIGURE 7.8: BAYESIAN MODEL FOR DEFENCES OF BOTH ENCLOSURES AT FORMOYLE HILLFORT, CO. CLARE (COURTESY KEVIN KEARNEY).

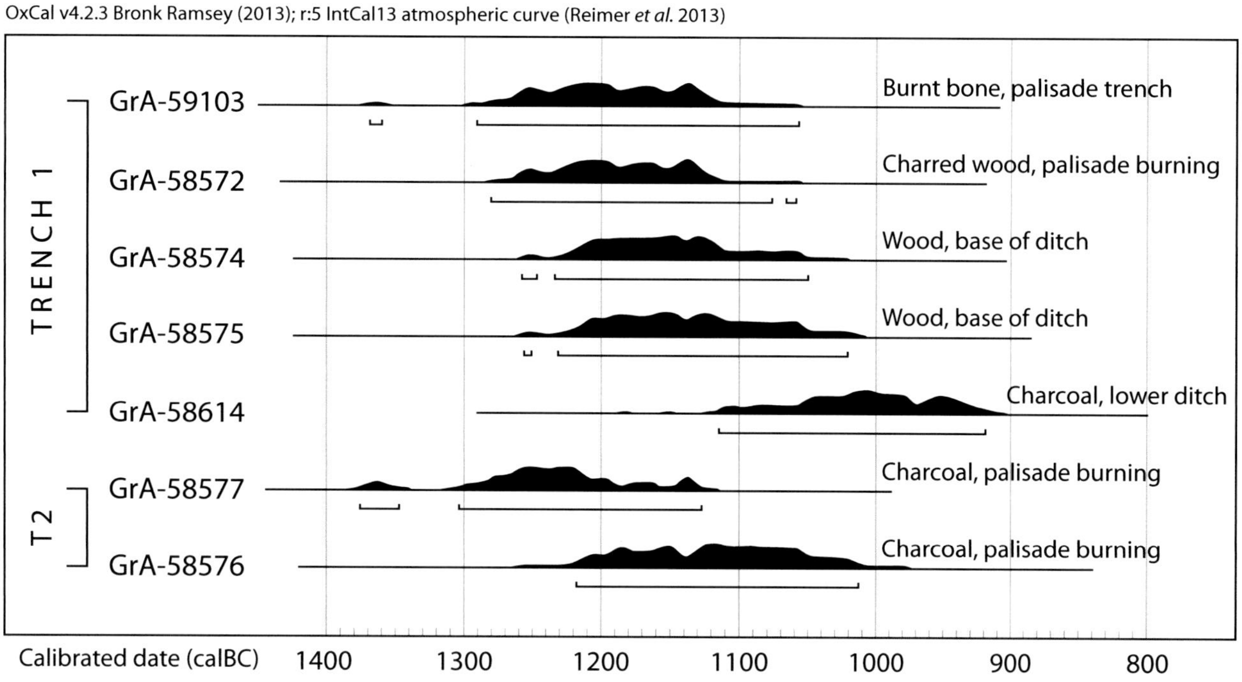

FIGURE 7.9: RADIOCARBON DATES FOR DEFENCES OF BOTH ENCLOSURES AT TOOR MORE HILLFORT, CO. KILKENNY (CALIBRATION AFTER OXCAL V.4.2.4). NOTE: GRA-59103 WAS LABELLED INCORRECTLY AS GRA-58713 IN O'BRIEN (2014-5, 21-2).

Bayesian analysis

Seven radiocarbon determinates were obtained from samples recovered during excavations at Toor More hillfort. Five dates, GrA-58572, GrA-58574, GrA-58575, GrA-58614 and GrA-59103), related to the inner enclosure, while the remaining dates, GrA-58576 and GrA-58577, related to the palisade of the outer enclosure. Two statistically consistent radiocarbon determinates (GrA-58572 and GrA-59103) (X2 Test: df=1: T'=0.0: T'(5%)=3.8) from the inner palisade and two statistically consistent radiocarbon determinates, GrA-58576 and GrA-58577, (X2 Test: df=1: T'=3.0: T'(5%)=3.8) from the outer palisade were included in the model. GrA-58574 and GrA-58575 from the basal and lower ditch fills of the inner ditch. were statistically consistent (X2-Test: df=3 T'=1.0; T'(5%)=7.8) with the dates from the palisade on the bank of the inner enclosure, and so probably relate to the construction of the enclosure.

These dates, were plotted using OxCal 4.2.4 (Bronk Ramsey 2009) to propose refined dates for the construction of the second enclosure at Toor More (Figure 7.10). Bayesian modelling returned a date range of 1320–1130 BC (95% probability), 1260–1160 BC (68% probability) for construction (Aoverall=113) of the hillfort.

Rathnagree, Co. Wicklow

A total of eight radiocarbon dates are available for the Class 2 hillfort (Figure 7.1). These include two samples from the enclosing elements of the inner enclosure (Trench 1); four from those of the middle enclosure (Trench 2); and two from those of the outer enclosure (Trench 3). Radiocarbon dates for the inner (1417–1135 BC), middle (1535–1126 BC), and outer palisaded enclosures (1411–1128 BC) indicate that this hillfort was built *c.*1400–1200 BC (Figure 7.11). The radiocarbon results suggest that the three palisaded enclosures of the Period 1 hillfort were broadly contemporary, an interpretation supported by their similar form and methods of construction.

The Period 1 radiocarbon results from Trench 2 are supported by the discovery of coarse ware pottery in the ditch of the middle enclosure. While this is a Period 2 context connected to re-building of those defences, the pottery find is probably residual from Period 1 activity. This is supported by the discovery of a sherd of similar pottery (14E227-20) in a burnt layer (C.30) under the Period 2 bank. A date of 1495–1415 BC for organic residue (unknown type) from one of the sherds in the ditch overlaps with the earliest date (1535–1450 BC) from the same burnt layer. No radiocarbon dates are available for the Period 2 defences, but this re-building is likely to have occured immediately after the burning event. This is indicated by the preservation of a distinct destruction layer (C.30) beneath the Period 2 bank.

Sruhaun, Co. Wicklow

There are two radiocarbon results from this Class 1 en-

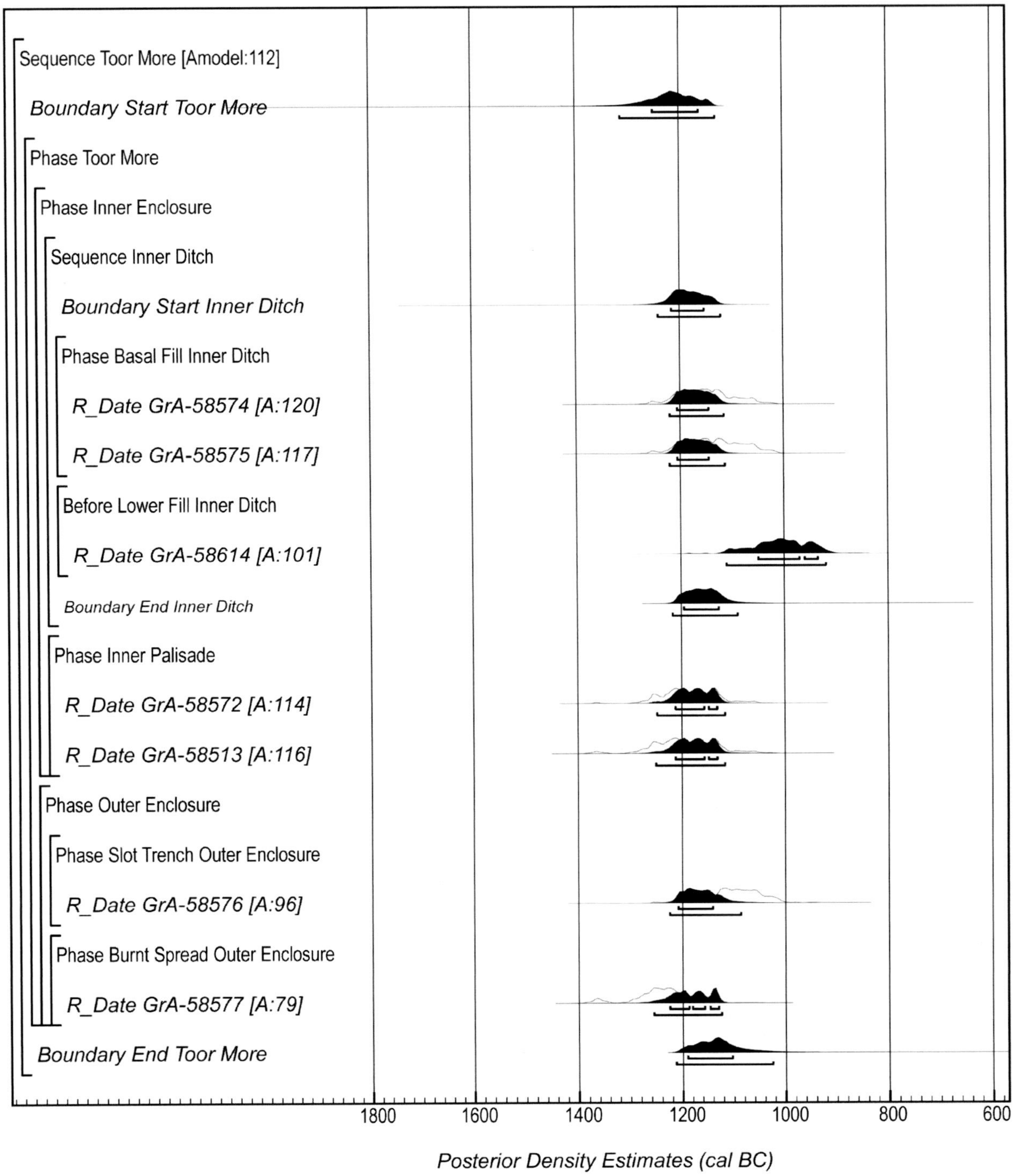

FIGURE 7.10: BAYESIAN MODEL FOR DEFENCES OF BOTH ENCLOSURES AT TOOR MORE HILLFORT, CO. KILKENNY (COURTESY KEVIN KEARNEY).

closure (Figure 7.1). A charcoal date 1405–1132 BC (GrA-64430) is probably (but not definitely) derived from the burning of a pre-enclosure fence (Figure 7.12). Whatever the source of the GrA-64430 charcoal, the stratigraphic record does not indicate a significant interval of time between the burning of this fence and the overlying enclosure bank. The dating of peat growth (GrA-64432) in the inner ditch suggests that feature dates to the early modern era.

Tinoran, Co. Wicklow

There are five radiocarbon results from this Class 2 hillfort (Figure 7.1). These indicate a date range of 1155–980 BC for construction of the third enclosure. This is based on the dating of organic residue on pottery found on the construction surface (GrA-64440), and on charcoal from construction sediment directly below the stone bank (GrA-64439). Both samples can be connected to

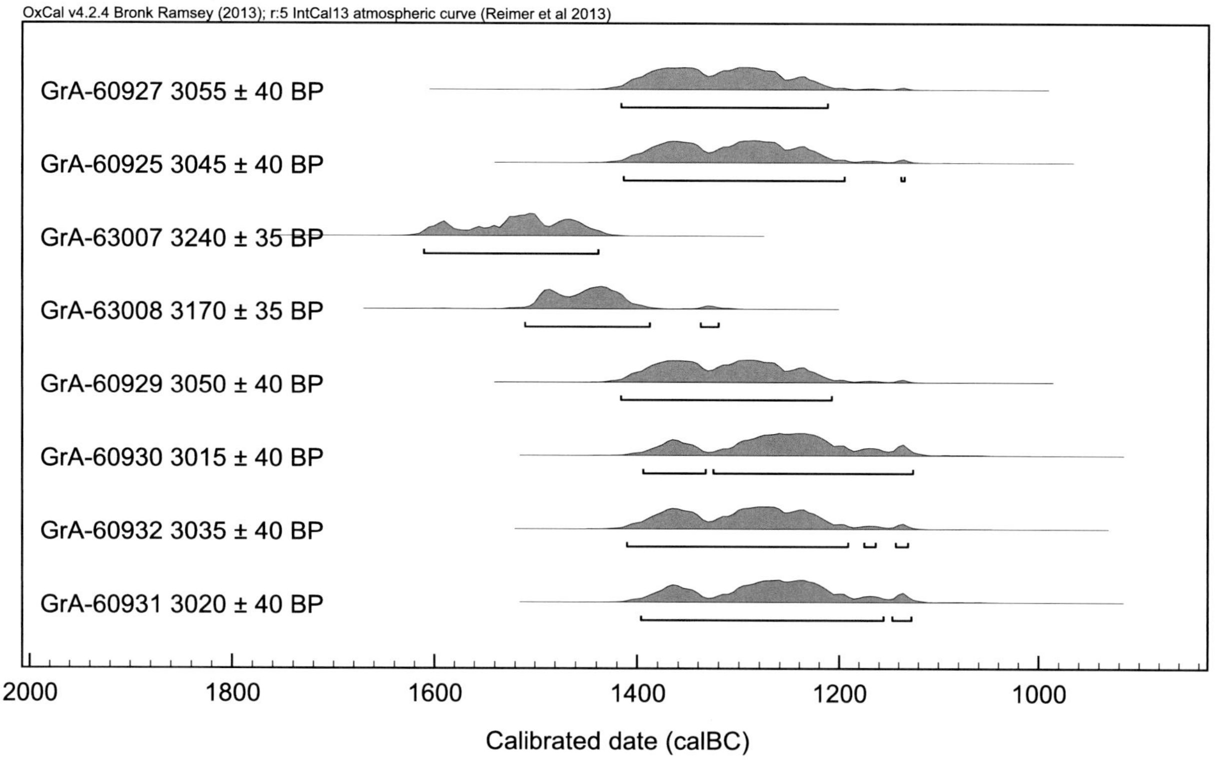

FIGURE 7.11: RADIOCARBON DATES FOR DEFENCES OF THE TWO ENCLOSURES OF RATHNAGREE HILLFORT, CO WICKLOW (CALIBRATION AFTER OXCAL V.4.2.4).

FIGURE 7.12: RADIOCARBON DATES FOR ENCLOSING ELEMENT OF SRUHAUN HILLFORT, CO WICKLOW (CALIBRATION AFTER OXCAL V.4.2.4).

habitation during construction of the enclosure bank (Figure 7.13). Radiocarbon dates for burnt bone (GrA-64571 and -64572) from a small hearth inside the bank are connected to continued occupation of the hillfort in the ninth century BC. This is supported by a single date 826–763 BC for charcoal (GrA-64438) from the base of the ditch of the fourth enclosure.

Hughstown, Co. Kildare

A total of eight radiocarbon dates are available for charcoal from this Class 2 hillfort (Figure 7.1). These include three samples from the defences of the second enclosure (Trench 1); three from those of the third enclosure (Trench 2); and two from those of the fourth (outer) enclosure (Trench 3). The results indicate that construction and/or use of the second enclosure at Hughstown occurred during the Early Neolithic, c.3694–3533 BC (Figure 7.14). A result of 3661–3521 BC (GrA-64434) provides a TAQ for the digging of the enclosure ditch, while a similar date range of 3694–3523 BC (GrA-64437) for charcoal in the slot trench is probably (but not certainly) part of the same construction event, as is the 3704–3533 BC (GrA-64436) date for an adjacent pit (posthole?). This is supported by the discovery of a single pottery sherd with parallels to burnished wares of the Early/Middle Neolithic.

The dating of charcoal from an inner slot trench (GrA-67382 and -67383) suggests that the third enclosure at Hughstown was built c.3629–3376 BC. This is suppor-

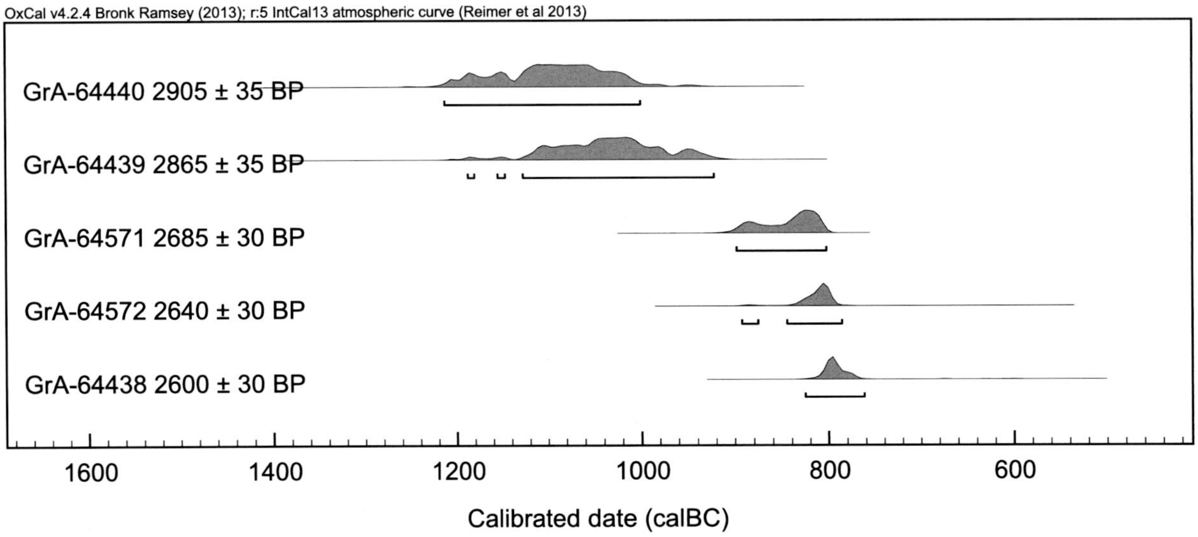

FIGURE 7.13: RADIOCARBON DATES FOR DEFENCES OF THE TWO ENCLOSURES OF TINORAN HILLFORT, CO WICKLOW (CALIBRATION AFTER OXCAL V.4.2.4).

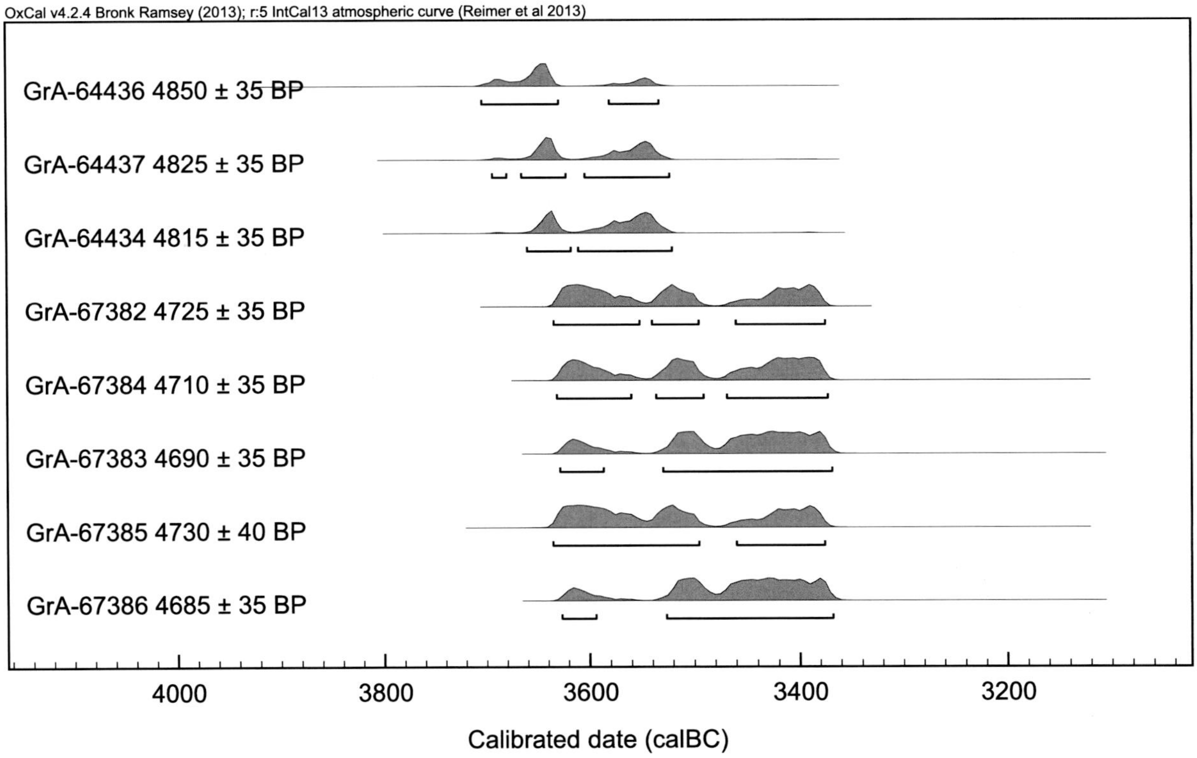

FIGURE 7.14: RADIOCARBON DATES FOR DEFENCES OF THREE ENCLOSURES OF HUGHSTOWN HILLFORT, CO KILDARE (CALIBRATION AFTER OXCAL V.4.2.4).

ted by a date range of 3632–3373 BC (GrA-67384) for charcoal from the lower fill of the adjacent ditch. Radiocarbon dating of charcoal (GrA-67385 and -67386) suggests that the ditch of the fourth enclosure was dug during or before 3627–3376 BC. In conclusion, while the nature of the Hughstown radiocarbon samples makes it difficult to assess the chronological relationship of those three enclosing elements, a date of *c*.3600–3400 BC can be proposed for occupation of this hill during the Early Neolithic.

Bayesian analysis

Eight radiocarbon dates were obtained from charcoal samples obtained during excavation at Hughstown. Three statistically consistent dates from the second enclosure, GrA-64434, GrA-64437 from the palisade, and GrA-64436 from the basal fill of the ditch (X2-Test: df=2; T'=0.5; T'(5%)=6.0), probably relate to the construction of the second enclosure. GrA-67382 and GrA-67383 from the palisade of the third enclosure, and GrA-

67384 from the basal fill of its ditch, also show statistical consistency (X2-Test: df=2; T'=0.5; T'(5%)=6.0). The dates from the fourth enclosure were excluded from the model for the reasons outline above.

These dates were plotted using OxCal 4.2.4 (Bronk Ramsey 2009) to propose refined dates for the defences of the second and third enclosure at Hughstown (Figure 7.15). Bayesian modelling returned a date range of 3780–3530 BC (95% probability), 3690–3550 BC (68% probability) for the construction of these defences (Aoverall=93).

Spinans Hill 1, Co. Wicklow

The date of this Class 1 hillfort relies on an age range of 3697–3527 BC for two samples of charcoal-flecked silt (GrA-67387 and -67389) from the base of the enclosing bank (Figure 7.16). Neither sample can be connected directly to the bank construction, or to occupation of the enclosure. As the possibility of surface burning from earlier activity cannot be ruled out, the age of this bank remains to be confirmed by further excavation. The results, however, do invite comparison with the Hughstown evidence.

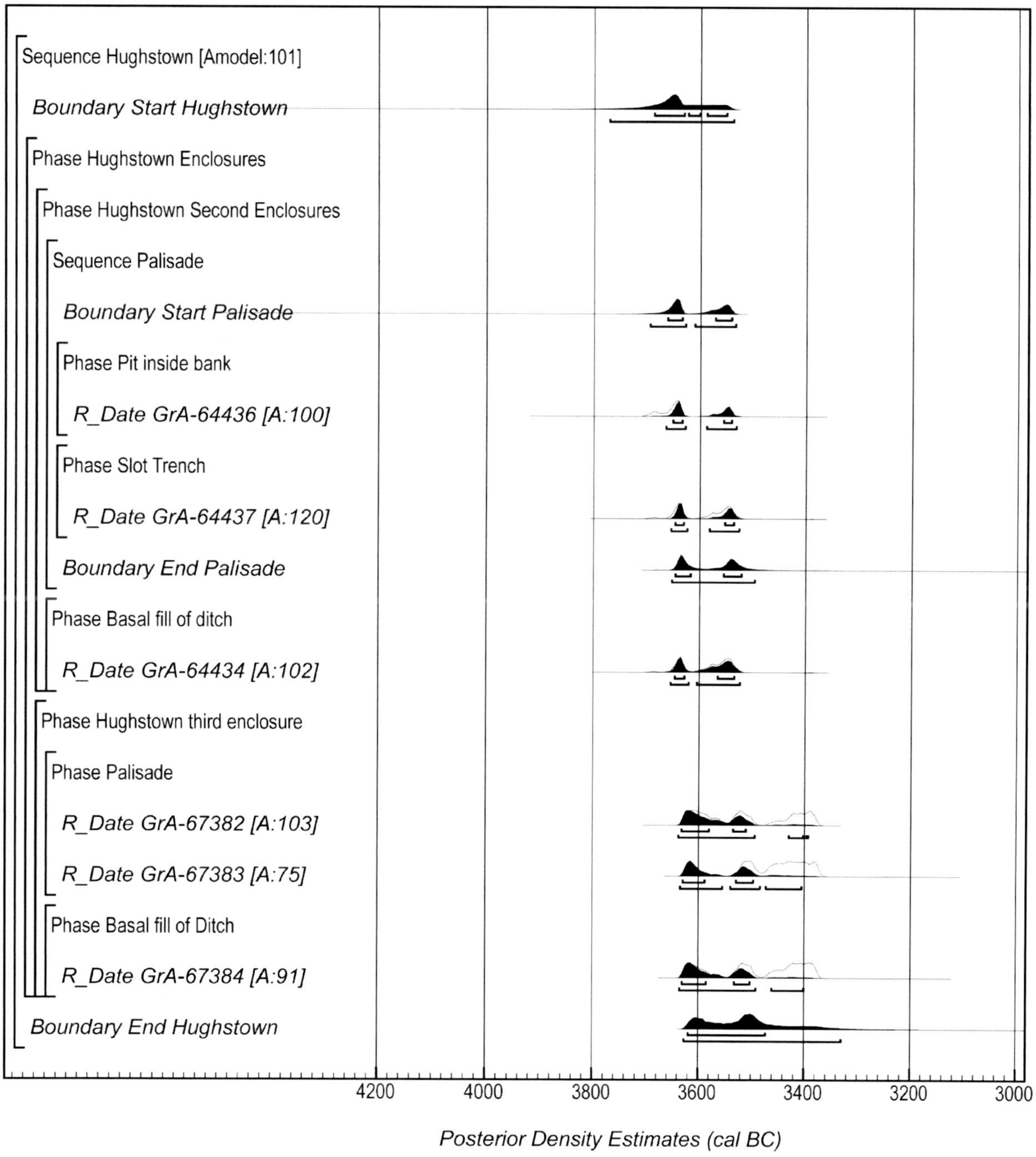

FIGURE 7.15: BAYESIAN MODEL FOR DEFENCES OF SECOND AND THIRD ENCLOSURES AT HUGHSTOWN, CO. KILDARE (COURTESY KEVIN KEARNEY).

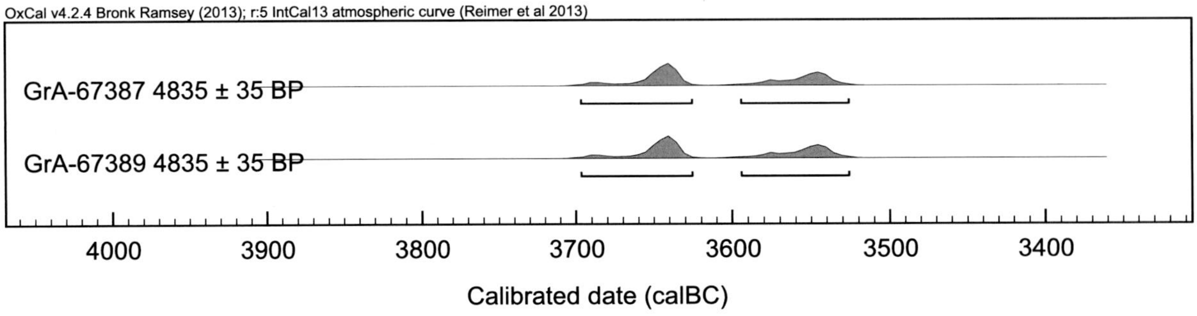

FIGURE 7.16: RADIOCARBON DATES FOR ENCLOSING BANK OF SPINANS HILL 1 HILLFORT, CO WICKLOW (CALIBRATION AFTER OXCAL V.4.2.4).

7.4 Discussion

As one expert observed, 'however much statistical analysis we do, radiocarbon dates are still reliant on the underlying assumptions of the radiocarbon method—any problems with the samples, their context, their association with each other, or with the calibration curve, will have implications for the accuracy of our chronologies.' (Bronk Ramsey 2009: 358). The Bayesian models for Clashanimud, Formoyle, Toor More and Hughstown have a rather large posterior density estimate for the construction of each of these hillforts. The long tails on the posterior density estimates arise as the models contain insufficient data to effectively assess and counteract the statistical scatter of radiocarbon dates. The absence of workable samples from each site that could be confidently included in the chronological models means it is not possible to refine the posterior density estimates for the construction of each hillfort to less than a few centuries.

Considering their large size and prominent landscape setting, it is not surprising to find evidence of earlier occupation at many hillforts. In some instances the presence of an ancient burial mound conveyed a special significance to that location, with the Neolithic passage tomb at Rathcoran in the Baltinglass complex, and the Early Bronze Age burial cairns at Freestone Hill, Co. Kilkenny, and Carntigherna, Co. Cork, being good examples. While no such associations were investigated in this project, evidence of earlier activity was found at two hillforts. These include an Early Bronze Age hearth at Clashanimud, and a wooden fence structure pre-dating the Sruhaun enclosure. The former has no connection with the building of the hillfort a thousand or so years later. The Sruhaun find is significant, as the burning of that fence was followed immediately by the building of the bank enclosure, with both structures likely to be used for animal enclosure on that side of Tuckmill Hill, probably by the occupants of nearby Rathnagree hillfort.

The recovery of construction dates for five Bronze Age sites in this project is very significant in terms of hillfort chronology in Ireland. While older excavations provide broad indications of construction date, these hillforts now have high quality radiocarbon dates for specific construction contexts. The results from Clashanimud, Formoyle, Toor More, Rathnagree and Tinoran are based on radiocarbon dating of wooden elements that were part of the original hillfort defences. The results from three other Class 2 hillforts, Glanbane, Ballylin, and Hughstown, provide important dates for primary occupation, though how close these are to construction is uncertain. Finally, the results from Sruhaun and Spinans Hill 1 are significant for the dating of univallate hillforts and hilltop enclosures in Ireland.

From this information, it is now possible to date the construction and/or primary occupation of eight Class 2 hillforts. This adds significantly to the number of hillforts dated in Ireland, while recognizing that further investigations are required to refine the internal chronology of the sites concerned. Another important result is that for the first time there is specific information available on the destruction and abandonment of individual hillforts. This has been examined in some detail for Clashanimud, where the interval between palisade construction and burning can be assessed. It is less clear for the burning of wooden defences at Formoyle, Toor More and Rathnagree, as in all three instances the radiocarbon results for burnt wood date the construction rather than the destruction event. Unfortunately, it was not possible to identify charcoal samples connected to fuel used in the burning of those hillforts. Any such fuel was probably consumed in the intense fires that ensued, with the only surviving charcoal coming from the final burning of the palisade posts. Similar problems apply to the dating of destruction at Glanbane and Hughstown, where the radiocarbon dates come from charcoal deposits and not wooden elements of the defences burnt *in situ*. The dates are significant for both sites, but again it is not possible to separate construction from destruction in the radiocarbon results.

While these investigations offer valuable information on defences, they provide little insight into the occupation history of these ten hillforts. The most comprehensive investigation was at Clashanimud, where there is no obvious record of occupation despite the apparent use of this site over two centuries or so. The radiocarbon record from the third and fourth enclosures at Tinoran suggests prolonged occupation of that hillfort, possibly lasting two to three centuries to around 800 BC. The extent of investigation in the other eight hillforts was too limited to recover details of site occupation and abandonment. Rathnagree is the only hillfort with evidence of re-building following destruction. That record is particularly interesting as the occupants chose to replace one of the three burnt palisades with a bank-and-ditch earthwork. There are no details as to the subsequent occupation of that site or its final abandonment.

There is no evidence that these ten hillforts were re-occupied in later periods. That is a feature of earlier excavations of Class 2 hillforts, including Mooghaun, Rahally and Rathgall, where there are strong records of early medieval occupation with ringfort-type enclosures. It is possible that the innermost enclosure ('Round-O') at Tinoran is of that period, and possibly also that at Hughstown, but this remains to be confirmed for both sites. It is notable that no artifacts connected to occupation in the Iron Age or early medieval period were recovered from any of the ten hillforts in this project.

Implications for hillfort chronology in Ireland

The results of this dating programme confirm that there is no chronological basis to Raftery's (1972) classification of Irish hillforts. The eight Class 2 hillforts investigated in this project have many design features in common, but range in date from the Early Neolithic (Hughstown) to the Middle Bronze Age (Rathnagree) and Late Bronze Age (Ballylin, Clashanimud, Glanbane, Formoyle, Tinoran and Toor More). The two Class 1 hillforts excavated are probably of Early Neolithic (Spinans Hill 1) and Middle Bronze Age (Sruhaun) date. Prior to these results, there was a growing acceptance in Ireland that multiple enclosure (Class 2) hillforts were Late Bronze Age in date, whereas univallate (Class 1) examples were more likely to be Iron Age. This generalisation is no longer tenable, which means that each hillfort must be independently dated.

It is now apparent that there was more than one prehistoric hillfort tradition in Ireland. The earliest of these can be linked to the first farming communities of the Early Neolithic. This is followed two millennia later by the emergence of the Bronze Age hillfort, a parallel phenomenon to developments in Britain and mainland Europe. These were first built in the Bishopsland Phase of the Middle Bronze Age *c.*1400–1200 BC, and in increasing numbers during the ensuing Roscommon Phase (1150–1000 BC) of the Late Bronze Age. A smaller number of hillforts were built and occupied in the next two centuries, during the Dowris Phase of the Late Bronze Age, with the use of hillforts declining sharply after 800 BC for reasons that remain unclear.

Neolithic hillforts

A small, but growing, number of hill-top enclosures of Neolithic date are recorded in Ireland. The first of these was excavated from 1937–51 at Lyles Hill, Co. Antrim, where Evans (1953) identified Neolithic occupation evidence that was initially linked to an earthen bank enclosure. Subsequent excavation in 1987–8 dated this bank to the Bronze Age, but obtained dates of 3330–2920 BC and 2600–2350 BC respectively for two parallel palisades that may have surrounded the hill during the Neolithic (Simpson and Gibson 1989: 215).

To the north of Lyles Hill is the Neolithic enclosure on Donegore Hill Co. Antrim. This Early Neolithic settlement was enclosed by two parallel rock-cut ditches with an inner palisade. There was prolonged occupation during the Neolithic, beginning *c.*3800–3400 BC, with some re-occupation during the Bronze age (Mallory *et al.* 2011). Reference can also be made to palisaded Neolithic settlements at Thornhill, Derry (Logue 2003) and Tullahedy, Co. Tipperary (Cleary and Kelleher 2011). Also relevant is the causewayed enclosure excavated at Magheraboy, Co. Sligo (Danaher 2007), where an area of 2ha was enclosed by a wooden palisade with irregular lengths of ditch outside it. There is evidence for prolonged use of this enclosure *c.*4000–3600 BC, possibly for both ceremonial and special purposes, but not for permanent residence.

There are parallels in design and date between the Hughstown site in this project and the Donegore and Magheraboy enclosures. These sites have obvious elements of protection, where defensive lines were created using wooden palisades with external ditches. The significance of the Early Neolithic enclosure on Spinans Hill 1, broadly contemporary with Hughstown in the Baltinglass complex, must also be considered. That site is different to Hughstown is design and enclosing elements, and so may have had a different purpose.

The function of these Neolithic enclosures is much debated, with comparisons made to causewayed enclosures in southern Britain used for assembly and ceremonial purposes. There is also evidence that some of these sites were fortified against attack; for example, Hambledon Hill, Dorset (Mercer 1988), Crickley Hill, Gloucestershire (Dixon 1988), Orsett, Essex (Hedges and Buckley 1978), and Hembury near Exeter (Liddell 1930). How Neolithic enclosures in Ireland related to the origins of the Bronze Age hillfort tradition is a subject for the final chapter of this book.

Bronze Age hillforts

The results of this project are significant for the dating of later Class 2 hillforts in Ireland. Prior to this, the accepted date range for Bronze Age hillforts in Ireland was 1200–800 BC. The new dates confirm that while the twelfth and eleventh centuries BC were certainly significant in terms of hillfort construction, these sites may have existed as early as the fourteenth century BC. The new consideration is the dating of Rathnagree to the Middle Bronze Age. Whether this means the Baltinglass complex, and the Middle Bronze Age activity at nearby Rathgall, was seminal in respect of hillfort origins in Ireland needs to be considered.

These results establish the Bishopsland phase of the Middle Bronze Age (*c.*1400–1150 BC), equivalent to Taunton (1400–1275 BC) and Penard phases (1275–1140 BC) in Britain, as an important period in the emergence of the Bronze Age hillforts in Ireland (typo-chronology after Becker 2012; Needham 1997; Waddell 2010). The building of these multiple enclosure hillforts intensified in the early part of the Roscommon phase (1150–1000 BC), which marks the beginning of the Late Bronze Age in Ireland and is equivalent to the Wilburton (1140–1020 BC) phase of metalworking in Britain. There is evidence for continued construction of Class 2 hillforts in the tenth and ninth centuries BC, during the transition from the Roscommon to the Dowris phase of the Late Bronze Age. Some hillforts continued to be occupied into the eighth century BC, but not thereafter, a situation often presented as an apparent collapse of Bronze Age society.

The results of this project cast some light on the internal chronology of Class 2 multiple enclosure hillforts. The sampling of these sites was specifically designed to address the question of '...whether these complex sites are the result of a single building phase or whether they acquired their multiple ramparts as a consequence of rebuilding and expansion.' (Raftery 1972: 45). Of the eight Class 2 hillforts investigated in this project, three sites have concentric enclosures that are closely contemporary in radiocarbon terms. These include Hughstown and Rathnagree with their three enclosures, and Toor More with two examples. Three other sites have concentric enclosures that are broadly contemporary within the same cultural period, two each in the case of Clashanimud and Formoyle, and two of the four or five enclosures at Tinoran. There are no dates for the outer enclosures of the remaining two sites, Ballylin and Glanbane.

The results confirm that Class 2 hillforts with two or three enclosures were probably built as a single design. The possibility that some sites were extended over time may apply to very large hillforts such as Tinoran, and possibly to some examples with three enclosures. The purpose of these multiple enclosures will be considered in Chapter 9.

The dating of Class I (univallate) hillforts is more uncertain, especially considering the results from two examples excavated in this project. The radiocarbon dates from Spinans Hill 1 suggest that some of these univallate enclosures date to the Neolithic. The Middle Bronze Age date for Sruhaun is relevant, but that site may be better regarded as a hill-top animal enclosure than a hillfort. Some Class 1 hillforts were certainly occupied during the Late Bronze Age. Freestone Hill in Kilkenny had intermittent activity from the Early Bronze Age to the Late Iron Age, and the enclosure itself was initially dated to the fourth century AD (Raftery 1969). A re-interpretation of coarse ware and glass bead finds, along with a single radiocarbon date, now suggests a Late Bronze Age (Dowris Phase) date for the enclosure, though questions remain (Raftery 1995; Ó Floinn 2000; Waddell 2010). The same uncertainty applies to the univallate enclosures at Downpatrick (Cathedral Hill), Co. Down (Proudfoot 1954; Raftery 1976) and Clogher, Co. Tyrone (Warner 2009), both of which have Bronze Age artefact associations. The dating of other excavated Class 1 hillforts is also uncertain, including an example at Knockacarrigeen Hill, Co. Galway (Carey 2002). Overall, it seems likely that Class 1 hillforts include sites from Neolithic to Iron Age date, with no obvious morphological distinction over that long period. The category also includes sites that should not be regarded as hillforts, but could have specific uses such as animal stockades or ceremonial enclosures. Some of these overlap with the category of hill-top enclosures discussed by Grogan (2005b). The dating of these smaller enclosures is very uncertain, even where there has been excavation, as at Clenagh, Co. Clare (Grogan and Daly 2005).

Finally, there is new evidence of Late Bronze Age occupation of inland promontory forts in Ireland. Recent excavations at Knockhu, Co. Antrim, uncovered significant occupation from the early tenth to the late ninth centuries BC, probably associated with the earthwork defences (McDonald 2016). This is the only Class 3 hillfort now dated, but the results are very significant for that class of monument.

Iron Age hillforts

Reference has already been made to the re-occupation of some Bronze Age hillforts during the early medieval period, a subject that is outside the scope of this volume. Given the history of research in Ireland, it is timely to re-visit the possibility of an Iron Age association. This is a subject that has emerged in post-excavation analysis of Rathgall, where some Iron Age occupation of the Bronze Age hillfort is now confirmed (Becker pers. comm.). The same is true for Dún Aonghasa (Cotter 2012) and probably Clogher (Warner 2009).

The investigation of ten sites in this project did not identify any evidence for the construction or occupation of hillforts during the Iron Age (*c.*600 BC–400 AD). Overall, there is little evidence that hillforts were built in Ireland during this period, though there was activity at some Bronze Age sites. This, of course, excludes consideration of the large univallate, internally ditched, enclosures of the Irish Iron Age, sites such as Rath na Riogh at Tara, Co. Meath (Roche 2002), Dún Ailinne (Johnston and Wailes 2007), and Navan Fort, Co. Armagh (Lynn 2003). These are generally regarded as ceremonial enclosures rather than hillforts, even though they do contain elements of fortification. While their exact use is uncertain, such sites are best treated separately from prehistoric hillforts.

A chronological model for the Baltinglass hillforts

The new picture of the Baltinglass complex presents a succession of hillforts and hill-top enclosures built at various times in the late prehistoric period, while also allowing for some overlap in the use of individual sites. The radiocarbon evidence from five of nine recorded sites points to distinct phases of construction over a 3000-year period. This commenced with the large enclosures built at Hughstown and Spinans Hill in the Early Neolithic (*c.*3700–3500 BC). Followed two millennia later by the construction of Rathnagree hillfort and the nearby Sruhaun enclosure during the Middle Bronze Age (*c.*1400–1100 BC). Tinoran hillfort was built in the early part of the Late Bronze Age (c.1100–1000 BC), and was occupied possibly as late as 900–800 BC. There is no evidence that hillforts were built in Baltinglass after this period, though this may change when the remaining four sites (Brusselstown Ring, Kilranlagh, Rathcoran and Spinans Hill 2) are eventually dated.

A number of these site histories may have overlapped, where they were occupied, or in some cases built, during the same period. This includes the Early Neolithic enclosures at Spinans Hill 1 and Hughstown, located on the eastern and western sides of the complex respectively. The two sites are very different in form, which may reflect differences in function. The same applies to Rathnagree and Sruhaun on Tuckmill Hill, which may have been in contemporaneous use during the Middle Bronze Age. Again, the morphological difference may be related to function, where Sruhaun was possibly used an animal enclosure by the occupants of Rathnagree hillfort.

This diachronic model has a spatial dimension across the Baltinglass landscape, where there are three main clusters of hillforts and enclosures. Each of these locales had a separate Neolithic and Bronze Age component, as follows:

1. The Early Neolithic hillfort of Hughstown and the Late Bronze Age hillfort of Tinoran are located on opposing ridges on the western side of the complex.

2. The undated hillfort of Rathcoran with its Early Neolithic passage tomb is located on Tuckmill Hill, where there are Middle Bronze Age enclosures at Rathnagree and Sruhaun.

3. The Early Neolithic enclosure of Spinans Hill 1 on the eastern side of the complex is on the same ridge as Brusselstown Ring hillfort, which may be Bronze Age in date. The date of the large Spinans Hill 2 enclosure, and nearby Kilranlagh hillfort, are both unknown.

While further research is required to date individual sites, it is possible to reach some conclusions as to the broad chronology of the Baltinglass complex. Mitchell and Ryan (1997: 240) suggested that these hillforts might be contemporary, representing defensive positions built by groups in competition with each other. The new radiocarbon evidence shows that these nine sites cannot all be contemporary. While the use of some sites may have overlapped, there is a clear separation in time between the Neolithic and Bronze Age sites, and between the Middle Bronze Age enclosures on Tuckmill Hill and the Late Bronze Age hillfort at Tinoran. This makes it very unlikely that the Baltinglass landscape was divided up into a series of small hillfort polities, but it does allow for perhaps more than one hillfort group in that area at the same time, during the Early Neolithic or later Bronze Age.

Mitchell and Ryan proposed a second scenario to explain this hillfort cluster at Baltinglass. This is where these sites were not contemporary, but were built by successive generations of the same community who moved their tribal centre from one hill to another across this landscape. This is certainly possible for sites from the same period, but cannot apply to the 3000 or so years of hillfort construction in the area (3700–800 BC), particularly when there is an apparent break of two millennia or so between the Neolithic and Bronze Age hillfort traditions. A modified version of this model would see Hughstown and Spinans Hill 1 occupied successively during the Early Neolithic, with a similar shift from Rathnagree/ Sruhaun on Tuckmill Hill to nearby Tinoran at the start of the Late Bronze Age. This will be discussed further in the next chapter where landscape setting of the Baltinglasss hillforts is explored.

8

Modelling the Baltinglass Hillfort Landsape

The importance of the Baltinglass landscape is attested by the sustained occupation of the region beginning during the Early Neolithic. The construction of the Early Neolithic enclosure at Hughstown and possibly Spinans Hill is important from a local perspective, in that it implies a large population base existed in the Baltinglass area during the 4th millennium BC. This is supported by other possible Early to Middle Neolithic monument types such as Linkardstown burials, stone axes found in the local region, and by the construction of burial cairns and passage tombs. The continued importance of the landscape during the Late Neolithic/Early Bronze Age is attested by the presence of the embanked stone circle at Castleruddery and possible cursus near Hughstown and approaching the summit of Keadeen Mountain. The Middle/Late Bronze Age saw a significant expansion in human activities in the area, with the construction of hillforts, stone circles, standing stones, barrows and other monument types. It is likely that this period saw the construction of many of the hillforts in the area.

This chapter will discuss the various surveys and excavations undertaken in the Baltinglass region as part of this project and contextualise this information with respect to the wider landscape. It will propose a number of models that attempt to explain the development of the forts and other monuments in the landscape. As well as explaining why these forts were built, we will also discuss how they were constructed, analysing the labour, resources, skills, techniques and social dynamic needed to build these monumental structures. Evidence for internal settlement and potential social structures are also discusses, as well as wider social concerns such as territoriality and land ownership.

8.1 Landscape Models for Hillfort Settlement: a Review

Mitchell and Ryan (1997: 240) proposed two scenarios to explain the remarkable clustering of hillforts near Baltinglass. The first suggests the hillforts are not contemporary, with the complex arising as a result of different generations of the same community moving their tribal centre from hilltop to hilltop over time. The second interprets the hillforts as broadly contemporary defensive structures built by opposing polities, the monuments acting as rival work of competition. Without a comprehensive set of radiocarbon samples to date the construction, occupation and abandonment of each site, it is difficult to interpret the clustering of these forts. The radiocarbon dates and excavation information available from this project can be used to argue a number of different interpretations. Two broad models will be presented. Model 1 considers whether some of the hillforts are broadly contemporary, such as Rathnagree and Sruhaun, and analyses why such a group may exist, while Model 2 discusses the evidence that indicates some forts are not contemporary, such as Rathnagree and Hughstown.

Model 1: Contemporary hillforts

The linear arrangement of some British hillforts on escarpments and near river valleys has been highlighted by researchers such as Bell and Lock (2000), Hamilton and Manley (2001), Corney and Payne (2006) and Sharples (2007: 64–70). This is often connected to a need for hillfort communities to control the movement of people and goods. However, such interpretations often ignore the significant morphological and chronological differences between nearby sites (Sharples 2010: 67), an excellent example being the hillforts of the Ridgeway in southern England. The Ridgeway is an east–west routeway at the edge of the Berkshire and Marlborough Downs. A series of hillforts are arranged approximately equidistant in a linear fashion, leading Cotton (1962), Bell and Lock (2000) and Lock *et al.* (2005) to suggest that they are broadly contemporary and were used to control the movement of people and animals. Conversely, Sharples (2010: 68) has argued that many escarpments could not have acted as routeways, stating that topographical barriers such as narrow valleys deter movement between sites.

Sharples' (2010: 68) principal issue is that the existence of structured routes implies regular long-distance movement, which he suggests did not occur in Britain during the Early Iron Age (*ibid.*: 68). However, this is a moot argument, considering the extensive temporal span of hillforts. For example, during the Late Bronze Age in Ireland, evidence for long-distance trade is attested by the foreign items and material recovered from the hillforts at Rathgall, Dún Aonghasa, Freestone Hill and Haughey's Fort. In Britain too, Late Bronze Age societies were immersed in extensive trade networks (Sharples 1991). The importance of this is manifested in the strategic positioning of both British and Irish Late Bronze Age hillforts along natural routeways.

Despite Sharples' reasonable caution, various researchers have suggested hillforts were used to control the movement of people and goods, regardless of their date. In some instances, the close siting of two or more hillforts has been interpreted as opposing, contemporary hillfort communities, competing to control a single routeway or resource. Brown (2009: 203), for example, suggested that the Iron Age hillforts of Barbury Castle and Liddington Castle in Wiltshire, England, are strategically placed on opposite hills at the northern end of the River Og Valley to control the direct route into Wiltshire from the north. Corney and Payne (2006: 135) also noted this pairing phenomenon, where hillforts positioned on opposing hilltops may be competing for control over a particular route or land-block. Similarly, Barker and Driver (2011: 83) highlighted the pairing of some Late Bronze Age/Early Iron Age coastal promontory forts in Wales, arguing these were contemporary and constructed by rivalling communities. Without dating evidence, however, it is impossible to interpret these sites with certainty.

Brown (2009: 205) notes a cluster of eight sites between Clywedog and Trannon on the eastern slopes of the Pumlumon massif, west of Caersws in Wales, which he argues were positioned to exploit silver and lead resources. A similar scenario has been identified on the Continent, where Winghart (2000: 152) identified a group of Middle/Late Bronze Age hillforts in the Alpine fringe that were probably positioned to control ore deposits and access routes of the Alpine valleys. Della Casa (2013: 714) has identified a concentration of hillfort sites in the Alpine Rhine Valley between Chur and Bregenz in Austria. These sites are usually located in commanding positions on large hillocks, along the edges of a valley that acts as an important natural routeway. Along the border of the eastern and western Alps the broad Alpine Rhine valley provides natural access to inner areas of the Alps. It also represents a major north–south axis of communication that extends to the southern periphery of the Alps into the plain of eastern upper Italy.

In Ireland, Doody (2008: 624) also associated the clustering of hillforts in several parts of the country with a common interest in controlling routeways. The area around the Silvermines Mountains in north Tipperary is an excellent example, with two hillforts, Knockadigeen and Ballincurra, on opposing hilltops separated approximately 1.4km apart (Figure 8.1). Neither site is dated and forestry prevents more detailed interpretation. Viewshed analysis reveals the hillforts have a high common field of visibility and that both overlook the same regional and local routeways, as well as extensive tracts of low-lying land to the north and south-east (Figure 8.2 and Figure 8.3). More importantly, both sites overlook the northern access point of the only break in the Silvermines Mountains connecting the fertile low-lands in the north with low-lying land in the south-east. Two other hillforts, Liss and Garrangreana Lower, command the south-eastern access point. These four hillforts could be seen to represent a number of contemporary political groups competing to control an important north–south route across the Silvermines Mountains, as well as the mineral wealth of that area and other natural resources they provided.

Similarly, in southeastern Tipperary, Ahenny and Curraghadobbin hillforts are positioned approximately 3.2km apart at the southern edge of the KnockMealdown Mountains (Figure 8.4). Both are large, strategically sited monuments, overlooking an important natural routeway extending east–west to connect Dungarvan Bay to the central Midlands, as well as more discrete north–south river valleys. The forts have strikingly similar viewsheds of the immediate landscape and in particular, the east–west natural routeway (Figure 8.5 and Figure 8.6).

Controlling the movement of people and access to goods may have been an important part of an elite maintaining power. Bradley (1990: 135) suggests that changes in access to exotic goods may have undermined the position of an elite, as communities in different areas competed for access to these artefacts. This may have forced elites and hillfort communities to strategically position themselves in areas that had access to exotic goods, to gain this material for themselves and to limit availability to rival groups. Control of these exchange networks would therefore be a principle cause of conflict and competition (Sharples 1991: 84). If this interpretation is correct, we could expect to see groups of contemporary hillforts in close proximity, potentially vying for strategic control over a single trade network or resource.

Despite their obvious strategic siting, Condit (1998: 19) has argued that there is a ritual element to the juxtaposition of hillforts, where one site incorporates an earlier burial monument. Condit infers that hillforts occurring as pairs were built by the same community, with one site being differentiated by a particular morphological layout and acting as a ritual centre. He cites Knockadigeen and Ballincurra hillforts as an example, noting that the former is a widely spaced bivallate fort and the latter is a univallate example with a central cairn. Ahenny and Curraghadobbin also follow this model, the former is univallate and the latter bivallate with a central cairn. A pair of hillforts in southern Offaly, Ballymacmurragh and Cumber Lower, are positioned 1.9km apart on opposing hilltops. Ballymacmurragh comprises two closely spaced banks and ditches, in contrast to Cumber Lower, with its two widely spaced enclosing elements and a central cairn. Although there seems to be a pattern emerging, this does not necessarily support Condit's thesis. The pairing phenomenon could equally be interpreted as two opposing communities competing for access to, or control of, a particular land-block or natural routeway. In an attempt to differentiate themselves and create a unique identity, both communities could have built distinctly

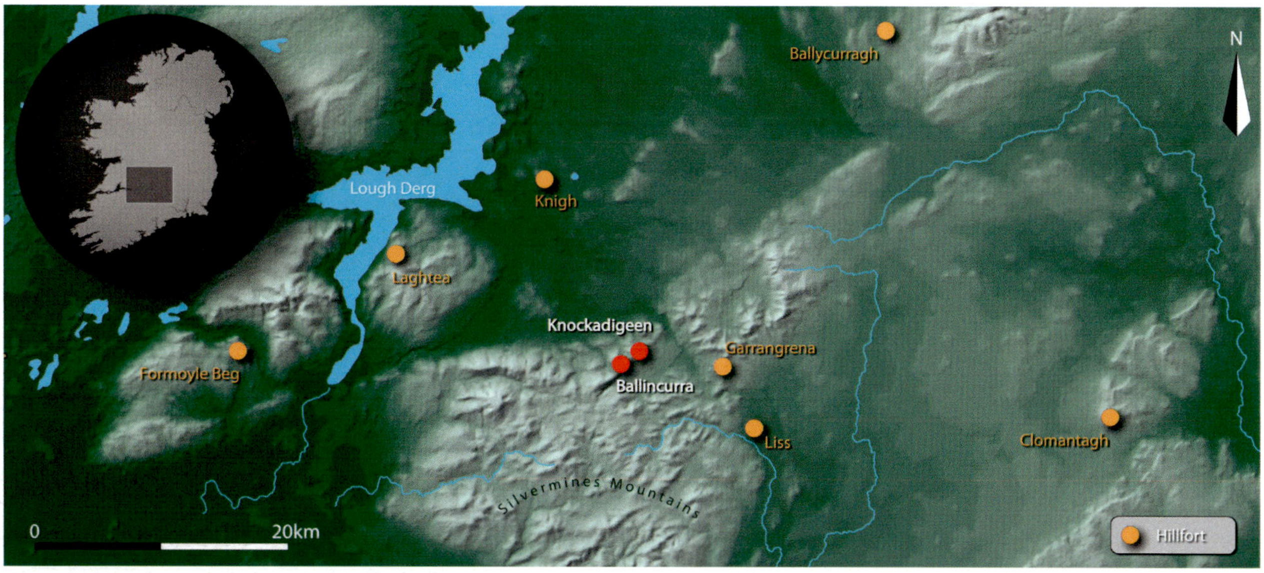

FIGURE 8.1: THE HILLFORTS OF KNOCKADIGEEN AND BALLINCURRA IN CO. TIPPERARY, LOCATED APPROXIMATELY 1.4KM APART.

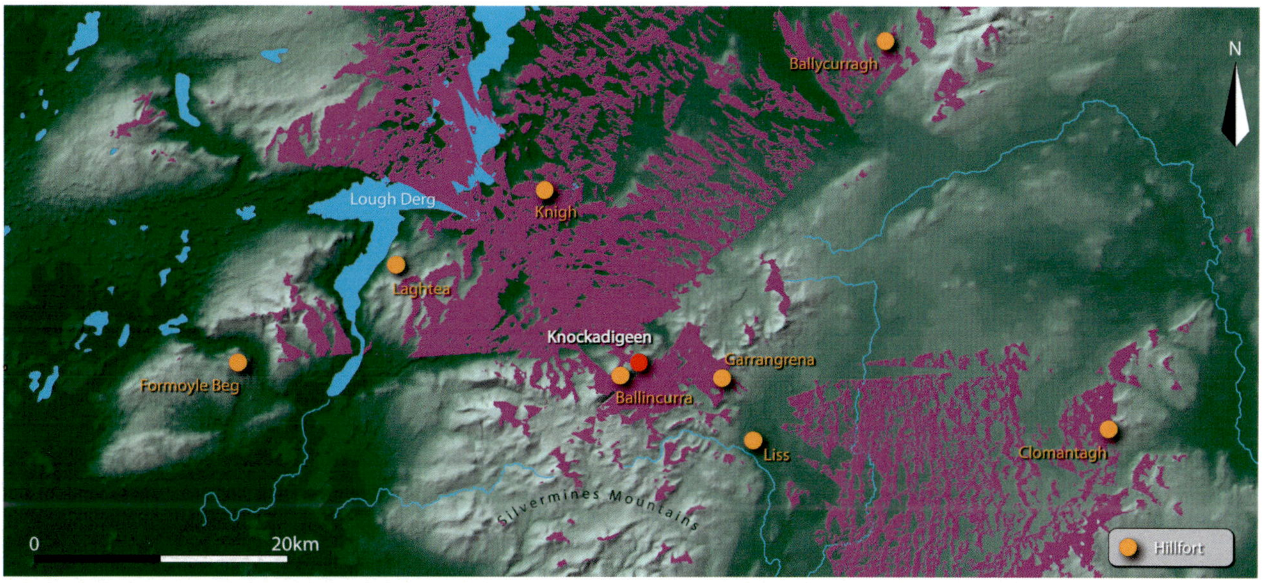

FIGURE 8.2: RESULTS OF VIEWSHED ANALYSIS AT KNOCKADIGEEN HILLFORT, CO. TIPPERARY.

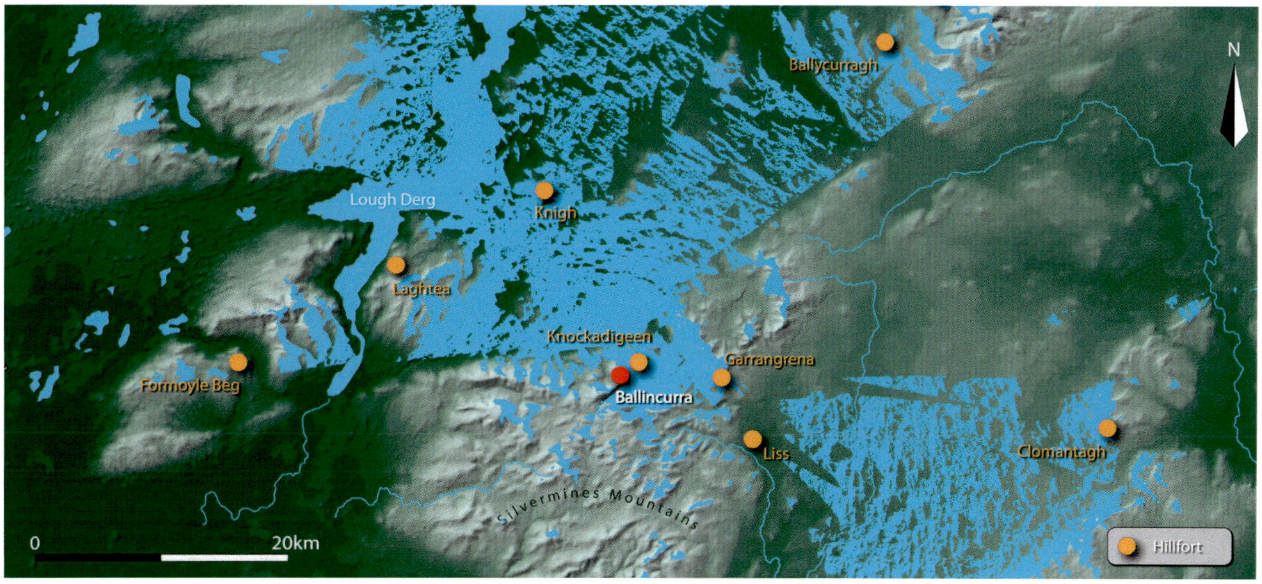

FIGURE 8.3: RESULTS OF VIEWSHED ANALYSIS AT BALLINCURRA HILLFORT, CO. TIPPERARY.

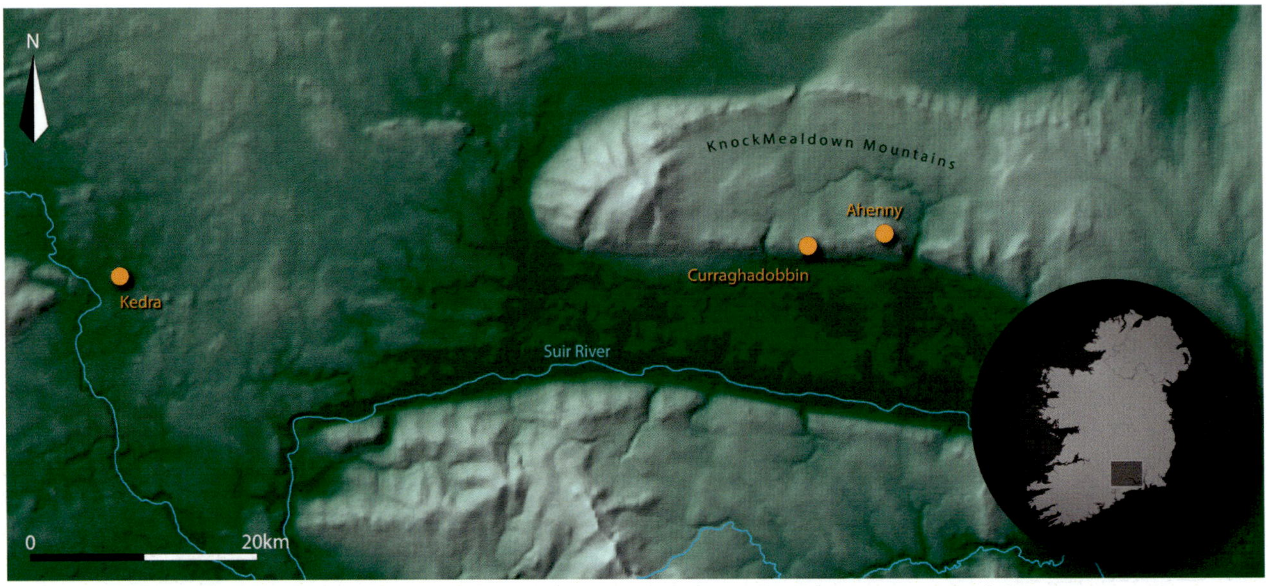

Figure 8.4: The hillforts of Curraghdobbin and Ahenny in Co. Tipperary, located 3.2km apart.

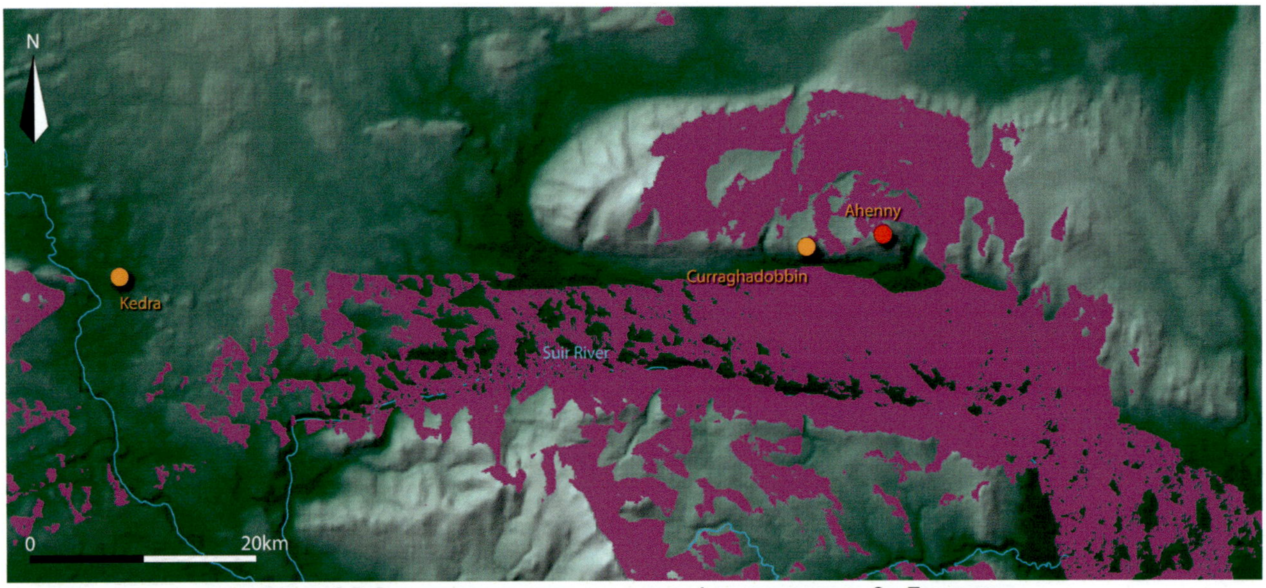

Figure 8.5: Results of viewshed analysis at Ahenny hillfort, Co. Tipperary.

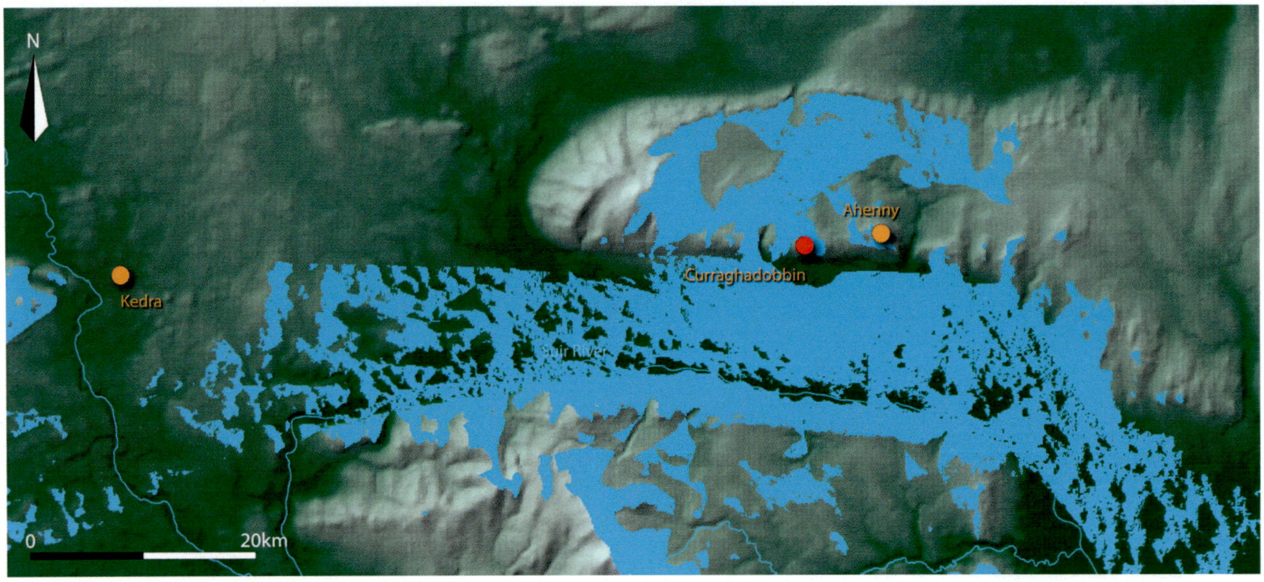

Figure 8.6: Results of viewshed analysis at Curraghdobbin hillfort, Co. Tipperary.

different hillforts. This can also be seen at larger groups such as the cluster of five hillforts (the Cwn Gwyddyl group) in the hill fringe zone bordering Cors Caron in Wales, sites that have different morphological features (Driver 2013: 52–53).

Conversely, there are examples of hillfort pairs that do not support this interpretation, such as the two hillforts on Friarstown Hill in Co. Limerick (Figure 2.5), and the adjacent Rathgall and Knockeen hillforts in Co. Wicklow (Figure 2.9). Rather than being positioned on opposing hilltops, the individual forts are located in close proximity on the same hill. Rathgall and Knockeen are separated by approximately 300m and the hillforts on Friarstown are less than 40m apart. As Condit (1998: 19) has noted, 'in purely defensive terms, it does not seem to make sense that two independent hillforts should be located so close together', an argument also made by Armit (2007: 35). The Friarstown hillforts are morphologically similar, both comprising a bank-ditch-counterscarp arrangement and are broadly equivalent in size. Aerial photographs have revealed a possible earthwork connecting the two enclosures, inferring both may be contemporary and possibly used by a single or two affiliated communities.

A similar morphological parallel is evident between Rathgall and Knockeen hillforts in Co. Wicklow. The Late Bronze Age enclosing elements at Rathgall likely comprise a bank-ditch-counterscarp bank separated from another bank and ditch by approximately 55m. Geophysical survey at Knockeen revealed a similar layout (Figure 8.7 and Figure 8.8; O'Driscoll 2014f). The upstanding remains consist of a bank and possible external ditch. The gradiometry survey identified a large counterscarp bank immediately outside this ditch (**G5**). Another concentric enclosing element, consisting of a bank and ditch, was identified approximately 50m outside the internal example (**G6** and **G7**).

The nearby Rathgall is one of the most intensively investigated hillforts in Ireland. Raftery recovered a substantial assemblage of crucible and clay moulds fragments, as well as various bronze, gold and amber objects that attest to the intensive production of prestige goods and long-distance trading during the Late Bronze Age. Contemporary burials were also recovered in the interior. Notably, there is no clear evidence that the site was extensively settled. In contrast, the geophysical survey at Knockeen revealed a number of ephemeral anomalies consisting of circular areas of uniformly 'quiet' magnetism, some of which are surrounded by a series of pit-like features that might represent post-holes (**G10–G36**). It is tempting to suggest that these represent hut structures and that the juxtaposition of Knockeen and Rathgall could represent the residence of an elite with prestige goods craftsmen under their patronage, with a larger domestic habitation site. The geophysical evidence is too ambiguous to state this with any certainty in the absence of excavation. Furthermore, an area of increased magnetic disturbance on the eastern side of the interior of Knockeen could represent a metalworking area similar to that found on the eastern portion of Rathgall (**G9**). In this respect, Rathgall and Knockeen could also be viewed as wholly identical in terms of the morphological layout of the enclosing elements, their internal layouts and function.

Hillfort groups could also represent areas where several communities interacted in a peaceful but competitive manner. In Arkush's (2011: 156–161) study of Colla hillforts in the Andes, she was able to reconstruct hypothetical networks of alliances by linking sites that were intervisible with regional pottery types. The results revealed that 'alliances' often clustered together in dense settlement patterns. Ralston (2006: 33–34) has also noted some regional hillfort concentrations that are of broadly regular form. Common architectural features in these clusters might suggest these groups formed alliances. The bastioned single-walled enclosures of southern France, where they show signs of being broadly of regular form, are an excellent example (*ibid.*: 33). The form and siting of the éperons tronqués forts along the valley of the Viroin near the Franco-Belgian border, also seems to indicate a particular 'fashion' (*ibid.*: 34) and may represent an alliance network in the area. In Ireland, the compelling evidence for long-distance trade could indicate that unions existed, as diplomatic or political alliances were needed for this to occur (Harding 2012: 268; Kristiansen and Larsson 2005: 50).

Cunliffe (1991: 537–538) has discussed the pairing of hillforts and suggests this phenomenon may be the archaeological manifestation of the Celtic system of partible inheritance. This was a particular feature of Early Welsh society that split the belongings of a father equally between his sons (Brown 2009: 225–226). Williams and Mytum (1998: 144) originally interpreted groups of closely sited hillforts as evidence for this this system. At a cluster of eight small hillforts in Llawhaden, Pembrokeshire, Wales, between two and four of the sites were occupied at any one time, which led Williams and Mytum (1998: 140; 144) to argue this interpretation. Harding (2012: 17) also views hillforts that occur in very close proximity on the same hilltop as reflecting the possible dual control of land by kin groups of equal status. To support his interpretation, Harding cites two mulltivallate forts at Eye Water in Berwickshire, England that are separated by less than 100m and two hillforts in Newhall Hill, Dumfreishire, Scotland that are located within 10m of each other.

Coles and Harding (1979: 11) have suggested that some hillfort groups could have been located in peripheral places marking the limits of adjacent territories. In some cases, these may have been peaceful areas with open so-

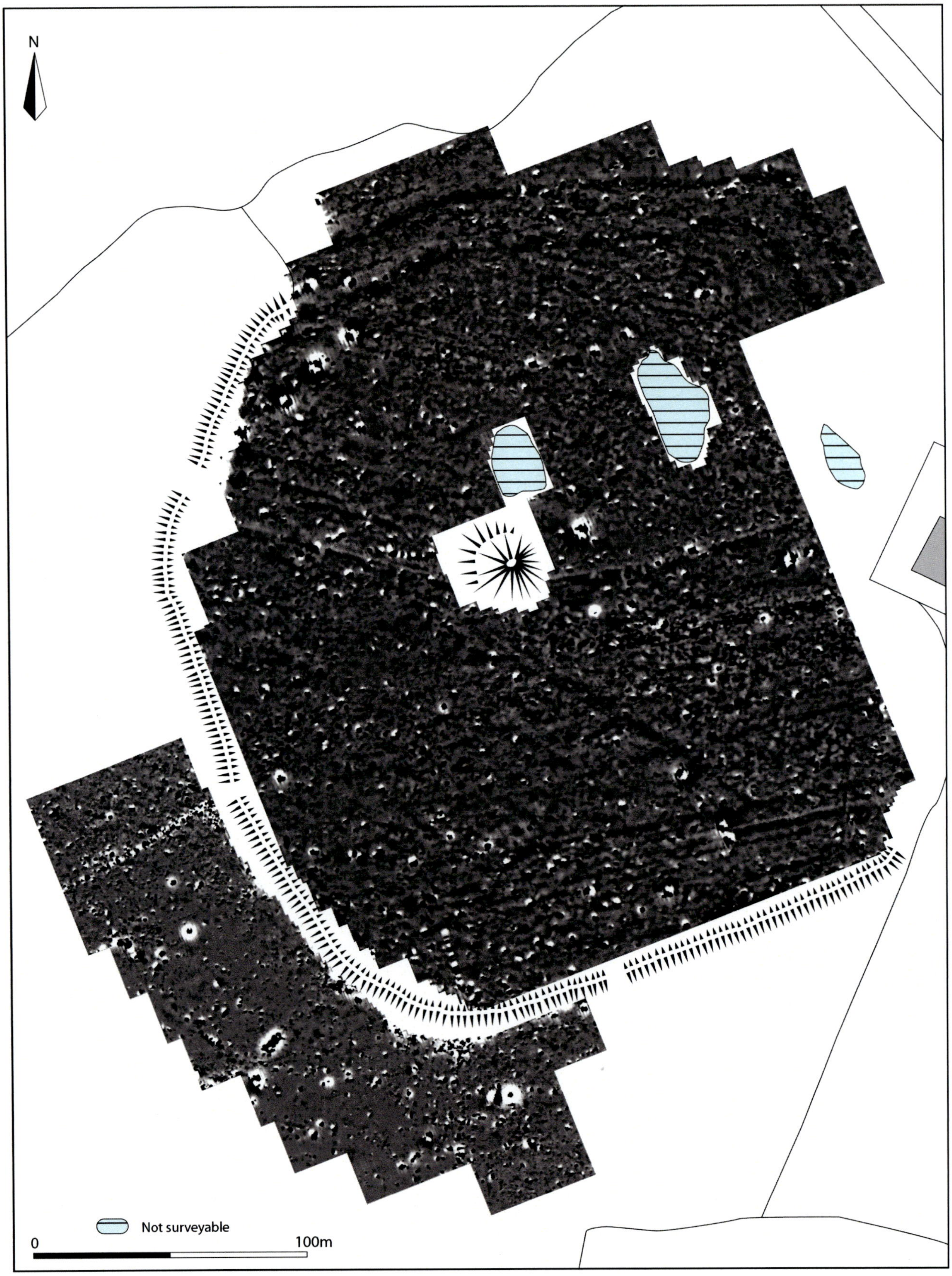

Figure 8.7: Results from geophysical survey (magnetic gradiometry) of Knockeen hillfort, Co. Wicklow.

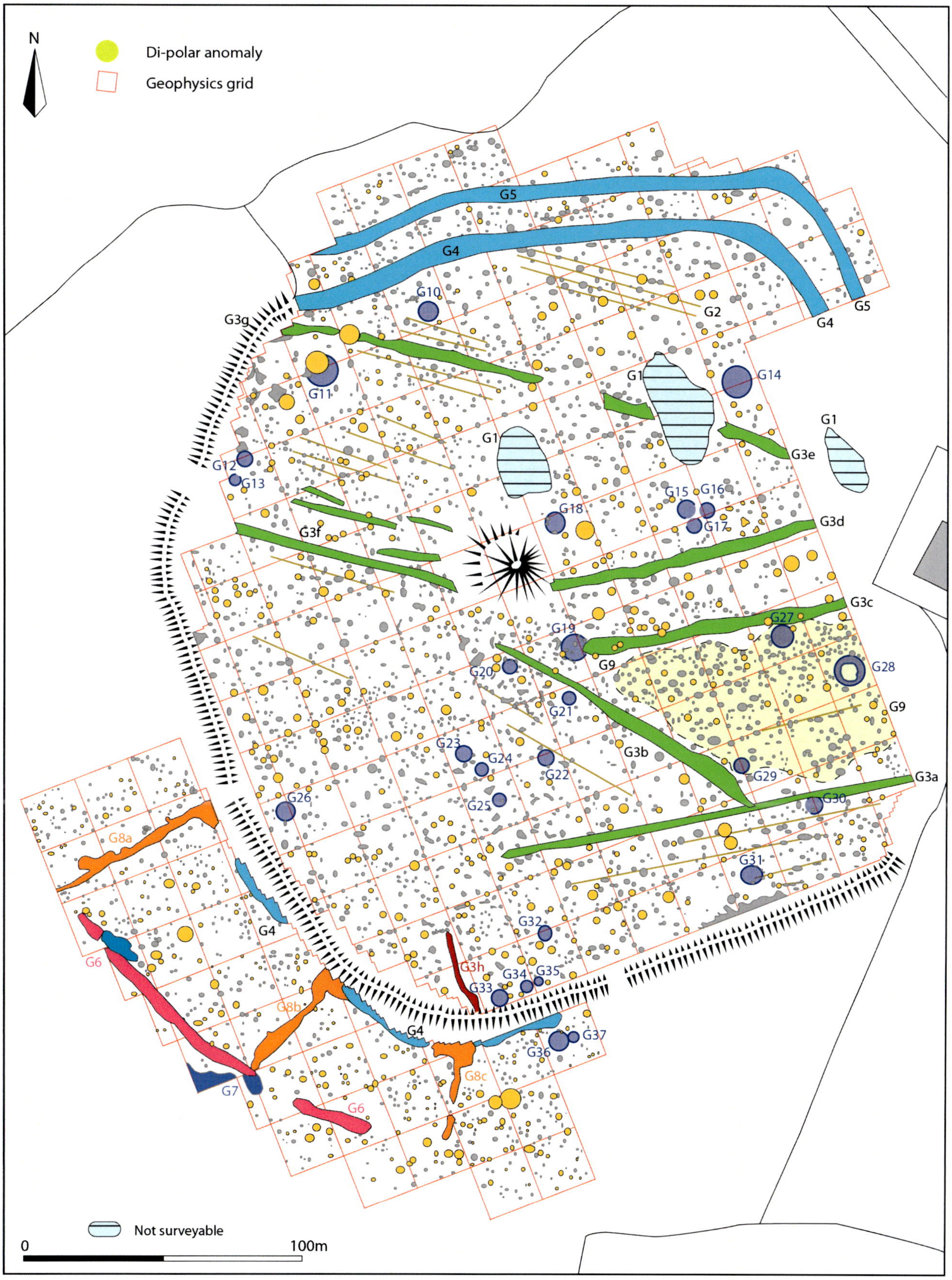

Figure 8.8: Interpretation of results from geophysical survey of Knockeen hillfort, Co. Wicklow.

cial systems where allied communities assembled. Brun (1993: 178) has identified a notable concentration of hillforts and fortified settlements within the buffer zone near the Paris Basin, separating the Late Bronze Age Urnfield and Atlantic cultures. He has convincingly argued that these forts were located to take advantage of both markets. Elites could procure raw material at low costs from multiple sources on both sides of the frontier and supply two economies (Brun 1993: 182). Atlantic-type bronze objects and North Alpine style pottery found at some of these sites infers a relatively open social system that supports this interpretation.

Conversely, Keeley (1996: 130–138) and Arksuh (2011: 65) argue that frontiers between different cultural or economic groups were often hostile areas subject to raids, intimidation and violent seizures of land. This assumption is based on ethnographic evidence from Maori cultures in New Zealand, and various central and North American societies. Keeley (1996: 130) explains that frontiers display things that people need or want just beyond the limits of their own social group and beyond easy acquisition. The temptation to gain these things through warfare could provoke aggressive behaviour. Communities in such areas are more inclined to retaliate to aggressive behaviour (Keeley 1996: 131–132), creating a vicious circle of aggressive acts and encouraging aggressive solutions to disputes (Arkush 2011: 13).

Model 1: The Baltinglass hillfort group

Model 1 proposes that most of the Baltinglass hillforts were broadly contemporary and were built by a number of communities. These communities may have competed for various natural resources or were positioned in a frontier zone, formed an alliance of communities or relate to partible inheritance. In some instances, the close siting of forts on the same hilltop could reflect the contemporary construction of multiple hillforts by the same community. Radiocarbon dates from Sruhaun and Rathnagree suggest that both were broadly contemporary in the Middle Bronze Age. Positioned within a few hundred metres of these sites, on the same hilltop, the undated Rathcoran could also be contemporary and the three monuments may have been constructed and occupied by the same community.

Cooney (2002: 75) has suggested that Rathcoran is a Neolithic causewayed enclosure due to the numerous breaks in the enclosing elements. Although the fort is undated, Cooney's interpretation is unlikely. There are two cairns at Rathcoran, one positioned at the highest point within the interior of the hillfort, the other abutting the exterior of the outer bank at the south-eastern side. The former was excavated by Walshe (1941) and revealed to be a passage tomb of Middle Neolithic date. This corresponds with Schulting *et al.* (2011: 2) and Cooney *et al.* (2011), who have proposed that passage tombs began to be constructed around the third quarter of the fourth millennium BC in the Middle Neolithic period.

This is important because there seems to be a distinct, if tentative, horizon for the construction of causewayed enclosures and large Neolithic enclosures in Ireland that pre-date complex passage tombs. The causewayed enclosures at Donegore in Co. Antrim and Maheraboy in Co. Sligo, were built around 3765–3695 BC (Whittle *et al.* 2011; Mallory *et al.* 2011: 221) and 4150–3935 BC (Whittle *et al.* 2011; Danaher 2007) respectively, with other large Neolithic enclosures such as Tullahedy in Co. Tipperary (Cleary and Kellaher 2011) constructed slightly after this, around 3700–3500 BC. Considering that Rathcoran was probably not constructed until after the two passage tombs, it is possible to suggest that the enclosure is Bronze Age, though this cannot be confirmed without more precise dating achieved through excavation. The large number of circular structures within the interior were probably constructed much later that the passage tomb, which again supports the identification of Rathcoran as a Bronze Age hillfort.

The radiocarbon dates from the third enclosing element at Tinoran are probably later than those from Rathnagree or Sruhaun although there is a slight overlap (Tinoran radiocarbon dates: 1188–923 BC, 1214–1001 BC; Rathnagree and Sruhaun dates range from 1417–1126 BC). Even if these were not contemporary, the Tinoran dates have prompted an interesting scenario. The fourth enclosing element is later then the third example, inferring that the defences were constructed over a protracted period during the Late Bronze Age, possibly by different generations of the same community (the inner most bank, 'The Round O', possibly being an Early Medieval addition). If the construction process began at the inner hillfort bank (the second enclosure), it could be argued that this enclosing element pre-dates the outer examples and could potentially be contemporary with the construction of Rathnagree and Sruhaun. It is interesting that Tinoran is possibly the only Irish hillfort that has produced potential evidence for the continued development of the defences over time, although it is important to note that the dates produced from the fourth enclosing element are a *terminus ante quem* and further excavation is needed to clarify its date. Whenever a multivallate hillfort has been excavated and reliable dates have been obtained for their construction or abandonment, they have shown they were broadly contemporary, the multiple circuits probably being planned and built at broadly the same time.

The dates obtained from the three enclosing elements at Hughstown, as well as Spinans Hill 1, date these enclosures to the Early Neolithic. The possibility, albeit tentative, of circular structures within Hughstown infers that the fort was reoccupied at a later stage. Early Neolithic structures in Ireland tend to be rectangular rather than circular, although the latter are found in the Later Neolithic (Smyth 2013: 301). Though this remains to be confirmed by excavation, the sequence may represent a symbolic attempt by later communities to both venerate the past and legitimate power and control of the landscape through visible links with the past and reoccupation of a much older site. The importance placed in such links in the Late Bronze Age is attested by approximately 25% of Irish hillforts surrounding earlier cairns or megalithic tombs. At Donegore Hill, circular structures inside the causewayed enclosure have been dated to the Late Bronze Age/Iron Age and attest to re-occupation of this Early Neolithic monument in this period (Mallory *et al.* 2011: 90).

Two of the enclosing elements on Spinans Hill (Brusselstown Ring and Spinans Hill 2) and Kilranlagh have not been dated. Widely spaced enclosing elements such as those found at Brusselstown Ring are more frequently found in the later prehistoric period, with large multivallate Early Neolithic enclosures in Ireland mostly comprising closely or moderately spaced enclosures. Brusselstown Ring could therefore be Late Bronze Age in date. Similar to the dated enclosing elements at Tinoran, the large Spinans Hill 2 enclosure could have been built after the construction of Brusselstown Ring and Spinans Hill 1 by a new generation of the same community. This interpretation is further supported by the outer enclosing elements of Brusselstown Ring being incorporated into the circuit of Spinans Hill 2. The Spinans Hill 1 enclosure surrounds a possible small passage tomb cemetery that could date to the Early/Middle Neolithic.

The above examples indicate that there are two types of groups; those where hillforts are positioned on opposing hilltops and those located on the same hilltop or in extremely close proximity. The former group can sometimes be differentiated by incorporating distinctly different morphological layouts or conversely, by adopting similar architectural elements. This may distinguish a cluster of communities competing for access or control of resources or routeways with a group of allied communities. The latter group probably represents a cluster of hillforts that were constructed and occupied by a single community or elites with a common ancestry and claims to the land. Both types of groups are evident in the Baltinglass cluster.

A number of hillforts on the same hilltop (Rathcoran, Rathnagree and Sruhaun are situated on Tuckmill Hill; Spinans Hill 2 and Brusselstown Ring are located on Spinans Hill) could suggest some communities in Baltinglass built more than one fort, or that an alliance of communities constructed hillforts on the same hill. Evidence suggests that the hillforts on Tuckmill Hill may have functioned as a defensive group (see Chapter 8.3) and a similar scenario might be suggested at Spinans Hill. Again, this remains to be clarified through excavation.

Model 2: A diachronic approach

The majority of researchers have tended to stress the relative contemporaneity of hillfort groups, despite the fact that, in most cases, there is no clear dating evidence. Although it is clear that the juxtaposition is deliberate, their construction and occupation could have been sequential. On the North Island of New Zealand, for example, some Pā sites (large forts of comparable dimensions to hillforts) were abandoned after the burial of a chief and new Pā were constructed close by, sometimes within a few hundred metres of the former (Armit 2007). The ritual nature of the abandonment might explain why the builders of the later fort did not take advantage of the pre-existing defences (*ibid.*: 35). Armit has proposed a similar scenario for the Iron Age multivallate hillforts on Doon Hill, East Lothian, which lie a few hundred metres from each other. A similar scenario could be proposed for the aforementioned hillfort clusters (see above) in southeastern Tipperary, north Tipperary, the Friarstown hillforts in Co. Limerick, or Rathgall and Knockeen hillforts in Co. Wicklow.

Sharples (2010: 62–64) has highlighted the pairing of hillforts on the same hilltop with particular reference to sites north of Salisbury and on Cranborne Chase in England. He suggests that such sites cannot be considered as autonomous communities as they would need close cooperation between the groups, particularly as they appear to have been farming the same fields. Instead, he argues that the sites may be better explained as not being contemporary.

Model 2: The Baltinglass hillfort group

Model 2 proposes that the Baltinglass hillforts are not all contemporary. This could have been a consequence of ritual abandonment and subsequent construction of new sites, or simply the construction of large enclosures over a protracted period in prehistory, which resulted in a palimpsest of sites. A speculative model of the evolution of the Baltinglass landscape is presented in Figure 8.9, Figure 8.10 and Figure 8.11. It may be difficult to identity short-term occupation, abandonment and construction of new sites associated with ritual abandonment, principally due to the ranges of radiocarbon determinations. An excellent example of this problem are the dates from Rathnagree which range approximately 1400–1130 BC. The dates from Tinoran tentatively show that the different enclosing elements could have been built at different times throughout the Bronze Age. This could be interpreted as different generations of the same community adding enclosing elements or the seasonal development of the hillfort over a protracted period of time. Regard-

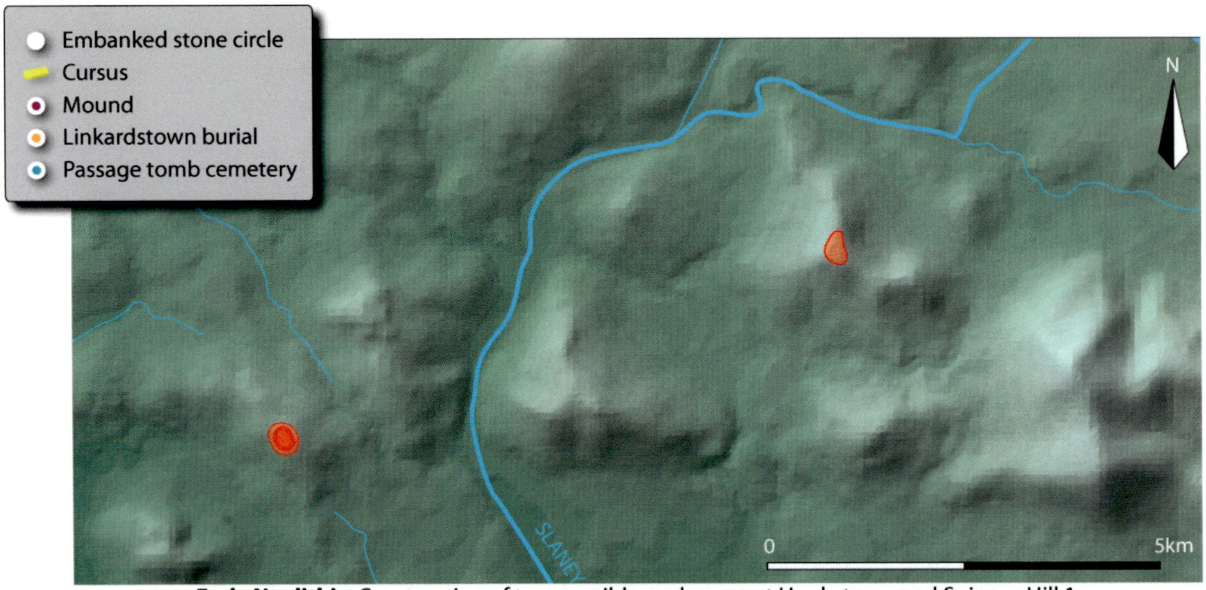

Early Neolithic: Construction of two possible enclosures at Hughstown and Spinans Hill 1.

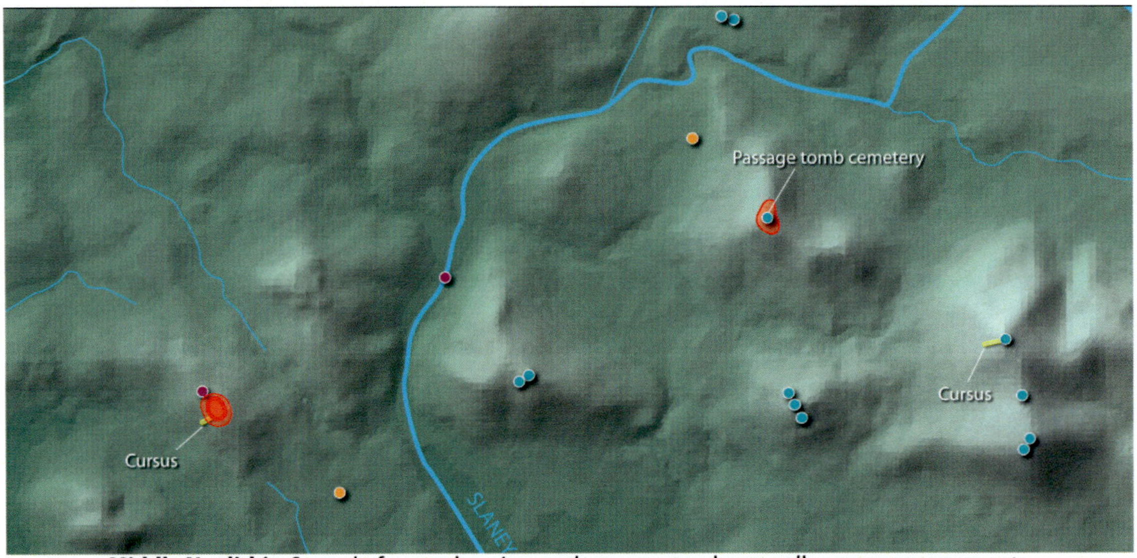

Middle Neolithic: Spread of mounds, cairns and passage-tombs as well as cursus monuments.

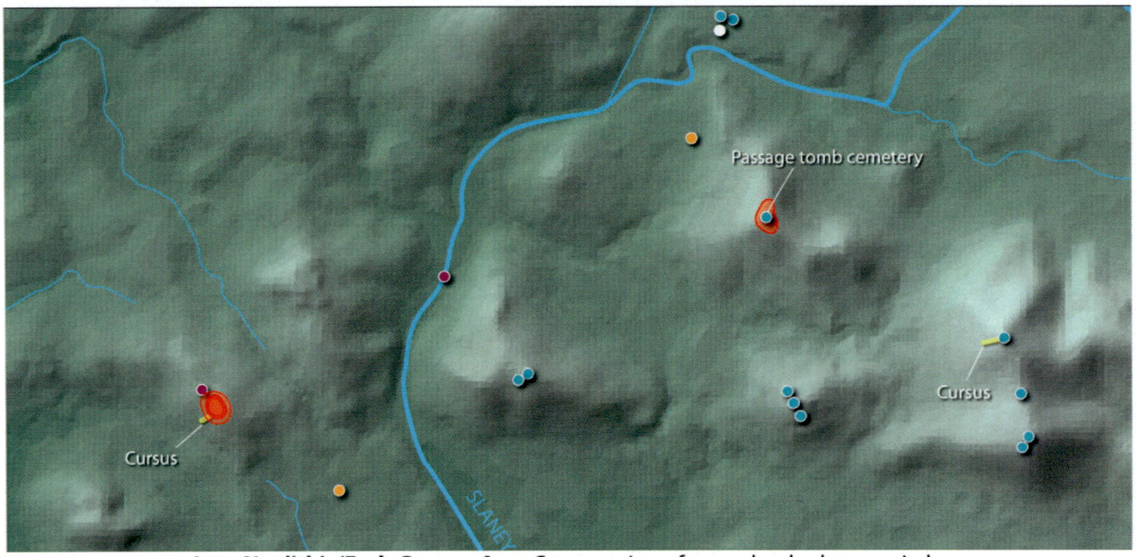

Late Neolithic/Early Bronze Age: Construction of an embanked stone circle.

Figure 8.9: Diachronic model of the Baltinglass landscape ranging from the Early Neolithic to Early Bronze Age.

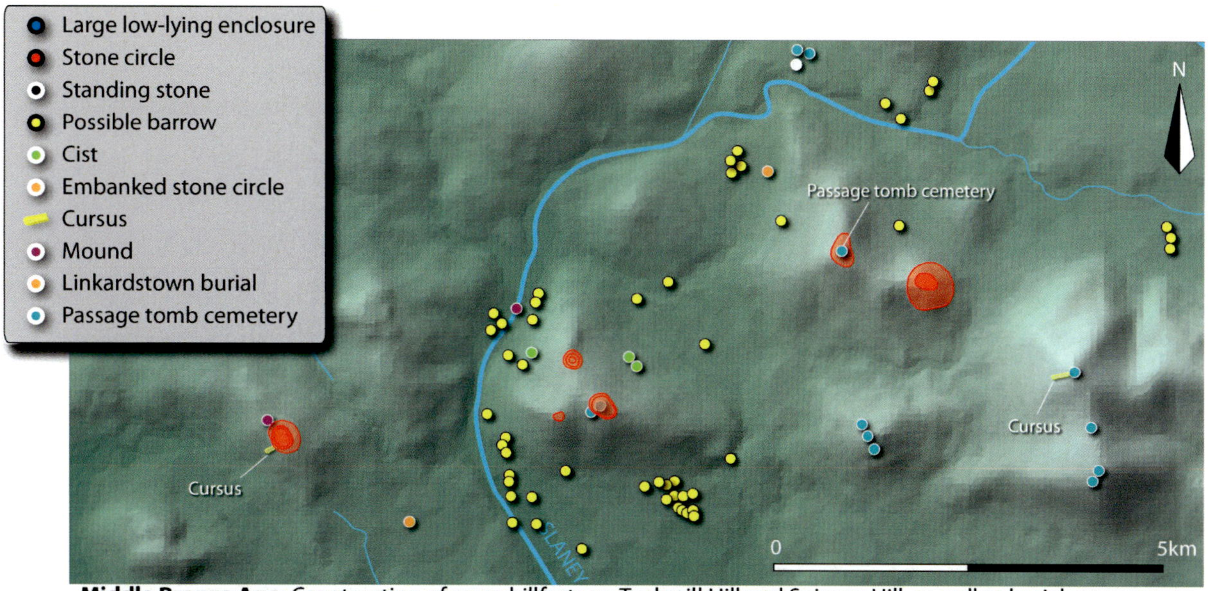

Middle Bronze Age: Construction of more hillforts on Tuckmill Hill and Spinans Hill, as well as burial monuments.

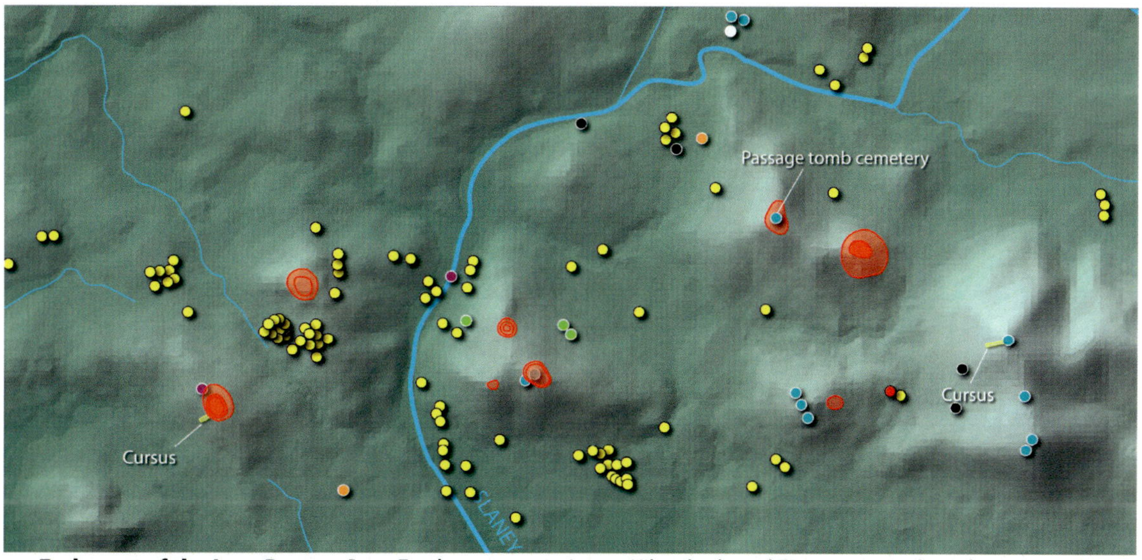

Early part of the Late Bronze Age: Further construction at Kilranlagh and Tinoran, more burial monuments.

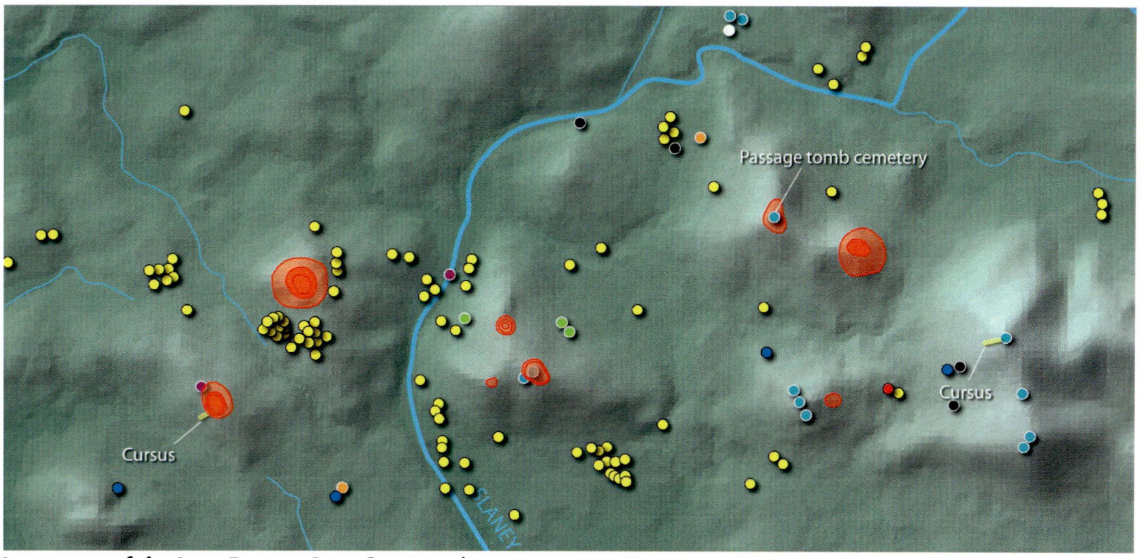

Later part of the Late Bronze Age: Continued construction at Tinoran and large low-lying enclosures

FIGURE 8.10: DIACHRONIC MODEL OF THE BALTINGLASS LANDSCAPE FROM MIDDLE TO LATE BRONZE AGE.

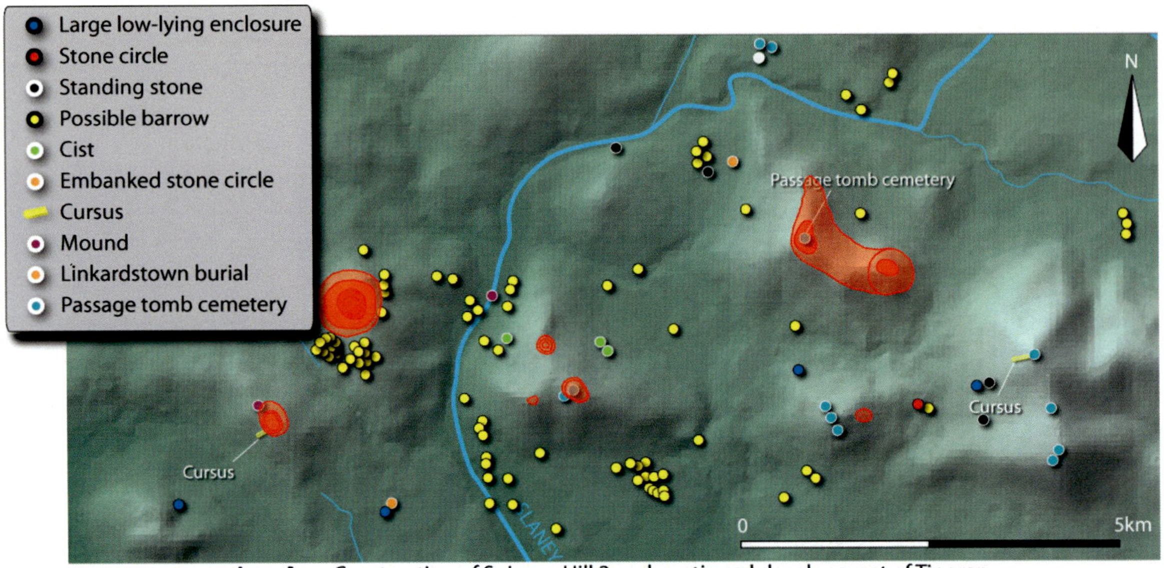

Iron Age: Construction of Spinans Hill 2 and continued development of Tinoran.

Figure 8.11: Diachronic model of the Baltinglass landscape in the Iron Age.

less, it confirms the continued use of the site over a prolonged period. Similarly, the multi-phase construction of Rathnagree might suggest its continued importance to a particular community over a period of time.

The Early Neolithic enclosures at Hughstown and Spinans Hill 1 provide an excellent example of the difficulties of interpreting this exceptional group of 'hillforts' without sufficient dating evidence. Prior to excavation, both sites had previously been interpreted as Late Bronze Age hillforts (see Condit 1992, 1998, Raftery 1994; Waddell 1998). However, the presence of two Early Neolithic enclosures, as well as a number of possible Neolithic monuments in the area is unequivocal, and is cause to re-evaluate the date of other large enclosures in the group.

Neolithic

Spinans Hill 1 is currently the largest Early Neolithic enclosure in Ireland at 11.11ha. The Neolithic enclosure at Hughstown is 8.22ha in size and is the second largest example discovered in Ireland to date. Prior to the identification of Hughstown and Spinans Hill 1, the largest Early Neolithic enclosure was Donegore in Co. Antrim which is 3.5ha in size. Donegore was probably built before Spinans Hill 1 and Hughstown, and it continued in use after both those sites were constructed (Mallory *et al.* 2011: 221).

The survey results and limited excavation at Hughstown suggest it may have comprised breaks or other features analogous with causewayed enclosures, although further excavation is needed to clarify this. Interestingly, survey at Spinans Hill 1 has not identified any obvious breaks, suggesting the multivallate Hughstown enclosure may have been structurally different to the contemporary univallate Spinans Hill 1. It is clear, however, that causewayed enclosures formed part of a broader suite of enclosure throughout Atlantic Europe during the Neolithic. Brophy (2004: 43) suggests causewayed enclosures and less complex single boundary enclosures found in Britain are contemporary. Darvill and Thomas (2001: 10) argue that there are a number of different types of Neolithic enclosures found in Britain, with the most numerous and widespread example actually being these simple 'non-causewayed' enclosures. There is an increasing number of these being identified, such as Carn Brea in Cornwall (Mercer 1981: 63). Bury Hill, West Sussex, and Beckhampton, Wiltshire, highlight that such enclosures existed within well-established groups of causewayed enclosures (Darvill and Thomas 2001: 10) and as such, communities must have made a conscious decision to build one type of enclosures over another. Cleary (2011: 415) commented on the challenge of finding comparisons for the Early Neolithic enclosure at Tullahedy in Co. Tipperary, suggesting that it is possibly a futile exercise to seek precise parallels as 'they may not exist in a Neolithic landscape that itself reflects considerable regionalism'. The variability in morphology and design further highlights the problems in identifying Early Neolithic enclosures without reliable dating evidence.

Large Early Neolithic enclosures have been interpreted in almost as many different ways as hillforts. In several cases, the recovery of arrowheads and evidence for destruction have been linked with warfaring practices of early farming communities. Some 700 arrowheads were recovered at Carn Brea in Cornwall, many of which were found within the enclosure wall (Mercer 2003). At Crickley Hill in Gloucestershire and Hambledon Hill in Dorset, leaf-shaped arrowheads were recovered and interpreted as evidence for an attack, with the entrance of the former site being destroyed by fire (Dixon 1976; Mercer 1980). In this regard, it is interesting to note the evidence for the destruction of the Hughstown enclosure by fire. In Ireland, these Early Neolithic enclosures provide some evidence for attack by archers. At Donegore, a substantial assemblage of projectiles implies some degree of violent activity. A cluster of arrowheads at Donegore, some of which were found along the exterior section of the enclosing elements, points to a possible attack (Mallory *et al.* 2011: 168). Similarly, at Thornhill in Co. Derry, a series of palisades enclosing an area of land were destroyed by fire, and seven arrowheads were recovered from the collapsed material which the excavator views as evidence for an attack (Logue 2003). Although there are no published radiocarbon dates, quantities of carinated bowl pottery from primary contexts imply a fourth millennium date (Sheridan 2001: 176). A high number of arrowheads recovered at Tullahedy in Co. Tipperary prompted Cleary (2011: 413) to suggest they could be linked with defence or warfare. There is also the presence of strong wooden palisading at the site, the location of which takes advantage of natural terrain.

Items associated with trade are often found at the enclosures. For example, Mercer (1981: 184) notes that both Carn Brea and Crickley Hill had imported 'gabbroic ware'. Imported porcellanite axe-heads and one axe-head from Great Langdale led Logue (2003: 154) to interpret Thornhill as an enclosure in a prominent position within an exchange network (*ibid.*: 154). Cooney *et al.* (2011) have similarly suggested that the palisaded enclosure at Thornhill may have played a key role in the distribution of stone resources. At Tullahedy, 105 polished stone axes or fragments that were probably not produced on-site are evidence for inter-regional exchange and implies Tullahedy was an important trading centre (Cleary 2011: 141). Evidence for trade corresponds with Evans *et al.*'s (1988: 82) suggestion that Neolithic enclosures, and in particular causewayed enclosures, had symbolic or religious functions and were often placed on the boundaries of community territory. Environmental data from the Neolithic enclosure at Maiden Castle in Dorset supports this theory (*ibid.*: 82). The data suggests that the site was relatively isolated, positioned in marginal land away from areas of agriculture. This is paralleled at other sites such as Windmill Hill in Wiltshire (Smith 1984). The construction of enclosures in marginal locations could be seen as an attempt to impose a structure on relationships between communities (Evans *et al.* 1988: 82; Bradley 1998: 197). Evans *et al.* (1988: 82) argue that the primary role of such contact was for exchange. They state that 'the peripheral position of these enclosures would be ideal for this role, as outsiders could be kept isolated and conflicts arising from contact could be contained away from the productive base'. Cleary (2011: 416) has similarly interpreted the 'somewhat' peripheral location of Tullahedy as a suitable contact point between different social groups. This is a fitting interpretation for the two Early Neolithic enclosures near Baltinglass. Considering their broad contemporaneity, their close landscape setting and distinct morphological layouts, we could suggest that these monuments were built by two different communities at the boundary between their respective territories, possibly functioning as trading centres. The destruction of Hughstown and the lack of evidence for such at Spinans Hill 1, is also interesting, and might suggest an attack on one community by the latter. This is speculation, as the morphological differences may also reflect differences in site function.

The period 3700–3570 BC is emerging as a very dynamic era in Ireland and Britain, with the initial use of court tombs and a strong peak in mortuary and settlement activity (Schulting *et al.* 2011: 1). Hughstown and Spinans Hill 1 are two of the earliest dated monuments in the Baltinglass landscape and it probably reflects a broad community base within the environs of the enclosures that were under some form of centralized social organisation. This corresponds with a concentration in that area of other ritual and burial monuments that broadly date to the Neolithic period. These include a Linkardstown burial identified at the northwestern base of Spinans Hill in Ballintruer More townland (Ryan 1973). Linkardstown burials comprise a group of inhumations in cists, accompanied by highly decorated bowls and are generally found under mounds. A crouched burial in the Ballintruer More grave produced a date of 3338–2910 BC and is therefore later than the Hughstown or Spinans Hill 1 enclosures. This date is consistent with Cooney *et al.*'s (2011: 634–637) Bayesian model, which places this burial tradition in the Middle Neolithic.

Other Neolithic burials have been identified in the area, including a site near the southern base of Hughstown in Rathmoon townland (Lucas 1960: 87). This comprised a circular mound 26m in diameter and 3.9m high. A rectangular cist at the southern edge produced cremated bone of a least three individuals, while a leaf-shaped arrowhead association typologically dates to the Early/Middle Neolithic. This monument, therefore, may represent another Linkardstown-type burial. The seven robbed-out cairns within the interior of Spinans Hill 1, all of which may have cist features, may represent Linkardstown burials or small passage tombs. Cooney *et al.* (2011) suggest both burial traditions are contemporary. Interestingly, all of these burials are either found within or near the base of Spinans Hill 1 and Hughstown. The concentration of cairns in the Baltinglass area certainly implies a dense Neolithic presence, with the identification of these important graves and large enclosures suggesting the existence of complex societies. This is further supported by the cluster of stone axeheads in low-lying terrain to the south-east of Baltinglass (Cooney and Mandal 1998).

Two possible cursus monuments have been identified in the Baltinglass area. The Keadeen cursus is positioned at the eastern edge of the landscape on the western slopes of Keadeen Mountain (Figure 8.12). It is located just off the summit where a large robbed-out cairn crowns the hilltop. It is tempting to suggest this was the focal point of the cursus (Corlett 2014). The second possible cursus is immediately outside Hughstown at the south-west. Both Newman (1999: 145) and Condit (1995; 1997) note that cursus monuments are often orientated on other ritual monuments such as passage tombs, pits, stone circles or henges. Nine of the ten recorded cursus monuments in Ireland are aligned on burial monuments such as barrows, cairns or passage graves. Cursus monuments are often built on sloping topography. This may have been deliberate, as Newman (2007: 428) has argued that obscuration and redirection are devices employed at many religious sites. The sloping terrain would have aided this. At Knockendrane, Co. Carlow, and Ballinvally, Co. Meath, the cursus monuments incorporate distinct 'dog-leg' turns, where the avenues suddenly change direction. Again, this was probably a deliberate attempt at obscuration. At Keadeen, the cairn was largely obscured from view until reaching the summit. Similarly, the possible cursus on the southwestern slopes of Hughstown obstruct visibility of the summit of the hilltop and the enclosing elements would have helped to obscure a large part of the interior of the enclosure. An unrecorded mound is positioned 45m from to the north of this possibly cursus.

Without radiocarbon evidence it is difficult to ascribe cursus monuments a specific date, and so the example at Hughstown might not be contemporary with the Neolithic enclosure. Based on evidence from examples in the Wessex area, these linear earthworks appear to date to the third millennium. Newman's (2007: 422) study of the Tech Midchúarta hints that some of these monuments could be Early Medieval.

The elaborate embanked stone circle surrounded by a ditch and a possible palisade at Castleruddery, near the northwestern base of Spinans Hill, may also date to the Neolithic period. Recent dating evidence from the embanked stone circle at Lough Gur suggests these types of monuments were constructed at the start of the Late Neolithic and a similar date could be ascribed to Castleruddery (O'Driscoll and Cleary 2016).

Bronze Age and Iron Age

The Bronze Age is strongly represented in the Baltinglass area (Figure 8.9 and Figure 8.10). Although a number of cist burials have been identified, these are not clearly dated. Rathnagree and Sruhaun are the earliest definitive Bronze Age features in the area and date to the end of the Middle Bronze Age. Rathcoran may also be contemporary with this phase of construction (see above for wider consideration of its dating). Near Tuckmill Hill, a bronze spearhead was recovered from the River Slaney. This is a socketed kite-shaped example with side loops and a blunt blade with mid-ridge and blade decoration. This type of spearhead dates to the Killymaddy/Acton Park Phase of the Middle Bronze Age *c.*1500–1350 and is probably of Irish origin.

FIGURE 8.12: CURSUS OFF THE SUMMIT OF THE WESTERN SLOPES OF KEADEEN MOUNTAIN.

During the Late Bronze Age, around 1150–1000 BC, the third enclosing element at Tinoran was constructed. This may be the primary phase of the monument, being built at the same time as the inner enclosure. Some time latter, possibly, *c.*900–800 BC, Tinoran hillfort may have been enlarged, possibly by a new generation of the same community who constructed the initial hillfort. The fifth enclosing element may be more recent again, representing the third and final stage of hillfort building in the area, although this remains to be confirmed by excavation.

The dating of Brusselstown Ring and Kilranlagh is not known at the present time. The widely spaced enclosing elements apparent at Brusselstown Ring are commonly found in the Late Bronze Age, therefore, such a date range may be applicable. It is difficult to fit the large, low-lying enclosures at Rathmoon, Kilranlagh, Corballis and Keadeen into this outline chronology, considering there is no independent dating or close comparative evidence for these sites. However, the widely spaced multivallation at Rathmoon, and the close siting of other possible Bronze Age monuments, such as standing stones, might tentatively suggest a Late Bronze Age date is appropriate.

The number of barrow monuments in the area that may broadly date to later prehistory imply a concentrated settlement base in the region that could have supported these building projects. The focus for burial may have shifted when a new hillfort was constructed and this may explain the dispersed pattern. The stone circle at Boleycarrigeen and the various standing stones may also be indicative of Late Bronze Age activity. The available evidence suggests that multiple stone circles in Cork and Kerry and some of the standing stones in that region broadly date to 1400–800 BC (O'Brien 2012a: 182).

Considering the enormous Spinans Hill 2 enclosure incorporates the outer enclosing elements of Brusselstown Ring, it is possible that this is a later feature. Flood (2009: 83) has argued that Knocknarea Mountain in Co. Sligo is the most comparable site to Spinans Hill 2, although there are a number of distinct differences that could imply they are not contemporary. Bergh (2000) discovered a system of discontinuous banks with deliberate breaks on the eastern side of Knocknarea, which effectively block off the summit from the lower eastern shoulder. Excavations concluded that the Knocknarea monument dates to the Neolithic period (Bergh 2002), although there are no radiocarbon dates, the early date being assumed because Neolithic material overlies the banks and does not occur within them. There are no obvious breaks in the enclosing elements at Spinans Hill 2, which is possibly later than Brusselstown Ring, for which a Late Bronze Age date has been proposed.

Another possibility is that the enormous Spinans Hill 2 enclosure is Iron Age. This site, and Brusselstown Ring, have been linked with the Iron Age fortress of Dún Bolg that features in a number of Early Medieval texts. The best known tale associated with this site is the Battle of the Pass of Dún Bolg in AD 596. This describes the battle between the Leinstermen and the Uí Néill, where the latter infiltrated the fort of the Ard Rí (High King), killed him and stopped the southern expansion of the Uí Néill. This tale is linked with a more extensive prose called The Bórama. It states Eochaid Doimlén of Ráth Imáil, the first-century King of Leinster, lived near the Glen of Imaal. Interestingly, Brusselstown Ring, Spinans Hill 1 and Spinans Hill 2 are the only large enclosures in the vicinity of the Glen. Spinans Hill 2 may have been built, or at least re-occupied during the Iron Age, but without dating evidence this is speculative.

While there are several Early Medieval ringforts in the Baltinglass area and a church site at Kilranlagh, there seems to be less intensive settlement during this period. The small enclosure ('The Round O') at the summit of Tinoran may be Early Medieval, as its slight banks and modest size are more suggestive of an Early Medieval ringfort than a later prehistoric enclosure. Similarly, the small enclosure at the centre of Hughstown is comparable to the ringfort class of monuments. Comparable evidence is found at Rathgall hillfort, where a large Early Medieval stone ringfort was constructed within a large multivallate hillfort of Late Bronze Age date. Apart from these two examples, there is no obvious evidence to suggest that Early Medieval settlers used older hillforts in the Baltinglass area. Even at Spinans Hill 2, which encloses an area of approximately 131 ha, there are no possible ringfort-type monuments inside the enclosure. Interestingly, there is a ringfort on the lower western slopes of Spinans Hill just outside the large hillfort. It may have been taboo to settle within the ancient forts of the area, unless you were a high status individual, as has been suggested for the Early Medieval occupants of Rathgall (Orpen 1911; 1916).

A Composite Model

Two broad models have been presented to explain the formation of a cluster of large enclosures and hillforts in the Baltinglass area. It is important to stress, however, that without extensive dating information from all of the enclosing elements of each fort, it is difficult to put forward a comprehensive chronology for the cluster. Model 1 proposes that most of the hillforts are broadly contemporary and were constructed during the Middle/Late Bronze Age transition, with additional elements being added to some sites throughout the Late Bronze Age. Model 2 considers that not all of the sites are contemporary and the group comprises a palimpsest of large enclosures. These were constructed from the Early Neolithic when Hughstown and Spinans Hill 1 were built, and after a prolonged temporal break, they continued to be constructed throughout the Bronze Age and possibly Iron Age. During the later prehistoric period, the sequential construction of these hillforts may have been undertaken by new generations of the same community.

It is likely that both models are somewhat correct. For example, the three forts on Tuckmill Hill may comprise a contemporary group of sites built by the same community. Similarly, the Spinans Hill 2 and Brusselstown Ring may also consist of a group of hillforts built at the same time but not necessarily contemporary with those on Tuckmill Hill.

Despite the ambiguity regarding the chronology of the cluster, the reasons for the convergence or persistent occupation of the landscape remains unclear. There are five principal reasons for hillforts to appear in groups. The clustering of forts in an alliance network and partible inheritance remain possible, however, without larger scale excavation to recover radiocarbon dates and sufficient amounts of material culture to compare these sites it is impossible to conclude. The Baltinglass group could be interpreted as a frontier zone where the borders of a number of communities overlap. However, it seems that the prevailing reason for clustering in other areas of Ireland and Britain relates to the control of natural routeways or resources. The Baltinglass group may have been positioned in a densely settled area with good quality agricultural land, allowing the elites in the area to gather larger groups of people to build and maintain the forts, as well as being able to produce larger quantities of surplus food stock for trade or to support the builders of the hillforts or craft-specialists. The possible presence of placer gold in the Wicklow Mountains could also have been a reason for the formation of the cluster; however, without definitive evidence, this remains speculative.

8.2 GIS Models of the Baltinglass Hillfort Landscapes

GIS (Geographical Information Systems) is a computer software system that is designed to capture, store, manipulate, analyse, manage and present data with a spatial or geographical component. The software is used by a wide range of industries and is being increasingly adopted for archaeological projects. GIS has largely been used in a data management capacity and for the creation of cartographic maps such as monument distribution plots. Recently, spatial analytical techniques have gained popularity among archaeologists with particular interest in viewshed, cumulative viewshed, Least-Cost-Path (LCP), aspect and slope analysis. These types of analysis can produce new quantifiable information based on different environmental variables. Their application is particularly useful for hillfort studies, a monument that is often interpreted as being a visible symbol of status and power positioned on or near natural routeways. Before the advent of GIS, it would have been difficult to support such interpretations with objective evidence. As such, these GIS techniques help to quantify what were previously subjective areas of research. GIS is also used in other capacities, such as to view LiDAR and GPS data as well as aerial and satellite imagery. In this regard, it has become an important tool for archaeologists. As many aspects of the following chapter centre on the application of GIS, the following is a short outline of the practical and theoretical parameters of analysis used.

Viewshed analysis is a technique that aims to 'identify those areas that can or cannot be seen from a single (or a set of) viewpoint(s) within a digital model of a terrain, either by calculating line-of-sights between pairs of point locations or via viewshed generation' (Paliou 2013: 2). Wheatley and Gillings (2001: 1) suggest that viewshed analysis is the most unique and valuable GIS application for archaeologists. It is argued that this type of analysis, being at its core 'a model of the field of vision of human actors', can help build and expand quantified generalizations and methodologies for archaeological research (Wheatley 2004: 11). Tschan *et al.* (2000: 33) describe viewshed analysis as a tool closely associated with the human capacity of sight as it attempts to explore past cognitive acts such as the movement of people and their perception of the contemporary landscape. While having obvious functionalist advantages, viewshed analysis has the potential to contribute to wider theoretical approaches, such as cognitive perception, culture/nature dichotomy, visualism and sensory primacy, temporality and directionality (Wheatley 2004: 11).

Others, such as Thomas (1993: 23), reject the 'functionalist' approach which GIS has often been associated with, primarily due to the seeming inability of such systems to accurately model past landscapes, or correctly incorporate human agency. The effect of vegetation in the past is a particular problem, as the height of tree canopies and the extent of forestry cannot be modelled with certainty. Ogburn (2006) discusses other problematic factors that influence visibility, such as the limits of human visual acuity, past environmental effects and the physical properties of objects and their surroundings, all important factors which are often not considered. In many cases, these problems can be compensated for. For example, he suggests that the limits of human recognition acuity for a 1m wide object is 6880m. Significant methodological issues such as visual reciprocity (Loots 1997), the quality of data (particularly the digital elevation model), and the modelling of 'fuzzy viewsheds' (Fisher 1996), need to be considered in order to create more robust visibility models, even if this is not always possible.

An excellent description of GIS methodology is provided by Wheatley (1995: 5). Two data-sets are needed to create a viewshed map, namely, point data and a raster terrain model. In each cell in the raster, a straight line is generated between the point data and every individual cell within the raster terrain model. The height of all the cells that occur on the straight line between the point data and largest cells is then obtained in order to ascertain whether or not the cell exceeds the height of the three dimensional line at that point. The result of each of these calculations is then transformed into either a positive (1: representing visible areas) or negative (0: representing not visible areas) cell, creating a binary image of visibility. A cumulative viewshed is the repetitive process of applying the former technique on the same raster terrain multiple times with different point data (i.e. different positions on the terrain). The multiple binary maps are then overlaid with cells visible from two different points combining and having a value of two, cells visible from three different points having a value of three, and so on. The resultant image is the sum of all the viewsheds, with the value of each cell corresponding with the number of points that can be seen from the cell. Wheatley (1995: 171) suggests that cumulative visibility can be used to make inferences about the relationships of intervisibility between related sites within a landscape.

LCP (Least-Cost Path) analysis can be described as the generation of the optimum path of travel between two chosen points. To pass between these points involves traversing terrain as well as natural and cultural features that impede movement (Howey 2007: 3–4). These impediments are classified and given a cost in the model (these are called 'cost surfaces'), which then selects the path that accumulates the least 'cost' connecting each point. Terrain is probably the most commonly used variable in LCP models because of the energy expenditure to traverse irregular terrain can be easily modelled (Bell and Lock 2000; Surface-Evans 2012: 137; Murrieta-Flores 2010: 254). Bell and Lock (2000) have contributed to the classification of elevation data by recognising that the cost of climbing a slope may not be directly proportional to the degree of slope, i.e. a 45 degree slope is not 45 times more difficult than moving through level terrain. The relationship between slope and effort is therefore not linear (Bell and Lock 2000: 88), and neither is it uniform in direction. Slope is anisotropic, meaning the cost of traversing a downhill slope is not equivalent to travelling uphill. Furthermore, travelling downhill is not necessarily an easier task due to the effects of gravity (Llobera 2000; Murrieta-Flores 2010). When interpreting routes through a landscape with an element of directionality, further calibration is required. In these cases an anisotropic cost algorithm may be used (see Bell and Lock 2000, De Silva and Pizziolo 2001). This algorithm incorporates the direction of force (i.e. downslope) in conjunction with its magnitude (slope). Effectively, an anisotropic algorithm will imply force against someone moving uphill and force with someone moving downhill. Whilst this is appropriate for most applications, there is no consideration of the implications of this over very rough terrain. Beyond certain thresholds in slope, effort moving downhill will ultimately become increased as the slope no longer assists movement. This type of cost analysis is also closely linked with catchment models, where the same 'cost surfaces' can be used to create catchment zones and model travel time.

Despite the advances in understanding slope, Llobera (2000) has emphasised the importance of additional 'cost' factors, suggesting a methodology based entirely on slope-dependant costs negates the importance of cultural factors that might strongly influence movement. Movement can be influenced by social, political or cultural factors, and also by religious beliefs and territoriality in the prehistoric period (Murrieta-Flores 2010: 258). These influences are often difficult to model, hence a reliance on physical factors such as slope. Modelling the physical environment, however, is also problematic. Palaeo-environmental information is often unavailable or too coarse to be able to effectively model woodland, wetland, vegetation cover, etc. Although it is best practice to include multi-criteria surface analysis for large spatial scales (Howey 2007: 1831), this is not always practical, particularly at a micro-landscape level.

Aspect analysis is used to assess the direction in a raster image, usually a terrain model. The technique identifies the downslope direction of the maximum rate of change in value from each cell to its neighbour. It essentially creates a pseudo TIN (Triangular Irregular Network) surface by connecting the edges of individual cells in a raster image to create a sloped surface. The angle of slope can then be measured and plotted against a colour gradient. Aspect is essentially the direction of slope and the values of the resultant analysis will be the compass direction of aspect. It is expressed in positive degrees from zero to 359.9 and flat areas are assigned a value of -1. As such, slope analysis works in a similar way. Slope information is extracted from an input TIN or raster terrain model. The resultant analysis produces a vector image of the severity of slope plotted against a colour gradient. For example, a minor slope of 4 degrees will have a lesser value than a slope of 25 degrees. For both analytical techniques, the quality and resolution of the original raster image or TIN is important.

Hillfort territories

Bradley (1990: 137) has argued that during the Late Bronze Age a concern with the definition of territory may be reflected in the siting of hillforts, with Kristiansen and Larsson (2005: 43) arguing that the idea of boundaries between inner and outer space, nature and culture, civilised and barbarians, them and us, is rooted in every society. A discussion of the Late Bronze Age of the North Munster region argued that the distributional pattern of hillforts suggests a strong element of territoriality, especially at a regional or sub-regional scale, and that this could be expanded to include the whole of Ireland (Grogan 2005a: 98). These territories would range from 225km² to 325km² and were divided into smaller territorial zones up to 21km² (also see Grogan 2014: 63) . Natural features defined these boundaries, with contemporary burial monuments often found in close vicinity.

Collens (1988) argues that Iron Age hillforts and enclosures of the Upper Severn Valley had a similar network of regularly spaced sites 6.5–9.2km apart, though with much smaller territories averaging 16–25km². Driver (2013: 145) argues for a similar territory size for Pen Dinas hillfort in Wales, although he has noted that smaller hillforts north of the Rheidol River in the North Ceredigion district have more limited zones of influence (*ibid.*,: 142–143). In Cunliffe's (2000) analysis of Danebury hillfort, the author reconstructs its territorial landscape at various periods in time. At the height of the hillfort phenomenon in Britain, around 300 BC, Danebury's territory was probably extended to a diameter of 20km (approximately 314.16km²), with hillforts of comparable size and status positioned just outside these limits. Conversely, in Baden-Württemberg, Germany, regularly spaced contemporary hillforts along river valleys, especially along the Danube and its tributaries, infer territories of only a few square kilometres in size (Harding 2000: 303). The reality is that hillfort territories probably varied in extent both regionally and chronologically.

Hillfort territories: a landscape approach

Cunliffe (1991: 510) views natural locations such as springs, streams or woodlands as religious and ritual locations. Stanford (1972: 313), and more recently Driver (2013: 141), have argued that rivers and other water courses may have formed 'ready-made' boundaries defining prehistoric territories. Fleming's (1978: 112) study of the Dartmoor reaves boundary systems highlighted the importance of rivers as functional and highly visible territorial markers. Similarly, Grogan (2005b: 140) has argued that rivers and streams were used to define territories in the Late Bronze Age. Murphy *et al.* (2007) and Driver (2013: 141–142) argue that these natural boundaries defined the territories of some hillforts in Wales. An example would be the spatial distribution of hillforts and smaller defended enclosures on either side of the Teifi River in Wales (Murphy *et al.* 2007). The importance of rivers in later prehistory is also emphasised by the significant number of prestige objects deposited within them. Rivers and other wetland locations are often interpreted as liminal places, where rituals of various types may have been conducted. Bradley (1990) suggests that the deposition of prestige goods in such locations supports the argument that rivers acted as 'tribal frontiers'. This is supported by the strong association of Late Bronze Age swords with rivers in Ireland (Eogan 1965).

Taking the Baltinglass landscape as an example, there are numerous streams and rivers cutting through the topography, many of which are tributaries of the Slaney River located at the centre of the hillfort cluster. The larger examples have created subtle valleys that have deeply affected the terrain and are distinct in the GIS slope analysis (Figure 8.13). These may have acted as 'ready-made' boundaries to the 'core' territories of each fort.

Located 400m to the south of Haughey's Fort, Conway (2006: 37) proposed that the Creeveroe linear earthworks, functioned as a territorial division and formed a key component of that Late Bronze Age landscape. He argues that linear earthworks often have a marked relationship with ring-barrows, and may have formed part of a territorial system with a less formal mode of definition. The earthworks essentially formed part of a boundary defining the core area dominated by Haughey's Fort (*ibid.*: 38). They are close to the find-spot of a Late Bronze Age neck-ring of Iberian origin (Warner 2006). This may have been deposited immediately outside the earthworks to enhance the ritual potency of the boundary. The Tamlaght hoard is located 600m to the south-west of Haughey's Fort and was deposited in a north–south river valley. This find contained some bronze bowls of Central European origin, as well as a sword (Warner 2006), and may have defined the south-western territorial boundary of the hillfort. The potential composite boundary would measure approximately 1.3km (east–west) by 1.6km (north–south) (2.08 km^2). The idea of a core boundary may be supported by environmental studies, which highlight the intensive clearance and exploitation of land immediately surrounding Irish hillforts. Major clearance episodes in the environs of Haughey's Fort seem to be

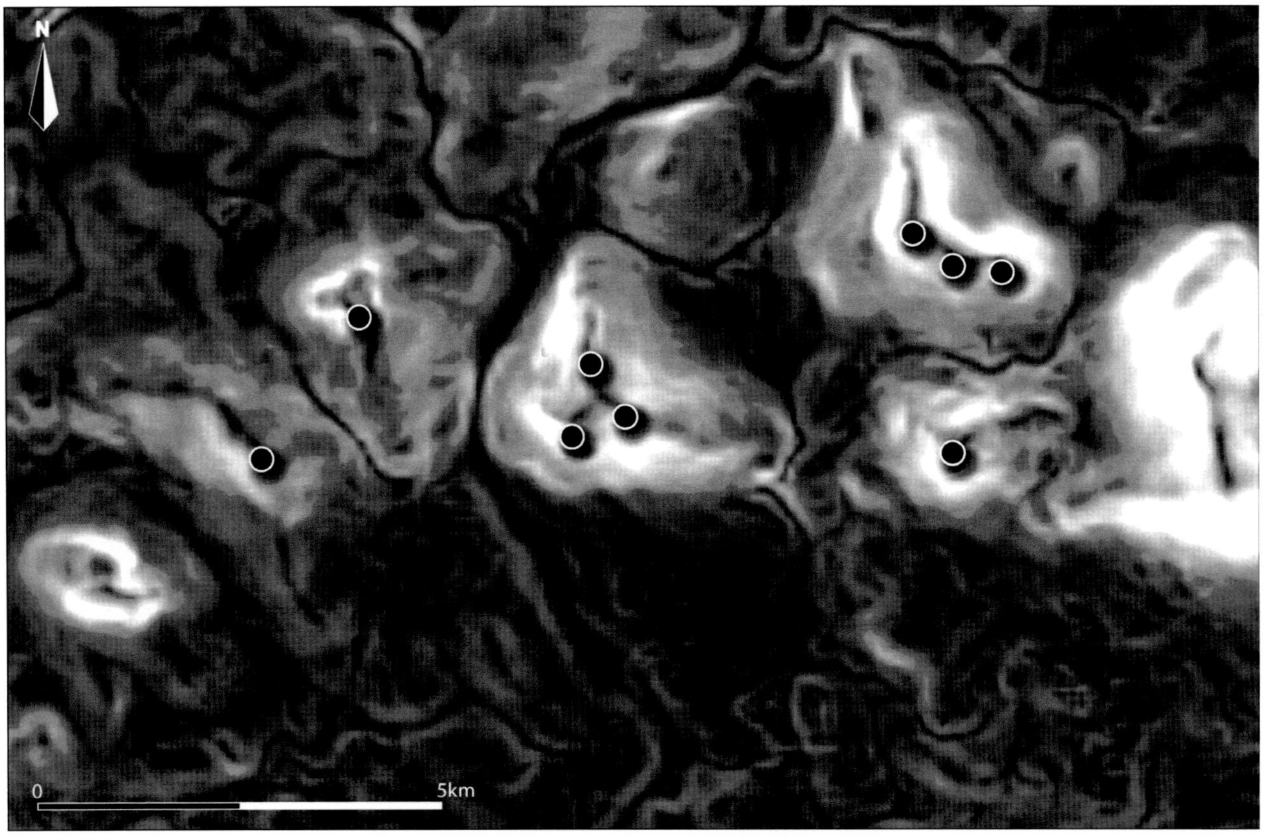

FIGURE 8.13: SLOPE ANALYSIS OF THE BALTINGLASS AREA.

contemporary with the construction and occupation of this hillfort (Weir 1987a; 1987b; 1993; 1994).

Boundaries may have been augmented by linear earthworks or other ritual monuments such as ring-barrows (Conway 2006: 38). This has been pointed out by Gosden and Lock (1998: 8) who argue that funerary monuments may have helped to loosely delineated later prehistoric territories. This corresponds with Woodward (2000) and Cooney's (2009: 376) interpretations that funerary barrows also functioned as 'landscape monuments', the latter arguing that barrow cemeteries were themselves a monument. The deliberate positioning of barrows in relation to each other demonstrates a marked concern with the past and the creation of ancestral history and lineage (*ibid.*: 378). It also facilitated the creation of group identity and social cohesion, as collective mourning and the sharing of funerary space are powerful bonding mechanisms (Grogan 2014: 61). Thomas (2007: 261) comments that in many traditional societies the knowledge of descent, genealogy, alliance and inheritance is an important form of power. Barrow cemeteries were significant as they could be used to visibly express legitimate rights to land or resources through patterns of actual or imagined lineage, which may have been particularly important at territorial margins.

In the Republic of Ireland approximately 73% of hillforts have at least one type of recorded barrow within 5km, and 50% have examples within 3km. Some hillforts have dense numbers of barrows in their environs, with seven examples having more than ten barrows within a 5km buffer zone. These include Knockainy, Co. Limerick; Grannagh, Co. Galway; Killeenadeema, Co. Roscommon; Sroove, Co. Roscommon; Mountfortesque, Co. Meath; Drumnagranshy, Co. Sligo and Knocknashee, Co. Sligo. Knockainy hillfort is positioned at the centre of an extensive group of barrows in the east Limerick plains. Another interesting example is the group of barrows near Grannagh hillfort in Co. Galway. Up to 30 barrows have been recorded with a 7km distance, most of these to the north of the hillfort. Outside of this buffer zone, there is a notable absence of barrow monuments, with only four additional examples within a 17km radius. A group of 31 barrows are located within 9km of Killeenadeema hillfort. These are mainly clustered in the east and south-east. A lesser number of barrows are scattered on the hilltops to the south. There is a clear restriction of other barrow monuments outside of this group. In Co. Roscommon, two hillforts approximately 13km apart sit on the eastern and western edge of upland terrain. Positioned between these hillforts are up to 116 barrows. These are distributed in an almost linear fashion, roughly orientated north-south. They may have been used to define the tribal territories of both hillforts (Figure 8.14).

In southeastern Slovenia, the appearance of hillforts in

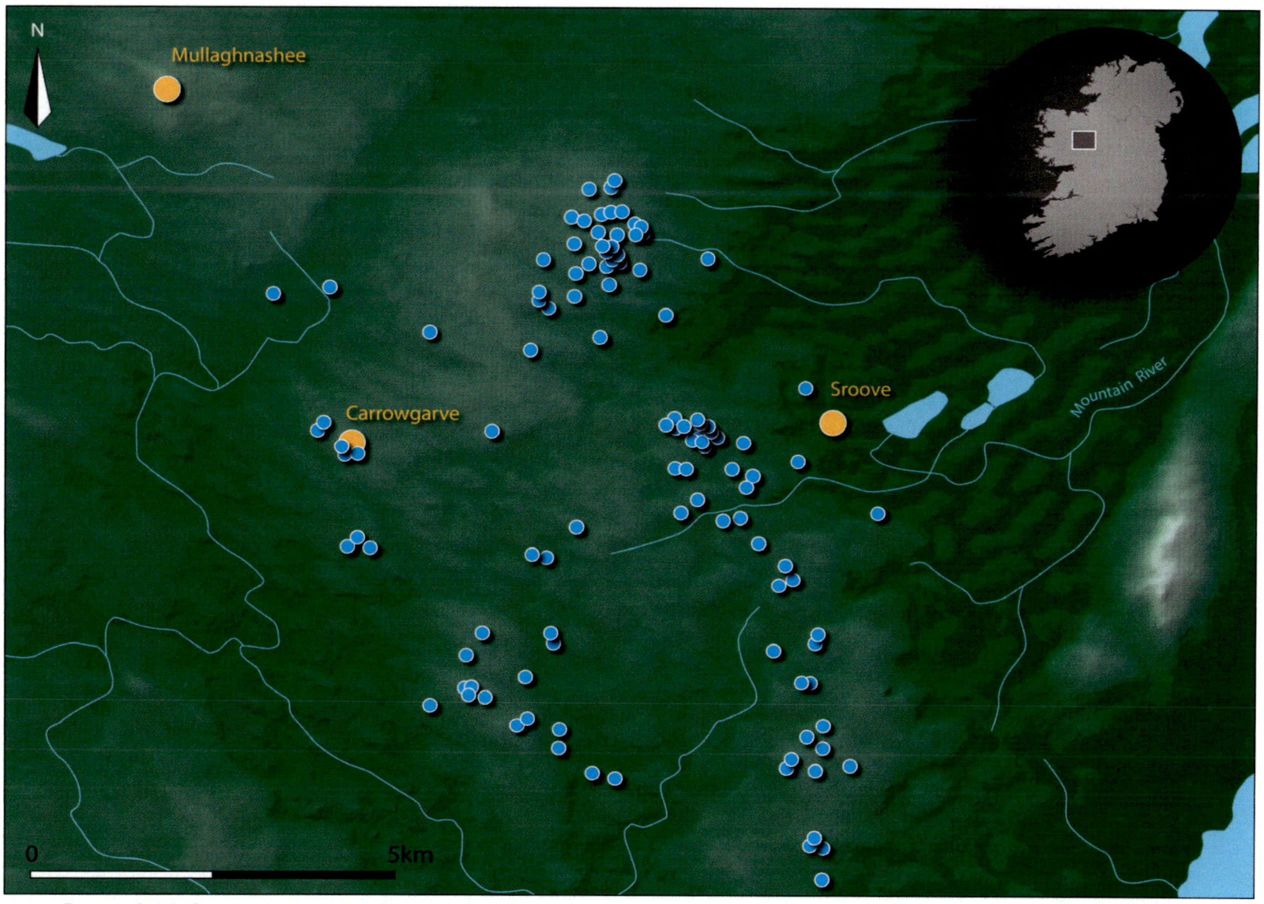

Figure 8.14: Carrowgarve and Sroove hillforts, Co. Roscommon seperated by a dense distribution of barrows.

the Early Iron Age coincided with the emergence of large barrow cemeteries that cluster in groups approximately 1km from contemporary hillforts. Mason (2013: 264–268) has demonstrated that these clusters were deliberately positioned on the main approach to a hillfort. This forced outsiders to progress past the tombs of the ancestors, 'ritually cleansing them' and allowing access to the interior. This procession would have been a powerful reminder of the legitimacy and legacy of the community and its leader. A similar interpretation could be applied to the Early Iron Age hillfort of Bel'sk in Eastern Ukraine, where a number of large barrow cemeteries surround the monument. Similarly, more than 50 burial mounds surround Heuneburg hillfort in southern Germany. These comprise two groups located 500m to the north-west and 3.5km to the west and include the Hohmichele mound, one of the largest of its type in Central Europe (Fernández-Götz and Krausse 2012: 29). The development of large barrow cemeteries in Central Europe at this time is not paralleled in Britain, although barrow groups have been identified near hillforts such as Maiden Castle in Dorset (Sharples 1991: 21).

Newman (2007: 431) noted the taboos relating to the kingship of Tara, which refer to the 'correct' direction one should enter and exit the complex, and suggests this to be a 'universal tradition of correct orientation towards the sacred, one not restricted solely to Tara'. The importance of accessing a site in the 'correct' way is therefore attested in many places throughout Europe in prehistory and the early historic period. In some cases, this may also have applied to Irish hillforts.

This may be evident in the Baltinglass area, where a considerable number of possible barrows, identified through aerial and satellite photography, as well as LiDAR survey, are located in low-lying areas, either at the base of hilltops with hillforts or adjacent to streams and rivers (Figure 5.54). There is a visible pattern in the placement of these burial monuments. Clusters of barrows appear at the base of Tuckmill Hill and Tinoran, whereas individual barrows or small groups of up to four are positioned near rivers and streams, or in other marginal locations. Barrow groups also appear near the most accessible slopes of the hilltops, such as at Tinoran and Tuckmill Hill.

On Tuckmill Hill, a group of possible barrows occur at the southeastern base at an excellent access point to the summit, where the gradient of slope is least severe. Other access routes outlined by Least-Cost-Path analysis to the west and north/north-west are close to smaller barrow groups (see Figure 8.45). Tuckmill Hill is also surrounded by a number of individual barrows and cist burials to the east and north-west. It seems that the base of the hill was surrounded by a dense number of possible burial monuments, with clusters of visible barrows in areas that allowed access to the summit. The latter could be viewed as an attempt to force visitors to progress past burial monuments that highlighted the legitimacy of the community and leader, while the former could be a reserved effort to placate local hilltop deities, ensuring the fertility of the land and its people, as well as spiritually demarcating the core territory of the hillfort. A similar scenario could be argued at Tinoran, where a cluster of possible barrows are positioned near the base of the hill at the easiest approach to the summit and individual barrows are located around the base in the east and north-east. At Hughstown, two unrecorded barrows and an embanked pond are positioned at an approach point near the base of the hill at the east/south-east. Barrows have also been identified surrounding the base of Spinans Hill and Kilranlagh, although in lesser numbers, though this may reflect the lack of available LiDAR data.

There is also a notable concentration of barrows near rivers and streams in the Baltinglass area. These monuments to the dead could have been placed near territorial boundaries to both physically and ritually demarcate a community's core tribal ground. Grogan (2005b: 140) infers that barrows and barrow cemeteries may have been positioned deliberately to emphasise natural boundaries such as rivers and streams. Mason (2013: 273) argues that some barrows in south-eastern Slovenia were constructed on or near important routeways as demonstrations of ownership. Similarly, Tilley (2010: 221) has proposed that barrow groups along the Wessex Ridgeway are invariably located with reference to transition points in the landscape, possibly indicating territorial division. For the same area Woodward (1991: 143) has argued that three separate 'territories' existed, each being defined by Bronze Age barrow cemeteries. At the Iron Age royal site of Rathcroghan in Co. Roscommon, Waddell *et al.* (2009: 198) have suggested that the burial monuments within the complex signify an important ancient burial place. They argue that the largest and most prominent ring-barrows, the Corrauneen and Dath-í's Mound, lie furthest from Rathcroghan Mound, the focal point of the complex, more or less at the northern and southern limits of the complex (*ibid.*: 205).

The number of possible barrows identified in the Baltinglass area suggests that this monument type was used for individuals that were seen as 'special' by their community. In this respect, Cunliffe (1991: 499) has pointed out an interesting difference between the recovery contexts of seventh- and sixth-century BC Hallstatt swords. On the Continent these are recovered from burial contexts in contrast to Britain, where all except one have been recovered from rivers. Cunliffe explains this phenomenon as a result of different burial rites, whereas in Britain, the dead were cremated and disposed of with their equipment in rivers. Similarly, in the southern Netherlands, Belgium and western Germany, swords were deposited in rivers during the Middle Bronze Age (Brück and Fontijn 2013: 119), with relatively few found in contemporary burial mounds. Kristiansen links the deposition of these artefacts in water contexts with the Celtic–Germanic–Greek ritual of sacrificing weapons after a victorious fight and argues that the deposition of a warriors most valued weapon should be regarded as a symbolic representation of the war party (*ibid.*: 329).

The deposition context of Irish Middle and Late Bronze Age swords (as well as in many parts of north-west Europe at this time), spearheads and axeheads in liminal areas such as rivers, streams and bogs could also be viewed in this way. Bradley (1990: 102; 107) has pointed out that the deposition of such items may be linked to funerary ritual and a new way of disposing of the dead. If such places were used to define territorial boundaries, the deposition of both prestige artefacts and the dead would have reinforced a community's sense of place and ownership of the land and solidified the ritual potency of territorial boundaries. The cremated remains of warriors may have been deposited in rivers with their weapons to defend the living from external threats, both living and dead, while visible burial monument such as barrows, positioned near these locations, could have acted as a physical means of defining and reinforcing territorial claims, with token deposits of the cremated individual. This may explain why, in Ireland, such weapons have never been found in association with human remains.

The 'power' of the ancestors played a significant role in the social and cosmological order of tribal societies (Waddell *et al.* 2009: 205). However, we must also consider the chronology of this type of burial monument. Barrows were being constructed as early as the Neolithic, and continued in use into the Iron Age as noted by Waddell (1998) and even into the Early Medieval period (Doody 2008). Even within a barrow group there can be a considerable chronological range. For example, both Raftery (1941) and Cooney (2009: 381) have pointed out an extensive sequence of activity at the barrow cemetery of Carrowjames II, Co. Mayo, that extended over 1500 years. This type of monument is, therefore, not necessarily contemporary with hillforts; however, their presence in numbers does indicate an area of exceptional importance.

This is further emphasised in the Baltinglass area by the numerous cairns and other ritual monuments such as Linkardstown burials and the embanked stone circle at Castleruddery, which are earlier in date (Figure 5.56). Of particular note is the possible passage tomb cemetery near the summit of Spinans Hill 1 (Figure 5.5). Rathcoran hillfort also encloses an earlier passage tomb, with a second cairn incorporated into the outer enclosing elements on the south-west side. Four cairns are positioned near the enclosing elements at Kilranlagh to the west. Thomas (2007: 261) argues that funerary structures that actually contained the remains of the dead would have been an important element of ritual and a means of securing legitimacy and power. This interpretation is supported by Kristiansen and Larsson (2005: 45), who suggest that a chief's 'access to origins', and the control of 'media' believed to be closely related to ancestry, were crucial to legitimate rule. Bradley (2002: 47) argues that the past in contemporary society was particularly important during periods when new regions were settled and new relationships were formed between people and the land. A physical link to the past in the form of an earlier burial cairn would have been a highly visible way to legitimate a community's real or perceived link to past generations and the land. Approximately 25% of Irish hillforts have recorded cairns or mounds and three hillforts surround recorded megalithic tombs. This indicates the perceived importance of this earlier monument to hillfort builders.

Sharples (2007: 180) suggests that hillfort communities were in competition to attract increasingly larger numbers of people to help in the construction of their hillfort. This, coupled with continued agricultural intensification may have brought about an increased sense of ownership of the land and a subsequent need to define and display that ownership. The wider territorial unit of a hillfort may have been defined by topographical features such as mountains and rivers. The construction and/or recognition of more constricted core zones has been noted at hillforts, such as Haughey's Fort in Co. Armagh. This may reflect a more common approach to defining core areas than a need to demarcate boundaries in a densely settled area. These zones were probably defined by natural features, such as rivers and streams, and were sometimes ritually reinforced by placing burial monuments close by, or by the deposition of weapons or prestige goods. These acted as physical claims to the land and so legitimised a community's right to the territory.

Hillfort territories: a GIS approach

In the late 1970's, there were several attempts to statistically define hillfort territories using Thiessen Polygons (Cunliffe 1971; Hogg 1971; Clarke 1972; Collis 1977). This technique generates polygons around a single sample point, located so that any point generated inside the polygon is closer to that sample point than other sample points on the map. There were a number of problems with this technique, primarily the assumption that the hillforts in question were contemporary, that the dataset is complete, and that the variables introduced by natural topography are not relevant. Despite these limitations, Thiessen-generated territories for second–first century BC hillforts in the Wiltshire chalklands hinted at the potential of statistical modelling. Cunliffe noted that the probable spheres of influence highlighted by the model usually bordered river valleys, comparing favourably with theoretical approaches and the clearly defined territories of contemporary hillforts on the Sussex Downs (Cunliffe 1971: 59–60; fig. 14). He concluded that somewhat evenly spaced territories averaging 90km² were the normal socio-economic unit for a single large hillfort on the southern chalkland.

Calculating the territorial boundaries based on distance from a single point is probably inappropriate. The cost factor should be weighted by cultural factors such as visibility, closeness to other hillforts, and by natural features such as rivers, streams and other topographical elements. As Driver (2013: 141) observed a 'flat' statistical calculation does not consider these factors, even though they probably exerted considerable influence on territorial layout. Some of these problems can be overcome using modern GIS techniques. The continued development of Path-Distance Catchment models is particularly important in this context. This analysis can generate more robust models that can quantitatively define accessibility and ease of movement. Importantly, anisotropic movement can be calculated using Tobler's hiking function, which assumes that the average person can walk 5km an hour in a flat landscape with no impediments (Tobler 1993). This determines the hiking speed with regard to the angle of slope in the terrain and can be used to determine walking time. An excellent review of this technique and other cost surface analysis has recently been published by Herzog (2014). This technique is important because it can incorporate terrain and other potential 'cost' features such as rivers and streams, bogs or even cultural attributes such as visibility.

Experimental studies have found that travel time is a major factor in a traveller's evaluation of subjective distance (Burnett 1978; Golledge and Zannaras 1973; MacEachren 1980; Livingwood 2012). Livingood (2012: 177) suggests that polity size of Southern Appalachian societies may be broadly defined as half a day's walk from the central monument, which he argues is the equivalent of 5–6 hours travel time. However other physical and cultural factors should also be considered, such as visibility to and from the site. The latter is particularly important, as it has been argued that Late Bronze Age hillforts were strategically positioned in the landscape to dominate and control trade routes and/or natural resources.

Taking one site dated by the present project, Ballylin hillfort in Co. Limerick, we might consider the above factors in attempting to define hillfort territory. Considering Ballyin is strategically positioned at the eastern edge of a north–south running escarpment overlooking a broad expanse of lowland to the east, with hilly terrain to the west (Figure 8.15), this will affect both travel time and visibility in different ways. Visibility from the hillfort is heavily obscured to the west, while to the east there are extensive views (Figure 8.16). Similarly, travel time and energy expenditure is adversely affected in the undulating territory to the west (Figure 8.16). This lowland zone mostly comprises well drained mineral soils, whereas, the upland terrain to the west consists

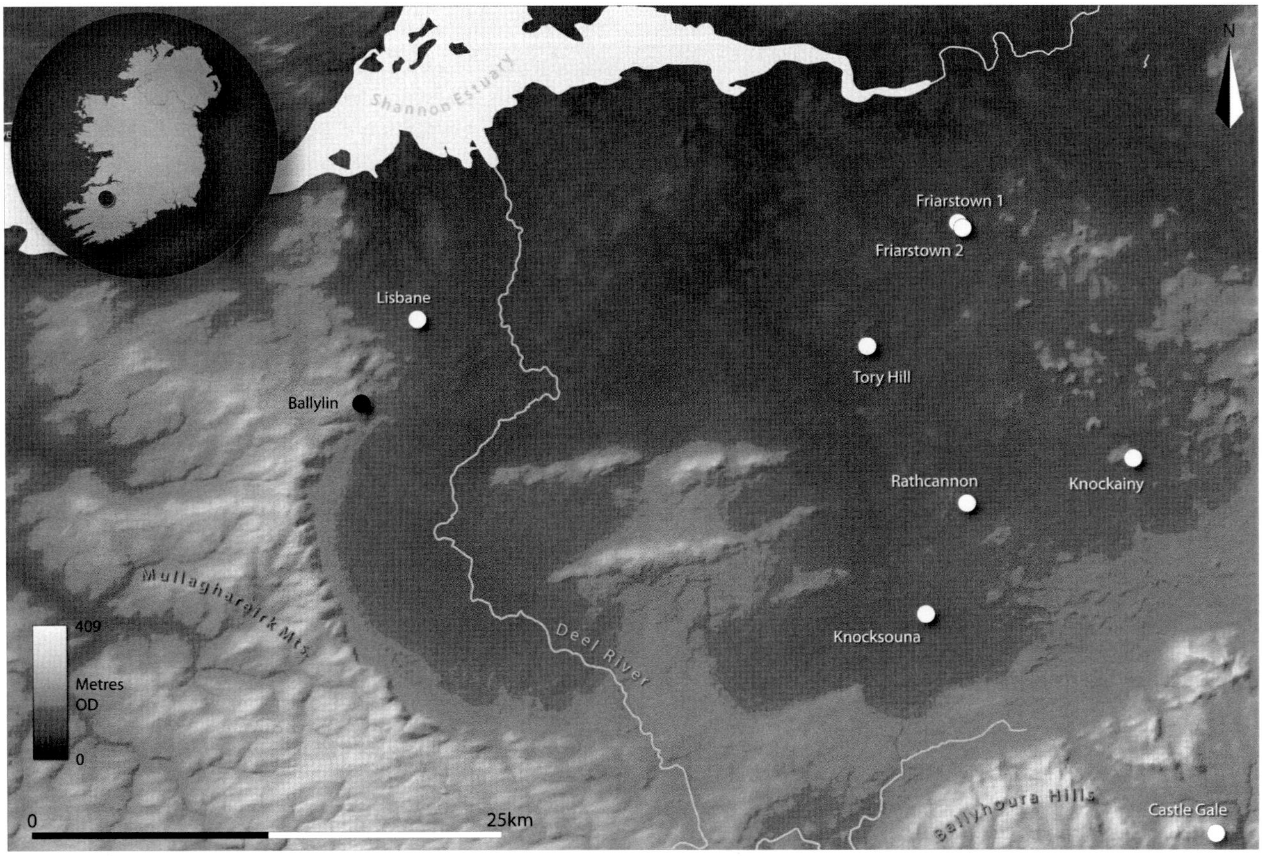

FIGURE 8.15: BALLYLIN AND THE HILLFORTS OF THE LIMERICK REGION.

of peats and poorly drained mineral soils less applicable to farming regimes. From a settlement perspective, the low-lying terrain to the east of Ballylin was probably more densely populated and, therefore, the social and economic territory likely expanded into this zone. Cumulative viewshed analysis supports this assumption (Figure 8.17). In this analysis, we populate the area with 630 randomly generated viewer points. Significantly, 98.5% of the 630 viewer points can see Ballylin hillfort, making it one of only four points in the landscape that is visible to that many points. If we restrict the viewer points to areas that are both visible from the hillfort and within six hour walking distance of the site, we see a partial rise in the percentage of points that can see the hillfort, 98.6%, however, in this case, it is the only position in the landscape that is visible to that many points. Interestingly, within the 6-hour isocline, the number of areas visible to a significant number of the viewer points increases dramatically, while beyond this boundary, the prominence of Ballylin begins to diminish. This might suggest that a combination of visibility and travel time can be used to broadly demarcate the territorial boundary of certain hillforts. In the case of Ballylin, this analysis suggests it controlled a considerable area of the Limerick lowlands, with an approximate territorial area of 370km^2, somewhat similar to the territorial sizes Grogan proposed for some Irish hillforts (Grogan 2005a: 87–99; Grogan 2014: 63). Although the proposed boundary does not correlate with any contemporary monuments or artefacts, it does broadly correspond with the physical attributes of the local landscape.

The siting of the Baltinglass hillforts

Using a basic Thiessen approach, the size of the hillfort territories in the Baltinglass cluster are presented in Figure 8.18. A more informative Path-Distance Catchment model was generated for all of the Baltinglass hillforts, to help define their territory and the area accessible to the hillfort communities (Figure 8.19). This identified five major zones of influence, each surrounding one or more hillforts. The three hillforts on Spinans Hill and the three hillforts on Tuckmill Hill each comprise a single zone. The zones are defined by topographical features, with rivers and streams comprising the principal boundaries. When this data is organised using quantile classification (a data classification method that distributes a set of values into groups that contain an equal number of values), major topographical impediments become more pronounced, allowing us to better define the potential catchment (Figure 8.19). This catchment is delineated to the east by the Wicklow Mountains, while to the north, undulating hilly terrain appears to be a significant cost factor for movement. Conversely, the comparatively flat terrain to the west and south is less costly for travel, with distance and travel time comprising the major 'barriers' or limits in this respect. A number of possible contemporary unenclosed settlements have been identified at the edge of this catchment area, including Mullamast, Burtown Little and Prumplestown Lower in Co. Kildare. This, however, may reflect more intensive archaeological investigation associated with the M8 motorway, contrasting with a lack of excavation in the environs of Baltinglass. More importantly, the paired hillforts at Rathgall and Knockeen are positioned at the southern extremity of this possible catchment zone.

Applying this Path-Distance Catchment approach to the individual hillforts at Baltinglass, we can begin to differentiate potential territories, catchments zones and areas of influence. The model generated for Hughstown (Figure 8.20) reveals a catchment area approximately 34km by 29km (944km^2), delineated in the east by the Wicklow Mountains and the north and north-east by undulating terrain. The southern and western portion of the potential catchment is more expansive because the land is flat and the boundary is determined by travel time rather than topographical impediments. Major topographical barriers include the hilltops of Spinans, Tuckmill and Kilranlagh, with the former hilltop located more than 6 hours walking distance from Hughstown. Tinoran Hill does not act as a major landscape impediment. The analysis suggests that Hughstown is more accessible from the north/north-west, where a more gradual incline ascends the hilltop. A second approach point is apparent at the east/south-east. This route corresponds with the entrance to the small internal enclosure on the summit of Hughstown, and is near two unrecorded ring-barrows and an embanked pond on the lower eastern side of the hill.

Viewshed analysis (Figure 8.21) corresponds with the Path-Distance Catchment model. The site dominates the eastern, southern and western surroundings of the hilltop and has particularly impressive views of the flat landscape to the south and south-east. There is direct line-of-sight visibility of the Castlecomer Hills, which are 23km south-west of Hughstown. This comprises a potential 1364km^2 of terrain visible from its interior. A ridge that extends towards the north-west of Hughstown blocks visibility beyond this area and prevents comprehensive visibility of the immediate slopes. Tinoran Hill prevents visibility upland to the north-east, while Tuckmill Hill and Spinans Hill obscures field of vision towards the west.

The Path-Distance Catchment model for Tinoran reveals easily accessible land to the immediate north and south, with major landscape impediments including Spinans Hill, Tuckmill Hill and Kilranlagh (Figure 8.22). The possible catchment area is defined by the Wicklow Mountains in the west, undulating terrain in the north and by travel time in the south and west. It measures approximately 28km east-west by 32km north-south (839km^2). The easiest access point for the site is to the south, where the gradual, elongated slope of the hill rises

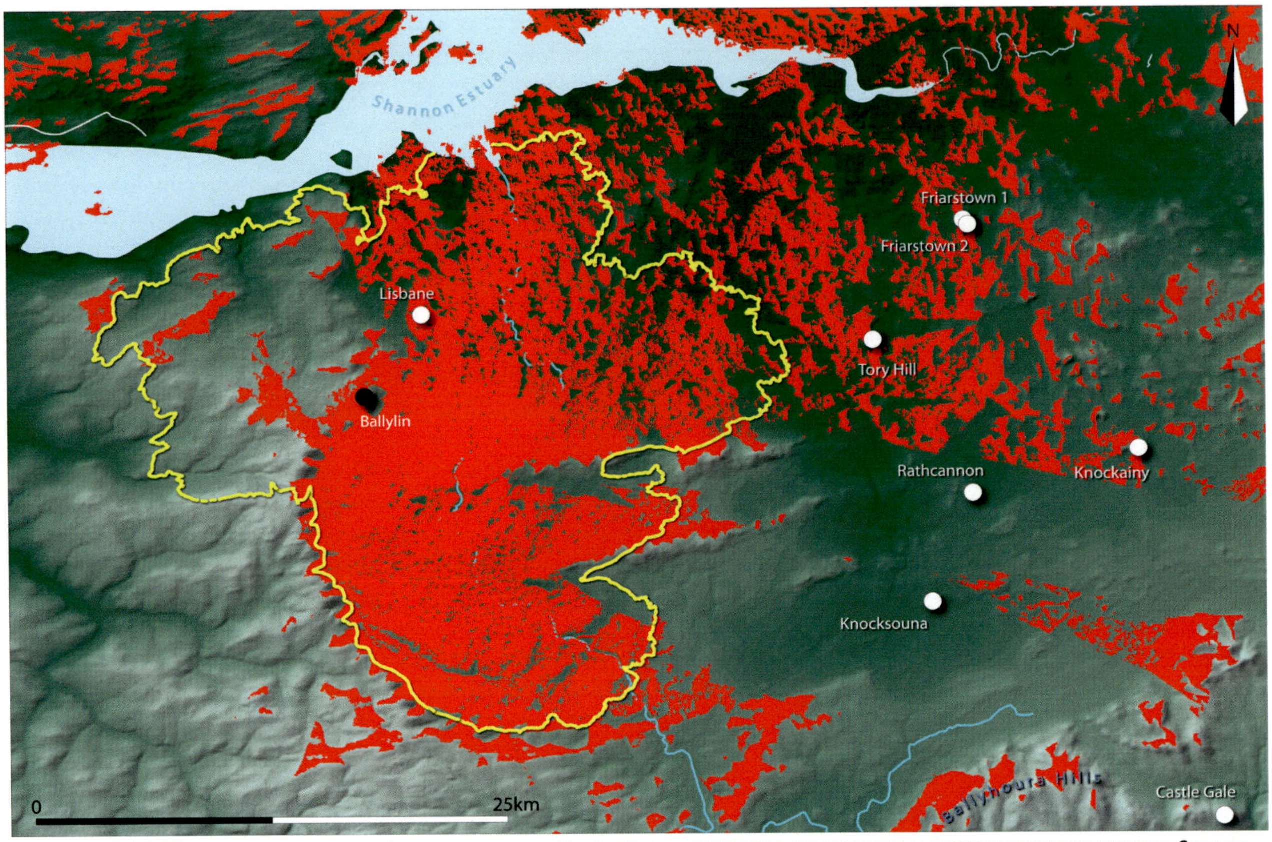

Figure 8.16: Viewshed analysis of Ballylin hillfort, Co. Limerick, with yellow isocline marking territory within 6 hour walking distance of the hillfort. Note the prominent escarpment hindering movement in the south-west.

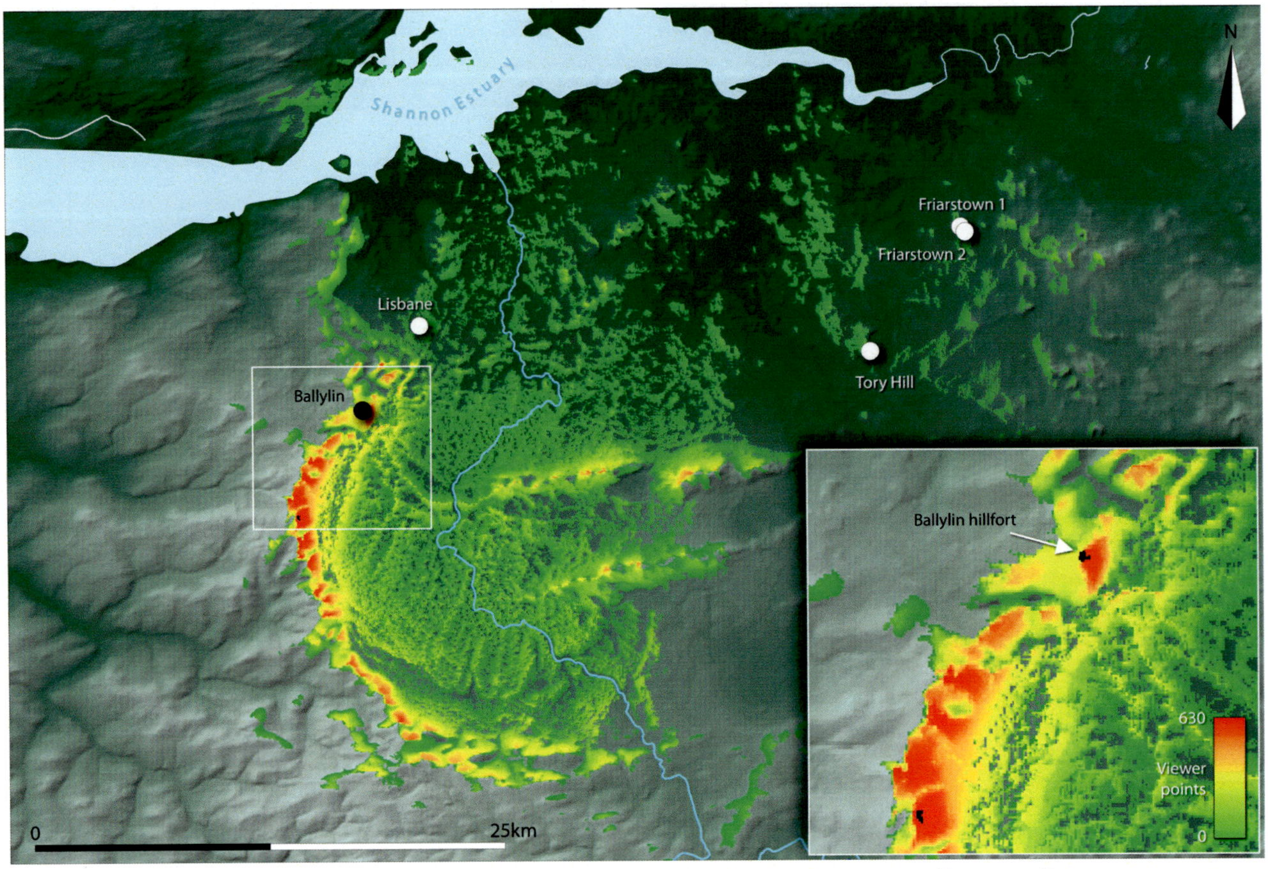

Figure 8.17: Cumulative viewshed analysis of lowlands to the east of Ballylin hillfort. Note that Ballylin hillfort is one of only two areas in this landscape that is visible to over 98 percent of the randomly generated viewer points. This highlights Ballylin's dominant visual position in this region.

to the summit.

Viewshed analysis broadly supports the catchment model. Tinoran hillfort has a potential 1435km² of terrain visible from its interior (Figure 8.23). There are extensive views of the immediate hill slopes and more expansive visibility of the flat terrain to the west and south. An elongated ridge to the south-east blocks visibility in that direction. Hughstown sits on the southern summit of a north-west/south-east running ridge 1.4km south-west of Tinoran and impedes visibility in this direction, although Corballis Hill is visible beyond Hughstown. Tuckmill Hill and Spinans Hill impede visibility to the east.

The Path-Distance Catchment model (Figure 8.24) for hillforts on Tuckmill Hill reveals a catchment area of approximately 29km east–west by 44km north–south (871km²). The possible catchment zone is defined by the Wicklow Mountains to the east, and to a lesser extent the north-east. The northwestern limit is delineated by undulating terrain, while the southern and western extent is defined by travel time. The three enclosures on Tuckmill Hill are positioned at the centre of the cluster and therefore are easily accessible to the other hillforts. There are no major topographical impediments preventing access to the other hillforts in the group. The three enclosures on Tuckmill Hill are within 15 minutes walking distance. The easiest access routes to the summit are to the north-east, overlooked by Rathnagree, the south-east, overlooked by Rathcoran, and to the west, overlooked by Sruhaun. The hillforts dominate the immediate hill-slopes and land surrounding it, with impressive views of terrain in the south. Viewsheds of the three hillforts suggest that land to the south was of primary importance (Figure 8.25, Figure 8.26 and Figure 8.27). This land, as well as low-lying areas to the north, is easily accessible from Tuckmill Hill.

Rathcoran has a potential 2082km² of terrain visible from the interior (Figure 8.25). The northern and western summits of Tuckmill Hill block immediate views of the slopes of the hilltop and its immediate environs, while other hilltops such as Spinans Hill, Hughstown and Tinoran impede visibility to the east and west. A series of

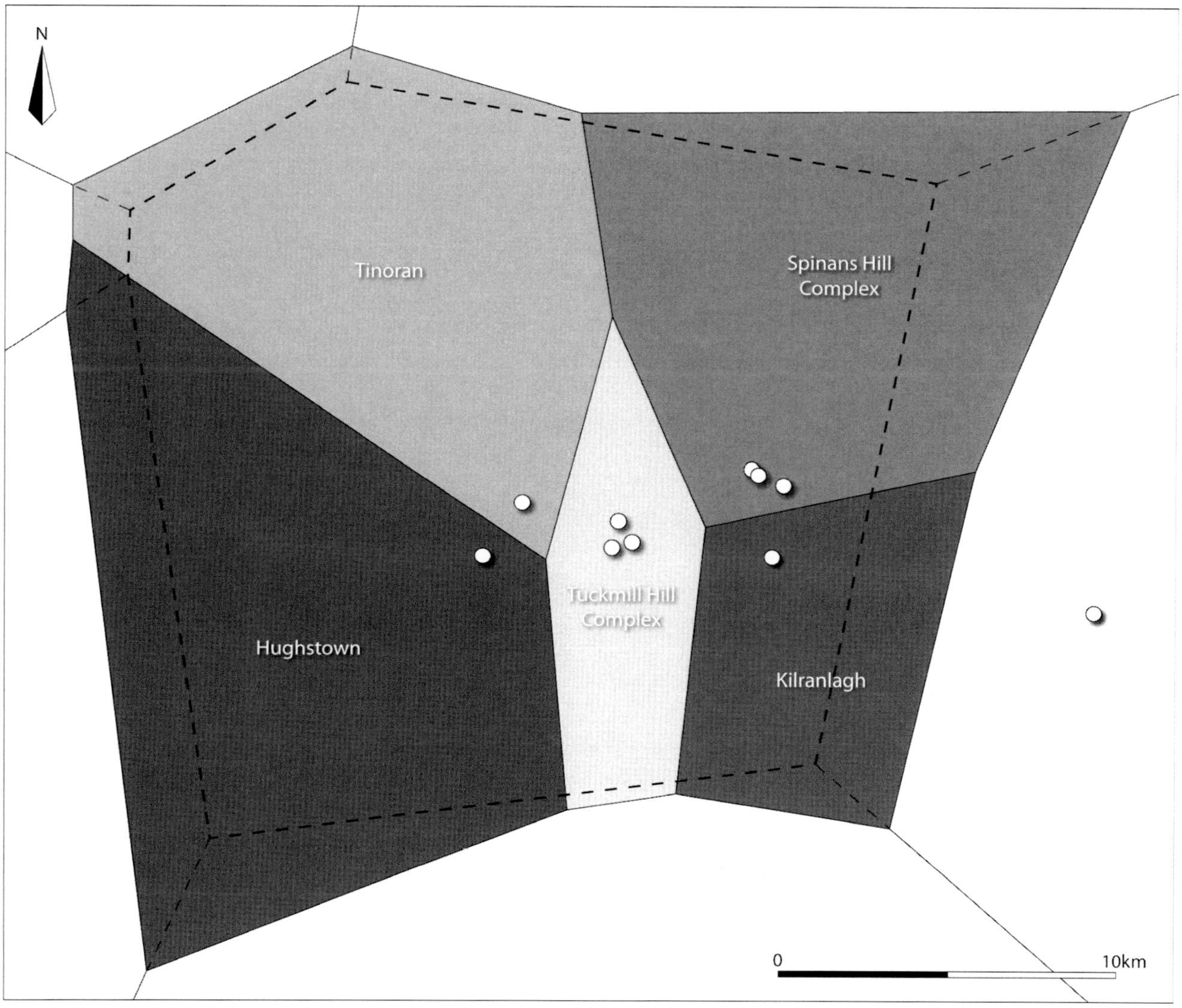

FIGURE 8.18: THIESSEN POLYGONS REFLECTING POTENTIAL TERRITORIAL BOUNDARIES IN THE BALTINGLASS AREA. THE DASHED LINE POSTULATES AN APPROXIMATE TERRITORY FOR A SINGLE ISOLATED FORT.

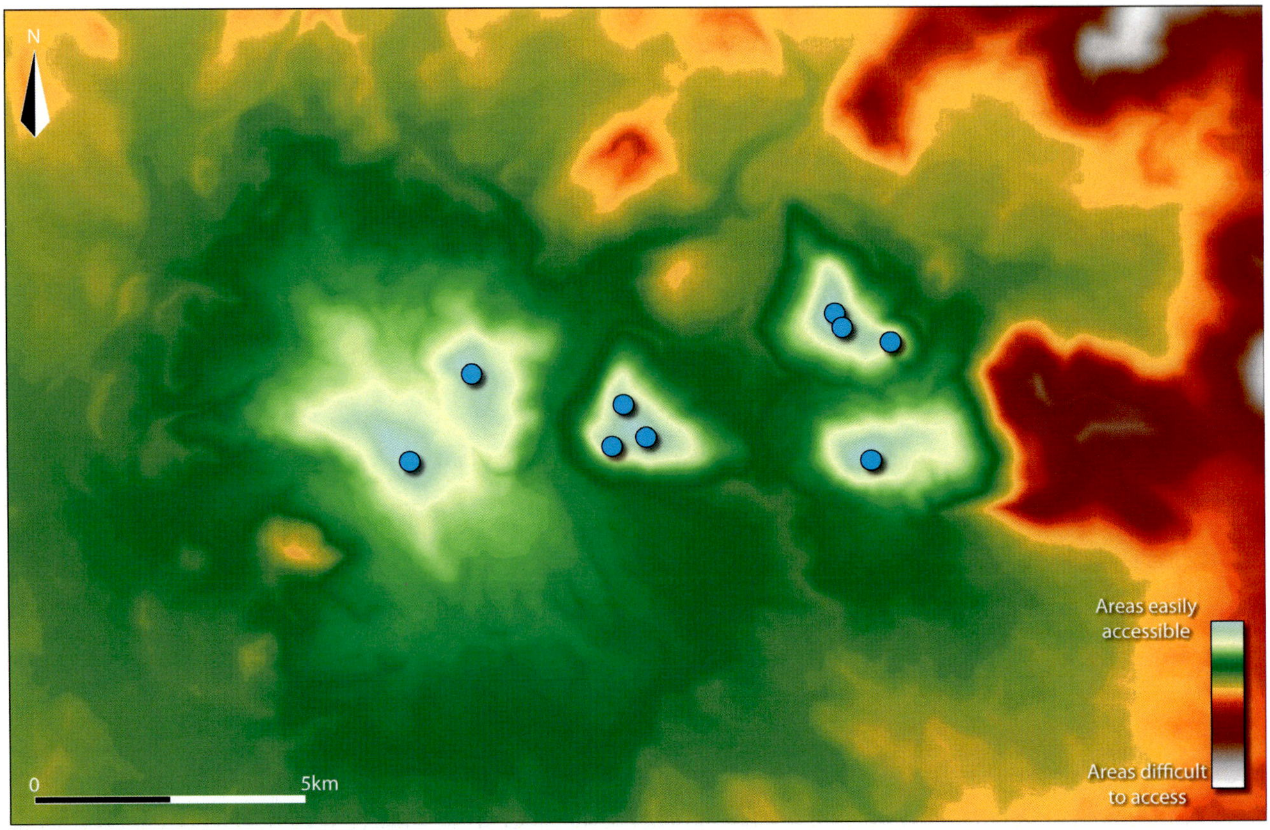

Figure 8.19: Path-Distance Catchment model of all the forts in the Baltinglass area.

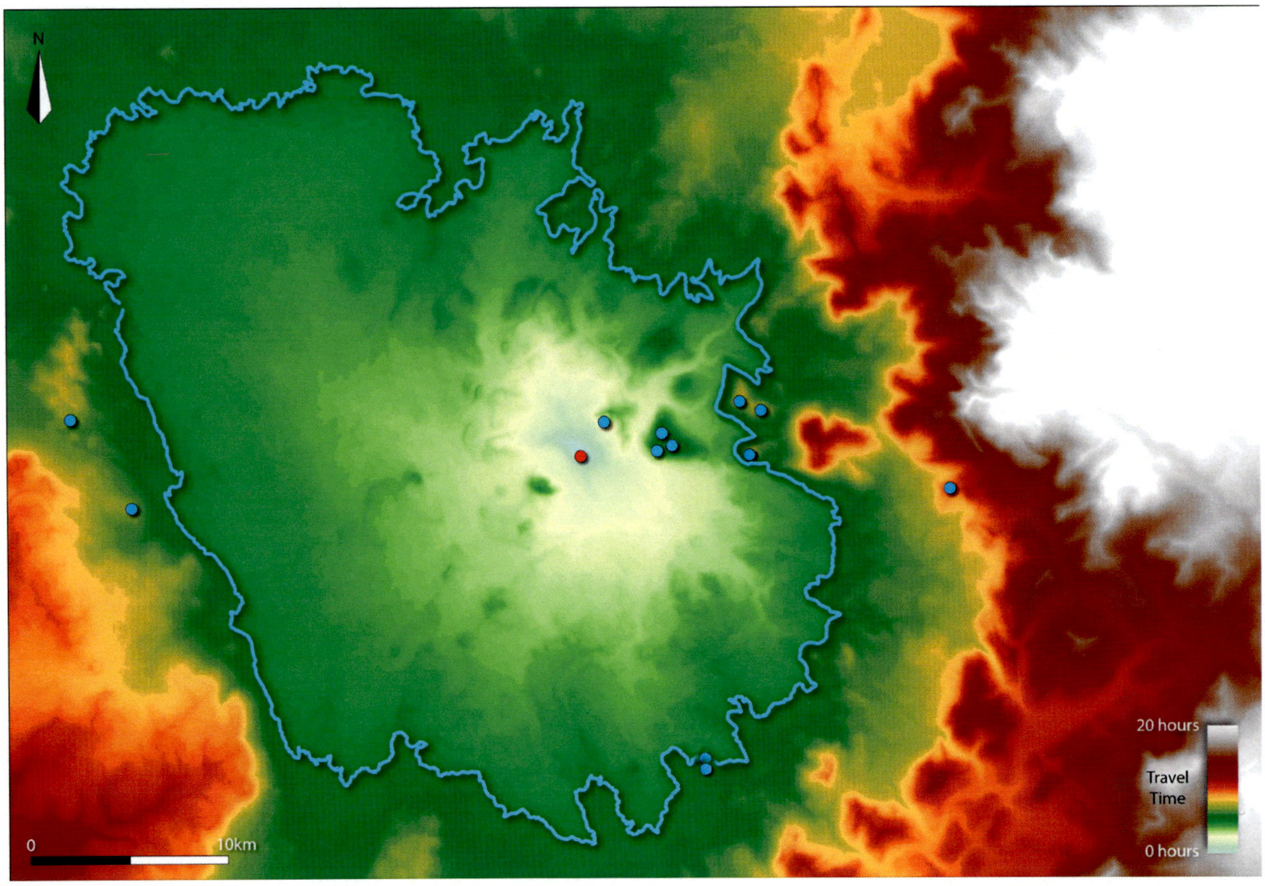

Figure 8.20: Path-Distance Catchment model of Hughstown, with blue isocline marking territory within 6 hour walking distance of the fort.

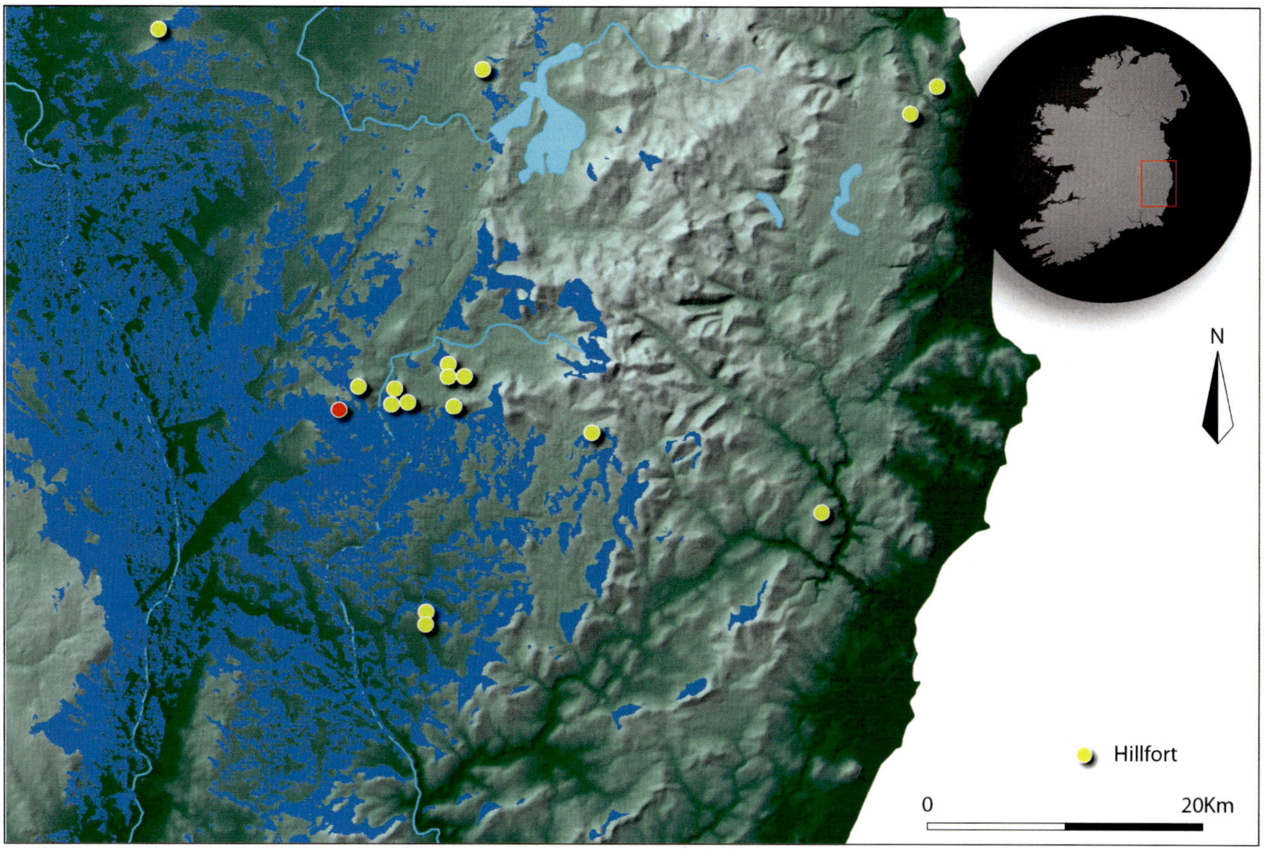

Figure 8.21: Viewshed analysis of Hughstown fort, Co. Kildare.

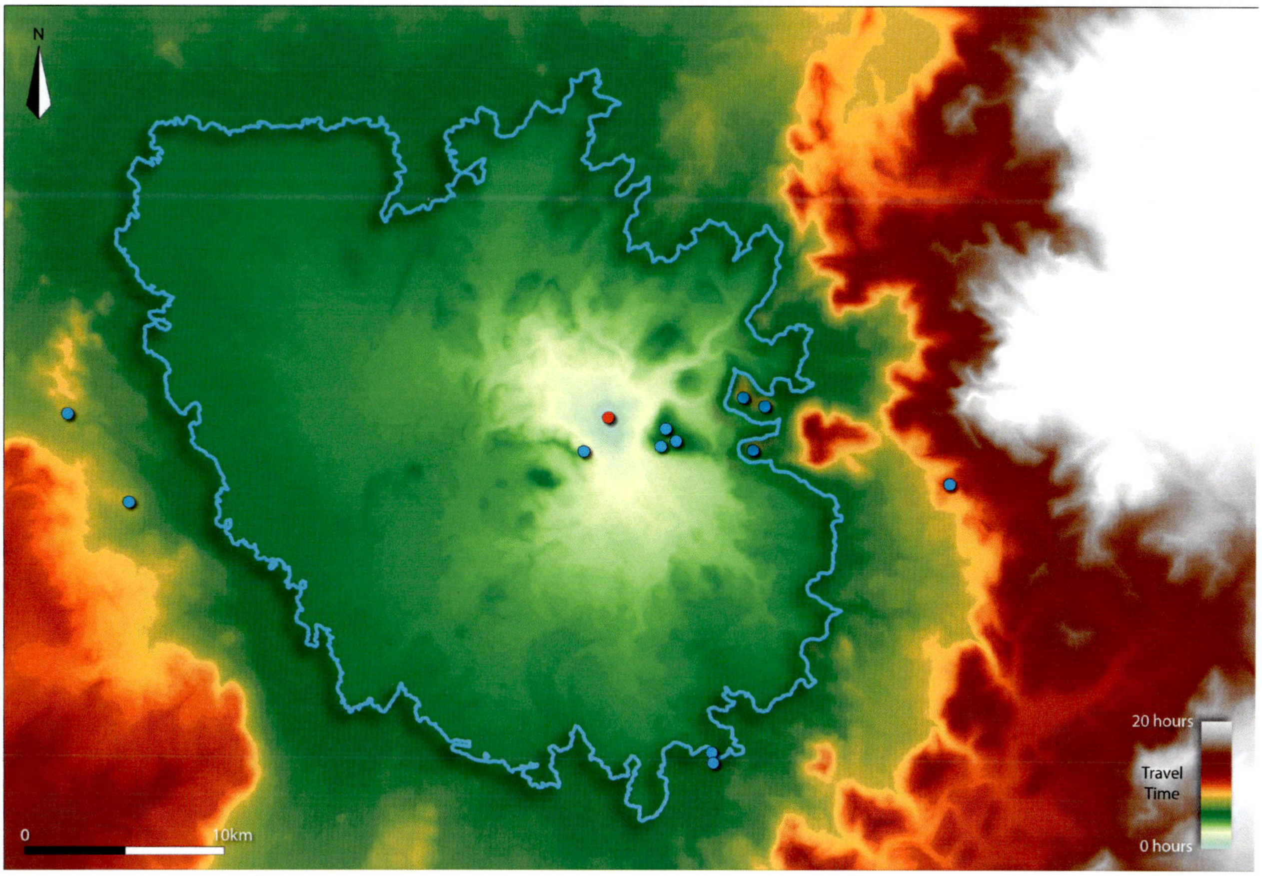

Figure 8.22: Path-Distance Catchment model of Tinoran, with blue isocline marking territory within 6 hour walking distance of the fort.

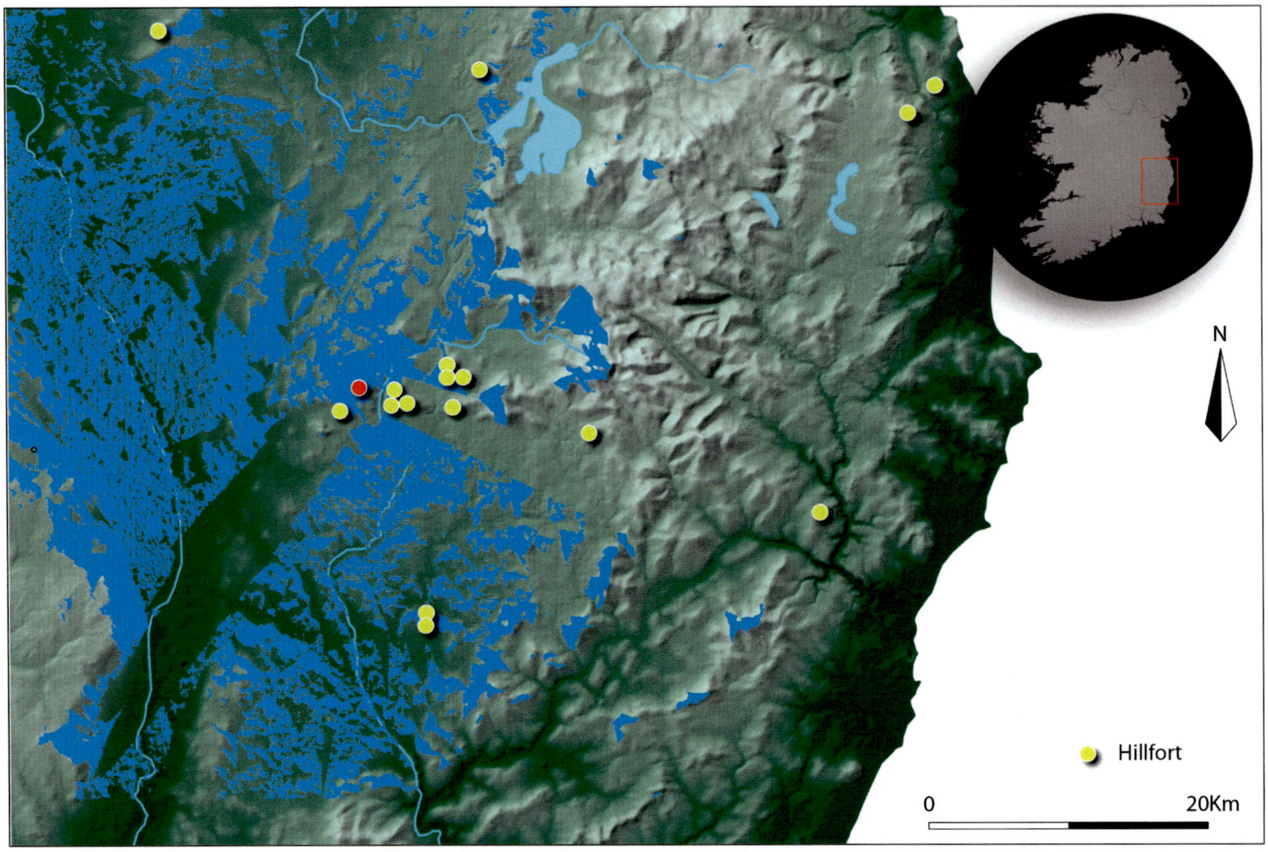

Figure 8.23: Viewshed analysis of Tinoran fort, Co. Wicklow.

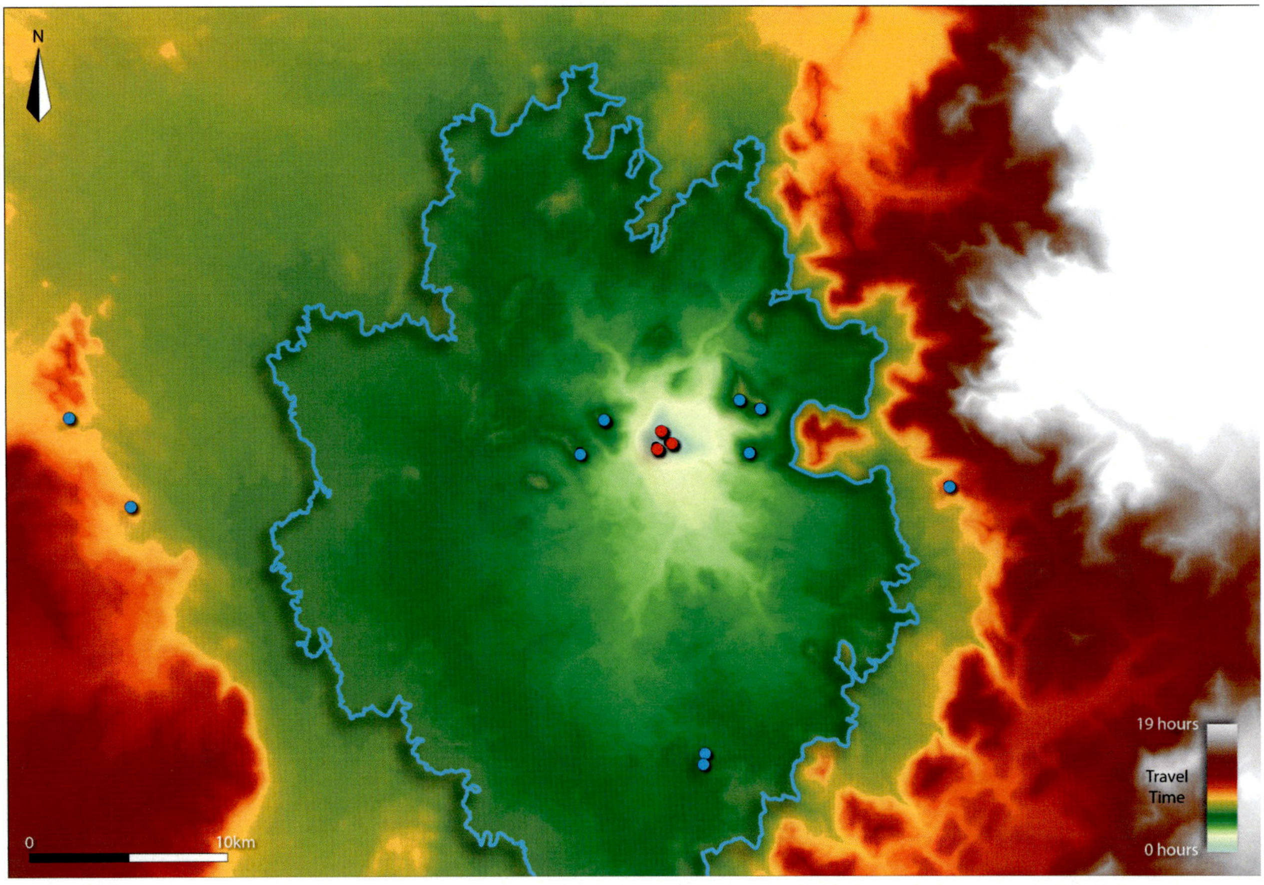

Figure 8.24: Path-Distance Catchment model of Tuckmill Hill, with blue isocline marking territory within 6 hour walking distance of the hilltop.

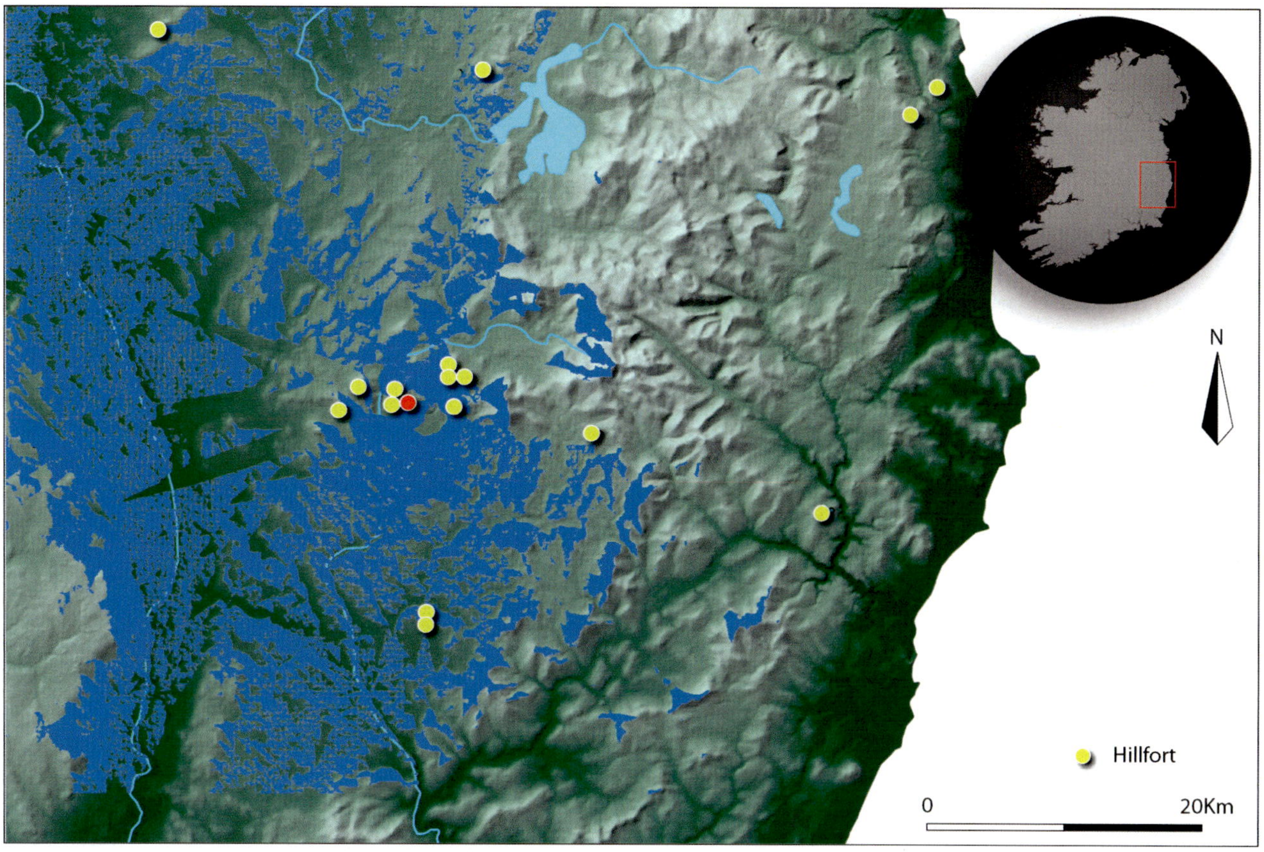

Figure 8.25: Viewshed analysis of Rathcoran fort, Co. Wicklow.

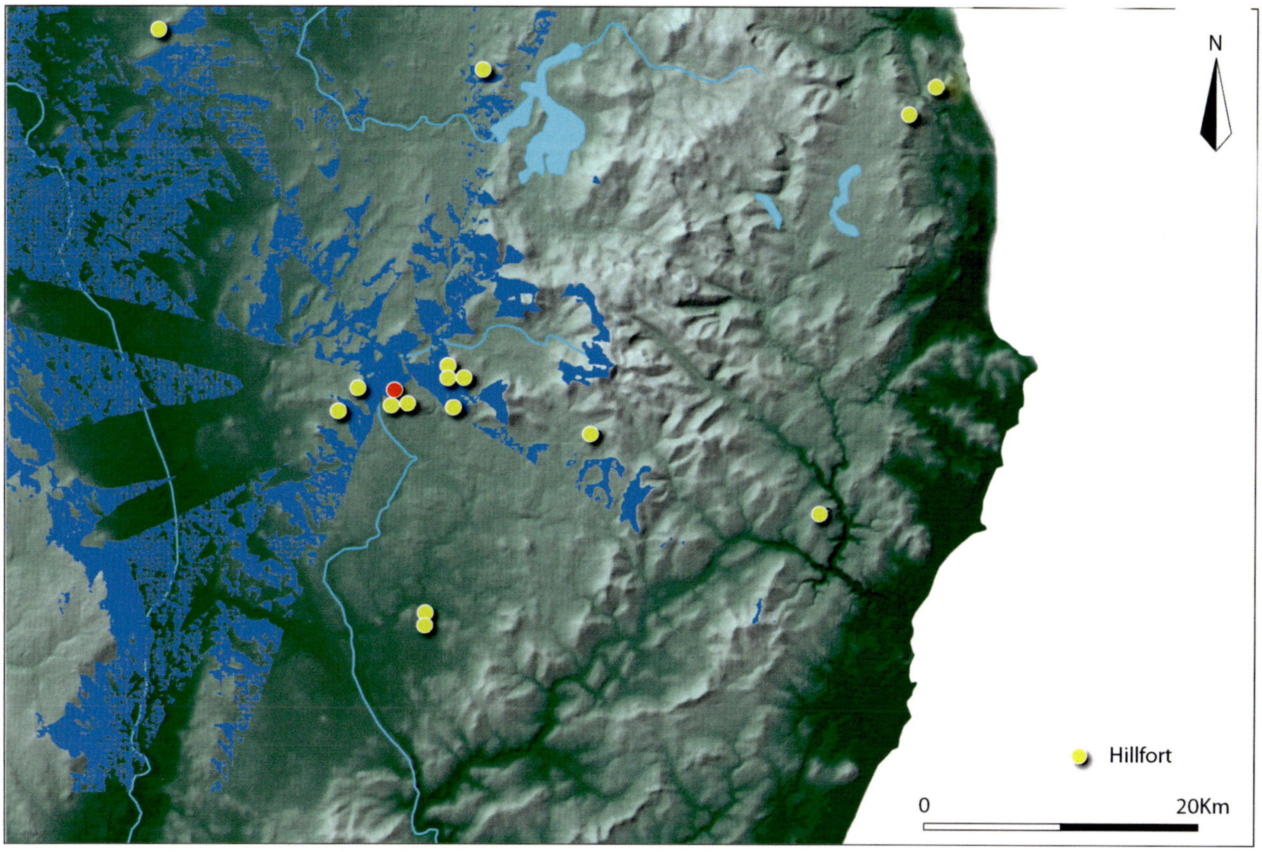

Figure 8.26: Viewshed analysis of Rathnagree fort, Co. Wicklow.

hilltops and upland terrain obscure visibility to the north. There is an unobstructed view of an extensive tract of land to the south, south-east and south-west. Visibility from Rathcoran is delimited by the southern extension of the Wicklow Mountains to the south-east, Mount Leinster and the Blackstair Mountains to the south and the Castlecomber Hills to the west.

The views from Rathnagree are excellent, but are more restricted than those from Rathcoran, with a potential 1134km² of terrain visible from the interior (Figure 8.26). Visibility to the south-east is largely restricted by the southern summit of Tuckmill Hill where Rathcoran is located. Visibility to the north, east and west is impeded by Spinans Hill, Tinoran and Hughstown. Notably, there are excellent views of the northern, eastern and western hillslopes and base of Tuckmill Hill.

Sruhaun is located in a commanding position overlooking Baltinglass town at the western base of Tuckmill Hill, with up to 1434km² of terrain visible from the interior (Figure 8.27). There are excellent views of the north-western, western and southern base of the hill and hillslopes, as well as unrestricted views of low-lying land to the south, south-east and south-west. Visibility in this area is limited by the southern extension of the Wicklow Mountains to the south-east, Mt. Leinster and the Blackstair Mountains to the south and the Castlecomber Hills to the west. Visibility to the east is blocked by the northern and southern summits of Tuckmill Hill and the ridge of higher ground that links the summits. The hilltops of Tinoran and Hughstown largely impede views of the land to the north-west and west.

Kilranlagh hillfort is located on the eastern edge of the group. The Path-Distance Catchment model (Figure 8.28) suggests that it had a catchment of 819km² over an area of approximately 30km (east–west) by 39km (north–south). Easy accessibility of flat terrain to the south means the catchment zone is much more expansive in that area, defined by travel time rather than topographical impediments. Viewshed analysis reveals extensive visibility of this area (Figure 8.29). The hillfort is in a topographically dominant landscape position overlooking extensive tracts of lowland to the south and south-west. It has a potential 2044km² of terrain visible from the interior. The unrestricted visibility to the south affords exceptional views of the low-lying terrain in this area, as well as the Barrow river valley and Castlecomber Hills to the west. Visibility to the west is largely restricted by Tuckmill Hill, Tinoran and Hughstown, while Spinans Hill and Keadeen Mountain block visibility to the north and east. The Wicklow Mountains define this possible catchment to the west and north-west, while undulating terrain delimits the zone in the north. Again, travel time defines the boundary to the west and south-west. There are no major topographical impediments obstructing access to other hillforts in the group. The easiest approach to Kilranlagh is from the east, where the slopes are less severe. It is notable that Boleycarrigeen stone circle and a ring-barrow are positioned on this path. Three large prehistoric cairns on the western slopes could imply that this was the main approach to the summit. There are no identified entrances in the enclosing elements of Kilranlagh to indicate a possible orientation for approaching the site.

The Path-Distance Catchment model for the forts on Spinans Hill (Figure 8.30) suggest a catchment area of approximately 729km² over an area about 23km (east–west) by 39km (north–south). Spinans Hill 1 and Brusselstown Ring are easily accessible to one another, taking less than 30 minutes to travel between sites. The perimeter of the large contour fort comprising Spinans Hill 2 is also easily accessible from both sites, always being, at most, 15 minutes walking distance from either fort. Unlike the other hillforts in the cluster, there is easier accessibility to land north and north-east of the hilltop, particularly the Glen of Imaal, a valley surrounded to the north, east and south by Lugnaquilla Mountain and its foothills. Viewshed analysis reveals extensive views of this area from all of the forts on Spinans Hill, but also indicates visibility of the lowland to the south was also important (Figure 8.31 and Figure 8.32). The significance of the Glen of Imaal may be inferred by the presence of the embanked stone circle at Castleruddery, 2km north of Spinans Hill, on the western fringes of the Glen.

Easy access to the south is partially restricted by prominent topography such as Kilranlagh and Tuckmill Hill, and so may have been controlled by the hillfort communities on these hilltops. Access to Spinans Hill 1 is easiest to the north. This site has a potential 2091km² of terrain visible from its interior (Figure 8.31). There are comprehensive views of the base of the hilltop; however, the slopes of the hill itself are largely obscured by the topography. There is a notable concentration of visibility towards the Glen of Imaal in the east and north-east. There are excellent views to the lowland in the south, although this is partially obscured by Kilranlagh. Tuckmill Hill, Hughstown and Tinoran restrict visibility to the west and south-west, while a series of hills and upland terrain obscure views to the north and north-west. There are comprehensive views of the base of the Spinans Hill 1 at the north, east and west.

Brusselstown Ring is equally accessible from the east, south and west, and possible multiple entrances in the inner enclosing elements could infer several routes to the interior (though these could be later openings). There are no significant topographical barriers blocking access to other hillfort, although there is increased difficulty in accessing Tinoran, Hughstown and Tuckmill Hill. Viewshed analysis reveals that there is a potential 1192km² of terrain visible from the interior (Figure 8.32). Visibility is concentrated on areas immediately

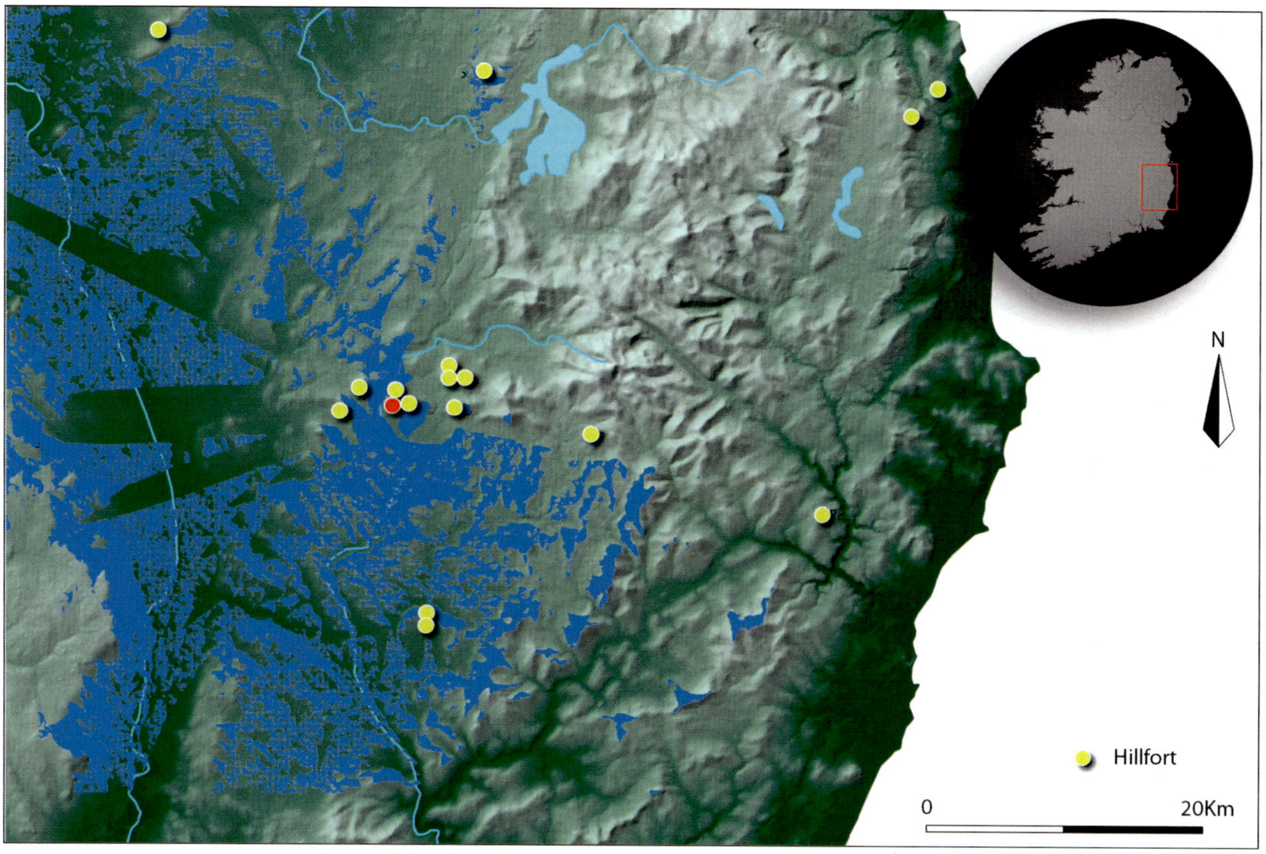

Figure 8.27: Viewshed analysis of Sruhaun fort, Co. Wicklow.

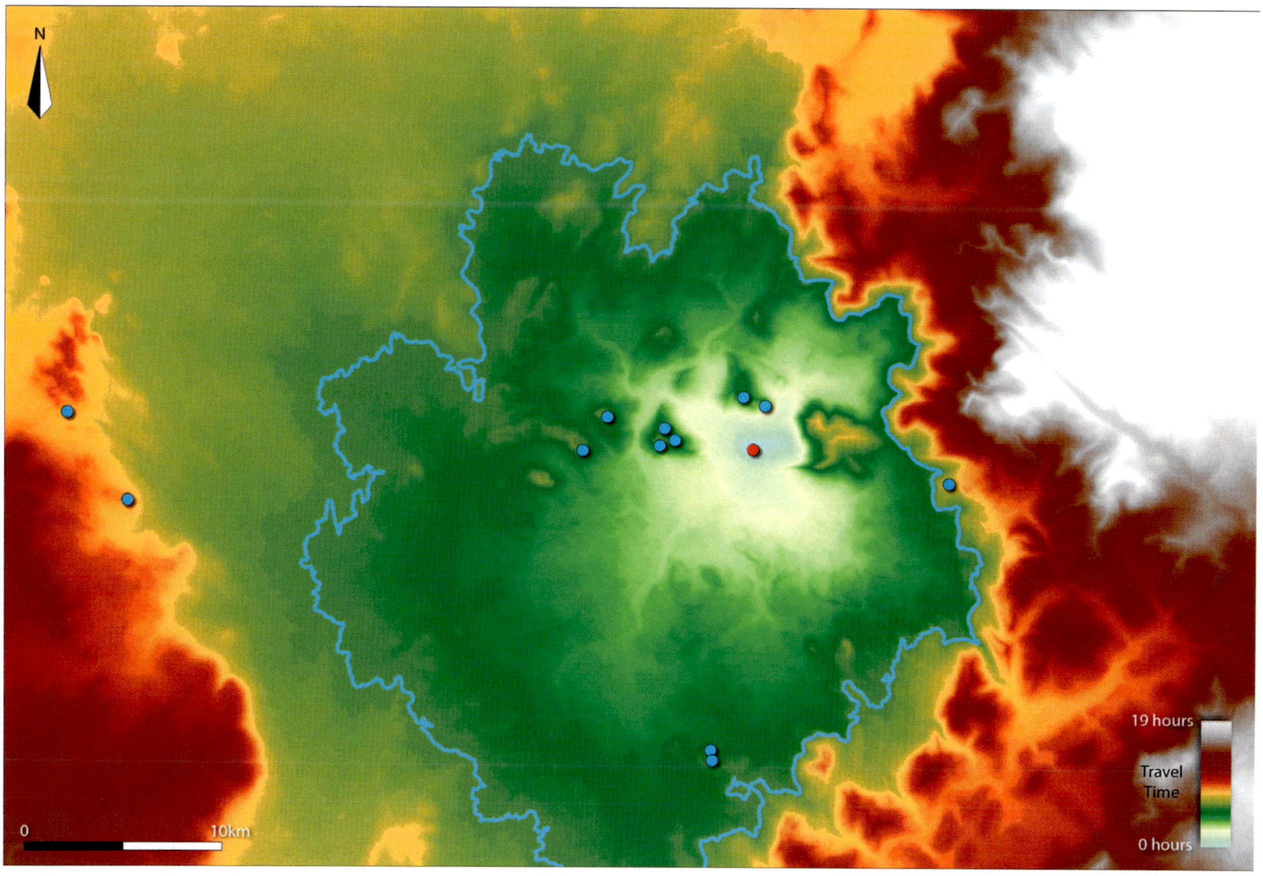

Figure 8.28: Path-Distance Catchment model of Kilranlagh, with blue isocline marking territory within 6 hour walking distance of the hilltop.

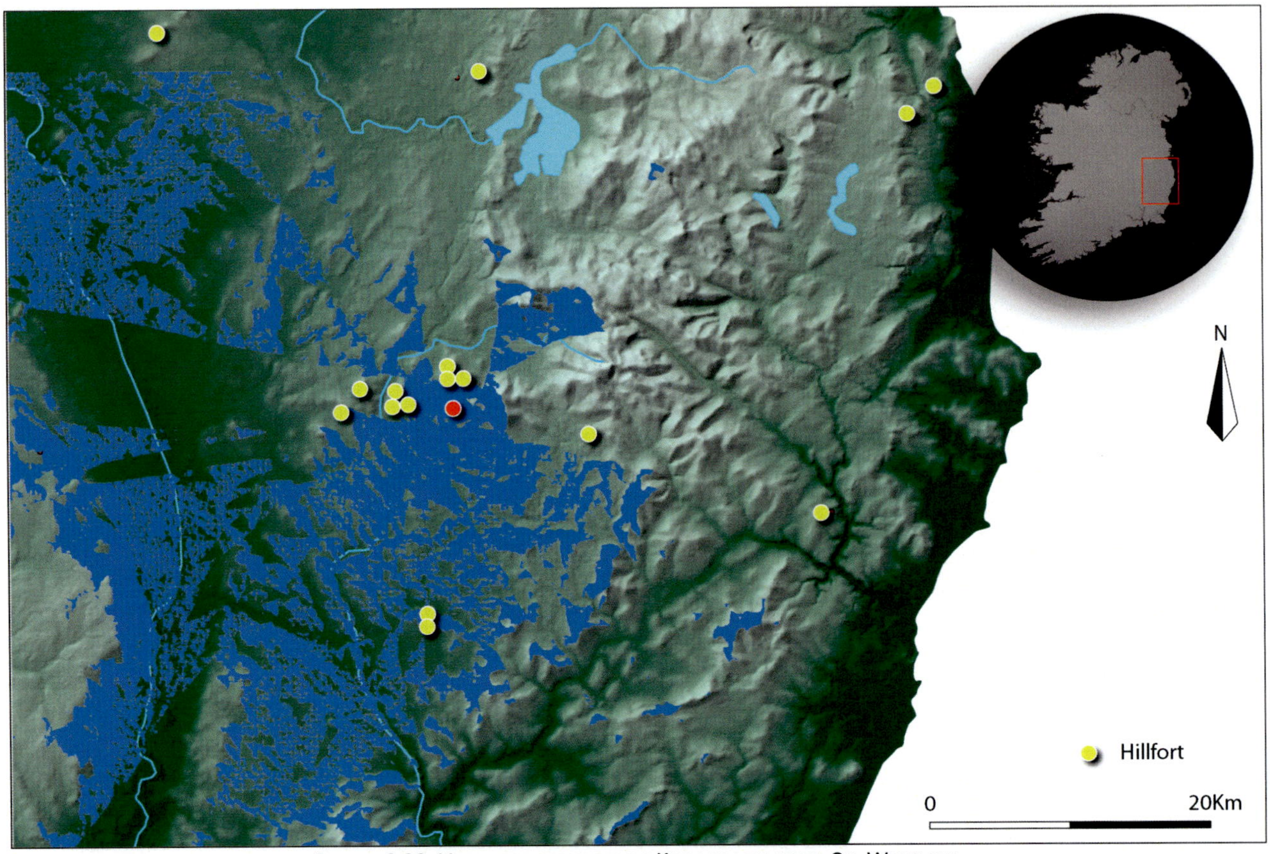

Figure 8.29: Viewshed analysis of Kilranlagh fort, Co. Wicklow.

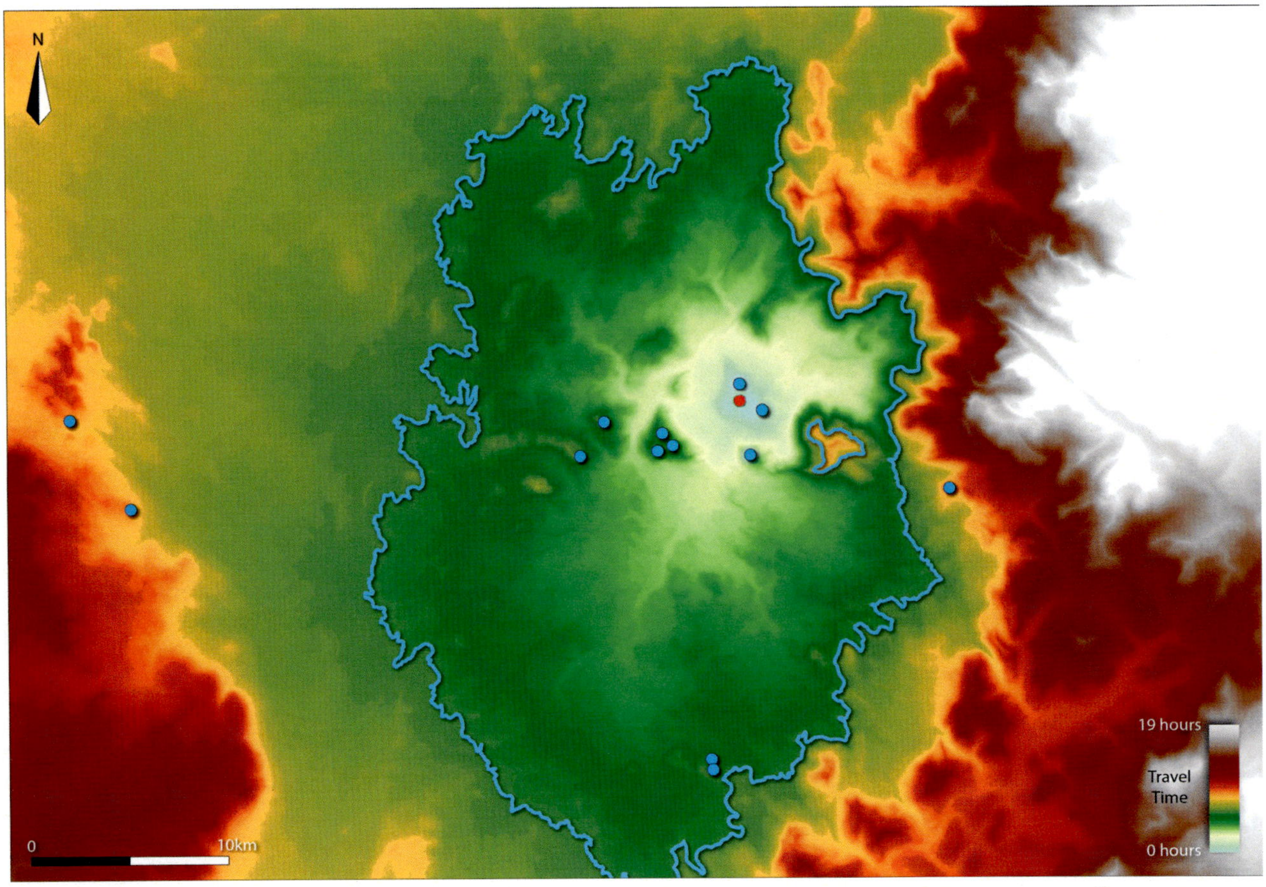

Figure 8.30: Path-Distance Catchment model of Spinans Hill, with blue isocline marking territory within 6 hour walking distance of the hilltop.

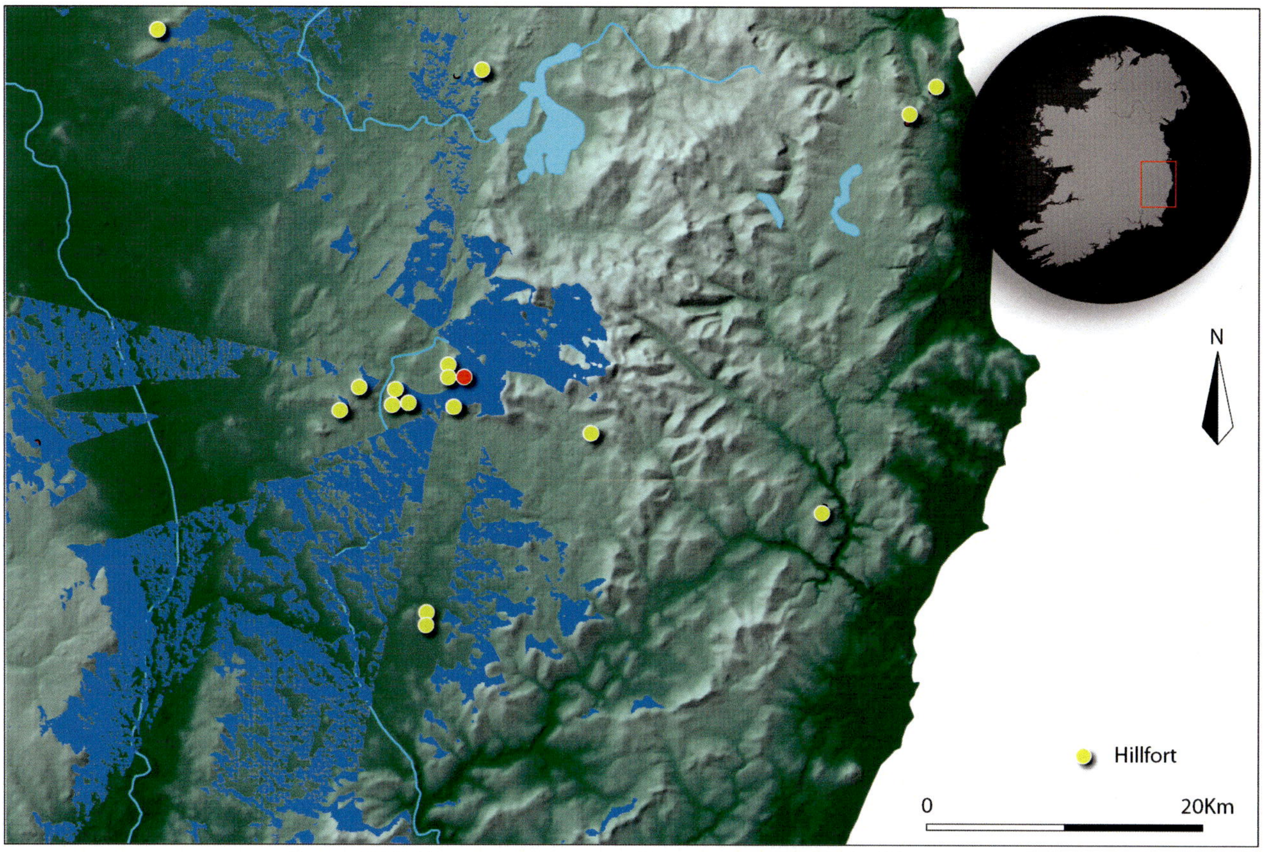

Figure 8.31: Viewshed analysis of Brusselstown Ring, Co. Wicklow.

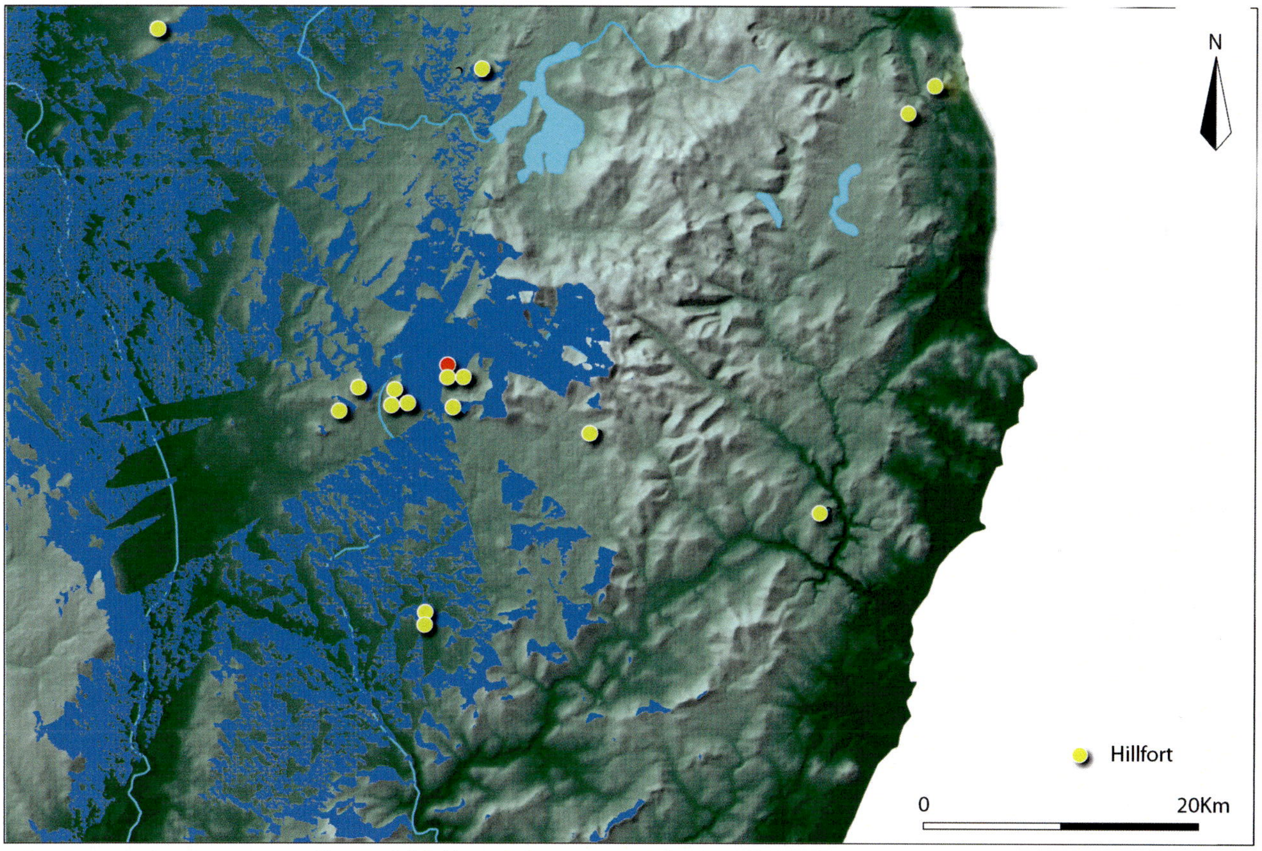

Figure 8.32: Viewshed analysis of Spinans Hill 1, Co. Wicklow.

surrounding the base of the hilltop and on the Glen of Imaal in the north-east. There are also excellent views of the low-lying terrain to the south-west. Kilranlagh Hill does obscure visibility to the south and south-east. Spinans Hill 1 blocks visibility of land to the north-west, while Tuckmill Hill, Tinoran and Hughstown restrict broader views to the west.

Interestingly, Thiessen Polygon analysis broadly corresponds with the data presented above (Figure 8.18). The polygons suggest that the territory of the Spinans Hill complex may have been primarily focused to the north and north-east in the Glen of Imaal. Kilranlagh hillfort dominates the southern flat lands and the hillfort community's territory may have been primarily in that area. The forts at Hughstown and Tinoran may have had territories extending to the south and north during the Neolithic and Late Bronze Age respectively. The Tuckmill Hill complex is particularly interesting because of its location, positioned in the middle of the Baltinglass hillfort cluster. Tuckmill Hill is bounded by the other hillforts and this produces a Thiessen Polygon that is much smaller than the aforementioned examples. This analysis may indicate the importance of controlling the land on and immediately around Tuckmill, with the territory and influence of the hillforts extending into the flat landscape to the south. It could also suggest that the hillforts in the group are not contemporary, and as such the confined Thiessen model is not as applicable as the Distance-Catchment model that supports a much larger territory. The size of the Path-Distance Catchment models broadly correspond with the large catchment zones proposed for other hillforts (Grogan 2005a; Cunliffe 2000).

Conversely, these Distance-Catchment models and visibility analysis could also be used to support the interpretation that some (tough not all) of these hillforts were contemporary. The individual sites each have a different focus in the landscape. If the hillforts represent different generations of the same community moving from hilltop to hilltop over time, we might expect that community to have a relatively stable focus with the hillfort being visible to those who built it. Instead, each hillfort (or group i.e. Spinans Hill or Tuckmill Hill) has a unique focus on different areas of the landscape.

The local settlement landscape

The evidence for settlement at hillforts in Ireland is diverse. At one extreme, there are those that show no signs of occupation or indeed any type of internal activity, such as Rahally hillfort in Co. Galway (Mullins 2008) and Clashanimud in Co. Cork. Conversely, some sites have revealed internal structures and evidence of habitation, such as Mooghaun in Co. Clare (Grogan 2005a; 2005b), Dún Aonghasa in Co. Galway (Cotter 2013a; 2013b), Knockdhu in Co. Antrim (Macdonald 2012) and most notably Rathgall hillfort, Co. Wicklow (Raftery 1976). A similar situation is evident in Britain and the Continent (Jockenhövel 2013: 741; Härke, 1979: 30). Mytum (2013, 741: 10) and Harding (2012: 206) argue that this diversity could reflect different functions; however, it could equally be a consequence of the small sample of hillforts excavated on a sufficiently large scale (Payne 2006: 5).

Ginn (2013) suggests that where settlement structures do exist, there is little to support the hierarchical model of Bronze Age society that is widely presented in the literature. What is apparent, however, is the clear divide between occupation evidence at hillfort sites and other settlements. This is supported by her study that shows two distinct social and economic classes: 'comfortable, independent farmers' and a 'minority, elite group', although she does not specifically link hillforts to the latter. In contrast to Ginn, Grogan (2005a: 87; 2014) has argued for a landscape organised in a hierarchical fashion, with a social ranking system comprising three primary classes: community, territory and chiefdom.

Most commentators would agree on a division between elites and non-elites which is important in the present context. The material culture from some hillforts, such as Rathgall or Haughey's Fort, clearly indicates an elite presence separate from the majority of domestic sites where there has been a paucity of artefactual wealth (Ginn 2013: 53; Grogan 2014: 65). Evidence for high-status occupation has also been identified at crannóg settlements such as Moynagh Lough, Co. Meath; Rathtinaun, Co. Sligo; Knocknalappa, Co. Clare, and Ballinderry 2 Co Meath. Contrasting with this, current evidence infers that habitation at such sites was not differentiated at least in terms of their functional architecture. This absence of demonstrably high status settlement led Ginn (2013: 53–54) to suggest that hillforts are not the homes of hierarchical groups. She argued that 'elites' may not exist in the perceived sense of the word. Rather, important people may have been regular members of society who were only differentiated for special occasions, although she does concede that in certain areas and in particular community's 'hierarchical systems' may have existed. The excavations of the large Middle/Late Bronze Age village at Corrstown in Co. Derry support Ginn's arguments. Here, approximately 73 structures of somewhat equal size are closely and uniformly spaced around a large metalled roadway and smaller tributary tracks (Ginn and Rathbone 2011). There is no obvious evidence for hierarchical settlement, though of course there may have been differences in status within that community that are not visible in archaeological terms.

Contrasting with this interpretation, the settlement evidence revealed on Tuckmill Hill and Spinans Hill point to a stratified social structure. At Brusselstown Ring, survey has identified up to 288 hut structures (Figure

5.8). The majority of the structures range 5–8m in diameter (Figure 8.33). This supports Cleary's examination of Irish Bronze Age structures which highlights the frequency of hut sites of comparable size (2007: 139). Additionally, there are a substantial number of structures ranging 3–5m at Brusselstown Ring. Cleary (2007: 139) suggests that small structures are commonly found associated with larger huts and could have formed ancillary structures. Fourteen structures, comprising approximately 4.5% of the known settlement, are 9–12m in diameter and only two structures were recorded over 12m. These fourteen hut sites are evenly distributed throughout the settlement, although it is notable that none are located at the centre of the hillfort. This, however, may be a consequence of the thick overgrowth within a large portion of the interior which may have obstructing identification of such features. Dense clusters of smaller huts often accompany larger examples at Brusselstown Ring. Cleary (2007: 141) suggests it is possible that the size variation of structures reflects an element of social stratification. It could be tentatively argued, therefore, that these clusters represent individual kin groups, with the head of each family differentiated by larger structures.

The largest cluster of hut sites at Brusselstown Ring is positioned immediately to the south of the west facing entrance and form a corridor for access to the hillfort interior. The terrain to the east and south falls away sharply and this area remains largely clear of habitation. Similarly, the area immediately to the south, east and north of the inner enclosing elements comprise severe slopes, covered with large glacial erratics that would have limited settlement space. Beyond these areas, in flatter terrain to the south and east, less condensed settlement occurs. Entrances in the inner enclosing elements of the hillfort at the north, east and south, aligned on terrain difficult to traverse, may, if original, have been largely symbolic features used to emphasise the perceived inclusiveness of the community.

There are no structures abutting or within 10m of the external face of the inner enclosing elements at Brusselstown Ring and it is unlikely that settlement was obstructed by a ditch. The bank is positioned at the edge of a sharp drop in slope at the south-east, east, north and north-west and this probably affected the distribution of structures in these areas. More suitable terrain is available in the south and south-west, however that area does not seem to have been settled. It may have been kept clear to allow better visibility of the defences from other hillforts in the area or from low-lying, settled regions in the landscape. Direct, unobstructed visibility of impressive displays of status and resource consumption would have been an important element of competitive display. In that respect, the positioning of hut structures around Brusselstown Ring may be significant in terms of social structures.

The southern and south-western slopes of Brusselstown Ring are highly visible from both Rathcoran and Kilran-

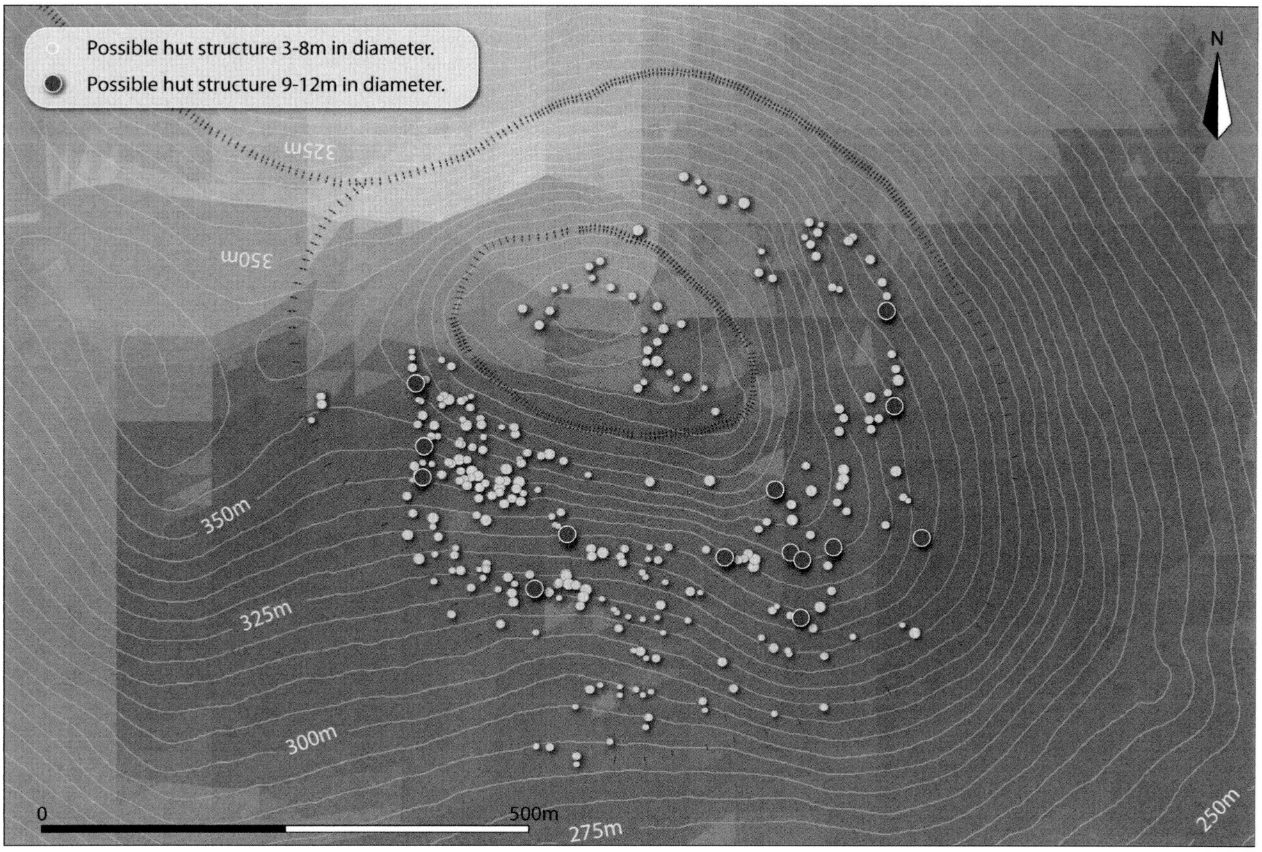

FIGURE 8.33: POSSIBLE HUT STRUCTURES IDENTIFIED BY GPS SURVEY AT BRUSSELSTOWN RING.

lagh. This is in contrast to the north-eastern, northern and north-western slopes of the hilltop, which are obscured by various topographical elements. The settlement, therefore, seems to be positioned in areas visible from other hilllforts. This may reflect topographic considerations, but could be viewed as an aspect of competitive display, where a substantial settlement, visible to rival hillforts reflected the labour force and potential manpower at the disposal of the community at Brusselstown Ring. Bowden and McOmish (1989: 13) have suggested that some British hillforts were deliberately placed on sloping ground to make activities within the interior visible to outsiders, while at the same time excluding them from participation. Driver (2013: 135) has developed this argument to suggest this would have facilitated the communication of strength, where the interior revealed a populated, well organised community. If we consider the Path-Distance Catchment models and viewshed analysis for Brusselstown Ring and the other settlements on Spinans Hill, these analyses show the Glen of Imaal positioned to the north-east was probably the main focus for the community. In this regard, if the hillforts were not contemporary and represent a palimpsest of enclosures, the layout of the settlement at Brusselstown Ring cannot be easily explained.

A similar pattern can be seen at Rathcoran (Figure 8.34). Approximately 124 circular hut structures have been revealed through LiDAR and geophysical survey (Figure 5.21 and Figure 5.24). Dense heather and gorse prevented collection of adequate LiDAR data at the south-west where there are few identifiable structures. A small portion of the hillfort is clear of vegetation and in this area there seems to be evidence of dense settlement. This variability probably reflects the collected data and ground conditions, and a similar density could be expected for much of the hillfort.

Approximately 89.9% of the potential structures at Rathcoran measure 5–8m in diameter, with a particular concentration of sites measuring 7–8m (Figure 8.34). A group of structures of approximately 5m diameter are clustered in the south-east of the interior where ground conditions were favourable for surveying. These could be interpreted as ancillary structures. There is a more uniform distribution of structures if these examples are removed. Comparable structures may exist in other areas obscured today by vegetation. Similar to Brusselstown Ring, a smaller number of structures, comprising 10.1% of the total settlement, are larger and are spread evenly throughout the interior. These are generally associated

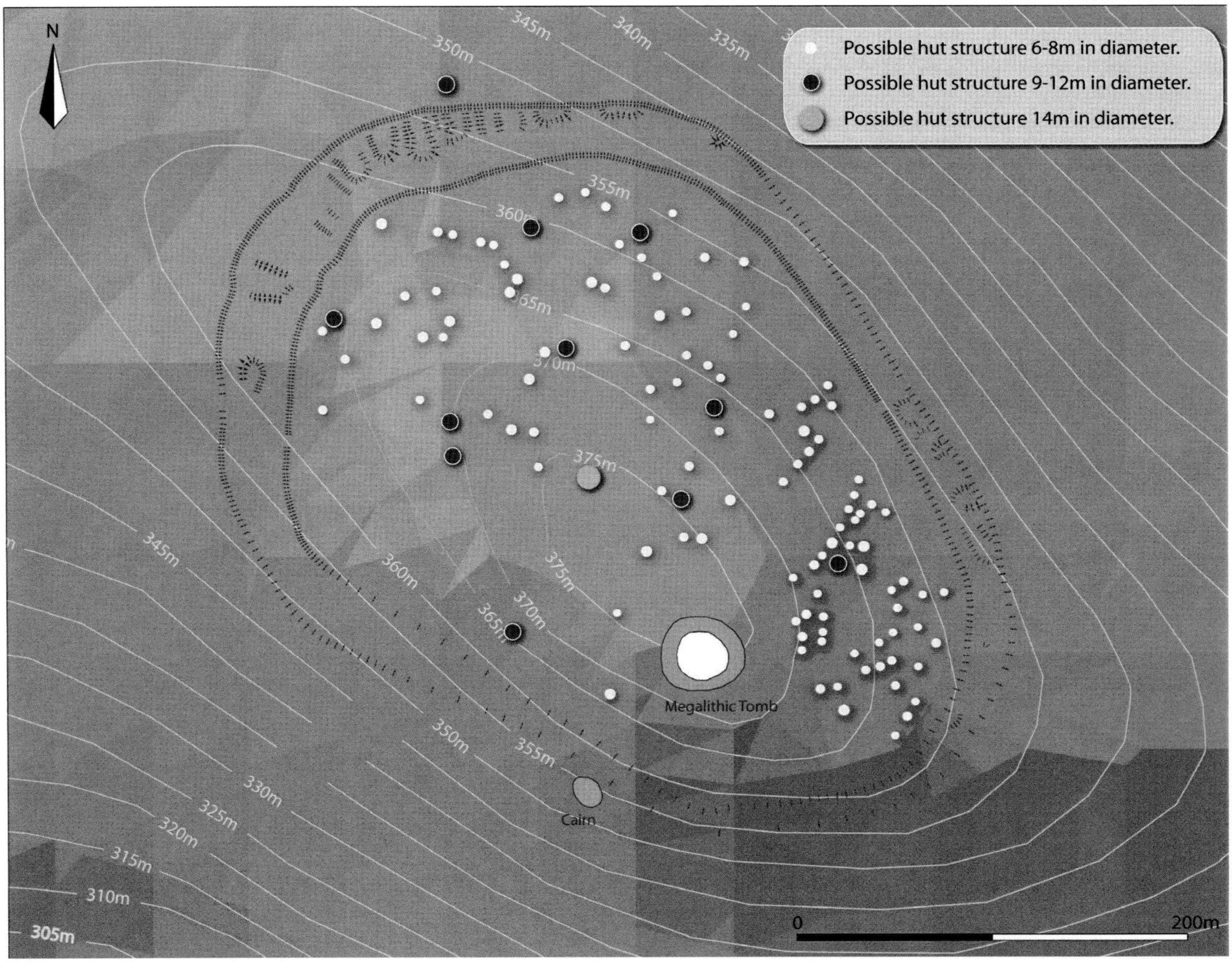

FIGURE 8.34: POSSIBLE HUT STRUCTURES IDENTIFIED BY LIDAR, GPS AND GEOPHYSICAL SURVEY AT RATHCORAN.

with more dense areas of occupation . Again, this distribution could be viewed as representing different kin groups present at the site.

There are no recorded structures within 30m of the passage tomb at Rathcoran. This area may have been kept clear of occupation to highlight the monument and differentiate it from normal occupation. It could also have been a sacred area which was taboo for everyday residence. The majority of structures are at least 10m from the inner bank of the hillfort. Only at the north-west, where the enclosing elements are largest, are there any examples of structures within this zone. If Rathcoran is an unfinished hillfort, the area abutting the enclosing elements may have remained clear of occupation while construction of the site continued.

One exceptional structure is seemingly the focal point of the interior and is distinguished from other possible hut sites by its prominence and size. It is positioned centrally within the interior and comprises a contiguous series of boulders approximately 14m in diameter (WI027-026007). It is the third highest hut within Rathcoran and is positioned strategically, overlooking the west, north, east and south-eastern portions of the interior, making it the most visible structure inside the fort (Figure 8.35). It seems to be deliberately separated from other hut sites, with no other examples identified within a 25m radius. The possible northern entrance of the hillfort is partially aligned on the structure. Although there are a number of hut sites between the large structure and the possible entrance, these are unlikely to have obstructed visibility, due to its commanding position and elevation of the structure. There is a path created by an absence of huts, extending from the entrance towards the central structure and this is lined by two substantial hut sites. Immediately outside the hillfort, approximately 10m north-east of the northern entrance, a third substantial structure may have been positioned to control access to the interior. It is tempting to suggest that the large, central structure was the residence of an important person/family. The remainder of the inhabitants may have comprised kin groups present to construct the hillfort, with more substantial structures housing the heads of each group. Grogan (2005a: 243) revealed structures built at Mooghaun during the initial construction stage of the hillfort were abandoned after its completion, inferring the use of somewhat permanent structures during the building process. A similar scenario could have taken place at Rathcoran. The structures could also reflect an earlier phase of enclosure at the site before it was later partially re-built, or could post-date the hillfort construction.

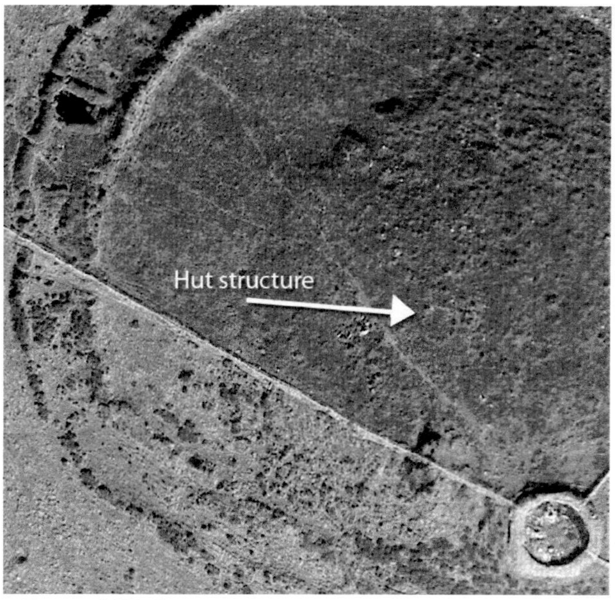

Figure 8.35: Aerial photograph of large hut structure within the interior of Rathcoran hillfort.

It is more difficult to assess the evidence for settlement structures at Hughstown, considering the ephemeral nature of the geophysical anomalies (Figure 5.41) and the earlier dates from the enclosing elements. Approximately 41 subtle magnetic anomalies were identified in the survey that might represent hut structures (Figure 8.36). Although the evidence is less comprehensive than Brusselstown Ring or Rathcoran, where the sites are visible on the ground and in LiDAR data, there are a number of similarities in density and distribution. The size range is higher than the previously examined sites. The majority of the possible structures range from 6–9m in diameter and there are a number of sites in the southern cluster that average 10m in diameter. There are four larger hut circles that range 11–13m in diameter and these are positioned at the edge of each cluster, with two large structures near the southern, largest group. This is similar to the distribution patterns at Brusselstown Ring and Rathcoran. Within the central enclosure at the summit of the hilltop, a substantial structure, 17m in diameter, is visible on the surface. This is apparent as a low-relief circle of covered stone approximately 0.7m in average width and up to 0.3m high. Geophysical survey revealed the structure was probably destroyed by fire (Figure 5.41). It was clearly differentiated from the smaller structures both in terms of its size and position at the summit of the hilltop. Similar to Rathcoran, this structure and the surrounding enclosure was probably a focal residence of the settlement and may have housed an elite. If correct, this suggests that significance was placed in the location of settlement structures and that people of higher status had more privilege to occupy structures in certain location. At Brusselstown Ring, hut sites located inside the inner enclosing elements may have been differentiated from those outside. The possible circular structures inside Hughstown may also hint that the hilltop was reused in the later prehistoric or Early Medieval period, as circular structures usually do not appear until the Later Neolithic and Bronze Age.

There is limited evidence for settlement at other hillforts in the area, principally due to the inability to carry

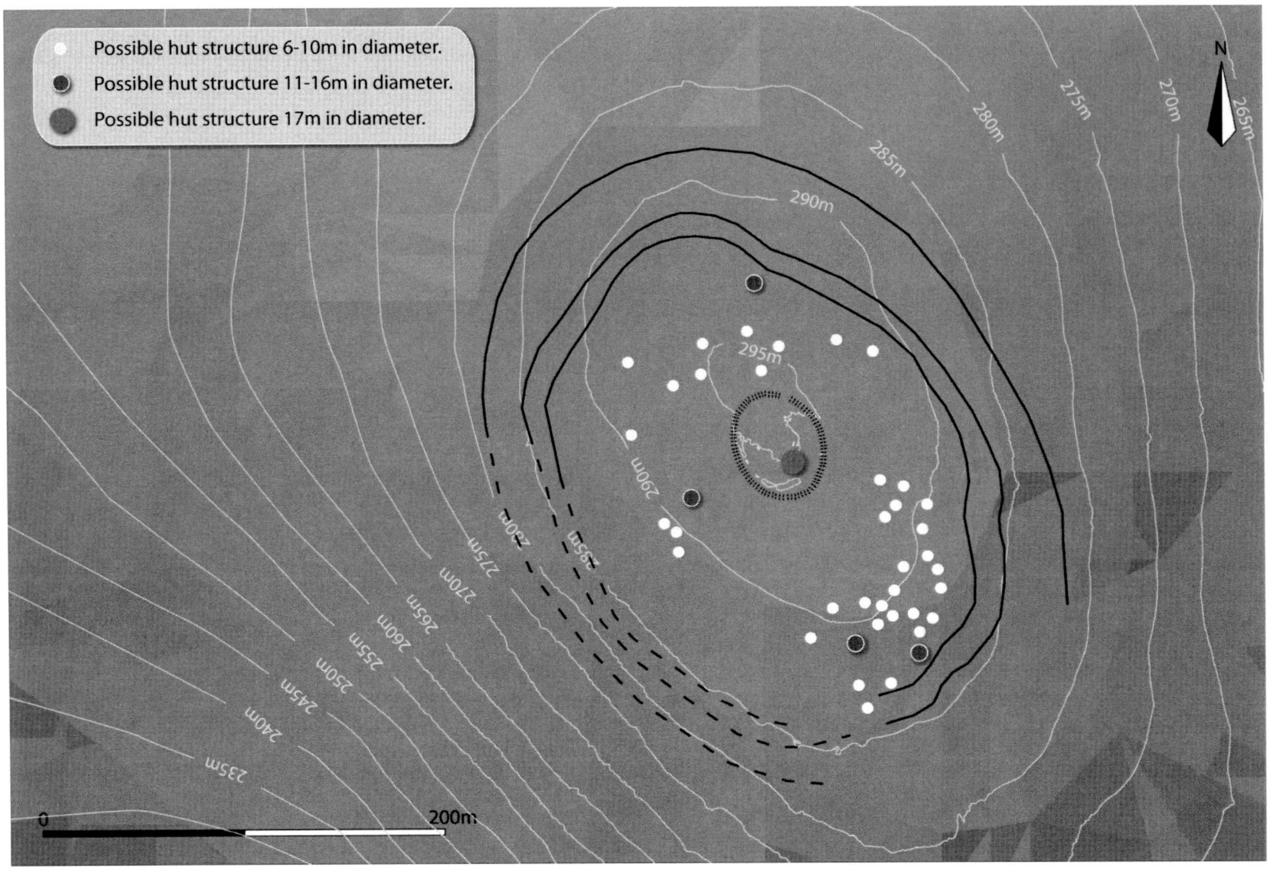

FIGURE 8.36: POSSIBLE STRUCTURES IDENTIFIED BY GEOPHYSICAL SURVEY AT HUGHSTOWN.

out geophysical surveys due to geology and vegetation cover as well as the lack of high resolution LiDAR data. At Tinoran, the dense tree cover obstructs both types of survey, although, prior to the area being forested a hut site was recorded inside the hillfort at the south-west (WI026-004001). No settlement features have been identified at Spinans 1 while dense forestry makes the recognition of such features at Kilranlagh difficult.

Geophysical survey at Sruhaun also revealed no internal features (Figure 5.32). This does not necessarily mean that there was no occupation of the interior, as negative results in geophysical surveys may be due to a number of different natural processes. Occupation features may be masked by background readings or could be to slight to be identified in the results. Sruhaun is much smaller than other hillforts in the area, and so could be a different type of enclosure, possibly used for stock management. However, the highly visible siting of the fort might also indicate that such a function is unlikely.

At Rathnagree up to 19 possible structures have been identified, but this is probably not representative of a true distribution due to issues with the LiDAR data and vegetation cover (Figure 5.27 and Figure 5.30). Trial excavation at Rathnagree also revealed potential evidence for settlement in the form of a possible arc of a structure in Trench 2 (Figure 6.21). A 'settlement cluster' was recorded by Condit (1992) on the north-eastern facing slopes of Spinans Hill, immediately outside Spinans Hill 2. Condit notes that settlement comprising enclosures, hut sites and field walls are evident in aerial photographs covering an area of 320m by 145m. Field walking by the present author identified a more defined settlement comprising two enclosures with associated hut sites and a series of field walls (Figure 8.37). These features may not necessarily be contemporary with the construction and occupation of the hillforts. The problem of dating highlights the difficulty in identifying convincing evidence for extra-mural settlement contemporary with hillforts in the area.

A large enclosure somewhat comparable in size with these hillforts was identified by Corlett at the western base of Keadeen Mountain (Corlett 2004; Figure 5.48). This comprises a sub-oval enclosure measuring 2.76ha. The bank of the enclosure is slight and consists of a collapsed stone wall 1.5–1.8m wide and 0.5m in height (*ibid.*: 80). A possible standing stone and a number of hut structures were recorded in the interior, though Corlett argues these were probably not contemporary with the enclosure. The size of the bank and the absence of identifiable contemporary settlement led Corlett to conclude that the enclosure was probably not defensive and may have served some ceremonial or ritual use. The location, at the edge of the possible 'core' boundary's

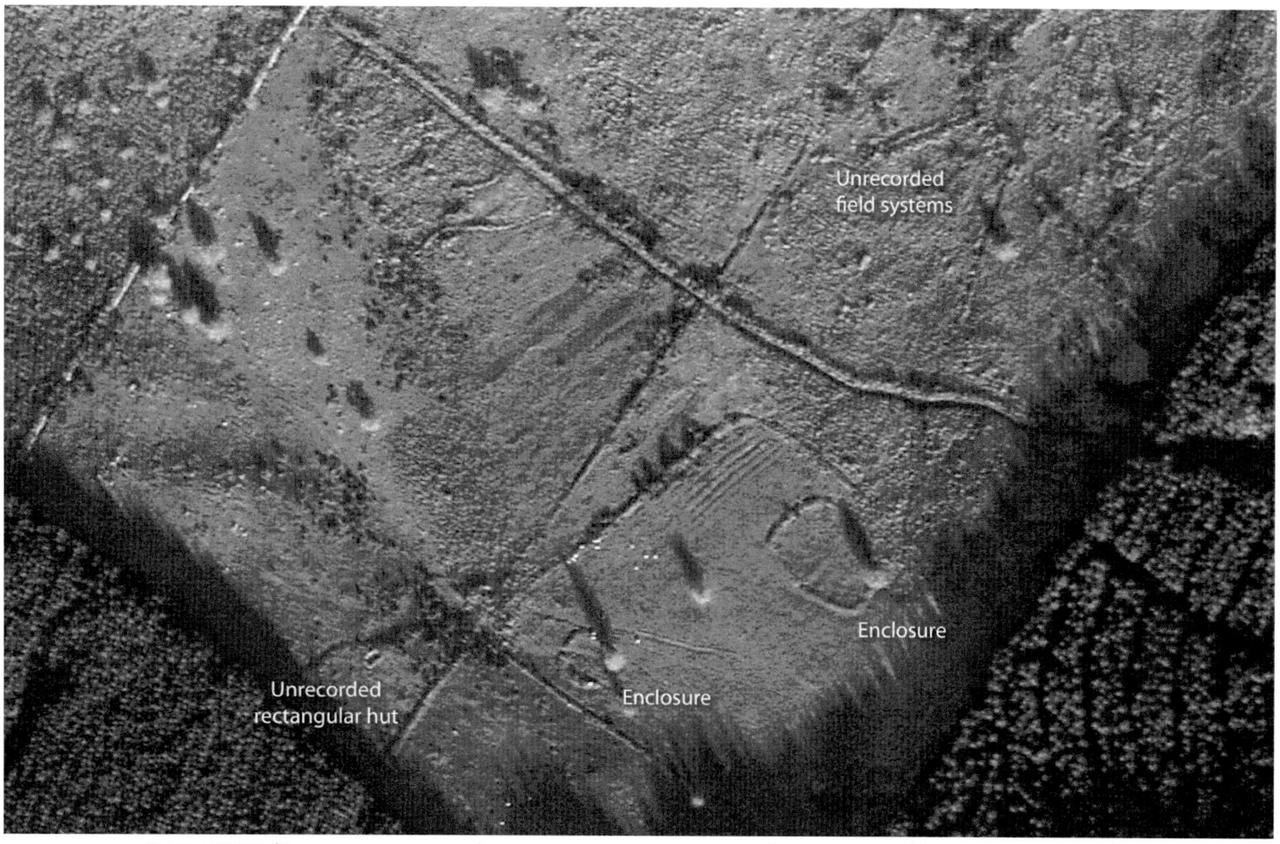

FIGURE 8.37: 'SETTLEMENT CLUSTER' AT SOUTH-EASTERN SLOPES OF SPINANS HILL 2 (GOOGLE EARTH 2017).

of Spinans Hill and Kilranlagh, might support this interpretation. Corlett suggests that there are potentially three original entrances, located on the east, south and north-west sides. These are simple, narrow breaks in the bank and reflect the morphology of many entrances found at Irish hillforts. Intriguingly, the southern and north-western breaks are orientated on Kilranlagh and Brusselstown Ring respectively, while the eastern entrance is aligned on a cursus monument near the top of Keadeen which extends towards the summit where a large, heavily robbed-out cairn is located. The similarities between the enclosing elements at Brusselstown Ring and Kilranlagh may hint at a possible affiliation between the two sites. If this is correct, the enclosure at the western base of Keadeen may have functioned as a gathering place for the two communities, who would then process towards the mountain summit.

Three other enclosures of comparable size and location have been identified in the Baltinglass area (Figure 5.48). At the north-west base of Kilranlagh, near the edge of its potential territorial boundary, Liam Price identified a large enclosure of 2.24ha extent (Corlett and Weaver 2002b: 539). Price describes the enclosing elements as comprising an outer ditch almost twelve paces wide with an internal bank seven paces wide and a possible internal ditch. He also notes a cairn inside the enclosure where a Late Bronze Age pottery vessel was found when the site was being levelled. Unfortunately the enclosure has been completely destroyed and forested and no other information regarded the site is available. Considering the potential ritual elements, i.e. the potential internal ditch, cairn and possible Late Bronze Age burial, the site could be regarded as a ceremonial or burial centre demarcated by a boundary.

A similar interpretation could be ascribed to Rathmoon, a large enclosure 1.8km south-east of Hughstown hillfort (Figure 5.50). Rathmoon is described by Grogan and Kilfeather (1997) as an approximately circular hilltop enclosure 120m in diameter. The lowland siting does not fit with a hillfort classification. Geophysical survey identified a much larger and more complex system of enclosing elements than previously identified. Four widely spaced enclosing elements were recorded, covering a total area of 1.71ha. The alignment of possible entrance openings in all four enclosures may suggest that they are contemporary. Entrances in the north-east and east are orientated on Tuckmill Hill, while there is an additional south/south-west facing break. Five circular features were identified within the two innermost enclosures and these could represent other burial monuments such as levelled ring-barrows. The elaborate form of the enclosing elements is reminiscent of the hillforts in the Baltinglass area, with the potential evidence for burials suggesting a possible funerary site. Again, the liminal location of the enclosure, just outside of the potential 'core' boundaries of Hughstown and the hillforts on Tuckmill Hill, is interesting. Rathmoon is roughly equidistant from both, although it is notable that the site is more accessible from Hughstown, taking approximately one hour to travel to, in contrast to two hours from Tuckmill Hill.

A fourth large enclosure recorded as a vegetation mark in aerial photography is located at the north-western base of Corballis Hill (Figure 5.48). The site is approximately 1.1 ha in size and is positioned immediately outside the possible 'core' boundary of Hughstown. Corballis Hill itself is a prominent topographical feature and comprises the westernmost hilltop of the Baltinglass hills. Unfortunately, it is densely forested and LiDAR data is not available, but it remains a possible location for another hillfort. The large enclosure at its base may have functioned in much the same way, or may have been used as a ceremonial or burial centre.

It is clear that these four large enclosures located in low-lying positions did not function as mundane settlement sites. Rather, the evidence, particularly from Rathmoon, suggests that these were ritual monuments that may have acted as sacred meeting places where burial and other ritual acts took place.

The majority of Late Bronze Age settlements in Ireland consist of one or two isolated domestic houses and are usually not enclosed (Ginn 2012: 27; Ginn 2014: 47; Grogan 2014: 60). This raises the possibility of significant extra-mural settlement in the Baltinglass area that has not been identified. Intensive extra-mural activity was probably focused on the hillslopes overlooked by the hillforts. This is supported by environmental analysis at other hillforts in Ireland, which have revealed substantial deforestation in areas immediately surrounding Rahally, Haughey's Fort and Mooghaun, among others. This could reflect extra-mural settlement, but could equally be associated with settlements within these hillforts. A similar scenario is likely at the hillforts in the Baltinglass area. The settlements at Brusselstown Ring, Rathcoran, and possibly Hughstown, represent settlement on a scale significantly greater than small domestic sites of the Middle and Late Bronze Age. This evidence opposes Ginn's (2013: 53–54) interpretation of Late Bronze Age society as largely egalitarian and instead supports the traditional hierarchical model.

8.3 Modelling Hillfort construction at Baltinglass

The identification of possible gang working at Rathcoran and Rathnagree brings into question how the building of a hillfort was organised. Corney (2006: 135) has suggested two scenarios: that discrete groups from a hillforts' hinterland contributed to the construction of the monument; or that a unified group built a hillfort in both cases over one or a number of seasons. Environmental analysis of Irish hillforts suggests that there was intensive use of the immediate surroundings, suggesting a large population connected to these sites. This population could have been augmented by people in a wider hinterland who identified with the hillfort community. The building project could have helped to consolidate social ties in an egalitarian community, as suggested by Lock (2011) and Sharples (2007; 2011), or could have been obligated labour serving an elite.

Labour estimates

Lock *et al.* (2005: 143) have provided labour estimates for Segsbury Camp in Oxfordshire, England, a multi-phase hillfort enclosing an area of approximately 11ha. It was calculated that nearly 19,800 cubic metres of chalk was quarried and piled to create the enclosing elements, representing 9,359 person days, or 212 people working for 44 days. This does not include the time it would take the hillfort builders to acquire, prepare and move wood included in the construction, which would have considerably increased the labour input (Sharples 2010: 116–117).

The enclosing elements at Segsbury are much larger than at Rathcoran, although the latter site has two banks. Approximately 8.4% of the area between the hillfort banks comprises pits, with an estimated 1384.76 cubic metres of material being extracted from these (Figure 5.23). This is a conservative estimate, as it does not account for the material that has partially infilled these features. If these estimates are extrapolated, the hillfort builders may have extracted 16485 cubic metres of material by the completion of the hillfort. Considering that loose stones and erratics from the interior would probably have been used to construct a portion of the bank, and an imposing wooden palisade was beginning to be constructed on the inner bank at the north-west (Figure 5.20), a labour force and time-scale proportionate to that at Segsbury may be an appropriate estimate. Approximately 124 possible hut sites have been identified within Rathcoran (Figure 5.24), and it is likely that more exist. If these are contemporary with the hillfort, even a conservative estimate of two people for every identified structure would accommodate the work-force needed to build the hillfort in the aforementioned timescale.

The incorporation of a wooden element necessitated considerable forethought on the part of the hillfort builders. Rathnagree hillfort, and possibly the hillforts at Rathcoran, Brusselstown Ring and Sruhaun, may have incorporated wooden elements, Rathnagree using closely spaced wooden posts over a perimeter distance of *c.*1.7km. Excavation revealed that these posts were positioned approximately 0.5m apart with a total estimate of 3406 posts needed for construction (Figure 6.18). Further wood may have been needed for stakes between these larger posts and for the construction of associated hut structures, further increasing labour and resource costs.

The intensive use of wood required careful management of local woodlands, which would also have been an important resource for hunting. Manning (1999) has estimated the approximate resources consumed by wooden-faced hillfort defences. For example, Pen Dinas hillfort in Aberystwyth, Wales, which is approximately 4ha in size, would have required 4680 trees equating to 76ha of woodland. This is a somewhat subjective analysis, as others have proposed significantly different estimates. Wainwright (1979: 237) suggests that 1600 posts would have been needed to construct the Neolithic palisaded enclosure at Mount Pleasant in Dorset, England, involving the exploitation of approximately 350ha of woodland. Conversely, Whittle suggests that only 15ha of forestry was needed, assuming 100–200 suitable trees per hectare. Gibson (2002b: 14) agrees that the latter estimations are more accurate but stresses that the size of the forestry required will depend on the type of available woodland.

The ratio of 1:3.5 has become widely accepted as the most accurate way of predicting the height of wooden posts (Whittle 1997: 8). This assumes that for every unit below ground, at least three and a half units could have stood above ground, i.e. a 1m post hole could have supported a post standing 3.5m above ground, the total length of the post itself being 4.5m. This calculation was developed by Mercer (1981: 149–150) who used posthole ramps at Neolithic sites to estimate the length of the post.

The post-holes at Rathnagree are approximately *c.*70cm deep, however, with the additional support of the stone footing at the base of the palisades, the true depth could have been over 1m. Using Mercer's estimates, this would equate to an above ground height of 3.5–4m. Gibson (2002b: 14) has suggested that a 6m long, 40cm wide post would weight about a tonne. The shorter posts at Rathnagree were probably lighter, however, the estimated 3406 posts requited to complete Phase 1 could still be equivalent to over 2000 tonnes of wood that needed to be felled, worked and transported to site before suitable post-holes were dug and the posts erected.

There are distinct differences between a bank and ditch arrangment, and a palisade (Lock *et al.* 2005: 142). The construction of a palisade requires a greater initial investment in labour and resources, but once constructed requires less maintenance than a bank and ditch, which involves considerable initial investment in labour and continued maintenance, but less natural resources. Obviously, wooden structures are not permanent, with Wainwright and Longworth (1971: 224–225) estimating that the rate of decay of an oak post is approximately 15 years for each 2.5cm of radius. Using this estimate, the palisades at Rathnagree may have lasted several generations if they had not been destroyed by fire. Palisades also required skilled labours to source, fell and work the wood, as well as unskilled workers and draught animals to transport the materials and erect the posts. This workforce would have been divided over a larger area. An earthen bank and ditch, however, requires fewer skilled workers, consolidating the workforce in a small area. In some cases the two situations were brought together where a palisade was constructed within a bank, as at Clashanimud, Co. Cork.

The extensive use of wood may have been another aspect of competitive display. The increased scarcity of this resource, through felling, use and eventual destruction by fire, might have depleted forestry in the area, forcing communities or different generations of the same community to construct monuments with earth and stone. The construction of an earthen bank and ditch comprising Phase 2 at Rathnagree, which replaced the burnt wooden palisade, may have been necessitated due to a lack of suitable wood, or to offset the threat of attack by fire. Manning (1999) has made a similar argument for the adoption of the glacis type defences in Britain. He suggests that a major catalyst for the change from wooden to earthen defences was the growing shortage of suitable wood within reasonable distance of the fort (*ibid.*: 28). This rarity would have invested trees and wood with importance, and the display of wooden elements would therefore have been a projection of status and power. Manning (1999: 24) has argued that the construction of wooden-framed hillforts and palisaded enclosures in Britain would have put considerable demands on woodland, and has pointed out that communities would have assumed some rights of ownership over these areas. Presumably, as these woodlands began to be depleted, they became more important to the communities in the area. The control of wood resources would have been vital to sustaining a community, as wood was the primary raw material on which a community depended (Mitchell and Ryan 1997: 232–233). The availability of this resource sets obvious limitations on the range of defensive architecture (Ralston 1981: 80–81), and as such, any excessive use might have been a visible display of resources, labour and power.

Construction process

Feachem (1971: 19) argues that there are many unfinished hillforts in Britain, with Ladle Hill (Figure 8.38) in North Hampshire the classic example (Piggott 1931). These unfinished sites provided the foundation for Feachem's model of hillfort construction. This model proposes a number of steps that the hillfort builders may have followed.

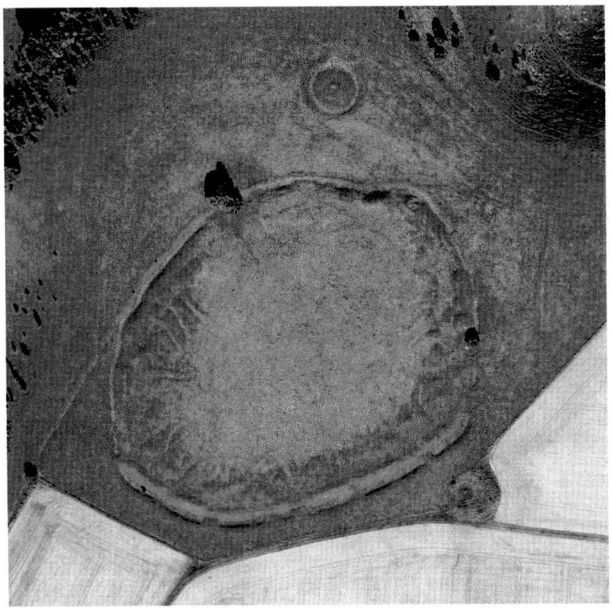

FIGURE 8.38: UNFINISHED HILLFORT AT LADLE HILL, NORTH HAMPSHIRE. (GOOGLE EARTH 2017).

• Firstly, a 'marker line' would have been constructed. This may have comprised a low bank, shallow ditch, or less permanent markers such as branches or stakes. A possible marker ditch is apparent at Ladle Hill, while at Bredon Hill in Worcestershire, Hencken (1938: 8) interpreted a row of stakes on the inner face of the bank as a possible marker. The need for a formal marker may have depended on the size and speed of the labour force (1971: 20–21). In many cases, these are unlikely to survive if the work is completed (Feachem 1971: 19).

• Following this, construction of the enclosing elements proper began, with the upper layers of loose soil and rock extracted from pits that would eventually become the ditch, being deposited around the pits or at a distance from the bank. This left the line of the proposed bank free from material, allowing for stone blocks quarried from the adjacent ditch and/or gather from field clearance to form the base, core and faces of the bank. Harding (2012: 87–88) has noted that although this 'doubling handling' process is labour intensive, it is not unique, and is apparent at other unfinished hillforts, such as Elsworthy Barrows in Somerset, England. This structure of this process depended on the type of enclosure being built, as a hillfort comprising a timber palisade, for example, would have had different stages of construction, though this is not noted by Feachem.

• Finally, the stockpiled loose soil was used to cap the bank or form a ramp abutting its inner face. Again, this is most vividly apparent at Ladle Hill.

Although there are a number of problems associated with the identification of 'unfinished' hillforts, possible construction features are apparent in hillforts of the Baltinglass group. GIS slope analysis, as well as excavation, have revealed that some of the enclosing elements at Rathcoran, Rathnagree and Tinoran were probably built on level platforms that could have been utilised when building the hillfort (Figure 5.23, Figure 5.29 and Figure 6.60), providing a level area to begin construction and could also have been used to mark the intended circuit of the defences (see Feachem 1971). Such a feature has been noted at other Irish hillforts, such as Mooghaun, where Grogan (2005a: 164) identified a 4–6m wide level platform along the inner edge of the middle rampart.

Excavation of the middle enclosure at Rathnagree revealed that none of the stone making up the core of the bank had the angular profile of quarried rock, with the prevalence of sub-rounded forms indicating the use of gathered stone. Similarly, excavation at Spinans Hill 1 revealed the hillfort bank mainly consisted of gathered stone, while the bank comprising the third enclosure at Tinoran was also field clearance. Grogan (2005a, 226) noted that loose surface stone was gathered and possibly used to form the core or 'marker line' at Mooghaun. The platforms identified at Rathcoran, Rathnagree, Tinoran and Mooghaun could also have provided a firm footing for a stone core. In some cases, such as Spinans Hill 1, enough stone may have been gathered to construct entire sections of the enclosure. Other hillforts, such as Rathcoran, may have used additional material to further augment the defences. Excavation revealed that the Phase 2 bank of the middle enclosing element at Rathnagree was capped with re-deposited sub-soil from the digging of the adjacent ditch and a stone wall, probably comprising blocks cut from the rock-cut ditch, was placed at its crest.

Evidence for 'gang working' is found at most unfinished examples (Feachem 1971), although such evidence is also apparent at many completed sites. At Ladle Hill for example, Piggott (1931) noted that up to 12 groups may have been working on the hillfort at any one time. Gang working, however, is a problematic term, as the same structural features used to identify this phenomenon could also be interpreted as evidence for seasonal construction by the same group over a prolonged period. Regardless of these issues, this evidence can still reveal some information about how a hillfort was created. For example, it is clear that many hillforts were built in sections and whether this is by one or more groups, the same amount of effort was needed to undertake the project. Of course, the overall labour input is a factor in terms of time of completion.

Gang working or seasonal construction can be identified a number of ways. At Perborough Castle, in Wessex, for example, the hillfort banks appear to have been created from a series of straight sections with angular changes in alignment, which has been interpreted as evidence for gang-working (Corney *et al.* 2006: 41). Similar evidence is found at Cherbury Camp, Oxfordshire (Bradford

1940), Chiselbury in Wiltshire (Pugh and Crittall 1957) and Mere Hill, Herefordshire (Ray and Hoverd 2000). There are often well-defined angles where the individual sections join, an excellent example being the hillfort of Castell Bwa-drain Camp in Wales (Murphy *et al.* 2006). Grogan's (2005a) study of Mooghaun hillfort in Co. Clare has revealed features that could be related to gang working. Topographical survey identified a series of slight angular joints in all three of the enclosing elements, with each section comprising 35–135m long segments (Grogan 2005a: 129). Differences in structural detail were also noted in adjoining bank sections.

In the middle enclosing element at Rathnagree, a series of straight sections ranging *c.*20–50m in length with angular changes in alignment are apparent (Figure 5.28 and Figure 5.29). Regular depressions at the crest of the bank may also relate to the irregular dumping of material by gang workers (Figure 5.29). This was also noted by Cunnington (1933) at Yarnbury Castle in Wiltshire.

These sections of bank would have been worked by a group or gang of people, who may have been further divided into smaller groups. This interpretation is supported by Dixon's excavations at Crickley Hill, Gloucestershire (Dixon 1994: 134–139). This identified a low bank with intermittent pits abutting its external face. These pits were only partially completed and were interpreted as an unfinished external ditch. The excavator suggested that the hillfort builders had begun working in separate pits with the intention of joining the features later. This assumption was confirmed by excavation, which revealed two such pits were subsequently joined.

At Breiddin hillfort in Powys, Wales, Musson suggests that the 'meandering' line of the bank could be divided into 8m long sections that could reflect different gangs (Musson 1991: 176). Even smaller sections were identified by Mytum (2013: 220) at Castell Henllys in Pembrokeshire, where bank sections of up to 2.2 and 2.4m were revealed by variations in the rear facing, suggesting small gang groups.

Rathcoran: an unfinished hillfort?

The impressive hillfort of Rathcoran in Baltinglass displays all of the aforementioned evidence for an unfinished hillfort. Similar to Ladle Hill and other unfinished hillforts in Britain, the enclosing elements seem to be in various stages of completion, some being almost finished while others have not yet started. Condit (1998), Waddell (1998) and Raftery (1994: 44) have interpreted Rathcoran as the only possible unfinished hillfort in Ireland, with the latter considering it a prime example to derive information regarding construction methods.

The construction of level platforms at Rathcoran could have been used as a marker lines and areas upon which to construct the banks. The core of these could have comprised gathered field stone, which would have the added benefit of clearing the hilltop of glacial drift. This is evidenced by the variation in composition of the enclosing elements (Figure 8.39). At the north, where the banks are largest, they are covered with soil, in contrast to the remainder of the defences which consist of stone (this was also noticed by Raftery 1994: 44; Grogan and Kilfeather 1997; Grogan and Hillery 1993: fig. 11).

Sub-rectangular pits are positioned abutting the inner edge of the outer bank of Rathcoran, at the north-west, north and south-east. There are low banks probably comprising quarried material along the sides of these pits. Condit (1992; 1998) has suggested that this material was intended for use in the hillfort banks. The loose soil overlying bedrock may have been stockpiled for later use. Blocks of bedrock, as well as stones from field clearance, may have been quarried to build the core of the bank and then capped with the remaining loose material.

The best comparison for these features is found at Old Oswestry in the Welsh Marshes, Shropshire, where up to eleven large rectangular pits outlined with low banks are positioned at either side of the eastern entrance (Hughes 1996). Various theories have been considered regarding their function, with more recent scholars suggesting they relate to the elaboration of the entrance and monumental display. The pits are positioned on sloping, east-facing terrain and are highly visible from that approach. In contrast, viewshed analysis highlights that the pits at Rathcoran are obscured from the immediate environs. Particularly at the most accessible point of the hilltop at the north-west and at the possible entrance in this area, the pits are not visually dominant like at Old Oswestry and are obscured by the moderately spaced enclosing elements. It is therefore unlikely that they functioned as an element of monumental display.

Late pre-Hispanic societies in the Andean highlands also built hilltop fortifications known as Pukaras, *c.* AD 1300–1450. Some of these had moderately spaced enclosing elements, separated 15–30m apart, which Arkush (2011: 84) suggests were utilized as 'killing alleys'. With regards Rathcoran, this is probably an erroneous interpretation and Least-Cost-Path analysis supports this non-defensive argument (Figure 8.40). Ninety six evenly distributed points were positioned at an average distance of 20m, 50m and 100m from the outer enclosing elements. The destination point was positioned near the highest point of the interior, outside the passage tomb, as the walls protecting the tomb affected the generation of the cost-path. The extensive number of points is used to offset the potential affect later field boundaries might have on the results, as well as alleviate discrepancies that generate if points are positioned too close to breaks in the enclosing elements. The results show that a large number

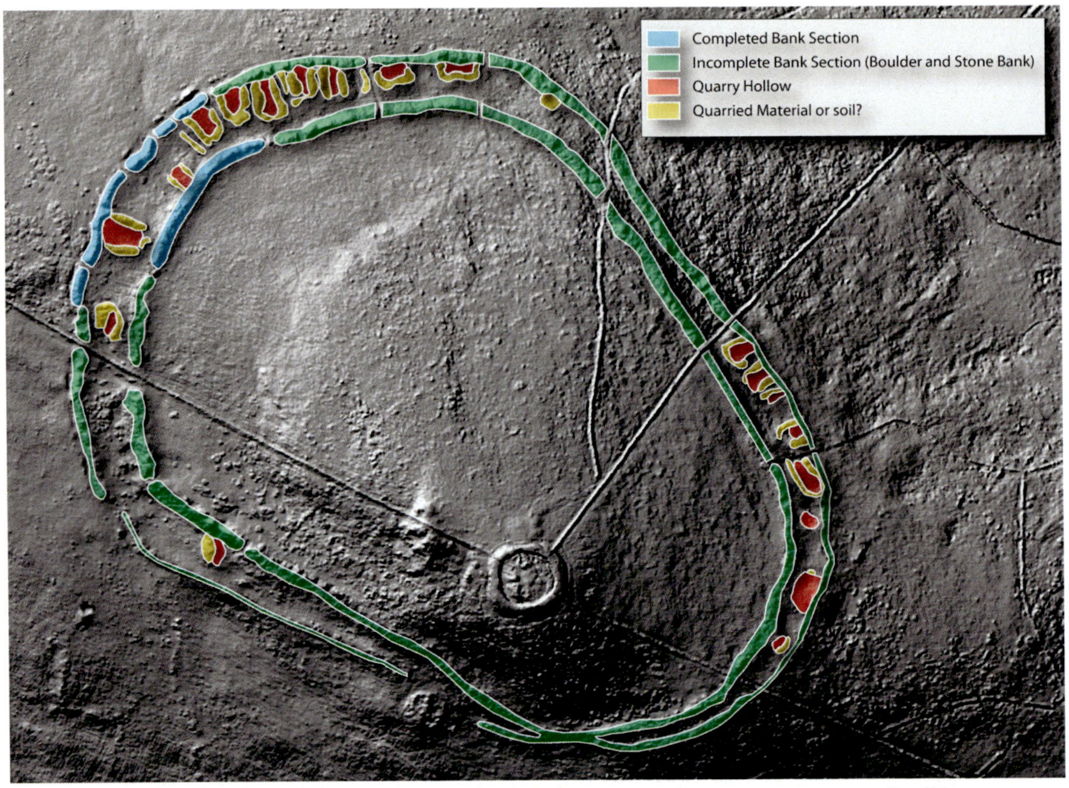

Figure 8.39: Different composition of enclosing elements at Rathcoran hillfort, Co. Wicklow.

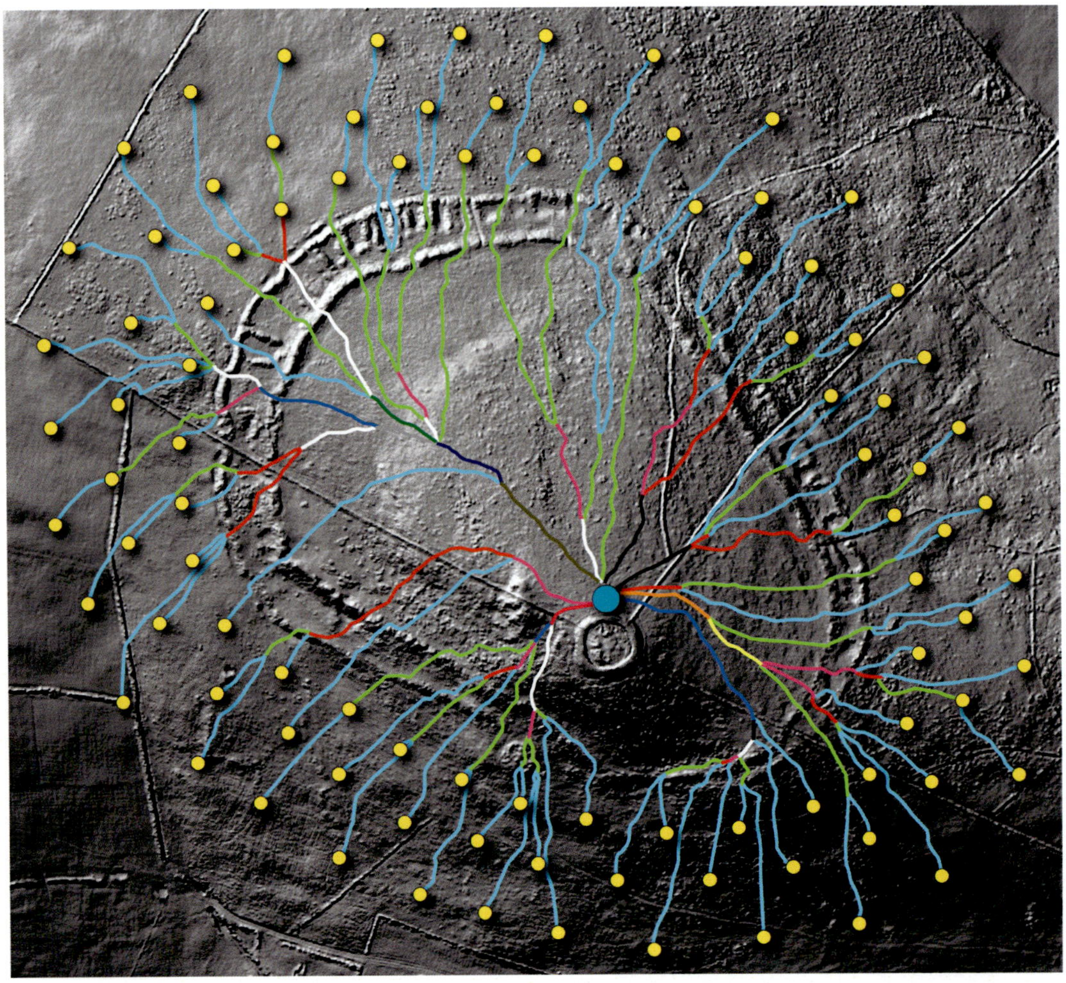

Figure 8.40: Least-Cost-Path analysis of Rathcoran highlighting the ineffectiveness of quarry pits as defensive features.

of paths traverse the area to the north-west, where the enclosing elements are largest and where there are no pit features. The basic assumption is that areas where paths converge and accumulate can be considered the most accessible and therefore, may be regarded as a natural routeway (Murrieta-Flores 2012: 108–109). The pits are ineffective as a defensive feature and largely fail to funnel paths, with some examples traversing through and alongside shallow pits. The failure of the pits to funnel paths is evident as a maximum of two paths converge at the north where the pits are most prominent. This is in contrast to a break in the outer bank at the north-west where there are no pits and six paths converge. Even when the possible palisade identified through geophysics is incorporated as a barrier, the paths converge at the same break and access the interior of the hillfort through a gap in the inner bank 30m to the north. This analysis also indicates the ineffectiveness of the northern entrance, where only two paths converge, with the numerous breaks in the hillfort banks acting as access points.

It is more plausible to suggest that Rathcoran is unfinished and that the enclosing elements at the north-west are the most complete sections. This is supported by LiDAR survey which identified the partial remains of two quarry pits abutting the outer face of the internal bank (Figure 8.41). The most extant example comprises a U-shaped bank 8m long and 12m wide, the banks being 5–6m wide and 0.6m high. This suggests a similar form of bank construction where pits were excavated for material to form the defences in this area. It also suggests that these pits, which mainly occur abutting the inside of the outer bank, were intended to be extended to the outer face of the inner bank.

Although this would have been a considerable undertaking, the creation of a wide, shallow ditch may be paralleled at other sites. Warner's excavations at Clogher in Co. Tyrone revealed a U-sectioned ditch approximately 2m wide and 1m deep (Warner 2009: 510). Profiles of the hillfort revealed the possibility that this was only an inner part of a much wider and shallower feature measuring 20m wide and 2m beneath the old ground surface. More recently, at the Hill of Ward in Co. Meath, at least three wide ditches were uncovered (some up to 15m in width), and dated to the Late Bronze Age (Davis pers. comm). Wide, flat bottomed ditches have been identified throughout Europe, one of the earliest examples being found at the fortified settlement of Bruszczewo in Poland dated to around 1800–1700 BC (Czebreszuk and Müller 2004; Müller and Czebreszuk 2010). An 11m wide and 4.7m deep ditch comprising part of the inner enclosing element was discovered at Corneşti-Iarcuri, a site dated to the beginning of the Late Bronze Age (Szentmiklosi *et al.* 2011: 824). A similar type of defensive arrangement, known as the Fécamp type, comprises a wide, shallow, flat-bottomed ditch with a large dump rampart. These sites are found in France and possibly southern Britain and date to around the first century BC (Cunliffe 1991: 366).

The partial construction of a palisade before the completion of the inner bank may have taken place at the north-western section at Rathcoran (Figure 5.20). Geo-

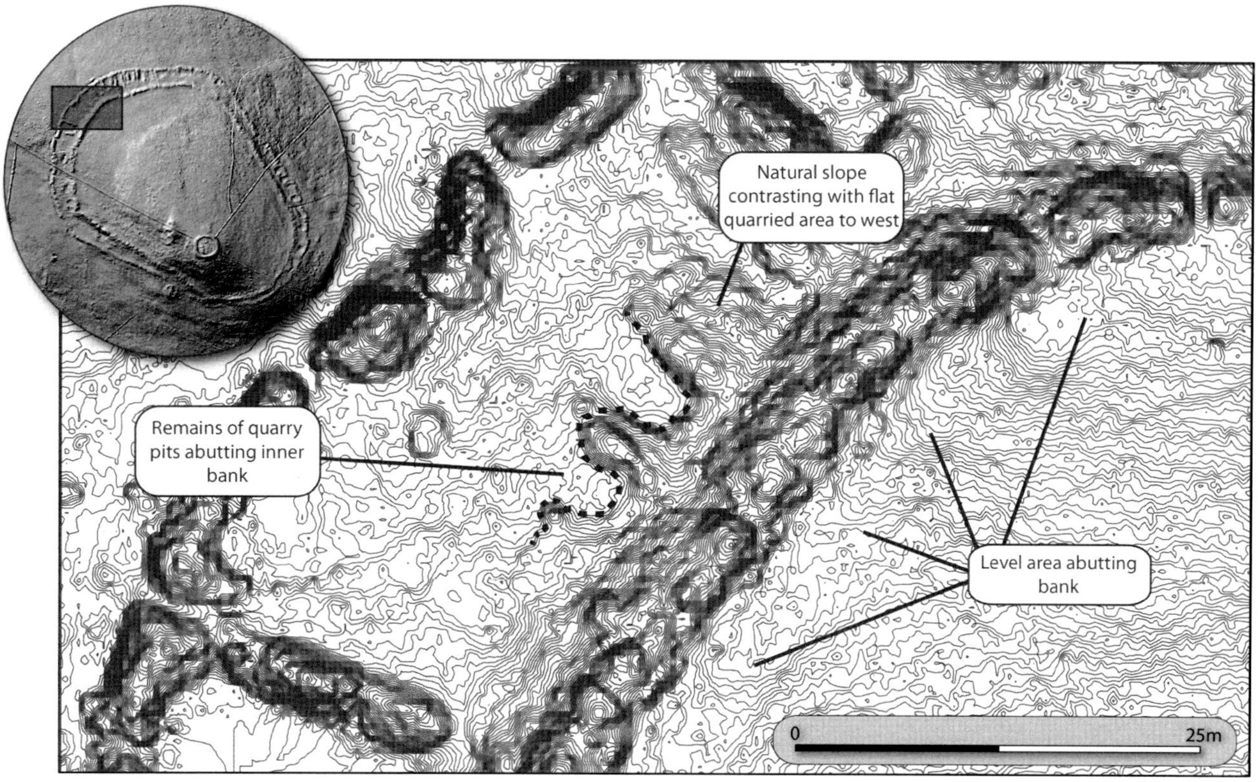

FIGURE 8.41: RATHCORAN 0.1M CONTOURS HIGHLIGHTING FINISHED QUARRY PITS AND LEVEL AREA INSIDE INNER BANK.

physical results suggest that the palisade may have been built at this phase to add height to the feature. There may also have been a practical element, negating the need to dig the considerable number of postholes that would have been necessary. Instead, material may have been piled around the posts when correctly positioned. Feachem's last phase of hillfort construction is reflected in the north-western section at Rathcoran, where the material surrounding the pits was probably used to cap the banks, erasing most of the evidence for the pits themselves.

Evidence for possible gang working or seasonal construction is also apparent at the site. The remains of the enclosing elements at Rathcoran seem to have been built in sections up to 70m in length, apparent as varying lengths of bank with different composition, alignment and dimensions. For example, at the north and north-west, where the defences are more substantial, sections are not well aligned, although the outer and inner banks correspond, in a manner that suggests they were constructed simultaneously (Figure 8.42). At the northern section where the enclosing elements begin to curve southwards, the hillfort banks are separated by 27.5m. Immediately to the west, there is a clear overlap between two sections of the outer bank and the separation between the hillfort defences narrows to 23.4m, a drop of 4.1m over 7m. After this overlap, the banks are notably much straighter on the western side. This section continues for approximately 33m at a uniform separation of around 27.5m and corresponds with a series of pits abutting the outer hillfort bank that are wider and shallower than examples further to the west.

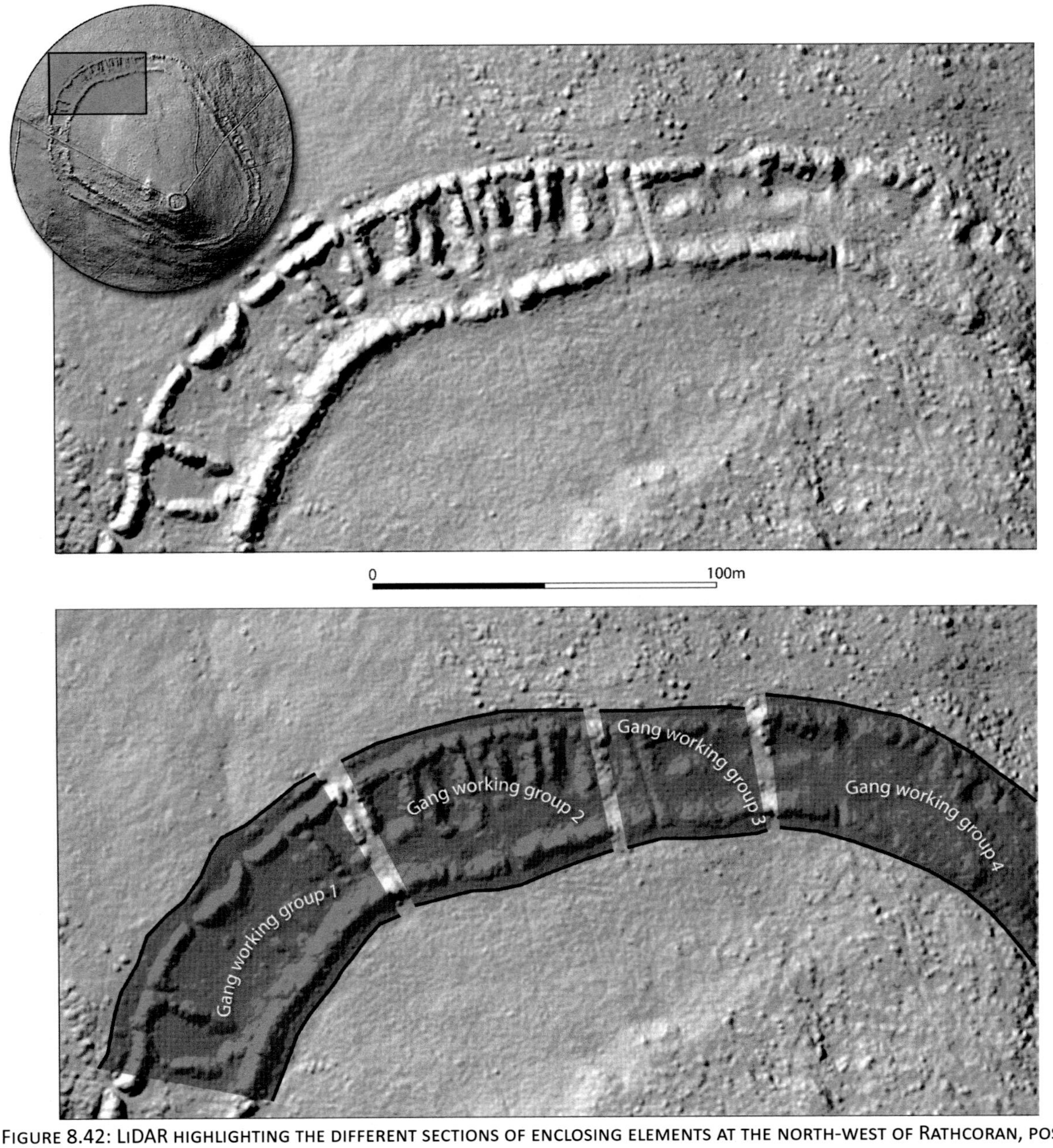

FIGURE 8.42: LIDAR HIGHLIGHTING THE DIFFERENT SECTIONS OF ENCLOSING ELEMENTS AT THE NORTH-WEST OF RATHCORAN, POSSIBLY INDICATING GANG-WORKING OR PHASED CONSTRUCTION, POSSIBLY OVER SEVERAL SEASONS.

A clear difference in alignment and separation is again visible to the west of the latter section. There, a length of approximately 70m is distinguished from the eastern section by more substantial banks, particularly the inner example which increases from 0.3m in internal height to 0.8m. This section is further distinguished by deeper, narrower and longer pits abutting the outer bank. There, the hillfort banks are slightly curved and a possible original entrance is positioned at the centre. The separation between the hillfort banks at this point is 37.5m. This was probably a deliberate attempt to make the space between the banks around the entrance area appear wider to visitors.

Abutting this section to the west is another well defined 71m length of banks. The inner bank is straighter than the aforementioned section and there is a clear step in internal height of the bank from an average of 0.8m to 1.2m. This section is also distinguished by the apparent lack of pits between enclosing elements, although the LiDAR has revealed slight remains of such features (Fig 7.4). The geophysical anomalies at the crest of the bank have been interpreted as evidence of a large wooden palisade. This series of anomalies extends along the bank at the north-west, but is confined to this 71m long stretch of bank. There are isolated anomalies along the length of the inner bank, suggesting that individual posts were positioned in certain areas, possibly to mark out the line of the uncompleted defences. It could be argued that this 71m section of the enclosing elements comprises the most completed part of the hillfort, possibly consisting of a wooden palisade within large banks capped with soil that may have been obtained from the initial digging of the quarry pits completed in that area between the inner and outer defences. To the south of this, a straight 50m section of the enclosing elements is differentiated from the former by a slight change in direction, and a reduction in the internal height of the inner bank from an average of 1.2m to 0.6m. Where the two sections of the inner bank join there is a clear angular joint. A similar connection is apparent in another 50m section of the outer bank to the south.

The remainder of the hillfort comprises straight lengths of banks, which follow the contours of the hilltop at the south-west, south and east. It is difficult to identify further evidence for phased construction or gang working in these areas. The evidence suggests that gangs of workers, or a small number of groups working seasonally, built sections of the two enclosing elements and were responsible for separate lengths of up to 70m, which presumably reflects the various sizes of those construction groups. These gangs would have been divided and given individual sections to extract material for the banks. This would have led to the creation of the closely spaced pits, which would subsequently have been joined together.

The evidence, therefore, supports three interpretations; that Rathcoran was completed, with the variable size and composition of the defences connected to competitive display; that it is unfinished; or that the site was partially rebuilt following an initial destruction and the disparity in the size of the enclosing elements is linked to different phasing. The latter two scenarios are more probable and the possible presence of a partially constructed wooden palisade may hint at why this hillfort was abandoned. The palisade could have been destroyed by fire, suggesting that the hillfort may have been attacked by rivals before its completion. In this respect, the evidence from Rathcoran is particularly significant in that it suggests hillforts may have been destroyed in acts of aggression and not as part of ritual and ceremonial deconstruction. None of this will be resolved without excavation, which it is hoped will be undertaken in the near future.

The Defensive Elements of the Baltinglass Hillforts

The purpose of enclosing elements has been a long-standing issue in regard to the function of hillforts. Three primary interpretations have been proposed; the enclosing elements formed a defensive barrier against a real or perceived threat; they were used to demarcate ritual or ceremonial areas; or they formed a physical representation of a community's strength, effectively acting as elements of monumental display. The evidence identified at the Baltinglass forts has highlighted the strategic and apparently defensive characteristics of the monuments and the extensive use of fire in apparently aggressive acts of calculated destruction. Against this, there are the practical considerations of defending enclosures with such long perimeters.

Smith and Cochrane's (2011: 80) study of chiefdom-level warfare in prehistoric Fiji and the Cauca Valley suggests that views of the immediate environs of defensive sites are the most important, allowing an approaching enemy to be seen and for adjacent agricultural lands to be overlooked. Rua *et al.* (2013: 2113) have argued that the ability to visually cover the surrounding landscape was an important factor for locating defensive structures since ancient times, stating that some of the key aspects for siting may have been the presence of comprehensive viewsheds, prominent look-out points and the surveillance of paths or approaches. Where evidence exists, it suggests that the immediate environs of Irish hillforts were heavily deforested and used intensively as agricultural land. This would also have aided visibility of approaching enemies. There has been no quantitative analysis of the defensive capabilities of hillforts in Ireland and in this regard GIS analysis has the potential to aid in the statistic investigation of visibility and optimal route selection. This is particularly applicable to Tuckmill Hill, where high resolution LiDAR data was attained for this project.

Figure 8.43 presents the viewsheds of some of the Baltinglass forts, with common areas of visibility being overlain and clipped. These are displayed in percentage format, where the common viewshed of one hillfort is given as a percentage in relation to the total viewshed of another. In relation to the hillforts on Tuckmill Hill, this analysis reveals the extensive visibility from Rathcoran, where up to 2082km² of land is visible from the interior. This contrasts with the more limited visibility from both Rathnagree hillfort (1134km²) and Sruhaun hillfort (1434km²). Significantly, 99% of the views from Rathnagree and Sruhaun are also visible from Rathcoran. It is only when we consider the immediate environs of these hillforts that there are clear distinctions in viewsheds.

The northern spur of Tuckmill Hill obscures the visibility of Rathcoran, blocking views of the north-west and eastern base of the hill. Rathnagree hillfort is strategically positioned to oversee views to the north-west, the 1% of unique views being visible from the fort (Figure 8.44). Similarly, Sruhaun is located at the break of a steep drop off to the south, allowing excellent views of the southern and eastern base of Tuckmill Hill. Again, it is these views that comprise the 1% of Sruhaun's viewshed that cannot be seen from Rathcoran. A similar situation occurs on Spinans Hill, where Brusselstown Ring has largely the same views as Spinans Hill 1. The contrasting views reflect differences in visibility of the immediate environs, and suggest that the hillforts on Spinans Hill were strategically positioned to overlook the base and slopes of the hilltop as well as access routes to the summit.

Tuckmill Hill is a tripartite hilltop with three distinct aspect. Rathcoran, Rathnagree and Sruhaun are positioned at the intersection of these aspects, allowing for maximum visibility of the hillslopes and immediate surroundings. The strategic setting of these forts is further emphasised by the Least-Cost-Path analysis (Figure 8.45). Twenty points were randomly generated surrounding the base of Tuckmill Hill and these form the starting points. The destination point is positioned near the northeastern entrance of Rathcoran, near the summit of Tuckmill Hill. The limited area being considered means that we do not have to consider the effect river systems or bogs would have on the resultant data, principally because there are none recorded in the area. Tree cover is also not considered, as where environmental evidence exists, it shows that the land immediately surrounding Irish hillforts was intensively cleared of forestry. Problems created by the high resolution of the LiDAR data are ironically the major factor affecting this analysis. Modern field boundaries create resistance while roads and other modern tracks funnel any generated paths. Fortunately, this only affected the data on the lower slopes of the hill. Field boundaries are somewhat evenly spaced and can therefore be seen to affect the generated paths equally, largely negating there effect.

The twenty generated paths converge at four distinct points in the landscape, creating four routes ascending the hill. Two of these paths traverse areas that are not visible to Rathcoran, but are visible to Rathnagree or Sruahun respectively. The GIS analysis implies that comprehensive views of the lands surrounding the base of the hill and control of the major routes to the summit were important contributing factors in the placement of these monuments. This could be viewed as an expression of defensibility and may also indicate that there was a significant threat (or perceived threat) to the community near the hilltop. It may also hint at the possibility that all three forts on Tuckmill Hill were contemporary (Rathnagree and Sruhaun were) and built by the same community or alliance of communities. It is important to state, however, that this does not mean the remainder of the forts in the Baltinglass group are contemporary. These results may also imply that Sruhaun could have functioned in a similar way to Rathnagree and Rathcoran, being located in a defensive manner on a prominent route to the summit of Tuckmill Hill and overlooking areas not visible to the other forts. Although Sruhaun may not have been used as a defensive enclosure, its strategic positioning could suggest it was meant to be viewed as such from a distance. It may have had more practical functions, such as being used as a stockade for cattle.

Unfortunately, the LiDAR data for Hughstown is too

B

A	Tinoran	Brusselstown Ring	Rathcoran	Rathnagree	Spinans Hill 1	Hughstown	Sruhaun
Tinoran		44%	89%	56%	78%	75%	73%
Brusselstown Ring	60%		81%	46%	93%	54%	64%
Rathcoran	72%	47%		55%	80%	62%	72%
Rathnagree	81%	48%	99%		85%	68%	69%
Spinans Hill 1	62%	54%	79%	48%		53%	59%
Hughstown	80%	43%	83%	51%	71%		70%
Sruhaun	82%	52%	99%	54%	83%	73%	

______% of **A**'s views are visible at **B**

FIGURE 8.43: INDIVIDUAL VIEWSHEDS OF THE BALTINGLASS FORTS IN RELATION TO ONE ANOTHER.

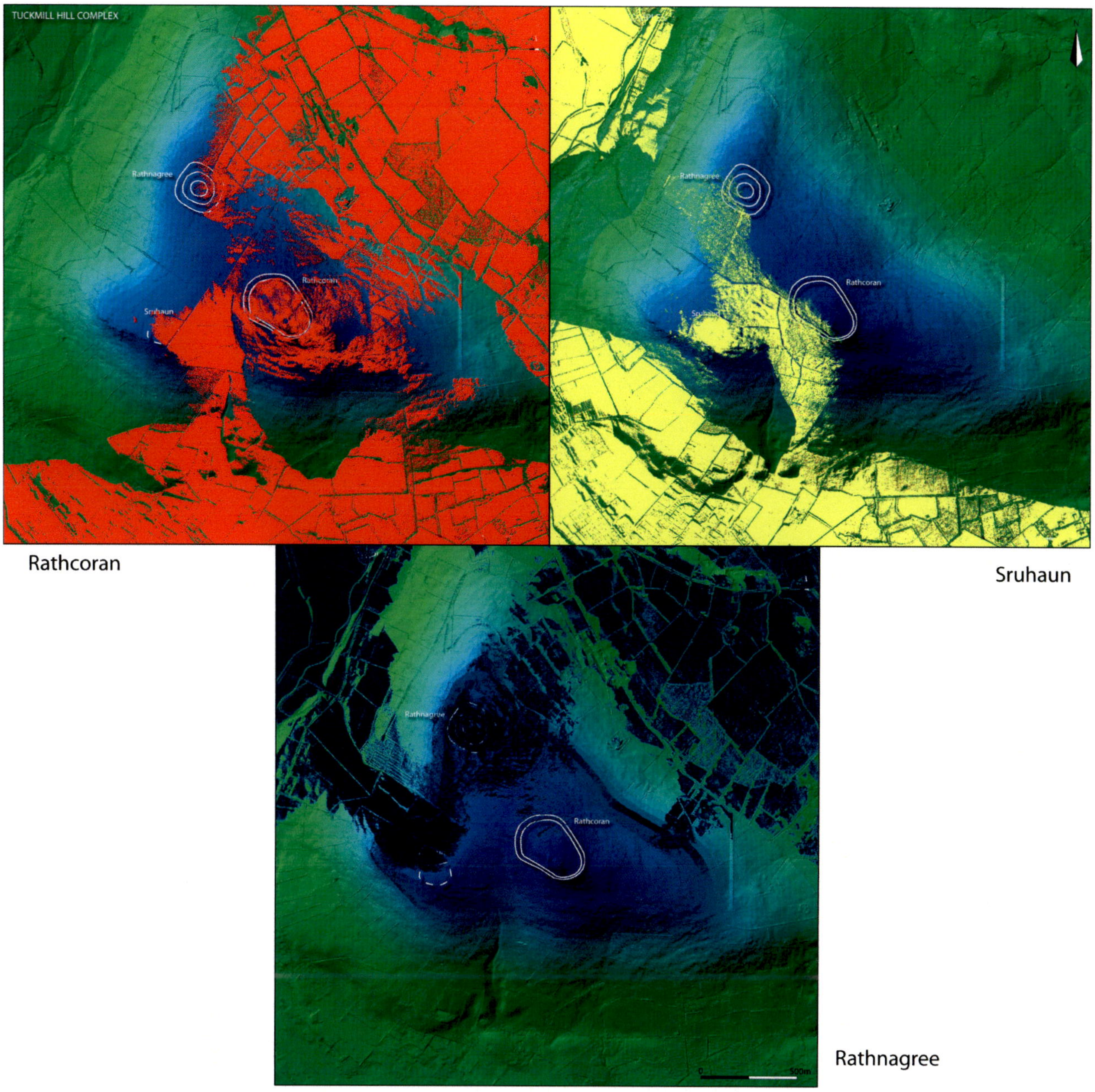

FIGURE 8.44: VIEWSHED ANALYSIS OF HILLFORTS ON TUCKMILL HILL SHOWING UNIQUE VIEWS OF THE IMMEDIATE ENVIRONS.

fragmented (Figure 5.42), and that for Tinoran severely affected by the extensive forestry (Figure 5.36), to allow detailed GIS analysis to be undertaken on these sites. Wider viewshed analysis does indicate a similar scenario on Spinans Hill, where two forts were positioned on the eastern and western summits to attain comprehensive views surrounding the immediate base of the hill and to facilitate control of the access routes to the summit. The dating of Spinans Hill 1 suggests it is probably Early Neolithic in date, while the date of Brusselstown Ring remains unknown.

8.4 Conclusion

The forts in the Baltinglass area form a unique cluster that is unparalleled in Ireland. Radiocarbon dating has revealed that not all of these were built at the same time. Some of the forts were contemporary, such as Rathnagree and Sruhaun, built at the end of the Middle Bronze Age, while others were much earlier, such as Spinans Hill 1 and Hughstown, both of which are Early Neolithic. Dating of individual enclosing elements also reveal that some were built over a prolonged period.

The construction of a hillfort was probably an important event for the people in the local landscape. Settlements recorded within Rathcoran, Brusselstown Ring and possibly Hughstown, suggest that there was a hierarchical layout of hut structures. The extensive number of recorded hut sites infers large populations which would have been necessary to construct these large monuments.

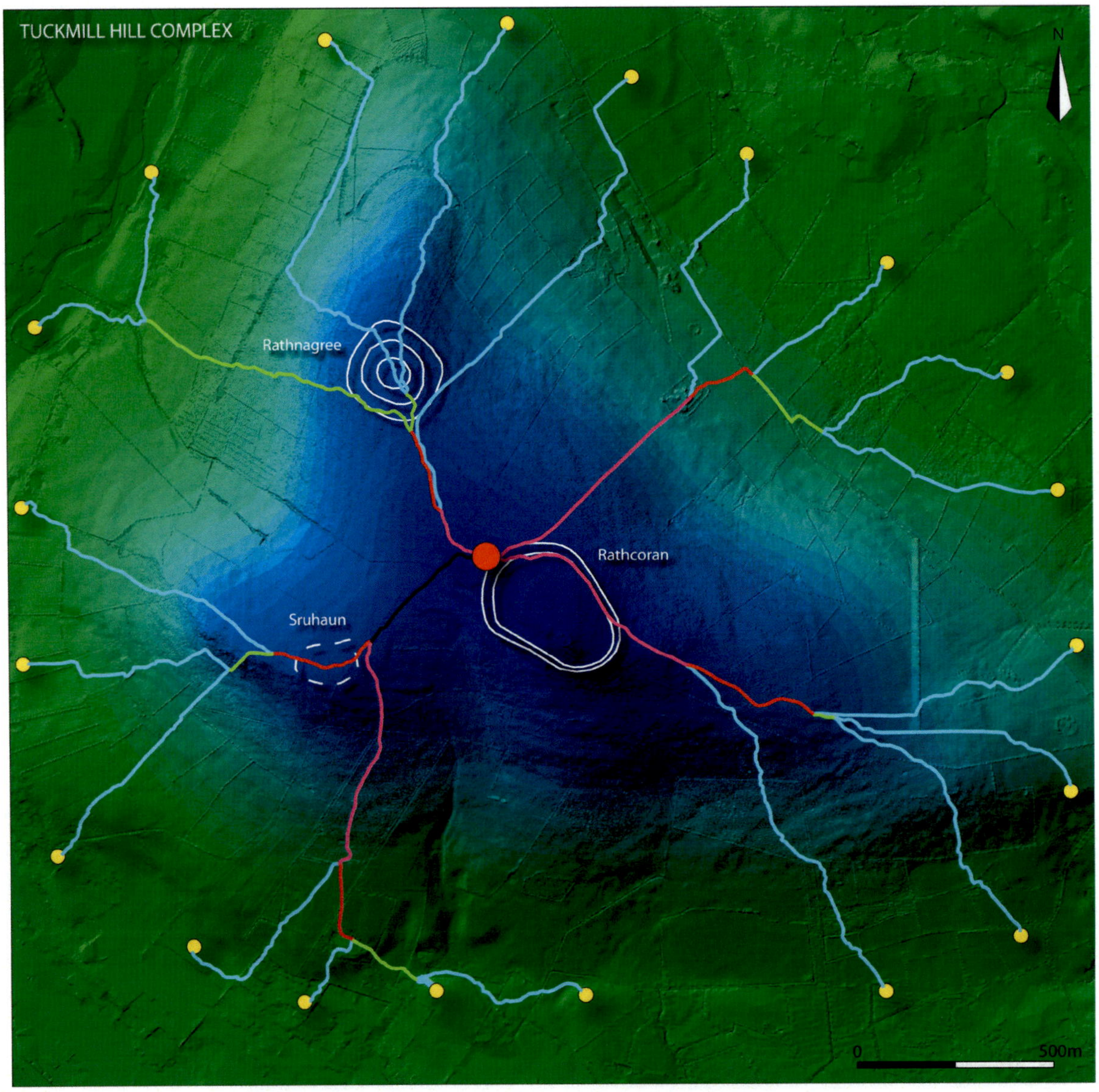

Figure 8.45: Least-Cost-Path analysis of Tuckmill Hill highlighting most accessible routes to the summit.

The evidence from Rathcoran, Rathnagree and Tinoran correspond with theoretical models of hillfort construction, which suggest that there were universally accepted ways and methods of constructing hillforts that spread throughout Britain, Ireland and probably the Continent. In this context Rathcoran hillfort is important. GIS analysis and geophysical survey support the interpretation that this is an unfinished hillfort. Breaks in the enclosing elements are probably not defensive. The destruction of a possible section of timber palisade at the crest of the most complete section of defences at the north-west imply that the monument was destroyed before it could be completed, possibly in an act of aggression by a rival group. The evidence for deliberate destruction of the nearby hillfort of Rathnagree may be relevant here.

Taking the hillforts on Tuckmill Hill as an example, GIS analysis indicates that these monuments were built in strategically important positions on that hill to oversee and control the immediate environs and its access routes. Defining and maintaining territories may also have been a concern for these communities, as the distribution of burial monuments near natural boundaries might suggest. These may have physically and ritually marked the territories of a hillfort community along with other physical landform such as rivers, bogs and mountains.

The need to define territories, oversee approach routes and land, as well as the hierarchial layout of settlements, infers a large population under the coercive power of elites. This occurred at a time when there was increased militarism and a European wide adoption of a warrior culture, as well as a dramatic increase in the exploitation of natural resources, maximisation of agricultural productivity and competition over trade routes (Earle 2002; Bruck and Fontijn 2013: 202). Therefore, the concerns shown by hillfort societies in Baltinglass correspond with the contemporary political and economic climate in Ireland and Europe.

9

Hillforts and Warfare in Bronze Age Ireland

As the name suggests, hillforts have long been interpreted as defensive structures built by prehistoric societies burdened by conflicts and disputes of various kinds. This is vividly illustrated by written accounts of hillfort warfare in Classical sources, notably Caesar's record of the Gallic wars in the first century BC, and by archaeological information for the Roman conquest of southern Britain, from such well-known sites as Maiden Castle, Dorset. The evidence of physical assault and destruction, massacres and cemeteries, which accompanied those military campaigns provides an insight into how hillforts were involved in warfare of the Roman Iron Age.

The close connection between hillforts and warfare has recently been questioned in respect of the limitations of these sites as defensive strongholds, with attention drawn instead to their broader meaning in symbolic terms (see Armit 2007 and Lock 2011 for opposing views). Harding (2012) suggests these recent criticisms of the defensive role of hillforts has more to do with a general objection to the prevalence of conflict in prehistory. In the case of hillforts, the focus of research has shifted to understanding the economic, political and other functions of these sites. This also applies to Ireland where a consideration of violence and military use is often absent from the interpretation of excavated hillforts. That has led to greater emphasis on the ceremonial and ritual use of hillforts, influenced in part by sustained research on the 'royal sites' of the Iron Age, such as Tara, Navan/Emain Macha, and Dún Aillinne, with their internally ditched hilltop enclosures. These changing perceptions of hillfort function are more shifts in emphasis than opposing interpretations, as most Irish researchers accept the multi-layered significance of these sites. That said, there continues to be some reluctance to engage with the military aspects of hillforts in Ireland, possibly because this might revive some association with debunked notions of Celtic invasions.

In recent years there has been renewed academic interest in the subject of ancient warfare. This chapter considers the phenomenon of war in Bronze Age Ireland, to examine the role hillforts may have played in such conflicts. While the geographical focus is narrow, parallels can be drawn with other parts of Europe where similar developments occurred during the second millennium BC.

9.1 War and Conflict in the Bronze Age

While violence has been a reality of human existence since earliest times, the Bronze Age is often associated with the first evidence of organized warfare on a significant scale in Europe (reviewed by Harding 2000 and Thorpe 2013). This is partly due to the archaeological visibility of specialised weapons, depictions of fighting on rock art, the building of fortifications, and most vivid of all, osteological evidence of human casualties. The second millennium BC witnessed the widespread adoption of swords and rapiers across Europe, produced in large numbers for the specific purpose of killing human beings. These were used together with throwing spears, thrusting lances, shields, body armour and helmets, as well as a range of daggers, axes and other tool-weapons.

This weapon panoply, with stylised representation on rock art and stelae in some regions (Figure 9.1), presents a particular persona of individuals of high standing who excelled in hand-to-hand combat. Such warriors are believed to have played a central role in the development of Bronze Age societies, and the emergence of complex social formations termed chiefdoms (Kristiansen 1999). These were not the professional soldiers and standing armies of historic times, but closer to the heroic figures of the Homeric tradition, and to mythologised warriors such as Cú Chulainn, a central figure in the Irish saga, the *Táin Bó Cúailgne*. Archaeology has famously shown how the tales of the Trojan War recounted in the Iliad have a basis in actual events during the Greek Bronze Age. This raises a question as to whether oral tradition recorded in medieval Irish literature has any relevance to the warrior culture of the Irish Bronze Age (see Mallory, 2016: 175–205 for discussion).

Understanding prehistoric warfare

Any brief survey of historical and ethnographic sources confirms the endless cycles of conflict and violence that have plagued human societies in the near or distant past. The writing of recent history tends to be punctuated by wars and rebellions, conflicts and political disputes of various kinds. While biological and evolutionary factors partly explain innate aggression in the human species, the expression of such tendencies through organized warfare is essentially a cultural phenomenon with complex origins and motivations. War refers to a state of armed conflict between societies. It lies at the extreme end of a scale of violence that begins with acts of individual aggression and personal feud at family and community level, and extends to depersonalised conflicts involving entire societies. War is often triggered by particular events, but is sustained by political, economic and other strategic objectives. The causes are many, often obscure and spontaneous, involving blood feuds connected to personal honour, disagreements over property and trade, right up to aggressive expansion, territorial conquest and appropriation of resources. The scale of these conflicts depends on root causes and the size of the groups involved, ranging from raids, skirmishes and reprisals to military engagements of short or long-term duration. It is precisely this variability of circumstance and causes that makes the phenomenon so difficult to explore.

War is generally portrayed by historians as rational and premeditated, representing what Clausewitz famously termed the continuation of politics by other means. Because of this political context, and the serious repercussions that follow, warfare in modern times tends to be highly organised and strategic in direction. Ancient warfare, often termed 'primitive war', in contrast, is viewed as limited in political ambition, localised, and chaotic in organization. Such warfare is often presented as highly ritualised, with various social restraints to limit the consequences for those involved. For many, this does not qualify as real war, but represents lower levels of conflict and aggression that were always present from early human origins. This raises the question of whether to believe that the distant past was relatively peaceful, and that any warfare that occurred was limited by ritual and social constraints, or else to face the possibility of total war without any such ideological restraints (Carman and Anthony 1999).

In 1996 Lawrence Keeley published 'War before Civilization', a highly influential work that argued all war is total, and that primitive warfare was often more deadly and frequent than its modern counterpart ('real war'). Supported by ethnographic examples, Keeley demonstrated the likely prevalence of warfare and violence in prehistoric societies. He deconstructed the unconscious pacification of the past that developed in the political climate of the post-war era. He also criticised the new directions in archaeological explanation in recent decades, such as post-processual emphasis on the symbolic meaning of material cultural, as opposed to historicist interpretations of weapons and other manifestations of war (Keeley 1996).

What Keeley calls the 'pacification of the past' applies to some extent to Ireland, where there has been relatively little research on prehistoric warfare. This is due mainly to problems of archaeological visibility, where the most tangible evidence of conflict such as massacre sites or battlefields is lacking. Against this, is the picture of endemic warfare and violence presented by annalistic sources in early medieval Ireland (Charles-Edwards 1996), which must caution against any Golden Age perception of the prehistoric past. While the heroic militarism of the ancient Celts was glorified in nationalist propaganda of recent centuries, such attitudes gradually changed in reaction to the legacy of the Irish Civil War, the recent 'Troubles' in Northern Ireland, and the historical revisionism of postmodern Ireland. The writing of Irish prehistory has also been modified by shifting paradigms in archaeological explanation, with older models of invasion and culture history replaced in the modern era by processual and post-processual perspectives, which are to a large extent ahistorical.

The nature of Bronze Age warfare

It has been observed that conflicts in prehistory were not war as such, but disorganised fighting with no clear motives beyond the resolution of local disputes. While this is probably true for earlier periods, the scale and direction of conflict does seem to have changed significantly during the Bronze Age, with the emergence of complex societies that had larger populations, hierarchical power structures, and greater economic power. In many instances this militarism was connected to a new type of social formation called the chiefdom. These were hierarchical societies controlled by a central figure, whose power was variously based on political, military, economic and even religious responsibilities. The chiefdom was usually made up of many different communities, often with blood ties, whose leaders were subservient to a paramount chief. Economic power was central to the rise of these powerful individuals and groups. This involved control of agricultural production, raw materials and technology, as well as the many opportunities for trade in this period. This concentration of power was accompanied by competitive and expansionist tendencies, which could be expressed in hostile acts against neighbouring groups.

True warfare requires a professional military class, that once created tended to sustain itself to become a major force in political relations. While the Bronze Age did not have professional soldiers or standing armies in a modern sense, the adoption of specialized weapons and armour across Europe during the later second millennium BC can be linked to the rise of a warrior aristocracy (Harding 1999; Kristiansen 1999). The iconic representation of these individuals in rock art and stelae (Figure 9.1) represents a new ideology of martial ideals that was central to many Bronze Age societies (Harrison 2004). Not all would concur with a militaristic, power-obsessed image

FIGURE 9.1: SCENES OF WARRIOR COMBAT ON BOUNDARIES, BRONZE AGE ROCK ART, TANUM, BOHUSLÄN, SOUTH-WEST SWEDEN.

of the Bronze Age, stressing instead the wider symbolism of the weapons concerned and the social contexts of performance and display (e.g. Neustupny 2006; Brück and Fontijn 2013). Yet, as often observed, for weapons to have symbolic meaning, this must be based on the terrible reality of their use.

Whatever about their intensity, most conflicts in the Bronze Age were short-lived and geographically confined. In the absence of written sources, it is not easy to understand the dynamics of such events from the perspective of a static archaeological record. The remarkable discovery of a Bronze Age battlefield along a 3km stretch of river at Tollense, north-east Germany (Jantzen *et al.* 2011), emphasizes the considerable gaps that exist in our understanding of such conflicts. As Vencl (1984: 118) observed, archaeologists tend to focus on the physical expressions of warfare, such as weapons and fortifications, and do not, or perhaps cannot, treat war as an historical phenomenon with social context, causes and consequences.

Some researchers have argued for a socio-biological approach, where aggression is an innate characteristic present from early human evolution. Brothwell (1999) makes the case that all warfare should be considered in epidemiological terms, as aberrant behaviour involving the suspension of reason and the blunting of conscience. Opinion varies from the philosophical position that humans are not responsible for their actions, which is instead a product of their environment, to socio-biological explanations of innate aggression and territorial behaviour. If biological determinism is excluded, war can be viewed as a product of human culture, one that increases in scale with increasingly complex social and economic relationships in society. In this social evolutionary approach, warfare and militarism can be regarded as an inevitable outcome of the way societies developed during the Bronze Age.

Written sources for early warfare indicate that the causes of conflict are many, but generally originate in specific historical contexts and social circumstances. In many cases this is rooted in a clash of cultures, where people of different ethnicity, religious orientation and political outlook have a fundamental fear and dislike of one another. There are numerous examples in ethnography of hyper-aggressive societies who wage war for its own sake and the personal prestige of those involved. In other instances, conflicts have a political or economic motivation, and involve disputes over territory, trade and resources. Factors that contribute to conflict can be both internal and external to a society, with an important distinction between the motivation of the aggressor and the response of the injured party. Keeley (1996: 116) argued that the precipitating causes of most wars, either primitive or civilized, were acts of violence, which in turn provoked further conflict in immediate defence or subsequent retaliation. These often had an origin in personal feuds or petty disputes that may have escalated without any particular design. While the outbreak of primitive war was generally triggered by such events, the underlying causes were usually connected to other factors, some of which may be accessible to archaeological enquiry.

Haas (1999: 24) argued that the root causes of warfare lie in demography, the environment and the economic conditions of different societies. This is a view also held by Keeley, who used ethnographic sources to demonstrate that primitive war was often economic in character. This could include competition for critical resources such as agricultural land, livestock, hunting and fishing grounds, slaves and women, mineral resources. It might extend from short-lived raiding to the seizure of territory and resources through longer-term conquest. Trade may also have been a significant factor. Osgood and Monks (2010: 147) observed that competition for exotic materials, so vital to prestige goods economies, was a significant factor in Bronze Age warfare. This is explored in a broader sense by Keeley who questioned the common assumption that societies involved in trade were more likely to maintain peaceful relations, suggesting that it was precisely those relationships that could lead to conflict. Observing that 'war is exchange gone bad, and exchange in war averted', he identified various ways that trading partners in close proximity can become enemies. These could include perceived slights in gift exchange, or discontent arising from the exercise of monopoly over desired commodities, leading to robbery, extortion and other types of forced exchange (Keeley 1996: 122–3). The problem often for the archaeologist is how to distinguish trade goods from plunder. Social distance is no guide, as Keeley observed that 'many societies tend to fight the people they marry, and marry those they fight, to raid the people with who they trade and to trade with their enemies' (Keeley 1996: 126).

Whether competition for territory was ever a motivation for warfare in the largely under-populated societies of Bronze Age Europe is debatable (see similar comments below in relation to warfare in medieval Ireland). There is much evidence of intensified agricultural production and land division during that period, with food shortages likely at different times. This could arise as a result of population growth, particularly when combined with short- or long-term environmental change that had a negative impact on agricultural production. Many subscribe to the Malthusian view that violent conflicts increase in frequency and intensity as human populations expand, with resulting pressure on food supply and other critical resources. While there can certainly be a connection between population pressure and warfare, Keeley (1996: 117) argued this is not straightforward, and in some instances may even have been the reverse, because modern civilised states had various mechanisms for avoiding war and minimizing casualties.

Moving to the social sphere, there are numerous examples throughout history of how war was used to advance the ambition and aggrandizement of elites. Political objectives can include the legitimization of leadership through prowess in war, plunder and the expansion of territory. The emergence of a warrior culture during the Bronze Age required outlets for aggression to build personal prestige. Ethnographic sources suggest that warfare was often waged to garner prestige and trophies. Other social causes include honour killings and revenge within or outside kin groups and marriage relationships. War-like pursuits such as raiding were significant in some societies as a rite of passage for young. Finally, as recent history shows, religious motivation and conflicting belief systems can be a significant driver of conflict.

There is generally more than one causal factor in the outbreak of any conflict leading to war. Using case-studies in the south-west United States, Hass (1999) argued that conflict and territorial behaviour is less likely to occur at times of low population and abundant resources, but more likely as those circumstances change. This makes the point that humans are not inherently bellicose, but that war is a final resort in circumstances of environmental pressure and economic stress. Citing other ethnographic sources, Osgood and Monks (2010: 5) contend that many small pre-state societies in prehistory found peace difficult to maintain, and possibly not even desirable, as the maintenance of a certain level of hostility was an important way of creating social relationships, maintaining connections between groups, and countering shortages and periods of risk.

For the Irish Bronze Age, it is likely that the outbreak of warfare was also caused by many different events and historical circumstances that will never be fully understood. Specific issues connected to personal honour, food supply, territorial disputes etc could be a pretext for war, but most conflicts probably had wider political and economic objectives. What was it about the populations of Middle to Late Bronze Age Ireland that made them more disposed to warfare? The answer lies in the type of society that evolved around that time –simple to complex chiefdoms with hierarchical power structures, controlled by leaders with aggrandizing tendencies. These societies had a strong organizational capacity, with large populations and a level of economic power required to engage in large-scale military conflicts. Most important, they had a warrior culture that encouraged certain aggressive tendencies and territorial behaviour.

War and conflict in the Bronze Age: the evidence

Evidence of prehistoric warfare tends to be very under-represented in the archaeological record, mostly due to the limited duration of those traumatic events and the equivocal nature of the physical remains. Weapons are obvious sources of information, but it is rarely possible to understand their use in battle as they tend to enter the archaeological record in other contexts. The occurrence of blunt force and projectile trauma on human skeletal remains is evidence of inter-personal violence, but this does not always explain the circumstances of that fatality. Not every act of violence constituted war, though the discovery of mass graves and massacre sites takes us closer to conflict on that scale.

As noted above, battlefield evidence is problematic,

given the dynamic nature of those engagements, and what happened afterward in terms of disposal of the dead and the gathering of weapons as spolia. This is also a problem for later periods; for example, there is almost no archaeological evidence for one of the most famous clashes in Irish history, the battle of Clontarf (AD 1014). Battles must also have been a key element of prehistoric warfare, albeit on a smaller scale, adding to problems of archaeological visibility. For this reason, the absence of battlefield archaeology cannot be used as evidence for the absence of war, especially when there are other indications of militarism. This is true of the Middle and Late Bronze Age, when specialised bronze weapons were produced in great quantities at the same time when hillforts with strong elements of fortification were built. The fact that such weapons are rarely found in hillforts is anomalous, as those sites would be defenceless without them, which would make the building of fortifications pointless for defensive purposes. While there is a danger of circular argument, the explanation lies in depositional practices connected to the symbolic importance of those weapons, as well as the usual variables of preservation and archaeological recovery.

Other sources of information are entirely absent in Ireland; for example, rock art with images of warriors found in Iberia, Italy and Sweden (see Harrison 2004; Ling and Cornell 2017). There is no human skeletal evidence of violence from later Bronze Age Ireland, mainly because cremation was the dominant burial rite at a time when weapons were not deposited as personal grave goods. No massacre sites or mass graves have been recorded near Irish hillforts, while the excavation of those sites has yielded very few human remains (see below). On a wider level, there may be indications of warfare and political instability in settlement patterns, metal hoarding, and religious practices involving votive deposition, but any such interpretations are usually controversial.

In conclusion, the study of warfare in archaeology represents research into a historical phenomenon that has left disproportionately little material evidence in view of its far-reaching social consequences (Vencl 1984: 131). Archaeology does have the potential to contribute to the history of warfare through its ability to interrogate the physical remains of conflict, what Keeley (1996) called the power of circumstantial evidence. While the physical record may limit our understanding of the many causes and conduct of warfare in the Bronze Age, the phenomenon can be explored in relation to the social and political environment that gave rise to these tumultuous events.

9.2 Hillforts and Warfare

'Fortifications are above all the materialised expression of the human fear of being attacked, and of losing life, freedom or property, which, in conditions of settled life and of accumulation of property, led to the development of defensive fighting tactics' (Vencl 1999: 67).

A defining characteristic of any hillfort, as opposed to other forms of hilltop enclosure, should be an emphasis on fortification, coupled with a visual symbolism connected to political and military power. The defences of a hillfort combined the protection of human life and property behind physical barriers with an imposing presence on the landscape. This served to deter would-be attackers, intimidate local communities, and display the social standing and political power of the occupants. A key concern of any defensive arrangement was to repel attack, and so protect the defenders, their families and property. In that sense the presence of a hillfort in any area was a statement of intent to defend and protect homeland, territory and resources.

The building of hillforts could suggest those communities felt vulnerable to attack, however the degree of protection afforded is often questioned in practical terms. The defensive potential of any fortification is based on the passive resistibility of the physical barriers and natural topography, and the active force of the defenders (after Vencl 1999: 66). The number of warriors, their experience, fighting spirit and motivation, and the quality of command, were critical factors in the defence of any hillfort. These human factors do not leave much physical evidence, which is why archaeological interpretations of hillforts tend to focus on the military effectiveness of the physical defences as a measure of site function (see Armit's 2007 discussion of this issue in relation to Maiden Castle).

The building of any fortification partly relates to the perceived threats to that society, and the frequency of those external attacks. It also relates to the internal dynamics of the group in question, and to the exercise of political and economic control. Defensive considerations were a feature of hillfort design, but that is only part of the significance of these sites. The building of these enormous sites was never an expression of insecurity, but rather a highly visual statement of military power and dominion over a surrounding territory. While defence is emphasized, hillforts may have played an important role in offensive warfare, and in some instances may have been used to consolidate territorial gains acquired through large-scale conquest. The concentration of military power at a hillfort meant it was not only a defensive position, but had the capability to launch attacks. These locations may have been important mustering points for raiding parties and military campaigns, where a military force was assembled from clan-like groups within that polity. The numbers involved are unknown, but may have been considerable if the construction of these enormous sites is any indication. A good example is the Class 2 hillfort in Ireland, the size of which reflects a considerable input of labour and materials, organized under some form of centralized leadership over a short period of construction. The ability to mobilize such resources must indicate a capability to muster an equally large fighting force at short notice.

Hillforts were not just about war, but were also instrumental in ensuring the peaceful co-existence of different groups. Their imposing presence on the landscape and visible concentration of military power had a significant deterrent value, which was central to the maintenance of peace in Bronze Age societies. Warfare in that period is unlikely to have been endemic, but there does seem to have been a prevailing insecurity in which the role of the hillfort as a deterrent was significant (Harding 2012: 178).

The location of hillforts also presents certain strategic advantages in respect of frontier defence, and the protection afforded to settlements within that territory vulnerable to raiding and enemy attack. Harding (2012: 178) observed that a hillfort was not able to control routeways in the way a hill fortified with artillery could in historic times. That said, their highly visible presence in the landscape had a significant deterrent effect that would have ensured the security of trade routes through that territory. Any consideration of hillfort defence must also examine its location within a wider settlement landscape. Many hillforts were surrounded by an outer defensive zone of settlements. This meant that surprise attack was near impossible, and that the initial military confrontations probably occurred well away from the hillfort, at or near a territorial boundary. In most instances hillforts were not the location of battles, but were probably drawn into prolonged military conflicts when they were targeted as centres of power with economic and strategic significance.

Class 2 hillfort design in Ireland

These Bronze Age hillforts were rarely built in inaccessible locations as mountain fortresses, but mostly in elevated settings overlooking large tracts of lowland from which where they are highly visible. For this reason, they were particularly unsuited as refuges, with few lines of retreat from what are highly exposed positions. That said, their elevated position, and the steep walk to many sites, did present defenders with advantages. Those sites that took most advantage of topography and elevation are the inland promontory and cliff-edge hillforts, such as Caherconree, Co. Kerry, and Dún Aonghasa, Co. Galway. The use of mountain spurs and sea cliffs reduced the defensive perimeter, while also removing the option of retreat, as in the stark choice faced by the defenders of Dún Aonghasa. That said, there are several well-known examples of Class 2 hillforts in Ireland in relatively low-lying locations, notably Haughey's Fort, Co. Armagh, Rathgall, Co. Wicklow, and Mooghaun, Co. Clare.

The design of Class 2 hillforts had certain tactical advantages in defensive terms, as well as some obvious disadvantages. These sites have some element of defence in depth, where a heavily fortified inner enclosure was shielded by an outer perimeter. This offers protection against surprise attacks, though these were unlikely given the protection afforded by the defensive shield of outlying settlements in that hillfort territory. As well as providing a physical barrier, many fortifications attempt to force assailants to concentrate on specific points, such as entrances, and in that way reduce any numerical advantage. How relevant this is to Class 2 hillforts is unclear as their large size means the direction of assault did not have to be restricted. The defenders were afforded protection from enemy weapons, and also enjoyed a screen of manoeuvre that made it difficult for attackers to see how the defenders were deployed.

If defence was the only consideration in design and location, Class 2 hillforts may never have been developed in Bronze Age Ireland. This is mainly because the tactical advantages presented by the elevated position, topography and enclosing elements were undermined by the sheer size of these hillforts, often having a defensive perimeter of several kilometres. This would require the use of sentinels and rapid deployment of defending forces to points of attack, though how these tactics were managed in the case of multiple enclosures is unclear. This may not have been a major concern in the Bronze Age, where instead of massed infantry attack or siege warfare the confrontations were on a smaller, more disorganised scale, that involved targeted attack on entrances and other points of weakness. There is no evidence of siege warfare at Irish hillforts, though this might be difficult to recognize in the archaeological record.

The use of multiple enclosures in Class 2 hillforts suggests some separation of activities combined with a layered defence strategy. One possibility is that the outer enclosure(s) was used for the stockading of livestock, with the innermost enclosure fortified for human protection. The reverse is also possible, though less likely for sites such as Rathgall and Haughey's Fort with evidence of human occupation in the innermost enclosure. The protection of cattle may have been a priority, with an ability to corral large herds inside these hillforts at short notice.

The physical defences

While there is a broad consistency in the layout of Class 2 hillforts, the artificial defences in those sites can vary considerably in design and construction. The many variations include stone walling; dump ramparts of soil and/

or stone, with or without revetments of wood and stone; heavy post palisades or light stake fencing inside or on the crest of a bank, or on their own; external ditches, both soil and rock-cut; and counterscarp banks. Entrances were usually simple openings in a bank protected by a wooden gate, with a causeway across an outer ditch. The closely-set multivallation and elaborate entrance arrangements in Iron Age hillforts in Britain is mostly absent in Irish sites.

The defences of some hillforts included in this project are rather slight, such as those at Ballylin, Co. Limerick, and Formoyle, Co. Clare. Other hillforts are more formidable, such as the stone walling used at Dún Aonghasa, or the 6–7m high palisaded earthwork of the inner enclosure at Clashanimud, Co. Cork (Figure 9.2). Wooden palisades created a strong barrier at some hillforts, whether built into (Clashanimud) or inside (Toor More, Co. Kilkenny) earthen banks, or used on their own (Rathnagree, Co. Wicklow). Some hillforts have impressive bank-and-ditch defences with no fencing, such the middle enclosures at Rathnagree and Rathgall (Figure 9.3). The dump ramparts of many stone-built hillforts are also imposing, such as those at Brusselstown Ring and Mooghaun (Figure 9.4).

Because of the variation in the enclosing elements, it is difficult to follow developments in hillfort design over the six centuries or so (1400–800 BC) of Class 2 hillfort construction in Ireland. Harding (2012: 198) notes an apparent shift in British hillfort design, from timber and stone faced ramparts in the Late Bronze Age/early Iron Age, to the use of dump ramparts in the later pre-Roman Iron Age. No clear trends are apparent in the Irish evidence. The use of timber palisades with or without ramparts seems to have been common in the Bishopsland/Roscommon phase (Clashanimud, Formoyle, Toor More, Rathnagree), whereas hillforts of the Dowris Late Bronze age (Tinoran, Mooghan, Dún Aonghasa) are of dump or stone wall construction. Whether this reflects lessons learned in the hillfort wars of the former period is uncertain, but may be the case at Rathnagree, where one of the enclosing palisades was replaced by a bank-and-ditch earthwork soon after that hillfort was destroyed by fire.

Reference must also be made to the stone chevaux-de-frise recorded at three stone forts in Ireland, namely Dún Aonghasa and Dún Dúchathair on Inishmore, Aran Islands, and Ballykinvarga, Co. Clare (Harbison 1971; see Casey 1999 for a re-interpretation of Doonamo, Co. Mayo). The most spectacular is the 17–38m wide band of several thousand sharp blocks of limestone, averaging 1–1.7m in height, which surround the middle enclosure

FIGURE 9.2: OAK PALISADE WITHIN STONE FACED BANK, CLASHANIMUD, CO. CORK.

FIGURE 9.3: EARTHWORK DEFENCES (BANK-DITCH-BANK) OF MIDDLE ENCLOSURE, RATHGALL, CO. WICKLOW.

FIGURE 9.4: DUMP RAMPART OF MIDDLE ENCLOSURE, MOOGHAUN HILLFORT, CO. CLARE.

at Dún Aonghasa. Recent excavation did not recover secure dating for this feature, with a suggested Late Bronze Age/Early Iron Age date based on supposed parallels outside of Ireland (Cotter 2012a: 197–212; table 6.4). Survey and excavation of other Bronze Age hillforts in Ireland, including the ten sites in this project, has uncovered no evidence that stone (or wooden) chevaux-de-frise were commonly used in Bronze Age hillforts in Ireland.

The *chevaux-de-frise* at Dún Aonghasa might be viewed in terms of visual display at a ceremonial centre (Rynne 1991), but was also a formidable impediment to any organised assault on the hillfort on foot, leaving aside the unlikely use of horses or wheeled vehicles in that terrain. The use of horses in Late Bronze Age warfare in Ireland is uncertain, even though this is probably the period when these animals were first present in any numbers (McCormick 2007, table 3; Bendry *et al.* 2013). There is no direct evidence for their use in war, and it is notable that the earliest bronze horse fittings are Iron Age (Raftery 1983). The use of chariots can be ruled out, as the only wheeled vehicles known from the Irish Bronze Age are heavy carts with wooden block-wheels, with the oldest example dated 1200–1000 BC from Edercloon, Co. Longford (Moore 2008).

While defence was an important consideration in Bronze Age hillforts, their design also incorporated elements of display connected to the visual symbolism of the monument. This is apparent at Class 2 hillforts in Ireland, where a layered defence strategy combined with an internal division of space that was significant in terms of access and the social standing of those within. These sites manifest authority and political power, as the permanent or occasional residence of a political elite, as places of assembly and ritual ceremony. The building of these enormous enclosures was a powerful statement of allegiance and solidarity by related groups who came together for this purpose. Such an act of communal endeavour would have been central to the symbolic construction of a hillfort polity.

Class 2 hillfort occupation and war

Any examination of the defensive role of hillforts must consider what exactly was being protected? The evidence from some Class 2 hillforts in Ireland points to permanent occupation. This is the case for Rathgall, Dún Aonghasa, Mooghaun, and Haughey's Fort, sites with occupation material and built structures that probably represent permanent residence over several centuries. The quality and quantity of this material, and its exotic origins in many instances, points more to elite residence than a large settlement. While some Bronze Age hillforts on the Continent have proto-urban characteristics in their layout, this is not the case for examples excavated in Ireland. Caution is required in any assessment of the size of hillfort settlements in Ireland, as only small areas were investigated in most of the excavated examples.

In some hillforts where a significant amount of excavation was carried out, very little evidence of occupation was uncovered. This is true of Clashanimud, and of Rahally, Co. Galway (Mullins 2008), and to a lesser extent Mooghaun, Co. Clare (Grogan 2005a). This might be explained by historical circumstances, where such hillforts were destroyed through warfare soon after they were built. It could also be explained by the use of these sites as refuges, as any occupation would be brief during times of crisis. Their design and large size is not consistent with this refuge theory. Given their size, it is unlikely that any of these Class 2 hillforts were built by a retreating army, or had any such temporary use.

Another explanation of the 'empty hillfort' phenomenon is that these sites were more places for assembly than residence. Hillforts may have been locations for periodic gatherings of extended population groups, coming from a wider settlement territory to a central place for socio-political, economic, or religious purposes, not unlike the use of óenach sites of the early medieval period (Gleeson 2014). A comparison can also be made with so-called royal sites of Iron Age Ireland, large, internally ditched, hilltop enclosures that are generally viewed as ceremonial centres rather than fortified residential sites (Newman 1998).

Archaeological excavation confirms that each hillfort had its own history of occupation and use. Some roles were part of the original hillfort design, while others developed over time in place of safety, political power and material wealth. While there was variability of use, the similarities in hillfort design does suggest some common purpose. Defence was important, but certainly not the only or even most important consideration. The use of hillforts for elite residence, refuge, specialised craftworking, and the storage of material wealth and livestock, made them obvious targets in any conflict involving other groups. Resources in the wider landscape also required protection, whether it was agriculture, trade routes, mineral resources. The economic wealth of hillforts such as Rathgall was attractive, but portable assets such as livestock and metalwork could be moved and hidden. Of greater significance was the hillfort itself, and what it meant in terms of the exercise of power in a region.

9.3 Waging War

While the type of warfare involving Class 2 hillforts was specific to Bronze Age cultures in Ireland, very similar conflicts occurred across Europe in that period. This is based on similarities in hillfort design, and in the type of weapons used. A consideration of the latter is important to understanding the dynamics of hillfort warfare in Ireland.

Weapons of war

The development of defended settlements and hillforts in Ireland during the Middle to Late Bronze Age transition (1400–1100 BC) coincided with a fundamental shift in weaponry. An earlier emphasis on archery, and various tool-weapons such as daggers and axes, gave way to specialised bronze weapons, beginning with the rapier and throwing spear, and followed by the slashing sword used with the shield, spear and lance. These new weapons were part of the symbolic panoply of the warrior, a central figure in Late Bronze Age society. The emphasis seems to be on short range combat with sword, shield and lance, or close quarter throwing of spears, with no use of long-distance fire involving either the bow or sling. There is no evidence for sling warfare, which seems to have been an important consideration for hillfort design in Iron Age in Britain (Avery 1986). This, together with the absence of archery, suggest the focus in the Irish Bronze Age was on hand-to-hand combat, which resonates with the portrayal of heroic warfare in early Irish epic literature.

While there has been no comprehensive study of Bronze Age warfare in Ireland, there have been several recent studies of weapon types from that period, including the halberd (O'Flaherty 2002; O'Flaherty *et al.* 2011), rapier (Ramsey 1993), sword (Molloy 2007) and shield (Molloy 2009; Uckelmann 2011). The production of weapons has been considered (Ó Faoláin and Northover 1998; Ó Faoláin 2004), along with use-wear (Bridgford 1997; Colquhoun 2011; Molloy 2011), and depositional practices (Bourke 2001), with several important corpus studies of different weapon types (e.g. Eogan 1965; Ramsey 1989; Eogan 2000; Lineen 2017).

Rapiers and swords

The development of Class 2 hillforts during the Middle Bronze Age, *c.*1500–1100 BC, coincided with the first use of specialised weaponry, beginning with rapiers and dirks, followed by the first swords. Rapiers are long narrow blades, known from Ireland, Britain and many parts of mainland Europe during the Middle Bronze Age. They can have mid-ribs, grooves, ribs and channels, with a riveted handle attached to a projecting tang. The handles were liable to break, which made these weapons most suitable for stabbing or thrusting, rather than a slashing motion (Burgess and Gerloff 1981). Rapiers are believed to have developed from daggers of the Early Bronze Age, along with variants under 30cm in length called dirks. They were first developed during the Killymaddy phase of the Middle Bronze Age, and continued in use into the Bishopsland phase to around 1200–1100 BC. The Irish examples are stray finds, with none coming from hillforts. Almost half of provenanced rapiers come from wet contexts, with 68% of these from rivers, 22% from bogs, and 10% from lakes (Cooney and Grogan 1994: figure 7.9).

Rapiers were gradually made redundant around 1100 BC with the introduction of the leaf-shaped sword from southern England. The first examples were the so-called Ballintober type, short swords 0.43–0.61m in length, which had organic handles riveted to projecting tangs (Eogan 1965; Waddell 2010). These were eventually replaced by the first flange-hilted swords, imported or copied forms of Erbenheim and Hemigkofen swords from the Continent, coming in again from southern England. The use of these weapons in Ireland expanded significantly after 1000 BC, when a native form of the flange-hilted, leaf-shaped sword (Eogan's class 4), known in Britain as the Ewart Park type, was produced in large quantities, mostly during the Dowris phase of the Late Bronze Age.

The militarism of the Middle and Late Bronze Age is evident in the considerable output of bronze weaponry during those periods. An estimated 660 bronze swords are recorded in Ireland, a density of 7.6 finds per 1000 km2 that is one of the highest in Europe (Eogan 1965, Figure 84; with additions). Allowing for survival and recovery factors, it is likely that these represent a tiny proportion of the total number of swords produced, which makes it likely that there were tens of thousands of these weapons in circulation. The fact that swords were not committed to graves, and were probably passed on through the generations, emphasizes the amount of weaponry available in that period. While swords did acquire special meanings that would have made them appropriate as 'gifts to the gods', this special significance was ultimately based on the reality of their use in warfare.

There is a general correlation between the distribution of Class 2 hillforts and Bronze Age swords, with the latter also found in parts of Ireland where hillforts are absent (Figure 9.5). These weapons are not found within or close to hillforts, but do occur in small numbers within 10–20km. Most provenanced finds come from rivers (estimated at 65%), with a small percentage from lakes and bogs (Eogan 1965; Cooney and Grogan 1994: figure 8:14). There are few archaeological contexts, and no confirmed grave associations.

Spearheads

The bronze spearhead was one of the most important weapon types during the period when hillforts were built in Ireland. Their development over a millennium or so

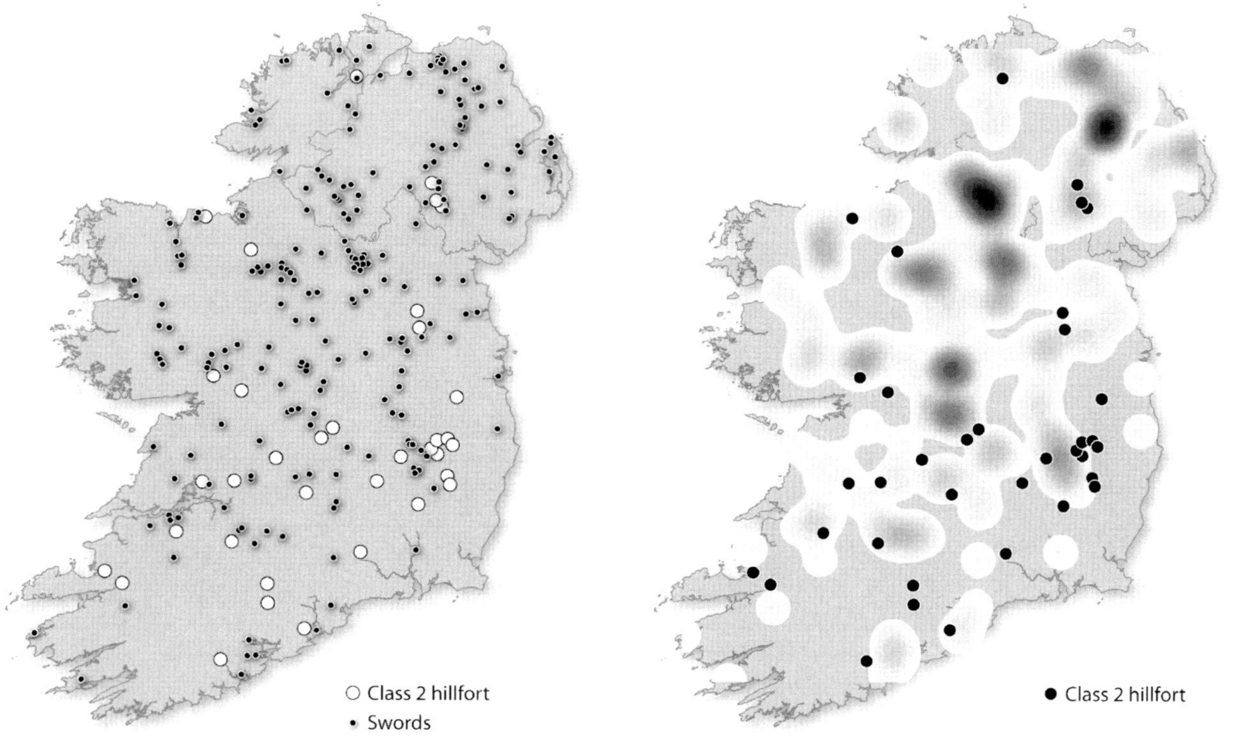

Figure 9.5: Distribution and density plot of Class 2 hillforts and Bronze Age swords in Ireland (source: Eogan 1965).

involved practical and stylistic changes in size, shape and hafting, from the early use of a tang, to the more common socketed examples, initially with loop attachments and later secured by rivets (Coffey 1894; Greenwell and Brewis 1909; Evans 1933; Ramsey 1989; Ramsey 1995; Davis 2006). The Irish and British spearheads have an insular character, with many similar styles and technical innovations shared across both islands. The earliest examples are tanged and end-looped types dating to the end of the Early Bronze Age, *c.*1700–1500 BC, followed by side-looped, basal-looped and protected-looped varieties of the Middle Bronze Age, with the adoption after 1100 BC of lunate and riveted forms during the Roscommon and Dowris phases of the Late Bronze Age (Figure 9.6).

A recent review lists some 1800 recorded Bronze Age spearheads found in Ireland, approximately half of which have no provenance (Lineen 2017). The scale of production is impressive, with records of 45 end-looped, 827 side-looped, 182 basal-looped, 56 protected-looped, 29 lunate, 7 basal-looped/riveted and 639 riveted leaf-shaped forms. The side-looped spearhead was manufactured in large numbers during the Middle Bronze Age, when the first Class 2 hillforts were built. These were replaced by riveted spearheads during the Roscommon phase of hillfort expansion, which became the main type used during the subsequent Dowris phase of hillfort activity.

An absence of contextual detail makes it difficult to understand the use and wider significance of bronze spearheads. There are only a few examples from excavated settlements, including two riveted examples from the lake settlement at Moynagh Lough, Co. Meath (Bradley 1996). Funerary contexts are rare, and include a number of old and recent finds. The former include a side-looped spearhead found in 1852 with human remains in a cist grave at Ballysadare, Co. Sligo (Lucas 1971), and another found near a cist with two inverted cinerary urns and human bone at Kilwatermoy Mountain, Co. Waterford (Power 1931). Modern excavated finds include a side-looped spearhead found near a pit cremation dated 1492–1316 BC at Mullamast, Co. Kildare (Hackett 2010). A broken spearhead found with a sword fragment and a small socketed chisel in Pit 31 at Rathgall, Co. Wicklow, is the only example from a hillfort (Raftery 1971; discussed below). The status of a 'spearhead' found in 1814 embedded in a human skull at Greenvale, Co. Kilkenny, is uncertain (*Transactions of the Kilkenny Archaeological Society* 1849, 30), as is the discovery in 1774 of six examples in a cairn in Offaly (Harbison 2004).

Spearheads do occur in the general vicinity of Class 2 hillforts, but there are no obvious concentrations close to these sites (Figures 9.7 and 9.8). They are also found in significant numbers in the Midlands and Ulster where there are few hillforts. As with swords, these weapons seem to have been deposited in different places in the landscape. Some 84% of recorded spearheads come from

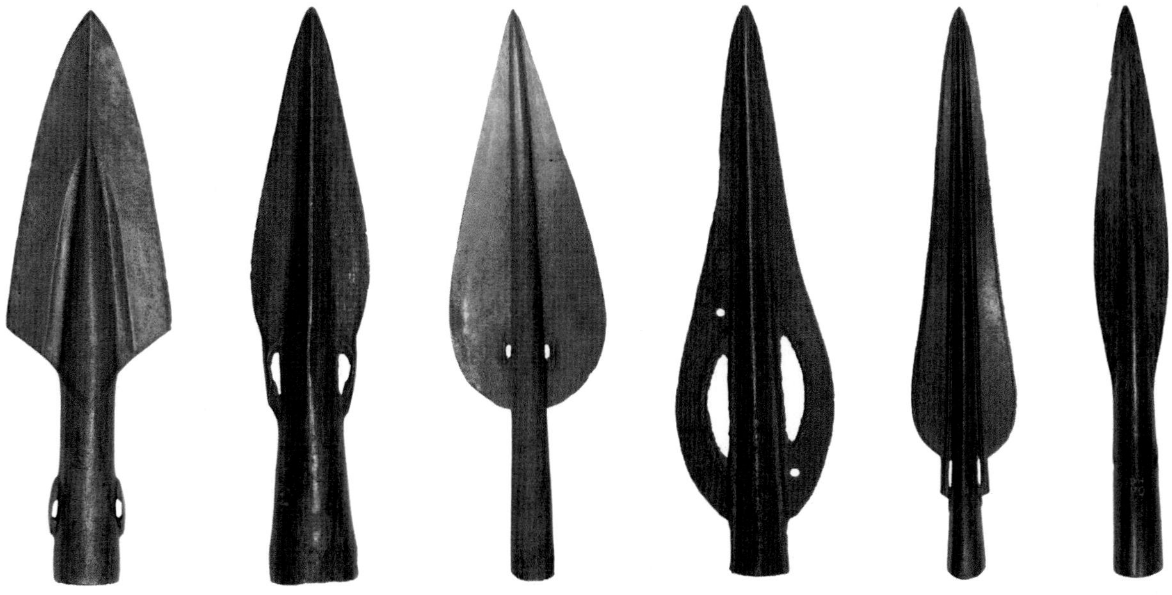

FIGURE 9.6: SELECTION OF MIDDLE AND LATE BRONZE AGE SPEARHEADS FROM IRELAND. LEFT TO RIGHT: SIDE-LOOPED, BASAL-LOOPED, PROTECTED-LOOPED, LUNATE, BASAL-LOOPED AND RIVETED EXAMPLES (SOURCE: LINEEN 2017).

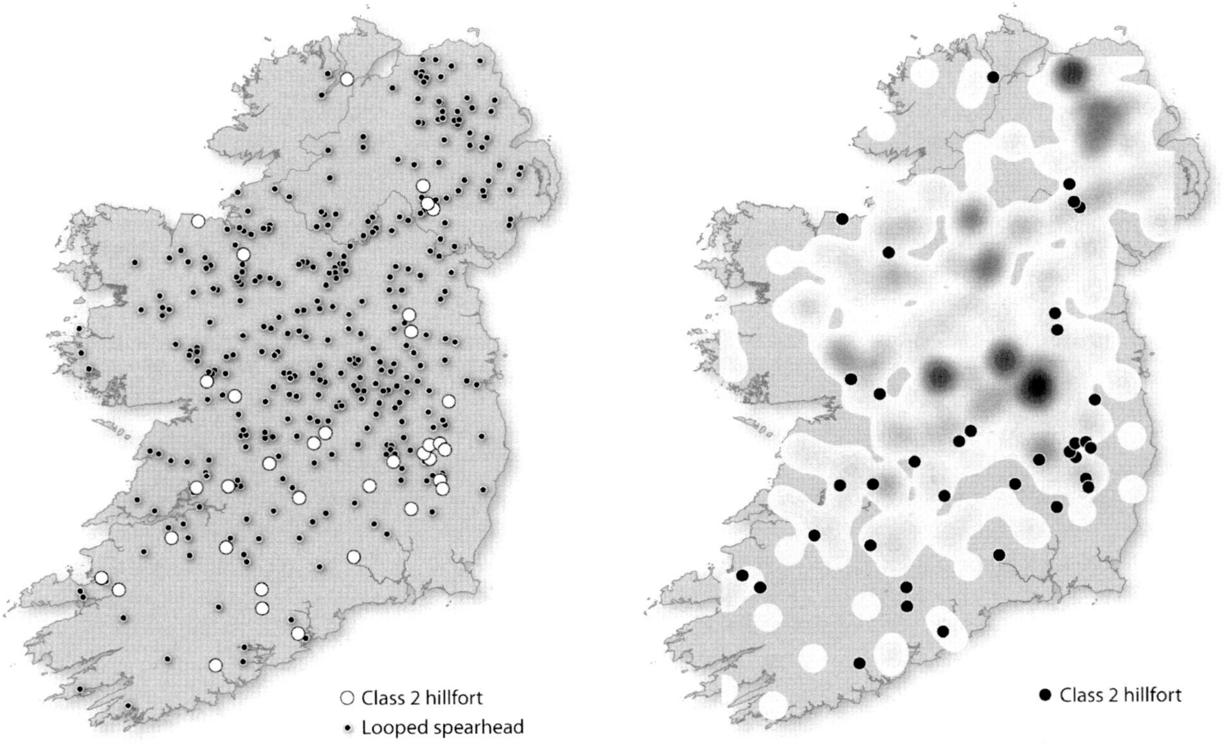

FIGURE 9.7: DISTRIBUTION AND DENSITY PLOT OF CLASS 2 HILLFORTS AND MIDDLE BRONZE AGE LOOPED SPEARHEADS IN IRELAND (SPEARHEAD INFORMATION: LINEEN 2017).

wet environments, namely rivers (34%), bogs (33%) and lakes (17%). A recent study of these finds confirms that most have evidence of use wear, but were still deposited in a usable condition (Lineen 2017). The author suggests those liminal locations were deliberately chosen for ritual deposition, connected to a symbolic decommissioning of weapons.

Shields and other weapons

Not surprisingly, the use of swords and the throwing or thrusting spear in close combat was accompanied by the adoption of the shield. A small number of circular shields made of wood, leather or bronze are recorded in Ireland. Leather shields may have been the most widely

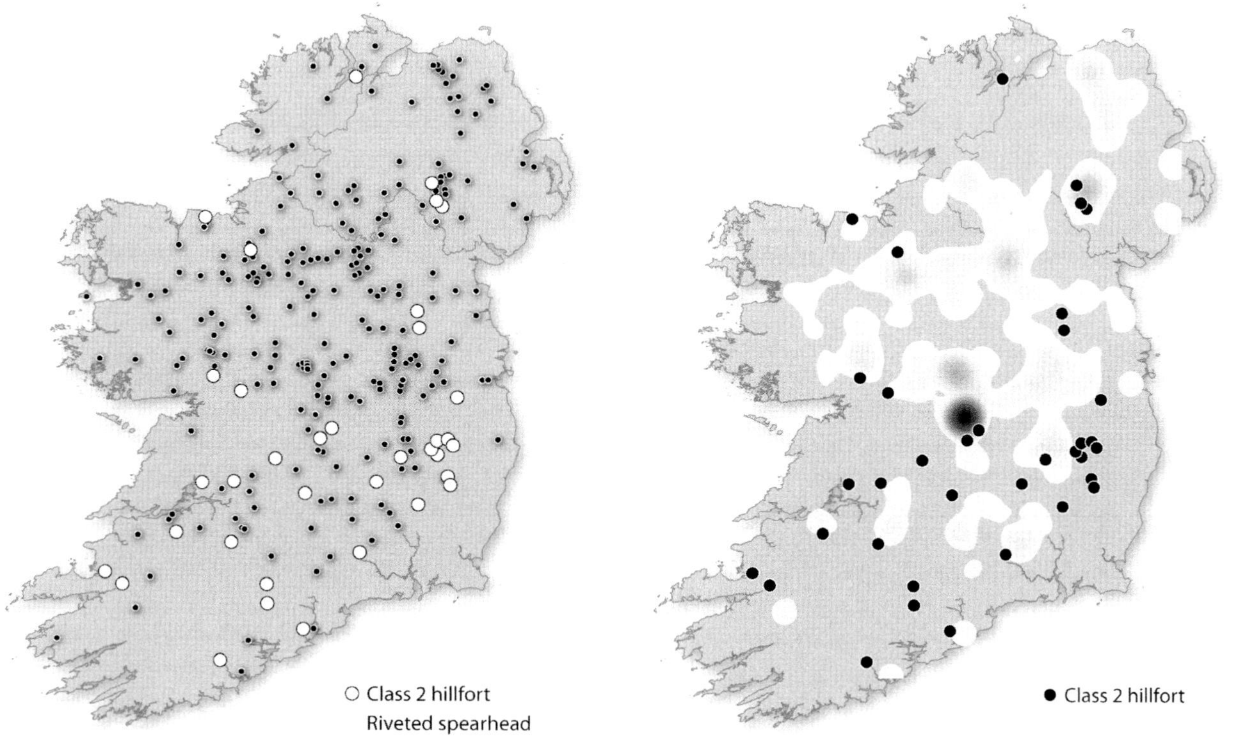

FIGURE 9.8: DISTRIBUTION AND DENSITY PLOT OF CLASS 2 HILLFORTS AND LATE BRONZE AGE RIVETED SPEARHEADS IN IRELAND (SPEARHEAD INFORMATION: LINEEN 2017).

used, such as the example from Cloonbrin, Co. Longford, produced using wooden moulds such as those from Churchfield, Co. Mayo, and Kilmahamogue, Co. Antrim (Coles 1962; Waddell 2010: 250–4). A radiocarbon date of 1950–1600 BC for the latter find (Hedges *et al.* 1991) suggests the first use of shields may have been connected to the development of the bronze spear and rapier during the Early to Middle Bronze Age transition. Wooden shields are also known, including examples from Annandale, Co. Leitrim, and an example from Cloonlara, Co. Mayo, dated 1630–1190 BC (Hedges *et al.* 1993).

Six bronze shields of Late Bronze Age date are recorded in Ireland, including three examples of type Yetholm, and three of type Athenry/Nipperwiese/Eynsham (Uckelmann 2011). One of the latter, from Athenry, Co. Galway, was possibly found with a spearhead (Eogan 1983: no. 82). There has been much discussion concerning the use of bronze shields in battle, but there can be no doubt of their effectiveness, along with their display value (see Molloy 2009). Finally, it should be noted that there are no examples of body armour or helmets recorded for the Irish Bronze Age, even though such equipment does occur in mainland Europe (Harding 2000: 287–291).

In addition to these specialised weapons, the use of bronze axes and daggers must also be considered. There are as many as 700 flanged axes and 400 palstaves recorded from the Middle Bronze Age in Ireland (Ramsey 1995: 56), with approximately 2000 socketed axeheads from the Late Bronze Age (Eogan 2000). As Ramsey observed, it is difficult to believe that in times of trouble axes used as work tools would not be lifted in anger. This is well attested from Bronze Age rock art in Sweden (Figure 9.1). The same may be true for dirks of the Middle Bronze Age (Burgess and Gerloff 1981), and socketed knives of the Late Bronze Age (Eogan 1964), and for the many implements of wood, antler and other organic materials that rarely survive. While contextual evidence for the use of tool-weapons in warfare is lacking, there are hoard associations with military equipment in Ireland. Eogan's (1983) corpus of Middle and Late Bronze Age hoards lists two examples where swords and socketed axeheads occur together, six hoards with spearheads and axeheads, three with swords, spearheads and axeheads, three with swords, spearheads, axeheads and socketed knives, and one hoard containing a spearhead and a socketed knife.

Weapons in water

The majority of Bronze Age rapiers, swords, spearheads and shields with recorded provenance and find circumstances come from 'wet' contexts in the natural landscape, seemingly removed from contemporary settlements and burial/ceremonial sites. A significant number were recovered from rivers and lakes, discovered by dredging and diving in the modern era, in deep-water locations where they could not have been easily retrieved or hidden with any certainty. While accidental loss cannot be ruled out, the widespread nature of this phenomenon in other parts of Europe points to deliberate and highly meaningful deposition during the later Bronze Age (see Bradley 1990). In Ireland, this practice began during the Killymaddy phase of the Middle Bronze Age with the majority of dirks and rapiers coming from rivers, lakes and bogs, a pattern that continued with sword deposition into the Late Bronze Age.

The motivation behind these irretrievable deposits is the subject of much debate, between those who favour sacred ('gifts to the gods') as opposed to profane interpretations. While the environmental setting may be similar, it would be a mistake to consider all metalwork finds from rivers and lakes as a coherent phenomenon, when there were probably many different circumstances behind their deposition. Bog finds are more complex, as those environments offer the possibility of recovery and so were suitable for the hiding of weapons and other valuables (see Becker 2008).

The tendency in modern research has been to interpret weapon finds from wet contexts as highly structured deposits of a symbolic nature, placed in liminal environments that have special significance in social and religious terms. The possibility of some direct or indirect connection with war has not received adequate consideration, particularly when the nature of the objects concerned (mostly weapons) is taken into account. There is also the interesting prospect that weapon finds from rivers and lakes have some connection with the political geography of warfare during the Bronze Age, confrontations that in some instances took place on what were territorial boundaries.

Several possible connections to warfare can be proposed for Bronze Age rapiers, swords and spearheads found in Irish rivers and lakes, some of which allow for votive deposition and religious intent. As territorial boundaries, rivers would be obvious settings for conflict, as illustrated by the Tollense discovery in Germany. The discovery of weapons may relate to confrontations at fording points, raising the possibility (at least for rapiers and swords) of loss in battle. These may also have been intentional deposits, connected to the death of a warrior in a battle near that location. The possibility they were made on boundaries may in itself represent '...an assertion of territory, an act of defiance, or an expression of ritualized violence' (Bourke 2001: 153). They may also signify the celebration of a military victory, involving a ritualized destruction of the weapons of the vanquished. While the circumstances of deposition remain unknown, these possibilities illustrate how the use of weapons as funerary or votive offerings does not preclude a close association with warfare.

Conclusions

The adoption of specialised bronze weaponry during the Middle Bronze Age, in the form of the rapier, dirk, sword, spear and shield, marked an important change in the way warfare was conducted in Ireland, with parallel developments in Europe at that time. This weapon panoply was connected to a particular warrior identity, individuals of high standing who excelled in hand-to-hand combat. Through these personal associations, some of these weapons may have acquired special significance over several generations of use, with some examples used for ceremonial display. When bronze axes and daggers are included with swords, spears and shields, there are an estimated 5000 bronze weapons recorded from the Middle and Late Bronze Age in Ireland. Taking survival and recovery factors into account, this suggests that there were hundreds of thousands of bronze weapons in circulation *c.* 1600–700 BC, leaving aside those made of organic materials and stone. This constitutes strong evidence of the militarism of that age, and provides an important context to understand the significance of hillforts.

The distribution of these bronze weapons may have a close association with warfare, connected to their loss in battle at river fords, and to ritualized destruction of weapons in wet contexts of special significance. The absence of finished weapons in excavated hillforts is a product of archaeological recovery and survival, but also to these special depositional conventions. The likelihood that bronze weapons were used at Class 2 hillforts is borne out by the evidence of weapon manufacture at several sites, notably Dún Aonghasa and Rathgall. Both sites have mould evidence for the casting of swords, spearheads, axeheads, knives and scabbard chapes in the Late Bronze Age (Cotter 2012b; Raftery 1971).

Is it possible that the design of Class 2 hillforts was influenced by these developments in weaponry during the Middle to Late Bronze Age? Did the size and layout of these hillforts counter the threat posed by these new weapon types? The staggered nature of these multiple enclosures might have been effective in countering the threat of archery or stoning, except there is no evidence either weapon was used in those centuries. The question then is whether the multiple enclosure design was effective against close quarter combat involving swords and shields, lances, daggers and axes, supported by use of javelins. Closely-set multivallation would have been more effective in this regard, but this is not a feature of Bronze Age hillforts in Ireland. The explanation probably lies in other uses made of the separate enclosures inside a Class 2 hillfort.

The conduct of Bronze Age warfare

The mass production of specialised weaponry is the

strongest indication that warfare was a common occurrence in the Irish Bronze Age. The amount of weaponry in circulation during the main period of hillfort construction (1200–800 BC) could be taken as evidence of endemic warfare, but this picture may be at odds with the picture of stable economies, agricultural intensification and extensive trade networks during the same period. It is more likely that war on a large scale was a relatively rare occurrence in Bronze Age societies that were otherwise peaceful. The threat of war, and the deterrent effect of weapons and hillforts, may have been more significant than actual fighting, with the latter reduced by political gift exchange and alliances. That said, the tens of thousands of bronze swords, spearheads and other weapons produced in those centuries were not solely for social display or votive deposition. As Osgood and Monks (1998: 149) observed, Bronze Age warfare was not simply a ceremonial activity, but rather a very real and deadly phenomenon. For the threat of violence to be real, it would have to occur with devastating consequences from time to time.

Historical analogy

While a direct comparison between medieval and Bronze Age Ireland is problematic, there may have been similarities in respect of the scale and type of warfare, and the broader context in which these conflicts occurred. Irish warfare of the Middle Ages was characterised by a general avoidance of pitched battle in favour of strategic retreat, counter-attack, the harrying of opposing forces, taking of hostages and raiding for cattle. The historian Katherine Simms considered the broader context of these conflicts, referring to the general under-population of Ireland during the thirteenth to sixteenth centuries. For that reason, seizure of territory was rarely a priority, but was more about establishing dominion over people and agricultural production. Simms concluded that 'a mode of warfare which aimed at killing large numbers of the enemy, while seizing their territory and securing possession by incastellation, could serve no purpose under Irish conditions. Instead the warlord required submission from people, the acquisition of additional subjects to render him tributes and services' (Simms 1975–6: 99–100).

Simms goes on to observe that there were only two viable solutions to the problem of how to conquer people without killing them, namely harrying and plundering. The former was a classic Viking strategy, where wanton destruction and pillage was designed to terrorize a people into submission and extort regular payments. An alternative was the traditional practice of cattle raiding, which survived in Ireland up to the sixteenth century. Cattle were the major commodity of value in medieval Ireland, and could be significant pawns in pursuit of military and political objectives. Simms observed that 'the commonest form of campaign was the cattle raid, in which the bare-footed, almost unarmed foot soldiers were chiefly employed in burning thatched houses and rounding up herds of cattle, while the bulk of the fighting fell to the armed horsemen, that is, the chieftain himself, his nobles and kinsmen, who rode first into enemy territory and last out of it' (Simms 1990: 608–9). She notes that the most honourable place for an Irish leader to die was at the rear of his army where many actual battles occurred, defending his plunder from counter-attack.

The fighting qualities and legitimacy of these leaders were extolled in bardic poetry, which portray a cult of reckless personal bravery, with the chief as war leader ever-vigilant sentinel, guarding his people and lands from attack (Simms 1990: 614). Any king with long-term ambitions to accumulate wealth and power did not engage in cattle raiding simply for its own sake, but was more connected to the subjugation of a territory, the payment of tribute, and the acquiring of a greater number of subjects (Simms 1975–6: 102). The taking of hostages was an important part of that process, to ensure the political submission of the new territory.

Annalistic sources indicate that raiding was also the most common form of warfare in the early medieval period. These present a similar picture of short-range sorties undertaken by a small body of warriors moving rapidly into enemy territory to seize and escape with as many cattle and other spoils as possible (see Lucas 1989). The prevalence of raiding was such that there is an entire genre of literature (*Táin*) devoted to the subject, of which the great epic *Táin Bó Cúailnge* is the best known. Sadowska (1997) has shown how that particular raid was essentially a pretext for a sustained military campaign with long-term political objectives. In many instances the seizure of cattle was an immediate outcome, rather than the long-term objective of those raids.

Raiding features in customary legal obligations in early legal texts, such as the institution of clientship (*célsine*) where the capture of livestock was a way of accumulating and dispersing wealth, or distraint (*athgabál*) where a raid was staged by a wronged party to seize an offender's property to compel him to submit to adjudication. There was also the royal raid (*crech rig*) that was part of an inauguration process, designed to demonstrate the prowess and popularity of a potential king (*ibid.*). As in the later medieval period, raiding was rarely carried out to acquire new territory, but was intended to subjugate a territory and then exact tribute (MacNiocaill 1972).

Whether these early medieval sources provide a 'window on the Irish Iron Age' (Jackson 1964), or indeed the Bronze Age, is controversial. Some comparison can be ventured between the type and scale of warfare in medieval Ireland and the conflicts that involved hillforts two thousand or so years later. Surprise, mobility and the tactical use of terrain were all probably important factors in Bronze Age warfare. Cattle were a major economic resource in that period, and so would have been a major prize in any conflict. It is not improbable that hillforts played an important role in the protection of such herds, with the design of the Class 2 (multiple enclosure) examples reflecting this important function. The use of the inner or outer enclosure(s) of these hillforts as stockades seems highly probable, given the large size of these sites and the evidence of limited human occupation. The absence of a water source at most hillforts meant the stockading of large herds would have lasted only for the duration of a raid, a strategy thwarted only by the element of surprise. The latter was generally prevented by a defensive shield of outlying settlements within the hillfort territory, allowing sufficient time for large herds of cattle to be placed inside the hillfort.

The historical parallels suggest other uses of the hillfort in warfare. Simms (1990) discussed the theme of mustering the host in medieval bardic poetry, where named contingents arrived in a place of assembly to prepare for military engagement. As the symbolic centre of a Bronze Age territory, the hillfort may also have been an rallying point for military campaigns, a connection that may have contributed in defeat to its eventual destruction (see below). The use of hillforts to protect wealth in periods of turmoil must on occasion have invited direct assault. This may have been exceptional, with early historical sources indicating that most conflicts connected to cattle raiding (*creach*) took place where a pursuing party (*toraigheacht*) attempted to recover their goods (Simms 1975–6: 104).

9.4 Consequences of War

As in other parts of Europe, it is difficult to identify direct evidence of warfare and conflict at Bronze Age hillforts in Ireland. Any consideration of warfare is generally a matter of interpretation rather than prima facie evidence of conflict. There is some evidence of conflict at Bronze Age hillforts in Europe, in the form of deliberate burning, weapon finds and human casualties (Harding 2000; Thorpe 2013). The record is limited in comparison to Neolithic enclosures, sites such as Crickley Hill and Hambledon Hill in England, where there are strong indications of assault in the form of arrowheads and human causalities (summarised in Mercer 1999; Heath 2009). Part of the difficulty of recognizing war at Bronze Age hillforts relates to shifts in weapon types and burial practice. Unlike the flint arrowheads of Neolithic warfare, bronze weapons were not easily lost and would have been collected after any such conflicts. The burning of bodies in the funerary traditions of the Middle and Late Bronze Age removes another potential source of information.

While the causes of Bronze Age warfare are not easily accessed through the archaeological record, it may be possible to explore some of the immediate and long-term consequences for the hillforts concerned. These include the destruction of hillforts, loss of life, and the hiding and loss of valuables.

The burning of hillforts

While evidence of direct assault on Bronze Age hillforts is lacking, the destruction of these sites by fire seems to have been commonplace (Härke 1979: 33; Primas 2002: 50; Osgood and Monks 2000). Some examples in Central Europe were rapidly destroyed, with artefact assemblages indicating a single phase of occupation rarely longer than 100 years (Harding 1994: 332). Evidence of hostile attacks is recorded at the hillforts of Velim in Bohemia; Heunischenburg near Kronach in Bavaria; and in the Welsh examples of Dinorben and the Breidden, amongst others (see Thorpe 2013: 240). These events are generally linked to warfare, where hillforts were targeted as strategic centres of power in their respective territories. It is also true that many hillforts have no visible signs of conflict, with instead indications of organized abandonment. Where evidence of deliberate destruction is found, the question is often asked whether this was an aggressive act or some esoteric performance connected to symbolic closure. In many cases the evidence is open to different interpretations, so as Harding (2012: 185–6) observed, we can only weigh the balance of possibilities for individual hillforts.

Even allowing for occasional lightning strikes on exposed heights, the accidental burning of hillfort defences would have been a rare event, if indeed it ever happened. The deliberate burning of wooden hillfort defences was identified at five Class 2 hillforts in this project. These include the Bronze Age hillforts of Clashanimud, Co. Cork; Formoyle, Co. Clare; Toor More, Co. Kilkenny, and Rathnagree, Co. Wicklow, as well as the early Neolithic hillfort of Hughstown, Co. Kildare. In these instances, wooden palisades were deliberately burnt down and, in the case of Toor More and Clashanimud, the hillforts were probably abandoned. In the case of Rathnagree, the adjacent fields were also possibly destroyed, as indicated by the burning of a stake fence of similar date at nearby Sruhaun. The latter was replaced soon after by a stone bank enclosure, while the middle enclosure at Rathnagree was re-built with a bank-and-ditch earthwork.

The burning of these hillforts must have taken considerable effort, particularly as the palisades were often made entirely of oak. A considerable amount of tinder and brushwood was required to ignite such heavy fencing, possibly assisted by the smearing of animal fat. Denis Harding observed that '..the more extensive and systematic the destruction, the more likely it is to have been the product of punitive razing after capture, whereas more limited evidence of burning, especially where concentrated around the gates, may be indicative of tactical use of fire in an attack on the hillfort itself.' (Harding 2012: 187). The latter may also indicate that an attack was successfully repelled, particularly if there is no evidence of destruction in the interior of the hillfort. The fact that the defences at Clashanimud, Formoyle, Toor More and Rathnagree were probably burnt along their entire perimeter points to punitive destruction after those hillfort were captured.

This raises the question of who burnt these hillforts and what was the motivation. These events may have been connected to an internal power struggle within a hillfort polity, but it is more likely that a victorious faction would seek to appropriate rather than destroy their symbolic centre of power. An alternative view is that hillforts were burnt by the defenders themselves, to prevent them falling into the hands of invading groups. Harding (2012: 186) cites an unusual (and probably unlikely) scenario where the burning of the defences of the Iron Age hillfort of Rainsborough, Northamptonshire, may have been deliberately fuelled by the defenders as a barrier of last resort, once they had failed to prevent those fires from taking hold.

In most cases, the burning of hillforts was most likely perpetrated by outsiders, connected to either a direct assault or was a consequence of events elsewhere. Whereas the firing of entrances or particular sections of defensive ramparts may have occurred in the course of a direct assault, the comprehensive burning of such defences, as illustrated in the examples above, was probably a punitive action. The use of fire was a very visible way of communicating the subordination of a rival group, while the ability to effect that destruction was no less impressive. Ralston (2006: 163) observed that the intense glow from a burning hillfort would have been a distinctly unnatural sight and a spectacular display of calculated destruction and power. Once alight, the ramparts could have burnt for days and nights, sending a dire signal for miles around and violating the communal sense of place that the hillfort embodied (Harding 2012: 189).

Taking Clashanimud as an example, the destruction of this hillfort may have been undertaken in one or two stages (Figure 9.9). The firing of the gated entrance and the burning of part of the defensive palisades could have been part of the military assault. The final burning of the palisades probably occurred after the capture of this hillfort, as this would not have been feasible or necessary during any direct attack. An alternative to this is that battles occurred elsewhere, and the victorious factions entered an abandoned hillfort, which they then destroyed prior to withdrawal. Less likely is that the hillfort was burnt by the occupants themselves, as an act of defiance in retreat. The burning of that heavy oak palisade would have taken a considerable amount of time and effort, resources that those fleeing a battlefield did not have, as such events may have unfolded over a matter of days.

An alternative interpretation is that the destruction of hillforts represents an intentional act of ritual destruction by the inhabitants (see Bowden and McOmish 1987: 78–79 for a discussion of the ritualized abandonment of so-called vitrified forts in Scotland). This may have been

Figure 9.9: Geophysical imaging (magnetic gradiometry) of burnt palisade, inner enclosure of Clashanimud hillfort, Co. Cork.

linked to the death of important individuals or some inauspicious events. Challis (1978: 23) suggests that the abandonment of some large Pā enclosures in New Zealand was linked with the burial of a chief. Some comparison might be made with the burning of Neolithic houses and enclosures in Europe, regarded by many as deliberate acts of ritualised destruction connected to the creation of memories of a place or event, with the goal of establishing group harmony and identity. It is difficult to compare the burning of hillforts and domestic buildings, as houses are vulnerable to accidental fire within a wooden structure. They can also be burnt down for reasons connected to the lives and beliefs of the occupants, to do with symbolic closure during site abandonment, purification connected to bereavement or disease, and for practical purposes to facilitate re-building.

As many commentators have observed, all warfare contains a ritual element, which in no sense diminishes its darker side. One of the outcomes of warfare in the Bronze Age may have been a type of ritual performance, where a victorious group burnt down a rival hillfort following the defeat of their enemy. This can be interpreted as a deliberate and calculated act of destruction by a rival group. This may have involved a direct attack on the hillfort, but could also have followed battles in the wider landscape. The highly visible destruction by fire can be considered an aggressive and highly symbolic act, designed to subjugate a rival group through the slighting of its main power centre. This was more than the destruction of a place, but rather of the identity of a group in their ancestral homeland. The kind of punitive destruction recorded at Bronze Age hillforts in this study is a form of ritual dismemberment of a symbolic location. The fact that some of these hillforts were not rebuilt or re-occupied may reflect the negative associations of those events in the collective memory. This may not have been immediately possible in the changed political landscape, where a rival hillfort polity had established dominion over that territory and its people.

Burying the dead

In certain cases, human remains can provide direct evidence of violence connected to warfare. Depending on its scale and duration, the consequences of warfare could be severe and long-lasting, extending far beyond the fate of a particular hillfort. They included the annihilation of entire populations through acts of genocide, or how their forced movement impacted on other groups. Slavery, loss of cultural identity, depopulation are well-known outcomes of warfare, what Vencl (1984) calls the second phase of warfare. These outcomes can be difficult to understand where there is weak differentiation in material culture between opposing hillfort groups.

No human remains were found in the ten hillforts investigated in this project. This must be considered against the limited extent of excavation at these sites, but also how and where any dead were disposed of. No examples of war cemeteries or massacres have been found in Irish hillforts, comparable to those found in Iron Age hillforts in Britain, sites such as Maiden Castle and Spetisbury Rings in Dorset; Sutton Walls, Herefordshire; Cadbury Castle, Somerset; Maiden Bower, Bedfordshire, and Fen Cop, Derbyshire, among others (Harding 2012: 179–185). None of the finds of human skeletal remains from Irish hillforts bear marks of injury and trauma that could be connected to violence. This need not have a bearing on the history of these sites, as archaeological visibility of on-site casualties would be poor due to formal disposal of human remains by cremation and other means.

Human remains are recorded from three excavated Irish hillforts. Excavations at Dún Aonghasa, Co. Galway, uncovered the scattered remains a small number of infant/juvenile burials, and one adult skeleton, dated to the Iron Age or Early Medieval period (Cotter 2012b: 196). There is a small number of undated human bones from Mooghaun hillfort, Co. Clare (Grogan 2005a: 304), but as with the Dún Aonghasa material, there is no evidence to regard these as causalities of war. The interpretation of such finds is problematic in terms of context and dating, but mainly because the circumstances of death are unknown.

The only evidence of formal burial in a hillfort comes from Rathgall, Co. Wicklow (Raftery 2004). Several cremation burials were found in four ring-ditch enclosures, two of which are inside the hillfort, and two others just outside. There are no burials of adult males in this funerary complex, suggesting that those interred were women and children of inherited or marital status, probably belonging to a chiefly lineage. One of the cremations is centrally placed inside a 34m wide circular enclosure (Ring-ditch 1), at the centre of the hillfort. This feature (Pit 119) contained the cremated remains of an infant dated 1290–1040 BC, accompanied by a penannular gold ring. A small circular enclosure (Ring-ditch 2) on the south-east side of Ring-ditch 1 contained three cremation burials, including that of a young adult at the centre of the enclosure, and a nearby pit containing the remains of a female and infant placed in a coarseware vessel, and dated 1041–838 BC (Becker *et al.* 2010). One of the pits inside Ring-ditch 2 contained fragments of a sword and spearhead, and a small socketed chisel, all of bronze, the only such weapons ever found inside an Irish hillfort.

The Rathgall evidence is exceptional, as most Irish hillforts were not places for formal burial. It is not possible to identify casualties of war, mass graves or graves containing weapons in the funerary record of Middle and Late Bronze Age Ireland (see Grogan 2004 for review). The prevalence of cremation and the general absence of grave-goods in that period are two factors that limit the visibility of warfare and conflict in the funerary record. There are very few weapon associations with burials, and no examples of what might be termed a 'warrior grave'. Eogan's (1965) corpus of swords does list six possible funerary associations, mostly from cairns and tumuli, but there are no details as to context. As discussed earlier, a small number of spearheads have possible funerary associations, but there is only limited information on these finds.

Knockatreenane: a warrior grave?

The most common prehistoric burial monument in the general vicinity of Irish hillforts is the barrow. They are small circular enclosures of earth and/or stone, where one or more burials, generally cremations, were placed in shallow pits under a low mound, within the level interior or in the enclosing ditch. Barrows occur in isolation or in cemetery groupings, and can be individually distinguished by their large size, prominent siting, multiple enclosing elements, and occasionally by stone settings (Waddell 2010). An estimated 3000 examples are recorded in the Republic of Ireland (source: www.archaeology.ie), representing funerary customs that developed over almost the entire Bronze Age and Iron Age.

As outlined in Chapter 3, in 2007 this project investigated a large earthen barrow 5km to the north of Clashanimud hillfort in Co. Cork. This C-shaped enclosure is 27m in overall diameter, comprising a low earthen bank and an internal ditch, with a flat central area (Figure 9.10). The monument was built by digging a flat-bottomed ditch to a depth of one metre, in a semi-circular shape that opens to the east. Soil and quarried rock from the ditch was piled close to its outer edge, to form a low external bank. The central platform was the focus for the funeral ceremony, which involved placing the cremated remains of an adult male cremation in a central pit. The burial is dated 901–811 BC, believed to be contemporary with construction of the barrow. It was initially thought the burial post-dated the Clashanimud occupation by several centuries (O'Brien 2016a: 22), but the possibility of overlap in the early ninth century BC can now be considered due to a recent radiocarbon result of 976–815 BC (GrA-67392) connected to the burning of that hillfort (Figure 7.3).

The Knockatreenane burial with its elaborate burial monument points the presence of powerful elites in the mid-Cork region during the Late Bronze Age. With this potential dating correlation, it is possible that the Knockatreenane chief was connected to Clashanimud, possibly even a victim of the war that led to the destruction of that hillfort. This is not a warrior grave as such, but the fact that weapons were not used as grave-goods in this period will always make it difficult to recognize such burials in Ireland.

Finally, mention can be made of another Bronze Age funerary monument in the Clashanimud area, namely the boulder-burial. These are an important element of the Cork/Kerry 'stone circle complex', a regional concentration of religious monuments that includes two types

Figure 9.10: Excavation of Knockatreenane barrow, Co. Cork (location of Clashanimud hillfort marked by arrow).

of axial stone circle, as well as short stone rows, stone pairs, single monoliths, boulder-burials and radial stone cairns. These monuments express in different ways the cult of sun worship that dominated religious belief in the Bronze Age. The earliest examples of these monuments were built around 1600 BC, with some of them erected as late as 1000–800 BC (O'Brien 2012).

Boulder-burials consist of a rough stone boulder, usually a rounded glacial erratic, placed on three or more smaller stones. They are interpreted as a form of monumental grave marker, based on the discovery of a pit cremation dated 1259–1024 BC at Bohonagh Co. Cork (Fahy 1961). This, together with the dating of an example at Cooradarrigan, Co. Cork to 1425–1266 BC, confirms a Middle Bronze Age date range for these monuments (O'Brien 1992). A total of 96 examples have been identified in Cork and Kerry, with 84 of these in Cork alone. There is a notable concentration of at least four boulder-burials within a 5km distance of Clashanimud hillfort (Figures 3.74 and 3.77). None of these have been excavated, but with the cremation at Bohonagh dated to the same period as Clashanimud, these boulder-burials may mark the burial place of local elites associated with that hillfort.

A climate of fear? Metal hoarding and hillfort warfare

The deliberate burial of hoards of metalwork was widespread during the European Bronze Age (see Bradley 1998 for discussion of the various manifestations). The practice began in Ireland during the Chalcolithic (Harbison 1968; O'Flaherty 1995), following on from an older tradition of stone axe deposition (Cooney 2004). The rate of hoard deposition fluctuated during the Bronze Age, with a notable decline during the later stages of the Early Bronze Age, followed by a resumption of hoarding during the Middle Bronze Age, and a very significant rise during the Late Bronze Age. Eogan (1983) records 161 metal hoards for the latter two periods, with a further 46 examples of uncertain association or date.

The interpretation of Bronze Age metal hoards is complex, mainly because this was not a coherent phenomenon in a chronological, cultural or depositional terms. Some hoards were of economic significance, connected to the supply and recycling of metal; others reflect a political climate in which it was necessary to hide valuables, while some deposits had a symbolic meaning in terms of social prestige or religious belief. Bronze Age hoards are often classified based on their composition into categories of ownership and use (merchant's hoards, founder's hoards, craftworker tool-kits, personal hoards), and by

FIGURE 9.11: HOARD OF BISHOPSLAND PHASE GOLD PERSONAL ORNAMENTS, CAPPEEN, CO. CORK (SOURCE: NATIONAL MUSEUM OF IRELAND).

the natural environment where they are found. For the latter, an important distinction is generally made between deposition on dry land, where objects could be retrieved if required, and those from wet contexts where recovery might be difficult, if not impossible.

There is a strong research tradition in northern Europe that regards Bronze Age metal hoards as ritual deposits (see Eogan 1983: 3–4 for review), representing graveless funerary offerings or 'gifts to the Gods' made with religious intent. This is partly due to the structured nature of these deposits, the range of items present and their condition, as well as irretrievable deposition in wet contexts. This is true of Ireland where approximately half of later Bronze Age hoards were recovered from bogs, and for that reason are generally considered in ritual terms. The fact that most bogs are accessible means that they are very suitable as hiding places for valuables in times of strife. This interpretation has not received enough attention, despite the many recorded instances of the hoarding of valuables during periods of war in historic times (e.g. Bradley 1998: Figure 3).

It is significant that the building of hillforts in Ireland during the Bishopsland phase of the Middle Bronze Age, *c.*1400–1100 BC, coincided with an upsurge in metal hoarding of a distinctive type. There are 25 hoards known from this period, all but two consisting of small collections of gold personal ornaments (Figure 9.11; Eogan 1983). These are novel forms, including bar and ribbon torcs, neck rings, penannular bracelets, armlets, earrings and tress rings, which represent new developments in goldworking (Eogan 1994: 47–63). There are find details for sixteen of these ornament hoards, twelve of which come from dryland contexts, with four from bogs. While the circumstances of deposition are unknown, the fact that they were buried in secret places where recovery was possible may point to the safeguarding of valuables during times of crisis.

The scale and type of metal hoarding increased significantly in Ireland during the Dowris phase of the Late Bronze Age, *c.*1000–600 BC. There was a considerable amount of metal in circulation, with a proliferation of new tool, weapon and ornament types that reflect influences from southern and western Britain, and the European mainland. It was a time of conspicuous wealth, with the consolidation of a warrior aristocratic society that had a liking for ostentatious display and depositional cult practices (Waddell 2010: 233). A total of 130 metal hoards are recorded from this period, representing 80% of such finds from Bronze Age Ireland (Eogan 1983). These include separate or mixed collections of weapons, tools, ornaments and other objects. There are find details for 89 of these, 52 (58%) recovered from wet contexts, mainly bogs, with 37 (42%) from dryland locations (Cooney and Grogan 1996, figures 8.11 and 8.12).

Dowris hoards are generally interpreted as ritual deposits, due mainly to their composition and the large number

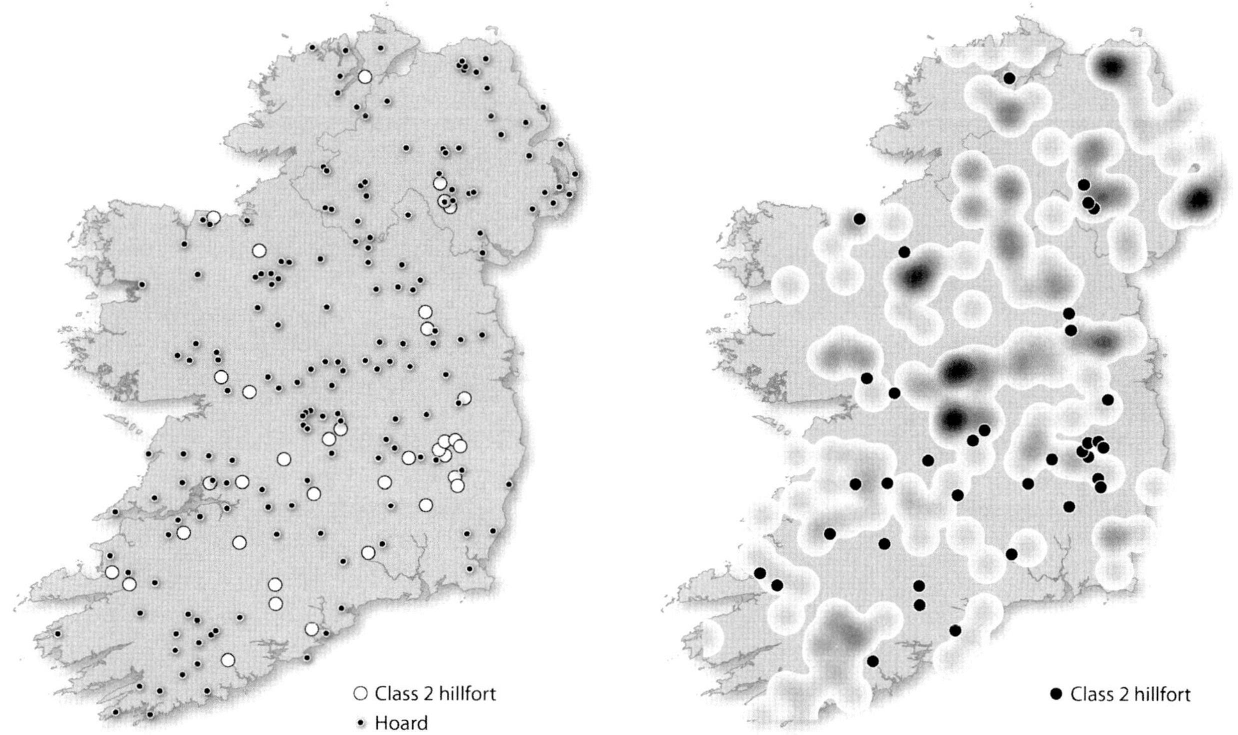

Figure 9.12: Distribution and density plot of Class 2 hillforts and later Bronze Age metal hoards in Ireland (source: Eogan 1983 and Cahill 2006, with additions).

of bog finds. Other considerations cannot be ruled out, as most of these bog and dryland deposits could be retrieved if required. A good example of the uncertainty surrounding their interpretation is the case of the 'Great Clare Find' of 1854, one of the largest discoveries of Bronze Age gold in Europe. This deposit was uncovered near the edge of a small lake, 750m north-east of the large hillfort of Mooghaun near Newmarket-on-Fergus, Co. Clare (Eogan 1983: 69–72). As this lake may have been larger in prehistory, the deposit has been interpreted as a votive deposit, with comparisons made to the connection between Haughey's Fort and the King's Stables in Co. Armagh (Cooney and Grogan 1999: 156; Grogan 2005a: 73; see also Condit 1996). Contemporary accounts refer to the discovery of this hoard in a cavity behind a large stone (Armstrong 1917), which is more consistent with deliberate burial on dryland than votive deposition in the lake. The wealth represented by the several hundred gold ornaments in this hoard can probably be connected to contemporary occupation of the nearby hillfort during the tenth or ninth centuries BC.

The distribution of Bronze Age metal hoards in Ireland reveals a general proximity to Class 2 hillforts (Figure 9.12). There is a notable occurrence of hoards close to some hillforts; for example, Haughey's Fort, Co. Armagh, and Toor More Co. Kilkenny. There is also a concentration of hoards in the hinterland of many sites; for example, to the west of Clashanimud, Co. Cork, and near the hillforts of the lower Shannon estuary, namely Ballylin, Mooghaun, and Formoyle. The fact these hoards do not occur at the hillforts themselves suggests they were hidden for safekeeping or used as votive deposits some distance away, but still within the territorial domain of the hillfort. The distribution pattern indicates that this wealth was concentrated near hillforts as the major centres of power, but also dispersed into wider settlement territories.

In conclusion, as with gold hoards of the Bishopsland phase, consideration must be given to the possibility that some Dowris deposits were buried for safekeeping during periods of turmoil. The possibility these hoards are connected to conflict in Bronze Age societies deserves greater consideration, with the Mooghaun example being possibly one such security deposit. It is notable that metal hoarding during the Middle and Late Bronze Age in Britain also coincided with the building of fortifications (see Burgess and Coombs 1979).

9.5 Conclusions: Hillforts and Bronze Age Warfare in Ireland

The apparent intensification of warfare during the Bronze Age can be linked to tensions arising out of growing social and economic complexity across Europe. The emergence of the hillfort coincided with a strengthening of regional interests, in a competitive climate where territorial and other disputes occasionally erupted into open war. This coincided with innovations in combat, involving the combined use of the sword, shield and thrusting/throwing spear, all part of a heroic warrior culture at the core of this new militarism.

As places of high-status residence, ceremony and assembly, hillforts were an important part of the visible display of political and military power in Bronze Age Ireland. This is often explained in terms of emergent chiefdom polities that controlled large regional territories. This seems to have been a competitive and hierarchical society, obsessed with power and prestige, with an underlying stability provided by agricultural settlement and economic prosperity over long periods. The latter broke down on occasion, where disputes of one kind or another, driven by the ambitions of warlords, led to conflicts of a brief, but intense, nature between regional hillfort polities. The deliberate burning of hillforts was a consequence of these conflicts, signifying in many cases a ritualised act of punitive destruction and the deliberate slighting of a symbolic centre of power. The burning of hillforts was not designed to render them unusable in a practical sense, but was a highly visible statement of victory that marked the subjugation of a vanquished group in their ancestral homeland.

This chapter has explored war and conflict as a special phenomenon in Bronze Age Ireland. The warfare of that period was determined by specific historical contexts and events, in societies whose political and economic relations reached new levels of complexity. While this historical contingency is not easy to understand using archaeological evidence, the study has attempted to connect new evidence for the deliberate destruction of hillforts to the growing militarism and social tensions of the later second millennium BC. This will be explored further in Chapter 10, to consider whether warfare was a key factor in the rise of regional chiefdom polities in Middle and Late Bronze Age Ireland.

10

The Hillfort in Bronze Age Ireland

The significance of Irish hillforts is often interpreted in relation to research in Britain, incorporating evidence from monuments built and used there during the Iron Age. This is despite a growing corpus of evidence for Late Bronze Age hillfort construction in Britain, and a lack of evidence for Iron Age examples in Ireland. This chronological issue is significant, considering the important changes that occur with the onset of the Iron Age, and the differences between Ireland and Britain during this period (Barrett 2012; Bradley 1980; Hodson 1964; Rowlands 1980). It is important, therefore, to consider the Irish evidence as a separate cultural phenomenon in the Late Bronze Age, before developing a broader discussion and synthesis. This is not to dismiss the very evident connections between Ireland and Britain, as well as Ireland and Atlantic Europe, at that time. Rather, by taking the Irish evidence in isolation, we can escape the constraints of the hillfort 'grand narrative' and associated spatial and temporal problems, and put forward new interpretations appropriate to Ireland.

Enclosure is a conscious act, involving the expenditure of resources that could have been employed elsewhere (Mytum 2013: 6). Neustupný (2006) considers the practical, social and symbolic significance of enclosure, concluding that prehistoric peoples may not have necessarily distinguished these as separate aspects of hillfort use. Although there is a general consensus that hillforts had a number of diverse functions that changed over time and space, recent debate has focused on two views (Armit 2007; Brown 2009; Harding 2012: 27; James 2007; Lock 2011). The first argues that some of these monuments functioned as practical, defensive enclosures. An alternative view criticizes this position, highlighting the inherent weaknesses in hillfort design and interpreting these sites as symbols of 'social isolation'. More recent studies stress the importance of monumental display in hillfort architecture and their role in the proclamation of power and status (Sharples 1991; Driver 2013).

While this study has made a case for a connection between hillforts and warfare in Bronze Age Ireland (see Chapter 9), the evidence is far from conclusive. It is important to consider other aspects of site function and their broader significance. Rather than viewing these in opposition, they can be seen as part of a multi-layered meaning that provides a more accurate understanding of these sites. This will be considered now in relation to two important aspects of these sites in Bronze Age Ireland: ritual and competitive display, and routeways and trade.

10.1 Ritual and Competitive Display

Conventionally, hillforts have been interpreted as defensive enclosures, but their disparate size, topographical setting and architectural form suggest that this falls short of a wholly adequate explanation (Coles and Harding 1979; Ralston 1996; Payne 2006: 1). Hamilton and Manley (2001: 13) argue that Early Iron Age hillforts acted as 'landscape coordinators' within intensive distributions of non-hillfort settlements. Hillfort ramparts 'have the appearance of being delimitators rather than substantial barriers' (Hamilton and Manley 2001: 13). Entrances are simple breaks directing people and animals through the enclosures and it is 'difficult to imagine security issues being a design intent' (*ibid.*: 13). Lock continued this theme by viewing hillforts as 'structures that mediated a peaceful and harmonious life within small scale agricultural communities' and argues against what he describes as 'the grand narrative of Iron Age warfare' (Lock 2011: 355). He argues that the defences of many hillforts are out of proportion to any possible threat posed (also see Driver 2008; 2013; Finney 2006: 81; Sharples 2007; 2010) and suggests that 'community building' offers a better explanation than a purely defensive rational (Lock 2011: 359). Lock suggests we should not under-estimate the importance of participation in communal work and social relationships this engendered. Scarre (2011: 17) aptly describes this as 'an act of social construction'. Sharples (1991: 83) considers that the construction of hillforts could have been an annual event which would attract an influx of people from the surrounding communities. Such an assembly would have added an important social function to hillfort construction, bringing together disparate groups and solidifying social ties through marriage arrangements and other relations.

In Ireland, evidence for assemblies and feasting has been identified at Dún Aonghasa and Haughey's Fort. At Haughey's Fort, an 18m section of the inner ditch produced an estimated 3000 animal bones, with a minimum number of 69 cattle, 43 pigs, six dogs, four sheep/goat and three horses (Mallory and Baban 2014: 25–26). Mallory and Baban (2014: 25–26) argue that unless there was an efficient method of preservation, the only sensible way to disperse such large quantities of meat was through communal feasting. The latter may explain the large number of *fulachtaí fia* water-boiling sites from that period (Hawkes 2015). McClatchie's (2014) study of the plant remains from Haughey's Fort suggests the range of weeds present and lack of chaff indicates cereals were processed from a variety of different environments before being brought to the hillfort. At Dún Aonghasa, the great cliff-edge hillfort dated 1300–810 BC (Figure 10.1), McCormick and Murphy (2012: 157–158; 166) recorded the presence of pig bone, even though the lack of tree cover on the island would not have been amenable to pigs, who would have seasonally relied on a diet of oak mast. This evidence might support the idea that disparate groups were congregating at the hillfort, bringing food stocks, possibly for communal feasting events. Etienne Rynne argues that Dún Aonghasa was built for ceremonial purposes such as communal gatherings, inaugurations or other ritual acts (Figure 10.1). He proposes that the internal terraces of the inner enclosure were 'much more suitable for looking inwards than for looking outwards, indicating that these monuments should more fittingly be regarded as amphitheatres rather than as forts', with the centrally placed natural platform at the edge of the cliff face acting as a focal point for ceremonies (Rynne 1992: 202).

The current data from Irish hillforts, although limited, seems to correspond with the recent narrative set out by Hawkes (2015), which indicates the prolific adoption of communal feasting during the Bronze Age. More extensive investigations of other hillforts are needed to support these interpretations.

The preparation of communal feasting requires long-term planning and the intensification or augmentation of subsistence activities for the accumulation of surpluses (Spielmann 2002: 197). The organiser of the feast may have used the gathering as a mechanism to maintain the *status quo*, to elevate their own status or create obligations among others (Leonard 2015). Dietler (1990: 363) argues that the guests who attend, enter into a reciprocal obligation of indebtedness. As such, communal feasting can become a highly competitive process and can also be highly ritualised. Leonard has suggested that the activities at Haughey's Fort and the nearby King's Stables in Co. Armagh could be related to celebrating the finest products of the region, such as the best barley, the largest animals, the most advanced ceramics or the best craftwork. The communal gathering of people to use such products and witness the deposition of others could be seen as ritual commensality in order to ensure the continued fertility of the land.

FIGURE 10.1: DÚN AONGHASA HILLFORT, INISHMORE, CO. GALWAY.

The importance of feasting and the champions portion is best illustrated in the Early Medieval text *Bricriu's Feast*. A large banquet was prepared by Bricriu for Conchobor and the Ulstermen. Bricriu incites the Ulstermen to contest the champions portion and they 'hacked at one another till half of the great house was an ambiance of fire with the clash of swords and spear edges'. The matter was not settled until the three heroes, Cú Chulainn, Conall Cernach and Lóegaire, travelled to the south of Ireland to Cú Roí mac Dári, who settled the dispute. The significance of feasting is attested by cauldrons and elaborate flesh-hooks dated to the Late Bronze Age. There are approximately 54 bronze cauldrons in Ireland with a concentrated distribution in the northern half of the island. In Ireland flesh-hooks and cauldrons have similar distributions (Needham and Bowman 2005: 93) and the two artefact types have been found together in the Spanish hoard at Hio (Gerloff 2010: 116). Their close association suggests that cauldrons were primarily used for boiling meat, a function they retained throughout the Late Bronze Age and probably the Iron Age (*ibid.*: 117). Cunliffe (2008: 255) has noted that the widespread distribution of Late Bronze Age cauldrons in Europe highlights the prevalence of elite feasting. Similarly, the dense distribution of *fulachtaí fia* in Ireland, a monument type that mostly dates to the Bronze Age, can be associated at least in part with communal feasting (Hawkes 2014), demonstrates the importance of feasting in prehistoric Ireland.

Important evidence of ritual activity at is found at the King's Stables near Haughey's Fort. The King's Stables is a man-made feature interpreted as a ritual pool, comprising a sunken hollow 25m in diameter and 3–4m deep (Lynn 1977: 43). Twigs preserved in the basal layers of the monument infer that the hollow was waterlogged soon after construction (*ibid.*: 50). Finds include 18 clay mould fragments for the manufacture of leaf-shaped bronze swords, two sherds of coarseware pottery, animal bones with a high proportion of red deer antlers and dog bone, and the anterior portion of a human skull (*ibid.*). The evidence indicates this was an artificial pool constructed for ritual activity and deposition. Radiocarbon results suggest that the pond was broadly contemporary with the Bronze Age occupation of Haughey's Fort (Lynn 1977: 48–54; Mallory 1995: 84; Weir and Conway 1988: 28; Mallory and Baban 2014). A 3m wide entrance flanked on either side by a palisade in the middle enclosing element of the hillfort is aligned with the King's Stables (Mallory 1995: 84; Conway 2006). On that basis, Mallory (1995, 84) suggests the community that constructed Haughey's Fort is likely to have created the votive pond of the King's Stables.

Structural evidence within Haughey's Fort offers further indications of contemporary ritual activity. A large 25–30m wooden structure, comprising an arc of three lines of stakes set outside larger posts, is dated 1250–900 BC (Mallory 1995: 75; Mallory and Baban 2014). Within this structure a series of large pits contained carbonized grain, Late Bronze Age pottery, fragments of quern stones, metal artefacts and fragments of bronze and gold (Mallory 1995: 78; Mallory and Warner 1988). The structure and internal deposits led Mallory (1995: 84) to suggest that Haughey's Fort, 'defended as it may be, was primarily the focus of ritual activities'.

Geophysical survey by the author at Glanbane hillfort, Co. Kerry, revealed a central wooden structure 38m in diameter, which truncates a larger (46m in diameter) enclosure (see Chapter 4.1). Both surround the highest point within the interior. Two linear settings of postholes radiating from inside the 38m structure may be associated with an entrance on the western side. The two linear features create a funnel-type avenue that narrows towards this entrance. It is tempting to interpret this as an elaborate entrance feature. The size and positioning of both structures suggests they were a central focus of the internal occupation of Glanbane. The Haughey's Fort and Glanbane structures, therefore, may be analogous ritual features associated with both hillforts, and may hint at the potential ritual uses of the monuments themselves.

Sharples (2007; 2010: 123) elaborates this theory, proposing that hillforts were the focus of community building and that hillfort ramparts acted as the mechanism for competitive display. The idea of monumental display has gained popularity in hillfort studies, not least because it can explain quite disparate forms of archaeological information. In a recent study of the hillforts in north Ceredigion, Wales, Driver argues that monumental display was the driving force of hillfort construction (Driver 2008; 2013). This study proposes that hillforts in this region were built using a complex suite of monumental devices to heighten the appearance of the defences from particular approaches (Driver 2013: 135). Although this limits the enclosing elements in strategic terms, it allowed the most important and more visible approaches to effectively communicate greater strategic strength than the hillfort actually possessed. This also prioritised labour output by focusing on more important sections of the enclosure. Sharples (2007: 180) suggests that if the construction process of a hillfort was related to the gift of labour and resources, then the building of even larger and more complicated enclosing elements is effectively the conspicuous consumption of resources. The 'strength' of these hillforts, therefore, may have been in the perceived threat of strength embodied in the monumentality of the main façade ramparts. As Driver (2013: 136) suggests, hillforts may have been a vital component of a chieftain's 'psychological armoury', acting as more permanent displays of power, less transitory than feasting, raiding or material deposition.

The concept of 'competitive display' can also be seen as a type of psychological warfare. Sharples (1991: 88) envisages ritualized display and threatening behaviour as warfare, although he views such behaviour as a deterrent, or a symbolisation of the nature of conflict, rather than its actual practice. This concept would fit well with the competitive Iron Age Wessex societies or the Late Bronze Age societies of Atlantic Europe (Hill 1995: 55). Bowden and McOmish (1989: 13) suggest that hillforts positioned on sloping ground, or in areas overlooked by higher ground, were non-defensive. They regard the positioning of such sites as a deliberate device to make activities within the interior visible to spectators outside the enclosure, while also excluding them from participation. Driver (2013: 135) has recently proposed that such sites may have facilitated the communication of strength through visibility, where the interior revealed a populous, well-organized community. The positioning of sites on sloping ground may also increase the visibility of the monument from certain positions. As such, this interpretation can be seen as another facet of competitive display. It can also be explained from a defensive standpoint, as Driver (2013: 109) notes that a hillfort that sought to command and/or control a population and/or territory would need to be highly visible.

Monumental display may explain the large defences of some hillforts, the size and composition of the enclosing elements acting as a physical imposition of power (Driver 2013: 109). For example, Sharples (2010: 123) sees the enclosing elements of Maiden Castle as symbols of competitive display. The size of the enclosing elements at Rathgall, Co. Wicklow, suggests a need for the ramparts to be visible and contrast in the local landscape. Here, the rather unimpressive location of the hillfort is substantially augmented by large banks.

As already noted, the few examples of excessive architecture, such as Dún Aonghasa, contrast with what at first glance seems to be the unimpressive nature of many Irish hillforts. This is also a feature of Late Bronze Age hillforts in Britain (Hamilton and Manley 2001). During that period, the topographical and strategic setting of these monuments was important and monumentality was emphasized by the creation of an enclosing element and the clearance of hill vegetation. Hillforts helped to monumentalize prominent topographic landmarks and heightened the appearance of artificiality, putting the hilltop at odds with the natural environment (Driver 2013: 91; Hamilton and Manley 2001: 29). Knockdhu and Lurigethan in Co. Antrim, are excellent examples of this. A concern with the display of power is also attested through the production, display and consumption of prestige goods. Monumentalization of the landscape through hillfort construction fed into this competitive social system. In many cases in Ireland, the strategic setting of hillforts may have derived from a need to be seen from and control strategic routes, with the hillfort declaring the communities' authority over this location.

Elements of competitive display are evident throughout Late Bronze Age society and in some instances can be directly related to hillforts. Animal remains from the ditch deposits at Haughey's Fort support evidence for competitive breeding of large animals (Murphy and McCormick 1996: 50; Stevens *et al.* 2010; Mallory and Baban 2014: 26). Domestic animals such as dogs, cattle and goat horn revealed some animals at the site were much larger than the average size of contemporary livestock (Mallory and Baban 2014: 26). In total, the remains of six canines were recovered including two canine skulls. The two skulls are the largest examples found in prehistoric Britain or Ireland (Mallory 1991: 24). Short-lived wood obtained around one of these skulls reveal the remains were contemporary with the occupation of the fort. Approximately 31% of the assemblage at the nearby ritual pool known as the King's Stables comprised dog bones, with three skulls recovered (Lynn 1977). The remains of a possible large dog were recovered at Freestone Hill (Raftery 1969) and an individual dog of large size, although not fully mature, was also identified at Rahally hillfort (Mullins and Bermingham 2009: 25–26). The competitive breeding of animals may have been another facet of this display of power and authority, expressions of which also feature in the early Irish epic, the *Táin Bó Cúailgne*, in respect of the importance of bulls.

Large dogs are often mentioned in ancient Irish texts and seem to be intertwined with hunter-warriors in insular Celtic literature (Bernhardt-House 2007: 14). For example, at the beginning of *Acallam na Senórach* the Irish manifestation of King Arthúr steals Finn's three famous hounds and flees across the Irish Sea (*ibid.*: 12). The importance of Finn's hounds is attested as they are given human ancestry in several tales. Chadbourne (2005: 29) has argued that the dogs represent the most cherished aspects of prehistoric warriors and their chosen life: free, wild, impulsive, heroic, quarrelsome, heedless, loyal, and untouched by Christian remorse, guilt or sin. The hounds themselves may be regarded as warriors in their own right, as the literature states that every warrior had at least one leashed hound and in some cases, more than one (*ibid.*: 31). Often the names of the great warriors of the Ulster Cycle are associated with the name or quality of a dog; Cu Chulainn is the 'hound' of Culann the smith, the divine hero Lugh is sometimes referred to as Mac Con, 'lad of hounds', or Con Mac, 'hound-lad', Conan Mac Morna translates as 'little dog' (*ibid.*: 37). The literature indicates that there often appears to be a correlation between the prowess and status of the dog and his owner (*ibid.*: 37). In several texts, such as *Duanaire Finn*, Finn is said to have fought dog-headed peoples and similar creatures appear in Arthurian legend. These creatures are often described as giants, or having equine features such as manes. For example, one of Conall Cernach's horses in the tales of Cu Culainn's death (*Brislech Mór Maige*

Murthemni) is described as having a hound's head. Large dogs accompanying warriors in battle may have been mythologised into such figures. The importance of dogs in prehistoric society may have encouraged competitive breeding and this may be visible in both the archaeological and literary records.

There can be a ritual and ceremonial component to acts of competitive display. The conspicuous consumption and deposition of bronze artefacts in watery contexts is a prime example. Single artefact deposition in the form of swords, spearheads, shields and cauldrons are well documented from the European and insular Bronze Age. The significant number of prestige objects found in rivers and bogs has led to the general consensus that these are deliberate ritual deposits not intended to be recovered. Rivers and bogs are often interpreted as liminal places and may mark territorial boundaries. The deposition of these objects on possible territorial boundaries is significant. They may have been essential in acts of conspicuous consumption, where the community and chieftain/powerful person displayed the resources under their control in front of neighbouring communities, while simultaneously worshiping and placating deities. The conspicuous consumption of prestige objects, therefore, provided a mechanism for competitive display, whereby, the amount, size or significance of the material deposited provided status to the owner(s), as well as obligations on the part of the other group.

Late Bronze Age hoards have been recovered from two hillforts in Ireland, namely Dún Aonghasa and Downpatrick. Four buffered bronze rings (Cotter 2012b: 48–49) were discovered at Dún Aonghasa. These are not 'typical' Late Bronze Age hoard objects, yet the deposit may still be seen as ritualistic, due to the find location close to the edge of a cliff face. Three hoards were located within the possible Late Bronze Age hillfort at Downpatrick, Co. Down. Hoard 1 was discovered in boulder clay within the interior of the hillfort and comprised five penannular bracelets with lozenge shaped bodies, six penannular bracelets with rounded bodies and a single penannular bracelet with an oval body. Hoard 2 was found in a similar context, 10m from Hoard 1 and comprised four penannular bracelets with a rounded body. A third hoard was found on the site but is otherwise unprovenanced and comprised three sleeve fasteners (Proudfoot 1955; 1957). Other hoards in close proximity to hillfort sites include the famous Mooghaun gold hoard (Figure 10.2), 1.9Km to the north of Mooghaun hillfort, comprising 157 penannular bracelets with rounded bodies, 11 gold collars, two gold rings, four neck-rings and two ingots; the Tamlaght hoard, comprising one sword, one ring, one sheet of copper and a pottery vessel located 763m south-east of Haughey's Fort. A possible hoard 2.4km to the north-east of Claraghatlea hillfort, Co. Cork is now lost, however, records suggest it contained rings and bracelets weighting a total of 3.98Kg (Cahill 2006).

FIGURE 10.2: THE GREAT CLARE GOLD FIND OF 1854, FROM VICINITY OF MOOGHAUN HILLFORT, CO. CLARE (COURTESY NATIONAL MUSEUM OF IRELAND).

The importance of watery places in Late Bronze Age Ireland and potential evidence for associated ritual activity on hillforts is attested at Rahally. This large trivallate hillfort is the most extensively excavated monument of its type in the country (Mullins 2008). About 53% of the interior has been excavated revealing no contemporary artefacts or structural remains. Only 31 hillforts in Ireland have visible structural features within their interiors, only nine of which show evidence for more than ten structures. Few of these have been excavated and proven to be contemporary with the construction and occupation of the hillforts. Brown (2009: 195) has noted a similar phenomenon in Britain, suggesting that the very presence of a hillfort on a prominent topographical feature would have been enough of a status enhancement not to warrant elaborate internal features, which might explain the seeming 'absence of life' at some sites.

Of further interest at Rahally is a conspicuous 30m break in the northern section of the inner enclosing element (Mullins and Bermingham 2009). Here, a wet marshy area extended northwards, the area being covered by colluvial deposits upon excavation. A late La Téne artefact, possibly some horse equipment, was recovered from this context. This marshy area may have been incorporated into the hillfort for ritual and ceremonial purposes, given the divinity and importance of such areas throughout prehistory. There is evidence for later activity at the site during the Iron Age in the form of a slot trench, large gully and bowl furnaces among other features.

10.2 Hillforts, Trade and Routeways

The European Bronze Age, and in particular the Late Bronze Age, is often considered to have seen a dramatic increase in the exploitation of natural resources, maximisation of agricultural productivity and competition over trade routes (Earle 2002; Bruck and Fontijn 2013: 202). The limited natural availability of ores such as gold, copper and tin provided a stimulus for the development of exchange networks and facilitated the evolution of politicised economies concerned with the production, display and consumption of prestige goods (Van De Noort 2013: 382; Yates 2007, 120). This type of economy drove social interaction through trade in the Atlantic zone, and is archaeologically visible in the distribution of common metalwork forms (Henderson 2007: 57; Yates 2007).

Prestige goods systems are essentially active growth-driven economies that depend on continued economic success to produce wealth. The political powers of the economic leaders was derived from their ability to accumulate, display and distribute this wealth. Ultimately, wealth resulted from the successful management of available resources and particularly agricultural produce (Yates 2007: 107). In this respect, Yates (2007: 4) suggests that intensive farming may have been the basis of rapid economic growth. This is supported by pollen analysis of contemporary environments surrounding hillforts such as Haughey's Fort, Co. Armagh, Rahally, Co. Galway and Mooghaun, Co. Clare, which indicate intensive land clearances that may have been part of a large expansion in farming activity associated with the construction and settlement of these hillforts. In Ireland, the possible collapse of this economy may have coincided with the cessation of hillfort construction, followed by a period of woodland regeneration. Elsewhere, Van de Veen and Jones (2007) have linked the 'decline of the Late Bronze Age elites' with the introduction of new iron technology and a reduction in long-distance trade. This suggests that long-distance exchange of metal supplies necessary for bronze production may have been an important driving mechanism for growth in agricultural production at this time, and also supports the palaeoenvironmental evidence that connects hillforts with this economy.

Trade and exchange

Sea, coastal and riverine transportation were important outlets for the circulation of artefacts, ideas and belief systems throughout the Bronze Age. Riverine transportation is particularly attested by the concentrated distribution of imported amber beads along the River Shannon and its tributaries. Amber provides one of the clearest indicators of long-distance trade in prehistoric Ireland. It is found in significant amounts in Poland, Kaliningrad, Lithuania and the coast of Jutland, Denmark. It also has a natural distribution spreading from the east coast of England and across northern Europe to the Black Sea (Feeney-Johnson 2012: 96; Harding, 2013: 374). Waddell (1998: 258) suggests that the limited amount of natural amber in eastern Britain means that it was probably imported from the Continent. Late Bronze Age amber is found in Ireland exclusively in bead form, indicating that these items were probably imported pre-made (Feeney-Johnson 2012: 93). During this period there is a significant increase in the use of amber throughout Ireland. This contrasts with the British evidence, where amber finds are comparatively scarce (Beck and Shennan 1991: 102). Feeney-Johnson (2012: 93) argues that this may suggest Britain was bypassed, with amber transported directly to the Irish markets.

The significance of coastal and sea travel is attested in the amber assemblage from Dún Aonghasa. This hillfort was strategically positioned at the mouth of Galway Bay, with access to coastal sea-routes to the north and south. Evidence for long-distance trade is apparent in nine complete and four incomplete amber beads, two probable bead fragments, and an object tentatively identified as a stud and a non-diagnostic scrap (Feeney-Johnson 2012: 94). Scientific analysis confirms that these amber finds originate from Baltic sources.Three amber beads and several fragments were recovered from Rathgall hillfort, Co. Wicklow, including a composite bead with gold mounting. A bronze bar toggle of probably Baltic origin also attests to trade links with this region (Raftery and Becker forthcoming).

A total of 88 complete and fragmentary glass beads from Rathgall also indicate that hillfort community was involved in long-distance exchange. Glass beads from three sites in Ireland, Rathgall, Lough Gur in Co. Limerick and Freestone Hill hillfort, Co. Kilkenny, are closely matched by examples from a small number of sites in Germany (Hartmann *et al.* 1997), France (Gratuze *et al.* 1998), Switzerland (Henderson 1988) and northern Italy (Henderson 1988, Brill 1992; Towel *et al.* 2001; Angelini et al. 2004, Angelini et al. 2009) and to a lesser extent Britain (Henderson 1988). These beads contain low magnesia (MgO) and high potassium oxide (K^2O) levels (LMHK) (Henderson 1988). The site of Frattesina (dated to 1200–1000 BC) in northern Italy produced semi-fused glass and other industrial by-products such as crucibles and large numbers of glass ingot fragments, strongly indicating that glass-working and/or production was taking place on-site (Brill 1992; Henderson 1988). This constitutes the only evidence of glass production in Late Bronze Age Europe to date (Angelini *et al.* 2009: 329). In total, 2651 glass finds, mostly comprising glass beads belonging to the LMHK mixed alkali glass group were recovered from the site (Angelini *et al.* 2009: 330). This constitutes the largest find of prehistoric glass in Europe. The evidence at Frattesina is indicative of a highly specialized glass workshop.

Excavations at Haughey's Fort recovered a possible handle from a Central European bronze bucket, and a possible bronze pin from northern Europe (Mallory 1991: 21; Warner 2006: 24; Mallory and Baban 2014: 26; Brandherm 2014). Approximately 700m south-west of Haughey's Fort, a hoard from the townland of Tamlaght, dated typologically to the Roscommon Phase, comprises a sword and bronze bowls that were probably imported from Central Europe (Warner 2006; 2013). An Iberian-style gold neck-ring found 600m east of Haughey's Fort probably dates to the Middle/Late Bronze Age transition (Warner 2013). The variety of finds indicates the hillfort had trading links with various regions of Continental Europe, with particularly strong links with Northern Europe. Part of a similar Iberian style neck ring was found in a hoard recovered within Downpatrick hillfort in Co. Down which possibly came from western France (Almagro-Gorbea 1995: 140; Eogan 1994; Waddell 1998: 198–199). A total of three hoards were found at Downpatrick and Warner (2013: 37) suggests that a number of these objects may have been imported from Iberia.

The artefactual evidence highlights contact between the Irish and Nordic zones, particularly during the early part of the Late Bronze Age *c.*1200–1000 BC, connections that continued until the end of the Bronze Age (Figure 10.3). This may have been direct, or more likely, through a complex coastal network along the northern and western coast of Scotland, avoiding to a large extent, southern Britain. The spread of LMHK glass and conical riveted vessels indicates contact with northern Italy and Switzerland. Links between this area, northern Germany and the Nordic zone may imply a route in which material from Italy, such as LMHK glass, acquired through a series of exchanges, ended in Rathgall and Freestone Hill. These contacts may have been stimulated by the lack of natural supplies of copper, tin or gold in the Nordic area (Eogan 1995: 128). This does not mean that exchange networks were not in place with the rest of Britain. Conversely, extensive links with the Thames Valley are attested by the distribution of Ballintober-type swords and Yetholm-type shields during this period, and such exchange routes may also have distributed Armorican artefacts into Ireland. Evidence for direct contact between Ireland and Iberia is also attested, although on a lesser scale (see O'Driscoll 2016: Chapter 9).

Centralisation

New patterns of interaction developed around the beginning of the Late Bronze Age *c.*1300 BC, with elite elements of ranked societies playing a central part in the exchange process. Their political power and status was seemingly linked with their ability to control the distribution of exotic goods (Waddell 1995: 162; Sharples 2007: 112). This surge in social interaction is attested by the distribution of various exotic objects in Ireland, Britain and the Continent, and by the spread of a warrior culture that manifests itself in weapons of strikingly similar form throughout Atlantic Europe (Cunliffe 2012: 252). To control this trade, elites may have constructed hilltop settlements in strategically significant positions in the landscape, acting as what Brown (2009) aptly describes as 'beacons in the landscape'. Hillforts, therefore, may have been regarded as topographically distinct nodes in the landscape, serving as central places synonymous with trade. The use of hillforts in this way may have continued in Britain during the Iron Age. In a passage in the Massaliote Periplus, a description of the sea routes around the Atlantic coast in the Early Iron Age, a passage refers to islands in the Atlantic called Oestrymnides 'rich in the mining of tin and lead. A vigorous tribe lives here, proud-spirited, energetic and skilful. On all the ridges trade is carried on'. The text locates this place as two days sailing from Ireland, which would place them in either Cornwall or Brittany (Cunliffe 1997: 149).

There seems little doubt that the ability to acquire prestige goods of exotic origin carried a considerable premium in socio-political terms (Bradley 1990: 133). This may have led to the centralisation of communities and economies to try and monopolise trade and pro-

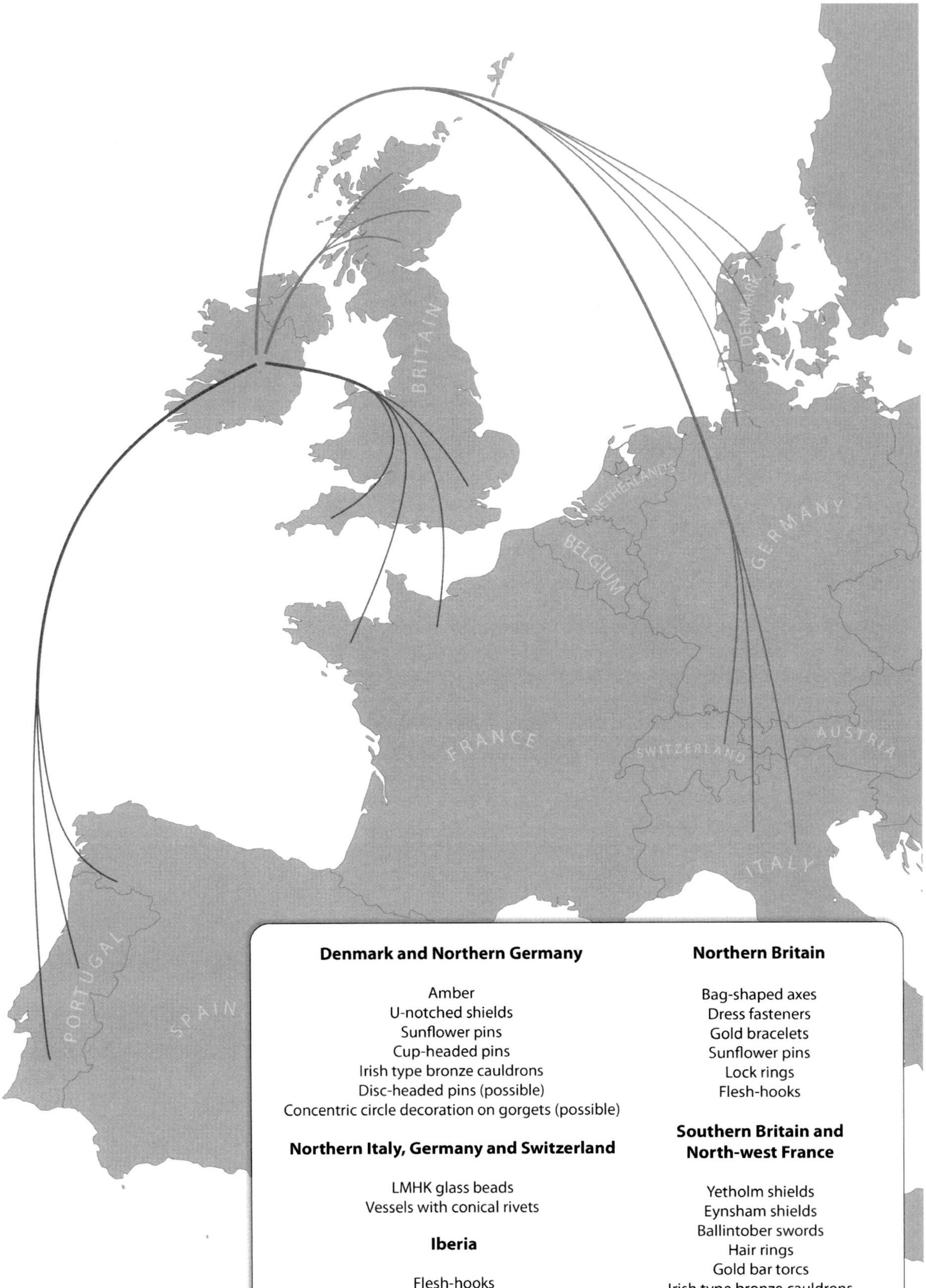

Figure 10.3: Some Bronze Age artefacts manufactured in Britain and the Continent found in Ireland.

duction of such items. Evidence for hillforts in Ireland and the Continent suggest that they provided a range of specialist economic and defensive functions that restricted access to high-status objects and centralized control over both agricultural and craft production (Brück and Fokkens 2013: 95). This corresponds with Cunliffe's argument that a hillfort functioned as a focal point in a redistribution network (Cunliffe 1995: 93). This was prompted by the 2400 or so grain storage pits excavated at Danebury hillfort (Cunliffe 2011: 99; 113–116). Renfrew and Bahn (2006: 215) note that an important indicator of centralised control of a society is the existence of permanent storage facilities for food and goods. This may be reflected in the archaeological record at a number of hillfort sites in Ireland.

More than a dozen clay or wattle-and-daub lined pits of varying size were excavated in the interior of Downpatrick hillfort (Proudfoot 1954: 98). At Haughey's Fort, large pits containing quantities of carbonized grain, as well as fragments of quern stones, coarseware pottery and metalwork were recorded (Mallory 1995: 78; Mallory and Warner 1988). These were interpreted as grain storage pits by the excavator (Mallory 1995: 79). The large volume of cereal remains at Haughey's Fort is unusual (McClatchie 2014: 40). Analysis of the plant remains highlights a lack of chaff and a variety of weed types, implying the cereals were obtained and processed in a variety of environments (McClatchie 2014). McClatchie has interpreted Haughey's Fort as a central place for the storage of seed corn and surplus produce, which may have been used for communal feasting. One could speculate that some of the magnetic anomalies at Toor More (Figure 4.58) and Ballylin (Figure 4.23) represent concentrations of possible pits within the interior of both sites. Bradley (1990: 137) states that there is evidence that food supply was regulated through centralized storage at Late Bronze Age hillforts in Britain. Interestingly, the Danebury Environs Programme has found that grain stored in the fort was not distributed to nearby sites, but was prepared and used by the occupants or possibly traded (Brown 2009: 207).

Centralized societies are often associated with increased intensification of farming (Renfrew and Bahn 2006: 215). This is attested in the pollen record at many Irish hillforts, where there is an intense tree clearance episode and increase in agricultural indicators contemporary with the construction and occupation of the hillfort. This may have been to acquire surplus stock for trade or to accommodate full-time craft specialists.

In some instances where extensive excavation has been undertaken, there is evidence for specialised and probably centralised craft-working at hillforts. At Dún Aonghasa, for example, over 460 moulds and crucible fragments were found (O'Carroll 2012: 28), while several thousand clay mould fragments were recovered at Rathgall (Raftery 1976: 345). Both assemblages are noteworthy for the range of artefacts being produced in comparison to any other Irish site (O'Carroll 2012: 41). Mould fragments from Rathgall indicate that weapons and tools were produced in that hillfort. This included socketed spearheads, spearheads with shallow lozenge-shaped cross-sections, swords, palstave axes, socketed bag-shaped axes and possibly rapiers (Raftery and Becker forthcoming). Other object, such as knives, razors and pins were also being cast. At Dún Aonghasa, a similar range of artefacts were manufactured, including two different types of socketed spearhead, swords and socketed axes, as well as knives, bracelets, pins and studs/buttons (O'Carroll 2012). Interestingly, two of three socketed axe moulds from that site had decoration near the socket, possibly indicating their use as ceremonial objects. At both sites there is evidence for long-distance trade, and it is tempting to suggest that they traded bronze weapons and goods for exotic materials such as amber, glass and other bronze and gold items.

Mallory (1995: 80–81) has posited that the small traces of gold found within pit features at the centre of Haughey's Fort may have been fragments of industrial waste, intended for use in personal ornaments. A gold stud in one of these pits dated 1260–910 BC is broadly contemporary with the construction and occupation of the hillfort. A total of 18 fragments of clay moulds used to produce leaf-shaped bronze swords were recovered from limited excavations of the nearby King's Stables (Lynn 1977). This is more substantial evidence linking the builders of the hillfort with the production of prestige goods. More recent analysis of the bronze and gold items by Brandherm (2014) and Warner (2014) reveals that there was probably a metal workshop within the hillfort. The remains clearly imply some specialist knowledge of bronze casting and gold working (Brandherm 2014: 65). Mallory and Baban (2014: 26) argue that sword moulds from in the nearby King's Stables indicate that casting of swords was probably undertaken by the residence of Haughey's Fort just outside the area enclosed by the outer ditch.

Beginning around 1400 BC, new centres of bronze and craft-working emerge in central and western Europe (Bowen 1972: 52). Jiran *et al.* (2013: 792) noted the high frequency of metalworking evidence at hillfort sites in the Czech Republic and Austria during the Late Bronze Age. A similar situation is apparent in France, where hillforts such as Fort-Harrouard and Saint-Pierre-en-Chastre were centres for the intensive production of prestige goods (Mohen 1987; Brun 1993: 178). Burgess and O'Connor (2008: 46–48) observe that an unusually large proportion of Late Bronze Age metal artefacts come from castros, inferring these hilltop sites were utilised as craft-working centres. Many contemporary German hillfort also have evidence for craft-working such as the Hunenburg hillfort near Waterstedt, Germany

(Heske 2007; Heske *et al.* 2010; Jockenhovel 2013: 741). Osgood and Monks (2000: 66) suggest that by the end of the Late Bronze Age, much of the production of goods seems to have taken place at fortified sites. This is reflected at some hillfort sites in Ireland, notably Dún Aonghasa, Haughey's Fort and Rathgall.

Routeways

The emerging emphasis on competition, trade and exchange, as well as the control of materials and land can be connected to the construction of hillforts. It is often proposed that a large number of Irish hillforts, and many early examples in Britain, are positioned to visually dominate natural route-ways and/or natural resources. This may represent an increasing need for control and competition (Hamilton and Manley 2001: 31; Bruck 2007: 31). The enclosing elements of these monuments and the clearance of the hilltop of vegetation effectively monumentalize and visually accentuate topographic landmarks, making them highly visible and helping them contrast with the natural environment. Such landmarks, along with other natural features such as rivers and mountains, would have been significant for long-distance travel and their augmentation by communities may have signaled their ability to trade or manufacture high status goods in the hope of attracting traders. This has recently been noted by Driver (2013: 59) who suggests that hillforts functioned as permanent, symbolic points of reference for travelers and acted as locales for embarkation and destination. It is likely that many hillforts were built in areas where natural topographic features were being exploited as natural routeway markers.

Brown (2009: 201) suggests large numbers of hillforts in England and Wales are located on escarpments and near river valleys, inferring that hillforts may have been used as 'trading nodes'. In Britain, many early interpretations were based on the assumption that hillforts may have acted as central places where storage and the redistribution of goods was based (Harding 2012: 203; Cunliffe 1995; Cunliffe 2006). Murrieta-Flores (2012: 114) proposed that natural corridors in the Sierra Morena region in Spain were heavily used during prehistory, noting that settlement and ritual activity is strongly linked to these natural route-ways. Similar evidence has been identified in central Portugal by Fonte *et al.* (2011), and in the Alpine region (Bruck and Fokkens 2013: 95). Many British hillforts are similarly positioned to control physical access to varied landscapes and resources (Hamilton and Manley 2001: 31).

A large proportion of Irish hillforts are located at strategic positions overlooking one or more natural 'corridors' in the landscape, suggesting that control of these areas contributed significantly to their positioning (Grogan 2005b; 2014: 68), Such observations are based on visual assessment of the topographic setting of a hillfort, and need to be tested using quantitative methods. This can be achieved using a combination of GIS techniques been previously described in Chapter 8 (see Figure 8.17). The remainder of this section will provide a number of other examples to demonstrate the ability of GIS analysis to contextualise and quantify the more subjective terms such as 'strategic' and 'prominent'.

The Shannon Estuary

Formoyle Beg is a large bivallate hillfort, positioned overlooking a deep, curving river valley defined by the Slieve Bearnagh mountains in the Broadford Gap of south-west Clare (Figure 10.4). Targeted excavation of its enclosing elements has dated the construction of this monument to the Late Bronze Age *c.*1200–1000 BC, and identified the composition of its bank and ditches (see Chapter 4). Both enclosing elements comprise a low earthen bank and shallow ditch with evidence for a light stake fence. The location takes advantage of natural terraces that exaggerate the size of the enclosing elements from the exterior. Considering the slight defences, it may be better to view this monument as a symbol of power viewed from a distance rather than a distinctly defensive structure (although that may have been a subsidiary function). In this respect, the small wooden posts could have augmented the visibility of the hillfort, making it significantly more visible in the landscape. These fences may also have had a practical element, keeping livestock protected and other types of defence.

The importance of visibility is highlighted by the viewshed analysis of Formoyle Beg (Figure 10.5). Significantly, the hillfort is highly visible from the river valley to the immediate north and east and is one of the most visible topographical features from the valley floor. The latter forms a natural route-way across the Slieve Bernagh Mountains which, together with Lough Derg to the east and the Slieve Aught Mountains to the north, form an extensive barrier to the Irish Midlands. The eastern terminal of the valley is near the southernmost fording point of Lough Derg (Killaloe) and adjacent to the southern edge of the lake, providing the most accessible point at which to cross this large natural barrier. This route-way may have been strategically and economically important, providing access to different marine resources including the fresh water lake of Lough Derg and sea water resources of the Shannon estuary, and controlling the movement of people and trade in the region. The valley may have acted as a significant trade-route during the Late Bronze Age, which may have prompted the construction of the hillfort.

The importance of this crossing point is attest as early as the beginnings of the Bronze Age, when a flat axehead was deposited here. Its importance increased over time,

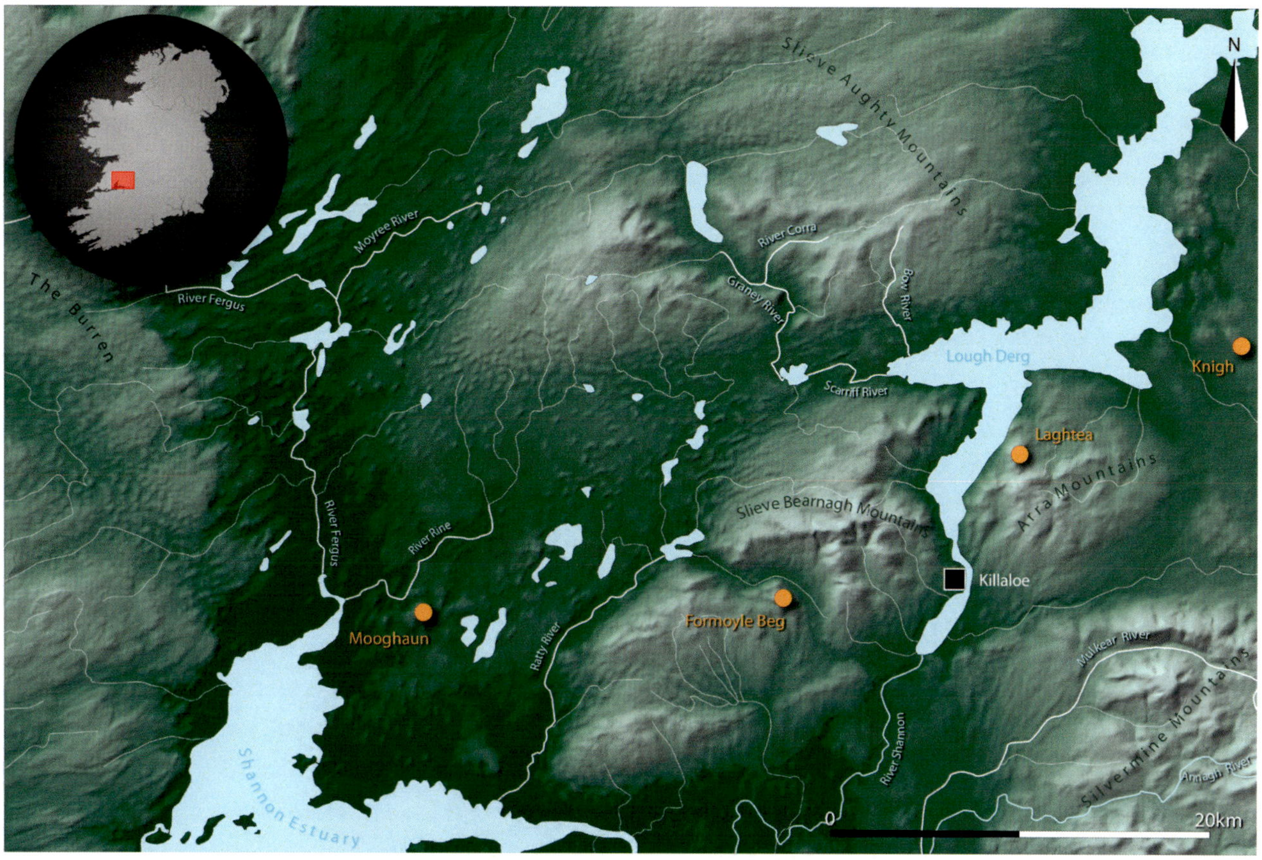

Figure 10.4: Hillforts in the Shannon Estuary region.

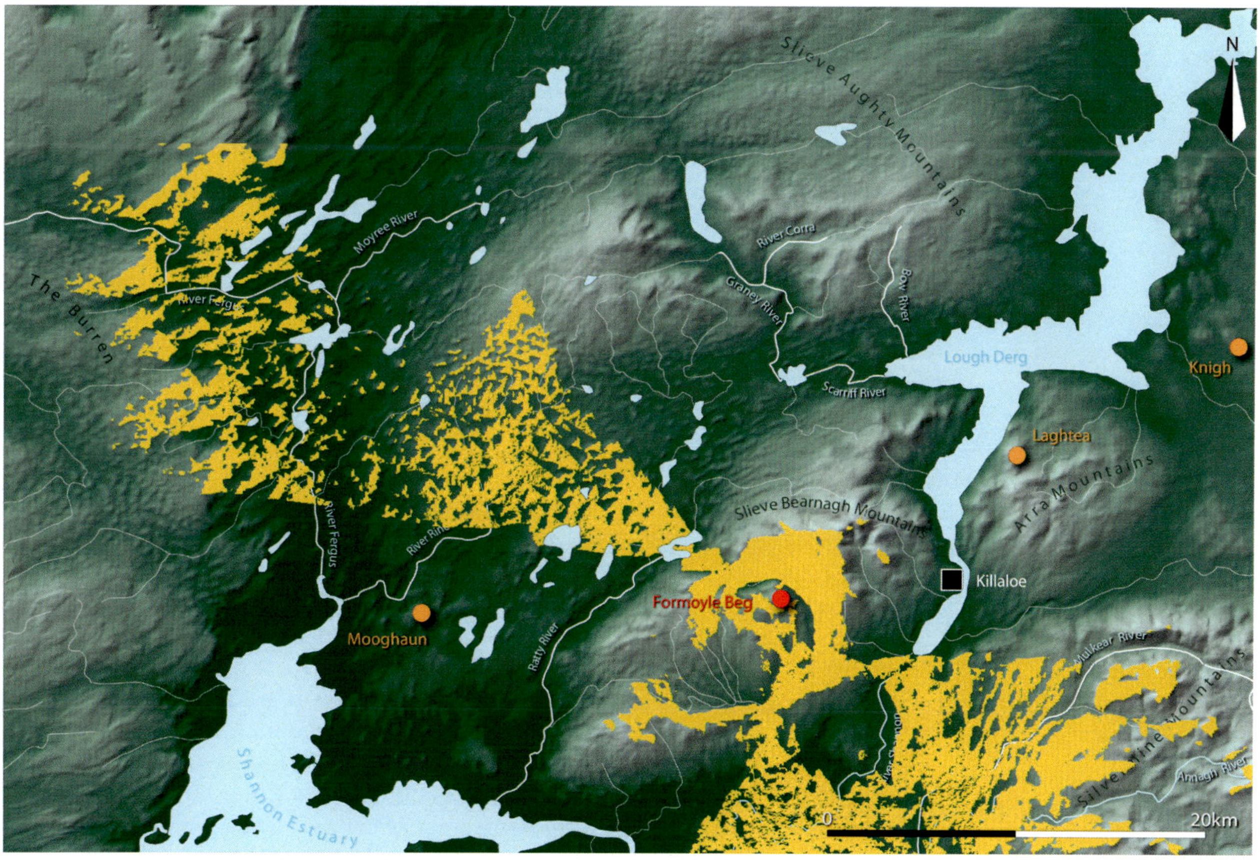

Figure 10.5: Viewshed analysis of Foymoyle Beg hillfort in Co. Clare.

as revealed by the deposition of three Middle Bronze Age spearheads, a Middle Bronze Age dirk and two rapiers, as well as a Late Bronze Age leaf-shaped lunate spearhead, a Class 4 sword, and a double-edged sickle (Burke 2001). Condit and O'Sullivan (1999: 37) have suggested that the weaponry deposits at Killaloe highlight the importance of warrior identity to the emerging communities of the region. Leonard (2015) further argues that these deposits were expressions of warrior identity 'tied to a particular location' and could be seen as symbols of ancestral entitlement to the resources of this particular region.

Least-Cost-Path (LCP) analysis highlights the importance of this river valley as a potential prehistoric trade route (Figure 10.6). Eighteen arbitrary start points were located to the west of Lough Derg and a single destination point was positioned at the southernmost fording point of the lake. Topography was chosen as the main cost factor for this analysis. Although this does not take into account other potential areas of cost such as forests and rivers or cultural and social boundaries, the analysis is still informative. The LCP demonstrates that the majority of the points (17 of the 18) traverse the river valley overlooked by Formoyle Beg, indicating that this may be the easiest route to the east. The viewshed and LCP analysis combined indicate that Formoyle Beg hillfort was positioned to take advantage of a significant natural route way linking the western areas of Lough Derg to the eastern Midlands.

To the west of Formoyle Beg, the large trivallate hillfort at Mooghaun dominates the lakeland zone to the north of the Shannon estuary (Figure 10.4). Similar to Formoyle Beg, the banks at Mooghaun largely follow the contours of the hill, taking advantage of the natural steep slopes to make the enclosing elements seem larger from the exterior. The large rubble limestone banks at that hillfort would have added to the contrast created by the clearance of the hilltop of vegitation. The northern extremity of the estuary is particularly visible from the hilltop, suggesting that Mooghaun may have been constructed primarily to control access to this important strategic and economic location (Figure 10.7). Waddell (2010: 269) observed that the site seems to be placed in respect to a natural routeway extending from the Fergus and Shannon estuaries to the eastern terminal of the Broadford river valley, which is dominated by the hillfort at Formoyle Beg. A dug-out canoe found in Clenagh townland, near the end of an overland routeway running north–south past Mooghaun to an inland fording point over the Ardsollus River (Grogan 2005b: 45; Leonard 2015), indicates that riverine travel was taking place in the immediate vicinity.

It is clear from the concentration of Late Bronze Age weapon deposits in the Shannon River, and a concentration of amber beads near this river and its tributaries (Feeney-Johnson 2012: 93), that this navigable river was a major focus for prehistoric societies and was being exploited for trade. The undated univallate hillfort at Laghtea, Co. Tipperary is located to overlook the southern opening to Lough Derg. At this fording point, two Late Bronze Age swords (Class 4 and Class 5) were recovered, further attesting to the significance of this location. Cunliffe (2008: 360) and Waddell (1998: 244) noted the unusually large number of Late Bronze Age gold artefacts found in the immediate region of Mooghaun, and have linked this with the hillfort, suggesting it may have formed a focal site in an elite system. There is little doubt that this concentration of gold artefacts reflects an area of importance and wealth (Grogan 1995). Eogan (1995: 134), however, stresses that the absence of foreign gold object types in the area 'prohibit us from considering North Munster as an Atlantic emporium or trading centre'. He proposed that the distribution of lock-rings infers land connections eastward, but this interpretation does not consider the large number of amber beads of Baltic origin in the area.

West Kerry

Glanbane hillfort is located next to a prominent natural routeway connecting Tralee and Dingle Bay, on the eastern edge of the Slieve Mish Mountains in west Co. Kerry (Figure 10.8). Excavation of the defences have dated its construction to the Late Bronze Age *c.*1150–900 (see Chapter 4). While the enclosing elements are not unimpressive in size, their stone revetments made the banks contrast more with the surrounding landscape. The more substantial rock-cut ditches were probably not visible from the low-lying land below the hilltop. However, the northern to eastern defences of the hillfort are positioned on sloping ground, which may have enhanced their visibility, particularly from the route-way. Geophysical survey of Glanbane has produced evidence for internal structures and two substantial enclosures at its centre (Figure 4.5 and Figure 4.6). Large, individual post-holes comprising a structure over 45m in diameter crowns the highest point of the hillfort and this seemingly truncates a 55m earthen enclosure. Both features would have created to a highly visible, topographical marker.

The dominant views from Glanbane are of the natural corridor connecting Tralee Bay with Dingle Bay to the south, which includes visibility of the Castle Island lowlands to the north and the Killarney region to the south (Figure 10.9). LCP analysis supports the presence of this route-way (Figure 10.10). Five arbitrary start points were positioned to the north of Tralee Bay and a single destination point was placed in the south-east. The LCP analysis indicates the easiest topographical route (5 of the 5 points) is through this valley. Geophysical survey identified a possible entrance to the fort on northern sloping ground. Cumulative viewshed analysis has identified

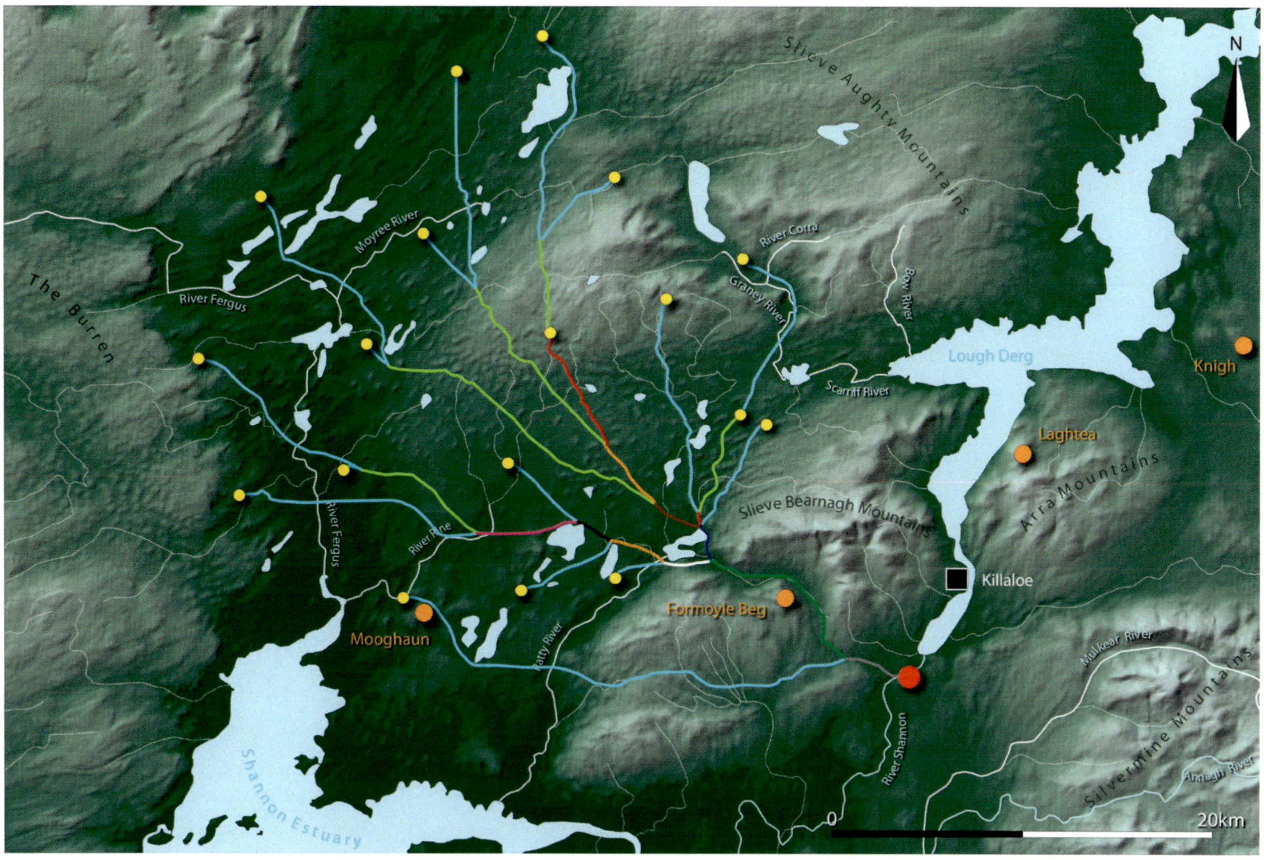

FIGURE 10.6: LCP ANALYSIS OF THE SHANNON ESTUARY REGION.

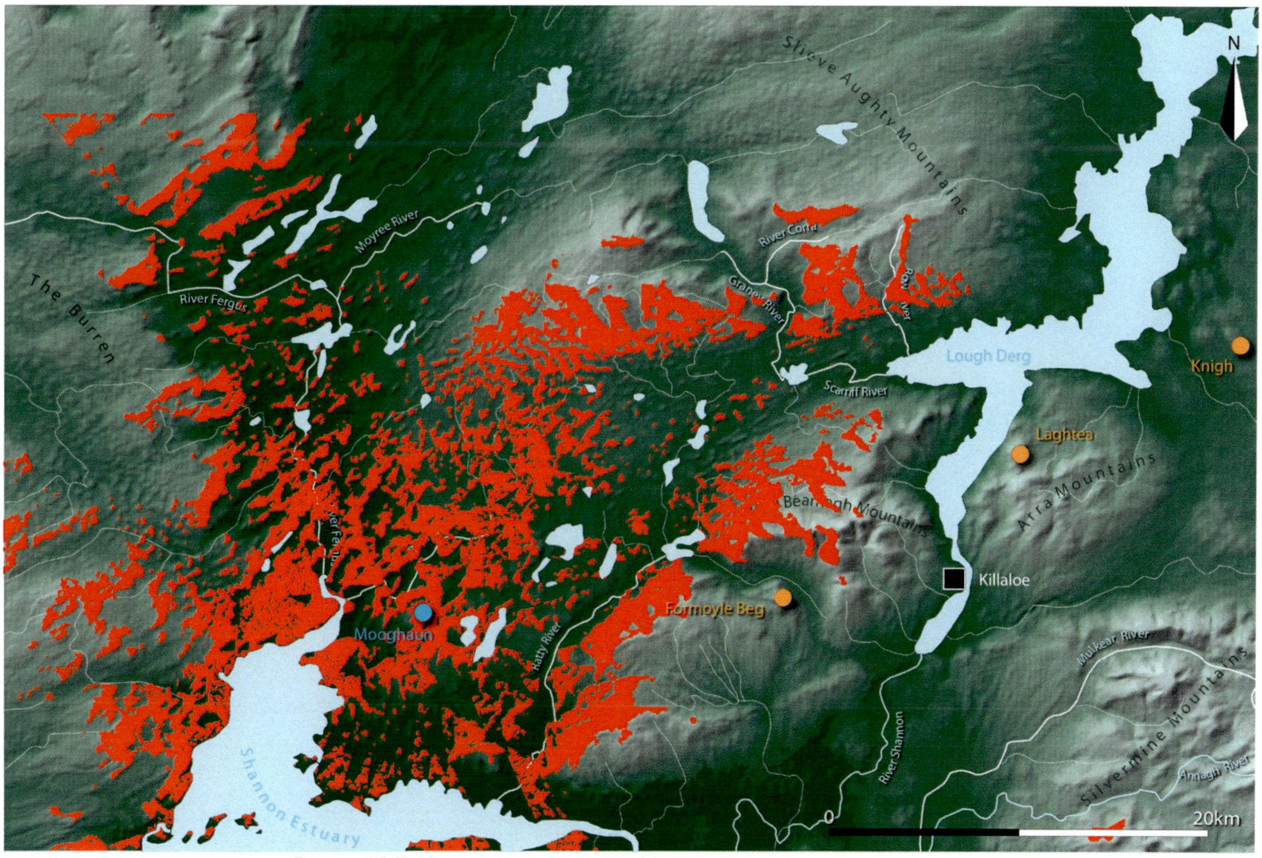

FIGURE 10.7: VIEWSHED ANALYSIS OF MOOGHAUN HILLFORT IN CO. CLARE.

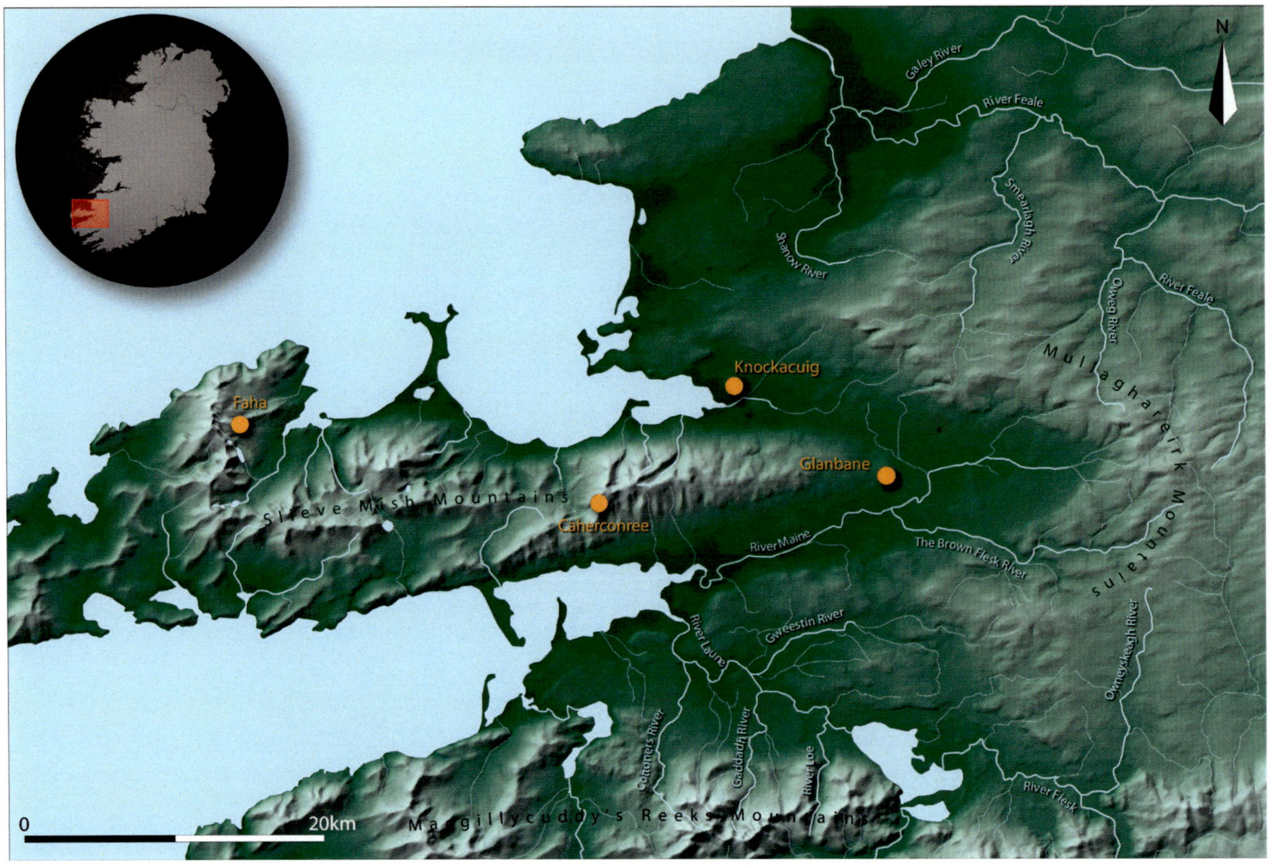

Figure 10.8: Hillforts in the West Kerry region.

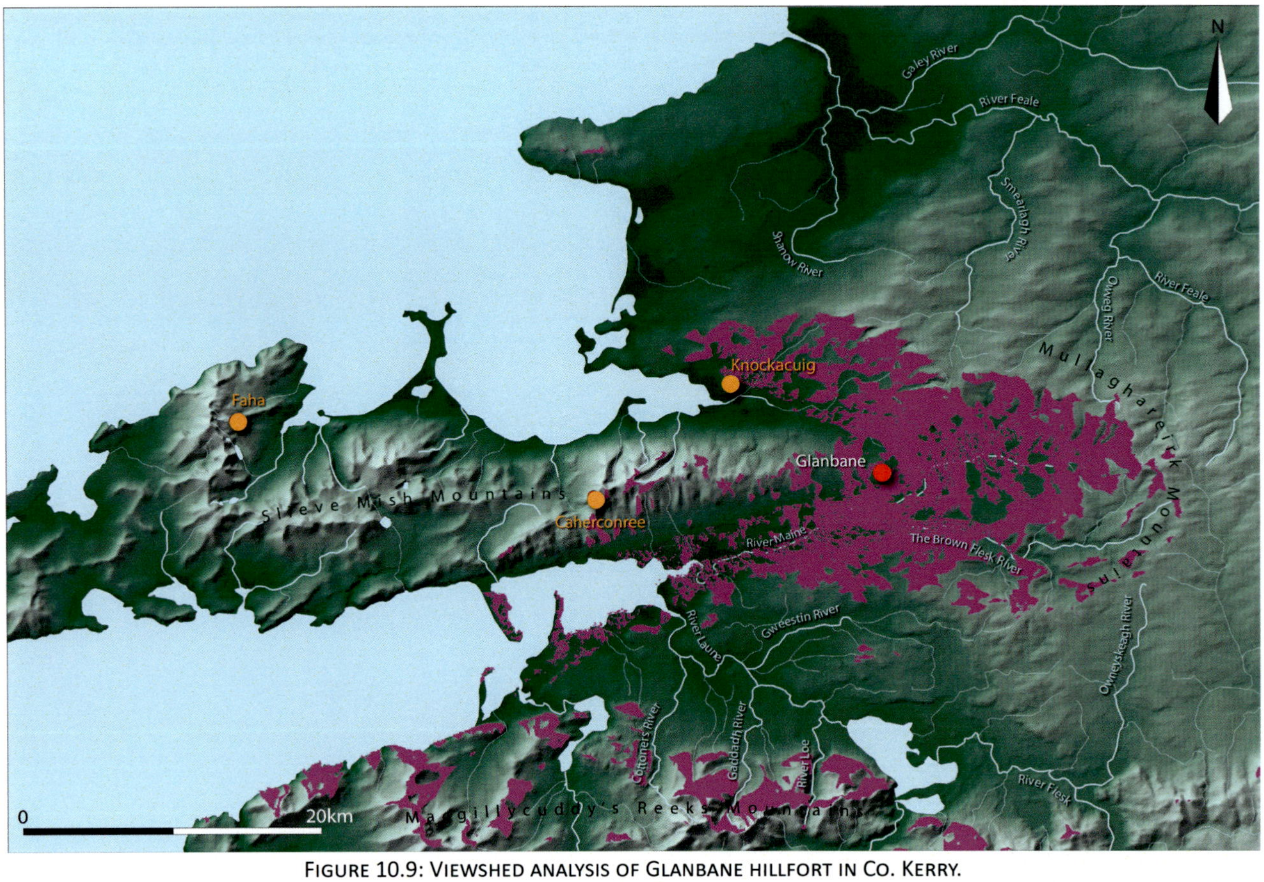

Figure 10.9: Viewshed analysis of Glanbane hillfort in Co. Kerry.

that Glanbane hillfort lies on the edge of land that is highly visible from both the generated LCP pathway and within the valley in general. Sitting at the edge of this high/low visibility area would help to further contrast the hillfort and the surrounding landscape.

Knockanacuig, a bivallate hillfort 7.21ha in maximum size, is positioned on a slight rise overlooking Tralee Bay 1.6km to the west. Viewshed analysis indicates that the dominant views from Knockanacuig are of the southern inlet of Tralee Bay, suggesting that it may have been located to command a sea route (Figure 10.11). Excavation of this monument ahead of a housing development retrieved Iron Age dates from the outer ditch of the monument; although the preliminary report indicates that there was substantial re-cutting of this feature (Dunne and Bartlett 2009). Without further contextual information, this cannot be securely dated to the Iron Age. The importance of Tralee Bay is further attested by the promontory fort at Faha in the Dingle Peninsula.

Positioned on a ridge near Brandon Mountain, on the western edge of the Slieve Mish Mountain range, at 822m OD, Faha is the highest recorded hillfort in Ireland or Britain. This almost inaccessible monument comprises two widely spaced drystone walls that defend the eastern edge of a ridge. Viewshed analysis highlights that the hillfort was primarily positioned to afford maximum views of Tralee Bay (Figure 10.12). It is located in a mountainous region, a setting that would have reduced its visibility when viewed from Tralee Bay.

Approximately 25km to the east of Faha, the island promontory fort of Caherconree is positioned in the heart of the Slieve Mish Mountains. The hillfort is situated on the edge of a west facing spur at 659m OD. The site comprises a substantial drystone wall that curves in an east-west direction for approximately 110m. A number of D-shaped structures abut both the internal and external face of the inner wall. No other features are visible within the interior, although deep blanket bog, up to 80cm in depth, may be overlying more extensive settlement evidence. The site itself is regarded in Early Medieval mythology as the fort of Cu Roi, one of the main antagonists to Cú Chulaind in the Ulster Cycle. The dominant views from Caherconree are of Dingle Bay, but a large proportion of Tralee Bay is also visible (Figure 10.13). The visibility of the monument is enhanced by the distinctive promontory which the site is built upon, which contrasts sharply with the natural landscape, creating what Smith (1756: 156) describes as 'a beacon' in the landscape. This setting was an important factor in the siting of the hillfort, particular considering the monument is immediately overlooked to the north-east by the mountain summit also known as Caherconree. This position leaves the site vulnerable, hinting that defence was not a primary concern, although one could consider the inaccessible location of the fort itself highly defensive. The locational setting of Caherconree may be related to a need to be highly visible but also stand-out in the natural landscape, have extensive views of both northern and southern sea-routes, and appear monumentally defensive.

In conclusion, these four hillforts in west Kerry were located in strategically significant locations in the landscape, overlooking important natural route-ways. The control of movement and trade, and the display of monumental structures in an attempt to assert authority over the landscape were an important elements in the location of these sites.

The Antrim Coast

Naturally conspicuous locations in the landscape were often chosen to build a hillfort, as long as they adhered to other strategic and defensive needs. Knockdhu and Lurigethan hillforts in Co. Antrim are prime examples. These sites impose their presence on the surrounding landscape, utilising impressive inland promontories overlooking the eastern Antrim coastline (Figure 10.14; Figure 10.15). These are highly contrasting topographical landmarks which make the sites highly visible in the local landscape. LiDAR survey of Knockdhu hillfort has identified up to 50 possible hut structures (McNeary 2012), which recent excavation has to the beginning of the Late Bronze Age (Macdonald 2012). Although Lurigethan hillfort remains undated, its striking similarities with Knockdhu might infer a similar date.

Hodges (1975) has previously noted the extensive views from Knockdhu, which overlooks the Irish Sea and the western coast of Scotland. Viewshed analysis has confirmed these broad views, but has also highlighted the restricted views of the immediate landscape (Figure 10.16). The lowlands to the immediate east are overlooked, possibly inferring that this was as an area of settlement controlled by the hillfort builders. Views to the west and most accessible route to the site are impeded by a slight knoll on slowly rising terrain. The viewshed suggests that an unrestricted view of the Irish Sea was more important than panoramic or defensive control of the land based routes in the immediate environs. Hodges (1975: 19) suggested that Knockdhu and Lurigethan may have been integral to the trading patterns of Ulster from as early as the Late Bronze Age and emphasised the potential for international trade in this area. The extensive settlement within Knockdhu may suggest that the monument was built and occupied by a large, thriving community controlling and exploiting sea routes between north-east Ireland and Scotland.

Lurigethan hillfort, 22km to the north-north-west of Knockdhu, is strikingly similar in both construction and siting. Aerial photography has revealed a number of hut structures within the fort and more may be waiting

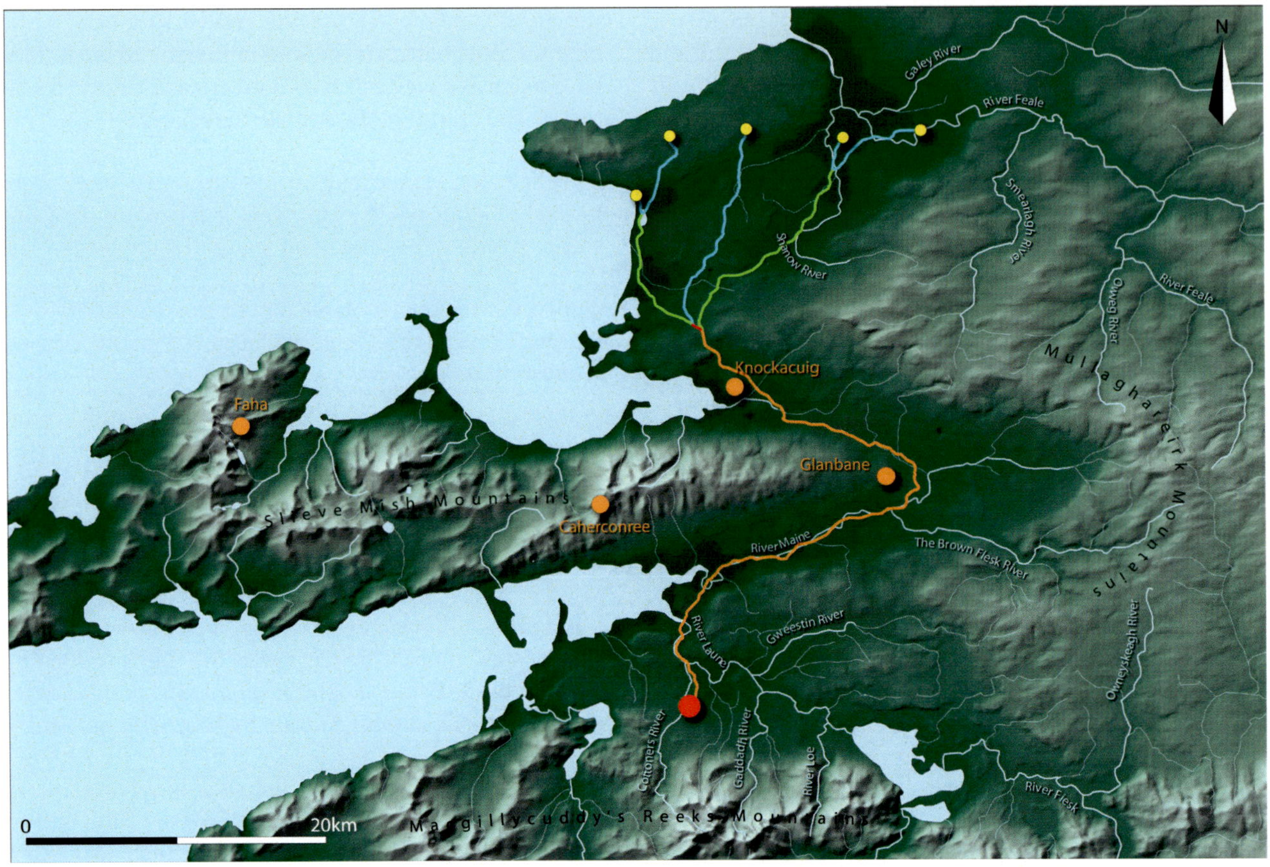

Figure 10.10: LCP analysis of the West Kerry region.

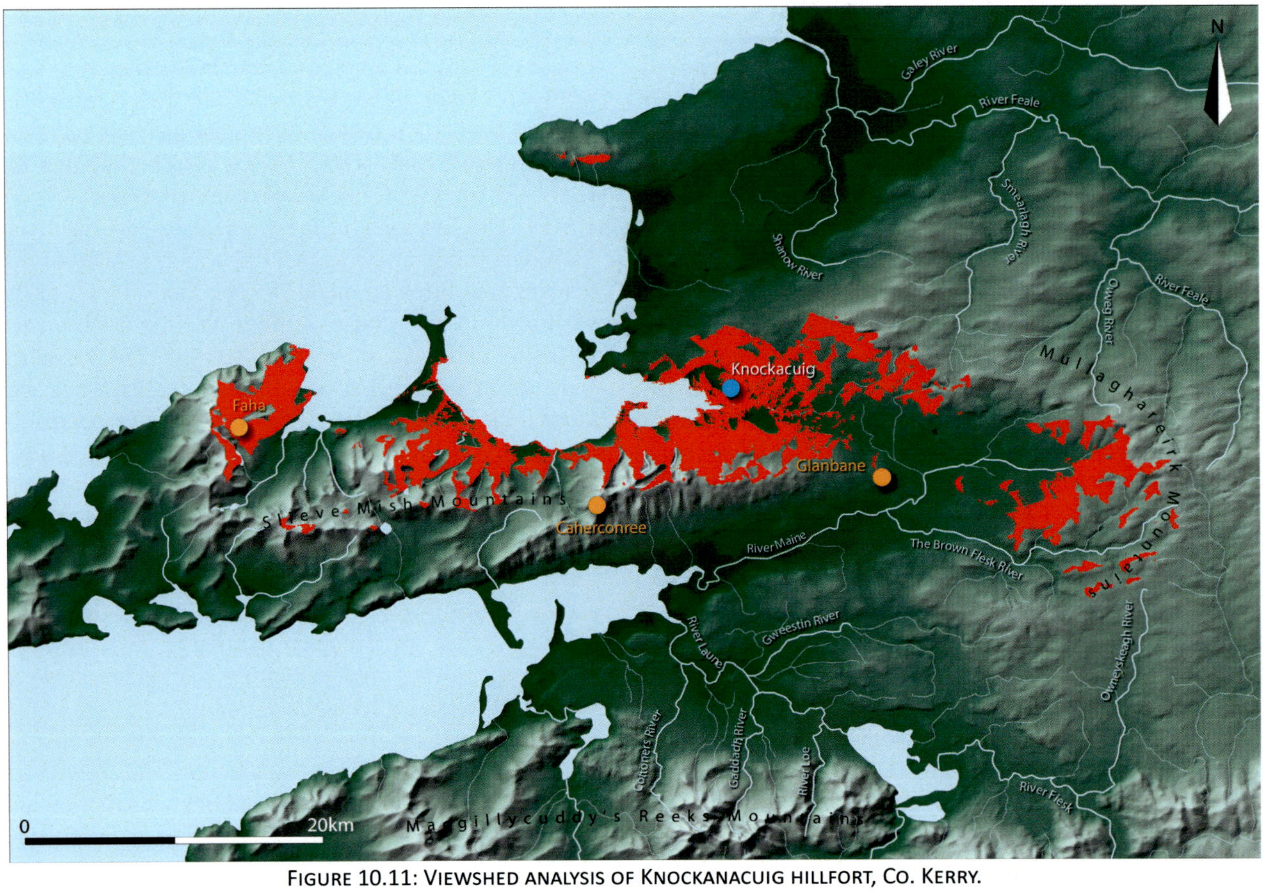

Figure 10.11: Viewshed analysis of Knockanacuig hillfort, Co. Kerry.

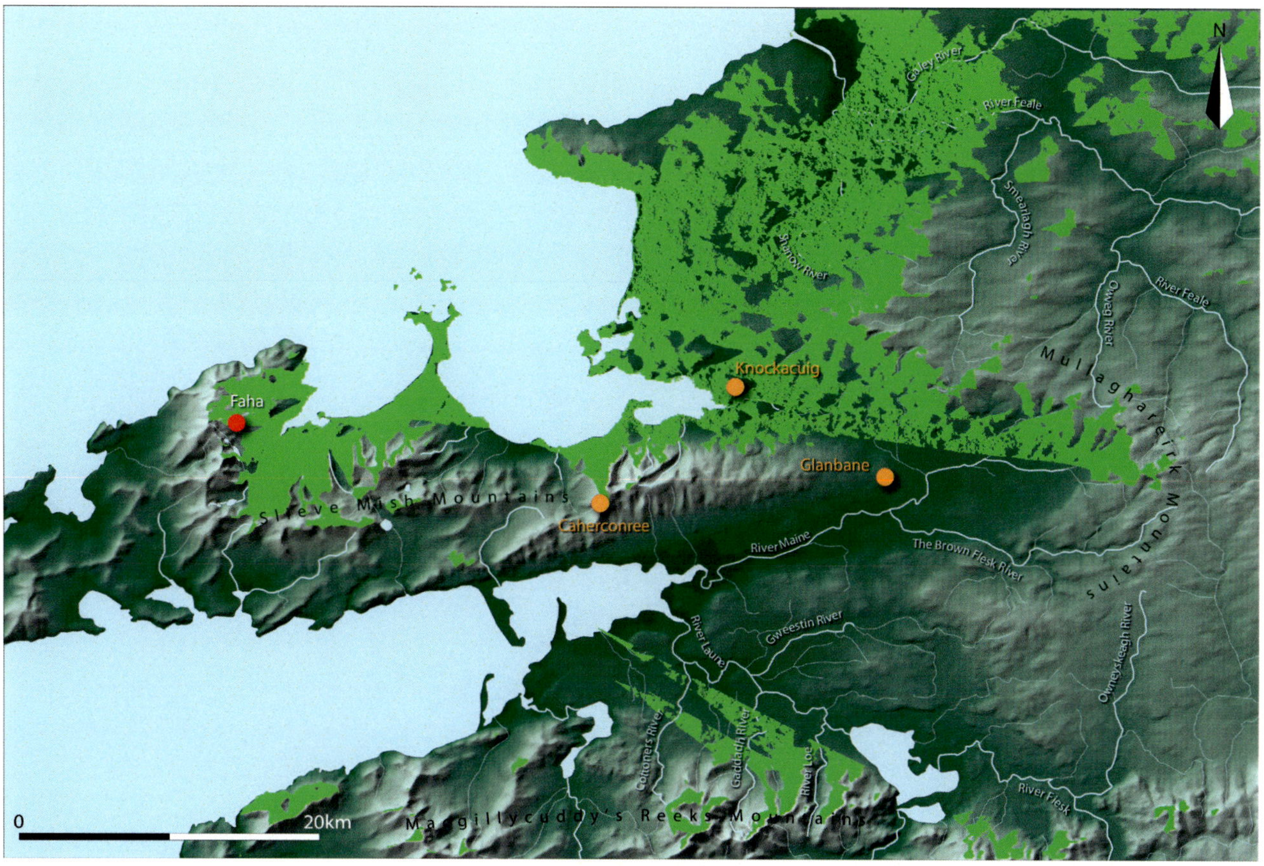

Figure 10.12: Viewshed analysis of faha hillfort, Co. Kerry.

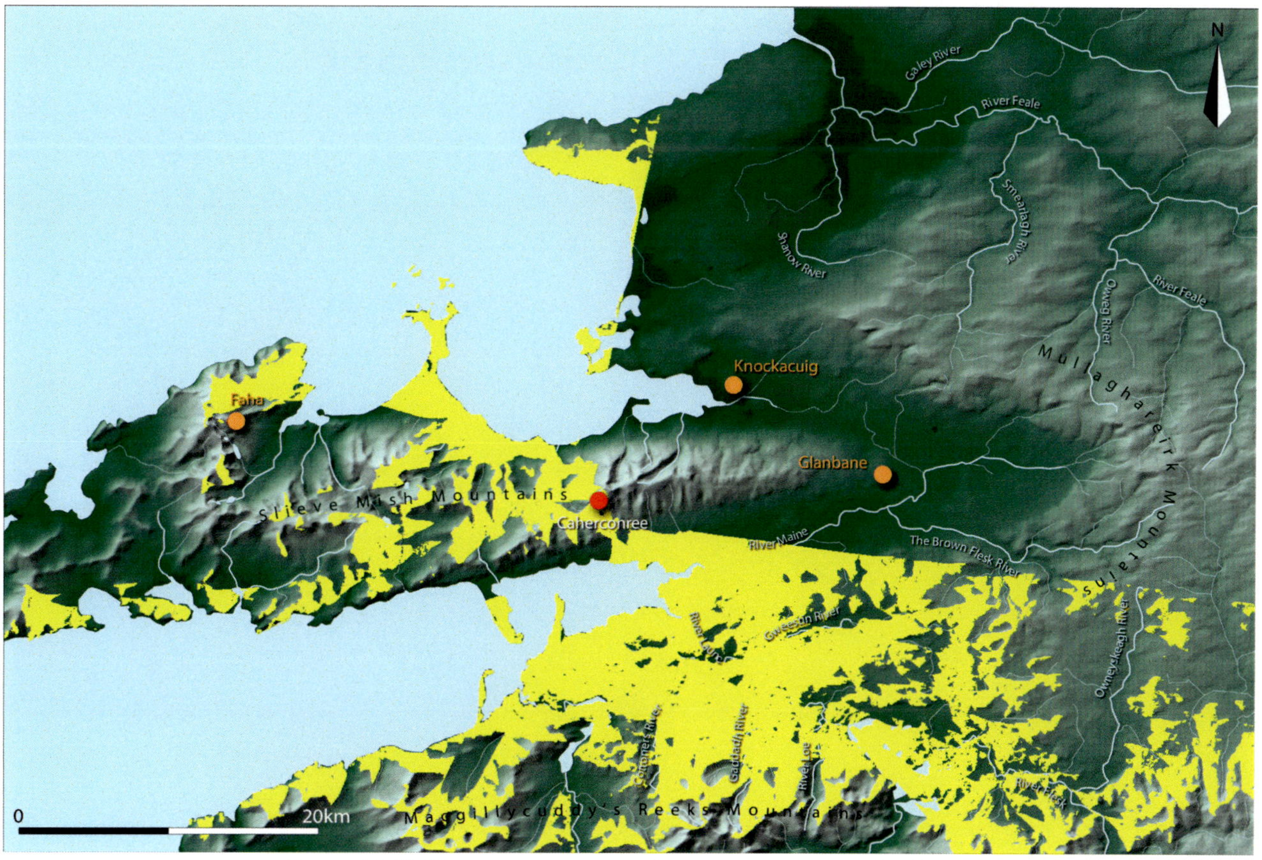

Figure 10.13: Viewshed analysis of Caherconree hillfort, Co. Kerry.

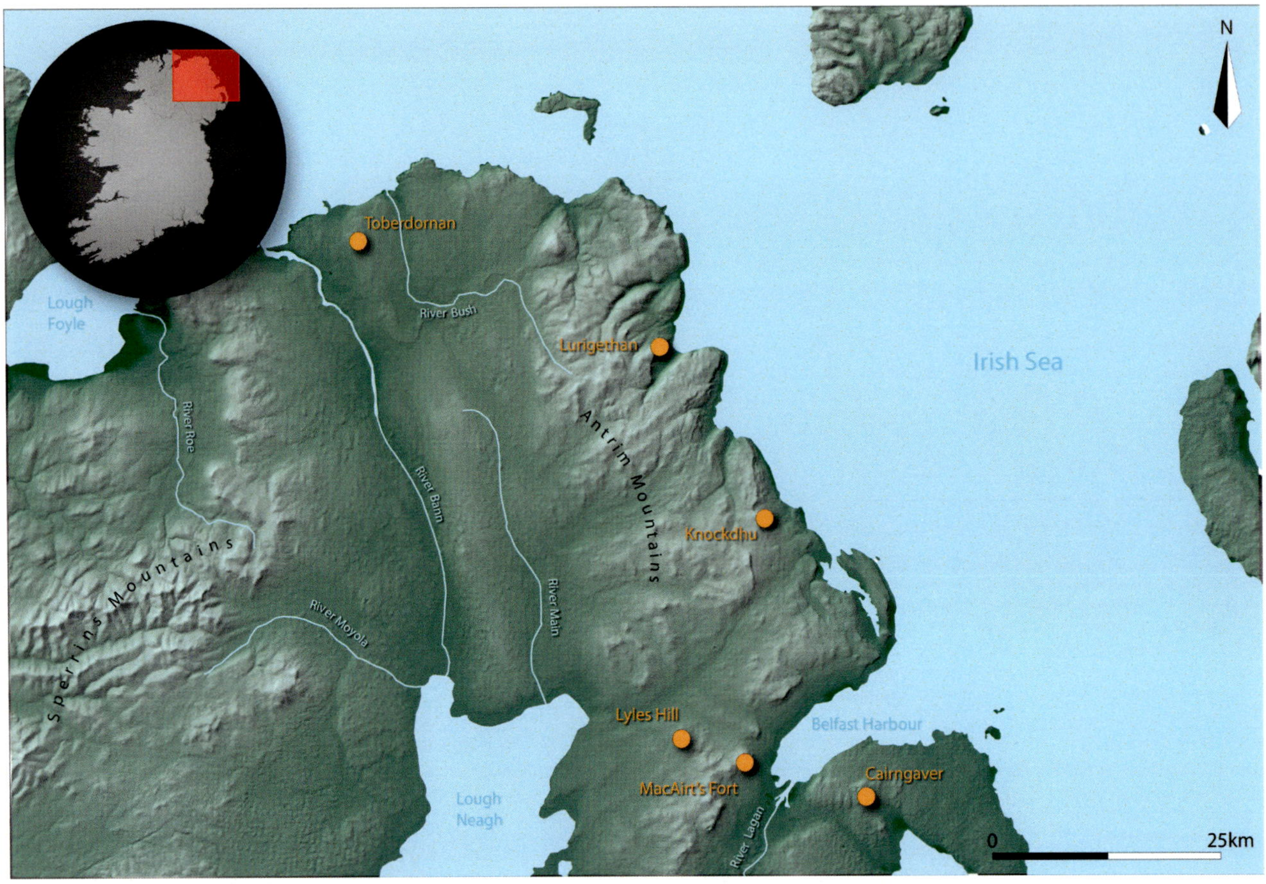

FIGURE 10.14: HILLFORTS IN THE ANTRIM COAST REGION.

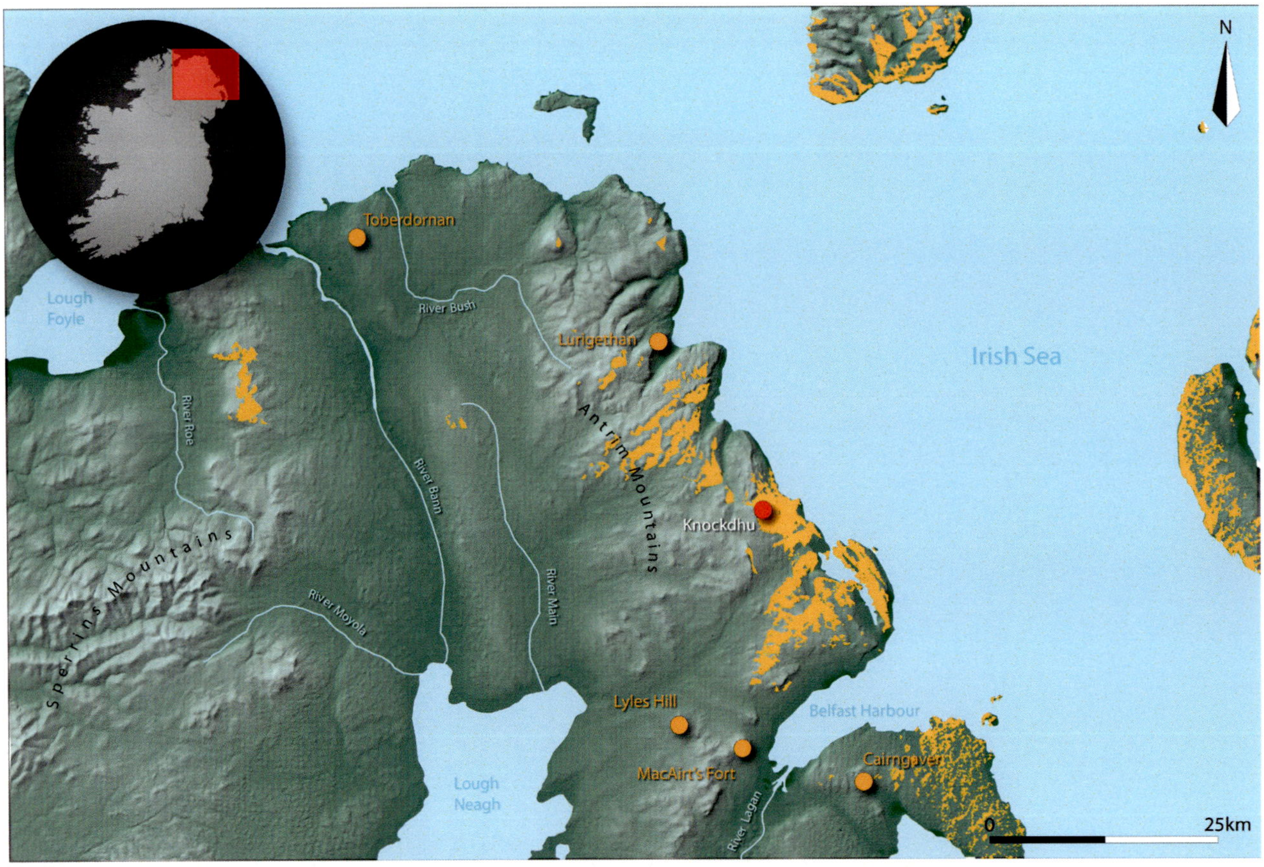

FIGURE 10.15: VIEWSHED ANALYSIS OF KNOCKDHU HILLFORT, CO. ANTRIM.

identification. Pollen analysis of a peat core (Weir 1993) 3.6km from Lurigethan has identified an intensification of activity, culminating in a major clearance episode at 1130–850 BC. A very low level of tree pollen at this time suggests that the local area was almost entirely cleared (Weir 1993: 22). Extensive woodland clearances associated with hillforts have been noted elsewhere in Ireland during the Late Bronze Age (Plunkett *et al.* 2009: 274). Late Bronze Age field systems at Galbolly Lower and Loughnatrosk, Co. Antrim attest to the significant intensification of activity in the environs of Lurigethan and the Antrim plateau during this period. Cunliffe (2012: 257–258) states that it is difficult to resist the suggestion that the prime cause of the appropriation of land for its productive capacity was the desire to produce agricultural surpluses that could be used in part for gift exchange. Certainly, the increased surpluses created by intensive farming are likely to have underpinned the elite class. Viewshed analysis suggests that the fort was located primarily to take advantage of the Irish–Scottish sea routes. Similar to Knockdhu, the views of the easily accessible western approach to this hillfort are severely restricted (Figure 10.17). This is in contrast to the extensive views of the lowlands immediately to the north, east and south of the site, and of the Scottish coast and the Irish Sea.

Knockdhu and Lurigethan are not inter-visible and share a limited composite viewshed, possibly indicating that these hillforts formed the focus of different, rival communities who competed for control of the Irish Sea and the trade and goods which it allowed access to. A third promontory fort, MacAirt's Fort, is situated overlooking Belfast city, and may be located to overlook both Belfast Harbour and the eastern coast of Scotland. This intensification of settlement activity in the area corresponds with an increase in trade between the Antrim coast and western Scotland, as evidenced by the northern Irish–western Scottish 'flesh-hook zone' (Needham and Bowman 2005), the heavily Irish–influenced Glentrool phase, and the appearance of Irish axe forms and Irish gold ornaments during the Ewart Park/Duddingston phase (Henderson 2007: 77). Sea and riverine travel in the Late Bronze Age were essential in consolidating local, regional and international trade and formed important trade routes. Knockdhu, Lurigethan and MacAirt's Fort may have had a similar role to the Late Bronze Age hillfort at Dún Aonghasa, which was strategically positioned to exploit and control the maritime resources and trade routes along the coast of western Ireland.

North Kilkenny

Two hillforts in Co. Kilkenny may also attest to the importance of controlling topographical and riverine routes during this period (Figure 10.18). Toor More sits on a north–south ridge at 244m above sea-level, overlooking the town of Ballyragget to the east, in north-west Co. Kilkenny. The hillfort comprises two enclosing elements visible on the ground as low relief banks. Geophysical survey identified potential palisade features on the crest of the banks and this was subsequently confirmed by excavation (Figure 4.58; see Chapter 4). Extensive views of the western lowlands and the valley of the River Nore are particularly evident from the site (Figure 10.19). A concentration of ring-ditches in this valley may highlight the importance of this region and the River Nore in later prehistory. It may be significant that nearly all of these ring-ditches and this section of the River Nore are highly visible from Toor More. LCP analysis underlines the importance of this river valley as both a land and riverine based route-way, connecting the Laois, Kilkenny and North Tipperary lowlands (Figure 10.20). Travelling south from a northern or western direction, 8 of 9 start points use the Nore valley, indicating this may be the easiest route to the south from both the north and west. Cumulative viewshed analysis suggests that Toor More is positioned in one of two areas visible to over 95% of the viewer points (Figure 10.19). Further cumulative analysis of the LCP pathway attains similar results. The circular shape and composition of the enclosing elements, which do not follow the contours, would have contrasted with the natural setting of the hilltop, making this highly visible area at odds with the local landscape.

Clomantagh hillfort, a univallate site of 3.25ha lies on the southwestern edge of a mountain ridge, overlooking a gap comprising the western approach to the Nore valley in north-west Kilkenny. The hillfort is situated at the highest point in the middle of this ridge. This is the only location on this ridge-top that affords extensive views of western lowlands and this gap. There is a concentration of up to 8 ring-ditches at the mouth of this opening, potentially identifying the importance of this route-way. This univallate hillfort has extensive views of this opening, as well as broad views of the western lowlands (Figure 10.21). Clomantagh Hill translates as 'Hill of the Gapped Stone' (logainm.ie), possibly hinting at an ancient association between the hilltop and natural route-way.

A third hillfort in Kilkenny, Freestone Hill, may have been positioned to control access to the southern openings to both the Nore and Barrow river valleys. Ó Floinn (2000: 15) notes that the hillfort overlooks the Pass of Gowran, which formed the principal route-way from Laigen (Leinster) into the buffer state of Osraige (between Leinster and Munster) during the Early Medieval period. Byrne (1973: 169) also notes the importance of this route, suggesting that access to Munster was restricted, the normal path from Leinster being guarded by the prehistoric hillfort of Freestone Hill. Evidence of long-distance trade is evident in the LMHK glass beads found at the hillfort (Raftery 1969). Scientific analysis of these beads suggests long-distance exchange between

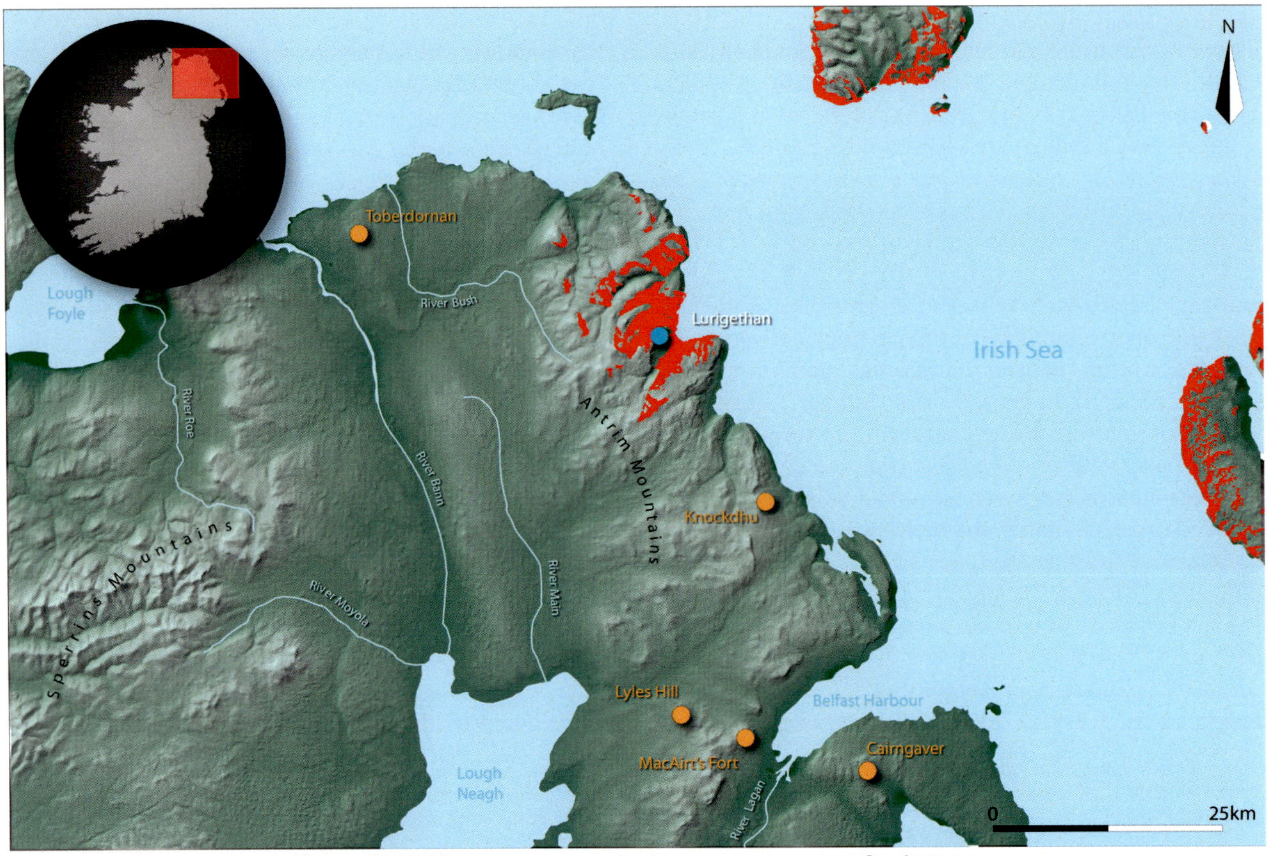

Figure 10.16: Viewshed analysis of Lurigethan hillfort, Co. Antrim.

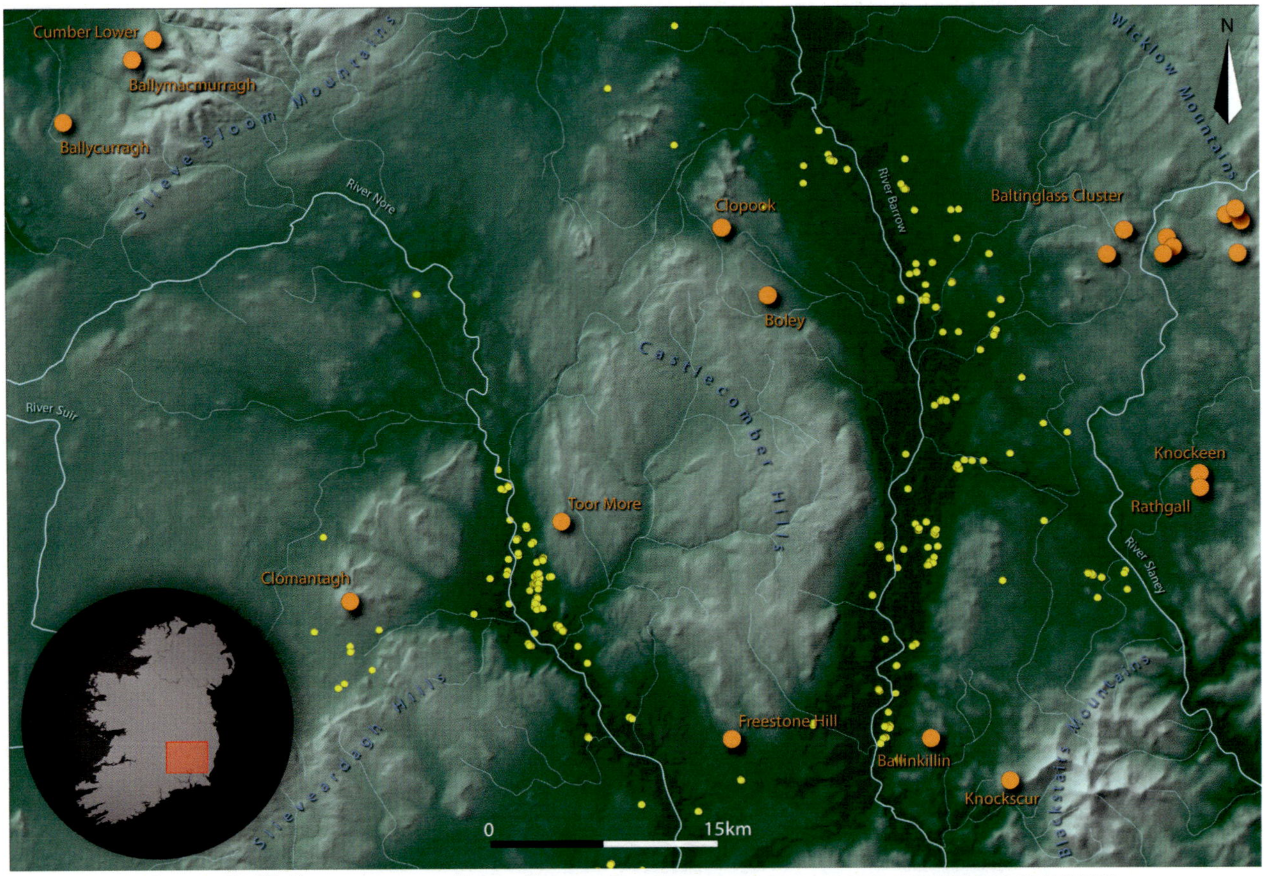

Figure 10.17: Hillforts of the North Kilkenny region with ring barrows highlighted in yellow.

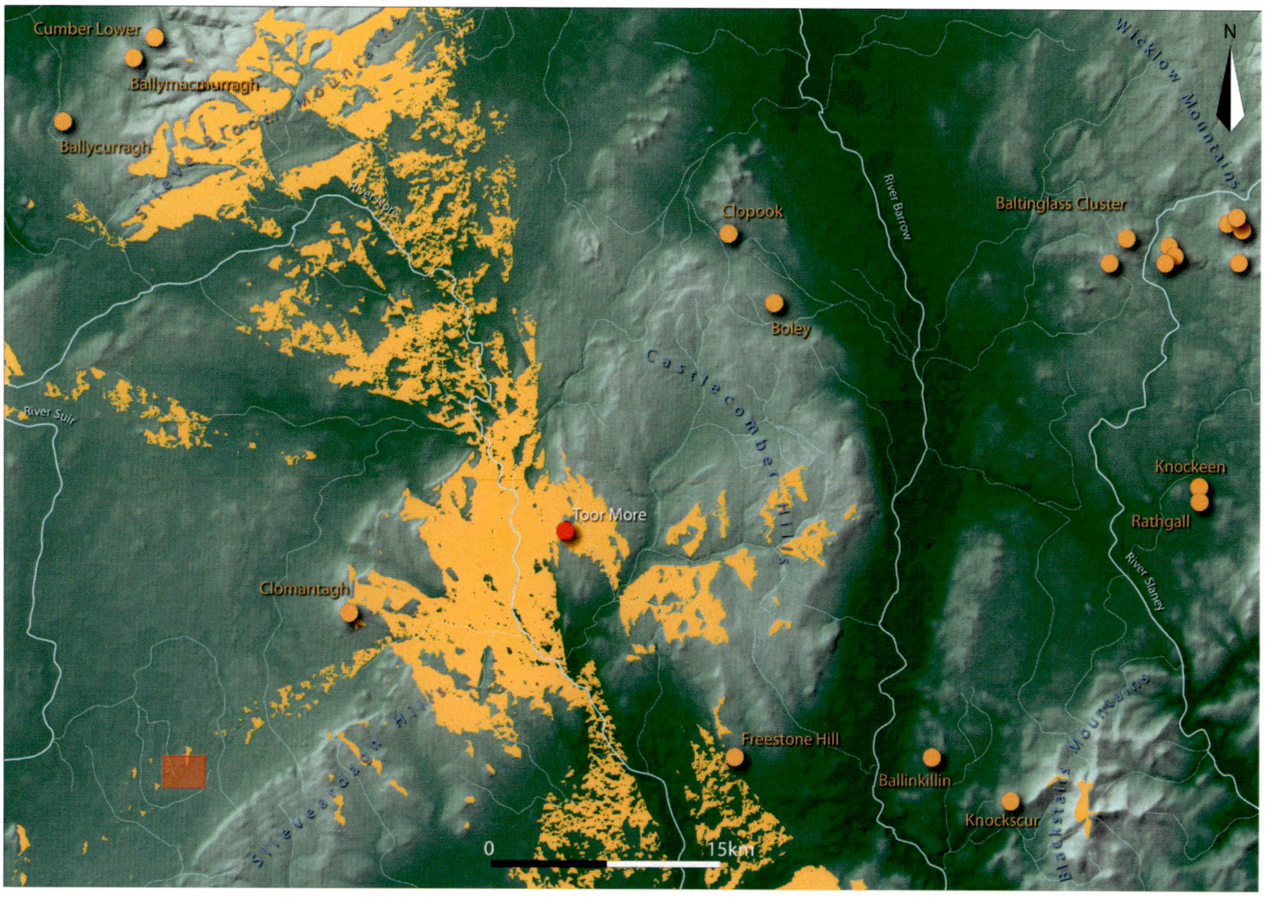

FIGURE 10.18: VIEWSHED ANALYSIS OF TOOR MORE HILLFORT, CO. KILKENNY.

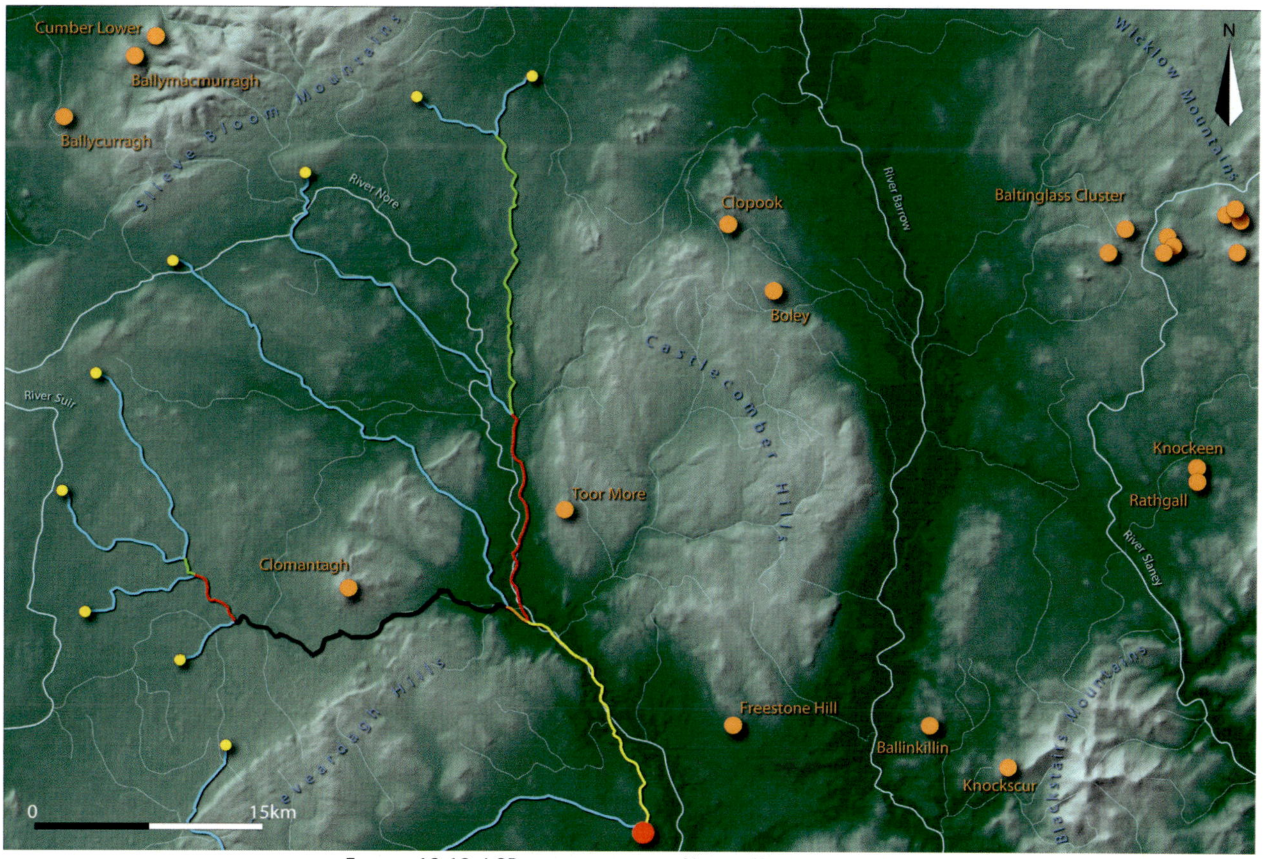

FIGURE 10.19: LCP ANALYSIS OF THE NORTH KILKENNY REGION.

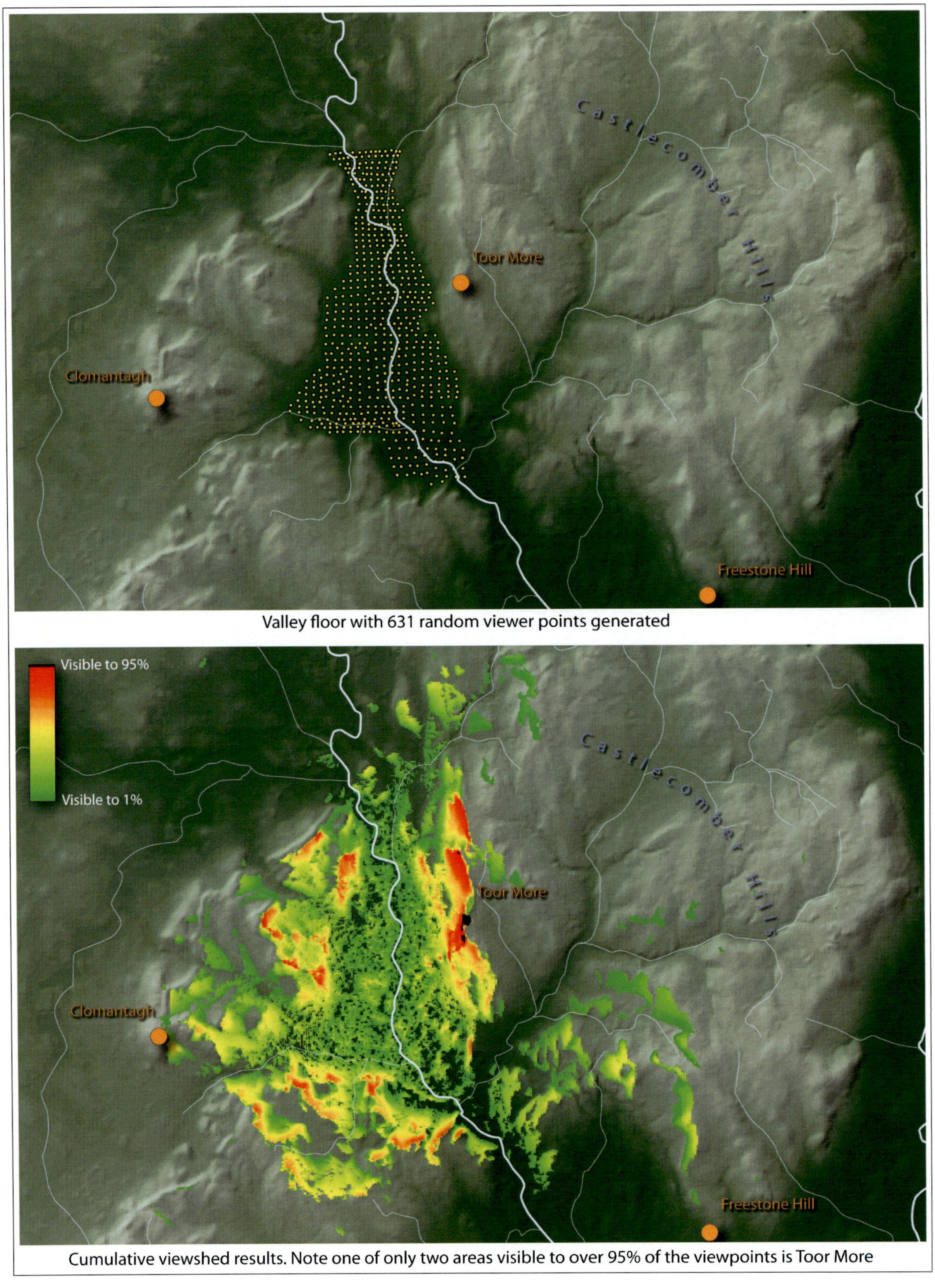

FIGURE 10.20: CUMULATIVE VIEWSHED ANALYSIS OF THE NORTH KILKENNY REGION, INDICATING THE PROMINANCE OF TOOR MORE FROM THE VALLEY BELOW THIS HILLFORT TO THE WEST AND SOUTH.

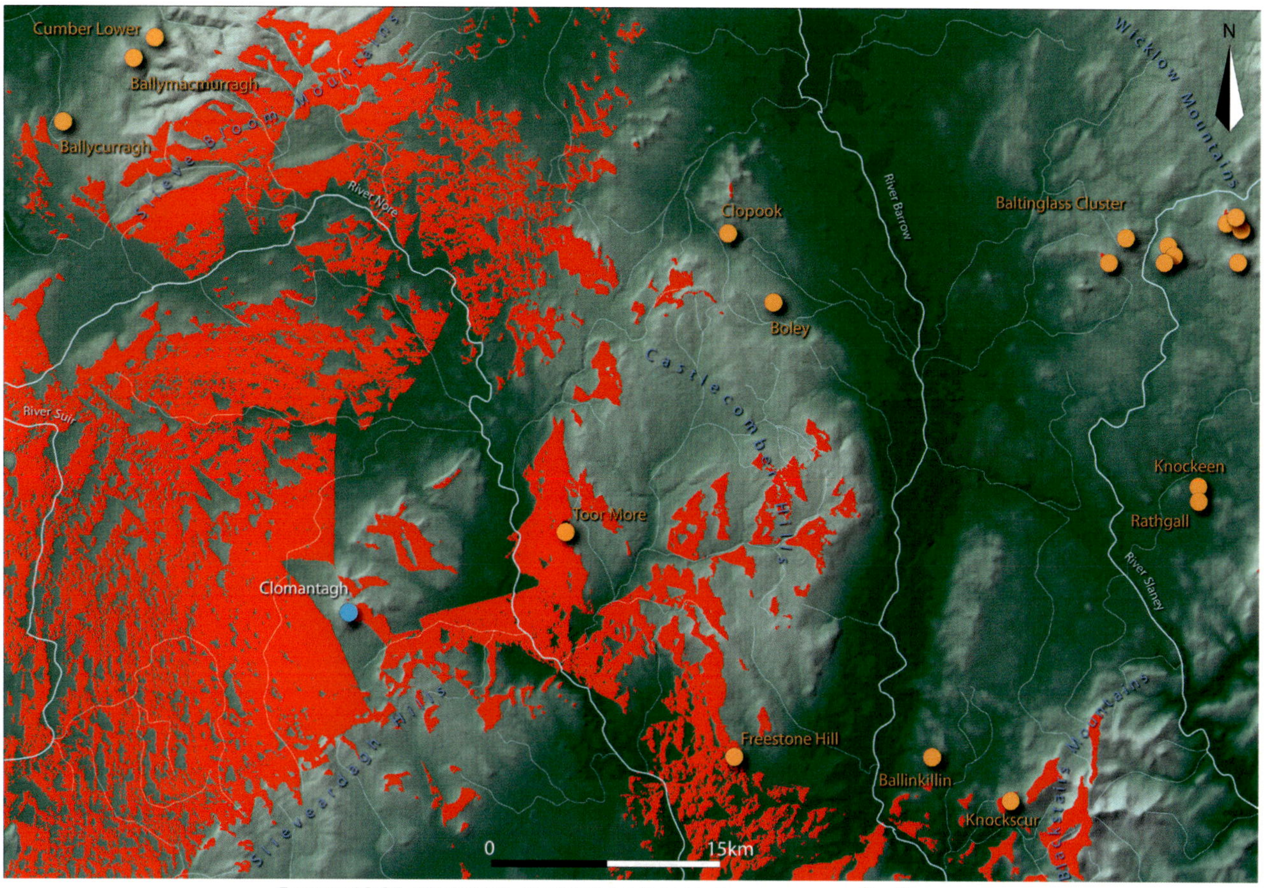

FIGURE 10.21: VIEWSHED ANALYSIS OF CLOMANTAGH HILLFORT, CO. KILKENNY.

this site and LMHK production centres in northern Italy and Switzerland.

Discussion

Viewshed and LCP analysis highlight the importance of maintaining strategic control of natural routeways by siting hillforts in highly visible locations. This is further highlighted when sections of some hillforts, such as Toor More, are positioned on partially sloping ground, making large portions of the interior visible from the adjacent routeway and increasing visibility of the entire monument. This evidence complements the studies of Fonte *et al.* (2011) and Sherratt (1996). Both have linked the distribution of hillforts with the control of movement and emphasise the importance of rivers in that regard. Similarly, Brown (2009: 197) argues that hillforts 'controlled inter-regional routes of traffic and trade [rather] than simply dominating their own immediate block of downland'. This has been challenged by Sharples (2010: 68), as it assumes a controlling relationship between rivers and hillforts that may not always have been present and does not explain the absence of sites on many apparently strategic rivers. Sherratt (1996) reduces the importance of overland transportation, seeing these routes used 'primarily between rivers' and stating that 'even if the river itself was not the means of transportation, it is likely that cross-country routes for pack animals or porters often followed the gentle slopes of riverine routes (*ibid.*: 225). While it is clear that river systems provided significant arteries for travel, overland routes also played important and independent roles in this system. This has recently been advanced by Driver (2013), who has identified significant Iron Age overland routes in the north Ceredigion region of Wales. Such a route is apparent in Ireland in Co. Limerick, where the Late Bronze Age hillfort at Ballylin is located on a northern plateau of an extensive and prominent north-south running escarpment.

A significant number of Irish hillforts also correspond with this proposed model, such as Carn Tighernagh in Co. Cork, Glanbane, Co. Kerry, or the cluster of hillforts in the Baltinglass area of Co. Wicklow (see O'Driscoll 2016). Those sites that cannot easily be linked with an obvious routeway may be located near more subtle routeways or natural resources. Haughey's Fort and Rahally, for example, are sited in lowland areas where there is little topographical variation or strong topographical markers. Palaeoenvironmental evidence suggests the construction of both hillforts was associated with intensive land clearance episodes and subsequent increases in agricultural activity. This is consistent with other hillfort sites such as Mooghaun, where pollen analysis has been undertaken. It may imply that Haughey's Fort and Rahally were used for a similar purpose by an agricultural community. Cleary (2007: 265) suggested that the deliberate backfilling of pits with a range of both domestic and high status material within Haughey's Fort may signify the importance of the monument for the exchange of commodities. As noted above, the variety of finds recovered within that hillfort and its environs indicates trading links with various parts of Continental Europe. There is clearly a link with long-distance trade even at hillfort sites in low-lying areas. In these lowland situations, river systems may have taken on an increasingly important role in the transportation and movement of goods and people.

It is interesting to note that both Haughey's Fort and Rahally overlook possible major Early Medieval routeways (Ó Lochlainn 1940). Although it is possible that Early Medieval roads had prehistoric origins, the routes proposed by Ó Lochlainn have been criticised for being influenced by 19th-century road networks (Ginn 2016: 154). However, of the 108 possible hillforts identified in Ireland, 33 are within 1.5km of one of Ó Lochlainn's possible routes and a total of 50 are within 3km, hinting that there may be an association between hillforts and these possible ancient routeways.

Ginn's analysis of Bronze Age settlement sites suggest that hillforts represented focal monuments that facilitated the connectivity and flow of power throughout the wider landscape, playing an important part in creating a global network of communication and trade (Ginn 2016: 176; 183). Although her catalogue of hillforts is not comprehensive, the addition of recently identified sites would probably strengthen her conclusions. Ginn's study may be supported by the artefactual evidence linking hillforts with long-distance exchange networks, as well as the strategic location of many sites in topographically and visually dominant landscape positions overlooking natural routeways.

Hillforts: A multi-layered interpretation

The archaeological evidence suggests that Irish hillforts fit into a model of a competitive Late Bronze Age society. These monuments represent highly visible displays of power, with their landscape position dominating trade routes, controlling the distribution of goods and the movement of peoples. It is proposed that the distinctive siting of hillforts was based on a need to control territory and routeways through visibility. This was particularly important, as many believe that elites created and maintained positions of social dominance by controlling the population and supply of prestige goods and metal (O'Brien 2015: 290). A large number of Irish hillforts are located at strategic positions in the landscape, at the interface between upland and lowland terrain and overlooking one or more natural corridors (Condit 1998: 22; Grogan 2005b; Waddell 1998: 269). The need to control these routeways, and to be seen from them, may have been a significant factor in choosing these locations. The importance of natural routeways has been noted by several researchers on the continent (see Chapter 2). Similarly, early hillforts in Britain are positioned to control physical access to varied landscapes and resources (Hamilton and Manley 2001: 31).

This does not exclude the communal aspect of hillfort building as presented by Lock (2011), or the potential defensive role of these monuments promoted by Armit (2007). Rather, it may be seen to amalgamate the two, in a multi-layered interpretation of these sites. A community may have built a hillfort primarily to convey their authority over a routeway and to provide a focus for trade. This construction process may have been important for consolidating a disparate social group and in the creation of group harmony and identity. During its lifecycle, a hillfort may have performed a number of diverse functions for the community. It may have been used as a defensive refuge, a central place for elites or craft specialists, or a meeting or assembly point at certain times in the year where social activities such as ritual feasting may have taken place.

Sharples (1991: 84) admits that control over exchange networks and the inter-community alliances that facilitated trade would be a principal cause of conflict and competition. The destruction of a hillfort would have been a striking visual way of undermining this authority. The archaeological evidence for the burning of hillfort defences is evident in a number of excavated and surveyed examples (e.g. Rathcoran, Rathnagree, Clashanimud, Toor More). Although some hillforts may not have been built to function primarily as defensive enclosures, they may still have been heavily linked with warfare practices in prehistory. Late Bronze Age hillforts may be seen as 'inevitable targets'. This term was used by Heath (2009: 51) to describe the Neolithic causewayed enclosures of Britain. Heath believes these enclosures must have been important locations that were in some way removed from the norm, and suggests they attracted 'the hostile intentions of 'foreign' communities who sought to usurp the material wealth and the resulting social power that this commanded'.

A hillfort may have been destroyed by a rival elite or community who were competing for the same resources or trade opportunities. While this had the practical function of eliminating a rival from competing in exotic goods and long-distance trade networks, the destruction of hillfort defences in acts of warfare could also have created vivid memories of subjugation for the community associated with the site and deconstructed their social order. Conversely, it would have reinforced the identity of the hostile group, solidifying social cohesiveness and creating social memory. A successful attack may have consolidated an elite's position and increased their status.

The life-cycle of the enclosing elements of a hillfort would therefore have been integral in the formation and consolidation of group identity on a number of levels. The construction of the hillfort could have allowed the builders to consolidate social cohesion and group identity. The 'active life' of the enclosing elements would have been essential in displaying this identity in the local landscape, and their destruction would have reinforced the identity of the aggressive community, while simultaneously deconstructing the social order of the building community.

The location and function of hillforts, and particularly those in Ireland, therefore, can be linked to the need to control the landscape and the movement of people and goods. This, in turn, would facilitate other potential functions such as ritual or assembly, the hillfort being highly visible in the landscape, yet decisively liminal within it. Similarly, the hillfort would have provided a special space for the display of status and power in the landscape, a visual statement consistent with the competitive society within which they were built.

10.3 Hillforts and Social Hierarchies

The review of chronology in Chapter 7 confirms that there was more than one hillfort tradition in prehistoric Ireland. The results from Hughstown, Co. Kildare demonstrate that the first hillforts were large multiple enclosures of the Hughstown type, connected to early farming communities in Neolithic Ireland, *c.*3600–3400 BC. These were followed two millennia or so later by the Bronze Age hillfort, a development with parallels in Britain and mainland Europe during the second millennium BC. The first of the Irish examples were built in the Bishopsland Phase of the Middle Bronze Age *c.*1400–1200/1100 BC, and in increasing numbers during the ensuing Roscommon Phase (1150–1000 BC) of the Late Bronze Age. A smaller number of hillforts were built and occupied over the following two centuries, during the Dowris Phase (1000/900–700 BC) of the Late Bronze Age, with the occupation of hillforts declining sharply after the eighth century BC for reasons that remain unclear.

While the hillfort has long been associated with the Late Bronze Age in Ireland, the results of this project show its origins lie within the Bishopsland phase of the Middle Bronze Age, with the main period of hillfort construction during the Roscommon phase of the twelfth and eleventh centuries BC. This was a period of great change in Ireland, with population growth and settlement expansion in many regions (Figure 10.22; see Waddell 2010: 187–289 for overview). Agriculture was the basis of these economies, with pollen records indicating ongoing

Early part of Middle Bronze Age (1600–1400 BC Killymaddy Phase)

Period of settlement expansion with rising population; technological innovation and growing demand for metal; intensification of agriculture with greater management and use of uplands; expansion of settlement, with growing number of roundhouse settlements (Figure 10.23) and burnt mounds (*fulachtaí fia*); greater use of protective enclosure, and the beginnings of village-type nucleation (Corrstown type).

Later part of Middle Bronze Age (1400–1200/1100 BC (Bishopsland Phase)

First hillforts (example: Rathnagree), connected to simple regional chiefdoms; intensification of economic production in agriculture and metalworking; technological innovation in gold and bronze; strong demand for metal with new reliance on imported bronze; settlement expansion with increased use of uplands and lake settlements; growing militarism (large-scale production of bronze spearheads).

Early part of Late Bronze Age (1150/1100–1000 BC; Roscommon Phase)

Continued construction of hillforts (examples: Ballylin, Clashanimud, Glanbane, Formoyle, Haughey's Fort, Toor More, Rahally, Rathgall); evidence of hillfort warfare; continued pressures on metal supply; strong evidence of militarism (first swords). Previously considered a period of recession (Eogan 1964) or 'a time of active adjustment between two active industrial phases' (Herity and Eogan 1977: 185); recent studies indicate 'a period of important social, economic and political re-organization' (Plunkett 2009: 292).

Later part of Late Bronze Age (1000–800/700 BC; Dowris Phase)

Continued construction of hillforts (examples: Dún Aonghasa and Mooghaun); period of stability and economic prosperity; major expansion of metal production (bronze and gold), with advanced craft specialization; general expansion of settlement (roundhouse settlements, burnt mounds); intensification of agricultural systems in pollen record (Plunkett 2009); consolidation of simple chiefdoms into complex chiefdoms; expansion of trade networks within and outside of Ireland; large-scale weapon production.

Bronze Age/Iron Age transition (800/700–500 BC; Dowris /Athlone Phase)

Collapse of hillfort society; dislocation of trade routes; replacement of bronze by iron; contraction of settlement and reduction in agriculture (Plunkett 2009).

Figure 10.22: Correlation of hillfort activity with major developments of the Middle and Late Bronze Age in Ireland.

deforestation and an intensification of farming that extended into uplands and other parts of the landscape not previously inhabited.

The demand for bronze increased significantly during the Bishopsland phase, at a time when there was only limited copper mining in Ireland (O'Brien 2013). This led to a greater reliance on imported metal supplies, which required participation in long-distance exchange networks. It was a period of innovation in metalworking, with the development of new fabrication methods, specialised tool-kits, the first bronze swords and new types of gold ornament. There was a further intensification of bronze and gold production across Ireland during the Dowris phase. The scale of production increased sharply, with exchange of Irish metalwork into Britain and the European mainland, from where various technical and stylistic influences originated. The growing demand for metal carried the seeds of exploitation, leading possibly to the emergence of powerful individuals or groups whose position was linked to a controlling interest in the supply of metal.

At one level, this was a fragmented society comprised of many small communities with dispersed settlement patterns (Ginn 2016). In such a society there were important social distinctions between different groups of farmers, depending on their material wealth, land and livestock. This was also a period of craft specialization, with division of labour into occupations and skills. The degree to which these local groups were autonomous is questionable, as the material culture points to higher levels of social organization involving a wealthy aristocracy that controlled significant economic resources and trade.

The type of society in Ireland during the Middle and Late Bronze Age is often characterized as a chiefdom, a social formation that is well known from ethnohistorical sources in many parts of the world (Earle 1987). These were hierarchical structures controlled by a central figure, whose power could be both hereditary and ascribed on the basis of certain political, military, economic and even religious responsibilities. They represent a concentration of power that was active in the consolidation of large regional territories. A chiefdom generally had central places of power, which is where an association can be made with Bronze Age hillforts.

Hillforts and chiefdoms

The concept of chiefdoms as a stage in general cultural evolution was first promoted by the American anthropologist, Elman Service (1962). The basic definition is an autonomous political unit that is hierarchically structured, comprised of several communities under the central control of a chief. It is a type of compound society, where previously autonomous villages have been aggregated into a larger territorial grouping. Chiefdoms vary considerably in size and political complexity, and are often categorised as simple, complex or so large and elaborate that they reach a new category called archaic states. They are regional polities that organize a population of a few thousand to tens of thousands of people (Earle 1999: 14). Chiefdoms are stratified societies, distinguished from lower levels of social organization by the presence of a permanent and effective means of political integration involving hierarchical power structures.

Renfrew (1973; 1974) lists 20 distinguishing features of a chiefdom, some of which find expression in archaeological evidence. The chiefdom is distinguished by the presence of centres that coordinate economic, social and religious activities. Chiefdoms are marked by greater population density, and higher levels of productivity and specialization. They have clearly defined territorial boundaries, and an ability to mobilize labour for large-scale monument construction. Those at the top of the social hierarchy are distinguished by dress and possessions, and have special roles in rituals and ceremonies. These individuals are usually related to one another, and often reside in separate communities. It is the nature of chiefdoms that those at the apex are more privileged than the rest of the population, and extract surplus for their own consumption through the exercise of power in various ways; these are the recognizable political strategies of exploitation (Renfrew 1982).

There are many different types of chiefdoms, varying significantly in size, wealth and organizational complexity. In relation to prehistoric Europe, Renfrew made a broad distinction between 'individualising chiefdoms" where personal wealth and a prestige goods economy was the basis of power, and 'group-orientated chiefdoms' with a focus on the construction of public monuments for communal use. The distinction is often made between 'simple' and 'complex' chiefdoms, or what Carneiro (1981) called 'minimal', 'typical' and 'maximal' chiefdoms, the latter approaching early state formation.

Drawing on ethnohistorical parallels (see Earle 1999), the chiefdoms of the Irish Middle and Late Bronze Age are likely to have been small polities associated with a single dominant hillfort. It is difficult to estimate population size, but this may have been in the low thousands for simple chiefdoms, and somewhat greater for complex chiefdoms. This was a politically centralized society, with a stratified structure reflected in a regional settlement hierarchy with higher and lower order settlements. These hillfort chiefdoms were self-sufficient in subsistence agriculture, with an ability to produce food surplus to acquire various commodities and valuable objects by participation in regional exchange networks. They had well defined territorial boundaries, which were defended aggressively when required, and could also be expanded through conquest warfare.

Figure 10.23: Enclosure of Early/Middle Bronze Age settlement (1700–1500 BC) at Ballybrowney Lower, Co. Cork. Upper image: Excavation of Enclosure 1 with internal roundhouse. Lower image: reconstruction of Ballybrowney Lower settlement (source: Digitale Archäologie, courtesy Eamon Cotter and Transport Infrastructure Ireland).

Sources of Power

Earle (1997) observed that a chiefdom society is first and foremost a political formation, created for the benefit of a particular group and sustained by manipulative social strategies. The sources of chiefly power are complex. Earle lists four: 1) social relationships (including kinship); 2) economic power (control of production and exchange; 3) military might, and 4) ideology (a code of social order that establishes an authority structure). He considers that the economy, military power and ideology all played a critical role in the emergence and shaping of these polities.

Chiefdoms are often characterised as kin-based societies, where a person's place in a kinship system determined their social standing and political position. While kinship with its political relationships was a fundamental basis of chiefly power, it is generally underpinned by strong economic foundations. This is where control over production and exchange of subsistence resources and wealth creates the basis for political power. Service (1962) regarded chiefdoms as re-distributional societies, where economic intensification and specialization required some degree of central management to organise the circulation of specialised products. Similar views were expressed by Gilman (1991) to explain the rise of social stratification in Bronze Age Europe, while Carneiro (1970) emphasized the ability of chiefs to manage internal pressures created by population growth and circumstances of resource availability.

Earle (1999) provides the example of the Thy region in Denmark, where the emergence of Bronze Age chiefdoms *c.*2300–1300 BC was linked to an intensification of the export economy based on a shift to intensive cattle herding. The surplus produced made it possible to trade for metal from foreign sources. This gave power to certain individuals who were able to control the specialised production and circulation of bronze. A similar model could be advanced for Middle Bronze Age Ireland, where agricultural intensification coincided with a strong demand for metal. This required the conversion of subsistence-based staple finance to wealth finance, in order to trade for imported metal and some domestic supply in regional exchange networks.

Chiefdoms are generally marked by a centralised accumulation of wealth, used to reward followers and to exercise monopoly over trade. This requires the creation and acquisition of surplus from the subsistence economy, which can be translated into other forms of exchangeable wealth. In modelling the concept of surplus, Earle (1997: 73–4) made a distinction between staple and wealth finance, the former based on subsistence production, while the latter involved the use of valuable objects as political currency. The creation of food surpluses through agricultural intensification provided a means to control the circulation of those luxury goods. This allowed small chiefdoms to participate in long-distance exchange networks, connections that seem to have been important for the maintenance of chiefly power. As Earle observes, 'control over the economy is a direct and material power over the lives of people' (1999: 67). This is a power that comes from voluntary or coercive control of key sectors of the economy.

Chiefdoms are often defined in economic terms, in relation to ecological constraints and demographic pressures that controlled their productive capacity. Recent research suggests that populations grew and declined erratically during the European Bronze Age, in cycles that are not obviously connected to patterns of economic progress. As Kristiansen (1998) observed, the dynamics behind population movements are constantly shifting and the key to understanding them lies in the specific political processes that chiefdoms chose to follow. It is therefore important to understand the historical circumstances at the time of chiefdom formation, but such information is difficult to glean from archaeological sources.

Economic power depends on two other sources of chiefly power: ideology to validate rights of unequal access and social distinction, and military might to create and defend such inequalities. Ideology refers here to a code of social order present in all societies, representing a shared view of the world and the place of people within it, one that supports a structure of political institutions and affirms certain rights and obligations. It can be materialized in different forms, such as the engraved stelae of the Iberian Bronze Age (Harrison 2004), or the weapon panoply of the Bronze Age warrior (Harding 2007). Hillforts are an obvious manifestation of ideology, representing a highly visible symbol of authority in the landscape. Hoarding is another type of ideological control, as is feasting and gift exchange when used as strategies of political power. In some instances religion may have influenced the development of a chiefdom as a theocracy, though Carneiro (1981) suggests its role was more to consolidate these structures than to create them.

In conclusion, in making a case for a multilinear evolutionary approach with different paths to complexity, Earle believes that there is no one critical factor in the rise of chiefdoms. He suggests that 'divergent sources of power exist according to specific historical contexts, and these sources can be put together in infinitely variable ways' (Earle 1999: 13). Once established, the growth of a chiefdom generally involved an increase in the size of that territory and its population, except where constrained by environmental circumstances. This means that the complexity of a chiefdom is related to the size of its territory and population. It can reach the point where a chiefdom is so large that it sub-divides into smaller units under the control of a paramount chief.

Ethnohistorical sources show that most chiefdoms go through cycles of expansion and decline over periods of 150–200 years (Carneiro 1981). Carneiro suggests that chiefdoms grow essentially by an accelerating process of accretion, observing that:

'Once chiefdoms begin to form in a region, the process proceeds rapidly. The military advantage that size alone confers on a society means that even a minimal chiefdom will have a significant edge over its neighbours if they are still independent villages. As a result, it will not be so long before autonomous villages as such will cease to exist. Either they will be defeated by and incorporated into one of the existing chiefdoms or they will join forces with other villages in a defensive alliance, which will itself tend to become a chiefdom' (Carneiro 1981: 66).

This implies that a certain level of coercion was necessary to the growth of any chiefdom, which brings us to the third source of chiefly power.

Hillfort warfare

The continued reluctance of many anthropologists and archaeologists to consider warfare as a driver of social change in prehistory was examined in Chapter 7. This was challenged by Carneiro (1970; 1981), who argued that warfare was a critical element in chiefly power strategies in early societies, where the reputation of a warrior was central to rank and political standing. War was an important outlet for warrior aggression, but as Earle observed, it can be a problematic source of power as it could ultimately bring down the very entities it created. 'Chiefdoms are continually at war and war is a critical element in chiefly power strategies. The power of force rips at the normal fabric, the institutions of society. To be effective as a power of centrality, coercive force must itself be controlled, a difficult task that is achieved by binding the military with economic and ideological tethers' (Earle 1997: 106).

Carneiro highlighted the essentially political nature of multi-community groups formed by the forceful incorporation of villages and other chiefdoms. He recognized that the formation of chiefdoms was not inevitable, and that certain conditions had to exist to turn autonomous villages into chiefdoms. He identified population growth and resource availability as causal factors, in what has become known as the Circumscription Theory. This is where an inability to support a growing population leads to fighting over land and resources, and to the resulting subjugation of villages into larger political entities. Carneiro argues that the aggregation of smaller groups into chiefdoms can only occur through war, either direct coercion or the threat of it. The latter is important as there can be a voluntary side to this aggregation, where villages and other communities come together for mutual protection.

Harrison (2004) suggests that fighting was endemic in the Bronze Age, and that many chiefly families had great difficulty in retaining power for more than a few generations before losing it to usurpers. There were constant threats to the position of chiefs, which often led to conflict and internecine warfare. While chiefs developed different strategies to retain power, involving a combination of force, ideology and economic strength, many Bronze Age chiefdoms may not have lasted much longer than the lifetimes of their founders, certainly if ethnographic sources are any guide.

Military force is, of course, a blunt instrument, and power in many chiefdom societies was probably exercised in a more pragmatic way, designed to achieve consensus across a broad social network. The threat of violence was important to the maintenance of social order, but to have real impact it would need to be exercised on occasion. As discussed in Chapter 9, the military power represented by a hillfort was a significant deterrent, not just against external attack, but also for the maintenance of chiefly power within that society.

Warfare in chiefdoms is often an attempt to control by force the staples and wealth on which a political economy is based (Earle 1999: 110). Disputes among warring chiefdoms can disrupt communications in a significant way that will affect the exchange of prestige goods and control of long-distance trade. For Earle the question still remains as to whether the warfare of chiefdoms represented the political failure of chiefs to organize stable regional systems, or was a successful strategy to build such systems (1999: 109). One of the ways that chiefdoms can emerge is in response to chaos and continuous conflict in society. This creates conditions where local leaders can emerge to positions of authority through offers of protection. Earle states that it is only with the evolution of complex chiefdoms that the nature of warfare changes fundamentally. It is then no longer an outcome of unregulated competition, but becomes a means of conquest, and a way of acquiring wealth by expanding a staple resource base.

10.4 'A Time of Trouble'

'*In the middle of the Bronze Age in Ireland there is a profound breach in continuity, no less real for all that its records, historical and archaeological, are of the vaguest. Nothing short of an overwhelming invasion can explain the facts; an invasion so devastating, that the invaders seemed very gods to the dispossessed, and as gods trod the soil.*' (Macalister 1935: 54).

As in many parts of Europe, the Bronze Age in Ireland was a formative period, when the organization of landscape, settlement, political economy and the structure of society, reached new levels of complexity. This is evident in the rise and fall of regional chiefdoms controlled by powerful individuals and families. These polities were built on a strong agricultural base, the intensification of which during the Middle and Late Bronze Age was partly connected to population growth, but also to a desire to create surplus for exchange purposes. This led to a concentration of wealth in those societies, which is archaeologically visible in the conspicuous consumption of prestige goods of bronze, gold and amber, many of which were obtained through distant trade connections.

The emergence of chiefdom societies in Bronze Age Ireland has generally been thought of in broad economic or social evolutionary terms, with little consideration given to the role of war. The direction of current academic discourse is relevant here, with the post-processual emphasis on the subjectivity of interpretation and the role of human agency. This has led to a largely pacified view of the Bronze Age, where instead of waging war social elites manipulated ideology to maintain economic and political control of their societies, where the symbolic meaning of artifacts were more potent than the terrible reality of their use. While invasionist thinking dominated narratives of the Irish Bronze Age to the 1970s (Waddell 1978; see above quotation from Macalister 1935), research has now moved to another extreme, one that largely ignores the role of warfare in that period.

These Bronze Age societies have long been portrayed by archaeologists as highly stratified, obsessed with personal status and the display of power through material culture. This is largely because of the extraordinarily rich record of prestige metalwork from the period, notably the gold of the Bishopsland and Dowris phases, but also the large number of specialised weapons and ceremonial objects (horns, cauldrons etc). Research in the modern era has linked this extravagant wealth to hillforts, through the excavations at Rathgall, and subsequently at Haughey's Fort and Dún Aonghasa, where important evidence of elite residence was uncovered. These discoveries support the interpretation of hillforts as centres of power in chiefdom societies.

This model of Late Bronze Age society received significant support from an important study of hillforts and settlement landscapes in the North Munster region, conducted in the 1990s by Eoin Grogan for the Discovery Programme. It was the first integrated analysis of hillfort territories in Ireland, and the first to consider the wider societal context of those sites in any detail, taking Mooghaun in south Clare as a major case-study (Grogan 2005a, 2005b). What is now known as the Mooghaun Model presents a three-tier organization of settlement corresponding to different levels of social hierarchy. The hillfort was at the apex of these complex chiefdom polities, occupied by an elite who exercised control over productive resources and a prestige goods economy. These centres represent a higher political structure overlying more local territorial patterns. The latter are represented by hill-top enclosures and lake settlements, occupied by communities of high status who controlled smaller territories. Within each territory there was a population of strong farming communities, based on single family occupation of enclosed farmsteads in the lowland zone (Figure 10.24).

Ginn's research provides an alternative to the social hierarchy approach of the Mooghaun Model. Her study examined domestic settlement patterns for the Middle to Late Bronze Age in Ireland, incorporating older site evidence with new data sources from recent development archaeology. The emphasis is placed on settlement at a local level, taken to represent a largely decentralized society of self-sufficient, autonomous, agricultural settlements dispersed across Ireland. The absence of obvious material wealth in these small farming communities suggests minimal differentiation in socio-economic terms at this level. The study revealed a considerable degree of local and regional variability in the settlement record. Ginn does recognize organization at a higher level, centred on community-based rituals at hillforts and enclosures. The hillfort represents a focus of community relations, 'arenas of exchange at the level of a local group of several hundred people.. where loose alignments were fostered and reformulated through commodity and community trading' (Ginn 2016: 215). While the likely existence of complex centralised societies of the Mooghaun type in some regions is acknowledged, warfare and warrior culture have no place in this study.

The Mooghaun Model continues to be very influential in its representation of chiefdom society and settlement organization. The model does have significant weaknesses, connected to the relative chronology of site and monument distributions in the cultural landscape, the significance of hill-top enclosures, the identification of lower-level settlements, and the relationship of sites such as barrows and *fulachtai fia* to different levels of society (see Ginn 2016: 16–17 for critique). The present study is convinced by many elements of Grogan's analysis, including the territorial approach to hillfort landscapes and the central position of those sites in stratified chiefdom societies.

The present study is influenced by Carneiro's (1970; 1981) view that warfare was a critical factor in the emergence of chiefdom polities in many parts of the world. There must have been many causes of conflict in the Bronze Age, from disputes over land, resources and trade, to personal honour slights and other social infractions. These were often the *casus belli*, but certain systemic factors must also be considered, such as the

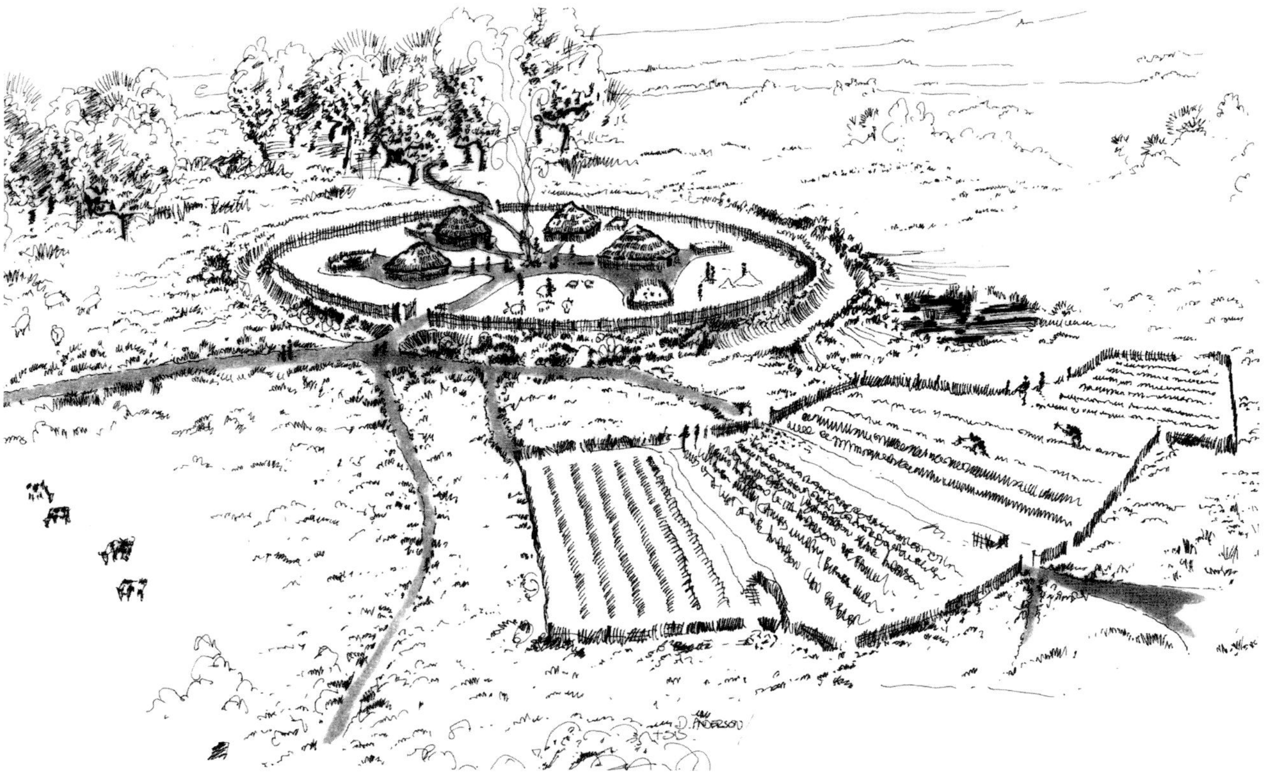

FIGURE 10.24: ARTIST RECONSTRUCTION OF ENCLOSED MIDDLE BRONZE AGE SETTLEMENT (1600–1300 BC) AT SITE A, CHANCELLORSLAND, CO. TIPPERARY (COURTESY MARTIN DOODY AND DONAL ANDERSON).

type of belligerent warrior culture that developed in that period and the aggrandising tendencies of elites. Many Bronze Age chiefdoms grew by accretion, which at times involved aggressive expansion and open warfare. This may have been relatively rare in the Irish Bronze Age, when much conflict was possibly confined to raiding and reprisal, leading to an aggressive defence of territory and an uneasy relationship between neighbouring chiefdoms. The military function was so important that the leaders of these simple and complex chiefdoms must have been warlords. Their power probably stemmed from their personal prowess in combat, but was more broadly based on a complex manipulation of economy, military strength and ideological control, the relative importance of which depended on historical contingencies.

One of the reasons why the visibility of warfare increased significantly in the Bronze Age is because the scale of conflict moved beyond the local and personal, to disputes that involved opposing political forces on an inter-regional level. This type of warfare was both a consequence and a driver of more complex cultural systems. As Haas observed, 'the higher frequency of warfare in states and chiefdoms is not necessarily a product of organizational complexity; rather, the economic and demographic conditions that are conducive to warfare are also conducive to the development of complex, centralised polities' (Haas 2001: 343). Violence was probably an integral part of the power structure of Bronze Age chiefdoms, the threat or reality of which was used to exercise control within those societies, and to protect their territories and resources from external attack.

Archaeological sources do not allow us to easily measure the prevalence of warfare in Bronze Age Ireland, but there is enough evidence in the form of destroyed hillforts and peaks in weapon production, interspersed with periods of sustained economic growth, to suggest these conflicts were frequent, short-lived and intense. The Late Bronze Age, in particular, has always been represented as 'a time of trouble' (Eogan 1964: 293). The underlying prosperity of those societies, as indicated by their material wealth and patterns of stable agricultural settlement, makes it unlikely that warfare was endemic. It did certainly erupt from time to time on different scales, due to a combination of historical circumstances, and political and socio-economic pressures. These conflicts are likely to have been of short duration once those same pressures eased, but also because these societies did not have the resources to sustain warfare over a long period. The enmity between neighbouring chiefdoms may have been eased by political alliances directed against other polities, and by marriage connections and other means. On occasion, this rivalry found expression in raiding, hostage taking and other activities that could escalate into open warfare.

To conclude, while some will see a focus on warfare as excessive, this study challenges current conceptions of hillfort societies in prehistoric Ireland as peaceful, ideologically driven, communities with economic priorities. While there are many layers of meaning, the hillfort phenomenon is another manifestation of the warrior culture that emerged in the Middle and Late Bronze Age, a period marked by cycles of economic expansion and contraction, as competing chiefdoms rose, and then faded. The building and use of Class 2 hillforts c.1400–800 BC may be explained in terms of emergent chiefdoms controlling large territories, where the hillfort was a centre for high-status residence, ceremony and assembly, representing an important visual display of power in the landscape. The use of these centres coincided with a strengthening of regional identities in a competitive political environment. The militarism of that era can be linked to a climate of territorial disputes and competition, where the aggrandizement and ambitions of warlords led to intermittent warfare, often with catastrophic consequences for individual hillfort communities.

The final collapse of hillfort chiefdoms in Ireland around the eighth century BC is not well understood. What emerges is an Iron Age in which there is no distinct hillfort tradition, something that sets Ireland apart from other parts of Europe in the later first millennium BC. While the spectre of Celtic invaders may have disappeared from academic discourse (though not popular culture), it is still possible that warfare played a significant part in the transformation of indigenous societies during that period. However, to quote Professor Macalister again, war on its own is never the full picture…

'*The Sword People had come with an invincible energy, and had subdued the land to themselves. They had established a complete social system, and had built their vast tumuli. But they reckoned without the climate. It was deteriorating annually during the whole time of their occupation, sapping their vitality and reducing them to impotence…The climate had not quite reached its worst when the Iron Men came in their turn.*' (Macalister 1935: 73).

Any archaeologist who has excavated hillforts in Ireland knows exactly how they felt!

Catalogue of Irish Hillforts

Catalogue number: 1
Hillfort name: Aghnahoo
Townland: Termonamonga
County: Tyrone
ITM coordinates: 621947, 880185
RMP number: TY023-016
Topographical position: Ridge
Elevation: 202m OD
Number of enclosing elements: 1 (Class 1)
Total area: 1.29ha
Shape: Circular
References:
Chart, D.A. 1940. *A Preliminary Survey of the Ancient Monuments of Northern Ireland*. Belfast, Stationery Office

Aghnahoo hillfort is positioned at the northeastern end of a hill ridge overlooking the Derg River valley to north. The site has a total footprint of approximately 1.3ha. The bank consists of stone covered in peat and heather and survives well throughout its circuit, although a portion of the perimeter at the northern side has been levelled. An enclosure at the south-west of the hillfort measures approximately 50m in diameter and comprises a collapsed stone wall 1m in height. Chart (1940: 228) notes that this may be an Early Medieval ringfort, as the enclosing elements are not concentric with the hillfort. Surrounding this is another oval bank 5m wide and 0.5m high. This truncates the hillfort bank at the south-west. There are a number of entrance breaks in the hillfort as well as the probably later enclosures to the south-west, although these are unlikely to be original (Chart 1940: 228). At least three rectangular houses are apparent within the interior. Considering the probably multiphase activity at the site, it is impossible to suggest a date for these hut sites.

Catalogue number: 2
Hillfort name: Ahenny
Townland: Ahenny
County: Tipperary
ITM coordinates: 640251, 629079
RMP number: TS079-027
Topographical position: Hill summit/ridge
Elevation: 296m OD
Number of enclosing elements: 1 (Class 1)
Total area: 8.4ha
Shape: Oval
References:
n/a

Ahenny is a contour fort surrounding the summit of a domed hill at the centre of a east–west running escarpment, overlooking the Linguan River and its valley. It is located 3.2km to the east of Curraghadobbin hillfort. Ahenny is univallate and has a total site footprint of 8.4ha. The ramparts survive well at the north and north-west, although the size of the enclosing elements vary considerably in this area. The bank is maximum 5m wide and 1m high and is composed of earth. There is a possible outer ditch at south measuring 1m wide and 0.2m deep. At north-east there is a possible internal ditch. This measures 1.2m wide and 0.9m deep though it is probably a modern feature. At the north, there is an external, V-shaped ditch 0.5m wide and 0.7m deep, with a counter scarp bank 1.4m wide and 0.9m high. The enclosing elements at south have been truncated by a modern road and are destroyed at the east. There are no recorded entrance features or any evidence for internal features on the surface. The southern half of the interior is under mature forestry. A large section of the enclosing elements at the south have been truncated by a forestry road. The northern half of interior is under scrub and bracken growth.

Catalogue number: 3
Hillfort name: Ardamagh
Townland: Ardamagh
County: Cavan
ITM coordinates: 646438, 812875
RMP number: CV016-003
Topographical position: Hill summit/ridge
Elevation: 123m OD
Number of enclosing elements: 1 (Class 1)
Total area: 1.07ha
Shape: Circular
References:
O'Donovan, P. 1995. *Archaeological Inventory of County Cavan*. Dublin, Stationary Office.

Contour fort surrounding the summit of hilltop, overlooking Coppony Lough and tributaries of the Annalee River. The site has a total footprint of approximately 1.1ha. The bank survives well at the north-east and eastern sides, but is otherwise ploughed flat. O'Donovan (1995) describes the enclosing elements as a low, narrow bank with shallow external ditch, although there are no exact measurements available. There are no obvious entrance features recorded or visible on the surface. No evidence for any internal features on the surface. Interior is currently under pasture.

Catalogue number: 4
Hillfort name: Ballincurra
Townland: Ballincurra
County: Tipperary
ITM coordinates: 192410, 169800
RMP number: TN027-140001
Topographical position: Hill summit
Elevation: 404m OD
Number of enclosing elements: 1 (Class 1)
Total area: 1.13ha
Shape: Oval
References:
Farrelly, J. and O'Brien, C. 2002. *Archaeological Inventory of County Tipperary Vol. 1: North Tipperary*. Dublin, Stationary Office.

Ballincurra is a univallate contour fort surrounding the domed summit of a mountain at the northern edge of the Silvermines Mountain range. Knockadiggeen hillfort is visible 1.4km to north-east. Ballincurra hillfort has a total footprint of approximately 1.1ha. It is univallate for the entire circuit. The enclosing elements survive best at north-east, where they comprise an earthen bank approximately 0.69m high and 1.8m wide, with a V-shaped external ditch approximately 3m wide, and 0.5m deep. There are no recorded entrance features. There is a heather covered cairn near the centre of the hillfort. This measures 18m in diameter and 2.2m in maximum height, and is positioned at the highest point of the interior. Commercial forestry plantation covers approximately two thirds of the hillfort. The remainder is under dense heather growth.

Catalogue number: 5
Hillfort name: Ballinkillin
Townland: Ballinkillin
County: Carlow
ITM coordinates: 672174, 656293
RMP number: CW019-027
Topographical position: Hill summit
Elevation: 149m OD
Number of enclosing elements: 2 (Class 2 possible)
Total area: 5.47ha
Shape: Sub-rectangular
References:
n/a

Sub-rectangular contour fort enclosing the flat summit of Ballinkillin Hill which is located on the southern summit of a north–south running ridge. There are panoramic views from the summit. The Barrow River is highly visible to the west and south. This hillfort has a total site footprint of 5.5ha. It comprises two earthen banks with an intervening ditch and is best preserved at the north-west. The outer bank is levelled through most of its length but is extant in the west and north-west and visible as a vegetation mark in the east. This suggests it may have originally formed a complete circuit. The interior of the site has recently been graded. No evidence for any entrance features. No evidence for internal features on the surface.

Catalogue number: 6
Hillfort name: Ballybreen
Townland: Ballybreen
County: Clare
ITM coordinates: 517053, 692638
RMP number: CL016-004
Topographical position: Hill summit/ridge
Elevation: 143m OD
Number of enclosing elements: 1 (Class 1)
Total area: 1.12ha
Shape: Oval
References:
n/a

Contour fort located on summit of Doon Hill near the village of Kilfenora. The site is univallate, with an approximate footprint of 1.1ha. The bank survives well throughout its circuit. Aerial photographs suggest the bank measures approximately 15m in width. An external ditch is apparent at the south-west, west and north-west. It likely extended for the full circuit of the rampart and has a maximum width of 17m. Simple entrance break in the enclosing elements recorded in the second edition Ordnance Survey maps. This is probably not original. No evidence for any internal features on the surface. The interior is overgrown with scrub and light tree cover.

Catalogue number: 7
Hillfort name: Ballybuckley
Townland: Ballybuckley
County: Wexford
ITM coordinates: 694900, 633424
RMP number: WX025-034
Topographical position: Hill summit
Elevation: 92m OD
Number of enclosing elements: 1 (Class 1)
Total area: 1.77ha
Shape: Circular
References:
Moore, M. 1996. *Archaeological Inventory of County Wexford.* Dublin, Stationary Office.

Ballybuckley is a circular contour fort surrounding the summit of Ballybuckley Hill (Figure 11.1). There are excellent views from summit, and particularly good visibility of the Slaney River to north-east, east and south-east. The enclosing elements form a complete circuit and have a total footprint of 1.8ha. The bank survives well throughout its circuit, although there is some partial destruction of the northern section which has been replaced by a modern field bank. The earthen bank measure approximately 11m in maximum width and 1m in maximum height. There is no evidence for a ditch. Three breaks in the enclosing elements are likely to be modern gaps. No evidence for any internal features on the surface. The interior is under pasture and is divided by a later field boundary.

Catalogue number: 8
Hillfort name: Ballycurragh
Townland: Ballycurragh
County: Offaly
ITM coordinates: 614177, 697994
RMP number: OF039-037
Topographical position: Hill slope
Elevation: 143m OD
Number of enclosing elements: 2 (Class 2 likely)
Total area: 4.91ha
Shape: Circular
References:
O'Brien, C. and Sweetman, D. 1997. *Archaeological Inventory of County Offaly*. Dublin, Stationary Office.

Circular multiple enclosure positioned in upland terrain on gently sloping western facing hillslope, overlooking Fuarawn River to west and south (Figure 11.2). The site has a total footprint of approximately 4.9ha. The site is bivallate for the entire circuit with widely spaced enclosing elements separated on average 45m apart. The inner enclosing elements comprise an earthen bank up to 3.5m in external height. The outer bank is approximately 4m wide and up to 4m in external height. The south-east sections of inner and outer enclosing elements are destroyed and the outer bank is quarried at south. There is light tree cover over the enclosing elements, though the interior is largely under pasture. No evidence for any entrance features or internal features visible on the surface.

Figure 11.1: Ballybuckley hillfort, Co. Wexford (Source: Google Earth 2017).

Figure 11.2: Ballycurragh hillfort, Co. Offaly (Source: Google Earth 2017).

Catalogue number: 9
Hillfort name: Ballylin
Townland: Ballylin
County: Limerick
ITM coordinates: 525748, 639522
RMP number: LI028-085
Topographical position: Hilltop
Elevation: 243m OD
Number of enclosing elements: 2 (Class 2 confirmed)
Total area: 20.5ha
Shape: Circular
References:
Cody, E. 1980. A hillfort at Ballylin, county Limerick, with a note on Mooghaun, County Clare. *Journal of the Royal Society of Antiquaries of Ireland* 111: 70–80.

O'Brien, W., Hogan, N. and O'Driscoll, J. 2016. Archaeological investigations at Ballylin hillfort, Co. Limerick. *Journal of the North Munster Archaeological Society* 56. 1–56.

Widely spaced multiple enclosure in commanding position on Ballylin Hill which is positioned on a partial spur in a north–south running escarpment. This provides panoramic views of the Limerick plains and Shannon estuary to the north, east and south. Ballylin is 20.5ha in size. It is bivallate with a slight in-turned entrance at the east side of the inner enclosure. There are two other breaks in the inner enclosure at the north-east and west. There are no obvious corresponding breaks in the outer enclosure. There is no evidence for any internal features on the surface. The enclosing elements survive well throughout much of its circuit, however, they are heavily overgrown in places and are under approximately 0.3m of peat. Excavation revealed that the inner enclosure comprised an internal bank with an external, partially rock-cut ditch and counter-scarp bank. The external enclosure consisted of an internal bank and ditch of slighter proportions than the inner example. Geophysical survey has identified a scattered distribution of possible pit features within the inner enclosing elements at the east. Late Bronze Age dates from basal fill of inner enclosing ditch (Chapter 4).

Catalogue number: 10
Hillfort name: Ballymacmurragh
Townland: Cumber Lower/Clonlee/ Ballymacmurragh
County: Offaly
ITM coordinates: 618816, 639522
RMP number: OF039-012
Topographical position: Hilltop
Elevation: 143m OD
Number of enclosing elements: 2 (Class 1)
Total area: 1.03ha
Shape: Circular
References:
O'Brien, C. and Sweetman, D. 1997. *Archaeological Inventory of County Offaly*. Dublin, Stationary Office.

Ballymacmurragh is a circular contour fort 1ha in size, in a commanding position surrounding the summit of a steep hilltop at the eastern edge of Slieve Bloom Mountains. It is strategically positioned overlooking tributaries of the Camcor River and is positioned 1.9km to the south-west of Cumber Lower hillfort. Ballymacmurragh has two closely spaced earthen banks with intervening and external ditches. The inner bank measures 1.1m wide and 1m in external height (0.4m internal height) and the outer bank measures approximately 3m wide and 1m in external height. The intervening ditch is 1m wide and the external ditch is 0.5m wide. The interior is covered in scrub. There is a possible original entrance at west-north-west comprising a simple gap and rectangular hut at the southwestern side of the interior.

Catalogue number: 11
Hillfort name: Belmont
Townland: Belmont
County: Galway
ITM coordinates: 535500, 763389
RMP number: GA015-016
Topographical position: Hilltop
Elevation: 92m OD
Number of enclosing elements: 2 (Class 1)
Total area: 2.03ha
Shape: Sub-circular
References:
Raftery, B. 1976-7. The hillfort at Belmont in Co. Galway. *Journal of the Galway Archaeological and Historical Society* 35: 89–95.
Alcock, O., de hÓra, K. and Gosling, P. 1995. *Archaeological Inventory of County Galway Vol. 2: North Galway*. Dublin, Stationary Office.

Contour fort in a commanding position surrounding the domed summit of Belmont Hill, overlooking tributary of River Clare to east (Figure 11.3). Belmont is a sub-circular hillfort defined by two closely spaced ramparts and external ditches. It has a total footprint of approximately 2ha. The internal bank survives well throughout and measures approximately 5m wide and 1m high with some evidence for internal stone facing at the east. The external ditch is flat bottomed, 5m wide and 0.5m wide at its base. There are the possible remains of a second bank and ditch immediately outside these enclosing elements, though these are truncated by a modern stone wall. There are two simple gaps in the enclosing elements at the south and north-west, however, Raftery (1976: 90–91) suggests that the break at the north-west is not original. Modern graveyard positioned at the centre of the hillfort. No evidence for any internal features on the surface that might be contemporary with the fort.

Catalogue number: 12
Hillfort name: Boley
Townland: Boley
County: Laois
ITM coordinates: 661408, 686287
RMP number: LA025-027001
Topographical position: Hilltop/edge of ridge
Elevation: 222m OD
Number of enclosing elements: 2 (Class 2 possible)
Total area: 28.12ha
Shape: Circular
References:
Sweetman, D., Alcock, O. and Moran, B. 1995. *Archaeological Inventory of County Laois*. Dublin, Stationary Office.

Large multiple enclosure surrounding the domed summit of Boley Hill, on the northeastern edge of the Castlecomber Hills. The site has widely spaced enclosing elements with a total footprint of approximately 28.1ha. The inner enclosure survives well throughout its circuit, however, it is covered in trees and gorse. It comprises a bank with an external ditch. A natural spring is located in the ditch of the inner enclosing elements at the east. The outer enclosing element survives as a curving field boundary in the west. This is concentric with the inner enclosing element. The remainder is likely to have been destroyed. There is a simple break in the south-west of the inner enclosing elements. No obvious break in the outer bank that might represent an original entrance. There is no evidence for any internal features on the surface within the hillfort. The interior is currently under pasture, with partial tree cover within the inner enclosure.

Catalogue number: 13
Hillfort name: Brandon Hill
Townland: Brandon Hill
County: Kilkenny
ITM coordinates: 669749, 639677
RMP number: KK033-008001
Topographical position: Hill slope
Elevation: 393m OD
Number of enclosing elements: 1 (Class 1)
Total area: 1.93ha
Shape: Sub-oval
References:
n/a

Hill slope fort positioned on severe west-south-west facing slopes of Brandon Hill, overlooking the source of the Ciodiagh River and a U-shaped glen formed by the mountain. The site is visible as a vegetation mark on aerial photographs. It is sub-oval in shape and occupies an area of 1.9ha. The enclosing elements have not been recorded, although they appear to be comprised of a single bank of stone with no apparent ditch. There is no recorded entrance features. There is a cairn within the hillfort to the east. There is no evidence for other internal features on the surface.

Catalogue number: 14
Hillfort name: Brodullagh South
Townland: Brodullagh South/Kinlough
County: Mayo
ITM coordinates: 525370, 751418
RMP number: MA123-041001
Topographical position: Hill summit
Elevation: 53m OD
Number of enclosing elements: 1 (Class 1)
Total area: 2.35ha
Shape: Circular
References:
n/a

Contour fort on southern shoulder of hilltop, surrounding the summit and overlooking the Black River to the east (Figure 11.4). The hillfort has a total footprint of approximately 2.3ha. Enclosing elements survives well throughout its circuit and consists of a circular stone bank, on average 12m in width and measuring approximately 180m in diameter. There is no indication of an associated ditch. Ordnance Survey mapping indicates three gaps in the bank to the north, east and west. It cannot be determined if these are original or later features. A possible hut structure was recorded within the interior. No other information relating to this structure is available. At the centre of the site, a circular mound of stones is apparent. This is not depicted in the historic mapping and may be modern. The maps do, however, suggest the presence of another enclosing element surrounding the centre of the interior, measuring approximately 70m in diameter. It is likely that this is a Medieval feature and its destruction may be connected to the appearance of the central mound of stone. Some tree cover on northern of side of the interior.

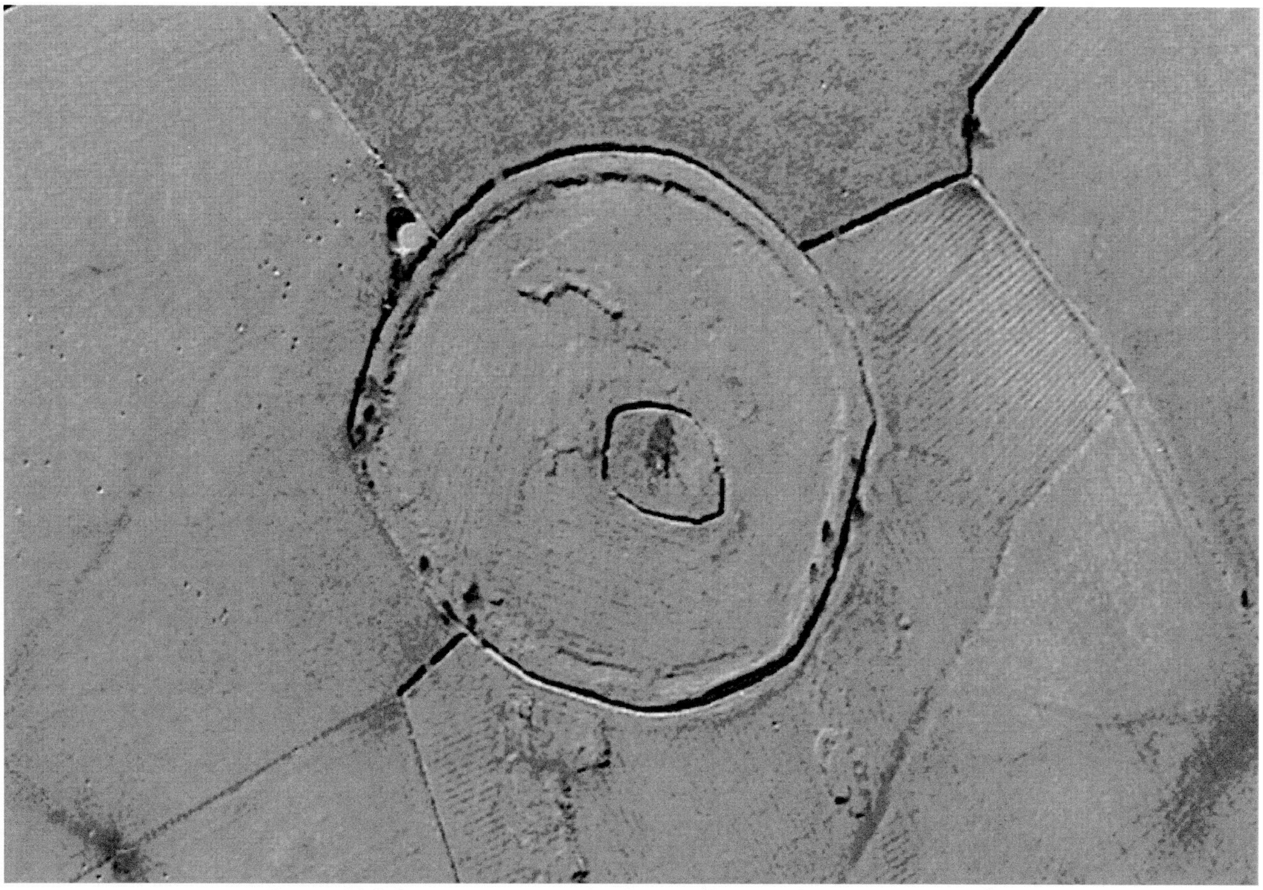

Figure 11.3: Belmont hillfort, Co. Galway (Source: Google Earth 2017).

Figure 11.4: The hillfort at Brodullagh South, Co. Mayo (Source: Google Earth 2017).

Catalogue number: 15
Hillfort name: Brusselstown Ring
Townland: Brusselstown
County: Wicklow
ITM coordinates: 692948, 691138
RMP number: WI027-018
Topographical position: Hilltop
Elevation: 402m OD
Number of enclosing elements: 2 (Class 2 likely)
Total area: 32.43ha
Shape: Oval
References:

Condit, T. 1992. Ireland's hillfort capital: Baltinglass, Co. Wicklow. *Archaeology Ireland* 6 (3): 16–20.

Grogan, E. and Kilfeather, A. 1997. *Archaeological Inventory of County Wicklow*. Dublin, Stationary Office.

Condit, T. 1998. Observations of the Baltinglass hillfort complex. In Corlett, C. and O'Sullivan, A. (eds), *Wicklow Archaeology and History* 1: 9–25.

Multiple enclosure surrounding the south-eastern summit of Spinans Hill at the south-west edge of the Wicklow Mountains, with panoramic views. Brusselstown Ring is one of nine forts comprising the Baltinglass hillfort group. It has a total footprint of 32.43ha making it one of the largest hillforts in Ireland. The inner enclosing elements form a complete circuit and survive almost intact. It comprises a stone bank approximately 12m wide and 1m high. There are four possible entrances comprising simple breaks in the inner bank at the north, east, south and west. The outer rampart has been damaged at the south-west but likely formed a complete circuit. It is currently covered by grass and heather but comprises a stone bank about 10m wide and up to 1.3m in height. There are no apparent entrance features in the outer enclosure. Two structures have been recorded within the inner enclosure and twenty three structures between the inner and outer defences (Grogan and Kilfeather 1997: 41). GPS survey (this volume) revealed an estimated 250 additional circular structures within the hillfort. The interior is mainly under pasture with pockets of scrub and gorse (Chapter 4).

Catalogue number: 16
Hillfort name: Caherconree
Townland: Ballyarkane Oughter
County: Kerry
ITM coordinates: 472643, 606700
RMP number: KE046-003
Topographical position: Hill spur
Elevation: 659m OD
Number of enclosing elements: 2 (Class 3)
Total area: 1.22ha
Shape: Triangular
References:

Lynch, P. 1899. Caherconree, Co. Kerry. *Journal of the Royal Society of Antiquaries of Ireland* 9: 5–17.

Lynch, P. 1910. A relic of Caherconree. *Journal of the Royal Society of Antiquaries of Ireland* 20: 357–360.

Caherconree is a high altitude inland promontory fort positioned on a western facing triangular spur off the summit of Caherconree Mountain in Co. Kerry (Figure 11.5). The enclosing elements are possibly bivallate and cut off the eastern approach. The remainder of the fort is protected by steep natural cliff edge at the north, west and south. The inner enclosing element survives as a drystone wall of Old Red Sandstone blocks. It is 110m long and survives best at the centre, measuring 3m in maximum height and 4.5m wide. An internal wall-walk is apparent throughout most of its length and comprises three steps surviving in good condition. A possible outer enclosure comprises a low bank and outer ditch 8–10m outside the inner example. Lynch (1899: 12–17) noted that the bank originally extended the full width of the promontory, however, only a small section to the north is visible today. Two possible original entrances are visible in the inner enclosing element at the north-east. No evidence for any internal features on the surface, although deep peat deposits may obscure possible activity. Five circular structures abut the interior and exterior of the inner enclosing wall. A possible stone trough was found in the interior (Lynch 1910).

Catalogue number: 17
Hillfort name: Caherdrinny
Townland: Caherdrinny
County: Cork
ITM coordinates: 579671, 607836
RMP number: CO019-097003
Topographical position: Hilltop
Elevation: 210m OD
Number of enclosing elements: 2 (Class 2 possible)
Total area: 12.59ha
Shape: Oval
References:
Doody, M. 2008. *The Ballyhoura Hills Project.* Bray, Wordwell.

Located near the town of Fermoy, an oval contour fort 12.5ha in size is positioned on an isolated hill overlooking the Blackwater River valley to the south and Fushion River valley to the north (Figure 11.6). The enclosing elements are partially preserved as two closely spaced banks with stepped profiles. The banks comprise a dump construction with external stone facing, built on and partially cut into a natural scarp. The defences are largely destroyed to the east. There are two possible entrance breaks at the north-west and south-west. The northwestern entrance comprises a simple 1.5m wide gap in the defences. The south-western entrance consists of a 6m wide gap through the enclosing elements. Three other breaks are likely to be later additions. Topographical survey by The Discovery Programme identified 14 hut structures within the interior to the north (Doody 2008). A ruined Medieval castle surrounded by an enclosure of unknown date is positioned at centre of the hillfort. The interior is under a mixture of pasture and gorse, the latter being particularly visible at the north and west.

Catalogue number: 18
Hillfort name: Cannakill/ Oldcroghan
Townland: Cannakill
County: Offaly
ITM coordinates: 647970, 733187
RMP number: OF010-004009
Topographical position: Hilltop
Elevation: 217m OD
Number of enclosing elements: 1 (Class 1)
Total area: 15.06ha
Shape: Oval
References:
n/a

Univallate contour fort in commanding location at summit of hill with panoramic views from the summit. The enclosing elements are almost completely destroyed, but are visible as a low-rise, oval shaped earthwork surrounding the domed summit of the interior. This bank measures up to 11m wide. There are no recorded entrance features or obvious breaks visible in the aerial or satellite imagery. There are no obvious internal features that might be contemporary with the hillfort. A number of prehistoric wooden trackways recorded near the hillfort to the east, north-east and north could have been connected to the hillfort. A church, graveyard and graveslabs are apparent in the interior. A gently sloping flat-topped mound is positioned at the highest point of the interior. This measures 30m in diameter and is 4m in maximum height. Two other mounds have been recorded at the base of the hilltop to the south. There have been no archaeological investigations of this hillfort.

Catalogue number: 19
Hillfort name: Carn Tigherna
Townland: Corrin Hill
County: Cork
ITM coordinates: 580624, 595936
RMP number: CO035-049001
Topographical position: Hilltop/spur
Elevation: 219m OD
Number of enclosing elements: 2 (Class 2 likely)
Total area: 5.28ha
Shape: Oval
References:
Borlase, W. 1897. *The Dolmens of Ireland.* London, Chapman and Hall Ltd.
Doody, M. 2008. *The Ballyhoura Hills Project.* Bray, Wordwell.

Carn Tigherna is an oval multiple enclosure 5.3ha in size (Figure 11.7). It is in a commanding position, overlooking the Blackwater and Bride River valleys at the eastern edge of the Nagle Mountains. The fort is bivallate with additional earthworks at the entrance in the west-north-west. The inner enclosure consists of a dump stone bank, 1.6m in maximum height with no obvious ditch. The outer enclosing element is best preserved to the west-south-west and is of similar composition. The additional earthworks at the entrance comprise 2–3 earthen banks with external ditches. A large cairn is positioned at the highest point in the interior. A Food Vessel burial was recovered after removal of some of the cairn in 1832 (Borlase 1897: 13). No evidence for other internal features on the surface. The Discovery Programme undertook an earthwork survey at the monument (Doody 2008).

Figure 11.5: Caherconree hillfort, Co. Kerry.

Figure 11.6: Caherdrinny hillfort, Co. Cork (Source: Google Earth 2017).

Catalogue number: 20
Hillfort name: Carrowgarve
Townland: Carrowgarve
County: Roscommon
ITM coordinates: 572903, 778152
RMP number: RO027-014001
Topographical position: Hilltop
Elevation: 152m OD
Number of enclosing elements: 1 (Class 1)
Total area: 3.48ha
Shape: Oval
References:
n/a

Oval contour fort surrounding domed summit and northwestern facing slopes of Mewlaghadooey Hill, overlooking Castleray town, as well as the Francis River and its tributaries to north-west. Univallate for its entire circuit with a total footprint of 3.5ha. Ramparts partially survive at western side as a low-rise bank measuring 0.1m high and 6m wide with a low scarp to the east. The remainder of the hillfort is visible as a vegetation mark on aerial photographs. There are no recorded entrance features. A large bowl barrow and ring-barrow are visible within the interior. A second-ring barrow is positioned on the enclosing elements at the south-east. The interior is currently under pasture.

Catalogue number: 21
Hillfort name: Carrownarush
Townland: Carrownarush
County: Sligo
ITM coordinates: 542674, 835047
RMP number: SL012-008001
Topographical position: Hilltop/edge of ridge
Elevation: 82m OD
Number of enclosing elements: 2 (Class 2 possible)
Total area: 1.56ha
Shape: Circular
References:
n/a

Contour fort at summit of hilltop at northeastern edge of steep slope, overlooking Sligo coastline with panoramic views from the summit (Figure 11.8). The hillfort is approximately 1.6ha in total size and comprises two closely set banks with an intervening ditch. The inner bank is largely destroyed and is best preserved at the north-west, measuring 4.5m wide. The intervening ditch measures 4m wide and up to 1.75m deep. The outer bank is approximately 7m wide and 1.4m wide. There is some scrub growth on these enclosure elements. There are also remnants of a possible second external ditch. A large enclosure at the centre of the hillfort is visible in aerial and satellite images. If contemporary, the hillfort may be more appropriately classed as a Class 2 example. A Napoleonic era signal tower at highest point within the interior.

Catalogue number: 22
Hillfort name: Carrowntemple/Knockacarrigeen
Townland: Carrowntemple
County: Galway
ITM coordinates: 537801, 748825
RMP number: GA043-033006
Topographical position: Hilltop
Elevation: 101m OD
Number of enclosing elements: 1 (Class 1)
Total area: 4.85ha
Shape: Oval
References:
Carey, A. 2002. Excavations at Knockacarrigeen Hill, Tuam Co. Galway. *Journal of the Galway Archaeological and Historical Society* 54: 55–71.

Oval hill slope fort of approximately 4.8ha, enclosing an area surrounding the summit and southern slopes of Knockacarrigeen Hill, overlooking low-lying terrain to the north, east and south. Knockacarrigeen is univallate and there are no recorded entrance features. The rampart survives as a rubble stone bank and is extant for much of its circuit. It is best preserved at the south and west where it is 1m in maximum height. Two cairns and an Early Medieval ringfort are located at the north of the interior. Excavation has revealed a small elongated stone enclosure within the interior, dated to the Neolithic/Early Bronze Age (Carey 2002). Much of the hillfort is under heavy gorse and scrub growth and a modern water reservoir was built at its summit in recent times. Although there were subsequent excavations by Carey (2002) in 1994, no radiocarbon dates relating to the construction of the hillfort were retrieved. Dates obtained from a small stone-built enclosure inside the hillfort indicate occupation during the Neolithic to Early Bronze Age.

Catalogue number: 23
Hillfort name: Carrowreagh/Grainán of Aileach
Townland: Carrowreagh
County: Donegal
ITM coordinates: 636598, 919735
RMP number: DG047-012005
Topographical position: Hilltop
Elevation: 241m OD
Number of enclosing elements: 3 (Class 2 possible)
Total area: 2.55ha
Shape: Oval
References:
Colby, T. 1837. *Ordnance Survey of Ireland, County of Derry, Vol. 1*. Dublin.

Multiple enclosure in commanding position at domed summit of Greenan Mountain, overlooking Lough Swilly. The site has a total footprint of approximately 2.6ha. Ramparts comprise low-rise earthen banks covered in heather. There are possible external ditches associated with the inner and external bank and a possible internal ditch with the middle enclosing element. The middle defences are not apparent at the south-east, but probably formed a complete circuit. There are no obvious entrance features within the interior. No features that might be contemporary with the hillfort are visible within the interior of the site. However, a substantial Early Medieval ringfort is positioned at the centre of the hillfort. This has been identified as the site of Aileach, the Early Medieval seat of the northern Uí Néill. This was surveyed by Petrie in 1835 (Colby 1837). A cairn and holy well are positioned between the inner and middle enclosing elements. The interior is covered in scrub and heather.

Catalogue number: 24
Hillfort name: Castle Gale
Townland: Darragh More
County: Limerick
ITM coordinates: 572098, 616003
RMP number: LI059-001
Topographical position: Hill spur
Elevation: 319m OD
Number of enclosing elements: 2 (Class 3)
Total area: 1.4ha
Shape: Triangular
References:
Doody, M. 2008. *The Ballyhoura Hills Project*. Bray, Wordwell.

Castle Gale is an inland promontory fort positioned on a north-facing triangular hill spur with panoramic views (Figure 11.9). The interior slopes from north to south and a steep drop at the northern side forms a natural defensive barrier. These defences are augmented with a bank and ditch approximately 10m from this cliff face. On the southern side, two closely spaced enclosing elements comprising a bank-ditch-bank-ditch arrangement form the defensive elements. A topographic survey by The Discovery Programme (Doody 2008) revealed that the banks consisted of earth and stone. There were two recorded entrances, one on the northern side and another at the south. At the highest point of the interior a small cairn is apparent, however, this has been disturbed in modern times with a trigonometrical station positioned on top. The interior is under dense heather and gorse growth.

Catalogue number: 25
Hillfort name: Claraghatlea
Townland: Claraghatlea South
County: Cork
ITM coordinates: 524973, 589149
RMP number: CO039-052002
Topographical position: Hilltop
Elevation: 452m OD
Number of enclosing elements: 1 (Class 1)
Total area: 1.05ha
Shape: Oval
References:
n/a

Contour fort positioned at the summit of the Claragh Mountain, overlooking the town of Millstreet. The oval enclosing element measures 122m in diameter and comprises a single bank of loose stone with no discernible ditch. This is best preserved at the north-north-east where it measures up to 6m wide and 0.6m high. It occupies a total area of 1.05ha. There is a possible original entrance at the west-north-west comprising a simple 8m wide break in the enclosing elements. Up to four breaks in the bank have been created in recent years. Near the centre of the interior, a sub-rectangular enclosure, 19m east–west, 14m north–south, is defined by a setting of stones. A cairn, 8m in diameter and 0.5m in maximum height is incorporated into the western section of the hillfort bank. Peat cutting at summit suggest an even blanket of peat approximately 0.2m in depth over the interior of the hillfort.

Catalogue number: 26
Hillfort name: Clashanimud
Townland: Clashanimud
County: Cork
ITM coordinates: 524973, 589149
RMP number: CO096-034
Topographical position: Hilltop
Elevation: 177m OD
Number of enclosing elements: 2 (Class 2 confirmed)
Total area: 8.51ha
Shape: Oval
References:
O'Brien, W. 2016b. Language shift and political context in Bronze Age Ireland: some implications of hillfort chronology. In John Koch and Barry Cunliffe (eds), *Celtic from the West 3: Atlantic Europe in the Metal Ages*: 219–246. Oxford, Oxbow Books.

Enclosing a hilltop on a partial spur in an east–west running ridge, Clashanimud is an oval bivallate multiple enclosure, 8.51ha in total size. The ramparts survive well throughout their circuits. The inner enclosing elements comprise a bank with external ditch and a low counterscarp bank. Excavation revealed that the main bank had exterior stone facing and was reveted on the inside by a timber fence. The remains of a timber palisade was identified at the crest of the bank. Stone quarrying near the inner enclosure to the west has partially destroyed the defences. The outer enclosure is incorporated into a modern field system. Excavation revealed it consisted of an earthen bank with a light timber fence and an external rock-cut ditch. An original entrance to the east comprises a simple 3–4m wide gap and excavations reveal evidence for a possible gate. No evidence for internal features has been identified. Excavations by O'Brien (2016b: 219–222) in 2004–2006 recovered a stone axe and a whetstone from the interior (Chapter 3). Geophysical survey was undertaken prior to the excavation. Late Bronze Age dates from excavation of ditch deposits and palisade features associated with enclosing elements.

Catalogue number: 27
Hillfort name: Clomantagh
Townland: Clomantagh
County: Kilkenny
ITM coordinates: 633212, 665532
RMP number: KK008-124002
Topographical position: Hilltop
Elevation: 349m OD
Number of enclosing elements: 1 (Class 1)
Total area: 3.24ha
Shape: Circular
References:
Manning, C. 1985. Prehistoric sites in the neighbourhood of Ardcroney. *Eile: Journal of the Roscrea Heritage Society* 2: 43–55.

Clomantagh is a circular contour fort surrounding the domed summit of Mount Garret which overlooks the town of Urlinford to the south-west and an east–west gap in the Slieveardagh Hills to the east (Figure 11.10). It is univallate with the enclosing elements surviving as a low rise earth and stone bank with evidence for external stone facing. The hillfort has a total site footprint of approximately 3.2ha. There are no recorded entrance features or obvious breaks in the enclosing elements. The remains of a probable megalithic structure is positioned at the highest point of the interior. Manning (1985: 53) suggests that this may be a possible Linkardstown-type burial. There are no other apparent surface features.

Catalogue number: 28
Hillfort name: Clopook
Townland: Clopook
County: Laois
ITM coordinates: 658387, 690736
RMP number: LA019-021001
Topographical position: Hilltop
Elevation: 193m OD
Number of enclosing elements: 1 (Class 1)
Total area: 1.71ha
Shape: Sub-circular
References:
Byrne, D. 1852. On the duns of Cloch-an-Phuca and Log-an-Chorain. *Transactions of the Kilkenny Archaeological Society* 1 (3): 298–300.
Sweetman, D., Alcock, O. and Moran, B. 1995. *Archaeological Inventory of County Laois*. Dublin, Stationary Office.

Clopook is a univallate contour fort located on top of a prominent rock outcrop with panoramic views from the summit. The site has a total footprint of 1.7ha. The enclosing elements comprise a bank, mostly of stone, with no evidence for an associated ditch. This measures up to 7m wide and 1.75m high. Grogan (2005b: 114) has identifed a possible outer enclosure but this has not been confirmed as being related to the hillfort. There is a simple entrance gap at the west and an eastern entrance with outworks. Here, there is a small outer bank immediately outside the main enclosing elements at the east, with a corresponding entrance gap acting like a barbican or defensive earthwork protecting the entrance into the interior (Sweetman *et al.* 1995: 17). A third bank abuts the exterior of the latter around the entrance gap. There is a possible hut structure recorded within the interior. A possible high Medieval tower house was identified within the interior at the east.

FIGURE 11.7: CARN TIGHERNA HILLFORT, CO. CORK.

FIGURE 11.8: CARROWNARUSH HILLFORT, CO. SLIGO (SOURCE: GOOGLE EARTH 2017).

Figure 11.9: Castle Gale hillfort, Co. Limerick.

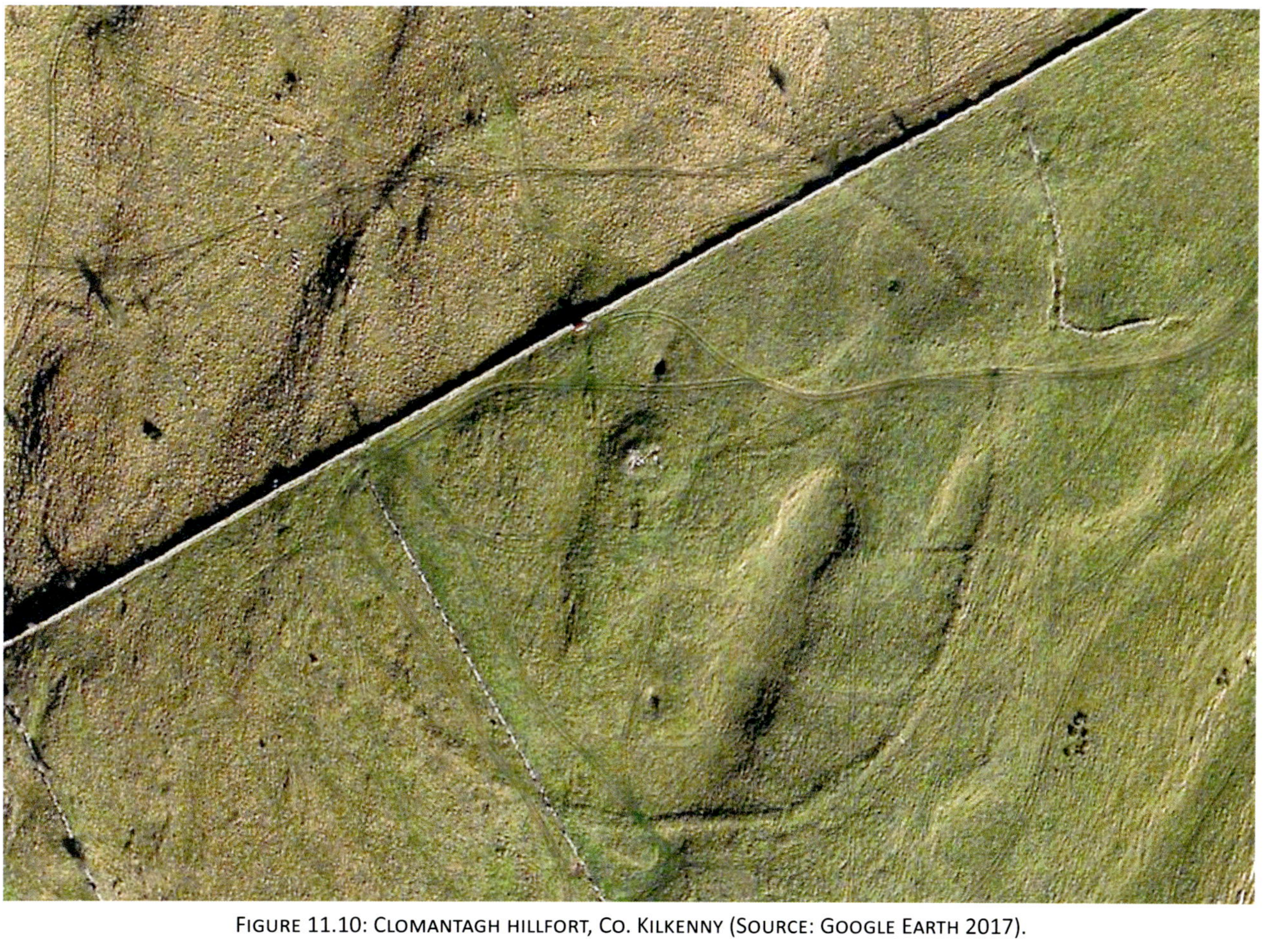

Figure 11.10: Clomantagh hillfort, Co. Kilkenny (Source: Google Earth 2017).

Catalogue number: 29
Hillfort name: Cluttahina
Townland: Cluttahina
County: Waterford
ITM coordinates: 658387, 690736
RMP number: WA021-008001
Topographical position: Hilltop/edge of ridge
Elevation: 143m OD
Number of enclosing elements: 1 (Class 1)
Total area: 12.58ha
Shape: Circular
References:
n/a

Cluttahina is a circular contour fort with a total site footprint of approximately 12.6ha. It is located on the summit and western slopes of a hill spur overlooking the Glenshelane River and valley to the immediate west. There is a possible bivallate Early Medieval ringfort at the centre of hillfort with an associated souterrain. The enclosing elements of the hillfort are on average 120m from the Early medieval enclosure and are visible in some aerial photographs as a vegetation mark. This enclosure was identified by the author and is most apparent in the 2005 Ordnance Survey aerial photographs. There are no obvious entrance features or any evidence for internal features on the surface.

Catalogue number: 30
Hillfort name: Commons of Lloyd
Townland: Commons of Lloyd
County: Meath
ITM coordinates: 672245, 776506
RMP number: ME016-054
Topographical position: Hilltop
Elevation: 129m OD
Number of enclosing elements: 3 (Class 3 confirmed)
Total area: 9.31ha
Shape: Oval
References:
Neary, P. 2004. *Archaeological excavations at Commons of Lloyd, Co. Meath.* Final Unpublished Report, prepared by Neary Archaeology Ltd.

Near the town of Kells, an oval multiple enclosure of approximately 9.3ha is located on a low, conical hill overlooking the River Blackwater. The hillfort is trivallate for its entire circuit with no recorded entrance features. The inner and middle enclosing elements are heavily truncated by later agricultural activity. These are visible on aerial photographs as vegetation marks. The defences are closely spaced at the south-west and west (separated by a minimum of 10m) and become widely spaced to the east (separated by up to 86m). The outer ramparts are integrated into a field system. There is no evidence for internal features that might be contemporary with the construction or occupation of the hillfort. Limited excavations by Neary (2004) prior to development of the interior. There is no dating evidence for the construction of the hillfort. Unpublished geophysical survey by The Discovery Programme in 2013. The area is mentioned in the Early Medieval text, 'The Táin', as being the site of a temporary camp (they spent a single night here) for Queen Maeve's army, who were marching from Connaught to Cooley. The site is currently under pasture.

Catalogue number: 31
Hillfort name: Coolagad
Townland: Kindlestown Upper
County: Wicklow
ITM coordinates: 727013, 712570
RMP number: WI008-015
Topographical position: Hilltop
Elevation: 219m OD
Number of enclosing elements: 1 (Class 1)
Total area: 28.2ha
Shape: Circular
References:
n/a

Partial contour fort surrounding the domed summit of steep hilltop. This prominent hilltop sits at the eastern edge of the Wicklow mountains overlooking Greystones town and the Wicklow coastline. Coolagad is positioned 2.8km to the north-east of Downshill hillfort in Co. Wicklow. Coolagad is a univallate site that forms a complete circuit and has a total footprint of 28.2ha. The rampart survives best at the east where it comprises a 4m wide and 1m high bank of earth. There is no obvious associated ditch feature. There are no recorded entrance features or breaks in the enclosing element. The majority of the interior is under mature forestry. This hillfort is not depicted in any historic mapping.

Catalogue number: 32
Hillfort name: Courthoyle New
Townland: Courthoyle New
County: Wexford
ITM coordinates: 682232, 626839
RMP number: WX030-058
Topographical position: Hill slope
Elevation: 90m OD
Number of enclosing elements: 1 (Class 1)
Total area: 1.09ha
Shape: Circular
References:
Moore, M. 1996. *Archaeological Inventory of County Wexford*. Dublin, Stationary Office.

Courthoyle New is a circular contour fort immediately east of the summit of a broad, low hill, overlooking the town of Raheen and Templeshelin Stream to the north. The site has a total footprint of approximately 1.1ha and is named 'Rathlyhar' in first and second edition Ordnance Survey maps. The earthen rampart of this univallate hillfort forms a complete circuit. It measures up to 5m wide and 1.3m high and has an external ditch that is up to 6m wide in places. First edition Ordnance Survey maps depict a second bank immediately outside the external ditch of the extant enclosing elements. This has subsequently been levelled and has not been previously recorded. A simple gap in the enclosing elements to the west is likely a modern entrance. There is no evidence for any internal features on the surface. The interior is currently under pasture with some tree cover over enclosing elements.

Catalogue number: 33
Hillfort name: Cumber Lower
Townland: Cumber Lower
County: Offaly
ITM coordinates: 620176, 703573
RMP number: OF036-062001
Topographical position: Hilltop
Elevation: 337m OD
Number of enclosing elements: 2 (Class 2 possible)
Total area: 12.19ha
Shape: Circular
References:
Cooke, T. 1875. *History of Birr*. Tullamore.

This large multiple enclosure is in a commanding position on the summit of a steep hilltop, at the eastern edge of the Slieve Bloom Mountains. The site overlooks the Camcor River to north and is located 1.9km to the northeast of Ballymacmurragh hillfort. Cumber Lower is most likely bivallate for the entire circuit and has a total footprint of approximately 12.2ha. The ramparts are largely obscured due to dense tree and scrub cover and have not been recorded in detail to date. There is no evidence for any internal features on the surface. A limited site description by Cooke (1875: 154) suggests that the monument 'stands high, and is a very conspicuous object, surrounded by large stones which appear to have undergone the action of fire'. Cooke also states that 'the ashes [are] plainly seen around wherever holes are dug for planting'. There are no recorded breaks in the enclosing elements.

Catalogue number: 34
Hillfort name: Curraghadobbin
Townland: Curraghadobbin
County: Tipperary
ITM coordinates: 636872, 628616
RMP number: TS079-024001
Topographical position: Hilltop
Elevation: 227m OD
Number of enclosing elements: 2 (Class 2 likely)
Total area: 4.06ha
Shape: Sub-circular
References:
n/a

Curraghadobbin is a multiple enclosure surrounding the summit and western facing slopes of Curraghadobbin Hill, at the centre of an east–west running escarpment. The site is likely to be bivallate for its entire length, although this cannot be confirmed due to destruction of the outer enclosing elements by modern forestry. The hillfort has a total footprint of 4.06ha. The inner enclosing elements have been heavily damaged by forestry clearance and its subsequent re-setting. They comprise a bank of sandstone boulders up to 1m high and 3.6m wide. There is no obvious associated ditch. The outer enclosure has been incorporated into later field boundaries or has been destroyed. They have not been recorded and are visible in aerial and satellite imagery, most notably the 2005 edition of the Ordnance Survey aerial photographs. There are no recorded entrance features. An oval cairn is positioned at the centre of the interior. There are no features visible on the surface that might be contemporary with the construction and occupation of the hillfort.

Catalogue number: 35
Hillfort name: Derrynaseer
Townland: Derrynaseer
County: Antrim
ITM coordinates: 710546, 863597
RMP number: ANT066-001
Topographical position: Hill summit/spur
Elevation: 35m OD
Number of enclosing elements: 1 (Class 1)
Total area: 1.77ha
Shape: Circular
References:
n/a

Positioned at the western edge of a ridge of hills, Derrynaseer is a univallate contour fort surrounding the slightly domed summit of a hill with excellent views in all directions. The site has a simple gap entrance at the south. The enclosing elements survive well at the south where they comprise a bank 1.2m high and 2.8m wide with no evidence for an associated ditch. There is no evidence for any internal features on the surface. The site is encroached upon at the north by a development that has extended into a large section of the interior of the fort. Another development abuts the hillfort at south. Derrynaseer hillfort is visible in the first edition Ordnance Survey maps.

Catalogue number: 36
Hillfort name: Donaghmore/Toor More/Corrandhu
Townland: Donaghmore/Toor More
County: Kilkenny
ITM coordinates: 647554, 671002
RMP number: KK010-007001
Topographical position: Hilltop
Elevation: 253m OD
Number of enclosing elements: 2 (Class 2 confirmed)
Total area: 8.94ha
Shape: Circular
References:
Carrigan, Rev. W. 1905. *The History and Antiquities of the Diocese of Ossory*. Dublin, (reprinted Kilkenny 1981). 4 Vols.

O'Brien, W., Hogan, N. and O'Driscoll, J. 2014–5. Archaeological investigations at Toor More (Corrandhu) hillfort, Co. Kilkenny. *Journal of The Royal Society of Antiquaries of Ireland* 144–5. 7–26.

Toor More is a large, widely spaced multivallate hillfort surrounding the summit of Corrandhu Hill, one of three summits in a north–south running ridge overlooking Ballyraggett town. The hillfort is draped over the narrow ridge, with the concentric enclosing elements ignoring the steep contours to the east and west, forming a circle in plan. The site has a total footprint of 8.9ha. There are three possible entrances at north-north-west and south-east identified through geophysical survey. The enclosing elements survive as low-rise banks. Excavation and geophysical survey revealed both enclosures consist of banks with external ditches with small palisades on the inside of the banks. The banks are made of soil and stone with a stone revetment. Samples from the palisades and basal ditch deposits returned Late Bronze Age dates (Chapter 4). There is no evidence for any internal features on the surface, though potential pits and three hut structures were identified by the geophysical survey. A possible cist burial from the interior (Carrigan 1905: 108) could pre-date the hillfort. This may have been associated with a levelled cairn (Carrigan 1905: 108).

Catalogue number: 37
Hillfort name: Downpatrick
Townland: Downpatrick
County: Down
ITM coordinates: 748127, 844471
RMP number: DOW037-027
Topographical position: Hilltop
Elevation: 21m OD
Number of enclosing elements: 1 (Class 1)
Total area: n/a ha
Shape: n/a
References:
Proudfoot, B. 1955a. Excavations at Cathedral Hill, Downpatrick, Co. Down: preliminary report on excavations in 1954. *Ulster Journal of Archaeology* 90: 57–72.

Hamlin, A. and Lynn, C. 1988. *Archaeological Excavations by the Department of the Environment for Northern Ireland 1970–1986*. Belfast, Crown.

Contour fort in commanding position on summit of Downpatrick Hill, with panoramic views. The site is visible as a vegetation mark in some aerial photographs. Excavations by Proudfoot (1954 and 1955) revealed the defences consisted of a ditch-bank-ditch arrangment, the internal ditch being slightly later in date. A series of post-holes abutting both faces of the bank, as well as tie-beams traversing the base, were also identified. Proudfoot (1955: 59) suggests these relate to a later refurbishment. No radiocarbon dates were obtained, though the artefactual evidence dates the site to the Late Bronze Age. Excavation by Hamlin and Lynn (1988) identified substantial evidence for reuse during the Medieval period. There are no obvious entrances. Three Late Bronze Age gold hoards were recovered from the interior. An excavated oval structure may be somewhat contemporary with the construction and occupation of the hillfort. This structure is truncated by later features and coarse pottery was found in close proximity (Proudfoot 1954: 97–99). More than a dozen clay or wattle and daub lined pits were excavated in the interior.

Catalogue number: 38
Hillfort name: Downshill
Townland: Downshill
County: Wicklow
ITM coordinates: 725213, 710151
RMP number: WI013-001
Topographical position: Hilltop
Elevation: 372m OD
Number of enclosing elements: 1 (Class 1)
Total area: 6.66ha
Shape: Sub-oval
References:
Grogan, E. and Kilfeather, A. 1997. *Archaeological Inventory of County Wicklow*. Dublin, Stationary Office.

Sub-oval shaped contour fort surrounding domed summit of Downshill. The site is in a commanding position at edge of the Glen of the Downs, overlooking the Wicklow coastline to the east. Coolagad hillfort is positioned 2.8km to north-east. Univallate for its entire circuit, it has a total footprint of 6.66ha. The enclosing elements comprise a stone faced earthen bank approximately 5m wide and up to 1.6m high. A 4m wide external ditch was discovered during ploughing at the south-east. The ramparts have been damaged by recent forestry. There are no recorded entrance features or evidence for any internal features on the surface. The interior is severely damaged by deep ridge and furrow associated with tree felling. A trial excavation of the enclosing elements in 2007 by University College Dublin produced no datable artefacts and no radiocarbon dates have been published.

Catalogue number: 39
Hillfort name: Drumnagranshy
Townland: Drumnagranshy
County: Sligo
ITM coordinates: 571226, 812590
RMP number: SL040-009
Topographical position: Hilltop
Elevation: 359m OD
Number of enclosing elements: 2 (Class 2 possible)
Total area: 2.87ha
Shape: Pear
References:
Egan, U., Byrne, E., Sleeman, M., Ronan, S. and Murphy, C. 2005. *Archaeological Inventory of Country Sligo, Vol 1: Sligo South*. Dublin, Stationary Office.

Kytmannow, T. 2005. New prehistoric discoveries in the Kesh Corran/Carrowkeel complex, Co. Sligo. *Archaeology Ireland* 19 (4): 20–23.

Drumnagranshy is a possible multiple enclosure surrounding the flat summit of Kesh Corann mountain (Figure 11.11). The site is approximately 2.9ha in size. The enclosing elements are on average 21m apart, with the inner example identified recently by the author. Aerial and satellite images suggest this comprises a stone bank. The external enclosing elements consist of a low, heather covered stone wall 2.5m wide and up to 0.5m high. At the north-west to east, the bank is built on the edge of a steep slope. The ramparts and the majority of the interior of the hillfort are covered in blanket bog and heather. An annex abutting the southern section of the enclosing elements has been interpreted as a possible entrance feature. A large cairn at the highest point in the interior measures 26m in diameter with a maximum height of 5m. This may be a passage tomb. A second cairn that could also be considered a passage tomb is visible within the interior. There are no other features visible on the surface.

Catalogue number: 40
Hillfort name: Dún Aonghasa
Townland: Kilmurvy
County: Galway
ITM coordinates: 481783, 709831
RMP number: GA110-039
Topographical position: Cliff edge
Elevation: 87m OD
Number of enclosing elements: 4 (Class 2 confirmed)
Total area: 5.85ha
Shape: D-shaped
References:
Cotter, C. 2012a. *The Western Stone Forts Project: Excavations at Dún Aonghasa and Dún Eoghanachta Vol. 1*. Dublin, Wordwell.

Dún Aonghasa is located on Inishmore, the largest of the Aran Islands in Co. Galway. It is 5.9ha in size and comprises up to four widely spaced enclosing elements that abut a sheer cliff face to the south. There were two main phases of construction. The fort was initially built at the beginning of the Late Bronze Age. A second phase of building and refurbishment took place later, possibly in Iron Age and Early Medieval times. This included the construction of *chevaux de frise* and a fourth enclosing element. There are three entrances that may date to the Late Bronze Age and up to seven entrances which were probably added during the Early Medieval period (Cotter 2012a: 55). The stone banks have been substantially rebuilt in modern times. Up to ten structures were identified within the interior during excavation. A wide range of artifacts were discovered including 40 bronze objects. Evidence for the casting of swords, spearheads and decorated socketed axe-heads were also recovered in the form of clay moulds. Excavations by Cotter in 1990s produced mainly Late Bronze Age dates.

Catalogue number: 41
Hillfort name: Dunmurry West
Townland: Dunmurry West
County: Kildare
ITM coordinates: 671402, 716918
RMP number: KD022-001001
Topographical position: Hilltop/hill slope
Elevation: 233m OD
Number of enclosing elements: 1 (Class 1)
Total area: 6.29ha
Shape: Oval
References:
n/a

Dunmurry West is an oval hill slope fort situated surrounding the summit and southeastern facing slopes of Dunmurry Hill, with panoramic views from the summit (Figure 11.12). The univallate fort has a total site footprint of 6.3ha. The enclosing element is a poorly preserved, grass-covered, stony bank, up to 6m wide and 0.5m high, with no obvious ditch feature. A mound (probably prehistoric), two possible hut structures and a small enclosure are apparent within the interior. The hut sites comprise circular platforms 5m and 7m in diameter and are defined by a circular band of grass covered stones. A larger enclosure has also been identified. This measures approximately 25m in diameter and is defined by a poorly preserved grass-covered stony bank. The interior is currently under pasture with patches of scrub and gorse.

Catalogue number: 42
Hillfort name: Faha
Townland: Begagh
County: Kerry
ITM coordinates: 447882, 612002
RMP number: KE034-048
Topographical position: Mountain ridge
Elevation: 822m OD
Number of enclosing elements: 2 (Class 3)
Total area: 13.46ha
Shape: Triangular
References:
Cuppage, J. 1986. *Archaeological Survey of the Dingle Peninsula*. Ballyferriter, Oidhreachta Chorca Dhuibhne.

Faha is an inland promontory fort on east–west mountain ridge, on the eastern side of Brandon Mountain in the Dingle Peninsula, Co. Kerry. The triangular promontory narrows to the west and is bounded at the north and south by steep cliffs. The site occupies a total area of 13.4ha. Two drystone walls define the most accessible approach to the east. The stone walls are separated by approximately 120m. The outer defences consist of a 7m wide stone bank that is up to 2.1m high and is approximately 134m long. There is some evidence for an internal wall walk consisting of two steps. A single entrance appears in the well preserved outer enclosing element, comprising a simple, stone faced gap, 2m in width. The inner enclosing element is not as well preserved. It comprises a collapsed stone bank 2.2m wide and up to 1.95m high and extends for a length of 55m. A simple entrance gap in the inner enclosing element comprises a 9m gap between the faced terminal of the stone bank and northern cliff face. There is no evidence for surface features in the interior, which is partially covered by vegetation scrub.

Catalogue number: 43
Hillfort name: Forkhill
Townland: Orior Upper
County: Antrim
ITM coordinates: 702309, 815358
RMP number: ANT031-025
Topographical position: Hilltop
Elevation: 263m OD
Number of enclosing elements: 1 (Class 1)
Total area: 4.24ha
Shape: Circular
References:
n/a

In commanding position overlooking the modern town of Forkill, a large circular contour fort around the domed summit of Forkill Mountain. The site is univallate for the entire circuit with no obvious entrance features. The rampart survives well throughout and is best preserved at the south. It comprises a substantial drystone wall up to 1m wide and 1.5m high. It is strategically positioned at the edge of steeply sloping ground, giving the impression of greater height from the exterior. A small cairn at the highest point of the interior measures 6.5m in diameter and up to 1.5m high. No other evidence for any internal features on the surface. Some tree cover and thick heather and scrub growth within the interior. Forestry surrounds the enclosing elements on all sides.

Figure 11.11: Drumnagranshy hillfort, Co. Sligo (Source: Google Earth 2017).

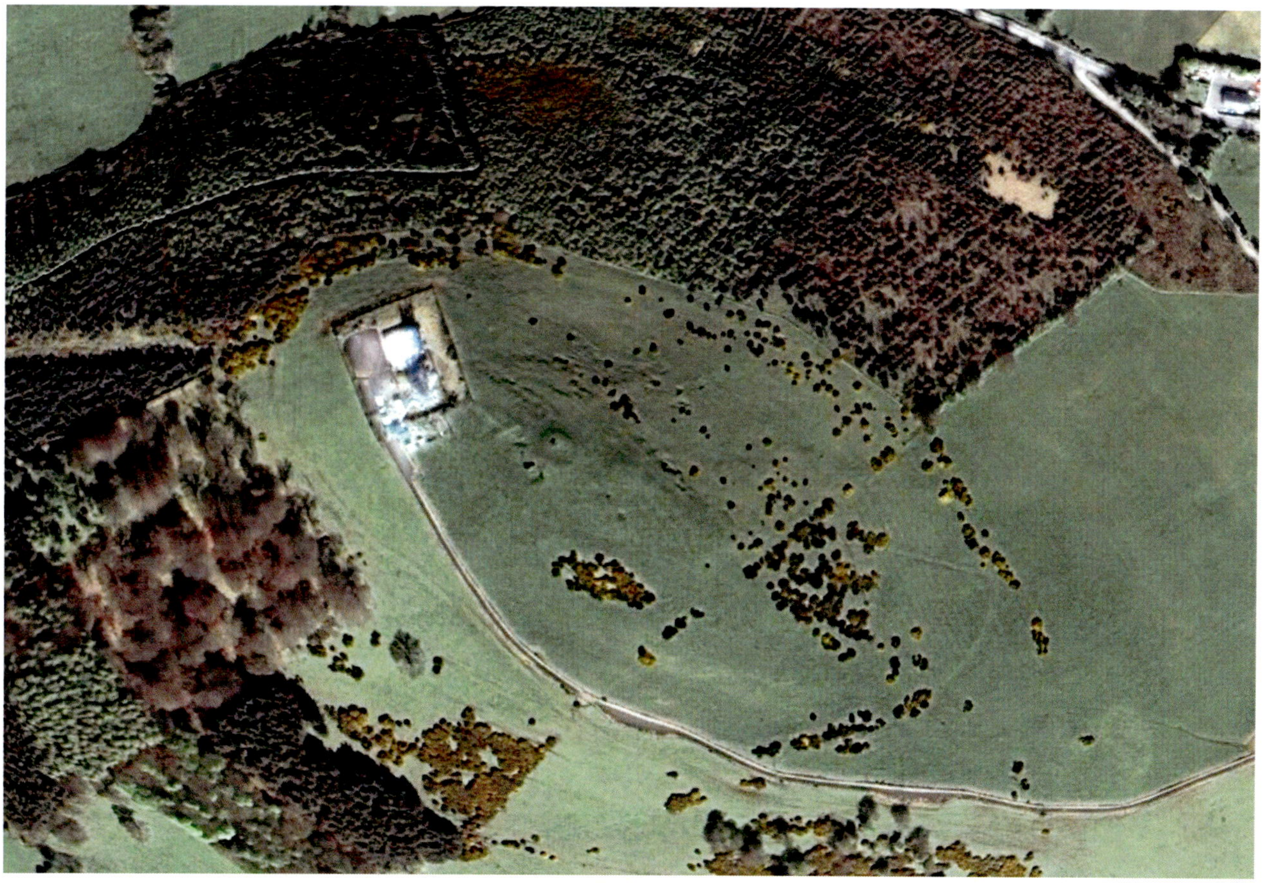

Figure 11.12: Dunmurry West hillfort, Co. Kildare (Source: Google Earth 2017).

Catalogue number: 44
Hillfort name: Formoyle Beg
Townland: Formoyle Beg
County: Clare
ITM coordinates: 560391, 671278
RMP number: CL044-085
Topographical position: Hilltop
Elevation: 242m OD
Number of enclosing elements: 2 (Class 2 confirmed)
Total area: 6.79ha
Shape: Oval
References:

Condit, T. 1995b. Hillfort discoveries near Killaloe, Co. Clare. *Archaeology Ireland* 9 (1): 34–37.

Hickey, L and Hogan, N. 2004. *Survey at Formoyle Beg Hillfort in Co. Clare*. Unpublished report, National University of Galway.

O'Brien, W. 2012c. *Report on archaeological excavation at Formoyle hillfort, Co. Clare (licence 12E145).* Unpublished report submitted to the National Monuments Service, Department of Arts, Heritage and the Gaeltacht. Dublin.

Formoyle Beg is a multivallate hillfort located in a commanding position overlooking a deep, curving river valley forming a pass through the Slieve Bearnagh Mountains. The site has a total footprint of approximately 6.79ha. It is bivallate for the entire circuit with widely spaced enclosing elements that are separated by a maximum of 62m. Excavation revealed both defences consisted of a low bank of earth and stone and a shallow outer ditch, with a small counterscarp bank. Evidence for a stake fence was found along the crest of the inner bank. On top and at the outer edge of this bank, a dense series of stake-holes were revealed through excavation. The ramparts of the fort survive well throughout but are covered in a layer of blanket bog. No obvious entrance features have been recorded. A possible cairn was identified by Condit (1995b: 37) at the summit of the hillfort, although this may not be an antiquity. No other evidence for internal features is visible on the surface. Excavations produced Late Bronze Age dates, indicating the hillfort was constructed during that period (Chapter 4). Condit and O'Sullivan (1999) suggest a third outer enclosure exists. This is not supported by recent excavation, which confirmed that the 'outlying ditch' identified by the latter is a modern drainage feature.

Catalogue number: 45
Hillfort name: Freestone Hill
Townland: Coolgrange
County: Kilkenny
ITM coordinates: 658829, 656234
RMP number: KK020-018002
Topographical position: Hilltop
Elevation: 134m OD
Number of enclosing elements: 1 (Class 1)
Total area: 1.52ha
Shape: Oval
References:

Raftery, B. 1969. Freestone Hill, Co. Kilkenny: an Iron Age and Bronze Age cairn. *Proceedings of the Royal Irish Academy* 68C: 1–108.

Ó Floinn, R. 2000. Freestone Hill, Co. Kilkenny: a re-assessment. In Smyth, A. (ed.), *Seanchas: Studies in Early and Medieval Irish Archaeology, History and Literature in Honour of Francis J. Byrne*: 12–29. Dublin, Four Courts Press.

Waddell, J. 2010 *(first edition 1998). The Prehistoric Archaeology of Ireland*. Bray, Wordwell.

Freestone Hill is a contour fort that surrounds a low-domed summit. The enclosing elements follow the 130m contour at the east, south and west. The hilltop is located at the southern foothills of the Castlecomber Hills, overlooking Kilkenny town. It also overlooks a north–south routeway through a gap in the Slieveardagh Hills and Castlecomber Hills. Freestone Hill is 1.5ha in size. The defenses comprise a low-rise bank with external ditch. Excavations were undertaken by Bersu in 1948–1949 and published by Raftery in 1969. This revealed that the ditch was rock-cut and varied from U- to V-shaped. It varies in width (1.3–2.5m) and depth (0.75–2m) (Raftery 1969: 33). The bank is composed of stone and gravel, and varies from 2.5–4m wide at its base, rising 0.5–1m above the old ground surface. The discovery of large blocks of stone may suggest some form of wall facing. A potential post-hole was identified on the crest of the bank, however, Raftery (1969: 34–35) suggests this is unlikely to relate to a timber palisade. The interior rises towards a flat centre where the partial remains of a circular wall, 18m in diameter, was surrounded by a 37m by 30m oval enclosure (Raftery 1969: 6). Underneath these enclosures, the remains of a cairn was identified. The site has been dated to the Late Bronze Age through association with Bronze Age coarse ware pottery, blue glass beads and other artefacts (Ó Floinn 2000).

Catalogue number: 46
Hillfort name: Friarstown 1
Townland: Friarstown
County: Limerick
ITM coordinates: 558317, 649328
RMP number: LI013-089
Topographical position: Hilltop
Elevation: 76m OD
Number of enclosing elements: 2 (Class 1)
Total area: 1.5ha
Shape: Circular
References:
Kelly, E. and Condit, T. 1998. Limerick's Tara. *Archaeology Ireland* 2: 18–22.

Friarstown 1 is a circular contour fort positioned on the low-domed summit of an isolated hill, 7.5km south of Limerick City (Figure 11.13). The hillfort has a total footprint of 1.5ha and there are panoramic views from the summit. Immediately to the north-east is a second hillfort, positioned to the east on a domed shoulder of the same hill. The enclosing elements comprise a pair of closely set banks with an intervening ditch. The outer bank is likely to be a counter scarp feature. There are no obvious entrance features recorded. No evidence for any internal features on the surface. Extensive plough damage has denuded the enclosing elements. The southern and western section of the enclosing features are under forestry. Kelly and Condit (1998: 19) have suggested that this is a large henge monument. However, the commanding position of the monument and the layout of its enclosing elements suggest that it is more likely to be a hillfort.

Catalogue number: 47
Hillfort name: Friarstown 2
Townland: Friarstown
County: Limerick
ITM coordinates: 558223, 649288
RMP number: LI013-094
Topographical position: Hilltop
Elevation: 83m OD
Number of enclosing elements: 1 (Class 1)
Total area: 2.11ha
Shape: Circular
References:
Kelly, E. and Condit, T. 1998. Limerick's Tara. *Archaeology Ireland* 2: 18–22.

Contour fort situated on the low-domed hilltop of an isolated hill, 7.5km south of Limerick City (Figure 11.13). Friarstown 2 hillfort has a total footprint of 2.1ha. There are extensive views to the north, east and south. Views to the west are blocked by the summit of Friarstown Hill. Immediately to the south-west is a second hillfort on Friarstown Hill. The enclosing elements comprise a pair of closely set banks with an intervening ditch. These survive best at the south-east and south-west. Here, the inner bank is 6m wide and is 1.7m above the bottom of the ditch. The ditch measures 2.5m wide. The outer bank is 3m wide and is 0.5m above the bottom of the ditch (Kelly and Condit 1998: 19). This may suggest it is a counterscarp. There are no recorded entrance features. No evidence for any internal features on the surface. Extensive plough damage has denuded the enclosing elements, which survive best to the south-east and south-west. Kelly and Condit (1998: 19) have suggested that this is a large henge monument. However, its commanding position and layout of its enclosing elements suggest it is more likely a hillfort.

Catalogue number: 48
Hillfort name: Garrangrena Lower
Townland: Garrangrena Lower
County: Tipperary
ITM coordinates: 600700, 669980
RMP number: TN028-070001
Topographical position: Hilltop
Elevation: 315m OD
Number of enclosing elements: 1 (Class 1)
Total area: 2.06ha
Shape: Sub-circular
References:
n/a

Garrangrena is positioned in a commanding location on the domed summit of a hill overlooking Moanamadra Lough to east and Fishmoyne River to east and south-east. The site has a total footprint of 2.1ha. It is univallate for its entire circuit and comprises two ditches with an intervening bank. The internal ditch is 1m wide and 0.2m deep. Immediately outside this is a 2m wide and 1m high earthen bank, with an external ditch 3m wide and 0.3m deep. The enclosing elements closely follow the contours of the hilltop. The ramparts survive well throughout its circuit. There is a possible entrance at the west comprising a simple 3m break in the enclosing elements. There are no other recorded entrance features. The interior is under blanket bog and heather.

Catalogue number: 49
Hillfort name: Glanbane
Townland: Glanbane
County: Kerry
ITM coordinates: 492247, 608504
RMP number: KE039-065
Topographical position: Hilltop/ridge edge
Elevation: 86m OD
Number of enclosing elements: 2 (Class 2 confirmed)
Total area: 6.43ha
Shape: Sub-oval
References:
O'Brien, W., O'Driscoll, J. and Hogan, N. 2016. Glanbane hillfort and the Bronze Age in Kerry. *Journal of the Kerry Archaeological and Historical Society* 16: 77–105.

Multiple enclosure in commanding position at the eastern edge of the Slieve Mish Mountains. Glanbane hillfort is situated just off the summit of a low-lying, flat hilltop. The hillfort is sub-oval in shape and bivallate for its entire circuit. The monument has been completely levelled and is only visible in aerial photographs and geophysical survey. It occupies a total area of 6.4ha. Excavation confirmed that each enclosure comprised an earthen bank with an external stone revetment. Deep external, U-shaped rock-cut ditches were also revealed by excavation. Geophysical survey has identified an out-turned entrance to the north where the separation between the two enclosing elements narrows from 25–30m to approximately 8m. There is a corresponding 10m wide gap in both enclosing elements. A number of possible hut structures and two large enclosures were identified in the survey, as well as post hillfort activity in the form of field boundaries. Radiocarbon dates from basal deposits of the hillfort ditches returned Late Bronze Age dates (see Chapter 4).

Catalogue number: 50
Hillfort name: Glasbolie
Townland: Glasbolie
County: Donegal
ITM coordinates: 589827, 867213
RMP number: DG103-029
Topographical position: Hilltop
Elevation: 147m OD
Number of enclosing elements: 1 (Class 1)
Total area: 5.51ha
Shape: Oval
References:
Cody, E. 2002. *Survey of the Megalithic Tombs of Ireland, vol. 6, Co. Donegal*. Dublin, Stationery Office.

Glasbolie is a large contour fort on the domed summit of Lurgan Hill, which sits at the western edge of upland terrain, overlooking lowland and the Donegal coastline to the west (Figure 11.14). The fort is univallate for its entire circuit, with a total footprint of 5.5ha. The rampart survives well at the south, west and north where it is defined by a collapsed stone wall. The eastern section is delimited by a steep natural scarp. No obvious entrance features have been recorded. An embanked enclosure surrounding a central mound 15m in diameter and 1m high was recorded at the centre of the hillfort by Cody (2002). This mound is called Lurgancarn in the first edition Ordnance Survey maps. Numerous possible circular hut sites are visible in aerial and satellite imagery in the interior.

Catalogue number: 51
Hillfort name: Granard
Townland: Granard
County: Longford
ITM coordinates: 632923, 780709
RMP number: LF010-080001
Topographical position: Hilltop
Elevation: 179m OD
Number of enclosing elements: 1 (Class 1)
Total area: 1.83ha
Shape: Oval
References:
n/a

Possible contour fort positioned on the summit of prominent hill, overlooking Granard town and River Rhine. The summit of the hill is occupied by a Medieval motte and bailey castle. The hillfort surrounds these later features and has a total footprint of 1.8ha. It is univallate for its entire circuit with a possible out-turned entrance at the north-west. The rampart survives well at the south-west where it measures 6m wide and up to 2.1m high. There are no apparent ditch features associated with this bank. The majority of the enclosing elements are incorporated into curvilinear field systems to the north, east and south. The interior is under pasture and forestry abuts the enclosing elements to the north.

Figure 11.13: Two hillforts of Friarstown 1 (left) and Friarstown 2 (right), Co. Limerick (Source: Google Earth 2017).

Figure 11.14: Glasbolie hillfort, Co. Donegal (Source: Google Earth 2017).

Catalogue number: 52
Hillfort name: Grannagh
Townland: Grannagh
County: Galway
ITM coordinates: 549611, 711162
RMP number: GA114-080
Topographical position: Hilltop
Elevation: 55m OD
Number of enclosing elements: 1 (Class 1)
Total area: 2.76ha
Shape: Oval
References:
n/a

Grannagh hillfort is a univallate contour fort surrounding the domed summit of a hillock positioned in low-lying terrain. Despite the fort being in a low-lying position, there are panoramic views from the summit. It has a total footprint of approximately 2.8ha. The rampart has been completely destroyed and is visible as a vegetation mark in some aerial photographs. There are no recorded entrance features or evidence for any internal features on the surface.

Catalogue number: 53
Hillfort name: Haughey's Fort
Townland: Tray
County: Armagh
ITM coordinates: 683458, 845300
RMP number: ARM012-013
Topographical position: Hilltop
Elevation: 74m OD
Number of enclosing elements: 3 (Class 2 confirmed)
Total area: 10.42ha
Shape: Circular
References:

Mallory, J. 1995. Haughey's Fort and the Navan Complex in the Late Bronze Age. In Waddell, J and Shee Twohig, E. (eds), *Ireland in the Bronze Age*: 73–86. Dublin, Stationary Office.

Mallory, J. and Baban, G. 2014. Excavations in Haughey's Fort East. *Emania* 22: 13–32.

Large, mostly levelled, trivallate hillfort, on a low-rise hill in Tray townland, County Armagh. The inner bank may survive as part of a modern field system. The middle and outer enclosures are visible in aerial photographs. Their presence has been confirmed by geophysics and excavation. Excavations by Mallory in 1987–1999 reveal that each of the three enclosures comprise an internal reveted bank and external V-shaped ditch ranging 2.3–3.2m deep (Mallory and Baban 2014). A portion of a large 30m diameter structure at the centre of the monument contained a concentration of pits with bronze and gold-work, Late Bronze Age pottery, lithics, animal remains and environmental remains such as charred cereal grain and worked wood. These features and artefacts were dated to the Late Bronze Age. A possible entrance in the internal enclosing element (15m in width) has been partially excavated. An entrance gap in the middle enclosing element to the north-east was excavated. It comprised a 3m wide entrance flanked on either side by a palisade and is aligned towards the King's Stables, a man-made ritual pool 300m to the north-east of Haughey's Fort. This has also been dated to the Late Bronze Age.

Catalogue number: 54
Hillfort name: Hill of Ward (Tlachta)
Townland: Mullaghstones
County: Meath
ITM coordinates: 673473, 764895
RMP number: ME030-038
Topographical position: Hilltop
Elevation: 111m OD
Number of enclosing elements: 3 (Class 2 confirmed)
Total area: n/a
Shape: Oval
References:
n/a

Surrounding the low, flat summit of Ward Hill in Co. Meath, this large multiple enclosure is strategically located overlooking flat terrain to the west and the Abhainn Atha Buí River, a southern tributary of the Boyne. The hillfort was identified by Davis through LiDAR. This survey indicated that the enclosing elements comprise a pair of largely levelled banks approximately 60m apart which are only visible on the northern side of the hill. Recent excavation of these features revealed a more complex series of enclosures. At least three wide ditches were uncovered (some up to 15m in width) and animal bones were extracted from the lower levels of these ditches. These produced Late Bronze Age radiocarbon dates, although the actual dates have not been published. At the centre of the hillfort is a large, earthwork monument identified as an Early Medieval royal assembly site (Tlachta). This comprises four closely spaced banks and ditches with a total diameter of 149m. LiDAR results suggest possible earlier features lie underneath the Early Medieval monument. The hillfort itself is largely levelled and is currently under pasture.

Catalogue number: 55
Hillfort name: Hughstown (Carrigeen Hill)
Townland: Hughstown
County: Kildare
ITM coordinates: 684012, 688926
RMP number: KD038-025001
Topographical position: Hilltop
Elevation: 298m OD
Number of enclosing elements: 3 (Class 2 confirmed)
Total area: 8.22ha
Shape: Oval
References:
Condit, T. 1998. Observations of the Baltinglass hillfort complex. In Corlett, C. and O'Sullivan, A. (eds), *Wicklow Archaeology and History* 1: 9–25.

Vegetation marks and low-relief features indicate the presence of a large, multiple enclosure surrounding the summit of Carrigeen Hill. Hughstown hillfort is one of nine large forts in the Baltinglass area of Co. Wicklow. It is situated at the southwestern edge of the Wicklow Mountains in a commanding position, with panoramic views from the summit. Roughly oval in plan, the fort has a total footprint of 8.2ha. Geophysical survey has revealed a complex system of enclosing elements. This includes an outer bank and ditch which surrounds a series of up to four closely set enclosing features. Some aerial photographs indicate associated ditch features and this was confirmed during excavation in 2015 and 2016. Excavation over the enclosing elements confirmed that each comprises an internal bank with external ditch. There is also evidence that wooden palisades were incorporated into the design of the enclosing elements. Radiocarbon dates reveal that all three enclosures date to the Early Neolithic (Chapter 6). Some possible hut structures were identified by the geophysical survey within the interior of the fort. No entrance features were identified. At the summit of the hillfort is an extant enclosure. The bank of this enclosure comprises a circular band of large boulders approximately 55m in diameter. Near the centre of this enclosure, a circular bank of grass covered stones 18m in diameter may be the remains of a hut structure.

Catalogue number: 56
Hillfort name: Kedrah
Townland: Kedrah
County: Tipperary
ITM coordinates: 606664, 627244
RMP number: TS075-039
Topographical position: Hilltop
Elevation: 62m OD
Number of enclosing elements: 1 (Class 1)
Total area: 2.21ha
Shape: Circular
References:
n/a

Kedrah is a contour fort on the summit of steep sided hilltop at the foothills on the eastern edge of the Galty Mountains (Figure 11.15). The site has a total footprint of 2.2ha. The enclosing elements survive well, but have been affected by quarrying at the south-east. They comprise a substantial, 3m wide internal ditch with a large external bank measuring 14m in width and up to 2.8m in height. At the west, there is evidence for a closely spaced bank, however, it remains to be confirmed if this is an original feature. There are two possible original entrances at the south-east and north-west which comprise simple breaks in the enclosing elements. Two other breaks are probably not original features. A possible structure was recorded abutting the northwestern section of the enclosing elements. There is no evidence for any other internal features on the surface.

Catalogue number: 57
Hillfort name: Kilcashel
Townland: Kilcashel
County: Wicklow
ITM coordinates: 719029, 681620
RMP number: WI035-062
Topographical position: Hilltop/hill slope
Elevation: 139m OD
Number of enclosing elements: 1 (Class 1)
Total area: 1.58ha
Shape: Oval
References:
n/a

Near the village of Ballygahan, an oval hill slope fort 1.6ha in size is positioned on sloping ground with steep break of slope to north, east and south. There are extensive views of the Avoca River valley from the interior. The hillfort is positioned at a major bend in the Avoca Valley. Kilcashel is adjacent to a disused copper mine. The ramparts have not been archaeologically recorded and their state is unknown. There are no recorded entrance features and there is no evidence for any internal features on the surface, though overgrowth may obscure low relief features. A possible mound, 25m in diameter, abuts the western section of the enclosing elements.

Catalogue number: 58
Hillfort name: Kill Hill
Townland: Kill Hill
County: Kildare
ITM coordinates: 694990, 722858
RMP number: KD020-001
Topographical position: Hilltop
Elevation: 153m OD
Number of enclosing elements: 3 (Class 2 likely)
Total area: 26.26ha
Shape: Circular
References:
n/a

Multiple enclosure around low domed summit and western slopes of Kill Hill (Figure 11.16). The site is situated in the northeastern foothills of the Wicklow Mountains and overlooks the town of Naas to the south-west. It comprises three widely spaced (78–109m apart) concentric enclosing elements which are circular in plan, measuring 593m in maximum diameter. The site has a total footprint of 26.3ha. The outer enclosing elements comprise earthen banks topped with modern hedges. The middle enclosing elements are apparent in the north, however, the remainder of its circuit and inner enclosing elements have been destroyed and are visible only in aerial photography. There are no recorded entrance features. The inner enclosing elements have been almost completely destroyed and are only visible in LiDAR survey. A possible bivallate ring-barrow is located between the inner and middle enclosing elements in the east.

Catalogue number: 59
Hillfort name: Killeenadeema
Townland: Killeenadeema
County: Roscommon
ITM coordinates: 587563, 754982
RMP number: RO044-025
Topographical position: Low rise
Elevation: 112m OD
Number of enclosing elements: 1 (Class 1)
Total area: 5.41ha
Shape: Sub-rectangular
References:
n/a

Killeenadeema is a sub-rectangular contour fort positioned on the summit of a flat, low-rise hilltop. The southwestern section of hillfort is positioned at the edge of a steep incline falling into a south-west–north-east running valley. There are excellent views of this valley from hillfort. The site has a total footprint of approximately 5.4ha. The rampart does not survive at ground level but is visible in some aerial photographs. There are no recorded entrance features or other information regarding the enclosing elements. There is no evidence for any internal features on the surface.

Catalogue number: 60
Hillfort name: Kilranlagh
Townland: Kilranlagh
County: Wicklow
ITM coordinates: 692599, 688901
RMP number: Unrecorded
Topographical position: Hilltop
Elevation: 385m OD
Number of enclosing elements: 1 (Class 1)
Total area: 5.33ha
Shape: Circular
References:
n/a

Possible univallate contour fort located in a commanding position surrounding the domed summit of Kilranlagh Hill at the southwestern edge of the Wicklow mountains. This is one of nine large forts in the Baltinglass area. The ramparts have been heavily affected by commercial forestry plantation. GPS survey by the author has identified a curving rubble stone bank measuring 14m wide and up to 0.7m high on the western side of the hill. This may be the remains of a possible hillfort. This corresponds with a curving section of bank on the eastern side of the hilltop, depicted in first edition Ordnance Survey maps, and with aerial photographs which indicates the possible presence of a large enclosure on the summit of Kilranlagh. There are no recorded entrance features and there is no evidence for any internal features on the surface. Three cairns, a stone circle and barrow are located on the hilltop, outside the possible hillfort. The interior is overgrown with scrub and is under light blanket bog and is in parts, covered by forestry (see Chapter 5).

Figure 11.15: Kedrah hillfort, Co. Tipperary.

Figure 11.16: Kill Hill hillfort, Co. Kildare (Source: Google Earth 2017).

Catalogue number: 61
Hillfort name: Kilriffin
Townland: Kilriffin
County: Meath
ITM coordinates: 687134, 789850
RMP number: ME006-062001
Topographical position: Hilltop
Elevation: 73m OD
Number of enclosing elements: 1 (Class 1)
Total area: 1.33ha
Shape: Circular
References:
n/a

Kilriffin is a contour fort in a commanding position surrounding the summit of Drumran Hill, overlooking a tributary of the Garra River to the north and west. The fort is visible as a vegetation mark in aerial photographs, though low level earthworks may survive on the north side. The site is univallate for the entire circuit, with aerial photographs indicating that it comprises an 8m wide bank with external ditch, with no apparent entrance features. It has a total site footprint of 1.3ha. A possible ring-ditch or hut structure is recorded at the centre of the hillfort. There is also a possible annex abutting the exterior of hillfort at the north.

Catalogue number: 62
Hillfort name: Kilskeagh
Townland: Kilskeagh
County: Galway
ITM coordinates: 548159, 735526
RMP number: GA071-046
Topographical position: Hilltop
Elevation: 103m OD
Number of enclosing elements: 2 (Class 2 likely)
Total area: 2.65ha
Shape: Oval
References:
Alcock, O., de hÓra, K. and Gosling, P. 1995. *Archaeological Inventory of County Galway Vol. 2: North Galway*. Dublin, Stationary Office.

Multiple enclosure surrounding the summit of Kilskeagh Hill. The site has a total footprint of 2.7ha. It is bivallate for its entire length, with widely spaced enclosing elements separated by 21m. The enclosing elements survive well throughout their circuit. The inner enclosing element survive as a scarp feature with an external ditch visible at the south. The external defences consist of a collapsed stone wall with external ditch. Alcock *et al.* (1995) suggest that corresponding 3m wide gap in both enclosing elements at south-east may be an original entrance. Two other breaks in the enclosing elements at the west are probably of later date. There is no evidence for any internal features on the surface. The interior is heavily overgrown with partial tree cover on the banks.

Catalogue number: 63
Hillfort name: Knigh
Townland: Knigh
County: Tipperary
ITM coordinates: 585772, 685357
RMP number: TN014-033002
Topographical position: Hilltop
Elevation: 125m OD
Number of enclosing elements: 2 (Class 2 likely)
Total area: 5.4ha
Shape: Circular
References:
Manning, C. 1985. Prehistoric sites in the neighbourhood of Ardcroney. *Eile, Journal of the Roscrea Heritage Society* 2: 43–55.

O'Driscoll, J. 2012c. *Geophysical Survey at Knigh Hillfort, Co. Tipperary*. Unpublished geophysical survey report, University College Cork.

Knigh is a multiple enclosure following natural contours of the hilltop, on southern summit of steep dome-shaped hill overlooking low-lying terrain. The hillfort overlooks Lough Eorna to east and Dromineer Bay is to the west. Geophysical survey by the author has identified that Knigh hillfort is probably bivallate. It has a total site footprint of 5.4ha. The enclosing elements are levelled and are visible on aerial photographs. Manning (1985: 48) recorded the monument before its destruction. He identified a bank and external ditch best preserved at the north. Both first and second edition Ordnance Survey mapping suggest that the inner defences were partially incorporated into a field system at its south-west, which is still present today. A possible second enclosing element was identified at the north, approximately 54m from the inner enclosing element. There are no recorded entrance features. A cairn (20m in diameter, 2.5m in height) and conjoined mound (20m in diameter and 0.8m high) are positioned at the centre of the hillfort. Geophysical survey has identified a number of potential pit features throughout the interior, and two possible structures (Figure 1.5).

Catalogue number: 64
Hillfort name: Knockadigeen
Townland: Knockadigeen
County: Tipperary
ITM coordinates: 593486, 670902
RMP number: TN027-098001
Topographical position: Hilltop
Elevation: 402m OD
Number of enclosing elements: 1 (Class 1)
Total area: 4.12ha
Shape: Circular
References:
Farrelly, J. and O'Brien, C. 2002. *Archaeological Inventory of County Tipperary Vol. 1: North Tipperary*. Dublin, Stationary Office.

Univallate contour fort surrounding the summit of a domed mountain at the northern edge of the Silvermines Mountains. Another hillfort, Ballincurra, is 1.4km to south-west on an adjacent hilltop. The enclosing elements of Knockadigeen comprise two ditches with an intervening bank and a possible outer bank at north-north-west (Farrelly and O'Brien 2002). Ramparts survive well throughout its circuit. There are no obvious entrance features recorded. There is a possible enclosure on the eastern side of the interior, visible on aerial photographs but not at ground level. No other features are visible on the surface, though this may be due to the interior being under dense gorse and heather growth.

Catalogue number: 65
Hillfort name: Knockainy
Townland: Knockainy
County: Limerick
ITM coordinates: 167703, 136450
RMP number: Unrecorded
Topographical position: Hilltop
Elevation: 155m OD
Number of enclosing elements: 1 (Class 1)
Total area: 10.37ha
Shape: Circular
References:
Grogan, 2005a. *The North Munster Project Vol. 1*. Dublin, Wordwell.

Possible univallate contour fort surrounding the summit of Knockainy Hill in Co. Limerick. The circular shaped enclosure is not visible on the ground or in any aerial photographs and was identified by Grogan (2005a). It has a total site footprint of approximately 10.4ha. There are no obvious entrance features, or structures visible on the surface or in aerial photographs. A number of barrows and a mound are recorded in the interior.

Catalogue number: 66
Hillfort name: Knockanacuig
Townland: Lohercannan
County: Kerry
ITM coordinates: 481947, 614652
RMP number: KE029-112
Topographical position: Low rise hill
Elevation: 30m OD
Number of enclosing elements: 2 (Class 2 possible)
Total area: 1.67ha
Shape: Circular
References:
Connolly, M. 2008. *The Prehistoric Settlement of the Lee Valley, Tralee, Co. Kerry: A Landscape Perspective*. Unpublished PhD thesis, University College Cork.

Dunne, L. and Bartlett, T. 2009. Knockanacuig/Lohercannon hillfort. In Bennett (ed.), *Excavations 2006*: 226–227. Dublin, Wordwell.

Situated on the summit of a low hill on the western edge of Tralee town, a circular multivallate hillfort encloses an area of approximately 1.67ha. Although at 30m OD, the site affords panoramic views from the summit, with particular emphasis on views of Tralee Bay. The site has been heavily disturbed by housing developments. Excavation reveals that the outer enclosure consists of a bank with external ditch. A single published radiocarbon sample from the basal fill of the ditch returned a Middle–Late Iron Age date. A possible entrance was excavated by Dunne and Bartlett (2009: 227), however, no information regarding its location is available. A possible Early Medieval ringfort is visible at the centre of the hillfort and a possible prehistoric mound within this has been destroyed. The site is described in the minutes of the County Kerry Field Club in November 1940 (Connolly 2008). A large mound, up to 5m in height, surrounded by a small enclosure was recorded. This is also depicted in first and second edition Ordnance Survey mapping. There is no surface indication of other internal features and excavation revealed only a single pit dated to the Early Medieval period.

Catalogue number: 67
Hillfort name: Knockash
Townland: Knockash
County: Galway
ITM coordinates: 564133, 711547
RMP number: GA115-042
Topographical position: Hilltop
Elevation: 204m OD
Number of enclosing elements: 1 (Class 1)
Total area: 4.56ha
Shape: Circular
References:
n/a

Univallate contour fort in commanding position at the summit of a domed hill, 5km south-east of Loughrea town in Co. Galway. The site is circular and has a footprint of 4.6ha. Knockash is not visible on the ground or in any available satellite or aerial photographs. There are no obvious entrance features. The interior is under pasture and has some overgrowth. The site is not depicted in any historic mapping. There are no obvious archaeological features visible within the interior on the surface.

Catalogue number: 68
Hillfort name: Knockbrack
Townland: Knockbrack
County: Dublin
ITM coordinates: 715350, 759428
RMP number: DU004-012006
Topographical position: Hilltop
Elevation: 176m OD
Number of enclosing elements: 1 (Class 1)
Total area: 9.11ha
Shape: Sub-circular
References:
Keeling, D. 1983. A group of tumuli and a hill-fort near Naul, County Dublin. *Journal of the Royal Society of Antiquaries of Ireland* 113: 67–74.

Univallate contour fort on the domed summit of isolated hilltop overlooking low-lying terrain in all directions. Knockbrack is visible in aerial photographs as a vegetation mark. It is univallate for its entire circuit, with a footprint of 9.1ha. Aerial photographs suggest there is an internal ditch. More recent aerial photographs show evidence for a possible inner palisade trench along the south-west and southeastern sections. No obvious entrance feature has been recorded. A barrow is positioned at the highest point of the interior. Four other barrows and a mound are recorded within the interior. There are no other features visible on the surface.

Catalogue number: 69
Hillfort name: Knockdhu
Townland: Knockdhu
County: Antrim
ITM coordinates: 734106, 906636
RMP number: ANT035-005
Topographical position: Spur of hill
Elevation: 362m OD
Number of enclosing elements: 3 (Class 3)
Total area: 8.21ha
Shape: Sub-rectangular
References:
Macdonald, P. 2016. Excavations at Knock Dhu promontory fort, Ballyhackett, Co. Antrim, 2008. *Emania* 23: 33–52.

Knockdhu is a large, multivallate, inland promontory fort on eastern edge of the Antrim plateau. The natural promontory is an impressive and commanding feature in the landscape, with particularly impressive views of the Antrim coastline and the Irish Sea to the east. The western approach is protected by a series of three banks and two ditches. The site has a footprint of approximately 8.2ha. The ramparts survive well throughout their length. Excavation of the enclosing elements in 2008 indicate the ditch was partially rock cut and there is evidence for a palisade on one of the banks. The site is dated to the Middle–Late Bronze Age by radiocarbon dating and flint tool associations (McNeary 2012). Near the southern edge of the enclosing elements, a simple corresponding gap in both the inner and outer banks is likely to be an original entrance. Evidence of round house structures in the interior has been confirmed by excavation. Four round-houses were excavated. Recent LiDAR commissioned by the Northern Ireland Environmental Agency has provided further evidence for internal occupation on site. This has added up to 50 new round-house structures to the 18 discovered in 2008 (McNeary 2012).

Catalogue number: 70
Hillfort name: Knockeen
Townland: Knockeen
County: Wicklow
ITM coordinates: 690170, 673699
RMP number: WI037-018
Topographical position: Spur of hill
Elevation: 123m OD
Number of enclosing elements: 2 (Class 2 likely)
Total area: 6.22ha
Shape: Sub-oval
References:
n/a

Possible multiple enclosure hillfort on the low-domed summit of a hilltop (Figure 11.17). This sub-oval fort closely follows the contours of the hill and takes advantage of a steep break of slope to north. It has a total footprint of 6.2ha and is 300m to the north of the large multiple hillfort of Rathgall. Aerial photographs has suggested that Knockeen is a bivallate multiple enclosure with widely spaced enclosing elements separated by approximately 50m. This has been confirmed by geophysics undertaken by the author. Ramparts survive well at the south and west, but are destroyed at the north and east. The inner example comprises a 5m wide bank of yellow earthy-clay and stands to a height of approximately 1.5m. The outer enclosing elements are partially visible in Cambridge University aerial photographs and the geophysical survey. There are three breaks through the inner enclosing elements that are probably modern. There is a large cairn positioned at the centre and highest point of the hillfort. Geophysical survey by the author has identified up to 20 possible hut structures within the interior. Possible pits and relict field systems have also been identified.

Catalogue number: 71
Hillfort name: Knocknacarragh
Townland: Knocknacarragh
County: Galway
ITM coordinates: 629773, 814975
RMP number: GA093-014
Topographical position: Spur of hill
Elevation: 28m OD
Number of enclosing elements: 1 (Class 1)
Total area: 1.46ha
Shape: Oval
References:
Gosling, P. 1993. *Archaeological Inventory of County Galway*. Dublin, Stationary Office.

Univallate contour fort on the domed summit of Gentian Hill, a prominent hilltop jutting out into Galway Bay and overlooking Galway City to the east. It has a total footprint of approximately 1.5ha. There are no recorded entrance features or evidence for any internal features on the surface. The hillfort is very poorly preserved. The enclosing elements are apparent at the east and south-east but are otherwise completely levelled.

Catalogue number: 72
Hillfort name: Knocknashee
Townland: Knocknashee
County: Sligo
ITM coordinates: 555592, 819076
RMP number: SL032-013001
Topographical position: Hilltop
Elevation: 276m OD
Number of enclosing elements: 1 (Class 1)
Total area: 21.5ha
Shape: Sub-oval
References:
Condit, T. and Gibbons, M. 1991. A glimpse of Sligo's prehistory. *Archaeology Ireland* 5 (3): 7–10.

Egan, U., Byrne, E., Sleeman, M., Ronan, S. and Murphy, C. 2005. *Archaeological Inventory of County Sligo, Vol 1*: Sligo South. Dublin, Stationary Office.

Sub-oval contour fort on flat summit of Knocknashee, a steep isolated mountain in otherwise low-lying terrain (Figure 11.18). The hillfort has a total footprint of approximately 21.5ha. The enclosing elements comprise a stone wall 3.8m wide and up to 1.5m high. There is no obvious ditch. A possible entrance was identified at the south comprising a gap with a passage-way/corridor. Within the interior, up to 30 circular hut structures are visible on the surface and in aerial photographs, clustered in the more sheltered eastern half of the hillfort. Two large cairns located within the hillfort to the north are passage tombs. A D-shaped enclosure abuts the inner bank of the hillfort. Condit *et al.* (1991) have suggested that various hollows and 'scoops' within the interior to the south may represent other settlement activity.

Figure 11.17: Knockeen hillfort, Co. Wicklow.

Figure 11.18: Knocknashee hillfort, Co. Sligo (Source: Google Earth 2017).

Catalogue number: 73
Hillfort name: Knockscur
Townland: Killoughterane
County: Carlow
ITM coordinates: 677393, 653534
RMP number: CW019-065
Topographical position: Spur of hill
Elevation: 265m OD
Number of enclosing elements: 1 (Class 1)
Total area: 1.04ha
Shape: Sub-oval
References:
Brindley, A. and Kilfeather, A. 1993. *Archaeological Inventory of County Carlow*. Dublin, Stationary Office.

Sub-oval contour fort with a total footprint of 1ha surrounding the summit of a hill in the north-west of the Blackstairs Mountains. The site overlooks a number of small river systems at the base of the hill. It is univallate for the entire circuit with a simple stone lined entrance break to the south. The ramparts survive well at the east where there is a single rubble bank with some stone facing. There is no obvious ditch feature apparent on the surface. At the northern section of the hillfort, the stones forming the bank have been used to create a field boundary which follows the course of the enclosing elements. There is no evidence for any internal features on the surface.

Catalogue number: 74
Hillfort name: Knocksouna
Townland: Knocksouna
County: Limerick
ITM coordinates: 556504, 627972
RMP number: LI047-092
Topographical position: Hilltop
Elevation: 103m OD
Number of enclosing elements: 1 (Class 1)
Total area: 2.82ha
Shape: Circular
References:
n/a

To the west of Killmallock village, a circular contour fort surrounding the summit of an isolated hill overlooks the Loobagh River 200m to the south. The site has a total footprint of approximately 2.8ha. The enclosing elements survives as a low lying bank with no evidence for an associated ditch feature. The bank is heavily overgrown at the east with scrub and trees. There are no recorded entrance features. Immediately outside the enclosing elements to the north are a number of earthworks and terraces which may comprise hut structures and relict field divisions. There have been no archaeological investigations of this hillfort.

Catalogue number: 75
Hillfort name: Laghtea
Townland: Laghtea
County: Tipperary
ITM coordinates: 573422, 679385
RMP number: LI047-092
Topographical position: Hilltop
Elevation: 322m OD
Number of enclosing elements: 2 (Class 1)
Total area: 7.83ha
Shape: Irregular shape
References:
Condit, T. 1995b. Hillfort discoveries near Killaloe, Co. Clare. *Archaeology Ireland* 9 (1): 34–37.

Irregular shaped contour fort surrounding the two summits of Laghtea Hill. The site is in a commanding position overlooking the southern fording point of Lough Derg, with panoramic views from the summit. The site has a total footprint of 7.8ha. It is bivallate for its entire perimeter. There is no separation between the inner and outer bank and a ditch separates the two features. The inner bank is approximately 2.5m wide and up to 0.9m high. The outer example measures 2.6m wide and 0.5m high. The enclosing elements are positioned at the base of a steep incline. Ramparts survive well throughout, though heavy overgrowth largely conceals the enclosing elements. There is a possible original entrance at the west (Condit 1995b: 37). A pathway breaks through enclosing elements at south and this is unlikely to have been an original feature. A low circular platform is visible within the interior to the north. There are no other features visible on the surface.

Catalogue number: 76
Hillfort name: Lisbancarney
Townland: Lisbancarney
County: Tyrone
ITM coordinates: 679714, 854690
RMP number: TYR061-027
Topographical position: Hilltop
Elevation: 79m OD
Number of enclosing elements: 2 (Class 2 possible)
Total area: 6.89ha
Shape: Sub-oval
References:
n/a

Possible multiple enclosure surrounding the domed summit of a prominent hillock in undulating terrain. Vegetation marks suggest that the fort was probably bivallate for the entire circuit. The enclosing elements mainly survive as concentric field boundaries following the contours of the hillock separated by a maximum of 89m. A simple 16m gap in the inner enclosing elements at the north-west is probably modern. No other evidence for any internal features on the surface or possible entrances. The interior is currently under pasture. There have been no archaeological investigations of this hillfort.

Catalogue number: 77
Hillfort name: Lisbane
Townland: Lisbane
County: Limerick
ITM coordinates: 528828, 644136
RMP number: LI019-127
Topographical position: Hilltop
Elevation: 71m OD
Number of enclosing elements: 2 (Class 2 possible)
Total area: 0.42ha
Shape: Circular
References:
Westropp, T. J. 1916–1917. On certain typical earthworks and ring-walls in Co. Limerick. *Proceedings of the Royal Irish Academy* 33C: 9–42.

Circular contour fort on summit of Kilbradran Hill. This hilltop dominates the surrounding flat, low-lying terrain. The summit offers panoramic views of the surrounding landscape. Lisbane has a total site footprint of 0.4ha. It is bivallate for most of its circuit, the north-east and eastern section of the enclosing elements have been truncated by a post-medieval road. The inner bank comprises of earth. Westropp (1916–1917: 29) noted that both the inner and outer faces of the bank were revetted. The inner bank survives best at the north. An external ditch is heavily infilled and measures 1.1m wide and 0.3m deep. Outer enclosing elements consist of an earthen bank, 3.1m wide and up to 2.6m in external height, with a shallow ditch, 1.3m wide and 0.1m deep. A possible annex to the north recorded by Westropp is now destroyed (1916–1917: 29). Four possible original entrances consisting of two simple gaps in the inner bank and two simple gaps in the outer enclosing elements. There is no evidence for any internal features on the surface.

Catalogue number: 78
Hillfort name: Lisbanoe
Townland: Lisbanoe
County: Armagh
ITM coordinates: 685459, 842351
RMP number: ARM016-001
Topographical position: Hilltop
Elevation: 72m OD
Number of enclosing elements: 2 (Class 2 possible)
Total area: 1.02ha
Shape: Sub-circular
References:
n/a

Multiple enclosure in commanding position surrounding the domed summit of Lisbanoe Hill, overlooking Callan River and Butler River to immediate east (Figure 11.19). The site is bivallate for its entire circuit and is just over 1ha in size. The ramparts survive well throughout and comprise two widely spaced features separated by an average of 20m. The inner feature comprises a steep scarp 2m in external height. The outer enclosing element consists of a scarp 1.7m high with an external ditch feature, 3.6m wide and 0.6m deep. There is some tree cover on the outer ramparts. A possible original entrance gap is apparent at the eastern side of the inner enclosing elements and consists of a simple gap. A break in the outer enclosing elements to the south is probably a modern gap. There is no evidence for any internal features on the surface.

Catalogue number: 79
Hillfort name: Lisdarush
Townland: Lisdarush
County: Leitrim
ITM coordinates: 591963, 845723
RMP number: LE008-004001
Topographical position: Hill slope/ridge
Elevation: 72m OD
Number of enclosing elements: 1 (Class 1)
Total area: 1.12ha
Shape: Sub-oval
References:
n/a

Univallate contour fort in commanding position overlooking Lough Melvin to the north. The fort occupies a slight spur of sloping ground and is located at the northern entrance to a break in the Darty Mountains in Co. Leitrim. The enclosing elements are defined by an earthen bank up to 0.3m high and 3m wide at the north and east. This is reduced to a scarp elsewhere. An external ditch is apparent at the east and south and this measures 4–7m wide. An external bank abutting the external face of the ditch is visible at the north and measures 3.2m wide and 1.2m in height. A modern road has truncated much of the enclosing elements at the east and north. There are no obvious entrance features. No other features visible on the surface. A ring-barrow and mound are recorded approximately 100m to the north of the site.

Catalogue number: 80
Hillfort name: Liss
Townland: Liss
County: Tipperary
ITM coordinates: 603219, 664661
RMP number: TN034-070
Topographical position: Low rise hill
Elevation: 101m OD
Number of enclosing elements: 2 (Class 2 possible)
Total area: 9.26ha
Shape: Sub-circular
References:
Farrelly, J. and O'Brien, C. 2002. *Archaeological Inventory of County Tipperary Vol. 1: North Tipperary*. Dublin, Stationary Office.

Multiple enclosure on a low hilltop at the eastern foothills of Silvermines Mountains, overlooking Cromoge River to east with panoramic views from the summit. Liss is possible bivallate with total footprint of 9.2ha. The inner enclosing elements are reduced to scarp and first edition Ordnance Survey mapping indicates the rampart was much more impressive than at present. It comprises a bank of earth 1.6m wide and 0.3m high with no obvious ditch. External drystone wall facing in some sections is likely to be of nineteenth-century date (Farrelly and O'Brien 2002). A possible outer enclosing element was identified on aerial photographs and first edition Ordnance Survey mapping. It is apparent to the north, north-east and west as a concentric bank approximately 125m from the inner enclosing elements. There are no recorded entrance features to either enclosure. There is no evidence for any internal features on the surface.

Catalogue number: 81
Hillfort name: Lurigethan
Townland: Layd
County: Antrim
ITM coordinates: 722630, 925529
RMP number: ANT020-008
Topographical position: Hill spur
Elevation: 343m OD
Number of enclosing elements: 6 (Class 3)
Total area: 9.74ha
Shape: Sub-rectangular
References:
Chart, D.A. 1940. *A Preliminary Survey of the Ancient Monuments of Northern Ireland*. Belfast, Stationery Office.

Lurigethan hillfort is a large multivallate inland promontory fort on the edge of the Antrim plateau (Figure 11.20). The natural promontory is an impressive and commanding feature in the landscape and affords panoramic views, with particularly impressive views of the Antrim coastline and the Irish Sea to the east. The site has a total footprint of approximately 9.7ha. Six closely spaced banks are visible in places, cutting off the western approach to the site. The remainder of the hillfort is protected by a sheer cliff face. The six closely spaced enclosing elements appear to merge into one another at various points throughout its length, although four banks are obvious at all times. Ramparts survive well throughout their length. There is a break through the enclosing elements at the south-west, comprising a simple gap. This probably comprises an original entrance. There is no evidence for any internal features on the surface, though possible roundhouse structures are apparent in aerial photographs inside the monument.

Figure 11.19: Lisbanoe hillfort, Co. Armagh (Source: Google Earth 2017).

Figure 11.20: Lurigethan hillfort, Co. Antrim (Source: Google Earth 2017).

Catalogue number: 82
Hillfort name: Lyles Hill
Townland: Ballymartin
County: Antrim
ITM coordinates: 724697, 882904
RMP number: ANT056-005
Topographical position: Hilltop
Elevation: 219m OD
Number of enclosing elements: 1 (Class 1)
Total area: 6.25ha
Shape: Pear-shaped
References:

Evans, E. 1953. *Lyles Hill: a Late Neolithic Site in County Antrim*. Belfast, Stationary Office.

Gibson, A. and Simpson, D. 1987. Lyles Hill, Co. Antrim. *Archaeology Ireland* 1 (2): 72–75.

Simpson, D. and Gibson, A. 1989. Lyles Hill. *Current Archaeology* 114: 214–215.

Pear-shaped partial contour fort surrounding the domed summit of Lyles Hill, near Belfast City. The site has a total footprint of approximately 6.3ha and is univallate for its entire circuit. The enclosing elements comprise a single bank up to 1m high with no associated ditch feature. It survives well throughout its circuit. Excavation recovered Late Bronze Age dates for the bank. There are four breaks in the enclosing elements. Two of these may be original and comprise simple breaks through the bank. A cairn is visible on the surface near the southern part of the interior. Pits, hearths, Neolithic pottery, stone tools, small stone ornaments, Bronze Age food Vessels and urns, as well as two palisade enclosures were found within the interior (Evans 1953; Gibson and Simpson 1987; Simpson and Gibson 1989). Most of this material dates to an earlier phase before the construction of the hillfort. There is also evidence for the reuse of the site during the Iron Age. The interior is currently under pasture. The site was excavations by Evans (1953) and Gibson and Simpson (1987).

Catalogue number: 83
Hillfort name: Magherintemple
Townland: Magherintemple
County: Cavan
ITM coordinates: 650990, 816468
RMP number: CV016-099001
Topographical position: Hilltop
Elevation: 126m OD
Number of enclosing elements: 1 (Class 1)
Total area: 3.06ha
Shape: Oval
References:

O'Donovan, P. 1995. *Archaeological Inventory of County Cavan*. Dublin, Stationary Office.

An oval contour fort with a total footprint of approximately 3.1ha, is located on a hilltop in undulating terrain overlooking a number of small river systems to the south and the Bunnoe River to the east and north-east. The site is univallate for its entire circuit with traces of an external counter-scarp bank in places. The enclosing elements have been levelled from north to east and from south to south-west but are still visible on the ground and in aerial photographs (O'Donovan 1995). A portion of the enclosing elements survive in the south-west and comprise a bank and external ditch with a small external counter-scarp. There are no obvious entrance features. There is a later graveyard and church within hillfort interior. There is no evidence for any internal features on the surface that may be contemporary with the hillfort.

Catalogue number: 84
Hillfort name: Mallabeny
Townland: Mallabeny
County: Cavan
ITM coordinates: 650730, 854110
RMP number: TYR058-007
Topographical position: Hilltop
Elevation: 176m OD
Number of enclosing elements: 1 (Class 1)
Total area: 1.19ha
Shape: Oval
References:

Warner, R. 2009. Clogher in late prehistory. In Cooney, G., Becker, K., Coles, J., Ryan, M. and Sievers, S. (eds), *Relics of Old Decency: Archaeological Studies in Later Prehistory*: 507–518. Dublin, Wordwell.

Univallate contour fort surrounding the domed summit of Mallabeny Hill, an isolated hilltop overlooking a broad valley to south. There are panoramic views from the summit. The ramparts survive as a scarp to the east, south and west, but are ploughed flat at the north, although still partially visible in aerial photographs. The enclosing elements are defined by a scarp, maximum 1.8m high. A 3.3m wide bank is positioned on top of this scarp and is approximately 0.3m in height. The remains of an internal ditch 3m wide and 0.7m deep is apparent. No obvious entrance features have been recorded and there is no evidence for any internal features on the surface.

Catalogue number: 85
Hillfort name: Mooghaun
Townland: Mooghaun
County: Clare
ITM coordinates: 540742, 670568
RMP number: CL042-074001
Topographical position: Hilltop
Elevation: 78m OD
Number of enclosing elements: 3 (Class 2)
Total area: 11.05ha
Shape: Oval
References:

Westropp, T. J. 1893. Prehistoric stone forts of central Clare–Moghane, and Langough, near Dromoland. *Journal of the Royal Society of Antiquities of Ireland* 23 (3): 281–291.

Grogan, E. 2005a. *The North Munster Project Vol. 1.* Dublin, Wordwell.

Near the village of Newmarket-on-Fergus, an oval multiple enclosure with a total site footprint of approximately 11.1ha is positioned in a commanding location overlooking low-lying terrain and the Shannon Estuary to the south and west. The site is trivallate for its entire circuit and the ramparts survive well throughout. They comprise three widely spaced limestone rubble banks that follow the contours of the hill, taking advantage of naturally steep slopes to make the defences seem higher from the exterior. Radiocarbon samples from underneath and within the bank returned Late Bronze Age dates around 1250–800 BC. Grogan (2005a: 128) suggests the three enclosing elements were likely contemporary. There are two possible original entrance features in the inner and outer enclosing elements. As many as nine other breaks in the banks of the hillfort may be modern. Up to nine hut structures, six enclosures and three cairns have been identified within the interior, attesting to pre-hillfort, post-hillfort and contemporary occupation of the hilltop. A number of quarry pits may also be contemporary with the construction of the fort. The site was excavated by Grogan from 1992–1995.

Catalogue number: 86
Hillfort name: Mountfortesque
Townland: Mountfortesque
County: Meath
ITM coordinates: 693809, 780031
RMP number: ME013-012001
Topographical position: Hill slope/ridge edge
Elevation: 213m OD
Number of enclosing elements: 1 (Class 1)
Total area: 2.29ha
Shape: Circular
References:

Ó Ríordáin, S. P. 1956. Small hill-fort and tumulus on Mountfortesque. *Journal of the Royal Society of Antiquaries of Ireland* 86 (1): 106–107.

Hill slope fort positioned surrounding the southern summit of a ridge of hills, overlooking the Devlin River and its tributaries. Mountfortesque is circular in shape and has a total footprint of 2.3ha. It is univallate for its entire circuit. The ramparts survive well at the east and south but have been destroyed at the north-east. The defences consist of a bank with a broad, rock-cut external ditch. The bank is largely composed of shale and earth from the digging of the ditch. In places, a counterscarp bank is present. The enclosing elements to the south-east and east have been altered and incorporated into modern field systems (Ó Ríordáin 1956). Ó Ríordáin has identified a possible original entrance at the north-east. A possible prehistoric burial mound is located at the highest point within the interior. There is no evidence for any internal features on the surface that might be contemporary with the construction or occupation of the hillfort.

Catalogue number: 87
Hillfort name: Mullaghnashee
Townland: Mullaghnashee
County: Roscommon
ITM coordinates: 567932, 788158
RMP number: RO014-078001
Topographical position: Hilltop
Elevation: 179m OD
Number of enclosing elements: 1 (Class 1)
Total area: 1.77ha
Shape: Oval
References:
n/a

Mullaghnashee is an oval contour fort located on the flat summit of Fairymount Hill, with panoramic views of the surrounding lowland from the summit. The site is univallate for its entire circuit with a total footprint of approximately 1.8ha. The ramparts survive well at south-east and north-west and comprise a grass covered stone rubble bank 3.5m in maximum width and 0.3m in maximum height. There is a modern wall built on bank at the north-east. The banks and large sections of interior have been destroyed by quarrying at south-east and by the construction of a reservoir at north-west. The northern and northeastern section of the enclosing elements are visible in second edition Ordnance Survey mapping as a curving boundary. There are no recorded entrance features or surface evidence for any internal features.

Catalogue number: 88
Hillfort name: Rahally
Townland: Rahally
County: Galway
ITM coordinates: 565965, 725900
RMP number: GA086-211
Topographical position: Low rise hill
Elevation: 104m OD
Number of enclosing elements: 3 (Class 2 confirmed)
Total area: 14.24ha
Shape: Circular
References:

Mullins, G. 2008. Three thousand years of human activity at Rahally, Co. Galway. In O'Sullivan, J. and Stanley, M. (eds), *Roads, Rediscovery and Research*: 25–35. Dublin, National Roads Authority.

The multiple enclosure of Rahally hillfort, Co. Galway, is positioned on a low-rise hill, though there is panoramic views from the summit. It was discovered in 2004–5 while archaeological testing was being undertaken in advance of the N6 Galway to East Ballinasloe scheme (Mullins 2008). This revealed a large trivallate hillfort with widely spaced enclosing elements, situated on the northwestern summit of a low glacial ridge. The road cut through the centre of the hillfort, necessitating excavation of over 50% of its interior and approximately 30% of the entire monument. Despite the large area excavated, there was a distinct lack of artifacts or features associated with the construction and occupation of the hillfort. There was a notable arrangement of parallel entrances running east–west through all three enclosures. The site was later re-occupied in the Early Medieval period when a number of ringforts were built within and abutting the enclosing elements of the hillfort. The site was excavated by Mullins in 2005. It revealed the enclosing elements comprised a series of banks with external ditches. Sherds of Late Bronze Age coarse-ware pottery and a damaged polished stone axe were recovered from the inner ditch, while a damaged bone needle and whetstone were found in the outer ditch (Mullins 2008: 26). Interestingly, animal bone was also recovered from the ditch fills, most notably dog bone and a complete deer skeleton (Mullins 2008). Radiocarbon samples and Late Bronze Age pottery from the ditch fills indicate the monument was built in the Late Bronze Age.

Catalogue number: 89
Hillfort name: Rath
Townland: Rath
County: Cork
ITM coordinates: 602415, 581055
RMP number: CO067-001001
Topographical position: Low rise hill
Elevation: 135m OD
Number of enclosing elements: 2 (Class 2 possible)
Total area: 4.91ha
Shape: Circular
References:

Power, D., Byrne, E., Egan, U., Lane, S. and Sleeman, M. 1994. *Archaeological Inventory of County Cork Vol. 2*. Dublin, Stationary Office.

Rath hillfort is a multiple enclosure fort located approximately 8.5km to the west-north-west of Youghal town. The site is strategically positioned on the summit of a low rise hill in Rath townland, with panoramic views from the summit. It is positioned at a bend in the Tourig River which flows along the base of the hilltop to the west and south. This river connects to Youghal Bay 7km to the east, which is also visible from the summit of the hillfort. The enclosing elements survive in varying states of preservation. The inner example survives to a height of 0.5m at the north-north-east and south-south-west and is ploughed out for the remainder of its circuit. The outer enclosing element, which is separated from the inner example by a maximum of 103m, is apparent as a series of modern earthen field boundaries at the south-west and north-west. There are no obvious entrance features recorded and there are no archaeological features visible on the surface of the interior. The majority of the interior of the inner enclosing element and northwestern portion of the total enclosed area is under dense scrub and bracken growth. The remainder of the site is currently under pasture.

Catalogue number: 90
Hillfort name: Rathcannon
Townland: Rathcannon
County: Limerick
ITM coordinates: 558662, 634045
RMP number: LI039-029
Topographical position: Low rise hill
Elevation: 105m OD
Number of enclosing elements: 2 (Class 2 possible)
Total area: 2.95ha
Shape: Sub-oval
References:
Condit, T. 1995b. Hillfort discoveries near Killaloe, Co. Clare. *Archaeology Ireland* 9 (1): 34–37.

Sub oval multiple enclosure at the summit of an isolated low-rise hill, with excellent views overlooking the surrounding low-lands. The site has a total footprint of approximately 2.9ha. It is bivallate for its entire circuit with no recorded entrance features. The enclosing elements are widely spaced and are separated by 23–200m. This variation is due to the outer enclosing element following the contours of the natural limestone plateau. There is no evidence for any internal features on the surface. The central enclosing element is depicted in the first and second editions of the Ordnance Survey maps.

Catalogue number: 91
Hillfort name: Rathcoran
Townland: Rathcoran
County: Wicklow
ITM coordinates: 688416, 689371
RMP number: WI027-026001
Topographical position: Hilltop
Elevation: 370m OD
Number of enclosing elements: 2 (Class 2 likely)
Total area: 10.06ha
Shape: Pear-shaped
References:
Condit, T. 1998. Observations of the Baltinglass hillfort complex. In Corlett, C. and O'Sullivan, A. (eds), *Wicklow Archaeology and History* 1: 9–25.

Waddell, J. 2010 *(first edition 1998). The Prehistoric Archaeology of Ireland.* Bray, Wordwell.

Rathcoran is a multiple enclosure positioned on the highest summit of Tuckmill Hill. It is one of nine forts comprising the Baltinglass hillfort cluster. This pear-shaped bi-vallate fort is approximately 10.1ha in size. The enclosing elements vary in size and are largest at the north-west, where the inner example is 16m wide and 2.4m high. The outer enclosure is 12m wide and 2.1m high. Geophysical survey has identified a possible palisade at the crest of the inner bank in this area (Chapter 5). There are a large number of breaks in the enclosing elements, however, many are probably modern. There are a number of quarry pits located between the inner and outer enclosures. LiDAR and geophysical survey have identified over 100 hut structures within the fort. A large Neolithic cairn was excavated within the hillfort interior in the 30s (Walshe 1941). A second cairn abuts the exterior of the outer enclosing elements at the south. Waddell (2010) and Condit (1998) have interpreted Rathcoran as an unfinished hillfort, due to the incomplete nature of the enclosing elements and intervening quarry features.

Catalogue number: 92
Hillfort name: Rathgall
Townland: Rathgall
County: Wicklow
ITM coordinates: 690144, 673198
RMP number: WI037-016
Topographical position: Hilltop
Elevation: 139m OD
Number of enclosing elements: 3 (Class 2 confirmed)
Total area: 6.08ha
Shape: Circular
References:
Orpen, G. 1911. Rathgall, County Wicklow. *The Journal of the Royal Society of Antiquaries of Ireland* 1 (2): 138–150.

Raftery, B. 1976. Rathgall and Irish hillfort problems. In Harding, D.W. (ed.) *Hillforts. Later Prehistoric Earthworks in Britain and Ireland*: 339–57. London, Academic Press.

Rathgall is a circular multiple enclosure surrounding the summit of a hilltop at the end of a prominent east–west shoulder of upland, overlooking a tributary of Derreen River to west. The multiple enclosure of Knockeen is situated 300m to north. Rathgall is 6.1ha is size and consists of four concentric enclosing elements, the inner example probably being an Early Medieval ringfort. The three large enclosures consist of two closely spaced banks with an intervening ditch and an outer enclosing element positioned approximately 50m away. Two gaps are apparent in the inner enclosing elements of hillfort (not the Early Medieval ringfort). One possible original entrance at the western side consists of a simple gap through the banks and causeway over the ditch. Excavation has revealed a large number of artifacts, pits, structures and four burials within the interior. A metalworking area was also identified. This produced a large number of artifacts associated with the manufacturing of bronze objects. Occupation structures dated to the Late Bronze Age were excavated immediately outside the hillfort to the south. The outer enclosing element has been destroyed at the north-east.

Catalogue number: 93
Hillfort name: Rathmicheal
Townland: Rathmicheal
County: Dublin
ITM coordinates: 723363, 721409
RMP number: DU026-048001
Topographical position: Hilltop
Elevation: 133m OD
Number of enclosing elements: 1 (Class 1)
Total area: 1.76ha
Shape: Circular
References:
n/a

Rathmicheal is a univallate contour fort surrounding the low domed summit of a hilltop at the eastern interface of mountainous terrain and low-lying agricultural land. It is univallate for its entire circuit with no obvious entrance feature recorded. Aerial photographs suggests that the ramparts survive well throughout the circuit and that the bank is approximately 5m in width. A small central enclosure, positioned at the summit of the interior may be a later earthwork dating to the Early Medieval period. There are no other features visible on the surface that might be contemporary with the construction and occupation of the hillfort.

Catalogue number: 94
Hillfort name: Rathnagree
Townland: Tuckmill Hill/Tuckmill Upper
County: Wicklow
ITM coordinates: 688005, 690013
RMP number: WI027-010
Topographical position: Hill spur
Elevation: 326m OD
Number of enclosing elements: 3 (Class 2 confirmed)
Total area: 5.78ha
Shape: Circular
References:

Condit, T. 1992. Ireland's hillfort capital: Baltinglass, Co. Wicklow. *Archaeology Ireland* 6 (3): 16–20.

Condit, T. 1998. Observations of the Baltinglass hillfort complex. In Corlett, C. and O'Sullivan, A. (eds), *Wicklow Archaeology and History* 1: 9–25.

Multiple enclosure positioned on a northern spur of Tuckmill Hill, 400m north-north-west of Rathcoran hillfort. Rathnagree is one of nine forts comprising the Baltinglass hillfort cluster. The name Rathnagree translates as 'rath of the king'. It has a total footprint of 5.8ha and comprises three widely spaced enclosing elements which do not follow the contours of the hill. The ramparts disregard topographical variation to form three circular enclosures. The ramparts survive best at north, north-east and north-west. Commercial woodland encroaches on the enclosing elements at the north and north-east. Geophysical survey suggests that the low rise stone banks of the inner and outer enclosing elements formed the footings for timber palisades. This has been confirmed by excavation. The inner and outer enclosures comprise low stone banks which excavation reveals provided the footing for substantial palisades. The middle enclosure consists of an earthen bank and external ditch with counter-scarp, although an earlier phase of construction consisted of a timber palisade similar to the inner and outer examples. Middle Bronze Age radiocarbon dates were returned from all three of the enclosing elements (Chapter 6). There are two possible original entrances in the middle enclosing elements at the north-north-east and north, comprising simple gaps. A number of possible hut structures were identified within the interior through geophysics and LiDAR surveys. The arc of a possible structure was identified by excavation abutting the middle enclosure.

Catalogue number: 95
Hillfort name: Sheemore
Townland: Sheemore
County: Leitrim
ITM coordinates: 599021, 804821
RMP number: LE027-054007
Topographical position: Hilltop
Elevation: 178m OD
Number of enclosing elements: 1 (Class 1)
Total area: 1.75ha
Shape: Sub-oval
References:

Moore, M.2003. *Archaeological Inventory of County Leitrim*. Dublin, Stationary Office.

Univallate contour fort surrounding the domed summit of Sheemore Hill, an isolated hilltop overlooking low-lying terrain, Ballinamore and Ballyconnell canal to north-west and Dooloughan Lough immediately to the north-east. The site has a total footprint of approximately 1.8ha. The hillfort comprises a sub-oval area defined by a single enclosing element comprising a grass covered stone bank best preserved at south, where it measures 0.9m wide and 0.55m high (Moore 2003). There are no recorded entrance features. The hillfort surrounds three possible megalithic tombs, a D-shaped enclosure and a hut site. The interior is currently under pasture.

Catalogue number: 96
Hillfort name: Sillagh
Townland: Sillagh
County: Kildare
ITM coordinates: 692151, 713625
RMP number: KD024-025
Topographical position: Low rise
Elevation: 174m OD
Number of enclosing elements: 1 (Class 1)
Total area: 3.52ha
Shape: Oval
References:
n/a

Univallate contour fort also known as 'The Ring' on a slight rise in low-lying terrain with panoramic views from the summit (Figure 11.21). The eastern half of the site had been completely ploughed out prior to the completion of the first edition Ordnance Survey programme. This is partially visible in some aerial photographs. The extant western portion of the enclosing elements survive well and comprise a 1.5m high, 6.4m wide bank, a 1.6m deep, 8.2m wide external ditch and an outer bank measuring 1.6m high and 8.2m wide. The entire site is under pasture, however, an extensive quarry pit abuts the site to the south.

Catalogue number: 97
Hillfort name: Slieveboy Lower
Townland: Slieveboy Lower
County: Wicklow
ITM coordinates: 702269, 687191
RMP number: Unrecorded
Topographical position: Hilltop
Elevation: 391m OD
Number of enclosing elements: 1 (Class 1)
Total area: 7.56ha
Shape: Circular
References:
n/a

Possible univallate contour fort in commanding hilltop position overlooking the entrance to a slight break in the north–south extension of the southern Wicklow Mountains. The site was first identified through aerial photography by the author in 2015. The possible hillfort is under commercial forestry plantation, although a portion of the southern perimeter and a larger section of the interior at the north have recently been felled. The enclosing elements are visible as a circular area of stunted tree growth. Where felling has been completed, the enclosing elements are apparent as a vegetation mark and this probably represents a ditch feature. The site has a total footprint of approximately 7.6ha.

Catalogue number: 98
Hillfort name: Spinans Hill 1
Townland: Ballyhubbock Upper
County: Wicklow
ITM coordinates: 691957, 691588
RMP number: WI027-078002
Topographical position: Hilltop
Elevation: 409m OD
Number of enclosing elements: 1 (Class 1)
Total area: 11.11ha
Shape: Irregular
References:

Condit, T. 1992. Ireland's hillfort capital: Baltinglass, Co. Wicklow. *Archaeology Ireland* 6 (3): 16–20.

Condit, T. 1998. Observations of the Baltinglass hillfort complex. In Corlett, C. and O'Sullivan, A. (eds), *Wicklow Archaeology and History* 1: 9–25.

Corlett, C. and Weaver, M. 2002b. *The Liam Price Notebooks: the Placenames, Antiquities and Topography of County Wicklow, Vol. 2*. Dublin, Department of Arts, Heritage and the Gaeltacht.

Spinans Hill 1 is a contour fort in a commanding location on the domed eastern summit of Spinans Hill, which is positioned at southwestern edge of the Wicklow mountains. Spinans Hill 1 is one of nine forts comprising the Baltinglass hillfort cluster. The site is univallate for its entire circuit and has a total footprint of approximately 11.1ha. The rampart forms an irregular-shaped enclosure with a peat-covered earth and stone bank. The bank is best preserved at the north and east and is largely levelled over the remainder of its perimeter (Grogan and Kilfeather 1997: 40–41). It was identified through aerial photography by Condit (1992). Price had previously noted a section of the enclosure but did not associated it with a hillfort (in Corlett and Weaver 2002: 538–539). Excavation revealed that the northern section of the enclosure consisted of a stone rubble bank with no evidence for an associated ditch (Chapter 6). There are no recorded entrance features to the fort. Condit (1992, 20; 1998, 20) has recorded what he interprets as a Neolithic passage tomb cemetery within the interior of the Spinans Hill 1. This comprises a large central cairn positioned at the summit, surrounded by five smaller examples. A seventh cairn was identified by the author. No other features are apparent within the fort, though this may be a result of heavy scrub and heather overgrowth throughout the site.

Catalogue number: 99
Hillfort name: Spinans Hill 2
Townland: Ballyhubbock Upper/Spinans Hill
County: Wicklow
ITM coordinates: 691977, 691520
RMP number: WI027-078001
Topographical position: Hilltop
Elevation: 409m OD
Number of enclosing elements: 2 (Class 1)
Total area: 131ha
Shape: Irregular
References:

Condit, T. 1992. Ireland's hillfort capital: Baltinglass, Co. Wicklow. *Archaeology Ireland* 6 (3): 16–20.

Condit, T. 1998. Observations of the Baltinglass hillfort complex. In Corlett, C. and O'Sullivan, A. (eds), *Wicklow Archaeology and History* 1: 9–25.

Corlett, C. and Weaver, M. 2002b. *The Liam Price Notebooks: the Placenames, Antiquities and Topography of County Wicklow, Vol. 2*. Dublin, Department of Arts, Heritage and the Gaeltacht.

Spinans Hill 2 is a contour fort surrounding all of Spinans Hill and enclosing the forts of Brusselstown Ring and Spinans Hill 1. Spinans Hill 2 is an extensive earthwork with a total footprint of 131ha. This is the largest hillfort in Ireland and is one of nine forts comprising the Baltinglass hillfort cluster. The ramparts survive well at the north and north-west where it comprises a double bank with an intervening ditch, 23m in total width. The southeastern section of Spinans Hill 2 integrates a large portion of the outer enclosing element of Brusselstown Ring. The southwestern section of Spinans Hill 2 has been destroyed. Condit (1992: 19) has noted that there are 'a number of breaches' to the north, which he believes are original entrance features. Bersu noted a possible roadway to the hillfort at the south-west corner of Brusselstown Ring (in Corlett and Weaver 2002: 504). There are up to 250 hut structures within the interior, though these may be associated with Brusselstown Ring. Condit (1992: 20; 1998: 20) has recorded a possible passage tomb cemetery within the interior of Spinans Hill 2, though these may be associated with Spinans Hill 1. Another cairn and enclosure have been recorded within the large contour fort (Condit 1992: 20).

Catalogue number: 100
Hillfort name: Sroove
Townland: Sroove
County: Roscommon
ITM coordinates: 586280, 778809
RMP number: RO028-094
Topographical position: Hill slope
Elevation: 60m OD
Number of enclosing elements: 1 (Class 1)
Total area: 2.03ha
Shape: Circular
References:
n/a

Contour fort of approximately 2ha enclosed area to the north-west of a broad low hill. The site is univallate for its entire circuit with two simple entrance gaps at the east and west. The ramparts survive well at north-east to south-west and are partially truncated by a modern road at the north-west. They comprise an earthen bank maximum 4m in width and 1m in maximum height. Outer ditch feature at north-east and north-west measuring 5m in maximum width and 0.2m deep. Possible original entrances at east and west comprising narrow simple gaps in the enclosing elements. No evidence for any internal features on the surface.

Catalogue number: 101
Hillfort name: Sruhaun
Townland: Sruhaun/Pinnacle
County: Wicklow
ITM coordinates: 687806, 689205
RMP number: Unrecorded
Topographical position: Hill spur
Elevation: 322m OD
Number of enclosing elements: 1 (Class 1)
Total area: 1.43ha
Shape: Sub-circular
References:
n/a

Univallate contour fort in commanding position on western ridge of Tuckmill Hill, a steep tripartite hilltop overlooking the modern town of Baltinglass. The hillfort is located on level terrain with a steep break of slope to the west. This fort is one of nine forts comprising the Baltinglass hillfort cluster and was identified by LiDAR and geophysical survey. The hillfort has a total site footprint of approximately 1.4ha. The ramparts are visible in the LiDAR data as a low-rise bank feature, although this is difficult to distinguish on the ground. Geophysical survey has confirmed the presence of the fort and revealed that the enclosing elements consisted of a low-rise bank (Chapter 5). This was subsequently confirmed through excavation (Chapter 6). There is a single 4m wide entrance feature at the north-west which may be original. Geophysical survey did not reveal archaeological features within the interior.

Catalogue number: 102
Hillfort name: The Doons
Townland: Fawnlion
County: Leitrim
ITM coordinates: 580516, 838826
RMP number: LE010-085005
Topographical position: Hilltop
Elevation: 255m OD
Number of enclosing elements: 1 (Class 1)
Total area: 1.29ha
Shape: Sub-circular
References:

Kytmannow, T., Kahlert, T., Hunt, C. 2010. The Doons Hillfort. *Archaeology Ireland* 24 (3): 18–21.

Contour fort on prominent hill at the southern edge of upland terrain. The site has a total footprint of 1.3ha. The enclosing elements form a complete circuit and enclose a flat plateau. Approximately 17m outside of this, the remains of a possible outer enclosure is apparent at the north and east, although further investigation is needed to confirms this as either a field boundary or a feature related to the hillfort. There is a possible original entrance at the east and west, both of which comprise a simple break in the enclosing elements. Aerial photography has identified a possible enclosure, two hut sites and a possible kerb circle inside the hillfort (Kytmannow *et al.* 2010).

Catalogue number: 103
Hillfort name: Tinoran
Townland: Tinoran
County: Wicklow
ITM coordinates: 685167, 690577
RMP number: WI026-004
Topographical position: Hilltop
Elevation: 312m OD
Number of enclosing elements: 4 (Class 2 confirmed)
Total area: 84.03ha
Shape: Sub-circular
References:

Condit, T. 1992. Ireland's hillfort capital: Baltinglass, Co. Wicklow. *Archaeology Ireland* 6 (3): 16–20.
Grogan, E. and Kilfeather, A. 1997. *Archaeological Inventory of County Wicklow*. Dublin, Stationary Office.
Condit, T. 1998. Observations of the Baltinglass hillfort complex. In Corlett, C. and O'Sullivan, A. (eds), *Wicklow Archaeology and History* 1: 9–25.

Multiple enclosure in commanding position surrounding the summit of Tinoran Hill. Tinoran is the second largest hillfort in Ireland with a total footprint of approximately 84ha. It is one of nine forts comprising the Baltinglass hillfort cluster. Tinoran can be translated as 'house of Odhrán'. It comprises up to four widely spaced enclosing elements and a central enclosure placed at its summit which is probably an Early Medieval ringfort. These do not form complete circuits, however, it is likely that they once did, but have subsequently been destroyed by agricultural processes. The ramparts have been heavily disturbed by commercial forestry plantation which covers most of this large hillfort. Recent excavation has dated the two middle enclosing elements. Radiocarbon dating confirms the hillfort is Late Bronze Age, but suggests the defences were built over a prolonged period (Chapter 6). There are no recorded entrance features. A single hut structure is located within the hillfort and a large barrow abuts the second middle enclosing element.

Catalogue number: 104
Hillfort name: Tobercurry/Clogher
Townland: Tobercurry
County: Tyrone
ITM coordinates: 653789, 851306
RMP number: TYR058-033
Topographical position: Hilltop
Elevation: 98m OD
Number of enclosing elements: 1 (Class 1)
Total area: 1.6ha
Shape: Sub-rectangular
References:

Evans, E. 1966. *Prehistoric and Early Christian Ireland: A Guide*. London, Batsworth.

Warner, R. 2009. Clogher in late prehistory. In Cooney, G., Becker, K., Coles, J., Ryan, M. and Sievers, S. (eds), *Relics of Old Decency: Archaeological Studies in Later Prehistory*. 507–518. Dublin, Wordwell.

Waddell, J. 2010 *(first edition 1998). The Prehistoric Archaeology of Ireland*. Bray, Wordwell.

A sub-rectangular univallate contour fort, 1.6ha in size, surrounds the upper part of a steep drumlin (Warner 2009: 510). The hillfort rampart comprises a 6m wide and 1m high bank with an external U-shaped ditch approximately 3m wide and 0.8m deep. It survives well at north-east, east and south-east, but is partially levelled at the west. Excavation revealed that the ditch may have comprised a much wider feature, measuring about 20m wide and 2m deep (Warner 2009: 510). Coarse ware pottery from the bank may date the hillfort to the Late Bronze Age (Waddell 1998: 270). Radiocarbon dates confirm occupation of the hilltop during this period (*ibid.*: 270; 277), although there is considerable evidence for later activity. A recent publication by Warner (2009) suggests that the hillfort is Iron Age, despite the author conceding that dating evidence for the earthwork itself is poor. There are up to eight breaks in the enclosing elements. It is unknown if these are original. A large ringfort and associated earthworks take up much of the interior. A well-preserved ring-barrow is positioned at the north-east of the interior. Pits and postholes were revealed through excavation of the interior.

Catalogue number: 105
Hillfort name: Toberdornan
Townland: Ballywillin
County: Antrim
ITM coordinates: 688867, 937089
RMP number: ANT006-004
Topographical position: Hilltop/edge of spur
Elevation: 125m OD
Number of enclosing elements: 1 (Class 1)
Total area: 1.43ha
Shape: Oval
References:
Chart, D.A. 1940. *A Preliminary Survey of the Ancient Monuments of Northern Ireland*. Belfast, Stationery Office.

Partial contour fort surrounding the flat-topped summit and eastern facing slopes of Dunmill Hill. The site has a total footprint of approximately 1.4ha and is univallate for the entire circuit. Aerial and satellite images suggest that the ramparts survive well, although there are no published record of their state. There are no obvious entrance features recorded. There are two enclosures partly visible on the surface within the interior of the fort and a number of possible hut sites visible in aerial photographs. There is dense tree cover over the enclosing elements and the interior is currently under pasture. The monument was surveyed in 1940 by Chart (1940: 9). The site is traditionally known as a pre-twelfth century stronghold of the O'Flynns. References to a chair and footprint stone suggest it may also have function as an Medieval inauguration site.

Catalogue number: 106
Hillfort name: Tory Hill
Townland: Tory Hill
County: Limerick
ITM coordinates: 553170, 642877
RMP number: LI022-111001
Topographical position: Hilltop
Elevation: 113m OD
Number of enclosing elements: 1 (Class 1)
Total area: 2.27ha
Shape: Oval
References:
Grogan, E. 2005b. *The North Munster Project Vol. 2*. Dublin, Wordwell.

Possible contour fort surrounding the summit of Tory Hill, an isolated hilltop situated in low-lying terrain, with extensive views from the summit. This possible hillfort overlooks a river to east. There is no available information regarding the enclosing elements. No obvious entrance features have been recorded or any evidence for internal features on the surface (Grogan 2005b: 113). There has been no archaeological investigation of this hillfort and further information is not available.

Catalogue number: 107
Hillfort name: Turlough Hill
Townland: Oughtmama
County: Clare
ITM coordinates: 531366, 707352
RMP number: CL003-036001
Topographical position: Hilltop
Elevation: 248m OD
Number of enclosing elements: 1 (Class 1)
Total area: 3.54ha
Shape: Sub-circular
References:
n/a

Sub-circular contour fort positioned on the eastern summit of Turlough Hill in Co. Clare (Figure 11.22). The hillfort is strategically positioned overlooking low-lying terrain to the east and north-east with excellent views of Galway Bay to the north. The fort comprises a single stone wall of thin slabs stacked up to 1m in height. It is 4.5m in maximum width. There are up to 16 evenly spaced breaks in the enclosing elements. These comprise simple narrow gaps in the stone wall and are evenly distributed around the perimeter. A large hilltop settlement on the western summit of Turlough Hill, comprising over 100 circular hut structures, may be somewhat contemporary with the hillfort. Turlough Hill has been recorded in the first and second edition Ordnance Survey maps.

Figure 11.21: Sillagh hillfort, Co. Kildare (Source: Google Earth 2017).

Figure 11.22: Turlough Hill, Co. Clare (Source: Google Earth 2017).

Catalogue number: 108
Hillfort name: Tycanny
Townland: Tycanny
County: Tyrone
ITM coordinates: 656149, 858039
RMP number: TYR052-029
Topographical position: Hilltop
Elevation: 210m OD
Number of enclosing elements: 1 (Class 1)
Total area: 1.38ha
Shape: Oval
References:
n/a

Partial contour fort surrounding the summit of Tycanny Hill with panoramic views from the summit. Univallate for the entire circuit, the hillfort has a total footprint of approximately 1.4ha. It is oval-shaped and consists of a bank and internal ditch. A modern track has truncated much of the bank. Where best preserved, the bank is 5m wide and approximately 2m high. The internal ditch is 2.3m in maximum width and 1.3m deep. The internal ditch survives well throughout the circuit. There are a number of breaks in the enclosing elements. A simple 2m wide gap in the bank and ditch at the east is likely to be an only original entrance. There is no evidence for any internal features on the surface.

Bibliography

Abels, B. 2002. *Die Heunischenburg bei Kronach. Eine späturnenfelderzeitliche Befestigung*. Regensburg, Univ.-Verl.

Ahern, S. 2012. *Ring-ditches of Later Prehistoric Ireland.* Unpublished MPhil thesis, University College Cork.

Aitchison, N. 1987. The Ulster cycle: heroic image and historical reality. *Journal of Medieval History* 13 (2): 87–116.

Aitchison, N. 1998. Late Bronze Age ritual at Haughey's Fort: the evidence of the deposited cup-and-ring marked stone. *Emania* 17: 31–39.

Alcock, L. 1972. *'By South Cadbury is that Camelot...' Excavations at Cadbury Castle, 1966–70*. London, Thames and Hudson.

Alcock, O., de hÓra, K. and Gosling, P. 1995. *Archaeological Inventory of County Galway Vol. 2: North Galway*. Dublin, Stationary Office.

Allen, T. Hayden, C. and Lamdin-Whymark, H. 2009. *From Bronze Age Enclosure to Anglo-Saxon Settlement: Archaeological Excavations at Taplow Hillfort, Buckinghamshire.* Oxford, Oxford University School of Archaeology.

Almagro-Gorbea, M. 1995. Ireland and Spain in the Bronze Age. In Waddell, J. and Shee Twohig, E. (eds), *Ireland in the Bronze Age*: 136–148. Dublin, Stationary Office.

Angelini, I., Artioli, G., Bellintani, P, Diella, V., Gemmi, M., Polla, A. and Rossi, A. 2004. Chemical analysis of Bronze Age glasses from Frattesina di Rovigo, Northern Italy. *Journal of Archaeological Science* 31: 1175–1184.

Angelini, I., Polla, A., Giussani, B., Bellintani, P. and Artioli, G. 2009. Final Bronze Age glass in northern and central Italy: is Frattesina the only glass production centre? In Moreau, J., Auger, R., Cahbot, J and Herzog, A. (eds), *36th Symposium International D'Archéometrie*: 329–337 Celat, Université Laval.

Arkush, E. 2011. *Hillforts of the Ancient Andes: Colla Warfare, Society, and Landscape.* Florida, University Press of Florida.

Armit, I. 2007. Hillforts at war: from Maiden Castle to Taniwaha Pã. *Proceedings of the Prehistoric Society* 73: 25–38.

Armit, I. 2012. *Head Hunting and the Body in Iron Age Europe*. Cambridge, Cambridge University Press.

Armit, I. and McKenzie, J. 2013. *An Inherited Place: Broxmouth Hillfort and the South-East Scottish Iron Age*. Edinburgh: Society of Antiquaries of Scotland.

Armstrong, E.C.R. 1917. The Great Clare Find of 1854. *Journal of the Royal Society of Antiquaries of Ireland* 47: 21–36.

Ashe FitzGerald, M. 2000. T*homas Johnson Westropp: An Irish Antiquary*. Dublin, University College Dublin.

Avery, M. 1976. Hillforts of the British Isles: a student's introduction. In Harding, D. (ed.), *Hillforts: Later Prehistoric Earthworks in Britain and Ireland*: 1–58. London, Routledge.

Avery, M. 1986. 'Stoning and fire' at hillfort entrances of southern Britain. *World Archaeology* 18: 216–230.

Avery, M. 1993. *Hillfort Defences of Southern Britain.* British Archaeological Report 231, Oxford, Archaeopress.

Baillie, M. and Brown, D. 1991. A dendro-date from Haughey's Fort. *Emania* 8: 39–40.

Baillie, M. and Brown, D. 1998. Further evidence confirms the twelfth century BC dendro-date from the inner ditch of Haughey's Fort. *Emania* 17: 45–6.

Barker, L. and Driver, L. 2011. Close to the edge: new perspectives on the architecture, function and regional geographies of the coastal promontory forts of the Castlemartin Peninsula, South Pembrokeshire, Wales. *Proceedings of the Prehistoric Society* 77: 65–87.

Barrett, J. 2012. Are models of prestige goods economies and conspicuous consumption applicable to the archaeology of the Bronze to Iron Age transition in Britain? In Jones, A., Pollard, J., Allen, M. and Gardiner, J. (eds),

Image, Memory and Monumentality. Archaeological Engagements with the Material World: 6–17. Oxford, Oxbow Books.

Bateson, D. 1973. Roman material from Ireland: a re-consideration. *Proceedings of the Royal Irish Academy* 73: 21–97.

Bayliss, A. 2007. Bayesian building: an introduction for the numerically challenged. *Vernacular Architecture* 38: 75–86.

Bayliss, A., Bronk Ramsey, C., Van der Plicht, J. and Whittle, A. 2007. Bradshaw and Bayes: towards a timetable for the Neolithic. *Cambridge Journal of Archaeology* 17.1: 1–28.

Bayliss, A., Van der Plicht, J., Bronk Ramsey, C., McCormack, G., Healy, F. and Whittle, A. 2011. Towards generational time-scales; the quantitative interpretation of archaeological chronologies. In Whittle, A., Healy, F. and Bayliss, A. (eds.) *Gathering Time: Dating the Early Neolithic Enclosures of Southern Britain and Ireland.* Oxford: Oxbow.

Beck, C. and Shennan, S. 1991. *Amber in Prehistoric Britain*. Oxford, Oxbow Books.

Becker, K. 2008. Left but not lost. *Archaeology Ireland* 22, (1): 12–15.

Becker, K. 2010. Rathgall, Co. Wicklow. *Archaeology Ireland Heritage Guide* 51. Dublin, Wordwell.

Becker, K. 2013. The dating of Late Bronze Age Dowris metalwork: a pilot study. *The Journal of Irish Archaeology* 21: 7–15.

Bell, T. and Lock, G. 2000. Topographic and cultural influences on walking the Ridgeway in later prehistoric times. In Lock, G. (ed.), *Beyond the Map: Archaeological and Spatial Technologies*: 85–100. The Netherlands, IOS Press.

Bellwood, P. 1971. Fortifications and economy in prehistoric New Zealand. *Proceedings of the Prehistoric Society* 37: 56–95.

Bellwood, P. 1972. Excavations at Otakanini Pā, South Kaipara Harbour. *Journal of the Royal Society of New Zealand* 2 (3): 259–191.

Bendry, R., Thorpe, N., Outram, A. and Van Wijngaarden-Bakker, L. 2013. The origins of domestic horses in north-west Europe: new direct dates on the horses of Newgrange, Ireland. *Proceedings of the Prehistoric Society* 79: 91–103.

Bentley, A. 2000. Provenience analysis of pottery from Fijian hillforts: preliminary implications for exchange with the archipelago. *Oceania* 35 (2): 82–91.

Bergh, S. 2000. Transforming Knocknarea. *Archaeology Ireland* 14 (2): 14–18.

Bergh, S. 2002. Knocknarea: the ultimate monument. In Scarre, C. (ed.), *Monuments and Landscape in Atlantic Europe*: 139–151. London, Routledge.

Bernhardt-House, P. 2007. Horses, hounds, and high kings: a shared Arthurian tradition across the Irish Sea? In Nagy, J. (ed.), *Myth in Celtic Literatures*: 11–21, Celtic Studies Association of North America Yearbook 6, Dublin, Four Courts Press.

Birch, J. 2010. Coalescence and conflict in Iroquois Ontario. *Archaeological Review from Cambridge* 25 (1): 29–48.

Bogucki, P. 2004. Late Bronze Age Urnfields of Central Europe. In Bogucki, P. and Crabtree, P. (eds), *Ancient Europe: 8000 BC–AD 1000, Encyclopaedia of the Barbarian World*: 86–91. New York, Charles Scribner's Sons.

Borlase, W. 1897. *The Dolmens of Ireland*. London, Chapman and Hall Ltd.

Bourke, L. 2001. *Crossing the Rubicon: Bronze Age Metalwork from Irish Rivers*. Bronze Age Studies 5, National University of Ireland, Galway.

Bowden, M. and McOmish, D. 1987. The required barrier. *Scottish Archaeological Review* 4: 76–84.

Bowden, M. and McOmish, D. 1989. Little boxes: more about hillforts. *Scottish Archaeological Review* 6: 12–15.

Bowen, E. 1972. *Britain and the Western Seaways*. London, Thames and Hudson.

Bradford, J. 1940. The excavations of Cherbury Camp, 1939. An interim report. *Oxonieisia* 5: 13–20.

Bradley, J. 2004. Moynagh Lough, Co. Meath, in the Late Bronze Age. In Roche, H., Grogan, E., Bradley, J., Coles, J. and Raftery, B. (eds), *From Megaliths to Metals*: 91–98. Oxford, Oxbow.

Bradley, R. 1971. Stock raising and the origins of the hillfort on the South Downs. *Antiquaries Journal* 51: 8–29.

Bradley, R. 1980. Subsistence, exchange and technology–a social framework for the Bronze Age in southern England. In Barrett, J. and Bradley, R. (eds), *Settlement and Society in the British Later Bronze Age*: 57–75. British Archaeological Report 83, Oxford, Archaeopress.

Bradley, R. 1990 (revised 1998). *The Passage of Arms: an Archaeological Analysis of Prehistoric Hoards and other Votive Deposits*. Cambridge, Cambridge University Press.

Bradley, R. 1998. Interpreting enclosures. In Edmonds, M. and Richards, C. (eds), *Understanding the Neolithic of North-Western Europe*: 188–203. Glasgow, Cruithne Press.

Bradley, R. 2002. *The Past in Prehistoric Societies*. London, Routledge.

Bradley, R. 2005. *The Moon and the Bonfire: An Investigation of Three Stone Circles in North-east Scotland. Edinburgh*, Society of Antiquaries of Scotland Monograph.

Bradley, R. and Ellison, A. 1975. *Rams Hill: a Bronze Age Defended Enclosure and its Landscape*. British Archaeological Report 19, Oxford, Archaeopress.

Brandherm, D. 2014. Late Bronze Age casting debris and other base metal finds from Haughey's Fort. *Emania* 22: 59–68.

Bridgford, S. 1997. Mightier than the pen? An edgewise look at Irish Late Bronze Age swords. In Carman, J. (ed.), *Material Harm: Archaeological Studies of War and Violence*: 95–115. Glasgow, Cruithne Press.

Bridgford, S. 2002. Bronze and the first arms race–cause, effect or coincidence? In Ottaway, B. and Wager, E. (eds), *Metals and Society: Papers from a Session Held at the European Association of Archaeologists Sixth Annual Meeting in Lisbon 2000*: 123–132. Oxford, Archaeopress.

Brill, R. 1992. Chemical analysis of some glasses from Frattesina. *The Journal of Glass Studies* 34: 11–22.

Brindley, A. and Kilfeather, A. 1993. *Archaeological Inventory of County Carlow. Dublin*, Stationary Office.

Brindley, A.L., Lanting, J.N. and Mook, W.G. 1989/90a. Radiocarbon dates from Irish *fulachta fiadh* and other burnt mounds. *The Journal of Irish Archaeology* 5: 25–33.

Brindley, A. and Lanting, J. 1989/1990b. Radiocarbon dates for Neolithic single burials. *The Journal of Irish Archaeology* 5: 1–7.

Brindley, A., Lanting, J. and Mook, W. 1983. Radiocarbon dates from the Neolithic burials at Ballintruer More, Co. Wicklow and Ardcrony, Co. Tipperary. *The Journal of Irish Archaeology* 1: 1–9.

Bronk Ramsey, C. 1995. Radiocarbon calibration and analysis of stratigraphy: the OxCal program. *Radiocarbon* 37: 425–30.

Bronk Ramsey, C. 1998. Probability and dating. *Radiocarbon* 40: 461–74.

Bronk Ramsey C. 2001. Development of the radiocarbon calibration program. *Radiocarbon* 43: 355–63.

Bronk Ramsey, C. 2009. Bayesian analysis of radiocarbon dates. *Radiocarbon* 51: 337–360.

Brothwell, Don. 1999. Biosocial and bioarchaeological aspects of conflict and warfare. In Carman, J. and Harding, A. (eds), *Ancient Warfare*: 25–38. Stroud, The History Press.

Brown, I. 2009. *Beacons in the Landscape: the Hillforts of England and Wales*. Oxford, Windgather Press.

Brück, J. 2007. The character of Late Bronze Age settlement in southern Britain. In Haselgrove, C. and Pope, R. (eds), *The Earlier Iron Age in Britain and the Near Continent*: 24–38. Oxford, Oxbow.

Brück, J and Fokkens, H. 2013. Bronze Age settlements. In Fokkens, H. and Harding, A (eds), *The Oxford Handbook of the European Bronze Age*: 82–101. Oxford, Oxford University Press.

Brück, J. and Fontijn, D. 2013. The myth of the chief: prestige goods, power, and personhood in the European Bronze Age. In Fokkens, H. and Harding, A. (eds), *The Oxford Handbook of the European Bronze Age*: 197–215. Oxford, Oxford University Press.

Brugge, D. 1978. A comparative study of Navajo mortuary practices. *American Indian Quaterly* 4: 309–338.

Brun, P. 1993. East-west relations in the Paris basin during the Late Bronze Age. In Scarre, C. and Healy, F. (eds), *Trade and Exchange in Prehistoric Europe*: 171–182. Oxford, Oxbow.

Buck, C. E., Cavanagh, W. G. & Litton, C. D. 1996. *Bayesian Approach to Interpreting Archaeological Data*. Chichester, Wiley.

Buckley, D. and Hedges, J. 1987. *The Bronze Age and Saxon Settlements at Springfield Lyons, Essex: and Interim Report*. Essex, Essex County Council.

Burgess, C. and Coombs, D. (eds) 1979. *Bronze Age Hoards: some Finds Old and New*. British

Archaeological Report 67, Oxford.

Burgess, C. and Gerloff, S. 1981. *The Dirks and Rapiers of Great Britain and Ireland*. Munich. Prähistorische Bronzefunde, abteilung IV, band 7. Stuttgart, Franz Steiner Verlag.

Burgess, C. and O'Connor, B. 2008. Iberia, the Atlantic Bronze Age and the Mediterranean. In Celestino, S., Rafel, N. and Armada, L. (eds), *Contacto cultural entre el Mediterráneo y el Atlántico (siglos XII–VIII ANE). La precolonización a debate*: 41–58. Madrid, Escuela Española de Historia y Arqueología en Roma-CSIC, Serie Arqueológica 11.

Byrne, D. 1852. On the duns of Cloch-an-Phuca and Log-an-Chorain. *Transactions of the Kilkenny Archaeological Society* 1 (3): 298–300.

Byrne, F. 1973. *Irish Kings and High-Kings*. Dublin, Four Courts Press.

Cahill, M. 2005. Bronze Age goldwork from Co. Kerry. In Connolly, M. (ed.), *Past Kingdoms: Recent Archaeological Research, Survey and Excavation in County Kerry*: 12–18. Tralee, The Heritage Council.

Cahill, M. 2006. John Windele's golden legacy: prehistoric and later gold ornaments from Co. Cork and Co. Waterford. *Proceedings of the Royal Irish Academy* 106C: 219–337.

Carey, A. 2002. Excavations at Knockacarrigeen Hill, Tuam, Co. Galway. *Journal of the Galway Archaeological and Historical Society* 54: 55–71.

Carman, J. 1997. Introduction: approaches to violence. In Carman, J. (ed.), Material Harm: Archaeological Studies of War and Violence: 1–23. Glasgow, Cruithne Press.

Carman, J. and Harding, A. 1999. Introduction. In Carman, J. and Harding, A. (eds), *Ancient Warfare*: 1–9. Stroud, The History Press.

Carneiro, R. 1981. The chiefdom: precursor of the state. In Jones, G. and Kautz, R. (eds), *The Transition to Statehood in the New World*: 37–75. Cambridge, Cambridge University Press.

Carrigan, Rev. W. 1905. *The History and Antiquities of the Diocese of Ossory*. Dublin, (reprinted Kilkenny 1981). 4 vols.

Casey, M. 1999. Excavation at the promontory fort at Doonamo, Aughernacallaigh, Co. Mayo. *Journal of the Galway Archaeological and Historical Society* 51: 65–76.

Caulfield, R. 1865. Untitled article in *Gentleman's Magazine* (1865, part 1): 707–710.

Caulfield, S. 1978. Neolithic fields: the Irish evidence. In Bowen, H. and Fowler, P. (eds), *Early Land Allotment in the British Isles: a Survey of Recent Work*: 137–143. British Archaeological Report, Oxford, Archaeopress.

Caulfield, S. 1983. The Neolithic settlement of North Connaught. In Reeves Smyth, T. and Hammons, F. (eds), *Landscape Archaeology in Ireland*: 195–216. British Archaeological Report, Oxford, Archaeopress.

Carey, A. 2002. Excavations at Knockacarrigeen Hill, Tuam Co. Galway. *Journal of the Galway Archaeological and Historical Society* 54: 55–71.

Chadbourne, K. 2005. Heroic dogs and men in the Finn ballads and tales. In Nagy, J. and Jones, L. (eds), *Heroic Poets and Poetic Heroes in Celtic Tradition: A Festschrift for Patrick K. Ford*: 28–41. Dublin, Four Courts Press.

Challis, A. 1978. *Motueka: an Archaeological Survey. Auckland*, Longman Paul.

Chapman, J. 1999. The origins of war in the prehistory of Central and Eastern Europe. In Carman, J. and Harding, A. (eds), *Ancient Warfare*: 101–142. Stroud, The History Press.

Chapple, R. 2013. https://sites.google.com/site/chapplearchaeology/irish-radiocarbon-dendrochronological-dates.

Charles-Edwards, T.M. 1996. Irish warfare before 1100. In Bartlett, T. and Jeffrey, K. (eds), *A Military History of Ireland*: 26–38. Cambridge, Cambridge University Press.

Chart, D.A. 1940. *A Preliminary Survey of the Ancient Monuments of Northern Ireland*. Belfast, Stationery Office.

Clarke, A. 2012. Coarse stone artefacts. In Cotter, C. *The Western Stone Forts Project: Excavations at Dún Aonghasa and Dún Eoghanachta*: 57–81. Dublin, Wordwell.

Clarke, D. 1972. A provisional model of an Iron Age society and its settlement systems. In Clarke, D. (ed.) *Models in Archaeology*: 801–870. London, Methuen.

Clarke, L. 2002. An early medieval enclosure and burials, Johnstown, Co. Meath. *Archaeology Ireland* 16 (3): 13–15.

Clarke, L. and Carlin, N. 2008. Living with the dead at Johnstown 1: an enclosed burial, settlement and industrial site. In Carlin, N., Clarke, L. and Walsh, F. (eds), *The Archaeology of Life and Death in the Boyne Floodplain: the Linear Landscape of the M4*: 55–86. Dublin, National Roads Authority.

Cleary, K. 2007. *Irish Bronze Age Settlements: Spatial Organisation and the Deposition of Material Culture.* Unpublished PhD thesis (2 vols), University College Cork.

Cleary, K. 2011. Neolithic landscape of Tullahedy. In Cleary, R. and Kelleher, H., *Archaeological Excavations at Tullahedy, Co. Tipperary: Neolithic Settlement in North Munster*: 122–144. Cork, Collins Press.

Cleary, K. (ed.) 2015. *Archaeological Networks. Excavations on Six Gas Pipelines in County Cork.* Cork, Collins Press.

Cleary, R.M. 1995. Late Bronze Age settlement and prehistoric burials, Lough Gur, Co. Limerick. *Proceedings of the Royal Irish Academy* 95C: 1–92.

Cleary, R.M. 2000. The potter's craft in prehistoric Ireland. In Desmond, A. *et al.* (eds), *New Agendas in Irish Prehistory*: 119–134. Dublin, Wordwell.

Cleary, R.M. 2003. Enclosed Late Bronze Age habitation site and boundary wall at Lough Gur, Co. Limerick. *Proceedings of the Royal Irish Academy* 103C: 97–189.

Cleary, R.M. 2008. The pottery from Site A. In M. Doody, *The Ballyhoura Hills Project*: 259–303. Discovery Programme Monograph 7, Bray, Wordwell.

Cleary, R.M. 2011. The pottery. In Cleary, R. and Kelleher. H. *Archaeological Excavations at Tullahedy, Co. Tipperary. Neolithic Settlement in North Munster*: 322–381. Cork, Collins Press.

Cleary, R.M. 2012. Pottery. In C. Cotter, *The Western Stone Forts Project: Excavations at Dún Aonghasa and Dún Eoghanachta, Vol 2*: 8–26. Dublin, Discovery Programme Monograph, Wordwell.

Cleary, R.M. and Kelleher, H. 2011. *Archaeological Excavations at Tullahedy, County Tipperary.* Cork, Collins Press.

Cleary, R.M. and O'Driscoll, J. 2014. Archaeological remains and geophysical surveys at Lough Gur and Grange stone circle. In Dalton, C. and O'Carroll, E. (eds), *Irish Quarternary Association Field Guide* 32: 31–44. Dublin, Irish Quaternary Association.

Cody, E. 1981. A hillfort at Ballylin, Co. Limerick, with a note on Mooghaun, Co. Clare. *Journal of the Royal Society of Antiquaries of Ireland* 111: 70–80.

Cody, E. 2002 *Survey of the megalithic tombs of Ireland, Vol. 6, Co. Donegal.* Dublin, Dublin Stationery Office.

Coffey, G. 1893-6. Notes on the classification of spearheads of the Bronze Age found in Ireland. *Proceedings of the Royal Irish Academy* 3, 486–510.

Colby, T. 1837. *Ordnance Survey of Ireland, County of Derry, Vol. 1.* Dublin.

Coles, J. 1962. European Bronze Age shields. *Proceedings of the Prehistoric Society* 28: 156–90.

Coles, J. and Harding, A. 1979. *The Bronze Age in Europe.* London, Methuen.

Collens, J. 1988. *Iron Age and Romano-British Settlement in the Upper Severn Valley.* Unpublished PhD thesis, Department of Ancient History and Archaeology, Faculty of Arts, University of Birmingham.

Collins, A. 1953. Excavations on Blewburton Hill, 1948 and 1949. *Berkshire Archaeological Journal* 57: 21–64.

Collis, J. 1977. An approach to the Iron Age. In Collis, J. (ed.), *The Iron Age in Britain: a Review*: 1–7. Sheffield, University of Sheffield.

Colquhoun, I. 2011. Irish swords: use and abuse. In Uckelmann, M. and Modlinger, M. (eds), *Bronze Age Warfare: Manufacture and Use of Weaponry*: 107–116. British Archaeological Report 2255, Oxford, Archaeopress.

Condit, T. 1992. Ireland's hillfort capital: Baltinglass, Co. Wicklow. *Archaeology Ireland* 6 (3): 16–20.

Condit, T. 1995. Hillfort discoveries near Killaloe, Co. Clare. *Archaeology Ireland* 9 (1): 34–37.

Condit, T. 1996. Gold and fulachta fiadh: the Mooghaun find, 1854. *Archaeology Ireland* 10 (1): 20–23.

Condit, T. 1997. The Newgrange cursus and the theatre of ritual. *Archaeology Ireland* 11 (3): 26–27.

Condit, T. 1998. Observations of the Baltinglass hillfort complex. In Corlett, C. and O'Sullivan, A. (eds), *Wicklow Archaeology and History* 1: 9–25.

Condit, T. and Gibbons, M. 1988. Two 'little known' hillforts in Co. Kilkenny. *Decies* 37: 47–54.

Condit, T. and Gibbons, M. 1991. A glimpse of Sligo's prehistory. *Archaeology Ireland* 5 (3): 7–10.

Condit, T. and Buckley, V. 1998. The Doon of Drumsna: an Iron Age frontier fortification in Connacht. *Archaeology Ireland Heritage Guide* 1. Dublin, Wordwell.

Condit, T. and O'Sullivan, A. 1996. Formoyle hillfort and later prehistoric landscapes in east Clare. *The Other Clare* 20: 39–45.

Condit, T. and O'Sullivan, A. 1999. Landscapes of movement and control: interpreting prehistoric hillforts and fording-places on the River Shannon. *Discovery Programme Reports 5*: 25–39. Dublin, Royal Irish Academy.

Connolly, M. 2008. *The Prehistoric settlement of the Lee Valley, Tralee, Co. Kerry: a Landscape Perspective.* Unpublished PhD thesis (2 vols), University College Cork.

Connolly, P. 2001. *Bandon, People and Places* (vol. 2). Cork.

Conway, M. 2006. Survey and excavation in the Navan environs with 'Time Team': Creeveroe, Haughey's Fort and Ballydoo. *Emania* 20: 29–52.

Cooke, T. 1875. *History of Birr*. Tullamore.

Cooney, G. 2002. From Lilliput to Brobdingnag: the traditions of enclosure in the Irish Neolithic. In Varndell, G. and Topping, P. (eds), *Enclosure in Neolithic Europe*: 69–82. Oxford, Oxbow.

Cooney, G. 2009. Tracing lines across landscapes: corporality and history in later prehistoric Ireland. In Cooney, G., Becker, K., Coles, J., Ryan, M. and Sievers, S. (eds), *Relics of Old Decency: Archaeological Studies in Later Prehistory*: 375–388. Dublin, Wordwell.

Cooney, G. and Grogan, E. 1999 (first edition 1994). Irish Prehistory: a Social Perspective. Dublin, Wordwell.
Cooney, G., Bayliss, A., Healy, F., Whittle, A., Danaher, E., Cagney, L., Mallory, J., Smyth, J., Kador, T. and O'Sullivan, M. 2011. Ireland. In Whittle, A., Bayliss, A. and Healy, F. (eds), *Gathering Time: Dating the Early Neolithic Enclosures of Southern Britain and Ireland*: 562–669. Oxford, Oxbow.

Corlett, C and Weaver, M. 2002a. *The Liam Price Notebooks: the Placenames, Antiquities and Topography of County Wicklow, Vol. 1*. Dublin, Department of Arts, Heritage and the Gaeltacht.

Corlett, C and Weaver, M. 2002b. T*he Liam Price Notebooks: the Placenames, Antiquities and Topography of County Wicklow, Vol. 2*. Dublin, Department of Arts, Heritage and the Gaeltacht.

Corlett, C. 2004. A prehistoric enclosure at Keadeen, Co. Wicklow. *Journal of the Royal Society of Antiquaries of Ireland* 134: 80–90.

Corlett, C. 2014. Some cursus monuments in south Leinster. *Archaeology Ireland* 28 (2): 20–25.

Corney, M. 2006. The hillforts of Wessex: their morphology and environs. In Payne, A., Corney, M. and Cunliffe, B., *The Wessex Hillforts Project: Extensive Survey of Hillfort Interiors in Central Southern England*: 131–143. London, English Heritage.

Corney, M. and Payne, A. 2006. The monuments and their setting. In Payne, A., Corney, M. and Cunliffe, B., *The Wessex Hillfort Project: Extensive Survey of Hillfort Interiors in Central Southern England*. English Heritage, London, 39–130.

Corns, A., Fenwick, J. and Shaw, R. 2008. More than meets the eye. *Archaeology Ireland* 22 (3): 34–38.

Cotter, C. 2012a. *The Western Stone Forts Project: Excavations at Dún Aonghasa and Dún Eoghanachta Vol. 1*. Dublin, Wordwell.

Cotter, C. 2012b. *The Western Stone Forts Project: Excavations at Dún Aonghasa and Dún Eoghanachta Vol. 2*. Dublin, Wordwell.

Cotton, M. 1962. Berkshire hillforts. *Berlshire Archaeological Journal* 60: 30–52.

Craig, R., Knüsel, C. and Carr, G. 2005. Fragmentation, mutilation and dismemberment: an interpretation of human remains on Iron Age sites. In Parker Pearson, M. and Thorpe, I. (eds), *Warfare, Violence and Slavery in Prehistory*: 165–170. British Archaeological Report 1374, Oxford, Archaeopress.

Cunliffe, B. 1971. Some aspects of hill-forts and their cultural environments. In Wheeler, M., Jesson, M. and Hill, D (eds), *The Iron Age and Hill-Forts*: 53–70. Southampton: University of Southampton.

Cunliffe, B. 1984a. *Danebury, an Iron Age Hillfort in Hampshire, Vol. 1: the Excavations 1969–1978: the Site*. Research Report 52a, London. Council for British Archaeology.

Cunliffe, B. 1984b. *Danebury, an Iron Age Hillfort in Hampshire, Vol. 2: the Excavations 1969–1978: the Finds*. Research Report 52b, London. Council for British Archaeology.

Cunliffe, B. and Poole, C. 1991a. *Danebury, an Iron Age Hillfort in Hampshire, Vol. 4: the Excavations 1979–1988: the Site*. Research Report 73a, London. Council for British Archaeology.

Cunliffe, B. and Poole, C. 1991b. *Danebury, an Iron Age Hillfort in Hampshire, Vol. 5: the Excavations 1979–1988: the Finds*. Research Report 73b, London. Council for British Archaeology.

Cunliffe, B. 1991c. *Iron Age Communities in Britain (Third Edition)*. London, Routledge.

Cunliffe, B. 1995. *Danebury, an Iron Age Hillfort in Hampshire, Vol. 6: A Hillfort Community in Perspective*. Research Report 102, London. Council for British Archaeology.

Cunliffe, B. 1997. *The Oxford Illustrated History of Prehistoric Europe*. Oxford, Oxford University Press.

Cunliffe, B. 2000. *The Danebury Environs Programme: The Prehistory of a Wessex Landscape, Vol. 1, Introduction*. Oxford, English Heritage and Oxford University Committee for Archaeology.

Cunliffe, B. 2001. *Facing the Ocean: The Atlantic and its Peoples, 8000 BC–AD 1500*. Oxford, Oxford University Press.

Cunliffe, B. 2006. Understanding hillforts: have we progressed? In Payne, A., Corney, M. and Cunliffe, B., *The Wessex Hillfort Project: Extensive Survey of Hillfort Interiors in Central Southern England*: 151–162. London, English Heritage.

Cunliffe, B. 2008. *Europe Between the Oceans: 9000 BC–AD 1000*. New Haven, Yale University Press.

Cunliffe, B. 2011. *Danebury Hillfort*. Gloucestershire, The History Press.

Cunliffe, B. 2013. *Britain Begins*. Oxford, Oxford University Press.

Cunnington, M. 1933. *Excavations at Yarnbury Castle. Wiltshire Archaeological and Natural History Magazine* 46: 198–221.

Cuppage, J. 1986. *Archaeological Survey of the Dingle Peninsula*. Ballyferriter, Oidhreachta Chorca Dhuibhne.

Czebreszuk, C. and Müller, J. (eds), 2004. *Bruszczewo. Ausgrabungen und Forschungen in einer prähistorischen Siedlungskammer Grosspolens/Badania mikroregionu z terenu Wielkopolski. Band/Tom I. Forschungsstand – Erste Ergebnisse – Das östliche Feuchtbodenareal/Stan badán – Pierwsze wyniki – Wschodnia, torfowa część stanowiska*. Poznań-Kiel-Rahden (Westf.), Verlag Marie Leidorf.

Danaher, E. 2007. Monumental Beginnings: the Archaeology of the N4 Sligo Inner Relief Road. Dublin, National Roads Authority.

Darvill, T. and Thomas, J. 2001. Introduction. In Darvill, T. and Thomas, J. (eds), *Neolithic Enclosures in Atlantic Northwest Europe*: 1–23. Oxford, Oxbow Books.

Davies, R. 2006. *Basal-looped Spearheads: Typology, Chronology and Use*. British Archaeological Report 1497, Oxford, Archaeopress.

Davies, R. 2012. *The Early and Middle Bronze Age Spearheads of Britain*. Prähistorische Bronzefunde, abteilung V, band 5. Stuttgart, Franz Steiner Verlag.

De Silva, M and Pizziolo, G. 2001. Setting up a 'human calibrated' anistropic cost surface for archaeological landscape investigation. In Stancic, Z. and Veljanovski, T. (eds), *Computing Archaeology for Understanding the Past: Computer Applications and Quantitative Methods in Archaeology*: 279–286. Proceedings of the 28th CAA Conference, Ljubjana, Slovenia. British Archaeological Report, Oxford, Archaeopress.

Della Casa, P. 2002. Landschaften, Siedlungen, Ressourcen–Langzeitszenarien menschlicher Aktivität in ausgewähten alpinen Gebieten der Schweiz, Italiens und Frankreichs. *Préhistoires* 6. Montagnac, Ēditions Monique Mergoil.

Della Casa, P. 2007. Transalpine pass routes in the Swiss Central Alps and the strategic use of topographic resources. *Prehistoria Alpina* 42: 109–118.

Della Casa, P. 2013. Switzerland and the central Alps. In Fokkens, H. and Harding, A. (eds), *The Oxford Handbook of the European Bronze Age*: 706–722 Oxford University Press.

Delrieu, F. 2013. Chronologie et statut des sites fortifiés de hauteur au Bronze final et au 1er Fer ancien dans le Nord-Ouestd e la France (Haute-Normandie, Basse-Normandie et Bretagne). In Krause, S., Colin, A., Gruel, K., Ralston, I. and Dechezleprêtre, T. (eds), *L'âge du Fer en Europe, Mélanges offerts à Olivier Buchsenschutz*: 131–146. Mémoires 32, Ausonius.

Diemer, G. 1995. *Der Bullenheimer Berg und seine Stellung im Siedlungsgefüge der Urnenfelderkultur Mainfrankens*. Materialh, Bayer.

Dietler, M. 1990. Driven by drink: the role of drinking in the political economy and the case of Early Iron Age France. *Journal of Anthropological Archaeology* 9 (4): 352–406.

Dixon, P. 1976. Crickley Hill, 1969–1972. In Harding, D. (ed.), *Hillforts: Later Prehistoric Earthworks in Britain and Ireland*: 162–175. London, Academic Press.

Dixon, P. 1988. The Neolithic settlements on Crickley Hill. In Burgess, C., Topping, P., Mordant, C. and Maddison, C. (eds), *Enclosures and Defences in the Neolithic of Western Europe*: 75–89. British Archaeological Reports 403, Oxford.

Dixon, P. 1994. *Crickley Hill: Vol. 1. The Hillfort Defences.* Nottingham, Crickley Hill Trust and Department of Archaeology, University Of Nottingham.

Doody, M. 2008. *The Ballyhoura Hills Project*. Dublin, Wordwell.

Driver, T. 2008. Hillforts and human movement: unlocking the Iron Age Landscapes of mid Wales. In Fleming, A. and Hingley, R. (eds), *Prehistoric and Roman Landscapes, Landscape History After Hoskins, Vol. 1*: 83–100. Bollington, Windgather Press.

Driver, T. 2013. *Architecture, Regional Identity and Power in the Iron Age Landscapes of Mid Wales: The Hillforts of North Ceredigion*. British Archaeological Report 583, Oxford, Archaeopress.

Dular, J. and Tomanič Jevremov, M. 2010. *Ormož. Utrjeno naselje iz pozne bronaste in starejše železne dobe*. Opera Instituti Archaeologici Sloveniae 18. Ljubljana, Založba ZRC.

Dunne, L. and Bartlett, T. 2009. Knockanacuig/Lohercannan hillfort. In Bennett, I. (ed.), *Excavations 2006*: 226–7. Dublin, Wordwell.

Earle, T. 1977. A reappraisal of redistribution: complex Hawaiian chiefdoms. In Earle, T. and Ericson (eds), *Exchange Systems in Prehistory*: 213–229. London, Academic Press.

Earle, T. 1987. Chiefdoms in archaeological and ethnohistorical perspective. *Annual Review of Anthropology* 16: 279–308.

Earle, T. 1997. *How Chiefs come to Power*. California, Stanford University Press.

Earle, T. 2002. *Bronze Age Economics: The Beginnings of Political Economies*. New York, Westview Press.

Ellis, C. and Rawlings, M. 2001. Excavations at Balksbury Camp, Andover 1995–1997, *Proceedings of the Hampshire Field Club and Archaeological Society* 56: 21–94.

Ellis, P. 1993. *Beeston Castle, Cheshire: A Report on the Excavations 1968–1985 by Laurence Keen and Peter Hough*. London, English Heritage Archaeological Report 23.

Egan, U., Byrne, E., Sleeman, M., Ronan, S. and Murphy, C. 2005. *Archaeological Inventory of Country Sligo, Vol 1: Sligo South*. Dublin, Stationary Office.

Eogan, G. 1964. The later Bronze Age in Ireland in the light of recent research. *Proceedings of the Prehistoric Society* 30: 268–351.

Eogan, G. 1965. *Catalogue of Irish Bronze Swords*. Dublin, Stationary Office.

Eogan, G. 1969. 'Lock-rings' of the Late Bronze Age. *Proceedings of the Royal Irish Academy* 67: 93–148.

Eogan, G. 1974. Pins of the Irish Late Bronze Age. *Journal of the Royal Society of Antiquaries of Ireland* 104: 74–119.

Eogan, G. 1981. The gold vessels of the Bronze Age in Ireland and beyond. *Proceedings of the Royal Irish Academy* 81: 345–382.

Eogan, G. 1983. *The Hoards of the Irish Later Bronze Age*. Dublin, University College Dublin.

Eogan, G. 1984. *Excavations at Knowth 1*. Dublin, Royal Irish Academy Monographs in Archaeology.

Eogan, G. 1994. *The Accomplished Art: Gold and Gold-Working in Britain and Ireland during the Bronze Age*. Oxford, Oxbow.

Eogan, G. 1995. Ideas, peoples and things: Ireland and the external world during the Later Bronze Age. In Waddell, J. and Shee-Twohig, E. (eds), *Ireland in the Bronze Age*: 128–135. Dublin, Stationary Office.

Eogan, G. 2000. *The Socketed Bronze Axes in Ireland.* Prähistorische Bronzefunde 9, 22. Stuttgart, Franz Steiner Verlag.

Evans, E. 1933.The bronze spear-head in Great Britain and Ireland. *Archaeologia* 83: 107–202.

Evans, E. 1953. *Lyles Hill: a Late Neolithic Site in County Antrim*. Archaeological Research Publications 2, Belfast, Her Majesty's Stationary Office.

Evans, E. 1966. *Prehistoric and Early Christian Ireland: A Guide*. London, Batsworth.

Evans, J., Rouse, A. and Sharples, N. 1988. The landscape setting of causewayed camps: recent work on the Maiden Castle enclosure. In Barrett, J. and Kinnes, I. (eds), *The Archaeology of Context in the Neolithic and Bronze Age: Recent Trends*: 73–84. Sheffield, University of Sheffield.

Evershed, R., Copley, M., Hansel, F. and Chivall, D. 2012. Organic residue analysis of pottery vessels. In Cotter, C., *The Western Stone Forts Project: Excavations at Dún Aonghasa and Dún Eoghanachta Vol. 2*: 28. Dublin, Wordwell.

Fahy, E. 1961. A stone circle, hut and dolmen at Bohonagh, Co. Cork. *Journal of the Cork Historical and Archaeological Society* 66: 93–104.

Farrelly, J. and O'Brien, C. 2002. *Archaeological Inventory of County Tipperary Vol. 1: North Tipperary*. Dublin, Stationary Office.

Feachem, R. 1971. Unfinished hill-forts. In Jesson, M. and Hill, D. (eds), *The Iron Age and its Hill-forts: Papers Presented to Sir Mortimer Wheeler*: 19–39. Southampton, Millbrook Press.

Feeney-Johnson, C. 2012. Amber beads. In Cotter, C., *The Western Stone Forts Project: Excavations at Dún Aonghasa and Dún Eoghanachta, Vol. 2*: 93–98. Dublin, Wordwell.

Fernández-Götz, M. and Krausse, D. 2012. Heuneburg: first city north of the Alps. *Current Archaeology* 55: 28–34.

Finney, J. 2006. *Middle Iron Age Warfare of the Hillfort Dominated Zone c.400 BC to c.150 BC*. British Archaeological Report, 423, Oxford, Archaeopress.

Fisher, P. 1996. Reconsideration of viewshed function in terrain modelling. *Geographical Systems* 3: 33–58.

FitzGerald, E. 1855. On St Declan's Oratory at Ardmore, County of Waterford, and the old Irish inscription built into its east end. *Journal of the Royal Society of Antiquaries of Ireland* 3: 223–231.

FitzGerald, M. 2012a. Bone pins and needles. In Cotter, C. *The Western Stone Forts Project: Excavations at Dún Aonghasa and Dún Eoghanachta, Vol. 2*: 118–134. Dublin, Wordwell.

FitzGerald, M. 2012b. Miscellaneous bone and antler artefacts. In Cotter, C. *The Western Stone Forts Project: Excavations at Dún Aonghasa and Dún Eoghanachta, Vol. 2*: 137–144. Dublin, Wordwell.

FitzGerald, M. 2012c. Iron objects. In Cotter, C. *The Western Stone Forts Project: Excavations at Dún Aonghasa and Dún Eoghanachta, Vol. 2*: 145–151. Dublin, Wordwell.

FitzGerald, M. and Warner, R. 2012. Blue glass beads. In Cotter, C., *The Western Stone Forts Project: Excavations at Dún Aonghasa and Dún Eoghanachta, Vol. 2*: 98–102. Discovery Programme Monograph, Wordwell, Dublin.

Fleming, A. 1978. The prehistoric landscape of Dartmoor, Part 1: South Dartmoor. *Proceedings of the Prehistoric Society* 44: 97–123.

Flood, R. 2009. *Aspects of the Irish Hillfort: a Reappraisal in Light of Recent Research in the Upper Slaney Valley*. Unpublished MLitt thesis. University College Dublin.

Fonte, J., Valdez, J., Lemos, F. and Cruz, G. 2011. Citânia de Briteiros e médio vale do ave (NW de Portugal): *SIG e análise arqueológica do território*. Anejos de AEspA, 359–366.

Gardner, W. and Savory, H. 1964. *Dinorben, a Hillfort Occupied in Early Iron Age and Roman Times*. Cardiff, National Museum of Wales.

Gerlach, S. 1998. Urnenfelderzeitliche Höhensiedlungen Nordbayerns in ihrem siedlungsgeschichtlichen Zusammenhang. In Schmotz, K. (ed.), *Vorträge des 16. Niederbayerischen Archäologentages*: 125–156. Rahden/Westf., Verlag Marie Leidorf.

Gerloff, S. 2010. *Atlantic Cauldrons and Buckets of the Late Bronze Age and Early Iron Ages in Western Europe*. Präehistorische Bronzefunde II, 18. Stuttgart, Franz Steiner Verlag.

Gibbons, M. The archaeology of early settlement in county Kilkenny. In Nolan, W. and Whelan, K. (eds), *Kilkenny-History and Society*: 1–32. Dublin, Geography Publications.

Gibson, A. 2002. The Later Neolithic palisaded sites of Britain. In Gibson, A. (ed.), *Behind Wooden Walls: Neolithic Palisaded Enclosures in Europe*: 5–23. British Archaeological Report, Oxford, Archaeopress.

Gibson, A. and Simpson, D. 1987. Lyles Hill, Co. Antrim. *Archaeology Ireland* 1 (2): 72–75.

Ginn, V. 2012. The fusion and identity in dispersed and nucleated settlements in Bronze Age Ireland. *The Journal of Irish Archaeology* 20: 27–44.

Ginn, V. 2013. Power to the people: re-interpreting Bronze Age society. *Emania* 21: 47–58.

Ginn, V. 2014. Who lives in a roundhouse like this? Going through the keyhole on Bronze Age domestic identity. In Ginn, V., Enlander, R. and Crozier, R. (eds), *Exploring Prehistoric Identity in Europe: Our Construct or Theirs?*: 72–84. Oxford, Oxbow.

Ginn, V. 2016. *Mapping Society: Settlement Structure in*

Later Bronze Age Ireland. Oxford, Archaeopress.

Ginn, V. and Rathbone, S. 2011. *Corrstown: A Coastal Community. Excavations of a Bronze Age Village in Northern Ireland*. Oxford, Oxbow.

Gogâltan, F. 2008. Fortified Bronze Age tell settlements in the Carpathian Basin. A general overview. In Czebreszuk, J., Kadrow, S. and Müller (eds), *Defensive Structures from Central Europe to the Aegean in the 3rd and 2nd Millennium BC*: 39–56. Poznań, Wydawnictwo Poznańskie.

Golledge, R. G., & Zannaras, G. 1973. Cognitive approaches to the analysis of human spatial behavior. In W. Ittelson (ed.), *Environment and Cognition*: 59–94. New York, Seminar Press.

Golson, J. 1957. Field Archaeology in New Zealand. *Polynesian Society* 66: 64–109.

González-Ruibal, A. 2004. *Facing the ocean: Mediterranean and Atlantic contacts in the north-west of Iberia in the first millennium BC*. Oxford Journal of Archaeology 23 (3): 287–317.

Gosden, C. and Lock, G. 1998. Prehistoric histories. *World Archaeology* 30 (1): 2–12.

Gosling, P. 1993. *Archaeological Inventory of County Galway*. Dublin: Stationary Office.

Gleeson, P. 2015. Kingdoms, communities and óenaig: Irish assembly practices in a northwest European context. *Journal of the North Atlantic* 8: 33-51.

Gratuze, B., Louboutin, C. and Billaud, Y. 1998. Les perles protohistoriques en verre de Musée des Antiquitiés Nationales. *Antiquitiés Nationales* 30: 13–24.

Graves, Rev. J. 1862. Untitled communication. *Journal of the Kilkenny and South-east of Ireland Archaeological Society* 4, 1: 93–102.

Greenwell, W. and Brewis, W. 1989. The origin, evolution and classification of the bronze spear-head in Great Britain and Ireland. *Archaeologia* 61: 439-72.

Gresham, C. 1939. Spettisbury Rings, Dorset. *Archaeological Journal* 96 (1): 114–131.

Grogan, E. 2004. Middle Bronze Age burial traditions in Ireland. In Roche, H., Grogan, E., Bradley, J., Coles, J. and Raftery, B. (eds), *From Megaliths to Metals*: 61–71. Oxford, Oxbow.

Grogan, E. 2005a. *The North Munster Project. Vol. 1: the Late Prehistoric Landscape of South-east Clare*. Dublin, Wordwell.

Grogan, E. 2005b. *The North Munster Project. Vol. 2: the Prehistoric Landscape of North Munster*. Dublin, Wordwell.

Grogan, E. 2014. High and low: identity and status in Late Bronze Age Ireland. In Ginn, V., Enlander, R. and Crozier, R. (eds), *Exploring Prehistoric Identity in Europe: Our Construct or Theirs?*: 60–71. Oxford, Oxbow.

Grogan, E. and Daly, A. 2005. Excavations at Clenagh, Co. Clare. In Grogan, E., *The North Munster Project. Vol. 1: the Late Prehistoric Landscape of South-east Clare*: 247–63. Dublin, Wordwell.

Grogan, E., Condit, T., O'Carroll, F., O'Sullivan, A. & Daly, A. 1996. Tracing the late prehistoric landscape in North Munster. *Discovery Programme Reports 4*: 26–46.

Grogan, E. and Eogan, G. 1987. Lough Gur excavations by Seán P. Ó Ríordáin: further Neolithic and Beaker habitations on Knockadoon. *Proceedings of the Royal Irish Academy 87C*: 299–506.

Grogan, E. and Hillery, T. 1993. *A Guide to the Archaeology of County Wicklow*. Greystones, Ross Enterprises.

Grogan, E. and Kilfeather, A. 1997. *Archaeological Inventory of County Wicklow. Dublin*, The Stationary Office.

Grogan, E. and Kilfeather, A. 1997. *Archaeological Inventory of County Wicklow*. Dublin, Stationary Office.

Grogan, E., O'Donnell, L. and Johnston, P. 2007. *The Bronze Age Landscapes of the Pipeline to the West*. Bray, Wordwell.

Grogan, E. and Roche, H. 2009. Clay and fire: the development and distribution of pottery traditions in prehistoric Ireland. In M. Stanley, E. Danagher and J. Eogan (eds), *Creative Minds: Production, Manufacture and Invention in Ancient Ireland*: 27–45. Dublin, National Roads Authority.

Guttmann, E. and Last, J. 2000. A Late Bronze Age landscape at South Hornchurch, Essex. *Proceedings of the Prehistoric Society* 66: 319–360.

Haas. J. 1999. The origins of war and ethnic violence. In Carman, J. and Harding, A. (eds), *Ancient Warfare*: 11–24. Stroud, The History Press.

Haas, J. 2001. Warfare and the evolution of culture. In Douglas Price, T. and Feinman, G. (eds), *Archaeology at the Millennium: a Sourcebook*: 329–350. New York,

Kluwer Academic/Plenum.

Hackett, L. 2010. Old to new. *Archaeology Ireland* 93: 10–12.

Haliday, S. and Ralston, I. 2009. How many hillforts are there in Scotland? In Cooney, G., Becker, K., Coles, J., Ryan, M. and Siever, S. (eds), *Relics of Old Decency: Archaeological Studies in Later Prehistory*: 455–469. Dublin, Wordwell.

Hamilton, D., McKenzie, J., Armit, I and Büster, L. 2013. Chronology: radiocarbon dating and Bayesian modelling. In Armit, I. and McKenzie, J. 2013. *An Inherited Place: Broxmouth Hillfort and the South-East Scottish Iron Age*: 191–224. Edinburgh, Society of Antiquaries of Scotland.

Hamilton, S. and Manley, J. 1997. Points of view: prominent enclosures in first millennium BC Sussex. *Sussex Archaeological Collections* 135: 93–112.

Hamilton, S. and Manley, J. 2001. Hillforts, monumentality and place: a chronological and topographic review of first millennium BC hillforts of south-east England. *Journal of European Archaeology* 4(1): 7–42.

Hamlin, A. and Lynn, C. 1988. *Pieces of the Past: Archaeological Excavations by the Department of the Environment for Northern Ireland 1970–1986*. Belfast, Her Majesty's Stationary Office.

Harbison, P. 1968. Catalogue of Irish Early Bronze Age associated finds containing copper or bronze. *Proceedings of the Royal Irish Academy* 67C, 35–91.

Harbison, P. 1971. Wooden and stone chevaux-de-frise in Central and Western Europe. *Proceedings of the Prehistoric Society* 37: 195–225.

Harbison, P. 2004. Three Midland megaliths as drawn and described in 1786 by J. Brownrigg, surveyor. In Roche, H., Grogan, E., Bradley, J., Coles, J. and Raftery, B. (eds), *From Megaliths to Metals*: 247–53. Oxford, Oxbow.

Harding, A. 1984. *The Mycenaeans and Europe*. London, Academic Press.

Harding, A. 1994. Reformation in Barbarian Europe, 1300–600 BC. In Cunlife, B. (ed.), *The Oxford Illustrated History of Prehistoric Europe*: 304–335. Oxford: Oxford University Press.

Harding, A. 1999. Warfare: a defining characteristic of Bronze Age Europe?. In Carman, J. and Harding, A. (eds), *Ancient Warfare*: 157–73. Stroud, The History Press.

Harding, A. 2000. *European Societies in the Bronze Age*. Cambridge, Cambridge University Press.

Harding, A. 2001. Reformation in Barbarian Europe. In Cunliffe, B. (ed.), *The Oxford Illustrated History of Prehistoric Europe*: 304–335. Oxford, Oxford University Press.

Harding, A. 2006. Enclosing and excluding in Bronze Age Europe. In A. Harding, S. Sievers and N. Venclová (eds), *Enclosing the Past: Inside and Outside in Prehistory*: 97–115. Sheffield, Collis Publications.

Harding, A. 2007. *Warriors and Weapons in Bronze Age Europe*. Budapest, Archaeolingua.

Harding, A. 2013. Trade and exchange. In Fokkens, H. and Harding, A. (eds), *The Oxford Handbook of the European Bronze Age*: 370–381. Oxford, Oxford University Press.

Harding, A., Šumberová, R., Outram, A. and Knüsel, C. 2007. *Velim: Violence and Death in Bronze Age Bohemia: the Results of Fieldwork 1992-95, with a Consideration of Peri-mortem Trauma and Deposition in the Bronze Age*. Prague, Prague Institute of Archaeology.

Harding, D. 2004. *The Iron Age in Northern Britain*. London, Routledge.

Harding, D. W. 2012. *Iron Age Hillforts in Britain and Beyond*. Oxford, Oxford University Press.

Härke, H. 1979. *Settlement Types and Patterns in the West Hallstatt Province*. British Archaeological Report 75, Oxford, Archaeopress.

Harrison, R.J. 2004. *Symbols and Warriors: Images of the European Bronze Age*. Bristol, Western Academic and Specialist Press.

Hartmann, G., Kappel, I., Grote, K. and Arnold, B. 1997. Chemistry and technology of prehistoric glass from Lower Saxony and Hesse. *Journal of Archaeological Science* 24: 547–559.

Hartnett, P. 1939. *A Survey of the Antiquities in the Barony of East Muskerry, Co. Cork*. Unpublished masters thesis, University College Cork.

Hartnett, P. 1952. Bronze Age burials in Co. Wicklow. *Journal of the Royal Society of Antiquaries of Ireland* 81: 153–162.

Haselgrove, C. and Moore, T. (eds), *The Later Iron Age of Britain and Beyond*. Oxford, Oxbow Books.

Hawkes, A 2014. The beginnings and evolution of the

fulacht fia tradition in early prehistoric Ireland. *Proceedings of the Royal Irish Academy* 114C: 89–139.

Hawkes, A. 2015. *Prehistoric Burnt Mound Archaeology in Ireland.* Unpublished PhD thesis (3 vols), University College Cork.

Heath, J. 2009. *Warfare in Prehistoric Britain.* Gloucestershire, Amberley Publishing.

Hedges, J. and Buckley, D. 1978. Excavations at a Neolithic causewayed enclosure, Orsett, Essex, 1975. *Proceedings of the Prehistoric Society* 44: 219–309.

Hedges, R.E.M., Houseley, R.A., Ramsey, C.B. and van Klinken, G.J. 1991. Radiocarbon dates from the Oxford AMS system: Archaeometry date-list 12. *Archaeometry* 33: 121–134.

Hedges, R.E.M., Houseley, R.A., Ramsey, C.B. and van Klinken, G.J. 1993. Radiocarbon dates from the Oxford AMS system: Archaeometry date-list 17. *Archaeometry* 35: 305–26.

Heizer, R. 1978. *Handbook of North American Indians: Vol. 8.* Washington DC, Smithsonian Institution.

Hencken, H. 1938. The excavation of the Iron Age camp on Bredon hill, *Gloucestershire Archaeological Journal* 92: 1–111.

Henderson, J. 1988. Glass production and Bronze Age Europe. *Antiquity* 62: 435–451.

Henderson, J. 2007. *The Atlantic Iron Age: Settlement and Identity in the First Millennium BC.* London, Routledge.

Herzog, I. 2014. A review of case studies in archaeological least-cost analysis. *Archeologia e Calcolatori* 25: 223–239.

Heske, I. 2007. Eine steinerne Sichelgussform aus der jungbronzezeitlichen Außensiedlung der Hünenburg bei Watenstedt, Ldkr. Helmstedt. *Nachrichten aus Niedersachsens Urgeschichte* 76: 29–39.

Heske, I., Grefen-Peters, S., Posselt, M. and Wiethold, J. 2010. Die jungbronzezeitliche Außensiedlung der Hünenburg“ bei Watenstedt, Lkr. Helmstedt. Vorbericht über die Ausgrabungen 2005–2007. *Praehistorische Zeitschrift*, 159–190.

Hickey, L. and Hogan, N. 2005. *Formoyle hillfort, Broadford, Co. Clare: Site Report.* Unpublished report for the National Monuments Service, Department of Arts, Heritage and the Gaeltacht.

Hill, J. 1995. How should we understand Iron Age societies and hillforts? A contextual study from southern Britain. In Hill, J. and Cumberpatch, C. (eds), *Different Iron Ages: Studies on the Iron Age in Temperate Europe*: 45–66. British Archaeological Report, Oxford, Archaeopress.

Hoaen, A. and Loney, H. 2013. Landesque capital and the development of the British uplands in later prehistory: investigating the accretion of cairns, carinfields, memories and myths in ancient agricultural landscapes. In Chadwick, A. and Gibson, C. (eds), *Memory, Myth and Long-term Landscape Inhabitation*: 124–145. Oxford, Oxbow.

Hodges, R. 1975. Knockdhu promontory fortress: an interpretation of its function in the light of some preliminary fieldwork. *Ulster Journal of Archaeology* 38: 19–24.

Hodson, F. 1964. Cultural groupings within the British pre-Roman Iron Age. *Proceedings of the Prehistoric Society* 30: 99–110.

Hogg, a. 1971. Some applications of surface fieldwork. In Hill, D. and Jesson, M. (eds), *The Iron Age and its Hill-forts*: 581–591. Southampton, Southampton University.

Hogg, A., 1975. *Hillforts of Britain.* London, Hart-Davis.

Holland, C. 2003. *The Irish Landscape: A Scenery to Celebrate.* Edinburgh, Dunedin Academic Press.

Howey, M. 2007. Using multi-criteria cost surface analysis to explore past regional landscapes: a case study of ritual activity and social interaction in Michigan, AD 1200–1600. *Journal of Archaeological Science* 34 (11): 1830–1846.

Hughes, G. 1996. Old Oswestry Hillfort. Excavations by W. J. Varley, 1939–40. *Archaeologia Cambrensis* 143: 46–91.

Hull, G. 2000. A Late Bronze Age ringwork, pits, and later features at Thrapston, Northamptonshire. *Northamptonshire Archaeology* 29: 73–92.

Jackson, K. 1964. *The Oldest Irish Tradition: A Window on the Iron Age.* Cambridge, Cambridge University Press.

Jackson, P., Parkes, M. and Simms, M. 2010. *Geology of Ireland: County by County.* Dublin, Trinity College Dublin.

James, S. 2007. A bloodless past: the pacification of Early Iron Age Britain. In Haselgrove, C. and Pope, R. (eds), *The Earlier Iron Age in Britain and the Near Con-*

tinent: 160–173. Oxford, Oxbow.

Jantzen, D., Brinker, U., Orschiedt, J. and Heinemeier, J. 2011. A Bronze Age battlefield? Weapons and Trauma in the Tollense Valley, north-eastern Germany. *Antiquity* 85: 417–433.

Jiráň, L., Salaš, M. and Krenn-Leeb, A. 2013. The Czech lands and Austria in the Bronze Age. In Fokkens, H. and Harding, A. (eds), *The Oxford Handbook of the European Bronze Age*: 785–812. Oxford, Oxford University Press.

Jockenhövel, A. 1975. Zu befestigten Siedlungen der Urnenfelderzeit aus Süddeutschland. *Fundber. Hessen* 14: 19–62.

Jockenhövel, A. 1990. Bronzezeitlicher Burgenbau in Mitteleuropa: Untersuchungen zur Struktur Frühmetallzeitlicher Gesellschaften. *Orientalisch-Ägäische Einflüsse in der Europäischen Bronzezeit, Bd.* 15: 209–228.

Jockenhövel, A. 2013. Germany in the Bronze Age. In Fokkens, H. and Harding, A. (eds), *The Oxford Handbook of the European Bronze Age*: 723–745. Oxford, Oxford University Press.

Johnson, S. and Wailes, B. 2007. *Dún Ailinne: Excavations at the Irish Royal Site, 1968–1975*. Philadelphia, University of Pennsylvania Museum of Archaeology and Anthropology.

Jones, C. 1998. The discovery and dating of the prehistoric landscape of Roughan Hill. *The Journal of Irish Archaeology* 9: 27–43.

Jones, M. and Bond, D. 1980. Later Bronze Age settlement at Mucking, Essex. In Barrett, J. and Bradley, R. (eds), *Settlement and Society in the British Later Bronze Age*: 471–482. British Archaeological Report, Oxford, Archaeopress.

Kalb, P. 1978. Senhora da Guia, Baiões. Die Ausgrabung 1977 auf einer Hõhensiedlung der Atlantischen Bronzezeit in Portugal. *Madrider Mitteilungen* 19: 112–138.

Keeley, L. 1996. *War Before Civilization: The Myth of the Peaceful Savage*. Oxford, Oxford University Press.

Keeling, D. 1983. A group of tumuli and a hill-fort near Naul, County Dublin. *Journal of the Royal Society of Antiquaries of Ireland* 113: 67–74.

Kelly, E. 1974. Aughinish Island. In Delaney, T. (ed.) *Excavations 1974*: 20–1. Belfast, Association of Young Irish Archaeologists.

Kelly, E. and Condit, T. 1998. Limerick's Tara. *Archaeology Ireland* 2: 18–22.

Kenyon, K. 1953. Excavations at Sutton Walls, Herefordshire, 1948–1951. *Archaeological Journal* 110: 1–87.

Kiely, J. 2007. Garraundarragh (04E0647). In Bennett, I. (ed.) *Excavations 2004*: 180–1. Dublin, Wordwell.

Kiely, J. and Dunne, L. 2005. Recent archaeological excavations in the Tralee area. In Connolly, M. (ed.) *Past Kingdoms: Recent Archaeological Research, Survey and Excavation in County Kerry*: 40–64. Tralee, The Heritage Council.

Kienlin, T. 2013. Copper and Bronze: Bronze Age metalworking in context. In Fokkens, H. and Harding, A. (eds), *The Oxford Handbook of the European Bronze Age*: 414–436. Oxford, Oxford University Press.

Kinsella, J. 2008. New discoveries and fresh insights: researching the early medieval archaeology of the M3 in County Meath. In O'Sullivan, J. and Stanley, M. (eds), *Roads, Rediscovery and Research*: 95–108. Dublin, National Roads Authority.

Koch, J. 1994. Windows on the Iron Age: 1964 – 1994. In Mallory, J. and Stockman, G. (eds), *Ulidia: Proceedings of the First International Conference on the Ulster Cycle of Tales*: 229–242 Belfast, December Publications.

Koch, J. 2013. Tartessian: Celtic in the South-west at the Dawn of History (second edition). *Celtic Studies* 13, Aberystwth.

Krause, R. 2003. Settlement archaeology and prehistoric mining: a new interdisciplinary research project in the Alpine Valley Montafon in Vorarlberg (Austria). *Prehistoric Alpina* 39: 211–218.

Krause, R. 2007. The prehistoric settlement of the inner-alpine valley of Montafon in Vorarlberg (Austria). *Prehistoric Alpina* 42: 119–136.

Krause, R. 2008. Bronze Age hillforts in the Alps. In Czebreszuk, J., Kadrow, S. and Müller (eds), *Defensive Structures from Central Europe to the Aegean in the 3rd and 2nd Millennium BC*: 65–84. Poznań, Wydawnictwo Poznańskie.

Kristiansen, K. 1993. Chiefdoms, states, and systems of social evolution. In Earle, T. (ed.), *Chiefdoms: Power, Economy, and Ideology*: 16–43. Cambridge, Cambridge University Press.

Kristiansen, K. 1999. The emergence of warrior aristocracies in later European prehistory and their long-term history. In Carman, J. and Harding, A. (eds), *Ancient Warfare*: 175–189. Stroud, The History Press.

Kristiansen, K. and Larsson, T. 2005. *The Rise of Bronze Age Society: Travels, Transmissions and Transformations.* Cambridge, Cambridge University Press.

Kytmannow, T. 2005. New prehistoric discoveries in the Kesh Corran/Carrowkeel complex, Co. Sligo. *Archaeology Ireland* 19 (4): 20–23.

Kytmannow, T., Kahlert, T., Hunt, C. 2010. The Doons Hillfort. *Archaeology Ireland* 24 (3): 18–21.

Leonard, K. 2015. *Ritual in Late Bronze Age Ireland.* Oxford, Archaeopress.

Lewis, S. 1837. A *Topographical Dictionary of Ireland.* Dublin, S. Lewis and Co.

Liddell, D.M. 1930. Report on the excavations at Hembury Fort, Devon, 1930. *Proceedings of the Devon Archaeological Exploration Society* 1: 40–63.

Lineen, J. 2016. *Spearheads in the Landscape: a Contextual Analysis.* MPhil thesis, University College Cork. Online publication: https://independent.academia.edu/JimLineen

Ling, J. and Cornell, P. 2017. Violence, warriors and rock art in Bronze Age Scandinavia. In Chacon, R. and Mendoza, R. (eds), *Feast, Famine or Fighting? Multiple Pathways to Social Complexity*: 15–33. New York, Springer International Publishing.

Lippert, A. 1992. *Der Götschenberg bei Bischofshofen, Eine ur- und frühgeschichtliche Höhensiedlung im Salzachpongau*, Mitteilungen der Prähistorischen Kommission der Österreichischen Akademie der Wissenschaften, Band 27, HG Herwig Friesinger.

Livingwood, P. 2012. No cows made mounds: do cost-distance calculations of travel time improve our understanding of Southern Appalachian polity size? In White, D. And Surface-Evans, S. (eds), *Least Cost Analysis of Social Landscapes: Archaeological Case Studies*: 174–187. Salt Lake City, University of Utah Press.

Llobera, M. 2000. Understanding movement: a pilot model towards the sociology of movement. In Lock, G. (ed.), *Beyond the Map: Archaeological and Spatial Technologies*: 65–84. The Netherlands, IOS Press.

Lock, G. 2011. Hillforts, emotional metaphors and the good life: a response to Armit. *Proceedings of the Prehistoric Society* 77: 355–62.

Lock, G., Gosden, C. and Daly, P. 2005. *Segsbury Camp: Excavations in 1996 and 1997 at an Iron Age Hillfort on the Oxfordshire Ridgeway.* Oxford, Oxford University School of Archaeology.

Logue, P. 2000. Ballycummin. In Bennett, I. (ed.) *Excavations 1998*: 128–9. Dublin, Wordwell.

Logue, P. 2003. Excavation at Thornhill, Co. Londonderry. In Armit, I., Murphy, E., Neilis, E. and Simpson, D. (eds), *Neolithic Settlement in Ireland and Western Britain*: 149–155. Oxford, Oxbow.

Loots, L. 1997. The use of projective and reflective viewsheds in the analysis of the Hellenistic city defence system at Sagalassos, Turkey. *Archaeological Computing Newsletter*: 12–16.

Lucas, A.T. 1960. Burial mound at Rathmoon, Co. Wicklow. *Journal of the Royal Society of Antiquaries of Ireland* 90: 84–88.

Lucas, A.T. 1971. National Museum of Ireland archaeological acquisitions in the year 1968. *Journal of the Royal Society of Antiquaries of Ireland* 101: 184–244.

Lucas, A.T. 1989. *Cattle in Ancient Ireland.* Suffolk, Boethius Press.

Lull, V., Micó, R., Rihuete Herrada, R. and Risch, R. 2013. Bronze Age Iberia. In Fokkens, H. and Harding, A. (eds), *The Oxford Handbook of the European Bronze Age*: 594–616. Oxford, Oxford University Press.

Lynch, F. Aldhouse-Green, S. and Davis, J. 2000. *Prehistoric Wales.* Gloucestershire, Sutton Publishing.

Lynch, P. 1899. Caherconree, Co. Kerry. J*ournal of the Royal Society of Antiquaries of Ireland* 9: 5–17.

Lynch, P. 1910. A relic of Caherconree. *Journal of the Royal Society of Antiquaries of Ireland* 20: 357–360.

Lynn, C. 1977. Trial excavations at the King's Stables, Tray townland, County Armagh. *Ulster Journal of Archaeology* 40: 42–62.

Lynn, C. 2003. *Navan Fort: Archaeology and Myth.* Bray, Wordwell.

Macalister, R.A.S. 1928. *The Archaeology of Ireland. London*, Methuen.

Macalister, R.A.S. 1935. *Ancient Ireland. A Study in the Lessons of Archaeology and History.* London, Methuen.

MacCana, P. 1995. Mythology and the oral tradition: Ireland. In Green, M. (ed.), *The Celtic World*: 779–784. London, Routledge.

Macdonald, P. 2008. *Knock Dhu, Ballyhackett, Antrim.* http://www.excavations.ie/report/2008/Antrim/0019062/

Macdonald, P. 2016. Excavations at Knock Dhu promontory fort, Ballyhackett, Co. Antrim, 2008. *Emania* 23: 33–52.

MacEachren, A. 1980. Travel time as the basis for cognitive distance. *Professional Geographer* 32 (1): 30–36.

MacNeill, Máire 1962. *The Festival of Lughnasa.* Oxford, Oxford University Press.

MacNiocaill, G. 1972. *Ireland before the Vikings.* Dublin, Gill and MacMillan.

MacSweeney, N. 2009. Beyond ethnicity: the overlooked diversity of group identities. *Journal of Mediterranean Archaeology* 22 (1): 101–126.

Mallory, J. 1988. Trial excavations at Haughey's Fort. *Emania* 4: 5–20.

Mallory, J. 1991. Excavations at Haughey's Fort: 1989–1990. *Emania* 8: 10–26.

Mallory, J. 1992. *Aspects of the Táin.* Belfast, December Publications.

Mallory, J. 1995. Haughey's Fort and the Navan Complex in the Late Bronze Age. In Waddell, J. and Shee Twohig, E. (eds), *Ireland in the Bronze Age*: 73–86. Dublin, The Stationary Office.

Mallory, J. 2000. Excavations of the Navan Ditch. *Emania* 18: 21–36.

Mallory, J. 2013. *The Origins of the Irish.* London, Thames and Hudson.

Mallory, J. 2016. *In Search of the Irish Dreamtime: Archaeology and Early Irish Literature.* London, Thames and Hudson.

Mallory, J.P. and Baban, G. 2014. Excavations in Haughey's Fort East. *Emania* 22: 13–32.

Mallory, J. and Warner, R. 1988. The date of Haughey's Fort. *Emania* 4: 36–40.

Mallory, J.P., Moore, D.G. & Canning, L.J. 1996. Excavations at Haughey's Fort 1991 and 1995. *Emania* 14: 5–20.

Mallory, J.P., Nelis, E. & Hartwell, B. 2011. *Excavations on Donegore Hill, Co. Antrim.* Dublin, Wordwell.

Manby, T. 1980. Bronze Age settlement in eastern Yorkshire. In Barrett, J. and Bradley, R. (eds), *Settlement and Society in the British Later Bronze Age*: 307–370. British Archaeological report 83, Oxford, Archaeopress.

Manby, T. 2007. Continuity of monumental traditions into the late Bronze Age? Henges to ring-forts, and shrines. In Burgess, C., Topping, P. and Lynch, F. (eds), *Beyond Stonehenge: Essays on the Bronze Age in Honour of Colin Burgess*: 403–424. Oxford, Oxbow.

Manning, C. 1985. Prehistoric sites in the neighbourhood of Ardcroney. *Eile: Journal of the Roscrea Heritage Society* 2: 43–55.

Manning, W. 1999. The use of timber in Iron Age defenses. *Studia Celtica* 33: 21–32.

Markova, K. and Ilon, G. 2013. Slovakia and Hungary. In Fokkens, H. and Harding, A. (eds), *The Oxford Handbook of the European Bronze Age*: 813–836. Oxford, Oxford University Press.

Mason, P. 2013. The power and the glory: hillforts, ironworking and the monumental landscape in the Early Iron Age of central and south eastern Slovenia. In Gheorghiu, D. and Nash, G. (eds), *Place as Material Culture: Objects, Geographies and the Construction of Time*: 258–276. Newcastle, Cambridge Scholars Publishing.

Masterson, B. 1999. A survey of Carn Tigherna hillfort. *Discovery Programme Reports 5*: 101–110.

Matuz, E. and Nováki, G. 2002. *Spätbronzezeitliche, früheisenzeitliche Erdwälle in Nordungarn. Inventaria praehistorica Hungariae* 10. Budapest, Magyar Nemzeti Múzeum.

McCarthy, M. 2012. Fish bone and sea mammal bone. In Cotter, C., *The Western Stone Forts Project: Excavations at Dún Aonghasa and Dún Eoghanachta, Vol. 2*: 167–174. Discovery Programme Monograph, Dublin, Wordwell.

McClatchie, M. 2014. Food production in the Bronze Age: analysis of plant macro-remains from Haughey's Fort, Co. Armagh. *Emania* 22: 33–48.

McConway, C. 2002. Excavations at Laytown reveal coastal settlement in Meath. *Archaeology Ireland* 16 (1): 16–19.

McCormick, F. 1991. The animal bones from Haughey's Fort: second report. *Emania* 8: 27–33.

McCormick, F. 2007. The horse in early Ireland. *Anthropozoologica* 42 (1): 85–104.

McCormick, F. and Murphy, E. 2012. Mammal bones.

In Cotter, C., *The Western Stone Forts Project: Excavations at Dún Aonghasa and Dún Eoghanachta, Vol. 2*: 153–166. Discovery Programme Monograph, Wordwell, Dublin.

McCormick, F. and Murray, E. 2005. Appendix A. The mammal bones from Mooghaun, Co. Clare: preliminary report. In Grogan, E. *The North Munster Project, Volume 1: The Later Prehistoric Landscape of South-east Clare*: 303–306. Bray, Wordwell.

McCorry, M 1997 Coarse ware pottery from Phase 3. In *D. M. Waterman Excavations at Navan Fort 1961–71*: County Armagh: 72–79 Belfast, The Stationary Office.

McGarry, T. 2009. Irish late prehistoric burial ring-ditches. In Cooney, G., Becker, K., Coles, J., Ryan, M. and Sievers, S. (eds), *Relics of Old Decency: Archaeological Studies in Later Prehistory*: 413–424. Dublin, Wordwell.

McNeary, R. 2012. *Archaeological applications of airborne LiDAR in Northern Ireland. Case study: Knockdhu, Co. Antrim*. http://www.archaeolandscapes.eu/index.php/ro/studii-de-caz/lidar/228.html.

McNeary. R. 2014. Lidar investigation of Knockdhu promontory and its environs, County Antrim. *Archaeological Prospection* 21: 263–76.

Mercer, R. 1988. Hambledon Hill, Dorset, England. In Burgess, C., Topping, P., Mordant, C. and Maddison, C. (eds), *Enclosures and Defences in the Neolithic of Western Europe*: 89–107. British Archaeological Reports 403, Oxford, Archaeopress.

Mercer, R. 1999. The origins of warfare in the British Isles. In Carman, J. and Harding, A. (eds), *Ancient Warfare*: 143–156. Stroud, The History Press.

Mercer, R. 1981. The excavations of a late Neolithic henge-type enclosure at Balfarg, Markinch, Fife, Scotland. *Proceedings of the Society of Antiquaries of Scotland* 111: 63–171.

Mercer, R. 2003. The early farming settlement of south-west England. In Armit, I., Murphy, E., Nelis, E. and Simpson, D. (eds), *Neolithic Settlement in Ireland and Western Britain*: 56–70. Oxford, Oxbow.

Metzner-Nebelsick, C. 2012. Social transition and spatial organisation: the problem of the Early Iron Age occupation of the strongholds in Northeast Hungary. In Anreiter, P., Bánffy, E., Bartosiewicz, L., Meid, W. and Metzner-Nebelsick, C. (eds), *Archaeological, Cultural and Linguistic Heritage: Festschrift for Erzsébet Jerem in Honor of her 70th Birthday*: 425–448. Vienna, Innsbrucker Beiträge zur Kulturwissenschaft.

Miles, B. 2011. *Heroic Saga and Classical Epic in Medieval Ireland*. Cambridge, D. S. Brewer.

Mitchell, G. and Ryan, M. 1997. *Reading the Irish Landscape (third Edition)*. Dublin, Country House.

Mohen, J. and Bailloud, G. 1987. La vie quotidienne : les fouilles du Fort-Harrouard. In Picard, J. (ed.), *Collection L'âge du Bronze en France*, 4. France, Picard.

Molloy, B. 2007. *The Cutting Edge: Studies in Ancient and Medieval Combat*. Stroud: Tempus.

Molloy, B. 2009. For Gods or Men? The use of European Bronze Age shields. *Antiquity* 83: 1052–1064.

Molloy, B. 2011. Use-wear analysis and use patterns of Bronze Age swords. In Uckelmann, M. and Modlinger, M. (eds), *Bronze Age Warfare: Manufacture and Use of Weaponry*: 67–84. British Archaeological Report 2255, Oxford, Archaeopress.

Molloy, K. 2005. Holocene vegetation and land-use history at Mooghaun, south-east Clare, with particular reference to the Bronze Age. In Grogan, E. *The North Munster Project, Volume 1: The Later Prehistoric Landscape of South-east Clare*: 255–287. Wicklow: Wordwell.

Mook, W. G. 1986. Business meeting: recommendations/resolutions adopted by the twelfth International Radiocarbon Conference. *Radiocarbon* 28: 799.

Moore, C. 2008. Old routes to new research: the Edercloon wetland excavations in County Longford. In O'Sullivan, J. and Stanley, M. (eds), *Roads, Rediscovery and Research*: 1–12. Dublin, National Roads Authority.

Moore, D. 2006. *Preliminary Report on Monitoring at Grianán of Aileach, Carrowreagh, Donegal*. http://www.excavations.ie/report/2006/Donegal/0015186/

Moore, M. 1996. *Archaeological Inventory of County Wexford*. Dublin, Stationary Office.

Moore, M. 2003. *Archaeological Inventory of County Leitrim*. Dublin, Stationary Office.

Moosauer, M. and Bachmaier, T. 2000. *Bernstorf. Die Versunkene Stadt Uas Der Bronzezeit*. Stuttgart, University of Stuttgart.

Müller, J. and Czebreszuk, C. 2010. Bruszczewo und Łęki Male – Ein frühbronzezeitliches Machtzentrum in Großpolen. In Meller, H. and Bertemes, F. (eds), *Der Griff Nach Den Sternen: Internationales Symposium in Halle (Saale) 2005*: 381–396. Halle, Tagungen Des Landesmuseums Für Vorgeschichte Halle.

Müller, R. 2006. A Várvölgy-Nagy-Lázhegyen feltárt későbronzkori magaslati településrészlet szerkezete. *Zalai Muzeum* 15: 189–201.

Müller, R. 2012. Késõbronzkori Arany Szalaggal Díszített Textíliák. *Archeometriai Mûhely*, 117–121.

Mullin, D. 2012. The river has never divided us: Bronze Age metalwork deposition in western Britain. *Oxford Journal of Archaeology* 31 (1): 47–57.

Mullins, C. 2012. Bone points. In Cotter, C. *The Western Stone Forts Project: Excavations at Dún Aonghasa and Dún Eoghanachta Vol. 2*: 104–117. Dublin, Wordwell.

Mullins, G. 2008. Three thousand years of human activity at Rahally, Co. Galway. In O'Sullivan, J. and Stanley, M. (eds), *Roads, Rediscovery and Research: Proceedings of a Public Seminar on Archaeological Discoveries on National Road Schemes, August 2007*: 25–35. Dublin, National Roads Authority.

Mullins, G. and Bermingham, N. 2009. *Archaeological excavations at Rahally, Go. Galway*. Final Unpublished Report, for CRDS Ltd.

Munsell, A. H. 1975 *The Munsell Book of Color*. Baltimore. Munsell.

Murphy, K, Ramsey, R. and Page, M. 2006. *A Survey of Defended Enclosures in Ceredigion 2006: Gazetteer of Ordnance Survey Grid Squares SNX, Project Report No. 2006:20, Project Record No. 54269*. Llandeilo, Cambria Archaeology.

Murphy, K., Wilson., H, Mytum, H. and Bosworth, L. 2007. Cropmark defended enclosures in south Ceredigion and north Pembrokeshire, 2006. *Archaeology in Wales* 46: 163–167.

Murrieta-Flores, P. 2010. Travelling in a prehistoric landscape: exploring the influences that shaped human movement. In Frischer, B., Webb Crawford, W. and Koller, D. (eds), *Making History Interactive. Computer Applications and Quantitative Methods in Archaeology*. Proceedings of the 37th International Conference: 258–276 British Archaeological Report 2079, Oxford, Archaeopress.

Murrieta-Flores, P. 2012. Understanding human movement through spatial technologies. The role of natural areas of transit in the late prehistory of south-western Iberia. *Trabajos de Prehistoria* 69 (1): 103–122.

Murray, E. and McCormick, F. 1996. The animal remains from the inner ditch of Haughey's Fort, Co. Armagh, 1991. *Emania* 14: 47–50.

Musson, C. 1991. *The Breiddin Hillfort: A Later Prehistoric Settlement in the Welsh Marshes*. London, Council for British Archaeology.

Mytum, H. 2013. *Monumentality in Later Prehistory: Building and Rebuilding Castell Henllys Hillfort*. New York, Springer.

Nairn, R. and Crowley, M. 1998. *Wild Wicklow: Nature in the Garden of Ireland*. Dublin, Townhouse.

National Folklore Collection 1937–8. Schools Manuscripts Scheme. *Innishannon parish* 254–55, 292.

Neary, P. 2004. *Archaeological excavations at Commons of Lloyd, Co. Meath*. Final Unpublished Report, prepared for Neary Archaeology Ltd.

Needham, S. 1996. Chronology and periodization in the Brtitish Bronze Age. *Acta Archaeologica* 67: 121–40.

Needham, S. and Ambers, J. 1994. Redating Rams Hill and reconsidering Bronze Age enclosure. *Proceedings of the Prehistoric Society* 60: 225–243.

Needham, S. and Bowman, S. 2005. Flesh hooks, technological complexity and the Atlantic Bronze Age feasting complex. *European Journal of Archaeology* 8 (2): 93–136.

Newman, C. 1998. Reflections on the making of a 'royal site' in early Ireland. *World Archaeology* 30: 127–141.

Neustupný, E. 2006. Enclosures and fortifications in Central Europe. In Harding, A., Sievers, S. and Venclová.N. (eds), *Enclosing the Past: Inside and Outside in Prehistory*: 1–4. Sheffield, J. R. Collis Publications.

Newman, C. 1999. Notes on four cursus-like monuments in Co. Meath, Ireland. In Barclay, A. and Harding, J. (eds), *Pathways and Ceremonies: The Cursus Monuments of Britain and Ireland*: 141–147. Oxford, Oxbow.

Newman, C. 2007. Procession and symbolism at Tara: analysis of Tech Midchurta (the Banqueting Hall) in context of the sacral campus. *Oxford Journal of Archaeology* 26 (4): 415–438.

Noble, G. 2006. *Neolithic Scotland: Timber, Stone, Earth and Fire*. Edinburgh, Edinburgh University Press.

O'Brien, C. and Sweetman, D. 1997. *Archaeological Inventory of County Offaly*. Dublin, Stationary Office.

O'Brien, W. 1992. Boulder-burials: a later Bronze Age megalith tradition in south-west Ireland. *Journal of the Cork Historical and Archaeological Society* 97: 11–35.

O'Brien, R. 2012. Bone spindle-whorls. In Cotter, C. *The Western Stone Forts Project: Excavations at Dún Aonghasa and Dún Eoghanachta*: 135–136. Dublin, Wordwell.

O'Brien, W. 2004. (Con)fusion of tradition? The circle henge in Ireland. In Gibson, A. and Sheridan, A. (eds), *From Sickles to Circles: Britain and Ireland at the Time of Stonehenge*: 323–338. Stroud, Tempus.

O'Brien, W. 2009. *Local Worlds: Early Settlement landscapes and Upland Farming in South-West Ireland.* Cork, Collins Press.

O'Brien, W. 2010. Knockatreenane and the prehistoric barrows of Cork. *Journal of the Cork Archaeological and Historical Society* 115: 31–62.

O'Brien, W. 2012a. *Report on archaeological excavation at Glanbane hillfort, Co. Kerry (licence 12E144).* Unpublished report submitted to the National Monuments Service, Department of Arts, Heritage and the Gaeltacht. Dublin.

O'Brien, W. 2012b. *Report on archaeological excavation at Ballylin hillfort, Co. Limerick (licence 12E146).* Unpublished report submitted to the National Monuments Service, Department of Arts, Heritage and the Gaeltacht. Dublin.

O'Brien, W. 2012c. *Report on archaeological excavation at Formoyle hillfort, Co. Clare (licence 12E145).* Unpublished report submitted to the National Monuments Service, Department of Arts, Heritage and the Gaeltacht. Dublin.

O'Brien, W. 2012d. *Iverni: a Prehistory of Cork.* Cork, Collins Press.

O'Brien, W. 2013a. *Report on archaeological excavation at Toor More hillfort, Co. Kilkenny (licence 13E268).* Unpublished report submitted to the National Monuments Service, Dublin.

O'Brien, W. 2013b. Later prehistoric settlement in mid and north Cork. In Hanley, K. and Hurley, M. (eds) *Generations: the Archaeology of Five National Road Schemes in County Cork: 178–199.* Dublin, National Roads Authority.

O'Brien, W. 2014. *Report on archaeological excavation at Rathnagree hillfort, Co. Wicklow (licence 14E227).* Unpublished report submitted to the National Monuments Service, Department of Arts, Heritage and the Gaeltacht. Dublin.

O'Brien, W. 2015a. *Report on archaeological excavation at Sruhaun hillfort, Co. Wicklow (licence 15E320).* Unpublished report submitted to the National Monuments Service, Department of Arts, Heritage and the Gaeltacht. Dublin.

O'Brien, W. 2015b. *Report on archaeological excavation at Tinoran hillfort, Co. Wicklow (licence 15E321).* Unpublished report submitted to the National Monuments Service, Department of Arts, Heritage and the Gaeltacht. Dublin.

O'Brien, W. 2015c. *Report on archaeological excavation (first season) at Hughstown hillfort, Co. Kildare (licence 15E322).* Unpublished report submitted to the National Monuments Service, Department of Arts, Heritage and the Gaeltacht. Dublin.

O'Brien, W. 2015d. *Archive report on archaeological excavation at Clashanimud (Cashel) Hillfort, Co. Cork (licence 11E110).* Unpublished report submitted to the National Monuments Service, Department of Arts, Heritage and the Gaeltacht. Dublin.

O'Brien, W. 2015e. *Prehistoric Copper Mining in Europe, 5500–500 BC.* Oxford University Press, Oxford.

O'Brien, W. 2016a. Clashanimud and the Bronze Age hillforts of Munster. *Emania* 23: 5–30.

O'Brien, W. 2016b. Language shift and political context in Bronze Age Ireland: some implications of hillfort chronology. In John Koch and Barry Cunliffe (eds), *Celtic from the West 3: Atlantic Europe in the Metal Ages*: 219–246. Oxford, Oxbow Books.

O'Brien, W. 2016c. *Report on archaeological excavation (second season) at Hughstown hillfort, Co. Kildare (licence 15E322).* Unpublished report submitted to the National Monuments Service, Department of Arts, Heritage and the Gaeltacht. Dublin.

O'Brien, W. 2016d. *Report on archaeological excavation at Spinans Hill 1 hillfort, Co. Wicklow (licence 16E338).* Unpublished report submitted to the National Monuments Service, Department of Arts, Heritage and the Gaeltacht. Dublin.

O'Brien, W., Hogan, N. and O'Driscoll, J. 2014–5. Archaeological investigations at Toor More (Corrandhu) hillfort, Co. Kilkenny. *Journal of The Royal Society of Antiquaries of Ireland* 144–5: 7–26.

O'Brien, W., Hogan, H. and O'Driscoll, J. 2016. Archaeological investigations at Ballylin hillfort, Co. Limerick. *North Munster Antiquarian Journal* 56: 1–26.

O'Brien, W., O'Driscoll, J. and Hogan, N. 2016. Glanbane hillfort and the Bronze Age in Kerry. *Journal of the Kerry Archaeological and Historical Society* 16:

77–105.

O'Callaghan, N. 2007. Garraundarragh (04E0646). In Bennett, I. (ed.) *Excavations 2004*: 181. Dublin, Wordwell.

O'Carroll, F. 2012a. Clay moulds. In Cotter, C., *The Western Stone Forts Project: Excavations at Dún Aonghasa and Dún Eoghanachta, Vol. 2*: 28–41. Discovery Programme Monograph, Dublin, Wordwell.

O'Carroll, F. 2012b. The crucible assemblage. In Cotter, C., *The Western Stone Forts Project: Excavations at Dún Aonghasa and Dún Eoghanachta, Vol. 2*: 42–44. Discovery Programme Monograph, Dublin, Wordwell.

O'Connell, M., Molloy, K. and McMahon, H. 2001. Reconstructing prehistoric farming activity and human impact at a fine spatial resolution: palaeoecological investigations at Mooghaun, Co. Clare, Western Ireland. In Schauer, P. (ed.), *Beiträge zur Siedlungsarchäologie und zum Landschaftwandel. Regensburger Beiträge zur Prähistorischen Archäologie*: 161–186. Regensburg, Universitätsverlag Regensburg.

O'Donovan, J. 1839. *Ordnance Survey Letters*. Dublin, Royal Irish Academy.

O'Donovan, P. 1995. *Archaeological Inventory of County Cavan*. Dublin, Stationary Office.

O'Driscoll J. 2012a. *Geophysical survey at Glanbane hillfort, Co. Kerry*. Unpublished report submitted to the National Monuments Service, Department of Arts, Heritage and the Gaeltacht.

O'Driscoll J. 2012b. *Geophysical survey at Ballylin hillfort, Co. Limerick*. Unpublished report submitted to the National Monuments Service, Department of Arts, Heritage and the Gaeltacht.

O'Driscoll J. 2012c. *Geophysical survey at Knigh hillfort, Co. Tipperary*. Unpublished report submitted to the National Monuments Service, Department of Arts, Heritage and the Gaeltacht.

O'Driscoll J. 2013. *Geophysical survey at Toor More, Co. Kilkenny*. Unpublished report submitted to the National Monuments Service, Department of Arts, Heritage and the Gaeltacht.

O'Driscoll J. 2014a. *Geophysical survey at Rathcoran hillfort, Co. Wicklow*. Unpublished report submitted to the National Monuments Service, Department of Arts, Heritage and the Gaeltacht.

O'Driscoll J. 2014b. *Geophysical survey at Rathnagree hillfort, Co. Wicklow*. Unpublished report submitted to the National Monuments Service, Department of Arts, Heritage and the Gaeltacht.

O'Driscoll J. 2014c. *Geophysical survey at Sruhaun hillfort, Co. Wicklow*. Unpublished report submitted to the National Monuments Service, Department of Arts, Heritage and the Gaeltacht.

O'Driscoll J. 2014d. *Geophysical survey at Hughstown hillfort, Co. Kildare*. Unpublished report submitted to the National Monuments Service, Department of Arts, Heritage and the Gaeltacht.

O'Driscoll J. 2014e. *Geophysical survey at Rathmoon, Co. Wicklow*. Unpublished report submitted to the National Monuments Service, Department of Arts, Heritage and the Gaeltacht.

O'Driscoll J. 2014f. *Geophysical survey at Knockeen hillfort, Co. Wicklow*. Unpublished report submitted to the National Monuments Service, Department of Arts, Heritage and the Gaeltacht.

O'Driscoll, J. 2016. *The Baltinglass Landscape and the Hillforts of Bronze Age Ireland*. PhD Thesis, University College Cork. https://cora.ucc.ie/handle/10468/3532.

O'Driscoll, J. 2017. Hillforts in prehistoric Ireland: a costly display of power? *World Archaeology* 49 (3): 1–20.

O'Driscoll, J. and Cleary, R. 2016. Grange stone circle, Lough Gur, Co. Limerick: geophysical survey at Stone Circles B, C and D and review of dating and phases of monument use of Circle B. *North Munster Antiquarian Journal* 56: 27–46.

O'Flaherty, R. 1995. An analysis of Irish Early Bronze Age hoards containing copper or bronze objects. *Journal of the Royal Society of Antiquaries of Ireland* 125: 10–45.

O'Flaherty, R. 2002. *A Consideration of the Early Bronze Age Halberd in Ireland: Function and Context*. Unpublished PhD thesis, University College Dublin.

O'Flaherty, R., Gilchrist, M.D., Cowie, T. 2011. Ceremonial or deadly serious? New insight into the function of Irish Early Bronze Age halberds. In Uckelmann, M. and Modlinger, M. (eds), *Bronze Age Warfare: Manufacture and Use of Weaponry*: 39–52. British Archaeological Report 2255, Oxford, Archaeopress.

O'Kelly, M. J. 1951. An Early Bronze Age ringfort at Carrigillihy, Co. Cork. *Journal of the Cork Historical and Archaeological Society* 51: 78–84.

O'Kelly, M. J. 1956. Review of Evans, E. 1953. Lyles Hill: a Late Neolithic Site in County Antrim. *Journal of the Royal Society of Antiquaries of Ireland* 86: 113–115.

O'Kelly, M. J. 1989. *Early Ireland*. Cambridge, Cambridge University Press.

O'Mahony, Canon 1908. Windele's papers on three prehistoric monuments in the County Cork. *Journal of the Ivernian Society* 1, 1: 77–88.

O'Neill, J. 2007. *Preliminary report on excavations at Downshill Co. Wicklow. School of Archaeology, University College Dublin*. Unpublished report (Licence 07E0596). Dublin, National Monuments Service, Department of Arts, Heritage and the Gaeltacht.

O'Sullivan, A. and Condit, T. 1998. Landscapes of movement and control: interpreting prehistoric hillforts and fording-places on the River Shannon. *Discovery Programme Reports 5*: 25–39.

Orpen, G. 1911. Rathgall, County Wicklow. T*he Journal of the Royal Society of Antiquaries of Ireland* 1 (2): 138–150.

Ó Drisceoil, C. 2003. Archaeological excavation of a Neolithic settlement at Coolfore, Co. Louth. In Armit, I., Murphy, E., Nelis, E. and Simpson, D. (eds), *Neolithic Settlement in Ireland and Western Britain*: 176–181. Oxford, Oxbow.

Ó Faoláin, S. 2004. *Bronze Artifact Production in Late Bronze Age Ireland: a Survey*. British Archaeological Report 382, Oxford, Archaeopress.

Ó Faoláin, S. and Northover, J.P. 1998. The technology of Late Bronze Age sword production in Ireland. *The Journal of Irish Archaeology* 9: 69–88.

Ó Floinn, R. 2000. Freestone Hill, Co. Kilkenny: a re-assessment. In Smyth, A. (ed.), *Seanchas: Studies in Early and Medieval Irish Archaeology, History and Literature in Honour of Francis J. Byrne*: 12–29. Dublin, Four Courts Press.

Ó Lochlainn, C. 1940. Roadways in ancient Ireland. In Ryan, J. (ed), *Féil-sgribhinn Eóin Mhic Néill: essays and studies presented to Professor Eoin MacNeill on the occasion of his seventieth birthday*: 465–474, Dublin, Three Candles.

Ó Nualláin, S. 1978. Boulder-burials. *Proceedings of the Royal Irish Academy* 78C: 75–100.

Ó Nualláin, S. 1988. Stone rows in the south of Ireland. *Proceedings of the Royal Irish Academy* 45C: 83–181.

Ó Ríordáin, A. 1972. Prehistoric burials and pottery. *Journal of the Royal Society of Antiquaries of Ireland* 102: 234–239.

Ó Ríordáin, S.P. 1935. The place names and antiquities of Kinalmeaky barony, Co. Cork. *Journal of the Cork Historical and Archaeological Society* 40: 49–52.

Ó Ríordáin, S. P. 1942. The excavation of a large earthen ringfort at Garranes, Co. Cork. *Proceedings of the Royal Irish Academy* 47C: 77–150.

Ó Ríordáin, S. P. 1943. A*ntiquities of the Irish Countryside*. Cork, Cork University Press.

Ó Ríordáin, S. P. 1952. Lough Gur excavations: the great stone circle (B) in Grange townland. *Proceedings of the Royal Irish Academy* 54: 37–74.

Ó Ríordáin, S. P. 1954 Lough Gur excavations: Neolithic and Bronze Age houses on Knockadoon, *Proceedings of the Royal Irish Academy* 56C: 297–459.

Ó Ríordáin, S. P. 1956. Small hill-fort and tumulus on Mountfortesque. *Journal of the Royal Society of Antiquaries of Ireland* 86 (1): 106–107.

Ogburn, D. 2006. Assessing the level of visibility of cultural objects in past landscapes. *Journal of Archaeological Science* 33: 405–413.

Orpen, G. 1911. Rathgall, County Wicklow. *Journal of the Royal Society of Antiquaries of Ireland* 1 (2): 138–150.

Orpen, G. 1916. Dún Galion and the 'Dunum' of Ptolemy. *Proceedings of the Royal Irish Academy* 32: 41–57.

Osgood, R. 1998. W*arfare in the Late Bronze Age of North Europe*. British Archaeological Report 694, Oxford, Archaeopress.

Osgood, R. 2006. The dead of Tormarton: Bronze Age combat victims? In Otto, T., Thrane, H. and Vandkilde H. (eds), *Warfare and Society. Archaeological and Social Anthropological Perspectives*: 331–340. Aarhus, Aarhus University Press.

Osgood, R. 2010. Northern and Western Europe. In Osgood, R. and Monks, S. (eds), *Bronze Age Warfare*: 9–36. Stroud, The History Press.

Osgood, R. and Monks, S. 2010. Introduction. In Osgood, R. and Monks, S. (eds), *Bronze Age Warfare*: 1–8. Stroud, The History Press.

Osgood, R. and Monks, S. 2010. Conclusions. In Osgood, R. and Monks, S. (eds), *Bronze Age Warfare*: 138–149. Stroud, The History Press.

Paliou, E. 2013. Reconsidering the concept of visualscapes: recent advances in three-dimensional visibility analysis. In Bevan, A. and Lake, M. (eds), *Computational Approaches to Archaeological Spaces*: 1–19. Walnut Creek, Left Coast Press.

Pardo, J., Castiñeira, J., Platas, I., Vidal, E. and Suárez, C. 2009. Radiocarbon and chronology of the Iron Age hillforts of northwestern Iberia. In Karl, R. and Leskovar, J. (eds), *Interpretierte Eisenzeiten. Fallstudien, Methoden, Theorie. Tagungsbeiträge der 3 Linzer Gespräche zur interpretativen Eisenzeitarchäologie. Studien zur Kulturgeschichte von Oberösterreich*, 22: 81–98. Linz, Oberösterreichischen Landesmuseum.

Parkinson, W. and Duffy, P. 2007. Fortifications and enclosures in European prehistory: a cross-cultural perspective. *Journal of Archaeological Research* 10: 97–141.

Parry, C. 1999. Excavations at Camp Gardens, Stow-on-the-Wold, Gloucestershire. *Transactions of the Bristol and Gloucestershire Archaeological Society* 117: 75–87.

Payne, A. 2006. Hillfort studies and the Wessex project. In Payne, A., Corney, M. and Cunliffe, B., *The Wessex Hillfort Project: Extensive Survey of Hillfort Interiors in Central Southern England*: 1–38. London, English Heritage.

Petrie, G. 1972. Aspects of George Petrie: an essay on military architecture in Ireland previous to the English invasion. *Proceedings of the Royal Irish Academy* 72: 219–269.

Piggott, S. 1931. Ladle Hill–an unfinished hillfort. *Antiquity* 5: 474–485.

Plunkett, G. 2006. Hekla 3, environmental downturn and Irish Late Bronze Age hillfort connections revisited. *Emania* 20: 62–67.

Plunkett, G. 2009. Land-use patterns and cultural change in the Middle to Late Bronze Age in Ireland: inferences from the pollen record. *Vegetation History and Archaeobotany* 18: 273–295.

Plunkett, G., Whitehouse, N., Hall, V., Charman, D., Blaauw, M., Kelly, E. and Mulhall, I. 2009. A multi-proxy palaeological investigation of the find-spot of an Iron Age bog body from Oldcroghan, Co. Offaly, Ireland. *Journal of Archaeological Science* 36 (2): 265–277.

Power, D. Byrne, E., Egan, U., Lane, S. and Sleeman, M. 1992. *Archaeological Survey of Co. Cork. Vol. 1*: West Cork. Dublin, Stationary Office.

Power, D., Byrne, E., Egan, U., Lane, S. and Sleeman, M. 1994. *Archaeological Inventory of County Cork. Vol. 2*: East and South Cork. Dublin, Stationary Office.

Power, D. Byrne, E., Egan, U., Lane, S. and Sleeman, M. 1997. *Archaeological Survey of Co. Cork. Vol. 3: Mid Cork*. Dublin, Stationary Office.

Power, Canon P. 1931. Some recent antiquarian finds in Munster. *Journal of the Royal Society of Antiquaries of Ireland* 61(1): 55–60.

Price, L. 1934. The ages of stone and bronze in Co. Wicklow. *Proceedings of the Royal Irish Academy* 42: 31–64.

Primas, M. 2002. Taking the high ground: continental hill-forts in Bronze Age contexts. *Proceedings of the Prehistoric Society* 68: 41–59.

Proudfoot, B. 1954. Excavations at the Cathedral Hill, Downpatrick, Co. Down, 1953. *Ulster Journal of Archaeology* 89: 97–102.

Proudfoot, B. 1955a. Excavations at Cathedral Hill, Downpatrick, Co. Down: preliminary report on excavations in 1954. *Ulster Journal of Archaeology* 90: 57–72.

Proudfoot, B. 1955b. *The Downpatrick Gold Find: a Hoard of Gold Objects from the Cathedral Hill, Downpatrick*. Belfast, Her Majesty's Stationary Office.

Proudfoot, B. 1957. A second gold find from Downpatrick. *Ulster Journal of Archaeology* 92: 70–72.

Pugh, R. and Crittall, E. 1957. *A History of Wiltshire (Vol. 1.1)*. London, Oxford University Press for the Institute of Historical Research.

Raftery, B. 1969. Freestone Hill, Co. Kilkenny: an Iron Age hillfort and Bronze Age cairn. *Proceedings of the Royal Irish Academy* 68C: 1–108.

Raftery, B. 1970a. The Rathgall hillfort, Co. Wicklow. *Antiquity* 44: 51–54.

Raftery, B. 1970b. A decorated strap-end from Rathgall, Co. Wicklow. *Journal of the Royal Society of Antiquaries of Ireland* 100: 200–211.

Raftery, B. 1971. Rathgall, Co. Wicklow: 1970 excavations. *Antiquity* 45: 296–298.

Raftery, B. 1972. Irish hill-forts. In Thomas, C. (ed.), *The Iron Age in the Irish Sea Province*: 37–58. London, Council for British Archaeology Research Report 9.

Raftery, B. 1973. Rathgall: a late Bronze Age burial in Ireland. *Antiquity* 47: 293–295.

Raftery, B. 1976. Rathgall and Irish hillfort problems. In Harding, D.W. (ed.) *Hillforts. Later Prehistoric Earthworks in Britain and Ireland*: 339–57. London, Academic Press.

Raftery, B. 1976-7. The hillfort at Belmont in Co. Galway. *Journal of the Galway Archaeological and Historical Society* 35: 89–95.

Raftery, B. 1983. *A Catalogue of Irish Iron Age Antiquities (2 vols)*. Marburg.

Raftery, B. 1988. Rath East (Rathgall) S902731 Hillfort. *Excavations Bulletin 1977–1979: Summary Account of Archaeological Excavations in Ireland*: 79. Dublin, Association of Young Irish Archaeologists.

Raftery, B. 1994. *Pagan Celtic Ireland*. London, Thames and Hudson.

Raftery, B. 1995. The conundrum of the Irish Iron Age pottery. In Raftery, B., Megaw, V. and Rigby, V. (eds), *Sites and Sights of the Iron Age. Essays on Fieldwork and Museum Research presented to Ian Matheson Stead*: 149–156. Oxford, Oxbow.

Raftery, B. 2004. Pit 119, Rathgall, Co. Wicklow. In Roche, H., Grogan, E., Bradley, J., Coles, J. and Raftery, B. (eds), *From Megaliths to Metals*: 83–90. Oxford, Oxbow.

Raftery, J. 1941. The tumulus cemetery of Carrowjames, Co. Mayo; Part II. *Journal of the Galway Archaeological and Historical Society* 19: 16–88.

Ralston, I. 1981. The use of timber in hillfort defences in France. In Guilbert, G. (ed.), *Hillfort Studies: Essays for A. H. A. Hogg*: 78–103. Leicester: Leicester University Press.

Ralston, I, 2006. *Celtic Fortifications*. Stroud, Tempus Publishing.

Ramsey, G. 1989. *Middle Bronze Age Weapons in Ireland*. Unpublished PhD thesis, Queen's University, Belfast.

Ramsey, G. 1993. Damaged butts and torn rivet-holes: the hafting and function of Middle Bronze Age 'dirks' and 'rapiers'. *Archaeomaterials* 7: 127–38.

Ramsey, G. 1995. Middle Bronze Age metalwork: are artefact studies dead and buried? In Waddell, J and Shee Twohig, E. (eds), *Ireland in the Bronze Age*: 73–86. Dublin, The Stationary Office.

Ray, K. and Hoverd, T. 2000. *Investigations at Mere Hill, Aynestrey, Herefordshire*. Hereford Archaeology Reports No. 2.

Redfern, R. 2011. A re-appraisal of the evidence for violence in the Late Iron Age human remains from Maiden Castle hillfort, Dorset, England. *Proceedings of the Prehistoric Society* 77: 111–138.

Renfrew, C. 1974. Beyond a subsistence economy: the evolution of social organization in prehistoric Europe. *Bulletin of the American Schools of Oriental Research, Supplementary Studies* 20: 69–88.

Renfrew, C. and Bahn, P. 2006. *Archaeology: Theories, Methods and Practice (fourth edition)*. London, Thames and Hudson.

Rind, M. 1999. *Der Frauenberg oberhalb Kloster Weltenburg. I: Höhenbefestigungen der Bronze- und Urnenfelderzeit. Regensburger Beiträge zur Prähistorischen Archäologie* 6. Bonn, Rudolf Habelt Verlag.

Roche, H. 1999. Later Iron Age activity at Tara, Co. Meath. *Ríocht na Midhe* 10: 18–30.

Roche, H. 2002. Excavations at Ráith na Ríg, Tara, Co. Meath, 1997. *Discovery Programme Reports 6*: 19–165.

Roche, H. 2004. The dating of the embanked stone circle at Grange, Co. Limerick. In Roche, H., Grogan, E., Bradley, J. and Raftery, B. (eds), *From Megaliths to Metals: Essays in Honour of George Eogan*: 109–116. Oxford, Oxbow.

Rowlands, M. 1980. Kinship, alliances and exchange in the European Bronze Age. In Barrett, J. and Bradley, R. (eds), *Settlement and Society in the British Later Bronze Age*: 15–55. British Archaeological Report, Oxford, Archaeopress.

Rua. H., Goncalves, A. and Figueiredo, R. 2013. Assessment of the lines of Torres Vedras defensive system with visibility analysis. *Journal of Archaeological Science* 40, 2113–2123.

Ryan, M.F. 1973. The excavation of a Neolithic burial mound at Jerpoint West, Co. Kilkenny. *Proceedings of the Royal Irish Academy* 73: 107–127.

Rynne, E. 1992. Dún Aengus and some similar Celtic ceremonial sites. In Bernelle, A. (ed.), *Decantations: a Tribute to Maurice Craig*: 196–207. Dublin, The Lilliput Press.

Sadowska, W. 1997. Horses led by a mare: martial aspects of Táin Bó Cúailnge. *Emania* 16: 4–48.

Savory, N. 1971. A Welsh Bronze Age Hillfort. *Antiquity* 45: 251–261.

Scarre, S. 2011. Monumentality. In Insoll, T. (ed.), *The Oxford Handbook of the Archaeology of Ritual and Religion*: 9–23. Oxford, Oxford University Press.

Schindler, R. 1968. Studien Zum Vorgeschichtlichen Siedlungs- und Befestigungswesen des Sarrlandes. Trier.
Schindler, R. 1974. Hallstättische Höhenburgen im Saar- und Moselraum. In Chropovsky, B. *Symposium zum Problemen der jüngeren Hallstattzeit in Mitteleuropa*: 435–446. Bratislava.

Schulting, R., Murphy, E., Jones, C. and Warren, G. 2011. New dates from the north and a proposed chronology for Irish court tombs. *Proceedings of the Royal Irish Academy* 113: 1–51.

Sharples, N. 1991. Warfare in the Iron Age of Wessex. *Scottish Archaeological Review* 8: 79–89.

Sharples, N. 2007. Building communities and creating identities in the first millennium BC. In Haselgrove, C. and Pope, R. (eds), *The Earlier Iron Age in Britain and the Near Continent*: 174–184. Oxford, Oxbow.

Sharples, N. 2010. *Social Relations in Later Prehistory. Wessex in the First Millennium BC*. Oxford, Oxford University Press.

Shennan, S. 1995. *Bronze Age Copper Producers of the Eastern Alps: Excavations at St. Veit-Klinglberg*. Universitätsforschungen zur prähistorischen Archäologie; Band 27. Bonn, Kommission be Dr. Rudolf Habelt GMBH.

Shepard A. O. 1968. *Ceramics for the Archaeologist*. Carnegie Institute of Washington Publication 609.

Sheridan, A. 2001. Donegore Hill and other Irish Neolithic enclosures: a view from outside. In Darvill, T. and Thomas, J. (eds), *Neolithic Enclosures in Atlantic Northwest Europe*: 171–180. Oxford, Oxbow.

Sherratt, A. 1996. Why Wessex? The Avon route and river transport in later British prehistory. *Oxford Journal of Archaeology* 15 (2): 221–234.

Silva, C. 1979. O Castro de Baiões (S. Pedro do Sul). Beira Alta. *Viseu* 38 (3): 509–531.

Simms, K. 1975. Warfare in the medieval Gaelic lordships. *Irish Sword* 12: 98–108.

Simms, K. 1990. Images of warfare in bardic poetry. *Celtica* 21: 608–19.

Simpson, D. and Gibson, A. 1989. Lyles Hill. *Current Archaeology* 114: 214–5.

Sleeman, A., McConnell, B. and Gately, S. 2004. *Understanding Earth Processes, Rocks and the Geological History of Ireland*. Dublin, Geological Survey of Ireland.

Smith, C. 1756. *The Ancient and Present State of the County Kerry*. Dublin, Bona Books.

Smith, C. and Cochrane, E. 2011. Is visibility important for defence?: a GIS analysis of sites in the Western Fijian Islands. *Archaeology in Oceania* 46 (2): 76–84.

Smith, R. 1984. The ecology of Neolithic farming systems as exemplified by the Avebury trigon of Wiltshire. *Proceedings of the Prehistoric Society* 50: 99–120.

Smyth, J. 2013. Tides of change? The house through the Irish Neolithic. In Hofmann, D. and Smyth, J. 2013. (eds), *Tracking the Neolithic House in Europe: Sedentism, Architecture and Practice*: 301–327. New York, Springer.

Smyth, J. 2014. *Settlement in Neolithic Ireland: New Discoveries on the Edge of Europe, Prehistoric Society Research Paper 6*. Oxford, The Prehistoric Society.

Spielmann, K. 2002. Feasting, craft specialization, and the ritual mode of production in small-scale societies. *American Anthropologist* 104 (1): 195–207.

Stanford, S. 1972. The function and population of hillforts in the Central Marches. In Lynch, F. and Burgess, C. (eds), *Prehistoric Man in Wales and the West: Essays in Honour of Lily F. Chitty*: 307–319. Bath, Adams and Dart.

Stead, I. 1968. An Iron Age hillfort at Grimthorpe, Yorkshire, England. *Proceedings of the Prehistoric Society* 4: 148–190.

Stevanović, M. 1997. The age of decay: the social dynamics of house destruction. *Journal of Anthropological Archaeology* 16: 334–395.

Stevens, R., Lightfoot, E., Hamilton, J., Cunliffe, B. and Hedges, R. 2010. Stable isotope investigations of the Danebury hillfort pit burials. *Oxford Journal of Archaeology* 29 (4): 407–428.

Stokes, W. 1868. *The Life and Labours in Art and Archaeology of George Petrie*. London, Longmans, Green and Co.

Stokes, W. (ed.) 1894. The Prose Tales from the Rennes Dindshenchas. *Revue Celtique* 15: 272 – 336.

Stuiver, M. and Reimer, P. J. 1986. A computer program for radiocarbon age calculation. *Radiocarbon* 28: 1022–30.

Stuiver, M. and Reimer, P. J. 1993. Extended 14C database and revised CALIB 3.0 14C age calibration program. *Radiocarbon* 35: 215-30.

Surface-Evans, S. 2012. A least cost path application for modelling hunter-gather land use. In White, D. and Surface-Evans (eds), *Least Cost Analysis of Social Landscapes*: 128–151. Utah, University of Utah Press.

Svensson, M. 2002. Palisade enclosures–second generation of enclosed sites in the Neolithic of Northern Europe. In Gibson, A. (ed.), *Behind Wooden Walls: Neolithic Palisaded Enclosures in Europe*: 5–23. British Archaeological Report, Oxford, Archaeopress.

Sweetman, D., Alcock, O. and Moran, B. 1995. *Archaeological Inventory of County Laois*. Dublin, Stationary Office.

Szentmiklosi, A., Heeb, B., Heeb, J., Harding, A., Krause, R. and Becker, H. 2011. Corneşti-Iarcuri–a Bronze Age town in the Romanian Banat? *Antiquity* 85: 819–838.

Tecchiati, U. 1998. *Sotciastel. Un Abitato Forticifato dell'etá del Bronzo in Val Badia*. Soprintendenza Provinciale ai Beni Culturali, Bolzano.

Teržan, B. 2013. The western Balkans in the Bronze Age. In Fokkens, H. and Harding, A. (eds), *The Oxford Handbook of the European Bronze Age*: 837–863. Oxford, Oxford University Press.

Thomas, J. 1993. The politics of vision and the archaeologies of landscape. In Bender, B. (ed.), *Landscape: Politics and Perspectives*: 19–48. Oxford, Berg.

Thomas, J. 2007. *Place and Memory: Excavations at the Pict's Knowe, Holywood and Holm Farm, Dumfries and Galloway*, 1994–8. Oxford, Oxbow.

Thorpe, N. 2013. Warfare in the European Bronze Age. In Fokkens, H. and Harding, A. (eds), *The Oxford Handbook of the European Bronze Age*: 235–247. Oxford, Oxford University Press.

Tilley, C. 2010. *Interpreting Landscapes: Geologies, Topographies and Identities*. Walnut Creek, Left Coast Press.

Tite, M. S. 1995 Firing temperature determinations - How and why? In Lindahl, A. and Stilborg, O. (eds), *The Aim of Laboratory Analyses of Ceramic in Archaeology*: 37–42 Kungl.

Vitterhets Historie och Antikvitets Akademien. Konferenser 34, Stockholm.

Tobler, W. 1993. Three presentations on geographic analysis and modelling. *National Centre for Geographic Information and Analysis, Technical Report*: 1–93.

Točík, A. 1981. *Nitriansky Hrádok Zámeček*. I-II. Nitra.

Towel, A., Henderson, J., Bellintani, P. and Gambacurta, G. 2001. Frattesina and Adria: repost of scientific analyses of early glass from the Veneto. *Padusa* 37: 7–68.

Tringham, R. 2005. Weaving house life and death into places: a blueprint for a hypermedia narrative. In Bailey, D., Whittle, A. and Cummings, V. (eds), *(Un)settling the Neolithic*: 98–111. Oxford, Oxbow.

Tschan, A., Rackowski, W. and Latalowa, M. 2000. Perception and viewsheds: Are they mutually inclusive? In Lock, G. (ed.), *Beyond the Map: Archaeology and Spatial Technologies*: 28–48. Amsterdam, IOS Press.

Uckelmann, M. 2011. The function of Bronze Age shields. In Uckelmann, M. and Modlinger, M. (eds), *Bronze Age Warfare: Manufacture and Use of Weaponry*: 187–200. British Archaeological Report 2255, Oxford, Archaeopress.

Van de Noort, R. 2013. Seafaring and riverine navigation in the Bronze Age of Europe. In Fokkens, H. and Harding, A. (eds), *The Oxford Handbook of the European Bronze Age*: 382–397. Oxford, Oxford University Press.

Van der Veen, M. and Jones G. 2007. The production and consumption of cereals: a question of scale. In Haselgrove, C. and Moore, T. (eds), *The Later Iron Age of Britain and Beyond*: 419–429. Oxford, Oxbow Books.

Vandkilde, H. 2004. Spiŝský Ŝtvrtok. In Bogucki, P. and Crabtree, P. Ancient Europe: 8000 BC–AD 1000. *Encyclopaedia of the Barbarian World*: 30–33. New York, Charles Scribner's Sons.

Vayda, A. 1960. *Maori Warfare*. Polynesian Society Maori Monograph 2, Wellington.

Vencl, S. 1984. War and warfare in archaeology. *Journal of Anthropological Archaeology* 3: 116–32.

Vencl, S. 1999. Stone Age warfare. In J. Carman and A. Harding (eds), *Ancient Warfare: Archaeological Perspectives*: 57–72. Stroud: Sutton.

Vines, G. 2007. The hunt for Wicklow gold. *New Scientist* 193 (2588): 48–49.

Waddell, J. 1978. The invasion hypothesis in Irish prehistory. *Antiquity* 52: 121–8.

Waddell, J. 1992. The Irish Sea in Prehistory. *The Journal of Irish Archaeology* 6: 29–40.

Waddell, J. 1995. Celts, celticisation and the Irish Bronze

Age. In Waddell, J. and Shee Twohig (eds), *Ireland in the Bronze Age*: 158–169. Dublin, The Stationary Office.

Waddell, J. 2010 *(first edition 1998). The Prehistoric Archaeology of Ireland*. Bray, Wordwell.

Waddell, J. 2011. Continuity, cult and contest. In Schot, R., Newman, C. and Bhreathnach, E. (eds), *Landscapes of Cult and Kingship*: 192–212. Dublin, Four Courts Press.

Waddell, J., Fenwick, J. and Barton, K. 2009. *Rathcroghan: Archaeological and Geophysical Survey in a Ritual Landscape*. Dublin, Wordwell.

Waddington, C. 2011. Massacre at Fin Cop: new evidence of an Iron Age hillfort at war. *Current Archaeology* 255: 20–27.

Wailes, B. 1982. The Irish royal sites in history and archaeology. *Cambridge Medieval Celtic Studies* 3: 1–29.

Wailes, B. 1990. Dún Ailinne: a summary excavation report. *Emania* 7: 10–21.

Wainwright, G. 1979. *Mount Pleasant, Dorset: Excavations 1970–71*. London, Society of Antiquaries of London.

Wainwright, G. and Davis, 1995. *Balksbury Camp, Hampshire excavations 1973 and 1981*. English Heritage, Archaeological Report 4, London.

Wainwright, G. and Longworth, I. 1971. *Durrington Walls: Excavations 1966–1968*. London, Society of Antiquaries of London.

Walshe, P. 1941. The excavation of a burial cairn on Baltinglass Hill, Co. Wicklow. *Proceedings of the Royal Irish Academy* 56: 221–236.

Warner, R. 1971. http://www.excavations.ie/Pages/Details.php?Year=&County=Meath&id=5473.

Warner, R. 2000. Keeping out the otherworld: the internal ditch at Navan and other Iron Age 'hengiform' enclosures. *Emania* 18: 39–44.

Warner, R. 2006. The hoard and the Creeveroe axe: two new finds of Late Bronze Age date from near Navan, Co. Armagh. *Emania* 20: 20–28.

Warner, R. 2009. Clogher in late prehistory. In Cooney, G., Becker, K., Coles, J., Ryan, M. and Sievers, S. (eds), *Relics of Old Decency: Archaeological Studies in Later Prehistory*: 507–518. Dublin, Wordwell.

Warner, R. 2012. The radiocarbon dates from Dún Aonghasa. In Cotter, C., *The Western Stone Forts Project: Excavations at Dún Aonghasa and Dún Eoghanachta, Vol 2*: 211–224. Discovery Programme Monograph, Wordwell, Dublin.

Warner, R. 2013. A lost, Iberian-style, Bronze Age gold neck-ring from near Navan, Co. Armagh. *Emania* 21: 36–39.

Warner, R. 2014. The gold fragments from Haughey's Fort, Co. Armagh: description and XRF analysis. *Emania* 22: 69–76.

Warner, R. 2015. The gold fragments from Haughey's Fort, Co. Armagh: description and XRF analysis. *Emania* 22: 69–76.

Webley, L., Timby, J. and Wilson, M. 2007. Fairfield Park, Stotfold, Bedfordshire: *Later Prehistoric Settlement in the Eastern Chilterns*. Oxford, Bedfordshire Archaeology Monograph 7.

Weir, D. 1987a. The earlier limits of Loughnashade. *Emania* 2: 25–28.

Weir, D. 1987b. Palynology and the environmental history of the Navan area: a preliminary study. *Emania* 3: 34–43.

Weir, D. 1993. Dark Ages and the pollen record. *Emania* 11: 21–30.

Weir, D. 1994. The environment of Emain Macha. In Mallory, J. and Stockman, G. (eds), *Ulidia: Proceedings of the First International Conference on the Ulster Cycle of Tales*: 171–180 Belfast.

Weir, D. and Conway, M. 1988. Haughey's Fort: a preliminary palaeobotanical analysis. *Emania* 4: 28–31.

Weston, G. 2008. *Bredon hillfort*. The 10th Annual Conference of the British Association of Biological Anthropology and Osteoarchaeology.

Westropp, T.J. 1893. Prehistoric stone forts of central Clare – Moghane, and Langough, near Dromoland. *Journal of the Royal Society of Antiquaries of Ireland* 23 (3): 281–291.

Westropp, T.J. 1896a. Prehistoric stone forts of northern Clare. *Journal of the Royal Society of Antiquaries of Ireland* 6 (2): 142–157.

Westropp, T.J. 1896b. Stone forts of northern Clare (Continued). *Journal of the Royal Society of Antiquaries of Ireland* 6 (4): 362–369.

Westropp, T.J. 1897. Stone forts of northern Clare (Continued). *Journal of the Royal Society of Antiquaries of Ireland* 7 (2): 343–367.

Westropp, T.J. 1901a. Prehistoric remains of north-western Clare (Continued). *Journal of the Royal Society of Antiquaries of Ireland* 31 (3): 273–292.

Westropp, T.J. 1901b. Prehistoric remains in north-western Clare. *Journal of the Royal Society of Antiquaries of Ireland* 31 (1): 1–17.

Westropp, T.J. 1902a. The ancient forts of Ireland: being a contribution towards our knowledge of their types, affinities and structural features. *Transactions of the Royal Irish Academy* 31: 579–730.

Westropp, T.J. 1902b. The cahers of county Clare: their names, features, and bibliography. *Proceedings of the Royal Irish Academy* 6: 415–449.

Westropp, T.J. 1908. Types of the ring-forts and similar structures remaining in eastern Clare (Quin, Tulla, Bodyke). *Proceedings of the Royal Irish Academy* 27C: 217–235.

Westropp, T.J. 1911. Prehistoric remains (forts and dolmens) in the Burren, Co. Clare (Continued). *Journal of the Royal Society of Antiquaries of Ireland* 41: 343–367.

Westropp, T.J. 1913. Types of the ring-forts remaining in eastern Clare (Clonlara, Broadford, Cullaun and Clooney). *Proceedings of the Royal Irish Academy* 32C: 58–77.

Westropp, T.J. 1916–1917. On certain typical earthworks and ring-walls in County Limerick. *Proceedings of the Royal Irish Academy* 33C: 9–42.

Westropp, T.J. 1919. The ancient places of assembly in the counties Limerick and Clare. *Journal of the Royal Society of Antiquaries of Ireland* 49: 1–24.

Wheatley, D. 1995. Cumulative viewshed analysis: A GIS-based method for investigating intervisibility, and its archaeological application. In Lock, G. and Stancic Z. (eds), *Archaeology and Geographical Information Systems: A European Perspective*: 171–185. London, Taylor and Francis.

Wheatley, D. 2004. Making space for an archaeology of place. *Internet Archaeology* 15. http://intarch.ac.uk/journal/issue15/wheatley_index.html.

Wheatley, D. and Gillings, M. 2001. Vision, perception and GIS: some notes on the development of enriched approaches to the study of archaeological visibility. In Lock, G. (ed.), *Beyond the Map: Archaeological and Spatial Technologies*: 1–27. The Netherlands, IOS Press.

Wheeler, R. 1943. *Maiden Castle*, Dorset. Oxford, Oxford University Press.

Whitehouse, N. J., Schultling, R. J., McClatchie, M., Barratt, P., McLaughlin, T. R., Bogaard, A., Colledge, S., Marchant, R., Gaffrey, J. and Buntinh, M. J. 2014. Neolithic agriculture on the European western frontier: the boom and bust of early farming in Ireland. *Journal of Archaeological Science*, 51: 181–205.

Whittle, A. 1997. *Sacred Mound Holy Rings. Silbury Hill and the West Kennet Palisade Enclosures: A Later Neolithic Complex in North Wiltshire*. Oxford, Oxbow.

Whittle, A., Bayliss, A. and Healy, F. 2011. *Gathering Time: Dating the Early Neolithic Enclosures of Southern Britain and Ireland*. Oxford, Oxbow.

Whittow, J. 1975. *Geology and Scenery in Ireland*. London, Penguin.

Williams, M. and Harper, D. 1999. *The Making of Ireland: Landscapes in Geology*. London, Immel Publishing.

Williams, M. and Mytum, H. 1998. *Llawhaden, Dyfed Excavations on a Group of Small Defended Enclosures, 1980–4*. British Archaeological Report 275, Oxford, Archaeopress.

Winghart, S. 2000. Mining, processing and distribution of bronze: reflections on the organisation of metal supply between the northern Alps and the Danube region. In Pare, C. (ed.), *Metals Make the World Go Round*: 151–159. Oxford, Oxbow.

Woodman, P., Anderson, E., and Finlay, N. 1999. *Excavations at Ferriter's Cove*, 1983–1995. Bray, Wordwell.

Woodward, A. 2000. *British Barrows: A Matter of Life and Death*. Stroud, Tempus.

Woodward, P. 1991. *The South Dorset Ridgeway: Survey and Excavations, 1977–84*. Dorset Natural History and Archaeological Society, Dorchester.

Yates, T. 2007. *Land, Power and Prestige: Bronze Age Field Systems in Southern England*. Oxford, Oxbow.